The
New York
State
Directory

2005-2006

The
New York
State
Directory

Grey House Publishing

MILLERTON, NY 12546

PUBLISHER: Leslie Mackenzie
EDITOR: Mai Shaikhanuar-Cota
EDITORIAL DIRECTOR: Laura Mars-Proietti

COMPOSITION: David Garoogian
RESEARCH ASSISTANTS: Jael Powell, Philip Rich, Bobbie-Jo Scutt

MARKETING DIRECTOR: Jessica Moody

Grey House Publishing, Inc.
185 Millerton Road
Millerton, NY 12546
518.789.8700
FAX 518.789.0545
www.greyhouse.com
e-mail: books @greyhouse.com

Publisher's Cataloging-In-Publication Data
(Prepared by The Donohue Group, Inc.)

The New York State directory. -- [1st ed.] (1983)-

    v. ; cm.
Annual
ISSN: 0737-1314

1. New York (State)--Officials and employees--Directories. 2. Government executives--New York (State)--Directories. 3. Legislators--New York (State)--Directories.

JK3430 .N52
353.9747002

2-Volume Set (*Directory* and *Profiles of New York*)   ISBN   1-59237-095-0
New York State Directory   ISBN   1-59237-093-4

TABLE OF CONTENTS

Introduction
Organization
Acronyms

NEW YORK STATE BRANCHES OF GOVERNMENT

POLICY AREAS

STATE & LOCAL PUBLIC INFORMATION

POLITICS

INTRODUCTION

The New York State Directory has come home! Published since 1983 by Walker's Research of San Mateo, California, the 2005/06 *Directory* is now part of Grey House Publishing in Millerton, New York.

The New York State Directory is a comprehensive and easy-to-use guide to accessing public officials and private sector organizations and individuals who influence public policy in the state of New York. This latest edition has been substantially updated and enhanced. You will find new information throughout the *Directory*, especially in the Lobbyists and Media chapters. A brand new feature is a section of four-color Demographic Maps from the most recent census, which includes employment and education levels, income distribution, and ethnic and racial population density.

Section One of *The New York State Directory* begins with an introduction to various offices and officers that form the executive, legislative, and judicial branches of the New York State government. This section includes important information on all New York State legislators and congressional representatives, key committee assignments, and staff rosters.

Section Two comprises twenty-five chapters covering the most significant public policy issue areas from Agriculture to Veterans & Military. Each chapter identifies the state, local, and federal agencies and officials that formulate or implement policy. At the end of each chapter is a list of private sector experts and advocates who influence the policy process.

Section Three provides information on state and local government, plus comprehensive sections on political party officials, lobbyists, political action committees, chambers of commerce, print and electronic media, colleges, universities, school district officials and a financial plan overview.

In addition, you'll find a comprehensive **Biographies** section that includes detailed biographical sketches of all 243 key state officials, including US Senators and House Representatives. Note that this edition has these biographies pulled together in one section, rather than spread out in five different sections throughout the book. Following the Biographies are **four Indexes** and a brand new section of 4-color **Demographic Maps**.

Every reasonable effort has been made to ensure that information in *The New York State Directory* is as easily accessible and as comprehensive as possible. Organizational and personnel entries in the *Directory* were updated before publication; follow-up verifications and editorial changes were made as late as May 2005. Continuing assistance and cooperation from state, regional, county, municipal, and federal officials and staff have helped make *The New York State Directory* a unique and valuable resource. We are grateful to these individuals and the private sector sources listed for their generous contributions of time and insight.

In addition to this latest edition of the *Directory*, Grey House is offering a companion volume, *Profiles of New York State,* which may be purchased separately or as a set with the *Directory.* This comprehensive volume, describing 2,307 counties and communities in New York State, is based on Grey House's four-volume *Profiles of America*. Each New York State community profile has data on education, health, housing, income, population, religion, and transportation. *Profiles of New York State* is based on 2000 Census data, 78% of which has been updated with 2004 data. In addition, it includes a new Comparative Statistics section.

— The Editors

ORGANIZATION of DATA

Section 1:
New York State Branches of Government

Executive Branch. Outlines key staff in the Governor's and Lieutenant Governor's offices and senior officials in New York state executive departments and agencies. Biographies for the five senior executive branch officials appear in the *Biographies* section at the back of the book.

Legislative Branch. Covers the state Senate and Assembly leadership, membership, administrative staff, and standing committees and subcommittees. Committee listings include the Chairperson, Ranking Minority Member, Majority and Minority committee members, committee staff, and key Senate or Assembly Majority and Minority staff assignments. Biographies with district office information for Senators and Assembly members appear in the *Biographies* section at the back of the book.

Judicial Branch. Identifies the state courts, judges who currently sit on these courts, and the clerk of each court. Includes the Court of Appeals, Appellate Division courts, Supreme Court, Court of Claims, New York City courts, county courts, district courts and city courts outside New York City. The county judge section identifies the specific court with which the judge is associated.

Section 2:
Policy Areas

This section classifies New York state government activity into 25 major policy areas. Each policy area lists key individuals in the New York state government, federal government, and the private sector who have expertise in the area of government activity. All entries show organization name, individual name, title, address, telephone number, and fax number. Internet and e-mail addresses are included where available. Each policy area includes the following information:

NEW YORK STATE

Governor's Office. Identifies the Governor's legal and program staff assigned to the policy area.

Executive Department & Related Agencies. Provides a complete organizational description of the primary state departments and agencies responsible for the policy area. Also includes those state departments and agencies whose activities relate to the policy area.

Corporations, Authorities & Commissions. Covers independent public and quasi-private sector agencies in the state, as well as intrastate bodies to which New York sends a representative official.

Legislative Standing Committees. Lists committees and subcommittees which oversee governmental activities in the policy area and their respective chairpersons and ranking minority members.

U.S. GOVERNMENT

Executive Departments & Related Agencies. Identifies federal departments and agencies located in or assigned to the New York region.

U.S. Congress. Lists congressional committees which oversee federal activities in the policy area, their respective chairpersons, ranking minority members, and members from the New York delegation.

PRIVATE SECTOR SOURCES
Includes an alphabetized list of public interest groups, trade and professional associations, corporations, and academia, with the associated individuals who have expertise in the policy area.

Section 3:
State & Local Government Public Information
Public Information Offices. Lists key contacts in state government public information offices and libraries.

U.S. Congress. Lists all New York State delegates to the Senate and the House of Representatives with their Washington, DC office, phone and fax numbers, and e-mail addresses. Biographies with district office information for each New York Senator and Representative appear in the *Biographies* section at the back of the book. Provides a comprehensive list of all Senate and House standing, select, and special committees and subcommittees. Each committee and subcommittee entry includes the chairperson, ranking minority member, and assigned members from the New York delegation.

County Government. Identifies senior government officials in all New York counties.

Municipal Government. Identifies senior public officials for cities, towns, and villages in New York with populations greater than 20,000. All New York City departments are included in the city listing.

Politics
Political Parties. Lists statewide party officials and county chairpersons for the Conservative, Democratic, Liberal and Republican parties.

Lobbyists. Identifies registered lobbyists and clients.

Political Action Committees. Lists registered political action committees and their treasurers.

Business
Chambers of Commerce. Lists contact information for chambers of commerce, and economic and industrial development organizations and their primary officials.

Media
Identifies daily and weekly newspapers in New York, major news services with reporters assigned to cover state government, radio stations with a news format, and television stations with independent news staff. Newspapers are categorized by the primary city they serve. Staff listings include managing, news, and editorial page editors, and political reporters. News service entries include bureau chiefs and reporters. Radio and television entries include the news director.

Education
SUNY and Other Universities and Colleges. Includes the board of trustees, system administration, the four University Centers, and all colleges and community colleges in the SUNY system; the central administration and all colleges in the CUNY system; and independent colleges and universities. Each college includes the name of its top official, usually the president or dean, as well as address, telephone number and Internet address.

Public School Administrators. Lists school district administrators by county and school district. The New York City School's subsection includes officials in the Chancellor's office. Following are BOCES District Superintendents by supervisory district and the education administrators of schools operated by the state or other public agencies.

Financial Plan Overview
Provides information excerpted from the New York State 2005-2006 Executive Budget, Appendix II, published January, 2005.

Biographies
Includes 243 political biographies of individuals representing New York state's Executive Branch, New York state Assembly members, New York state Senate members, US Senators from New York, and US Representatives from New York

INDEXES
Name Index. Includes every official and executive name listed in **The New York State Directory**.

Organizations Index. Includes the names of the top three organization levels in all New York state executive departments and agencies, as well as public corporations, authorities, and commissions. In addition, this index includes all organizations listed in the Private Sector Sources segment of each policy chapter, as well as lobbyist organizations and political action committees, chambers of commerce, newspapers, news services, radio and television stations, SUNY and CUNY locations, and private colleges.

Geographic Index. Includes the organizations listed in the *Government and Private Sector Organizations Index* (see above) arranged by the city location.

World Wide Web (URL) Index. Provides Internet addresses for all organizations listed in the *Directory*.

DEMOGRAPHIC MAPS
Four-color maps, generated by the US Census Bureau, include the following topics:
    Metropolitan Areas, Counties, and Central Cities
    Total Population
    Percent White Population
    Percent Black Population
    Percent Asian Population
    Percent Hispanic Population
    Median Age
    Median Household Income
    Percent in Poverty
    Percent Foreign Born
    Percent Speaking Language Other Than English
    Percent High School Education Only
    Percent Bachelor's Degree or Higher
    Percent Female Labor Force Participation
    Percent Disabled
    Percent Commuting via Public Transportation

ACRONYMS

AFL-CIO	American Federation of Labor/Congress of Industrial Organizations
AFSCME	American Federation of State, County & Municipal Employees
BAC	Bricklayers & Allied Craftsmen
BOCES	Board of Cooperative Educational Services
CIO	Chief Information Officer (Office of the)
COPE	Committee on Political Education
CPB	Customs & Border Protection
CSD	Central School District
CUNY	City University of New York
DHS	Department of Homeland Security
FEMA	Federal Emergency Management Agency
HFA	Housing Finance Agency
IBPAT	International Brotherhood of Painters & Allied Trades
IBT	International Brotherhood of Teamsters
ILGWU	International Ladies' Garment Workers' Union
IOLA	Interest on Lawyers Account
IUE	International Union of Electrical, Radio & Machine Workers
IUOE	International Union of Operating Engineers
MBBA	Municipal Bond Bank Agency
NOW	National Organization for Women
NYC	New York City
NYS	New York State
NYSHESC	New York State Higher Education Services Corp
NYU	New York University
PAC	Political Action Committee
PACE	Political Action for Candidates' Election
PAF	Political Action Fund
PAT	Political Action Team
PBA	Patrolmen's Benevolent Association
PEF	Political Education Fund
SEMO	Emergency Management Office (NYS)
SONYMA	State of New York Mortgage Agency
SUNY	State University of New York
USWA	United Steel Workers of America
VESID	Vocational & Educational Services for Individuals with Disabilities Office

Section 1:
BRANCHES OF GOVERNMENT

EXECUTIVE BRANCH

This chapter provides a summary of officials in the Executive Branch. For a more detailed listing of specific executive and administrative departments and agencies, refer to the appropriate policy area in Section 2 or to the Organizations Index. Biographies for the five senior Executive Branch officials appear in a separate section in the back of the book.

New York State

Governor (also see Governor's Office):
George E Pataki **518-474-8390**
Lieutenant Governor (also see Lieutenant Governor's Office):
Mary Donohue . . . . **518-474-4623 or 212-681-4532**
Chief Information Officer (also see Technology, Office of):
James T Dillon **518-474-3421**
Comptroller (also see State Comptroller, Office of the):
Alan G Hevesi **518-474-4040**
Attorney General (also see Law Department):
Eliot Spitzer **518-474-7330**
Secretary of State (also see State Department):
Randy A Daniels **518-474-0050**

Governor's Office
Executive Chamber
State Capitol
Albany, NY 12224
518-474-8390 Fax: 518-474-1513
Web site: www.state.ny.us

Governor:
George E Pataki 518-474-8390
Executive Director:
Kara Lanspery 518-474-8390

Administration
Director, Administrative Services:
Teresa A Brennan 518-474-3036
Chief, Computer Services:
Thomas Irvin 518-473-5632
Secretarial Services:
Cheryl Dumicich 518-474-0467

Appointments
Deputy Secretary, Appointments & Intergovernmental Affairs:
Robert D Bulman 518-474-0491
Deputy Appointments Secretary:
Mandi Loss 518-474-0491
Senior Assistant Counsel to Appointments Secretary:
John Mancini 518-474-0491
Assistant Counsel to Appointments Secretary:
Michael DeMartino 518-474-0491

Communications
Director, Communications:
Catalfamo David 518-474-8418
Press Secretary:
Kevin Quinn 518-474-8418
Deputy Press Secretary:
Todd Alhardt 518-474-8418

Director, Special Projects:
Joseph Conway 518-408-2588
Press Officer:
Jennifer Meicht 518-474-8418
Press Officer:
Andrew Rush 518-474-8418
Director, Scheduling:
Audra Viscusi 518-474-4727
Director, Correspondence:
Tricia Curley 518-474-3612
Citizens Services:
Linda Boyd 518-474-1041

Counsel
Counsel to the Governor-Attorney General, Budget:
Richard Platkin 518-474-8343
Deputy Counsel to the Governor-Appointments, Elections, Ethics, FOIL Appeals, Lobbying Commission, Governor's Office of Regulatory Reform:
W Brooks Debow 518-474-8343
Senior Asst Counsel to the Governor-Indian Affairs, Lottery, State Liquor Authority, Racing & Wagering Board:
Greg Allen 518-474-2266
Senior Asst Counsel to the Governor-Banking, Insurance, State Insurance Fund, Tort Reform, Uniform Laws, Workers' Compensation Board:
Christopher McCarthy 518-474-2294
Senior Asst Counsel to the Governor-Criminal Justice Services, Inspector General, Office of Public Security, Special Prosecutors, State Investigation Commission:
Roger McDonough 518-474-1291
Senior Asst Counsel to the Governor-Council on Arts, Dormitory Authority, Education, Higher Education, Office for Technology, Real Property, Rent Control, CUNY, SUNY:
Martin Bienstock 518-474-1310
Senior Asst Counsel to the Governor-Energy Research & Development, Environmental Conservation, Long Island Power Authority, NY Power Authority, Public Service Commission:
Carl Patka 518-474-8327
Asst Counsel to the Governor-Athletic Commn, Court Admin, Judiciary, Tax Tribunal, Taxation & Finance, FOIL Appeals:
Ryan McAllister 518-474-8494
Asst Counsel to the Governor-Economic Development, Empire State Dev Corp, Jacob Javits Conv Center, NYSTAR, Olympic Regional Dev Auth, Tourism:
Robert Ryan 518-474-2266
Asst Counsel to the Governor-Clemency, Crime Vics, Correcs, Correc Svcs, Disaster, Extrads, Military/Naval/SEMO, Parole, Domestic Viol, Probatn/Correc Alts, Veterans:
Gerald Connolly 518-474-8494
Asst Counsel to the Governor-Adirondack Pk Agency, Agric & Markets, Bond Act Coord, Consumer Protection Bd, Environ Facilities Corp, Parks & Recreation, State & Local Govt, OGS:
James Walsh 518-474-8327

Offices and agencies appear in alphabetical order.

Asst Counsel to the Governor-Aging, Advocate for Persons with Disabilities, Commission on Quality of Care, Health, Mental Health, OASAS, OMRDD:
   Mark Ustin 518-474-8494
Asst Counsel to the Gov-Battery Pk, Child/Family Svcs, Child/Family Council, Family, Housing, Human Rts, Roosevelt Is, Temp/Disabl, Women, HFA/MBBA/SONYMA:
   Carolyn Betz Kerr. 518-474-1310
Asst Counsel to the Governor-Civil Svc, Elections, Empl Relations, Labor, Motor Veh, Niagara Fr, Port Auth, Retirement/Pensions, Transp, Thruway, Waterfr, MTA, PERB:
   Christopher Staszak 518-474-1310

Legislative & Intergovernmental Relations
Director, State & Local Government Affairs:
   John Haggerty. 518-486-9896
Director, Intergovernmental Affairs:
   Michael Elmendorf. 518-408-2555
Deputy Director, Legislative Affairs:
   Joanne Fernandez. 518-486-6672
Assistant Director, Legislative Affairs:
   Saleem Cheeks. 518-486-6672

New York City Office
633 Third Ave, 38th Fl, New York, NY 10017
Director:
   Ann McConnachie 212-681-4580
Executive Assistant to the Governor:
   Amy Holden 212-681-4580
Assistant to the Governor for NYC Issues:
   Doug Blais 212-681-4580
Director, Community Affairs:
   James Barcia. 212-681-4580
Director, Legislative Affairs-NYC:
   James Harding 212-681-4580
Senior Advisor to the Governor for Women's Issues:
   Lynn Rollins. 212-681-4580
New York City Press Secretary:
   Lynn Rasic. 212-681-4580/fax: 212-681-4608

New York State Office of Federal Affairs
444 N Capitol St NW, Washington, DC 20001
Director & Counsel:
   James Mazzarella 202-434-7100
Deputy Director:
   Kerry O'Hare 202-434-7100

Office of the Secretary
Secretary to the Governor:
   John P Cahill. 518-474-4246
Senior Assistant to the Secretary:
   Susan Myers. 518-474-4246
Senior Policy Advisor to the Governor:
   Jeffrey Lovell 518-486-9671
First Deputy Secretary to the Governor:
   William Howard. 518-474-3522
Deputy Secretary to the Governor:
   William McGahay 518-474-3522
Deputy Secretary to the Governor for Administration & Operations:
   Carolyn Ahl 518-408-2800
Deputy Secretary to the Governor for Public Authorities, Finance & Housing:
   Adam Barsky 518-473-2610
Deputy Secretary to the Governor for Appointments & Intergovernmental Affairs:
   Robert Bulman 518-474-0491
Deputy Secretary to the Governor for Energy, Environment & Transportation:
   Charles Fox. 518-474-0411
Deputy Secretary to the Governor for Health & Human Services:
   Mark Kissinger. 518-408-2500

Deputy Secretary to the Governor for Transportation:
   Thomas Madison 518-408-2552
Director, Energy Programs:
   James Austin. 518-474-0351
Director, Environmental Programs:
   Matthew Millea 518-473-5442
Director, Health Programs:
   Megan Kearney 518-408-2500
Director, Human Services Programs:
   Timothy Dunn 518-408-4079
Director, Social Services Programs:
   Renee Rider 518-486-4079

Lieutenant Governor's Office
Executive Chamber
State Capitol
Albany, NY 12224
518-474-4623 Fax: 518-486-4170

633 Third Ave
38th Fl
New York, NY 10017
212-681-4532
Fax: 212-681-4533

Lieutenant Governor:
   Mary O Donohue . . . . 518-474-4623 or 212-681-4532
Counsel to Lt Governor:
   John Watson. 518-474-4623
Acting Chief of Staff:
   Karin Kennett. 518-474-4623
Director, Scheduling:
   Dan Sandowski. 518-474-4623
Executive Secretary:
   Jane Burhans. 518-474-4623

EXECUTIVE DEPARTMENTS AND RELATED AGENCIES

Advocate for Persons with Disabilities, Office of
One Empire State Plaza
Suite 1001
Albany, NY 12223-1150
518-473-4538 Fax: 518-473-6005
Web site: www.oapwd.org

State Advocate:
   Richard Warrender. 518-473-4129
Deputy Advocate, Counsel & Public Info Officer:
   Gregory Jones. 518-473-4609
   e-mail: oapwdinfo@oapwd.org

Aging, Office for the
Two Empire State Plaza
5th Floor
Albany, NY 12223-1251
518-474-5731 Fax: 518-474-0608
Web site: www.aging.state.ny.us

Acting Director:
   Neal Lane. 518-474-4425/fax: 518-474-1398

Offices and agencies appear in alphabetical order.

Deputy Director, Executive Division:
Laurie Pferr. 518-473-4275
Secretary to Acting Director:
Christine E Reilly. 518-474-7012
Deputy Director, Finance & Administration:
Robert A Bush. 518-474-2631/fax: 518-474-0608
Assistant Director, Finance & Administration:
James Foy. 518-473-4808
Deputy Director, Local Program Operations:
Franklin DeMarinis 518-473-5705/fax: 518-474-0608
Assistant Deputy Director, Local Program Operations:
Marcus Harazin 518-473-5705/fax: 518-474-0608
Director, Targeting Services & EOP Programs:
Carmen V Cunningham 518-474-5041
Counsel:
Vacant 518-473-5796
Public Information Officer:
Thomas Gallagher 518-474-7158/fax: 518-473-6565
e-mail: tom.gallagher@ofa.state.ny.us
Director, Communications:
David R Murray 518-473-2950
Director, Information Technology Systems:
Rebecca Stegman 518-474-8896

Agriculture & Markets Department

10 B Airline Dr
Albany, NY 12235
800-554-4501 or 518-457-3880 Fax: 518-457-3087
e-mail: info@agmkt.state.ny.us
Web site: www.agmkt.state.ny.us

Commissioner:
Nathan Rudgers 518-457-8876
First Deputy Commissioner:
Ruth A Moore. 518-457-2771
Deputy Commissioner:
Margaret Becker. 518-485-7728
Deputy Commissioner:
Rick Zimmerman 518-457-0752
Counsel:
Joan A Kehoe 518-457-1059
Executive Assistant:
Tim Pezzolesi. 518-485-7728
Public Information Officer:
Jessica Chittenden 518-457-3136
e-mail: jessica.chittenden@agmkt.state.ny.us

Alcoholic Beverage Control, Division of

105 W 125th St
4th Fl
New York, NY 10027
212-961-3835 Fax: 212-961-8299
Web site: www.abc.state.ny.us

84 Holland Ave
Albany, NY 12208
518-486-4767
Fax: 518-402-4015

Chair:
Edward F Kelly. . . . . 212-961-8347 or 518-473-6559
Commissioner:
Lawrence Gedda. 212-961-8347

Commissioner:
Joseph Zarriello 518-474-0810
Counsel:
Thomas McKeon 212-961-8317
Deputy Commissioner, Administration & Public Affairs:
J Mark Anderson 518-486-4767
Deputy Commissioner, NYC:
Fred Gioffre 212-961-8301

Alcoholism & Substance Abuse Services, Office of

1450 Western Ave
Albany, NY 12203
518-473-3460 Fax: 518-457-5474
Web site: www.oasas.state.ny.us

501 7th Ave
8th Fl
New York, NY 10018
646-728-4533

Associate Commissioner, Administration:
Michael Lawler. 518-457-5312
Associate Commissioner Prevention Services Division:
Frances M Harding 518-485-6022
Acting Associate Commissioner, Treatment Services Division:
Timothy P Williams 518-485-2322
Associate Commissioner, Standards & Quality Assurance:
Neil Grogin. 518-485-2257
Counsel:
Henry F Zwack. 518-485-2312
Director, Communications:
Jennifer Farrell 518-485-1768
e-mail: jenniferfarrell@oasas.state.ny.us
Public Information Officer:
Joseph Morrissey 518-485-1768
e-mail: josephmorrissey@oasas.state.ny.us

Banking Department

One State Street
New York, NY 10004-1417
212-709-5470
Web site: www.banking.state.ny.us

5 Empire State Plaza
Ste 2310
Albany, NY 12223-1555
518-473-6160
Fax: 518-473-7204

Superintendent of Banks:
Diana L Taylor 212-709-3501/fax: 212-709-3585
e-mail: barbara.kent@banking.state.ny.us
First Deputy Superintendent:
Daniel Muccia 212-709-3502
Secretary to the Board:
Sam L Abram. 212-709-1658
Director, Consumer Affairs & Financial Products:
Barbara Kent. 212-709-3503
Deputy Superintendent & Counsel:
Sara Kelsey. 212-709-1640
Deputy Superindent & Counsel:
Sara Kelsey. 212-709-1640

Offices and agencies appear in alphabetical order.

Chief Information Officer:
Connie Van Decker 212-709-5400
Deputy Superintendent, Consumer Services Division:
Edward B Kramer 212-709-3560/fax: 212-709-3582
Deputy Superintendent, Community & Regional Banks Division:
Manuel Kursky. 212-709-1610
Deputy Superintendent, Communications & Media Relations:
Catie Marshall 212-709-1691
e-mail: catie.marshall@banking.state.ny.us

Budget, Division of the
State Capitol
Albany, NY 12224
518-473-3885
e-mail: dobinfo@budget.state.ny.us
Web site: www.state.ny.us/dob

Director:
John F Cape 518-474-2300
Deputy Director:
Ron Rock 518-474-6323
Deputy Director:
Al Kaplan 518-474-6300
Administrative Officer:
Karen Bodnar. 518-474-6324/fax: 518-402-2298
Director, Communications:
Michael Marr 518-474-3885
Press Officer:
Peter Constantakes 518-473-3885
Press Officer:
Scott Reif 518-473-3885
Legislative Liaison:
Christina Kidera. 518-474-7953/fax: 518-473-7243

CIO Office & Office for Technology
State Capitol, SEP
PO Box 2062
Albany, NY 12202-0062

CIO Office
Web site: www.cio.state.ny.us
Chief Information Officer:
James T Dillon. 518-474-3421/fax: 518-402-2976
e-mail: cio@cio.state.ny.us
Deputy Chief Information Officer:
Michael Mittleman 518-408-2140/fax: 518-402-2976

Office for Technology
Web site: www.oft.state.ny.us
Director:
Michael McCormack. 518-473-9450/fax: 518-402-2976
Chief Administrative Officer:
Meg Levine 518-408-2476/fax: 518-402-2976
Deputy Director & Counsel:
Susan Zeronda. 518-473-2807/fax: 518-402-2976
Chief Operating Officer:
David Swits 518-473-7041/fax: 518-402-2976
Deputy Director, Applications:
Ellen Kattleman 518-402-2010/fax: 518-486-4344
Deputy Director, Networking:
Dave Runyon. 518-486-9200/fax: 518-408-4693

Children & Family Services, Office of
52 Washington St
Rensselaer, NY 12144
518-473-7793 Fax: 518-486-7550
Web site: www.dfa.state.ny.us

Commissioner:
John A Johnson. 518-473-8437
Executive Deputy Commissioner:
Roger Biagi. 518-474-7688
Assistant Commissioner, Public Affairs:
Sandra A Brown 518-402-3130
e-mail: cfspio@dfa.state.ny.us
Deputy Commissioner & General Counsel:
Gail Gordon 518-473-8418
Deputy Commissioner, Administration:
Susan Costello 518-486-7218
Deputy Commissioner, Development & Prevention Services:
Larry Brown 518-402-3108
Deputy Commissioner, Rehabilitative Services:
Ed Ausborn. 518-473-1786
Associate Commissioner, Human Resources:
Nicole McCulloch 518-473-8453
Assistant Commissioner, Office of Youth Development:
Sally Herrick. 518-473-8455
Deputy Commissioner, Information Technology:
William E Travis, Jr 518-402-3194
Assoc Commissioner, Commn for Blind & Visually Handicapped:
Thomas A Robertson 518-473-1801

Civil Service Department
State Campus
Bldg 1
Albany, NY 12239
518-457-2487 Fax: 518-457-7547
Web site: www.cs.state.ny.us

Commissioner:
Daniel E Wall. 518-457-3701
Executive Deputy Commissioner:
John F Barr 518-457-6212
Deputy Commissioner:
Regina M DuBois. 518-485-7515
Director, Civil Service Operations & Administrations:
Patricia Hite 518-485-0340
Special Counsel:
Thomas F Brennan 518-485-7278
Counsel:
Brian S Reichenbach 518-457-3177
Director, Workforce & Occupational Planning:
Nancy B Kiyonaga 518-485-9274
Director, Employee Benefits:
Robert Dubois 518-457-9391/fax: 518-485-8952
Director, Public Information:
Marc E Carey. 518-457-9375/fax: 518-457-6654
e-mail: mec5@cs.state.ny.us
Public Records Access Officer:
Jane Prus 518-457-6875/fax: 518-457-6654

Civil Service Commission
President:
Daniel E Wall. 518-457-3701
Commissioner:
Margaret Dadd 518-457-3504

Offices and agencies appear in alphabetical order.

Commissioner:
Leo J Kesselring 518-457-5444

Consumer Protection Board
5 Empire State Plaza
Ste 2101
Albany, NY 12223-1556
518-474-8583 or 800-NYS-1220 Fax: 518-486-3936
Web site: www.consumer.state.ny.us

5 Penn Plaza
5th Fl
New York, NY 10001
212-268-6199
Fax: 212-268-7124

Chairperson & Executive Director:
Teresa A Santiago. 518-474-3514
Deputy Executive Director:
Corinne Biviano 518-474-1471
General Counsel:
Lisa Harris 518-486-3934
Director, Education:
Gina Pinos 518-459-8852
Director, Consumer Services:
Cyndee D Berlin. 518-474-1471
Director, Marketing & Public Relations:
Jon Sorensen 518-473-9472/fax: 518-474-2986
Director, Strategic Programs & Utility Intervention:
Doug Elfner 518-486-6532

Correctional Services Department
1220 Washington Ave, Bldg 2
Albany, NY 12226-2050
518-457-8126 Fax: 518-457-7252
Web site: www.docs.state.ny.us

Commissioner:
Glenn S Goord 518-457-8126
Executive Assistant to Commissioner:
Edward McSweeney. 518-457-1281
Secretary to the Commissioner:
Diane Rowen 518-457-8126
Executive Deputy Commissioner:
John R Patterson, Jr 518-457-1748
Deputy Commissioner & Counsel:
Anthony Annucci 518-457-4951
Inspector General:
Richard D Roy 518-457-2653
Deputy Commissioner, Administrative Services:
Charles Devane. 518-457-8188
Deputy Commissioner, Correctional Facility Operations:
Lucien LeClaire 518-457-8138
Deputy Commissioner, Health Services Division / Chief Medical Officer:
Lester Wright 518-457-7073
Deputy Commissioner, Program Services:
John Nuttall 518-457-5555
Assoc Commissioner, Inspector General, Population Management:
Richard D Roy 518-457-7261
Public Information Officer:
James Flateau. 518-457-8182/fax: 518-457-7070

Council on Children & Families
5 Empire State Plaza
Ste 2810
Albany, NY 12223
518-473-3652 Fax: 518-473-2570
e-mail: council@ccf.state.ny.us
Web site: www.ccf.state.ny.us

Chief Exec Director:
Alana M Sweeny 518-474-5522
e-mail: alana.sweeny@ccf.state.ny.us
Counsel:
Beth O'Connor. 518-473-3652
Public Information & Personnel:
Donna Ned. 518-474-5522/fax: 518-473-7568
e-mail: donna.ned@ccf.state.ny.us

Council on the Arts
175 Varick St
3rd Fl
New York, NY 10014
212-627-4455 or TDD: 800-895-9838 Fax: 212-620-5911
Web site: www.nysca.org

Chair:
Richard J Schwartz. 212-627-4440
Vice Chair:
Debra R Black 212-627-4440
Acting Executive Director:
Richard J Schwartz. 212-627-8686
e-mail: rschwartz@nysca.org
Deputy Director:
Al Berr 212-627-8444
e-mail: aberr@nysca.org
Deputy Director:
Jack Lindahl 212-627-3338
e-mail: glindahl@nysca.org
Deputy Director:
Debby Silverfine. 212-627-7778
e-mail: dsilverfine@nysca.org
Public Information Officer:
Margaret Keta. 212-627-3131
e-mail: mketa@nysca.org

Crime Victims Board
55 Hanson Place
10th Fl
Brooklyn, NY 11217
718-923-4325 Fax: 718-923-4352
e-mail: cvbinfo@cvb.state.ny.us
Web site: www.cvb.state.ny.us

845 Central Ave
Rm 107
Albany, NY 12206-1504
518-457-8727
Fax: 518-457-8658

65 Court Street
Buffalo, NY 14202

Offices and agencies appear in alphabetical order.

716-847-7992
Fax: 716-847-7995

Chairwoman:
 Joan A Cusack 718-923-4331
Commissioner:
 Christina Hernandez 518-485-5719
Commissioner:
 Charles F Marotta 718-923-4336
Commissioner:
 Jacqueline C Mattina 716-847-7948
Commissioner:
 Benedict J Monachino 718-923-4400
General Counsel:
 Everett Mayhew, Jr. 518-457-8066
Executive Director:
 Virginia A Miller 518-457-9320
Director, MIS:
 David Loomis 518-457-8050
Contract Supervisor:
 Ron Dickens 518-485-2763

Criminal Justice Services, Division of

Four Tower Place
Albany, NY 12203-3764
518-457-1260 Fax: 518-457-3089
Web site: www.criminaljustice.state.ny.us

Commissioner & Director:
 Chauncey G Parker 518-457-1260
Executive Deputy Commissioner:
 Martin Cirincione 518-457-6091
Deputy Commissioner:
 Roger Jeffries 518-485-7433
Director, Administration Office:
 Paula Steigman 518-457-6100
Deputy Commissioner & Counsel, Legal Svcs & Forensic Svcs Ofc:
 Kimberly O'Conner 518-457-4181
Deputy Commissioner, Public Safety Office:
 James DeLapp 518-457-6101
Deputy Commissioner, Systems & Operations Office:
 Daniel Foro 518-485-2995
Director, Funding & Program Assistance Office:
 AnneMarie Strano 518-457-8462
Director, Justice Research & Innovation Bureau:
 Donna Hall 518-457-7301
Director, Communications:
 Lynn Rasic 518-485-0857
Director, Operations Office:
 William Sillery 518-457-6050
Public Information Officer:
 Lyle Hartog 518-485-2465/fax: 518-485-2467

Developmental Disabilities Planning Council

155 Washington Ave
2nd Fl
Albany, NY 12210
518-486-7505 or 800-395-DDPC Fax: 518-402-3505
e-mail: ddpc@ddpc.state.ny.us
Web site: www.ddpc.state.ny.us

Executive Director:
 Sheila M Carey 518-486-7505

Deputy Executive Director:
 Anna Lobosco 518-486-7505
Secretary to Exec Director:
 Lois M Goodwill 518-486-7505
Public Information Officer:
 Thomas F Lee 518-486-7505

Education Department

State Education Bldg
89 Washington Ave
Albany, NY 12234
518-474-3852 Fax: 518-486-5631
Web site: www.nysed.gov

Commissioner, University President:
 Richard P Mills 518-474-5844
 e-mail: rmills@mail.nysed.gov
Assistant to the Commissioner:
 Peggy Rivers 518-474-5845
 e-mail: privers@mail.nysed.gov
Counsel & Deputy Commissioner, Legal Affairs:
 Kathy A Ahearn 518-474-6400
 e-mail: kahearn@mail.nysed.gov
Deputy Commissioner, Cultural Education Office:
 Carole F Huxley 518-474-5976/fax: 518-474-2718
 e-mail: chuxley@mail.nysed.gov
Deputy Commissioner, Higher Education:
 Johanna Duncan-Poitier 518-474-5851/fax: 518-486-2175
 e-mail: hedepcom@mail.nysed.gov
Deputy Commissioner, Office of Elementary, Middle, Secondary, Continuing
 Education:
 James A Kadamus 518-474-5915/fax: 518-486-2233
 e-mail: jkadamus@mail.nysed.gov
Deputy Commissioner, Office of the Professions:
 Johanna Duncan-Poitier 518-474-3817 x470
 e-mail: jpoitier@mail.nysed.gov
Deputy Commissioner, Vocational & Educational Services for Individuals
 with Disabilities Office:
 Rebecca Cort 518-474-2714
 e-mail: rcort@mail.nysed.gov
Deputy Commissioner & COO, Management Services:
 Theresa E Savo 518-474-2547/fax: 518-473-2827
Director, Communications:
 R Alan Ray 518-474-1201/fax: 518-473-2977
 e-mail: aray@mail.nysed.gov

Elections, State Board of

40 Steuben St
Albany, NY 12207-2109
518-474-8100 or TTY: 800-533-8683 Fax: 518-486-4068
Web site: www.elections.state.ny.us

Chair:
 Carol Berman 518-474-8113
Vice Chair:
 Neil W Kelleher 518-474-8113
Commissioner:
 Evelyn Aquila 518-474-8113
Commissioner:
 Helena M Donohue 518-474-8113
Executive Deputy Director:
 Peter S Kosinski 518-474-6236
 e-mail: pkosinski@elections.state.ny.us
Special Counsel:
 Todd D Valentine 518-474-6367

Offices and agencies appear in alphabetical order.

Counsel for Enforcement:
  Stanley L Zalen 518-474-2063
Chief Investigator, Election Law Enforcement:
  Vacant 518-474-2371
Director, Election Operations:
  Anne E Svizzero 518-473-5086
Director, Public Information:
  Lee Daghlian 518-474-1953/fax: 518-473-8315
  e-mail: ldaghlian@elections.state.ny.us
Coordinator, Registration Operations:
  Gregory Fiozzo 518-474-1953

Emergency Management Office, NYS (SEMO)
1220 Washington Ave
Bldg 22, Ste 101
Albany, NY 12226-2251
518-457-8900
Web site: www.nysemo.state.ny.us

Director:
  James W Tuffey 518-457-2222
First Deputy Director:
  Andrew X Feeney 518-457-9996
Deputy Director, Support Services:
  Tom Rinaldi 518-457-8130
Counsel:
  Lai Sun Yee 518-457-8901
Program Asst:
  Judy Williams 518-457-2222/fax: 518-457-9995

Administration
Chief Budget Analyst:
  Susan Mutch 518-457-9994
Manager Recovery Section:
  Les Radford 518-457-5285

Community Affairs
Asst Director:
  Dennis J Michalski 518-485-5666
Public Information Officer:
  Donald L Maurer 518-485-6011/fax: 518-457-4923
  e-mail: donald.maurer@semo.state.ny.us

Operations
Chief, Operations:
  Kevin Neary 518-457-9933

Preparedness
Chief, Special Operations:
  Robert Olazagasti 518-457-8916
Chief, Training/Exercises:
  William Campbell 518-457-8917
Chief Planning:
  Radeph Anderson 518-457-9941

Technology
Chief, Information Technology Services:
  Vacant 518-485-0194
Chief, Logistics:
  Robert Olazagasti 518-457-9927
Communications Officer:
  Kenneth Goetz 518-457-9938

Empire State Development
30 South Pearl St
Albany, NY 12245

518-292-5100
Web site: www.empire.state.ny.us

633 Third Ave
New York, NY 10017
212-803-3100

Commissioner:
  Charles A Gargano 212-803-3700
Executive Deputy Commissioner/Chief Operating Officer:
  Eileen Mildenberger 212-803-3730
Executive Vice President:
  Michael Wilton 518-292-5101
Senior VP & Sr Deputy Commissioner, Corp Marketing:
  Neville Bugwadia 212-803-2244
Senior Vice President, Economic Revitalization:
  Christine Glassner 212-803-3727/fax: 212-803-3236
Senior Vice President, Legal & General Counsel:
  Anita W Laremont 212-803-3750
Deputy Commissioner & Counsel:
  Donald Ross 518-292-5120
Senior VP & Deputy Commissioner for Policy & Research:
  John Bacheller 518-292-5115/fax: 518-292-5812
Deputy Commissioner, Business Marketing, Advertising & Tourism:
  Suzanne Morris 518-292-5360/fax: 518-292-5802
Deputy Commissioner, Governor's Office of Motion Picture & TV
    Development:
  Patricia Kaufman 212-803-2334/fax: 212-803-2339
Senior VP, Deputy Commissioner & Chief Administrative Officer:
  Joseph J LaCivita . . . . 212-803-3158 or 518-292-5102
  fax: 518-292-5812
Chief Financial Officer:
  Frances Walton 212-803-3510
Senior VP, Operations:
  Susanna Stein 212-803-3641
Communications Director:
  Ron Jury 212-803-3740/fax: 212-803-3735
  e-mail: rjury@empire.state.ny.us
Senior VP, Strategic Business:
  Ray Richardson 518-292-5340
Deputy Commissioner, Business Services:
  Amy Schoch 518-292-5340
Senior VP, Market Development:
  Christine Glassner 212-803-3727

Employee Relations, Governor's Office of
Two Empire State Plaza, Ste 1201
Albany, NY 12223
518-474-6988 Fax: 518-473-6795
e-mail: info@goer.state.ny.us
Web site: www.goer.state.ny.us

Director:
  George Madison 518-474-6988/fax: 518-486-7304
General Counsel:
  Walter J Pellegrini 518-474-4090
Director, Administration:
  Paul Shatsoff 518-473-3467/fax: 518-473-6725
  e-mail: pshatsoff@goer.state.ny.us
Public Information Officer:
  Michelle McDonald 518-474-4800/fax: 518-486-7304
  e-mail: mgmcdonald@goer.state.ny.us

Offices and agencies appear in alphabetical order.

Environmental Conservation Department

625 Broadway
Albany, NY 12233-4500
518-474-2121 Fax: 518-402-9016
Web site: www.dec.state.ny.us

Acting Commissioner:
Denise M Sheehan 518-402-8540
e-mail: dsheeha@gw.dec.state.ny.us
Deputy Commissioner & General Counsel:
James H Ferreira 518-402-2794/fax: 518-485-8484
Deputy Commissioner, Air & Waste Management:
Carl Johnson 518-402-8549
Assistant Commissioner, Hearings & Mediation Services Office:
Louis Alexander 518-402-8537
Deputy Commissioner, Natural Resources & Water Quality:
Lynette Stark 518-402-8560
Assistant Commissioner, Administration:
Jack McKeon 518-402-9401
Assistant Commissioner, Public Protection:
Henry Hamilton 518-402-8552
Assistant Commissioner of Media Relations:
Michael Frazer 518-402-8000/fax: 518-402-2209
Public Information Officer:
Maureen Wren 518-402-8000

Freshwater Wetlands Appeals Board

625 Broadway
Rm 145
Albany, NY 12233-1070
518-402-0566 Fax: 518-402-0588

Chairwoman:
Rhonda K Amoroso 518-402-0566
Counsel:
Michele M Stefanucci 518-402-0566
Counsel:
Pamela J Norrix 518-402-0566
Docket Clerk:
Carol A Goldstein 518-402-0566

General Services, Office of

Corning Tower, 41st Fl
Empire State Plaza
Albany, NY 12242
518-474-3899 Fax: 518-474-1546
Web site: www.ogs.state.ny.us

633 Third Ave
New York, NY 10017
212-681-4580
Fax: 212-681-4558

Commissioner:
Daniel D Hogan 518-474-5991
e-mail: daniel.hogan@ogs.state.ny.us
First Deputy Commissioner:
Robert J Fleury 518-473-6953
e-mail: robert.fleury@ogs.state.ny.us
Special Asst to the Commissioner:
Nita Chicatelli 518-473-7345
Deputy Commissioner, Administration:
Charles E Stanley 518-474-7483

Deputy Commissioner, Design & Construction:
William F O'Connor, AIA 518-474-0335
Deputy Commissioner, Information Technology & Procurement Services:
Barrett Russell 518-473-3933
e-mail: barrett.russell@ogs.state.ny.us
Deputy Commissioner, Legal Services:
Richard Reed 518-474-5988/fax: 518-473-4973
Deputy Commissioner, Support Services:
John J Spano 518-474-5390
e-mail: john.spano@ogs.state.ny.us
Deputy Commissioner, Real Estate Planning & Development Group:
Bart Bush 518-473-8550
e-mail: bart.bush@ogs.state.ny.us
Assistant Commissioner, Public Affairs:
Jennifer L Morris 518-474-5987/fax: 518-474-3187
e-mail: jennifer.morris@ogs.state.ny.us

Health Department

Corning Tower
Empire State Plaza
Albany, NY 12237
518-474-7354
Web site: www.health.state.ny.us

Commissioner:
Antonia C Novello 518-474-2011
Executive Deputy Commissioner:
Dennis P Whalen 518-473-0458
Deputy Commissioner, Operations:
William Van Slyke 518-474-3384
Deputy Commissioner, Medicaid Management Office:
Kathryn Kuhmerker 518-474-3018/fax: 518-486-6852
Deputy Commissioner, Planning, Policy & Resource Development:
Judith Arnold 518-474-0180/fax: 518-474-3295
Assistant Commissioner, Governmental Affairs:
Martha McHugh 518-473-1124/fax: 518-473-9674
General Counsel:
Donald P Berens, Jr 518-474-7553/fax: 518-473-2802
Chief Counsel, Professional Medical Conduct:
Brian M Murphy 518-402-0855
Director, Executive & Advisory Council Operations:
Kelly Seebold 518-474-8009
Director, AIDS Institute:
Guthrie S Birkhead 518-473-7542/fax: 518-486-1455
Director, Center for Community Health:
Guthrie S Birkhead 518-474-5073/fax: 518-486-1455
Director, Center for Environmental Health:
Ronald Tramontano 518-402-7500/fax: 518-402-7509
Director, Health Facilities Management:
Donald Brown 518-474-2772/fax: 518-474-0611
Director, The Wadsworth Center:
Lawrence S Sturman 518-474-7592/fax: 518-474-3439
Director, Public Affairs Group:
Vacant 518-474-7354/fax: 518-473-7071

Housing & Community Renewal, Division of

Hampton Plaza
38-40 State St
Albany, NY 12207
866-275-3427
Web site: www.dhcr.state.ny.us

Offices and agencies appear in alphabetical order.

25 Beaver St
New York, NY 10004-2319
866-275-3427

Commissioner:
   Judith A Calogero 518-473-8384/fax: 518-473-9462
First Deputy Commissioner:
   Donald A Clarey 518-473-0632
Executive Assistant:
   Ellen DeVane 518-473-0632
General Counsel:
   Marcia P Hirsch 212-480-6709/fax: 212-480-6711
Deputy Commissioner, Administration:
   Mary Beth Labate 518-486-3370/fax: 518-473-9462
Deputy Commissioner, Community Development:
   Joan F Hoover 518-480-6446/fax: 518-480-7450
Deputy Commissioner, Housing Operations:
   David Cabrera 212-480-6440/fax: 212-480-7169
Deputy Commissioner, Policy & Intergovernmental Relations:
   Lorrie Pizzola 518-474-9553/fax: 518-473-9462
Deputy Commissioner, Rent Administration:
   Paul Roldan 718-262-4822/fax: 718-262-4008
Assistant Commissioner, Fair Housing & Equal Opportunity:
   Providence Baker 518-474-6157/fax: 518-473-3173
Director, Communications:
   Jennifer Farina 518-402-3728/fax: 518-474-5752
Press Secretary:
   Peter Moses 212-480-6732/fax: 212-480-6737

Hudson River Valley Greenway

Capitol Bldg, Rm 254
Albany, NY 12224
518-473-3835 Fax: 518-473-4518
e-mail: hrvg@hudsongreenway.state.ny.us
Web site: www.hudsongreenway.state.ny.us

Greenway Conservancy for the Hudson River Valley
Board Chair:
   Kevin J Plunkett 518-473-3835
Executive Director:
   Carmella R Mantello 518-473-3835

Hudson River Valley Greenway Communities Council
Board Chair:
   Barnabas McHenry 518-473-3835
Executive Director:
   Carmella R Mantello 518-473-3835

Human Rights, State Division of

1 Fordham Plaza
4th Fl
Bronx, NY 10458-5871
718-741-8400 Fax: 718-741-3214
Web site: www.nysdhr.com

Commissioner:
   Michelle Cheney Donaldson 718-741-8326
Executive Assistant to the Commissioner:
   Tammy Collins 718-741-8328
Executive Deputy Commissioner:
   Edward A Friedland 718-741-8330
General Counsel:
   Gina M Lopez-Summa 718-741-8398

Deputy Commissioner, Administration:
   Martha B Furlong 718-741-8358
Deputy Commissioner, Federal Programs:
   Edward A Watkins 718-741-8440
Deputy Commissioner, Regional Affairs:
   Michele Heitzner 718-741-8332
Deputy Commissioner, Public Affairs:
   Denise L Ellison 718-741-8459
   e-mail: dellison@dhr.state.ny.us

Inspector General (NYS), Office of the

61 Broadway, 12th Fl
New York, NY 10006
212-635-3150 Fax: 212-809-6287
Web site: www.ig.state.ny.us

Executive Chamber
State Capitol
Albany, NY 12224
518-474-1010
Fax: 518-486-3745

State Inspector General:
   Jill Konviser-Levine . . . . 212-635-3150 or 518-474-1010
   e-mail: inspector.general@ig.state.ny.us
First Deputy Inspector General:
   Michael Boxer 212-635-3150
Executive Deputy Inspector General/Special Counsel:
   Ralph A Rossi, III 518-474-1010
Director, Administration:
   Cindy Haskins 518-474-1010
Director, Communications:
   Stephen Del Giacco 518-474-1010
   e-mail: steve.delgiacco@ig.state.ny.us

Insurance Department

25 Beaver St
New York, NY 10004
212-480-6400
Web site: www.ins.state.ny.us

One Commerce Plaza
Albany, NY 12257
518-474-4567
Fax: 518-473-4600

Acting Superintendent:
   Howard Mills 518-474-4567
First Deputy Superintendent, Consumer Services, Fraud & Licensing:
   Louis W Pietroluongo 212-480-2306
Senior Deputy Superintendent:
   Peter J Molinaro 518-474-4567
Deputy Superintendent, Property:
   Joseph A DeMauro 212-480-2296
Director, Administration & Operations:
   Joseph J Burns 518-474-6848/fax: 518-486-6600
Deputy Superintendent & Chief Info Systems & Technology Bureau:
   Ronald Minafri 212-480-2332
Deputy Superintendent & General Counsel:
   Audrey M Samers 212-480-5259
Director, Public Affairs & Research:
   Michael Barry 212-480-5262/fax: 212-480-6077
   e-mail: public-affairs@ins.state.ny.us

Offices and agencies appear in alphabetical order.

Insurance Fund (NYS)

199 Church St
New York, NY 10007
888-875-5790
Web site: www.nysif.com

Executive Director/CEO:
Kenneth J Ross 212-312-7001
Deputy Executive Director & Marketing Director:
Ann F Formel 518-437-1879
Deputy Executive Director:
Christopher Barclay 518-437-5220
Deputy Executive Director:
Stephen D Nelson 518-437-6196
Special Assistant to Executive Director:
Kurt Rumpler 518-437-6196
Chief Fiscal Officer & Actuary:
Susan D Sharp 518-437-6168
Public Information Officer:
Robert Lawson 518-437-3504/fax: 518-437-1849
General Attorney:
Douglas J Hayden 212-342-7093
Special Counsel:
Jacob H Weintraub 212-312-7872
Assistant Director:
Jane Burgdorf 212-312-7001
Director, Administration:
Albert K Di Meglio 212-312-7020

Insurance Fund Board of Commissioners

Chair:
Terence L Morris 212-312-7001
Vice Chair:
Robert H Hurlbut 212-312-7001
Secretary to the Board:
Christopher Barclay 212-437-5220

Labor Department

Building 12, Room 500
State Campus
Albany, NY 12240
518-457-2741 Fax: 518-457-6908
e-mail: nysdol@labor.state.ny.us
Web site: www.labor.state.ny.us

345 Hudson St, Ste 8301
Box 662, Mail Stop 01
New York, NY 10014-0662
212-352-6000
Fax: 212-352-6824

Commissioner:
Linda Angello 518-457-2746
Executive Deputy Commissioner:
Dennis Ryan 518-457-4318
Counsel:
Jerome A Tracy 518-457-7069
Inspector General:
Brian Sanvidge 518-457-7012
Deputy Commissioner, Administration & Public Affairs:
Mary L Hines 518-457-3905
Deputy Commissioner, Labor & Planning Technology:
Michael Nevins 518-457-7994

Deputy Commissioner, Workforce Protection, Standards & Licensing:
Connie Varcasia 518-457-4317
Associate Commissioner, Human Resources:
James W Leary 518-457-9570
Director, Communications:
Robert Lillpopp 518-457-5519/fax: 518-485-1126

Law Department

State Capitol
Albany, NY 12224-0341
518-474-7330 Fax: 518-402-2472
Web site: www.oag.state.ny.us

120 Broadway
New York, NY 10271-0332
212-416-8000
Fax: 212-416-8942

Attorney General:
Eliot Spitzer 518-474-7330/fax: 518-402-2472
First Deputy Attorney General:
Michele Hirshman 212-416-8050
Assistant First Deputy Attorney General:
Francine James 212-416-8050
Chief of Staff:
Richard Baum 212-416-8050
Counsel to Attorney General:
David Nocenti 212-416-8050
Deputy Attorney General:
Beth L Golden 212-416-8050
Deputy Attorney General, Criminal Division:
Peter B Pope 212-416-8058/fax: 212-416-8026
Acting Deputy Attorney General, Public Advocacy Division:
Terryl Brown Clemens 212-416-8041/fax: 212-416-8068
Deputy Attorney General, Regional Offices:
Martin Mack 315-448-4880/fax: 315-448-4899
Deputy Attorney General, State Counsel Division:
Richard Rifkin 518-473-7190
Solicitor General, Appeals & Opinions:
Caitlin J Halligan 212-416-8069/fax: 212-416-8962
Director, Communications:
Darren Dopp 518-473-5525/fax: 518-473-9907
Director, Public Information & Correspondence:
Peter A Drago 518-474-7330/fax: 518-402-2472

Lottery, Division of

One Broadway Center
PO Box 7500
Schenectady, NY 12301-7500
518-388-3300 Fax: 518-388-3403
Web site: www.nylottery.org

Director:
Nancy A Palumbo 518-388-3400
Deputy Director:
Susan E Miller 518-388-3404
Director, Communications:
Jennifer Mauer 518-388-3415
General Counsel:
Robert J McLaughlin 518-388-3408
Director, Operations:
Joe Seeley 518-388-3411
Director, Financial Administration:
Gardner Gurney 518-388-3404

Offices and agencies appear in alphabetical order.

Director, Advertising:
  Michael Flanagan 518-388-3430
Director, Administration:
  Art DelSignore 518-388-3404
  e-mail: claverty@lottery.state.ny.us

Mental Health, Office of

44 Holland Ave
Albany, NY 12229
518-474-4403 Fax: 518-474-2149
Web site: www.omh.state.ny.us

Commissioner:
  Sharon E Carpinello 518-474-4403
Executive Deputy Commissioner:
  Barbara Cohn 518-474-7056
Deputy Commissioner & Counsel:
  John Tauriello. 518-474-1331
Chief Medical Office, Interim Director:
  Lewis Opler 518-476-4327
Deputy Commissioner, Investigation & Audit:
  Michael Dufresne 518-473-5940

Mental Retardation & Developmental Disabilities, Office of

44 Holland Avenue
Albany, NY 12229
518-474-6601 or TDD: 518-474-3964 Fax: 518-474-1335
Web site: www.omr.state.ny.us

Commissioner:
  Thomas A Maul 518-473-1997
Special Assistant to Commissioner:
  Tracy Durfee. 518-473-1997
Executive Deputy Commissioner:
  Helene DeSanto 518-474-8115
General Counsel:
  Paul R Kietzman. 518-474-7700
Deputy Commissioner, Administration & Revenue Support:
  James F Moran 518-473-2747
Deputy Commissioner, Quality Assurance:
  Jan Abelseth 518-474-3625
Associate Commissioner, NYC Regional Office:
  Kathleen M Broderick 212-229-3231/fax: 212-229-3234
Associate Commissioner, Upstate Support:
  Peter F Pezzolla 518-474-9897
Director, Public Affairs:
  Deborah Sturm Rausch. 518-474-6601

Military & Naval Affairs, Division of

330 Old Niskayuna Rd
Latham, NY 12110-2224
518-786-4500 Fax: 518-786-4325
Web site: www.dmna.state.ny.us

Adjutant General:
  Maj Gen Thomas P Maguire, Jr 518-786-4502
Deputy Adjutant General:
  Col F David Sheppard 518-786-4502
Inspector General, Federal:
  Col James D McDonough, Jr 518-786-4426
Legal Counsel:
  Robert G Conway, Jr 518-786-4541

Director, Government Affairs:
  Scott Hommel 518-786-4580
Director, Public Affairs:
  Kent Kisselbrack 518-786-4581/fax: 518-786-4649
  e-mail: kent.kisselbrack@ny.ngb.army.mil
Director, Resource Management:
  Robert A Martin 518-786-4513

Motor Vehicles Department

Swan Street Building 6
Empire State Plaza
Albany, NY 12228
518-474-0841 or 800-225-5368
Web site: www.nysdmv.com

Commissioner:
  Raymond P Martinez. 518-474-0841/fax: 518-474-0712
  e-mail: rpmart@dmv.state.ny.us
Executive Deputy Commissioner:
  Renato Donato 518-474-0846/fax: 518-474-0712
Deputy Commissioner, Administration:
  Gregory J Kline 518-474-6876
Deputy Commissioner, Counsel:
  Jill A Dunn 518-474-1003
Deputy Commissioner, Operations & Customer Service:
  John C Hilliard 518-473-5127
Deputy Commissioner, Safety, Consumer Protection & Clean Air:
  Donald F Savage. 518-402-4860
Executive Director, Traffic Safety:
  Kenneth H Carpenter 518-474-5111
Assistant Commissioner, Traffic Safety:
  Vacant 518-474-0972
Director, Driver Program Regulation:
  Barbara Askham 518-486-5572
Director, Driver Program Regulation:
  Kevin P O'Brien 518-474-0855
Associate Commissioner, Communications:
  Joe Picchi. 518-473-7000/fax: 518-473-1930
  e-mail: jpicc@dmv.state.ny.us

Parks, Recreation & Historic Preservation, NYS Office of

Empire State Plaza
Bldg 1
Albany, NY 12238
518-486-1868 Fax: 518-486-2924
Web site: www.nysparks.com

Commissioner:
  Bernadette Castro 518-474-0443
Executive Deputy Commissioner:
  Christopher Pushkarsh 518-473-5385
Deputy Commissioner, Hudson Valley Operations:
  James F Moogan. 518-474-0440
Deputy Commissioner, Upstate Operations:
  Dominic Jacangelo 518-474-0402
Chief Counsel:
  Paul Laudato. 518-474-0430
Assistant Commissioner, Public Affairs:
  Wendy Gibson 518-486-1868

Offices and agencies appear in alphabetical order.

Parole, Division of

97 Central Ave
Albany, NY 12206
518-473-9400 Fax: 518-473-6037
e-mail: nysparole@parole.state.ny.us
Web site: parole.state.ny.us

314 W 40th St
New York, NY 10018
212-239-6000
Fax: 212-239-6160

Executive Director:
 Anthony G Ellis, II 518-473-9672
Chief Counsel:
 Terrence X Tracy. 518-473-5671/fax: 518-473-9760
Chair, Parole Board:
 Robert Dennison. 518-473-9548
Public Information Offficer:
 Scott E Steinhardt 518-486-4631/fax: 518-473-6037
Secretary to the Chair:
 Felix M Rosa 518-473-5424
Director, Administrative Services:
 Steven H Philbrick 518-473-9531
Director, Operations:
 Angela Jiminez. 518-473-5421
Director, Strategic Planning:
 Mary Ellen Flynn 518-473-5766

Prevention of Domestic Violence, Office for the

80 Wolf Rd
Ste 406
Albany, NY 12205
518-457-5800 Fax: 518-485-5140
Web site: www.opdv.state.ny.us

Executive Director:
 Sherry Frohman 518-457-5800
General Counsel & Agency Affairs:
 Wendy Jaracka-Maher 518-457-5800
Director, Training & Policy Development Unit:
 Gwen Wright 518-457-5916
Administrative Officer:
 Linda Cassidy. 518-457-7995
Public Information Officer:
 Suzanne Cecala. 518-457-5744
  e-mail: suzanne.cecala@opdv.state.ny.us

Probation & Correctional Alternatives, Division of

80 Wolf Rd
Ste 501
Albany, NY 12205
518-485-7692 Fax: 518-485-5140
Web site: www.dpca.state.ny.us

State Director:
 Sara Tullar Fasoldt 518-485-7692
Secretary to the Director:
 Barbara J Flanigan 518-485-7692
Executive Deputy Director:
 Robert Maccarone 518-485-7692

General Counsel:
 Linda Valenti 518-485-2394
Administrative Officer:
 Howard Bancroft 518-485-5145/fax: 518-485-2401

Public Employment Relations Board

80 Wolf Rd
Albany, NY 12205
518-457-2854 Fax: 518-457-2664
Web site: www.perb.state.ny.us

Chair:
 Michael R Cuevas. 518-457-2578
Member:
 Vacant 518-457-2578
Member:
 John T Mitchell. 518-457-2578
Executive Director:
 James R Edgar 518-457-2676
Deputy Chair & Counsel:
 Robert A DePaula. 518-457-2614
Secretary to the Board:
 Sheila Talavera. 518-457-2578
Director, Conciliation:
 Richard A Curreri. 518-457-2690
Director, Employment Practices & Representation:
 Monte Klein 518-457-5973

Public Service Department

Three Empire State Plaza
Albany, NY 12223-1350
518-474-7080 Fax: 518-474-2838
Web site: www.dps.state.ny.us

90 Church St
New York, NY 10007-2919
212-417-2378

295 Main St
Buffalo, NY 14203
716-847-3400

Commissioner:
 Thomas J Dunleavy. 212-290-4416/fax: 212-290-4362
Commissioner:
 Neal N Galvin 518-474-2503/fax: 518-473-2838
Commissioner:
 Leonard A Weiss. 518-474-2503/fax: 518-473-2838
Executive Deputy:
 Paul Powers 518-473-4544/fax: 518-473-2838
General Counsel:
 Dawn Jablonski Ryman. 518-474-2510/fax: 518-486-5710
Director, Retail Market Development:
 Ronald Cerniglia 518-474-1540/fax: 518-473-5685
  e-mail: ormd@dps.state.ny.us
Director, Consumer Services Office:
 Sandra Sloane 518-474-3280/fax: 518-486-7868
  e-mail: csd@dps.state.ny.us
Director, Electricity & Environment Office:
 James Gallagher. 518-473-7248/fax: 518-486-1672
Director, Gas & Water Office:
 Thomas Dvorsky 518-473-6080/fax: 518-473-4992
Director, Office of Administration:
 Debra Renner. 518-474-2508/fax: 518-474-0413

Offices and agencies appear in alphabetical order.

Director, Public Affairs:
  David C Flanagan 518-474-7080/fax: 518-473-2838
Director, Telecommunications:
  Robert H Mayer. 518-474-1668/fax: 518-474-5616
Chair, Public Service Commission:
  William M Flynn. 518-474-2523/fax: 518-473-2838
Secretary to the Commission:
  Jaclyn A Brilling 518-474-6530/fax: 518-486-6081
  e-mail: secretary@dps.state.ny.us

Racing & Wagering Board
1 Watervliet Ave Ext
Ste 2
Albany, NY 12206-1668
518-453-8460 Fax: 518-453-8867
e-mail: info@racing.state.ny.us
Web site: www.racing.state.ny.us

Chair:
  Michael J Hoblock, Jr. 518-453-8460
Member:
  Cheryl Ritchko-Buley. 518-453-8460
Executive Director:
  Edward J Martin 518-453-8460
Counsel:
  Robert A Feuerstein 212-290-4401
Secretary to the Board:
  Erin E Dahlmeyer. 518-453-8460
Public Information Officer:
  Stacy Clifford 518-453-8640 x3311/fax: 518-453-8867

Real Property Services, Office of
16 Sheridan Ave
Albany, NY 12210-2714
518-486-5446 Fax: 518-474-9276
Web site: www.orps.state.ny.us

Chair, State Board of Real Property Services:
  Ifigenia Brown 518-474-5711
Executive Director, Board Secretary:
  Thomas G Griffen. 518-474-5711
  e-mail: thomas.griffen@orps.state.ny.us
Executive Deputy Director:
  Thomas Bellard 518-473-6914
  e-mail: tom.bellard@orps.state.ny.us
Chief Appraiser:
  Jeff Jordan 518-474-2854
  e-mail: jeff.jordan@orps.state.ny.us
Counsel:
  Richard J Sinnott 518-474-6753
  e-mail: richard.sinnott@orps.state.ny.us
Director, Public Information:
  Geoffrey T Gloak 518-486-5446
  e-mail: geoffrey.gloak@orps.state.ny.us

Regulatory Reform, Governor's Office of
Agency Bldg 1, 4th Fl
Empire State Plaza, PO Box 2107
Albany, NY 12220-0107
518-486-3292 Fax: 518-473-9342
Web site: www.gorr.state.ny.us

Acting Director:
  David S Bradley 518-473-8197
Deputy Director:
  David S Bradley 518-473-8197
Counsel:
  Amelia Stern. 518-473-0620
Public Information Officer:
  David Pietrusza. 518-486-3292
Director, Administration:
  Sandra L Curry 518-473-8197

Science, Technology & Academic Research, Office of
30 South Pearl St
11th Fl
Albany, NY 12207
518-292-5700 Fax: 518-292-5780
Web site: www.nystar.state.ny.us

Executive Director:
  Russell W Besette. 518-292-5700
Director, Operations:
  James A Denn 518-292-5700/fax: 518-292-5798
Director, Programs:
  Kathleen J Wise 518-292-5700
Director, Finance:
  Edward J Hamilton. 518-292-5700
General Counsel:
  Robert Beshaw 518-292-5700
Director, Public Information:
  James A Denn 518-292-5700/fax: 518-292-5780
  e-mail: jdenn@nystar.state.ny.us

Small Cities, Governor's Office for
Agency Building 4, 6th Fl
Empire State Plaza
Albany, NY 12223
518-474-2057 Fax: 518-474-5247
Web site: www.nysmallcities.com

Director:
  Glen King 518-474-2057
Associate Counsel:
  Brian McCartney 518-474-2057
First Deputy Director:
  Albert J Jurezynski. 518-474-2057
Deputy Director:
  Kenneth J Flood 518-474-2057
Public Information Officer:
  Tracey McNerney. 518-474-2057
  e-mail: tmcnerney@nyssmallcities.com

State Comptroller, Office of the
110 State St, 15th Fl
Albany, NY 12236-0001
518-474-4040 Fax: 518-473-3004
Web site: www.osc.state.ny.us

633 Third Ave, 31st Fl
New York, NY 10017-6754
212-681-4491
Fax: 212-681-4468

Offices and agencies appear in alphabetical order.

State Comptroller:
Alan G Hevesi . . . . 518-474-4040 or 212-681-4491
Chief of Staff:
Jack Chartier 212-681-4498
First Deputy Comptroller:
Thomas Sanzillo 518-473-4333
Executive Deputy:
Diana Jones Ritter 518-474-3610
Deputy Chief of Staff:
Dalia Schapiro 212-681-4540
Director, Correspondence Unit:
Ellen J Evans 518-473-1323
Deputy Comptroller, Office of Budget & Policy Analysis:
Kim Fine 518-473-4333
Deputy Comptroller, Division of Investigations:
Robert Brackman . . . . 212-681-4474 or 518-402-4926
Deputy Comptroller, Division of Intergovernmental Affairs & Community Relations:
Myrna Santiago 212-383-2662
State Deputy Comptroller for New York City:
Kenneth Bleiwas 212-383-3900
Counsel:
Alan Lebowitz . . . . 518-474-3444 or 212-681-6069
Deputy Comptroller, Administration:
Harris Lirtzman 518-402-4884
Deputy Comptroller, Local Government Services & Economic Development Division:
Mark P Pattison 518-474-4037
Deputy Comptroller, Payroll & Revenue Services:
Daniel Berry 518-408-4149
Deputy Comptroller, Pension Investment & Public Finance:
David Loglisci 518-474-4003
Deputy Comptroller, Retirement Services:
Laura Anglin 518-474-2600
Deputy Comptroller, State Audit Group:
Lynn Canton 518-474-5598
Director, Communications:
David Neustadt 518-474-4015/fax: 518-473-8940
e-mail: dneustadt@osc.state.ny.us
Chief Information Officer:
Jeffrey Grunwald 518-473-3004
Press Secretary:
Jeffrey Gordon 518-474-4015
e-mail: jgordon@osc.state.ny.us

State Department
123 William St
New York, NY 10038
212-417-5801 Fax: 212-417-5805
Web site: www.dos.state.ny.us

41 State St
Albany, NY 12231
518-474-0050
Fax: 518-474-4765

Secretary of State:
Randy A Daniels 518-474-0050
First Deputy Secretary of State:
Frank P Milano 518-474-0050
Counsel:
Glen Bruening 518-474-6740/fax: 518-473-9211
Deputy Secretary of State, Public Affairs:
Eamon Moynihan 212-417-5800

Deputy Secretary of State, Business & Licensing Services Division:
Keith W Stack 518-474-4429/fax: 518-473-6648
e-mail: licensing@dos.state.ny.us
Deputy Secretary of State, Local Government & Community Services:
Matthew Andrus 518-486-9888/fax: 518-474-6572
Assistant Secretary of State for Communications:
Lawrence Sombke 518-474-4752/fax: 518-474-4597
e-mail: info@dos.state.ny.us

State Police, Division of
Bldg 22, State Campus
1220 Washington Ave
Albany, NY 12226-2252
518-457-6811 Fax: 518-457-3207
Web site: www.troopers.state.ny.us

Superintendent:
Wayne E Bennett 518-457-6721
First Deputy Superintendent:
Preston L Felton 518-457-6711/fax: 518-485-7505
Counsel:
Glenn P Valle 518-457-6137/fax: 518-485-1164
Deputy Superintendent, Administration:
David L Christler 518-457-6621/fax: 518-485-5051
Deputy Superintendent, Employee Relations:
Deborah J Campbell 518-457-3572/fax: 518-485-7505
Deputy Superintendent, Field Command:
William DeBlock 518-457-5936/fax: 518-457-4779
Deputy Superintendent, Internal Affairs:
Harry J Corbitt 518-485-6018/fax: 518-485-1493
Technical Lieutenant, Public Information:
Glenn R Miner 518-457-2180/fax: 518-485-7818
Crime Prevention Coordinator:
Sgt Kern Fwoboda 518-457-2180/fax: 518-485-7818

Tax Appeals, Division of
Riverfront Professional Tower
500 Federal St, 4th & 5th Fl
Troy, NY 12180
518-266-3000 Fax: 518-271-0886
Web site: www.nysdta.org

Administrative Law Judges & Officers
Chief Administrative Law Judge:
Andrew Marchese 518-266-3000
Assistant Chief Administrative Law Judge:
Daniel Ranalli 518-266-3000
Secretary & Administrative Officer:
Robert P Rivers . . . . 518-266-3036 or 518-266-3062

Tax Appeals Tribunal
President:
Donald C Dewitt 518-266-3050
Commissioner:
Caroll Jenkins 518-266-3051
Counsel:
Donna M Gardiner 518-266-3052

Taxation & Finance Department
State Campus
Bldg 9
Albany, NY 12227

Offices and agencies appear in alphabetical order.

518-457-4242 Fax: 518-457-2486
Web site: www.tax.state.ny.us

Commissioner:
Andrew S Eristoff 518-457-2244
Executive Deputy Commissioner:
Barbara G Billet 518-457-7358
Deputy Commissioner & Counsel:
Christopher C O'Brien 518-457-3746/fax: 518-457-8247
Deputy Commissioner & Treasurer:
Aida Brewer. 518-474-4250/fax: 518-402-4118
Deputy Commissioner, Tax Enforcement:
Peter Farrell 518-457-9693
Deputy Commissioner, Tax Operations:
Robert Gola 518-485-2863
Deputy Commissioner, Tax Policy Analysis:
Michelle A Cummings 518-457-4357
Chief Financial Officer:
Robert F Tangorre 518-457-4261
Director, Communications:
Thomas Bergin 518-457-4242

Temporary & Disability Assistance, Office of

40 N Pearl St
Albany, NY 12243
518-474-9003 Fax: 518-474-7870
e-mail: nyspio@dfa.state.ny.us
Web site: www.otda.state.ny.us

Commissioner:
Robert Doar. 518-474-4152/fax: 518-486-6255
Deputy Commissioner, Child Support Enforcement:
Margot Bean. 518-474-9081
Deputy Commissioner, Disability Determinations:
David Avenius 518-473-0070
Director, Budget Management & Finance:
Mike Normile 518-474-0183
Deputy Commissioner, Program Support & Quality Improvement:
Mary Meister 518-473-3912
Deputy Commissioner, Information Technology:
Robert Mastro. 518-473-7858
Deputy Commissioner, Temporary Assistance:
Russell Sykes 518-474-9222
Legal/Acting General Counsel:
John Bailly 518-474-9502
Director, Office of Intergovernmental & External Affairs:
Lisa Irving 518-474-7420
Assistant Commissioner, Public Information:
John B Madden 518-474-9516/fax: 518-486-6935
e-mail: nyspio@dfa.state.ny.us

Transportation Department

1220 Washington Ave
Albany, NY 12232
518-457-5100 Fax: 518-457-5583
Web site: www.dot.state.ny.us

Commissioner:
Joseph H Boardman 518-457-4422
e-mail: jboardman@dot.state.ny.us
First Deputy Commissioner:
Brian O Rowback 518-457-4422
Assistant Commissioner, Budget & Finance Office:
Lawrence M Knapek 518-457-2226

Deputy Commissioner & Chief Engineer:
Paul T Wells 518-457-4430
Assistant Commissioner, Human Resources Office:
Lisa Wright. 518-457-6300
Acting Assistant Commissioner & Chief Counsel:
Peter Loomis. 518-457-7097
Assistant Commissioner, Operations Office:
Clifford A Thomas 518-457-7475
Asst Commissioner, Passenger & Freight Transportation Office:
John F Guinan. 518-457-2320
Director, Resource & Risk Management Bureau:
Richard D Albertin 518-485-8236
Director, Public Affairs:
Jennifer Post 518-457-6400/fax: 518-457-6506
e-mail: jpost@dot.state.ny.us

Veterans' Affairs, Division of

5 Empire State Plaza
Ste 2836
Albany, NY 12223
518-474-6114 Fax: 518-473-0379
Web site: www.veterans.state.ny.us

Director:
George P Basher. 518-474-6114
Executive Deputy Director:
Harvey J McCagg. 518-474-6784
Counsel:
William J Brennan 518-474-6114

Welfare Inspector General, Office of NYS

22 Cortland St
11th Fl
New York, NY 10007
212-417-5822 Fax: 212-417-5849

40 No Pearl St, Sect 10B
Albany, NY 12224
518-474-9636
Fax: 518-486-6148

Inspector General:
Paul Balukas. 212-417-5840
Deputy Inspector General:
Pasqualino Russo 212-417-5860
Counsel:
Andrew J Weiss 212-417-2395
Chief Investigator:
Joseph R Bucci. 212-417-2026

Workers' Compensation Board

20 Park Street
Albany, NY 12207
518-474-6670 Fax: 518-473-1415
Web site: www.wcb.state.ny.us

Chair, Board of Commissioners:
David Wehner. 518-474-6670
Vice Chair:
Jeffrey R Sweet. 518-474-6670
Secretary to the Board:
Susan M Olson 518-402-6071

Offices and agencies appear in alphabetical order.

Executive Director:
 Richard A Bell 518-474-6670
Deputy Executive Director, Adminstration:
 Glenn Warren 518-473-8900/fax: 518-486-6411
Deputy Executive Director, Operations:
 Marsha Orndorff 518-486-7143/fax: 518-474-9367
Deputy Executive Director, Systems Modernization:
 Nancy Mulholland 518-486-7143/fax: 518-474-9367

General Counsel:
 Vacant 518-486-9564/fax: 518-473-2233
Director, Public Information:
 Jon A Sullivan 518-474-6670/fax: 518-473-1415
Advocate for Injured Workers:
 Edwin Ruff 800-580-6665/fax: 518-486-7510
Fraud Inspector General:
 John Burgher 888-363-6001/fax: 518-402-1059

Offices and agencies appear in alphabetical order.

LEGISLATIVE BRANCH SENATE

Members of the Senate welcome e-mail correspondence from the public. They may reply by e-mail, or by mail when more extensive follow-up is necessary. Please include both an e-mail and mailing address in all correspondence. Biographies of Legislative Branch Senate and Assembly Members appear in a separate section in the back of the book.

State Senate Leadership

State Capitol
Albany, NY 12247
Web site: www.senate.state.ny.us

Majority Leadership

Joseph L Bruno (R) 518-455-3191
e-mail: bruno@senate.state.ny.us
Title: President Pro Tempore & Majority Leader

Owen H Johnson (R) 518-455-3411
e-mail: ojohnson@senate.state.ny.us
Title: Chair of Senate Finance Committee

Frank Padavan (R) 518-455-3381
e-mail: padavan@senate.state.ny.us
Title: Vice President Pro Tempore

Dean G Skelos (R) 518-455-3171
e-mail: skelos@senate.state.ny.us
Title: Deputy Majority Leader for Legislative Operations

Nicholas A Spano (R) 518-455-2231
e-mail: spano@senate.state.ny.us
Title: Senior Asst Majority Leader/Liaison to the Executive Branch

John J Marchi (R) 518-455-3215
e-mail: marchi@senate.state.ny.us
Title: Assistant Majority Leader on Conference Operations

Thomas W Libous (R) 518-455-2677
e-mail: senator@senatorlibous.com
Title: Assistant Majority Leader for House Operations

Kenneth P LaValle (R) 518-455-3121
e-mail: lavalle@senate.state.ny.us
Title: Chair of Majority Conference

Caesar Trunzo (R) 518-455-2111
e-mail: trunzo@senate.state.ny.us
Title: Chair of Majority Program Development Committee

Hugh T Farley (R) 518-455-2181
e-mail: farley@senate.state.ny.us
Title: Majority Whip

Dale M Volker (R) 518-455-3471
e-mail: volker@senate.state.ny.us
Title: Vice Chair of Majority Conference

James L Seward (R) 518-455-3131
e-mail: seward@senate.state.ny.us
Title: Secretary of Majority Conference

Serphin R Maltese (R) 518-455-3281
e-mail: maltese@senate.state.ny.us
Title: Deputy Majority Whip

William J Larkin, Jr (R) 518-455-2770
e-mail: larkin@senate.state.ny.us
Title: Chair of Majority Steering Committee

Kemp Hannon (R) 518-455-2200
e-mail: hannon@senate.state.ny.us
Title: Assistant Majority Whip

Stephen M Saland (R) 518-455-2411
e-mail: saland@senate.state.ny.us
Title: Deputy Majority Leader for State/Federal Relations

John DeFrancisco (R) 518-455-3511
e-mail: defrancisco@senate.state.ny.us
Title: Deputy Majority Leader for Intergovernmental Affairs

James W Wright (R) 518-455-2346
e-mail: wright@senate.state.ny.us
Title: Deputy Majority Leader for Policy

Majority Staff

Kenneth E Riddett 518-455-2675/fax: 518-426-6830
Title: Counsel to the Majority

Francis J Gluchowski 518-455-2563/fax: 518-426-2265
Title: Legislative Counsel to the Majority

Richard Burdick 518-455-2381/fax: 518-426-6818
Title: Director, Majority District Operations

Robert J Hess 518-455-2591/fax: 518-426-6979
Title: Bill Clerk

Offices and agencies appear in alphabetical order.

Peter L Rupert................... 518-455-2578/fax: 518-426-6803
Title: Home Rule Counsel

Louise Guiliano................... 518-455-2595/fax: 518-426-6996
Title: Special Projects Coordinator

Janet L Reilly.................... 518-455-2589/fax: 518-426-6815
Title: Majority Calendar Clerk

Laurie Axenfeld-Lankford 202-624-5880
e-mail: axenfeld@senate.state.ny.us
Title: Federal Liaison (Washington)

Mary Louise Mallick............. 518-455-3198/fax: 518-426-6958
Title: Secretary to the Finance Committee

Robert Mujica.................. 518-455-2880/fax: 518-426-6836
Title: Director, Majority Budget Studies

Magaret Law 518-455-2567/fax: 518-426-6936
Title: Director, Majority Correspondence

Robert Hotz 518-455-2741/fax: 518-426-6932
Title: Director, Majority Fiscal Studies

John E McArdle 518-455-2264/fax: 518-455-2260
Title: Director, Majority Communications

Linda Marano 518-455-3541/fax: 518-426-6917
Title: Director, Majority Media Services

Edward S Lurie................. 518-455-2550/fax: 518-426-6835
Title: Director, Majority Member Services

Matthew Walter 518-455-2264/fax: 518-455-2448
Title: Assistant Majority Press Secretary

Minority Leadership

David A Paterson (D)........................... 518-455-2701
e-mail: paterson@senate.state.ny.us
Title: Minority Leader

Eric T Schneiderman (D)...................... 518-455-2041
e-mail: schneide@senate.state.ny.us
Title: Deputy Minority Leader

Neil D Breslin (D) 518-455-2225
e-mail: breslin@senate.state.ny.us
Title: Ranking Minority Member of Senate Finance Committee

Martin M Dilan (D) 518-455-2177
e-mail: dilan@senate.state.ny.us
Title: Assistant Minority Leader for Conference Operations

Ada L Smith (D) 518-455-3531
e-mail: smith@senate.state.ny.us
Title: Assistant Minority Leader for Policy & Administration

Velmanette Montgomery (D) 518-455-3451
e-mail: montgome@senate.state.ny.us
Title: Assistant Minority Leader for Floor Operations

Byron W Brown (D)............................ 518-455-3371
e-mail: bbrown@senate.state.ny.us
Title: Assistant Minority Leader for Intergovernmental Affairs

Efrain Gonzalez, Jr (D)........................ 518-455-3395
e-mail: gonzalez@senate.state.ny.us
Title: Chair of Minority Conference

George Onorato (D) 518-455-3486
e-mail: onorato@senate.state.ny.us
Title: Vice Chair of Minority Conference

Carl Kruger (D)............................... 518-455-2460
e-mail: kruger@senate.state.ny.us
Title: Secretary of Minority Conference

Carl Andrews (D) 518-455-2431
e-mail: andrews@senate.state.ny.us
Title: Minority Whip

Suzi Oppenheimer (D).......................... 518-455-2031
e-mail: oppenhei@senate.state.ny.us
Title: Deputy Minority Whip

Toby Ann Stavisky (D) 518-455-3461
e-mail: stavisky@senate.state.ny.us
Title: Assistant Minority Whip

Ruth Hassell-Thompson (D) 518-455-2061
e-mail: hassellt@senate.state.ny.us
Title: Chair of Minority Policy Committee

Liz Krueger (D) 518-455-2297
e-mail: lkrueger@senate.state.ny.us
Title: Chair of Minority Program Development

Minority Staff

Michael Jones-Bey............... 518-455-2071/fax: 518-426-6933
Title: Chief of Staff to the Minority Leader

Francisco Moya.................. 518-455-2701/fax: 518-455-6933
Title: Secretary to the Minority Leader

Edward Wasserman 518-455-3401/fax: 518-426-6844
Title: Counsel to the Minority

Mary K Berger 518-455-2636/fax: 518-455-2816
Title: Director, Minority Operations

Michael Weber 518-455-2641/fax: 518-426-6839
Title: Secretary to Minority Finance Committee

Mamadou Ahmed Diomande...... 518-558-2641/fax: 518-426-6839
Title: Director, Minority Budget Studies

Offices and agencies appear in alphabetical order.

Jannette Rondo 518-455-2948/fax: 518-426-6839
Title: Director, Public Affairs

Maureen McCandless 518-455-2966/fax: 518-426-3980
Title: Director, Minority Policy Development

Valerie Berlin 518-455-2701/fax: 518-426-6933
Title: Director, Communications to the Minority

David Johnson 518-455-2701/fax: 212-678-0001
Title: Director, Minority Special Projects

Paul Burns 518-455-2551/fax: 518-426-6845
Title: Director, Minority Bill Operations

Tracey Pierce-Smith 518-455-2501/fax: 518-426-6930
Title: Director, Minority Conference Services

Vincent Lonergan 202-624-7853/fax: 202-624-8448
Title: Director, Minority Federal Relations Office (Washington)

Mitzi Hart 518-455-2953/fax: 518-426-6845
Title: Minority Calendar Coordinator

James Plastiras 518-455-2415/fax: 518-426-6933
Title: Secretary to the Press Office

Senate Administration

Steven M Boggess 518-455-2051/fax: 518-455-3332
Title: Secretary of the Senate

Gail M Skelos 518-455-2201/fax: 518-426-6978
Title: Director, Appointments Office

General Information . . . . 800-342-9860 or 518-
Title: Bill Status Hotline

Chris J Cook 518-455-2318/fax: 518-426-6841
Title: Director, Document Room

Thomas A Testo 518-455-2245/fax: 518-426-6842
Title: Journal Clerk

Paul Graffeo 518-455-3216/fax: 518-426-6813
Title: Supervisor, Legislative Assistance & Services

Ellen Breslin 518-455-2468/fax: 518-426-6901
Title: Legislative Librarian, Legislative Library

James Giliberto 518-455-2468/fax: 518-426-6901
Title: Legislative Librarian, Legislative Library

Ed Stahr 518-455-2558/fax: 518-426-6911
Title: Director, Constituent Relations

Rosemary Vogt 518-455-2173/fax: 518-455-3552
Title: Director, Senate Research Services

William C Martin 518-455-2338/fax: 518-455-3332
Title: Sergeant-at-Arms

James A Utermark 518-455-2611/fax: 518-432-5470
Title: Director, Student Programs Office

Tracy Starr 518-455-3145/fax: 518-426-6831
Title: District Office Coordinator

Edward S Lurie 518-455-2550/fax: 518-426-6835
Title: Director, Legislative Services

Frank W Patience 518-455-3376/fax: 518-426-6927
Title: Personnel Officer

James Bell 518-455-2313/fax: 518-455-7339
Title: Director, Technology Services

State Senate Roster

Multiple party abbreviations following the names of legislators indicate that those legislators ran as the Senate candidate for each identified party. Source: NYS Board of Elections. Party abbreviations: Conservative (C), Democrat (D), Green (G), Independent (I), Liberal (L), Republican (R), Working Families (WF)

James S Alesi (R-C) 518-455-2015/fax: 518-426-6968
District: 55   *Room:* 905 LOB   *e-mail:* alesi@senate.state.ny.us
Committees: Banks; Commerce, Economic Development & Small Business (Chair); Crime Victims, Crime and Correction; Energy & Telecommunications; Higher Education; Insurance; Labor; Tourism, Recreation and Sports Development
Senior Staff: Melissa Pugliese

Carl Andrews (D-I-L-WF) 518-455-2431/fax: 518-426-6856
District: 20   *Room:* 413 LOB   *e-mail:* andrews@senate.state.ny.us
Title: Minority Whip
Committees: Banks; Civil Service & Pensions (Ranking Minority Member); Commerce, Economic Development & Small Business; Energy & Telecommunications; Health; Insurance; Judiciary
Senior Staff: Wendy Rost

Michael A L Balboni (R-I-C) 518-455-2471/fax: 518-426-6817
District: 7   *Room:* 803 LOB   *e-mail:* balboni@senate.state.ny.us
Committees: Aging; Environmental Conservation; Higher Education; Insurance; Judiciary; Labor
Senior Staff: James M Sherry

Offices and agencies appear in alphabetical order.

John J Bonacic (R-C) 518-455-3181/fax: 518-426-6948
District: 42   *Room:* 815 LOB   *e-mail:* bonacic@senate.state.ny.us
Committees: Banks; Codes; Commerce, Economic Development & Small
Business; Judiciary; Labor; Local Government
Senior Staff: Langdon Chapman

Neil D Breslin (D-I-L-WF) 518-455-2225/fax: 518-426-6807
District: 46   *Room:* 414 CAP   *e-mail:* breslin@senate.state.ny.us
Committees: Agriculture; Banks; Codes; Finance (Ranking Minority
Member); Insurance (Ranking Minority Member); Judiciary; Labor
Senior Staff: Jim Clancy

Byron W Brown (D-L) 518-455-3371/fax: 518-426-6969
District: 60   *Room:* 615 LOB   *e-mail:* bbrown@senate.state.ny.us
Title: Assistant Minority Leader for Intergovernmental Affairs
Committees: Aging; Cities (Ranking Minority Member); Commerce,
Economic Development & Small Business; Finance; Higher Education;
Labor; Tourism, Recreation & Sports Development (Ranking Minority
Member)
Senior Staff: Steven M Casey

Joseph L Bruno (R-I-C) 518-455-3191/fax: 518-455-2448
District: 43   *Room:* 909 LOB   *e-mail:* bruno@senate.state.ny.us
Title: President Pro Tempore & Majority Leader; ex officio member of all
committees
Committees: Rules (Chair)
Senior Staff: Rick Burdick

Martin Connor (D-L-WF) 518-455-2625/fax: 518-426-6956
District: 25   *Room:* 408 LOB   *e-mail:* connor@senate.state.ny.us
Committees: Elections; Judiciary; Local Government (Ranking Minority
Member); Mental Health & Developmental Disabilities; Tourism, Recreation
& Sports Development; Veterans, Homeland Security & Military Affairs
Executive Assistant: Charlene Gilooly

John A DeFrancisco (R-I-C) 518-455-3511/fax: 518-426-6952
District: 50   *Room:* 307 LOB   *e-mail:* jdefranc@senate.state.ny.us
Title: Deputy Majority Leader, Intergovernmental Affairs
Committees: Banks; Codes; Energy & Telecommunications; Finance; Health;
Tourism, Recreation & Sports Development
Senior Staff: Carole Luther

Ruben Diaz, Sr. (D) 518-455-2511/fax: 518-426-6945
District: 32   *Room:* 304 LOB   *e-mail:* diaz@senate.state.ny.us
Committees: Aging; Children & Families; Crime Victims, Crime &
Correction; Higher Education; Mental Health & Developmental Disabilities;
Social Services; Veterans, Homeland Security & Military Affairs
Senior Staff: Kelli Herndon

Martin M Dilan (D) 518-455-2177/fax: 518-426-6947
District: 17   *Room:* 606 LOB   *e-mail:* dilan@senate.state.ny.us
Title: Assistant Minority Leader for Conference Operations
Committees: Banks; Civil Service & Pensions; Education; Elections (Ranking
Minority Member); Finance; Judiciary; Transportation
Senior Staff: Lorenda Harris

Thomas K Duane (D-L-WF) 518-455-2451/fax: 518-426-6846
District: 29   *Room:* 711B LOB   *e-mail:* duane@senate.state.ny.us
Committees: Civil Service & Pensions; Codes (Ranking Minority Member);
Crime Victims, Crime & Correction (Ranking Minority Member); Finance;
Health; Judiciary; Rules
Senior Staff: Mark Furnish

Hugh T Farley (R-C-I) 518-455-2181/fax: 518-455-2271
District: 44   *Room:* 412 LOB   *e-mail:* farley@senate.state.ny.us
Title: Majority Whip
Committees: Aging; Banks (Chair); Codes; Ethics; Finance; Health;
Judiciary; Rules
Senior Staff: David Smigler

John J Flanagan (R-I-C) 518-455-2071/fax: 518-426-6904
District: 2   *Room:* 817 LOB   *e-mail:* flanagan@senate.state.ny.us
Committees: Aging; Elections (Chair); Higher Education; Insurance; Labor;
Transportation; Veterans, Homeland Security & Military Affairs
Senior Staff: Raymond Bennardo

Charles J Fuschillo, Jr (R-I-C) 518-455-3341/fax: 518-426-6823
District: 8   *Room:* 947 LOB   *e-mail:* fuschill@senate.state.ny.us
Committees: Civil Service & Pensions; Commerce, Economic Development
& Small Business; Consumer Protection (Chair); Education; Health; Labor;
Transportation
Senior Staff: Barbara Lee Steigerwald

Martin J Golden (R-C) 518-455-2730/fax: 518-426-6910
District: 22   *Room:* 946 LOB   *e-mail:* golden@senate.state.ny.us
Committees: Aging (Chair); Cities; Codes; Crime Victims, Crime &
Correction; Education; Investigations & Government; Taxation &
Government Operations; Tourism, Recreation & Sports Development;
Veterans, Homeland Security & Military Affairs
Senior Staff: Walter A Pacholczak

Efrain Gonzalez, Jr (D) 518-455-3395/fax: 518-426-6858
District: 33   *Room:* 420 CAP   *e-mail:* gonzalez@senate.state.ny.us
Title: Chair, Minority Conference
Committees: Banks; Commerce, Economic Development & Small Business
(Ranking Minority Member); Corporations, Authorities & Commissions;
Finance; Insurance; Labor
Senior Staff: Amy Class

Kemp Hannon (R-I-C) 518-455-2200
District: 6   *Room:* 501 CAP   *e-mail:* hannon@senate.state.ny.us
Committees: Codes; Corporations, Authorities & Commissions; Elections;
Finance; Health (Chair); Judiciary; Rules
Senior Staff: Jane Preston

Ruth Hassell-Thompson (D-WF) . . 518-455-2061/fax: 518-426-6998
District: 36   *Room:* 613 LOB   *e-mail:* hassellt@state.senate.ny.us
Title: Chair of Minority Policy Committee
Committees: Banks (RM); Commerce, Economic Development & Small
Business; Consumer Protection (Ranking Minority Member); Environ
Conservation; Housing, Construction & Community Development; Rules;
Veterans, Homeland Security & Military Affairs (RM)
Senior Staff: Jerry W Williams

Owen H Johnson (R-I-C) 518-455-3411/fax: 518-426-6973
District: 4   *Room:* 913 LOB   *e-mail:* ojohnson@senate.state.ny.us
Committees: Banks; Children & Families; Consumer Protection;
Environmental Conservation; Finance (Chair); Rules; Social Services;
Transportation
Senior Staff: Rory P Whelan

Jeffrey Klein (D) 518-455-3595/fax: 518-426-6887
District: 34   *Room:* 415 LOB   *e-mail:* jdklein@senate.state.ny.us
Committees: Agriculture; Codes; Consumer Protection (Ranking Minority
Member); Health; Investigations & Government Operations; Judiciary; Labor
Senior Staff: Shelley Adrews

Offices and agencies appear in alphabetical order.

Liz Krueger (D-G-WF) 518-455-2297/fax: 518-426-6874
District: 26 *Room:* 302 LOB *e-mail:* lkrueger@senate.state.ny.us
Title: Chair of Minority Program Development
Committees: Banks; Consumer Protection; Finance; Higher Education; Housing, Construction & Community Development (Ranking Minority Member); Rules
Senior Staff: Brad Usher

Carl Kruger (D-R-L) 518-455-2460/fax: 518-426-6855
District: 27 *Room:* 608 LOB *e-mail:* kruger@senate.state.ny.us
Committees: Aging (Ranking Minority Member); Crime Victims, Crime & Correction; Energy & Telecommunications; Finance; Insurance; Veterans, Homeland Security & Militiary Affairs (Ranking Minority Member)
Senior Staff: Jason Koppel

Kenneth P LaValle (R-C) 518-455-3121/fax: 518-426-6826
District: 1 *Room:* 806 LOB *e-mail:* lavalle@senate.state.ny.us
Title: Chair of Majority Conference
Committees: Agriculture; Education; Finance; Higher Education (Chair); Insurance; Judiciary; Rules
Senior Staff: Ann Eisenhut

William J Larkin, Jr (R-C) 518-455-2770/fax: 518-426-6923
District: 39 *Room:* 612 LOB *e-mail:* larkin@senate.state.ny.us
Title: Chair of Majority Steering Committee
Committees: Elections; Finance; Health; Insurance; Racing, Gaming & Wagering (Chair); Transportation; Veterans, Homeland Security & Military Affairs
Senior Staff: Jennifer Downs

Vincent L Leibell, III (R-I-C) 518-455-3111/fax: 518-426-6977
District: 40 *Room:* 609 LOB *e-mail:* leibell@senate.state.ny.us
Committees: Aging; Civil Service & Pensions; Corporations, Authorities & Commissions (Chair); Elections; Environmental Conservation; Housing, Construction & Community Development; Insurance; Veterans, Homeland Security & Military Affairs
Senior Staff: Lynne Klein

Thomas W Libous (R-C) 518-455-2677/fax: 518-455-2065
District: 52 *Room:* 512 LOB *e-mail:* senator@senatorlibous.com
Title: Asst. Majority Leader, House Operations
Committees: Finance; Health; Insurance; Mental Health & Developmental Disabilities; Racing, Gaming & Wagering; Transportation (Chair); Rules
Senior Staff: Robert N Nielson Jr

Elizabeth O'Connor Little (R-I-C) 518-455-2811/fax: 518-426-6873
District: 45 *Room:* 903 LOB *e-mail:* little@senate.state.ny.us
Committees: Aging; Crime Victims, Crime & Correction; Education; Environmental Conservation; Local Government (Chair); Racing, Gaming & Wagering; Tourism, Recreation & Sports Development
Senior Staff: Rebecca Marino

Serphin R Maltese (R-I-C) 518-455-3281/fax: 518-426-6951
District: 15 *Room:* 413 CAP *e-mail:* maltese@senate.state.ny.us
Title: Deputy Majority Whip
Committees: Cities (Chair); Civil Service & Pensions; Codes; Finance; Higher Education; Investigations & Government Operations; Judiciary; Rules
Senior Staff: Victoria Vattimo

Carl L Marcellino (R-I-C) 518-455-2390/fax: 518-426-6975
District: 5 *Room:* 812 LOB *e-mail:* marcelli@senate.state.ny.us
Committees: Children & Families; Civil Service & Pensions; Consumer Protection; Education; Environmental Conservation (Chair); Labor; Mental Health & Developmental Disabilities; Social Services
Legislative Director/Press Coordinator: Kirk Ives

John J Marchi (R-C) 518-455-3215/fax: 518-426-6852
District: 24 *Room:* 416 CAP *e-mail:* marchi@senate.state.ny.us
Title: Assistant Majority Leader, Conference Operations
Committees: Cities; Environmental Conservation; Finance; Housing, Construction & Community Development; Investigations & Government Operations; Judiciary; Rules
Senior Staff: Ann M Spratt

George D Maziarz (R-I-C-WF) . . . 518-455-2024/fax: 518-426-6987
District: 62 *Room:* 915 LOB *e-mail:* maziarz@senate.state.ny.us
Committees: Aging; Commerce, Economic Development & Small Business; Crime Victims, Crime & Correction; Energy & Telecommunications; Health; Housing, Construction & Community Development; Labor (Chair)
Senior Staff: Renea Molineaux

Raymond A Meier (R-C) 518-455-3334/fax: 518-426-6921
District: 47 *Room:* 944 LOB *e-mail:* meier@senate.state.ny.us
Committees: Banks; Children & Families; Codes; Education; Energy & Telecommunications; Investigations & Government Operations; Judiciary; Social Services (Chair)
Senior Staff: Dwight Evans

Velmanette Montgomery (D-WF) . 518-455-3451/fax: 518-426-6854
District: 18 *Room:* 306 LOB *e-mail:* montgome@senate.state.ny.us
Title: Asst Minority Leader for Floor Operations
Committees: Children & Families (Ranking Minority Member); Crime Victims, Crime & Correction; Education; Finance; Health; Mental Health & Developmental Disabilities (Ranking Minority Member); Rules; Social Services
Senior Staff: Nancy M Santiago

Thomas P Morahan (R-C-I-WF) . . 518-455-3261/fax: 518-455-2959
District: 38 *Room:* 848 LOB *e-mail:* morahan@senate.state.ny.us
Committees: Agriculture; Banks; Education; Elections; Housing, Construction & Community Development; Local Government; Mental Health & Developmental Disabilities (Chair); Veterans, Homeland Security & Military Affairs
Senior Staff: Catherine McDougall

Michael F Nozzolio (R-I-C) 518-455-2366/fax: 518-426-6953
District: 54 *Room:* 409 LOB *e-mail:* nozzolio@senate.state.ny.us
Committees: Banks; Consumer Protection; Crime Victims, Crime & Correction (Chair); Finance; Racing, Gaming & Wagering; Tourism, Recreation & Sports Development; Transportation
Senior Staff: Justin J McCarthy

George Onorato (D) 518-455-3486/fax: 518-426-6929
District: 12 *Room:* 315 LOB *e-mail:* onorato@senate.state.ny.us
Title: Vice Chair of Minority Conference
Committees: Banks; Energy & Telecommunications; Ethics; Health; Insurance (Ranking Minority Member); Operations; Labor; Racing, Gaming & Wagering
Senior Staff: Candyce Propper

Offices and agencies appear in alphabetical order.

Suzi Oppenheimer (D-WF)........ 518-455-2031/fax: 518-426-6860
District: 37   *Room:* 515 LOB   *e-mail:* oppenhei@senate.state.ny.us
Committees: Cities; Education (Ranking Minority Member); Environmental
Conservation; Ethics; Finance; Higher Education; Transportation
Senior Staff: Steven Otis

Frank Padavan (R-I-C).......... 518-455-3381/fax: 518-455-2008
District: 11   *Room:* 505 CAP   *e-mail:* padavan@senate.state.ny.us
Title: Vice President Pro Tempore; ex officio member of all committees
Committees: Cities; Energy & Telecommunication; Finance; Mental Health
& Developmental Disabilities; Transportation; Veterans, Homeland Security
& Military Affairs
Senior Staff: John C Googas, Jr

Kevin S Parker (D-WF).......... 518-455-2580/fax: 518-426-6843
District: 21   *Room:* 517 LOB   *e-mail:* parker@senate.state.ny.us
Committees: Commerce, Economic Development & Small Business; Energy
& Telecommunications (Ranking Minority Member); Environmental
Conservation; Finance; Higher Education; Insurance; Veterans, Homeland
Security & Military Affairs)
Senior Staff: Glynda Carr

David A Paterson (D-WF-L)...... 518-455-2701/fax: 518-455-2816
District: 30   *Room:* 907 LOB   *e-mail:* paterson@senate.state.ny.us
Title: Minority Leader; ex officio member of all committees
Committees: Rules (Ranking Minority Member)
Senior Staff: Michael Jones-Bey

Mary Lou Rath (R-C-I).......... 518-455-3161/fax: 518-426-6963
District: 61   *Room:* 310 LOB   *e-mail:* rath@senate.state.ny.us
Committees: Elections; Finance; Health; Higher Education; Local
Government; Racing, Gaming & Wagering; Tourim, Recreation & Sports
Development (Chair)
Senior Staff: Sharon Rich

Joseph E Robach (R)............. 518-455-2909/fax: 518-426-6938
District: 56   *Room:* 902 LOB   *e-mail:*
Committees: Banks; Civil Service & Pensions(chair); Commerce, Economic
Development & Small Business; Consumer Protection; Higher Education;
Labor; Tourism, Recreation & Sports Development; Transportation
Senior Staff: Judi DeMarco

John D Sabini (D)................ 518-455-2529/fax: 518-426-6906
District: 13   *Room:* 513 LOB   *e-mail:* sabini@senate.state.ny.us
Committees: Consumer Protection; Education; Elections; Environmental
Conservation; Rules; Racing, Gaming & Wagering (Ranking Minority
Member); Transportation
Senior Staff: Katharine Pichardo-Erskine

Stephen M Saland (R-C)......... 518-455-2411/fax: 518-426-6920
District: 41   *Room:* 708 LOB   *e-mail:* saland@senate.state.ny.us
Title: Deputy Majority Leader for State/Federal Relations
Committees: Banks; Codes; Education (Chair); Finance; Insurance; Judiciary
Senior Staff: Toni Dickinson

John L Sampson (D)............. 518-455-2788/fax: 518-426-8806
District: 19   *Room:* 506 LOB   *e-mail:* sampson@senate.state.ny.us
Committees: Codes; Health (Ranking Minority Member); Judiciary; Racing,
Gaming & Wagering; Veterans, Homeland Security & Military Affairs
Senior Staff: Michelle Trotman

Diane Savino (D).................. 518-455-2437/fax: 518-426-6943
District: 23   *Room:* 406 LOB   *e-mail:* savino@senate.state.ny.us
Committees: Civil Service & Pensions; Environmental Conservation;
Housing, Construction & Community Development; Judiciary; Labor
(Ranking Minority Member); Tourism, Recreation & Sports Development;
Transportation
Senior Staff: Robert Cataldo

Eric T Schneiderman (D-WF)..... 518-455-2041/fax: 518-426-6847
District: 31   *Room:* 313 LOB   *e-mail:* schneide@senate.state.ny.us
Title: Deputy Minority Leader; ex officio member of all committees
Committees: Codes; Education; Investigations & Government Operations;
Judiciary; Mental Health & Developmental Disabilities; Rules
Senior Staff: Michael Clements

Jose Serrano (D).................. 518-455-2795/fax: 518-426-6946
District: 28   *Room:* 706 LOB   *e-mail:*
Committees: Aging, Education, Environmental Conservation; Higher
Education; Local Government, Tourism, Recreation & Sports Development
(Ranking Minority Member)
Senior Staff: Linda Russ

James L Seward (R-I-C).......... 518-455-3131/fax: 518-455-3123
District: 51   *Room:* 917 LOB   *e-mail:* seward@senate.state.ny.us
Title: Secretary of Majority Conference
Committees: Agriculture; Commerce, Economic Development & Small
Business; Education; Energy & Telecommunications; Finance; Higher
Education; Insurance (Chair); Rules; Social Services
Senior Staff: Duncan Davie

Dean G Skelos (R-I-C)............ 518-455-3171/fax: 518-426-6950
District: 9   *Room:* 503 CAP   *e-mail:* skelos@senate.state.ny.us
Title: Deputy Majority Leader for Legislative Operations; ex officio member
of all committees
Committees: Civil Service & Pensions; Codes; Finance; Insurance;
Investigations & Government Operations; Judiciary; Rules
Senior Staff: Tracy Lloyd

Malcolm A Smith (D-R-WF-C) ... 518-455-2195/fax: 518-426-6805
District: 14   *Room:* 508 LOB   *e-mail:* masmith@senate.state.ny.us
Committees: Codes; Education; Finance; Health; Judiciary (Ranking Minority
Member); Rules; Transportation
Senior Staff: Patricia Rubens

Ada L Smith (D-WF-I-L)......... 518-455-3531/fax: 518-426-6859
District: 10   *Room:* 808 LOB   *e-mail:* asmith@senate.state.ny.us
Title: Asst Minority Leader, Policy Administration
Committees: Banks; Codes; Corporations, Authorities & Commissions
(Ranking Minority Member); Finance; Insurance; Rules; Transportation
Senior Staff: Claude Nelson

Nicholas A Spano (R-I-C-WF) 518-455-2231/fax: 518-426-6906
District: 35   *Room:* 509 LOB   *e-mail:* spano@senate.state.ny.us
Title: Senior Asst Majority Leader, Liaison to Exec Branch
Committees: Investigations & Government Operations (Chair)
Senior Staff: Claire Wainwright

William T Stachowski (D-I-C-WF) 518-455-2426/fax: 518-426-6851
District: 58   *Room:* 604 LOB   *e-mail:* stachows@senate.state.ny.us
Committees: Agriculture; Ethics (Ranking Minority Member); Finance;
Insurance; Investigations & Government Operations (Ranking Minority
Member); Labor; Racing, Gaming & Wagering; Rules
Senior Staff: Millie Powers

Offices and agencies appear in alphabetical order.

Toby Ann Stavisky (D-WF) 518-455-3461/fax: 518-426-6857
District: 16 *Room:* 504 LOB *e-mail:* stavisky@senate.state.ny.us
Title: Assistant Minority Whip
Committees: Aging; Cities; Civil Service & Pensions; Education; Finance; Tourism, Recreations & Sports Development; Transportation
Senior Staff: Marilyn Dyer

Caesar Trunzo (R-I-C) 518-455-2111/fax: 518-455-2113
District: 3 *Room:* 711 LOB *e-mail:* trunzo@senate.state.ny.us
Title: Chair, Majority Program Development Committee
Committees: Civil Service & Pensions; Corporations, Authorities & Commissions; Environmental Conservation; Finance; Local Government; Rules; Transportation
Senior Staff: Christopher Molluso

David J Valesky (D) 518-455-2838/fax: 518-426-6885
District: 49 *Room:* 707 LOB *e-mail:* valesky@senate.state.ny.us
Committees: Agriculture (Ranking Minority Member); Energy & Telecommunications; Environmental Conservation (Ranking Minority Member); Higher Education; Local Gocernment; Tourism, Recreation & Sports Development; Transportation
Senior Staff: Cort Ruddy

Dale M Volker (R-I-C) 518-455-3471/fax: 518-426-6949
District: 59 *Room:* 427 CAP *e-mail:* volker@senate.state.ny.us
Title: Vice Chair of Majority Conference
Committees: Cities; Codes (Chair); Crime Victims, Crime & Correction; Finance; Judiciary; Mental Health & Developmental Disabilities; Rules
Senior Staff: John R Drexielius

George H Winner Jr (R) 518-455-2091/fax: 518-426-6976
District: 53 *Room:* 802 LOB *e-mail:* winner@senate.state.ny.us
Committees: Agriculture; Consumer Protection; Crime Victims, Crime & Correction; Energy & Telecommunication; Health; Higher Education; Judiciary
Senior Staff: Sperry J Navone

James W Wright (R-C-I) 518-455-2346/fax: 518-455-2365
District: 48 *Room:* 811 LOB *e-mail:* wright@senate.state.ny.us
Committees: Commerce, Economic Development & Small Business; Crime Victims, Crime & Correction; Energy & Telecommunications (Chair); Finance; Labor; Tourism, Recreation & Sports Development; Veterans, Homeland Security & Military Affairs
Senior Staff: Graham Wise

Catherine M Young 518-455-5241/fax: 518-455-5869
District: 57 *Room:* 443 LOB *e-mail:* youngc@senate.state.ny.us
Title: Chair, Agriculture & Markets
Committees: Aging; Environmental Conservation; Higher Education; Housing, Construction & Community Development; Mental Health & Developmental Disabilities; Social Services Children & Families
Senior Staff: Jessica Proud

State Senate Standing Committees

Aging
Chair:
   Martin J Golden (R) 518-455-2730
Ranking Minority Member:
   Carl Kruger (D) 518-455-2460

Committee Staff
Executive Assistant & Committee Clerk:
   Patricia Donnelly 518-455-2730
Director, Legislation:
   Robert Herz 518-455-2730

Key Senate Staff Assignments
Senate Majority Counsel/Program Services/Program Associate:
   Michelle Di Bacco 518-455-2597
Senate Research Service Analyst:
   Kim VanNortwick 518-455-2146
Senate Minority Policy Development & Counsel Staff:
   Cathy Bern 518-455-2957

Membership

Majority
Michael A L Balboni	Hugh T Farley
John J Flanagan	Vincent L Leibell, III
George D Maziarz	Catherine M Young

Minority
Ruben Diaz, Sr	Jose E Serrano
Byron W Brown	Toby Ann Stavisky

Agriculture
Chair:
   Catherine M Young 518-455-5241
Ranking Minority Member:
   David J Valeski (D) 518-455-2426

Committee Staff
Clerk:
   Lynne Swedick 518-455-2665
Agritourism & Education Coordinator:
   Loretta Switzer 518-455-5400

Key Senate Staff Assignments
Senate Majority Counsel/Program Services Assistant Counsel:
   Karen Moreau 518-455-3413
Senate Research Service Analyst:
   Todd Kusnierz 518-455-2153
Senate Minority Policy Development & Counsel Staff:
   Jim Watson 518-455-2977

Membership

Majority
George H Winner, Jr	Kenneth P LaValle
Elizabeth O'Connor Little	Thomas P Morahan
James L Seward	

Minority
Neil D Breslin	William T Stachowski
Jeffrey D Klein	

Offices and agencies appear in alphabetical order.

Alcoholism & Drug Abuse

Chair:
  Vacant 518-455-3563
Ranking Minority Member:
  Ruben Diaz, Sr (D) 518-455-2511

Committee Staff

Legislative Director:
  Alison Woytowich 518-455-3563
Clerk:
  Catherine Mural 518-455-3563

Key Senate Staff Assignments

Senate Majority Counsel/Program Services/Program Associate:
  Michael Fox 518-455-7924
Senate Research Service Analyst:
  Michael Cartenuto 518-455-2154
Senate Minority Policy Development & Counsel Staff:
  Edna Jackson 518-455-2972

Membership

Majority

Charles J Fuschillo, Jr	Kemp Hannon
Mary Lou Rath	Carl L Marcellino
Michael F Nozzolio	Frank Padavan
James W Wright	

Minority

Martin Connor	Carl Kruger
Velmanette Montgomery	Kevin S Parker

Banks

Chair:
  Hugh T Farley (R) 518-455-2181
Ranking Minority Member:
  Ruth Hassell-Thompson (D) 518-455-2061

Committee Staff

Director:
  Peter A Edman 518-455-2181
Clerk:
  Tracy Cullen 518-455-2181

Key Senate Staff Assignments

Senate Majority Counsel/Program Services Principal Program Assoc:
  Bernard McGarry 518-455-2986
Senate Research Service Analyst:
  Art DiLello 518-455-2296
Senate Minority Policy Development & Counsel Staff:
  Michael Broderick 518-455-2988

Membership

Majority

James S Alesi	John J Bonacic
John A DeFrancisco	Owen H Johnson
Martin J Golden	Raymond A Meier
Thomas P Morahan	Michael F Nozzolio
Joseph E Robach	Stephen M Saland

Minority

Neil D Breslin	Martin M Dilan
Efrain Gonzalez, Jr	Liz Krueger
George Onorato	Ada L Smith
Carl Andrews	

Children & Families

Chair:
  Mary Lou Rath (R) 518-455-3161
Ranking Minority Member:
  Velmanette Montgomery (D) 518-455-3451

Committee Staff

Counsel:
  Michael Hettler 518-455-3161
Director:
  Carol Cybulski 518-455-3161
Clerk:
  Dede Morrissey 518-455-3161

Key Senate Staff Assignments

Senate Majority Counsel/Program Services Program Associate:
  Michelle DiBacco 518-455-2597
Senate Research Service Analyst:
  Kim VanNortwick 518-455-2146
Senate Minority Policy Development & Counsel Staff:
  Francis McKearin 518-455-2975

Membership

Majority

Michael A L Balboni	Charles J Fuschillo, Jr
Kenneth P LaValle	Thomas P Morahan
Stephen M Saland	

Minority

Ruben Diaz, Sr	Liz Krueger
Seymour P Lachman	

Cities

Chair:
  Serphin R Maltese (R) 518-455-3281
Ranking Minority Member:
  Byron W Brown (D) 518-455-3371

Committee Staff

Counsel:
  Susan T Aron 518-455-3281
Clerk:
  Kristin Brown 518-455-3281

Key Senate Staff Assignments

Senate Majority Counsel/Program Home Rule Counsel:
  Peter Rupert 518-455-2578
Senate Research Service Analyst:
  Chris Anderson 518-455-3501
Senate Minority Policy Development & Counsel Staff:
  Edna Jackson 518-455-2972

Membership

Majority

Dale M Volker	John J Marchi
Frank Padavan	

Minority

Suzi Oppenheimer

Civil Service & Pensions

Chair:
  Joseph E Robach (R) 518-455-2909
Ranking Minority Member:
  Carl Andrews (D) 518-455-2431

Offices and agencies appear in alphabetical order.

Committee Staff

Counsel:
Judi DeMarco 518-455-2909
Clerk:
Denise Keyes 518-455-2909

Key Senate Staff Assignments

Senate Majority Counsel/Program Services Assistant Counsel:
Edward Bartholomew 518-455-2424
Senate Research Service Analyst:
Steven Koczak 518-455-2295
Senate Minority Policy Development & Counsel Staff:
Lowell Siegel 518-455-2987

Membership

Majority

Vincent L Leibell, III	Serphin R Maltese
Carl L Marcellino	Dean G Skelos
Charles J Fuschillo, Jr	Caesar Trunzo

Minority

Thomas K Duane	Carl Andrews
Martin M Dilan	Toby Ann Stavisky

Codes

Chair:
Dale M Volker (R) 518-455-3471
Ranking Minority Member:
Thomas K Duane (D) 518-455-2451

Committee Staff

Counsel:
J R Drexelius 518-455-3471
Clerk:
Colleen Purcell 518-455-3471
Minority Counsel:
Mark Furnish 518-455-2451

Key Senate Staff Assignments

Senate Majority Counsel/Program Services Assistant Counsel:
Joseph Messina 518-455-2342
Senate Research Service Analyst:
Kandi Corey-Terry 518-455-2134
Senate Minority Policy Development & Counsel Staff:
Keith St John 518-455-2842

Membership

Majority

John J Bonacic	John A DeFrancisco
Martin J Golden	Kemp Hannon
Serphin R Maltese	Raymond A Meier
Stephen M Saland	Dean G Skelos

Minority

Neil D Breslin	Jeffrey D Klein
John L Sampson	Eric T Schneiderman
Ada L Smith	Malcolm A Smith

Commerce, Economic Development & Small Business

Chair:
James S Alesi (R) 518-455-2015
Ranking Minority Member:
Efrain Gonzalez, Jr (D) 518-455-3395

Committee Staff

Counsel:
Melissa Pugliese 518-455-2015
Clerk:
Michelle Larango 518-455-2015

Key Senate Staff Assignments

Senate Majority Counsel/Program Services Assistant Counsel:
Heather Briccetti 518-455-3413
Senate Research Service Analyst:
Jason Wheatley 518-455-2151
Senate Minority Policy Development & Counsel Staff:
Graham Ennis 518-455-2879

Membership

Majority

John J Bonacic	Charles J Fuschillo, Jr
George D Maziarz	Joseph E Robach
William J Larkin, Jr	James W Wright

Minority

Carl Andrews	Ruth Hassell-Thompson
Byron W Brown	Kevin S Parker

Consumer Protection

Chair:
Charles J Fuschillo, Jr (R) 518-455-3341
Ranking Minority Member:
Jeffrey D Klein (D) 518-455-2061

Committee Staff

Counsel:
Barbara Lee Steigerwald 518-455-3341
Clerk:
Kathy Farrell 518-455-3341

Key Senate Staff Assignments

Senate Majority Counsel/Program Services Assistant Counsel:
Marcus Ferguson 518-455-7924
Senate Research Service Analyst:
Art DiLello 518-455-2296
Senate Minority Policy Development & Counsel Staff:
Michael Broderick 518-455-2972

Membership

Majority

Joseph E Robach	Owen H Johnson
George H Winner, Jr	Carl L Marcellino
Michael F Nozzolio	

Minority

Ruth Hassell-Thompson	Liz Krueger
John D Sabini	

Corporations, Authorities & Commissions

Chair:
Vincent L Leibell, III 518-455-3111
Ranking Minority Member:
Ada L Smith (D) 518-455-3531

Committee Staff

Counsel:
Robert Farley 518-455-3111
Clerk:
Marianne Reilly 518-455-3111

Offices and agencies appear in alphabetical order.

Key Senate Staff Assignments
Senate Majority Counsel/Program Services Assistant Counsel:
David Reid 518-455-3413
Senate Research Service Analyst:
Tracey Tudor 518-455-2546
Senate Minority Policy Development & Counsel Staff:
Keith St John 518-455-2842

Membership

Majority

Kemp Hannon	Caesar Trunzo

Minority

Ada L Smith	Efrain Gonzales, Jr

Crime Victims, Crime & Correction
Chair:
Michael F Nozzolio (R) 518-455-2366
Ranking Minority Member:
Thomas K Duane (D) 518-455-2451

Committee Staff
Director:
Justin McCarthy 518-455-2366
Clerk:
Meagan Fitzgerald 518-455-2366

Key Senate Staff Assignments
Senate Majority Counsel/Program Assistant Counsel:
Kennedy Connolly 518-455-2342
Senate Research Service Analyst:
Kandi Corey-Terry 518-455-2134
Senate Minority Policy Development & Counsel Staff:
Christina Dickinson 518-455-2823

Membership

Majority

James S Alesi	Martin J Golden
Elizabeth O'Connor Little	George D Maziarz
Raymond A Meier	George H Winner, Jr
Dale M Volker	James W Wright

Minority

Ruth Hassell-Thompson	Ruben Diaz, Sr
Carl Kruger	John L Sampson
Velmanette Montgomery	

Education
Chair:
Stephen M Saland (R) 518-455-2411
Ranking Minority Member:
Suzi Oppenheimer (D) 518-455-2031

Committee Staff
Deputy Director:
Tina Marlow 518-455-2631
Clerk:
Darlene Murray 518-455-2631

Key Senate Staff Assignments
Senate Majority Counsel/Program Services Program Associate:
Michael Fox 518-455-7924
Senate Research Service Analyst:
Ken Kienzle 518-455-3397
Senate Minority Policy Development & Counsel Staff:
Greg Roberts 518-455-2870

Membership

Majority

Charles J Fuschillo, Jr	Martin J Golden
Raymond A Meier	Kenneth P LaValle
Elizabeth O'Connor Little	Carl L Marcellino
Thomas P Morahan	James L Seward
Nicholas A Spano	

Minority

Martin M Dilan	Malcolm A Smith
Velmanette Montgomery	John D Sabini
Eric T Schneiderman	Toby Ann Stavisky
Jose E Serrano	

Elections
Chair:
Thomas P Morahan (R) 518-455-3261
Ranking Minority Member:
Martin M Dilan (D) 518-455-2177

Committee Staff
Counsel:
Steven G Natoli 518-455-3261

Key Senate Staff Assignments
Senate Majority Counsel/Program Services Assistant Counsel:
Michael Melkonian 518-455-3413
Senate Research Service Analyst:
Tracey Tudor 518-455-2546
Senate Minority Policy Development & Counsel Staff:
Jim Long. 518-455-2965

Membership

Majority

Kemp Hannon	William J Larkin, Jr
Thomas P Morahan	Mary Lou Rath

Minority

Martin Connor	John D Sabini

Energy & Telecommunications
Chair:
James W Wright (R) 518-455-2346
Ranking Minority Member:
Kevin S Parker (D) 518-455-2580

Committee Staff
Counsel:
Frank Moroney 518-455-2346
Director:
Carlene Pacholczak 518-455-2346

Key Senate Staff Assignments
Senate Majority Counsel/Program Services Principal Program Assoc:
Bernard McGarry 518-455-2986
Senate Research Service Analyst:
Todd Kusnierz 518-455-2153
Senate Minority Policy Development & Counsel Staff:
Marcy Palmer. 518-455-2830

Membership

Majority

James S Alesi	John A DeFrancisco
George D Maziarz	Raymond A Meier
Frank Padavan	George H Winner

Minority

Carl Andrews	Carl Kruger
George Onorato	David J Valesky

Environmental Conservation

Chair:
Carl L Marcellino (R).............................518-455-2390
Ranking Minority Member:
David J Valesky (D)...............................518-455-2838

Committee Staff

Director:
Deborah Peck Kelleher............................518-455-2390

Key Senate Staff Assignments

Senate Majority Counsel/Program Services Program Associate:
Darren Suarez....................................518-455-3413
Senate Research Service Analyst:
Glenda Denison 518-455-2192
Senate Minority Policy Development & Counsel Staff:
Marcy Palmer.....................................518-455-2830

Membership

Majority

Michael A L Balboni	Owen H Johnson
Vincent L Leibell, III	Elizabeth O'Connor Little
John J Marchi	Caesar Trunzo
Catherine M Young	

Minority

Suzi Oppenheimer	Kevin S Parker
Martin Connor	John D Sabini
Diane J Savino	Jose E Serrano

Ethics

Chair:
George H Winner (R)..............................518-455-2091
Ranking Minority Member:
William T Stachowski (D)..........................518-455-2426

Key Senate Staff Assignments

Senate Majority Counsel/Program Services Legislative Counsel:
Francis Gluchowski 518-455-2563
Senate Minority Policy Development & Counsel Staff:
Keith St John 518-455-2842

Membership

Majority

Hugh T Farley	Stephen M Saland

Minority

George Onorato	Suzi Oppenheimer

Finance

Chair:
Owen H Johnson (R) 518-455-3411
Ranking Minority Member:
Neil D Breslin (D) 518-455-2225

Committee Staff

Secretary to the Committee:
Mary Louise Mallick 518-455-2754
Assistant Secretary:
David J Natoli...................................518-455-2417
Counsel:
Thomas N Cioffi.................................518-455-2333

Communications Director:
Kathleen O'Neill 518-455-3411
Clerk:
Louis Sitrin.....................................518-455-3232

Key Senate Staff Assignments

Senate Majority Finance Budget Studies Director:
Robert Mujica....................................518-455-2880
Senate Majority Fiscal Studies Director:
Robert Hotz......................................518-455-2741
Secretary to Minority Finance:
Jennifer McCormick...............................518-455-2641
Senate Minority Finance Budget Studies Director:
Michael Weber....................................518-455-2641
Senate Minority Finance Fiscal Studies Director:
Ahmed Diomande 518-455-2641

Membership

Majority

Hugh T Farley	Kemp Hannon
John D DeFrancisco	Michael F Nozzolio
William J Larkin, Jr	Kenneth P LaValle
Thomas W Libous	Serphin R Maltese
John J Marchi	James W Wright
Frank Padavan	Stephen M Saland
James L Seward	Dean G Skelos
Nicholas A Spano	Caesar Trunzo
Mary Lou Rath	Dale M Volker

Minority

Byron W Brown	Thomas K Duane
Efrain Gonzalez, Jr	Carl Kruger
Neil D Breslin	Velmanette Montgomery
Suzi Oppenheimer	Kevin S Parker
Ada L Smith	Malcolm A Smith
William T Stachowski	Martin M Dilan
Liz Krueger	Toby Ann Stavisky

Health

Chair:
Kemp Hannon (R) 518-455-2200
Ranking Minority Member:
John L Sampson (D)...............................518-455-2788

Committee Staff

Executive Director:
Jane Preston 518-455-2200
Clerk:
Lori Gradwell....................................518-455-2200

Key Senate Staff Assignments

Senate Majority Counsel/Program Services Principal Program Assoc:
Caron O'Brien Crummey...........................518-455-2597
Senate Research Service Analyst:
Tom Wickham....................................518-455-2809
Senate Minority Policy Development & Counsel Staff:
Cathy Bern 518-455-2957

Membership

Majority

John A DeFrancisco	Hugh T Farley
Charles J Fuschillo, Jr	William J Larkin, Jr
Thomas W Libous	George D Maziarz
George H Winner, Jr	Mary Lou Rath
Nicholas A Spano	

Minority

Carl Andrews	Thomas K Duane

Offices and agencies appear in alphabetical order.

Velmanette Montgomery	George Onorato
Malcolm Smith	Jeffrey D Klein

Higher Education
Chair:
　Kenneth P LaValle (R) 518-455-3121
Ranking Minority Member:
　Toby Ann Stavisky (D) 518-455-3461

Committee Staff
Director:
　John D'Agati 518-455-3121
Counsel:
　Nicole Burckard 518-455-3121

Key Senate Staff Assignments
Senate Majority Counsel/Program Services Assistant Counsel:
　David Reid 518-455-3413
Senate Research Service Analyst:
　Ken Kienzle 518-455-3397
Senate Minority Policy Development & Counsel Staff:
　Greg Roberts 518-455-2870

Membership

Majority
Michael A L Balboni	John J Flanagan
James S Alesi	Serphin R Maltese
George H Winner, Jr	Mary Lou Rath
Joseph E Robach	James L Seward
Catherine M Young	

Minority
Byron W Brown	Ruben Diaz, Sr
Liz Krueger	Suzi Oppenheimer
Kevin S Parker	Jose E Serrano
David J Valesky	

Housing, Construction & Community Development
Chair:
　John J Bonacic (R) 518-455-3181
Ranking Minority Member:
　Liz Krueger (D) 518-455-2297

Committee Staff
Director/Counsel:
　Langdon Chapman 518-455-3181
Asst Director/Clerk:
　Darlene Leder 518-455-3181

Key Senate Staff Assignments
Senate Majority Counsel/Program Services Principal Program Assoc:
　Bernard McGarry 518-455-2986
Senate Research Service Analyst:
　Jason Wheatley 518-455-2151
Senate Minority Policy Development & Counsel Staff:
　Dorsey Whitehead 518-455-2824

Membership

Majority
Vincent L Leibell, III	George D Maziarz
John J Marchi	Thomas P Morahan
Catherine M Young	

Minority
Ruth Hassell-Thompson	Diane J Savino

Insurance
Chair:
　James L Seward (R) 518-455-3131
Ranking Minority Member:
　George Onorato (D) 518-455-3486

Committee Staff
Director:
　Andrew Jewett 518-455-3131
Counsel:
　Kristina Baldwin. 518-455-3131
Clerk:
　Bernadette Phillips 518-455-3131

Key Senate Staff Assignments
Senate Majority Counsel/Program Services Assistant Counsel:
　Kristen Sukatos 518-455-2986
Senate Research Service Analyst:
　Art DiLello. 518-455-2296
Senate Minority Policy Development & Counsel Staff:
　Michael Broderick 518-455-2988

Membership

Majority
James S Alesi	Michael A L Balboni
John J Flanagan	William J Larkin, Jr
Kenneth P LaValle	Vincent L Leibell, III
Thomas W Libous	Stephen M Saland
Dean G Skelos	

Minority
Carl Andrews	Efrain Gonzalez, Jr
Neil D Breslin	Ada L Smith
William T Stachowski	Carl Kruger
Kevin S Parker	

Investigations & Government Operations
Chair:
　Nicholas A Spano (R) 518-455-2231
Ranking Minority Member:
　William T Stachowski (D) 518-455-2426

Committee Staff
Director:
　John Turoski 518-455-2231
Clerk:
　Jamie Smith 518-455-2231

Key Senate Staff Assignments
Senate Majority Counsel/Program Services Assistant Counsel:
　Heather Briccetti 518-455-3413
Senate Research Service Analyst:
　Tracey Tudor 518-455-2546
Senate Minority Policy Development & Counsel Staff:
　Christina Dickinson 518-455-2823

Membership

Majority
Martin J Golden	John J Marchi
Raymond A Meier	Dean G Skelos

Minority
Jeffrey D Klein	Eric T Schneiderman

Judiciary
Chair:
　John A DeFrancisco (R) 518-455-3511

Offices and agencies appear in alphabetical order.

Ranking Minority Member:
  Malcolm A Smith (D)............................518-455-2195

Committee Staff
Senior Counsel:
  David Gruenberg 518-455-3511
Clerk:
  Carole Luther 518-455-3511

  Key Senate Staff Assignments
  Senate Majority Counsel/Program Services Assistant Counsel:
    John Cahill 518-455-2342
  Senate Research Service Analyst:
    Tracey Tudor 518-455-2546
  Senate Minority Policy Development & Counsel Staff:
    Keith St John 518-455-2864

Membership

  Majority

Michael A L Balboni	John J Bonacic
Hugh T Farley	Kemp Hannon
Kenneth P LaValle	Serphin R Maltese
John J Marchi	Raymond A Meier
Stephen M Saland	Dean G Skelos
George H Winner, Jr	Dale M Volker

  Minority

Carl Andrews	Neil D Breslin
Martin Connor	Martin M Dilan
Thomas K Duane	John L Sampson
Eric T Schneiderman	Jeffrey D Klein
Diane J Savino	

Labor
Chair:
  George D Maziarz (R) 518-455-2024
Ranking Minority Member:
  Diane J Savino (D)................................518-455-2437

Committee Staff
Legislative/Committee Director:
  Sue Schmidt 518-455-3264

  Key Senate Staff Assignments
  Senate Majority Counsel/Program Services Assistant Counsel:
    Edward Bartholomew.............................518-455-2424
  Senate Research Service Analyst:
    Steven Koczak 518-455-2295
  Senate Minority Policy Development & Counsel Staff:
    Lowell Siegel 518-455-2987

Membership

  Majority

James S Alesi	Michael A L Balboni
John J Bonacic	John J Flanagan
Charles J Fuschillo, Jr	Carl L Marcellino
Joseph E Robach	James W Wright

  Minority

Neil D Breslin	Byron W Brown
Efrain Gonzalez, Jr	Jeffrey D Klein
George Onorato	William T Stachowski

Local Government
Chair:
  Elizabeth O'Connor Little (R) 518-455-2811
Ranking Minority Member:
  Martin Connor (D) 518-455-2625

Committee Staff
Clerk:
  Mary Pat McDonald 518-455-2811

  Key Senate Staff Assignments
  Senate Majority Counsel/Program Services Home Rule Counsel:
    Peter Rupert 518-455-2578
  Senate Research Service Analyst:
    Chris Anderson.................................518-455-3501
  Senate Minority Policy Development & Counsel Staff:
    Jim Watson.....................................518-455-2977

Membership

  Majority

John J Bonacic	Thomas P Morahan
Mary Lou Rath	Caesar Trunzo

  Minority

Jose E Serrano	David J Valesky

Mental Health & Developmental Disabilities
Chair:
  Thomas P Morahan (R) 518-455-3261
Ranking Minority Member:
  Ruben Diaz, Sr (D)................................518-455-2511

Committee Staff
Legislative Director:
  Aaron M Martin 518-455-2674
Legislative Assistant:
  Phillip J Bach 518-455-2677
Legislative Assistant:
  David J Austin 518-455-2677

  Key Senate Staff Assignments
  Senate Majority Counsel/Program Services Program Associate:
    Michael Fox 518-455-7924
  Senate Research Service Analyst:
    Tom Wickham 518-455-2809
  Senate Minority Policy Development & Counsel Staff:
    Cathy Bern 518-455-2957

Membership

  Majority

Thomas W Libous	Carl L Marcellino
Frank Padavan	Nicholas A Spano
Dale M Volker	Catherine M Young

  Minority

Martin Connor	Velmanette Montgomery
Eric T Schneiderman	

Racing, Gaming & Wagering
Chair:
  William J Larkin, Jr (R) 518-455-2770
Ranking Minority Member:
  John D Sabini (D).................................518-455-2529

Committee Staff
Director:
  Charlotte Johnson.................................518-455-2775
Counsel:
  J Stephen Casscles 518-455-2770

  Key Senate Staff Assignments
  Senate Majority Counsel/Program Services Program Associate:
    Jon McCloskey..................................518-455-3413

Offices and agencies appear in alphabetical order.

Senate Research Service Analyst:
Jason Wheatley. 518-455-2151
Senate Minority Policy Development & Counsel Staff:
Jim Long. 518-455-2965

Membership

Majority

Thomas W Libous	Elizabeth O'Connor Little
Michael F Nozzolio	Mary Lou Rath
Nicholas A Spano	

Minority

George Onorato	John L Sampson
William T Stachowski	

Rules

Chair:
Joseph L Bruno (R) 518-455-3191
Ranking Minority Member:
David A Paterson (D). 518-455-2701

Membership

Majority

Hugh T Farley	Kemp Hannon
Owen H Johnson	Kenneth P LaValle
John J Marchi	Thomas W Libous
Frank Padavan	James L Seward
Dean G Skelos	Nicholas A Spano
Caesar Trunzo	Serphin R Maltese
Dale M Volker	

Minority

Thomas K Duane	Ruth Hassell-Thompson
Liz Krueger	Velmanette Montgomery
John D Sabini	Eric T Schneiderman
Ada L Smith	Malcolm A Smith
William T Stachowski	

Social Services

Chair:
Raymond A Meier (R) 518-455-3334
Ranking Minority Member:
Velmanette Montgomery (D). 518-455-3451

Committee Staff

Policy Analyst:
Kristin Sinclair 518-455-3334

Key Senate Staff Assignments

Senate Majority Counsel/Program Services Program Assoc:
Michelle DiBacco. 518-455-2597
Senate Research Service Analyst:
Kim VanNortwick 518-455-2146
Senate Minority Policy Development & Counsel Staff:
Francis McKearin. 518-455-2975

Membership

Majority

Owen H Johnson	Carl L Marcellino
Catherine M Young	

Minority

Ruben Diaz, Sr

Tourism, Recreation & Sports Development

Chair:
Mary Lou Rath (R) 518-455-3161
Ranking Minority Member:
Jose E Serrano (D) 518-455-2795

Committee Staff

Director:
Gary Rouleau 518-455-2024
Clerk:
Jean Boyd 518-455-2024

Key Senate Staff Assignments

Senate Majority Counsel/Program Services Assistant Counsel:
Karen Moreau. 518-455-3413
Senate Research Service Analyst:
Jason Wheatley. 518-455-2151
Senate Minority Policy Development & Counsel Staff:
Marcy Palmer. 518-455-2830

Membership

Majority

James S Alesi	John J Bonacic
John A DeFrancisco	Martin J Golden
Nancy Larraine Hoffmann	Elizabeth O'Connor Little
George D Maziarz	Michael F Nozzolio
Joseph E Robach	James W Wright

Minority

Martin M Dilan	Efrain Gonzalez, Jr
Ruth Hassell-Thompson	John D Sabini
Toby Ann Stavisky	

Transportation

Chair:
Thomas W Libous (R) 518-455-2677
Ranking Minority Member:
John D Sabini (D). 518-455-2529

Committee Staff

Legislative Director:
Aaron M Martin 518-455-2091
Deputy Director:
David J Austin 518-455-2091
Legislative Asst:
Rebecca L Reeder. 518-455-2091
Chief Counsel:
Teresa Rossi 518-455-2091

Key Senate Staff Assignments

Senate Majority Counsel/Program Services Assistant Counsel:
Michael Melkonian 518-455-3413
Senate Research Service Analyst:
Michael Cartenuto 518-455-2154
Senate Minority Policy Development & Counsel Staff:
Graham Ennis. 518-455-2879

Membership

Majority

John J Flanagan	Charles J Fuschillo, Jr
Owen H Johnson	William J Larkin, Jr
Michael F Nozzolio	Frank Padavan
Joseph E Robach	James L Seward
Caesar Trunzo	

Minority

Martin M Dilan	Malcolm A Smith
Suzi Oppenheimer	Ada L Smith

Offices and agencies appear in alphabetical order.

Toby Ann Stavisky   Diane J Savino

David J Valesky

Veterans, Homeland Security & Military Affairs

Chair:
Michael A L Balboni (R) 518-455-2471
Ranking Minority Member:
Ruth Hassell-Thompson (D) 518-455-2061

Committee Staff

Counsel:
James Sherry 518-455-2471
Clerk:
Mary Lee Cohen 518-455-2471
Legislative Director:
James Kirkwood 518-455-2471

Key Senate Staff Assignments
Senate Majority Counsel/Program Services Assistant Counsel:
Richard Consentino 518-455-2424
Senate Majority Counsel/Program Svcs Asst Counsel:
Kenneth Connolly 518-455-2341
Senate Research Service Analyst:
Kim VanNortwick 518-455-2146
Senate Minority Policy Development & Counsel Staff:
Dorsey Whitehead 518-455-2824

Membership

Majority
John J Flanagan   Martin J Golden
William J Larkin, Jr   Vincent L Leibell, III
Thomas P Morahan   Frank Padavan

James W Wright

Minority
Martin Connor   Ruben Diaz, Sr
Kevin S Parker   John L Sampson
Carl Kruger

SENATE SELECT & SPECIAL COMMITTEES & SPECIAL TASK FORCES

Arts & Cultural Affairs, Special Committee on the

Chair:
Serphin R Maltese (R) 518-455-3281
Legislative Director:
Kristin Brown 518-455-3281

Disabled, Select Committee on the

Chair:
Thomas W Libous (R) 518-455-2677
Director:
Aaron Martin 518-455-2677

Interstate Cooperation, Select Committee on

Chair:
Hugh T Farley (R) 518-455-2181
Director:
Robert W Geddis 518-455-2181/fax: 518-455-2271

Joint Legislative Commissions

Administrative Regulations Review, Legislative Commission on

Senate Co-Chair:
John J Flanagan (R) 518-455-2071
Assembly Co-Chair:
Ruben Diaz, Jr (D) 518-455-5514
Senate Director:
John Koury 518-455-2731/fax: 518-426-6820
Assembly Program Manager:
Rich Murphy 518-455-5091/fax: 518-455-4175

Critical Transportation Choices, Legislative Commission on

Senate Chair:
John R Kuhl, Jr (R) 518-455-2091
Assembly Vice Chair:
Vacant 518-455-0000
Program Manager:
Heidi Kromphardt 518-455-4031/fax: 518-455-4859

Demographic Research & Reapportionment, Legislative Task Force on

Senate Co-Chair:
Dean G Skelos (R) 518-455-3171
Assembly Co-Chair:
William B Hoyt, III (D) 518-455-4886

Senate Co-Executive Dir:
Debra A Levine 212-618-1100/fax: 212-618-1135
Assembly Co-Executive Dir:
Lewis M Hoppe 212-618-1100/fax: 212-618-1135

Ethics Committee, Legislative

Senate Co-Chair:
John J Flanagan (R) 518-455-2071
Assembly Co-Chair:
Mark Weprin (D) 518-455-5806
Program Manager/Counsel:
Melissa Ryan 518-455-2142/fax: 518-426-6850

Government Administration, Legislative Commission on

Senate Vice-Chair:
Owen H Johnson (R) 518-455-3411
Assembly Chair:
Joan Millman (D) 518-455-5426
Program Manager:
Philip Johnson 518-455-3632/fax: 518-455-4574

Health Care Financing, Council on

Senate Chair:
Joseph L Bruno (R) 518-455-3191
Assembly Vice Chair:
Alexander B Grannis (D) 518-455-5282

Offices and agencies appear in alphabetical order.

Executive Director:
  Al Cardillo 518-455-2067/fax: 518-426-6925

Rural Resources, Legislative Commission on

Senate Chair:
  Vacant 518-455-3563
Assembly Chair:
  David R Koon (D) 518-455-5784
Senate Executive Dir:
  Ronald C Brach 518-455-2544/fax: 518-426-6960
Assembly Director:
  Susan Bartle 518-455-3999/fax: 518-455-4175
Counsel:
  Donald A Walsh 518-455-2544

Science & Technology, Legislative Commission on

Assembly Chair:
  Adele Cohen (D) 518-455-4811
Senate Vice Chair:
  Kenneth P LaValle (R) 518-455-3121
Program Manager:
  Philip Johnson 518-455-3632/fax: 518-455-4574

Solid Waste Management, Legislative Commission on

Assembly Chair:
  William Colton (D) 518-455-5828

Senate Vice Chair:
  Nicholas A Spano (R) 518-455-2231
Program Manager:
  Richard D Morse, Jr 518-455-3711/fax: 518-455-3837

Toxic Substances & Hazardous Waste, Legislative Commission on

Senate Chair:
  Vacant 518-455-0000
Assembly Vice Chair:
  David R Koon (D) 518-455-5784
Program Manager:
  Richard D Morse, Jr 518-455-3711/fax: 518-455-3837

Water Resources Needs of New York State & Long Island, Legislative Commission

Assembly Co-Chair:
  Thomas P DiNapoli (D) 518-455-5192
Senate Co-Chair:
  Michael A L Balboni (R) 518-455-2471
Program Manager:
  Richard D Morse, Jr 518-455-3711/fax: 518-455-3837

Offices and agencies appear in alphabetical order.

LEGISLATIVE BRANCH ASSEMBLY

State Assembly Leadership

Members of the Assembly welcome e-mail correspondence from the public. They may reply by e-mail, or by mail when more extensive follow-up is necessary. Please include both an e-mail and mailing address in all correspondence.

State Capitol
Albany, NY 12248
Web site: www.assembly.state.ny.us

Assembly Administration

June Egeland 518-455-4242/fax: 518-455-4935
Title: Clerk of the Assembly

Wayne P Jackson 518-455-3797/fax: 518-455-4445
Title: Sergeant-at-Arms, Chamber

John Longo 518-455-5767/fax: 518-455-4963
Title: Director, Communication & Information Services

John P Wellspeak 518-455-4411/fax: 518-455-4298
Title: Director, Administration

Patricia R Bolek 518-455-4999/fax: 518-455-4989
Title: District Office Administrator

James Murphy 518-455-4704/fax: 518-455-4705
Title: Director, Internship Program

Donald Poleto 518-455-5165/fax: 518-455-4741
Title: Superintendent, Document Room

Sharon Walsh 518-455-4218/fax: 518-455-5175
Title: Public Information Officer

Ellen Breslin 518-455-2468/fax: 518-426-6901
Title: Reference Librarian, Legislative Library

Barbara VanNortwick 518-455-2468/fax: 518-455-6901
Title: Reference Librarian

Joseph E O'Brien 518-455-5190/fax: 518-455-4517
Title: Director, Operations

Majority Leadership

Sheldon Silver (D) 518-455-3791
e-mail: speaker@assembly.state.ny.us
Title: Speaker

Ivan C Lafayette (D) 518-455-4545
e-mail: lafayei@assembly.state.ny.us
Title: Speaker Pro Tempore

Harvey Weisenberg (D) 518-455-3028
e-mail: weisenh@assembly.state.ny.us
Title: Assistant Speaker Pro Tempore

Paul A Tokasz (D) 518-455-5921
e-mail: tokaszp@assembly.state.ny.us
Title: Majority Leader

Clarence Norman, Jr (D) 518-455-5262
e-mail: normanc@assembly.state.ny.us
Title: Deputy Speaker

Rhoda S Jacobs (D) 518-455-5385
e-mail: jacobsr@assembly.state.ny.us
Title: Assistant Speaker

William L Parment (D) 518-455-4511
e-mail: parmenw@assembly.state.ny.us
Title: Chair, Committee on Standing Committees

Aurelia Greene (D) 518-455-5671
e-mail: greenea@assembly.state.ny.us
Title: Deputy Majority Leader

Earlene Hooper (D) 518-455-5871
e-mail: hoopere@assembly.state.ny.us
Title: Assistant Majority Leader

Vivian E Cook (D) 518-455-4203
e-mail: cookv@assembly.state.ny.us
Title: Majority Whip

Dov Hikind (D) 518-455-5721
e-mail: hikindd@assembly.state.ny.us
Title: Deputy Majority Whip

Barbara Clark (D) 518-455-4711
e-mail: clarkb@assembly.state.ny.us
Title: Assistant Majority Whip

N Nick Perry (D) 518-455-4171
e-mail: perryn@assembly.state.ny.us
Title: Chair, Majority Conference

Adriano Espaillat (D) 518-455-5807
e-mail: espaila@assembly.state.ny.us
Title: Vice Chair, Majority Conference

Offices and agencies appear in alphabetical order.

William B Magnarelli (D) 518-455-4826
e-mail: magnaw@assembly.state.ny.us
Title: Secretary, Majority Conference

John J McEneny (D) 518-455-4178
e-mail: mcenenj@assembly.state.ny.us
Title: Chair, Majority Steering Committee

William Colton (D) 518-455-5828
e-mail: coltonw@assembly.state.ny.us
Title: Vice Chair, Majority Steering Committee

Anthony S Seminerio (D) 518-455-4621
e-mail: seminea@assembly.state.ny.us
Title: Chair, Majority Program Committee

Herman D Farrell, Jr (D) 518-455-5491
e-mail: farrelh@assembly.state.ny.us
Title: Chair, Ways & Means Committee

Majority Staff

Judy R Rapfogel 212-312-1400/fax: 212-312-1418
Title: Chief of Staff to the Speaker

Charles Carrier 518-455-3888/fax: 518-455-3858
Title: Press Secretary/Acting Director of the Speaker's Communications

Kevin C McGraw 518-455-4303/fax: 518-455-4380
Title: First Deputy to the Speaker for Majority Program & Policy

Karen McCann 518-455-4736/fax: 518-455-5428
Title: Director, Legislative Services

John Hudder 518-455-4386/fax: 518-455-5573
Title: Director, Program Development

Bill Collins 518-455-4191/fax: 518-455-4103
Title: Counsel to the Majority

Dean Fuleihan 518-455-3786/fax: 518-455-4445
Title: Secretary to the Majority Committee on Ways & Means

Minority Leadership

Charles H Nesbitt (R) 518-455-3751
e-mail: nesbitc@assembly.state.ny.us
Title: Minority Leader

Willis H Stephens, Jr (R) 518-455-5783
e-mail: stephew@assembly.state.ny.us
Title: Minority Leader Pro Tempore

vacant 518-455-5241
e-mail: youngc@assembly.state.ny.us
Title: Assistant Minority Leader Pro Tempore

Nancy Calhoun (R) 518-455-5441
e-mail: calhoun@assembly.state.ny.us
Title: Ranking Minority Member, Committee on Standing Committees

Robert C Oaks (R) 518-455-5655
e-mail: oaksr@assembly.state.ny.us
Title: Deputy Minority Leader

James N Tedisco (R) 518-455-5811
e-mail: tediscj@assembly.state.ny.us
Title: Assistant Minority Leader

G Christian Ortloff (R) 518-455-5943
e-mail: ortlofc@assembly.state.ny.us
Title: Assistant Minority Leader

James P Hayes (R) 518-455-4618
e-mail: hayesj@assembly.state.ny.us
Title: Minority Whip

Daniel J Burling (R) 518-455-5314
e-mail: burlind@assembly.state.ny.us
Title: Deputy Minority Whip

James G Bacalles (R) 518-455-5791
e-mail: bacallj@assembly.state.ny.us
Title: Assistant Minority Whip

David R Townsend, Jr (R) 518-455-5334
e-mail: townsed@assembly.state.ny.us
Title: Chair, Minority Conference

Patricia Acampora (R) 518-455-5294
e-mail: acampop@assembly.state.ny.us
Title: Vice-Chair, Minority Conference

Gary Finch (R) 518-455-5878
e-mail: finchg@assembly.state.ny.us
Title: Secretary, Minority Conference

Donna Ferrara (R) 518-455-4684
e-mail: ferrard@assembly.state.ny.us
Title: Chair, Minority Joint Conference Committee

Fred W Thiele, Jr (R) 518-455-5997
e-mail: thielef@assembly.state.ny.us
Title: Vice Chair, Minority Joint Conference Committee

Patrick R Manning (R) 518-455-5177
e-mail: manninp@assembly.state.ny.us
Title: Chair, Minority Steering Committee

Clifford W Crouch (R) 518-455-5741
e-mail: crouchcw@assembly.state.ny.us
Title: Vice Chair, Minority Steering Committee

Brian M Kolb (R) 518-455-5772
e-mail: kolbb@assembly.state.ny.us
Title: Chair, Minority Program Committee

William A Barclay (R) 518-455-5841
e-mail: barclaw@assembly.state.ny.us
Title: Vice Chair, Minority Program Committee

Offices and agencies appear in alphabetical order.

Thomas F Barraga (R) 518-455-4611
e-mail: barragt@assembly.state.ny.us
Title: Ranking Minority Member, Ways & Means

Minority Staff

Kimberly Galvin 518-455-3751/fax: 518-455-3750
Title: Chief of Staff/Minority Leader's Counsel

Kelliann Cummings 518-455-3756/fax: 518-455-3750
Title: Director, Minority Communications

Gregory Amorosi 518-455-3761/fax: 518-455-3750
Title: Director, Conference Operations

Jean McDonnell 518-455-3751/fax: 518-455-3750
Title: Counsel to the Minority

Harry MacAvoy 518-455-5002/fax: 518-455-5829
Title: Director, Minority Research & Program Development

Rebecca D'Agati 518-455-5161/fax: 518-455-4550
Title: Director, Minority Ways & Means Staff

Judith A Skype 518-455-4211/fax: 518-455-3758
Title: Director, Minority Administration & Personnel

State Assembly Roster

Multiple party abbreviations following the names of legislators indicate that those legislators ran as the Assembly candidate for each identified party. Source: NYS Board of Elections. Party abbreviations: Conservative (C), Democrat (D), Green (G), Independent (I), Liberal (L), Republican (R), Right to Life (RL), Veterans (VE), Working Families (WF)

Peter J Abbate, Jr (D-I) 518-455-3053/fax: 518-455-5524
District: 49 *Room:* 839 LOB *e-mail:* abbatep@assembly.state.ny.us
Committees: Aging; Banks; Consumer Affairs & Protection; Governmental
Employees (Chair); Labor
Senior Staff: Barbara M O'Neill

Patricia L Acampora (R-I-C-WF) . 518-455-5294/fax: 518-455-4740
District: 1 *Room:* 404 LOB *e-mail:* acampop@assembly.state.ny.us
Title: Vice Chair, Minority Conference
Committees: Banks; Governmental Employees; Labor (Ranking Minority
Member)
Senior Staff: Robert Parker

Thomas W Alfano (R-I-C-WF) 518-455-4627/fax: 518-455-4643
District: 21 *Room:* 721 LOB *e-mail:* alfanot@assembly.state.ny.us
Committees: Corporations, Authorities & Commissions; Judiciary (Ranking
Minority Leader); Labor
Senior Staff: M Scott Cushing

Carmen E Arroyo (R-D-L) 518-455-5402/fax: 518-455-4681
District: 84 *Room:* 734 LOB *e-mail:* arroyoc@assembly.state.ny.us
Committees: Aging; Alcoholism and Drug Abuse; Children & Families;
Education
Senior Staff: Richard Izquierdo

Darrel J Aubertine (D-I-G-WF) . . . 518-455-5545/fax: 518-455-5751
District: 118 *Room:* 602 LOB *e-mail:* aubertd@assembly.state.ny.us
Committees: Agriculture; Economic Development, Job Creation, Commerce
& Industry; Energy; Higher Education; Transportation; Veterans Affairs
Senior Staff: Ed Gaffney

Jeffrion L Aubry (D-L-WF) 518-455-4561/fax: 518-455-4565
District: 35 *Room:* 526 LOB *e-mail:* aubry@assembly.state.ny.us
Committees: Cities; Correction (Chair); Economic Development, Job
Creation, Commerce & Industry; Governmental Employees; Housing; Social
Services
Senior Staff: Indira Noel

James G Bacalles (R-C) 518-455-5791/fax: 518-455-4644
District: 136 *Room:* 439 LOB *e-mail:* bacallj@assembly.state.ny.us
Title: Assistant Minority Whip
Committees: Corporations, Authorities & Commissions (Ranking Minority
Member); Health; Social Services; Transportation
Senior Staff: Robin Lettimer

William A Barclay (R-I-C) 518-455-5841/fax: 518-455-5362
District: 124 *Room:* 938 LOB *e-mail:* barclaw@assembly.state.ny.us
Title: Vice-Chair, Minority Program Committee
Committees: Corporations, Authorities & Commissions; Election Law; Ethics
& Guidance; Insurance (Ranking Minority Member); Judiciary
Senior Staff: Dan Sweetland

Robert D Barra (R-I-C) 518-455-4656/fax: 518-455-4337
District: 14 *Room:* 723 LOB *e-mail:* barrar@assembly.state.ny.us
Committees: Consumer Affairs & Protection; Corporations, Authorities &
Commissions; Mental Health; Racing & Wagering (Ranking Minorty
Member)
Senior Staff: Rosemary Pugliese

Thomas F Barraga (R-I-C-RL-WF) 518-455-4611/fax:
518-455-5258
District: 8 *Room:* 444 CAP *e-mail:* barragt@assembly.state.ny.us
Title: Ranking Minority Member, Ways & Means Committee
Committees: Rules; Ways & Means (Ranking Minority Member)
Senior Staff: Mary Lou Curro

Michael Benedetto 518-455-5296/fax: 518-455-4641
District: 82 *Room:* 919 LOB *e-mail:* benedm@assembly.state.ny.us
Committees: Agriculture; Consumer Affairs & Protection; Education;
Governmental Operations; Housing; Labor
Senior Staff: John Collazzi

Michael A Benjamin (D-R-WF) . . . 518-455-5272/fax: 518-455-5925
District: 79 *Room:* 548 LOB *e-mail:* benjami@assembly.state.ny.us
Committees: Banks; Children & Families; Correction; Election Law;
Housing; Libraries & Education Technology
Senior Staff: Kennedy Benjamin

Offices and agencies appear in alphabetical order.

Jonathan L Bing (D) 518-455-4794/fax: 518-455-4629
District: 73   *Room:* 827 LOB   *e-mail:* bingj@assembly.state.ny.us
Committees: Banks; Health, Housing; Judiciary; Social Services; Tourism, Arts & Sports Development
Senior Staff: Julie Hendricks

William F Boyland, Jr (D-L) 518-455-4466/fax: 518-455-3894
District: 55   *Room:* 324 LOB   *e-mail:* boylanw@assembly.state.ny.us
Committees: Aging; Banks; Economic Development, Job Creation, Commerce & Industry; Housing; Local Goverment
Senior Staff: Tamecca Greene

Adam T Bradley (D-I-WF) 518-455-5397/fax: 518-455-5041
District: 89   *Room:* 529 LOB   *e-mail:* bradlea@assembly.state.ny.us
Committees: Children & Families; Corporations, Authorities & Commissions; Election Law; Environmental Conservation; Judiciary; Veterans' Affairs
Senior Staff: Jonathan Lemle

James F Brennan (D-WF) 518-455-5377/fax: 518-455-5592
District: 44   *Room:* 641 LOB   *e-mail:* brennaj@assembly.state.ny.us
Committees: Codes; Corporations, Authorities & Commissions; Education; Oversight, Analysis & Investigation (Chair); Real Property Taxation
Senior Staff: Lorrie Smith

Richard L Brodsky (D-I-WF) 518-455-5753/fax: 518-455-5920
District: 92   *Room:* 422 LOB   *e-mail:* brodskr@assembly.state.ny.us
Committees: Banks; Corporations, Authorities & Commissions (Chair); Tourism, Arts & Sports Development
Senior Staff: Kelly MacMillan

Jeffrey D Brown (R) 518-455-4505/fax: 518-455-5523
District: 121   *Room:* 628 LOB   *e-mail:* brownj@assembly.state.ny.us
Committees: Commerce & Industry; Economic Development; Environmental Conservation; Job Creation; Health; Veterans' Affairs
Senior Staff: Tammy Rosanio

Daniel J Burling (R-I-C) 518-455-5314/fax: 518-455-5691
District: 147   *Room:* 329 LOB   *e-mail:* burlind@assembly.state.ny.us
Title: Deputy Minority Whip
Committees: Environmental Conservation; Housing; Veterans' Affairs; Ways & Means
Senior Staff: Barbara Finke

Marc W Butler (R-I-C) 518-455-5393/fax: 518-455-5889
District: 117   *Room:* 318 LOB   *e-mail:* butlerm@assembly.state.ny.us
Title: Chair, Minority Program Committee
Committees: Agriculture; Economic Development, Job Creation, Commerce & Industry (Ranking Minority Member); Higher Education
Senior Staff: Laurel D Corby

Kevin A Cahill (D-I-WF) 518-455-4436/fax: 518-455-5576
District: 101   *Room:* 557 LOB   *e-mail:* cahillk@assembly.state.ny.us
Title: Vice Chair, Majority Steering Committee
Committees: Economic Development, Ethics (Chair); Job Creation, Commerce & Industry; Health; Higher Education; Ways & Means
Senior Staff: Kathy Keyser

Nancy Calhoun (R-I-C) 518-455-5441/fax: 518-455-5884
District: 96   *Room:* 525 LOB   *e-mail:* calhoun@assembly.state.ny.us
Title: Ranking Minority Member, Committee on Standing Committees
Committees: Insurance; Labor; Rules; Ways & Means
Senior Staff: Marianne D Crary

Ronald J Canestrari (D-I) 518-455-4474/fax: 518-455-4727
District: 106   *Room:* 717 LOB   *e-mail:* canestr@assembly.state.ny.us
Committees: Banks; Higher Education (Chair); Labor; Local Government; Rules; Ways & Means
Senior Staff: Cathy Krasnopolski

Ann-Margaret E Carrozza (D-WF) 518-455-5425/fax: 518-455-4648
District: 26   *Room:* 656 LOB   *e-mail:* carroza@assembly.state.ny.us
Committees: Aging; Banks; Governmental Employees; Insurance
Senior Staff: Evelyn R Lewis

Pat M Casale (R-C-RL) 518-455-5777/fax: 518-455-5923
District: 108   *Room:* 320 LOB   *e-mail:* casalep@assembly.state.ny.us
Committees: Economic Development, Job Creation, Commerce & Industry; Housing
Senior Staff: Linda G Quillinan

Joan K Christensen (D-WF-VE) . . 518-455-5383/fax: 518-455-5417
District: 119   *Room:* 502 LOB   *e-mail:* christj@assembly.state.ny.us
Committees: Housing; Insurance; Labor; Real Property Taxation; Small Business
Senior Staff: Sally Drake

Barbara M Clark (D-L-WF) 518-455-4711/fax: 518-455-3740
District: 33   *Room:* 702 LOB   *e-mail:* clarkb@assembly.state.ny.us
Title: Assistant Majority Whip
Committees: Children & Families; Education; Environmental Conservation; Labor; Libraries & Education Technology
Senior Staff: Christiana Akwari

Adele Cohen (D-WF) 518-455-4811/fax: 518-455-5654
District: 46   *Room:* 435 LOB   *e-mail:* cohena@assembly.state.ny.us
Title: Chair, Commission on Science & Technology
Committees: Aging; Agriculture; Cities; Energy; Insurance; Judiciary
Senior Staff: Rosemary Lategano

William Colton (D-L-WF) 518-455-5828/fax: 518-455-5706
District: 47   *Room:* 733 LOB   *e-mail:* coltonw@assembly.state.ny.us
Title: Vice Chair, Majority Steering Committee
Committees: Correction; Environmental Conservation; Governmental Employees; Labor; Ways & Means
Senior Staff: Alice M Raab

James D Conte (R-I-C) 518-455-5732/fax: 518-455-5553
District: 10   *Room:* 635 LOB   *e-mail:* contej@assembly.state.ny.us
Committees: Education (Ranking Minority Member); Health; Higher Education
Senior Staff: Jenifer J Pratico

Vivian E Cook (D-L) 518-455-4203/fax: 518-455-3606
District: 32   *Room:* 331 LOB   *e-mail:* cookv@assembly.state.ny.us
Title: Majority Whip
Committees: Alcoholism & Drug Abuse; Codes; Corporations, Authorities & Commissions; Housing; Insurance; Ways & Means
Senior Staff: Joyce Corker

Clifford W Crouch (R) 518-455-5741/fax: 518-455-5864
District: 107   *Room:* 545 LOB   *e-mail:* crouchc@assembly.state.ny.us
Committees: Agriculture (Ranking Minority Member); Economic Development, Job Creation, Commerce & Industry; Governmental Operations; Labor
Senior Staff: Kathleen Moore

Offices and agencies appear in alphabetical order.

Michael J Cusick (D-I-C-WF). 518-455-5526/fax: 518-455-4760
District: 63 *Room:* 727 LOB *e-mail:* cusikm@assembly.state.ny.us
Committees: Governmental Employees; Higher Education; Mental Health;
Transportation; Veterans' Affairs
Senior Staff: Philip Maravojo

Steven H Cymbrowitz (D-WF). . . 518-455-5214/fax: (518) 455-5738
District: 45 *Room:* 538 LOB *e-mail:* cymbros@assembly.state.ny.us
Committees: Agriculture; Environmental Conservation; Health; Housing;
Insurance
Senior Staff: Peg Donahue

Francine DelMonte (D-I-WF). 518-455-5284/fax: 518-455-5694
District: 138 *Room:* 553 LOB *e-mail:* delmonf@assembly.state.ny.us
Committees: Agriculture; Economic Development, Job Creation, Commerce
& Industry; Local Governments; Racing & Wagering; Tourism, Arts &
Sports Development; Transportation
Senior Staff: Valerie Pillo

RoAnn M Destito (D-I-WF). 518-455-5454/fax: 518-455-5928
District: 116 *Room:* 621 LOB *e-mail:* destitr@assembly.state.ny.us
Committees: Aging; Agriculture; Economic Development, Job Creation,
Commerce & Industry; Governmental Operations (Chair); Ways & Means
Senior Staff: Stephen M Longo

Thomas P DiNapoli (D-I-L-WF). . 518-455-5192/fax: 518-455-4921
District: 16 *Room:* 625 LOB *e-mail:* dinapot@assembly.state.ny.us
Committees: Education; Environmental Conservation (Chair); Rules;
Veterans' Affairs; Ways & Means
Senior Staff: Diane C Lombardi

Luis M Diaz (D). 518-455-5511/fax: 518-455-5449
District: 86 *Room:* 921 LOB *e-mail:* diazl@assembly.state.ny.us
Committees: Aging; Banks; Higher Education; Housing; Social Services
Senior Staff: Suzy A Lind

Ruben Diaz, Jr (D). 518-455-5514/fax: 518-455-5827
District: 85 *Room:* 419 LOB *e-mail:* diazr@assembly.state.ny.us
Committees: Children & Families; Education; Environmental Conservation;
Housing; Ways & Means
Senior Staff: Paul DelDuca

Jeffrey Dinowitz (D-L-WF). 518-455-5965/fax: 518-455-4437
District: 81 *Room:* 627 LOB *e-mail:* dinowij@assembly.state.ny.us
Committees: Alcoholism & Drug Abuse (Chair); Consumer Affairs &
Protection; Election Law; Environmental Conservation; Health; Judiciary;
Mental Health
Senior Staff: Ryan Miday

Patricia A Eddington (D-I-WF). . . 518-455-4901/fax: 518-455-5908
District: 3 *Room:* 639 LOB *e-mail:* eddingp@assembly.state.ny.us
Committees: Education; Government Operations; Health; Higher Education;
Labor; Veterans Affairs
Senior Staff: Donna Lent

Steven C Englebright (D-I-G-WF) 518-455-4804/fax: 518-455-5795
District: 4 *Room:* 824 LOB *e-mail:* engles@assembly.state.ny.us
Committees: Aging (Chair); Agriculture; Education; Energy; Higher
Education; Tourism, Arts & Sports Development
Senior Staff: Maria Weisenberg

Joseph A Errigo (R-C). 518-455-5662/fax: 518-455-5918
District: 130 *Room:* 427 LOB *e-mail:* errigoj@assembly.state.ny.us
Committees: Banks; Children & Families (Ranking Minority Member);
Housing
Senior Staff: Eileen Collins

Adriano Espaillat (D-L-WF). 518-455-5807/fax: 518-455-4908
District: 72 *Room:* 652 LOB *e-mail:* espaila@assembly.state.ny.us
Title: Vice-Chair, Majority Conference
Committees: Alcoholism & Drug Abuse; Corporations, Authorities &
Commissions; Environmental Conservation; Insurance; Social Services;
Ways & Means
Senior Staff: Giovanni Puello

Herman D Farrell, Jr (D). 518-455-5491/fax: 518-455-5776
District: 71 *Room:* 923 LOB *e-mail:* farrellh@assembly.state.ny.us
Title: Chair, Ways & Means Committee
Committees: Rules; Ways & Means (Chair)
Senior Staff: Marcia Coleman

Donna Ferrara (R-I-C-WF). 518-455-4684/fax: 518-455-5477
District: 15 *Room:* 322 LOB *e-mail:* ferrard@assembly.state.ny.us
Title: Chair, Minority Joint Conference Committee
Committees: Judiciary; Libraries & Education Technology (Ranking Minority
Member); Oversight, Analysis & Investigation (Ranking Minority Member)
Senior Staff: Carol A Cardell

Ginny Fields (D-WF). 518-455-5937/fax: 518-455-4784
District: 5 *Room:* 432 LOB *e-mail:* fieldsg@assembly.state.ny.us
Committees: Aging; Consumer Affairs & Protection; Corporations,
Authorities & Commissions; Oversight; Analysis & Investigation; Real
Property Taxation; Tourism, Arts & Sports Development
Senior Staff: Kathleen Koppenhoefer

Gary D Finch (R-I-C). 518-455-5878/fax: 518-455-3895
District: 123 *Room:* 718 LOB *e-mail:* finchg@assembly.state.ny.us
Committees: Agriculture; Energy; Economic Development, Job Creation,
Commerce & Industry
Senior Staff: Suzanne Redmond

Michael J Fitzpatrick (R-C-RL). . . 518-455-5021/fax: 518-455-4394
District: 7 *Room:* 544 LOB *e-mail:* fitzpam@assembly.state.ny.us
Committees: Higher Education; Local Government; Small Business;
Tourism, Arts & Sports Development (Ranking Minority Member)
Senior Staff: James B Teese

Sandra R Galef (D-I-WF). 518-455-5348/fax: 518-455-5728
District: 90 *Room:* 540 LOB *e-mail:* galefs@assembly.state.ny.us
Committees: Corporations Authorities & Commissions; Election Law;
Governmental Operations; Health; Libraries & Education Technology (Chair)
Senior Staff: Nicole Haff

David F Gantt (D). 518-455-5606/fax: 518-455-5419
District: 133 *Room:* 830 LOB *e-mail:* ganttd@assembly.state.ny.us
Committees: Corporations, Authorities & Commissions; Economic
Development, Job Creation, Commerce & Industry; Local Government;
Rules; Transportation (Chair); Ways & Means
Senior Staff: Robert Cook

Offices and agencies appear in alphabetical order.

Michael N Gianaris (D-WF). 518-455-5014/fax: 518-455-4044
District: 36   *Room:* 742 LOB   *e-mail:* gianarm@assembly.state.ny.us
Committees: Banks; Consumer Affairs & Protection; Election Law;
Environmental Conservation; Judiciary; Tourism, Arts & Sports
Development
Senior Staff: Michael Sais

Deborah J Glick (D-WF). 518-455-4841/fax: 518-455-4649
District: 66   *Room:* 844 LOB   *e-mail:* glickd@assembly.state.ny.us
Committees: Children & Families; Environmental Conservation; Higher
Education; Social Services (Chair); Ways & Means
Senior Staff: Theresa Swidorski

Diane M Gordon (D). 518-455-5912/fax: 518-455-3891
District: 40   *Room:* 441 LOB   *e-mail:* gordond@assembly.state.ny.us
Committees: Alcoholism & Drug Abuse; Corporations, Authorities &
Commissions; Correction; Health; Real Property Taxation; Social Services
Senior Staff: Nancy Lewis

Richard N Gottfried (D-L-WF) . . . 518-455-4941/fax: 518-455-5939
District: 75   *Room:* 822 LOB   *e-mail:* gottfrr@assembly.state.ny.us
Committees: Health (Chair); Higher Education; Rules
Senior Staff: Richard Conti

Alexander B Pete Grannis (D-WF) 518-455-5676/fax: 518-455-5282
District: 65   *Room:* 712 LOB   *e-mail:* grannis@assembly.state.ny.us
Committees: Environmental Conservation; Health; Housing; Insurance
(Chair); Rules; Ways & Means
Senior Staff: Peter J Newell

Roger L Green (D-WF) 518-455-5325/fax: 518-455-3684
District: 57   *Room:* 523 LOB   *e-mail:* greenr@assembly.state.ny.us
Committees: Cities; Environmental Conservation; Higher Education; Labor
Senior Staff: Rhonda VanNess

Aurelia Greene (D-WF). 518-455-5671/fax: 518-455-5461
District: 77   *Room:* 939 LOB   *e-mail:* greenea@assembly.state.ny.us
Title: Deputy Majority Leader
Committees: Cities; Education; Rules; Social Services; Ways & Means
Senior Staff: Sarah Curry-Cobb

Aileen M Gunther (D-C) 518-455-5355/fax: 518-455-5239
District: 98   *Room:* 428 LOB   *e-mail:* gunthea@assemby.state.ny.us
Committees: Agriculture; Environmental Conservation; Racing & Wagering;
Real Property Taxation; Tourism, Arts & Sports Development
Senior Staff: Steven wilkinson

James P Hayes (R-C-WF). 518-455-4618/fax: 518-455-5023
District: 148   *Room:* 458 LOB   *e-mail:* hayesj@assembly.state.ny.us
Title: Deputy Minority Whip
Committees: Banks; Election Law; Ethics & Guidance; Local Government;
Ways & Means
Senior Staff: Mary Jo Tamburlin

Carl E Heastie (D-WF). 518-455-4800/fax: 518-455-5103
District: 83   *Room:* 417 LOB   *e-mail:* heastic@assembly.state.ny.us
Committees: Aging; Children & Families; Corporations, Authorities &
Commissions; Housing; Labor; Small Business
Senior Staff: Paul Upton

Andrew Hevesi (D-WF) 518-455-4926/fax: 518-455-5173
District: 28   *Room:* 833 LOB   *e-mail:* hevesia@assembly.state.ny.us
Committees: Alcoholism & Drug Abuse; Consumer Affairs & Protection;
Corporations, Authorities & Commissions; Energy; Labor; Racing &
Wagering
Senior Staff: Todd Ferrara

Dov Hikind (D-R). 518-455-5721/fax: 518-455-5948
District: 48   *Room:* 551 LOB   *e-mail:* hikindd@assembly.state.ny.us
Title: Deputy Majority Whip
Committees:
Senior Staff: Marc B Kroneberg

Daniel L Hooker (R) 518-455-5363/fax: 518-455-5856
District: 127   *Room:* 937 LOB   *e-mail:* hookerd@assembly.state.ny.us
Committees: Agriculture; Veterans' Affairs
Senior Staff: Chuck Kaiser

Earlene Hooper (D-I-L). 518-455-5861/fax: 518-455-4329
District: 18   *Room:* 744 LOB   *e-mail:* hoopere@assembly.state.ny.us
Title: Assistant Majority Leader
Committees: Economic Development, Job Creation, Commerce & Industry;
Education; Housing; Labor; Rules
Senior Staff: Arndreia M Goodbee

William B Hoyt, III (D-I-L-WF) . . 518-455-4886/fax: 518-455-4890
District: 144   *Room:* 454 LOB   *e-mail:* hoyts@assembly.state.ny.us
Committees: Children & Families; Energy; Tourism, Arts & Sports
Development; Transportation; Ways & Means
Senior Staff: Sarah Kolberg

Vincent Ignizio (R). 518-455-4495/fax: 518-455-4501
District: 62   *Room:* 531 LOB   *e-mail:*
Committees: Children & Families; Corporations, Authorities &
Commissions; Social Services (Ranking Minority Member)
Senior Staff: Joseph Bovelli

Rhoda S Jacobs (D-L). 518-455-5385/fax: 518-455-3881
District: 42   *Room:* 736 LOB   *e-mail:* jacobsr@assembly.state.ny.us
Title: Assistant Speaker
Committees: Banks; Health; Higher Education; Insurance; Rules
Senior Staff: Mary-Jo Ehrlich

Susan V John (D) 518-455-4527/fax: 518-455-5342
District: 131   *Room:* 522 LOB   *e-mail:* johns@assembly.state.ny.us
Committees: Education; Energy; Judiciary; Labor (Chair); Libraries &
Education Technology
Senior Staff: Patricia L Rzepka

Ryan S Karben (D-I). 518-455-5118/fax: 518-455-5119
District: 95   *Room:* 637 LOB   *e-mail:* karbenr@assembly.state.ny.us
Committees: Alcoholism & Drug Abuse; Corporations, Authorities &
Commissions; Energy; Insurance; Judiciary; Local Goverment
Senior Staff: Arron Troodler

Thomas J Kirwan (R-C-RL) 518-455-5762/fax: 518-455-5593
District: 100   *Room:* 725 LOB   *e-mail:* kirwant@assembly.state.ny.us
Committees: Alcoholism & Drug Abuse; Cities (Ranking Minority Member);
Codes; Education
Senior Staff: Thilde Rafferty

Offices and agencies appear in alphabetical order.

Brian M Kolb (R-I-C-RL) 518-455-5772/fax: 518-455-4650
District: 129 *Room:* 720 LOB *e-mail:* kolbb@assembly.state.ny.us
Title: Chair, Minority Program Committee
Committees: Energy (Ranking Minority Member); Higher Education; Labor;
Tourism; Arts & Sports Development
Senior Staff: Doug Finch

David R Koon (D-I-WF) 518-455-5784/fax: 518-455-4639
District: 135 *Room:* 643 LOB *e-mail:* koond@assembly.state.ny.us
Committees: Alcoholism & Drug Abuse; Economic Development, Job
Creation, Commerce & Industry; Libraries & Education Technology; Local
Government; Small Business
Senior Staff: Elizabeth Hoffman

Ivan C Lafayette (D-L-WF) 518-455-4545/fax: 518-455-4547
District: 34 *Room:* 646 LOB *e-mail:* lafayei@assembly.state.ny.us
Title: Speaker, Pro Tempore
Committees: Banks; Insurance; Rules; Transportation; Ways & Means
Senior Staff: Evan Schneider

George Latimer (D) 518-455-4897/fax: 518-455-4861
District: 91 *Room:* 820 LOB *e-mail:*
Committees: Environmental Conservation; Governmental Operations;
Insurance; Labor; Local Governments; Transportation
Senior Staff: Vacant

John W Lavelle (D-WF) 518-455-4677/fax: 518-455-5946
District: 61 *Room:* 833 LOB *e-mail:* lavellj@assembly.state.ny.us
Committees: Education; Governmental Employees; Mental Health; Social
Services; Transportation; Veterans' Affairs
Senior Staff: Keith Parascandola, COS

Charles Lavine (D) 518-455-5456/fax: 518-455-5467
District: 13 *Room:* 325 LOB *e-mail:* lavinec@assembly.state.ny.us
Committees: Alcoholism & Drug Abuse; Codes; Economic Development;
Local Government; Social Services; Transportation
Senior Staff: Carol Hammond

Joseph R Lentol (D) 518-455-4477/fax: 518-455-4599
District: 50 *Room:* 632 LOB *e-mail:* lentolj@assembly.state.ny.us
Committees: Codes (Chair); Election Law; Ethics & Guidance; Rules; Ways
& Means
Senior Staff: Catherine E Peake

Barbara S Lifton (D-WF) 518-455-5444/fax: 518-455-4640
District: 125 *Room:* 821 LOB *e-mail:* liftonb@assembly.state.ny.us
Committees: Agriculture; Economic Development, Job Creation, Commerce
& Industry; Environmental Conservation; Higher Education; Mental Health
Senior Staff: Susan Pratt

Vito J Lopez (D-L) 518-455-5537/fax: 518-455-5789
District: 53 *Room:* 943 LOB *e-mail:* lopezv@assembly.state.ny.us
Committees: Economic Development, Job Creation, Commerce & Industry;
Housing (Chair); Rules; Social Services
Senior Staff: Jonathan Harkavy

Donna Lupardo (D) 518-455-5431/fax: 518-455-5693
District: 126 *Room:* 834 LOB *e-mail:* lupardd@assembly.state.ny.us
Committees: Election Law; Environmental Conservation; Higher Education;
Libraries & Education Technology; Mental Health; Transportation
Senior Staff: Michael Kennerknecht

William Magee (D-I) 518-455-4807/fax: 518-455-5237
District: 111 *Room:* 828 LOB *e-mail:* mageew@assembly.state.ny.us
Committees: Aging; Agriculture (Chair); Banks; Higher Education; Local
Government
Senior Staff: Troy Waffner

William B Magnarelli (D-WF-VE) 518-455-4826/fax: 518-455-5498
District: 120 *Room:* 519 LOB *e-mail:* magnarw@assembly.state.ny.us
Title: Secretary, Majority Conference
Committees: Economic Development, Job Creation, Commerce & Industry;
Education; Health; Oversight, Analysis & Investigation; Veterans' Affairs
Senior Staff: Susan McSweeney

Patrick R Manning (R) 518-455-5177/fax: 518-455-5418
District: 103 *Room:* 402 LOB *e-mail:* manninp@assembly.state.ny.us
Title: Chair, Minority Steering Committee
Committees: Banks; Environmental Conservation (Ranking Minority
Member); Transportation (Ranking Minority Member)
Senior Staff: Paula K Odegard

Margaret M Markey (D) 518-455-4755/fax: 518-455-5032
District: 30 *Room:* 654 LOB *e-mail:* markeym@assembly.state.ny.us
Committees: Agriculture; Consumer Affairs & Protection; Governmental
Operations; Labor; Racing & Wagering; Tourism, Arts & Sports
Development
Senior Staff: Gussie Motta

Nettie Mayersohn (D-L-WF) 518-455-4404/fax: 518-455-5408
District: 27 *Room:* 746 LOB *e-mail:* mayersn@assembly.state.ny.us
Committees: Health; Labor
Senior Staff: Mary A Schlotter

Roy J McDonald (R-I-C) 518-455-5404/fax: 518-455-3727
District: 112 *Room:* 426 LOB *e-mail:* mcdonar@assembly.state.ny.us
Committees: Agriculture; Banks (Ranking Minority Member); Veterans
Affairs; Ways & Means
Senior Staff: Mark Luciano

David G McDonough (R-C-I) 518-455-4633/fax: 518-455-5559
District: 19 *Room:* 533 LOB *e-mail:* mcdond@assembly.state.ny.us
Committees: Consumer Affairs & Protection (Ranking Minority Member);
Education; Transportation
Senior Staff: Lynette Liverani

John J McEneny (D-I-L-WF) 518-455-4178/fax: 518-455-5737
District: 104 *Room:* 648 LOB *e-mail:* mcenenj@assembly.state.ny.us
Title: Chair, Majority Steering Committee
Committees: Agriculture; Ethics & Guidance; Governmental Employees;
Social Services; Tourism, Arts & Sports Development; Ways & Means
Senior Staff: Joe Galu

Brian M McLaughlin (D-L-WF) .. 518-455-5172/fax: 518-455-5479
District: 25 *Room:* 704 LOB *e-mail:* mclaugb@assembly.state.ny.us
Committees: Aging; Alcoholism & Drug Abuse; Cities; Real Property
Taxation (Chair); Transportation; Ways & Means
Senior Staff: Kathleen Conroy

Jimmy Meng (D) 518-455-5411/fax: 518-455-4995
District: 22 *Room:* 920 LOB *e-mail:* mengj@assembly.state.ny.us
Committees: Aging; Education; Consumer Affairs & Protection;
Corporations, Authorities & Commissions; Education; Small Business;
Transportation
Senior Staff: Vacant

Offices and agencies appear in alphabetical order.

Joel M Miller (R-C).............. 518-455-5725/fax: 518-455-5729
District: 102   *Room:* 722 LOB   *e-mail:* millerj@assembly.state.ny.us
Committees: Education; Higher Education (Ranking Minority Member);
Social Services
Senior Staff: Rachel Tolliver

Joan L Millman (D-WF)......... 518-455-5426/fax: 518-455-4787
District: 52   *Room:* 510 CAP   *e-mail:* millmaj@assembly.state.ny.us
Committees: Aging; Corporations, Authorities & Commissions; Labor;
Libraries & Education Technology; Small Business; Transportation
Senior Staff: Corri Freedman

Matthew Mirones (R-I-C-RL)..... 518-455-5716/fax: 518-455-5970
District: 60   *Room:* 429 LOB   *e-mail:* mironem@assembly.state.ny.us
Committees: Cities; Corporations, Authorities & Commissions; Health;
Mental Health (Ranking Minority Member); Transportation
Senior Staff: Georgea Kay

Joseph D Morelle (D) 518-455-5373/fax: 518-455-5647
District: 132   *Room:* 716 LOB   *e-mail:* morellj@assembly.state.ny.us
Committees: Economic Development, Job Creation, Commerce & Industry;
Higher Education; Libraries & Education Technology; Local Government;
Tourism, Arts, & Sports Development (Chair)
Senior Staff: Kristin Anderson

Louis Mosiello (R) 518-455-3662/fax: 518-455-5499
District: 93   *Room:* 431 LOB   *e-mail:* mosiell@assembly.state.ny.us
Committees: Cities; Education; Governmental Operations (Ranking Minority
Member)
Senior Staff: Mary Allen

Charles H Nesbitt (R-I-C)........ 518-455-3751/fax: 518-455-3750
District: 139   *Room:* 933 LOB   *e-mail:* nesbitc@assembly.state.ny.us
Title: Minority Leader
Committees: Rules (Ranking Minority Member); ex officio to all committees
Senior Staff: Darlene Moore

Catherine T Nolan (D-WF) 518-455-4851/fax: 518-455-3847
District: 37   *Room:* 424 LOB   *e-mail:* nolanc@assembly.state.ny.us
Committees: Banks (Chair); Corporations, Authorities & Commissions;
Rules; Veterans' Affairs; Ways & Means
Senior Staff: Anne-Marie G Baumann-Weiss

Clarence Norman, Jr (D-WF)..... 518-455-5262/fax: 518-455-5768
District: 43   *Room:* 739 LOB   *e-mail:* normanc@assembly.state.ny.us
Title: Deputy Speaker
Committees: Banks; Codes; Election Law; Rules; Ways & Means
Senior Staff: Nancy Ramos

Maureen C O'Connell (R-I-C) 518-455-5341/fax: 518-455-4346
District: 17   *Room:* 326 LOB   *e-mail:* oconnem@assembly.state.ny.us
Committees: Ethics & Guidance; Health (Ranking Minority Member);
Insurance; Judiciary
Senior Staff: Eileen O'Donnell

Daniel J O'Donnell (D-WF) 518-455-5603/fax: 518-455-3812
District: 69   *Room:* 819 LOB   *e-mail:* odonned@assembly.state.ny.us
Committees: Codes; Environmental Conservation; Judiciary; Local
Government; Oversight, Analysis & INvestigation; Tourism, Arts & Sports
Development
Senior Staff: Elizabeth Ball

Tom O'Mara (R) 518-455-4538/fax: 518-455-5922
District: 137   *Room:* 433 LOB   *e-mail:*
Committees: Aging; Correction (Ranking Minority Member); Economic
Development, Job Creation, Commerce & Industry; Tourism, Arts & Sports
Development
Senior Staff: Michael Fuller

Robert C Oaks (R)............... 518-455-5655/fax: 518-455-5407
District: 128   *Room:* 437 LOB   *e-mail:* oaksr@assembly.state.ny.us
Title: Deputy, Minority Leader
Committees: Aging; Ethics & Guidance (Ranking Minority Member);
Insurance; Labor; Rules
Senior Staff: Laurie Levine

Felix W Ortiz (D-I-L-WF) 518-455-3821/fax: 518-455-3828
District: 51   *Room:* 542 LOB   *e-mail:* ortizf@assembly.state.ny.us
Committees: Banks; Correction; Economic Development, Job Creation,
Commerce & Industry; Energy; Labor; Rules
Senior Staff: Linda A Buckley

George Christian Ortloff (R-I-C).. 518-455-5943/fax: 518-455-5761
District: 114   *Room:* 450 LOB   *e-mail:* ortlofc@assembly.state.ny.us
Title: Assistant Minority Leader
Committees: Election Law; Environmental Conservation; Rules;
Transportation
Senior Staff: Anthony L Rivera

William L Parment (D-I)......... 518-455-4511/fax: 518-455-4328
District: 150   *Room:* 547 LOB   *e-mail:* parmenw@assembly.state.ny.us
Title: Chair, Committee on Standing Committees
Committees: Education; Environmental Conservation; Mental Health;
Veterans' Affairs; Ways & Means
Senior Staff: Amy Abbati

Amy R Paulin (D-I-WF) 518-455-5585/fax: 518-455-5409
District: 88   *Room:* 327 LOB   *e-mail:* paulina@assembly.state.ny.us
Committees: Children & Families; Education; Health; Higher Education;
Veterans' Affairs
Senior Staff: Nancy Fisher

Crystal D Peoples (D-I-L) 518-455-5005/fax: 518-455-5471
District: 141   *Room:* 619 LOB   *e-mail:* peoplec@assembly.state.ny.us
Committees: Alcoholism & Drug Abuse; Consumer Affairs & Protection;
Environmental Conservation; Health; Insurance; Social Services
Senior Staff: Karla Thomas

Jose R Peralta (D-WF)........... 518-455-4567/fax: 518-455-5375
District: 39   *Room:* 528 LOB   *e-mail:* peraltj@assembly.state.ny.us
Committees: Banks; Cities; Consumer Affairs & Protection; Correction;
Election Law; Labor
Senior Staff: Yonel Letellier

N Nick Perry (D-WF) 518-455-4166/fax: 518-455-5478
District: 58   *Room:* 452 LOB   *e-mail:* perryn@assembly.state.ny.us
Title: Chair, Majority Conference
Committees: Banks; Energy; Insurance; Labor; Transportation; Ways &
Means
Senior Staff: Jeanine Johnson

Audrey I Pheffer (D-L-WF) 518-455-4292/fax: 518-455-4723
District: 23   *Room:* 941 LOB   *e-mail:* pheffea@assembly.state.ny.us
Committees: Aging; Consumer Affairs & Protection (Chair); Higher
Education; Rules; Veterans' Affairs
Senior Staff: JoAnn Shapiro

Offices and agencies appear in alphabetical order.

Adam Clayton Powell, IV (D-L-WF) 518-455-4781/fax: 518-455-3893
District: 68   *Room:* 527 LOB   *e-mail:* powella@assembly.state.ny.us
Committees: Corporations, Authorities & Commissions; Housing; Insurance; Small Business
Senior Staff: France Blanco-Bardia

J Gary Pretlow (D-I-WF) 518-455-5291/fax: 518-455-5447
District: 87   *Room:* 845 LOB   *e-mail:* pretloj@assembly.state.ny.us
Committees: Cities; Codes; Insurance; Racing & Wagering (Chair); Social Services; Ways & Means
Senior Staff: Janet E Edwards

Jack Quinn (R) 518-455-4462/fax: 518-455-5560
District: 146   *Room:* 543 LOB   *e-mail:* quinnj@assembly.state.ny.us
Committees: Alcoholism & Drug Abuse (Ranking Minority Member), Small Business; Transportation; Small Business;
Senior Staff: Mary Lou Palmer

Annie Rabbitt (R-C) 518-455-5991/fax: 518-455-5929
District: 97   *Room:* 532 LOB   *e-mail:*
Committees: Aging; Consumer Affairs & Protection; Local Governments (Ranking Minority Member)
Senior Staff: Susan Stammel

Andrew P Raia (R-C) 518-455-5952/fax: 518-455-5804
District: 9   *Room:* 629 LOB   *e-mail:* raiaa@assembly.state.ny.us
Committees: Aging (Ranking Minority Member); Housing; Local Government; Social Services
Senior Staff: Judy Van Amburgh

Philip R Ramos (D-WF) 518-455-5185/fax: 518-455-5236
District: 6   *Room:* 650 LOB   *e-mail:* ramosp@assembly.state.ny.us
Committees: Aging; Economic Development, Job Creation, Commerce & Industry; Education; Housing; Local Government
Senior Staff: Luis Montes

William Reilich (R-C-I) 518-455-4664/fax: 518-455-3093
District: 134   *Room:* 940 LOB   *e-mail:* reilicw@assembly.state.ny.us
Committees: Aging; Banks; Education; Small Business
Senior Staff: Michelle Marini

Robert Reilly (D) 518-455-5931/fax: 518-455-5840
District: 109   *Room:* 430 LOB   *e-mail:* reillyr@assembly.state.ny.us
Committees: Agriculture; Corporations, Authorities & Commissions; Education; Governmental Operations; Racing & Wagering; Tourism, Arts & Sports Development
Senior Staff: Tim Nichols

Peter M Rivera (D) 518-455-5102/fax: 518-455-3693
District: 76   *Room:* 826 LOB   *e-mail:* riverap@assembly.state.ny.us
Committees: Agriculture; Consumer Affairs & Protection; Judiciary; Mental Health (Chair); Rules

Naomi Rivera (D) 518-455-5844/fax: 518-455-5596
District: 80   *Room:* 530 LOB   *e-mail:* naomirivera2004@aol.com
Committees: Children & Families; Cities; Health; Real Property Taxation; Tourism, Arts & Sports Development
Senior Staff: Guillermo A Martinez
Senior Staff: Michelle Dolgow

Jose Rivera (D-L) 518-455-5414/fax: 518-455-5322
District: 78   *Room:* 536 LOB   *e-mail:* riveraj@assembly.state.ny.us
Committees: Aging; Insurance; Small Business
Senior Staff: Edwina Townes

Annette M Robinson (D-WF) 518-455-5474/fax: 518-455-5857
District: 56   *Room:* 729 LOB   *e-mail:* robinsa@assembly.state.ny.us
Committees: Children & Families; Housing; Oversight, Analysis & Investigation; Real Property Taxation; Small Business
Senior Staff: Adrienne Johnson

Joseph S Saladino (R-C-I) 518-455-5305/fax: 518-455-5024
District: 12   *Room:* 534 LOB   *e-mail:* saladij@assembly.state.ny.us
Committees: Education; Environmental Conservation; Governmental Employees (Ranking Minority Member)
Senior Staff: Barbara Nolan-Murphy

Steven Sanders (D-L-WF) 518-455-5506/fax: 518-455-4801
District: 74   *Room:* 836 LOB   *e-mail:* sanders@assembly.state.ny.us
Committees: Cities; Education (Chair); Housing; Rules
Senior Staff: John A Frederick

Teresa R Sayward (R) 518-455-5565/fax: 518-455-5710
District: 113   *Room:* 633 LOB   *e-mail:* saywart@assembly.state.ny.us
Committees: Children & Families; Correction (Ranking Minority Member); Education; Environmental Conservation (Ranking Minority Member)
Senior Staff: Meg Wood

William D Scarborough (D-L-WF) 518-455-4451/fax: 518-455-5522
District: 29   *Room:* 622 LOB   *e-mail:* scarbow@assembly.state.ny.us
Committees: Banks; Corporations, Authorities & Commissions; Correction; Education; Energy
Senior Staff: Robyn L Montgomery

Robin L Schimminger (D-I-C) 518-455-4767/fax: 518-455-4724
District: 140   *Room:* 847 LOB   *e-mail:* schimmr@assembly.state.ny.us
Committees: Codes; Economic Development, Job Creation, Commerce & Industry (Chair); Health; Ways & Means
Senior Staff: Kenneth L Berlinski

Mark Schroeder (D) 518-455-4691/fax: 518-455-5238
District: 145   *Room:* 323 LOB   *e-mail:* schroem@assembly.state.ny.us
Committees: Insurance; Local Governments; Mental Health; Oversight, Analysis & Investigation; Small Business; Veterans Affairs
Senior Staff: Patrick Curry

Dierdre K Scozzafava (R-C) 518-455-5797/fax: 518-455-5289
District: 122   *Room:* 532 LOB   *e-mail:* scozzad@assembly.state.ny.us
Committees: Banking; Codes (Ranking Minority Member); Ethics & Guidance; Ways & Means
Senior Staff: Dayle B Burgess

Frank R Seddio (D-I) 518-455-5211/fax: 518-455-5043
District: 59   *Room:* 555 LOB   *e-mail:* seddiof@assembly.state.ny.us
Committees: Aging; Banks; Insurance; Transportation; Ways & Means
Senior Staff: Alan Maisel

Anthony S Seminerio (D-C) 518-455-4621/fax: 518-455-5361
District: 38   *Room:* 818 LOB   *e-mail:* seminea@assembly.state.ny.us
Title: Chair, Majority Program Committee
Committees: Banks; Cities; Governmental Employees; Higher Education; Racing & Wagering
Senior Staff: Jody Rickert

Offices and agencies appear in alphabetical order.

Sheldon Silver (D-L-WF) 518-455-3791/fax: 518-455-5459
District: 64 *Room:* 932 LOB *e-mail:* speaker@assembly.state.ny.us
Title: Speaker
Committees: Rules (Chair); ex officio to all committees
Senior Staff: Judy R Rapfogel

Willis H Stephens, Jr (R-I-C) 518-455-5783/fax: 518-455-5543
District: 99 *Room:* 446 LOB *e-mail:* stephew@assembly.state.ny.us
Title: Minority Leader, Pro Tempore
Committees: Judiciary; Rules; Ways & Means
Senior Staff: Dottie Pohlid

Scott M Stringer (D-L-WF) 518-455-5802/fax: 518-455-5015
District: 67 *Room:* 842 LOB *e-mail:* strings@assembly.state.ny.us
Committees: Cities (Chair); Education; Higher Education; Housing; Judiciary
Senior Staff: Susannah Vickers

Robert K Sweeney (D-I-WF) 518-455-5787/fax: 518-455-3976
District: 11 *Room:* 837 LOB *e-mail:* sweeney@assembly.state.ny.us
Committees: Education; Environmental Conservation; Local Government (Chair); Transportation; Veterans' Affairs
Senior Staff: Stephen Liss

James N Tedisco (R-I-C) 518-455-5811/fax: 518-455-5558
District: 110 *Room:* 521 LOB *e-mail:* tediscj@assembly.state.ny.us
Title: Assistant Minority Leader Pro Tempore
Committees: Banks; Racing & Wagering; Rules; Ways & Means
Senior Staff: Howard Becker

Fred W Thiele, Jr (R-I-WF) 518-455-5997/fax: 518-455-5963
District: 2 *Room:* 550 LOB *e-mail:* thielef@assembly.state.ny.us
Title: Vice-Chair, Minority Joint Conference Committee
Committees: Environmental Conservation; Election Law (Ranking Minority Member); Ways & Means
Senior Staff: McGrory Housing

Michele R Titus (D-L-WF) 518-455-5668/fax: 518-455-3892
District: 31 *Room:* 741 LOB *e-mail:* titusm@assembly.state.ny.us
Committees: Children & Families; Codes; Ethics & Guidance; Judiciary; Local Government; Small Business
Senior Staff: Richard A McKoy

Paul A Tokasz (D-I-C-WF) 518-455-5921/fax: 518-455-3962
District: 143 *Room:* 926 LOB *e-mail:* tokaszp@assembly.state.ny.us
Title: Majority Leader
Committees: Rules; ex officio to all committees
Senior Staff: Margaret McGovern

Paul D Tonko (D-L-I-WF) 518-455-5197/fax: 518-455-5435
District: 105 *Room:* 713 LOB *e-mail:* tonkop@assembly.state.ny.us
Committees: Agriculture; Education; Energy (Chair); Transportation
Senior Staff: John B Howard

Darryl C Towns (D-I-L-WF) 518-455-5821/fax: 518-455-5591
District: 54 *Room:* 841 LOB *e-mail:* townsd@assembly.state.ny.us
Committees: Banks; Economic Development, Job Creation, Commerce & Industry; Health; Mental Health; Veterans' Affairs (Chair)
Senior Staff: Natashua Rice

David R Townsend, Jr (R-C-I-WF) 518-455-5334/fax: 518-455-5391
District: 115 *Room:* 329 LOB *e-mail:* townsed@assembly.state.ny.us
Title: Chair, Minority Conference
Committees: Codes; Labor; Local Governments; Rules
Senior Staff: vacant

Helene E Weinstein (D-WF) 518-455-5462/fax: 518-455-5752
District: 41 *Room:* 831 LOB *e-mail:* weinsth@assembly.state.ny.us
Committees: Aging; Codes; Judiciary (Chair); Rules; Ways & Means
Senior Staff: Joan T Byalin

Harvey Weisenberg (D-I-L) 518-455-3028/fax: 518-455-5769
District: 20 *Room:* 731 LOB *e-mail:* weisenh@assembly.state.ny.us
Title: Assistant Speaker Pro Tempore
Committees: Banks; Correction; Education; Environmental Conservation; Mental Health; Transportation
Senior Staff: Marie Curley

Mark Weprin (D-L-WF) 518-455-5806/fax: 518-455-5977
District: 24 *Room:* 626 LOB *e-mail:* weprinm@assembly.state.ny.us
Committees: Aging; Codes; Insurance; Judiciary; Small Business (Chair)
Senior Staff: Ruth Wimpfheimer

Sandra Lee Wirth (R-C-RL) 518-455-4601/fax: 518-455-5257
District: 142 *Room:* 546 LOB *e-mail:* wirths@assembly.state.ny.us
Committees: Aging; Codes; Insurance; Real Property Taxation (Ranking Minority Member); Rules
Senior Staff: Carl R Wawrzyniak

Keith L T Wright (D-L-WF) 518-455-4793/fax: 518-455-3890
District: 70 *Room:* 749 LOB *e-mail:* wrightk@assembly.state.ny.us
Committees: Codes; Correction; Election Law (Chair); Housing; Judiciary; Labor
Senior Staff: Terence Tolbert

Kenneth P Zebrowski (D) 518-455-5735
District: 94 *Room:* 631 LOB *e-mail:* zebrowk@assembly.state.ny.us
Committees: Aging; Codes; Corporations, Authorities & Commissions; Governmental Employees; Judiciary; Racing & Wagering
Senior Staff: Ken Ingenito

State Assembly Standing Committees

Aging
Chair:
    Steven C Englebright (D) 518-455-4804
Ranking Minority Member:
    Andrew P Raia (R) 518-455-5952

Committee Staff
Clerk:
    Elizabeth Nostrand 518-455-4804

Key Assembly Staff Assignments
Majority Program & Counsel Legislative Analyst:
    Debra Holland 518-455-4371

Offices and agencies appear in alphabetical order.

Majority Program & Counsel Associate Counsel:
Elana Marton 518-455-4371
Minority Associate Counsel:
Heather A Mogan 518-455-4265
Minority Research & Program Development Legislative Analyst:
Jessica C Howard 518-455-5002

Membership

Majority

Peter J Abbate, Jr	Carmen E Arroyo
William F Boyland, Jr	Ann-Margaret E Carrozza
Adele H Cohen	RoAnn M Destito
Luis M Diaz	Ginny Fields
Carl E Heastie	William Magee
Brian M McLaughlin	Jimmy K Meng
Joan L Millman	Audrey I Pheffer
Philip R Ramos	Jose Rivera
Frank R Seddio	Mark Weprin
Helene E Weinstein	Kenneth P Zebrowski

Minority

Robert C Oaks	Thomas F O'Mara
Ann G Rabbitt	William Reilich
Sandra Lee Wirth	

Agriculture

Chair:
William Magee (D) 518-455-4807
Ranking Minority Member:
Clifford W Crouch (R) 518-455-5741

Committee Staff

Clerk:
Lisa Chakmakas 518-455-4807

Key Assembly Staff Assignments
Majority Program & Counsel Legislative Analyst:
William Ketzer 518-455-4355
Majority Program & Counsel Associate Counsel:
Elizabeth Hogan 518-455-4355
Minority Associate Counsel:
Anne S Tarpinian 518-455-4285
Minority Research & Program Development Legislative Analyst:
Elizabeth Bough-Martin 518-455-5002

Membership

Majority

Darrel J Aubertine	Michael Benedetto
Adele H Cohen	Steven Cymbrowitz
Francine DelMonte	RoAnn M Destito
Steven C Englebright	Aileen M Gunther
Barbara S Lifton	Margaret M Markey
John J McEneny	Robert P Reilly
Peter M Rivera	Paul D Tonko

Minority

Marc W Butler	Gary D Finch
Daniel L Hooker	Roy J McDonald

Alcoholism & Drug Abuse

Chair:
Jeffrey Dinowitz (D) 518-455-5965
Ranking Minority Member:
Jack Quinn (R) 518-455-4462

Committee Staff

Clerk:
Dan Katz 518-455-5965

Key Assembly Staff Assignments
Majority Program & Counsel Legislative Analyst:
William Eggler 518-455-4371
Majority Program & Counsel Associate Counsel:
Elana Marton 518-455-4371
Minority Associate Counsel:
Henry C Meier 518-455-4515
Minority Research & Program Development Legislative Analyst:
Kristin Zielinksi 518-455-5002

Membership

Majority

Carmen E Arroyo	Adriano Espaillat
Diane Gordon	Andrew Hevesi
Ryan S Karben	David R Koon
Charles D Lavine	Brian M McLaughlin
Crystal D Peoples	

Minority

Thomas J Kirwan

Banks

Chair:
Catherine T Nolan (D) 518-455-4851
Ranking Minority Member:
Roy J McDonald (R) 518-455-5404

Committee Staff

Clerk:
Nisha Thomas 518-455-4851

Key Assembly Staff Assignments
Majority Program & Counsel Legislative Analyst:
Brian Quiara 518-455-4928
Majority Program & Counsel Associate Counsel:
Teri Kleinmann 518-455-4928
Minority Associate Counsel:
Henry C Meier 518-455-4515
Minority Research & Program Development Legislative Analyst:
Angelo Cafaro 518-455-5002

Membership

Majority

Peter J Abbate, Jr	Michael Benjamin
Jonathan L Bing	William F Boyland, Jr
Richard L Brodsky	Ronald J Canestrari
Ann-Margaret E Carrozza	Luis M Diaz
Michael N Gianaris	Rhoda S Jacobs
Ivan C Lafayette	William Magee
Clarence Norman, Jr	Felix W Ortiz
Jose R Peralta	N Nick Perry
William D Scarborough	Frank R Seddio
Anthony S Seminerio	Darryl C Towns
Harvey Weisenberg	

Minority

Patricia L Acampora	Joseph A Errigo
James P Hayes	Patrick R Manning
Roy J McDonald	William Reilich
Deirdre K Scozzafava	James N Tedisco

Offices and agencies appear in alphabetical order.

Children & Families

Chair:
William Scarborough (D) 518-455-4451
Ranking Minority Member:
Joseph A Errigo (R) 518-455-5662

Committee Staff

Clerk:
Elizabeth Vedder 518-455-5325

Key Assembly Staff Assignments
Majority Program & Counsel Legislative Analyst:
Judi West 518-455-4371
Majority Program & Counsel Associate Counsel:
Jacqueline Greene 518-455-4371
Minority Associate Counsel:
Danielle C Rathbun 518-455-4264
Minority Research & Program Development Legislative Analyst:
Erin M Hynes 518-455-5002

Membership

Majority

Carmen E Arroyo	Michael A Benjamin
Adam T Bradley	Barbara M Clark
Ruben Diaz, Jr	Deborah J Glick
Carl E Heastie	William B Hoyt, III
Amy Paulin	Naomi Rivera
Annette M Robinson	Michele R Titus

Minority

Vincent Ignizio	Teresa R Sayward

Cities

Chair:
Scott M Stringer (D) 518-455-5802
Ranking Minority Member:
Thomas J Kirwan (R) 518-455-5762

Committee Staff

Clerk:
Deshawanda Maklin 518-455-5802

Key Assembly Staff Assignments
Majority Program & Counsel Legislative Analyst:
Julia Donnaruma 518-455-4363
Majority Program & Counsel Associate Counsel:
Julia Mallalieu 518-455-4363
Minority Associate Counsel:
Edmund V Wick 518-455-4262
Minority Research & Program Development Legislative Analyst:
Angela Cafaro 518-455-5002

Membership

Majority

Jeffrion L Aubry	Adele H Cohen
Roger L Green	Aurelia Greene
Brian M McLaughlin	Jose R Peralta
James G Pretlow	Naomi Rivera
Steven Sanders	Anthony S Seminerio

Minority

Matthew Mirones	Louis A Mosiello

Codes

Chair:
Joseph R Lentol (D) 518-455-4477

Ranking Minority Member:
Dierdre K Scozzafava 518-455-5797

Committee Staff

Clerk:
Wilda Lang 518-455-4484

Key Assembly Staff Assignments
Majority Program & Counsel Legislative Analyst:
Veronica Ebhuoma 518-455-4313
Majority Program & Counsel Legislative Analyst:
Seth Agata 518-455-4313
Majority Program & Counsel Legislative Analyst:
Kathleen O'Keefe 518-455-4313
Majority Program & Counsel Senior Team Counsel:
Tracey Brooks 518-455-4313
Minority Associate Counsel:
Heather A Mogan 518-455-4265
Minority Research & Program Development Principal Legislative Analyst:
Kim Halayko 518-455-5002

Membership

Majority

James F Brennan	Vivian E Cook
Steven Cymbrowitz	Charles D Lavine
Clarence Norman, Jr	Daniel J O'Donnell
James G Pretlow	Robin L Schimminger
Michele R Titus	Mark Weprin
Keith L Wright	Kenneth P Zebrowski

Minority

Thomas J Kirwan	David R Townsend, Jr
Sandra Lee Wirth	

Consumer Affairs & Protection

Chair:
Audrey I Pheffer (D) 518-455-4292
Ranking Minority Member:
David G McDonough (R) 518-455-4633

Committee Staff

Clerk:
Kim Lease 518-455-4292

Key Assembly Staff Assignments
Majority Program & Counsel Legislative Analyst:
Todd Gold 518-455-4355
Majority Program & Counsel Associate Counsel:
Elizabeth Hogan 518-455-4355
Minority Associate Counsel:
Edmund V Wick 518-455-4262
Minority Research & Program Development Legislative Analyst:
Marc G Lundberg 518-455-5002

Membership

Majority

Peter J Abbate, Jr	Michael Benedetto
Jeffrey Dinowitz	Ginny Fields
Michael N Gianaris	Andrew Hevesi
Margaret M Markey	Jimmy K Meng
Jose R Peralta	Peter M Rivera

Minority

Robert D Barra	Ann G Rabbitt

Corporations, Authorities & Commissions

Chair:
Richard L Brodsky (D) 518-455-5753

Offices and agencies appear in alphabetical order.

Ranking Minority Member:
James G Bacalles (R) 518-455-5791

Committee Staff

Clerk:
Arnold Farber 518-455-5753

Key Assembly Staff Assignments
Majority Program & Counsel Legislative Analyst:
Mara Elliott 518-455-4881
Majority Program & Counsel Associate Counsel:
William Thornton 518-455-4881
Minority Associate Counsel:
Danielle C Rathbun 518-455-4264
Minority Research & Program Development Legislative Analyst:
Angelo Cafaro 518-455-5002

Membership

Majority

Adam T Bradley	James F Brennan
Vivian E Cook	Adriano Espaillat
Ginny Fields	Sandra R Galef
David F Gantt	Diane Gordon
Carl E Heastie	Andrew Hevesi
Ryan S Karben	Jimmy K Meng
Joan L Millman	Catherine T Nolan
Adam Clayton Powell, IV	Robert P Reilly
William D Scarborough	Kenneth P Zebrowski

Minority

Thomas W Alfano	William A Barclay
Robert D Barra	Vincent Ignizio
Matthew Mirones	

Correction

Chair:
Jeffrion L Aubry (D) 518-455-4561
Ranking Minority Member:
Thomas F O'Mara (R) 518-455-4538

Committee Staff

Clerk:
Indira Noel 518-455-4548

Key Assembly Staff Assignments
Majority Program & Counsel Legislative Analyst:
Richard McDonald 518-455-4313
Majority Program & Counsel Legislative Analyst:
Dominique Tauzin 518-455-4313
Majority Program & Counsel Senior Team Counsel:
Tracey Brooks 518-455-4313
Minority Associate Counsel:
Heather A Mogan 518-455-4265
Minority Research & Program Development Principal Legislative Analyst:
Kim Halayko 518-455-5002

Membership

Majority

Michael A Benjamin	William Colton
Diane Gordon	Felix W Ortiz
Jose R Peralta	William D Scarborough
Harvey Weisenberg	Keith L Wright

Minority

Thomas F O'Mara

Economic Development, Job Creation, Commerce & Industry

Chair:
Robin L Schimminger (D) 518-455-4767
Ranking Minority Member:
Marc W Butler (R) 518-455-5393

Committee Staff

Clerk:
Judi Giuliano 518-455-4773

Key Assembly Staff Assignments
Majority Program & Counsel Legislative Analyst:
Erik Trojian 518-455-4928
Majority Program & Counsel Associate Counsel:
Teri Kleinmann 518-455-4928
Minority Associate Counsel:
Douglas L Goldman 518-455-4637
Minority Research & Program Development Legislative Analyst:
Erin M Hynes 518-455-5002

Membership

Majority

Darrel J Aubertine	Jeffrion L Aubry
William F Boyland, Jr	Kevin A Cahill
Francine DelMonte	RoAnn M Destito
David F Gantt	Earlene Hooper
David R Koon	Charles D Lavine
Barbara S Lifton	Vito J Lopez
William B Magnarelli	Joseph D Morelle
Felix W Ortiz	Philip R Ramos
Darryl C Towns	

Minority

Jeffrey Brown	Pat M Casale
Clifford W Crouch	Gary D Finch
Thomas F O'Mara	

Education

Chair:
Steven Sanders (D) 518-455-5506
Ranking Minority Member:
James D Conte (R) 518-455-5732

Committee Staff

Clerk:
Debra Triblet 518-455-4722

Key Assembly Staff Assignments
Majority Program & Counsel Legislative Analyst:
Norrieda Reyes 518-455-4881
Majority Program & Counsel Associate Counsel:
Sabrina Ty 518-455-4881
Minority Associate Counsel:
Henry C Meier 518-455-4515
Minority Research & Program Development Legislative Analyst:
Matthew S Baer 518-455-5002

Membership

Majority

Carmen E Arroyo	Michael Benedetto
James F Brennan	Barbara M Clark
Ruben Diaz, Jr	Thomas P DiNapoli
Patricia A Eddington	Steven C Englebright
Aurelia Greene	Earlene Hooper
Susan V John	John W Lavelle
William B Magnarelli	Jimmy K Meng

Offices and agencies appear in alphabetical order.

William L Parment	Amy R Paulin
Philip R Ramos	Robert P Reilly
Scott M Stringer	Robert K Sweeney
Paul D Tonko	Harvey Weisenberg

Minority

Thomas J Kirwan	David G McDonough
Joel M Miller	Louis A Mosiello
William Reilich	Joseph S Saladino
Teresa R Sayward	

Election Law

Chair:
Keith L Wright (D) 518-455-4793
Ranking Minority Member:
Fred W Thiele, Jr (R) 518-455-5997

Committee Staff

Clerk:
Laurie Barone 518-455-3073

Key Assembly Staff Assignments
Majority Program & Counsel Legislative Analyst:
Stanley Schlein 518-455-4313
Majority Program & Counsel Legislative Analyst:
Brian Quail 518-455-4313
Majority Program & Counsel Associate Counsel:
Tracey Brooks 518-455-4313
Minority Associate Counsel:
Kevin J Engel 518-455-5230
Minority Research & Program Development Legislative Analyst:
Khai Gibbs 518-455-5002

Membership

Majority

Michael A Benjamin	Adam T Bradley
Jeffrey Dinowitz	Sandra R Galef
Michael N Gianaris	Joseph R Lentol
Donna Lupardo	Clarence Norman, Jr
Jose R Peralta	

Minority

Chris Ortloff	Fred W Thiele, Jr

Energy

Chair:
Paul D Tonko (D) 518-455-5197
Ranking Minority Member:
Brian M Kolb (R) 518-455-5772

Committee Staff

Clerk:
Brian Cechnicki 518-455-4779

Key Assembly Staff Assignments
Majority Program & Counsel Associate Counsel:
Julia Mallalieu 518-455-4363
Minority Associate Counsel:
Anne S Tarpinian 518-455-4285
Minority Research & Program Development Legislative Analyst:
Angelo Cafaro 518-455-5002

Membership

Majority

Darrel J Aubertine	Adele H Cohen
Steven C Englebright	Andrew Hevesi
William B Hoyt, III	Susan V John
Ryan S Karben	Felix W Ortiz

N Nick Perry	William D Scarborough

Minority

Gary D Finch	Catharine M Young

Environmental Conservation

Chair:
Thomas P DiNapoli (D) 518-455-5172
Ranking Minority Member:
Teresa R Sayward (R) 518-455-5565

Committee Staff

Clerk:
Grisel Davis 518-455-5192

Key Assembly Staff Assignments
Majority Program & Counsel Legislative Analyst:
Alexander Roth 518-455-4363
Majority Program & Counsel Associate Counsel:
Julia Mallalieu 518-455-4363
Minority Associate Counsel:
Anne S Tarpinian 518-455-4285
Minority Research & Program Development Legislative Analyst:
Elizabeth Bough-Martin 518-455-5002

Membership

Majority

Adam T Bradley	Barbara M Clark
William Colton	Steven Cymbrowitz
Ruben Diaz, Jr	Jeffrey Dinowitz
Adriano Espaillat	Michael N Gianaris
Deborah J Glick	Alexander B Grannis
Roger L Green	Aileen M Gunther
George S Latimer	Barbara S Lifton
Daniel J O'Donnell	William L Parment
Crystal D Peoples	Donna Lupardo
Robert K Sweeney	Harvey Weisenberg

Minority

Jeffrey D Brown	Daniel J Burling
Chris Ortloff	Joseph S Saladino
Teresa R Sayward	Fred W Thiele, Jr

Ethics & Guidance

Chair:
Kevin A Cahill (D) 518-455-5806
Ranking Minority Member:
Robert C Oaks (R) 518-455-5655

Membership

Majority

Joseph R Lentol	John J McEneny
Michele R Titus	

Minority

William A Barclay	Robert C Oaks
Maureen C O'Connell	Dierdre K Scozzafava

Governmental Employees

Chair:
Peter J Abbate, Jr (D) 518-455-3053
Ranking Minority Member:
Joseph S Saladino 518-455-5305

Committee Staff

Clerk:
Christine Epplemann 518-455-3053

Offices and agencies appear in alphabetical order.

Key Assembly Staff Assignments
Majority Program & Counsel Associate Counsel:
  Tony Cantore 518-455-4311
Minority Associate Counsel:
  Douglas L Goldman 518-455-4637
Minority Research & Program Development Legislative Analyst:
  Jason M Kehoe 518-455-5002

Membership

Majority

Jeffrion L Aubry	Ann-Margaret E Carrozza
William Colton	Michael J Cusick
John W Lavelle	John J McEneny
Anthony S Seminerio	Kenneth P Zebrowski

Minority

Patricia L Acampora

Governmental Operations

Chair:
  RoAnn M Destito (D) 518-455-5454
Ranking Minority Member:
  Louis A Mosiello (R) 518-455-3662

Committee Staff

Clerk:
  Liza Setticase 518-455-5436

Key Assembly Staff Assignments
Majority Program & Counsel Legislative Analyst:
  Cheryl Couser 518-455-4355
Majority Program & Counsel Associate Counsel:
  Elizabeth Hogan 518-455-4355
Minority Associate Counsel:
  Charles E Crandall 518-455-4626
Minority Research & Program Development Principal Legislative Analyst:
  Mark G Lundberg 518-455-5002

Membership

Majority

Michael Benedetto	Patricia A Eddington
Sandra R Galef	George S Latimer
Margaret M Markey	Nettie Mayersohn
Robert P Reilly	

Minority

Clifford W Crouch

Health

Chair:
  Richard N Gottfried (D) 518-455-4941
Ranking Minority Member:
  Maureen C O'Connell (R) 518-455-5341

Committee Staff

Executive Director:
  Richard Conti 518-455-4941
Clerk:
  Helen Dong 518-455-4941

Key Assembly Staff Assignments
Majority Program & Counsel Legislative Analyst:
  Elsie Chun 518-455-4371
Majority Program & Counsel Associate Counsel:
  Elana Marton 518-455-4371
Minority Associate Counsel:
  John B Robeson 518-455-4258

Minority Research & Program Development Legislative Analyst:
  Kristin Zielinski 518-455-5002

Membership

Majority

Jonathan L Bing	Kevin A Cahill
Steven Cymbrowitz	Jeffrey Dinowitz
Patricia A Eddington	Sandra R Galef
Diane M Gordon	Alexander B Grannis
Aileen M Gunther	Rhoda S Jacobs
William B Magnarelli	Nettie Mayersohn
Amy R Paulin	Crystal D Peoples
Naomi Rivera	Robin L Schimminger
Darryl C Towns	

Minority

James G Bacalles	Jeffrey D Brown
James D Conte	

Higher Education

Chair:
  Ronald J Canestrari (D) 518-455-4474
Ranking Minority Member:
  Joel M Miller (R) 518-455-5725

Committee Staff

Clerk:
  Nancy Jordan 518-455-4594

Key Assembly Staff Assignments
Majority Program & Counsel Legislative Analyst:
  Mark Casellini 518-455-4881
Majority Program & Counsel Associate Counsel:
  William Thornton 518-455-4881
Minority Associate Counsel:
  Henry C Meier 518-455-4515
Minority Research & Program Development Legislative Analyst:
  Matthew S Baer 518-455-5002

Membership

Majority

Darrel J Aubertine	Kevin A Cahill
Michael J Cusick	Luis M Diaz
Patricia A Eddington	Steven C Englebright
Deborah J Glick	Richard N Gottfried
Roger L Green	Rhoda S Jacobs
Barbara S Lifton	Donna Lupardo
William Magee	Joseph D Morelle
Amy R Paulin	Audrey I Pheffer
Scott M Stringer	

Minority

Marc W Butler	James D Conte
Michael J Fitzpatrick	James P Hayes
Brian M Kolb	

Housing

Chair:
  Vito J Lopez (D) 518-455-5537
Ranking Minority Member:
  vacant 518-455-5241

Committee Staff

Chief of Staff:
  Jonathan Harkavy 518-455-5537
Clerk:
  Patrice Mago 518-455-5537

Offices and agencies appear in alphabetical order.

Key Assembly Staff Assignments
Majority Program & Counsel Legislative Analyst:
Linda Camoin. 518-455-4355
Majority Program & Counsel Associate Counsel:
Don Lebowitz. 518-455-4355
Minority Associate Counsel:
Edmund V Wick. 518-455-4262
Minority Research & Program Development Legislative Analyst:
Mark G Lundberg. 518-455-5002

Membership

Majority
Jeffrion L Aubry	Michael Benedetto
Michael Benjamin	Jonathan L Bing
William F Boyland, Jr	Joan K Christensen
Vivian E Cook	Steven Cymbrowitz
Luis M Diaz	Ruben Diaz, Jr
Alexander B Grannis	Carl E Heastie
Earlene Hooper	Adam Clayton Powell, IV
Philip R Ramos	Annette M Robinson
Steven Sanders	Scott M Stringer
Keith L Wright	

Minority
Daniel J Burling	Pat M Casale
Joseph A Errigo	Andrew P Raia
Fred W Thiele, Jr	

Insurance
Chair:
Alexander B Grannis (D) 518-455-5676
Ranking Minority Member:
William A Barclay (R) 518-455-5841

Committee Staff
Director:
Peter Newell 518-455-5676
Executive Clerk:
Debbie Hicks 518-455-5677

Key Assembly Staff Assignments
Majority Program & Counsel Legislative Analyst:
LouAnn Ciccone 518-455-4928
Majority Program & Counsel Associate Counsel:
Teri Kleinmann 518-455-4928
Minority Associate Counsel:
John B Robeson 518-455-4258
Minority Research & Program Development Legislative Analyst:
Harry J MacAvoy. 518-455-5002

Membership

Majority
Ann-Margaret E Carrozza	Joan K Christensen
Adele H Cohen	Vivian E Cook
Steven H Cymbrowitz	Adriano Espaillat
Rhoda S Jacobs	Ryan S Karben
Ivan C Lafayette	George S Latimer
Crystal D Peoples	N Nick Perry
Adam Clayton Powell, IV	James G Pretlow
Jose Rivera	Mark J Schroeder
Frank R Seddio	Mark Weprin

Minority
Robert D Barra	Nancy Calhoun
Maureen C O'Connell	Robert C Oaks
Sandra Lee Wirth	

Judiciary
Chair:
Helene E Weinstein (D) 518-455-5462
Ranking Minority Member:
Thomas W Alfano (R) 518-455-4627

Committee Staff
Advisory Counsel:
Ken Munnelly. 518-455-5462
Clerk:
Sarah Beaver. 518-455-5462

Key Assembly Staff Assignments
Majority Program & Counsel Legislative Analyst:
Richard Ancowitz. 518-455-4313
Majority Program & Counsel Legislative Analyst:
Lisa Seemann 518-455-4313
Majority Program & Counsel Senior Team Counsel:
Vacant 518-455-4313
Minority Associate Counsel:
Kevin J Engel 518-455-5230
Minority Research & Program Development Legislative Analyst:
Khai H Gibbs 518-455-5002

Membership

Majority
Jonathan L Bing	Adam Bradley
Adele H Cohen	Jeffrey Dinowitz
Michael N Gianaris	Susan V John
Ryan S Karben	Daniel J O'Donnell
Peter M Rivera	Scott M Stringer
Michele R Titus	Mark Weprin
Keith L Wright	Kenneth P Zebrowski

Minority
Donna Ferrara	Maureen C O'Connell
Willis H Stephens, Jr	

Labor
Chair:
Susan V John (D) 518-455-4527
Ranking Minority Member:
Patricia L Acampora (R) 518-455-5294

Committee Staff
Clerk:
Vacant 518-455-4527

Key Assembly Staff Assignments
Majority Program & Counsel Legislative Analyst:
Glen Casey 518-455-4311
Majority Program & Counsel Legislative Analyst:
Harry Bronson 518-455-4311
Majority Program & Counsel Associate Counsel:
Tony Cantore 518-455-4311
Minority Associate Counsel:
Douglas L Goldman. 518-455-4637
Minority Research & Program Development Legislative Analyst:
Jason M Kehoe. 518-455-5002

Membership

Majority
Peter J Abbate, Jr	Michael Benedetto
Ronald J Canestrari	Joan K Christensen
Barbara M Clark	William Colton
Patricia A Eddington	Roger L Green
Carl E Heastie	Andrew Hevesi
Earlene Hooper	George S Latimer

Offices and agencies appear in alphabetical order.

Margaret M Markey
Joan L Millman
Jose R Peralta
Keith L Wright

Nettie Mayersohn
Felix W Ortiz
N Nick Perry

Minority

Thomas W Alfano
Clifford W Crouch
Robert C Oaks

Nancy Calhoun
Brian M Kolb
David R Townsend, Jr

Libraries & Education Technology

Chair:
Sandra R Galef (D)................................518-455-5348

Committee Staff

Clerk:
Nicole Haff..518-455-5348

Key Assembly Staff Assignments

Majority Program & Counsel Legislative Analyst:
Julie Marlette...................................518-455-4881
Majority Program & Counsel Associate Counsel:
William Thornton................................518-455-4881
Minority Associate Counsel:
Henry C Meier...................................518-455-4515
Minority Research & Program Development Legislative Analyst:
Matthew S Baer..................................518-455-5002

Membership

Majority

Michael A Benjamin
Susan V John
Donna Lupardo
Joseph D Morelle

Barbara M Clark
David R Koon
Joan L Millman

Local Government

Chair:
Robert K Sweeney (D)..........................518-455-5787
Ranking Minority Member:
Ann G Rabbitt (R).............................518-455-5991

Committee Staff

Clerk:
Steve Liss.......................................518-455-5787
Clerk:
Rebecca Rasmussen..............................518-455-5787

Key Assembly Staff Assignments

Majority Program & Counsel Legislative Associate:
Michelle Milot...................................518-455-4363
Majority Program & Counsel Associate Counsel:
Julia Mallalieu.................................518-455-4363
Minority Associate Counsel:
Charles E Crandall.............................518-455-4626
Minority Research & Program Development Legislative Analyst:
Elizabeth Bough-Martin.........................518-455-5002

Membership

Majority

William F Boyland, Jr
David F Gantt
Ryan S Karben
George S Latimer
William Magee
Daniel J O'Donnell
Mark J Schroeder

Ronald J Canestrari
Francine DelMonte
David R Koon
Charles D Lavine
Joseph D Morelle
Philip R Ramos
Michele R Titus

Minority

Michael J Fitzpatrick
David R Townsend, Jr

Andrew P Raia

Mental Health

Chair:
Peter M Rivera (D)............................518-455-5102
Ranking Minority Member:
Matthew Mirones (R)..........................518-455-5716

Committee Staff

Clerk:
Anton Konev....................................518-455-5102

Key Assembly Staff Assignments

Majority Program & Counsel Legislative Analyst:
Carl Letson, Jr................................518-455-4371
Majority Program & Counsel Associate Counsel:
Elana Marton...................................518-455-4371
Minority Associate Counsel:
John B Robeson.................................518-455-4258
Minority Research & Program Development Legislative Analyst:
Kristin Zielinski..............................518-455-5002

Membership

Majority

Michael J Cusick
John W Lavelle
Donna Lupardo
Mark J Schroeder
Harvey Weisenberg

Jeffrey Dinowitz
Barbara S Lifton
William L Parment
Darryl C Towns

Minority

Robert D Barra

Oversight, Analysis & Investigation

Chair:
James F Brennan (D)...........................518-455-5377
Ranking Minority Member:
Donna Ferrara (R).............................518-455-4684

Committee Staff

Majority Committee Counsel:
Thomas J Fox...................................518-455-3039
Minority Associate Counsel:
Edmund V Wick..................................518-455-4262

Membership

Majority

Ginny Fields
Daniel J O'Donnell
Mark J Schroeder

William B Magnarelli
Annette Robinson

Racing & Wagering

Chair:
James G Pretlow (D)...........................518-455-5291
Ranking Minority Member:
Robert D Barra (R)............................518-455-4656

Committee Staff

Clerk:
Anne Richmond..................................518-455-5735

Key Assembly Staff Assignments

Majority Program & Counsel Legislative Analyst:
Stephen Bochnak................................518-455-4311

Offices and agencies appear in alphabetical order.

Legislative Branch

Majority Program & Counsel Associate Counsel:
Tony Cantore 518-455-4311
Minority Associate Counsel:
Edmund V Wick 518-455-4262
Minority Research & Program Development Legislative Analyst:
Erin M Hynes 518-455-5002

Membership

Majority

Michael Benedetto	Francine DelMonte
Aileen Gunther	Andrew Hevesi
Margaret M Markey	Robert P Reilly
Anthony S Seminerio	Kenneth P Zebrowski

Minority

James N Tedisco

Real Property Taxation

Chair:
Brian M McLaughlin (D) 518-455-5172
Ranking Minority Member:
Sandra Lee Wirth (R) 518-455-4601

Committee Staff

Clerk:
Kathy Conroy 518-455-5172
Clerk:
Anne Rua 518-455-5172

Key Assembly Staff Assignments
Majority Program & Counsel Legislative Analyst:
Karen Smeaton 518-455-4311
Majority Program & Counsel Associate Counsel:
Tony Cantore 518-455-4311
Minority Associate Counsel:
Kevin J Engel 518-455-5230
Minority Research & Program Development Legislative Analyst:
Erin M Hynes 518-455-5002

Membership

Majority

James F Brennan	Joan K Christensen
Ginny Fields	Diane M Gordon
Aileen M Gunther	Naomi Rivera
Annette M Robinson	

Rules

Chair:
Sheldon Silver (D) 518-455-3791
Ranking Minority Member:
Charles H Nesbitt (R) 518-455-3751

Committee Staff

Majority Committee Counsel:
Dan Conviser 518-455-3760
Minority Chief Counsel:
Kimberly Galvin 518-455-3751

Membership

Majority

Ronald J Canestrari	Thomas P DiNapoli
Herman D Farrell, Jr	David F Gantt
Richard N Gottfried	Alexander B Grannis
Aurelia Greene	Earlene Hooper
Rhoda S Jacobs	Ivan C Lafayette
Joseph R Lentol	Vito J Lopez
Catherine T Nolan	Clarence Norman, Jr

Felix W Ortiz	Audrey I Pheffer
Peter M Rivera	Steven Sanders
Paul A Tokasz	Helene E Weinstein

Minority

Thomas F Barraga	Nancy Calhoun
Robert C Oaks	Chris Ortloff
Wilis H Stephens, Jr	James N Tedisco
David R Townsend, Jr	

Small Business

Chair:
Mark S Weprin (D) 518-455-5806
Ranking Minority Member:
William Reilich (R) 518-455-4664

Committee Staff

Clerk:
Jenny Rodriguez 518-455-5821

Key Assembly Staff Assignments
Majority Program & Counsel Legislative Analyst:
Yolanda Bostic 518-455-4928
Majority Program & Counsel Associate Counsel:
Teri Kleinmann 518-455-4928
Minority Associate Counsel:
Douglas L Goldman 518-455-4637
Minority Research & Program Development Legislative Analyst:
Mark G Lundberg 518-455-5002

Membership

Majority

Joan K Christensen	Carl E Heastie
David R Koon	Jimmy K Meng
Joan L Millman	Adam Clayton Powell, IV
Jose Rivera	Annette M Robinson
Mark J Schroeder	Michele R Titus

Minority

Michael J Fitzpatrick	Jack Quinn

Social Services

Chair:
Deborah J Glick (D) 518-455-4841
Ranking Minority Member:
Vincent Ignizio (R) 518-455-4656

Committee Staff

Clerk:
Susan Nowogrodski 518-455-4841

Key Assembly Staff Assignments
Majority Program & Counsel Legislative Analyst:
Amy Nickson 518-455-4371
Majority Program & Counsel Associate Counsel:
Jacqueline Greene 518-455-4371
Minority Associate Counsel:
Danielle C Rathbun 518-455-4264
Minority Research & Program Development Legislative Analyst:
Erin M Hynes 518-455-5002

Membership

Majority

Jeffrion L Aubry	Jonathan L Bing
Luis M Diaz	Adriano Espaillat
Diane M Gordon	Aurelia Greene
John W Lavelle	Charles D Lavine
Vito J Lopez	John J McEneny

Offices and agencies appear in alphabetical order.

Crystal D Peoples   James G Pretlow

Minority
James G Bacalles   Joel M Miller
Andrew P Raia

Tourism, Arts & Sports Development
Chair:
Joseph D Morelle (D) 518-455-5373
Ranking Minority Member:
Michael J Fitzpatrick (R) 518-455-5021

Committee Staff
Clerk:
Dan Farfaglia 518-455-5373

Key Assembly Staff Assignments
Majority Program & Counsel Legislative Analyst:
Brendan Fitzgerald 518-455-4928
Majority Program & Counsel Associate Counsel:
Teri Kleinmann 518-455-4928
Minority Associate Counsel:
Heather A Mogan 518-455-4265
Minority Research & Program Development Legislative Analyst:
Jessica C Howard 518-455-5002

Membership

Majority
Jonathan L Bing	Richard L Brodsky
Francine DelMonte	Steven C Englebright
Ginny Fields	Michael N Gianaris
Aileen M Gunther	William B Hoyt, III
Margaret M Markey	John J McEneny
Daniel J O'Donnell	Robert P Reilly
Naomi Rivera	

Minority
Brian M Kolb	David G McDonough
Thomas F O'Mara	

Transportation
Chair:
David F Gantt (D) 518-455-5606
Ranking Minority Member:
Patrick R Manning (R) 518-455-5177

Committee Staff
Clerk:
Janet Crist 518-455-5606

Key Assembly Staff Assignments
Majority Program & Counsel Legislative Analyst:
Julie Barney 518-455-4881
Majority Program & Counsel Associate Counsel:
William Thornton 518-455-4881
Minority Associate Counsel:
Danielle C Rathbun 518-455-4264
Minority Research & Program Development Legislative Analyst:
Jessica C Howard 518-455-5002

Membership

Majority
Darrel J Aubertine	Michael J Cusick
Francine DelMonte	William B Hoyt, III
Ivan C Lafayette	George S Latimer
John W Lavelle	Charles D Lavine
Donna Lupardo	Brian M McLaughlin
Jimmy K Meng	Joan L Millman

N Nick Perry   Frank R Seddio
Robert K Sweeney   Paul D Tonko
Harvey Weisenberg

Minority
James G Bacalles   Patrick R Manning
David G McDonough   Matthew Mirones
Chris Ortloff   Jack Quinn

Veterans' Affairs
Chair:
Darryl C Towns (D) 518-455-5821
Ranking Minority Member:
Jeffrey Brown (R) 518-455-4505

Committee Staff
Clerk:
Rebecca Southard 518-455-4897

Key Assembly Staff Assignments
Majority Program & Counsel Legislative Analyst:
Joanne Martin 518-455-4355
Majority Program & Counsel Legislative Counsel:
Elizabeth Hogan 518-455-4355
Minority Associate Counsel:
Charles E Crandall 518-455-4626
Minority Research & Program Development Legislative Analyst:
Mark G Lundberg 518-455-5002

Membership

Majority
Darrel J Aubertine	Adam T Bradley
Michael J Cusick	Thomas P DiNapoli
Patricia A Eddington	John W Lavelle
William B Magnarelli	Catherine T Nolan
William L Parment	Amy R Paulin
Audrey I Pheffer	Mark J Schroeder
Robert K Sweeney	

Minority
Jeffrey D Brown	Daniel J Burling
Roy J McDonald	

Ways & Means
Chair:
Herman D Farrell, Jr (D) 518-455-5491
Ranking Minority Member:
Thomas F Barraga (R) 518-455-4611

Committee Staff
Executive Director:
Marcia Coleman 518-455-5491
Secretary to the Committee:
Dean Fuleihan 518-455-3786
Deputy Secretary to the Committee:
Roman Hedges 518-455-4049
Counsel to the Chair:
Francis G Hoare 518-455-5491
Clerk:
Emma Leigh 518-455-4026
Clerk:
Deb Devine 518-455-4026

Key Assembly Staff Assignments
Majority Tax & Fiscal Studies Director:
Steven Pleydle 518-455-4051
Majority Chief Economist/Director of Research:
Vacant 518-455-4006

Offices and agencies appear in alphabetical order.

Majority Director of Budget Studies:
Stephen M August 518-455-4054
Majority Deputy Budget Director (Education & General Government):
Jocelyn Dax 518-455-4053
Majority Deputy Budget Director (Economic Development, Environment
& Higher Education):
Matthew Howard 518-455-4053
Majority Deputy Budget Director (General Government, Labor & Budget
Initiatives):
Victor Franco 518-455-4052
Majority Deputy Budget Director (Health, Mental Hygiene, Children &
Families):
Mary Ann Donnaruma 518-455-5979
Majority Deputy Budget Director (Infrastructure, Criminal Justice &
Social Services):
Lou Tobias 518-455-4053
Majority Counsel (Taxation):
Brien R Downes 518-455-3933
Majority Deputy Fiscal Director (Taxation):
Scott Palladino 518-455-3933
Majority Deputy Fiscal Director (State & Local Finance):
Phillip Fields 518-455-4051
Majority Principal Economist:
InBong Kang 518-455-4006
Minority Ways & Means Director:
Rebecca P D'Agati 518-455-5161
Minority Ways & Means First Deputy Director:
Michael A Lawler 518-455-5161
Minority Deputy Directory for Economic Development:
Vacant 518-455-5161
Minority Deputy Director of Budget Studies:
Edward V Golden 518-455-5161

Membership

Majority

Kevin A Cahill	Ronald J Canestrari
William Colton	Vivian E Cook
RoAnn M Destito	Ruben Diaz, Jr
Thomas P DiNapoli	Adriano Espaillat
David F Gantt	Deborah J Glick
Alexander B Grannis	Aurelia Greene
William B Hoyt, III	Ivan C Lafayette
Joseph R Lentol	John J McEneny
Brian M McLaughlin	Catherine T Nolan
Clarence Norman, Jr	William L Parment
N Nick Perry	James G Pretlow
Robin L Schimminger	Frank R Seddio
Helene E Weinstein	

Minority

Thomas F Barraga	Daniel J Burling
Nancy Calhoun	James P Hayes
Roy J McDonald	Dierdre K Scozzafava
Willis H Stephens, Jr	James N Tedisco
Fred W Thiele, Jr	

Food, Farm & Nutrition, Task Force on
Chair:
Felix W Ortiz (D) 518-455-3821
Program Manager:
Robert Stern 518-455-5203

Legislative Women's Caucus
Chair:
Aurelia Greene (D) 518-455-5671
Executive Director:
Shirley Tranholm 518-455-4347/fax: 518-455-4537

Puerto Rican/Hispanic Task Force
Chair:
Peter M Rivera (D) 518-455-5102
Executive Director:
Vacant 518-455-5102/fax: 518-455-3693

Skills Development & Career Education, Legislative Commission on
Assembly Chair:
Joan K Christensen (D) 518-455-5383
Program Manager:
Brenda Carter 518-455-4865/fax: 518-455-4175

State-Local Relations, Legislative Commission on
Assembly Chair:
Vacant 518-455-0000
Program Manager:
William Kraus 518-455-5035/fax: 518-455-5396

University-Industry Cooperation, Task Force on
Chair:
William B Magnarelli (D) 518-455-4826
Coordinator:
Maureen Schoolman 518-455-4884/fax: 518-455-4175

Women's Issues, Task Force on
Chair:
Joan L Millman (D) 518-455-5426
Coordinator:
Jean Emery 518-455-3632/fax: 518-455-4574

Joint Legislative Commissions

Administrative Regulations Review, Legislative Commission on
Assembly Co-Chair:
Ruben Diaz, Jr (D) 518-455-5514
Senate Co-Chair:
John J Flanagan (R) 518-455-2071

Senate Director:
John Koury 518-455-2731/fax: 518-426-6820
Assembly Program Manager:
Rich Murphy 518-455-5091/fax: 518-455-4175

Offices and agencies appear in alphabetical order.

Critical Transportation Choices, Legislative Commission on

Senate Chair:
John R Kuhl, Jr (R)...............................518-455-2091
Assembly Vice Chair:
Vacant...518-455-0000
Program Manager:
Heidi Kromphardt.................................518-455-4031

Demographic Research & Reapportionment, Legislative Task Force on

Assembly Co-Chair:
William B Hoyt, III (D)...........................518-455-4886
Senate Co-Chair:
Dean G Skelos (R)................................518-455-3171
Assembly Co-Executive Director:
Lewis M Hoppe...................212-618-1100/fax: 212-618-1135
Senate Co-Executive Director:
Debra A Levine..................212-618-1100/fax: 212-618-1135

Ethics Committee, Legislative

Assembly Co-Chair:
Kevin A Cahill (D)...............................518-455-4436
Senate Co-Chair:
George H Winner, Jr (R)..........................518-455-2091
Program Manager/Counsel:
Melissa Ryan.................518-455-2142/fax: 518-426-6850

Government Administration, Legislative Commission on

Assembly Chair:
Joan Millman (D).................................518-455-5426
Senate Vice Chair:
Owen H Johnson (R)...............................518-455-3411
Program Manager:
Philip Johnson.................518-455-3632/fax: 518-455-4574

Health Care Financing, Council on

Senate Chair:
Joseph L Bruno (R)...............................518-455-3191
Assembly Vice-Chair:
Alexander B Grannis (D)..........................518-455-5676
Executive Director:
Al Cardillo....................518-455-2067/fax: 518-426-6925

Rural Resources, Legislative Commission on

Assembly Chair:
David R Koon (D).................................518-455-5784

Senate Chair:
Vacant...518-455-3563
Senate Executive Director:
Ronald C Brach.................518-455-2544/fax: 518-426-6960
Assembly Director:
Susan Bartle...................518-455-3999/fax: 518-455-4175
Counsel:
Donald A Walsh..................................518-455-2544

Science & Technology, Legislative Commission on

Assembly Chair:
Adele Cohen (D).................................518-455-4811
Senate V Chair:
Kenneth P LaValle (R)..........518-455-3121/fax: 518-455-4859
Program Manager:
Philip Johnson.................518-455-5081/fax: 518-455-4859

Solid Waste Management, Legislative Commission on

Assembly Chair:
William Colton (D)..............................518-455-5828
Senate Vice Chair:
Nicholas A Spano (R)............................518-455-2231
Program Manager:
Richard D Morse, Jr............518-455-3711/fax: 518-455-3837

Toxic Substances & Hazardous Wastes, Legislative Commission on

Senate Chair:
Vacant..518-455-0000
Assembly Vice Chair:
David R Koon (D)................................518-455-5784
Program Manager:
Richard D Morse, Jr............518-455-3711/fax: 518-455-3837

Water Resource Needs of NYS & Long Island, Legislative Commission on

Assembly Co-Chair:
Thomas P DiNapoli (D)...........................518-455-5192
Senate Co-Chair:
Michael A L Balboni (R).........................518-455-2471
Program Manager:
Richard D Morse, Jr............518-455-3711/fax: 518-455-3837

Offices and agencies appear in alphabetical order.

JUDICIAL BRANCH

Court of Appeals

The Court of Appeals is the highest court in New York State, hearing both civil and criminal appeals. This court consists of the Chief Judge and six Associate Judges. Judges are appointed by the Governor for fourteen-year terms or until age seventy, whichever comes first. The Court of Appeals receives direct appeal on matters where the only question relates to the constitutionality of a State or Federal statute. The Court also establishes policy for administration of the New York State Unified Court System.

Court of Appeals
Court of Appeals Hall
20 Eagle St
Albany, NY 12207-1905
518-455-7700

Clerk of the Court:
Stuart M Cohen. 518-455-7810
e-mail: coa@courts.state.ny.us

Public Information Officer:
Gary Spencer 518-455-7711
Judith S Kaye: 2007   Chief Judge

Associate Judges
Carmen Beauchamp Ciparick: 2007   Victoria A Graffeo: 2010
Susan Phillips Read: 2016   Albert M Rosenblatt: 2006
George Bundy Smith: 2006   Robert S Smith: 2014

Appellate Divisions

The Appellate Divisions of the Supreme Court exist for each of New York State's four Judicial Departments. Each Judicial Department is comprised of one or more of the State's twelve judicial districts and has Governor appointed Presiding and Associate Justices. The Presiding Justice serves the duration of his/her term as a Supreme Court Justice. Associate Justices serve for the shorter of a five-year term or the balance of their term. Supreme Court Justices are required to retire at age seventy, unless they become "Certificated" by the Administrative Board of the Courts. Justices may serve after age seventy under Certification for two-year terms, until age seventy-six. The Appellate Divisions review appeals from the Superior Court decisions in civil and criminal cases, and from Appellate Terms and County Courts in civil cases.

1st Department
Judicial Districts 1, 12
Courthouse
27 Madison Ave
New York, NY 10010
212-340-0400 Fax: 212-889-4412

Clerk of the Court:
Catherine O'Hagan Wolfe 212-340-0418
John T Buckley: 2006   Presiding Justice

Associate Justices
Richard T Andrias: 2013   James M Catterson: 2012
Betty W Ellerin (Cert): 2005   David Friedman: 2011
Luis A Gonzalez: 2010   George Marlow: 2011
Angela M Mazzarelli: 2006   Eugene Nardelli (Cert): 2006
David B Saxe: 2018   Joseph P Sulllivan (Cert): 2005
John W Sweeny: 2013   Peter Tom: 2018
Milton L Williams (Cert): 2006

2nd Department
Judicial Districts 2, 9, 10, 11
718-875-1300 Fax: 718-858-2446

Clerk of the Court:
James E Pelzer 718-875-1300
A Gail Prudenti: 2014   Presiding Justice

Associate Justices
Thomas A Adams: 2006   Barry A Cozier: 2006
Stephen G Crane: 2017   Steven Fisher: 2006
Anita R Florio: 2006   Gloria Goldstein (Cert): 2005
Gabriel Krausman (Cert): 2005   Robert A Lifson: 2008
Daniel F Luciano (Cert): 2006   William F Mastro: 2006
Howard Miller: 2018   Sondra Miller (Cert): 2005
David S Ritter (Cert): 2006 Reinaldo E Rivera: 2005
Fred T Santucci (Cert): 2006 Robert W Schmidt: 2007
Peter B Skelos: 2012   Nancy E Smith: 2011
Robert A Spolzino: 2015

3rd Department
Judicial Districts 3, 4, 6
Justice Bldg, Capitol Station
PO Box 7288
Albany, NY 12224-7288
518-474-3609

Offices and agencies appear in alphabetical order.

Clerk of the Court:
    Michael Novak 518-474-3609
Anthony V Cardona: 2018   Presiding Justice

Associate Justices

Anthony J Carpinello: 2008	D Bruce Crew III: 2007
Anthony T Kane: 2009	John A Lahtinen: 2011
Thomas E Mercure: 2009	Carl J Mugglin: 2007
Karen K Peters: 2009	Robert S Rose: 2013
Edward O Spain: 2005	

4th Department
Judicial Districts 5, 7, 8

50 East Ave
Rochester, NY 14604-2214
585-530-3100 Fax: 585-530-3247

Clerk of the Court:
    JoAnn M Wahl 585-530-3100
Eugene F Pigott, Jr: 2011   Presiding Justice

Associate Justices

Jerome C Gorski: 2016	Leo F Hayes (Cert): 2006
Robert G Hurlbutt: 2009	L Paul Kehoe: 2006
John F Lawton (Cert): 2005	Salvatore R Martoche: 2010
Elizabeth W Pine (Cert): 2006	Henry J Scudder: 2010

Supreme Court

The Supreme Court consists of twelve Judicial Districts, which are comprised of County Courts within NYS (See County Court information in related section). Justices are elected by their Judicial Districts for fourteen-year terms, unless they reach age seventy before term expiration. Justices may serve beyond age seventy if Certificated (see Apellate Divisions for definition). The Supreme Court generally hears cases outside the jurisdiction of other courts, such as: civil matters with monetary limits exceeding that of the lower courts; divorce, separation and annulment proceedings; equity suits; and criminal prosecutions of felonies.

1st Judicial District
New York County
Chief Clerk, Civil Branch:
    John F Werner 212-374-4422
Chief Clerk, Criminal Branch:
    Alan Murphy 212-374-4984
Jacqueline W Silberman: 2004   Administrative Judge
Micki A Scherer: 2008   Administrative Judge

Judges

Sheila Abdus-Salaam: 2007	Rolando T Acosta: 2016
Eileen Bransten: 2013	Richard F Braun: 2017
Herman Cahn (Cert): 2006	William J Davis (Cert): 2007
Leland G De Grasse: 2016	Carol R Edmead: 2016
Nicholas Figueroa (Cert): 2005	Helen E Freedman: 2016
Emily Jane Goodman: 2018	Budd G Goodman (Cert): 2005
Sherry Klein Heilter: 2014	Carol E Huff: 2016
Phyllis Gangel Jacob (Cert): 2004	Marcy L Kahn: 2008
Barbara Kapnick: 2015	Edward H Lehner: 2005
Doris Ling-Cohan: 2005	Joan Lobis: 2006
Richard B Lowe: 2016	Joan Madden: 2011
William P McCooe (Cert): 2005	Donna Marie Mills: 2013
Karla Moskowitz: 2005	Eduardo Pardo: 2015
Charles E Ramos: 2007	Rosalyn H Richter: 2016
Alice Schlesinger: 2013	Martin Schoenfeld: 2008
Stanley L Sklar (Cert): 2004	John EH Stackhouse: 2017
Lucindo Suarez: 2009	Milton A Tingling: 2014
Edwin Torres (Cert): 2005	Laura Visitacion-Lewis: 2011
Troy K Webber: 2016	Lottie E Wilkins: 2005
James A Yates: 2011	Louis B York: 2014

2nd Judicial District
Richmond & Kings Counties
Acting Chief Clerk, Civil Division:
    James Imperatrice 718-643-7086
Chief Clerk, Criminal Division:
    James Imperatrice 718-643-7086
Neil Jon Firetog: 2009   Administrative Judge

Judges

Thomas P Aliotta: 2015	Bruce M Balter: 2017
Betsy Barros: 2011	Bernadette Bayne: 2017
Ariel Belen: 2008	Michael J Brennan: 2011
Bert A Bunyan: 2010	Cheryl E Chambers: 2012
Anthony J Cutrona: 2008	Gloria Dabiri: 2008
Carolyn E Demarest: 2005	Patricia DiMango: 2015
Lewis L Douglass (Cert): 2006	Deborah A Dowling: 2010
Anne G Feldman (Cert): 2006	Michael J Garson: 2006
Abraham G Gerges (Cert): 2006	Robert Gigante: 2013
Raymond Guzman: 2017	L Priscilla Hall: 2007
Ira B Harkavy (Cert): 2005	Gerald S Held (Cert): 2006
Sylvia O Hinds-Radix: 2018	Allen Z Hurkin-Torres: 2015
M Randolph Jackson: 2016	Laura Lee Jacobson: 2016
Diana A Johnson: 2014	Theodore T Jones: 2017
Lawrence S Knipel: 2011	Herbert Kramer: 2017
John M Leventhal: 2008	Joseph S Levine (Cert): 2006
Yvonne Lewis: 2005	Plummer E Lott: 2008
Louis John Marrero: 2018	Larry D Martin: 2007
Christopher Mega (Cert): 2006	Philip G Minardo: 2009
Mark I Partnow: 2016	Michelle Weston Patterson: 2018
Michael L Pesce: 2017	Eric I Prus: 2018
Gustin L Reichbach: 2012	Francois A Rivera: 2010
Gerard H Rosenberg: 2013	Leon Ruchelsman: 2016
Howard A Ruditzky: 2014	Wayne P Saitta: 2018
Arthur M Schack: 2017	Martin Schneier (Cert): 2006
Martin M Solomon: 2017	James G Starkey: 2005
Marsha Steinhardt: 2008	James P Sullivan: 2016
Albert Tomei: 2007	David B Vaughan: 2005

3rd Judicial District
Albany, Columbia, Greene, Rensselaer, Schoharie, Sullivan & Ulster Counties
George B Ceresia Jr: 2007   Administrative Judge
Executive Assistant to Administrative Judge:
    Felicia D LaReau 518-445-7867

Judges

Louis C Benza (Cert): 2005	Vincent Bradley: 2009

Offices and agencies appear in alphabetical order.

James B Canfield: 2005
Nicholas A Clemente (Cert): 2005
E Michael Kavanagh: 2012
William E McCarthy: 2018
Leslie E Stein: 2015

Joseph Cannizzaro: 2013
John G Connor (Cert): 2005
Bernard J Malone: 2012
Thomas J Spargo: 2013
Joseph C Teresi: 2007

4th Judicial District
Counties: Clint, Essex, Frankln, Fultn, Hamiltn, Montg, St Lawr, Saratga, Schenectady, Warren & Wash
Vito C Caruso
Executive Assistant to Administrative Judge:
Marilyn F Jordon 518-587-3019/fax: 518-587-3179

Judges
Richard T Aulisi: 2012
Vito C Caruso: 2008
David R Demarest: 2007
David B Krogmann: 2017
Vincent J Reilly: 2012
Frank B Williams: 2007

Robert P Best (Cert): 2005
James P Dawson: 2008
Stephen A Ferradino: 2008
Thomas D Nolan: 2013
Joseph M Sise: 2012

5th Judicial District
Herkimer, Jefferson, Lewis, Oneida, Onondaga & Oswego Counties
James C Tormey: 2009   Administrative Judge
Executive Assistant to Administrative Judge:
John R Voninski 315-671-2111/fax: 315-671-1175

Judges
Edward D Carni: 2015
Michael E Daley: 2015
Hugh A Gilbert: 2017
John Grow (Cert): 2006
Robert F Julian: 2014
Joseph D McGuire: 2014
Thomas J Murphy (Cert): 2006
William R Roy (Cert): 2005
Anthony F Shaheen: 2011

John V Centra: 2013
Brian F De Joseph: 2014
Donald A Greenwood: 2018
Samuel D Hester: 2011
Deborah H Karalunas: 2016
James P Murphy: 2018
Anthony J Paris: 2013
Norman W Seiter Jr: 2017

6th Judicial District
Broome, Chemung, Chenango, Cortland, Delaware, Madison, Otsego, Schuyler, Tioga & Tompkins Counties
Judith F O'Shea: 2013   Administrative Judge
Executive Assistant to Administrative Judge:
G Russell Oechsle 607-721-8541/fax: 607-721-8634

Judges
Kevin M Dowd: 2012
Robert C Mulvey: 2014
Walter J Relihan Jr (MB): 2006
Jeffrey A Tait: 2017

Joseph P Hester: 2009
William F O'Brien: 2010
Philip R Rumsey: 2007

7th Judicial District
Cayuga, Livingston, Monroe, Ontario, Seneca, Steuben, Wayne & Yates Counties
Thomas M Van Strydonck: 2012   Administrative Judge
Executive Assistant to Administrative Judge:
Harry Salis 585-454-4242/fax: 716-325-1396

Judges
Francis A Affronti: 2017
David M Barry: 2012
David D Egan: 2014
Evelyn Frazee: 2006

John J Ark: 2007
Raymond E Cornelius: 2006
Kenneth R Fisher: 2009
Harold Galloway: 2005

Robert J Lunn: 2008
Matthew A Rosenbaum: 2005
Ann Marie Taddeo: 2018

William P Polito: 2008
Thomas A Stander: 2018
Joseph D Valentino: 2015

8th Judicial District
Allegany, Cattaraugus, Chautauqua, Erie, Genesee, Niagara, Orleans & Wyoming Counties
Sharon S Townsend: 2017   Administrative Judge
Executive Assistant to Administrative Judge:
Harold J Brand 716-852-2850

Judges
Ralph A Boniello, III: 2014
John M Curran: 2018
Vincent E Doyle (Cert): 2006
Paula L Ferdeto: 2018
Amy J Fricano: 2013
John P Lane (Cert): 2006
Frederick J Marshall: 2014
Joseph D Mintz: 2005
Peter Notaro: 2005
Erin M Peradotto: 2017
Rose H Sconiers: 2007
Donna M Siwek: 2014

Christopher J Burns: 2009
Kevin M Dillon: 2010
Eugene M Fahey: 2010
Joseph Forma: 2012
Joseph R Glownia: 2018
Joseph G Makowski: 2012
John A Michalek: 2008
Patrick H Nemoyer: 2011
John F O'Donnell: 2009
Janice M Rosa: 2016
Frank A Sedita: 2005
Penny Wolfgang: 2013

9th Judicial District
Dutchess, Orange, Putnam, Rockland & Westchester Counties
Francis A Nicolai: 2014   Administrative Judge
Executive Assistant to Administrative Judge:
Tomme Berg 914-995-4100/fax: 914-285-4111

Judges
Lester B Adler: 2018
Louis A Barone (Cert): 2005
George M Bergerman (Cert): 2006
Nicholas Colabella: 2006
Thomas A Dickerson: 2016
W Denis Donovan (Cert): 2006
William J Giacomo: 2018
Linda S Jamieson: 2016
Joan B Lefkowitz: 2018
J Emmett Murphy: 2010
Andrew P O'Rourke: 2005
Peter C Patsalos (Cert): 2005
Kenneth W Rudolph: 2006
Mary H Smith: 2016
Bruce E Tolbert: 2018

Daniel D Angiolillo: 2013
Orazio Bellantoni: 2009
James V Brands: 2016
Janet Di Fiore: 2016
Mark Dillon: 2013
Margaret Garvey: 2017
Lawrence I Horowitz: 2017
John R Lacava: 2012
John McGuirk: 2013
Aldo Nastasi (Cert): 2006
Joseph G Owen (Cert): 2005
Peter P Rosato (Cert): 2006
William E Sherwood: 2007
Christine A Sproat: 2017
Alfred Weiner: 2018

10th Judicial District
Nassau & Suffolk Counties
Executive Assistant to Administrative Judge, Nassau:
Susan Sharp 516-571-2400/fax: 516-571-3653
Anthony F Marano: 2013   Administrative Judge, Nassau
Executive Assistant to Administrative Judge, Suffolk:
Thomas F Lorito 631-853-7742/fax: 631-853-7741

Judges
Bruce D Alpert: 2006
Paul J Baisley: 2011
Howard Berler (Cert): 2006
Donald R Blydenburgh: 2010
Peter Fox Cohalan: 2008
Joseph Covello: 2013
Kenneth A Davis: 2008

Leonard B Austin: 2012
Ruth C Balkin: 2018
John C Bivona: 2009
Stephen A Bucaria: 2009
Ralph F Costello: 2010
Robert B Cozzens: 2011
Joseph A DeMaro: 2007

Arthur M Diamond: 2017
John P Dunne (Cert): 2005
Anthony Falanga: 2005
Patrick Henry (Cert): 2005
John J J Jones, Jr: 2013
William J Kent: 2008
William R Lamarca: 2005
Roy S Mahon: 2011
Edward W McCarty: 2005
Denise F Molia: 2012
Robert W Oliver (Cert): 2005
Thomas P Phelan: 2009
Arthur G Pitts: 2013
Robert Roberto (Cert): 2006
Marvin E Segal (Cert): 2004
Joseph P Spinola: 2017
Melvyn Tanenbaum: 2005
Mary M Werner: 2005
Thomas F Whelan: 2014
Michele M Woodard: 2014

Robert W Doyle: 2005
Elizabeth H Emerson: 2009
Thomas Feinman: 2017
Zelda Jonas (Cert): 2006
Burton S Joseph (Cert): 2005
Ute W Lally: 2005
Daniel J Loughlin (Cert): 2006
Edward G McCabe: 2005
Marion T McNulty: 2018
Geoffrey J O'Connell: 2007
Anthony L Parga: 2011
Emily Pines: 2015
William B Rebolini: 2017
Robert A Ross: 2015
Sandra L Sgroi: 2014
Elaine J Stack (Cert): 2005
Ira B Warshawsky: 2011
Ira H Wexner (Cert): 2005
F Dana Winslow: 2010

11th Judicial District
Queens County
Leslie G Leach: 2017   Administrative Judge
Chief Clerk:
   Anthony D'Angelis 718-298-1150

Judges
Augustus C Agate: 2018
Laura D Blackburne: 2007
Evelyn L Braun: 2006
Arthur J Cooperman (Cert): 2005
Joseph P Dorsa: 2006
David Elliot: 2017
William M Erlbaum: 2018
Phyllis Orlikoff Flug: 2017
Joseph G Golia: 2008
Robert J Hanophy: 2017
Ronald D Hollie: 2014

Michael B Aloise: 2017
Valerie Brathwaite Nelson: 2018
Richard Lance Buchter: 2006
James P Dollard (Cert): 2005
Roberta L Dunlop: 2005
Randall T Eng: 2018
Timothy J Flaherty (Cert): 2006
James J Golia: 2018
Marguerite A Grays: 2016
Duane A Hart: 2015
Richard D Huttner: 2014

Peter Joseph Kelly: 2016
Robert C Kohm: 2006
Leslie G Leach: 2017
Daniel Lewis: 2009
James M McGuire: 2018
Thomas V Polizzi (Cert): 2005
Jaime Antonio Rios: 2008
Martin E Ritholtz: 2015
Roger N Rosengarten: 2007
Frederick D R Sampson: 2008
Martin J Schulman: 2008
Sidney F Strauss: 2008
Charles J Thomas (Cert): 2006
Allan B Weiss: 2011

Orin R Kitzes: 2008
Gregory L Lasak: 2017
Alan Levine (Cert): 2005
Robert J McDonald: 2013
Peter O'Donoghue: 2015
Arnold N Price (Cert): 2005
Joseph J Risi (Cert): 2005
Sheri S Roman: 2008
Seymour Rotker (Cert): 2005
Patricia P Satterfield: 2012
Mark H Spires (Cert): 2006
Janice A Taylor: 2011
Jeremy S Weinstein: 2013

12th Judicial District
Bronx County
Gerald V Esposito: 2005   Administrative Judge
John P Collins: 2007   Administrative Judge
Chief Clerk, Criminal:
   Steven B Clark 718-590-3985
Tracy Pardo

Judges
John A Barone: 2014
Janice L Bowman: 2010
Edward Davidowitz (Cert): 2006
Joseph Fisch (Cert): 2005
Yvonne Gonzalez: 2013
Bertram Katz (Cert): 2006
Latia W Martin: 2016
Richard L Price: 2016
Nelson Roman: 2016
Robert A Sackett: 2017
George D Salerno (Cert): 2005
Howard R Silver (Cert): 2006
David Stadtmauer (Cert): 2006
Kenneth Thompson, Jr: 2009
Alison Y Tuitt: 2017

Lawrence H Bernstein (Cert): 2006
Mary Briganti-Hughes: 2018
Laura G Douglas: 2013
Mark Friedlander: 2015
Alexander W Hunter: 2008
Sallie Manzanet: 2015
Douglas E McKeon: 2017
Dianne T Renwick: 2015
Norma Ruiz: 2013
Alan J Saks (Cert): 2005
Barry Salman: 2018
Harold Silverman (Cert): 2005
Betty Owen Stinson: 2013
Robert E Torres: 2018
Paul A Victor (Cert): 2005

Court of Claims

The Court of Claims is a special trial court that hears and determines only claims against the State of New York. Court of Claims judges are appointed by the Governor for nine-year terms. Certain judges of this court, as designated herein by an *, also serve as acting Supreme Court Justices for the assigned judicial district.

Court of Claims
Justice Bldg
Capitol Station
PO Box 7344
Albany, NY 12224
518-432-3437 Fax: 518-432-3483

Clerk of the Court:
   David B Klingaman 518-432-3411/fax: 518-432-3483
Administrative Judge:
   Richard E Sise 518-432-3435/fax: 518-432-3428

Judges
Michael R Ambrecht*: 2008
Edward D Burke*: 2008
Gregory Carro*: 2004

John J Brunetti*: 2010
Russell P Buscaglia*: 2006
Thomas J Carroll*: 2004

Caesar Cirigliano*: 2006
Robert J Collini*: 2004
Michael A Corriero*: 2008
Vincent M DelGuidice*: 2004
Diane L Fitzpatrick: 2007
Philip M Grella*: 2010
Alan L Honorof*: 2004
John G Ingram*: 2004
James J Lack: 2003
Ferris D Lebous: 2005
Joseph J Maltese*: 2004
Martin Marcus*: 2008
Daniel Martin*: 2004
Thomas J McNamara: 2004
Stephen J Mignano: 2011
Richard Molea*: 2006
S Michael Nadel: 2009

Margaret L Clancy*: 2004
Francis T Collins: 2006
Matthew J D'Emic*: 2005
William C Donnino*: 2010
Anthony Giacobbe*: 2004
Judith A Hard: 2009
Michael E Hudson: 2006
Richard C Kloch*: 2004
Dan Lamont*: 2004
Albert Lorenzo*: 2009
Guy J Mangano, Jr*: 2010
Alan C Marin: 2006
Dominic R Massaro*: 2004
Nicholas V Midey Jr: 2010
Renee Forgensi Minarik: 2008
Michael F Mullen*: 2004
Victor M Ort*: 2004

Offices and agencies appear in alphabetical order.

Philip J Patti: 2011
Mario J Rossetti*: 2005
Thomas H Scuccimarra: 2006
Richard E Sise: 2004

Stephen J Rooney*: 2004
Terry J Ruderman: 2006
Norman I Siegel*: 2006
Lewis Bart Stone*: 2008

Charles J Tejada*: 2008
Rena K Uviller*: 2007
William A Wetzel*: 2008
Ronald A Zweibel*: 2010

Ronald H Tills*: 2010
Alton R Waldon, Jr: 2006
Maxwell T Wiley*: 2009

New York City Courts

New York City has its own Civil, Criminal and Family courts, separate from the County Court system. The NYC Civil Court hears civil cases involving amounts up to $25,000, and its judges are elected for ten-year terms. The NYC Criminal Court conducts trials of misdemeanors and violations. Criminal Court judges act as magistrates for all criminal offenses and are appointed by the City's Mayor for ten-year terms. The NYC Family Court hears matters involving children and families, such as: child protection, delinquency, domestic violence, guardianship, parental rights and spousal and child support. Family Court judges are appointed by the City's Mayor for ten-year terms.

Civil Court, NYC
Chief Clerk:
    Jack Baer 646-386-5409/fax: 212-374-5709

Bronx County
851 Grand Concourse, Bronx, NY 10451
Joseph Monastra

Kings County
141 Livingston St, Brooklyn, NY 11201
Stewart Feigel

New York County
111 Centre St, New York, NY 10013
Mary Lee Andronaco

Queens County
89-17 Sutphin Blvd, Jamaica, NY 11435
Thomas Touhey

Richmond County
927 Castleton Ave, Staten Island, NY 10310
Lorraine Stergious

Judges
Sharon A Aarons: 2013
Harold Adler: 2011
Loren Baily-Schiffman: 2008
Johnny Lee Baynes: 2014
Miriam R Best: 2005
Arthur Birnbaum: 2006
John A K Bradley: 2004
Raymond L Bruce: 2011
Abraham L Clott: 2005
Raul Cruz: 2012
Catherine M DiDomenico: 2005
Monica Drinane: 2005
Gerald J Dunbar: 2014
Laura Safer Espinoza: 2010
Saralee Evans: 2013
Anthony J Ferrara: 2005
Kathryn E Freed: 2013
Robin S Garson: 2012
Ellen Frances Gesmer: 2013
Ira R Globerman: 2005
Ferne J Goldstein: 2005
Stephen S Gottlieb: 2013
Desmond A Green: 2013
Wilma Guzman: 2008
Barbara Jaffe: 2011
Deborah A Kaplan: 2011

Rachel Amy Adams: 2009
Francis M Alessandro: 2009
Jack M Battaglia: 2010
Harold B Beeler: 2007
Lucy Billings: 2007
Arlene P Bluth: 2014
Dorothy K Chin Brandt: 2007
Denis J Butler: 2011
Matthew F Cooper: 2010
Anna Culley: 2013
Marylin G Diamond: 2010
Timothy J Dufficy: 2012
Arthur F Engoron: 2012
Joseph J Esposito: 2014
Paul G Feinman: 2006
Fern A Fisher: 2007
Marcy S Friedman: 2013
Darrell L Gavrin: 2012
Judith J Gische: 2013
Lila P Gold: 2013
Lizbeth Gonzalez: 2014
Bernard J Graham: 2014
Stanley Green: 2009
Shlomo S Hagler: 2013
Debra A James: 2014
Joan M Kenney: 2010

Cynthia S Kern: 2009
Kathy J King: 2013
Shirley W Kornreich: 2004
Donald Scott Kurtz: 2009
Howard G Lane: 2013
Robert D Lippmann: 2013
Nelida Maleve: 2014
Charles J Markey: 2010
Lee A Mayersohn: 2014
Manuel J Mendez: 2013
Peter H Moulton: 2013
Ann E O'Shea: 2013
Paula J Omansky: 2004
Barbara I Panepinto: 2006
Steven W Paynter: 2005
Diccia T Pineda-Kirwan: 2012
Julia I Rodriguez: 2013
Alice Fisher Rubin: 2008
Saliann Scarpulla: 2011
David Schmidt: 2005
Marilyn Shafer: 2013
Martin Shulman: 2004
Marcia J Sikowitz: 2007
George J Silver: 2014
ShawnDya L Simpson: 2013
Karen Smith: 2005
Jane S Solomon: 2006
Ellen M Spodek: 2012
Philip S Straniere: 2006
Fernando Tapia: 2012
Walter Tolub: 2009
Margarita Lopez Torres: 2012
George R Villegas: 2012
Edgar G Walker: 2010
Betty J Williams: 2010
Geoffrey D Wright: 2007

Kevin Kerrigan: 2009
Stephen A Knopf: 2006
Sarah L Krauss: 2014
Evelyn J LaPorte: 2014
Diane A Lebedeff: 2012
Karen I Lupuloff: 2005
Ira H Margulis: 2013
Milagros A Matos: 2014
Judith N McMahon: 2012
Esther M Morgenstern: 2005
Eileen N Nadelson: 2008
Jeffrey K Oing: 2013
Jose A Padilla: 2014
Kibbie F Payne: 2012
Geraldine Pickett: 2014
Eileen A Rakower: 2006
Karen B Rothenberg: 2007
Debrarose Samuels: 2012
Larry S Schachner: 2013
Matthew Sciarrino Jr: 2005
Howard E Sherman: 2009
Bernice Daun Siegal: 2011
Debra Silber: 2007
Joseph Silverman: 2007
Anil C Singh: 2012
Ruth E Smith: 2005
Faviola Soto: 2013
Michael D Stallman: 2006
Peter Paul Sweeney: 2011
Delores J Thomas: 2012
Analisa Torres: 2009
Wavny Toussaint: 2012
Eric N Vitaliano: 2011
Dolores L Waltrous: 2008
John H Wilson: 2014
Alex J Zigman: 2005

Housing Court Judges
Paul L Alpert: 2005
Gilbert Badillo: 2007
Joseph E Capella: 2009
Oymin Chin: 2008
Mitchell Danzinger: 2009
Timmie E Elsner: 2007
Anthony J Firoella: 2008
James R Grayshaw: 2007
Sheldon J Halprin: 2008
Douglas E Hoffman: 2006
Dawn M Jimenez: 2009

Ava P Alterman: 2005
Ronni D Birnbaum: 2006
Ernest J Cavallo: 2007
David B Cohen: 2009
Marian C Doherty: 2006
Marc Finkelstein: 2009
Thomas M Fitzpatrick: 2009
Arlene H Hahn: 2009
George M Heymann: 2006
Pam B Jackman-Brown: 2008
Anne Katz: 2008

Offices and agencies appear in alphabetical order.

Jerald R Klein: 2007
Lydia C Lai: 2008
Laurie L Lau: 2008
Ulysses B Leverett: 2009
Gary F Marton: 2004
Margaret P McGowan: 2008
Inez Muniz-Hoyos: 2008
Eardell J Rashford: 2005
Jose Rodriguez: 2006
Jean T Schneider: 2007
Brenda S Spears: 2006
Elizabeth J Yalin Tao: 2009
Deighton S Waithe: 2009

Bruce Marc Kramer: 2009
John S Lansden: 2008
Gerald Lebovits: 2006
Jaya Madhavan: 2009
Kevin C McClanahan: 2007
Maria Milin: 2007
Michael J Pinckney: 2004
Maria Ressos: 2006
Bruce E Scheckowitz: 2009
Michelle D Schreiber: 2009
John Stanley: 2010
Pierre B Turner: 2006
Peter M Wendt: 2008

Criminal Court, NYC

Chief Clerk:
  William H Etheridge 646-386-4600/fax: 212-374-4835

Bronx County
215 E 161st St., Bronx, NY 10451
William Kalish

Kings County
120 Schermerhorn St, Brooklyn, NY 11201
John Hayes

New York County
100 Centre St, New York, NY 10013
Serena Springle

Queens County
125-01 Queens Blvd, Kew Gardens, NY 11415
Brian Wynne

Richmond County
67 Targee St, Staten Island, NY 10304
Andrew Hassell

Judges

Bruce Allen: 2005
Allen G Alpert: 2012
Efrain L Alvarado: 2010
Steven Lloyd Barrett: 2008
Peter J Benitez: 2011
Joel L Blumenfeld: 2010
James M Burke: 2012
Alexander Calabrese: 2006
Richard D Carruthers: 2012
John Cataldo: 2008
Darcel D Clark: 2008
John P Collins: 2007
Joseph J Dawson: 2008
Ralph A Fabrizio: 2007
Joann Ferdinand: 2011
Daniel P Fitzgerald: 2011
William E Garnett: 2009
Lenora Gerald: 2011
Arlene D Goldberg: 2008
Ethan Greenberg: 2010
Michael A Gross: 2013
Josephe Gubbay: 2008
Gerald Harris: 2008
Charles J Heffernan: 2007
Douglas E Hoffman: 2012
Melissa C Jackson: 2007
Eileen Koretz: 2005
John B Latella: 2005
Jeffrey Lebowitz: 2014
Judith S Lieb: 2011

Richard N Allman: 2007
Herbert I Altman: 2006
Jeffrey M Atlas: 2009
A Kirke Bartley: 2008
Carol Berkman: 2008
Denis J Boyle: 2011
John N Byrne: 2006
Fernando M Camacho: 2008
John W Carter: 2012
Danny K Chun: 2008
Ellen M Coin: 2013
Miriam Cyrulnik: 2005
Laura E Drager: 2011
Thomas A Farber: 2011
Neil Jon Firetog: 2009
Bernard J Fried: 2009
Michael A Gary: 2010
James D Gibbons: 2012
Joel M Goldberg: 2012
James P Griffin: 2005
Joseph A Grosso: 2012
William M Harrington: 2012
Roger S Hayes: 2011
Patricia E Henry: 2006
Nicholas Iacovetta: 2005
Diane R Kiesel: 2008
Barry Kron: 2006
Leslie G Leach: 2012
Judith A Levitt: 2005
Gene R Lopez: 2008

Alan D Marrus: 2012
Robert C McGann: 2007
Joseph K McKay: 2013
Suzanne J Melendez: 2010
William Miller: 2012
Salvatore J Modica: 2005
Suzanne M Mondo: 2008
Pauline Mullings: 2014
Juanita B Newton: 2004
Mary O'Donoghue: 2014
Eugene Oliver: 2005
Ruth Pickholz: 2009
Donna A Recant: 2005
Neil E Ross: 2008
Robert G Seewald: 2013
Brenda S Soloff: 2009
Michael R Sonberg: 2011
Robert M Stoltz: 2012
Joan C Sudolnik: 2009
Megan Tallmer: 2014
Laura A Ward: 2013
Renee A White: 2007
Bonnie G Wittner: 2010
Alvin M Yearwood: 2005

Seth L Marvin: 2011
William L McGuire Jr: 2013
Edward J McLaughlin: 2012
Alan J Meyer: 2012
Deborah S Modica: 2008
William I Mogulescu: 2009
John S Moore: 2010
Barbara F Newman: 2006
Patricia M Nunez: 2012
Michael J Obus: 2005
Sheryl L Parker: 2008
Robert M Raciti: 2007
Leonard P Rienzi: 2011
Matthew Sciarrino Jr: 2005
Arlene Silverman: 2008
Charles H Solomon: 2009
Larry R Stephen: 2007
Robert H Straus: 2000
Ruth L Sussman: 2006
John P Walsh: 2008
Richard M Weinberg: 2007
Patricia Anne Williams: 2009
Douglas S Wong: 2011
Joseph A Zayas: 2009

Family Court, NYC

Chief Clerk:
  James E Kenny . . . . 646-386-5170 or 646-386-5200
  fax: 212-374-3257

Bronx County
900 Sheridan Ave, Bronx, NY 10451
Paul Moriarity

Kings County
283 Adams St, Brooklyn, NY 11201
Robert Ratanski

New York County
60 Lafayette St, New York, NY 10013
Evelyn Hasanoeddin

Queens County
151-20 Jamaica Ave, Jamaica, NY 11432
George Cafasso

Richmond County
100 Richmond Terrace, Staten Island, NY 10301
William Quirk

Judges

Jody Adams: 2012
Mary E Bednar: 2005
Robert F Clark: 2007
Alma Cordova: 2005
Tandra L Dawson: 2015
Lee Hand Elkins: 2005
Nora L Freeman: 2012
Sidney Gribetz: 2009
Bryanne A Hamill: 2011
John M Hunt: 2006
Susan K Knipps: 2007
Joseph M Lauria: 2008
Fran L Lubow: 2018
Myrna Martinez-Perez: 2012
Terrence J McElrath: 2005
Martin P Murphy: 2006
Jane Pearl: 2009
Clark V Richardson: 2014

Michael A Ambrosio: 2012
Stephen J Bogacz: 2005
Rhoda J Cohen: 2012
Susan S Danoff: 2011
Guy P DePhillips: 2012
Maryellen Fitzmaurice: 2010
Rhea G Friedman: 2008
Paul H Grosvenor: 2010
Paula J Hepner: 2010
George L Jurow: 2008
Susan R Larabee: 2009
Arnold Lim: 2009
Harold J Lynch: 2006
Ruben A Martino: 2012
Maureen A McLeod: 2011
Emily M Olshansky: 2007
Ralph J Porzio: 2005
Edwina G Richardson: 2014

Offices and agencies appear in alphabetical order.

Marybeth S Richroath: 2011
Barbara Salinitro: 2013
Marian R Shelton: 2007
Betty E Staton: 2011

Gayle P Roberts: 2006
Sara P Schechter: 2008
Gloria Sosa-Lintner: 2012
Carol Ann Stokinger: 2009

Helen C Sturm: 2009
Daniel Turbow: 2005
Virginia E Yancey: 2005

Jeffrey S Sunshine: 2013
Stewart H Weinstein: 2010

County Courts

NYS has three types of courts designated at a county level: County Court, Family Court and Surrogate's Court. The County Court is authorized to handle criminal prosecutions of offenses committed within the county and hears civil cases involving amounts up to $25,000. County Court judges are elected for ten-year terms. The Family Court hears matters involving children and families (for types of court matters see NYC Courts). Family Court judges are elected for ten-year terms. The Surrogate's Court hears cases involving the affairs of decedents, including the probate of wills, and administration of estates and adoptions. Surrogates are elected for ten-year terms. This section also includes Supreme Court clerks and their addresses. Additional information and a list of judges for the NYS Supreme Court is provided in the related Section.

Albany County

Judges
Thomas A Breslin: 2012
W Dennis Duggan: 2013
Gerard E Maney: 2011

Cathryn M Doyle: 2010
Stephen W Herrick: 2011
Margaret T Walsh: 2014

Family Court
1 Van Tromp St, Albany, NY 12207-2209
William J Person

Supreme, County & Surrogate's Courts
Courthouse, 16 Eagle St, Albany, NY 12207
Charles Diamond
Stacy L Pettit

Allegany County

Judges
Thomas Paul Brown: 2009
James E Euken: 2007

Supreme, County, Family & Surrogate's Courts
Courthouse, 7 Court St, Belmont, NY 14813
Kathleen C Johnson
Carolyn J Miller

Bronx County

Judges
Lee L Holzman: 2011

COUNTY & FAMILY COURTS: See New York City Courts

Supreme & Surrogate's Courts
851 Grand Concourse, Bronx, NY 10451
Steven B Clark
Tracy Pardo
Michael L Prisco

Broome County

Judges
Pater P Charnetsky: 2014
Patrick H Mathews: 2007
Spero Pines: 2013

Mary Rita Connerton: 2011
Eugene E Peckman: 2010
Martin E Smith: 2010

Family Court
Justice Bldg, 65 Hawley St, Binghamton, NY 13901-4708
Joan Goode

Supreme, County & Surrogate's Courts
Courthouse, 92 Court St, Binghamton, NY 13901-3301
Michael P Husar
Marilyn A Vescio

Cattaraugus County

Judges
Larry M Himelein: 2012
Michael L Nenno: 2011

Family Court
1701 Lincoln Ave, Ste 1140, Olean, NY 14760-1152
Ruth Dickerson

Supreme, County & Surrogate's Courts
Courthouse, 303 Court St, Little Valley, NY 14755
M Kathryn Smith
Sandra A Wogick

Cayuga County

Supreme, County & Surrogate's Courts
Courthouse, 154 Genesee St, Auburn, NY 13021

Family Court
Old Historic PO Bldg, 157 Genesee St, Auburn, NY 13021-3476
Barbara A Carmody
Anne B Delaney
Kelly J Wejko

Judges
Peter E Corning: 2006
Mark H Fandrich: 2011

Chautauqua County

Judges
Stephen W Cass: 2009
John T Ward: 2012

Judith S Claire: 2008

Family & Surrogate's Courts
Gerace Bldg, 3 N Erie St, Mayville, NY 14757
D Gallagher
Lydia Romer

Supreme & County Courts
Courthouse, 1 N Erie St, Mayville, NY 14757
Judith Helman

Offices and agencies appear in alphabetical order.

Chemung County

Judges
David M Brockway: 2010   Peter C Buckley: 2006
James T Hayden: 2009

Family Court
    203-209 William St, Elmira, NY 14901-0558
Marie Brewer

Supreme Court
    Hazlett Bldg, 203 Lake St, PO Box 588, Elmira, NY 14901-0588
John A Buturla

Surrogate's & County Courts
    Courthouse, 224 Lake St, Elmira, NY 14901
Patricia Kreitzer

Chenango County

Judges
W Howard Sullivan: 2009

Supreme, County, Family & Surrogate's Courts
    5 Court St, Norwich, NY 13815-1676
Linda Burke   Carole S Dunham
Catherine Schell

Clinton County

Judges
Timothy J Lawliss: 2008   Patrick R McGill: 2009
Kevin K Ryan: 2006

Supreme, County, Family & Surrogate's Courts
    Government Ctr, 137 Margaret St, Plattsburgh, NY 12901
Bonnie Dorman   Jan M Lavigne
Patricia A LeClerc

Columbia County

Judges
Paul Czajka: 2014   Jonathan D Nichols: 2013

Supreme, County, Family & Surrogate's Courts
    Courthouse, 401 Union St, Hudson, NY 12534
Elizabeth Bennett   Dorothy Prest
Ronald D Wiley

Cortland County

Judges
William F Ames: 2008   Julie A Campbell: 2013

Supreme, County, Family & Surrogate's Courts
    Courthouse, 46 Greenbush St, Ste 301, Cortland, NY 13045-2725
Laurie L Case   Christina DeMass
Maxine Ripley

Delaware County

Judges
Carl F Becker: 2012

Supreme, County, Family & Surrogate's Courts
    Courthouse, 3 Court St, Delhi, NY 13753
Allison Barnes   Nancy A Smith

Donna Torma

Dutchess County

Judges
Damian J Amodeo: 2008   Thomas J Dolan: 2012
Peter M Forman: 2009   Gerald V Hayes: 2010
James D Pagones: 2008   Valentino T Sammarco: 2013

Family Court
    50 Market St, Poughkeepsie, NY 12601
Peter A Palladino

Supreme, County & Surrogate's Courts
    Courthouse, 10 Market St, Poughkeepsie, NY 12601
John J Atherton   Ronald Varricchio

Erie County

Judges
Rosalie Bailey: 2013   Paul G Buchanan: 2013
Kevin M Carter: 2012   Michael L Damico: 2006
James H Dillon: 2010   Sheila Ditullio: 2005
Timothy J Drury: 2007   Barbara Howe: 2013
Patricia Anne Maxwell: 2011   Michael F Pietruszka: 2008
Margaret O Szczur: 2014   Shirley Troutman: 2012

Family Court
    One Niagara Plz, Buffalo, NY 14202
Frank J Boccio

Supreme, County & Surrogates Court
    Erie County Hall, 92 Franklin St, Buffalo, NY 14202
Nicholas G Baich   Katen Bolm
Paul Smaldone

Essex County

Judges
Andrew Halloran: 2005

Supreme, County, Family & Surrogate's Courts
    Courthouse, 100 Court St, PO Box 217, Elizabethtown, NY 12932
Mary Anne Allen   Darlene K Gough
Darlene Kahler

Franklin County

Judges
Robert G Main, Jr: 2007

Supreme, County, Family & Surrogate's Courts
    Courthouse, 355 W Main St, Malone, NY 12953-1817
Martha A LaBarge   Martha A LaBarge
Gertrude Matthews

Fulton County

Judges
Richard C Giardino: 2006   Polly A Hoye: 2011
David F Jung: 2009

Family Court
    County Ofc Bldg, 11 N William St, Johnstown, NY 12095
Geraldine Kussius

Supreme, County & Surrogate's Courts
    County Ofc Bldg, 223 W Main St, Johnstown, NY 12095

Offices and agencies appear in alphabetical order.

Patricia Caravella   Barbara Shattuck

Genesee County

Judges
Eric R Adams: 2010   Robert C Noonan: 2006

Supreme, County, Family & Surrogate's Courts
County Courts Facility, 1 W Main St, Batavia, NY 14020-2019
Kathleen Blake   Nelson L Green
Colleen Kelly

Greene County

Judges
Daniel K Lalor: 2010   George J Pulver, Jr: 2005

Supreme, County, Family & Surrogate's Courts
Courthouse, 320 Main St, Catskill, NY 12414
Donna M Anderson   Kathleen Barry Gorczyca
Brenda Van Der Mark

Hamilton County

Judges
S Peter Feldstein: 2009

Supreme, County, Family & Surrogate's Courts
County Ofc Bldg, White Birch Ln, PO Box 780, Indian Lake, NY
     12842-0780
Catherine Linton

Herkimer County

Judges
Patrick L Kirk: 2011   Henry A LaRaia: 2014

Family Court
County Office Bldg, 109-111 Mary St, Herkimer, NY 13350
Eleanor Tucker

Supreme, County & Surrogate's Courts
Courthouse, 301 N Washington St, Herkimer, NY 13350
Constance A Vertucci

Jefferson County

Judges
R V Hunt: 2014   Kim H Martusewicz: 2009
Peter A Schwerzmann: 2010

Family & Surrogate's Courts
175 Arsenal St, Watertown, NY 13601
Tanice A Gebo   Bonnie S Johnston

Supreme & County Courts
195 Arsenal St, 10th Fl, Watertown, NY 13601
Wayne J Schreck

Kings County

Judges
Michael H Feinberg: 2010

COUNTY & FAMILY COURTS: See New York City Courts

Supreme Court
Civic Ctr, 360 Adams St, Brooklyn, NY 11201
James Imperatrice   James Imperatrice

Surrogate's Court
2 Johnson St, Brooklyn, NY 11201
Stephen Chepiga

Lewis County

Judges
Charles C Merrell: 2012

Supreme, County, Family & Surrogate's Courts
Courthouse, 7660 N State St, Lowville, NY 13367-1396
Judy Meekins   Lori Pfendler
Bart R Pleskach

Livingston County

Judges
Gerard J Alonzo: 2005   Ronald Cicoria: 2005

Supreme, County, Family & Surrogate's Courts
Courthouse, 2 Court St, Geneseo, NY 14454
Robert Lewis   Toni Moore
Diane Murphy

Madison County

Judges
Biagio J DiStefano: 2007   Dennis K McDermott: 2012

Supreme, County, Family & Surrogate's Courts
Courthouse, N Court St, Wampsville, NY 13163-0545
Marianne Kincaid   Andrea Slivinski

Monroe County

Judges
Elma A Bellini: 2010   Edmund A Calvaruso: 2009
John J Connell: 2014   Gail A Donofrio: 2008
Frank P Geraci: 2008   Richard A Keenan: 2010
Joan S Kohout: 2008   Patricia D Marks: 2014
Marilyn L O'Connor: 2007   Alex R Renzi: 2012
John J Rivoli: 2010   Dandrea L Ruhlmann: 2013
Anthony J Sciolino: 2006

Supreme, County, Family & Surrogate's Courts
Hall of Justice, 99 Exchange Blvd, 5th Fl, Rochester, NY 14614
William Brongo   James Hendricks
Ronald W Pawelczak

Montgomery County

Judges
Felix J Catena: 2009   Philip V Cortese: 2012
Guy P Tomlinson: 2005

Supreme, County, Family & Surrogate's Courts
Courthouse, 58 Broadway, PO Box 1500, Fonda, NY 12068-1500
Ella Bowerman   Flora Onorato
Timothy J Riley

Offices and agencies appear in alphabetical order.

Judicial Branch

Nassau County

Judges

David J Ayres: 2013	Meryl J Berkowitz: 2009
Lawrence J Brennan: 2006	Jeffrey S Brown: 2009
Joseph Calabrese: 2013	Jerald S Carter: 2007
Julianne S Eisman: 2007	Carnell Foskey: 2008
John M Galasso: 2007	Frank A Gulotta: 2005
Angela G Iannacci: 2013	Steven M Jaeger: 2014
John L Kase: 2013	Richard Lapera: 2007
Richard S Lawrence: 2007	John G Marks: 2012
George R Peck: 2012	John B Pessala: 2006
John B Riordan: 2010	Tammy S Robbins: 2014
David P Sullivan: 2012	Claire I Weinberg: 2005
Hope Schwartz Zimmerman: 2014	

County & Surrogate's Courts
262 Old Country Rd, Mineola, NY 11501
Katharine A Cunningham   Albert W Petraglia

Family Court
1200 Old Country Rd, Westbury, NY 11590
Rosalie Fitzgerald

Supreme Court
Supreme Court Bldg, 100 Supreme Court Dr, Mineola, NY 11501
Kathryn D Hopkins

New York County

Judges
Eve M Preminger: 2018   Renee R Roth: 2008

COUNTY & FAMILY COURTS: See New York City Courts

SUPREME COURT, Civil Term
60 Centre St, New York, NY 10007
John Werner

SUPREME COURT, Criminal Term
100 Centre St, New York, NY 10013
Alan Murphy

Surrogate's Court
31 Chambers St, New York, NY 10007
Jane Passenant

Niagara County

Judges
John F Batt: 2007   Peter L Broderick: 2007
David E Seaman: 2012   Sara S Sperrazza: 2010

County, Family & Surrogate's Courts
Courthouse, 175 Hawley St, Lockport, NY 14094
William F McCarthy   Mary Ellen Florian
Ronald A Sutton

Supreme Court
775 3rd St, PO Box 1710, Niagara Falls, NY 14302
Mary Ellen Florian

Oneida County

Judges
Frank S Cook: 2013   Barry M Donalty: 2013
Michael L Dwyer: 2005   James R Griffith: 2008

John G Ringrose: 2005   Bernadette T Romano: 2010

Supreme & County Courts
Courthouse, 200 Elizabeth St, 1st Fl, Utica, NY 13501
Joseph Panella

Family Court
Courthouse, 301 W Dominick St, Rome, NY 13440
Barbara L Tokarski

Surrogate's Court
County Office Bldg, 800 Park Ave, 8th Fl, Utica, NY 13501
Martha R Hoffman

Onondaga County

Judges
Anthony F Aloi: 2009	Joseph E Fahey: 2006
Michael Hanuszczak: 2010	Bryan R Hedges: 2014
Martha Walsh Hood: 2010	David G Klim: 2005
Robert J Rossi: 2007	William D Walsh: 2010
Peter N Wells: 2008	

Supreme, County, Family & Surrogate's Courts
Courthouse, 401 Montgomery St, Syracuse, NY 13202
Bobette Morin   Patricia Noll
Ava Raphael

Ontario County

Judges
Craig Doran: 2009   James R Harvey: 2009
Frederick G Reed: 2011

Supreme, County, Family & Surrogate's Courts
Courthouse, 27 N Main St, Canandaigua, NY 14424-1459
Donna Crudele   Michael R Morrisey
Kathleen D Sweeney

Orange County

Judges
Jeffrey G Berry: 2010	Andrew P Bivona: 2008
Nicholas DeRosa: 2007	Debra Kiedaisch: 2005
Carol S Klein: 2010	Stewart Rosenwasser: 2009
Elaine Slobod: 2014	

Supreme, County & Family Courts
Government Ctr, 255-275 Main St, Goshen, NY 10924
Thomas Adams   Elizabeth Holbrook

Surrogate's Court
Courthouse, 30 Park Pl, Goshen, NY 10924
Lorraine Ryerson

Orleans County

Judges
James P Punch: 2010

Supreme, County, Family & Surrogate's Courts
Courthouse, 243 S Main St, Albion, NY 14411-1497
Patricia J Beach   Elsie M Boring
Barbara Hale

Offices and agencies appear in alphabetical order.

Oswego County

Judges

John Elliott: 2008
James W McCarthy: 2012

Walter W Hafner, Jr: 2008
David J Roman: 2008

Family Court

Public Safety Ctr, 39 Churchill Rd, Oswego, NY 13126
Sherryl Waldron

Supreme, County & Surrogate's Courts

Courthouse, 25 E Oneida St, Oswego, NY 13126
Judy Cooper   Theres Stephens

Otsego County

Judges

Brian D Burns: 2010   Michael V Coccoma: 2004

Supreme, County, Family & Surrogate's Courts

197 Main St, Cooperstown, NY 13326
Gloria Chandler   Jeanne Johnson
Judy McBrearty

Putnam County

Judges

Robert E Miller: 2006   James T Rooney: 2010

Supreme, County, Family & Surrogate's Courts

County Ofc Bldg, 40 Gleneida Ave, Carmel, NY 10512
Karen O'Connor   Leonard A Pace
Linda M VanderWoulde

Queens County

Judges

Robert L Nahman: 2005

COUNTY & FAMILY COURTS: See New York City Courts

Supreme & Surrogate's Courts

88-11 Sutphin Blvd, Jamaica, NY 11435
Anthony D'Angelis   Alicemarie E Rice

Rensselaer County

Judges

Catherine Cholakis: 2012
Christian F Hummel: 2011

Linda C Griffin: 2013
Patrick J McGrath: 2013

Family Court

1504 5th Ave, Troy, NY 12180-4107
Patricia Beeler

Supreme, County & Surrogate's Courts

Courthouse, 72 Second St, Troy, NY 12180
Paul Morgan, Jr   Richard Reilly

Richmond County

Judges

John A Fusco: 2007

COUNTY & FAMILY COURTS: See New York City Courts

Supreme & Surrogate's Courts

County Courthouse, 18 Richmond Terrace, Staten Island, NY 10301
Ronald M Cerrachio   Joseph Como

Rockland County

Judges

Linda Christopher: 2014
William K Nelson: 2005
William P Warren: 2008

William A Kelly: 2007
Kenneth H Resnik: 2010

Supreme, County, & Family Courts

Courthouse, 1 S Main St, New City, NY 10956
Carol Deery   Eileen Stanford

Surrogate's Court

18 New Hempstead Rd, New York City, NY 10956
Virginia Athens

Saratoga County

Judges

Gilbert L Abramson: 2010
Jerry J Scarano Jr: 2014

Courtenay W Hall: 2008
Harry W Seibert: 2012

Family Court

Municipal Ctr, Bldg 2, 35 W High St, Ballston Spa, NY 12020
Susan P Janczak

Supreme, County & Surrogate's Courts

30 McMaster St, Ballston Spa, NY 12020
Debra D Baker   Carolyn Hall

Schenectady County

Judges

Jo Anne Assini: 2010
Barry D Kramer: 2013

Karen A Drago: 2014
Mark L Powers: 2011

Family Court

County Office Bldg, 620 State St, Schenectady, NY 12305
James C Armour

Supreme, County & Surrogate's Courts

Courthouse, 612 State St, Schenectady, NY 12305
Margaret J Datz   Sharon Sheffer

Schoharie County

Judges

George R Bartlett, III: 2005

Supreme, County, Family & Surrogate's Courts

Courthouse, 300 Main St, 669, Schoharie, NY 12157-0669
Lynda Haggart   Christian F Spies

Schuyler County

Judges

J C Argetsinger: 2007

Supreme, County, Family & Surrogate's Courts

Courthouse, 105 9th St, Unit 35, Watkins Glen, NY 14891
Lynda Lo Presti   Karen H Morgan
Frances Pierce

Offices and agencies appear in alphabetical order.

Judicial Branch

Seneca County

Judges
Dennis F Bender: 2013

Supreme, County, Family & Surrogate's Courts
Courthouse, 48 W Williams St, Waterloo, NY 13165
Conchetta M Brown   Rosemarie Capozzi
Elizabeth C Young

St Lawrence County

Judges
Barbara R Potter: 2011   Jerome J Richards: 2014
Kathleen Martin Rogers: 2008

Supreme, County, Family & Surrogate's Courts
Courthouse, 48 Court St, Canton, NY 13617-1169
Mary B Curran   William Murphy
Patricia Roda

Steuben County

Judges
Peter C Bradstreet: 2012   Marianne Furfure: 2007
Joseph W Latham: 2008

Supreme, County, Family & Surrogate's Courts
Courthouse, 13 Pulteney Sq E, Bath, NY 14810-1598
Bill Deninger   Christine Lavarnway
Peggy Plank

Suffolk County

Judges
Gregory J Blass: 2005   Stephen L Braslow: 2010
Andrew A Crecca: 2005   John M Czygier, Jr: 2011
James F X Doyle: 2012   Joseph Farnetti: 2008
David Freundlich: 2008   Ralph T Gazzillo: 2006
Joan M Genchi: 2012   C Randall Hinrichs: 2011
James C Hudson: 2010   Barbara Kahn: 2015
John Kelly: 2013   Martin J Kerins: 2008
Dudley L Lehman: 2008   Barbara Lynaugh: 2010
Carol McKenzie: 2014   Ettore Simeone: 2007
Jeffrey Arlen Spinner: 2008   Patrick A Sweeney: 2011
Gary J Weber: 2012

County Court
210 Center Dr, Riverhead, NY 11901
Victor Rossomano

Family Court
Courthouse, 400 Carleton Ave, Central Islip, NY 11722
Robert O'Mara

Supreme Court
235 Griffing Ave, Riverhead, NY 11901
Michael Scardino

Surrogate's Court
320 Center Dr, Riverhead, NY 11901
Michael Cipollino

Sullivan County

Judges
Frank J Labuda: 2006   Burton Ledina: 2007
Mark M Meddaugh: 2012

Family & Surrogate's Courts
Government Ctr, 100 North St, Monticello, NY 12701
Cathy Emerson   LuAnn Hering

Supreme & County Courts
Courthouse, 414 Broadway, Monticello, NY 12701
Earl L Lilley

Tioga County

Judges
Vincent Sgueglia: 2012

Family & Surrogate's Courts
Court Annex, 20 Court St, Owego, NY 13827
Denise Marsili   Primrose M Shafer

Supreme & County Courts
Courthouse Sq, 16 Court St, Owego, NY 13827
Deborah Epstein

Tompkins County

Judges
John C Rowley: 2010   M John Sherman: 2013

Supreme, County, Family & Surrogate's Courts
Courthouse, 320 N Tioga St, Ithaca, NY 14850
Constance L Delaney   Nancy M Joch
Donna Srnka

Ulster County

Judges
J Michael Bruhn: 2013   Marianne O Mizel: 2013
Mary MacMaster Work: 2014

Family Court
16 Lucas Ave, Kingston, NY 12401
Katrina Hansen

Supreme & County Courts
Courthouse, 285 Wall St, Kingston, NY 12401
Florence Brandt

Surrogate's Court
240 Fair St, PO Box 1800, Kingston, NY 12401-3806
Mary Ellen Sullivan

Warren County

Judges
J Timothy Breen: 2009   John S Hall Jr: 2013

Supreme, County, Family & Surrogate's Courts
Municipal Ctr, 1340 State Rte 9, Lake George, NY 12845
Regina Ellis   Shirley Friday
Joseph R Hughes

Washington County

Judges
Philip A Berke: 2012   Stanley L Pritzker: 2014

Supreme, County, Family & Surrogate's Courts
Courthouse, 383 Broadway, Fort Edward, NY 12828-1015
Kathleen M LaBelle   Patricia A Ross
Barbara Smith

Offices and agencies appear in alphabetical order.

Wayne County

Judges
Dennis M Kehoe: 2005
Stephen R Sirkin: 2009
John B Nesbitt: 2010

Supreme, County, Family & Surrogate's Courts
Hall of Justice, 54 Broad St, Rm 106, Lyons, NY 14489-1199
Suzanne M Allan
Kelly Wejko
Shirley Comella

Westchester County

Judges
Joseph S Alessandro: 2013
Joan O Cooney: 2012
Robert M Di Bella: 2013
Nilda Morales Horowitz: 2010
Gerald E Loehr: 2015
Anthony A Scarpino: 2010
Barbara G Zambelli: 2007
Rory J Bellantoni: 2013
Kathie E Davidson: 2013
Sandra B Edlitz: 2006
David Klein: 2010
Francis Nicolai: 2009
Sam D Walker: 2012

Supreme, County & Family Courts
111 Dr Martin Luther King Jr Blvd, White Plains, NY 10601

James McAllister
Donna Minort

Surrogate's Court
140 Grand St, White Plains, NY 10601-4831
John W Kelly

Wyoming County

Judges
Mark H Dadd: 2013
Michael F Griffith: 2011

Supreme, County, Family & Surrogate's Courts
Courthouse, 147 N Main St, Warsaw, NY 14569
William D Beyer
Rebecca Miller

Yates County

Judges
W Patrick Falvey: 2008

Supreme, County, Family & Surrogate's Courts
Courthouse, 415 Liberty St, Penn Yan, NY 14527-1191
Michelle Covert
Roxanne R Lynn
Margaret D Dimartino

District Courts

District Courts exist in Nassau County and in five western towns of Suffolk County. District Courts have civil jurisdiction up to $15,000, and criminal jurisdiction for misdemeanors, violations and lesser offenses. Judges are elected for six-year terms by their judicial districts.

Nassau County
Chief Clerk:
Eileen Bianchi 516-572-2157

1st, 2nd & 3rd District Courts
99 Main St, Hempstead, NY 11550
Michael Beganskas
Kenneth Roll
Dona Pratesi

Judges
Anna Anzalone: 2009
Valerie Bullard: 2006
Sharon Commissiong: 2005
Vito M Destefano: 2009
Kenneth L Gartner: 2005
Dana M Jaffe: 2008
Randy Sue Marber: 2007
Martin J Massell: 2008
Adam H Moser: 2005
Sondra K Pardes: 2009
Christopher G Quinn: 2010
Francis Ricigliano: 2008
Denise L Sher: 2007
Joel K Asarch: 2006
Bonnie P Chaikin: 2010
Alfred D Cooper, Sr: 2005
Scott Fairgrieve: 2006
David Gross: 2005
Susan T Kluewer: 2006
Edward A Maron: 2005
Howard S Miller: 2007
William J O'Brien: 2006
Erica L Prager: 2007
Margaret C Reilly: 2010
Lea Ruskin: 2008
Norman St George: 2010

Suffolk County
Chief Clerk:
Roger Huguenin 631-853-4530

1ST DISTRICT COURT, Civil Term . . . . fax: 631-854-9681
3105 Veterans Memorial Hwy, Ronkonkoma, NY 11779
631-854-9676 Fax: 631-854-9681

1ST DISTRICT COURT, Criminal Term . . . fax: 631-853-5889
Courthouse, 400 Carleton Ave, Central Islip, NY 11722
631-853-7500 Fax: 631-853-5889

2nd District Court
375 Commack Rd, Deer Park, NY 11729
631-854-1950

3rd District Court . . . . fax: 631-854-1956
1850 New York Ave, Huntington Station, NY 11746
631-854-4545 Fax: 631-854-1956

4th District Court
Veterans' Memorial Highway, North Cty Complex Bldg 158, Hauppauge, NY 11787
631-853-5408

5th District Court . . . . fax: 631-854-9681
3105 Veterans Memorial Hwy, Ronkonkoma, NY 11779
631-854-9676 Fax: 631-854-9681

6th District Court
150 W Main St, Patchogue, NY 11772
631-854-1440

Judges
Salvatore A Alamia: 2010
Patrick J Barton: 2007
Stephen M Behar Sr: 2009
William J Burke, III: 2007
Lawrence Donohue: 2010
Patricia M Filiberto: 2009
James P Flanagan: 2009
Paul M Hensley: 2008
W Gerard Asher: 2010
Toni A Bean: 2010
Howard M Bergson: 2008
Kevin J Crowley: 2007
Martin I Efman: 2010
Madeleine A Fitzgibbon: 2009
C Steven Hackeling: 2008
Steven A Lotto: 2009

Offices and agencies appear in alphabetical order.

Gaetan B Lozito: 2007
Joseph A Santorelli: 2010

Glenn A Murphy: 2009
Anthony A Tafuri: 2010

John J Toomey, Jr: 2008
Georgia A Tschiember: 2008

Hertha C Trotto: 2008

City Courts Outside New York City

City Courts outside New York City have civil jurisdiction up to $15,000 and criminal jurisdiction over misdemeanors or lesser offenses. City Court judges are either elected or appointed for terms of ten years for full-time judges and six years for part-time judges.

Albany

Judges
William A Carter: 2012
Helena Heath-Roland: 2005
Gary F Stiglmeier: 2014

John Egan: 2006
Thomas K Keefe: 2012

Civil Court
24 Eagle St, 2nd Fl, Albany, NY 12207-1905
Linda File

Criminal Court
Public Safety Bldg, 1 Morton Ave, Albany, NY 12202
Janice Celucci

Traffic Court
Basement, City Hall, 24 Eagle St, Albany, NY 12207-1905
Victoria McManus

Amsterdam

Judges
Howard M Aison: 2008

Paul L Wollman: 2005

Civil & Criminal Courts
Public Safety Bldg, Rm 208, 1 Guy Park Ave Ext, Amsterdam, NY 12010
Melanie Hartman

Auburn

Judges
Michael F McKeon: 2008

Thomas J Shamon: 2008

Civil & Criminal Courts
157 Genesee St, Auburn, NY 13021-3423
Deborah L Robillard

Batavia

Judges
Robert J Balbick: 2010

Michael A Delplato: 2009

Civil & Criminal Courts
Genesee County Courts Facility, 1 W Main St, Batavia, NY 14020-2019
Linda M Giambrone

Beacon

Judges
Rebecca S Mensch (Acting): 2005

Timothy G Pagones: 2005

Civil & Criminal Courts
1 Municipal Plz, Beacon, NY 12508
Debra Antonelli

Binghamton

Judges
Mary Anne Lehmann: 2006
William C Palella: 2014

Robert C Murphy: 2008

Civil & Criminal Courts
Governmental Plz, 38 Hawley St, 5th Fl, Binghamton, NY 13901
Catherine R Maloney

Buffalo

Judges
Thomas P Amodeo: 2014
Diane Devlin: 2010
Thomas P Franczyk: 2007
Kevin J Keane: 2013
David M Manz: 2011
Henry J Nowak, Jr: 2012
Robert T Russell: 2011

Patrick M Carney: 2014
Joseph A Fiorella: 2011
Debra L Givens: 2013
Sharon M LoVallo: 2012
James A McLeod: 2008
E Jeanette Ogden: 2005

Civil & Criminal Courts
50 Delaware Ave, Buffalo, NY 14202
Sharon A Thomas

Canandaigua

Judges
Stephen D Aronson: 2009

John A Schuppenhauer (Acting): 2007

Civil & Criminal Courts
City Hall, 2 N Main St, Canandaigua, NY 14424
Lisa Schutz

Cohoes

Judges
Richard R Maguire: 2010

Stephen J Vanullen: 2009

Civil, Criminal & Traffic Courts
97 Mohawk St, Cohoes, NY 12047
Janet LeBeau

Corning

Judges
Robert H Cole, Jr: 2009

David B Kahl: 2008

Civil & Criminal Courts
City Hall, 12 Civic Ctr Plz, Corning, NY 14830-2884
Julie L Callahan

Offices and agencies appear in alphabetical order.

Cortland

Judges
Elizabeth Burns: 2007   Thomas A Meldrim: 2009

Civil & Criminal Courts
City Hall, 25 Court St, Cortland, NY 13045
Kelly L Preston

Dunkirk

Judges
Walter F Drag: 2007   John M Kuzdale (Acting): 2011

Civil & Criminal Courts
City Hall, 342 Central Ave, Dunkirk, NY 14048-2122
Jean Dill

Elmira

Judges
Steven W Forrest: 2009   Thomas E Ramich: 2006

Civil & Criminal Courts
City Hall, 317 E Church St, 2nd Fl, Elmira, NY 14901-2790
Teresa B Seeley

Fulton

Judges
Spencer J Ludington: 2008   Jerome A Mirabito (Acting): 2005

Civil & Criminal Courts
Municipal Bldg, 141 S First St, Fulton, NY 13069
Maureen Ball

Geneva

Judges
Timothy J Buckley: 2009   Walter C Gage: 2007
Elisabeth A Toole: 2009

Civil & Criminal Courts
Public Safety Bldg, 255 Exchange St, Geneva, NY 14456
Josephine Guard

Glen Cove

Judges
Richard J McCord: 2006   Joel B Meirowitz: 2006

Civil & Criminal Courts
13 Glen St, Glen Cove, NY 11542
Hedy Amstel

Glens Falls

Judges
Gary C Hobbs (Acting): 2005   Richard P Tarantino: 2014

Civil & Criminal Courts
42 Ridge St, 3rd Fl, Glens Falls, NY 12801
Theresa S LaPoint

Gloversville

Judges
Vincent Desantis: 2005   Mario J Papa: 2005

Civil & Criminal Courts
City Hall, 3 Frontage Rd, Gloversville, NY 12078
Jodi L Ferguson

Hornell

Judges
Joseph E Damrath: 2007   David A Shults: 2009

Civil & Criminal Courts
PO Box 627, 82 Main St, Hornell, NY 14843-0627
Laura Beltz

Hudson

Judges
William F Cranna: 2008   Barry Sacks: 2008

Civil & Criminal Courts
427 Warren St, Hudson, NY 12534
Karen De Benedetto

Ithaca

Judges
Marjorie Z Olds (Acting): 2007   Judith A Rossiter: 2010

Civil & Criminal Courts
118 E Clinton St, Ithaca, NY 14850
James R Jecen

Jamestown

Judges
John J LaMancuso: 2013   George Panebianco (Acting): 2010

Civil & Criminal Courts
Municipal Bldg, 200 E 3rd St, Jamestown, NY 14701-5494
Cheryl Dove

Johnstown

Judges
Frederick R Stortecky: 2006   Thomas C Walsh: 2007

Civil & Criminal Courts
City Hall, 33-41 E Main St, Johnstown, NY 12095
Stephen Russo

Kingston

Judges
Edward T Feeney: 2006   James P Gilpatric: 2005

Civil & Criminal Courts
1 Garraghan Dr, Kingston, NY 12401
Janet Strauss

Offices and agencies appear in alphabetical order.

Lackawanna

Judges
Joseph V Deren (Acting): 2008   Frederic J Marrano: 2007

Civil & Criminal Courts
   City Hall, 714 Ridge Rd, Lackawanna, NY 14218
Kim Delmont

Little Falls

Judges
Bart M Carrig (Acting): 2007   Edward J Rose: 2007

Civil & Criminal Courts
   City Hall, 659 E Main St, Little Falls, NY 13365
Jane B Fortuna

Lockport

Judges
William J Watson: 2005   David R Wendt: 2007

Civil & Criminal Courts
   Municipal Bldg, 1 Locks Plz, Lockport, NY 14094-3694
Cynthia M Russell

Long Beach

Judges
Stanley A Smolkin: 2009   Roy Tepper: 2013

Civil & Criminal Courts
   1 W Chester St, Long Beach, NY 11561
Joann Spiritis

Mechanicville

Judges
James F Hughes (Acting): 2008   Joseph W Sheehan: 2009

Civil & Criminal Courts
   City Hall, 36 N Main St, Mechanicville, NY 12118
Francine Baker

Middletown

Judges
Richard J Guertin: 2013   Michael Schwartz: 2010

Civil & Criminal Courts
   2 James St, Middletown, NY 10940
Linda Padden

Mount Vernon

Judges
Brenda L Dowery: 2009   Colleen Duffy: 2008
William Edwards: 2013   Adam Seiden: 2006

Civil & Criminal Courts
   30 Roosevelt Sq East, Mount Vernon, NY 10550-2060
Lawrence E Darden, Jr

New Rochelle

Judges
John P Colangelo: 2012   Gail B Rice: 2008
Preston S Scher: 2005

Civil & Criminal Courts
   475 North St, New Rochelle, NY 10801
James Generoso

Newburgh

Judges
Peter M Kulkin: 2014   B Harold Ramsey: 2013

Civil & Criminal Courts
   Public Safety Bldg, 57 Broadway, Newburgh, NY 12550
Sharon Reed

Niagara Falls

Judges
Angelo J Morinello: 2012   Robert M Restaino: 2011
Mark A Violante: 2005

Civil & Criminal Courts
   Public Safety Bldg, 520 Hyde Park Blvd, Niagara Falls, NY 14302
Martha J Farbo-Lincoln

North Tonawanda

Judges
R Thomas Burgasser: 2011   William R Lewis: 2011

Civil & Criminal Courts
   City Hall, 216 Payne Ave, North Tonawanda, NY 14120-5446
Sheila D McQuade

Norwich

Judges
Maureen A Byrne (Acting): 2006   James Downey: 2005

Civil & Criminal Courts
   1 Court Plz, Norwich, NY 13815
Linda Roys-Jones

Ogdensburg

Judges
A Michael Gebo: 2005   George Silver: 2005

Civil & Criminal Courts
   330 Ford St, Ogdensburg, NY 13669
Lisa Marie Meyer

Olean

Judges
William H Mountain III: 2006   Daniel R Palumbo (Acting): 2011

Civil & Criminal Courts
   Municipal Bldg, 101 E State St, PO Box 631, Olean, NY 14760-0631
Rhonda J Deckman

Offices and agencies appear in alphabetical order.

Oneida

Judges
Anthony P Eppolito: 2007   Michael J Misiaszek (Acting): 2008

Civil & Criminal Courts
Municipal Bldg, 109 N Main St, Oneida, NY 13421
Lynne Mondrick

Oneonta

Judges
Lucy P Bernier: 2009   Walter L Terry: 2009

Civil & Criminal Courts
Public Safety Bldg, 81 Main St, Oneonta, NY 13820
Ann Lane

Oswego

Judges
James M Metcalf: 2005   Thomas A Reynolds (Acting): 2007

Civil & Criminal Courts
Conway Municipal Ctr, 20 W Oneida St, Oswego, NY 13126
Vacant

Peekskill

Judges
Thomas R Langan (Acting): 2010   William L Maher: 2013

Civil & Criminal Courts
2 Nelson Ave, Peekskill, NY 10566
Janice Laughlin

Plattsburgh

Judges
Penelope D Clute: 2012   Mark J Rogers (Acting): 2007

Civil & Criminal Courts
24 US Oval, Plattsburgh, NY 12903
Robin Germain

Port Jervis

Judges
Victoria B Campbell: 2008   Robert A Onofry: 2008

Civil & Criminal Courts
20 Hammond St, Port Jervis, NY 12771-2495
Edwina Wulff

Poughkeepsie

Judges
John B Garrity: 2010   Ronald J McGaw: 2006

Civil & Criminal Courts
62 Civic Ctr Plz, PO Box 300, Poughkeepsie, NY 12601
Jean Jicha

Rensselaer

Judges
Kathleen L Robichaud: 2007

Civil & Criminal Courts
City Hall, 505 Broadway, Rensselaer, NY 12144
Patricia Wiesmaier

Rochester

Civil Court
Hall of Justice, 99 Exchange Blvd, Rm 6, Rochester, NY 14614

Criminal Court
123 Public Safety Bldg, Rochester, NY 14614
Sandra Petrella

Judges
Melchor E Castro: 2011   John E Elliott: 2013
Teresa D Johnson: 2009   Roy W King: 2007
Stephen K Lindley: 2012   Thomas R Morse: 2009
Ann E Pfeiffer: 2005   John R Schwartz: 2013
Ellen Yacknin: 2012

Rome

Judges
John C Gannon: 2005   Daniel C Wilson: 2013

Civil & Criminal Courts
100 W Court St, Rome, NY 13440
Eleanor T Coniglio

Rye

Judges
John L Alfano: 2007   Peter Lane: 2009

Civil & Criminal Courts
21 McCullough Pl, Rye, NY 10580
Antoinette Cipriano

Salamanca

Judges
William J Gabler (Acting): 2010   William H Mountain: 2010

Civil & Criminal Courts
Municipal Bldg, 225 Wildwood Ave, Salamanca, NY 14779
Stella Johnston

Saratoga Springs

Judges
James E Doern (Acting): 2010   Douglas C Mills: 2008

Civil & Criminal Courts
City Hall, 474 Broadway, Ste 3, Saratoga Springs, NY 12866
Elizabeth M Thornhill

Schenectady

Judges
Christine Clark: 2005   Guido A Loyola: 2008
Vincent W Versaci: 2008

Offices and agencies appear in alphabetical order.

Civil Court
City Hall, 105 Jay St, Schenectady, NY 12305
Patricia Jordan

Criminal Court
531 Liberty St, Schenectady, NY 12305
Patricia Jordan

Sherrill

Judges
Neal P Rose: 2008

Civil & Criminal Courts
373 Sherrill Rd, Sherrill, NY 13461
Carol A Shea

Syracuse

Judges
James H Cecile: 2007   Stephen J Dougherty: 2012
Thomas W Higgins: 2010   Langston C McKinney: 2007
Jeffrey R Merrill: 2013   Kate Rosenthal: 2010
Karen M Uplinger: 2011   Kevin G Young: 2005

Civil & Criminal Courts
Public Safety Bldg, 505 S State St, Rm 130, Syracuse, NY 13202-2179
Lucia Sander

Tonawanda

Judges
Joseph J Cassata: 2011   Salvatore M Rua: 2007

Civil & Criminal Courts
City Hall, 200 Niagara St, Tonawanda, NY 14150
Elizabeth Ciambrone

Troy

Judges
Christopher T Maier: 2014   Matthew J Turner: 2010

Civil & Criminal Court
51 State St, Troy, NY 12180
Diane Hulett

Utica

Judges
John S Balzano: 2008   Ralph J Eannace, Jr: 2013
Gerald J Popeo: 2010

Civil & Criminal Courts
411 Oriskany St W, Utica, NY 13502
Steven V Pecheone

Watertown

Judges
James C Harberson: 2006   Eugene R Renzi: 2008

Civil & Criminal Courts
Municipal Bldg, 245 Washington St, Watertown, NY 13601
Agnes Zaremba

Watervliet

Judges
Thomas Lamb: 2010   Susan B Reinfurt: 2010

Civil & Criminal Courts
City Hall, 2 - 15th St, Watervliet, NY 12189
Eugenia R Robillard

White Plains

Judges
JoAnn Friia: 2006   Brian Hansbury: 2009
Barbara A Leak: 2007   Eric P Press: 2009

Civil & Criminal Courts
77 S Lexington Ave, White Plains, NY 10601
Patricia Lupi

Yonkers

Judges
Robert C Cerrato: 2010   Thomas R Daly: 2010
Arthur J Doran: 2012   Arthur J Doran III: 2013
Richard B Liebowitz: 2005   Michael A Martinelli: 2005

Civil & Criminal Courts
R W Cacace Justice Ctr, 100 S Broadway, 2nd Fl, Yonkers, NY 10701
Marissa Garcia

Offices and agencies appear in alphabetical order.

Section 2:
POLICY AREAS

AGRICULTURE

New York State

GOVERNOR'S OFFICE

Governor's Office
Executive Chamber
State Capitol
Albany, NY 12224
518-474-8390 Fax: 518-474-1513
Web site: www.state.ny.us

Governor:
Ĝeorge E Pataki 518-474-8390
Executive Director:
Kara Lanspery 518-474-8390
Secretary to the Governor:
John P Cahill. 518-474-4246
Senior Policy Advisor to the Governor:
Jeffrey Lovell 518-486-9671
Counsel to the Governor-Attorney General, Budget:
Richard Platkin. 518-474-8343
Director, Communications:
David Catalfamo. 518-474-8418
Asst Counsel to the Governor-Adirondack Pk Agency, Agric & Markets,
Bond Act Coord, Consumer Protection Bd, Environ Facilities Corporation,
Parks & Recreation, State & Local Govt, OGS:
James Walsh. 518-474-8327

EXECUTIVE DEPARTMENTS AND RELATED AGENCIES

Agriculture & Markets Department
10B Airline Dr
Albany, NY 12235
518-457-3880 Fax: 518-457-3087
e-mail: info@agmkt.state.ny.us
Web site: www.agmkt.state.ny.us

Commissioner:
Nathan Rudgers 518-457-8876
First Deputy Commissioner:
Ruth A Moore. 518-457-2771
Deputy Commissioner:
Margaret Becker. 518-485-7728
Assistant Commissioner:
Thomas Lindberg 518-485-7728
Deputy Commissioner:
Rick Zimmerman 518-457-0752
Special Assistant:
Edward Biel 518-457-2771
Special Assistant:
Raymond Christensen. 518-457-3136
Special Assistant:
Carol Cybulski 518-457-2771
Special Assistant:
William Jordan 518-457-0752

Special Assistant:
Kate Lane 518-457-3136
Executive Assistant:
Tim Pezzolesi 518-485-7728
Public Information Officer:
Jessica Chittenden 518-457-3136
e-mail: jessica.chittenden@agmkt.state.ny.us

Agricultural Protection & Development Svcs
Director:
William Kimball 518-457-7076/fax: 518-457-2716

Agricultural Child Care
Program Administrator:
Steven Greenberg. 518-457-7076

Agricultural Protection Unit
Chief:
Bob Somers 518-457-2713

Animal Industry . . . . fax: 518-485-7773
Director:
John Huntley. 518-457-3502
Assistant Director:
Bruce Ackey. 518-457-3502
Companion Animal & Dog Licensing:
Roberta Brooks. 518-485-7965
Milk Ring Tests:
Erin Bond 518-457-7757
DAHP & Pullorum:
Mary Beth Dobrucki. 518-457-5558
NYSCHAP, Tuberculosis & Brucellosis:
Sandy McKay. 518-457-5365
Animal Exports & Imports:
Suzy Berry 518-457-3971
Veterinarian Accreditation:
Sherry Coffinger. 518-457-2886

Counsel's Office . . . . fax: 518-457-8842
Counsel:
Joan A Kehoe 518-457-1059
Supervising Attorney:
Michael McCormick. 518-457-2449
Penalty Litigation Unit:
Nancy Bogaard. 518-485-8741

Fiscal Management . . . . fax: 518-485-7750
Director:
Lucy Roberson 518-457-2080

Food Laboratory . . . . fax: 518-485-8097
Director:
Daniel Rice. 518-457-4477
Associate Bacteriologist:
Kurt Mangione 518-457-2453
Food Chemist:
Virginia Greene 518-485-8098

Food Safety & Inspection. . . . . fax: 518-485-8986
Director:
Joseph Corby 518-457-4492

Offices and agencies appear in alphabetical order.

Policy Areas

Assistant Director:
  Curtis Vincent.................................... 518-457-5382
Director, Field Operations:
  Steve Stich 518-457-5380
Food Products Quality Manager:
  Stephen Biehler 518-457-2090
Supervisor, Compliance:
  vacant 518-457-2840
Poultry, Fruit & Vegetable Inspector:
  Michael Jones.................................... 518-457-2090

Field Operations
  Brooklyn .... fax: 718-722-2836
    55 Hanson Place, Rm 378, Brooklyn, NY 11217-1583
    Chief Inspector:
      Richard Olson 718-722-2838
  Buffalo .... fax: 716-847-3155
    Donovan St Ofc Bldg, 125 Main St, Buffalo, NY 14203
    Supervising Inspector:
      Dan Gump 716-847-3185
  Hauppauge .... fax: 631-952-3390
    Suffolk State Office Bldg, Veteran's Memorial Hwy, Hauppauge, NY 11787-5532
    Farm Prod Grading Inspector 3:
      John Cross 631-952-3079
  Rochester .... fax: 585-424-1248
    900 Jefferson Rd, Rochester, NY 14623
    Supervising Food Inspector:
      Evelyn Miles 585-427-2273
    Chief Inspector:
      Earl Flint 716-427-0200
  Syracuse
    Art & Home Center, New York State Fairgrounds, Syracuse, NY 13209
    Supervising Food Regional Supervisor:
      John Luker 315-487-0852/fax: 315-487-1064

Human Resources .... fax: 518-457-8852
Director:
  Karen Stenard................................... 518-457-3216

Information Systems........................ fax: 518-457-7815
Director:
  Dolores C Dybas................................. 518-457-7368

Internal Audit .... fax: 518-457-3087
Director:
  Lawrence J Emminger 518-457-4418

Milk Control & Dairy Services.............. fax: 518-485-8730
Director:
  Will Francis 518-457-1772
Assistant Director:
  James Fitts 518-457-5731
Supervisor, Milk Licensing:
  Charles Huff 518-457-5731
Compliance Officer:
  Carol McClenahan 518-457-4142

New York City Office...................... fax: 718-722-2836
  55 Hanson Place, Brooklyn, NY 11217-1583
Chief, Food Safety & Inspection:
  Rich Olson 718-722-2876
Office Manager:
  Melba Delgado 718-722-2850
Director, Kosher Law Enforcement:
  Luzer Weiss 718-722-2852
Director, Kosher Food Marketing:
  Felise G Gross 718-722-2834

Plant Industry .... fax: 518-457-1204
Director:
  Robert J Mungari 518-457-2087

Soil & Water Conservation Committee ..... fax: 518-457-3412
  10B Airline Dr, Albany, NY 12235
  518-457-3738 Fax: 518-457-3412
  Web site: www.nys-soilandwater.org
Chair:
  Dennis Hill 518-457-3738
Director:
  Ron Kaplewicz 518-457-3738
    e-mail: ron.kaplewicz@agmkt.state.ny.us
Assistant Director:
  Mike Latham 518-457-3738
    e-mail: michael.latham@agmkt.state.ny.us
Coordinator, Agricultural Environmental Management Program:
  Jeff Ten Eyck 518-457-3738
    e-mail: jeff.teneyck@agmkt.state.ny.us

State Fair .... fax: 315-487-9260
  581 State Fair Blvd, Syracuse, NY 13209
  315-487-7711 Fax: 315-487-9260
  Web site: www.nysfair.org/2004
Director:
  Peter Cappuccilli, Jr........................ 315-487-7711 x1200
Assistant Director:
  Michael Sommers 315-487-7711 x1210

Statistics .... fax: 518-453-6564
  Fax: 518-453-6564
  Web site: www.nass.usda.gov/ny
State Statistician:
  Stephen C Ropel................................. 518-457-5570
Deputy State Statistician:
  Blair Smith 518-487-5870

Weights & Measures .... fax: 518-457-5693
Director:
  Ross Andersen 518-457-3146
Metrologist:
  William Fishman 518-485-8377
Metrologist:
  Edward Szesnat 518-457-4781

NEW YORK STATE LEGISLATURE

See Legislative Branch in Section 1 for additional Standing Committee and Subcommittee information.

Assembly Standing Committees

Agriculture
Chair:
  William Magee (D)............................... 518-455-4807
Ranking Minority Member:
  Clifford W Crouch (R)........................... 518-455-5741

Assembly Task Force

Food, Farm & Nutrition Policy, Task Force on
Chair:
  Felix W Ortiz (D)............................... 518-455-3821
Program Manager:
  Robert Stern 518-455-5203

Offices and agencies appear in alphabetical order.

Senate Standing Committees

Agriculture
Chair:
  Catherine M Young 518-455-5241
Ranking Minority Member:
  David J Valesky (D). 518-455-2838

Senate/Assembly Legislative Commissions

Rural Resources, Legislative Commission on
Senate Chair:
  Vacant 518-455-3563
Assembly Vice Chair:
  David R Koon (D) 518-455-5784
Senate Executive Director:
  Ronald C Brach 518-455-2544/fax: 518-426-6960
Assembly Director:
  Susan Bartle. 518-455-3999/fax: 518-455-4175

Counsel:
  Donald A Walsh 518-455-2544

Toxic Substances & Hazardous Wastes, Legislative Commission on
Senate Chair:
  Vacant 518-455-0000
Assembly Vice Chair:
  David R Koon (D) 518-455-5784
Program Manager:
  Richard D Morse, Jr 518-455-3711/fax: 518-455-3837

Water Resource Needs of NYS & Long Island, Legislative Commission on
Assembly Co-Chair:
  Thomas P DiNapoli (D) 518-455-5192
Senate Co-Chair:
  Michael A L Balboni (R) 518-455-2471
Program Manager:
  Richard D Morse, Jr 518-455-3711/fax: 518-455-3837

U.S. Government

Policy Areas

EXECUTIVE DEPARTMENTS AND RELATED AGENCIES

Commodity Futures Trading Commission
Web site: www.cftc.gov

Eastern Region
140 Broadway, New York, NY 10005
Regional Coordinator:
  Marvin Jackson 646-746-9700/fax: 646-746-9938

US Commerce Department
Web site: www.doc.gov

National Oceanic & Atmospheric Administration

National Weather Service, Eastern Region
630 Johnson Ave, Ste 202, Bohemia, NY 11716
Web site: www.nws.noaa.gov
Director:
  Dean Gulezian. 631-244-0100/fax: 631-244-0109
Deputy Director:
  Mickey J Brown. 631-244-0102
Public Affairs Specialist:
  Marcie Katcher 631-244-0149/fax: 631-244-0167
Chief, Meteorological Services Division:
  John Guiney. 631-244-0121
Chief, Regional Hydrology Division:
  Peter Garbrielsen 631-244-0111
Chief, Scientific Services Division:
  Kenneth Johnson 631-244-0136

US Department of Agriculture
Web site: www.usda.gov

Agricultural Marketing Service

Dairy Programs
Web site: www.ams.usda.gov
  Northeast Marketing Area . . . . fax: 518-464-6468
  1 Columbia Circle, Albany, NY 12203

Assistant Market Administrator:
  John F Poole 518-452-4410

Fruit & Vegetable Division
  Fresh Products Branch - Bronx Field Office . . . . . . fax: 718-589-5108
  465B NYC Terminal Market, Bronx, NY 10474
  Officer-in-Charge:
    Cathy Hance 718-991-7665
  Market News Branch—New York State . . . . fax: 718-378-0891
  NYC Terminal Market, Rm 4A, Bronx, NY 10474
  Federal Supervisor:
    Edward Martello 718-542-2225

USDA-AMS Poultry Grading Branch
  Gastonia Region—New York Office . . . . fax: 518-459-5163
  21 Aviation Rd, Albany, NY 12205
  Federal-State Supervisor:
    Dennis McAuliffe 518-459-5487

Agricultural Research Service

North Atlantic Area
  Ithaca NY Research Units
  Plant Genetic Resources Unit . . . . fax: 315-787-2339
  USDA, 630 W North St, Geneva, NY 14456-0462
  Research Leader:
    Philip Forsline 315-787-2356

Animal Plant Health Inspection Service
Web site: www.aphis.usda.gov

Plant Protection Quarantine (PPQ) Programs-Eastern Region . . . . fax: 919-716-5656
  920 Main Campus Dr, Ste 200, Raleigh, NC 27606-5213
  Eastern Regional Director:
    Jerry L Fowler 919-716-5576
    e-mail: jerry.l.fowler@aphis.usda.gov
  Avoca Work Unit . . . . fax: 607-566-2081
    8237 Kanona Rd, Avoca, NY 14809-9729
    Director:
      Daniel J Kepich 607-566-2212
      e-mail: daniel.j.kepich@aphis.usda.gov
  Batavia Work Station . . . . fax: 585-343-5538
    29 Liberty St, Ste 1, Batavia, NY 14020

Offices and agencies appear in alphabetical order.

PPQ Officer:
    Lewis Tandy 585-343-9167 x1033
    e-mail: lewis.tandy@aphis.usda.gov

Big Flats Work Station . . . . fax: 607-562-3470
USDA Plant Material Ctr, 3266-B State Rte 352, Corning, NY 14830
PPQ Officer:
    Lawrence R Kershaw 607-562-3459

Canandaigua Work Station . . . . fax: 585-394-8367
3037 County Rd 10, Canandaigua, NY 14424
Senior PPQ Officer:
    Cynthia A Estey 585-394-0525 x5
    e-mail: cynthia.a.estey@aphis.usda.gov

JFK International Airport Inspection Station
230-59 Intl Airport Ctr Blvd, Jamaica, NY 11413
Supervising PPQ Officer:
    Lubomira Rydl 718-553-1732/fax: 718-553-0060

New York State Office . . . . fax: 518-438-7675
500 New Karner Rd, Albany, NY 12205
State Plant Health Director:
    Yvonne Demrino 518-869-5540

Oneida Work Station
248 Main St, 1st Fl, Oneida, NY 13421
Senior PPQ Officer:
    Paul F Wrege 315-361-4281/fax: 315-363-3657
    e-mail: paul.f.wrege@usda.gov

Westhampton Beach Work Station . . . . fax: 631-288-6021
4 Stewart Ave, Westhampton Beach, NY 11978-1103
PPQ Officer:
    Willy Hsiang 631-288-4191

Veterinary Services
NY Animal Import Center
200 Drury Lane, Rock Tavern, NY 12575
Veterinarian-in-Charge:
    Dr Kenneth Davis 845-564-2950/fax: 845-564-1075
New York Area Office . . . . fax: 518-869-6135
500 New Karner Rd, 2nd FL, Albany, NY 12205
518-869-9007 Fax: 518-869-6135
Veterinarian-in-Charge, New York Area:
    Roxanne C Mullaney 518-453-0187/fax: 518-453-0213

Cornell Cooperative Extension Service
Roberts Hall, Rm 365, Cornell University, Ithaca, NY 14853-5905
State Director:
    Helene Dillard 607-255-2237/fax: 607-255-0788

Farm Service Agency, New York State Office . . . . fax: 315-477-6323
441 S Salina St, Rm 536, Syracuse, NY 13202-2455
Executive Director:
    Ron Robbins 315-477-6303

Food & Nutrition Service

Albany Field Office . . . . fax: 518-431-4271
O'Brien Federal Bldg, Rm 752, Clinton Ave & N Pearl St, Albany, NY 12207
Officer-in-Charge:
    Claudia Ortiz 518-431-4274
    e-mail: claudia.ortiz@FNS.usda.gov

New York City Field Office . . . . fax: 212-620-6948
201 Varick St, Rm 609, New York, NY 10014
Assistant Director:
    Angela Mackey 212-620-7360

Rochester Field Office
Federal Bldg, 100 State St, Rm 318, Rochester, NY 14614
Officer in Charge:
    Claudia Ortiz 585-263-6748/fax: 585-263-5807

Food Safety & Inspection Service
Web site: www.fsis.usda.gov

Field Operations - Albany District Office . . . . fax: 518-452-3118
230 Washington Ave Ext, Albany, NY 12203-5388
District Manager:
    Louis C Leny 518-452-6870

National Agricultural Statistics Service-NYS Office . . . . fax: 518-485-8719
10B Airline Dr, Albany, NY 12235
800-591-3834 Fax: 518-485-8719
State Statistician:
    Stephen C Ropel 518-457-5570

Office of the Inspector General, Northeast Region . . . . . . fax: 212-264-8416
26 Federal Plaza, Room 1409, New York, NY 10278
Special Agent-in-Charge, Investigation:
    Brian L Haaser 212-264-8400
Assistant Special Agent-in-Charge, Investigation:
    Bruce A Bethka 212-264-8400

Rural Development
Web site: www.rurdev.usda.gov/ny

New York State Office
The Galleries of Syracuse, 441 S Salina St, Ste 357, 5th Fl, Syracuse, NY 13202-2425
TDD: 315-477-6447
State Director:
    Patrick H Brennan 315-477-6400/fax: 315-477-6438
Special Projects Representative:
    Joel Weirick 315-477-6433/fax: 315-477-6438
Program Director, Rural Business-Cooperative Service:
    Walter D Schermerhorn 315-477-6425
    e-mail: walter.schermerhorn@ny.usda.gov
Program Director, Rural Utilities Service:
    David Miller 315-477-6427/fax: 315-477-6448
    e-mail: david.miller@ny.usda.gov
Program Director, Rural Housing Service:
    George Von Pless 315-477-6419/fax: 315-477-6468
    e-mail: george.vonpless@ny.usda.gov
Human Resources Manager:
    Ora Giles 315-477-6405/fax: 315-477-6440
    e-mail: ora.giles@ny.usda.gov

USDA/GIPSA, Packers & Stockyards Pgms-Atlantic Region . . . . fax: 404-562-5848
75 Spring St, Ste 230, Atlanta, GA 30303
Regional Manager:
    Elkin Parker 404-562-5840

US Department of Homeland Security (DHS)
Web site: www.dhs.gov

Customs & Border Protection (CBP)
Web site: www.cbp.gov

Agricultural Inspections (AI)
Brooklyn, Port of
6405 7th Ave, 3rd Fl, Brooklyn, NY 11220
Supervising Ag Specialist:
    Willie J Martin 718-340-5225/fax: 718-340-5224
Buffalo, Port of
1 Peace Bridge Plaza, Room 316, Buffalo, NY 14213
Agriculture Specialist:
    Samra Boukadida 716-884-5701/fax: 716-884-5679
Champlain, Port of
234 West Service Rd, Suite 2, Champlain, NY 12919

Offices and agencies appear in alphabetical order.

Agriculture Specialist:
Vacant. 518-298-4332

JFK International Airport Area Office
JFK Int'l Airport, Bldg #77, 2nd Fl, Jamaica, NY 11430
Port Director:
Camille Polimeni. 718-487-5164
Canine Kennel:
James Armstrong. 718-553-1659
Agriculture Supervisor:
Robert Redes 718-487-2619
Director:
Mary E Benzie. 718-553-1643

Plum Island Animal Disease Center
PO Box 848, Greenport, NY 11944
Director:
Beth Lautner 631-323-3202/fax: 631-323-3295

U.S. CONGRESS

See U.S. Congress Chapter for additional Standing Committee and Subcommittee information.

House of Representatives Standing Committees

Agriculture
Chair:
Robert Goodlatte (R-VA). 202-225-2171
Ranking Minority Member:
Collin C Peterson (D-MN). 202-225-2165

Appropriations
Chair:
Jerry Lewis (R-CA) 202-225-5861
Ranking Minority Member:
David R Obey (D-WI) 202-225-3365
New York Delegate:
Maurice D Hinchey (D) 202-225-6335

New York Delegate:
Nita M Lowey (D) 202-225-6506
New York Delegate:
Jose E Serrano (D) 202-225-4361
New York Delegate:
John E Sweeney (R) 202-225-5614
New York Delegate:
James T Walsh (R) 202-225-3705

Subcommittee
Agriculture, Rural Development, Food & Drug Administration & Related Agencies
Chair:
Henry Bonilla (R-TX) 202-225-4511
Ranking Minority Member:
Rosa L DeLauro (D-CT) 202-225-3661
New York Delegate:
Maurice D Hinchey (D). 202-225-6335

Senate Standing Committees

Agriculture, Nutrition & Forestry
Chair:
C Saxby Chambliss (R-GA). 202-224-3521
Ranking Minority Member:
Tom Harkin (D-IA) 202-224-3254

Appropriations
Chair:
Thad Cochran (R-MS) 202-224-5054
Ranking Minority Member:
Robert C Byrd (D-WV) 202-224-3954

Subcommittee
Agriculture, Rural Development & Related Agencies
Chair:
Robert Bennett (R-UT) 202-224-5444
Ranking Minority Member:
Herbert Kohl (D-WI). 202-224-5653

Private Sector

NYS Bar Association, Animals & the Law Cmte
1 Elk Street, Albany, NY 12207
518-463-3200 Fax: 518-463-4276
e-mail: hkennedypassantino@woh.com
Web site: www.nysba.org
Holly Kennedy-Passantino, Chair

Agricultural Affiliates
638 Lake St, PO Box 10, Wilson, NY 14172-0010
716-751-9331 Fax: 716-751-6141
e-mail: agaffiliat@aol.com
Peter Russell, President
Advise & inform agriculture industry on labor issues & related public policy

Agway Inc
PO Box 4933, Syracuse, NY 13221-4933
315-449-7061 Fax: 315-449-6281
e-mail: info@agway.com
Web site: www.agway.com
Mike Hopsicker, President & Chief Executive Officer
Farm cooperative

American Farmland Trust, Northeast Regional Office
6 Franklin Square, Ste E, Saratoga Springs, NY 12866
518-581-0078 Fax: 518-581-0079
e-mail: neaft@farmland.org
Web site: www.farmland.org
Jeremiah P Cosgrove, Northeast Regional Director
Advocacy & education to protect farmland & promote environmentally sound farming practices

Offices and agencies appear in alphabetical order.

American Society for the Prevention of Cruelty to Animals (ASPCA)
424 E 92nd St, New York, NY 10128
212-876-7700 x4552 Fax: 212-360-6875
e-mail: government@aspca.org
Web site: www.aspca.org
Lisa Weisberg, Senior Vice President, Government Affairs & Public Policy, Senior Policy Advisor
Promoting humane treatment of animals, education & advocacy programs & conducting statewide anti-cruelty investigation & enforcement

Associated New York State State Food Processors Inc
16 Loretta Dr, Ste 100, Spencerport, NY 14559
585-352-7766 Fax: 585-349-2334
e-mail: jackie@nyfoodprocessors.org
Web site: www.nyfoodprocessors.org
Jacqueline J Arnold, Executive Secretary

Birds Eye Foods Inc
PO Box 1116, Comfort, TX 78013
830-995-3493 Fax: 830-995-3597
e-mail: siwanicki@birdseyefoods.com
Web site: www.birdseyefoods.com
Stan Iwanicki, Vice President-Science & Technology
Produces & markets processed food products

CSA-Farm Network Project
130 Ruckytucks Rd, Stillwater, NY 12170
518-583-4613
e-mail: sgilman@netheaven.com
Steve Gilman, Coordinator
Survey consumer supported agriculture (CSA) practices & report findings

Christmas Tree Farmers Association of New York Inc
646 Finches Corners Rd, Red Creek, NY 13143
315-754-8132 Fax: 315-754-8499
e-mail: bnorris@redcreek.net
Web site: www.christmastreesny.org
Robert D Norris, Executive Director
Fresh Christmas trees & evergreen wreaths

Consumers Union
101 Truman Ave, Yonkers, NY 10703-1057
914-378-2000 Fax: 914-378-2900
Web site: www.consumerreports.org; www.consumersunion.org
James A Guest, President
Food safety issues including genetically engineered food, microbial safety of food, toxic chemical issues, pesticides, integrated pest management, sustainable agriculture

Cornell Cooperative Extension
365 Roberts Hall, Cornell University, Ithaca, NY 14853-5905
607-255-2237 Fax: 607-255-0788
e-mail: cedir@cornell.edu
Web site: www.cce.cornell.edu
Helene Dillard, Director
Extension educational system & outreach

Cornell Cooperative Extension, Community & Rural Development Institute
43 Warren Hall, Cornell University, Ithaca, NY 14853
607-255-9510 Fax: 607-255-2231
Web site: www.cardi.cornell.edu
Donald Tobias, Director
Provides research, education & policy analysis on critical community & rural development issues

Cornell Cooperative Extension, New Farmers/New Markets Program
Cornell University, 16 East 34th St, New York, NY 10016
212-340-2946 Fax: 212-340-2908
e-mail: jma20@cornell.edu
Web site: www.cce.cornell.edu
John Ameroso, Extension Educator
Farmer recruitment & training for urban farmers' markets; community gardens advisory; food access/food security policy

Cornell Cooperative Extension, Pesticide Management Education Program
5123 Comstock Hall, Cornell University, Ithaca, NY 14853-0901
607-255-1866 Fax: 607-255-3075
e-mail: rdg5@cornell.edu
Web site: pmep.cce.cornell.edu
Ronald D Gardner, Senior Extension Associate

Cornell University, College of Agriculture & Life Sciences, Animal Science
Morrison Hall, Rm 149, Ithaca, NY 14853
607-255-2862 or 607-255-5497 Fax: 607-255-9829
e-mail: awb6@cornell.edu
Web site: www.ansci.cornell.edu
Alan Bell, Department Chair
Nutritional physiology

Cornell University, Community, Food & Agriculture Program
Dept of Rural Sociology, 216 Warren Hall, Ithaca, NY 14853
607-255-0417 Fax: 607-254-2896
e-mail: hmm1@cornell.edu
Web site: www.cfap.org
Heidi Mouillesseaux-Kunzman, Program Coordinator
To support food & agriculture based community development in NY & the Northeast through integrated, multi-disciplinary & participating teaching, research & extension activities

Cornell University, Department of Applied Economics & Management
357 Warren Hall, Ithaca, NY 14853-7801
607-255-4534 Fax: 607-255-1589
e-mail: ell4@cornell.edu
Web site: www.aem.cornell.edu/profiles/ladue.htm
Eddy L LaDue, W I Myers Professor of Agricultural Finance
Agricultural finance

Offices and agencies appear in alphabetical order.

Cornell University, Development Sociology
Community Food & Agriculture Program, 216 Warren Hall, Ithaca, NY 14853
607-255-9832 Fax: 607-254-2896
e-mail: dlh3@cornell.edu
Web site: www.cfap.org
Duncan Hilchey, Agricultural Development Specialist
Ethnic markets, cooperatives, farmers' markets, agritourism, agricultural marketing, regional identity

Cornell University, FarmNet Program
Dept of Applied Economics & Management, 415 Warren Hall, Ithaca, NY 14853-7801
607-255-4121 or 800-547-3276 Fax: 607-254-7435
e-mail: nyfarmnet@cornell.edu
Web site: www.nyfarmnet.org
Steve Richards, Program Director
Farm family resource library; financial & family consultations; workshops for agricultural services professionals & farmers

Cornell University, Program on Dairy Markets & Policy
Agriculture & Life Sciences, 602 Warren Hall, Ithaca, NY 14853-7801
607-255-7602 Fax: 607-255-9984
e-mail: amn3@cornell.edu
Web site: www.cpdmp.cornell.edu
Andrew Novakovic, Director

Dairylea Cooperative Inc
PO Box 4844, Syracuse, NY 13221-4844
315-433-0100 Fax: 315-433-2345
e-mail: clyde.rutherford@dairylea.com
Web site: www.dairylea.com
Clyde Rutherford, President

Empire State Honey Producers Association
273 Randall Rd, Lisbon, NY 13658
315-322-4208
e-mail: harmonydeb@starband.net
Web site: www.eshpa.org
Deborah Kalicin, Secretary/Treasurer
Promote & protect the interests of beekeepers in NYS

Empire State Potato Growers Inc
PO Box 566, Stanley, NY 14561-0566
585-526-5356 Fax: 585-526-6576
e-mail: mwickham@empirepotatogrowers.com
Web site: www.empirepotatogrowers.com
Melanie Wickham, Executive Secretary
To foster the potato industry in NYS

FARMEDIC National Training Center
Cornell University-FARMEDIC, 777 Warren Rd, Ithaca, NY 14850
800-437-6010 Fax: 607-257-5041
e-mail: farmedic@cornell.edu
Web site: www.farmedic.com
Daryl Nydam, Extension Field Service Section
Training programs for emergency providers & agricultural workers to reduce mortality, injury & property loss from agricultural emergencies

Farm Sanctuary
PO Box 150, Watkins Glen, NY 14891
607-583-2225 Fax: 607-583-2041
e-mail: info@farmsancturary.org
Web site: www.farmsanctuary.org
Gene Bauston, President
Farm animal rescue; public information programs & advocacy for the humane treatment of animals

Farmers' Market Federation of NY NYS Farmers Direct Marketing Association
2100 Park St, Syracuse, NY 13208
315-475-1101 Fax: 315-362-5012
e-mail: diane99@dreamscape.com
Web site: www.nyfarmersmarket.com; www.nysfdma.com
Diane Eggert, Director
Education & services to NY's farm direct marketers

Food Industry Alliance of New York State Inc
130 Washington Ave, Albany, NY 12210
518-434-1900 Fax: 518-434-9962
e-mail: michael@fiany.com
Web site: www.fiany.com
Michael Rosen, Vice President for Government Relations & General Counsel
Assn of retail grocery, wholesale & supplier/manufacturer food companies

Fund for Animals (The)
200 W 57th St, New York, NY 10019
212-757-3425 Fax: 212-246-2633
Web site: www.fund.org
Marian Probst, Chair
Working to protect all animals through education, legislation, litigation & hands-on care

New York State Flower Industries Inc
Garden Gate Greenhouse
11649 W Perrysburg Rd, Perrysburg, NY 14129
716-532-6282 Fax: 716-532-0396
Gary Patterson, President
Greenhouse plant production

Global Gardens Program, New York Botanical Garden (The)
200th St & Southern Blvd, Bronx, NY 10458-5126
718-817-8700 Fax: 718-817-8178
e-mail: emccarthy@nybg.org
Web site: www.nybg.org
Toby Adams, Family Garden Manager Ext 8126
Promoting understanding of ethnic diversity & the interconnectedness of cultures through gardening

GreenThumb
c/o NYC Parks & Recreation Dept, 49 Chambers St, Rm 1020, New York, NY 10007
212-788-8070 Fax: 212-788-8052
e-mail: edie@greenthumbnyc.org
Web site: www.greenthumbnyc.org
Edie Stone, Director
Development & preservation of community gardens; reclamation of urban land for green space

Offices and agencies appear in alphabetical order.

Greenmarket/Council on the Environment of NYC
51 Chambers Street, Room 228, New York, NY 10007
212-788-7900 Fax: 212-788-7913
e-mail: conyc@cenyc.org
Web site: www.cenyc.org
Tom Strumolo, Director
Direct to consumer farmers' markets, sustainable agriculture

Hill & Gosdeck
99 Washington Ave, Ste 400, Albany, NY 12210-2823
518-463-5449 x3102 Fax: 518-463-0947
e-mail: tjgosdeck@aol.com
Thomas J Gosdeck, Partner
Food industry regulation

Humane Society of the United States, Mid Atlantic Regional Office
Bartley Square, 270 Route 206, Flanders, NJ 07836
973-927-5611 Fax: 973-927-5617
e-mail: maro@hsus.org
Web site: www.hsus.org
Nina Austenberg, Regional Director

Long Island Farm Bureau
104 Edwards Ave, Calverton, NY 11923
631-727-3777 Fax: 631-727-3721
e-mail: askus@lifb.com
Web site: www.lifb.com
Joseph M Gergela, III, Executive Director

Long Island Nursery & Landscape Association Inc
PO Box 1792, Southold, NY 11971
631-765-5113 Fax: 631-765-5113
e-mail: linla@optonline.net
Margot Bridgen, Secretary

National Potato Board
McCormick Farms Inc
4189 Route 78, Bliss, NY 14024
585-322-7274 Fax: 585-322-7495
James P McCormick, NYS Delegate

My-T Acres Inc
8127 Lewiston Rd, Batavia, NY 14020
585-343-1026 Fax: 585-343-2051
Peter Call, Co-Owner
Vegetable crops & grain

NOFA-NY Certified Organic LLC
840 Upper Front St, Binghamton, NY 13905-1542
607-724-9851 Fax: 607-724-9853
e-mail: certifiedorganic@nofany.org
Web site: www.nofany.org
Carol King, Program Representative
Organic farming certification

NY Farms!
125 Williams Rd, Candor, NY 13743
607-659-3710
e-mail: nyfarms@nyfarms.info
Web site: www.nyfarms.info
Jim Barber, President
Campaign to promote farming & protect farmland in NYS

NYS Agricultural Society
493 Charlton Rd, Ballston Spa, NY 12020
518-384-1715 Fax: 518-384-1715
e-mail: pennyh@nycap.rr.com
Web site: www.nysagsociety.org
Penny Heritage, Executive Secretary
To improve the condition of agriculture through education, leadership development & recognition programs

NYS Arborists
PO Box 306, Pawling, NY 12564-0306
845-855-0225 Fax: 845-855-0387
e-mail: execsec@newyorkstatearborists.com
Web site: www.newyorkstatearborists.com
David Hayner, Executive Secretary
Professional arborists & educators; promote public interest, foster research & education in the care & benefits of trees, shrubs & their environment

NYS Association For Food Protection
Cornell University, Dept of Food Science, 172 Stocking Hall, Ithaca, NY 14853
607-255-2892 Fax: 607-255-7619
e-mail: jgg3@cornell.edu
Web site: www.foodscience.cornell.edu/nysfsanit/index.html
Janene Lucia, Executive Secretary

NYS Association of Veterinary Technicians Inc
119 Washington Ave, 2ND Floor, Albany, NY 12210
518-426-7920 Fax: 518-432-5902
e-mail: nysavt@associationresources.org
Jan Dorman, Executive Director

NYS Berry Growers Association
14 State Street, Bloomfield, NY 14469
585-657-5328 Fax: 585-657-4642
e-mail: goodberries@frontiernet.net
Web site: www.nysbga.org
Jim Altemus, Executive Secretary

NYS Cheese Manufacturers Association, Department of Food Science
Cornell University, 413 Stocking Hall, Ithaca, NY 14853
607-255-3111 Fax: 607-254-4868
e-mail: kjb4@cornell.edu
Web site: www.newyorkcheese.org
Kathryn Boor, Secretary & Scientific Advisor
Cheese manufacturing education & product promotion

Offices and agencies appear in alphabetical order.

NYS Grange
100 Grange Place, Cortland, NY 13045
607-756-7553 Fax: 607-756-7757
e-mail: nysgrange@nysgrange.com
Web site: www.nysgrange.com
Bruce Croucher, President
Advocacy, education & services for farm, rural & suburban families

NYS Horticultural Society
Hedrick Hall, Box 462, Geneva, NY 14456
315-787-2404 Fax: 315-787-2216
e-mail: wilsonk36@hotmail.com
George Lamont, Executive Director
Advocacy, education & member services for the fruit industry

NYS Nursery/Landscape Association
PO Box 657, 2115 Downer Street Rd, Baldwinsville, NY 13027
315-635-5008 Fax: 315-635-4874
e-mail: nysnla@aol.com; suzannemm@nycap.rr.com
Web site: www.nysnla.org
Suzanne M Maloney, Executive Director
Trade Association

NYS Turfgrass Association
PO Box 612, 4 Youngs Place, Latham, NY 12110
518-783-1229 Fax: 518-783-1258
e-mail: nysta@nysta.org
Web site: www.nysta.org
Beth Seme, Executive Director
Grow & manage turf for golf courses, ball fields & landscape

NYS Vegetable Growers Association Inc
PO Box 70, Kirkville, NY 13082-0070
315-687-5734 Fax: 315-687-5734
e-mail: nysvga@twcny.rr.com
Jeff & Lindy Kubecka, Co-Contacts

NYS Weights & Measures Association
5427 Trinity Ave, Lowville, NY 13367
315-376-5397 Fax: 315-376-5874
e-mail: bcooper@lewiscountyny.org
Barbara J Cooper, Secretary
Promote uniformity in measure accuracy, enforcement standards & legal requirements

National Coffee Association
15 Maiden Ln, Ste 1405, New York, NY 10038
212-766-4007 Fax: 212-766-5815
e-mail: info@ncausa.org
Web site: www.ncausa.org
Robert F Nelson, President & Chief Executive Officer

National Grape Cooperative-Welch Foods Inc
575 Virginia Rd, 3 Concord Farms, Concord, MA 01742-9101
978-371-1000 Fax: 978-371-3707
Web site: www.welchs.com
Dan Dillon, President & Chief Executive Officer

New York Agriculture in the Classroom
Cornell University, Dept of Education, 422 Kennedy Hall, Ithaca, NY 14853
607-255-9253 or 607-255-9252 Fax: 607-255-7905
e-mail: nfw3@cornell.edu
Web site: www.cerp.cornell.edu/aitc
Nancy Schaff, Director
An agricultural literacy program providing resources and professional development opportunities for teachers to facilitate the integration of food and fiber systems education into the curriculum

New York Apple Association Inc
7645 Main St, PO Box 350, Fishers, NY 14453
585-924-2171 Fax: 585-924-1629
e-mail: jimallen@nyapplecountry.com
Web site: www.nyapplecountry.com
James Allen, President
Promote NYS apples & apple products

New York Beef Industry Council Inc
PO Box 250, Westmoreland, NY 13490
315-339-6922 Fax: 315-339-6931
e-mail: cgillis@nybeef.org
Web site: www.nybeef.org
Carol Gillis, Executive Director
Producer-directed & funded organization conducting beef promotion & information programs

New York Center for Agricultural Medicine & Health, Bassett Healthcare
1 Atwell Rd, Cooperstown, NY 13326
607-547-6023 or 800-343-7527 Fax: 607-547-6087
e-mail: info@nycamh.com
Web site: www.nycamh.com
John May, Director
Occupational health & medicine in agriculture

New York Farm Bureau
159 Wolf Road, PO Box 5330, Albany, NY 12205-0330
518-436-8495 or 800-342-4143 Fax: 518-431-5656
e-mail: nyphooker@fb.org
Web site: www.nyfb.org
Patrick Hooker, Director, Public Policy
Resources, education, advocacy, services & programs for the farming industry & community

New York Field Corn Growers Association
2269 DeWindt Rd, Newark, NY 14513
315-331-7791 Fax: 315-331-1294
e-mail: kswar10462@yahoo.com
Web site: www.nycorn.org
Kevin Swartley, President

New York Holstein Association
957 Mitchell St, Ithaca, NY 14850
607-273-7591 or 800-834-4644 Fax: 607-273-7612
e-mail: pgifford@nyholsteins.com
Web site: www.nyholsteins.com
Patricia G Gifford, Executive Manager
Promoting the Holstein breed for the economic & social benefit of junior & senior members

Policy Areas

Offices and agencies appear in alphabetical order.

New York Pork Producers Coop
12 North Pork Street, Seneca Falls, NY 13141
315-568-2750 Fax: 315-568-2752
Gerald Swartley, President
Education & promotion of pork industry in NY

New York Seed Improvement Project, Cornell University, Plant Breeding Depar
103 Leland Lab, Cornell University, Ithaca, NY 14853
607-255-9869 Fax: 607-255-9048
e-mail: aaw4@cornell.edu; nysip@cornell.edu
Web site: SeedPotato.NewYork.cornell.edu
Alan Westra, Manager
Official seed certifying agency for the state of NY & foundation seedstocks agency

New York State Association of Agricultural Fairs Inc
67 Verbeck Ave, Schaghticoke, NY 12154
518-753-4956 Fax: 518-753-0208
e-mail: carousels4@aol.com
Web site: www.nyfairs.org
Norma W Hamilton, Executive Secretary

New York State Dairy Foods Inc
201 S Main St, Suite 302, North Syracuse, NY 13212
315-452-6455 Fax: 315-452-1643
Web site: www.nysdfi.org
Bruce W Krupke, Executive Vice President
Full service trade association representing dairy processing/distribution industry

New York State Maple Producers Association Inc
6242 Swiss Rd, Castorland, NY 13620
315-346-1034 Fax: 315-346-1662
e-mail: swisser@twcny.rr.com
Barbara Zehr, Secretary
Promoting quality maple products through education & research

New York State Veterinary Medical Society
9 Highland Ave, Albany, NY 12205
518-437-0787 or 800-876-9867 Fax: 518-437-0957
e-mail: info@nysvms.org
Web site: www.nysvms.org
Julie Lawton, Executive Director

New York Thoroughbred Breeders Inc
Saratoga Spa State Park, 19 Roosevelt Drive, Saratoga Springs, NY 12866
518-580-0100 Fax: 518-580-0500
e-mail: nybreds@nybreds.com
Web site: www.nybreds.com
Barry Ostrager, President

New York Wine & Grape Foundation
350 Elm St, Penn Yan, NY 14527
315-536-7442 Fax: 315-536-0719
e-mail: info@newyorkwines.org
Web site: www.newyorkwines.org
James Trezise, President
Promotion of winery products & tours; research for wine & grape related products

NYS Bar Assn, Food, Drug & Cosmetic Law Section
North Shore-Long Island Jewish Health System
Office of Legal Affairs, 150 Community Dr, Great Neck, NY 11021
516-465-8379 Fax: 516-465-8105
e-mail: cmcgowan2@nshs.edu
Coreen McGowan, Esquire

Northeast Organic Farming Association of New York
PO Box 880, Cobleskill, NY 12043
518-922-7937 Fax: 518-922-7646
e-mail: office@nofany.org
Web site: www.nofany.org
Sarah Johnston, Executive Director
Education for farmers, gardeners & consumers; organic certification program

Public Markets Partners / Baum Forum
5454 Palisade Ave, Bronx, NY 10471
718-884-5716 Fax: 718-884-2724
e-mail: hilarybaum@aol.com
Web site: www.baumforum.org
Hilary Baum, President
Partnerships with communities to develop & manage public markets to revitalize urban areas & promote regional agriculture; educational programs

Regional Farm & Food Project
295 Eighth Street, Troy, NY 12180
518-271-0744 Fax: 518-271-0745
e-mail: billie@farmfood.org
Web site: www.farmfood.org
Billie Best, Executive Director
Farmer to farmer & public education; community development creating new opportunities for family-scale, sustainable agriculture

Rural Housing Action Corporation
400 East Ave, Rochester, NY 14607-1910
585-340-3366 Fax: 585-340-3309
e-mail: lbeaulac@ruralinc.org
Web site: www.ruralinc.org
Lee Beaulac, President
Housing & related assistance for farmworkers, seniors & the rural poor

Rural Opportunities Inc
400 East Ave, Rochester, NY 14607
585-340-3300 Fax: 585-340-3335
e-mail: smitchell@ruralinc.org
Web site: www.ruralinc.org
Stuart J Mitchell, President & Chief Executive Officer
Advance self-sufficiency of farm workers, low-income & other disenfranchised people & communities through advocacy & programs including Training & Employment, Child Development, Health & Safety, Home Ownership, Economic Dev, Housing & Property Mgmt

Offices and agencies appear in alphabetical order.

Seneca Foods Corporation
3736 South Main St, Marion, NY 14505
315-926-8100 Fax: 315-926-8300
e-mail: webmaster@senecafoods.com
Web site: www.senecafoods.com
Susan Boeding, Senior Vice President of Technical Services
Vegetable food products

Tea Association of the USA Inc
420 Lexington Ave, New York, NY 10170
212-986-9415 Fax: 212-697-8658
e-mail: info@teausa.com
Web site: www.teausa.com
Joe Simrany, President
Trade association for the tea industry

United Dairy Cooperative Services Inc
12 North Park St, Seneca Falls, NY 13148
315-568-2750 Fax: 315-568-2752
e-mail: unitedag@flare.net
James G Patsos, Chief Executive Officer
Management, accounting & payroll services to agriculture industry

Upstate Farms Cooperative Inc
25 Anderson Rd, Buffalo, NY 14225
716-892-3156 Fax: 716-892-3157
Web site: www.upstatefarms.com
Bob Hall, General Manager & Chief Executive Officer

Venture Vineyards Inc
8830 Upper Lake Rd, Lodi, NY 14860
607-582-6774 Fax: 607-582-6342
e-mail: venturev@capital.net
Melvin P Nass, President
Produce wholesaler of grapes/juices

Policy Areas

BANKING AND FINANCE

New York State

GOVERNOR'S OFFICE

Governor's Office
Executive Chamber
State Capitol
Albany, NY 12224
518-474-8390 Fax: 518-474-1513
Web site: www.state.ny.us

Governor:
  George E Pataki 518-474-8390
Executive Director:
  Kara Lanspery 518-474-8390
Secretary to the Governor:
  John P Cahill. 518-474-4246
Senior Policy Advisor to the Governor:
  Jeffrey Lovell 518-486-9671
Deputy Secretary to the Governor for Public Authorities, Finance & Housing:
  Adam Barsky 518-473-2610
Counsel to the Governor-Attorney General, Budget:
  Richard Platkin 518-474-8343
Senior Assistant Counsel to the Governor-Banking, Tort Reform, Insurance,
    State Insurance Fund, Uniform Laws, Workers' Compensation Board:
  Christopher McCarthy 518-474-2294
Asst Counsel to the Governor-Battery Pk, Child/Family Svcs, Child/Family
    Council, Family, Housing, Human Rts, Roosevelt Is, Temp/Disabl,
    Women, HFA/MBBA/SONYMA:
  Carolyn Betz Kerr. 518-474-1310
Director, Communications:
  David Catalfamo. 518-474-8418

EXECUTIVE DEPARTMENTS AND RELATED AGENCIES

Banking Department
One State St
New York, NY 10004-1417
212-709-5470
Web site: www.banking.state.ny.us

5 Empire State Plaza
Ste 2310
Albany, NY 12223-1555
518-474-2364
Fax: 518-473-7204

Superintendent of Banks:
  Diana L Taylor 212-709-3501/fax: 212-709-3585
  e-mail: diana.taylor@banking.state.ny.us
First Deputy Superintendent of Banks:
  Daniel Muccia 212-709-3502
Director, Consumer Affairs & Financial Products:
  Barbara Kent. 212-709-3503

Deputy Superintendent & Counsel:
  Sara Kelsey. 212-709-1640
Acting Director, Criminal Investigations Bureau:
  John Dinin 212-709-3540
Deputy, Communications & Media Relations:
  Catie Marshall 212-709-1691
Chief Information Officer:
  Connie Van Decker 212-709-5400
Information Security Officer:
  Walter Jones 212-709-1535
Information Security Officer:
  Karen Sorady 518-474-0192
Secretary, NYS Banking Board:
  Sam L Abram 212-709-1658

Communication & Media Relations
Deputy Superintendent:
  Catie Marshall 212-709-1691

Community and Regional Banks Division
Deputy Superintendent:
  Manuel Kursky. 212-709-1610

Consumer Services Division
Deputy Superintendent:
  Edward B Kramer 212-709-3560/fax: 212-709-3582

Criminal Investigations Bureau
Acting Director:
  John Dinin 212-709-3540/fax: 212-709-3555

Foreign and Wholesale Banks Division
Acting Deputy Superintendent:
  David Fredsall 212-709-1551

Human Resources Management Division
Director:
  Linda P Wilson 212-709-5440/fax: 212-709-5450

Information Technology Division
Director:
  Connie Van Decker 212-709-5400/fax: 212-709-5427

Large Complex Banks
Deputy Superintendent:
  Michael Lesser. 212-709-1550/fax: 212-709-1586

Licensed Financial Services Division
Deputy Superintendent:
  Regina A Stone 212-709-5500/fax: 212-709-5513

Mortgage Banking Division
Deputy Superintendent:
  Kenneth Bielemeier. 212-709-5540/fax: 212-709-5555

Regional Offices

Albany Office
  5 Empire Plaza, Suite 2310, Albany, NY 12223
  518-473-6160

Offices and agencies appear in alphabetical order.

London Office
Sardinia House, 52 Lincoln's Inn Fields, London, UK WC2A 3LZ
011 44-20-7405-5475

Upstate Office . . . . fax: 315-428-4052
333 E Washington St, 5th Fl, Syracuse, NY 13202

Research & Technical Assistance Division
Assistant Deputy Superintendent:
   Robert Woods. 212-709-1613

Law Department
State Capitol
Albany, NY 12224-0341
518-474-7330 Fax: 518-402-2472
Web site: www.oag.state.ny.us

120 Broadway
New York, NY 10271-0332
212-416-8000
Fax: 212-416-8942

Attorney General:
   Eliot Spitzer 518-474-7330
First Deputy Attorney General:
   Michele Hirshman 212-416-8050
Director, Public Information & Correspondence:
   Peter A Drago 518-474-7330/fax: 518-402-2472

Public Advocacy Division
Acting Deputy Attorney General:
   Terryl Brown Clemons 212-416-8041/fax: 212-416-8068
Special Counsel:
   Mary Ellen Burns 212-416-6155

Consumer Fraud & Protection Bureau
Bureau Chief:
   Thomas G Conway 518-474-2374/fax: 518-474-3618

Investment Protection Bureau
Bureau Chief:
   David Brown. 212-416-8198/fax: 212-416-6377

CORPORATIONS, AUTHORITIES AND COMMISSIONS

Municipal Assistance Corporation for the City of New York
420 Lexington Avenue
Room 1756
New York, NY 10170
212-840-8255 Fax: 212-840-8570
e-mail: macnyc@earthlink.net

Chairman:
   Jonathan A Ballan. . . . . 212-840-8255 or 212-692-6772
Executive Director:
   Nancy H Henze. 212-840-8255

New York State Housing Finance Agency (HFA)
641 Lexington Ave
New York, NY 10022

212-688-4000 Fax: 212-872-0678
Web site: www.nyhomes.org

Chair:
   Jerome M Becker 212-688-4000
President & CEO:
   Stephen J Hunt 212-688-4000
Senior VP, COO & CFO:
   Ralph J Madalena. 212-688-4000
Senior VP & Counsel:
   Justin Driscoll. 212-688-4000
Senior VP & Special Assistant to President/CEO for Policy Development & Programs:
   James P Angley 212-688-4000
Senior VP, Debt Issuance:
   Bernard Abramowitz. 212-688-4000 x530
Vice President, Director of Development:
   Jonathan Cortrell 212-688-4000 x688
Vice President, Policy & Planning:
   Tracy A Oats 212-688-4000 x678
Vice President, Intergovernmental Relations:
   Michael Houseknecht 518-434-2118/fax: 518-432-7158

Affordable Housing Corporation
Senior VP & Special Assistant to Pres/CEO for Policy Development & Programs:
   James P Angley 212-688-4000

New York State Mortgage Loan Enforcement & Administration Corporation
633 Third Ave
35th Fl
New York, NY 10017-6754
212-803-3530 Fax: 212-803-3535
Web site: www.empire.state.ny.us

President & CEO:
   Garry P Ryan 212-803-3530
General Counsel:
   Anita W Laremont 212-803-3750
Chief Financial Officer:
   Frances Walton. 212-803-3510
Public Affairs Officer:
   Deborah Wetzel. 212-803-3740/fax: 212-803-3735
   e-mail: dwetzel@empire.state.ny.us

New York State Project Finance Agency
641 Lexington Ave
New York, NY 10022
212-688-4000 Fax: 212-872-0678

Chair:
   Jerome M Becker 212-688-4000
President & CEO:
   Stephen J Hunt 212-688-4000
Senior VP, COO & CFO:
   Ralph J Madalena. 212-688-4000
Senior VP & General Counsel:
   Justin Driscoll. 212-688-4000
Senior VP, Debt Issuance:
   Bernard Abramowitz. 212-688-4000 x530
Vice President, Director of Development:
   Jonathan Cortrell 212-688-4000 x688
Vice President, Policy & Planning:
   Tracy A Oats 212-688-4000 x678

Offices and agencies appear in alphabetical order.

Policy Areas

State of New York Mortgage Agency (SONYMA)

641 Lexington Ave
New York, NY 10022
212-688-4000 Fax: 212-872-0678
Web site: www.nyhomes.org

Chair:
  Joseph Strasburg...................................212-688-4000
President & CEO:
  Stephen J Hunt....................................212-688-4000
Senior VP & Special Assistant to Pres/CEO for Policy Development & Programs:
  James P Angley....................................212-688-4000
Senior VP, COO & CFO:
  Ralph J Madalena..................................212-688-4000
Senior VP & General Counsel:
  Justin Driscoll...................................212-688-4000
Vice President/Director, SONYMA Mortgage Insurance Fund:
  Michael Friedman..........................212-688-4000 x714
Senior VP, Single Family Programs & Financing:
  Charles Rosenwald.........................212-688-4000 x531
Vice President, Policy & Planning:
  Tracy A Oats..............................212-688-4000 x678
Vice President, Intergovernmental Relations:
  Michael Houseknecht..............518-434-2118/fax: 518-434-7158

State of New York Municipal Bond Bank Agency (MBBA)

641 Lexington Ave
New York, NY 10022
212-688-4000 Fax: 212-872-0678
Web site: www.nymbba.org

Chair:
  Jerome M Becker...................................212-688-4000

President & CEO:
  Stephen J Hunt....................................212-688-4000
Senior VP, CFO, COO:
  Ralph J Madalena..................................212-688-4000
Senior VP & Counsel:
  Justin Driscoll...................................212-688-4000
Senior VP & Special Assistant to Pres/CEO for Policy Development & Programs:
  James P Angley....................................212-688-4000
Senior VP, Debt Issuance:
  Bernard Abramowitz........................212-688-4000 x530
Vice President, Policy & Planning:
  Tracy A Oats..............................212-688-4000 x678

NEW YORK STATE LEGISLATURE

See Legislative Branch in Section 1 for additional Standing Committee and Subcommittee information.

Assembly Standing Committees

Banks
Chair:
  Catherine T Nolan (D).............................518-455-4851
Ranking Minority Member:
  Roy McDonald (R)..................................518-455-5404

Senate Standing Committees

Banks
Chair:
  Hugh T Farley (R).................................518-455-2181
Ranking Minority Member:
  Ruth Hassell-Thompson (D).........................518-455-2061

U.S. Government

EXECUTIVE DEPARTMENTS AND RELATED AGENCIES

Export Import Bank of the United States
Web site: www.exim.gov

Northeast Regional Office
20 Exchange Pl, 40th Fl, New York, NY 10005
Regional Director:
  Thomas Cummings.................212-809-2650/fax: 212-809-2646
  e-mail: thomas.cummings@exim.gov
Business Development Officer, Rockland & Westchester Counties:
  Sharyn Koenig.....................................212-809-2653
  e-mail: sharyn.koenig@exim.gov
Business Development Assistant:
  Jennifer Drakes...................................212-809-2649
  e-mail: jennifer.drakes@exim.gov

Federal Deposit Insurance Corporation
Web site: www.fdic.gov

Division of Supervision & Consumer Protection........fax: 917-320-2919
  20 Exchange Place, 4th Fl, New York, NY 10005
Regional Director:
  Christopher J Spoth...............................917-320-2570

Federal Reserve System

Federal Reserve Bank of New York
33 Liberty St, New York, NY 10045-0001
Web site: www.newyorkfed.org
President:
  Timothy F Geithner................................212-720-5000
Senior Vice President, Public Information:
  Peter Bakstansky..................212-720-6136/fax: 212-720-6628
  e-mail: peter.bakstansky@ny.frb.org
Assistant Vice President:
  Rae Rosen.........................212-720-1935/fax: 212-720-6628
  e-mail: rae.rosen@ny.frb.org

Buffalo Branch
40 Fountain Plaza, Ste 650, Buffalo, NY 14202

Offices and agencies appear in alphabetical order.

Senior Vice President & Branch Manager:
Kausar Hamdani 716-849-5000

National Credit Union Administration

Albany Region
9 Washington Sq, Washington Ave Ext, Albany, NY 12205
Acting Regional Director:
Mark A Treichel 518-862-7400/fax: 518-862-7420

US Treasury Department
Web site: www.ustreas.gov

Comptroller of the Currency
Web site: www.occ.treas.gov

Northeastern District
1114 Avenue of the Americas, Ste 3900, New York, NY 10036
Deputy Comptroller:
Toney Bland 212-790-4001/fax: 212-790-4058
Assistant Deputy Comptroller:
Michael Carnovali 212-790-4025/fax: 212-790-4058
Assistant Deputy Comptroller:
Beverly Cole 212-790-4003
Assistant Deputy Comptroller:
William Reinhardt 212-790-4020
District Counsel:
Jonathan Rushdoony 212-790-4010

Office of Thrift Supervision
Web site: www.ots.treas.gov

Northeast Region (serving NY)
Harborside Financial Center, Plaza 5, Suite 1600, Jersey City, NJ 07311
Regional Director:
Robert C Albanese 201-413-1000/fax: 201-413-7543

US Mint . . . . fax: 845-446-6258
Rt 218, PO Box 37, West Point, NY 10996
Fax: 845-446-6258
Web site: www.usmint.gov
Superintendent:
Ellen McCullom 845-446-6201
Administrative Officer:
Vacant 845-446-6203
Chief, Mint Police:
Robert Beck 845-446-6234

See U.S. Congress Chapter for additional Standing Committee and Subcommittee information.

House of Representatives Standing Committees

Financial Services
Chair:
Michael G Oxley (R-OH) 202-225-2676
Ranking Minority Member:
Barney Frank (D-MA) 202-225-5931
New York Delegate:
Gary L Ackerman (D) 202-225-2601
New York Delegate:
Joseph Crowley (D) 202-225-3965
New York Delegate:
Vito Fossella (R) 202-225-3371
New York Delegate:
Steve Israel (D) 202-225-3335
New York Delegate:
Sue W Kelly (R) 202-225-5441
New York Delegate:
Peter T King (R) 202-225-7896
New York Delegate:
Carolyn B Maloney (D) 202-225-7944
New York Delegate:
Carolyn McCarthy (D) 202-225-5516
New York Delegate:
Gregory W Meeks (D) 202-225-3461
New York Delegate:
Nydia M Velasquez (D) 202-225-2361

Senate Standing Committees

Banking, Housing & Urban Affairs
Chair:
Richard C Shelby (R-AL) 202-224-5744
Ranking Minority Member:
Paul S Sarbanes (D-MD) 202-224-4524
New York Delegate:
Charles E Schumer (D) 202-224-6542

Private Sector

Alliance Bank
Tower II, 120 Madison St, Syracuse, NY 13202
315-475-2100 Fax: 315-473-9684
Web site: www.alliancebankna.com
Jack H Webb, President & Chief Executive Officer

American Express Company
200 Vesey St, 48th Fl, New York, NY 10285
212-640-3216 Fax: 212-640-0331
Web site: www.americanexpress.com
Teresa Jennings, Director, State & Government Affairs
Consumer lending, travel services, proprietary database marketing, insurance underwriting & investment services

American International Group Inc
70 Pine St, 36th Fl, New York, NY 10270
212-770-6114 Fax: 212-785-4214
e-mail: ned.cloonan@aig.com
Web site: www.aig.com
Edward T Cloonan, Vice President International & Corporate Affairs
International business, government & financial services

Offices and agencies appear in alphabetical order.

Policy Areas

Antalek & Moore Insurance Agency
340 Main St, Beacon, NY 12508
845-831-4300 or 866-894-1026 Fax: 845-831-5631
e-mail: fantalek@antalek-moore.com
Web site: www.antalek-moore.com
Frederick N Antalek, Sr, President
NYS Banking Board member

Apple Banking for Savings
122 East 42nd St, 9th Fl, New York, NY 10168
212-224-6410 Fax: 212-224-6580
Web site: www.applebank.com
Alan Shamoon, President & Chief Executive Officer
NYS Banking Board member

**Community Bankers Assn of NY State, Banking Law &
Regulations Cmte**
Astoria Federal Savings & Loan
1 Astoria Federal Plaza, Lake Success, NY 11042-1085
516-327-3000 Fax: 516-327-7860
e-mail: banking@astoriafederal.com
Web site: www.astoriafederal.com
Alan P Eggleston, Member

Community Bankers Assn of NY State
Astoria Federal Savings & Loan
19 Dove St, #102, Albany, NY 12210
518-434-3555 Fax: 518-434-1576
e-mail: gbrody@cbanys.org
Web site: www.cbanys.org
Gary Brody, Senior Vice President/Director, State & Local
  Government

Bank of Akron
46 Main St, Akron, NY 14001
716-542-5401 Fax: 716-542-5510
Web site: www.bankofakron.com
E Peter Forrestel, II, President & Chief Executive Officer
*NYS Banking Board member/ Director - Independent Bankers
Association of New York State (IBANYS)*

Bear Stearns & Co Inc
383 Madison Ave, 11th Fl, New York, NY 10179
212-272-2000 Fax: 212-272-5188
e-mail: bforan@bear.com
Web site: www.bearstearns.com
James E Cayne, Chairman & Chief Executive Officer
Public finance

Bond Market Association (The)
360 Madison Ave, Ste 18, New York, NY 10017-7111
646-637-9200 Fax: 646-637-9126
e-mail: namiel@bondmarkets.com
Web site: www.bondmarkets.com
Jon Teall, Vice President, Media Relations
*Represent securities firms & banks that underwrite, trade & sell debt
securities*

**Brown Brothers Harriman & Co, Bank Asset Management
Group**
140 Broadway, New York, NY 10005-1101
212-493-5502 Fax: 212-493-7657
e-mail: carl.terzer@bbh.com
Web site: www.bbh.com
Carl E Terzer, Senior Vice President & Marketing Director

Canandaigua National Bank & Trust Co
72 S Main St, Canandaigua, NY 14424
585-394-4260 or 800-724-2621 Fax: 585-396-1355
e-mail: ghamlin@cnbank.com
Web site: www.cnbank.com
George W Hamlin, President
Full service banking

Citigroup
399 Park Avenue, New York, NY 10043
212-559-5248 or 800-285-3000 Fax: 212-793-8011
e-mail: thomsonte@citi.com
Web site: www.citigroup.com
Terri Thomson, Director, State Civic Affairs

Citigroup Inc
399 Park Ave, 2nd Fl, New York, NY 10043
212-793-0141 Fax: 212-793-2008
e-mail: schleinm@citigroup.com
Web site: www.citigroup.com
Michael Schlein, Senior Vice President, Global Corporate Affairs,
  Human Resources & Business Practices
Commercial & retail banking

City National Bank & Trust Company
10-24 N Main St, PO Box 873, Gloversville, NY 12078
518-773-7911 Fax: 518-725-2730
e-mail: wsmith@citynatlbank.com
Web site: www.citynatlbank.com
William N Smith, President
Commercial banking

Community Bankers Association of NYS
655 3rd Ave, Ste 816, New York, NY 10017
212-573-5500 Fax: 212-573-5509
e-mail: mdonath@cbanys.org
Web site: www.cbanys.org
Mariel O Donath, President & Chief Executive Officer

Cornell University, Economics Department
450 Uris Hall, Ithaca, NY 14853-7601
607-255-6283 Fax: 607-255-2818
e-mail: dae3@cornell.edu
Web site: www.arts.cornell.edu/econ
David Easley, Professor
Microeconomic theory, financial economics

Credit Advocate Counseling Corporation
237 First Ave, Ste 305, New York, NY 10003
212-260-2776 Fax: 646-218-4599
e-mail: info@creditadvocates.com
Web site: www.creditadvocates.com
Steve Burman, President
Advice & assistance in eliminating credit card debt by consolidating & handling bill payments while reducing interest rates

Deutsche Bank
345 Park Ave, New York, NY 10154
212-454-7170 Fax: 212-454-0500
e-mail: thomas.curtis@db.com
Web site: www.db.com
Thomas Curtis, Global Head of Business Development

Evergreen Bank
237 Glen St, PO Box 318, Glens Falls, NY 12801
518-792-1151 Fax: 518-792-4837
e-mail: dburke@banknorth.com
Web site: www.banknorth.com
Dan Burke, President & Chief executive Officer
Commercial, retail & investment banking

Federal Home Loan Bank of New York
101 Park Ave, New York, NY 10178-0599
212-681-6000 Fax: 212-441-6890
Web site: www.fhlbny.com
Alfred A DelliBovi, President

Financial Services Forum
708 3RD Avenue, 17TH Floor, New York, NY 10015
212-692-0828 Fax: 212-692-0830
Web site: www.estandardsforum.com
George J Vojta, Chairman, Estandardsforum Inc
NYS Banking Board member; organization of CEOs of twenty one of the largest & most diversified financial institutions

Goldman Sachs & Co
101 Constitution Avenue NW, Suite 1000 East, Washington, DC 20001
202-637-3700 Fax: 202-637-3773
Web site: www.gs.com
Judah C Sommer, Managing Director & Head of Global Government Affairs

Community Bankers Assn of NY State, Accounting & Taxation Cmte
GreenPoint Bank
275 Broadhollow Road, Melville, NY 11747
631-844-1004
Web site: www.greenpoint.com
Aurelie Campbell, Co-Chair

HSBC Bank USA
452 Fifth Ave, New York, NY 10018
212-525-6533 Fax: 212-525-8447
e-mail: janetlburak@ushsbc.com
Janet L Burak, General Counsel

HSBC USA Inc
452 Fifth Ave, New York, NY 10018
212-525-3800 Fax: 212-525-0109
e-mail: linda.stryker-luftig@us.hsbc.com
Linda Stryker-Luftig, Executive Vice President, Group Public Affairs
Bank holding company

IRX Therapeutics Inc
140 West 57th, Ste 9-C, New York, NY 10019
212-582-1199 Fax: 212-582-3659
e-mail: jhwang@immunorx.com
Web site: www.irxtherapeutics.com
Jeffrey Hwang, Chief Financial Officer
NYS Banking Board member

Independent Bankers Association of NYS
125 State St, Albany, NY 12207
518-436-4646 Fax: 518-436-4648
e-mail: williamc@ibanys.net
Web site: ibanys.net
William Y Crowell, III, Executive Director
Representing New York's community banks

Kudlow & Company LLC
One Dag Hammarskjold Plaza, 885 Second Ave @ 48TH Street, 26TH Floor, New York, NY 10017
212-644-8610 Fax: 212-588-1636
Web site: www.kudlow.com
James Higgins, Managing Director
NYS Banking Board member

Lake Shore Savings
128 East Fourth St, Dunkirk, NY 14048
716-366-4070 Fax: 716-366-2965
e-mail: dave.mancuso@lakeshoresavings.com
Web site: www.lakeshoresavings.com
David C Mancuso, President & Chief Executive Officer
NYS Banking Board member

Law Offices of Wesley Chan
641 Lexington Ave, 20th Fl, New York, NY 10022
212-751-7100 Fax: 212-371-6632
e-mail: wchenlaw@aol.com
Wesley Chen, Attorney
NYS Banking Board member

M&T Bank Corporation
One M&T Plaza, Buffalo, NY 14203-2399
716-842-5425 Fax: 716-842-5220
e-mail: rwilmers@mandtbank.com
Web site: www.mandtbank.com
Robert G Wilmers, Chairman, Chief Executive Officer & President
Commercial, savings & mortgage banking services

Policy Areas

Offices and agencies appear in alphabetical order.

MBIA Insurance Corporation
113 King St, Armonk, NY 10504
914-273-4545 Fax: 914-765-3555
e-mail: ethel.geisinger@mbia.com
Web site: www.mbia.com
Ethel Z Geisinger, Vice President, Government Relations
Insure municipal bonds & structured transactions

Mallory Factor Inc
555 Madison Ave, New York, NY 10022
212-350-0000 Fax: 212-350-0022
Mallory Factor, President
NYS Banking Board member

Merrill Lynch & Co Inc
222 Broadway, 16th Fl, New York, NY 10038-2510
212-670-0302 Fax: 212-670-4501
e-mail: andrew_kandel@ml.com
Andrew Kandel, First Vice President & Assistant General Counsel,
    State Regulation, Legislation
Securities, capital markets & financial services

Morgan Stanley
1585 Broadway, New York, NY 10036
212-761-4000 Fax: 212-762-7994
Web site: www.morganstanley.com
Phillip J Purcell, Chairman & Chief Executive Officer
Investment banking

Municipal Credit Union
22 Cortlandt St, New York, NY 10007-3107
212-238-3361 Fax: 212-416-7050
Thomas G Siciliano, General Counsel
NYS Banking Board member

NBT Bancorp Inc
PO Box 351, Norwich, NY 13815
607-337-6416 Fax: 607-336-6545
e-mail: customerservice@nbtbank.com
Web site: www.nbtbank.com
Martin A Dietrich, Chairman & Chief Executive Officer
Commercial banking

NYS Credit Union League
19 British American Blvd, Latham, NY 12110
518-437-8100 Fax: 518-782-4212
e-mail: akramer@nyscul.org
Web site: www.nyscul.org
Amy Kramer, Vice President/Governmental Affairs
Serving & support credit unions

National Federation of Community Development Credit Unions
120 Wall St, 10th Fl, New York, NY 10005
212-809-1850 Fax: 212-809-3274
e-mail: info@natfed.org
Web site: www.natfed.org
Cliff Rosenthal, Executive Director

New York Bankers Association
99 Park Ave, 4th Fl, New York, NY 10016-1502
212-297-1664 Fax: 212-297-1622
e-mail: bbosies@nyba.com
Web site: www.nyba.com
William J Bosies, Senior Vice President, Legislation & Regulation
Advocacy for commercial banking industry

Community Bankers Assn of NY State, Mortgages & Real Estate Cmte
New York Community Bank
615 Merrick Ave, Westbury, NY 11590
516-683-4100 Fax: 516-683-8344
Web site: www.mynycb.com
Joseph R Ficalora, President & Chief executive Officer

New York State Credit Union League Inc
19 British American Blvd, Latham, NY 12110
800-342-9835 Fax: 518-782-4285
e-mail: mlanotte@nyscul.org
Web site: www.nyscul.org
Michael A Lanotte, Senior Vice President, Governmental &
    Regulatory Affairs
*Trade association for over 600 not-for-profit, member owned credit
unions in New York*

New York Stock Exchange
Government Relations, 11 Wall St, 6th Fl, New York, NY 10005
212-656-3000 Fax: 212-656-5605
e-mail: pagurto@nyse.com
Web site: www.nyse.com
Richard G Ketchum, Chief Regulatory Officer

Norddeutsche Landesbank Girozentrale
1114 Ave of the Americas, 37th Fl, New York, NY 10036
212-812-6800 Fax: 212-812-6860
e-mail: jens.westrick@nordlb.com
Web site: www.nordlbnewyork.com
Jens A Westrick, EVP, North America & General Manager
NYS Banking Board member

Community Bankers Assn of NY State, Bank Operations & Admin Cmte
North Country Savings Bank
127 Main St, Canton, NY 13617
315-386-4533 Fax: 315-386-3739
Web site: www.northcountrysavings.com
Michael A Noble, Chair

Community Bankers Assn of NY State, Government Relations Cmte
Pioneer Savings Bank
21 Second St, Troy, NY 12180
518-274-4800 Fax: 518-274-1060
e-mail: troybranch@pioneersb.com
Web site: www.pioneersb.com
Dawn Gendron, Sales Development Officer/Senior Branch Manager

Securities Industry Association (SIA)
120 Broadway, 35th Fl, New York, NY 10271
212-618-0533 Fax: 212-968-0703
e-mail: ndonohoelancia@sia.com
Web site: www.sia.com
Nancy Donohoe Lancia, Vice President & Director, State
  Government Affairs

Securities Industry Association (SIA)
120 Broadway, 35th Fl, New York, NY 10271
212-618-0532 Fax: 212-968-0703
e-mail: kutsey@sia.com
Web site: www.sia.com
Keith Utsey, Vice President & Managing Director/Counsel, State
  Government Affairs

Sullivan & Cromwell
125 Broad St, New York, NY 10004
212-558-3534 Fax: 212-558-3588
H Rodgin Cohen, Partner & Chairman
Bank regulation & acquisition law

The Clearing House Association, LLC
100 Broad St, New York, NY 10004
212-612-9205 Fax: 212-612-9253
e-mail: norm.nelson@theclearinghouse.org
Web site: www.theclearinghouse.org
Norman R Nelson, General Counsel
Electronic funds transfer

Tompkins Trustco Inc
110 N Tioga St, PO Box 460, Ithaca, NY 14851
607-273-3210 Fax: 607-273-0063
e-mail: chairmansoffice@tompkinstrust.com
Web site: www.tompkinstrustco.com
James J Byrnes, Chairman & Chief Executive Officer

Ulster Savings Bank
180 Schwank Dr, Kingston, NY 12401
845-338-6322 Fax: 845-339-9008
Web site: www.ulstersavings.com
Clifford Miller, President & Chief Executive Officer
NYS Banking Board member

Union State Bank
100 Dutch Hill Rd, Orangeburg, NY 10962
845-365-4605 Fax: 845-365-4659
Web site: www.unionstate.com
Thomas E Hales, Pres & Chief Executive Officer
NYS Banking Board member

Valley National Bank
275 Madison Ave, New York, NY 10016
973-916-2250 Fax: 973-779-7563
e-mail: fcosentino@valleynationalbank.com
Web site: www.valleynationalbank.com
Frank T Cosentino, FVP-Corporate & Government Services
*Full-service banking, cash management, municipal leasing & public
finance*

Washington Mutual
340 Ave of the Americas, 3rd Fl, New York, NY 10011
212-353-6230 Fax: 212-673-5118
Donna Wilson, Senior Vice President, Regional President
*National financial services company that provides a diversified line
of products to consumers & small to mid-sized businesses*

White & Case LLP
1155 Ave of the Americas, New York, NY 10036
212-819-8200 Fax: 212-354-8113
e-mail: dwall@whitecase.com
Web site: www.whitecase.com
Duane D Wall, Managing Partner
*Advises domestic & foreign banks on the nature & structure of their
operations & activities in the US & abroad*

Wilber National Bank
245 Main St, PO Box 430, Oneonta, NY 13820
607-432-1700 Fax: 607-433-4161
e-mail: whitteas@wilberbank.com
Web site: www.wilberbank.com
Alfred S Whittet, Vice Chairman & Chief Executive Officer
Commercial & retail banking

Policy Areas

Offices and agencies appear in alphabetical order.

COMMERCE, INDUSTRY & ECONOMIC DEVELOPMENT

New York State

GOVERNOR'S OFFICE

Governor's Office
Executive Chamber
State Capitol
Albany, NY 12224
518-474-8390 Fax: 518-474-1513
Web site: www.state.ny.us

Governor:
  George E Pataki 518-474-8390
Executive Director:
  Kara Lanspery 518-474-8390
Secretary to the Governor:
  John P Cahill. 518-474-4246
Senior Policy Advisor to the Governor:
  Jeffrey Lovell 518-486-9671
Counsel to the Governor-Attorney General, Budget:
  Richard Platkin. 518-474-8343
Senior Assistant Counsel to the Governor-Indian Affairs, Lottery, Racing &
  Wagering, State Liquor Authority:
  Greg Allen 518-474-2266
Asst Counsel to the Governor-Battery Pk, Child/Family Svcs, Child/Family
  Council, Family, Housing, Human Rts, Roosevelt Is, Temp/Disabl,
  Women, HFA/MBBA/SONYMA:
  Carolyn Betz Kerr. 518-474-1310
Asst Counsel to the Governor-Economic Development, Empire State
  Development Corporation, Jacob Javits Convention Center, NYSTAR,
  Olympic Regional Development Authority, Tourism:
  Robert Ryan 518-474-2266
Director, Communications:
  David Catalfamo. 518-474-8418

EXECUTIVE DEPARTMENTS AND RELATED AGENCIES

Alcoholic Beverage Control, Division of
84 Holland Ave
Albany, NY 12208
518-486-4767 Fax: 518-402-4015

105 W 125th St
4th Fl
New York, NY 12208
212-961-8385
Fax: 212-961-8299

Chair:
  Edward F Kelly. . . . . 212-961-8347 or 518-473-6559
Commissioner:
  Joseph Zarriello 518-474-0810

Counsel:
  Thomas McKeon 212-961-8317

Administration
Deputy Commissioner, Administration & Public Affairs:
  J Mark Anderson 518-486-4767
Director, Financial Administration:
  Franklin Hecht 518-474-4546
Director, Human Resources:
  Dan Cunningham 518-473-5995

Licensing

Albany (Zone II)
84 Holland Ave, 2nd Fl, Albany, NY 12208
Director, Licensing:
  Kerri O'Brien. 518-474-7604
Associate Counsel:
  Leslie Trebby 518-474-6750
Assistant Director, ABC Compliance:
  Richard Mann 518-474-0385/fax: 518-473-7527
Supervising Beverage Control Investigator:
  Thomas Pascucci. 518-474-0385/fax: 518-473-7527

Buffalo (Zone III)
Donovan State Office Bldg, 125 Main St, Buffalo, NY 14203
716-847-3035
Executive Officer:
  Brandon Noyes. 716-847-3060
Associate Counsel:
  Gerald Greenan 716-847-3057
Supervising Beverage Control Investigator:
  Thomas Cocker 716-847-3039/fax: 716-847-5020

New York City (Zone I)
317 Lenox Avenue, New York, NY 10027
212-961-8385
Deputy Commissioner:
  Fred Gioffre 212-961-8301
Supervising Attorney:
  Stephen Kalinsky 212-961-8351
Assistant Director, ABC Compliance:
  Richard Mann 212-961-8376/fax: 212-961-8381

Budget, Division of the
State Capitol
Albany, NY 12224
518-473-3885
e-mail: dobinfo@budget.state.ny.us
Web site: www.state.ny.us/dob

Director:
  John F Cape 518-474-2300
Deputy Director:
  Al Kaplan 518-474-6300

Offices and agencies appear in alphabetical order.

Deputy Director:
    Ron Rock 518-474-6323
Administrative Officer:
    Karen Bodnar 518-474-6324
Director, Communications:
    Michael Marr 518-474-3885
Press Officer:
    Peter Constantakes 518-473-3885
Press Officer:
    Scott Reif 518-473-3885
Legislative Liaison:
    Christina Kidera 518-474-7953/fax: 518-473-7243

Consumer Protection Board

5 Empire State Plaza
Ste 2101
Albany, NY 12223-1556
518-474-8583 Fax: 518-486-3936
Web site: www.consumer.state.ny.us

5 Penn Plaza
5th Fl
New York, NY 10001
212-268-6199
Fax: 212-268-7124

Chairperson & Executive Director:
    Teresa A Santiago 518-474-3514
Executive Deputy Director:
    Caroline Quartararo 518-474-3514
General Counsel:
    Lisa R Harris 518-474-2348
Director, Marketing & Public Relations:
    Jon Sorensen 518-473-9472/fax: 518-474-2896
Director, Consumer Education:
    Gina Pinos 212-459-8852
Director, Consumer Services:
    Cyndee D Berlin 518-474-8583

Strategic Programs Office

Director Strategic Programs & Utility Intervention:
    Douglas Elfner 518-486-4137
Chief Economist, Utility Intervention:
    Tariq Niazi 518-486-4137

Long Island Region
333 Earle Ovington Blvd, Ste 403, Uniondale, NY 11553
Regional Outreach Specialist:
    Christine Sculti 516-470-2954/fax: 516-470-2955

New York City Office
1740 Broadway, 15th Fl, New York, NY 10019
Assistant to the Chairperson:
    Carmen Castro 212-459-8850/fax: 212-459-8855
Regional Outreach Specialist:
    James Dees 212-459-8851/fax: 212-459-8855

Upstate New York Office
5 Empire State Plaza, Ste 2101, Albany, NY 14604
Regional Outreach Specialist:
    Cindy Connors-DeSimone 518-474-3563/fax: 518-286-4177

Western New York Region
340 East Main St, Rochester, NY 14604
Deputy Director, Consumer Education:
    Joan Mueller 585-262-2180/fax: 585-262-3748

Empire State Development Corporation

30 South Pearl St
Albany, NY 12245
518-292-5100
Web site: www.empire.state.ny.us

633 Third Ave
New York, NY 10017
212-803-3100

Commissioner:
    Charles A Gargano 212-803-3700
Executive Deputy Commissioner, Chief Operating Officer:
    Eileen Mildenberger 212-803-3730
Senior Vice President, Legal & General Counsel:
    Anita W Laremont 212-803-3750
Communications Director:
    Ron Jury 212-803-3740/fax: 212-803-3735
    e-mail: rjury@empire.state.ny.us
Deputy Commissioner & Counsel:
    Donald Ross 518-292-5120
Chief Financial Officer:
    Frances Walton 212-803-3510
Senior Vice President, Design & Construction:
    Frances Huppert 212-803-3255
Senior Vice President, Loans & Grants:
    Doug Wehrle 212-803-3640
Senior Vice President, Privatization:
    Vacant 212-803-3680
Senior Vice President, Transportation & Infrastructure:
    Vacant 212-803-3516

Administration

Senior Vice President, Deputy Commissioner & Chief Administrative
    Officer:
    Joseph J LaCivita . . . . 212-803-3158 or 518-292-5102
    fax: 518-292-5812

Advertising, Marketing & Tourism

Web site: www.iloveny.state.ny.us
Senior Vice President & Senior Deputy Commissioner, Corporate Marketing:
    Neville Bugwadia 212-803-2244
Deputy Commissioner, Business Marketing, Advertising & Tourism:
    Suzanne Morris 518-292-5360/fax: 518-292-5802

Business Development

Senior Vice President, Business Development:
    Ray Richardson 212-292-5101

International
Senior Vice President:
    Maureen Caldwell 212-803-3704

Regional Economic Development
Deputy Commissioner, Regional Office Administration:
    Carrie Laney 518-292-5273
Capital Region
Rensselaer Technology Park, 385 Jordan R, Troy, NY 12180
Director:
    James E Scripps 518-283-1010/fax: 518-283-1112
    e-mail: nys-capitaldist@empire.state.ny.us
Central New York Region
620 Erie Blvd West, Ste 112, Syracuse, NY 13204
Director:
    Thomas E Gillson 315-425-9110/fax: 315-425-7156
    e-mail: nys-centralny@empire.state.ny.us
Finger Lakes Region
400 Andrews St, Ste 710, Rochester, NY 14604

Director:
> Jack Kinnicutt 585-325-1944/fax: 585-325-6505
> e-mail: nys-fingerlakes@empire.state.ny.us

Long Island Region
150 Motor Parkway, Hauppauge, NY 11788
Director:
> Henry A Mund 631-435-0717/fax: 631-435-3399
> e-mail: nys-longisland@empire.state.ny.us

Mid-Hudson Region
33 Airport Center Dr, Ste 201, New Windsor, NY 12553
Director:
> Ronald Hicks 845-567-4882/fax: 845-567-6085
> e-mail: nys-midhudson@empire.state.ny.us

Mohawk Valley Region
207 Genesee St, Utica, NY 13501
Director:
> Anthony J Picente, Jr 315-793-2366/fax: 315-793-2705
> e-mail: nys-mohawkval@empire.state.ny.us

New York City Region
633 Third Ave, 34th Fl, New York, NY 10017
Director:
> Kelly Jones 212-803-2340/fax: 212-803-2409
> e-mail: nys-nyc@empire.state.ny.us

North Country Region (Plattsburgh)
West Bay Plaza, Ste 401, Plattsburgh, NY 12901
Director:
> Randy Beach. 518-561-5642/fax: 518-561-8831
> e-mail: nys-northcountry@empire.state.ny.us

North Country Region (Watertown)
Dulles State Ofc Bldg, 317 Washington St, 2nd Fl, Watertown, NY 13601
Director:
> Douglas B Schelleng 315-785-7907/fax: 315-785-7935
> e-mail: nys-northcountry@empire.state.ny.us

Southern Tier Region (Binghamton)
State Office Bldg, Rm 1508, 44 Hawley St, Binghamton, NY 13901
Director:
> Robert J Moppert 607-721-8605/fax: 607-721-8613
> e-mail: nys-southerntier@empire.state.ny.us

Southern Tier Region (Elmira)
400 E Church St, Elmira, NY 14901
Director:
> Joe Roman 607-733-6513/fax: 607-734-2698
> e-mail: nys-southerntier@empire.state.ny.us

Western New York Region
420 Main St, Ste 717, Buffalo, NY 14202
Director:
> Timothy Doolittle. 716-856-8111/fax: 716-856-1744
> e-mail: nys-westernny@empire.state.ny.us

Strategic Business Division
Senior Vice President:
> Ray Richardson 518-292-5201

Business Products

Empire Zones Program
Deputy Commissioner:
> Carrie Laney 518-292-5240/fax: 518-292-5811

Environmental Services Unit (Environ Invest Pgm/EIP & Small Business Environ Ombudsman/SBEO)
Deputy Commissioner:
> Amy Schoch. . . . . 518-292-5340 or 800-782-8369
> fax: 518-292-5802

Small Business Services
Assistant Deputy Commissioner:
> Jeff Boyce 518-292-5220/fax: 518-292-5884

Economic Revitalization

Senior Vice President:
> Christine Glassner 212-803-3727/fax: 212-803-3236

Vice President, Empowerment Zones:
> James Ilako 212-803-3237/fax: 212-803-3235

Vice President, Renewal Communities:
> James Ilako 212-803-3237/fax: 212-803-3235

Director, Metropolitan Economic Revitalization Fund (MERF):
> Michael Searles 212-803-2417/fax: 212-803-2459

Director, Division of Minority & Women's Business Development:
> Jorge Vidro 212-803-3228/fax: 212-803-3223

Director, Entrepreneurial Assistance Program:
> Joyce Smith 212-803-3234/fax: 212-803-3235

Director, Puerto Rican & Latino Business Development Program:
> Martha Otero 212-803-3227/fax: 212-803-3235

Director, Business & Economic Development:
> Huey-Min Chuang 212-803-3238/fax: 212-803-3235

Director, Capital Access & Technical Assistance Program:
> Issac J Elliston 212-803-2317/fax: 212-803-2459

Governor's Office of Motion Picture & Television Development

Deputy Commissioner:
> Patricia Kaufman. 212-803-2334/fax: 212-803-2339

Policy & Research

Deputy Commissioner/Senior Vice President:
> John Bacheller 518-292-5115/fax: 518-292-5812

State Data Center
Chief Demographer:
> Robert Scardamalia 518-292-5300/fax: 518-292-5806

Special Projects & Subsidiaries

Harlem Community Development Corp
163 West 125th St, New York, NY 10027
President:
> Diane P Phillpotts 212-961-4156/fax: 212-961-4143

Penn Station Redevelopment Corp
633 Third Ave, New York, NY 10017
President:
> Michael Royce 212-803-3647/fax: 212-803-3660

Queens West Development Corp
633 Third Ave, New York, NY 10017
President:
> Alex Federbush 212-803-3600/fax: 212-803-3631

USA Niagara Development Corp
345 Third St, Ste 505, Niagara Falls, NY 14303
President:
> Meredith Bahr-Andreucci 716-284-2556/fax: 716-284-2917

Law Department
120 Broadway
New York, NY 10271-0332
212-416-8000 Fax: 212-416-8942

State Capitol
Albany, NY 12224-0341
518-474-7330
Fax: 518-402-2472

Attorney General:
> Eliot Spitzer 518-474-7330

Offices and agencies appear in alphabetical order.

First Deputy Attorney General:
  Michele Hirshman 212-416-8050
Chief of Staff:
  Richard Baum...................................... 212-416-8050
Director, Public Information & Correspondence:
  Peter A Drago 518-474-7330/fax: 518-402-2472
Director, Communications:
  Darren Dopp 212-416-8060/fax: 212-416-6005

Public Advocacy Division
Acting Deputy Attorney General:
  Terryl Brown Clemons 212-416-8041/fax: 212-416-8068
Special Counsel:
  Mary Ellen Burns 212-416-6155

Antitrust Bureau
Bureau Chief:
  Jay L Himes..................... 212-416-8282/fax: 212-416-6015

Consumer Fraud & Protection Bureau
Bureau Chief:
  Thomas G Conway 518-472-2374/fax: 518-474-3618

Internet Bureau
Bureau Chief:
  Kenneth Dreifach 212-416-8433/fax: 212-416-8369

Investment Protection Bureau
Bureau Chief:
  David Brown................... 212-416-8198/fax: 212-416-6377

State Counsel Division
Deputy Attorney General:
  Richard Rifkin 518-473-7190
Assistant Deputy Attorney General:
  Patricia Martinelli 518-473-0648/fax: 518-486-9777
Assistant Deputy Attorney General:
  Susan L Watson................... 212-416-8579/fax: 212-416-6001

Claims Bureau
Bureau Chief:
  Susan Pogoda 212-416-8516/fax: 212-416-8946

Regulatory Reform, Governor's Office of
Agency Bldg 1, 4th Fl, Empire State Plz
PO Box 2107
Albany, NY 12220-0107
518-486-3292 Fax: 518-473-9342
Web site: www.gorr.state.ny.us

Acting Director:
  David S Bradley.................................... 518-473-8197
Deputy Director:
  David S Bradley.................................... 518-473-8197
Counsel:
  Amelia Stern...................................... 518-473-0620
Public Information Officer:
  David Pietrusza.................................... 518-486-3292
Director, Administration:
  Sandra L Curry.................................... 518-473-8197

Science, Technology & Academic Research, Office of
30 South Pearl St
11th Fl
Albany, NY 12207

518-292-5700 Fax: 518-292-5780
Web site: www.nystar.state.ny.us

Executive Director:
  Russell W Bessette................................. 518-292-5700
Deputy Executive Director:
  Joshua B Toas, Esq................................. 518-292-5700
Director, Operations:
  James A Denn 518-292-5700/fax: 518-292-5798
Director, Programs:
  Kathleen J Wise 518-292-5700
General Counsel:
  Robert Beshaw 518-292-5700
Director, Finance:
  Edward J Hamilton................................. 518-292-5700
Director, Public Information:
  James A Denn 518-292-5700/fax: 518-292-5780
  e-mail: jdenn@nystar.state.ny.us

Centers for Advanced Technology

Center for Advanced Ceramic Technology at Alfred University
352 McMahon Engineering Bldg, 2 Pine St, Alfred, NY 14802-1296
Director:
  Vasantha Amarakoon 607-871-2486/fax: 607-871-3469

Center for Advanced Materials Processing at Clarkson University
Box 5665, Potsdam, NY 13699-5665
Director:
  S V Babu...................... 315-268-2336/fax: 315-268-7615

Center for Advanced Technology in Biomedical & Bioengineering
SUNY at Buffalo, 162K Farber Hall, 3435 Main St, Buffalo, NY 14214-3092
Director:
  William M Mihalko............... 716-829-2982/fax: 716-829-3945

Center for Advanced Technology in Diagnostic Tools & Sensor Systems
SUNY Stony Brook, 214 Old Chemistry Bldg, 2nd FL, Stony Brook, NY 11794-3717
Director:
  Serge Luryi 631-632-1368/fax: 631-632-8529

Center for Advanced Technology in Electronic Imaging Systems
Univ of Rochester, Taylor Hall, 260 Hutchinson Rd, Rochester, NY 14627-0194
Director:
  Eby Friedman 585-275-1022/fax: 585-276-0200

Center for Advanced Technology in Info Mgmt
Columbia University, 630 W 168th St, PH-15-1501, New York, NY 10032
Director:
  Edward H Shortliffe 212-305-2944/fax: 212-305-0196

Center for Advanced Technology in Life Science Enterprise
Cornell University, 130 Biotechnology Bldg, Ithaca, NY 14853-2703
Director:
  Stephen Kresovich 607-255-2300/fax: 607-255-6249

Center for Advanced Technology in Photonic Applications
Dept of Physics, City College of CUNY, 138th St & Convent Ave Rm J419, New York, NY 10031
Director:
  Robert R Alfano 212-650-5531/fax: 212-650-5530

Center for Advanced Technology in Telecommunications at Polytechnic Unv
5 MetroTech Center, Room LC 208, Brooklyn, NY 11201
Director:
  Shivendra S Panwar 718-260-3050/fax: 718-260-8687

Policy Areas

Offices and agencies appear in alphabetical order.

Center for Automation Technologies at Rensselaer
CII Bldg, Rm 8015, Troy, NY 12180-3590
Director:
    Ray Puffer . . . . 518-276-8990 or 518-276-8087
    fax: 518-276-4897

Center for Biotechnology
SUNY at Stony Brook, Psychology A, 3rd Fl, Stony Brook, NY
    11794-2580
Director:
    Clinton T Rubin. 631-632-8521/fax: 631-632-8577

Center for Computer Applications & Software Engineering
Syracuse University, 2-212 Ctr for Science & Tech, Syracuse, NY 13244
Director:
    Shui-Kai Chin 315-443-1060/fax: 315-443-4745

Center in Nanomaterials and Nanoelectronics
Albany Institue for Materials, CESTM Bldg, 251 Fuller Rd, Rm B110,
    Albany, NY 12203
Director:
    Alain E Kaloyeros 518-437-8686/fax: 518-437-8687

Future Energy Systems CAT at Rensselaer Polytechnic Inst
Ctr for Integrated Electronics and, 9023 Low Ctr for Industrial Innovation,
    110 8th St, Troy, NY 12180
Director:
    Omkaram Nalamasu 518-276-3290/fax: 518-276-2990

Integrated Electronics Engineering Center
Thomas J Watson School of Engineering, S, Vestal Pkwy East, PO Box
    6000, Binghamton, NY 13902-6000
Director:
    Bahgat Sammakia 607-777-4332/fax: 607-777-4683

Regional Technology Development Centers

Alliance for Manufacturing & Technology
59 Court St, 6th Fl, State St Entrance, Binghamton, NY 13901
Executive Director:
    Edward Gaetano 607-774-0022 x304/fax: 607-774-0026

Center for Economic Growth
63 State St, Albany, NY 12207
President:
    Kelly Lovell 518-465-8975/fax: 518-465-6681

Central New York Technology Development Organization
1201 E Fayette St, Syracuse, NY 13210
President:
    Robert I Trachtenberg 315-425-5144/fax: 315-233-1259

Council for International Trade, Technology, Education & Communication
Peyton Hall, Rm 101, Main St, Potsdam, NY 13676
Executive Director:
    Thomas Plastino 315-268-3778 x24/fax: 315-268-4432

High Technology of Rochester
Chamber of Commerce Bldg, 5 Bragdon Pl, Rochester, NY 14604
Executive Director:
    Paul Wettenhall 585-327-7920/fax: 585-327-7931

Hudson Valley Technology Development Center
300 Westage Business Ctr, Ste 130, Fishkill, NY 12524
Executive Director:
    Thomas J Phillips, Sr 845-896-6934 x3006/fax: 845-896-7006

Industrial & Technology Assistance Corp
253 Broadway, Rm 302, New York, NY 10007
President:
    Sara Garretson 212-442-2990/fax: 212-442-4567

Long Island Forum for Technology
111 West Main St, Bayshore, NY 11706
Executive Director:
    Patricia Howley 631-969-3700/fax: 631-969-4489

Mohawk Valley Applied Technology Corp
207 Genesee St, Ste 405, Utica, NY 13501
President:
    Paul MacEnroe 315-793-8050/fax: 315-793-8057

Western New York Technology Development Center
726 Exchange St, Ste 620, Buffalo, NY 14210
President:
    Robert J Martin 716-636-3626/fax: 716-845-6418

Small Cities, Governor's Office for
Agency Building 4, 6th Fl
Empire State Plaza
Albany, NY 12223
518-474-2057 Fax: 518-474-5247
Web site: www.nysmallcities.com

Director:
    Glen King 518-474-2057
Executive Assistant to the Director:
    Patricia Longstaff 518-474-2057
First Deputy Director:
    Albert P Jurczynski 518-474-2057
Deputy Director:
    Kenneth J Flood 518-474-2057
Associate Counsel:
    Brian McCartney 518-474-2057
Public Information Officer:
    Tracey McNerney 518-474-2057
    e-mail: tmcnerney@nysmallcities.com

State Department
41 State Street
Albany, NY 12231
518-474-0050 Fax: 518-474-4765
Web site: www.dos.state.ny.us

123 William St
New York, NY 10038
212-417-5801
Fax: 212-417-5805

Secretary of State:
    Randy A Daniels 518-474-0050
First Deputy Secretary of State:
    Frank P Milano 518-474-0050
Deputy Secretary of State, Public Affairs:
    Eamon Moynihan 212-417-5800
Assistant Secretary of State for Communications:
    Lawrence Sombke 518-474-4752/fax: 518-474-4597
    e-mail: info@dos.state.ny.us
Counsel:
    Glen Bruening 518-474-6740/fax: 518-473-9211
Deputy Secretary of State, Local Government & Community Services:
    Matthew Andrus 518-486-9888/fax: 518-474-6572

Business & Licensing Services Division
Deputy Secretary of State:
    Keith W Stack 518-474-4429/fax: 518-473-6648
    e-mail: licensing@dos.state.ny.us

Offices and agencies appear in alphabetical order.

Administrative Rules Division
Director:
Deborah Ritzko 518-474-6957/fax: 518-473-9055
e-mail: adminrules@dos.state.ny.us

Cemeteries Division
Director:
Richard D Fishman . . . . 518-474-6226 or 212-417-5713
fax: 518-473-0876
e-mail: cemeteries@dos.state.ny.us

Corporations, State Records & UCC Division
Director:
Daniel E Shapiro 518-473-2492/fax: 518-474-1418
e-mail: corporations@dos.state.ny.us

Taxation & Finance Department
State Campus
Bldg 9, Rm 227
Albany, NY 12227
518-457-4242 Fax: 518-457-2486
Web site: www.tax.state.ny.us

Commissioner:
Andrew S Eristoff 518-457-2244
Executive Deputy Commissioner:
Barbara G Billet 518-457-7358
Deputy Commissioner & Counsel:
Christopher C O'Brien 518-457-3746/fax: 518-457-8247
Special Assistant to Commissioner for Business:
Holly Chamberlin 518-485-5080
Director, Conciliation & Mediation Services:
Barry M Bresler 518-485-8063
Director, Executive Correspondence Control Unit:
Elizabeth Amodeo 518-457-8193
Director, Legislative Affairs:
John Evers 518-457-2398
Director, Communications:
Thomas Bergin 518-457-4242

Enterprise Services Division
Director:
Brian Digman 518-457-4362

Office of Administration (OOA)
Deputy Commissioner:
Harry VanWormer 518-457-4900

Human Resources Management
Director:
Deborah S Dammer 518-457-2786

Operations Support Bureau
Director:
Thomas Beckstein 518-485-7891

Office of Budget & Management Analysis
Chief Financial Officer:
Robert F Tangorre 518-457-1000

Bureau of Fiscal Services
Director:
Donald J Kohn 518-457-8235

Planning & Management Analysis Bureau
Director:
Kiaran M Johnson 518-457-8660

Tax Enforcement, Office of
Deputy Commissioner:
Peter Farrell 518-457-9693

Tax Operations, Office of
Deputy Commissioner:
Robert Gola 518-485-2863

Audit Division
Director, Tax Audits:
Nonie Manion 518-457-2750

Tax Compliance Division
Director:
Joseph F Gecewicz 518-457-1138

Tax Policy Analysis, Office of
Deputy Commissioner:
Michelle A Cummings 518-457-4357

Technical Services Division
Director:
Marilyn M Kaltenborn 518-457-1153

Taxpayer Services & Revenue Division
Director:
Jamie Woodward 518-457-2261

Treasury Division
Deputy Commissioner & Treasurer:
Aida Brewer 518-474-4250/fax: 518-402-4118

e-MPIRE
Director:
Terry Atwater 518-457-7924

CORPORATIONS, AUTHORITIES AND COMMISSIONS

Central New York Regional Market Authority
2100 Park St
Syracuse, NY 13208
315-442-8647 Fax: 315-442-6897

Executive Director:
Benjamin Vitale 315-422-8647
Counsel:
Robert Scalione 315-422-1311

Development Authority of the North Country
Dulles State Office Bldg, 4th Fl
317 Washington St
Watertown, NY 13601
315-785-2593 Fax: 315-785-2591
Web site: www.danc.org

Chair:
Douglas L Murray 315-785-2593
Executive Director:
Robert S Juravich 315-785-2593
e-mail: juravich@danc.org
Engineer:
Carrie M Tuttle 315-782-8661
e-mail: ctuttle@danc.org

Policy Areas

Offices and agencies appear in alphabetical order.

Deputy Executive Director:
Thomas R Sauter 315-785-2593
e-mail: tsauter@danc.org
Fiscal Officer:
John D Donaghy 315-785-2592
e-mail: jdonaghy@danc.org
Solid Waste Management Facilities General Manager:
E William Seifried 315-232-3236
Director, Project Development:
Kevin J Jordan 315-785-2593
e-mail: kjordan@danc.org
Technical Services Supervisor:
John J Condino 315-232-3236

Empire State Development Corporation

30 South Pearl St
Albany, NY 12245
800-782-8369 or 518-292-5100

633 Third Ave
New York, NY 10017-6706
212-803-3100
Fax: 212-803-3735

Chair & Chief Executive Officer:
Charles A Gargano 212-803-3700
Executive Vice President & Chief Operating Officer:
Eileen Mildenberger 212-803-3730
Executive Vice President:
Michael Wilton 518-292-5100
Communications Director:
Ron Jury 212-803-3740/fax: 212-803-3735
e-mail: rjury@empire.state.ny.us
Senior Vice President, General Counsel:
Anita W Laremont 212-803-3750
Senior Vice President, Chief Administrative Officer:
Joseph J LaCivita 518-292-5102
Senior Vice President, Policy & Research:
John Bacheller 518-292-5115
Senior Vice President, Marketing, Tourism, Advertising, International:
Neville Bugwadia 212-803-2244

Great Lakes Commission

2805 S Industrial Hwy
Ste 100
Ann Arbor, MI 48104-6791
734-971-9135 Fax: 734-971-9150
e-mail: glc@great.lakes.net
Web site: www.glc.org

Chair:
Thomas E Huntley 651-296-2228
Vacant
Vacant
Interim Executive Director:
Thomas R Crane 734-971-9135
Program Manager, Resource Management:
Thomas R Crane 734-971-9135 x123
Program Manager, Transportation & Sustainable Development:
Dave Knight 734-971-9135 x131
Program Manager, Communications & Internet Technology:
Christine Manninen 734-971-9135 x112
Program Manager, Data & Information Management:
Roger Gauthier 734-971-9135 x113

Program Manager, Environmental Quality:
Matthew Doss 734-971-9135 x104

New York State Liquor Authority

84 Holland Ave
Albany, NY 12208
518-473-6559 Fax: 518-402-4015
Web site: www.abc.state.ny.us

Chairman:
Edward F Kelly 518-473-6559
Commissioner:
Lawrence J Gedda 212-961-8347
Commissioner:
Joseph C Zarriello 518-474-0810
Counsel:
Thomas G McKeon 212-961-8317
Deputy Commissioner, Licensing, NYC:
Fred J Gioffre 212-961-8301
Deputy Commissioner, Administration:
J Mark Anderson 518-486-4767
Public Information Officer:
Kimberly Morella 212-961-8331

United Nations Development Corporation

Two United Nations Plaza, 27th Fl
New York, NY 10017-4403
212-888-1618 Fax: 212-588-0758
Web site: www.undc.org

Chair, Board of Directors:
George Klein 212-888-1618
President & Chief Operating Officer:
Roy M Goodman 212-888-1618
Executive Vice President, Director of Development:
Jeffrey Feldman 212-888-1618
Senior Vice President, Controller:
Rudy C Montenegro 212-888-1618
Senior Vice President, Operations:
Robert M Preissner 212-888-1618

NEW YORK STATE LEGISLATURE

See Legislative Branch in Section 1 for additional Standing Committee and Subcommitee information.

Assembly Standing Committees

Cities
Chair:
Scott M Stringer (D) 518-455-5802
Ranking Minority Member:
Thomas J Kirwan (R) 518-455-5762

Consumer Affairs & Protection
Chair:
Audrey I Pheffer (D) 518-455-4292
Ranking Minority Member:
David G McDonough (R) 518-455-4633

Corporations, Authorities & Commissions
Chair:
Richard L Brodsky (D) 518-455-5753

Offices and agencies appear in alphabetical order.

Ranking Minority Member:
James G Bacalles (R) 518-455-5791

Economic Development, Job Creation, Commerce & Industry
Chair:
Robin L Schimminger (D) 518-455-4767
Ranking Minority Member:
Marc Butler (R) 518-455-5393

Small Business
Chair:
Mark Weprin (D) 518-455-5806
Ranking Minority Member:
William Reilich (R) 518-455-4664

Assembly Task Forces

University-Industry Cooperation, Task Force on
Chair:
William B Magnarelli (D) 518-455-4826
Program Manager:
Maureen Schoolman 518-455-4884/fax: 518-455-4175

Senate Standing Committees

Cities
Chair:
Serphin R Maltese (R) 518-455-3281
Ranking Minority Member:
Byron W Brown (D). 518-455-3371

Commerce, Economic Development & Small Business
Chair:
James S Alesi (R) 518-455-2015

Ranking Minority Member:
Efrain Gonzalez, Jr (D). 518-455-3395

Consumer Protection
Chair:
Charles J Fuschillo, Jr (R) 518-455-3341
Ranking Minority Member:
Efrain Gonzalez, Jr (D). 518-455-3395

Corporations, Authorities & Commissions
Chair:
Vincent L Leibell, III (R) 518-455-3111
Ranking Minority Member:
Ada L Smith (D). 518-455-3531

Senate/Assembly Legislative Commissions

Rural Resources, Legislative Commission on
Senate Chair:
Vacant 518-455-3563
Assembly Vice Chair:
David R Koon (D) 518-455-5784
Assembly Program Manager:
Susan Bartle. 518-455-3999/fax: 518-455-4175
Senate Program Manager:
Ronald C Brach 518-455-2544/fax: 518-426-6960
Counsel:
Donald A Walsh. 518-455-2544

Science & Technology, Legislative Commission on
Assembly Chair:
Adele Cohen (D). 518-455-4811
Senior Vice Chair:
Kenneth P LaValle (R) 518-455-3121/fax: 518-455-4859
Program Manager:
Philip Johnson 518-455-5081

U.S. Government

EXECUTIVE DEPARTMENTS AND RELATED AGENCIES

Commodity Futures Trading Commission
Web site: www.cftc.gov

Eastern Region
140 Broadway, New York, NY 10005
Regional Coordinator:
Marvin Jackson 646-746-9700/fax: 646-746-9937

Consumer Product Safety Commission
Web site: www.cpsc.gov

Eastern Regional Center . . . . fax: 212-620-5338
201 Varick St, Rm 903, New York, NY 10014
Acting Director:
Beverly Kohen 212-620-6180

Export Import Bank of the United States
Web site: www.exim.gov

Northeast Regional Office
20 Exchange PL, 40th Fl, New York, NY 10005
Regional Director:
Thomas Cummings 212-809-2650/fax: 212-809-2646
e-mail: thomas.cummings@exim.gov
Business Development Officer, Rockland & Westchester Counties:
Sharyn Koenig 212-809-2653
e-mail: sharyn.koenig@exim.gov
Business Development Assistant:
Jennifer Drakes. 212-809-2649
e-mail: jennifer.drakes@exim.gov

Federal Trade Commission
Web site: www.ftc.gov

Northeast Regional Office . . . . fax: 212-607-2822
1 Bowling Green, Ste 318, New York, NY 10004
Regional Director:
Barbara Anthony 212-607-2829
Senior Assistant Regional Director:
Thomas Cohn 212-607-2829

Small Business Administration
Web site: www.sba.gov

Offices and agencies appear in alphabetical order.

Region II New York . . . . fax: 212-264-0038
26 Federal Plaza, Rm 3108, New York, NY 10278
Regional Administrator:
    William Mangler Jr. 212-264-1450
Regional Advocate:
    Alan Steinberg 212-264-7750

District Offices
Buffalo
    111 W Huron St, Ste 1311, Buffalo, NY 14202
    District Director:
        Franklin J Sciortino 716-551-4301/fax: 716-551-4418
New York City
    26 Federal Plaza, Ste 3100, New York, NY 10278
    District Director:
        Jose Sifontes 212-264-1318/fax: 212-264-4963
Syracuse
    401 S Salina St, 5th Fl, Syracuse, NY 13202
    District Director:
        Bernard J Paprocki 315-471-9393/fax: 315-471-9288

New York Business Information Center
1 Computer Dr South, Albany, NY 12205
Director:
    Daniel O'Connell 518-446-1118 x231/fax: 518-446-1228
    e-mail: daniel.oconnel@sba.gov

US Commerce Department
Web site: www.doc.gov

Census Bureau
Web site: www.census.gov

Boston Region (includes upstate New York)
4 Copley Pl, Ste 301, PO Box 9108, Boston, MA 02117-9108
Regional Director:
    Kathleen Ludgate 617-424-0547/fax: 617-424-4501

New York Region
395 Hudson St, Ste 800, New York, NY 10014-7451
Regional Director:
    Lester A Farthing 212-584-3400/fax: 212-478-4800

Economic Development Administration
Web site: www.doc.gov/eda/

Philadelphia Region (includes New York)
Curtis Ctr, Ste 140 South, Independence Sq West, Philadelphia, PA 19106
Representative, NYC & Long Island:
    Edward Hummel 215-597-6767/fax: 215-597-6669

Upstate New York Office
620 Erie Blvd W, Ste 104, Syracuse, NY 13204-2442
Representative:
    Harold J Marshall 315-448-0938/fax: 315-448-0939

Minority Business Development Agency
Web site: www.mbda.gov

New York Region
26 Federal Plaza, Rm 3720, New York, NY 10278
Regional Director:
    Heyward B Davenport. 212-264-3262/fax: 212-264-0725

National Oceanic & Atmospheric Administration

National Weather Service, Eastern Region
630 Johnson Ave, Ste 202, Bohemia, NY 11716
Web site: www.nws.noaa.gov

Director:
    Dean Gulezian. 631-244-0100/fax: 631-244-0109
    e-mail: dean.gulezian@noaa.gov
Deputy Director:
    Mickey J Brown 631-244-0102
Public Affairs Specialist:
    Marcie Katcher 631-244-0149/fax: 631-244-0167
Chief, Meteorological Services Division:
    John Guiney 631-244-0121
Chief, Regional Hydrology Division:
    Peter Gabrielsen 631-244-0111
Chief, Scientific Services Division:
    Kenneth Johnson 631-244-0136

US Commercial Service - International Trade Administration
Web site: www.export.gov

Buffalo US Export Assistance Center
111 W Huron St, Ste 1304, Buffalo, NY 14202
Director:
    James C Mariano. 716-551-4191/fax: 716-551-5290
    e-mail: james.mariano@mail.doc.gov

Harlem US Export Assistance Center
163 West 125th St, Ste 901, New York, NY 10027
Director:
    K L Fredericks. 212-860-6200/fax: 212-860-6203
    e-mail: office.harlem@mail.doc.gov
International Trade Specialist:
    Fernando Sanchez 212-860-6200

Long Island US Export Assistance Center
400 County Seat Dr, Ste 046, Mineola, NY 11501
Acting Director:
    Gil Hatchadoorian 516-739-1765/fax: 516-739-3310
    e-mail: office.longisland@mail.doc.gov

New York US Export Assistance Center
20 Exchange Pl, 40th Fl, New York, NY 10005
Director, NY-NJ Hub:
    William D Spitler 212-809-2675/fax: 212-809-2687
    e-mail: office.newyork@mail.doc.gov

Rochester US Export Assistance Center
400 Andrews St, Ste 710, Rochester, NY 14604
Web site: www.export.gov
Director:
    Erin Cole 585-263-6480/fax: 585-325-6505
    e-mail: erin.cole@mail.doc.gov

Westchester US Export Assistance Center
707 Westchester Ave, Ste 209, White Plains, NY 10604
Director:
    Joan Kanlian 914-682-6712/fax: 914-682-6698
    e-mail: joan.kanlian@mail.doc.gov

US Department of Agriculture

Rural Development
Web site: www.rurdev.usda.gov/ny

New York State Office
The Galleries of Syracuse, 441 S Salina St, Ste 357, 5th Fl, Syracuse, NY 13202-2425
TDD: 315-477-6447
State Director:
    Patrick H Brennan 315-477-6400/fax: 315-477-6438
Special Projects Representative:
    Joel Weirick 315-477-6433/fax: 315-477-6438

Offices and agencies appear in alphabetical order.

Program Director, Rural Business-Cooperative Service:
Walter D Schermerhorn 315-477-6425
e-mail: walter.schermerhorn@ny.usda.gov

US Justice Department
Web site: www.usdoj.gov

Antitrust Division-New York Field Office
26 Federal Plaza, Rm 3630, New York, NY 10278-0096
Chief:
Ralph T Giordano 212-264-0391/fax: 212-264-7453
e-mail: ralph.giordano@usdoj.gov
Assistant Chief:
Philip F Cody 212-264-0394/fax: 212-264-7453

Civil Division-Commercial Litigation Branch
26 Federal Plz, Rm 346, New York, NY 10278
Attorney-in-Charge:
Barbara S Williams 212-264-9240/fax: 212-264-1916

Community Relations Service-Northeast & Carribean Region
26 Federal Plaza, Ste 36-118, New York, NY 10278
Regional Director:
Reinaldo Rivera, Jr 212-264-0700/fax: 212-264-2143

US Securities & Exchange Commission
Web site: www.sec.gov

Northeast Region . . . . fax: 646-428-1981
233 Broadway, New York, NY 10279
Deputy Regional Director:
Linda Hoshall 646-428-1630

Broker-Dealer Inspection Program
Associate Regional Director:
Robert A Sollazzo 646-728-1620

Enforcement Division
Associate Regional Director:
Barry Rashkover. 646-428-1856
Associate Regional Director:
Mark Schonfeld 646-428-1650
Associate Regional Director:
Robert B Blackburn 646-428-1610

Investment Management
Associate Regional Director:
Douglas Scarff 646-428-1660

U.S. CONGRESS

See U.S. Congress Chapter for additional Standing Committee and Subcommittee information.

House of Representatives Standing Committees

Energy & Commerce
Chair:
Joe Barton (R-TX) 202-225-2002
Ranking Minority Member:
John D Dingell (D-MI). 202-225-4071
New York Delegate:
Eliot L Engel (D) 202-225-2464

New York Delegate:
Vito Fossella (R). 202-225-3371
New York Delegate:
Edolphus Towns (D). 202-225-5936

International Relations
Chair:
Henry J Hyde (R-IL) 202-225-4561
Ranking Minority Member:
Tom Lantos (D-CA). 202-225-3531
New York Delegate:
Gary L Ackerman (D) 202-225-2601
New York Delegate:
Joseph Crowley (D) 202-225-3965
New York Delegate:
Eliot L Engel (D) 202-225-2464
New York Delegate:
Amory Houghton (R) 202-225-3161
New York Delegate:
Peter T King (R). 202-225-7896
New York Delegate:
Gregory W Meeks (D) 202-225-3461

Small Business & Entrepreneurship
Chair:
Olympia J Snowe (R-ME) 202-225-5344
Ranking Minority Member:
John F Kerry (D-MA). 202-225-2742

Joint Senate & House Standing Committees

Economic Committee, Joint
Vice Chair:
Sen Robert Bennett (R-UT) 202-224-5444
Chair:
Rep Jim Saxton (R-NJ). 202-225-4765
Ranking Minority Member:
Carolyn Maloney (D-NY) 202-225-7944
Ranking Minority Member:
Jack Reed (D-RI) 202-224-4642

Senate Standing Committees

Commerce, Science & Transportation
Chair:
Ted Stevens (R-AK). 202-224-3004
Ranking Minority Member:
Daniel K Inouye (D-HI). 202-224-3934

Finance
Chair:
Charles E Grassley (R-IA) 202-224-3744
Ranking Minority Member:
Max Baucus (D-MT) 202-224-2651

Foreign Relations
Chair:
Richard G Lugar (R-IN). 202-224-4814
Ranking Minority Member:
Joseph R Biden, Jr (D-DE). 202-224-5042

Small Business & Entrepreneurship
Chair:
Olympia J Snowe (R-ME) 202-224-5344
Ranking Minority Member:
John F Kerry (D-MA). 202-224-2742

Policy Areas

Offices and agencies appear in alphabetical order.

Private Sector

AeA New York Council
472 Westfield Avenue, Suite LL3, Clark, NJ 07066
732-340-1500 Fax: 908-561-7954
e-mail: linda_klose@aeanet.org
Web site: www.aeanet.org
Linda Klose, Executive Director
Electronics, software & information technology industries; support of high tech industry goals

Altria Corporate Services
120 Park Ave, 16th Fl, New York, NY 10017
917-663-4000
Web site: www.altria.com
Louis C Camilleri, Chairman & Chief Executive Officer
Manufacturing & marketing of foods, tobacco, alcoholic beverages

American Chemistry/American Plastics Council
One Commerce Plaza, 99 Washington Ave, Ste 701, Albany, NY 12210
518-432-7835 Fax: 518-426-2276
e-mail: steve_rosario@americanchemistry.com
Web site: www.americanchemistry.com
Stephen Rosario, Director

American Council of Engineering Companies of NY (ACECNY)
6 Airline Drive, Albany, NY 12205
518-452-8611 Fax: 518-452-1710
e-mail: acecny@acecny.org
Web site: www.acecny.org
Jay J Simson, Executive Director
Business association for consulting engineering & land surveying companies

American Institute of Architects (AIA) New York State Inc
235 Lark St, Albany, NY 12210
518-449-3334 Fax: 518-426-8176
e-mail: aianys@aianys.org
Web site: www.aianys.org
Barbara J Rodriguez, Executive Vice President/Chief Executive
    Officer
Architectural regulations & state policy

American Management Association International
1601 Broadway, New York, NY 10019
212-586-8100 or 800-262-9699 Fax: 212-903-8168
Web site: www.amanet.org
Edward T Reilly, President & Chief Executive Officer
Business education & management development programs for individuals & organizations

Associated Builders & Contractors, Empire State Chapter
6369 Collamer Dr, East Syracuse, NY 13057-1115
315-463-7539 Fax: 315-463-7621
e-mail: empire@abcnys.org
Web site: www.abc.org/newyork
Rebecca Meinking, President
Merit shop construction trade association

Associated General Contractors of America, NYS Chapter
10 Airline Dr, Ste 203, Albany, NY 12205-1025
518-456-1134 Fax: 518-456-1198
e-mail: agcadmin@agcnys.org
Web site: www.agcnys.org
A J Castelbuono, President & Chief Executive Officer

Association Development Group Inc
119 Washington Ave, Ste 100, Albany, NY 12210
518-465-7085 Fax: 518-427-9495
e-mail: info@adgcommunications.com
Web site: www.adgcommunications.com
Kathleen A Van De Loo, President
Association management, communications, education & training, strategic planning, graphic design, web design, database design

Association for a Better New York
355 Lexington Ave, 11th Fl, New York, NY 10017
212-370-5800 Fax: 212-661-5877
e-mail: info@abny.org
Web site: www.abny.org
Michelle Adams, Executive Director
Business recruitment & retention, NYC public policy issues forums & committees

Association of Graphic Communications
330 Seventh Ave, 9th Fl, New York, NY 10001
212-279-2100 x108 Fax: 212-279-5381
e-mail: spindrvrk@agcomm.org
Web site: www.agcomm.org
Vicki R Keenan, Executive Vice President
Promote the economic well-being & public perception of printing & graphic communications within the NY/NJ/CT metro area

Better Business Bureau of Metropolitan New York
257 Park Ave South, 4th Fl, New York, NY 10010
212-533-6200 Fax: 212-477-4912
e-mail: inquiry@newyork.bbb.org
Web site: www.newyork.bbb.org
Ronna D Brown, President
Membership organization promoting ethical business practices

NYS Bar Assn, Public Relations Cmte
Brown & Kelly, LLP
1500 Liberty Bldg, Buffalo, NY 14202-3615
716-854-2620 Fax: 716-854-0082
e-mail: phassett@brownkelly.com
Paul Michael Hassett, Chair

Building Contractors Association
451 Park Ave South, 4th Fl, New York, NY 10016
212-683-8080 Fax: 212-683-0404
e-mail: nybca1@aol.com
Web site: www.ny-bca.com
Paul J O'Brien, Managing Director
Commercial contractors

Offices and agencies appear in alphabetical order.

Building Industry Association of NYC Inc
406 Forest Ave, Staten Island, NY 10301
718-720-3070 Fax: 718-720-3088
e-mail: jfortino@webuildnyc.com
Web site: www.webuildnyc.com
Jessica Fortino, Executive Vice President

Business Council for International Understanding
1212 Ave of the Americas, 10th Fl, New York, NY 10036
212-490-0460 Fax: 212-697-8526
Web site: www.bciu.org
Peter J Tichansky, President & Chief Executive Officer
Promoting dialogue & action between the business & government communities to expand international commerce

Business Council of New York State Inc
152 Washington Ave, Albany, NY 12210
518-465-7511 Fax: 518-465-4389
e-mail: dan.walsh@bcnys.org
Web site: www.bcnys.org
Daniel B Walsh, President & Chief Executive Officer
Create an economic renaissance for NYS & its people

Business Training Institute Inc (The)
200 Genesee St, Utica, NY 13502
315-733-9848 Fax: 315-733-0247
e-mail: nywbc@aol.com
Web site: www.nywbc.org
Donna L Rebisz, Project Director, Women's Business Center
Dedicated to helping women reach their entrepreneurial goals & aspirations

Center for Economic Growth Inc
63 State Street, Albany, NY 12207
518-465-8975 Fax: 518-465-6681
e-mail: ceg@ceg.org
Web site: www.ceg.org
Kelly A Lovell, President/Chief Executive Officer
Business membership nonprofit promoting economic & business development in the Capital Region

Columbia University, Science & Technology Venture
80 Clearmont Avenue, 4TH Floor, New York, NY 10027
212-854-6777 Fax: 212-854-8463
Web site: www.stv.columbia.edu
Michael Cleare, Executive Director
Identify & patent new inventions & copyright materials; interact with industry to setup collaborative research agreements

Conference Board (The)
845 Third Ave, New York, NY 10022
212-339-0300 Fax: 212-836-3805
e-mail: gail.fosler@conference-board.org
Web site: www.conference-board.org
Gail Fosler, Executive Vice President & Chief Economist
Research for business

Construction Contractors Association of the Hudson Valley Inc
330 Meadow Ave, Newburgh, NY 12550
845-562-4280 Fax: 845-562-1448
Web site: www.constructioncontractorsassociation.com
Richard O'Beirne, Executive Director

Consumers Union
101 Truman Ave, Yonkers, NY 10703-1057
914-378-2000 Fax: 914-378-2905
Web site: www.consumerreports.org; www.consumersunion.org
James A Guest, President
Publisher of Consumer Reports magazine; independent, nonprofit testing & information organization serving only consumers

Cornell University, Economics Department
450 Uris Hall, Ithaca, NY 14853-7601
607-255-6283 Fax: 607-255-2818
e-mail: dae3@cornell.edu
Web site: www.arts.cornell.edu/econ
David Easley, Professor
Microeconomic theory, financial economics

Dale Carnegie & Associates Inc
290 Motor Parkway, Hauppauge, NY 11788-5102
631-415-9300 Fax: 631-415-9358
e-mail: peter_handal@dale-carnegie.com
Web site: www.dale-carnegie.com
Peter Handal, President & Chief Executive Officer
Executive leadership training

Davis Polk & Wardwell
450 Lexington Ave, New York, NY 10017
212-450-4284 Fax: 212-450-5545
e-mail: hking@dpw.com
Henry L King, Senior Counsel
Securities litigation & antitrust law

Decision Strategies Group
One Commerce Plaza, Ste 2001, Albany, NY 12210
518-436-0607 Fax: 518-432-4359
e-mail: lynnmueller@dsgny.com
Web site: www.decisionstrategiesgroup.com
I Lynn Mueller, President
Strategic planning & communications consulting

Development Counsellors International
461 Park Ave South, 12th Floor, New York, NY 10016
212-725-0707 Fax: 212-725-2254
e-mail: alevine@dc-intl.com
Web site: www.aboutdci.com
Andrew T Levine, President
Marketing services for economic development & tourism

Policy Areas

Offices and agencies appear in alphabetical order.

EVCI
1 Van Der Donck St, Yonkers, NY 10701-7049
914-623-0700 Fax: 914-964-8222
e-mail: info@evcinc.com
Web site: www.evcinc.com
John J McGrath, President/Chief Executive Officer
Own & operate accredited career & college centers in NY
emphasizing business, technology & allied health programs

Eastern Contractors Association Inc
6 Airline Dr, Albany, NY 12205-1095
518-869-0961 Fax: 518-869-2378
e-mail: acceca@nycap.rr.com
Web site: www.easterncontractorsassn.org
Anthony C Caropreso, Managing Director
Commercial development & construction

Eastman Kodak Company
1250 H Street, Ste 800, Washington, DC 20005
202-857-3474 Fax: 202-857-3401
e-mail: stephen.ciccone@kodak.com
Web site: www.kodak.com
Stephen J Ciccone, Director & Vice President of Public Affairs
Manufactures & markets imaging systems & related services

Empire State Restaurant & Tavern Association Inc
40 Sheridan Ave, Albany, NY 12210
518-436-8121 Fax: 518-436-7287
e-mail: esrta@capital.net
Web site: www.esrta.org
Scott Wexler, Executive Director

Empire State Society of Association Executives Inc
275-1/2 Lark Street, Albany, NY 12210
518-463-1755 Fax: 518-463-5257
e-mail: penny@essae.org
Web site: www.essae.org
Penny Murphy, President & Chief Executive Officer
Education, information, research & networking for professional staff
of not-for-profit trade business & professional associations

Eric Mower & Associates
500 Plum St, Syracuse, NY 13204
315-466-1000 Fax: 315-466-2000
e-mail: jhuppertz@eric.mower.com
Web site: www.mower.com
Tim Green, Senior Managing Partner
Marketing communications & issues management

NYS Bar Assn, Antitrust Law Section
Federal Trade Commission
One Bowling Green, Ste 318, New York, NY 10004
212-607-2828 Fax: 212-607-2822
e-mail: banthony@ftc.gov
Barbara Anthony, Chair

Food Industry Alliance of New York State Inc
130 Washington Ave, Albany, NY 12210
518-434-8144 Fax: 518-434-9962
e-mail: michael@fiany.com
Web site: www.fiany.com
Michael Rosen, Vice President for Government Relations & General
    Counsel
Assn of retail grocery, wholesale & supplier/manufacturer food
companies

General Building Contractors of NYS/AGC
6 Airline Dr, Albany, NY 12205
518-869-2207 Fax: 518-869-0846
e-mail: jeffz@gbcnys.agc.org
Web site: www.gbcnys.agc.org
Jeffrey J Zogg, Executive Director

General Contractors Association of NY
60 East 42nd St, Rm 3510, New York, NY 10165
212-687-3131 Fax: 212-986-4746
e-mail: ritas@mindspring.com
Rita Schwartz, Director, Government Relations
Heavy construction, transportation

Geto & deMilly Inc
130 E 40th St, New York, NY 10016
212-686-4551 Fax: 212-213-6850
e-mail: pr@getodmilly.com
Ethan Geto, President
Public & government relations

Gilbert Tweed Associates Inc
415 Madison Ave, 20th Fl, New York, NY 10017
212-758-3000 Fax: 212-832-1040
e-mail: spinson@gilberttweed.com
Web site: www.gilberttweed.com
Stephanie L Pinson, President
Executive searches & recruitment in public transit, transportation,
energy, utilities, communication & insurance

NYS Bar Assn, Intellectual Property Law Section
Hartman & Winnicki, PC
115 W Century Rd, Paramus, NJ 7654
201-967-8040 Fax: 201-967-0590
e-mail: rick@ravin.com
Richard L Ravin, Chair

IBM Corporation
80 State St, Albany, NY 12207
518-487-6733 Fax: 518-487-6679
Web site: www.ibm.com
Jim Costa, Director, Government Affairs

Intermagnetics General Corporation
450 Old Niskyuna Rd, PO Box 461, Latham, NY 12110-0461
518-782-1122 Fax: 518-786-8216
e-mail: ir@igc.com
Web site: www.igc.com
Kathy Sheehan, Vice President & General Counsel

Offices and agencies appear in alphabetical order.

International Flavors & Fragrances Inc
521 West 57th Street, New York, NY 10019-2960
212-765-5500 Fax: 212-708-7132
Web site: www.iff.com
Dennis M Meany, Senior Vice President, General Counsel &
  Secretary
Create & manufacture flavors & fragrances for consumer products

Macy's East Inc
151 W 34th St, 18th Fl, New York, NY 10001
212-494-5568 Fax: 212-494-1857
e-mail: egoldberg@fds.com
Edward Jay Goldberg, Senior Vice President Government &
  Consumer Affairs
Retail department/specialty stores

Manhattan Institute for Policy Research
52 Vanderbilt Avenue, 2nd Floor, New York, NY 10017
212-599-7000 x315 Fax: 212-599-3494
e-mail: communications@manhattan-institute.org
Web site: www.manhattan-institute.org
Lindsay M Young, Executive Director, Communications
Think-tank promoting the development & dissemination of new ideas
that foster greater economic choice & individual responsibility

Manufacturers Association of Central New York
One Webster's Landing, 5th Fl, Syracuse, NY 13202-1044
315-474-4201 or 1-800-272-9175 Fax: 315-474-0524
e-mail: macny@macny.org
Web site: www.macny.org
Kristen M Heath, Director, Communications & Government
  Relations
Training, education, compensation data & government relations
services, HR services, consulting, purchasing consortiums

NYS Bar Assn, Business Law Section
Menaker & Herrmann LLP
10 East 40th Street, New York, NY 10016
212-545-1900 Fax: 212-545-1656
e-mail: sfa@mhjur.com
Samuel F Abernathy, Chair

Mid-Hudson Pattern for Progress
6 Albany Post Rd, Newburgh, NY 12550-1439
914-565-4900 Fax: 914-565-4918
e-mail: mditullo@pfprogress.org
Web site: www.pattern-for-progress.org
Michael J DiTullo, President & Chief Executive Officer
Regional planning, research & policy development

NYS Bar Assn, Commercial & Federal Litigation Section
Montclare & Wachtler
110 Wall St, New York, NY 10005
212-509-3900 Fax: 212-509-7239
e-mail: ljwachtler@montclarewachtler.com
Lauren J Wachtler, Chair

NY Society of Association Executives Inc (NYSAE)
322 Eighth Avenue, Suite 1400, New York, NY 10001-8001
212-206-8230 Fax: 212-645-1147
e-mail: jdolci@nysaenet.org
Web site: www.nysaenet.org
Joel Dolci, President & Chief Executive Officer

NYS Association of Electrical Contractors
16 Wade Rd, Latham, NY 12110
518-785-3676 Fax: 518-785-0912
Web site: www.nysaec.org
George Ternent, Managing Director

NYS Builders Association Inc
One Commerce Plaza, Ste 704, Albany, NY 12207
518-465-2492 Fax: 518-465-0635
e-mail: phill@nysba.com
Web site: www.nysba.com
Philip A Larocque, Executive Vice President
Advocate for building industry on all legislative & regulatory issues
impacting builders

NYS Building & Construction Trades Council
71 West 23 St, New York, NY 10010
212-647-0700 Fax: 212-647-0705
Edward J Malloy, President

NYS Clinical Laboratory Association Inc
62 William St, 2nd Fl, New York, NY 10005
212-664-7999 Fax: 212-248-3008
e-mail: info@nyscla.com
Web site: www.nyscla.com
Tom Rafalsky, President
Promote the common business interests & seek to improve the
business conditions of clinical laboratories located or operated
within the state

NYS Economic Development Council
19 Dove Street, Ste 101, Albany, NY 12210
518-426-4058 Fax: 518-426-4059
e-mail: mcmahon@nysedc.org
Web site: www.nysedc.org
Brian McMahon, Executive Director
Economic development professionals membership organization

NYS Society of Certified Public Accountants
3 Park Ave, 18th Fl, New York, NY 10016-5991
212-719-8300 Fax: 212-719-4759
e-mail: lgrumet@nysscpa.org
Web site: www.nysscpa.org
Louis Grumet, Executive Director

NYS Trade Adjustment Assistance Center
117 Hawley St, Binghamton, NY 13901
607-771-0875 Fax: 607-724-2404
Web site: www.nystaac.org
Louis G McKeage, Director
Advises US manufacturers on competing with foreign imports

Offices and agencies appear in alphabetical order.

National Association of Black Accountants, NY Chapter
PO Box 2791, Grand Central Station, New York, NY 10163
212-969-0560 Fax: 646-349-9620
e-mail: info@nabany.org
Web site: www.nabany.org
Tyrone Browne, President
Represents the interest of African Americans & other minorities in accounting, auditing, business, consulting, finance & information technology

National Federation of Independent Business
1 Commerce Plaza, Ste 1119, Albany, NY 12260-1000
518-434-1262 Fax: 518-426-8799
e-mail: mark.alesse@nfib.org
Web site: www.nfib.org
Mark Alesse, State Director
Small business advocacy; supporting pro-small business candidates at the state & federal levels

New York Association of Convenience Stores
130 Washington Ave, Suite 300, Albany, NY 12210-2219
518-432-1400 Fax: 518-432-7400
e-mail: info@nyacs.org
Web site: www.nyacs.org
Jim Calvin, President
Retail & small business issues

New York Biotechnology Association (The)
30 Rockefeller Plaza, 27TH Floor, New York, NY 10112
212-332-4395 Fax: 212-332-4398
e-mail: info@nyba.org
Web site: www.nyba.org
Karin A Duncker, Executive Director
Development & growth of NYS-based biotechnology-related industries & institutions; strengthen competitiveness of the state as a location for biotech/biomed research, education & industry

New York Building Congress
44 W 28th St, 12th Fl, New York, NY 10001-4212
212-481-9230 Fax: 212-447-6037
e-mail: rtanders55@aol.com
Web site: www.buildingcongress.com
Richard T Anderson, President
Coalition of design, construction & real estate organizations

New York Business Development Corporation
50 Beaver St, 6th Fl, Albany, NY 12207
518-463-2268 Fax: 518-463-0494
e-mail: rlazar@nybdc.com
Web site: www.nybdc.com
Robert W Lazar, President & Chief Executive Officer
Small business lending

New York Mercantile Exchange Inc
1 North End Ave, New York, NY 10282-1101
212-299-2000 Fax: 212-301-4568
Web site: www.nymex.com
Mitchell Steinhause, Chair
Commodity trading

New York State Auto Dealers Association
37 Elk St, Albany, NY 12207
518-463-1148 x204 Fax: 518-432-1309
e-mail: bob@nysada.com
Web site: www.nysada.com
Robert Vancavage, President

New York State Restaurant Association
409 New Karner Rd, Albany, NY 12205
518-452-4222 Fax: 518-452-4497
e-mail: ricks@nysra.org
Web site: www.nysra.org
Rick J Sampson, President & Chief Executive Officer

New York University, Faculty of Arts & Science
Dept of Economics, 269 Mercer St, Rm 323, New York, NY 10003
212-998-8943 Fax: 212-995-3932
e-mail: william.baumol@nyu.edu
William J Baumol, Professor of Economics
Productivity growth, downsizing, scale economies; trade, anti-trust; economics of industry, the environment & the arts

Northeast Equipment Dealers Association Inc
128 Metropolitan Park Dr, Liverpool, NY 13088
315-457-0314 Fax: 315-451-3548
e-mail: rgaiss@ne-equip.com
Web site: www.ne-equip.com
Ralph F Gaiss, Executive Vice President & Chief Executive Officer
Agricultural, industrial & outdoor power equipment

Partnership for New York City
One Battery Park Plaza, 5th Fl, New York, NY 10004-1479
212-493-7570 Fax: 212-493-7778
e-mail: dmele@pfnyc.org
Web site: www.partnershipfornyc.org
Don Mele, Vice President for State Affairs and Tax Issues
Government Affairs; Business organization working in partnership with government, labor & the nonprofit sector to enhance the NYC economy

Pepsi-Cola Company
700 Anderson Hill Rd, MD 3/1-311, Purchase, NY 10577
914-253-2609 Fax: 914-249-8203
e-mail: pwilcox@pepsi.com
Web site: www.pepsi.com
Peter G Wilcox, Director, Government Affairs
Manufacture, sell & distribute soft drinks, concentrates & syrups

Perry Davis Associates
25 W 45th St, Suite 1405, New York, NY 10036
212-840-1166 Fax: 212-840-1514
e-mail: perry@perrydavis.com
Web site: www.perrydavis.com
Perry Davis, President
Economic development & fundraising & management consulting for nonprofit organizations

NYS Bar Assn, Multi-jurisdictional Practice Cmte
Proskauer Rose LLP
1585 Broadway, New York, NY 10036-8200
212-969-3245 Fax: 212-969-2900
e-mail: keppler@proskauer.com
Web site: www.proskauer.com
Klaus Eppler, Co-Chair

Public Policy Institute of NYS Inc
152 Washington Ave, Albany, NY 12210
518-465-7511 Fax: 518-432-4537
e-mail: david.shaffer@bcnys.org
Web site: www.ppinys.org
David Shaffer, President
Conduct & publish research on NYS economic development issues

Regional Plan Association
4 Irving Place, 7th Fl, New York, NY 10003
212-253-2727 Fax: 212-253-5666
e-mail: yaro@rpa.org
Web site: www.rpa.org
Robert D Yaro, President
Develops & implements land-use, transportation, open-space preservation, economic development & social equity proposals

Retail Council of New York State
258 State St, PO Box 1992, Albany, NY 12201
518-465-3586 Fax: 518-465-7960
e-mail: info@retailcouncilnys.com
Web site: www.retailcouncilnys.com
James R Sherin, President & Chief Executive Officer

Sawchuk Brown Associates
41 State St, Ste 500, Albany, NY 12207
518-462-0318 Fax: 518-462-0688
e-mail: info@sawchukbrown.com
Web site: www.sawchukbrown.com
Sean Casey, Vice President, Public Affairs
Public affairs, public relations, marketing, association communication

Society of Professional Engineers Inc (NYS)
RPI Technology Park, 385 Jordan Rd, Troy, NY 12180-7620
518-283-7490 Fax: 518-283-7495
Web site: www.nysspe.org
Kelly K Norris, Executive Director

Software & Information Industry Association
11 Penn Plaza, 5th Fl, New York, NY 10001
212-946-2283 Fax: 212-946-2792
Web site: www.siia.net
Ken Wasch, President
Issues affecting the software & information industry, in particular electronic commerce & the digital marketplace

Support Services Alliance Inc
107 Prospect St, PO Box 130, Schoharie, NY 12157
800-322-3920 or 518-295-7966 Fax: 518-295-8556
e-mail: scole@ssamembers.com
Web site: www.smallbizgrowth.com
Steven Cole, President
Provides representation & group purchasing for small businesses

The Empire Center for New York State Policy
PO Box 7113, Albany, NY 12224
518-434-3100
e-mail: info@empirecenter.org
Web site: www.empirecenter.org/index.php
E J McMahon, Director
An independent nonpartisan research organization dedicated to fostering greater economic growth, opportunity, and individual responsibility in the Empire State. The Empire Center is a project of the Manhattan Inst for Policy Research.

Urbach, Kahn & Werlin Advisors Inc
66 State St, Albany, NY 12207
518-449-3166 Fax: 518-449-5832
e-mail: kotlow@ukw.com
Web site: www.ukw.com
Richard Kotlow, Chief Executive Officer
Accounting, tax & consulting services for private industry, not-for-profits & government

Wegmans Food Markets Inc
1500 Brooks Ave, PO Box 30844, Rochester, NY 14603-0844
585-464-4760 Fax: 585-464-4669
e-mail: comments@wegmans.com
Web site: www.wegmans.com
Mary Ellen Burris, Senior Vice President, Consumer Affairs

Women's Venture Fund Inc
240 West 35th St, Ste 501, New York, NY 10001
212-563-0499 Fax: 212-868-9116
e-mail: info@wvf-ny.org
Web site: www.womensventurefund.org
Maria Otero, President & Founder
Micro-lender that targets women entrepreneurs in under-served urban communities

Zogby International
901 Broad St, Utica, NY 13501
315-624-0200 Fax: 315-624-0210
e-mail: mail@zogby.com
Web site: www.zogby.com
John Zogby, President
Political polling & analysis; social science research; business & consumer public opinion surveys & market research

Offices and agencies appear in alphabetical order.

CORPORATIONS, AUTHORITIES & COMMISSIONS

New York State

Adirondack Park Agency
Rte 86
PO Box 99
Ray Brook, NY 12977
518-891-4050 Fax: 518-891-3938
Web site: www.apa.state.ny.us

Chair:
    Ross Whaley..518-891-4050
Executive Director:
    Daniel T Fitts......................................518-891-4050
    e-mail: dfitts@gw.dec.state.ny.us
Counsel:
    John S Banta..518-891-4050
Associate Counsel:
    Barbara A Rottier...................................518-891-4050
Public Information Director:
    Keith McKeever......................................518-891-4050

Agriculture & NYS Horse Breeding Development Fund
90 State St
Albany, NY 12207
518-436-8713 Fax: 518-426-1490
Web site: www.nysirestakes.com

Executive Director:
    Peter Goold..518-436-8713
Counsel:
    Steven Losquadro...................................518-436-8713

Albany County Airport Authority
Administration Bldg, 2nd Fl
Albany International Airport
Albany, NY 12211-1507
518-242-2222 x1 Fax: 518-242-2641
e-mail: info@albanyairport.com
Web site: www.albanyairport.com

Chief Executive Officer:
    John A O'Donnell............................518-242-2222 x1
Chief Fiscal Officer:
    J Dwight Hadley.............................518-242-2222 x1
Director, Public Affairs:
    Doug Myers..................................518-242-2222 x4
Counsel:
    Peter F Stuto..............................518-242-2222 x5
Airport Planner:
    Stephen A Iachetta.........................518-242-2222 x3
Purchasing Agent:
    Mary Ann Mysliwiec.........................518-242-2222 x2

Administrative Services Manager:
    Ginger Olthoff.............................518-242-2222 x1

Albany Port District Commission
Administration Bldg Port of Albany
Albany, NY 12202
518-463-8763 Fax: 518-463-8767
e-mail: portofalbany@portofalbany.com
Web site: www.portofalbany.com

Chair:
    Robert F Cross.....................................518-463-8763
General Manager:
    Frank W Keane......................................518-463-8763
Counsel:
    Thomas Owens.......................................518-463-1004

Atlantic States Marine Fisheries Commission
1444 Eye St, NW
6th Floor
Washington, DC 20005
202-289-6400 Fax: 202-289-6051
e-mail: info@asmfc.org
Web site: www.asmfc.org

Chair & Administrative Commissioner, North Carolina:
    Preston P Pate, Jr.................................252-726-7021
Administrative Commissioner, New York:
    Gordon C Colvin....................................631-444-0433
Governor's Appointee, New York:
    Pat Augustine......................................631-928-1524
Legislative Commissioner, New York:
    Senator Owen H Johnson.............................631-669-9200
Executive Director:
    John V O'Shea......................................202-289-6400
    e-mail: voshea@asmfc.org
Public Affairs & Resource Specialist:
    Tina Berger..202-289-6400
    e-mail: tberger@asmfc.org

Battery Park City Authority (Hugh L Carey)
One World Financial Center, 24th Fl
New York, NY 10281
212-417-2000 Fax: 212-417-2001
e-mail: info@bpcauthor.org
Web site: www.batteryparkcity.org

Chairman:
    James F Gill.......................................212-417-3192
Vice Chairman:
    Charles J Urstadt..................................212-417-2000

Offices and agencies appear in alphabetical order.

President & Chief Executive Officer:
   Timothy S Carey 212-417-4205/fax: 212-417-4153
   e-mail: careyt@bpcauthor.org
Member:
   David B Cornstein 212-417-2000
Press Liaison:
   Leticia M Remauro 212-417-2276/fax: 212-417-2279
   e-mail: remaurol@bpcauthor.org

Brooklyn Navy Yard Development Corporation

63 Flushing Ave, Unit #300
Bldg 292, 3rd Fl
Brooklyn, NY 11205-1054
718-907-5900 Fax: 718-643-9296
Web site: www.brooklynnavyyard.com

Chair:
   Alan H Fishman 718-907-5900
President & Chief Executive Officer:
   Eric Deutsch 718-907-5900
Senior Vice President, External Affairs:
   Richard Drucker 718-907-5936
   e-mail: rdrucker@brooklynnavyyard.com

Buffalo & Fort Erie Public Bridge Authority (Peace Bridge Authority)

One Peace Bridge Plaza
Buffalo, NY 14213-2494
716-884-6744 Fax: 716-884-2089
Web site: www.peacebridge.com

Chair (American):
   Paul J Koessler 716-884-6744
Vice Chair (Canadian):
   John A Lopinski 716-884-6744
General Manager:
   Ron Rienas 716-884-6744

Capital Defender Office

217 Broadway, 9th Fl
New York, NY 10007
212-608-3352 Fax: 212-608-4558
Web site: www.nycdo.org

Capital Defender:
   Kevin Doyle. 212-608-3352 x208
First Deputy Capital Defender, Albany Office:
   Mark Harris 518-473-9521
First Deputy Capital Defender, New York City Office:
   Susan Salomon 212-608-3352 x206
First Deputy Capital Defender, Rochester Office:
   William Easton 716-232-5480
Counsel to Board of Directors:
   Peter Sistrom 212-608-3352 x209

Capital District Regional Off-Track Betting Corporation

510 Smith St
Schenectady, NY 12305
518-344-5200 Fax: 518-370-5460
Web site: www.capitalotb.com

Chair:
   Marcel Webb 518-344-5225
President & Chief Executive Officer:
   Michael J Connery 518-344-5225
Vice President:
   John F Signor 518-344-5224
Executive Assist to the President:
   Tod Grenci 518-344-5408
Secretary:
   G James Traub 518-482-5615
Chief Fiscal Officer:
   Nancy Madrian 518-344-5233
General Counsel:
   Robert Hemsworth. 518-344-5298/fax: 518-370-0558

Capital District Regional Planning Commission

One Park Place
Suite 102
Albany, NY 12205-1606
518-453-0850 Fax: 518-453-0856
e-mail: cdrpc@cdrpc.org
Web site: www.cdrpc.org

Executive Director:
   Rocco Ferraro 518-453-0850

Capital District Transportation Authority

110 Watervliet Ave
Albany, NY 12206
518-482-1125 Fax: 518-689-3090
Web site: www.cdta.org

Chair:
   David M Stackrow 518-482-1125
Vice Chair:
   James Cappiello 518-482-1125
Executive Director:
   Stephen G Bland. 518-482-1125
Deputy Executive Director, Development:
   Jack Reilly 518-482-4199
General Counsel:
   David Winans 518-482-6359
Chief Fiscal Officer:
   Milt Pratt. 518-482-6258
Chief of Staff & Director, Marketing:
   Carm Basile 518-482-3371/fax: 518-446-0675

Catskill Off-Track Betting Corporation

PO Box 3000
Pomona, NY 10970
845-362-0400 Fax: 845-362-0419
e-mail: otb@interbets.com
Web site: www.interbets.com

President:
   Donald J Groth 845-362-0400

Central New York Regional Market Authority

2100 Park St
Syracuse, NY 13208
315-422-8647 Fax: 315-422-6897

Offices and agencies appear in alphabetical order.

Policy Areas

Executive Director:
  Benjamin Vitale 315-422-8647
Counsel:
  Robert Scalione 315-422-1311

Central New York Regional Transportation Authority
200 Cortland Ave
PO Box 820
Syracuse, NY 13205-0820
315-442-3300 Fax: 315-442-3337
Web site: www.centro.org

Chair, Board of Directors:
  Robert E Colucci 315-442-3300
Executive Director:
  Frank Kobliski 315-442-3360
  e-mail: fkoblisk@centro.org
Senior Vice President, Finance & Administration:
  Steven M Share. 315-442-3358
Senior Vice President, Corporate Operations:
  John Renock 315-442-3388

Central Pine Barrens Joint Planning & Policy Commission
PO Box 587
3525 Sunrise Hwy, 2nd Fl
Great River, NY 11739
631-224-2604 Fax: 631-224-7653
e-mail: info@pb.state.ny.us
Web site: www.pb.state.ny.us

Governor's Appointee & Reg 1 Director DEC:
  Peter A Scully. 631-224-2604
Executive Director:
  Ray Corwin. 631-224-2604
Chair & Suffolk County Executive:
  Steven A Levy 631-224-2604
Member & Brookhaven Town Supervisor:
  John Jay LaValle 631-224-2604
Member & Riverhead Town Supervisor:
  Philip J Cardinale 631-224-2604
Member & Southampton Town Supervisor:
  Patrick A Heaney 631-224-2604

City University Construction Fund
555 W 57th St, 10th Fl
New York, NY 10019
212-541-0171 Fax: 212-541-0401

Chair:
  Harvey Auerbach 212-541-0171
Executive Director:
  Emma Espino Macari. 212-794-5315
  e-mail: emma.macari@mail.cuny.edu
Counsel:
  Frederick Schaffer 212-794-5506
Chief Fiscal Officer:
  Catherine Yang. 212-541-0458
  e-mail: catherine.yang@mail.cuny.edu
Fiscal Coordinator:
  Denise Phillips 212-541-0190
  e-mail: denise.phillips@mail.cuny.edu

Delaware River Basin Commission
25 State Police Drive
PO Box 7360
West Trenton, NJ 08628-0360
609-883-9500 Fax: 609-883-9522
Web site: www.drbc.net

Chair:
  George Pataki. 518-474-8390
Executive Director:
  Carol R Collier 609-883-9500 x200
  e-mail: carol.collier@drbc.state.nj.us
Secretary:
  Pamela Bush 609-883-9500 x203
  e-mail: pamela.bush@drbc.state.nj.us
General Counsel:
  Kenneth J Warren 215-977-2276
Communications Manager:
  Clarke Rupert. 609-883-9500 x260

Development Authority of the North Country
Dulles State Office Bldg, 4th Fl
317 Washington St
Watertown, NY 13601
315-785-2593 Fax: 315-785-2591
Web site: www.danc.org

Chair:
  Douglas L Murray 315-785-2593
Executive Director:
  Robert S Juravich. 315-785-2593
  e-mail: juravich@danc.org
Engineer:
  Carrie M Tuttle. 315-782-8661
  e-mail: ctuttle@danc.org
Deputy Executive Director:
  Thomas R Sauter 315-785-2593
  e-mail: tsauter@danc.org
Fiscal Officer:
  John D Donaghy. 315-785-2593
  e-mail: jdonaghy@danc.org
Solid Waste Management Facility General Manager:
  E William Seifried 315-232-3236
Director, Project Development:
  Kevin J Jordan 315-785-2593
  e-mail: kjordan@danc.org
Technical Services Supervisor:
  John J Condino 315-232-3236

Empire State Development Corporation
633 Third Ave
New York, NY 10017-6706
212-803-3100 Fax: 212-803-3735
e-mail: esd@empire.state.ny.us
Web site: www.empire.state.ny.us

30 South Pearl St
Albany, NY 12245
518-292-5100

Chair & Chief Executive Officer:
  Charles A Gargano. 212-803-3700

Offices and agencies appear in alphabetical order.

Executive Vice President & Chief Operating Officer:
  Eileen Mildenberger.................................212-803-3730
Executive Vice President:
  Michael Wilton.....................................518-292-5100
Communications Director:
  Ron Jury........................212-803-3740/fax: 212-803-3735
  e-mail: rjury@empire.state.ny.us
Senior Vice President, General Counsel:
  Anita W Laremont...................................212-803-3750
Senior Vice President, Chief Administrative Officer:
  Joseph J LaCivita..................................518-292-5102
Senior Vice President, Policy & Research:
  John Bacheller.....................................518-292-5115
Senior Vice President, Marketing, Tourism, Advertising, International:
  Neville Bugwadia...................................212-803-2244

Great Lakes Commission

2805 S Industrial Hwy
Ste 100
Ann Arbor, MI 48104-6791
734-971-9135 Fax: 734-971-9150
e-mail: glc@glc.org
Web site: www.glc.org

Chair:
  Thomas E Huntley 651-296-2228
Vice Chair:
  vacant 734-971-9135
Chair, New York State Delegation:
  vacant 734-971-9135
Interim Executive Director:
  Thomas R Crane.....................................734-971-9135
Program Manager, Resource Management:
  Thomas R Crane 734-971-9135 x123
Program Manager, Transportation & Sustainable Development:
  Dave Knight....................................734-971-9135 x131
Program Manager, Communications & Internet Technology:
  Christine Manninen.............................734-971-9135 x112
Program Manager, Data & Information Management:
  Roger Gauthier 734-971-9135 x113
Program Manager, Environmental Quality:
  Matthew Doss 734-971-9135 x104

Hudson River-Black River Regulating District

350 Northern Blvd
Albany, NY 12204
518-465-3491 Fax: 518-432-2485
e-mail: hrbrrd@choiceonemail.com
Web site: www.hrbrrd.com

Chair:
  Anne B McDonald 518-465-3491
Executive Director:
  Richard Lefebvre 518-465-3491
Chief Engineer:
  Robert S Foltan....................................518-465-3491
Counsel:
  Shari Calnero 518-465-3491

Interest on Lawyer Account (IOLA) Fund of the State of NY

11 East 44th St
Ste 1406
New York, NY 10017-0055
646-865-1541 Fax: 646-865-1545
e-mail: iolaf@iola.org
Web site: www.iola.org

Chair:
  William R Nojay....................................646-865-1541
Executive Director:
  Lorna Blake 646-865-1541
  e-mail: lblake@iola.org
General Counsel:
  Stephen Brooks.....................................646-865-1541
  e-mail: sbrooks@iola.org
Assistant Director & Director of Administration:
  Odette M McNeil 646-865-1541
  e-mail: omcneil@iola.org

Interstate Environmental Commission

311 W 43rd St, Ste 201
New York, NY 10036
212-582-0380 Fax: 212-581-5719
e-mail: iecmail@iec-nynjct.org
Web site: www.iec-nynjct.org

Chair:
  John Walsh...212-582-0380
Executive Director & Chief Engineer:
  Howard Golub 212-582-0380
General Counsel:
  Eileen D Millett 212-582-0380

Interstate Oil & Gas Compact Commission

PO Box 53127
Oklahoma City, OK 73152-3127
405-525-3556 Fax: 405-525-3592
e-mail: iogcc@iogcc.state.ok.us
Web site: www.iogcc.state.ok.us

Chair (Governor of NM):
  Bill Richardson....................................505-476-2200
Vice Chair:
  Donald L Mason.....................................614-466-3905
Executive Director:
  Christine Hansen 405-525-3556
New York State Official Representative:
  Bradley J Field 518-402-8076

Lake George Park Commission

Fort George Rd
PO Box 749
Lake George, NY 12845-0749
518-668-9347 Fax: 518-668-5001
e-mail: info@lgpc.state.ny.us
Web site: www.lgpc.state.ny.us

Chair:
  Bruce E Young......................................518-668-9347

Policy Areas

Offices and agencies appear in alphabetical order.

Vice Chair:
Anthony P Reale 518-668-9347
Executive Director:
Michael P White 518-668-9347
Secretary/Treasurer:
Margaret M Stewart 518-668-9347

Lawyers' Fund for Client Protection

119 Washington Ave
Albany, NY 12210
518-434-1935 Fax: 518-434-5641
e-mail: info@nylawfund.org
Web site: www.nylawfund.org

Chair:
Eleanor Breitel Alter 518-434-1935
Vice Chair:
Bernard F Ashe 518-434-1935
Executive Director & Counsel:
Timothy O'Sullivan 518-434-1935
Deputy Counsel:
Michael J Knight 518-434-1935

Legislative Bill Drafting Commission

Capitol, Rm 308
Albany, NY 12224
518-455-7500 Fax: 518-455-7598

Commissioner:
Ronald H Backer 518-455-7501
e-mail: backer@lbdc.state.ny.us
Commissioner:
Randall G Bluth 518-455-7506
e-mail: bluth@lbdc.state.ny.us
Counsel:
Jamie-Lynne Elacqua 518-455-7538
e-mail: elacqua@lbdc.state.ny.us

Legislative Retrieval System . . . . fax: 518-455-7679
55 Elk St, Albany, NY 12210
800-356-6566 Fax: 518-455-7679
Director:
Barbara Lett 518-455-7673
e-mail: lett@lbdc.state.ny.us

Long Island Power Authority

333 Earle Ovington Blvd, Ste 403
Uniondale, NY 11553
516-222-7700 Fax: 516-222-9137
e-mail: info@lipower.org
Web site: www.lipower.org

Chair:
Richard M Kessel 516-222-7700
General Counsel:
Stanley Klimberg 516-222-7700
Vice President, Communications:
Bert Cunningham 516-222-7700
e-mail: bcunningham@lipower.org
Director, Government Relations:
William Davidson 516-719-9852

MTA (Metropolitan Transportation Authority)

347 Madison Ave
New York, NY 10017
212-878-7000 Fax: 212-878-7030
Web site: www.mta.info

Chairman & Chief Executive Officer:
Peter S Kalikow 212-878-7200
Executive Director/Chief Operating Officer:
Katherine N Lapp 212-878-7274
Deputy Executive Director, Director of Security:
William Morange 212-878-7155
Deputy Executive Director, Corporate & Community Affairs:
Christopher P Boylan 212-878-7160
Deputy Executive Director, Policy/Special Advisor on Safety &
Environmental Issues:
Linda Kleinbaum 212-878-7206
Director, Labor Relations:
Gary Dellaverson 212-878-7438
Director, Budgets & Financial Management:
Gary Lanigan 212-878-7236
Director, Finance:
Patrick McCoy 212-878-7278
Director, Human Resources:
Margaret M Connor 212-878-7017
Director, Government Affairs:
Michelle Goldstein 212-878-7313/fax: 212-878-7050
MTA Chief of Police:
Thomas Lawless 212-878-1146
Press Secretary:
Tom Kelly 212-878-7440

MTA Bridges & Tunnels

Triborough Station, PO Box 35
New York, NY 10035
646-252-7000 Fax: 646-252-7408
Web site: www.mta.info/bandt

Chairman & Chief Executive Officer:
Peter S Kalikow 212-878-7200
President:
Michael C Ascher 212-360-3100
Vice President & Chief Engineer:
Stanley C Vonasek 212-360-3080
Vice President, Labor Relations:
Sharon Gallo-Kotcher 212-360-3015
Vice President, Operations:
Martha Walther 212-360-3060
Vice President, Procurement & Materials:
Roy Parks 646-252-7084
Vice President, Staff Services & Chief of Staff:
Catherine T Sweeney 646-252-7421
Chief Financial Officer:
David Moretti 646-252-7100
Chief Technology Officer:
Tariq Habib 646-252-7230
General Counsel:
Robert O'Brien 646-252-7617
Director, Public Affairs:
Frank Pascual 646-252-7416

MTA Long Island Bus

700 Commercial Ave
Garden City, NY 11530

Offices and agencies appear in alphabetical order.

516-542-0100 Fax: 516-542-1428
Web site: www.mta.info/libus

Chairman & Chief Executive Officer:
   Peter S Kalikow 212-878-7200
President:
   Neil S Yellin 516-542-0100 x4525
Senior Vice President, Operations:
   William Norwich 516-542-0100 x4334
Vice President, Finance:
   Joseph Pokorny 516-542-0100 x4439
Vice President, Adminstration:
   James R Campbell 516-542-0100 x4345
General Counsel:
   Cheryl Hartell 516-542-0100 x4429

MTA Long Island Rail Road

Jamaica Station
Jamaica, NY 11435
718-558-7400 Fax: 718-558-8212
Web site: www.mta.info/lirr

Chairman & Chief Executive Officer:
   Peter S Kalikow 212-878-7200
President:
   James J Dermody 718-558-8252
   e-mail: jjdermo@lirr.org
Executive Vice President:
   Albert Cosenza 718-558-7993
   e-mail: accosen@lirr.org
Chief Information Officer:
   Joseph M DeCarlo 718-588-8166
   e-mail: jmdecar@lirr.org
Vice President & Chief Fiscal Officer:
   Nicholas DiMola 718-558-7777
   e-mail: ndimola@lirr.org
Vice President, General Counsel & Secretary:
   Mary J Mahon. 718-558-8264
   e-mail: mmahon@lirr.org
Vice President, Labor Relations:
   Jerry Moran 718-558-7405
   e-mail: gmmoran@lirr.org
Vice President, Market Development & Public Affairs:
   Brian P Dolan 718-558-7301
   e-mail: bpdolan@lirr.org
Vice President, Service, Planning, Technology & Capital Program
   Management:
   John Coulter 718-558-7363
   e-mail: jwcoult@lirr.org
Vice President, System Safety:
   Jose R Fernandez 718-558-7711
   e-mail: jrferna@lirr.org
Chief Fire Marshal:
   Louis Scida. 718-558-3007

MTA Metro-North Railroad

347 Madison Ave
New York, NY 10017
212-340-2677 Fax: 212-340-4995
Web site: www.mta.info/mnr

Chairman & Chief Executive Officer:
   Peter S Kalikow 212-878-7200
President:
   Peter A Cannito 212-340-2677

Executive Vice President:
   Genevieve Firnhaber 212-340-2636
Vice President & General Counsel:
   Richard Bernard 212-340-4933
Vice President, Human Resources & Diversity:
   Gregory Bradley 212-340-2172
Vice President, Operations:
   George Walker 212-499-4300
Vice President, Planning & Development:
   Howard Permut. 212-340-2500
Director, Corporate & Media Relations:
   Donna Evans 212-672-1201/fax: 212-672-1220
Director, Government & Community Relations:
   Mark Mannix 212-340-3024

MTA New York City Transit

370 Jay St
Brooklyn, NY 11201
718-330-3000 Fax: 718-596-2146
Web site: www.mta.info/nyct

Chairman & Chief Executive Officer:
   Peter S Kalikow 212-878-7200
President:
   Lawrence G Reuter. 718-243-4321
Executive Vice President:
   Barbara R Spencer 718-243-3052
Senior Vice President, Buses:
   Millard Seay. 718-243-4186
Senior Vice President, Capital Program Management:
   Cosema Crawford. 646-252-3034
Senior Vice President, Corp Communications:
   Paul Fleuranges 718-243-8881
Senior Vice President, Subways:
   Michael Lombardi 718-243-4567
Senior Vice President, System Safety:
   Cheryl Kennedy 718-243-4780
Vice President & General Counsel:
   Martin Schnabel 718-694-3900
Vice President, Labor Relations:
   Ralph Agritelley 718-243-3218
Chief Officer, Staten Island Railway:
   John McCabe 718-876-8239

MTA Office of the Inspector General

111 West 40th St
5th Fl
New York, NY 10018
800-682-4448 Fax: 212-878-0003
e-mail: complaints@mtaig.org
Web site: www.mtaig.state.ny.us

Inspector General:
   Matthew D Sansverie 212-878-0007
   e-mail: msansver@mtaig.org
1st Deputy Inspector General:
   Stephen M Spahr 212-878-0030
Deputy Inspector General, Intergovernmental & Public Affairs:
   James Bono. 212-878-0000
   e-mail: jbono@mtaig.org
General Counsel:
   Carl Copertino 212-878-0074
   e-mail: copertino@mtaig.org

Offices and agencies appear in alphabetical order.

Policy Areas

Municipal Assistance Corporation for the City of New York

420 Lexington Avenue
Room 1756
New York, NY 10170
212-840-8255 Fax: 212-840-8570
e-mail: macnyc@earthlink.net

Chairman:
Jonathan A Ballan.................212-840-8255 or 212-692-6772
Executive Director:
Nancy H Henze....................................212-840-8255

Nassau Regional Off-Track Betting Corporation

220 Fulton Ave
Hempstead, NY 11550
516-572-2800 Fax: 516-572-2840
e-mail: webmaster@nassauotb.com
Web site: www.nassauotb.com

President:
Lawrence Aaronson 516-572-2800
Executive Director of Operations:
Richard T Bennett, Jr.......................516-572-2800 x155
Director, Public Affairs:
Joseph Galante................................516-572-2800 x152
Comptroller:
Kevin R Conroy...............................516-572-2800 x141

New England Interstate Water Pollution Control Commission

116 John St
Lowell, MA 01852-1124
978-323-7929 Fax: 978-323-7919
e-mail: mail@neiwpcc.org
Web site: www.neiwpcc.org

Chair:
Glenn Haas......................................617-292-5748
Vice Chair:
Harry Stewart 603-271-3308
Acting Commissioner, New York State:
Denise M Sheehan 518-485-8940
Executive Director:
Ronald F Poltak 978-323-7929
Deputy Director:
Susan Sullivan 978-323-7929

New York City Housing Development Corp

110 William St
10th FL
New York, NY 10038
212-227-5500 Fax: 212-227-6865
e-mail: info@nychdc.com
Web site: www.nychdc.com

Chairperson:
Shaun Donovan 212-863-6100
President:
Emily Youssouf 212-227-3600

Executive Vice President, Chief of Staff:
John Crotty 212-227-6846/fax: 212-227-9807
Senior Vice President & General Counsel:
Richard Froehlich................................212-227-7435
Senior Vice President, Portfolio Management:
Teresa Gigliello 212-227-9133
Senior Vice President & Chief Fiscal Officer:
Carol Kostik.....................212-227-7494/fax: 212-227-6757
Director, Marketing & Public Affairs:
Tracy Paurowski 212-227-9496/fax: 212-227-6846

New York City Residential Mortgage Insurance Corporation

Chair:
Shaun Donovan 212-863-6100
President:
Emily Youssouf 212-227-3600
Board Member:
Gina Bolden-Rivera 718-802-1212
Board Member:
Harry E Gould 212-227-5500
Board Member:
Michael W Kelly 212-227-5500
Board Member:
Pater Madonia....................................212-788-2728
Board Member:
Charles G Moerdler 212-227-5500
Board Member:
Mark Page..212-788-5900
Board Member:
Martha E Stark 212-669-4855

New York City Off-Track Betting Corp

1501 Broadway
New York, NY 10036-5572
212-221-5200 Fax: 212-221-8025
Web site: www.nycotb.com

President:
Raymond V Casey 212-704-5101
Executive Vice President/Chief Operating Officer:
John Van Lindt...................................212-704-5108
Chief of Staff:
Denise DePrima 212-704-5107
Executive Vice President/Chief Fiscal Officer:
Peter Aranow................................212-221-5200 x5214
Executive Vice President/General Counsel:
Ira H Block 212-221-5200 x5311
Executive Director, Legislative Affairs:
Daniel Wray.................................212-221-5200 x5230
Inspector General:
Robert E Unger 212-704-5642/fax: 212-221-8479
Senior Vice President, Marketing, Media & Communications:
Ron Ceisler 212-704-5152/fax: 212-704-5141
Senior Vice President, New Business, Real Estate, Facilities & Community Affairs:
Denis McManus.............................212-221-5200 x5583
Vacant

New York City School Construction Authority

30-30 Thomson Ave
Long Island City, NY 11101-3045
718-472-8000 Fax: 718-472-8840
Web site: www.nycsca.org

Offices and agencies appear in alphabetical order.

Chair/Chancellor:
    Joel I Klein 718-472-8000
President & Chief Executive Officer:
    William H Goldstein 718-472-8001/fax: 718-472-8009
Vice President & General Counsel:
    Ross J Holden 718-472-8220/fax: 718-472-8088
Senior Director, Real Estate:
    Lorraine Grillo. 718-472-8216/fax: 718-472-8040
Corporate Secretary:
    Michael Szabaga 718-472-8302/fax: 718-472-8088

New York Convention Center Operating Corp

655 W 34th St
New York, NY 10001-1188
212-216-2000 Fax: 212-216-2588
e-mail: moreinfo@javitscenter.com
Web site: www.javitscenter.com

President & Chief Executive Officer:
    Gerald T McQueen. 212-216-2130
Vice President, Operations:
    Myles McGrane 212-216-2211
Director, Public Affairs:
    Michael Eisgrau. 212-216-2176/fax: 212-216-2895

New York Metropolitan Transportation Council

199 Water St
New York, NY 10038
212-383-7200 Fax: 212-383-2418
Web site: www.nymtc.org

Executive Director:
    Joel Ettinger 212-383-7363
Deputy Director, Administration Group:
    Alan Borenstein 212-383-7363
    e-mail: aborenstein@dot.state.ny.us
Assistant Director, Planning Group:
    Gerard J Bogacz. 212-383-7260
Assistant Director, Technical Group:
    Kuo-Ann Chiao 212-383-7212

New York Power Authority

30 South Pearl St
Albany, NY 12207
518-433-6700 Fax: 518-433-1406

123 Main St
White Plains, NY 10601
914-681-6200
Fax: 914-390-8190

Chairman:
    Louis P Ciminelli 518-433-6700
President & Chief Executive Officer:
    Eugene W Zeltmann. 518-433-6719
Senior Vice President, Public & Government Affairs:
    Peter Barden 914-390-8160/fax: 914-390-8190
Director, Community Relations:
    Paul Finnegan. 518-433-6740
Director, Public Relations:
    Jack Murphy 914-390-8198/fax: 914-390-8190
    e-mail: jack.murphy@nypa.gov

New York State Assn of Fire Districts

PO Box 99
Mastic, NY 11950
800-520-9594 or 631-281-4577 Fax: 631-399-0873
Web site: www.firedistnys.com

President:
    Frank A Nocerino 516-799-8575/fax: 516-799-2516
First Vice President:
    Kenneth Hoffarth. 914-946-2599/fax: 914-682-5208
Second Vice President:
    Randall Rider. 716-875-0183/fax: 716-876-9566
Secretary & Treasurer:
    John F Dolezal. 800-520-9594/fax: 631-399-0873
Counsel:
    William N Young 800-349-2904/fax: 518-869-5142

New York State Athletic Commission

123 William St
20th Fl
New York, NY 10038-3804
212-417-5700 Fax: 212-417-4987
e-mail: athletic@dos.state.ny.us
Web site: www.dos.state.ny.us/athletic.html

Chair:
    Ron Scott Stevens. 212-417-5700
Secretary:
    Robert Limerick 212-417-5700

New York State Board of Law Examiners

Corporate Plaza Bldg 3
254 Washington Ave Ext
Albany, NY 12203
518-452-8700 Fax: 518-452-0175
Web site: www.nybarexam.org

Chair:
    Diane F Bosse. 518-452-8700
Executive Director:
    John J McAlary. 518-452-8700

New York State Bridge Authority

Mid-Hudson Bridge Plaza
PO Box 1010
Highland, NY 12528
845-691-7245 Fax: 845-691-3560
Web site: www.nysba.net

Chair:
    Edmund A Fares. 845-691-7245
Vice Chair:
    Morton Marshak 845-691-7245
Executive Director:
    George C Sinnott 845-691-7245
Deputy Executive Director:
    James J Bresnan 845-691-7245
    e-mail: jbresnan@nysba.state.ny.us
General Counsel:
    Carl Whitbeck. 518-828-4107

Policy Areas

Offices and agencies appear in alphabetical order.

Public Information Officer, Director Planning & Public Relations:
   Mark Sheedy 845-691-7245/fax: 845-691-3636
   e-mail: msheedy@nysba.state.ny.us

New York State Commission of Correction

30 Wolfe Road
4th FL
Albany, NY 12205
518-485-2346 Fax: 518-485-2467
e-mail: infoscoc@scoc.state.ny.us
Web site: www.scoc.state.ny.us

Chair/Commissioner:
   Alan J Croce 518-485-2346
Assistant to Chair:
   Patricia Amati 518-485-2330
Special Counsel to Chair:
   Michael F Donegan 518-485-2346
Director, Human Resource Management:
   Marylyn Sullivan 518-457-6110
Director, Operations:
   James Lawrence 518-485-2346
Chair, Medical Review Board:
   Frederick C Lamy 518-485-2346
Press Secretary:
   Jessica Scaperotti 518-485-2346

New York State Commission on Judicial Nomination

c/o Phillips Nizer LLP
666 Fifth Ave, 28th Fl
New York, NY 10103-0084
212-841-0715 Fax: 212-262-5152

Chair:
   John F O'Mara 607-733-4635
Counsel:
   Stuart A Summit 212-977-9700
   e-mail: ssummit@phillipsnizer.com
Assistant Counsel:
   Stephen P Younger 212-336-2000

New York State Commission on Quality of Care for the Mentally Disabled

401 State St
Schenectady, NY 12305-2397
518-388-2888 Fax: 518-388-2800
Web site: www.cqc.state.ny.us

Chair:
   Gary D O'Brien 518-388-1281
Commissioner:
   Elizabeth W Stack 518-388-2888
Executive Assistant:
   Mindy Becker 518-388-1281
Press Officer:
   Gary W Masline 518-388-1270/fax: 518-388-1275

Administrative Services Bureau

Director:
   Richard H Schaefer 518-388-2804

Advisory Council

Chair:
   Vacant 518-388-1277
Secretary:
   Darlene Stefani 518-388-1270/fax: 518-388-1275

Advocacy Services Bureau

Director:
   Marcel Chaine 518-388-2892

Counsel, Policy Analysis, Fiscal Investigations

Counsel/Director:
   Robert J Boehlert 518-388-1270

Medical Review Board

Executive Secretary:
   Thomas Harmon 518-388-1281

Quality Assurance

Director:
   Mark Keegan 518-388-2888

Surrogate Decision-Making Committees Program

Program Director:
   Thomas Fisher 518-388-2820

New York State Commission on the Restoration of the Capitol

Corning Tower, 40th Fl
Empire State Plaza
Albany, NY 12242
518-473-0341 Fax: 518-486-5720

Executive Director:
   Andrea J Lazarski 518-473-0341
   e-mail: andrea.lazarski@ogs.state.ny.us

New York State Disaster Preparedness Commission

Building 22, Suite 101
1220 Washington Ave
Albany, NY 12226-2251
518-457-2222 Fax: 518-457-9930
Web site: www.nysemo.state.ny.us

Executive Director:
   James W McMahon 518-402-2227
Chief of Operations, NYSEMO:
   Robert Olazagasti 518-457-9987/fax: 518-457-9930

New York State Dormitory Authority

539 Franklin St
Buffalo, NY 14202-1109
716-884-9780 Fax: 716-884-9787

One Penn Plaza
52nd Fl
New York, NY 10119-0098
212-273-5000
Fax: 212-273-5121

515 Broadway
Albany, NY 12207-2964

Offices and agencies appear in alphabetical order.

518-257-3000
Fax: 518-257-3100

Chair:
 Gail H Gordon .518-257-3180/fax: 518-257-3183
Executive Director:
 Maryanne Gridley 518-257-3180/fax: 518-257-3183
Deputy Executive Director:
 Michael T Corrigan 518-257-3192/fax: 518-257-3183
Chief Fiscal Officer:
 John G Pasicznyk 518-257-3630/fax: 518-257-3100
 e-mail: jpasiczn@dasny.org
General Counsel:
 Jeffrey M Pohl .518-257-3120/fax: 518-257-3101
 e-mail: jpohl@dasny.org
Associate General Counsel:
 Debbie Drescher 518-257-3120
Associate General Counsel:
 George Weissman 518-257-3120
Associate General Counsel:
 Deborah Paden 518-257-3120
Managing Director, Construction:
 Douglas M Van Vleck 518-257-3200/fax: 518-257-3100
 e-mail: dvanvlec@dasny.org
Managing Director, Policy & Program Development:
 Lora K Lefebvre 518-257-3163/fax: 518-257-3387
 e-mail: llefebvr@dasny.org
Managing Director, Public Finance:
 Cheryl Ishmael 518-257-3362/fax: 518-257-3100
 e-mail: cishmael@dasny.org
Director, Communications & Marketing:
 Paul Burgdorf .518-257-3380/fax: 518-257-3387
 e-mail: pburgdor@dasny.org
Press Officer:
 Claudia Hutton 518-257-3382/fax: 518-257-3387
 e-mail: chutton@dasny.org

New York State Energy Research & Development Authority

17 Columbia Circle
Albany, NY 12203-6399
518-862-1090 Fax: 518-862-1091
Web site: www.nyserda.org

Chairman:
 Vincent A DeIorio 518-862-1090
President:
 Peter R Smith 518-862-1090 x3220
 e-mail: prs@nyserda.org
General Counsel:
 Roger D Avent 518-862-1090 x3333
 e-mail: rda@nyserda.org
Vice President, Administration:
 Wendy M Shave 518-862-1090 x3226
 e-mail: wms@nyserda.org
Vice President, Programs:
 Robert Callender 518-862-1090 x3233
 e-mail: rgc@nyserda.org
Treasurer:
 Jeffrey J Pitkin 518-862-1090 x3223
 e-mail: jjp@nyserda.org
Director, Communications:
 Thomas G Collins 518-862-1090 x3250/fax: 518-464-8249
 e-mail: tgc@nyserda.org

New York State Environmental Facilities Corp

625 Broadway
Albany, NY 12207-2997
518-402-6924 or 800-882-9721 Fax: 518-486-9323
Web site: www.nysefc.org

Chair:
 Denise M Sheehan 518-402-6924
President:
 Thomas J Kelly 518-402-6924
Executive Vice President:
 David Sterman 518-402-6924
General Counsel:
 James R Levine 518-402-6969
Chief Financial Officer:
 James T Gebhardt 518-402-6985
Director, Corporate Communications & Records Access Officer:
 Susan Mayer 518-402-6957
Director, Corporate Operations:
 Barbara Wayman 518-486-9267
Director, Engineering & Program Management:
 Robert Davis 518-402-7396
Director, Technical Advisory Services:
 Frederick McCandless 518-402-7461

New York State Ethics Commission

39 Columbia Street
4th FL
Albany, NY 12207-2717
518-432-8207 Fax: 518-432-8255
e-mail: ethics@dos.state.ny.us
Web site: www.dos.state.ny.us/ethc/ethics.html

Chair:
 Paul Shechtman 518-432-8208
Commissioner:
 Robert J Giuffra, Jr 518-432-8208
Commissioner:
 Carl H Loewenson, Jr 518-432-8208
Commissioner:
 Lynn Millane 518-432-8208
Commissioner:
 Susan E Shepard 518-432-8208
Executive Director:
 Karl J Sleight 518-432-8208
Counsel:
 Bruce A Androphy 518-432-8250
Public Information Officer:
 Walter C Ayres 518-432-8210
 e-mail: wayres@dos.state.ny.us

New York State Financial Control Board

123 William St
23rd Fl
New York, NY 10038-3804
212-417-5046 Fax: 212-417-5055
e-mail: nysfcb@fcb.state.ny.us
Web site: www.fcb.state.ny.us

Acting Executive Director:
 Jeffrey Sommer 212-417-5066
Deputy Director, Expenditure Analysis:
 Dennis DeLisle 212-417-5069

Offices and agencies appear in alphabetical order.

121

Deputy Director, Financial & Capital Analysis:
  Jewel A Douglas 212-417-5067
Acting Deputy Director, Economic & Revenue Analysis:
  Martin Fischman. 212-417-5068
Associate Director:
  Mattie W Taylor 212-417-5053

New York State Higher Education Services Corp (NYSHESC)

99 Washington Ave
Albany, NY 12255
518-473-7087 or 888-697-4372 Fax: 518-474-2839
Web site: www.hesc.org

President & Chief Executive Officer:
  Michael R Wilton, Jr 518-474-5592
  e-mail: mwilton@hesc.org
Executive Vice President:
  Pierre L Alric 518-474-5775
  e-mail: palric@hesc.org
Senior Vice President, Corporate Finance & Chief Fiscal Officer:
  Lisa Smith. 518-473-1200
  e-mail: lsmith@hesc.org
Deputy Counsel:
  Marin Gibson 518-474-3219
  e-mail: mgibson@hesc.org
Senior Vice President, Corporate Relations:
  Robert E Butler. 518-473-2523
  e-mail: rbutler@hesc.org
Senior Vice President, Communications:
  Ronald Kermani 518-402-3349
  e-mail: rkermani@hesc.org
Senior Vice President, Information Technology:
  Victor Stucchi. 518-474-7083
  e-mail: vstucchi@hesc.org
Senior Vice President, Customer Relations:
  Thomas Dalton 518-473-0733
  e-mail: tdalton@hesc.org
Acting Director, Human Resources Management:
  Linda Dillon 518-474-0510
  e-mail: ldillon@hesc.org

New York State Housing Finance Agency (HFA)

641 Lexington Ave
New York, NY 10022
212-688-4000 Fax: 212-872-0678
Web site: www.nyhomes.org

Chair:
  Jerome M Becker 212-688-4000
President & Chief Executive Officer:
  Stephen J Hunt 212-688-4000
Senior Vice President, Chief Operating Officer & Chief Fiscal Officer:
  Ralph J Madalena. 212-688-4000
Senior Vice President & Counsel:
  Justin Driscoll. 212-688-4000
Senior Vice President & Special Assistant to President/Chief Executive
  Officer for Policy Development & Programs:
  James P Angley 212-688-4000
Senior Vice President, Debt Issuance:
  Bernard Abramowitz 212-688-4000 x530
Vice President, Director of Development:
  Jonathan Cortrell 212-688-4000 x688
Vice President, Policy & Planning:
  Tracy A Oats 212-688-4000 x678

Vice President, Intergovernmental Affairs:
  Michael R Houseknecht 518-434-2118/fax: 518-432-7158

Affordable Housing Corporation
Senior Vice President & Special Assistant to President/Chief Executive
  Officer for Policy Development & Programs:
  James P Angley 212-688-4000

New York State Judicial Conduct Commission

61 Broadway
12th Floor
New York, NY 10006
212-809-0566 Fax: 212-949-8864
e-mail: webmaster@scjc.state.ny.us
Web site: www.scjc.state.ny.us

Henry T Berger
Robert H Tembeckjian
Chief Attorney, Albany Office:
  Cathleen Cenci 518-474-5617
John J Postel
Jean M Savanyu

New York State Law Reporting Bureau

One Commerce Plaza, Ste 1750
Albany, NY 12210
518-474-8211 Fax: 518-463-6869
Web site: www.courts.state.ny.us/reporter

State Reporter:
  Gary D Spivey 518-474-8211
Deputy State Reporter:
  Charles A Ashe. 518-474-8211
  e-mail: cashe@courts.state.ny.us

New York State Law Revision Commission

80 New Scotland Rd
Albany, NY 12208
518-472-5858 Fax: 518-445-2303
Web site: www.lawrevision.state.ny.us

Chairman:
  Robert M Pitler. 518-472-5858
Executive Director:
  Rose Mary Bailly 518-472-5858

New York State Liquor Authority

84 Holland Ave
Albany, NY 12208
518-473-6559 Fax: 518-402-4015
Web site: www.abc.state.ny.us

Chairman:
  Edward F Kelly. 518-473-6559
Commissioner:
  Lawrence J Gedda 212-961-8347
Commissioner:
  Joseph C Zarriello. 518-474-0810
Counsel:
  Thomas G McKeon 212-961-8317
Deputy Commissioner, Licensing, NYC:
  Fred J Gioffre 212-961-8301

Offices and agencies appear in alphabetical order.

Deputy Commissioner, Administration:
  J Mark Anderson 518-486-4767

New York State Mortgage Loan Enforcement & Administration Corporation
633 Third Ave, 35th Fl
New York, NY 10017-6754
212-803-3530 Fax: 212-803-3535
Web site: www.empire.state.ny.us

President & Chief Executive Officer:
  Garry P Ryan 212-803-3530
General Counsel:
  Anita W Laremont 212-803-3750
Chief Financial Officer:
  Frances Walton 212-803-3510
Public Affairs Officer:
  Deborah Wetzel 212-803-3740/fax: 212-803-3735
  e-mail: dwetzel@empire.state.ny.us

New York State Olympic Regional Development Authority
Olympic Center, 218 Main St
Lake Placid, NY 12946
518-523-1655 Fax: 518-523-9275
e-mail: info@orda.org
Web site: www.orda.org

Chair:
  Charles A Gargano 212-803-3700
President & Chief Executive Officer:
  Ted Blazer 518-523-1655 x201
Senior Vice President:
  Jeffrey Byrne 518-523-1655 x203
Olympic Center Manager:
  Denny Allen 518-523-1655 x222
Marketing Director:
  Fran Sayers 518-523-1655 x209
Director, Events:
  Jim Goff 518-523-1655 x212
Director, Finance:
  Kathy Bushy 518-523-1655 x208
Director, Communications:
  Sandy Caligiore 518-523-1655 x213
  e-mail: sandyc@orda.org

New York State Teachers' Retirement System
10 Corporate Woods Dr
Albany, NY 12211-2395
518-447-2666 Fax: 518-447-2695
Web site: www.nystrs.albany.ny.us

Executive Director:
  George M Philip 518-447-2666
  e-mail: execdir@nystrs.state.ny.us
General Counsel:
  Wayne Schneider 518-447-2722
Actuary:
  Lawrence A Johansen 518-447-2611
Director, Administration:
  William S O'Brien 518-447-2730
Director, Member Relations, Public Relations:
  David Daly 518-447-2910/fax: 518-447-2875

Real Estate Investment Officer:
  James D Campbell 518-447-2752
Securities Investment Officer:
  Joseph N Vet 518-447-2921

New York State Temporary Commission of Investigation
59 Maiden Lane, 31st Fl
New York, NY 10038
212-344-6660 Fax: 212-344-6868
Web site: www.sic.state.ny.us

Chair:
  Dineen A Riviezzo 212-344-6660
Chief Investigator:
  Anthony Hellmer 212-344-6660
Deputy Commissioner/Chief Counsel:
  Anthony T Cartusciello 212-344-6670

New York State Temporary Commission on Lobbying
2 Empire State Plaza, Ste 1701
Albany, NY 12223-1254
518-474-7126 Fax: 518-473-6492
e-mail: lobcom@attglobal.net
Web site: www.nylobby.state.ny.us

Commissioner:
  Joseph Dunn 518-474-7126
Chair:
  Bartley Livolsi 518-474-7126
Commissioner:
  Kenneth Barr 518-474-7126
Vice Chair:
  Patrick Bulgaro 518-474-7126
Commissioner:
  Andrew Cecci 518-474-7126
Commissioner:
  Peter Moschetti 518-474-7126
Executive Director:
  David M Grandeau 518-474-7126
Director, Program & Finance Administration:
  Jeannine M Clemente 518-474-7126
Public Information Officer:
  Kris Thompson 518-474-7126

New York State Thoroughbred Breeding & Development Fund
One Penn Plaza
Ste 725
New York, NY 10119
212-465-0660 Fax: 212-465-8205
Web site: www.nybreds.com

Chair:
  William A Levin 212-465-0660
Executive Director:
  Martin G Kinsella 212-465-0660

Offices and agencies appear in alphabetical order.

Policy Areas

123

New York State Thruway Authority

200 Southern Blvd
Albany, NY 12209
518-436-2700 Fax: 518-436-2899
Web site: www.thruway.state.ny.us

Chair:
  John L Buono 518-436-3000
Executive Director:
  Michael R Fleischer 518-436-2900
General Counsel:
  Sharon O'Conor 518-436-2840
Deputy Counsel:
  Katherine McCartney 518-436-3188
Director, Government Relations:
  Pamela Davis 518-436-2860/fax: 518-471-4340
Director, Public Information:
  Dan Gilbert 518-436-2983/fax: 518-426-3995
  e-mail: publicinfo@thruway.state.ny.us

New York State Canal Corporation

  Web site: www.canals.state.ny.us
Acting Director:
  Lawrence Frame 518-436-3055

New York State Tug Hill Commission

Dulles State Office Bldg
317 Washington St
Watertown, NY 13601
315-785-2380 Fax: 315-785-2574
e-mail: tughill@tughill.org
Web site: www.tughill.org

Chair:
  Arnold E Talgo 315-785-2380
Executive Director:
  John K Bartow, Jr 315-785-2380
  e-mail: john@tughill.org
Counsel:
  James P McClusky 315-232-4551

Niagara Falls Bridge Commission

PO Box 1031
Niagara Falls, NY 14302
716-285-6322 Fax: 716-282-3292
e-mail: general_inquiries@niagarafallsbridges.com
Web site: www.niagarafallsbridges.com

Chair:
  Robert E Lewis 716-285-6322
Vice Chair:
  Christine Whyte 716-285-6322
General Manager & Secretary/Treasurer:
  Thomas E Garlock 716-285-6322

Niagara Frontier Transportation Authority

181 Ellicott St
Buffalo, NY 14203
716-855-7300 Fax: 716-855-6655
e-mail: info@nfta.com
Web site: www.nfta.com

Chair:
  Luiz F Kahl 716-855-7233
Executive Director:
  Lawrence M Meckler 716-855-7369
  e-mail: lawrence_meckler@nfta.com
Chief Financial Officer:
  Deborah Leous 716-855-7250
General Counsel:
  David M Gregory 716-855-7230
Director, Aviation:
  William Vanecek 716-630-6030
Director, Employee Services:
  Ruth McManus 716-855-7373
Director, Surface Transportation:
  Walter D Zmuda 716-855-7252
General Manager, Engineering:
  Harold Matuszak 716-855-7383
Director, Public Affairs:
  C Douglas Hartmayer 716-855-7420

Northeastern Forest Fire Protection Commission

21 Parmenter Terrace
PO Box 6192
China Village, ME 04926-6192
207-968-3782 Fax: 207-968-3782
e-mail: necompact@pivot.net
Web site: www.nffpc.org

Chair of Commissioners:
  Bernard Drolet 418-647-3367
Past Chair of Commissioners:
  David Wight 207-968-3782
Executive Director:
  Thomas G Parent 207-968-3782
New York State Fire Supervisor:
  Col Andrew Jacob 518-457-5740
New York State Forester:
  Robert Davies 518-402-9405

Northeastern Queens Nature & Historical Preserve Commission

Bldg 635, Bayside St, Box 5
Fort Totten, NY 11359-1012
718-229-8805 Fax: 718-229-6131
e-mail: sneq@aol.com
Web site: www.sneq.com

Chair:
  Lucile Helfat 718-229-8805
Vice Chair:
  Bernard Haber 718-229-8805
Executive Director:
  Joan M Vogt 718-229-8805

Ogdensburg Bridge & Port Authority

One Bridge Plaza
Ogdensburg, NY 13669
315-393-4080 Fax: 315-393-7068
e-mail: obpa@ogdensport.com
Web site: www.ogdensport.com

Offices and agencies appear in alphabetical order.

Chair:
Connie G Augsbury 315-393-2636
Executive Director:
Joseph E Tracy 315-393-4080
e-mail: jtracy@ogdensport.com

Ohio River Valley Water Sanitation Commission
5735 Kellogg Ave
Cincinnati, OH 45228-1112
513-231-7719 Fax: 513-231-7761
Web site: www.orsanco.org

New York State Commissioner:
Douglas E Conroe.................................. 513-231-7719
New York State Commissioner:
Thomas L Servatius 513-231-7719
Acting New York State Commissioner:
Denise Sheehan 518-457-3446
Executive Director:
Alan H Vicory 513-231-7719
Legal Counsel:
Thomas D Heekin................................... 513-231-7719
Public Information Programs Manager:
Jeanne Ison 513-231-7719
e-mail: jison@orsanco.org

Port Authority of New York & New Jersey
225 Park Ave South
18th Fl
New York, NY 10003
212-435-7000 Fax: 212-435-6543
Web site: www.panynj.gov

Chair, NJ:
Anthony R Coscia.................................. 212-435-7000
Vice Chair, NY:
Charles A Gargano................................. 212-435-7000
Executive Director:
Kenneth J Ringler................................. 212-435-7271
Deputy Executive Director:
James P Fox 212-435-6667
Director, Government & Community Relations:
Arthur Cifelli 212-435-6903
Chief of Staff:
Edmond Schorno 212-435-6688
General Counsel:
Darrell Buchbinder................................ 212-435-3515
Chief Financial Officer:
A Paul Blanco..................................... 212-435-7738
Chief Administrative Officer:
Louis J LaCapra 212-435-8140
Chief Operating Officer:
Ernesto Butcher 212-435-7887
Chief of Public & Government Affairs:
Michael A Petralia 212-435-6502
Chief Engineer:
Francis J Lombardi................................ 212-435-7449
Director, Public Affairs:
Kayla M Bergeron 212-435-8041
Office of Secretary:
Karen E Eastman 212-435-6528

Port of Oswego Authority
1 East Second St, PO Box 387
Oswego, NY 13126
315-343-4503 Fax: 315-343-5498
e-mail: shipping@dreamscape.com
Web site: www.portoswego.com

Chairman:
Steven Thomas 315-343-8095
Executive Director:
Thomas McAuslan 315-343-4503
Counsel:
Timothy Fennell................................... 315-343-6363

Rochester-Genesee Regional Transportation Authority
1372 E Main St
PO Box 90629
Rochester, NY 14609
585-654-0200 Fax: 585-654-0224
Web site: www.rgrta.com

Chair:
John G Doyle 585-654-0200
Chief Executive Officer:
Mark R Aesch...................................... 585-654-0200
Chief Operating Officer:
Stephen W Hendershott 585-654-0200
Chief Financial Officer:
Robert W Frye 585-654-0200
Director, Transit Operations:
Bruce G Philpott.................................. 585-654-0200

Roosevelt Island Operating Corporation (RIOC)
591 Main St
Roosevelt Island, NY 10044
212-832-4540 Fax: 212-832-4582
e-mail: info@roosevelt-island.ny.us
Web site: www.rioc.com

President:
Herbert E Berman.................................. 212-832-4540
Vice President, Operations:
Sari Halper Dickson 212-832-4540
Chairperson, Board of Directors (ex officio):
Judith A Calogero 518-473-8384/fax: 518-473-9462
Commissioner's Designate to Board of Directors:
Mary Beth Labate.................................. 518-486-3370
General Counsel:
Kenneth A Leitner............................. 212-832-4540 x311
Chief Financial Officer:
Vacant 212-832-4540
Public Information Officer:
John Melia 212-832-4540

State University Construction Fund
353 Broadway
Albany, NY 12246
518-689-2500 Fax: 518-689-2634
Web site: www.sucf.suny.edu

Offices and agencies appear in alphabetical order.

General Manager:
   Philip W Wood 518-689-2501
Acting General Counsel:
   William K Barczak 518-689-2514/fax: 518-689-2634

State of New York Mortgage Agency (SONYMA)

641 Lexington Ave
New York, NY 10022
212-688-4000 Fax: 212-872-0678
Web site: www.nyhomes.org

Chair:
   Joseph Strasburg 212-688-4000
President & Chief Executive Officer:
   Stephen J Hunt 212-688-4000
Senior Vice President & Special Assistant to President/Chief Eececutive
   Officer for Policy Development & Programs:
   James P Angley 212-688-4000
Senior Vice President, Chief Operating Officer & Chief Fiscal Officer:
   Ralph J Madalena 212-688-4000
Senior Vice President & General Counsel:
   Justin Driscoll 212-688-4000
Vice President/Director, SONYMA Mortgage Insurance Fund:
   Michael Friedman 212-688-4000 x714
Senior Vice President, Single Family Programs & Financing:
   Charles Rosenwald 212-688-4000 x531
Vice President, Policy & Planning:
   Tracy A Oats 212-688-4000 x678
Vice President, Intergovernmental Affairs:
   Michael R Houseknecht 518-434-2118/fax: 518-432-7158

State of New York Municipal Bond Bank Agency (MBBA)

641 Lexington Ave
New York, NY 10022
212-688-4000 Fax: 212-872-0678
Web site: www.nymbba.org

Chair:
   Jerome M Becker 212-688-4000
President & Chief Executive Officer:
   Stephen J Hunt 212-688-4000
Senior Vice President & Special Assistant to President/Chief Executive
   Officer for Policy Development & Programs:
   James P Angley 212-688-4000
Senior Vice President, Chief Fiscal Officer & Chief Operating Officer:
   Ralph J Madalena 212-688-4000
Senior Vice President & Counsel:
   Justin Driscoll 212-688-4000
Vice President, Policy & Planning:
   Tracy A Oats 212-688-4000 x678

Suffolk Regional Off-Track Betting Corp

5 Davids Dr
Hauppauge, NY 11788-2004
631-853-1000 Fax: 631-853-1086
e-mail: srotb@suffolkotb.com
Web site: www.suffolkotb.com

President/Chief Executive Officer:
   Anthony F Apollaro 631-853-1000

Vice President:
   Jeffrey A Casale 631-853-1000
Associate Counsel/Director, Executive Administration:
   Neil H Tiger 631-853-1000
Public Information:
   DuWayne Gregory 631-853-1000 x3512/fax: 631-853-1086
Comptroller/Director, Finance:
   Celine M Gazes 631-853-1000

Thousand Islands Bridge Authority

PO Box 428
Alexandria Bay, NY 13607
315-482-2501 or 315-658-2281 Fax: 315-482-5925
Web site: www.tibridge.com

Chair:
   Donald J Grant 315-482-2501
Executive Director:
   Robert G Horr, III. 315-482-2501
   e-mail: roberthorr@tibridge.com
Legal Counsel:
   Anderson Wise 315-482-2501

Uniform State Laws Commission

c/o Coughlin & Gerhart LLP, 20 Hawley St
East Tower
Binghamton, NY 13902-2039
607-584-4193 Fax: 607-723-1530

Chair:
   Richard B Long 607-584-4193
   e-mail: rlong@cglawllp.com
Member:
   Sandra Stern 212-207-8150

United Nations Development Corporation

Two United Nations Plaza, 27th Fl
New York, NY 10017-4403
212-888-1618 Fax: 212-588-0758
Web site: www.undc.org

Chair, Board of Directors:
   George Klein 212-888-1618
President & Chief Executive Officer:
   Roy M Goodman 212-888-1618
Executive Vice President/Director of Development:
   Jeffrey Feldman 212-888-1618
Senior Vice President, Controller:
   Rudy C Montenegro 212-888-1618
Senior Vice President, Operations:
   Robert M Preissner 212-888-1618

Waterfront Commission of New York Harbor

39 Broadway, 4th Fl
New York, NY 10006
212-742-9280 Fax: 212-480-0587
Web site: www.wcnyh.org

Commissioner, NY:
   Michael C Axelrod 212-742-9280
Commissioner, NJ:
   Michael J Madonna 212-742-9280

Offices and agencies appear in alphabetical order.

Executive Director:
　　Thomas De Maria. 212-742-9280

Western Regional Off-Track Betting Corp

700 Ellicott St
Batavia, NY 14020
585-343-1423 Fax: 585-343-6873
Web site: www.westernotb.com

Chair:
　　Gregory L Davis. 585-343-1423

President & Chief Executive Officer:
　　Martin C Basinait 585-343-1423
Executive Vice President:
　　Patrick T Murphy 585-343-1423
Vice President, Administration:
　　Michael Kane 585-343-1423
General Counsel & Secretary:
　　Timothy A McCarthy 585-343-1423
Comptroller:
　　Nicholas A Noce. 585-343-1423

Offices and agencies appear in alphabetical order.

CRIME & CORRECTIONS

Governor's Office

Executive Chamber
State Capitol
Albany, NY 12224
518-474-8390 Fax: 518-474-1513
Web site: www.state.ny.us

Governor:
  George E Pataki 518-474-8390
Executive Director:
  Kara Lanspery 518-474-8390
Secretary to the Governor:
  John P Cahill. 518-474-4246
Counsel to the Governor-Attorney General, Budget:
  Richard Platkin. 518-474-8343
Senior Assistant Counsel to the Governor-Criminal Justice, Inspector
  General, Public Security, Special Prosecutors, State Investigation:
  Roger McDonough. 518-474-1291
Asst Counsel to the Governor-Clemency, Crime Vics, Correcs, Correc Svcs,
  Disaster, Extrads, Military/Naval/SEMO, Parole, Domestic Viol,
  Probatn/Correc Alts, Veterans:
  Gerald Connolly 518-474-8494
Director, Communications:
  David Catalfamo. 518-474-8418

EXECUTIVE DEPARTMENTS AND RELATED AGENCIES

Correctional Services Department

1220 Washington Ave
Bldg 2 State Campus
Albany, NY 12226-2050
518-457-8126 Fax: 518-457-7252
Web site: www.docs.state.ny.us

Commissioner:
  Glenn S Goord 518-457-8126
Executive Deputy Commissioner:
  John R Patterson, Jr 518-457-1748
Deputy Commissioner & Counsel:
  Anthony Annucci 518-457-4951
Inspector General:
  Richard D Roy 518-457-2653
Executive Assistamt to Commissioner:
  Edward McSweeney. 518-457-1281
Secretary to the Commissioner:
  Diane Rowen 518-457-8126
Public Information Officer:
  James Flateau. 518-457-8182/fax: 518-457-7070

Administrative Services

Deputy Commissioner:
  Charles Devane. 518-457-8188

Budget & Finance Division
Assistant Commissioner:
  Russell Di Bello 518-457-7135

Diversity Management
Director:
  Charlie R Harvey 518-435-9494
ADA Coordinator:
  Donna Masterson 518-435-9494

Human Resources Management Division
Personnel Bureau
  Director:
    Daniel Martuscello 518-457-5393
Support Operations Division
  550 Broadway, Menands, NY 12204
  Director:
    Stewart Kidder. 518-436-7886

Inmate Grievance
Director:
  Thomas Eagen 518-457-1885

Internal Controls
Director:
  Deborah Coons. 518-485-1394

Labor Relations Bureau
Director:
  Peter Brown 518-457-7383

Training Academy
  1134 New Scotland Rd, Albany, NY 12208
Director:
  Bruce Olsen 518-489-9072

Workers' Compensation Investigation Unit
Director:
  Paul DiMura. 518-457-3112

Board of Examiners of Sex Offenders
Chair:
  Elizabeth Devane 518-457-4185

Correctional Facility Operations
Deputy Commissioner:
  Lucien LeClaire 518-457-8138
Assistant Commissioner:
  Diane Van Buren 518-457-5902
Assistant Commissioner:
  Clair F Bee 518-457-5902
Assistant Commissioner:
  Paul Kikendall 518-457-4118

Agri-Business
  Eastern NY Correctional Facility, Box 333, Napanoch, NY 12458
Director:
  James Marion. 914-647-7400

Correctional Industries Division . . . . fax: 518-436-6007
  Corcraft Products, 550 Broadway, Albany, NY 12204
  Fax: 518-436-6007
  Web site: www.corcraft.org
Director:
  James Hoffman. 518-436-6321

Facilities
Adirondack Correctional Facility
  Box 110, Ray Brook, NY 12977-0110
  Superintendent:
    Alan Roberts. 518-891-1343/fax: 518-891-3299

Offices and agencies appear in alphabetical order.

Albion Correctional Facility
3595 State School Rd, Albion, NY 14411
Superintendent:
    Anginell Andrews 585-589-5511/fax: 585-589-1247

Altona Correctional Facility
555 Devil's Den Rd, Box 125, Altona, NY 12910-0125
Acting Superintendent:
    Deborah Keysor 518-236-7841

Arthur Kill Correctional Facility
2911 Arthur Kill Rd, Staten Island, NY 10309-1197
Superintendent:
    Dennis Breslin 718-356-7333

Attica Correctional Facility
Box 149, Attica, NY 14011-0149
Superintendent:
    James Conway 585-591-2000

Auburn Correctional Facility
135 State St, Auburn, NY 13021
Superintendent:
    John Burge 315-253-8401

Bare Hill Correctional Facility
Caller Box #20 181 Brand Rd, Malone, NY 12953
Superintendent:
    John Donelli 518-483-8411

Bayview Correctional Facility
550 West 20th St, New York, NY 10011-2878
Superintendent:
    Delores Thornton 212-255-7590

Beacon Correctional Facility
PO Box 780, Beacon, NY 12508-0780
Superintendent:
    Gail Thomas 845-831-4200

Bedford Hills Correctional Facility
247 Harris Rd, Bedford Hills, NY 10507-2499
Superintendent:
    Ada Perez 914-241-3100

Buffalo Correctional Facility
PO Box 300, Alden, NY 14004
Superintendent:
    William Powers 716-937-3786/fax: 716-937-3789

Butler ASACTC
PO Box 400, Red Creek, NY 13143
Superintendent:
    James Morrissey 315-754-8001

Butler Correctional Facility
PO Box 388, Rt 370, Red Creek, NY 13143
Superintendent:
    James Morrissey 315-754-6216

Camp Gabriels
Box 100, Gabriels, NY 12939-0100
Superintendent:
    Michael Corcoran 518-327-3111

Camp Georgetown
RD #1, Box 48, Georgetown, NY 13072-9307
Superintendent:
    Scott C Carlsen 315-837-4446

Camp Pharsalia
486 Center Rd, South Plymouth, NY 13844-6777
Superintendent:
    Leo Payant 607-334-2264

Cape Vincent Correctional Facility
Route 12E, Box 599, Cape Vincent, NY 13618
Superintendent:
    Warren D Barkley 315-654-4100/fax: 315-654-4103

Cayuga Correctional Facility
PO Box 1150, Moravia, NY 13119-1150
Superintendent:
    Joseph E McCoy 315-497-1110/fax: 315-497-3617

Chateaugay Correctional Facility
PO Box 320, Route 11, Chateaugay, NY 12920
Superintendent:
    R W Santor 518-497-3300/fax: 497-3300 x2099

Clinton Correctional Facility
PO Box 2000, Dannemora, NY 12929
Superintendent:
    Dale Artus 518-492-2511 x2099/fax: 518-492-7892

Collins Correctional Facility
PO Box 490, Taylor Hollow Rd, Collins, NY 14034-0490
Superintendent:
    James Berbary 716-532-4588

Coxsackie Correctional Facility
Box 200, West Coxsackie, NY 12051-0200
Superintendent:
    Gary Filion 518-731-2781

Downstate Correctional Facility
PO Box 445, Fishkill, NY 12524-0445
Superintendent:
    Frank J Tracy 845-831-6600

Eastern NY Correctional Facility
Box 338, Napanoch, NY 12458-0338
Superintendent:
    David L Miller 845-647-7400

Edgecombe Correctional Facility
611 Edgecombe Ave, New York, NY 10032-4398
Superintendent:
    William J Connolly 212-923-2575

Elmira Correctional Facility
Box 500, Elmira, NY 14902-0500
Superintendent:
    Calvin West 607-734-3901

Fishkill Correctional Facility
PO Box 307, Beacon, NY 12508
Superintendent:
    William Mazzuca 845-831-4800

Five Points Correctional Facility
Caller Box 400, State Rte 96, Romulus, NY 14541
Superintendent:
    Thomas Poole 607-869-5111

Franklin Correctional Facility
PO Box 10, Malone, NY 12953
Superintendent:
    Michael Allard 518-483-6040

Fulton Correctional Facility
1511 Fulton Ave, Bronx, NY 10457-8398
Superintendent:
    Eduardo Nieves 718-583-8000

Gouverneur Correctional Facility
PO Box 370, Gouverneur, NY 13642-0370
Superintendent:
    Justin Taylor 315-287-7351

Gowanda Correctional Facility
PO Box 350, South Rd, Gowanda, NY 14070-0350
Superintendent:
    Timothy Murray 716-532-0177

Great Meadow Correctional Facility
Box 51, Comstock, NY 12821
Superintendent:
    Gary Greene 518-639-5516

Green Haven Correctional Facility
Rte 216, Stormville, NY 12582
Acting Superintendent:
    William E Phillips 845-221-2711

Greene Correctional Facility
PO Box 8, Coxsackie, NY 12051-0008
Superintendent:
    Joseph David 518-731-2741/fax: 518-731-9377

Policy Areas

Offices and agencies appear in alphabetical order.

Groveland Correctional Facility
Route 36, Sonyea Rd, Sonyea, NY 14556-0001
Superintendent:
Michael Rabideau 585-658-2871

Hale Creek ASACTC
279 Maloney Rd, Johnstown, NY 12095
Superintendent:
Hazel Lewis. 518-736-2094

Hudson Correctional Facility
Box 576, Hudson, NY 12534-0576
Superintendent:
Herbert McLaughlin 518-828-4311/fax: 518-828-5559

Lakeview Shock Incarceration Correctional Facility
PO Box T, Brocton, NY 14716
Superintendent:
Ronald Moscicki. 716-792-7100/fax: 792-7197 x3099

Lincoln Correctional Facility
31-33 West 110th St, New York, NY 10026-4398
Superintendent:
Joseph Williams. 212-860-9400

Livingston Correctional Facility
Route 36, Sonyea Rd, Sonyea, NY 14556-0049
Acting Superintendent:
Edward J Hamill 585-658-3710

Lyon Mountain Correctional Facility
Box 276, Lyon Mountain, NY 12952-0276
Superintendent:
Lawrence Sears 518-735-4546

Marcy Correctional Facility
PO Box 5000, Marcy, NY 13403
Superintendent:
William Lape 315-768-1400/fax: 315-768-1419

Mid-Orange Correctional Facility
900 Kings Hwy, Warwick, NY 10990-0900
Superintendent:
Susan Schultz. 845-986-2291

Mid-State Correctional Facility
PO Box 216, Marcy, NY 13403-0216
Superintendent:
Kenneth Perlman 315-768-8581

Mohawk Correctional Facility
6100 School Rd, PO Box 8450, Rome, NY 13440
Superintendent:
Leo E Payant 315-339-5232 x2000/fax: 339-5232 x2099

Monterey Shock Incarceration Correctional Facility
2150 Evergreen Hill Rd, RD #1, Beaver Dams, NY 14812-9718
Superintendent:
Malcolm Cully. 607-962-3184

Moriah Shock Incarceration Correctional Facility
PO Box 999, Mineville, NY 12956-0999
Superintendent:
Leo J Bisceglia. 518-942-7561 x2000/fax: 942-7561 x2099

Mt McGregor Correctional Facility
1000 Mt McGregor Rd, PO Box 2071, Wilton, NY 12831-5071
Superintendent:
Harold McKinney 518-587-3960

Ogdensburg Correctional Facility
One Correction Way, Ogdensburg, NY 13669-2288
Superintendent:
Dana Smith 315-393-0281

Oneida Correctional Facility
6100 School Rd, Rome, NY 13440
Superintendent:
Susan Connell 315-339-6880

Orleans Correctional Facility
35-31 Gaines Basin Rd, Albion, NY 14411
Superintendent:
David Unger 585-589-6820

Otisville Correctional Facility
Box 8, Otisville, NY 10963-0008
Superintendent:
Robert J Ebert 845-386-1490

Queensboro Correctional Facility
47-04 Van Dam St, Long Island City, NY 11101-3081
Superintendent:
Dennis Crowley. 718-361-8920

Riverview Correctional Facility
PO Box 158, Ogdensburg, NY 13669
Superintendent:
Ekpe D Ekpe. 315-393-8400/fax: 315-394-1189

Rochester Correctional Facility
470 Ford St, Rochester, NY 14608-2499
Superintendent:
William Powers 585-454-2280/fax: 585-454-3412

Shawangunk Correctional Facility
PO Box 750, Wallkill, NY 12589-0750
Superintendent:
Joseph Smith 845-895-2081

Sing Sing Correctional Facility
354 Hunter St, Ossining, NY 10562-5442
Superintendent:
Brian Fischer 914-941-0108

Southport Correctional Facility
236 Bob Masia Drive, PO Box 2000, Pine City, NY 14871
Superintendent:
Michael McGinnis. 607-737-0850

Sullivan Correctional Facility
PO Box 116, Riverside Dr, Fallsburg, NY 12733-0116
Superintendent:
James Walsh 845-434-2080

Summit Shock Incarceration Correctional Facility
RFD, Dibbles Rd, Summit, NY 12175-9608
Superintendent:
Bruce Yelich. 518-287-1721/fax: 518-287-1241

Taconic Correctional Facility
250 Harris Rd, Bedford Hills, NY 10507-2498
Superintendent:
Alexandreena Dixon 914-241-3010

Ulster Correctional Facility
Berme Rd, PO Box 800, Napanoch, NY 12458
Superintendent:
Scott C Carlsen 845-647-1670

Upstate Correctional Facility
PO Box 2000, 309 Bare Hill Rd, Malone, NY 12953
Superintendent:
Roy Girdich. 518-483-6997

Wallkill Correctional Facility
Box G, Wallkill, NY 12589-0286
Superintendent:
Paul W Annetts 845-895-2021

Washington Correctional Facility
Box 180, Comstock, NY 12821-0180
Superintendent:
Israel Rivera 518-639-4486/fax: 518-639-4073

Watertown Correctional Facility
23147 Swan Rd, Watertown, NY 13601-9340
Superintendent:
Christ T Mellas 315-782-7490

Wende Correctional Facility
3622 Wende Rd, PO Box 1187, Alden, NY 14004-1187
Superintendent:
Anthony Zon. 716-937-4000/fax: 937-4000 x2099

Willard Drug Treatment Center
7116 County Route 132, PO Box 303, Willard, NY 14588
Superintendent:
Melvin L Williams 607-869-5500

Offices and agencies appear in alphabetical order.

Woodbourne Correctional Facility
Riverside Dr, Woodbourne, NY 12788
Superintendent:
Raymond Cunningham 845-434-7730
Wyoming Correctional Facility
Dunbar Rd, PO Box 501, Attica, NY 14011
Superintendent:
Michael Giambruno 585-591-1010

Facilities Planning & Development
One Watervliet Ave Extension, Albany, NY 12206
Director:
Frank Sheridan 518-435-9477

Security Staffing Unit
One Watervliet Ave Extension, Albany, NY 12206
Director:
Kathy Austin 518-435-9487

Special Operations
Director, Crisis Intervention Unit:
Mike Hogan 518-457-2006
Director, Corrections Emergency Response Team (Cert):
Mark Vann 518-457-2006
Director, Shock Incarceration Program:
Cheryl Clark 518-457-8144
Director, Special Housing/Inmate Disciplinary Program:
Donald Selsky 518-457-2337

Health Services Division
Deputy Commissioner, Chief Medical Officer:
Lester Wright 518-457-7072
Assistant Commissioner:
John Sheridan 518-457-7072

Correctional Health Services
Director:
Theresa Wuerdeman 518-457-7072

Dental Services
Director:
Robert McArdle 518-457-7072

Mental Health
Director:
John Culkin 518-457-5067

Nursing & Ancillary Services
Director:
Donna Constant 518-457-7072

Population Management
Associate Commissioner, Inspector General:
Richard D Roy 518-457-7261

Classification & Movement/Transportation
Director:
Terry Knapp-David 518-457-6022

Management Information Services
Director:
G Ronald Courington 518-457-2540

Program Planning, Research & Evaluation
Assistant Director:
Paul Korotkin 518-457-3007

Temporary Release
Director:
Debra Joy 518-457-2655

Program Services
Deputy Commissioner:
John Nuttall 518-457-5555

Education
Director:
Linda Hallman 518-457-8142

Guidance & Counseling
Director:
Jim Granger 518-457-5652

Library Services
Supervising Librarian:
Jean Clancy-Botta 518-485-7109

Ministerial & Family Services
Director:
Mark Leonard 518-457-8106

Substance Abuse Treatment Services
Director:
Dwight Bradford 518-485-7903

Volunteer Services
Director:
Mark Leonard 518-485-1851

Crime Victims Board
845 Central Ave
Rm 107
Albany, NY 12206-1504
518-457-8727 or 800-247-8035 Fax: 518-457-8658
e-mail: cvbinfo@cvb.state.ny.us
Web site: www.cvb.state.ny.us

55 Hanson Place
Room 1000
Brooklyn, NY 11217-1523
718-923-4325
Fax: 718-923-4352

65 Court St
Rm 308
Buffalo, NY 14202-3406
716-847-7992
Fax: 716-847-7995

Chairwoman:
Joan A Cusack 718-923-4331
Commissioner:
Benedict J Monachino 718-923-4400
Commissioner:
Charles F Marotta 718-923-4336
Commissioner:
Christina Hernandez 518-485-5719
Commissioner:
Jacqueline C Mattina 716-847-7948
Executive Director:
Virginia A Miller 518-457-9320
Contract Supervisor:
Ron Dickens 518-485-2763
General Counsel:
Everett Mayhew, Jr. 518-457-8066
Director, MIS:
David Loomis 518-457-8050

Offices and agencies appear in alphabetical order.

Policy Areas

Criminal Justice Services, Division of

Four Tower Place
Albany, NY 12203-3764
518-457-1260 Fax: 518-457-3089
Web site: www.criminaljustice.state.ny.us

Commissioner & Director:
   Chauncey G Parker. 518-457-1260
Executive Deputy Commissioner:
   Martin Cirincione. 518-457-6091
Affirmative Action Officer:
   G Bernett Marion 518-457-6110
Director, Communications:
   Lynn Rasic 518-485-0857
Public Information Officer:
   Lyle Hartog 518-485-2465/fax: 518-485-2467

Administration Office

Director, Administration:
   Paula Steigman. 518-457-6100

Administrative Operations
Director:
   Phyllis M Foster. 518-457-1696

Human Resources Management
Director:
   Alyce Ashe. 518-457-6110

State Finance & Budget
Acting Director, Financial Administration:
   Kimberly J Szady. 518-457-6105
Director, Internal Audit & Compliance:
   William Gritsavage 518-457-1417

Advisory Groups

Juvenile Justice Advisory Group
15 Van Dyke Ave, Amsterdam, NY 12010
Acting Chair:
   Michael Elmendorf. 518-474-7516

NYS Motor Vehicle & Insurance Fraud Prevention Board
Chair/Commissioner & Director:
   Chauncey G Parker 518-457-1260

Legal Services & Forensic Services Office

Deputy Commissioner & Counsel:
   Kimberly O'Conner 518-457-4181

Missing & Exploited Children Clearinghouse
Director:
   Kenneth R Buniak 518-485-7632

Office of Forensic Services
Director:
   John Hicks 518-457-7287

Sex Offender Registry
Director:
   Jeanne Sample 518-457-7985

Office of Criminal Justice Operations

Deputy Commissioner:
   Daniel Foro. 518-485-2995
Executive Director:
   James Shea 518-457-8724

Information Technology Development Group
Director:
   Thomas Meyer. 518-457-9716

Information Technology Services Group
Director:
   Alex Roberts. 518-457-3743

Office of Operations
Director:
   William J Sillery 518-457-6050
Assistant Bureau Director:
   Michael Tymeson. 518-457-6050
Chief, Records Management Bureau:
   James Stanco 518-457-6051
Chief, Civil Identification Bureau:
   Ann Sammons 518-485-5763

Office of Public Safety

Deputy Commissioner:
   James DeLapp 518-457-6101
Director:
   Mark R Lindsay 518-457-2667
Assistant Director:
   John R Digman. 518-485-1414
Chief of Administrative Services:
   David H Mahany 518-457-4135
Chief of Program Services:
   Dennis W McCarty. 518-485-1410

Advisory Groups
Law Enforcement Accreditation Council
Deputy Commissioner:
   James DeLapp 518-457-6101
Municipal Police Training Council
Deputy Commissioner:
   James DeLapp 518-457-6101
Security Guard Advisory Council
Chief:
   David H Mahany. 518-457-6101
State Cmte for Coordination of Police Services for the Elderly (TRIAD)
Deputy Commissioner:
   James DeLapp 518-457-6101
Statewide Law Enforcement Telecommunications Cmte
Deputy Commissioner:
   James DeLapp 518-457-6101

Office of Strategic Planning

Deputy Commissioner:
   Roger Jeffries 518-485-7433

Bureau of Justice Research & Innovation
Director:
   Donna Hall. 518-457-7301
Crime Reductions Strategies Unit
Chief:
   Thomas Mitchell 518-457-7301
Justice Statistics & Performance Unit
Chief:
   Susan Jacobsen 518-457-8381
Justice Systems Analysis Unit
Chief:
   David vanAlstyne 518-457-7301
Offender Management Analysis Unit
Chief:
   Bruce Frederick. 518-457-3724

Funding & Program Assistance Office
Director:
   AnneMarie Strano 518-457-8462

Offices and agencies appear in alphabetical order.

Inspector General (NYS), Office of the

Executive Chamber
State Capitol
Albany, NY 12224
518-474-1010 Fax: 518-486-3745

61 Broadway
12th Fl
New York, NY 10006
212-635-3150
Fax: 212-809-6287

State Inspector General:
  Jill Konviser-Levine . . . . 212-635-3150 or 518-474-1010
  e-mail: inspector.general@ig.state.ny.us
First Deputy Inspector General:
  Michael Boxer 212-635-3150
Executive Deputy Inspector General/Special Counsel:
  Ralph A Rossi, III. 518-474-1010
Director, Administration:
  Cindy Haskins 518-474-1010
Director, Communications:
  Stephen Del Giacco 518-474-1010
  e-mail: steve.delgiacco@ig.state.ny.us

Executive District Office

  65 Court St, Buffalo, NY 14202
Deputy Inspector General:
  Joseph Giglio. 716-847-7118/fax: 716-847-7156

Law Department

120 Broadway
New York, NY 10271-0332
212-416-8000 Fax: 212-416-8942

State Capitol
Albany, NY 12224-0341
518-474-7330
Fax: 518-402-2472

Attorney General:
  Eliot Spitzer 518-474-7330
First Deputy Attorney General:
  Michele Hirshman 212-416-8050
Director, Public Information & Correspondence:
  Peter A Drago 518-474-7330/fax: 518-402-2472

Appeals & Opinions Division

Solicitor General:
  Caitlin J Halligan. 212-416-8016/fax: 212-416-8942
Deputy Solicitor General:
  Michael Belohlavek. 212-416-8028/fax: 212-416-8962
Deputy Solicitor General:
  Wayne L Benjamin 518-474-7138/fax: 518-473-8963
Deputy Solicitor General:
  Michelle Aronowitz. 212-416-8027/fax: 212-416-8962
Deputy Solicitor General:
  Daniel Smirlock. 518-473-0903/fax: 518-486-3176
Legal Records:
  Cynthia Bogardus. 518-474-5241

Law Library

Chief, Library Services:
  Sarah Brown 518-474-3840/fax: 518-402-2271

Senior Librarian, New York City Office:
  Franette Sheinwald 212-416-8012/fax: 212-416-6130

Criminal Division

Deputy Attorney General:
  Peter B Pope 212-416-8058/fax: 212-416-8026
Assistant Deputy Attorney General:
  Karen Lupuloff 212-416-8090/fax: 212-416-8026

Criminal Prosecutions Bureau

Chief:
  Janet Cohn. 518-474-4096/fax: 518-474-3364
Deputy Bureau Chief, NYC:
  Zachary Weiss. 212-416-6095/fax: 212-416-8026
Deputy Bureau Chief, Albany:
  Viola Abbitt. 518-474-4096/fax: 518-474-3364

Investigations Bureau

Chief Investigator:
  William M Casey . . . . 212-416-6328 or 518-486-4540

Medicaid Fraud Control Unit

  120 Broadway, 13th Fl, New York, NY 10271-0007
Deputy Attorney General-in-Charge:
  William J Comisky 212-417-5250/fax: 212-417-5274
First Deputy Attorney General:
  Peter M Bloch 212-417-5261/fax: 212-417-5274
Assistant Deputy Attorney General:
  George Quinlan 716-853-8584
Regional Director, Albany:
  Steven Krantz 518-473-8350/fax: 518-474-4519
Deputy Regional Director, Buffalo:
  Gary A Baldauf. 716-853-8507/fax: 716-853-8525
Regional Director, Long Island:
  Alan Buonpastore 631-952-6400/fax: 631-952-6382
Regional Director, NYC:
  Richard Harrow. 212-417-5391/fax: 212-417-4725
Regional Director, Rochester:
  Jerry Solomon 716-262-2860/fax: 716-262-2866
Regional Director, Syracuse:
  Ralph Tortora, III 315-423-1121/fax: 315-423-1120
Deputy Regional Director, Westchester/Rockland:
  Anne Jardine 845-732-7500/fax: 845-732-7555
Regional Director for Special Projects Unit:
  Pat Lupinetti 845-732-7550/fax: 845-732-7557

Organized Crime Task Force

Deputy Attorney General-in-Charge:
  J Christopher Prather. 518-474-1620/fax: 518-474-7258

Public Advocacy Division

Acting Deputy Attorney General:
  Terryl Brown Clemons 212-416-8041/fax: 212-416-8068
Special Counsel:
  Mary Ellen Burns 212-416-6155

Antitrust Bureau

Bureau Chief:
  Jay L Himes. 212-416-8282/fax: 212-416-6015

Charities Bureau

Bureau Chief:
  William Josephson 212-416-8401/fax: 212-416-8393

Civil Rights Bureau

Bureau Chief:
  Dennis Parker 212-416-8250/fax: 212-416-8074

Consumer Frauds & Protection Bureau

Bureau Chief:
  Thomas G Conway 518-474-2374/fax: 518-474-3618

Offices and agencies appear in alphabetical order.

Environmental Protection Bureau
Bureau Chief:
Peter Lehner 212-416-8450/fax: 212-416-6007

Healthcare Bureau
Bureau Chief:
Joseph R Baker, III 212-416-8521/fax: 212-416-8034

Internet Bureau
Bureau Chief:
Kenneth Dreifach 212-416-8433/fax: 212-416-8369

Investment Protection Bureau
Bureau Chief:
David Brown 212-416-8198/fax: 212-416-8816

Telecommunications & Energy Bureau
Bureau Chief:
Susanna M Zwerling 212-416-8333/fax: 212-416-8877

State Counsel Division
Deputy Attorney General:
Richard Rifkin 518-473-7190
Assistant Deputy Attorney General:
Patricia Martinelli 518-473-0648/fax: 518-486-9777
Assistant Deputy Attorney General:
Susan L Watson 212-416-8579/fax: 212-416-6001

Civil Recoveries Bureau
Assistant Attorney General in Charge:
Mary E House 518-474-7131/fax: 518-473-1635

Claims Bureau
Bureau Chief, NYC:
Susan Pogoda 212-416-8516/fax: 212-416-8946

Labor Bureau
Bureau Chief:
M Patricia Smith 212-416-8710

Litigation Bureau
Bureau Chief, Albany:
Bruce D Feldman 518-473-8328/fax: 518-473-1572
Bureau Chief, NYC:
James B Henley 212-416-8523/fax: 212-416-6075

Real Property Bureau
Assistant Attorney General in Charge:
Henry A DeCotis 518-474-7151/fax: 518-473-5106

Parole, Division of
97 Central Ave
Albany, NY 12206
518-473-9400 Fax: 518-473-6037
e-mail: nysparole@parole.state.ny.us
Web site: parole.state.ny.us

314 W 40th St
New York, NY 10018
212-239-6000
Fax: 212-239-6160

Administrative Services
Director:
Steven H Philbrick 518-473-9531
Deputy Director, Financial Management:
Jeffrey W Nesich 518-473-3901
Director, Finance:
J Dennis Casey 518-473-9419

Director, Human Resource Management:
Jose Burgos 518-473-6041
Labor Relations Representative:
Robert Oeser 518-474-5612
Director, Support Operations:
George Hemstead 518-473-5790

Board of Parole
Chairman:
Robert Dennison 518-473-9548/fax: 518-402-3456
Secretary to the Board:
Felix M Rosa 518-473-5424/fax: 518-402-3456

Clemency Unit
845 Central Ave, Albany, NY 12206
Director:
Felix M Rosa 518-485-8953

Executive Office . . . . fax: 518-486-5858
Executive Director:
Anthony G Ellis, II 518-473-9672
Deputy Exec Director:
Thomas J Herzog 518-473-0852
Public Information Officer:
Scott E Steinhardt 518-486-4631
Director, Office of Pro Responsibility:
Theodore Cook III 518-473-5470

Information Services
Chief:
Thomas J Herzog 518-445-7558

Office of Counsel
Chief Counsel:
Terrence X Tracy 518-473-5671/fax: 518-473-9760
Associate Counsel:
William Nowak 518-473-5673/fax: 518-473-9760

Parole Operations Unit
Director, Operations:
Angela Jiminez 518-473-5421
Assistant Deputy Director of Operations:
William Barhold 518-473-4064
Director, Bureau of Special Services:
Vicent Defilippis 212-239-6158
Director, Parole Violations Unit:
Gerald McCord 212-239-5176
Director, Strategic Planning:
Mary Ellen Flynn 212-239-5766
Director, ACCESS:
Robert Smith 212-239-5735
Regional Dir-Region I:
Lou Cali 212-736-9880
Regional Dir-Region II:
James Dress 718-254-2007
Regional Dir-Region III:
Michael Burdi 914-654-8691
Regional Dir-Region IV:
Michael Hayden 518-459-7469
Regional Dir-Region V:
Timothy Wolcott 585-232-6927

Policy Analysis
Director:
Michael R Buckman 518-445-6071

Victim Impact Unit . . . . fax: 518-493-9659
Parole Officer:
William Lynn Hamilton 518-486-4400

Offices and agencies appear in alphabetical order.

Parole Officer:
Barbara Tobin. 518-486-4400

Prevention of Domestic Violence, Office for the
80 Wolf Road
Ste 406
Albany, NY 12205
518-457-5800 Fax: 518-457-5810
Web site: www.opdv.state.ny.us

Executive Director:
Sherry Frohman 518-457-5800
General Counsel & Agency Affairs:
Wendy Juracka-Maher. 518-457-5800
Director, Training & Policy Development Unit:
Gwen Wright 518-457-5916
Administrative Officer:
Linda Cassidy. 518-457-7995
Public Information Officer:
Suzanne Cecala. 518-457-5744
e-mail: suzanne.cecala@opdv.state.ny.us

Probation & Correctional Alternatives, Div of
80 Wolf Rd
Ste 501
Albany, NY 12205
518-485-7692 Fax: 518-485-5140
Web site: www.dpca.state.ny.us

State Director:
Sara Tullar Fasoldt. 518-485-7692
Secretary to the Director:
Barbara J Flanigan 518-485-7692
Executive Deputy Director:
Robert Maccarone 518-485-7692
General Counsel:
Linda Valenti 518-485-2394
Administrative Officer:
Howard Bancroft. 518-485-5145/fax: 518-485-2401

Interstate/Intrastate Transfers Unit
Supervisor:
Sandra Layton .518-485-2399/fax: 518-485-7198

New York State Probation Commission
Chair/State Director:
Sara Tullar Fasoldt. 518-485-7692
Chief Administrative Judge:
Jonathan Lippman 212-428-2812
Member:
Wayne D'Arcy 518-485-7692

State Police, Division of
Building 22, State Campus
1220 Washington Ave
Albany, NY 12226-2252
518-457-6811 Fax: 518-457-3207
Web site: www.troopers.state.ny.us

Superintendent:
Wayne E Bennett 518-457-6721
First Deputy Superintendent:
Preston L Felton 518-457-6711/fax: 518-485-7505

Counsel:
Glenn P Valle .518-457-6137/fax: 518-485-1164

Administration
Deputy Superintendent:
David L Christler. 518-457-6621/fax: 518-485-5051

Forensic Investigation Center
Director, Staff Inspector:
Gerald M Zeosky. 518-457-2466/fax: 518-457-2477

Public Information
Director, Technical Lieutenant:
Glenn R Miner. 518-457-2180/fax: 518-485-7818
e-mail: piooffice@troopers.state.ny.us
Crime Prevention Coordinator:
Sgt Kern Fwoboda. 518-457-2180/fax: 518-485-7818

Employee Relations
Deputy Superintendent:
Deborah J Campbell 518-457-3572/fax: 518-485-7505

Human Resources
Assistant Deputy Superintendent:
James L Harney. 518-485-5044/fax: 518-485-2293

State Police Academy
Director:
Major Ellwood A Sloat, Jr 518-457-7254/fax: 518-485-1454

Field Command
Deputy Superintendent:
William DeBlock. 518-457-5936/fax: 518-457-4779

Internal Affairs
Deputy Superintendent:
Joseph F Loszynski 518-485-6018/fax: 518-485-1493

CORPORATIONS, AUTHORITIES AND COMMISSIONS

Capital Defender Office
217 Broadway
9th Fl
New York, NY 10007
212-608-3352 Fax: 212-608-4558
Web site: www.nycdo.org

Capital Defender:
Kevin Doyle. 212-608-3352 x208
Frist Deputy Capital Defender, Albany Office:
Mark Harris 518-473-9521
First Deputy Capital Defender, New York City Office:
Susan Salomon 212-608-3352 x206
First Deputy Capital Defender, Rochester Office:
William Easton. 716-232-5480
Counsel to Board of Directors:
Peter Sistrom 212-608-3352 x209

New York State Commission of Correction
30 Wolfe Road
4th FL
Albany, NY 12205
518-485-2346 Fax: 518-485-2467
e-mail: infoscoc@scoc.state.ny.us
Web site: www.scoc.state.ny.us

Offices and agencies appear in alphabetical order.

Policy Areas

Chair/Commissioner:
Alan J Croce 518-485-2346
Assistant to Chair:
Patricia Amati 518-485-2330
Special Counsel to Chair:
Michael F Donegan 518-485-2346
Director, Human Resource Management:
Marylyn Sullivan 518-457-6110
Director, Operations:
James Lawrence 518-485-2346
Chair, Medical Review Board:
Frederick C Lamy 518-485-2346
Press Secretary:
Jessica Scaperotti 518-485-2346

NEW YORK STATE LEGISLATURE

See Legislative Branch in Section 1 for additional Standing Committee and Subcommittee information.

Assembly Standing Committees

Alcoholism & Drug Abuse
Chair:
Jeffrey Dinowitz (D) 518-455-5965
Ranking Minority Member:
Jack Quinn (R) 518-455-4462

Codes
Chair:
Joseph R Lentol (D) 518-455-4477
Ranking Minority Member:
Dierdre Scozzafava (R) 518-455-5797

Correction
Chair:
Jeffrion L Aubry (D) 518-455-4561
Ranking Minority Member:
Thomas O'Mara (R) 518-455-4538

Senate Standing Committees

Alcoholism & Drug Abuse
Chair:
Vacant 518-455-3563
Ranking Minority Member:
Ruben Diaz, Sr (D) 518-455-2511

Codes
Chair:
Dale M Volker (R) 518-455-3471
Ranking Minority Member:
Thomas K Duane (D) 518-455-2451

Crime Victims, Crime & Correction
Chair:
Michael F Nozzolio (R) 518-455-2366
Ranking Minority Member:
Thomas K Duane (D) 518-455-2451

U.S. Government

EXECUTIVE DEPARTMENTS AND RELATED AGENCIES

US Justice Department
Web site: www.usdoj.gov

Bureau of Alcohol, Tobacco, Firearms & Explosives
Web site: www.atf.gov

New York Field Division . . . . fax: 718-650-4001
241 37th St, Brooklyn, NY 11232
718-650-4000 Fax: 718-650-4001
Special Agent-in-Charge:
William McMahon 718-650-4000/fax: 718-650-4071
Public Information Officer:
Joseph G Green 718-650-4000

Drug Enforcement Administration - New York Task
Force . . . . fax: 212-337-3978
99 Tenth Ave, New York, NY 10011
Fax: 212-337-3978
Web site: www.usdoj.gov/dea/deahome.html
Special Agent-in-Charge:
John P Gilbride 212-337-2912
Associate Special Agent-in-Charge:
Wilbert L Plummer 212-337-2901
Associate Special Agent-in-Charge:
Derex S Maltz 212-620-4910
Associate Special Agent-in-Charge:
T Glen Coughlin 212-337-2903

Federal Bureau of Investigation - New York Field Offices
Web site: www.fbi.gov

Albany . . . . fax: 518-431-7463
200 McCarty Ave, Albany, NY 12209
Special Agent-in-Charge:
William Chase 518-465-7551

Buffalo . . . . fax: 716-843-5288
One FBI Plaza, Buffalo, NY 14202
Special Agent-in-Charge:
Peter J Ahearn 716-856-7800

New York City . . . . fax: 212-384-2745
26 Federal Plaza, 28th Fl, New York, NY 10278
Assistant Director-in-Charge:
Pasquale J Damuro 212-384-1000

Federal Bureau of Prisons
Web site: www.bop.gov

Brooklyn Metropolitan Detention Center
100 29th St, Brooklyn, NY 11232
Warden:
Michael Zenk 718-840-4200/fax: 718-840-5005

Federal Correctional Institution at Otisville
PO Box 600, Otisville, NY 10963
Warden:
Craig Parker 845-386-5855/fax: 845-386-1030

Metropolitan Correctional Center
150 Park Row, New York, NY 10007-1779

Offices and agencies appear in alphabetical order.

Warden:
Marvin D Morrison 646-836-6423/fax: 646-836-7751

Ray Brook Federal Correctional Institution
PO Box 300, Ray Brook, NY 12977
Warden:
T.R. Craig 518-897-4000/fax: 518-897-4216

Secret Service - New York Field Offices

Albany
39 N Pearl St, Ste 2, Albany, NY 12207-2785
Resident Agent-in-Charge:
William Leege 518-436-9600/fax: 518-436-9635

Buffalo
610 Main St, Ste 300, Buffalo, NY 14202
Special Agent-in-Charge:
Michael Bryant 716-551-4401/fax: 716-551-5075

JFK/LGA . . . . fax: 718-553-7626
JFK International Airport, Bldg 75, Ste 246, Jamaica, NY 11430
Resident Agent-in-Charge:
J Mark Bartlett 718-553-0911

Melville . . . . fax: 631-293-4389
145 Pinelawn Rd, Ste 200N, Melville, NY 11747
Resident Agent-in-Charge:
Kenneth Pleasant 631-293-4028

New York City . . . . fax: 718-840-1001
335 Adams St, Brooklyn, NY 11201
Special Agent-in-Charge:
A T Smith 718-840-1000

Rochester
1820 HSBC Plaza, 100 Chestnut St, Rochester, NY 14604
Resident Agent:
Michael de Stefano 585-232-4160/fax: 585-232-4662

Syracuse . . . . fax: 315-448-0302
100 S Clinton St, PO Box 7006, Syracuse, NY 13261
Resident Agent-in-Charge:
Timothy Kirk 315-448-0304

White Plains
140 Grand St, White Plains, NY 10601
Resident Agent-in-Chg:
Milton D Johnson 914-682-6300/fax: 914-682-6182

US Attorney's Office - New York

Eastern District
147 Pierrepont St, Brooklyn, NY 11201
718-254-7000
US Attorney:
Roslynn R Mauskopf 718-254-6260/fax: 718-254-6319
Chief Assistant United States Attorney:
Andrew C Hruska 718-254-6210/fax: 718-254-6300
Executive Assistant United States Attorney:
William J Muller 718-254-6258/fax: 718-254-6329
Administrative Assistant United States Attorney:
John Lenior 718-254-6255
Chief Assistant United States Attorney, Criminal Division:
Daniel Alonso 718-254-6238/fax: 718-254-6150
Chief Assistant United States Attorney, Civil Division:
Susan Riley 718-254-6037/fax: 718-254-7483
Chief Assistant United States Attorney, Appeals Division:
Peter Norling 718-254-6280
Deputy Administrative Officer:
Peter Kurtin 718-254-6569/fax: 718-254-6550

Northern District
Albany
James T Foley US Courthouse, #218, 455 Broadway, Albany, NY 12207
Supervising Assistant United States Attorney:
Grant C Jaquith 518-431-0247/fax: 518-431-0249
Binghamton
US Courthouse, Ste 304, 15 Henry St, Binghamton, NY 13901
Supervising Assistant United States Attorney:
Thomas P Walsh 607-773-2887/fax: 607-773-2901
Syracuse
J F Hanley Fed Bldg, 100 S Clinton St, Rm 900, Syracuse, NY 13261
United States Attorney:
Glenn Suddaby 315-448-0672
First Assistant United States Attorney:
Joseph A Pavone 315-448-0672
Assistant United States Attorney, Chief Criminal Division:
Andrew T Baxter 315-448-0672
Assistant United States Attorney, Chief Civil Division:
William H Pease 315-448-0672
Administrative Officer:
Martha Stratton 315-448-0672/fax: 315-448-0689

Southern District
New York City
United States Attorney:
David N Kelley 212-637-2573
Associate United States Attorney:
John M McEnany 212-637-2571
Chief United States Appellate Attorney:
Gary Stein 212-637-1065
Chief, Civil Division:
James Cott 212-637-2695
Chief, Criminal Division:
Karen Patten Seymour 212-637-2508
Administrative Officer:
Edward Tyrrell 212-637-2269/fax: 212-637-0084
White Plains . . . . fax: 914-682-3392
300 Quarropas St, 3rd Fl, White Plains, NY 10601
914-993-1900 Fax: 914-682-3392
Chief Assistant United States Attorney:
Maria A Barton 914-993-1909

Western District
Buffalo . . . . fax: 716-551-3052
138 Delaware Ave, Buffalo, NY 14202
716-843-5700 Fax: 716-551-3052
United States Attorney:
Michael A Battle 716-843-5814
First Assistant United States Attorney:
Kathleen M Mehltretter 716-843-5817
Assistant United States Attorney, Civil Division Chief:
Mary Pat Fleming 716-843-5867
Assistant United States Attorney, Narcotics & Violent Crime Division Chief:
Joseph M Guerra, III 716-843-5824
Assistant United States Attorney, Strike Force Division Chief:
Anthony M Bruce 716-843-5886
Assistant United States Attorney, White Collar & General Crimes Division Chief:
Paul J Campana 716-843-5819
Administrative Officer:
Barbara A Sweitzer 716-843-5826/fax: 716-551-3170
Rochester . . . . fax: 585-263-6226
620 Federal Bldg, 100 State St, Rochester, NY 14614
585-263-6760 Fax: 585-263-6226
Assistant United States Attorney-in-Charge:
Bradley E Tyler 585-263-5717

Offices and agencies appear in alphabetical order.

Policy Areas

US Marshals' Service - New York

Eastern District
225 Cadman Plaza East, Ste G-80, Brooklyn, NY 11201
718-254-6700
United States Marshal:
Eugene J Corcoran 718-254-6701/fax: 718-254-6720

Northern District
Albany
US Courthouse, 2nd Fl, 445 Broadway, Albany, NY 12207
United States Marshal:
James J Parmley 518-431-0101/fax: 518-431-0100
Syracuse
Federal Bldg, 100 S Clinton St, 10th Fl, PO Box 7260, Syracuse, NY 13261
Unitede States Marshal:
James J Parmley 315-448-0341/fax: 315-448-0343

Southern District
500 Pearl St, Ste 400, New York, NY 10007
United States Marshal:
Joseph R Guccione 212-331-7000/fax: 212-637-6130

Western District
Buffalo
Courthouse Bldg, Rm 129, 68 Court St, Buffalo, NY 14202
United States Marshal:
Peter Lawrence 716-551-4851/fax: 716-551-5505
Rochester
US Courthouse, Rm 284, 100 State St, Rochester, NY 14614
United States Marshal:
Peter Lawrence 585-263-5787/fax: 585-263-6741

US Parole Commission
5550 Friendship Blvd, Ste 420, Chevy Chase, MD 20815
Chairman:
Edward F Reilly. 301-492-5990/fax: 301-492-5543

See U.S. Congress Chapter for additional Standing Committee and Subcommittee information.

House of Representatives Standing Committees

Judiciary
Chair:
F James Sensenbrenner, Jr (R-WI). 202-225-5101
Ranking Minority Member:
John Conyers, Jr (D-MI). 202-225-5126
New York Delegate:
Jerrold Nadler (D). 202-225-5635
New York Delegate:
Anthony D Weiner (D). 202-225-6616

Subcommittee
Crime, Terrorism & Homeland Security
Chair:
Howard Coble (R-NC) 202-225-3926
Ranking Minority Member:
Robert C Scott (D-VA) 202-225-8351

Senate Standing Committees

Judiciary
Chair:
Arlen Specter (R-PA). 202-224-4254
Ranking Minority Member:
Patrick J Leahy (D-VT) 202-224-4242
New York Delegate:
Charles E Schumer (D). 202-224-6542

Private Sector

NYS Bar Assn, Justice & the Community Cmte
299 Broadway, Ste 607, New York, NY 10007
212-619-4662 Fax: 212-619-4630
e-mail: rcuyler778@aol.com
Renaye B Cuyler, Chair

Ackerman, Levine. Cullen, Brickman & Limmer LLP
175 Great Neck Road, Great Neck, NY 11021
516-829-6900 Fax: 516-829-6966
e-mail: slupkin@alcllp.comspx.com
Web site: www.ackermanlevine.com
Stanley N Lupkin, White Collar Criminal Defense
Corporate, criminal & financial investigations

American Society for the Prevention of Cruelty to Animals (ASPCA)
424 E 92nd St, New York, NY 10128
212-876-7700 x4552 Fax: 212-360-6875
e-mail: government@aspca.org
Web site: www.aspca.org
Lisa Weisberg, Sr VP, Government Affairs & Public Policy, Sr Policy Advisor
Promoting humane treatment of animals, education & advocacy programs & conducting statewide anti-cruelty investigation & enforcement

Associated Licensed Detectives of New York State
575 Madison Avenue, Suite 1006, New York, NY 10022
646-320-0143 Fax: 212-605-0222
e-mail: info@aldonys.org
Web site: www.aldonys.org
William C Vassell, President
Licensed NYS private investigators & watch, guard & patrol license holders

Offices and agencies appear in alphabetical order.

Berkshire Farm Center & Services for Youth
13640 Route 22, Canaan, NY 12029
518-781-4567 Fax: 518-781-4577
e-mail: jdecker@berkshirefarm.org
Web site: www.berkshirefarm.org
Rose W Washington, Executive Director
Multi-function agency for troubled youth & families

CUNY John Jay College of Criminal Justice
899 10th Ave, Room 625, New York, NY 10019
212-237-8600 Fax: 212-237-8607
e-mail: president@jjay.cuny.edu
Web site: www.jjay.cuny.edu
Jeremy Travis, President
Criminal justice, police & fire science, clinical psychology & forensic psychology, human dignity & human rights

Center for Alternative Sentencing & Employment Services (CASES)
346 Broadway, 3rd Fl, New York, NY 10013
212-732-0076 Fax: 212-571-0292
e-mail: jcopperman@cases.org
Web site: www.cases.org
Joel Copperman, President/Chief Executive Officer
Advocacy for the use of community sanctions that are fair, affordable & consistent with public safety

Center for Law & Justice
Pine West Plaza, Bldg 2, Washington Ave Ext, Albany, NY 12205
518-427-8361 Fax: 518-427-8362
e-mail: cflj@knick.net
Web site: www.timesunion.com/communities/cflj
Alice P Green, Executive Director
Advocacy for fair treatment of poor people & communities of color by the legal & criminal justice systems; referral, workshops, community lawyering & education

Coalition Against Domestic Violence, NYS
350 New Scotland Ave, Albany, NY 12208
518-482-5465 Fax: 518-482-3807
e-mail: newell@nyscadv.org
Web site: www.nyscadv.org
Patti Jo Newell, Director, Public Policy

Coalition Against Sexual Assault (NYS)
63 Colvin Ave, Albany, NY 12206
518-482-4222 Fax: 518-482-4248
e-mail: lafo@nyscasa.org
Web site: www.nyscasa.org
Anne Liske, Executive Director
Advocacy, public education, technical assistance & training

Correctional Association of New York
135 E 15th St, New York, NY 10003
212-254-5700 Fax: 212-473-2807
e-mail: rgangi@correctionalassociation.org
Web site: www.correctionalassociation.org
Robert Gangi, Executive Director
Drug law reform/improved prison conditions

NYS Bar Assn, Public Trust & Confidence in the Legal System
Debevoise & Plimpton LLP
919 Third Ave, New York, NY 10022
212-909-6096 Fax: 212-909-6836
e-mail: elieberman@debevoise.com
Ellen Lieberman, Chair

Education & Assistance Corporation Inc
50 Clinton St, Ste 107, Hempstead, NY 11550
516-539-0150 Fax: 516-539-0160
e-mail: lelder@eacinc.org
Web site: www.eacinc.org
Lance W Elder, President & CEO
Rehabilitation for nonviolent offenders; advocacy, education & counseling programs for youth, elderly & families

Fortune Society (The)
53 W 23rd St, 8th Fl, New York, NY 10010
212-691-7554 x501 Fax: 212-255-4948
e-mail: jpfortune@aol.com
Web site: www.fortunesociety.org
JoAnne Page, Executive Director
Education & vocational training for ex-offenders, alternatives to incarceration, counseling, drug treatment & HIV/AIDS services & referrals & transitional housing facility

Hofstra University, School of Law
121 Hofstra University, Hempstead, NY 11549-1210
212-864-6092
e-mail: lawdny@hofstra.edu
Web site: www.hofstra.edu/law
David N Yellen, Emeritus Professor of Law
Antitrust, criminal law, evidence

Legal Action Center of the City of NY Inc
153 Waverly Place, New York, NY 10014
212-243-1313 Fax: 212-675-0286
e-mail: lacinfo@lac.org
Web site: www.lac.org
Paul N Samuels, President & Director
Legal & policy issues, alcohol/drug abuse, AIDS & criminal justice

Legal Aid Society
49 Thomas St, New York, NY 10013
212-298-5215 Fax: 212-693-1149
e-mail: jpreble@legal-aid.org
Web site: www.legal-aid.org
Judith Preble, Supervising Attorney, Criminal Defense Division
Criminal defense & appeals

NYS Bar Assn, Criminal Justice Section
Michael T Kelly, Esq
1217 Delaware Ave, Apt 1003, Buffalo, NY 14209
716-886-1922 Fax: 716-886-1922
e-mail: mkelly1005@aol.com
Michael T Kelly, Chair

Offices and agencies appear in alphabetical order.

Policy Areas

Mothers Against Drunk Driving (MADD) of NYS

476 Troy-Schenectady Rd, Latham, NY 12110
518-785-6233 Fax: 518-782-1806
e-mail: madd@nycapp.rr.com
Web site: www.madd.org
Donna Kopec, Executive Director
Advocacy, public education & victim support

NYS Association of Chiefs of Police Inc

2697 Hamburg Street, Schenectady, NY 12303
518-355-3371 Fax: 518-356-5767
e-mail: nysacop@nycap.rr.com
Web site: www.nychiefs.org
John Grebert, Executive Director

NYS Correctional Officers & Police Benevolent Association Inc

102 Hackett Blvd, Albany, NY 12209
518-427-1551 Fax: 518-426-1635
Web site: www.nyscopba.org
Richard Harcrow, President

NYS Council of Probation Administrators

c/o Council of Community Svcs of NYS, Box 2, 272 Broadway,
Albany, NY 12204-2941
518-434-9194 Fax: 518-434-0392
e-mail: president@nyscopa.org
Web site: www.nyscopa.org
Robert A Sudlow, President
Provide supervision & investigation services to courts

NYS Defenders Association

194 Washington Ave, Ste 500, Albany, NY 12210-2314
518-465-3524 Fax: 518-465-3249
e-mail: info@nysda.org
Web site: www.nysda.org
Jonathan E Gradess, Executive Director
Criminal defense

NYS Deputies Association Inc

61 Laredo Dr, Rochester, NY 14624
585-247-9322 Fax: 585-247-6661
e-mail: tross1@rochester.rr.com
Web site: www.nysdeputy.org
Thomas H Ross, Executive Director

NYS Law Enforcement Officers Union, Council 82, AFSCME, AFL-CIO

Hollis V Chase Bldg, 63 Colvin Ave, Albany, NY 12206
518-489-8424 Fax: 518-435-1523
e-mail: c82@council82.org
Web site: www.council82.org
James Lyman, President

NYS Sheriffs' Association

27 Elk St, Albany, NY 12207-1002
518-434-9091 Fax: 518-434-9093
e-mail: pkehoe@nysheriffs.org
Web site: www.nysheriffs.org
Peter R Kehoe, Counsel & Executive Director

Osborne Association/South Forty

36-31 38th St, Long Island City, NY 11101
718-707-2600 Fax: 718-707-3103
e-mail: info@osborneny.org
Web site: www.osborneny.org
Anne McLaughlin, Senior Director of Employment & Training
Career/educational counseling, job referrals & training for recently released prisoners

Pace University, School of Law, John Jay Legal Services Inc

80 N Broadway, White Plains, NY 10603-3711
914-422-4333 Fax: 914-422-4391
e-mail: vmerton@law.pace.edu
Web site: www.law.pace.edu
Vanessa Merton, Assoc Dean for Clinical Edu & Exec Dir for John Jay Legal Svcs, Inc
Health law, poverty law, elder law, securities arbitration, immigration

Palladia Inc

10 Astor Pl, New York, NY 10003
212-979-8800 Fax: 212-979-0100
e-mail: info@palladiainc.org
Web site: www.palladiainc.org
Susan Ohanesian, Vice President, Residential Services
Outpatient treatment, substance abuse treatment & counseling, alternatives to incarceration & parole transitional services

Patrolmen's Benevolent Association

40 Fulton St, 17th Fl, New York, NY 10038
212-233-5531 Fax: 212-233-3952
e-mail: union@nycpba.org
Web site: www.nycpba.org
Patrick Lynch, President
NYC patrolmen's union

Police Conference of NY Inc (PCNY)

112 State St, Ste 1120, Albany, NY 12207
518-463-3283 Fax: 518-463-2488
Web site: www.pcny.org
Edward W Guzdek, President
Advocacy for law enforcement officers

Prisoners' Legal Services of New York

114 Prospect St, Ithaca, NY 14850-5616
607-273-2283 Fax: 607-272-9122
e-mail: jwein@frontiernet.net
Jerry Wein, Executive Director

Remove Intoxicated Drivers (RID-USA Inc)

1013 Nott St, PO Box 520, Schenectady, NY 12301
518-372-0034 or 518-393-4357 Fax: 518-370-4917
e-mail: ridusa@netzero.net
Web site: www.rid-usa.org
Doris Aiken, President
Victims' rights, alcohol policy & public awareness

Offices and agencies appear in alphabetical order.

Pearls' Prison Families of NY
Rochester Interfaith Jail Ministry Inc
130 Plymouth Avenue South, Rochester, NY 14614
585-428-3802
e-mail: rochesterjail/ministry@yahoo.com
Harry Bronson, Executive Director
Support services for ex-offenders, the incarcerated & their families

SUNY at Stony Brook, NY State Drinking Driver Program
Social & Behavioral Sciences, Rm North 231, Stony Brook, NY 11794-4326
631-632-7060 Fax: 631-632-4224
e-mail: pbrennan@notes.cc.sunysb.edu
Patricia Brennan, Director
Drinking & driving education & prevention

Stillman & Friedman PC
425 Park Ave, New York, NY 10022
212-223-0200 Fax: 212-223-1942
e-mail: cstillman@stillmanfriedman.com
Charles A Stillman, Partner
White collar criminal law

Trooper Foundation-State of New York Inc
3 Airport Park Blvd, Latham, NY 12110-1441
518-785-1002 Fax: 518-785-1003
e-mail: rmincher@nystf.org
Web site: www.nystrooperfoundation.org
Rachel L Mincher, Foundation Administrator
Supports programs & services of the NYS Police

Vera Institute of Justice
233 Broadway, 12th Fl, New York, NY 10279-1299
212-334-1300 Fax: 212-941-9407
e-mail: mgolden@vera.org
Web site: www.vera.org
Michael Jacobson, Director
Research, design & implementation of demonstration projects in criminal justice & social equity in partnership with governmental community organizations

Women's Prison Association & Home Inc
110 Second Ave, New York, NY 10003
212-674-1163 Fax: 212-677-1981
Web site: www.wpaonline.org
Ann Jacobs, Executive Director
Community corrections & family preservation programs

Policy Areas

Offices and agencies appear in alphabetical order.

EDUCATION

New York State

GOVERNOR'S OFFICE

Governor's Office
Executive Chamber
State Capitol
Albany, NY 12224
518-474-8390 Fax: 518-474-1513
Web site: www.state.ny.us

Governor:
George E Pataki 518-474-8390
Executive Director:
Kara Lanspery 518-474-8390
Secretary to the Governor:
John P Cahill. 518-474-4246
Senior Policy Advisor to the Governor:
Jeffrey Lovell 518-486-9671
Counsel to the Governor-Attorney General, Budget:
Richard Platkin. 518-474-8343
Senior Assistant Counsel to the Governor-Council on Arts, Dormitory
Authority, Education, Higher Education, Ofc for Technology, Real
Property, Rent Control, CUNY, SUNY:
Martin Bienstock 518-474-1310
Director, Communications:
David Catalfamo. 518-474-8418

EXECUTIVE DEPARTMENTS AND RELATED AGENCIES

Board of Regents
State Education Bldg, 89 Washington Ave
Rm 110
Albany, NY 12234
518-474-5889 Fax: 518-486-2405
Web site: www.regents.nysed.gov

Chancellor:
Robert M Bennett (2010) 716-694-6783
Vice Chancellor:
Adelaide L Sanford (2010). 718-722-2796
Commissioner, University President:
Richard P Mills. 518-474-5844
e-mail: rmills@mail.nysed.gov
Secretary to the Board:
David Johnson 518-474-5889
e-mail: djohnson@mail.nysed.gov
Member:
Carol Bellamy (2010). 212-326-7028
Member:
Anthony S Bottar (2006) 315-422-3466
Member:
Joseph E Bowman, Jr (2009) 518-442-4987
Member:
John Brademas (2007) 212-998-2407

Member:
Geraldine Chapey (2008) 718-634-8471
Member:
Milton L Cofield (2007). 585-248-8494
Member:
Saul B Cohen 914-633-7889
Member:
Lorraine A Cortes-Vasquez (2008) 212-233-8955
Member:
James C Dawson (2010). 518-643-9289
Member:
Arnold B Gardner (2009) 716-845-6000
Member:
Harry Phillips, III (2010) 914-948-2228
Member:
James R Tallon, Jr (2007). 212-494-0777
Member:
Meryl H Tisch (2006). 212-879-9414
Member:
Roger B Tilles (2010). 516-364-2533

Children & Family Services, Office of
52 Washington St
Rensselaer, NY 12144
518-473-7793 Fax: 518-486-7550
Web site: www.dfa.state.ny.us

Commissioner:
John A Johnson. 518-473-8437
Executive Deputy Commissioner:
Roger Biagi. 518-474-7768
Assistant Commissioner, Public Affairs:
Sandra A Brown 518-402-3130
e-mail: cfspio@dfa.state.ny.us
Director, Strategic Planning & Policy Development:
Nancy Martinez 518-473-1776
Director, Equal Employment & Diversity Development:
Mikki Ward-Harper 518-474-3715

Office of Youth Development
Assistant Commissioner:
Sally Herrick. 518-473-8544

Advantage AfterSchool Program
Director:
Carole Miller 518-473-4463

Bureau of Compliance
Director:
Matt Murell 518-402-3830

Office of National & Community Service - Americorps

Youth Development Field Operations
Director:
Larry Pasti 518-561-8740

Offices and agencies appear in alphabetical order.

Education Department

State Education Bldg, Rm 124
89 Washington Ave
Albany, NY 12234
518-474-3852 Fax: 518-486-5631
Web site: www.nysed.gov

Commissioner, University President:
Richard P Mills.....................518-474-5844
e-mail: rmills@mail.nysed.gov
Assistant to the Commissioner:
Peggy Rivers.......................518-474-5845
e-mail: privers@mail.nysed.gov
Counsel & Deputy Commissioner, Legal Affairs:
Kathy A Ahearn....................518-474-6400
e-mail: kahearn@mail.nysed.gov

Cultural Education Office

10A 33 Cultural Education Center, Madison Avenue, Albany, NY 12230
Web site: www.oce.nysed.gov
Deputy Commissioner:
Carole F Huxley..........518-474-5976/fax: 518-474-2718
e-mail: chuxley@mail.nysed.gov

Educational TV & Public Broadcasting Services
Director:
Robert Reilly.....................518-474-5862
e-mail: rreilly@mail.nysed.gov

State Archives
Assistant Commissioner & State Archivist:
Christine Ward....................518-473-7091
e-mail: cward@mail.nysed.gov
Archival Services
Principal Archivist:
Kathleen Roe....................518-473-4254
Government Records Services
Chief:
Robert Arnold...................518-474-6926
Public Programs & Outreach
Coordinator:
Judy Hohmann...................518-473-9098
Records Center
Chief:
John Welter....................518-457-4801
Training & Grants Support Services
Chief:
vacant.........................518-474-5834

State Library
Empire State Plaza, Cultural Education Center, Albany, NY 12230
Web site: www.nysl.nysed.gov
State Librarian & Assistant Commissioner for Libraries:
Janet Welch.....................518-474-5930
e-mail: jwelch2@mail.nysed.gov
Public Information Officer:
Valerie Chevrette..........518-474-5961/fax: 518-486-2152
Research Library
Interim Director:
Mary Redmond..................518-473-1189
Statewide Library Services
Coordinator Statewide Library Services:
Carol Desch....................518-474-7196

State Museum Office
Assistant Commissioner & Director:
Clifford A Siegfried............518-474-5812
e-mail: csiegfri@mail.nysed.gov

Exhibit Design, Division of Exhibits / Public & Educational Svcs
Director, Exhibits:
Mark Schaming..................518-486-2031
Exhibit Production
Supervisor:
David LaPlante.................518-402-5531
Floor Services
Director:
John Krumdieck.................518-474-0076
Museum Education - Public Programs & Visitor Services
Chief:
Jeanine Grinage................518-486-2003
Research & Collections
Director:
John Hart......................518-474-5813
Acting State Geologist:
William Kelly..................518-474-5816
Museum Services:
Vacant.........................518-486-2037

Office of Elementary, Middle, Secondary, Continuing Education

89 Washington Ave, EBA, Rm 875, Albany, NY 12234
Web site: www.emsc.nysed.gov
Deputy Commissioner:
James A Kadamus.........518-474-5915/fax: 518-486-2233
e-mail: jkadamus@mail.nysed.gov
Lead Contact, District Superintendent's Office:
Raymond Kesper.........518-474-8076/fax: 518-473-2860
e-mail: rkesper@mail.nysed.gov
Lead Contact, Administrative Support Group:
Merril-Lee Lenegar.............518-486-1544

Curriculum & Instructional Support
Assistant Commissioner:
Jean Stevens...........518-474-8892/fax: 518-474-0319
e-mail: jstevens@mail.nysed.gov
Adult Education & Workforce Development
Lead Contact:
Thomas Orsini..................518-474-8940
Career & Technical Education
Lead Contact:
Konrad Raup....................518-486-1547
Curriculum, Instruction & Instructional Technology
Lead Contact:
Anne Schiano...........518-402-5544/fax: 518-486-1385
Summer School of the Arts
Lead Contact:
Mary Daley.....................518-474-8773

School Improvement & Community Services (NYC) fax: 718-722-4559
55 Hanson Place, Brooklyn, NY 11217
Associate Commissioner:
Shelia Evans-Tranumn......718-722-2796 or 518-474-4715
e-mail: sevans-tra@mail.nysed.gov
Coordinator, School Accountability Workgroup:
Ira Schwartz...................718-722-2796
e-mail: ischwart@mail.nysed.gov
Early Education & Reading Initiatives
89 Washington Ave, EBA, Rm 381, Albany, NY 12234
Lead Contact:
Cynthia Gallagher.......518-474-5807/fax: 518-486-7290
NYC Intra/Interagency Group
Lead Contact:
Sandra Herndon.................718-722-2784
NYC School Improvement
Lead Contact:
Sandra Norfleet................718-722-2636

Offices and agencies appear in alphabetical order.

Title I School & Community Services
Lead Contact:
    Roberto Reyes 518-473-0295

School Improvements & Community Services (Regional)
Assistant Commissioner:
    James Butterworth 518-474-4817
    e-mail: jbutterw@mail.nysed.gov
Native American Education
Lead Contact:
    Adrian Cooke. 518-474-0537
Nonpublic School Services
Lead Contact:
    Tom Hogan 518-474-3879
Planning & Professional Development
Lead Contact:
    Laurie Rowe 518-473-7155
Public School Choice
Lead Contact:
    Darlene Mengel 518-474-1762
Regional School Services
Lead Contact:
    James Viola 518-474-5923
Student Support Services
Lead Contact:
    Rebecca Gardner 518-486-6090/fax: 518-474-8299

School Operations & Management Services
Coordinator:
    Charles Szuberla. 518-474-2238
Coordinator, State Aid Workgroup:
    Deborah Cunningham 518-402-5286
Child Nutrition Program Administration
Lead Contact:
    Frances O'Donnell. 518-473-8781
Facilities & Management Services
Lead Contact:
    Carl Thurnau 518-474-3906

Standards, Assessment & Reporting
Assistant Commissioner:
    David Abrams 518-473-7880
    e-mail: dabrams@mail.nysed.gov
Bilingual Education
Lead Contact:
    Carmen Perez-Hogan. 518-474-8775
Information & Reporting Services
Lead Contact:
    Martha Musser. 518-474-7965
    e-mail: mmusser@mail.nysed.gov
State Assessment
Lead Contact, Administration:
    Steven Katz 518-474-5099
Lead Contact, Development:
    Deborah Hogan 518-474-5900

Office of Higher Education
89 Washington Ave, 2nd Fl Mezzanine, EB West, Albany, NY 12234
Web site: www.highered.nysed.gov
Deputy Commissioner:
Johanna Duncan-Poitier. 518-474-3862/fax: 518-473-2056
e-mail: hedepcom@mail.nysed.gov

Office of K-16 Initiatives & Access Programs
Executive Coordinator:
    Stanley S Hansen, Jr 518-474-3719/fax: 518-474-7468
    e-mail: shansen2@mail.nysed.gov
Collegiate Development Programs Unit
Supervisor:
    James Donsbach 518-474-5313

Pre-Collegiate Preparation Programs Unit
Supervisor:
    Lewis Hall 518-486-2976
Scholarship & Grants Administration
Supervisor:
    Lewis Hall 518-486-2976
Teacher Development Programs
Director:
    Hector Millan. 518-486-6042
    e-mail: hmillan@mail.nysed.gov

Office of Quality Assurance
Assistant Commissioner:
    Joseph P Frey. 518-486-3633
College & University Evaluation
Coordinator:
    Barbara D Meinert. 518-474-1551
Proprietary School Supervision
Chief:
    Carole Yates 518-474-3969
Research & Information Systems
Manager:
    Glenwood Rowse. 518-474-5091
    e-mail: growse@mail.nysed.gov

Office of Teaching Initiatives
Teacher Certification
Executive Director:
    Robert G Bentley 518-474-3817 x340
    e-mail: rbentley@mail.nysed.gov
Teacher Policy Unit & Office of School Personnel Review & Accountability
Executive Director:
    Joseph B Porter 518-474-6440
    e-mail: jporter@mail.nysed.gov

Office of Management Services
Web site: www.oms.nysed.gov
Deputy Commissioner/COO:
Theresa E Savo 518-474-2547/fax: 518-473-2827

Administration
Director, Communications:
    R Alan Ray 518-474-1201/fax: 518-473-2977
    e-mail: aray@mail.nysed.gov
Legislative Coordinator (State):
    Claudia Alexander 518-486-5644
Diversity, Ethics & Access:
    Steven Earle 518-474-1265
Facilities & Business Services:
    George Webb 518-474-7770
Human Resources Management:
    Gayle Bowden 518-474-5883

Fiscal Services
Chief Financial Officer:
    Theresa E Savo. 518-474-2387
    e-mail: tsavo@mail.nysed.gov
Budget Coordination:
    Lenton D Simms 518-474-6571
Education Finance Director:
    Burt Porter 518-474-8825
Fiscal Management:
    Michael DiVirgilio. 518-474-7751
Child Nutrition Reimbursement:
    John H Feldkamp 518-474-3926
Categorical Aid:
    Margaret Zollo 518-473-4815
Program Services Reimbursement:
    Thomas Hamel 518-486-2991

Offices and agencies appear in alphabetical order.

STAC (Systems to Track & Account for Children):
Harold Matott 518-474-7116

Information Technology Services
Chief Information Officer:
David Walsh. 518-486-1702
Information Technology Services (ITS) Director:
Richard Melita 518-474-4640

Planning & Policy Development
Associate Commissioner:
Thomas E Sheldon 518-474-5836
e-mail: tsheldon@mail.nysed.gov
Audit Services:
Michael Abbott. 518-473-4516
Organizational Effectiveness:
Rebecca Kennard 518-486-5289
Secretary to the Board of Regents:
David Johnson 518-474-5889
e-mail: djohnson@mail.nysed.gov

Office of the Professions . . . . fax: 518-473-2056
89 Washington Ave, EB, 2nd Fl, West Mezz, Albany, NY 12234
Fax: 518-473-2056
Web site: www.op.nysed.gov
Deputy Commissioner:
Johanna Duncan-Poitier. 518-474-3817 x470
e-mail: opdepcom@mail.nysed.gov
Director, Management Operations:
Leslie E Templeman. 518-474-3862
Coordinator, Customer Service:
Tony Lofrumento. 518-474-3817 x570
e-mail: op4info@mail.nysed.gov

Office of Professional Responsibility
Executive Director:
Frank Munoz. 518-474-3817 x440
e-mail: opexdir@mail.nysed.gov
Office of Special Projects & Legislation
Coordinator:
Cynthia Laks. 518-474-3817 x190
Professional Assistance Program
Acting Executive Secretary:
Lawrence DeMers 518-474-3817 x480
Professional Discipline
475 Park Ave South, New York, NY 10016
Director:
Louis Catone 212-951-6400
Director, Investigations:
Daniel Kelleher 212-951-6400
Director, Legal Services:
Christopher Lefkarites. 212-951-6550
Director, Prosecutions:
Vacant. 212-951-6400
State Review
Chief:
Paul Kelly 518-485-9373

Professional Education Program Review
Supervisor:
Gail Rosettie 518-474-3817 x360
e-mail: opprogs@mail.nysed.gov

Professional Licensing Services
Director:
Robert G Bentley. 518-474-3817 x340
e-mail: opdpls@mail.nysed.gov
Chief, Office of Comparative Education:
Leonard Lapinski 518-474-3817 x300

State Boards for the Professions
Acupuncture, Occupational Therapy, Speech-Language Pathology & Audiology
Executive Secretary:
Vacant 518-474-3817 x100
Architecture & Landscape Architecture
Executive Secretary:
Robert Lopez 518-474-3817 x110
Chiropractic
Executive Secretary:
Cynthia T Laks. 518-474-3817 x190
Dentistry & Optometry
Executive Secretary:
Milton Lawney. 518-474-3817 x550
Engineering & Land Surveying & Interior Design
Executive Secretary:
Jane Blair 518-474-3817 x140
Medicine, Dietetics-Nutrition, Athletic Training, Medical Physics & Veterinary Medicine
Executive Secretary:
Thomas J Monahan. 518-474-3817 x560
Nursing & Respiratory Therapy
Executive Secretary:
Barbara Zittel 518-474-3817 x120
Pharmacy & Midwifery
Executive Secretary:
Lawrence H Mokhiber 518-474-3817 x130
Psychology & Massage Therapy
Executive Secretary:
Kathleen M Doyle 518-474-3817 x150
Public Accountancy & Certified Shorthand Reporting
Executive Secretary:
Daniel J Dustin. 518-474-3817 x160
Social Work & Mental Health Practitioners
Executive Secretary:
David Hamilton 518-474-3817 x450

Vocational & Educational Services for Individuals With Disabilities Office (VESID) . . . . fax: 518-474-8802
One Commerce Plaza, Rm 1606, Albany, NY 12234
Fax: 518-474-8802
Web site: www.vesid.nysed.gov
Deputy Commissioner:
Rebecca Cort 518-474-2714
e-mail: rcort@mail.nysed.gov
Assistant Commissioner:
Edward Placke 518-473-4818

Fiscal & Administrative Services
Coordinator:
Rosemary Ellis Johnson. 518-486-4038
Manager, Data Collection:
Inni Barone. 518-486-4678
Manager, Contracts & Grants:
Jack LaFrank 518-486-6585
Manager, Support Services:
Michael Plotzker 518-473-4823
Manager, Budget & Finance:
William Keane 518-473-4824
Manager, Technology:
Lori Scalera 518-486-4609
Manager, Vendor Review:
Lisa Kowalik 518-474-5411
Quality Assurance - Statewide Special Education
Acting Statewide Coordinator:
Daniel Johnson 518-486-6221
Upstate Regional Coordinator:
Daniel Johnson 518-486-6221

Policy Areas

Offices and agencies appear in alphabetical order.

State School for the Blind at Batavia
2A Richmond Ave, Batavia, NY 14020
Superintendent:
Jennifer Spas Ervin 716-343-5384
State School for the Deaf at Rome
401 Turin St, Rome, NY 13340
Interim Superintendent:
Gregory Carey 315-337-8400

Program Development & Support Svcs / Special Ed Policy & Partnerships
Coordinator:
Fredric DeMay 518-486-7462
Manager, Deaf & Hard of Hearing Services:
Dorothy Steele 518-474-2925
Supervisor, Lifelong Services:
Daniel J Ryan 518-486-7462
Supervisor, Special Education Policy & Partnerships:
Candace Shyer 518-473-2878

Special Education Quality Assurance Regional Offices
Central Regional Office
State Office Bldg, 333 E Washington St, Syracuse, NY 13202
Region Office Supervisor:
Jackie Bumbalo 315-428-3287/fax: 315-428-3286
Eastern Regional Office
One Commerce Plaza, Rm 1623, Albany, NY 12234
Regional Office Supervisor:
James DeLorenzo 518-486-6366/fax: 518-486-7693
Hudson Valley Regional Office
1950 Edgewater St, Yorktown Heights, NY 10598
Regional Office Supervisor:
Christine Efner 518-473-1185/fax: 518-402-3582
Long Island Regional Office
The Kellum Education Center, 887 Kellum St, Lindenhurst, NY 11757
Regional Office Supervisor:
Stephen Berman 631-884-8530/fax: 631-884-8540
New York City Regional Office
55 Hanson Place, Rm 545, Brooklyn, NY 11217-1580
NYC Regional Coordinator:
Patricia Shubert 718-722-4544/fax: 718-722-2032
Western Regional Office
2A Richmond Ave, Batavia, NY 14020
Regional Office Supervisor:
Phyllis Powers 716-821-7360/fax: 716-821-7364

Vocational Rehabilitation Operations
Acting Director, District Office Administration:
Debora Brown-Grant 518-473-1626
e-mail: dbrowngr@mail.nysed.gov
Director, Operations-District Office Administration:
William Deschenes 518-486-4035
e-mail: wdeschen@mail.nysed.gov
Manager, Independent Living Centers:
Robert Gumson 518-474-2925
Albany District Office
80 Wolf Road, Albany, NY 12205
Regional Director:
David Segalla 518-473-8097
Bronx District Office
1215 Zerega Ave, Bronx, NY 10462
District Office Manager:
Mary Faulkner 718-931-3500
Brooklyn District Office
55 Hanson Pl, Brooklyn, NY 11217-1578
District Office Manager:
Frank Stechel 718-722-6700
Buffalo District Office
508 Main St, Buffalo, NY 14202

Regional Coordinator:
Susan Piper 716-848-8001
Hauppauge District Office
State Office Bldg, Veterans Memorial Hwy, Hauppauge, NY 11788-5127
District Office Manager:
Ingo Gloeckner 631-952-6357
Hempstead District Office
50 Clinton St, Rm 708, Hempstead, NY 11550
District Office Manager:
Alex Jacobs 518-483-6510
Malone District Office
209 W Main St, Malone, NY 12953
District Office Manager:
Steve Novacich 518-483-3530
Manhattan District Office
116 West 32nd St, 6th Fl, New York, NY 10001
Regional Coordinator:
William Ursillo 212-630-2300
Mid-Hudson District Office
Manchester Mill Ctr, 301 Manchester Rd, Ste 200, Poughkeepsie, NY 12603
District Office Manager:
Bruce Solomkin 845-452-5325
Queens District Office
One LeFrak City Plaza, 20th Fl, 59-17 Junction Blvd, Corona, NY 11368
Regional Coordinator:
Aurora Farrington 718-271-9346
Rochester District Office
Wilson Bldg, 109 S Union St, 2nd Fl, Rochester, NY 14607
District Office Manager:
Nicolette Leathersich 585-238-2900
Southern Tier District Office
44 Hawley St, Binghamton, NY 13901
Regional Coordinator:
Richard Bohman 607-721-8400
Syracuse District Office
333 E Washington St, 2nd Fl, Rm 230, Syracuse, NY 13202-1428
Regional Coordinator:
John Emperor 315-428-4179
Utica District Office
207 Genesee St, Rm 801, Utica, NY 13501-2812
District Office Manager:
John Tracy 315-793-2536
White Plains District Office
75 South Broadway, 1st Fl, White Plains, NY 10601
District Office Manager:
Mark Ridgeway 914-946-1313

Science, Technology & Academic Research, Office of
30 South Pearl St
11th Fl
Albany, NY 12207
518-292-5700 Fax: 518-292-5780
Web site: www.nystar.state.ny.us

Executive Director:
Russell W Bessette 518-292-5700
Director, Operations:
James A Denn 518-292-5700/fax: 518-292-5798
Director, Programs:
Kathleen J Wise 518-292-5700
General Counsel:
Robert Beshaw 518-292-5700

Offices and agencies appear in alphabetical order.

Director, Finance:
Edward J Hamilton. 518-292-5700
Director, Public Information:
James A Denn 518-292-5700/fax: 518-292-5780
e-mail: jdenn@nystar.state.ny.us

Centers for Advanced Technology

Center for Advanced Ceramic Technology at Alfred University
352 McMahon Engineering Bldg, 2 Pine St, Alfred, NY 14802-1296
Director:
Vasantha Amarakoon 607-871-2486/fax: 607-871-3469

Center for Advanced Materials Processing at Clarkson University
Box 5665, Potsdam, NY 13699-5665
Director:
S V Babu. 315-268-2336/fax: 315-268-7615

Center for Advanced Technology in Biomedical & Bioengineering
SUNY at Buffalo, 162K Farber Hall, 3435 Main St, Buffalo, NY
14214-3092
Director:
William M Mihalko. 716-829-2982/fax: 716-829-3945

Center for Advanced Technology in Diagnostic Tools & Sensor Systems
SUNY at Stony Brook, 214 Old Chemistry Bldg, 2nd Fl, Stony Brook,
NY 11794-3717
Director:
Serge Luryi 631-632-1368/fax: 631-632-8529

Center for Advanced Technology in Electronic Imaging Systems
Univ of Rochester, Taylor Hall, 260 Hutchison Rd, Rochester, NY 14627
Director:
Eby Friedman 585-275-1022/fax: 585-276-0200

Center for Advanced Technology in Information Management
Columbia University, 630 W 168th St, PH-15-1501, New York, NY
10032
Director:
Edward H Shortliffe 212-305-2944/fax: 212-305-0196

Center for Advanced Technology in Life Science Enterprise
Cornell University, 130 Biotechnology Bldg, Ithaca, NY 14853-2703
Director:
Stephen Kresovich 607-255-2300/fax: 607-255-6249

Center for Advanced Technology in Photonic Applications
Dept of Physics, City College of CUNY, 138th St & Convent Ave Rm
J419, New York, NY 10031
Director:
Robert R Alfano 212-650-5531/fax: 212-650-5530

Center for Automation Technologies at Rensselaer Polytechnic Inst
CII Bldg, Rm 8015, Troy, NY 12180-3590
Director:
Ray Puffer . . . . 518-276-8990 or 518-276-8087
fax: 518-276-4897

Center for Biotechnology
SUNY at Stony Brook, Psychology A, 3rd Fl, Stony Brook, NY
11794-2580
Director:
Clinton T Rubin. 631-632-8521/fax: 631-632-8577

Center for Computer Applications & Software Engineering
Syracuse University, 2-212 Ctr for Science & Tech, Syracuse, NY 13244
Director:
Shui-Kai Chin 315-443-1060/fax: 315-443-4745

Center in Nanomaterials and Nanoelectronics
Albany Institue for Materials, CESTM Bldg, 251 Fuller Rd, Rm B110,
Albany, NY 12203

Director:
Alain E Kaloyeros. 518-437-8686/fax: 518-437-8687

Ctr for Advanced Technology in Telecommunications at Polytechnic U
5 MetroTech Center, Rm LC 208, Brooklyn, NY 11201
Director:
Shivendra S Panwar 718-260-3050/fax: 718-260-3074

Future Energy Systems CAT at Rensselaer Polytechnic Inst
Ctr for Integrated Electronics and, 9023 Low Ctr for Industrial Innovation,
110 8th St, Troy, NY 12180
Director:
Omkaram Nalamasu 518-276-3290/fax: 518-276-2990

Integrated Electronics Engineering Center
Thomas J Watson School of Engineering, S, Vestal Pkwy East, PO Box
6000, Binghamton, NY 13902-6000
Director:
Bahgat Sammakia 607-777-4332/fax: 607-777-4683

Regional Technology Development Centers

Alliance for Manufacturing & Technology
59 Court St, 6th Fl, State St Entrance, Binghamton, NY 13901
Executive Director:
Edward Gaetano. 607-774-0022 x304/fax: 607-774-0026

Center for Economic Growth
63 State St, Albany, NY 12207
President:
Kelly Lovell 518-465-8975/fax: 518-465-6681

Central New York Technology Development Organization
1201 E Fayette St, Syracuse, NY 13210
President:
Robert I Trachtenberg. 315-425-5144/fax: 315-233-1259

Council for International Trade, Technology, Education & Communication
Peyton Hall, Rm 101, Main St, Potsdam, NY 13676
Executive Director:
Thomas Plastino. 315-268-3778 x24/fax: 315-268-4432

High Technology of Rochester
Chamber of Commerce Bldg, 5 Bragdon Pl, Rochester, NY 14604
Executive Director:
Paul Wettenhall. 585-327-7920/fax: 585-327-7931

Hudson Valley Technology Development Center
300 Westage Business Ctr, Ste 130, Fishkill, NY 12524
Executive Director:
Thomas J Phillips, Sr 845-896-6934 x3006/fax: 845-896-7006

Industrial & Technology Assistance Corp
253 Broadway, Rm 302, New York, NY 10007
President:
Sara Garretson. 212-442-2990/fax: 212-442-4567

Long Island Forum for Technology
111 West Main St, Bayshore, NY 11706
Executive Director:
Patricia Howley. 631-969-3700/fax: 631-969-4489

Mohawk Valley Applied Technology Corp
207 Genesee St, Ste 405, Utica, NY 13501
President:
Paul MacEnroe 315-793-8050/fax: 315-793-8057

Western New York Technology Development Center
726 Exchange St, Ste 620, Buffalo, NY 14210
President:
Robert J Martin 716-636-3626/fax: 716-845-6418

Offices and agencies appear in alphabetical order.

CORPORATIONS, AUTHORITIES AND COMMISSIONS

City University Construction Fund
555 W 57th St
10th Fl
New York, NY 10019
212-541-0171 Fax: 212-541-0401

Chair:
Harvey Auerbach 212-541-0171
Executive Director:
Emma Espino Macari. 212-794-5315
e-mail: emma.macari@mail.cuny.edu
Counsel:
Frederick Schaffer 212-794-5506
Chief Fiscal Officer:
Catherine Yang. 212-541-0458
e-mail: catherine.yang@mail.cuny.edu
Fiscal Coordinator:
Denise Phillips 212-541-0190
e-mail: denise.phillips@mail.cuny.edu

New York City School Construction Authority
30-30 Thomson Ave
Long Island City, NY 11101-3045
718-472-8000 Fax: 718-472-8840
Web site: www.nycsca.org

Chair/Chancellor:
Joel I Klein 718-472-8000
President & Chief Executive Officer:
William H Goldstein 718-472-8001/fax: 718-472-8009
Vice President, General Counsel:
Ross J Holden 718-472-8220/fax: 718-472-8088
Senior Director, Real Estate:
Lorraine Grillo. 718-472-8216/fax: 718-472-8040
Corporate Secretary:
Michael Szabaga 718-472-8302/fax: 718-472-8088

New York State Dormitory Authority
515 Broadway
Albany, NY 12207-2964
518-257-3000 Fax: 518-257-3100
e-mail: dabonds@dasny.org
Web site: www.dasny.org

One Penn Plaza
52nd Fl
New York, NY 10119-0098
212-273-5000
Fax: 212-273-5121

539 Franklin St
Buffalo, NY 14202-1109
716-884-9780
Fax: 716-884-9787

Chair:
Gail H Gordon. 518-257-3180/fax: 518-257-3183

Executive Director:
Maryanne Gridley 518-257-3180/fax: 518-257-3183
Deputy Executive Director:
Michael T Corrigan 518-257-3192/fax: 518-257-3183
Chief Fiscal officer:
John G Pasicznyk 518-257-3630/fax: 518-257-3100
e-mail: jpasiczn@dasny.org
General Counsel:
Jeffrey M Pohl. 518-257-3120/fax: 518-257-3101
e-mail: jpohl@dasny.org
Managing Director, Construction:
Douglas M VanVleck 518-257-3200/fax: 518-257-3100
e-mail: dvanvlec@dasny.org
Managing Director, Policy & Program Development:
Lora K Lefebvre 518-257-3163/fax: 518-257-3387
e-mail: llefebvr@dasny.org
Managing Director, Public Finance:
Cheryl Ishmael. 518-257-3362/fax: 518-257-3100
e-mail: cishmael@dasny.org
Director, Communications & Marketing:
Paul Burgdorf 518-257-3380/fax: 518-257-3387
e-mail: pburgdor@dasny.org
Press Officer:
Claudia Hutton. 518-257-3382/fax: 518-257-3387
e-mail: chutton@dasny.org

New York State Higher Education Services Corp (NYSHESC)
99 Washington Ave
Albany, NY 12255
518-473-7087 or 888-697-4372 Fax: 518-474-2839
Web site: www.hesc.org

President & Chief Executive Officer:
Michael R Wilton, Jr 518-474-5592
e-mail: mwilton@hesc.org
Executive Vice President:
Pierre L Alric 518-474-5775
e-mail: palric@hesc.org
Senior Vice President, Corporate Finance & Chief Fiscal Officer:
Lisa Smith. 518-473-1200
e-mail: lsmith@hesc.org
Deputy Counsel:
Marin Gibson 518-474-3219
e-mail: mgibson@hesc.org
Senior Vice President, Corporate Relations:
Robert E Butler. 518-473-2523
e-mail: rbutler@hesc.org
Senior Vice President, Communications:
Ronald Kermani 518-402-3349
e-mail: rkermani@hesc.org
Senior Vice President, Information Technology:
Victor Stucchi. 518-474-7083
e-mail: vstucchi@hesc.org
Senior Vice President, Customer Relations:
Thomas Dalton 518-473-0733
e-mail: tdalton@hesc.org
Acting Director, Human Resources Management:
Linda Dillon 518-474-0510
e-mail: ldillon@hesc.org

New York State Teachers' Retirement System
10 Corporate Woods Dr
Albany, NY 12211-2395

Offices and agencies appear in alphabetical order.

518-447-2666 Fax: 518-447-2695
Web site: www.nystrs.albany.ny.us

Executive Director:
  George M Philip 518-447-2666
    e-mail: execdir@nystrs.state.ny.us
General Counsel:
  Wayne Schneider 518-447-2722
Actuary:
  Lawrence A Johansen 518-447-2611
Director, Administration:
  William S O'Brien 518-447-2730
Director, Member Relations, Public Relations:
  David Daly 518-447-2910/fax: 518-447-2875
Real Estate Investment Officer:
  James D Campbell 518-447-2752
Securities Investment Officer:
  Joseph N Vet 518-447-2921

State University Construction Fund

353 Broadway
Albany, NY 12246
518-689-2500 Fax: 518-689-2634
Web site: www.sucf.suny.edu

General Manager:
  Philip W Wood 518-689-2501
Acting General Counsel:
  William K Barczak 518-689-2514/fax: 518-689-2634

NEW YORK STATE LEGISLATURE

See Legislative Branch in Section 1 for additional Standing Committee and Subcommittee information.

Assembly Standing Committees

Education
Chair:
  Steven Sanders (D) 518-455-5506
Ranking Minority Member:
  James D Conte (R) 518-455-5732

Higher Education
Chair:
  Ronald J Canestrari (D) 518-455-4474

Ranking Minority Member:
  Joel M Miller (R) 518-455-5725

Libraries & Education Technology
Chair:
  Sandra R Galef (D) 518-455-5348
Ranking Minority Member:
  Donna Ferrara (R) 518-455-4684

Assembly Task Forces

Skills Development & Career Education, Legislative Commission on
Assembly Chair:
  Joan K Christensen (D) 518-455-5283
Program Manager:
  Brenda Carter 518-455-4865/fax: 518-455-4175

University-Industry Cooperation, Legislative Task Force on
Chair:
  William B Magnarelli (D) 518-455-4826
Staff Coordinator:
  Maureen Schoolman 518-455-4884/fax: 518-455-4175

Senate Standing Committees

Education
Chair:
  Stephen M Saland (R) 518-455-2411
Ranking Minority Member:
  Suzi Oppenheimer (D) 518-455-2031

Subcommittee
Libraries
  Chair:
    Hugh T Farley (R) 518-455-2181
  Legislative Associate:
    Marian Crounse 518-455-2181/fax: 518-455-2271

Higher Education
Chair:
  Kenneth P LaValle (R) 518-455-3121
Ranking Minority Member:
  Toby Ann Stavisky (D) 518-455-3461

U.S. Government

EXECUTIVE DEPARTMENTS AND RELATED AGENCIES

National Archives & Records Administration

Franklin D Roosevelt Presidential Library & Museum
  4079 Albany Post Rd, Hyde Park, NY 12538
  Web site: www.fdrlibrary.marist.edu
Director:
  Cynthia M Koch 845-486-7770/fax: 845-486-1147
    e-mail: roosevelt.library@nara.gov

US Defense Department

US Military Academy
  West Point, NY 10996
  845-938-4011
  Web site: www.usma.edu
Superintendent:
  Lt Gen William J Lennox, Jr 845-938-2610
Director, Public Affairs:
  LTC Kent Cassella 845-938-3808/fax: 845-446-5820

Offices and agencies appear in alphabetical order.

US Education Department

Web site: www.ed.gov

Region 2 - NY, NJ, PR, Vi . . . . fax: 212-264-4427
75 Park Pl, 12th Fl, New York, NY 10007
Secretary's Regional Representative:
 Valarie Smith 212-637-6283
 e-mail: valarie.smith@ed.gov
Deputy Secretary's Regional Representative:
 Orysia Dmytrenko 212-637-6284

Civil Rights
Regional Director:
 Randolph Wills 212-637-6332/fax: 212-264-3803
 e-mail: randolph.wills@ed.gov
Chief Civil Rights Attorney:
 Steven Pereira. 212-637-6336
 e-mail: steven.pereira@ed.gov

Federal Student Aid
NY Team Area Case Director:
 William Swift 212-637-6418/fax: 212-264-5025
 e-mail: william.swift@ed.gov
Director, Loan Client Accoumt Management Group Team Leader:
 David A Sola 617-565-5810/fax: 617-565-8636
 e-mail: david.sola@ed.gov

Financial Partner Services
Director, Eastern Regions:
 AnnMaria Fusco 212-637-6432/fax: 212-264-0772
 e-mail: ann.maria.fusco@ed.gov

Office of Inspector General
Regional Inspector General, Audit:
 Daniel Schultz 212-637-6271/fax: 212-264-5228
 e-mail: daniel.schultz@ed.gov
Regional Inspector General, Investigations:
 Gary Mathison. 212-264-4104/fax: 212-637-0603
 e-mail: gary.mathison@ed.gov

Regional Grants Representative
Regional Grants Representative:
 Earl Williams 212-637-6397
 e-mail: earl.williams@ed.gov

Rehabilitation Services Administration
Regional Commissioner:
 Allen Kropp. 212-223-4577/fax: 212-264-3029
 e-mail: allen.kropp@ed.gov
Assistant Regional Commissioner, Management & Support Services:
 Gennaro Iodice 212-637-6449
 e-mail: gennaro.iodice@ed.gov

US Transportation Department

US Merchant Marine Academy . . . . fax: 516-773-5774
300 Steamboat Road, Kings Point, NY 11024-1699
516-773-5000 Fax: 516-773-5774
Web site: www.usmma.edu
Superintendent:
 VAdm Joseph D Stewart 516-773-5348/fax: 516-773-5347

U.S. CONGRESS

See U.S. Congress Chapter for additional Standing Committee and Subcommittee information.

House of Representatives Standing Committees

Education & the Workforce
Chair:
 John A Boehner (R-OH). 202-225-6205
Ranking Minority Member:
 George Miller (D-CA) 202-225-2095
New York Delegate:
 Timothy H Bishop (D) 202-225-3826
New York Delegate:
 Carolyn McCarthy (D) 202-225-5516
New York Delegate:
 Major R Owens (D) 202-225-6231

Subcommittee
Education Reform
 Chair:
  Michael N Castle (R-DE) 202-225-4165
 Ranking Minority Member:
  Lynn Woolsey (D-CA) 202-225-5161

Senate Standing Committees

Health, Education, Labor & Pensions
Chair:
 Michael Enzi (R-WY) 202-224-3424
Ranking Minority Member:
 Edward M Kennedy (D-MA) 202-224-4543
New York Delegate:
 Hillary Rodham Clinton (D). 202-224-4451

Private Sector

ASPIRA of New York Inc
520 Eighth Ave, 22nd Fl, New York, NY 10018
212-564-6880 Fax: 212-564-7152
e-mail: hgesualdo@ny.aspira.org
Web site: www.nyaspira.org
Hector Gesualdo, Executive Director
Foster the social advancement of the PuertoRican/Latino community by supportig its youth through community & leadership development

Advocates for Children of New York Inc
151 West 30th St, 5th Fl, New York, NY 10001
212-947-9779 Fax: 212-947-9790
e-mail: info@advocatesforchildren.org
Web site: www.advocatesforchildren.org; www.insideschools.org
Jill Chaifetz, Executive Director
Advocacy for public school students

Offices and agencies appear in alphabetical order.

Africa-America Institute (The)
420 Lexington Ave, Rm 1706, New York, NY 10170-0007
212-949-5666 Fax: 212-682-6174
e-mail: aainy@aaionline.org
Web site: www.aaionline.org
Mora McLean, President & Chief Executive Officer
Promoting enlightened engagement between Africa & America through education, training & dialogue

After-School Corporation (The)
925 Ninth Ave, New York, NY 10019
212-547-6950 Fax: 212-548-6983
e-mail: info@tascorp.org
Web site: www.tascorp.org
John P Albert, Vice President, External Relations
Non-profit organization dedicated to enhancing the quality, availability & sustainability of in-school, after-school programs in NYS

Agudath Israel of America
42 Broadway, 14th Fl, New York, NY 10004
212-797-7385 Fax: 646-254-1650
e-mail: dzwiebel@agudathisrael.org
David Zwiebel, Executive Vice President, Government & Public
   Affairs
Religious school education; Orthodox Judaism

American Higher Education Development Corporation
Two Penn Plaza, Ste 1500, New York, NY 10121
212-292-5658 Fax: 212-292-4957
e-mail: jmdevaney@earthlink.net
James M Devaney, President
Acquisition of & investment in post-secondary education institutions

Assciation of Presidents of Public Community Colleges
c/o Tompkins-Cortland CC, 170 North St, POB 139, Dryden, NY 13053
607-844-8211 x4368 Fax: 607-844-6545
Carl Haynes, Executive Committee

Associated Medical Schools of New York
10 Rockefeller Plaza, Suite 1120, New York, NY 10020
212-218-4610 Fax: 212-218-5644
e-mail: jo.wiederhorn@amsny.org
Web site: www.amsny.org
Jo Wiederhorn, Executive Director
AMS is a consortium of the fourteen public and private medical schools in New York State. Our mission is to support quality health care in New York State through the continual strengthening of medical education, medical care, and medical research.

Association of Proprietary Colleges
1259 Central Ave, Albany, NY 12205
518-437-1867 Fax: 518-437-1048
e-mail: lnhol@aol.com
Web site: www.apc-colleges.org
Ellen Hollander, President

Board of Jewish Education of Greater New York
520 - 8th Ave, New York, NY 10018
212-245-8200 Fax: 212-247-6562
e-mail: judyopp@bjeny.org
Chaim Lauer, Executive Vice President

Campaign for Fiscal Equity, Inc
35 Maiden Ln, 3RD Floor, Albany, NY 12207
518-810-0031 Fax: 518-810-0108
e-mail: cfeinfo@cfequity.org
Web site: www.cfequity.org
Michael Rebell, Executive Director & Counsel

Catholic School Administrators Association of NYS
406 Fulton St, Ste 512, Troy, NY 12180
518-273-1205 Fax: 518-273-1206
e-mail: nysadm@csdsl.net
Web site: www.csaanys.org
Carol Geddis, Executive Director

Center for Educational Innovation - Public Education Association
28 W 44th St, Ste 300, New York, NY 10036-6600
212-302-8800 Fax: 212-302-0088
e-mail: info@pea-online.org
Web site: www.cei-pea.org
Judy Roth Berkowitz, Chairman
Advocacy & public information for NYC public education

Cerebral Palsy Associations of New York State
330 W 34th St, New York, NY 10001
212-947-5770 Fax: 212-356-0746
e-mail: sconstantino@cpofnys.org
Web site: www.cpofnys.org
Susan Constantino, Executive Director
Advocate & provide direct services with & for individuals with cerebral palsy & other significant disabilities, & their families

Coalition of New York State Career Schools (The)
437 Old Albany Post Rd, Garrison, NY 10524
845-788-5070 Fax: 845-788-5071
e-mail: tzaleski@sprynet.com
Web site: www.coalitionofnewyorkstatecareerschools.com
Terence M Zaleski, Special Counsel
Licensed post-secondary proprietary career schools

Commission on Independent Colleges & Universities
17 Elk St, PO Box 7289, Albany, NY 12224
518-436-4781 Fax: 518-436-0417
e-mail: abe@cicu.org
Web site: www.cicu.org
Abraham M Lackman, President
Represent public policy interests of member colleges & universities

Conference of Big 5 School Districts
One Steuben Place, 5th Fl Loft, Albany, NY 12207-2106
518-465-4274 Fax: 518-465-0638
e-mail: big5@nycap.rr.com
Georgia Asciutto, Executive Director

Offices and agencies appear in alphabetical order.

Cornell University
114 Day Hall, Ithaca, NY 14853
607-254-4636 Fax: 607-255-5396
e-mail: spj2@cornell.edu
Web site: www.cornell.edu
Stephen Philip Johnson, Assistant Vice President for Government &
Community Relations

Cornell University, Rural Schools Association of NYS
114 Kennedy Hall, Ithaca, NY 14853
607-255-8056 or 607-255-8709 Fax: 607-254-3350
e-mail: lak35@cornell.edu
Web site: www.education.cornell.edu/rsp
Lawrence Kiley, Executive Director
Advocacy for small & rural schools throughout New York

Cornell University, School of Industrial & Labor Relations
390 Ives Hall, Ithaca, NY 14853-3901
607-255-2742 or 607-257-1402 Fax: 607-255-1836
e-mail: jhb5@cornell.edu
Web site: www.ilr.cornell.edu
John Bishop, Professor
*Education, workforce preparedness; student peer culture, employee
training, recruitment & selection practices*

Council of School Supervisors & Administrators
16 Court St, 4th Fl, Brooklyn, NY 11241
718-852-3000 Fax: 718-403-0278
e-mail: jill@csa-nyc.org
Web site: www.csa-nyc.org
Jill Levy, President

**Council on the Environment of NYC, Environmental
Education**
51 Chambers St, Rm 228, New York, NY 10007
212-788-7900 or 212-788-7932 Fax: 212-788-7913
e-mail: cenyctso@hotmail.com
Web site: www.cenyc.org
Michael Zamm, Program Director
Environmental education & action training programs for students

Fordham University
Admin Bldg, 441 E Fordham Rd, Rm 117, Bronx, NY 10458
718-817-3023 Fax: 718-817-5722
e-mail: massiah@fordham.edu
Web site: www.fordham.edu
Lesley A Massiah, Assistant Vice President, Government Relations

Learning Leaders
352 Park Ave South, 13th Fl, New York, NY 10010-1709
212-213-3370 Fax: 212-213-0787
e-mail: jinnies@learningleaders.org
Web site: www.learningleaders.org
Jinnie Spiegler, Program Director
*Recruit, screen & train school volunteers for grades K through 12;
assist schools with program monitoring & evaluation*

MDRC
16 East 34th St, 19TH Floor, New York, NY 10016-4326
212-532-3200 Fax: 212-684-0832
e-mail: information@mdrc.org
Web site: www.mdrc.org
Gordon Berlin, President
*Nonprofit research & field testing of education & employment
programs for disadvantaged adults & youth*

**NYC Board of Education Employees, Local 372/AFSCME,
AFL-CIO**
125 Barclay Street, 6th Fl, New York, NY 10007
212-815-1372 Fax: 212-815-1347
Web site: www.local372.com
Veronica Montgomery-Costa, President, District Council 37/372

NYS Alliance for Arts Education
PO Box 2217, Albany, NY 12220-0217
800-ARTS-N-ED or 518-473-0823 Fax: 518-486-7329
e-mail: info@nysaae.org
Web site: www.nysaae.org
Amy Williams, Executive Director
*State & local advocacy, professional development, technical
assistance & information for educators, organizations, artists,
parents & policymakers*

**NYS Association for Health, Physical Education, Recreation
& Dance**
77 North Ann St, Little Falls, NY 13365
315-823-1015 Fax: 315-823-1012
e-mail: ccorsi@nysahperd.org
Web site: www.nysahperd.org
Colleen Corsi, Executive Director
*Promoting, educating & creating opportunites for physical
education, health, recreation & dance professionals*

NYS Association for the Education of Young Children
230 Washington Ave Ext, Albany, NY 12203-5390
518-867-3517 Fax: 518-867-3520
e-mail: nysaeyc@capital.net
Web site: www.nysaeyc.org
Patricia A Myers, Executive Director
*Supporting the development of professionals to promote quality care
& education for the well-being of all young children & their families*

NYS Association of Library Boards
PO Box 11048, Albany, NY 12211
518-445-9505 Fax: 518-426-8240
Web site: www.nysalb.org
Margaret Malicki, Association Manager

NYS Association of School Business Officials
7 Elk St, #1, Albany, NY 12207-1002
518-434-2281 Fax: 518-434-1303
e-mail: steve@nysasbo.org
Web site: www.nysasbo.org
Steve Van Hoesen, Director of Governement Relations
Leadership in the practice of school business management

Offices and agencies appear in alphabetical order.

NYS Head Start Association
230 Washington Ave Ext, Albany, NY 12203
518-452-0897 Fax: 518-452-0898
e-mail: nyshsa@capital.net
Web site: www.nysheadstart.org
Steven Moskowitz, Executive Director
Educational program designed to meet the needs of low-income children & their families

NYS Public High School Athletic Association
88 Delaware Ave, Delmar, NY 12054
518-439-8872 Fax: 518-475-1556
e-mail: nvanerk@nysphsaa.org
Web site: www.nysphsaa.org
Nina Van Erk, Executive Director
Provide equitable & safe competition through interschool athletic activities at secondary schools

NYS Reading Association
PO Box 874, Albany, NY 12201-0874
518-434-4748 Fax: 518-434-4748
e-mail: information@capital.net
Web site: www.nysreading.org
Stan Cianfarano, President
Literacy education advocacy & professional development programs for educators

National Education Association of New York
217 Lark St, Albany, NY 12210
518-462-6451 Fax: 518-462-1731
e-mail: dbutler@neany.org
Web site: www.neany.org
Denis M Butler, Legislative & Educational Policy Coord
Public school employees union

Nelson A Rockefeller Inst of Govt, Higher Education Program
411 State St, Albany, NY 12203
518-443-5835 or 518-443-5843 Fax: 518-443-5845
e-mail: burkejo@rockinst.org
Web site: www.rockinst.org/higheduc.htm
Joseph C Burke, Director
Accountability & autonomy in public higher education; system governance; performance funding, budgeting, reporting & assessment

New York Community College Trustees (NYCCT)
State University Plaza, FB #10, Albany, NY 12246-0001
518-443-5136 Fax: 518-443-5100
Arthur Anthonisen, President
Trustee education, legislative advocacy & communication

New York Library Association (The)
252 Hudson Ave, Albany, NY 12210-1802
518-432-6952 Fax: 518-427-1697
e-mail: director@nyla.org
Web site: www.nyla.org
Michael J Borges, Executive Director
Library funding/services; advocacy for public schools and academic librarians and libraries on funding and public policy issues

New York State Association of Independent Schools
12 Jay St, Schenectady, NY 12305-1913
518-346-5662 Fax: 518-346-7390
e-mail: hq@nysais.org
Web site: www.nysais.org
Frederick C Calder, Executive Director

New York State Catholic Conference
465 State St, Albany, NY 12203-1004
518-434-6195 Fax: 518-434-9796
e-mail: info@nyscatholic.org
Web site: www.nyscatholic.org
Richard E Barnes, Executive Director
Identify, formulate & implement public policy objectives of the NYS Bishops in health, education, welfare, human & civil rights

New York State Congress of Parents & Teachers Inc
One Wembley Square, Albany, NY 12205-3830
518-452-8808 Fax: 518-452-8105
e-mail: office@nypta.com
Web site: www.nypta.com
Penny Leask, President
Advocating education, health, welfare of children & parent involvement

New York State Council of School Superintendents
7 Elk St, 3rd Floor, Albany, NY 12207-1002
518-449-1063 Fax: 518-426-2229
Web site: www.nyscoss.org
Thomas L Rogers, Executive Director

New York State School Boards Association
24 Century Hill Drive, Ste 200, Latham, NY 12110-2125
518-783-0200 Fax: 518-783-0211
e-mail: info@nyssba.org
Web site: www.nyssba.org
Timothy G Kremer, Executive Director
Public school leadership advocates

New York State School Music Association (NYSSMA)
718 The Plain Rd, Westbury, NY 11590-5931
888-697-7621 Fax: 516-997-1700
e-mail: nyssmaexec@nyssma.org
Web site: www.nyssma.org
Bert Nelson, Executive Administrator
Advocacy for a quality school music education for every student

New York State United Teachers/AFT, AFL-CIO
800 Troy-Schenectady Road, Latham, NY 12110-2455
518-213-6000 or 800-342-9810
Web site: www.nysut.org
Richard Iannuzzi, President
Representing employees & retirees of NY's schools, colleges & healthcare facilities

New York University
25 West 4th St, 5th Fl - Rm 503, New York, NY 10012
212-998-6840 Fax: 212-995-4021
e-mail: john.beckman@nyu.edu
Web site: www.nyu.edu
John Beckman, Vice President of Public Affairs

Offices and agencies appear in alphabetical order.

Niagara University
Alumni Hall, Niagara University, NY 14109-2014
716-286-8360 Fax: 716-286-8349
e-mail: dfo@niagara.edu
Web site: www.niagara.edu
Rev Daniel F O'Leary, Associate Vice President for Academic
 Affairs

ProLiteracy Worldwide
1320 Jamesville Ave, Syracuse, NY 13210-4224
315-422-9121 Fax: 315-422-6369
e-mail: info@proliteracy.org
Web site: www.proliteracy.org
Rochelle A Cassella, Director, Corporate Communications
Sponsors educational programs & services to empower adults &
families through the acquisition of literacy skills & practices

Rensselaer Polytechnic Institute
110 8th St, Troy, NY 12180-3590
518-276-6000 Fax: 518-276-6091
e-mail: bourgt@rpi.edu
Web site: www.rpi.edu
Theresa Bourgeois, Director, Media Relations

Research Foundation of SUNY
State University Plz, Albany, NY 12246
518-434-7066 Fax: 518-434-9108
e-mail: cathy.kaszluga@rfsuny.org
Web site: www.rfsuny.org
Cathy Kaszluga, Vice President, Corporate Communications
Facilitate research, education & public service at SUNY campuses

Rochester School for the Deaf
1545 St Paul St, Rochester, NY 14621
585-544-1240 Fax: 585-544-0383
e-mail: hmowl@rsdeaf.org
Web site: www.rsdeaf.org
Harold Mowl, Jr, Superintendent
Complete educational program for deaf children to age 21

SCAA - Schuyler Center for Analysis & Advocacy
150 State St, 4th Fl, Albany, NY 12207-1626
518-463-1896 x25 Fax: 518-463-3364
e-mail: kschimke@scaany.org
Web site: www.scaany.org
Karen Schimke, President & Chief Executive Officer
Advocacy, analysis & forums on education, child welfare, health,
economic security, mental health, revenue & taxation issues

School Administrators Association of NYS
8 Airport Park Blvd, Latham, NY 12110
518-782-0600 Fax: 518-782-9552
e-mail: rthomas@saanys.org
Web site: www.saanys.org
Richard J Thomas, Executive Director

Sports & Arts in Schools Foundation
58-12 Queens Blvd, Suite 1 - 59th Entrance, Woodside, NY 11377
718-786-7110 Fax: 718-786-7635
e-mail: info@sasfny.org
Web site: www.sasfny.org
James R O'Neill, Executive Director
After-school, summer camps & clinics, winter-break festival

**Syracuse University, Office of Government & Community
Relations**
Room 2-212, Center for Science & Technology, Syracuse, NY
13244-4100
315-443-3919 Fax: 315-443-3676
e-mail: earougeu@syr.edu
Web site: govt-comm.syr.edu
Elizabeth A Rougeux, Executive Director, Government &
 Community Relations

Teachers College, Columbia University
525 W 120th St, Box 7, New York, NY 10027
212-678-3782 Fax: 212-678-3682
e-mail: ts171@columbia.edu
Web site: www.tc.columbia.edu
Thomas Sobol, Professor
Education policy

Teaching Matters Inc
475 Riverside Dr, Ste 1270, New York, NY 10115-0122
212-870-3505 Fax: 212-870-3516
e-mail: lguastaferro@teachingmaters.org
Web site: www.teachingmatters.org
Lynette Guastaferro, Executive Director
Technology planning & professional development for NYC public
schools

United Federation of Teachers
52 Broadway, New York, NY 10004
212-777-7500 Fax: 212-260-6393
e-mail: rweigarte@aol.com
Web site: www.uft.org
Randi Weingarten, President

United University Professions
PO Box 15143, Albany, NY 12212-5143
518-640-6600 Fax: 518-640-6698
e-mail: contact@uupmail.org
Web site: www.uupinfo.org
William E Scheuerman, President
SUNY labor union of academic & other professional faculty

Western New York Library Resources Council
4455 Genesee, Buffalo, NY 14225-0400
716-633-0705 Fax: 716-633-1736
e-mail: gstaines@wnylrc.org
Web site: www.wnylrc.org;
www.wnylibraries.org;www.askus247.org
Gail M Staines, Executive Director
Dedicated to enhancing access to information, encouraging resource
sharing & promoting library interests

Offices and agencies appear in alphabetical order.

ELECTIONS

New York State

GOVERNOR'S OFFICE

Governor's Office
Executive Chamber
State Capitol
Albany, NY 12224
518-474-8390 Fax: 518-474-1513
Web site: www.state.ny.us

Governor:
  George E Pataki 518-474-8390
Executive Director:
  Kara Lanspery 518-474-8390
Secretary to the Governor:
  John P Cahill. 518-474-4246
Counsel to the Governor-Attorney General, Budget:
  Richard Platkin. 518-474-8343
Director, Communications:
  David Catalfamo. 518-474-8418
Director, State & Local Government Affairs:
  John Haggerty. 518-486-9896
Deputy Counsel to the Governor-Appointments, Elections, Ethics, FOIL
  Appeals, Lobbying Commission, Regulatory Reform:
  W Brooks Debow 518-474-8343
Asst Counsel to the Governor-Civil Svc, Elections, Empl Relations, Labor,
  Motor Veh, Niagara Fr, Port Auth, Retirement/Pensions, Thruway, Transp,
  Waterfr, MTA, PERB:
  Christopher Staszak 518-474-1310
Citizens Services:
  Linda Boyd. 518-474-1041

New York City Office
633 Third Ave, 38th Fl, New York, NY 10017
Director:
  Ann McConnachie 212-681-4580
Executive Assistant to the Governor:
  Amy Holden 212-681-4580/fax: 212-681-4608
Assistant to the Governor for NYC Issues:
  Doug Blais 212-681-4580
Director, Community Affairs:
  James Barcia. 212-681-4580
Director, Legislative Affairs - NYC:
  James Harding 212-681-4580
Senior Advisor to the Governor for Women's Issues:
  Lynn Rollins 212-681-4580
New York City Press Secretary:
  Lyn Rasic. 212-681-4580/fax: 212-681-4608

EXECUTIVE DEPARTMENTS AND RELATED AGENCIES

Elections, State Board of
40 Steuben St
Albany, NY 12207-2108

518-474-6220 or TTY: 800-367-8683 Fax: 518-486-4068
Web site: www.elections.state.ny.us

Chair:
  Carol Berman 518-474-8113
Vice Chair:
  Neil W Kelleher 518-474-8113
Commissioner:
  Evelyn Aquila. 518-474-8113
Commissioner:
  Helena M Donohue. 518-474-8113
Acting Executive Director:
  Peter S Kosinski 518-474-8100
Deputy Executive Director:
  Peter S Kosinski 518-474-6236
Director, Public Information:
  Lee Daghlian 518-474-1953/fax: 518-473-8315
  e-mail: ldaghlian@elections.state.ny.us

Administrative Services
Administrative Officer:
  Patricia Tracey 518-474-6336
Special Counsel:
  Todd D Valentine. 518-474-6367
Deputy Counsel:
  Patricia L Murray 518-474-6367

Campaign Finance
Senior Accountant:
  Josephine Jackson. 518-474-8200

Counsel/Enforcement
Counsel:
  Stanley L Zalen. 518-474-2063

County Boards of Elections

Albany . . . . fax: 518-487-5077
 Co Court House, 16 Eagle St, Rm 38, Albany, NY 12207
Commissioner:
  John A Graziano, Sr (R). 518-487-5060
Commissioner:
  Michael J Monescalchi (D) 518-487-5060
Deputy Commissioner:
  Catherine F Rogowski (R) 518-487-5060
Deputy Commissioner:
  Karen A Shea (D). 518-487-5060

Allegany . . . . fax: 585-268-9406
 6 Schuyler Street, Belmont, NY 14813
Commissioner:
  James Gallman (R). 585-268-9294
Commissioner:
  Diane Martin (D) 585-268-9296
Deputy Commissioner:
  Elaine Herdman (R) 585-268-9294
  e-mail: herdmae@allegany.co.com
Deputy Commissioner:
  Catherine Lorow (D) 585-268-9295
  e-mail: lorowem@allegany.co.com

Offices and agencies appear in alphabetical order.

Policy Areas

Broome . . . . fax: 607-778-2174
44 Hawley St, PO Box 1766, Binghamton, NY 13902
Commissioner:
   Catherine C Schaewe (R). 607-778-2172
Commissioner:
   John Perticone (D) 607-778-2172
Deputy Commissioner:
   John Sejan (R) 607-778-2172
Deputy Commissioner:
   Barbara Paoletti (D) 607-778-2172

Cattaraugus . . . . fax: 716-938-6347
302 Court Street, Little Valley, NY 14755
Fax: 716-938-6347
Web site: www.co.cattaraugus.ny.us
Commissioner:
   Sue A Fries (R) 716-938-9111 x2405
   e-mail: suefri@cattco.org
Commissioner:
   Kevin Burleson (D). 716-938-9111 x2404
Deputy Commissioner:
   Kristie L Dustman (R). 716-938-9111 x2401
Deputy Commissioner:
   Karen L Byrne (D) 716-938-9111 x2403

Cayuga . . . . fax: 315-253-1289
10 Court St, Auburn, NY 13021
Fax: 315-253-1289
Web site: www.co.cayuga.ny.us/election
Commissioner:
   Cherl Heary (R) 315-253-1285
Commissioner:
   Dennis Sedor (D) 315-253-1285

Chautauqua . . . . fax: 716-753-4111
3 North Erie St, Mayville, NY 14757
716-753-4580 Fax: 716-753-4111
e-mail: vote@co.chautauqua.ny.us
Web site: www.votechautauqua.com
Commissioner:
   Terry Niebel (R). 716-753-4226
Commissioner:
   Norman P Green (D) 716-753-4580
Deputy Commissioner:
   Phyllis Clute (R). 716-753-4240
Deputy Commissioner:
   Janet Jankowski George (D) 716-753-4250

Chemung . . . . fax: 607-737-5499
425 Pennsylvania Ave, PO Box 588, Elmira, NY 14902-0588
607-737-5475 Fax: 607-737-5499
Web site: www.chemungcounty.com
Commissioner:
   Martin T Kain (R) 607-737-5475
   e-mail: dpeters@co.chemung.ny.us
Commissioner:
   Keith H Osborne (D) 607-737-5475
   e-mail: kosborne@co.chemung.ny.us
Deputy Commissioner:
   Linda A Forrest (R) 607-737-5475
   e-mail: lforrest@co.chemung.ny.us
Deputy Commissioner:
   Mary Dell (D). 607-737-5475
   e-mail: modell@co.chemung.ny.us

Chenango . . . . fax: 607-337-1766
5 Court Street, Norwich, NY 13815
607-337-1760 Fax: 607-337-1766
e-mail: boe@co.chenango.ny.us
Web site: www.chenango.ny.us

Commissioner:
   Harriet L Jenkins (R) 607-337-1764
Commissioner:
   Carol A Franklin (D) 607-337-1765

Clinton . . . . fax: 518-565-4508
County Gov't Center, 137 Margaret St, Ste 104, Plattsburgh, NY 12901
Fax: 518-565-4508
Web site: www.clintoncountygov.com
Commissioner:
   Judith C Layhee (R) 518-565-4740
Commissioner:
   John Brunell (D). 518-565-4740
Deputy Commissioner:
   Lois M McShane (R) 518-565-4740
Deputy Commissioner:
   Debra L Bruno (D). 518-565-4740

Columbia . . . . fax: 518-828-2624
401 State St, Hudson, NY 12534
Commissioner:
   Thomas D Fisher (R) 518-828-3115
Commissioner:
   Francis J Blake, Jr (D) 518-828-3115
Deputy Commissioner:
   Michael P Nabozny (R) 518-828-3115
Deputy Commissioner:
   Ann W Vedder (D). 518-828-3115

Cortland . . . . fax: 607-758-5513
County Court House, 60 Central Ave, Ste 102, Cortland, NY 13045-2746
Commissioner:
   Robert C Howe (R) 607-753-5031
Commissioner:
   Richard C VanDonsel (D) 607-753-5033

Delaware . . . . fax: 607-746-6516
3 Gallant Ave, Delhi, NY 13753
Fax: 607-746-6516
e-mail: elec@co.delaware.ny.us
Web site: www.co.delaware.ny.us
Commissioner:
   William J Campbell (R) 607-746-2315
Commissioner:
   William J Buccheri (D) 607-746-2315
Deputy Commissioner:
   Robin L Alger (R) 607-746-2315
Deputy Commissioner:
   Janice G Burdick (D) 607-746-2315

Dutchess . . . . fax: 845-486-2483
47 Cannon St, Poughkeepsie, NY 12601
Fax: 845-486-2483
Web site: www.dutchesselections.com
Commissioner:
   David J Gamache (R). 845-486-2473
   e-mail: dgamache@co.dutchess.ny.us
Commissioner:
   Frances A Knapp (D). 845-486-2473
   e-mail: fknapp@co.dutchess.ny.us
Deputy Commissioner:
   John M Kennedy (R) 845-486-2473
   e-mail: jkennedy@co.dutchess.ny.uc
Deputy Commissioner:
   John P Ballo (D). 845-486-2473
   e-mail: jballo@co.dutchess.ny.us

Erie . . . . fax: 716-858-8282
134 West Eagle St, Buffalo, NY 14202
Commissioner:
   Ralph M Mohr (R) 716-858-8891

Offices and agencies appear in alphabetical order.

Commissioner:
Dennis Ward (D) 716-858-8891
Deputy Commissioner:
Dennis V Ryan (R). 716-858-8891
Deputy Commissioner:
Alonzo W Thompson (D). 716-858-8891

Essex . . . . fax: 518-873-3479
7551 Court Street, PO Box 217, Elizabethtown, NY 12932
518-873-3474 Fax: 518-873-3479
Web site: www.co.essex.ny.us/elect.html
Commissioner:
Lewis W Sanders (R) 518-873-3478
Commissioner:
Edward P Hatch (D). 518-873-3475
Deputy Commissioner:
Patti L Doyle (R) 518-873-3476
Deputy Commissioner:
Steven W Laundree (D) 518-873-3477

Franklin . . . . fax: 518-481-6018
335 West Main St, Malone, NY 12953-1821
Commissioner:
Beverly C Mills (R) 518-481-1661
e-mail: bmills@co.franklin.ny.us
Commissioner:
Kathy M Fleury (D) 518-481-1662
e-mail: kfleury@co.franklin.ny.us
Deputy Commissioner:
Veronica B King (R) 518-481-1663
e-mail: vking@co.franklin.ny.us
Deputy Commissioner:
Cheryl A Dumas (D) 518-481-1664
e-mail: cdumas@co.franklin.ny.us

Fulton . . . . fax: 518-736-1612
2714 State Highway 29, Ste 1, Johnstown, NY 12095-9946
Commissioner:
Dexter J Risedorph (R). 518-736-5526
Commissioner:
Marilyn J Cornell (D). 518-736-5526
Deputy Commissioner:
Linda M Madison (R). 518-736-5526
Deputy Commissioner:
Linda L Coons (D). 518-736-5526

Genesee. . . . . fax: 585-344-8562
County Bldg One, 15 Main St, PO Box 284, Batavia, NY 14021
Fax: 585-344-8562
Web site: www.co.genesee.ny.us
Commissioner:
Richard Siebert (R) 585-344-2550
Commissioner:
Dawn E Cassidy (D). 585-344-2550
Deputy Commissioner:
Sharon E White (R) 585-344-2250
Deputy Commissioner:
Karen S Gannon (D). 585-344-2250

Greene . . . . fax: 518-719-3784
411 Main St, 4th Fl, #437, POB 307, Catskill, NY 12414
Commissioner:
Frank DeBenedictus (R). 518-719-3550
Commissioner:
Thomas J Burke (D). 518-719-3550
Deputy Commissioner:
Mary L Dwyer (R) 518-719-3550
Deputy Commissioner:
Marie Metzler (D) 518-719-3550

Hamilton. . . . . fax: 518-548-6345
County Complex, Rte 8, PO Box 175, Lake Pleasant, NY 12108
Commissioner:
Judith L Peck (R). 518-548-4684
Commissioner:
Cathleen E Rogers (D). 518-548-4684
Deputy Commissioner:
Deborah A O'Rourke (R). 518-548-4684
Deputy Commissioner:
William Parslow (D) 518-548-4684

Herkimer . . . . fax: 315-867-1106
109 Mary Street, Suite 1306, Herkimer, NY 13350
Commissioner:
Marty L Smith (R) 315-867-1104
e-mail: msmith@herkimercounty.org
Commissioner:
Toni M Scalise (D). 315-867-1103
e-mail: tmscalise@herkimercounty.org

Jefferson. . . . . fax: 315-785-5197
175 Arsenal St, Watertown, NY 13601
Fax: 315-785-5197
Web site: www.co.jefferson.ny.us
Commissioner:
James E Fitzpatrick (R) 315-785-3027
Commissioner:
Sean M Hennessey (D). 315-785-3027
Deputy Commissioner:
Sandra Corey (R) 315-785-3027
e-mail: sandyc@co.jefferson.ny.us
Deputy Commissioner:
Cindy Corbett (D) 315-785-3027
e-mail: cindyc@co.jefferson.ny.us

Lewis. . . . . fax: 315-376-2860
7660 N State St, Lowville, NY 13367
Commissioner:
Ann M Nortz (R) 315-376-5329
Commissioner:
Elaine M McLear (D). 315-376-5330

Livingston. . . . . fax: 585-243-7015
County Government Ctr, 6 Court St, Rm 104, Geneseo, NY 14454-1043
Commissioner:
Gerald L Smith (R). 585-243-7090
e-mail: gsmith@co.livingston.ny.us
Commissioner:
Susan N Guenther (D) 585-243-7090
e-mail: sguenther@co.livingston.ny.us
Deputy Commissioner:
Nancy L Leven (R). 585-243-7090
e-mail: nleven@co.livingston.ny.us
Deputy Commissioner:
Laura M Schoonover (D). 585-243-7090
e-mail: lschoonover@co.livingston.ny.us

Madison . . . . fax: 315-366-2532
North Court St, County Office Bldg, PO Box 666, Wampsville, NY 13163
Commissioner:
Lynne M Jones (R) 315-366-2231
Commissioner:
Laura P Costello (D) 315-366-2231

Monroe
39 Main St West, Rochester, NY 14614
Web site: www.monroe.county.gov
Commissioner:
Peter M Quinn (R). 585-428-4550/fax: 585-428-2158
e-mail: mcboe@monroecounty.gov

Policy Areas

Commissioner:
Thomas F Ferrarese (D) 585-428-4550/fax: 585-428-2590
Deputy Commissioner:
Douglas E French (R). 585-428-4550
Deputy Commissioner:
Sheila Fleischauer (D) 585-428-4550

Montgomery. . . . . fax: 518-853-8392
Old Court House, Park St, PO Box 1500, Fonda, NY 12068-1500
518-853-8180 Fax: 518-853-8392
Commissioner:
Arlene S Macek (R) 518-853-8183
Commissioner:
Deborah L Tessiero (D) 518-853-8184
Deputy Commissioner:
Lyn A May (R). 518-853-8182
Deputy Commissioner:
Joan M Grainer (D) 518-853-8181

Nassau. . . . . fax: 516-571-2058
New Administration Bldg, 400 County Seat Dr, Mineola, NY 11501
Commissioner:
John A DeGrace (R). 516-571-2411
Commissioner:
Jeffrey M Stein (D) 516-571-2411
Deputy Commissioner:
Carol Demauro Busketta (R) 516-571-2411
Deputy Commissioner:
Eleanor Sciglibaglio (D) 516-571-2411

New York City. . . . . fax: 212-487-5349
32 Broadway, 7th Fl, New York, NY 10004
Fax: 212-487-5349
Web site: www.vote.nyc.ny.us
Executive Director:
John Ravitz (R) 212-487-5412
Deputy Executive Director:
George Gonzalez (D) 212-487-5409
Administrative Manager:
Pamela Green Perkins (D) 212-487-5406
Bronx
1780 Grand Concourse, Bronx, NY 10457
Commissioner:
Joseph Savino (R) 718-299-9017
Commissioner:
Nero Graham, Jr (D) 718-299-9017
Chief Clerk:
Vico Tosi 718-299-9017
Chief Clerk:
Naomi Rivera. 718-299-9017
Kings. . . . . fax: 718-522-6227
345 Adams St, Brooklyn, NY 11201
Commissioner:
Nancy Mottola Schacher (R). 718-797-8800
Commissioner:
Jeannette Gadson (D) 718-797-8800
Deputy Chief Clerk:
Diane Haslett Rudiano. 718-797-8800
Chief clerk:
Kathy King 718-797-8800
New York
200 Varick St, New York, NY 10014
Commissioner:
Frederic M Umane (R) 212-886-2100
Commissioner:
Douglas A Kellner (D) 212-886-2100
Deputy Chief Clerk:
Rosanna Rahmouni 212-886-2100
Chief Clerk:
Al Taylor 212-886-2100

Queens
126-06 Queens Blvd, Kew Gardens, NY 11415
Commissioner:
Stephen H Weiner (R) 718-730-6730
Commissioner:
Terrance C O'Connor (D) 718-730-6730
Deputy Chief Clerk:
Kathryn James. 718-730-6730
Chief Clerk:
Barbara Conacchio 718-730-6730
Richmond
1 Edgewater Plaza, Staten Island, NY 10305
Commissioner:
Michael J Cilmi (R). 718-876-0079
Commissioner:
Mark B Herman (D) 718-876-0079
Deputy Chief Clerk:
Maryann Yennella. 718-876-0079
Chief Clerk:
Barbara Kett. 718-876-0079

Niagara. . . . . fax: 716-438-4054
111 Main Street, Ste 100, Lockport, NY 14094
Fax: 716-438-4054
Web site: www.elections.niagara.ny.us
Commissioner:
Scott P Kiedrowski (R) 716-438-4040
Commissioner:
Nancy L Smith (D). 716-438-4041
Deputy Commissioner:
Mary Ann Casamento (R) 716-438-4040
Deputy Commissioner:
Lora A Allen (D) 716-438-4041

Oneida . . . . fax: 315-798-6412
Union Station, 321 Main St, 3rd Fl, Utica, NY 13501
Fax: 315-798-6412
Web site: www.oneidacounty.org
Commissioner:
Patricia Ann DiSpirito (R) 315-798-5765
Commissioner:
Angela Pedone Longo (D) 315-798-5765
Deputy Commissioner:
Catherine A Dumka (R) 315-798-5765
Deputy Commissioner:
Carolann Cardone (D) 315-798-5765

Onondaga . . . . fax: 315-435-8451
Civic Center, 421 Montgomery St, 15th Fl, Syracuse, NY 13202
Fax: 315-435-8451
e-mail: elemail@nyset.net
Web site: www.ongov.net
Commissioner:
Helen M Kiggins (R) 315-435-3312
Commissioner:
Edward J Szczesniak (D) 315-435-3312

Ontario . . . . fax: 585-393-2941
20 Ontario St, Canandaigua, NY 14424
Fax: 585-393-2941
Web site: www.co.ontario.ny.us/elections
Commissioner:
Michael J Northrup (R) 585-396-4005
Commissioner:
Mary Q Salotti (D). 585-396-4005
Deputy Commissioner:
Elaine Mallaber (R) 585-396-4005
Deputy Commissioner:
Joan F Luther (D). 585-396-4005

Offices and agencies appear in alphabetical order.

Orange . . . . fax: 845-291-2437
25 Court Lane, PO Box 30, Goshen, NY 10924
Commissioner:
    David C Green (R) 845-291-2444
Commissioner:
    Susan Bahren (D) 845-291-2444
Deputy Commissioner:
    Courtney Canfield Greene (R) 845-291-2444
Deputy Commissioner:
    Ellouise S Raffo (D) 845-291-2444

Orleans . . . . fax: 585-589-2771
County Admin Bldg, 14016 State Rte 31, Albion, NY 14411
Commissioner:
    Dennis Piedimonte (R) 585-589-3274
Commissioner:
    Helen L Zelazny (D) 585-589-3274
Deputy Commissioner:
    Clara L Martin (R) 585-589-3274
Deputy Commissioner:
    Janice E Grabowski (D) 585-589-3274

Oswego . . . . fax: 315-349-8357
46 E Bridge St, Oswego, NY 13126
Commissioner:
    Donald M Wart (R) 315-349-8350
Commissioner:
    William W Scriber (D) 315-349-8350

Otsego . . . . fax: 607-547-4248
197 Main St, Cooperstown, NY 13326
Commissioner:
    Charlotte Konluto (R) 607-547-4247
Commissioner:
    Henry J Nicols (D) 607-547-4325
Deputy Commissioner:
    Sheila M Ross (R) 607-547-4247
Deputy Commissioner:
    Lucinda A Jarvis (D) 607-547-4325

Putnam . . . . fax: 845-278-6798
One Geneva Rd, Brewster, NY 10509
Commissioner:
    Anthony G Scannapieco, Jr (R) 845-278-6970
Commissioner:
    Robert J Bennett (D) 845-278-6970
Deputy Commissioner:
    Nancy M Quis (R) 845-278-6970
Deputy Commissioner:
    Amy Schleimer (D) 845-278-6970

Rensselaer . . . . fax: 518-270-2909
Ned Pattison Gov Cen, 1600 Seventh Ave, Troy, NY 12180
Commissioner:
    Larry A Bugbee (R) 518-270-2990
Commissioner:
    Edward G McDonough (D) 518-270-2990

Rockland . . . . fax: 845-638-5196
11 New Hempstead Rd, New City, NY 10956
Fax: 845-638-5196
Web site: www.co.rockland.ny.us
Commissioner:
    Joan M Silvestri (R) 845-638-5172
Commissioner:
    Ann Marie Kelly (D) 845-638-5172
Deputy Commissioner:
    Ruth A Vezzetti (R) 845-638-5172
Deputy Commissioner:
    Kathleen Pietanza (D) 845-638-5172

Saint Lawrence . . . . fax: 315-386-2737
48 Court St, Canton, NY 13617
Fax: 315-386-2737
Web site: www.co.st-lawrence.ny.us
Commissioner:
    Deborah J Pahler (R) 315-379-2202
Commissioner:
    Robin M St Andrews (D) 315-379-2202
Deputy Commissioner:
    Cathy A Marich (R) 315-379-2202
Deputy Commissioner:
    Sandra Ragan (D) 315-379-2202

Saratoga . . . . fax: 518-884-4751
50 W High St, Ballston Spa, NY 12020
Fax: 518-884-4751
e-mail: saraboe@govt.co.saratoga.ny.us
Web site: www.co.saratoga.ny.us
Commissioner:
    Diane Wade (R) 518-885-2249
Commissioner:
    William Fruci (D) 518-885-2249
Deputy Commissioner:
    Kathleen Anderson (R) 518-885-2249
Deputy Commissioner:
    Carol Turney (D) 518-885-2249

Schenectady . . . . fax: 518-377-2716
388 Broadway, Ste E, Schenectady, NY 12305-2520
Fax: 518-377-2716
Web site: www.schenectadyelections.com
Commissioner:
    Armando G Tebano (R) 518-377-2469
Commissioner:
    Robert A Brehm (D) 518-377-2469
Deputy Commissioner:
    Anna Marie Guida (R) 518-377-2469
Deputy Commissioner:
    Marie M Woodward (D) 518-377-2469

Schoharie . . . . fax: 518-295-8419
County Office Bldg, 284 Main St, PO Box 99, Schoharie, NY 12157
Commissioner:
    Lewis L Wilson (R) 518-295-8388
Commissioner:
    Clifford C Hay (D) 518-295-8388
Deputy Commissioner:
    Anne W Hendrix (R) 518-295-8388
Deputy Commissioner:
    Diane J Becker (D) 518-295-8388

Schuyler . . . . fax: 607-535-8364
County Ofc Bldg, 105 Ninth St, Unit 13, Watkins Glen, NY 14891-9972
Commissioner:
    Joseph Fazzary (R) 607-535-8195
Commissioner:
    John L Vona (D) 607-535-8195
Deputy Commissioner:
    Bonnie G Herzig (R) 607-535-8195
Deputy Commissioner:
    Carolyn Elkins (D) 607-535-8195

Seneca . . . . fax: 315-539-3710
1 DiPronio Dr, Waterloo, NY 13165
Fax: 315-539-3710
Web site: www.co.seneca.ny.us/boe
Commissioner:
    Elaine M Catanise (R) 315-539-1762
    e-mail: ecatanise@co.seneca.ny.us

Policy Areas

Offices and agencies appear in alphabetical order.

Commissioner:
Ruth V Same (D) 315-539-1763
e-mail: rsame@co.seneca.ny.us
Deputy Commissioner:
Joan P Mooney (R). 315-539-1760
e-mail: jmooney@co.seneca.ny.us
Deputy Commissioner:
Barbara R McCann (D) 315-539-1761
e-mail: bmccann@co.seneca.ny.us

Steuben . . . . fax: 607-664-1200
3 E Pulteney Square, Bath, NY 14810
Fax: 607-664-1200
Web site: www.steubencony.org
Commissioner:
Sharlene J Thompson (R). 607-664-2261
Commissioner:
Allan C Johnson (D). 607-664-2262
e-mail: allanj@co.steuben.ny.us
Deputy Commissioner:
Penny Ruest (R) 607-664-2260
Deputy Commissioner:
Kelly Austin (D). 607-664-2263

Suffolk . . . . fax: 631-852-4590
Yaphank Ave, PO Box 700, Yaphank, NY 11980
Commissioner:
Robert L Garfinkle (R). 631-852-4500
Commissioner:
Anita S Katz (D). 631-852-4500
Deputy Commissioner:
Linda Powell (R) 631-852-4500
Deputy Commissioner:
Jeanne O'Rourke (D) 631-852-4500

Sullivan . . . . fax: 845-794-0183
Government Ctr, 100 North St, PO Box 5012, Monticello, NY
12701-5192
845-794-3000 x5024 Fax: 845-794-0183
Commissioner:
Fran Thalmann (R). 845-794-3000 x3392/3
e-mail: fran.thalmann@co.sullivan.ny.us
Commissioner:
Timothy E Hill (D). 845-794-3000 x3390/3
e-mail: timothy.hill@co.sullivan.ny.us
Deputy Commissioner:
Joanne Clements (R). 845-794-3000 x3385
e-mail: joanne.clements@co.sullivan.ny.us
Deputy Commissioner:
Faith Kaplan (D) 845-794-3000 x3385
e-mail: faith.kaplan@co.sullivan.ny.us

Tioga . . . . fax: 607-687-6348
County Office Bldg, 56 Main St, Owego, NY 13827
607-687-8261 Fax: 607-687-6348
Web site: www.tiogacountyny.com/boardofelections.asp
Commissioner:
Phyllis A Blackman (R) 607-687-8220
e-mail: blackmanp@co.tioga.ny.com
Commissioner:
Joann K Lindstrom (D) 607-687-8217
Deputy Commissioner:
Bernadette M Toombs (R) 607-687-8218
e-mail: toombsb@co.tioga.ny.com
Deputy Commissioner:
Cinda Lou Goodrich (D) 607-687-8219
e-mail: goodrichc@co.tioga.ny.com

Tompkins . . . . fax: 607-274-5533
Court House Annex, 128 E Buffalo St, Ithaca, NY 14850

Fax: 607-274-5533
Web site: www.tompkins-co.org/boe
Commissioner:
Elizabeth W Cree (R). 607-274-5522
e-mail: ecree@tompkins-co.org
Commissioner:
Stephen M DeWitt (D). 607-274-5522
e-mail: sdewitt@tompkins-co.org
Deputy Commissioner:
Kathryn L Bortz 607-274-5522
Deputy Commissioner:
Thomas M Paolangeli 607-274-5522

Ulster . . . . fax: 845-334-5434
284 Wall Street, Kingston, NY 12401
Commissioner:
Thomas F Turco (R). 845-334-5470
Commissioner:
Harry M Castiglione (D) 845-334-5470
Deputy Commissioner:
Joan M Millham (R) 845-334-5470
Deputy Commissioner:
Kathleen C Mihm (D) 845-334-5470

Warren . . . . fax: 518-761-6480
County Municipal Center, 1340 State Rte 9, Lake George, NY 12845
Commissioner:
Mary Beth Casey (R) 518-761-6458
e-mail: caseym@co.warren.ny.us
Commissioner:
Lois A Montfort (D). 518-761-6459
e-mail: monfortl@co.warren.ny.us
Deputy Commissioner:
Constance L Service (R) 518-761-6457
e-mail: servicec@co.warren.ny.us
Deputy Commissioner:
M Suzanne O'Dea (D) 518-761-6456
e-mail: odeas@co.warren.ny.us

Washington . . . . fax: 518-746-2179
383 Broadway, Fort Edward, NY 12828
Commissioner:
Donna English (R) 518-746-2181
e-mail: denglish@co.washington.ny.us
Commissioner:
Patricia A Haley (D). 518-746-2183
e-mail: phaley@co.washington.ny.us
Deputy Commissioner:
Linda Falkouski (R) 518-746-2180
Deputy Commissioner:
Jeffrey J Curtis (D). 518-746-2182

Wayne . . . . fax: 315-946-7409
157 Montezuma St Ext, PO Box 636, Lyons, NY 14489
Fax: 315-946-7409
Web site: www.co.wayne.ny.us
Commissioner:
Richard E Clark (R) 315-946-7400
Commissioner:
Thomas F Healy (D). 315-946-7400
Deputy Commissioner:
Kelley M. Borrelli (R) 315-946-7400
Deputy Commissioner:
Joyce A Krebbeks (D) 315-946-7400
e-mail: jkrebbeks@co.wayne.ny.us

Westchester . . . . fax: 914-995-3190
25 Quarropas Street, White Plains, NY 10601
Commissioner:
Carolee C Sunderland (R) 914-995-5700

Offices and agencies appear in alphabetical order.

Commissioner:
Reginald A LaFayette (D) 914-995-5700
Deputy Commissioner:
Melissa Nacerino (R) 914-995-5700
Deputy Commissioner:
Jeannie L Palazola (D) 914-995-5700

Wyoming . . . . fax: 585-786-8843
76 N Main St, Warsaw, NY 14569-1329
Fax: 585-786-8843
Web site: www.wyoming.co.net
Commissioner:
James E Schlick (R) 585-786-8931
Commissioner:
Norman R George (D) 585-786-8931
Deputy Commissioner:
Wendy Simpson (R) 585-786-8931
e-mail: wlsimpson@frontiernet.net
Deputy Commissioner:
Jeanne M Williams (D) 585-786-8931
e-mail: jewilliams@frontiernet.net

Yates . . . . fax: 315-536-5523
417 Liberty St, Ste 1124, Penn Yan, NY 14527
Commissioner:
Pamela A Welker (R) 315-536-5135
Commissioner:
Wendy S Gibson (D) 315-536-5135
Deputy Commissioner:
Helen J Scarpechi (R) 315-536-5135
Deputy Commissioner:
Patricia Selwood (D) 315-536-5135

Election Law Enforcement
Investigator:
Javan Owens 518-474-2371

Election Operations
Director:
Anna E Svizzero 518-473-5086

General Information
Coordinator of Registration Operations:
Gregory Fiozzo 518-474-1953

Information Technology Unit
Supervisor:
George Stanton 518-473-4803

CORPORATIONS, AUTHORITIES AND COMMISSIONS

New York State Temporary Commission on Lobbying
2 Empire State Plaza
Ste 1701
Albany, NY 12223-1254

518-474-7126 Fax: 518-473-6492
e-mail: lobcom@attglobal.net
Web site: www.nylobby.state.ny.us

Commissioner:
Joseph Dunn 518-474-7126
Vice Chair:
Bartley Livolsi 518-474-7126
Commissioner:
Andrew Cecci 518-474-7126
Commissioner:
Peter Moschetti 518-474-7126
Commissioner:
Kenneth Baer 518-474-7126
Vice Chair:
Patrick Bulgaro 518-474-7126
Executive Director:
David M Grandeau 518-474-7126
Director, Program & Finance Administration:
Jeannine M Clemente 518-474-7126
Public Information Officer:
Kris Thompson 518-474-7126

NEW YORK STATE LEGISLATURE

See Legislative Branch in Section 1 for additional Standing Committee and Subcommittee information.

Assembly Standing Committees

Election Law
Chair:
Keith L Wright (D) 518-455-4793
Ranking Minority Member:
Fred Thiele (R) 518-455-5997

Senate Standing Committees

Elections
Chair:
John Flanagan (R) 518-455-2071
Ranking Minority Member:
Martin Malave Dilan (D) 518-455-2177

Senate/Assembly Legislative Commissions

Demographic Research & Reapportionment, Legislative Task Force on
Assembly Co-Chair:
William B Hoyt, III (D) 518-455-4886
Senate Co-Chair:
Dean G Skelos (R) 518-455-3171
Assembly Program Manager:
Lewis M Hoppe 212-618-1100/fax: 212-618-1135
Senate Program Manager:
Debra A Levine 212-618-1110/fax: 212-618-1135

Offices and agencies appear in alphabetical order.

Policy Areas

U.S. Government

EXECUTIVE DEPARTMENTS AND RELATED AGENCIES

Federal Election Commission
999 E St NW
Washington, DC 20463
202-694-1100 or 800-424-9530 Fax: 202-219-8504
Web site: www.fec.gov

Vice Chair:
  Ellen L Weintraub 202-694-1000
Member:
  Michael E Toner. 202-694-1000
General Counsel:
  Lawrence Norton 202-694-1000
Inspector General:
  Lynne A McFarland 202-694-1015
Director, Congressional, Legislative & Intergovernmental Affairs:
  Tina VanBrakle 202-694-1006
Acting Press Officer:
  Robert Biersack. 202-694-1220/fax: 202-501-3283

US Commission on Civil Rights
Web site: www.usccr.gov

EASTERN REGION (includes New York State)
624 9th St NW, Rm 500, Washington, DC 20425
Acting Regional Director:
  Ivy Davis 202-376-7533/fax: 202-376-7548

U.S. CONGRESS

See U.S. Congress Chapter for additional Standing Committee and Subcommittee information.

House of Representatives Standing Committees

Government Reform
Chair:
  Thomas M Davis, III (R-VA). 202-225-1492

Ranking Minority Member:
  Henry A Waxman (D-CA) 202-225-3976
New York Delegate:
  Carolyn B Maloney (D) 202-225-7944
New York Delegate:
  John R McHugh (R). 202-225-4611
New York Delegate:
  Major R Owens (D) 202-225-6231
New York Delegate:
  Edolphus Towns (D). 202-225-5936

  Subcommittee
  Federal Workforce & Agency Organization
    Chair:
      Jon Potter (R-NV) 202-225-3252
    Ranking Minority Member:
      Danny K Davis (D-IL). 202-225-5006
    New York Delegate:
      Major R Owens (D). 202-225-6231

Standards of Official Conduct
Chair:
  Doc Hastings (R-WA) 202-225-5816
Ranking Minority Member:
  Alan B Mollohan (D-WV) 202-225-4172

Senate Standing Committees

Ethics, Select Committee on
Chair:
  George V Voinovich (R-OH). 202-224-3353
Vice Chair:
  Tim Johnson (D-SD) 202-224-5842

Governmental Affairs
Chair:
  Susan Collins (R-ME) 202-224-2523
Ranking Minority Member:
  Joseph I Lieberman (D-CT) 202-224-4041

Private Sector

Arthur J Finkelstein & Associates Inc
16 N Astor, Irvington, NY 10533
914-591-8142 Fax: 914-591-4013
Arthur J Finkelstein, President
Election polling & consulting

Branford Communications
611 Broadway, New York, NY 10012
212-260-9905 Fax: 212-260-9908
Ernest Lendler, Principal
Media consulting; print production & advertising

Bynum, Thompson, Ryer
44 Travis Corners, Garrison, NY 10524
845-424-4300 Fax: 845-424-3850
e-mail: bynum@btrsc.com
Web site: www.btrsc.com
Peter Bynum, President
Campaign communication, strategy & media production

Offices and agencies appear in alphabetical order.

CUNY Graduate School, Center for Urban Research
365 5th Ave, New York, NY 10016-4309
212-817-2046 Fax: 212-817-1575
e-mail: jmollenkopf@gc.cuny.edu
John Hull Mollenkopf, Director
Political participation, voting behavior, NYC politics & urban economic & demographic change

Century Foundation (The)
41 East 70th St, New York, NY 10021
212-535-4441 Fax: 212-535-7534
e-mail: info@tcf.org
Web site: www.tcf.org
Christy Hicks, Vice President, Public Affairs
Sponsor the Federal Election Reform Network; co-organizer of the National Commission on Federal Election Reform; provide policymakers with new ideas to address challenges facing the nation

Citizen Action of New York
94 Central Ave, Albany, NY 12206
518-465-4600 x113 Fax: 518-465-2890
e-mail: rkirsch@citizenactionny.org
Web site: www.citizenactionny.org
Richard Kirsch, Executive Director
Campaign finance reform; health care advocacy & consumer protection; education

Columbia Law School, Legislative Drafting Research Fund
435 W 116th St, New York, NY 10027-7297
212-854-2640 Fax: 212-854-7946
e-mail: rb34@columbia.edu
Web site: www.law.columbia.edu
Richard Briffault, Professor of Legislation
State & local government law, property law & election law

Common Cause/NY
155 Ave of the Americas, 4th Fl, New York, NY 10013
212-691-6506 Fax: 212-807-1809
e-mail: cocauseny@aol.com
Web site: www.commoncause.org/ny
Rachel Leon, Executive Director
Campaign finance reform, ballot access, political gift disclosure & public interest lobbying

Conservative Party of NYS
325 Parkview Dr, Schenectady, NY 12303
518-356-7882 Fax: 518-356-3773
e-mail: cpnys@nycap.rr.com
Web site: www.cpnys.org
Shaun Marie Levine, Executive Director
Campaign consulting services & funding for Conservative Party political candidates

Cookfair Media Inc
536 Buckingham Ave, Syracuse, NY 13210
315-478-3359 Fax: 315-478-5236
e-mail: cookfair@aol.com
John R Cookfair, III, President
Campaign media production, print production & advertising

Democratic Congressional Campaign Committee
430 South Capitol St, SE, Washington, DC 20003
202-863-1500 Fax: 202-485-3512
Web site: www.dccc.org
Rahm Emanuel, Chair
Funding for Democratic congressional candidates; campaign strategy

Election Computer Services Inc
197 County Route 7, Pine Plains, NY 12567-9664
212-750-8844 or 518-398-8844 Fax: 518-398-9370
e-mail: ecs37@aol.com
Margo Marabon, President
Computer services, voter lists & direct mail

Emily's List
1120 Connecticut Ave NW, Ste 1100, Washington, DC 20036-3949
202-326-1400 Fax: 202-326-1415
Web site: www.emilyslist.org
Karen White, Political Director
Political network for pro-choice Democratic women political candidates

Garth Group Inc (The)
1 W 67th St, #206, New York, NY 10023-6200
212-838-8800 Fax: 212-873-5252
e-mail: garthgroup@aol.com
David Garth, Chairman
Political & media consulting

Harris Interactive Inc
135 Corporate Woods, Rochester, NY 14623-1457
585-272-8400 or 800-866-7655 Fax: 585-272-8763
e-mail: info@harrisinteractive.com
Web site: www.harrisinteractive.com
Greg Novak, President & Chief Executive Officer
Market research

League of Women Voters of New York State
35 Maiden Lane, Albany, NY 12207-2712
518-465-4162 Fax: 518-465-0812
e-mail: rob@lwvny.org
Web site: www.lwvny.org
Rob Marchiony, Executive Director
Public policy issues forum; good government advocacy

Marist Institute for Public Opinion
Marist College, 3399 North Road, Poughkeepsie, NY 12601
845-575-5050 Fax: 845-575-5111
e-mail: lee.miringoff@marist.edu
Web site: www.maristpoll.marist.edu
Lee M Miringoff, Director
Develops & conducts nonpartisan public opinion polls on elections & issues

Offices and agencies appear in alphabetical order.

NY League of Conservation Voters/NY Conservation Education Fund
29 Broadway, Rm 1100, New York, NY 10006-3201
212-361-6350 x208 Fax: 212-361-6363
e-mail: mbystryn@nylcv.org
Web site: www.nylcv.org
Marcia Bystryn, Executive Director
Endorsement of pro-environmental candidates; environmental advocacy & education statewide

NYC Campaign Finance Board
40 Rector St, 7th Fl, New York, NY 10006-1705
212-306-7100 Fax: 212-306-7143
e-mail: info@nyccfb.info
Web site: www.nyccfb.info
Nicole A Gordon, Executive Director
Public funding of candidates for NYC elective offices

NYS Republican Party
315 State St, Albany, NY 12210
518-462-2601 Fax: 518-449-7443
Web site: www.nygop.org
Ryan Moses, Executive Director

NYS Right-to-Life Committee
41 State St, Ste 100, Albany, NY 12207
518-434-1293 Fax: 518-426-1200
e-mail: infonysrighttolife.org
Web site: www.nysrighttolife.org
Lori Kehoe, Executive Director

National Organization for Women, NYS
1500 Central Avenue, Albany, NY 12205
518-452-3944 Fax: 518-452-3861
e-mail: newyorkstatenow@aol.com
Web site: www.nownys.com
Marcia Pappas, President
Campaign assistance & funding for political candidates who support feminist agenda; legislative lobbying on women's issues

New School University, Department of Political Science
65 5th Ave, New York, NY 10011
212-229-5784 Fax: 212-807-1669
e-mail: hattamv@newschool.edu
Web site: www.newschool.edu
Victoria Hattam, Associate Professor of Political Science
Business unionism in the US; political parties & elections

New York State Democratic Committee
60 Madison Ave, Ste 1201, New York, NY 10010
212-725-8825 Fax: 212-725-8867
e-mail: rodneyc@nysdems.org
Web site: www.nydems.org
Rodney S Capel, Executive Director

New York University, Departmentt of Politics
726 Broadway, New York, NY 10003-9580
212-998-8500 Fax: 212-995-4184
e-mail: russell.hardin@nyu.edu
Web site: www.nyu.edu/gsas/dept/politics
Russell Hardin, Professor of Politics
Ethics in public life; collective action & social movements; nationalism & ethnic conflict

New York University, Graduate School of Journalism
10 Washington Place, New York, NY 10003
212-998-7965 Fax: 212-995-4148
e-mail: jr3@nyu.edu
Web site: www.journalism.nyu.edu
Jay Rosen, Chair, Journalism Department
Political role of the press

New York Wired
One Commerce Plz, Ste 301, PO Box 3945, Albany, NY 12203
518-462-1780 x211
Web site: www.newyorkwired.com
Tom Owens, Consulting & Legal

Nostradamus Advertising
884 West End Ave, Ste 2, New York, NY 10025
212-581-1362 Fax: 212-662-8625
e-mail: nos@nostradamus.net
Web site: www.nostradamus.net
Barry N Sher, President
Print production, media consulting, direct mail development

PinPoint Communications Group Inc
1223 Peoples Ave, Ste 1200, Troy, NY 12180-3511
518-276-8050 Fax: 518-276-8086
e-mail: stan@pinpointc.com
Web site: www.pinpointc.com
Stanley Wright, President
Grassroots lobbying & letter writing campaigns; database mgmt & fundraising; Internet lobbying; web news feed services

Public Agenda
6 East 39th St, 9th Fl, New York, NY 10016
212-686-6610 Fax: 212-889-3461
e-mail: info@publicagenda.org
Web site: www.publicagenda.org
Claudia Feurey, Vice President, Communications & External Relations
Nonpartisan, nonprofit organization dedicated to conducting unbiased public opinion research & producing fair-minded citizen education materials

SUNY at Albany, Nelson A Rockefeller College
135 Western Ave, Albany, NY 12222
518-442-5378 Fax: 518-442-5298
e-mail: zimmer@albany.edu
Web site: www.albany.edu/rockefeller
Joseph F Zimmerman, Professor
Intergovernmental relations; NY state & local government; ethics in government; election systems & voting

Offices and agencies appear in alphabetical order.

SUNY at New Paltz, College of Liberal Arts & Sciences
614 Faculty Tower, New Paltz, NY 12561-2499
845-257-3520 Fax: 845-257-3517
e-mail: benjamig@newpaltz.edu
Web site: www.newpaltz.edu
Gerald Benjamin, Dean & Professor of Political Science
Local & state government process & structure; regionalism; politics & election law

Sheinkopf Communications
152 Madison Avenue, Suite 1603, New York, NY 10016
212-725-2378 Fax: 212-725-6896
e-mail: info@scheinkopf.com
Henry A Sheinkopf, President
Strategic message counseling for corporate & political clients

US Term Limits Foundation
240 Waukegan Road, Suite 200, Glenview, IL 60025
847-657-7429 or 800-733-6440 Fax: 847-657-7502
e-mail: howrch@cs.com
Web site: www.ustermlimits.org
Howard Rich, President
Publishers of

Women's Campaign Fund
734 15th St NW, Ste 500, Washington, DC 20005
202-393-8164 or 800-446-8170 Fax: 202-393-0649
e-mail: susanmedalie@wcfonline.org
Web site: www.wcfonline.org
Ilana Goldman, Executive Director
Training, education & funding for pro-choice women political candidates

Women's City Club of New York
33 West 60th St, 5th Fl, New York, NY 10023-7905
212-353-8070 Fax: 212-228-4665
e-mail: info@wccny.org
Web site: www.wccny.org
Blanche E Lawton, President
Nonpartisan, nonprofit which fosters active, responsible citizen participation in shaping public policy decisions affecting the NYC community

Working Families Party
88 Third Ave, 4th Flr, Brooklyn, NY 11217
718-222-3796 Fax: 718-246-3718
e-mail: wfp@workingfamiliesparty.org
Web site: www.workingfamiliesparty.org
Dan Cantor, Executive Director

Zogby International
901 Broad St, Utica, NY 13501
315-624-0200 Fax: 315-624-0210
e-mail: mail@zogby.com
Web site: www.zogby.com
John Zogby, President
Political polling & analysis; social science research; business & consumer public opinion surveys & market research

Policy Areas

Offices and agencies appear in alphabetical order.

ENERGY, UTILITY & COMMUNICATION SERVICES

New York State

GOVERNOR'S OFFICE

Governor's Office
Executive Chamber
State Capitol
Albany, NY 12224
518-474-8390 Fax: 518-474-1513
Web site: www.state.ny.us

Governor:
George E Pataki 518-474-8390
Executive Director:
Kara Lanspery 518-474-8390
Secretary to the Governor:
John P Cahill. 518-474-4246
Senior Policy Advisor to the Governor:
Jeffrey Lovell 518-486-9671
Counsel to Governor-Attorney General, Budget:
Richard Platkin. 518-474-8343
Deputy Secretary to the Governor for Energy, Environment, Transportation:
Charles Fox. 518-474-0411
Senior Asst Counsel to the Governor-Energy Research & Development,
Environmental Conservation, Long Island Power Authority, NY Power
Authority, Public Service Commission:
Carl Patka 518-474-8327
Director, Energy Programs:
James Austin. 518-474-0351
Director, Communications:
David Catalfamo. 518-474-8418
Citizens Services:
Linda Boyd. 518-474-1041

EXECUTIVE DEPARTMENTS AND RELATED AGENCIES

CIO Office & Office for Technology
State Capitol, ESP
PO Box 2062
Albany, NY 12220-0062

CIO Office
Web site: www.cio.state.ny.us
Chief Information Officer:
James T Dillon. 518-474-3421/fax: 518-402-2976
e-mail: cio@cio.state.ny.us
Deputy Chief Information Officer:
Michael Mittleman 518-408-2140/fax: 518-402-2976

Office for Technology
Web site: www.oft.state.ny.us
Director:
Michael McCormack. 518-473-9450/fax: 518-402-2976
e-mail: nyoft@oft.state.ny.us

Administration
Chief Administrative Officer:
Meg Levine 518-408-2476/fax: 518-402-2976
Administrative Support:
Max Morehouse 518-402-2202/fax: 518-402-2019
Budget & Fiscal Administration:
Kevin Nephew. 518-402-4874/fax: 518-402-4807
Human Resources:
Elaine Ehlinger 518-473-1935/fax: 518-402-4924

Counsel
Deputy Director & Counsel:
Susan Zeronda. 518-473-2807/fax: 518-402-2976
Deputy Counsel:
Darlene Van Sickle 518-473-5115/fax: 518-486-7923

Operations
Chief Operating Officer:
David Swits. 518-473-7041/fax: 518-402-2976
Deputy Director, Customer Service:
Dan Healy 518-473-2658/fax: 518-474-1196
Director, Enterprise Help Desk:
Igor Koroluk 518-474-1179/fax: 518-473-0832
Deputy Director, Applications:
Ellen Kattleman. 518-402-2010/fax: 518-486-4344
Deputy Director, Networking:
Dave Runyon. 518-486-9200/fax: 518-408-4693
Director, Telecom:
Daniel Corcoran 518-474-3019/fax: 518-473-7145
Deputy Director, Computing:
Peter Poleto 518-474-8345/fax: 518-402-2976
Data Center/Technical Support:
Glenn Kreig. 518-485-9556/fax: 518-457-8936
Data Center/Operations:
Allan Goldsmith 518-473-0927/fax: 518-474-9108

Statewide Initiatives
HIPAA Coord:
Anne Marie Rainville 518-474-0683/fax: 518-473-3389
NYS Technology Academy:
Terri Daly 518-474-0683/fax: 518-473-3389

Statewide Wireless Network
Director:
Hanford Thomas 518-443-2042/fax: 518-443-2787
Assistant Deputy Director:
Jim Sciacca. 518-443-2042

Strategic Policies Acquisitions & e-Commerce (SPAC)
Deputy Director:
Susan Zeronda. 518-473-2807/fax: 518-402-2976

Consumer Protection Board
5 Empire State Plaza
Ste 2101
Albany, NY 12223-1556

Offices and agencies appear in alphabetical order.

518-474-8583 or 800-NYS-1220 Fax: 518-486-3936
Web site: www.consumer.state.ny.us

5 Penn Plaza, 5th Fl
New York, NY 10001
212-268-6199
Fax: 212-268-7124

Chairperson & Executive Director:
   Teresa A Santiago. 518-474-3514
Deputy Executive Director:
   Corinne Biviano 518-474-1471
General Counsel:
   Lisa Harris 518-486-3934
Director, Marketing & Public Relations:
   Jon Sorensen 518-473-9472/fax: 518-474-2986
Director, Education:
   Gina Pinos 518-459-8852
Director, Consumer Services:
   Cyndee D Berlin. 518-474-1471

Strategic Programs Office
Director Strategic Programs & Utility Intervention:
   Douglas Elfner 518-486-6532
Chief Economist, Utility Intervention:
   Tariq Niazi 518-486-3932

Long Island Region
   333 Earle Ovington Blvd, Ste 403, Uniondale, NY 11553
Regional Outreach Specialist:
   Christine Scuti. 516-470-2954/fax: 516-470-2955

New York City Office
   1740 Broadway, 15th Fl, New York, NY 10019
Assistant to the Chairperson:
   Carmen Castro. 212-459-8850/fax: 212-459-8859
Regional Outreach Specialist:
   James Dees 212-459-8850/fax: 212-459-8855

Western New York Office
   340 East Main St, Rochester, NY 14604
Deputy Director, Consumer Education:
   Joan Mueller 585-262-2180/fax: 585-262-3748

Law Department
120 Broadway
New York, NY 10271-0332
212-416-8000 Fax: 212-416-8942

State Capitol
Albany, NY 10271-0332
518-474-7330
Fax: 518-402-2472

Attorney General:
   Eliot Spitzer 518-474-7330
First Deputy Attorney General:
   Michele Hirshman 212-416-8050
Director, Public Information & Correspondence:
   Peter A Drago 518-474-7330/fax: 518-402-2472

Public Advocacy Division
Acting Deputy Attorney General:
   Terryl Brown Clemons 212-416-8041/fax: 212-416-8068
Special Counsel:
   Mary Ellen Burns 212-416-6155

Internet Bureau
Bureau Chief:
   Kenneth Dreifach 212-416-8433/fax: 212-416-8369

Telecommunications & Energy Bureau
Bureau Chief:
   Susanna M Swerling 212-416-8333/fax: 212-416-8877

Public Service Department
Three Empire State Plaza
Albany, NY 12223-1350
518-474-7080 Fax: 518-473-2838
Web site: www.dps.state.ny.us

90 Church St
New York, NY 10007-2919
212-417-2378

295 Main St
Buffalo, NY 14203
716-847-3400

Chair:
   William M Flynn. 518-474-2523/fax: 518-486-1947
Executive Deputy:
   Paul Powers 518-473-4544/fax: 518-473-2838
General Counsel:
   Dawn Jablonski Ryman. 518-474-2510/fax: 518-486-5710
Director, Public Affairs:
   David C Flanagan 518-474-7080/fax: 518-473-2838

Accounting & Finance Office
Director:
   Charles M Dickson 518-474-4508/fax: 518-486-7524

Consumer Services Office
Director:
   Sandra Sloane 518-474-3280/fax: 518-486-7868
   e-mail: csd@dps.state.ny.us

Electricity & Environment Office
Director:
   James Gallagher. 518-473-7248/fax: 518-486-1672
Chief, Administration & Planning:
   Frederick Carr 518-486-2892/fax: 518-473-2420
Chief, Energy Resources & The Environment:
   Douglas K May 518-474-5368/fax: 518-474-5026
Chief, Rates & Retail Choice:
   Harvey Arnett 212-290-4385/fax: 212-290-4228
Chief, Distribution Systems & Generation:
   Charles F Puglisi 518-486-2899/fax: 518-472-2420
Chief, Bulk Transmission Systems:
   Howard A Tarler 518-486-2483/fax: 518-473-2420

Gas & Water Office
Director:
   Thomas Dvorsky 518-473-6080/fax: 518-473-4992
Chief, Gas Rates:
   Frank Berak 518-474-1372/fax: 518-473-4992
Acting Chief, Safety Sector:
   Gavin S Nicoletta 518-486-2496/fax: 518-473-5625
Chief, Policy Section:
   Sheila A Rappazzo 518-486-1645/fax: 518-473-4992
Chief, Water Rates:
   Arthur Gordon 518-474-8656/fax: 518-473-5625

Offices and agencies appear in alphabetical order.

Policy Areas

Hearings & Alternative Dispute Resolution Office

Chief Administrative Law Judge:
Judith Lee 518-474-4520/fax: 518-473-3263

Office of Administration

Director:
Debra Renner. 518-474-2508/fax: 518-474-0413
Adminstrative Management:
Kathryn Norton 518-474-1990/fax: 518-474-0413
Finance & Budget:
Sorelle Brauth 518-474-2516/fax: 518-473-9990
Human Resources:
Barbara Herbert 518-486-2633/fax: 518-473-9990
Information Services Director:
Jane Craig 518-486-4960/fax: 518-473-7815
Internal Audit:
Steve Suriano. 518-473-2079/fax: 518-474-0413

Office of Economic Development & Policy Coordination (OEDPC)

Director:
John P Reese 518-474-2530/fax: 518-473-2838

Office of Retail Market Development (ORMD)

Director:
Ronald Cerniglia 518-474-1540/fax: 518-473-5685
e-mail: ormd@dps.state.ny.us
Manager, Consumer Education:
Richard Gifford 518-402-5014/fax: 518-473-5685

Office of Telecommunications

Director:
Robert H Mayer. 518-474-1668/fax: 518-474-5616
Deputy Director, Cable:
Chad Hume 518-474-1939/fax: 518-486-5727

Public Service Commission

Chair:
William M Flynn 518-474-2523/fax: 518-486-1947
vacant
Secretary to the Commission:
Jaclyn A Brilling 518-474-6530/fax: 518-486-6081
e-mail: secretary@dps.state.ny.us

Regulatory Economics Office

Director:
Robert Whitaker 518-474-1522/fax: 518-473-5204
Chief:
Mark Reeder. 518-474-8267

Utility Security Office

Director:
John J Sennett 518-473-0547/fax: 518-473-1498

CORPORATIONS, AUTHORITIES AND COMMISSIONS

Interstate Oil & Gas Compact Commission

PO Box 53127
Oklahoma City, OK 73152-3127
405-525-3556 Fax: 405-525-3592
e-mail: iogcc@iogcc.state.ok.us
Web site: www.iogcc.state.ok.us

Chair (Governor of NM):
Bill Richardson. 505-476-2200

Vice Chair:
Donald L Mason. 614-466-3905
Executive Director:
Christine Hansen 405-525-3556
New York State Official Representative:
Bradley J Field 518-402-8076

Long Island Power Authority

333 Earle Ovington Blvd
Ste 403
Uniondale, NY 11553
516-222-7700 Fax: 516-222-9137
e-mail: info@lipower.org
Web site: www.lipower.org

Chair:
Richard M Kessel. 516-222-7700
General Counsel:
Stanley Klimberg 516-222-7700
Vice President, Communications:
Bert Cunningham 516-222-7700
e-mail: bcunningham@lipower.org
Director, Government Relations:
William Davidson. 516-719-9852

New York Power Authority

123 Main St
White Plains, NY 10601
914-681-6200 Fax: 914-390-8190

30 S Pearl St
Albany, NY 12207
518-433-6700
Fax: 518-433-1406

Chairman:
Louis P Ciminelli 518-433-6700
President & Chief Executive Officer:
Eugene W Zeltmann. 518-433-6719
Senior Vice President, Public & Government Affairs:
Peter Barden 914-390-8160/fax: 914-390-8190
Director, Community Relations:
Paul Finnegan. 518-433-6740
Director, Public Relations:
Jack Murphy 914-390-8198/fax: 914-390-8190
e-mail: jack.murphy@nypa.gov

New York State Energy Research & Development Authority

17 Columbia Circle
Albany, NY 12203-6399
518-862-1090 Fax: 518-862-1091
Web site: www.nyserda.org

Chairman:
Vincent A Delorio 518-862-1090
President:
Peter R Smith. 518-862-1090 x3220
e-mail: prs@nyserda.org
General Counsel:
Roger D Avent. 518-862-1090 x3333
e-mail: rda@nyserda.org

Offices and agencies appear in alphabetical order.

Vice President, Administration:
  Wendy M Shave 518-862-1090 x3226
  e-mail: wms@nyserda.org
Vice President, Programs:
  Robert Callender 518-862-1090 x3233
Treasurer:
  Jeffrey J Pitkin. 518-862-1090 x3223
  e-mail: jjp@nyserda.org
Director, Communications:
  Thomas G Collins. 518-862-1090 x3250/fax: 518-464-8249
  e-mail: tgc@nyserda.org

NEW YORK STATE LEGISLATURE

*See Legislative Branch in Section 1 for additional Standing Commit-
tee and Subcommittee information.*

Assembly Standing Committees

Energy
Chair:
  Paul D Tonko (D). 518-455-5197
Ranking Minority Member:
  Brian Kolb (R) 518-455-5772

Senate Standing Committees

Energy & Telecommunications
Chair:
  James W Wright (R). 518-455-2346
Ranking Minority Member:
  Kevin S Parker (D). 518-455-2580

U.S. Government

EXECUTIVE DEPARTMENTS AND RELATED AGENCIES

Federal Communications Commission
Web site: www.fcc.gov

Office of Media Relations
445 12th St SW, Rm CY-C314, Washington, DC 20554
Director:
  David Fiske. 202-418-0500

Nuclear Regulatory Commission
Web site: www.nrc.gov

REGION I (includes New York State)
475 Allendale Rd, King of Prussia, PA 19406-1415
Regional Administrator:
  Samuel J Collins 610-337-5299/fax: 610-337-5241
Senior Public Affairs Officer:
  Diane P Screnci 610-337-5330
Public Affairs Officer:
  Neil A Sheehan. 610-337-5331

US Department of Agriculture
Web site: www.usda.gov

Rural Development
Web site: www.rurdev.usda.gov/ny

New York State Office
The Galleries of Syracuse, 441 S Salina St, Ste 357, 5th Fl, Syracuse, NY
  13202-2425
TDD: 315-477-6447
State Director:
  Patrick H Brennan. 315-477-6400/fax: 315-477-6438
Special Projects Representative:
  Joel Weirick 315-477-6433/fax: 315-477-6438
Program Director, Rural Utilities Service:
  David Miller 315-477-6427/fax: 315-477-6448
  e-mail: david.miller@ny.usda.gov

US Department of Energy
Web site: www.doe.gov

Federal Energy Regulatory Commission

New York Regional Office
19 W 34th St, Ste 400, New York, NY 10001
Regional Engineer:
  Anton J Sidoti 212-273-5990/fax: 212-631-8124
Hydropower Licensing & Analysis Supervisor:
  Peter Valeri. 212-273-5930

Office of External Affairs
888 First St NE, Washington, DC 20426
Director:
  J. Mclane Layton. 202-502-8004/fax: 202-208-2106

Laboratories

Brookhaven National Laboratory
Brookhaven Group
53 Bell Ave, Bldg 464, Upton, NY 11973-5000
Area Manager:
  Michael Holland. 631-344-3424/fax: 631-344-3444
Community Involvement/Public Affairs
35 Brookhaven Ave, Upton, NY 11973
Assistant Lab Director:
  Margaret Lynch 631-344-4747/fax: 631-344-5004
Media & Communications Manager:
  Mona Rowe 631-344-5056/fax: 631-344-3368
Office of the Director
40 Brookhaven Ave, Bldg 460, Upton, NY 11973-5000
Director:
  Praveen Chaudhari 631-344-2772/fax: 631-344-5803

Knolls Atomic Power Laboratory- KAPL Inc
PO Box 1072, Schenectady, NY 12301-1072
General Manager:
  Michael F Quinn 518-395-4200/fax: 518-395-6469

U.S. CONGRESS

*See U.S. Congress Chapter for additional Standing Committee and
Subcommittee information.*

Offices and agencies appear in alphabetical order.

House of Representatives Standing Committees

Appropriations
Chair:
    Jerry Lewis (R-CA) 202-225-5861
Ranking Minority Member:
    David R Obey (D-WI) 202-225-3365
New York Delegate:
    Maurice D Hinchey (D) 202-225-6335
New York Delegate:
    Nita M Lowey (D) 202-225-6506
New York Delegate:
    Jose E Serrano (D) 202-225-4361
New York Delegate:
    John E Sweeney (R) 202-225-5614
New York Delegate:
    James T Walsh (R) 202-225-3701

Subcommittee
Energy & Water Development
Chair:
    David L Hobson (R-OH)...................... 202-225-4324
Ranking Minority Member:
    Peter J Visclosky (D-IN) 202-225-2461

Energy & Commerce
Chair:
    Joe Barton (R-TX) 202-225-2002
Ranking Minority Member:
    John D Dingell (D-MI)......................... 202-225-4071
New York Delegate:
    Eliot L Engel (D) 202-225-2464
New York Delegate:
    Vito Fossella (R)............................... 202-225-3371
New York Delegate:
    Edolphus Towns (D)........................... 202-225-5936

Subcommittee
Energy & Air Quality
Chair:
    Ralph M Hall (R-TX) 202-225-6673
Ranking Minority Member:
    Rick Boucher (D-VA)........................... 202-225-3861
New York Delegate:
    Eliot L Engel (D)............................... 202-225-2464
New York Delegate:
    Vito Fossella (R) 202-225-3371

Resources
Chair:
    Richard W Pombo (R-CA)....................... 202-225-2761
Ranking Minority Member:
    Nick J Rahall, II (D-WV) 202-225-3452

Subcommittees
Energy & Mineral Resources
Chair:
    Jim Gibbons (R-NV)......................... 202-225-6155
Ranking Minority Member:
    Raul Grisalva (D-AZ) 202-225-2435

Water & Power
Chair:
    George Radanovich (R-CA) 202-225-4540
Ranking Minority Member:
    Grace Napolitano (D-CA)..................... 202-225-5256

Science
Chair:
    Sherwood L Boehlert (R-NY) 202-225-3665
Ranking Minority Member:
    Bart Gordon (D-TN)........................... 202-225-4231

Subcommittee
Energy
Chair:
    Judy Biggert (R-IL)......................... 202-225-3515
Ranking Minority Member:
    Mike Honda (D-CA) 202-225-2631

Senate Standing Committees

Appropriations
Chair:
    Thad Cochran (R-MS) 202-224-5054
Ranking Minority Member:
    Robert C Byrd (D-WV) 202-224-3954

Subcommittee
Energy & Water Development
Chair:
    Peter V Domenici (R-NM) 202-224-6621
Ranking Minority Member:
    Harry Reid (D-NV) 202-224-3542

Commerce, Science & Transportation
Chair:
    Ted Stevens (R-AK)............................ 202-224-3004
Ranking Minority Member:
    Daniel K Inouye (D-HI) 202-224-3934

Subcommittee
Aviation
Chair:
    Conrad R Burns (R-MT) 202-224-2644
Ranking Minority Mbr:
    John D Rockefeller, IV (D-WV) 202-224-6472
Science & Space
Chair:
    Kay Bailey Hutchison (R-TX)................. 202-224-5922
Ranking Minority Member:
    Bill Nelson (D-FL) 202-224-5274

Energy & Water Development
Chair:
    Pete V Domenici (R-NM) 202-224-6621
Ranking Minority Member:
    Harry Reid (D-NV)............................ 202-224-3542

Offices and agencies appear in alphabetical order.

Private Sector

AT&T Corporation
One AT&T Way, Bedminster, NJ 7921
908-532-1835 Fax: 908-532-1702
e-mail: morrisse@lga.att.com
Michael Morrissey, Vice President, Law & Government Affairs
Telecommunications services & systems

AeA New York Council
472 Westfield Avenue, Suite LL3, Clark, NJ 07066
732-340-1500 Fax: 908-561-7954
e-mail: linda_klose@aeanet.org
Web site: www.aeanet.org
Linda Klose, Executive Director
Electronics, software & information technology industries; support of high tech industry goals

Amerada Hess Corporation
1185 Ave of the Americas, New York, NY 10036
212-997-8500 Fax: 212-536-8390
Web site: www.hess.com
John B Hess, Chief Executive Officer
Manufacture & market petroleum products; operate gasoline outlets

Association of Public Broadcasting Stations of NY Inc
33 Elk St, Ste 200, Albany, NY 12207
518-462-1590 Fax: 518-462-1390
e-mail: apbs@wxxi.org
Peter Repas, Executive Director
Public television

Boralex Operation Inc
39 Hudson Falls Road, South Glens Falls, NY 12803
518-747-0930 Fax: 518-747-2409
e-mail: daubute@cascades.com
Web site: www.boralex.com
Denis Aubute, GM, Hydro Operations
Independent energy producer

Business Council of New York State Inc
152 Washington Ave, Albany, NY 12210
518-465-7511 x223 Fax: 518-465-4389
e-mail: anne.vanburen@bcnys.org
Web site: www.bcnys.org
Anne Van Buren, Director, Telecommunications & Transmission Policy
Telecommunications, small business, financial services, insurance

CBS Corporation
51 W 52nd St, New York, NY 10019
212-975-4321 Fax: 212-975-6035
Web site: www.cbs.com
Martin Franks, Executive Vice President, CBS Television & Senior Vice President, Viacom
TV & radio broadcasting, news, entertainment

Cable Telecommunications Association of New York Inc
80 State St, 10th Fl, Albany, NY 12207
518-463-6676 Fax: 518-463-0574
e-mail: cttany@nycap.rr.com
Web site: www.cabletvny.com
Richard F Alteri, President
Advocate & represent the interests of the cable television industry

Cablevision Systems Corporation
1111 Stewart Ave, Bethpage, NY 11714-3581
516-803-2580 Fax: 516-803-2585
e-mail: lrosenbl@cablevision.com
Lisa Rosenblum, Senior Vice President, Government Relations
Own & operate cable television systems & programming networks, telecommunications, Madison Square Garden, Radio City Music Hall, pro sports teams

Central Hudson Gas & Electric Corporation
284 South Ave, Poughkeepsie, NY 12601
845-486-5218 Fax: 845-486-5544
e-mail: jglusko@cenhud.com
Web site: www.cenhud.com
John P Glusko, Director, Governmental Affairs & Economic Development
Governmental relations, corporate relocations & economic development

Consolidated Edison Energy
4 Irving Pl, Rm 1650S, New York, NY 10003
212-460-2706 Fax: 212-614-1821
e-mail: banksjo@coned.com
Web site: www.coned.com
John H Banks, Vice President, Government Relations

Constellation NewEnergy Inc
551 Fifth Ave, Ste 400, New York, NY 10176
212-883-5880 Fax: 212-883-5888
e-mail: brian.hayduk@constellation.com
Web site: www.newenergy.com
Brian Hayduk, Vice President
Retail energy supply & energy services

Crane, Parente, Cherubin & Murray
90 State Street, Ste 1515A, Albany, NY 12207
518-432-8000 Fax: 518-432-0086
e-mail: jcrane@cpcmlaw.com
James B Crane, II, Managing Partner
Governmental relations, banking & financial services, corporate law, construction law, energy, utilities, communications, land use, environmental & wireless telecommunications law

Educational Broadcasting Corporation
450 West 33rd St, New York, NY 10001
212-560-2072 Fax: 212-560-3045
e-mail: rae@thirteen.org
Web site: www.thirteen.org
Kathleen Rae, Director Governmental Affairs

Offices and agencies appear in alphabetical order.

Empire State Petroleum Association Inc
111 Washington Ave, Ste 203, Albany, NY 12210
518-449-0702 Fax: 518-449-0779
e-mail: tpeters@espa.net
Web site: www.espa.net
Thomas J Peters, Executive Vice President
Petroleum industry lobby & trade association

Energy Association of New York State
111 Washington Ave, Suite 601, Albany, NY 12210
518-449-3440 Fax: 518-449-3446
Howard Shapiro, President & Chief Executive Officer
Electric & gas utility companies

Entek Power Services
11 Satterly Rd, East Setauket, NY 11733
631-751-9800 Fax: 631-980-3759
e-mail: info@entekpower.com
Web site: www.entekpower.com
Harry Davitian, President
Energy consulting

Entergy Nuclear Northeast
440 Hamilton Ave, White Plains, NY 10601
914-272-3200 Fax: 914-272-3205
Web site: www.entergy.com
Michael R Kansler, President
Second largest operator of nuclear power plants in the US

Exxon Mobil Corporation
1400 Old Country Rd, Ste 203, Westbury, NY 11590
516-333-3177 Fax: 516-333-3428
e-mail: donald.l.clarke@exxonmobil.com
Web site: www.exxonmobil.com
Donald L Clarke, Manager, Public Affairs Northeast

Frontier, A Citizens Communications Co
145 North Main St, Monroe, NY 10950
845-783-5217 Fax: 845-782-9937
Web site: www.frontieronline.com
Jen Memmelaar, Operations Director
Full service telecommunications provider

Fund for the City of New York, Center for Internet Innovation
121 Ave of the Americas, 6th Fl, New York, NY 10013
212-925-6675 Fax: 212-925-5675
e-mail: mmccormick@fcny.org
Web site: www.fcny.org
Mary McCormick, President
Developing technology systems & applications that help nonprofits & government streamline operations, expand services, improve performance

Getty Petroleum Marketing Inc
1500 Hempstead Turnpike, East Meadow, NY 11554
516-542-5055 Fax: 516-832-8443
e-mail: mlewis@getty.com
Web site: www.getty.com
Michael G Lewis, Vice President & General Counsel
Petroleum products sales & distribution

NYS Bar Assn, Electronic Communications Task Force
Heslin Rothenberg Farley & Mesiti PC
5 Columbia Cir, Albany, NY 12203
518-452-5600 Fax: 518-452-5579
e-mail: dpm@hrfmlaw.com
David P Miranda, Chair

NYS Bar Assn, Media Law Committee
Hogan & Hartson LLP
875 3rd Ave, 25th Fl, New York, NY 10022
212-918-3637 Fax: 212-918-3100
e-mail: srmetcalf@hhlaw.com
Slade R Metcalf, Chair

Independent Oil & Gas Association of New York
5743 Walden Drive, Lake View, NY 14085
716-627-4250 Fax: 716-627-4375
e-mail: bgill@iogany.org
Web site: www.iogany.org
Bradley Gill, Executive Director
Trade association representing oil & natural gas producers, drillers & affiliated service companies

Independent Power Producers of NY Inc
19 Dove Street, Ste 302, Albany, NY 12210
518-436-3749 Fax: 518-436-0369
e-mail: gavin@ippny.org
Web site: www.ippny.org
Gavin J Donohue, President & Chief Executive Officer
Companies developing alternative, environmentally friendly electric generating facilities

KeySpan Corporation
175 E Old Country Rd, Hicksville, NY 11801
516-545-4449 Fax: 516-545-5065
e-mail: tdejesu@keyspanenergy.com
Thomas DeJesu, Director, Government Relations
Electric generation & gas utility

Komanoff Energy Associates
636 Broadway, Rm 602, New York, NY 10012-2623
212-260-5237
e-mail: kea@igc.org
Charles Komanoff, Director
Energy, utilities & transportation consulting

MCI
100 Park Ave, 13th Flr, New York, NY 10166
212-547-3232 Fax: 212-478-6202
Web site: www.mci.com
Evlyn Tsimis, Director, Northeast Region Public Policy

Mechanical Technology Inc
431 New Karner Road, Albany, NY 12205
518-533-2200 Fax: 518-533-2201
Web site: www.mechtech.com
Dale W Church, Chairman & Chief Executive Officer
New energy technologies, precision measurement & testing instruments

Offices and agencies appear in alphabetical order.

Municipal Electric Utilities Association
445 Electronics Pkwy, Ste 207, Liverpool, NY 13088-6001
315-453-7851 Fax: 315-453-7849
e-mail: info@meua.org
Web site: www.meua.org
Robert Mullane, Executive Director

NY Oil Heating Association
14 Penn Plaza, Ste 1102, New York, NY 10122
212-695-1380 Fax: 212-594-6583
e-mail: nyoilheating@nyoha.org
Web site: www.nyoha.org
John Maniscalco, Executive Vice President
Fuel dealers & auxiliary industries

NY Press Association
1681 Western Ave, Albany, NY 12203
518-464-6483 Fax: 518-464-6489
e-mail: mkrea@nynewspapers.com
Web site: www.nynewspapers.com
Michelle Rea, Executive Director
Weekly community & ethnic newspaper publishers

NY Propane Gas Association
PO Box 152, Rensselaer, NY 12144
518-218-1810 Fax: 518-765-5762
e-mail: nypga1@aol.com
Web site: www.nypropane.org
Stephanie O'Grady, Executive Director

NYS Broadcasters Association
1805 Western Ave, Albany, NY 12203
518-456-8888 Fax: 518-456-8943
Web site: www.nysbroadcastersassn.org
Joseph Reilly, President
Trade association for NYS Broadcasters

NYS Technology Enterprise Corporation (NYSTEC)
100 State St, Ste 330, Albany, NY 12207
518-431-7020 Fax: 518-431-7037
e-mail: nystec@nystec.com
Web site: www.nystec.com
Geoff Plante, Director, Business Development
Technology acquisition, technology management & engineering services to government clients

National Economic Research Associates
308 N Cayuga St, Ithaca, NY 14850
607-277-3007 Fax: 607-277-1581
e-mail: alfred.kahn@nera.com
Web site: www.nera.com
Alfred E Kahn, Professor Emeritus & Special Consultant
Utility & transportation regulation, deregulation & antitrust

National Energy Group
111 Washington Ave, Ste 403, Albany, NY 12203
518-432-8725 Fax: 518-432-0587
Web site: www.neg.pge.com
Daniel Whyte, Director External Relations & Permitting

National Fuel Gas
800 North 3rd Street, Ste 410, Box 1145, Harrisburg, PA 17108
717-232-7236 Fax: 717-232-8238
e-mail: morrisong@nat.fuel.com
Web site: www.nationalfuel.com
Gary L Morrison, General Manager, Government Affairs

NYS Bar Assn, Public Utility Law Committee
National Fuel Gas Distribution
Legal Department, 6363 Main Street, Buffalo, NY 14221
716-857-7313
Michael W Reville, Chair

Nelson A Rockefeller Inst of Government, NY Forum for Info
411 State St, Albany, NY 12203-1003
518-443-5001 Fax: 518-443-5006
e-mail: gbenson@nysfirm.org
Web site: www.nysfirm.org
Gregory M Benson Jr, Executive Director
Information management; public access to government information; privacy & confidentiality; intellectual property

New York Independent System Operator - Not For Profit
290 Washington Ave Extension, Albany, NY 12203
518-356-8728 or 518-356-6253 Fax: 518-356-7524
e-mail: cmurphy@nyiso.com
Web site: www.nyiso.com
Carol E Murphy, Vice President of Government Affairs & Communications
Grid operator

New York Newspaper Publishers Association
120 Washington Ave, Albany, NY 12210
518-449-1667 Fax: 518-449-5053
Web site: www.nynpa.com
Diane Kennedy, President

New York Press Photographers Association
225 E 36th St, Ste 1-P, New York, NY 10016
212-889-6633 Fax: 212-889-6634
e-mail: nyppa@aol.com
Web site: www.nyppa.org
Bernie Nunez, President

New York State Electric & Gas Corporation (NYSEG)
18 Link Drive, Box 5224, Binghamton, NY 13902-5224
607-762-7310 Fax: 607-762-8751
e-mail: ctchadwick@nyseg.com
Web site: www.nyseg.com
Cindy T Chadwick, Manager, Public Affairs

New York State Petroleum Council
150 State St, Albany, NY 12207
518-465-3563 Fax: 518-465-4022
e-mail: nyspc@nycap.rr.com
Web site: www.api.org
Michael R Doyle, Executive Director
Petroleum industry lobby

Policy Areas

Offices and agencies appear in alphabetical order.

New York State Telecommunications Association Inc
100 State St, Ste 650, Albany, NY 12207
518-443-2700 Fax: 518-443-2810
e-mail: rpuckett@nysta.com
Web site: www.nysta.com
Robert R Puckett, President

Niagara Mohawk - A National Grid Company
300 Erie Blvd West, Syracuse, NY 13202
315-428-5430 Fax: 315-428-3406
e-mail: susan.crossett@us.ngrid.com
Susan Crossett, Vice President, Public Affairs

Northeast Gas Association
75 Second Ave, Ste 510, Needham, MA 02494-2824
781-455-6800 Fax: 781-455-6828
e-mail: tkiley@northeastgas.org
Web site: www.northeastgas.org
Thomas M Kiley, President
Gas utility companies

Oil Heat Institute of Long Island
601 Veterans Memorial Highway, Suite 180, Hauppauge, NY 11788
631-360-0200 Fax: 631-360-0781
e-mail: info@ohili.org
Web site: www.ohili.org
Kevin M Rooney, Chief Executive Officer
Heating oil industry association

Orange & Rockland Utilities Inc
One Blue Hill Plz, Pearl River, NY 10965
845-352-6000 Fax: 845-577-6914
e-mail: struckr@oru.com
Web site: www.oru.com
John D McMahon, President & Chief Executive Officer
New business development

Plug Power Inc
968 Albany-Shaker Rd, Latham, NY 12110
518-782-7700 x1970 Fax: 518-782-7884
Web site: www.plugpower.com
Gerard L Conway, Jr, General Counsel
Fuel cell research & development for small stationary applications

Public Utility Law Project of New York Inc
90 State St, Ste 601, Albany, NY 12207-1715
518-449-3375 Fax: 518-449-1769
e-mail: info@pulp.tc
Web site: www.pulp.tc
Gerald A Norlander, Executive Director
Advocacy of universal service, affordability & customer protection for residential utility consumers

Rochester Gas & Electric Corporation
89 East Ave, Rochester, NY 14649
585-771-2230 Fax: 585-724-8799
e-mail: marion@rge.com
Web site: www.rge.com
Dick Marion, Manager, Corporate Communications

Sithe Energies Inc
335 Madison Ave, New York, NY 10017
212-351-0266 Fax: 212-351-0800
Web site: www.sithe.com
Frank Gomez, Office Manager
Independent electric power producer & generator

Spanish Broadcasting System Network Inc
26 W 56th St, New York, NY 10019
212-541-9200 Fax: 212-541-8535
Web site: www.lamusica.com
Luis A Miranda, Jr, Director, Public Affairs
Spanish language FM radio stations

Sunwize Technologies LLC
1155 Flatbush Rd, Kingston, NY 12401
845-336-0146 x124 Fax: 845-336-0457
e-mail: sunwize@besicorp.com
Web site: www.sunwize.com
Bruce Gould, Vice President, Sales
Solar electric energy development & product distribution

Verizon Communications
158 State St, Rm 900C, Albany, NY 12207
518-396-1086 Fax: 518-436-0141
Web site: www.verizon.com
David Lamendola, Director, Government Affairs-State of NY
Telecommunications services for northeastern US

Viacom Inc
1501 M St NW, Ste 1100, Washington, DC 20005
202-785-7300 Fax: 202-785-6360
Web site: www.viacom.com
Sumner M Redstone, Chairman & Chief Executive Officer
International media, entertainment

Wall Street Journal (The)
200 Liberty St, New York, NY 10281
212-416-2000 Fax: 212-416-2720
e-mail: paul.steiger@dowjones.com
Web site: www.wsj.com
Paul E Steiger, Managing Editor

Offices and agencies appear in alphabetical order.

ENVIRONMENT & NATURAL RESOURCES

New York State

GOVERNOR'S OFFICE

Governor's Office
Executive Chamber
State Capitol
Albany, NY 12224
518-474-8390 Fax: 518-474-1513
Web site: www.state.ny.us

Governor:
  George E Pataki 518-474-8390
Executive Director:
  Kara Lanspery 518-474-8390
Secretary to the Governor:
  John P Cahill. 518-474-4246
Deputy Secretary to the Governor for Energy, Environment & Transportation:
  Charles Fox. 518-474-0411
Senior Policy Advisor to the Governor:
  Jeffrey Lovell 518-486-9671
Counsel to the Governor-Attorney General, Budget:
  Richard Platkin 518-474-8343
Senior Asst Counsel to the Governor-Energy Research & Development,
  Environmental Conservation, Long Island Power Auth, NY Power Auth,
  Public Service Commn:
  Carl Patka 518-474-8327
Asst Counsel to the Governor-Adirondack Pk Agency, Agric & Markets,
  Bond Act Coord, Consumer Protection Bd, Environ Facilities Corp, Parks
  & Recreation, State & Local Govt, OGS:
  James Walsh 518-474-8327
Director, Environmental Programs:
  Matthew Millea 518-473-5442
Director, Communications:
  David Catalfamo. 518-474-8418

EXECUTIVE DEPARTMENTS AND RELATED AGENCIES

Empire State Development
30 South Pearl St
Albany, NY 12245
518-292-5100
Web site: www.empire.state.ny.us

633 Third Ave
New York, NY 10017
212-803-3100

Commissioner:
  Charles A Gargano 212-803-3700
Executive Deputy Commissioner, Chief Operating Officer:
  Eileen Mildenberger 212-803-3730

Deputy Commissioner & Counsel:
  Donald Ross 518-292-5120
Communications Director:
  Ron Jury. 212-803-3740/fax: 212-803-3735
  e-mail: rjury@empire.state.ny.us

Business Products

**Environ Svcs Unit (Environ Invest Program/EIP & Small Busi
Environ Ombudsman/SBEO)**
30 S Pearl St, Albany, NY 12245
Deputy Commissioner:
  Amy Schoch . . . . 518-292-5340 or 800-782-8369
  fax: 518-292-5802

Environmental Conservation Department
625 Broadway, 2nd Fl
Albany, NY 12233-4500
518-474-2121 Fax: 518-402-9016
Web site: www.dec.state.ny.us

Acting Commissioner:
  Denise M Sheehan 518-402-8540
  e-mail: dsheeha@gw.dec.state.ny.us

Air & Waste Management Office
Deputy Commissioner:
  Carl Johnson 518-402-8549

Air Resources Division
Director:
  David Shaw 518-402-8452/fax: 518-402-9035

Environmental Remediation Division
Director:
  Dale Desnoyers 518-402-9706/fax: 518-402-9020

Solid & Hazardous Materials Division
Director:
  Stephen Hammond 518-402-8651/fax: 518-402-9024

General Counsel's Office
Deputy Commissioner & General Counsel:
  James H Ferreira 518-402-2794/fax: 518-485-8484

Environmental Enforcement Division
Director:
  Charles Sullivan 518-402-9509/fax: 518-402-9019

Environmental Justice Division
Environmental Justice Coordinator:
  Monica L Kreshik 518-402-8556/fax: 518-402-9018

Legal Affairs Division
Director:
  Alison Crocker 518-402-9184/fax: 518-402-9018

Offices and agencies appear in alphabetical order.

175

Policy Areas

Hearings & Mediation Services Office
Asst Commissioner:
Louis Alexander 518-402-8537
Chief Administrative Law Judge:
James McClymonds............... 518-402-9003/fax: 518-402-9037

Legislative Affairs Office
Asst Commissioner:
Thomas O'Connor................. 518-402-8533/fax: 518-402-9016
Legislative Counsel:
Maureen Coleman 518-402-2797

Natural Resources & Water Quality Office
Deputy Commissioner:
Lynette Stark 518-402-8560

Fish, Wildlife & Marine Resources Division
Director:
Gerald Barnhart................. 518-402-8924/fax: 518-402-8925

Lands & Forests Division
Director:
Robert Davies 518-402-9405/fax: 518-402-9028

Mineral Resources Division
Director:
Bradley J Field 518-402-8076/fax: 518-402-8060

Water Division
Director:
Sandra Allen 518-402-8233/fax: 518-402-8230

Office of Administration
Asst Commissioner:
Jack McKeon 518-402-9401

Environmental Permits Division
Director:
Jeffrey Sama 518-402-9182/fax: 518-402-9168

Information Services Division
Director:
Eugene Pezdek 518-402-9860/fax: 518-402-9031

Management & Budget Services Division
Director:
Nancy Lussier 518-402-9228/fax: 518-402-9230

Operations Division
Director:
Michael Turley 518-402-9055/fax: 518-402-9053

Public Affairs & Education Division
Director:
Laurel Remus 518-402-8049/fax: 518-402-8050

Office of Employee Relations
Director:
Joe Lattanzio 518-402-9388/fax: 518-486-9957

Office of Media Affairs
Asst Commissioner of Media Relations:
Michael Fraser.................. 518-402-8000/fax: 518-402-2209
Public Information Officer:
Maureen Wren 518-402-8000

Freedom of Information Law
Records Access Officer:
Ruth Earl 518-402-8000

Public Protection Office
Asst Commissioner:
Henry Hamilton 518-402-8552

Forest Protection & Fire Management Division
Director:
Andrew T Jacob 518-402-8839/fax: 518-402-8840

Law Enforcement Division
Director:
vacant 518-402-8829/fax: 518-402-8830

Regional Offices

Region 1
SUNY - Bldg 40, Rm 121, Stony Brook, NY 11790-2356
Director:
Peter A Scully 631-444-0345/fax: 631-444-0349

Region 2
One Hunters Pt Plaza, 47-40 21st St, Long Island City, NY 11101-5407
Director:
Thomas Kunkel.................. 718-482-4949/fax: 718-482-4954

Region 3
21 S Putt Corners Rd, New Paltz, NY 12561-1696
Director:
Marc Moran..................... 845-256-3000/fax: 845-255-3042

Region 4
1150 N Westcott Rd, Schenectady, NY 12306-2014
Director:
Steve Schassler 518-357-2068/fax: 518-357-2087

Region 5
Rte 86, PO Box 296, Ray Brook, NY 12977
Director:
Stuart Buchanan 518-897-1220/fax: 518-897-1394

Region 6
317 Washington St, Watertown, NY 13601-3787
Director:
Sandra L LeBarron 315-785-2239/fax: 315-785-2242

Region 7
615 Erie Blvd West, Syracuse, NY 13204-2400
Director:
Kenneth Lynch 315-426-7403/fax: 315-426-7408

Region 8
6274 E Avon-Lima Rd, Avon, NY 14414-9519
Director:
Sean Hanna 585-226-2466/fax: 585-226-9485

Region 9
270 Michigan Ave, Buffalo, NY 14203-2999
Director:
Gerald Mikol.................... 716-851-7000/fax: 716-851-7211

Special Programs

Great Lakes Program
Region 9 NYS DEC, 270 Michigan Ave, Buffalo, NY 14203
Coordinator:
Donald Zelazny.................. 716-851-7220/fax: 716-851-7226

Hudson River Estuary Program
Region 3 NYS DEC, 21 S Putt Corners Rd, New Paltz, NY 12561
Special Asst:
Frances Dunwell 845-256-3016/fax: 845-255-3649
e-mail: hrep@gw.dec.state.ny.us

New York Natural Heritage Program
625 Broadway, 5th Fl, Albany, NY 12233-4757
Director:
David Van Leuven 518-402-8935/fax: 518-402-8925

Offices and agencies appear in alphabetical order.

Freshwater Wetlands Appeals Board

625 Broadway
Rm 145
Albany, NY 12233-1070
518-402-0566 Fax: 518-402-0588

Chairwoman:
  Rhonda K Amoroso 518-402-0566
Counsel:
  Michele M Stefanucci. 518-402-0566
Counsel:
  Pamela J Norrix 518-402-0566
Docket Clerk:
  Carol A Goldstein. 518-402-0566

Health Department

Corning Tower
Empire State Plaza
Albany, NY 12237
518-474-7354
Web site: www.health.state.ny.us

Commissioner:
  Antonia C Novello 518-474-2011
Executive Deputy Commissioner:
  Dennis P Whalen 518-473-0458
Deputy Commissioner, Operations:
  William Van Slyke. 518-474-3384

Administration & Public Affairs

Deputy Commissioner:
  William Van Slyke. 518-474-3384

Center for Environmental Health . . . . fax: 518-402-7509
  547 River St, Troy, NY 12180
Director:
  Ronald Tramontano 518-402-7500

Division of Environmental Health Investigation
Associate Director:
  G Anders Carlson. 518-402-7501

Environmental Health Assessment Division
Director:
  Nancy Kim. 518-402-7511
Associate Director:
  John Wilson 518-402-7511

Environmental Protection
Director:
  Richard W Svenson 518-402-7510

Wadsworth Center
Director:
  Lawrence S Sturman 518-474-7592/fax: 518-474-3439
Deputy Director:
  David Martin 518-474-3157
Director, Education:
  Kathy Zdeb 518-474-6713/fax: 518-474-5049
Director, Extramural Funding:
  Martin Sorin. 518-486-3882/fax: 518-474-3439
Director, Policy & Planning:
  Ann Willey 518-486-2523/fax: 518-474-3439
Director, Quality Assurance:
  Richard Jenny 518-474-2133/fax: 518-474-3439
Director, Research:
  Robert Trimble 518-474-5511/fax: 518-402-5540

Environmental Disease Prevention
Director:
  George Eadon 518-474-4170/fax: 518-486-1505
Deputy Director:
  Laurence Kaminsky 518-474-4920

Hudson River Valley Greenway

Capitol Building, Rm 254
Albany, NY 12224
518-473-3835 Fax: 518-473-4518
e-mail: hrvg@hudsongreenway.state.ny.us
Web site: www.hudsongreenway.state.ny.us

Greenway Conservancy for the Hudson River Valley
Board Chair:
  Kevin J Plunkett 518-473-3835
Executive Director:
  Carmella R Mantello 518-473-3835

Hudson River Valley Greenway Communities Council
Board Chair:
  Barnabas McHenry. 518-473-3835
Executive Director:
  Carmella R Mantello 518-473-3835

Law Department

120 Broadway
New York, NY 10271-0332
212-416-8000 Fax: 212-416-8942

State Capitol
Albany, NY 12224-0341
518-474-7330
Fax: -18-402-2472

Attorney General:
  Eliot Spitzer 518-474-7330
First Deputy Attorney General:
  Michele Hirshman 212-416-8050
Asst Deputy Attorney General, Program Development:
  Daniel Feldman 212-416-8167
Asst Attorney General, Legislative Bureau:
  Kathy Bennett. 518-486-3000
Director, Public Information & Correspondence:
  Peter Drago 518-474-7330/fax: 518-402-2472

Public Advocacy Division
Acting Deputy Attorney General:
  Terryl Brown Clemons 212-416-8041/fax: 212-416-8068
Special Counsel:
  Mary Ellen Burns 212-416-6155

Environmental Protection Bureau
Bureau Chief:
  Peter Lehner 212-416-8450/fax: 212-416-6007

Parks, Recreation & Historic Preservation, NYS Office of

Empire State Plaza
Bldg 1
Albany, NY 12238
518-486-1868 Fax: 518-486-2924
Web site: www.nysparks.com

Offices and agencies appear in alphabetical order.

Commissioner:
    Bernadette Castro 518-474-0443
Executive Deputy Commissioner:
    Christopher Pushkarsh 518-473-5385
Deputy Commissioner, Upstate Operations:
    Dominic Jacangelo 518-474-0402
Deputy Commissioner, Hudson Valley Operations:
    James F Moogan. 518-474-0440
Counsel:
    Paul Laudato. 518-474-0430
Asst Commissioner, Public Affairs:
    Wendy Gibson 518-486-1868
Director, Natural Heritage Trust:
    Kevin Carey 518-474-2997
Director, Natural Resources: *
    Ralph Odell. 845-889-4100
Chief, Park Police:
    Michael Daly 518-474-4029

Advisory Groups

State Board for Historic Preservation
Chairman:
    Robert MacKay 631-692-4664

State Council of Parks, Recreation & Historic Preservation
Chairman:
    Edward Cox 212-336-2029
Agency Contact:
    Bernadette Castro. 518-486-1868

Historic Preservation
Counsel:
    Paul Laudato. 518-486-0447

Field Services
Peebles Island, Waterford, NY 12118
Director & Deputy State Historic Preservation Officer:
    Ruth Pierpont 518-237-8643

Historic Sites Bureau
Peebles Island, Waterford, NY 12118
Director:
    James P Gold 518-237-8643

Marine & Recreational Vehicles
Director:
    Brian Kempf. 518-474-0445

Resource Management

Environmental Management
Director:
    Thomas Lyons 518-474-0409

Planning & Development
Director:
    Robert W Reinhardt 518-474-0415

State Comptroller, Office of the
110 State St, 15th Fl
Albany, NY 12236-0001
518-474-4040 Fax: 518-473-3004
Web site: www.osc.state.ny.us

633 Third Ave
31st Fl
New York, NY 10017-0001

212-681-4491
Fax: 212-681-4468

State Comptroller:
    Alan G Hevesi . . . . 518-474-4040 or 212-681-4491

Executive Office
Chief of Staff:
    Jack Chartier. 212-681-4498
First Deputy:
    Thomas Sanzillo 518-474-2909
Executive Deputy:
    Diana Jones Ritter. 518-474-3610
Deputy Chief of Staff:
    Dalia Schapiro 212-681-4540

Oil Spill Fund Office
Executive Director:
    Anne Hohenstein 518-474-6657

State Department
123 William St
New York, NY 10038
212-417-5801 Fax: 212-417-5805
Web site: www.dos.state.ny.us

41 State St
Albany, NY 12231
518-474-0050
Fax: 518-474-4765

Secretary of State:
    Randy A Daniels. 518-474-0050
First Deputy Secretary of State:
    Frank P Milano. 518-474-0050
Asst Secretary of State for Communications:
    Lawrence Sombke 518-474-4752/fax: 518-474-4597
    e-mail: info@dos.state.ny.us
Deputy Secretary of State, Public Affairs:
    Eamon Moynihan 212-417-5800
Counsel:
    Glen Bruening 518-474-6740/fax: 518-473-9211

Local Government & Community Services
Deputy Secretary of State:
    Matthew Andrus 518-486-9888/fax: 518-474-6572

Coastal Resources & Waterfront Revitalization Division
Director:
    George Stafford. 518-474-6000/fax: 518-473-2464
    e-mail: coastal@dos.state.ny.us

Community Services Division
Director:
    Evelyn M Harris 518-474-5741/fax: 518-486-4663
    e-mail: commserv@dos.state.ny.us

Fire Prevention & Control Office
State Fire Administrator:
    James A Burns. 518-474-6746/fax: 518-474-3240
    e-mail: fire@dos.state.ny.us
    New York State Academy of Fire Science
      600 College Ave, Montour Falls, NY 14865-9634
      Director:
        Richard Nagle. 607-535-7136/fax: 607-535-4841

Offices and agencies appear in alphabetical order.

CORPORATIONS, AUTHORITIES AND COMMISSIONS

Adirondack Park Agency
Rte 86
PO Box 99
Ray Brook, NY 12977
518-891-4050 Fax: 518-891-3938
Web site: www.apa.state.ny.us

Chair:
   Ross Whaley.................................518-891-4050
Executive Director:
   Daniel T Fitts...............................518-891-4050
   e-mail: dfitts@gw.dec.state.ny.us
Counsel:
   John S Banta................................518-891-4050
Associate Counsel:
   Barbara A Rottier............................518-891-4050
Public Information Director:
   Keith McKeever..............................518-891-4050

Atlantic States Marine Fisheries Commission
1444 Eye St NW
6th Fl
Washington, DC 20005
202-289-6400 Fax: 202-289-6051
e-mail: info@asmfc.org
Web site: www.asmfc.org

Chair & Administrative Commissioner, North Carolina:
   Preston P Pate, Jr...........................252-726-7021
Administrative Commissioner, New York:
   Gordon C Colvin.............................516-444-0433
Governor's Appointee, New York:
   Pat Augustine...............................516-928-3540
Legislative Commissioner, New York:
   Senator Owen H Johnson......................516-669-9200
Executive Director:
   John V O'Shea...............................202-289-6400
   e-mail: voshea@asmfc.org
Public Affairs & Resource Specialist:
   Tina Berger.................................202-289-6400
   e-mail: tberger@asmfc.org

Central Pine Barrens Joint Planning & Policy Commission
PO Box 587
3525 Sunrise Hwy, 2nd Fl
Great River, NY 11739
631-224-2604 Fax: 631-224-7653
e-mail: info@pb.state.ny.us
Web site: www.pb.state.ny.us

Governor's Appointee & Reg 1 Director DEC:
   Peter A Scully..............................631-224-2604
Executive Director:
   Ray Corwin..................................631-224-2604
Chair & Suffolk County Exec:
   Steven A Levy...............................631-224-2604
Member & Brookhaven Town Supervisor:
   John Jay LaValle............................631-224-2604

Member & Riverhead Town Supervisor:
   Philip J Cardinale..........................631-224-2604
Member & Southampton Town Supervisor:
   Patrick A Heaney............................631-224-2604

Delaware River Basin Commission
25 State Police Dr
PO Box 7360
West Trenton, NJ 08628-0360
609-883-9500 Fax: 609-883-9522
Web site: www.drbc.net

Chair:
   George Pataki...............................518-474-8390
Executive Director:
   Carol R Collier.........................609-883-9500 x200
   e-mail: carol.collier@drbc.state.nj.us
Secretary:
   Pamela Bush.............................609-883-9500 x203
   e-mail: pamela.bush@drbc.state.nj.us
General Counsel:
   Kenneth J Warren............................215-977-2276
Communications Manager:
   Clarke Rupert...........................609-883-9500 x260

Great Lakes Commission
2805 S Industrial Hwy
Ste 100
Ann Arbor, MI 48104-6791
734-971-9135 Fax: 734-971-9150
e-mail: glc@great.lakes.net
Web site: www.glc.org

Chair:
   Thomas E Huntley............................651-296-2228
Vacant
Vacant
Interim Exec Director:
   Thomas R Crane..............................734-971-9135
Program Manager, Communications & Internet Technology:
   Christine Manninen......................734-971-9135 x112
Program Manager, Data & Information Management:
   Roger Gauthier..........................734-971-9135 x113
Program Manager, Environmental Quality:
   Matthew Doss............................734-971-9135 x104
Program Manager, Resource Management:
   Thomas R Crane..........................734-971-9135 x123
Program Manager, Transportation & Sustainable Development:
   Dave Knight.............................734-971-9135 x131

Hudson River-Black River Regulating District
350 Northern Blvd
Albany, NY 12204
518-465-3491 Fax: 518-432-2485
e-mail: hrbrrd@choicemail.com
Web site: www.hrbrrd.com

Chair:
   Anne B McDonald.............................518-465-3491
Executive Director:
   Richard Lefebvre............................518-465-3491
Chief Engineer:
   Robert S Foltan.............................518-465-3491

Offices and agencies appear in alphabetical order.

Counsel:
Shari Calnero 518-465-3491

Interstate Environmental Commission

311 W 43rd St
Ste 201
New York, NY 10036
212-582-0380 Fax: 212-581-5719
e-mail: iecmail@iec-nynjct.org
Web site: www.iec-nynjct.org

Chair:
John Walsh 212-582-0380
Executive Director & Chief Engineer:
Howard Golub 212-582-0380
General Counsel:
Eileen D Millett 212-582-0380

Interstate Oil & Gas Compact Commission

PO Box 53127
Oklahoma City, OK 73152-3127
405-525-3556 Fax: 405-525-3592
e-mail: iogcc@iogcc.state.ok.us
Web site: www.iogcc.state.ok.us

Chair (Governor of NM):
Bill Richardson 505-476-2200
Vice Chair:
Donald L Mason 614-466-3905
Executive Director:
Christine Hansen 405-525-3556
New York State Official Representative:
Bradley J Field 518-402-8076

Lake George Park Commission

Fort George Rd
PO Box 749
Lake George, NY 12845-0749
518-668-9347 Fax: 518-668-5001
e-mail: info@lgpc.state.ny.us
Web site: www.lgpc.state.ny.us

Chair:
Bruce E Young 518-668-9347
Vice Chair:
Anthony P Reale 518-668-9347
Executive Director:
Michael P White 518-668-9347
Secretary/Treasurer:
Margaret M Stewart 518-668-9347

New England Interstate Water Pollution Control Commission

Boott Mills South
100 Foot of John St
Lowell, MA 01852-1124
978-323-7929 Fax: 978-323-7919
e-mail: mail@neiwpcc.org
Web site: www.neiwpcc.org

Chair:
Glenn Haas 617-292-5748
Vice Chair:
Harry Stewart 603-271-3308
Acting Commissioner, New York State:
Denise M Sheehan 518-485-8940
Executive Director:
Ronald F Poltak 978-323-7929
Deputy Director:
Susan Sullivan 978-323-7929

New York State Energy Research & Development Authority

17 Columbia Circle
Albany, NY 12203-6399
518-862-1090 Fax: 518-862-1091
Web site: www.nyserda.org

Chairman:
Vincent A DeIorio 518-862-1090
President:
Peter R Smith 518-862-1090 x3220
e-mail: prs@nyserda.org
General Counsel:
Roger D Avent 518-862-1090 x3333
e-mail: rda@nyserda.org
Vice President, Administration:
Wendy M Shave 518-862-1090 x3226
e-mail: wms@nyserda.org
Vice President, Programs:
Robert Callender 518-862-1090 x3233
Treasurer:
Jeffrey J Pitkin 518-862-1090 x3223
e-mail: jjp@nyserda.org
Director, Communications:
Thomas G Collins 518-862-1090 x3250/fax: 518-464-8249
e-mail: tgc@nyserda.org

New York State Environmental Facilities Corp

625 Broadway
Albany, NY 12207-2997
518-402-6924 or 800-882-9721 Fax: 518-486-9323
Web site: www.nysefc.org

Chair:
Denise M Sheehan 518-402-6924
President:
Thomas J Kelly 518-402-6924
Executive Vice President:
David Sterman 518-402-6924
General Counsel:
James R Levine 518-402-6969
Chief Financial Officer:
James T Gebhardt 518-402-6985
Director, Corporate Communications & Records Access Officer:
Susan Mayer 518-402-6957
Director, Corporate Operations:
Barbara Wayman 518-486-9267
Director, Engineering & Program Management:
Robert Davis 518-402-7396
Director, Technical Advisory Services:
Frederick McCandless 518-402-7461

Offices and agencies appear in alphabetical order.

New York State Tug Hill Commission

Dulles State Office Bldg
317 Washington St
Watertown, NY 13601
315-785-2380 Fax: 315-785-2574
e-mail: tughill@tughill.org
Web site: www.tughill.org

Chair:
   Arnold E Talgo...................................315-785-2380
Executive Director:
   John K Bartow, Jr..............................315-785-2380
   e-mail: john@tughill.org
Counsel:
   James P McClusky..............................315-232-4551

Northeastern Forest Fire Protection Commission

21 Parmenter Terr
PO Box 6192
China Village, ME 04926-6192
207-968-3782 Fax: 207-968-3782
e-mail: necompact@pivot.net
Web site: www.nffpc.org

Chair of Commissioners:
   Bernard Drolet 418-647-3367
Past Chair of Commissioners:
   David Wight....................................207-968-3782
Executive Director:
   Thomas G Parent...............................207-968-3782
New York State Fire Supervisor:
   Col Andrew Jacob 518-457-5740
New York State Forester:
   Robert Davies..................................518-402-9405

Northeastern Queens Nature & Historical Preserve Commission

Bldg 635, Bayside St
Box 5
Fort Totten, NY 11359
718-229-8805 Fax: 718-229-6131
e-mail: sneq@aol.com
Web site: www.sneq.com

Chair:
   Lucile Helfat...................................718-229-8805
Vice Chair:
   Bernard Haber 718-229-8805
Executive Director:
   Joan M Vogt....................................718-229-8805

Ohio River Valley Water Sanitation Commission

5735 Kellogg Ave
Cincinnati, OH 45228-1112
513-231-7719 Fax: 513-231-7761
Web site: www.orsanco.org

New York State Commissioner:
   Douglas E Conroe..............................513-231-7719
New York State Commissioner:
   Thomas L Servatius............................513-231-7719
New York State Commissioner, Acting:
   Denise M Sheehan.............................518-457-3446
Executive Director:
   Alan H Vicory..................................513-231-7719
Legal Counsel:
   Thomas D Heekin..............................513-231-7719
Public Information Programs Manager:
   Jeanne Ison....................................513-231-7719
   e-mail: jison@orsanco.org

NEW YORK STATE LEGISLATURE

See Legislative Branch in Section 1 for additional Standing Committee and Subcommittee information.

Assembly Standing Committees

Environmental Conservation
Chair:
   Thomas P DiNapoli (D) 518-455-5192
Ranking Minority Member:
   Teresa Sayward (R) 518-455-5565

Senate Standing Committees

Environmental Conservation
Chair:
   Carl L Marcellino (R)...........................518-455-2390
Ranking Minority Member:
   David J Valesky (D).............................518-455-2838

Senate/Assembly Legislative Commissions

Rural Resources, Legislative Commission on
Senate Chair:
   Vacant 518-455-3563
Assembly Vice Chair:
   David R Koon (D) 518-455-5784
Senate Exec Director:
   Ronald C Brach...................518-455-2544/fax: 518-426-6960
Assembly Director:
   Susan Bartle.....................518-455-3999/fax: 518-455-4175
Counsel:
   Donald A Walsh................................518-455-2544

Solid Waste Management, Legislative Commission on
Assembly Chair:
   William Colton (D)..............................518-455-5828
Senate Vice Chair:
   Nicolas A Spano (R).............................518-455-2231
Program Manager:
   Richard D Morse, Jr 518-455-3711/fax: 518-455-3837

Toxic Substances & Hazardous Wastes, Legislative Commission on
Senate Chair:
   Vacant 518-455-0000
Assembly Vice Chair:
   David R Koon (D) 518-455-5784
Program Manager:
   Richard D Morse, Jr 518-455-3711/fax: 518-455-3837

Policy Areas

Offices and agencies appear in alphabetical order.

Water Resource Needs of NYS & Long Island, Legislative Commission on
Assembly Co-Chair:
   Thomas P DiNapoli (D) 518-455-5192

Senate Co-Chair:
   Michael A L Balboni (R) 518-455-2471
Program Manager:
   Richard D Morse, Jr 518-455-3711/fax: 518-455-3837

U.S. Government

EXECUTIVE DEPARTMENTS AND RELATED AGENCIES

US Commerce Department
Web site: www.doc.gov

National Oceanic & Atmospheric Administration

National Marine Fisheries Service, Northeast Region
Headquarters . . . . fax: 978-281-9207
 One Blackburn Dr, Gloucester, MA 1930
 Regional Administrator:
   Patricia A Kurkul 978-281-9250

National Weather Service, Eastern Region
 630 Johnson Ave, Ste 202, Bohemia, NY 11716
 Web site: www.nws.noaa.gov
 Director:
   Dean Gulezian 631-244-0100/fax: 631-244-0109
   e-mail: dean.gulezian@noaa.gov
 Deputy Director:
   Mickey J Brown 631-244-0102
 Public Affairs Specialist:
   Marcie Katcher 631-244-0149/fax: 631-244-0167
 Chief, Meteorological Services Division:
   John Guiney 631-244-1021

US Defense Department

Army Corps of Engineers
Web site: www.usace.army.mil

Great Lakes & Ohio River Division (Western NYS)
 550 Main St, PO Box 1159, Cincinnati, OH 45201-1159
 Commander:
   BG Steven R Hawkins 513-684-3002/fax: 513-684-2085
   Buffalo District Office . . . . fax: 716-879-4195
     1776 Niagara St, Buffalo, NY 14207-3199
     District Engineer:
       Maj R Brian Phillips 716-879-4200
     Deputy District Commander:
       LTC Timothy B Touchette 716-879-4201

North Atlantic Division
 302 General Lee Ave, Ft Hamilton Military Cmty, Brooklyn, NY 11252
 Commander:
   BG Bo Temple 718-765-7000
 Deputy Commander:
   Francis Kosich 718-765-7001
 Executive Officer:
   Steve Sattinger 718-765-7002
 Emergency Mgmt Specialist:
   John Hasselman 718-765-7074
 Public Affairs Officer:
   David J Lipsky 718-765-7018/fax: 718-765-7173

Program Directorate
 Acting Director of Programs:
   Stuart Piken 718-765-7129
 Supervisory Civil Engineer, Civil Works Integration Div:
   Larry Petrosino 718-765-7060
 Supervisory Civil Engineer, Military Integration Div:
   Bob Mawhinney 718-765-7120
 Supervisory Civil Engineer, Program Support Div:
   Joseph Vietri 718-765-7080
Regional Business Directorate
 Regional Business Director:
   Mohan Singh 718-765-7055
 Director/Financial Manager:
   Irma Nanez 718-765-7033
 Supervisory Program Manager, Business Mgmt Div:
   John Sassi 718-765-7127
 Supervisory Civil Engineer, Business Technical Div:
   John Bianco 718-765-7086

US Department of Agriculture

Forest Service-Northeastern Area State & Private Forestry
 11 Campus Blvd, Ste 200, Newtown Square, PA 19073
 Area Director:
   Kathryn P Maloney 610-557-4103/fax: 610-557-4177
 Deputy Director:
   John O Nordin 610-557-4103/fax: 610-557-4177
 Asst Director, Forest Health & Economics:
   Kenneth H Knauer 610-557-4139/fax: 610-557-4136
 Asst Director, Fire Management:
   Vacant 610-557-4152/fax: 610-557-4154
 Asst Director, Forest Management:
   N Robin Morgan 610-557-4124/fax: 610-557-4136
 Asst Director, Information Management & Analysis:
   Susan E Lacy 610-557-4114/fax: 610-557-4177

Forest Service-Northeastern Research Station
 11 Campus Blvd, Ste 200, Newton Square, PA 19073
 Director:
   Michael T Rains 610-557-4017
 Asst Director, Continuing Research:
   Roy Patton 610-557-4107

Forest Service-Region 9
Web site: www.fs.fed.us

Green Mountain & Finger Lakes
 231 N Main St, Rutland, VT 5701
 Forest Supervisor:
   Paul Brewster 802-747-6704/fax: 802-747-6766
   Finger Lakes National Forest . . . . fax: 607-546-4474
     5218 State Route 414, Hector, NY 14841
     District Ranger:
       Martha Twarkins 607-546-4470

Natural Resources Conservation Service . . . . fax: 315-477-6550
 441 S Salina St, Suite 354, Syracuse, NY 13202-2450

Offices and agencies appear in alphabetical order.

Fax: 315-477-6550
Web site: www.ny.nrcs.usda.gov
State Conservationist:
Joseph R DelVecchio 315-477-6504

US Department of Homeland Security (DHS)

Environmental Measurements Laboratory
201 Varick St, 5th Fl, New York, NY 10014-7447
Web site: www.eml.doe.gov
Director:
Mitchell D Erickson 212-620-3619/fax: 212-620-3651
e-mail: erickson@eml.doe.gov
Deputy Director:
Catherine S Klusek. 212-620-3231
e-mail: klusek@eml.doe.gov

Administration
Director:
Joseph J Caroli 212-620-3604/fax: 212-620-3600
e-mail: jcaroli@eml.doe.gov

Environmental Science
Director:
Kevin M Miller 212-620-3572/fax: 212-620-3600
e-mail: kmiller@eml.doe.gov

Quality Assurance/Metrology
Acting Director:
Richard J Larsen 212-620-3524/fax: 212-620-3600

Technical Program Services
Acting Director:
Merrill Heit 212-620-3623/fax: 212-620-3600

US Department of the Interior
Web site: www.doi.gov

Bureau of Land Management
Web site: www.blm.gov

Eastern States Office (includes New York State) . . . . fax: 703-440-1701
7450 Boston Blvd, Springfield, VA 22153
State Director:
Michael D Nedd 703-440-1711

Fish & Wildlife Service
Web site: www.fws.gov

Northeast Region (includes New York State) . . . . fax: 413-253-8308
300 Westgate Center Dr, Hadley, MA 1035
Regional Director:
Marvin E Moriarty 413-253-8300

Geological Survey
Web site: ny.usgs.gov

Water Resources Division - New York State District Office
425 Jordan Rd, Troy, NY 12180-8349
District Chief:
Rafael W Rodriguez 518-285-5659/fax: 518-285-5601
Coram Sub-District Office . . . . fax: 631-736-4283
2045 Rte 112, Bldg 4, Coram, NY 11727
Sub-District Chief:
Bronius Nemickas 631-736-0783 x102
Ithaca Sub-District Office . . . . fax: 607-266-0521
30 Brown Rd, Ithaca, NY 14850-1573
Sub-District Chief:
Edward Bugliosi 607-266-0217 x3005

National Park Service-Northeast Region
200 Chestnut St, US Custom House, Philadelphia, PA 19106
Web site: www.nps.gov
Acting Northeast Regional Director:
Mary A Bomar. 215-597-7013/fax: 215-597-0815

Fire Island National Seashore
120 Laurel St, Patchogue, NY 11772
Superintendent:
Michael Reynolds 631-289-4810/fax: 631-289-4898

Office of the Secretary, Environmental Policy & Compliance

Northeast Region (includes New York State)
408 Atlantic Ave, Rm 142, Boston, MA 02210-3334
Regional Environmental Officer:
Andrew L Raddant 617-223-8565/fax: 617-223-8569

Office of the Solicitor

Northeast Region (includes New York State) . . . . fax: 617-527-6848
One Gateway Center, Ste 612, Newton, MA 2458
Regional Solicitor:
Anthony R Conte 617-527-3400
Deputy Regional Solicitor:
James E Epstein 617-527-3400
Attorney Advisor:
Martha F Ansty 802-872-0629 x17
Attorney Advisor:
Mark D Barash 617-527-3400
Attorney Advisor:
Marcia F Gittes. 617-527-3400
Attorney Advisor:
J Robin Lepore 617-527-3400
Attorney Advisor:
Joris Naiman. 617-527-3400
Attorney Advisor:
David Rothstein 617-527-3400
Attorney Advisor:
Kathryn Costenbader 617-527-3400
Attorney Advisor:
Andrew Tittler 617-527-3400

US Environmental Protection Agency
Web site: www.epa.gov

Region 2 - New York . . . . fax: 212-637-3526
290 Broadway, New York, NY 10007
212-637-3000 Fax: 212-637-3526
Regional Administrator:
Kathleen Callahan 212-637-5000
Acting Deputy Regional Administrator:
George Pavlou 212-637-5000

Caribbean Environmental Protection Division (CEPD)
Director:
Carl-Axel P Soderberg 787-977-5814

Division of Enforcement & Compliance Assistance (DECA)
Director:
Dore LaPosta 212-637-4031

Division of Environmental Planning & Protection (DEPP)
Director:
Walter Mugdan. 212-637-3725

Division of Environmental Science & Assessment (DESA)
2890 Woodbridge Ave, Edison, NJ 08837-3679

Offices and agencies appear in alphabetical order.

Director:

Barbara A Finazzo 732-321-6754

e-mail: finazzo.barbara@epa.gov

Emergency & Remedial Response Division (ERRD)

Acting Director:

William McCabe 212-637-4391

Inspector General, Office of (OIG)

Divisional Inspector General, Investigation:

Paul Zammit 212-637-3042/fax: 212-637-3071

e-mail: zammit.paul@epa.gov

OCEFT/Criminal Investigations Division

Special-Agent-In-Charge:

William V Lometti 212-637-3610

e-mail: lometti.william@epa.gov

Policy & Management, Office of

Asst Regional Administrator for Policy & Management:

Donna Vizian 212-637-3581

Public Affairs Division (PAD)

Director:

Bonnie Bellow. 212-637-3660/fax: 212-637-5046

e-mail: bellow.bonnie@epa.gov

Regional Counsel, Office of (ORC)

Deputy Regional Counsel:

Eric Schaff 212-637-3107

e-mail: schaaf.eric@epa.gov

U.S. CONGRESS

See U.S. Congress Chapter for additional Standing Committee and Subcommittee information.

House of Representatives Standing Committees

Agriculture

Chair:

Robert Goodlatte (R-VA) 202-225-2171

Ranking Minority Member:

Collin C Peterson (D-MN) 202-225-2165

Subcommittees

Department Operations, Oversight, Nutrition & Forestry

Chair:

Gil Gutknecht (R-OK) 202-225-2472

Ranking Minority Member:

Joe Baca (D-CA) 202-225-6161

General Farm Commodities & Risk Management

Chair:

Jerry Moran (R-KS) 202-225-2715

Ranking Minority Member:

Bob Etheridge (D-NC) 202-225-4531

Livestock & Horticulture

Chair:

Robert (Robin) Hayes (R-NC) 202-225-3715

Ranking Minority Member:

Ed Case (D-HI) 202-225-4906

Specialty Crops & Foreign Agriculture Programs

Chair:

William Jenkins (R-TN) 202-225-6356

Ranking Minority Member:

Mike McIntyre (D-NC) 202-225-2731

Energy & Commerce

Chair:

Joe Barton (R-TX) 202-225-2002

Ranking Minority Member:

John D Dingell (D-MI). 202-225-4071

New York Delegate:

Eliot L Engel (D) 202-225-2464

New York Delegate:

Vito Fossella (R). 202-225-3371

New York Delegate:

Edolphus Towns (D). 202-225-5936

Subcommittees

Energy & Air Quality

Chair:

Ralph M Hall (R-TX) 202-225-6673

Ranking Minority Member:

Rick Boucher (D-VA) 202-225-3861

New York Delegate:

Eliot L Engel (D). 202-225-3371

New York Delegate:

Vito Fossella (R) 202-225-3371

Environment & Hazardous Materials

Chair:

Paul E Gillmor (R-OH) 202-225-6405

Ranking Minority Member:

Hilda L Solis (D-CA) 202-225-5464

New York Delegate:

Vito Fossella (R) 202-225-3371

Resources

Chair:

Richard W Pombo (R-CA) 202-225-2761

Ranking Minority Member:

Nick J Rahall, II (D-WV) 202-225-3452

Science

Chair:

Sherwood L Boehlert (R-NY) 202-225-3665

Ranking Minority Member:

Bart Gordon (D-TN). 202-225-4231

Subcommittee

Energy

Chair:

Judy Biggert (R-IL) 202-225-3515

Ranking Minority Member:

Mike Honda (D-CA) 202-225-2631

Transportation & Infrastructure

Chair:

Don Young (R-AK) 202-225-5765

Ranking Minority Member:

James L Oberstar (D-MN) 202-225-6211

New York Delegate:

Timothy Bishop (D) 202-225-3826

New York Delegate:

Sherwood Boehlert (R). 202-225-3665

New York Delegate:

Brian M Higgins (D) 202-225-3306

New York Delegate:

Sue W Kelly (R). 202-225-5441

New York Delegate:

John R (Randy) Kuhl (R) 202-225-3161

New York Delegate:

Jerrold Nadler (D). 202-225-5635

New York Delegate:

Anthony Weiner (D). 202-225-6616

Offices and agencies appear in alphabetical order.

Subcommittee

Water Resources & Environment

Chair:
John J Duncan, Jr (R-TN) 202-225-5435
Ranking Minority Member:
Eddie Bernice Johnson (D-TX) 202-225-8885
New York Delegate:
Timothy Bishop (D) 202-225-3826
New York Delegate:
Sherwood L Boehlert (R) 202-225-3665
New York Delegate:
Brian M Higgins (D) 202-225-3306
New York Delegate:
Sue W Kelly (R) 202-225-5441

Senate Standing Committees

Agriculture, Nutrition & Forestry

Chair:
C Saxby Chambliss (R-GA) 202-224-3521
Ranking Minority Member:
Tom Harkin (D-IA) 202-224-3254

Subcommittee

Forestry, Conservation & Rural Revitalization

Chair:
Michael D Crapo (R-ID) 202-224-6142
Ranking Minority Member:
Blanche Lincoln (D-AR) 202-224-4843

Commerce, Science & Transportation

Chair:
Ted Stevens (R-AK) 202-224-3004
Ranking Minority Member:
Daniel K Inouye (D-HI) 202-224-3934

Subcommittee

Fisheries & Coast Guard

Chair:
Olympia J Snowe (R-ME) 202-224-5344
Ranking Minority Member:
Maria Cantwell (D-WA) 202-224-3441

Energy & Natural Resources

Chair:
Pete V Domenici (R-NM) 202-224-6621
Ranking Minority Member:
Jeff Bingaman (D-NM) 202-224-5521

Environment & Public Works

Chair:
James M Inhofe (R-OK) 202-224-4721
Ranking Minority Member:
James Jeffords (I-VT) 202-224-5141
New York Delegate:
Hillary Rodham Clinton (D) 202-224-4451

Policy Areas

Private Sector

Adirondack Council Inc (The)

103 Hand Ave, Ste 3, Box D-2, Elizabethtown, NY 12932
518-873-2240 Fax: 518-873-6675
e-mail: info@adirondackcouncil.org
Web site: www.adirondackcouncil.org
Brian L Houseal, Executive Director
Environmental advocacy & education

Adirondack Mountain Club Inc

301 Hamilton Street, Albany, NY 12210-1738
518-449-3870 Fax: 518-449-3875
e-mail: nwoodwor@nycap.rr.com; miannac1@nycap.rr.com
Web site: www.adk.org
Neil F Woodworth, Executive Director
Hiking, nonmotorized recreation, conservation & education

American Museum of Natural History

Central Park West at 79th St, New York, NY 10024-5192
212-769-5100 Fax: 212-769-5018
e-mail: info@amnh.org
Web site: www.amnh.org
Ellen V Futter, President
Education, exhibition & scientific research

Audubon New York

200 Trillium Lane, Albany, NY 12203
518-869-9731 Fax: 518-869-0737
e-mail: nasny@audubon.org
Web site: ny.audubon.org
David J Miller, Executive Director
Protecting birds, other wildlife & their habitats

Audubon Society of NYS Inc (The) / Audubon International

Hollyhock Hollow Sanctuary, 46 Rarick Rd, Selkirk, NY 12158
518-767-9051 x20 Fax: 518-767-0069
e-mail: hjack@auduboninternational.org
Web site: www.auduboninternational.org
Howard A Jack, Vice President & Chief Operating Officer
Wildlife & water conservation; environmental education; sustainable land management

Brooklyn Botanic Garden

1000 Washington Ave, Brooklyn, NY 11225-1099
718-623-7200 Fax: 718-857-2430
e-mail: judithzuk@bbg.org
Web site: www.bbg.org
Judith D Zuk, President
Comprehensive study of plant biodiversity in metropolitan New York; home gardener's resource center

Offices and agencies appear in alphabetical order.

Business Council of New York State Inc
152 Washington Ave, Albany, NY 12210
518-465-7511 x205 Fax: 518-465-4389
e-mail: ken.pokalsky@bcnys.org
Web site: www.bcnys.org
Kenneth J Pokalsky, Director, Environmental & Manufacturing
    Programs
Environment, manufacturing, economic development

CWM Chemical Services LLC
1550 Balmer Rd, PO Box 200, Model City, NY 14107
716-754-8231 Fax: 716-754-0211
e-mail: cwmmdc@wm.com
Web site: www.cwmmodelcity.com
Dick Sturges, District Manager
Hazardous waste treatment, storage & disposal

Catskill Center for Conservation & Development
PO Box 504, Route 28, Arkville, NY 12406-0504
845-586-2611 Fax: 845-586-3044
e-mail: cccd@catskillcenter.org
Web site: www.catskillcenter.org
Tom Alworth, Executive Director
*Advocacy for environmental & economic health of the Catskill
Mountain region*

Center for Environmental Information Inc
55 St Paul St, Rochester, NY 14604-1314
585-262-2870 Fax: 585-262-4156
e-mail: ceiroch@frontiernet.net
Web site: www.ceinfo.org
Elizabeth Thorndike, Executive Director
Public information & education on environmental topics

Citizens' Environmental Coalition
543 Franklin St, Suite 200, Buffalo, NY 14202
716-885-6848 Fax: 716-885-6845
e-mail: cecmike@choiceonemail.com
Web site: www.cectoxic.org ; www.kodakstoxicolors.org
Michael Schade, Western NY Director
*Organizing & assistance for communities concerned about toxic
waste, air & water contamination & pollution prevention*

Colgate University, Department of Geology
13 Oak Dr, Hamilton, NY 13346
315-228-7949 Fax: 315-228-7187
e-mail: bselleck@mail.colgate.edu
Web site: departments.colgate.edu/geology
Bruce Selleck, Chair of Geology
Marine geology; coastal geology

**Columbia University, MPA in Environmental Science &
Policy**
420 W 118th St, Rm 1314, New York, NY 10027
212-854-4445 or 212-854-3142 Fax: 212-864-4847
e-mail: sc32@columbia.edu
Web site: www.columbia.edu/~sc32
Steven Cohen, Director
Urban & environmental policy; public management

Commodore Applied Technologies Inc
150 East 58th St, Ste 3238, New York, NY 10155-0001
212-308-5800 Fax: 212-753-0731
e-mail: jdeangelis@commodore.com
Web site: www.commodore.com
James DeAngelis, Senior Vice President/Chief Financial &
    Administration Officer
*Develops technologies for destroying hazardous waste, PCBs,
dioxins, mixed waste & chemical weapons*

**Cornell Cooperative Extension, Environment & Natural
Resources Initiative**
108 Fernow Hall, Cornell University, Ithaca, NY 14853
607-255-2115 Fax: 607-255-2815
e-mail: dlt5@cornell.edu
Web site: www.dnr.cornell.edu/extension
Diana Bryant, Department Extension Leader
*Working to improve the quality & sustainability of human
environments & natural resources*

Cornell Cooperative Extension, NY Sea Grant
Cornell University, 112 Rice Hall, Ithaca, NY 14853-5905
607-255-2832 Fax: 607-255-2812
e-mail: drb17@cornell.edu
Web site: www.nyseagrant.org
Dale Baker, Program Leader
*Research, education & training related to ocean, coastal & Great
Lakes resources*

Cornell University Center for the Environment
200 Rice Hall, Ithaca, NY 14853-5601
607-255-7535 Fax: 607-255-0238
Web site: environment.cornell.edu
Mark B Bain, Director
Environmental research

Council on the Environment of NYC (The)
51 Chambers St, Rm 228, New York, NY 10007
212-788-7900 Fax: 212-788-7913
e-mail: conyc@cenyc.org
Web site: www.cenyc.org
Lys McLaughlin, Executive Director
*Promotes environmental awareness & develops solutions to
environmental problems*

Dakota Software Corporation
95 Allens Creek Rd, #2-302, Rochester, NY 14618
585-244-3300 Fax: 585-244-3301
e-mail: info@dakotasoft.com
Web site: www.dakotasoft.com
Arlene Davidson, Marketing Director
Environmental health & safety regulatory software systems design

Dionondehowa Wildlife Sanctuary & School - Not For Profit
148 Stanton Rd, Shushan, NY 12873
518-854-7764 Fax: 518-854-3648
e-mail: dionondehowa@yahoo.com
Web site: www.dionondehowa.org
Bonnie Hoag, Director
*Conservation & land use issues, conscious living, nature studies &
healing & expressive arts*

Offices and agencies appear in alphabetical order.

ENSR International
360 Linden Oaks, Rochester, NY 14625
585-381-2210 Fax: 585-381-5392
e-mail: pnielsen@ensr.com
Web site: www.ensr.com
Peter Nielsen, Senior Program Manager
Environmental consulting, engineering, remediation & related services

Ecology & Environment Inc
368 Pleasant View Dr, Lancaster, NY 14086-1397
716-684-8060 Fax: 716-684-0844
e-mail: dcastle@ene.com
Web site: www.ene.com
Gerhard J Neumaier, President
Environmental scientific & engineering consulting; field monitoring & analytical laboratory services

Empire State Forest Products Association
828 Washington Ave, Albany, NY 12203-1622
518-463-1297 x2 Fax: 518-426-9502
e-mail: kking@esfpa.org
Web site: www.esfpa.org
Kevin S King, Executive Vice President

Environmental Advocates of New York
353 Hamilton St, Albany, NY 12210
518-462-5526 x224 Fax: 518-427-0381
Web site: www.eany.org
Patti Kelly, Assistant Director
Environmental health & protection of New York's natural resources

Environmental Business Association of NYS Inc
126 State St, 3rd Fl, Albany, NY 12207-1637
518-432-6400 x226 Fax: 518-432-1383
e-mail: ira@eba-nys.org
Web site: www.eba-nys.org
Ira S Rubenstein, Executive Director
Supports businesses that provide products & services to prevent, monitor, control or remediate pollution or conserve and/or recycle energy & resources

Environmental Defense
257 Park Ave South, 17th Fl, New York, NY 10010
212-505-2100 Fax: 212-505-2375
e-mail: adarrell@environmentaldefense.org
Web site: www.environmentaldefense.org
Andrew Darrell, NY Regional Director

Ethan C Eldon Associates Inc
1315 Broadway, Ste 612, New York, NY 10018
212-967-5400 Fax: 212-967-2747
e-mail: eceaethan@aol.com
Ethan C Eldon, President
Environmental, EIS, traffic, hazardous & solid waste consulting

NYS Bar Assn, Environmental Law Section
Farrell Fritz, C.P.
EAB Plaza, Uniondale, NY 11556-1320
516-227-0607 Fax: 516-227-0777
Web site: www.farrellfritz.com
Mariam Villani, Chair

Great Lakes United
Buffalo State College, Cassety Hall, 1300 Elmwood Ave, Buffalo, NY 14222
716-886-0142 Fax: 716-886-0303
e-mail: glu@glu.org
Web site: www.glu.org
Derrick Stack, Executive Director
Great Lakes & St Lawrence River issues

GreenThumb
c/o NYC Parks & Recreation Dept, 49 Chambers St, Rm 1020, New York, NY 10007
212-788-8070 Fax: 212-788-8052
e-mail: edie@greenthumbnyc.org
Web site: www.greenthumbnyc.org
Edie Stone, Director
Development & preservation of community gardens; reclamation of urban land for green space

Greene County Soil & Water Conservation District
907 County Office Building, Cairo, NY 12413
518-622-3620 Fax: 518-622-0344
e-mail: rene@gcswcd.com
Web site: www.gcswcd.com
Rene Van Schaack, Executive Director
Natural resource conservation & water quality programs & public access to Hudson River, stormwater management, wetland mitigation

Hawk Creek Wildlife Center Inc
PO Box 662, East Aurora, NY 14052
716-652-8646 Fax: 716-652-8646
e-mail: hawkcreek@aol.com
Web site: www.hawkcreek.org
Loretta C Jones, President
Hawk Creek's mission is to create understanding & knowledge of the natural world & its relationship to humankind through conservation, environmental education & research

Hofstra University, School of Law
121 Hofstra University, Hempstead, NY 11549
212-864-6092
William R Ginsberg, Emeritus Professor of Law
Land use & environmental law

Hudson River Environmental Society
6626 Stitt Road, Altamont, NY 12009-4523
518-861-8020 Fax: 518-861-8020
e-mail: hres@nycap.rr.com
Web site: www.hres.org
Stephen Wilson, Executive Director
Facilitates & coordinates research in the physical & biological sciences, environmental engineering & resource management in the Hudson River region

Offices and agencies appear in alphabetical order.

Policy Areas

Hudson River Sloop Clearwater Inc
112 Little Market St, Poughkeepsie, NY 12601
845-454-7673 Fax: 845-454-7953
e-mail: office@clearwater.org
Web site: www.clearwater.org
Andre P Mele, Executive Director
Hudson River water quality, environmental education & advocacy

Hudson Valley Grass Roots Energy & Environmental Network
PO Box 208, Red Hook, NY 12571
845-486-7070
e-mail: hvgreentimes@hotmail.com
Brian Reid, Board Member
Public environmental education & journalism

INFORM Inc
120 Wall Street, 14th Flr, New York, NY 10005-4001
212-361-2400 Fax: 212-361-2412
e-mail: inform@informinc.org
Web site: www.informinc.org
Joanna D Underwood, President
Advocacy, research & education on practical methods to protect natural resources & public health

Institute of Ecosystem Studies
PO Box R, Millbrook, NY 12545
845-677-5359 Fax: 845-677-6455
e-mail: quillenl@ecostudies.org
Web site: www.ecostudies.org
Gene E Likens, Director & President
Ecosystem research; curriculum development & on-site ecology education

Land Trust Alliance Northeast Program
110 Spring St, PO Box 792, Saratoga Springs, NY 12866
518-587-0774 Fax: 518-587-6467
e-mail: newyork@lta.org
Web site: www.lta.org
Ezra Milchman, Program Director
Promotes voluntary land conservation; provides leadership, information, skills & resources needed by land trusts

Messinger Woods Wildlife Care & Education Center Inc
PO Box 508, Orchard Park, NY 14127
716-648-8091
e-mail: mike@messingerwoods.org
Web site: www.messingerwoods.org
Michael Olek, President
Promoting community awareness, education, instruction, involvement, understanding, appreciation & acceptance of our wildlife in order to conserve it

Modutank Inc
41-04 35th Ave, Long Island City, NY 11101
718-392-1112 Fax: 718-786-1008
e-mail: info@modutank.com
Web site: www.modutank.com
Reed Margulis, President
Rent & sell modular storage tanks for potable water, wastewater & liquid chemicals

NY League of Conservation Voters/NY Conservation Education Fund
29 Broadway, Suite 1100, New York, NY 10006-3201
212-361-6350 x208 Fax: 212-361-6363
e-mail: info@nylcv.org
Web site: www.nylcv.org
Marcia Bystryn, Executive Director
Endorsement of pro-environmental candidates; environmental advocacy & education statewide

NYC Neighborhood Open Space Coalition
232 E 11th St, New York, NY 10003
212-228-3126 Fax: 212-471-9987
e-mail: nosc@treebranch.com
Web site: www.treebranch.com; www.walkny.org
David Lutz, Executive Director
Works to preserve/expand NYC's parks, waterfront, community gardens & other public open space

NYS Association of Solid Waste Management
PO Box 13461, Albany, NY 12212
518-736-5501 Fax: 518-762-2859
e-mail: info@newyorkwaste.org
Web site: www.newyorkwaste.org
Jeffrey Bouchard, President
Waste management & recycling professionals providing advocacy & education for responsible integrated solid waste management

NYS Corps Collaboration
One Pine West Plaza, Ste 105, Albany, NY 12205-5531
518-464-2676 Fax: 518-464-2677
e-mail: info@nyscc.net
Web site: www.nyscc.net
Linda J Cohen, Executive Director
Statewide youth service & conservation corps; buiding self-esteem, a sense of civic responsibility & leadership skills

NYS Water Resources Institute of Cornell University
Cornell University, 207 Rice Hall, Ithaca, NY 14853-5601
607-255-5941
e-mail: nyswri@cornell.edu
Web site: wri.eas.cornell.edu
Keith S Porter, Director
Education, research, investigation & technical assistance to agencies & communities concerned with water resources

National Wildlife Federation
1400 16th Street NW, Suite 501, Washington, DC 20036
202-797-6635 Fax: 202-797-6646
e-mail: spencer@nwf.org
Web site: www.nwf.org
Rick Spencer, Regional Representative
Conservation education, litigation & advocacy for policies to restore habitat & return wildlife to natural environs

Natural Resources Defense Council
40 W 20th St, 11th Fl, New York, NY 10011
212-727-2700 Fax: 212-727-1773
e-mail: nrdcinfo@nrdc.org
Web site: www.nrdc.org
John H Adams, President
Litigation, legislation advocacy & public education to preserve & protect the environment & public health

Nature Conservancy (The)
415 River St, 4th Fl, Troy, NY 12180
518-273-9408 Fax: 518-273-5022
Web site: www.nature.org
Henry Tepper, New York State Director
Preserve plants, animals & natural communities by protecting the land & water which they need to survive

New York Forest Owners Association Inc
PO Box 541, Lima, NY 14485
800-836-3566
e-mail: nyfoainc@hotmail.com
Web site: www.nyfoa.org
Alan White, President
Promote & nurture private woodland owners stewardship

New York Public Interest Research Group
9 Murray St, 3rd Fl, New York, NY 10007
212-349-6460 Fax: 212-349-1366
e-mail: nypirg@nypirg.org
Web site: www.nypirg.org
Christopher Meyer, Executive Director
Environmental preservation, public health, consumer protection & government reform

New York State Conservation Council
8 E Main St, Ilion, NY 13357-1899
315-894-3302 Fax: 315-894-2893
e-mail: nyscc@nyscc.com
Web site: www.nyscc.com
Howard O Cushing, Jr, President
Promotes conservation & wise use & management of natural resources

New York State Woodsmen's Field Days Inc
PO Box 123, 118-120 Main St, Boonville, NY 13309
315-942-4593 Fax: 315-942-4452
e-mail: fielddays@aol.com
Web site: www.starinfo.com/woodsmen/
Phyllis W White, Executive Coordinator
Promoting the forest products industry

New York Water Environment Association Inc (NYWEA)
126 N Salina St, Ste 200, Syracuse, NY 13202
315-422-7811 Fax: 315-422-3851
e-mail: pcr@nywea.org
Web site: www.nywea.org
Patricia Cerro-Reehil, Executive Director
Water quality education, protection & enhancement

Northeastern Loggers' Association
PO Box 69, Old Forge, NY 13420
315-369-3078 Fax: 315-369-3736
e-mail: nela@northernlogger.com
Joseph E Phaneuf, Executive Director & Treasurer

Open Space Institute
1350 Broadway, Rm 201, New York, NY 10018-7799
212-629-3981 Fax: 212-244-3441
Web site: www.osiny.org
Christopher J Elliman, Chief Executive Officer
Conserves land in NYS for public recreation & scenic & historic value; sponsors citizen action groups; loans for land acquisition

Pace University, School of Law Center for Environmental Legal Studies
78 N Broadway, White Plains, NY 10603
914-422-4244 Fax: 914-422-4261
e-mail: nrobinson@law.pace.edu
Web site: www.law.pace.edu
Nicholas Robinson, Co-Director
US & international environmental law

Proskauer Rose LLP
1585 Broadway, 23rd Fl, New York, NY 10036-1507
212-969-3280 Fax: 212-969-2900
e-mail: rkafin@proskauer.com
Web site: www.proskauer.com
Robert J Kafin, Chief Operating Partner
Environmental law

Radiac Environmental Services
261 Kent Ave, Brooklyn, NY 11211
718-963-2233 Fax: 718-388-5107
e-mail: jtekin@radiacenv.com
John V Tekin, Jr, Operations Manager
Radioactive & chemical waste disposal, decontamination & remediation

Radon Testing Corp of America Inc
2 Hayes St, Elmsford, NY 10523
914-345-3380 or 800-457-2366 Fax: 914-345-8546
e-mail: rtca97@att.net
Web site: www.rtca.com
Nancy Bredhoff, President
Radon detection services for health departments, municipalities, homeowners; manufacture canister detectors

Rensselaer Polytechnic Institute, Ecological Economics, Values & Policy Pro
Dept of Science & Tech Studies, 110 Eighth St, Troy, NY 12180
518-276-8515 Fax: 518-276-2659
e-mail: breyms@rpi.edu
Web site: www.rpi.edu/dept/sts/eevp
Steve Breyman, Professor & Director
Educating leaders for a sustainable future

Policy Areas

Offices and agencies appear in alphabetical order.

Riverhead Foundation for Marine Research & Preservation (The)
467 E Main St, Riverhead, NY 11901
631-369-9840 Fax: 631-369-9826
Web site: www.riverheadfoundation.org
Kimberly Durham, Rescue Program Director/Biologist
Preservation & protection of the marine environment through education, rehabilitation & research

Riverkeeper Inc
PO Box 130, Garrison, NY 10524
845-424-4149 Fax: 845-424-4150
e-mail: info@riverkeeper.org
Web site: www.riverkeeper.org
Alex Matthiessen, Executive Director
Nonprofit member supported environmental organization protecting the ecological integrity of the Hudson and its tributaries, also safeguards NYC drinking water supply watershed.

Rural Water Association
PO Box 487, Claverack, NY 12513-0487
518-828-3155 Fax: 518-828-0582
Patricia C Scalera, Executive Director

SCS Engineers PC
140 Rte 303, Valley Cottage, NY 10989-1923
845-353-5727 Fax: 845-353-5731
e-mail: pkuniholm@scsengineers.com
Web site: www.scsengineers.com
Peter Kuniholm, Vice President
Environmental consulting

SUNY at Cortland, Center for Environmental & Outdoor Education
PO Box 2000, Cortland, NY 13045
607-753-5488 Fax: 607-753-5985
e-mail: sheltmirej@cortland.edu
Web site: www.cortland.edu
Jack Sheltmire, Director

Scenic Hudson
1 Civic Center Plaza, #200, Poughkeepsie, NY 12601
845-473-4440 Fax: 845-473-2648
e-mail: info@scenichudson.org
Web site: www.scenichudson.org
Ned Sullivan, President
Environmental advocacy, air & water quality, riverfront protection, land/historic preservation, smart growth planning

Sierra Club, Atlantic Chapter
353 Hamilton St, Albany, NY 12210-1709
518-426-9144
e-mail: john.stouffer@sierraclub.org
Web site: www.sierraclub.org/chapters/ny/
John Stouffer, Legislative Director
Environmental protection advocacy & education; outdoor recreation

Spectra Environmental Group Inc
19 British American Blvd, Latham, NY 12110
518-782-0882 Fax: 518-782-0973
e-mail: gsovas@spectraenv.com
Web site: www.spectraenv.com
Gregory H Sovas, Vice President, Government Affairs
Environmental & infrastructure engineering, architecture, surveying, air quality & power generation consulting & services

St John's University, School of Law
8000 Utopia Pkwy, Jamaica, NY 11439
718-990-6628 Fax: 718-990-6649
e-mail: weinberp@stjohns.edu
Philip Weinberg, Professor
Environmental law

Syracuse University Press
621 Skytop Rd, Syracuse, NY 13244-5290
315-443-5543 Fax: 315-443-5545
e-mail: msevans@syr.edu
Web site: www.syracuseuniversitypress.syr.edu
Mary Selden Evans, Executive Editor
Adirondack & regional NYS studies series

Syracuse University, Maxwell School of Citizenship & Public Affairs
400 Eggers Hall, Syracuse, NY 13244-1020
315-443-1890 Fax: 315-443-1075
e-mail: whlambri@maxwell.syr.edu
Web site: www.maxwell.syr.edu
W Henry Lambright, Director & Professor
Environmental policy; science, technology & public policy

Trees New York
51 Chambers St, Ste 1412A, New York, NY 10007
212-227-1887 Fax: 212-732-5325
e-mail: treesny@treesny.com
Web site: www.treesny.com
Barbara Eber-Schmid, Executive Director
Planting, preserving & protecting street trees; urban forestry resources & reference materials & programs in NYC

University of Rochester School of Medicine
Box EHSC, Rochester, NY 14642
585-275-3911 Fax: 585-256-2591
e-mail: tom_clarkson@urmc.rochester.edu
Web site: www2.envmed.rochester.edu
Thomas Clarkson, Professor, Department of Environmental Medicine
Mercury poisoning

Upstate Freshwater Institute
PO Box 506, Syracuse, NY 13214
315-431-4962 Fax: 315-431-4969
e-mail: sweffler@upstatefreshwater.org
Web site: www.upstatefreshwater.org
Steven Effler, Executive Director
Freshwater water quality research

Offices and agencies appear in alphabetical order.

Waterkeeper Alliance
828 S Broadway, Ste 100, Tarrytown, NY 10591
914-674-0622 Fax: 914-674-4560
e-mail: info@waterkeeper.org
Web site: www.waterkeeper.org
Steve Fleischli, Executive Director
Protect & restore the quality of the world's waterways

Whiteman Osterman & Hanna LLP
One Commerce Plaza, Albany, NY 12260
518-487-7619 Fax: 518-487-7777
e-mail: druzow@woh.com
Web site: www.woh.com
Daniel A Ruzow, Senior Partner
Environmental & zoning law

Wildlife Conservation Society
2300 Southern Blvd, Bronx, NY 10460
718-220-7139 Fax: 718-220-6890
e-mail: jcalvelli@wcs.org
Web site: www.wcs.org
John Calvelli, Senior Vice President, Public Affairs

Offices and agencies appear in alphabetical order.

GOVERNMENT OPERATIONS

New York State

GOVERNOR'S OFFICE

Governor's Office

Executive Chamber
State Capitol
Albany, NY 12224
518-474-8390 Fax: 518-474-1513
Web site: www.state.ny.us

Governor:
  George E Pataki 518-474-8390
Executive Director:
  Kara Lanspery 518-474-8390
Secretary to the Governor:
  John P Cahill. 518-474-4246
First Deputy Secretary to the Governor:
  William Howard. 518-474-3522
Deputy Secretary to the Governor for Admin & Operations:
  Carolyn Ahl 518-408-2800
Deputy Secretary to the Governor for Appointments & Intergovernmental
  Affairs:
  Robert Bulman 518-474-0491
Asst Counsel to the Governor-Clemency, Crime Vics, Correcs, Correc Svcs,
  Disaster, Extrads, Military/Naval/SEMO, Parole, Domestic Viol,
  Probatn/Correc Alts, Veterans:
  Gerald Connolly 518-474-8494
Counsel to the Governor-Attorney General, Budget:
  Richard Platkin. 518-474-8343
Deputy Counsel to the Governor-Appointments, Elections, Ethics, FOIL
  Appeals, Lobbying Commission, Regulatory Reform:
  W Brooks Debow 518-474-8343
Senior Asst Counsel to the Governor-Indian Affairs, Lottery Racing &
  Wagering Bd, State Liquor Auth:
  Greg Allen 518-474-2266
Asst Counsel to the Gov-Battery Pk, Child/Family Svcs, Child/Family
  Council, Family, Housing, Human Rts, Roosevelt Is, Temp/Disabl,
  Women, HFA/MBBA/SONYMA:
  Carolyn Betz Kerr. 518-474-1310
Asst Counsel to the Governor-Civil Svc, Elections, Empl Relations, Labor,
  Motor Veh, Niagara Fr, Port Auth, Retirement/Pensions, Transp, Thruway,
  Waterfr, MTA, PERB:
  Christopher Staszak 518-474-1310
Director, Intergovernmental Affairs:
  Michael Elmendorf. 518-474-8390
Director, State & Local Government Affairs:
  John Haggerty. 518-486-9896
Director, Communications:
  David Catalfamo. 518-474-8418

New York City Office

633 Third Ave, 38th Fl, New York, NY 10017
Director:
  Ann McConnachie 212-681-4580
Executive Assistant to the Governor:
  Amy Holden. 212-681-4580
Asst to the Governor for NYC Issues:
  Doug Blais 212-681-4580

Director for Community Affairs:
  James Barcia. 212-681-4580
Director, Legislative Affairs-NYC:
  James Harding 212-681-4580
NYC Press Secretary:
  Lynn Rasic. 212-681-4580/fax: 212-681-4608

New York State Office of Federal Affairs

444 N Capitol St NW, Washington, DC 20001
Director & Counsel:
  James Mazzarella 202-434-7100
Deputy Director:
  Kerry O'Hare 202-434-7100

Lieutenant Governor's Office

Executive Chamber State Capitol
Albany, NY 12224
518-474-4623 Fax: 518-486-4170

633 Third Ave
38th Fl
New York, NY 10017
212-681-4532
Fax: 212-681-4533

Lieutenant Governor:
  Mary Donohue . . . . 518-474-4623 or 212-681-4532
Counsel to Lt Governor:
  John Watson 518-474-4623
Acting Chief of Staff:
  Karin Kennett. 518-474-4623
Executive Secretary:
  Jane Burhans. 518-474-4623
Director, Scheduling:
  Dan Sandowski. 518-474-4623

EXECUTIVE DEPARTMENTS AND RELATED AGENCIES

Budget, Division of the

State Capitol
Albany, NY 12224
518-473-3885
e-mail: dobinfo@state.ny.us
Web site: www.budget.state.ny.us

Director:
  John F Cape 518-474-2300
Deputy Director:
  Al Kaplan 518-474-6300
Deputy Director:
  Ron Rock 518-474-6323
Administrative Officer:
  Karen Bodnar 518-474-6324

Offices and agencies appear in alphabetical order.

Director, Communications:
  Michael Marr 518-473-3885
Press Officer:
  Peter Constantakes 518-473-3885
Press Officer:
  Scott Reif 518-473-3885
Legislative Liaison:
  Christina Kidera 518-474-7953/fax: 518-473-7243

CIO Office & Office for Technology

State Capitol, ESP
PO Box 2062
Albany, NY 12220-0062

CIO Office

Web site: www.cio.state.ny.us
Chief Information Officer:
  James T Dillon 518-474-3421/fax: 518-402-2976
  e-mail: cio@cio.state.ny.us
Deputy Chief Information Officer:
  Michael Mittleman 518-408-2140/fax: 518-402-2976

Office for Technology

Web site: www.oft.state.ny.us
Director:
  Michael McCormack 518-473-9450/fax: 518-402-2976
  e-mail: nyoft@oft.state.ny.us

Administration

Chief Administrative Officer:
  Meg Levine 518-408-2476/fax: 518-402-2976
Administrative Support:
  Max Morehouse 518-402-2202/fax: 518-402-2019
Budget & Fiscal Admin:
  Kevin Nephew 518-402-4874/fax: 518-402-4807
Human Resources:
  Elaine Ehlinger 518-473-1935/fax: 518-402-4924

Counsel

Deputy Director & Counsel:
  Susan Zeronda 518-473-2807/fax: 518-402-2976
Deputy Counsel:
  Darlene Van Sickle 518-473-5115/fax: 518-486-7923

Operations

Chief Operating Officer:
  David Swits 518-473-7041/fax: 518-402-2976
Deputy Director, Customer Service:
  Dan Healy 518-473-2658/fax: 518-474-1196
Director, Enterprise Help Desk:
  Igor Koroluk 518-474-1179/fax: 518-473-0832
Deputy Director, Applications:
  Ellen Kattleman 518-402-2010/fax: 518-486-4344
Deputy Director, Networking:
  Dave Runyon 518-486-9200/fax: 518-408-4693
Director, Telecom:
  Daniel Corcoran 518-474-3019/fax: 518-473-7145
Deputy Director, Computing:
  Peter Poleto 518-474-8345/fax: 518-402-2976
Data Center/Technical Support:
  Glenn Kreig 518-485-9556/fax: 518-457-8936
Data Center/Operations:
  Allan Goldsmith 518-473-0927/fax: 518-474-9108

Statewide Initiatives

HIPAA Coord:
  Anne Marie Rainville 518-474-0683/fax: 518-473-3389
NYS Technology Academy:
  Terri Daly 518-474-0683/fax: 518-473-3389

Statewide Wireless Network

Director:
  Hanford Thomas 518-443-2042/fax: 518-443-2787
Asst Deputy Director:
  Jim Sciacca 518-443-2042

Strategic Policies Acquisitions & e-Commerce (SPAC)

Deputy Director:
  Susan Zeronda 518-473-2807/fax: 518-402-2976

Emergency Management Office, NYS (SEMO)

1220 Washington Ave
Bldg 22, Ste 101
Albany, NY 12226-2251
518-457-8900
Web site: www.nysemo.state.ny.us

Director:
  James W Tuffey 518-457-2222
First Deputy Director:
  Andrew X Feeney 518-457-9996
Deputy Director, Support Services:
  Tom Rinaldi 518-457-8130
Deputy Director, Preparedness:
  Thomas Fargione 518-457-9982
Deputy Director, Administration:
  John A Agostino 518-457-9994
Counsel:
  Lai Sun Yee 518-457-8901
Program Asst:
  Judy Williams 518-457-4875/fax: 518-457-9995

Administration

Chief Budget Analyst:
  Susan Mutch 518-457-5285
Manager, Recovery Section:
  Les Radford 518-485-0853

Community Affairs

Asst Director:
  Dennis J Michalski 518-485-5666
Public Information Officer:
  Donald L Maurer 518-485-6011/fax: 518-457-4923
  e-mail: donald.maurer@semo.state.ny.us

Preparedness

Chief, Special Operations:
  Robert Olazagasti 518-457-8916
Chief, Training/Exercises:
  William Campbell 518-457-9981
Chief, Planning:
  Radeph Anderson 518-457-9941

Support Services

Acting Manager, Technology:
  Kevin Ross 518-485-0194
Manager, Supply Services:
  John Zobel 518-457-9926

General Services, Office of

Corning Tower, 41st Fl
Empire State Plaza
Albany, NY 12242
518-474-3899 Fax: 518-474-1546
Web site: www.ogs.state.ny.us

Offices and agencies appear in alphabetical order.

633 Third Ave
New York, NY 10017
212-681-4580
Fax: 212-681-4558

Commissioner:
Daniel D Hogan 518-474-5991
e-mail: daniel.hogan@ogs.state.ny.us
First Deputy Commissioner:
Robert J Fleury. 518-473-6953
e-mail: robert.fleury@ogs.state.ny.us
Deputy Commissioner, Legal Services:
Richard Reed. 518-474-5988/fax: 518-473-4973
Special Asst to Commissioner:
Nita Chicatelli. 518-473-7345
Asst Commissioner, Public Affairs:
Jennifer Morris 518-474-5987/fax: 518-474-3187
e-mail: jennifer.morris@ogs.state.ny.us

Administration
Deputy Commissioner:
Charles E Stanley 518-474-7483
Director, Administration:
Franklin A Hecht. 518-474-4546/fax: 518-473-2844
Director, Financial Administration:
Linda Decker 518-474-4546
Director, Food Services:
Vincent Brewer. 518-474-1606
Director, Human Resources Management:
Dan Cunningham. 518-474-5995/fax: 518-473-8610
Director, Personnel:
Mary Beth Metzger. 518-408-1497
Acting Director, Bureau of Risk & Insurance Management:
Tomlynn Yacono. 518-474-4725/fax: 518-474-7867

Empire State's Convention & Cultural Events Office
Director:
Heather Flynn. 518-474-3195
Manager, Convention Center:
Dick Hallocks. 518-474-0558
Director, Marketing:
Michael J Snyder 518-474-0538
Director, Curatorial & Tour Services:
Dennis Anderson 518-473-7521
Curator, NYS Vietnam Memorial:
Robert Allyn 518-473-5546/fax: 518-474-3465

Design & Construction
Deputy Commissioner:
William F O'Connor, AIA 518-474-0335
Director, Construction:
Robert Palmer 518-474-0333/fax: 518-474-8201
Director, Contract Administration:
John D Lewyckyj. 518-474-0201/fax: 518-486-1650
Director, Design:
James M Davies, AIA. 518-474-0337

Information Technology & Procurement Services
Deputy Commissioner:
Barrett Russell 518-473-3933
e-mail: barrett.russell@ogs.state.ny.us

Information Resource Management
Director:
William Jurgens 518-473-4788
Asst Director, Technical Services:
Kevin Baxter 518-473-4788
Asst Director, Applications Services/Web Unit:
Barbara Draiss. 518-473-4788/fax: 518-474-1997

Information Security Officer:
Brett Lewis 518-474-5502/fax: 518-486-9166
Procurement Services Group
Director:
Walter Bikowitz 518-474-6710/fax: 518-486-6099
Deputy Director:
Jerry Gerard. 518-474-3695/fax: 518-486-6099
Asst Director, Customer Services & Admin:
Dixon J Ross 518-474-3855/fax: 518-474-2437
Asst Director:
Donald R Greene 518-474-3418
Asst Director:
Bruce Hallenbeck. 518-408-1705
Asst Director:
James Mastromarchi. 518-474-3416

Real Estate Planning & Development Group
Deputy Commissioner:
Bart Bush 518-473-8550
e-mail: bart.bush@ogs.state.ny.us
Director, Real Estate Planning & Development:
Joseph F Stellato. 518-474-4944
Asst Director, Real Estate Planning & Development:
Daniel Kennedy 518-474-4944
Asst Director, Real Estate Planning & Development:
Amy Chevalier 518-474-4944
Bureau Chief, Land Management:
Lee C Kiernan. 518-474-2195
Bureau Chief, Space Planning & Lease Construction & Compliance:
Anne M Carr. 518-473-9887
Bureau Chief, Space Planning & Lease Construction & Compliance:
John T Culliton 518-473-9887
Bureau Chief, Real Estate Planning - Upstate:
Joseph V Luvera. 518-486-1484
Bureau Chief, Real Estate Planning - Upstate:
Timothy J Leonard 518-486-1484
Bureau Chief, Special Projects:
Vacant 518-473-9887
Bureau Chief, Real Estate Planning - Downstate:
Robert Lazarou 518-474-7963

Real Property Management Group
Deputy Commissioner:
Bart Bush 518-473-8550
e-mail: bart.bush@ogs.state.ny.us
Director:
Martin J Gilroy 518-474-6057/fax: 518-474-1523
Manager, Capital Planning:
Richard Stock 518-473-3927/fax: 518-474-1523
Director, Construction Management:
Thomas Tedisco. 518-402-5279/fax: 518-474-1312
Director, Downstate Regional Buildings:
Glenn P Winski 212-681-4556/fax: 212-681-4558
Director, Empire State Plaza & Downtown Buildings:
Thomas E Casey 518-474-8894/fax: 518-474-4182
Director, Upstate Harriman State Office Campus:
James Lynch 518-457-2290/fax: 518-457-8297
Director, Utilities Management:
Robert Lobdell. 518-474-3249/fax: 518-402-5682

Support Services
Deputy Commissioner:
John J Spano. 518-474-5390
e-mail: john.spano@ogs.state.ny.us
Director, Operations:
Brian Moody. 518-402-5557
Director, Food Distribution & Warehousing:
Tom Osterhout 518-474-5122

Offices and agencies appear in alphabetical order.

Director, Properties & Fleet Administration:
Ronald Ottman 518-457-1744
Bureau Chief, Parking Management:
Dennis Moffre 518-486-5945
Director, Central Printing & Copy Center:
James Walls 518-457-6593
Director, Clean Fueled Vehicles Program:
Gerald King 518-473-6594
Distribution Ctr Mgr: Mail & Freight Security:
James Cerone 518-402-5750

Inspector General (NYS), Office of the

Executive Chamber
State Capitol
Albany, NY 12224
518-474-1010 Fax: 518-486-3745

61 Broadway
12th Fl
New York, NY 10006
212-635-3150
Fax: 212-809-6287

State Inspector General:
Jill Konviser-Levine . . . . 212-635-3150 or 518-474-1010
e-mail: inspector.general@ig.state.ny.us
First Deputy Inspector General:
Michael Boxer 212-635-3150
Executive Deputy Inspector General/Special Counsel:
Ralph A Rossi, III. 518-474-1010
Director, Administration:
Cindy Haskins 518-474-1010
Director, Communications:
Stephen Del Giacco 518-474-1010
e-mail: steve.delgiacco@ig.state.ny.us

Executive District Office
65 Court St, Buffalo, NY 14202
Deputy Inspector General:
Joseph Giglio 716-847-7118/fax: 716-847-7156

Law Department

120 Broadway
New York, NY 10271-0332
212-416-8000 Fax: 212-416-8942

State Capitol
Albany, NY 10271-0332
518-474-7330
Fax: 518-402-2472

Attorney General:
Eliot Spitzer 518-474-7330
Asst Attorney General, Legislative Bureau:
Kathy Bennett 518-486-3000

Administration
Agency Bldg 4, Empire State Plaza, Albany, NY 12224-0341
Executive Director for Administration:
Sylvia Hamer 518-473-7900/fax: 518-474-0680
Asst Dir:
Jean M Woodard 518-473-7900/fax: 518-474-0680

Intergovernmental Relations
Director:
Lila Kirton 212-416-6044/fax: 212-416-8539
Deputy Director:
Daniel Perkins 212-416-8078/fax: 212-416-8539
Asst Director:
Amy Solomon 518-402-2185/fax: 518-474-4290

Regulatory Reform, Governor's Office of

Agency Bldg 1, 4th Fl
Empire State Plaza
Albany, NY 12220-0107
518-486-3292 Fax: 518-473-9342
Web site: www.gorr.state.ny.us

Acting Director:
David S Bradley 518-473-8197
Deputy Director:
David S Bradley 518-473-8197
Counsel:
Amelia Stern 518-473-0620
Public Information Officer:
David Pietrusza 518-486-3292
Director, Administration:
Sandra L Curry 518-473-8197

State Comptroller, Office of the

110 State St
15th Fl
Albany, NY 12236-0001
518-474-4040 Fax: 518-473-3004
Web site: www.osc.state.ny.us

633 Third Ave, 31st Fl
New York, NY 10017-6754
212-681-4491
Fax: 212-681-4468

State Comptroller:
Alan G Hevesi . . . . 518-474-4040 or 212-681-4491

Administration
Deputy Comptroller:
Harris Lirtzman 518-402-4884

Financial Administration
Director:
Larry Appel 518-474-7574

Information Technology Services
Director:
Richard Green 518-474-7476

Management Services
Director:
Paul Capobianco 518-473-0675

Oil Spill Fund Office
Executive Director:
Anne Hohenstein 518-474-6657

Division of Intergovernmental Affairs & Community Relations
Deputy Comptroller:
Myrna Santiago 212-383-2662

Offices and agencies appear in alphabetical order.

Policy Areas

Director, Intergovernmental Affairs:
Douglas Forand 518-473-2449
Director, Intergovernmental Affairs, Upstate & Long Island Rural Liais:
Victor Mallison. 518-473-2449
Director, Intergovernmental Affairs, NYC, Brooklyn & Staten Island:
Samuel Nicolas. 212-383-2672

Division of Investigations
Deputy Comptroller:
Robert Brackman . . . . 212-681-4474 or 518-402-4926
Asst Comptroller for Internal Audit & Division Operations:
Stephen R Hillerman 518-286-2622 x105
Chief Investigative Counsel:
Samantha Biletsky . . . . 212-681-4475 or 518-486-3501
Director, Internal Audit:
Robert Kosky. 518-286-2622 x110

Division of Local Govt Services & Economic Development
Deputy Comptroller:
Mark P Pattison 518-474-4037/fax: 518-486-6479
Asst Comptroller:
Steve Hancox 518-474-4037
Asst Comptroller:
John Clarkson. 518-474-4037
Albany Area
22 Computer Dr West, Albany, NY 12205
Chief Examiner:
Thomas J Kelly. 518-438-0093/fax: 518-438-0367
Binghamton Area
44 Hawley St, Rm 1701, Binghamton, NY 13901-4455
Chief Examiner:
Patrick Carbone 607-721-8306/fax: 607-721-8313
Buffalo Area
Ellicott Sq Bldg, Rm 1050, 295 Main St, Buffalo, NY 14203
Chief Examiner:
Robert Meller 716-847-3647/fax: 716-847-3643
Glens Falls Area
One Broad Street Plaza, Glens Falls, NY 12801
Chief Examiner:
Karl Smoczynski 518-793-0057/fax: 518-793-5797
Hauppauge Area
State Ofc Bldg, #3A10, Veterans Mem Hwy, Hauppauge, NY 11788-5533
Chief Examiner:
Richard Rennard. 631-952-6534/fax: 631-952-6530
Rochester Area
Powers Bldg, 16 West Main St, Ste 522, Rochester, NY 14614
Chief Examiner:
Edward Grant 585-454-2460/fax: 585-454-3545
Syracuse Area
State Office Bldg, 333 E Washington St, Syracuse, NY 13202-1440
Chief Examiner:
Debora Wagner. 315-428-4192/fax: 315-426-2119

Division of State Services
Deputy Comptroller:
Lynn Canton. 518-474-5598

State Audit Group
Asst Comptroller:
Lynn Canton. 518-474-5598
Director, Administration:
Bob Blot 518-474-3271
Director, Audit:
Steve Sossei 518-474-3271
Director, Audit:
David R Hancox 518-474-3271

State Financial Services Group
Asst Comptroller:
Joan Sullivan 518-402-4103
Director, Accounting Operations Bureau:
Tom Mahoney 518-474-4017
Director, Accounting Systems Bureau:
Bob Campano. 518-474-8657

Executive Office
Chief of Staff:
Jack Chartier. 212-681-4498
First Deputy:
Thomas Sanzillo. 518-474-2909
Executive Deputy:
Diana Jones Ritter. 518-474-3610
Deputy Chief of Staff:
Dalia Schapiro 212-681-4540
Director, Correspondence Unit:
Ellen J Evans 518-473-1323
Chief Information Officer:
Jeffrey Grunfeld 518-473-3004

Human Resources & Affirmative Action Office
Asst Comptroller:
Jacquelyn J Hawkins 518-474-5512
Director, Affirmative Action:
Celia Gonzalez 518-473-1368
Director, Personnel:
Jay Canetto 518-474-7662
Director, Employee Relations & Training Services:
Steve Masterson 518-473-7317
Assistant Director, Personnel:
Gregory Hurd 518-474-0010
EAP Coordinator:
Joe Quinlan. 518-473-8838

Legal Services
Counsel:
Alan Lebowitz . . . . 518-474-3444 or 212-681-6069
Deputy Counsel:
Helen Fanshawe 518-474-5242
Counsel, Division of Retirement Services:
George King 518-474-3592
Associate Counsel, Finance:
Maurice Peaslee 518-474-5426
Associate Counsel, Local:
Mitchell Morris. 518-474-5586
Associate Counsel, State:
John K Dalton. 518-474-6011
Associate Counsel, State Audit:
Albert Brooks. 518-474-5490
Associate Counsel, Legislative Policy & Research:
William Murray 518-474-9024

Office of Budget & Policy Analysis
Deputy Comptroller:
Kim Fine. 518-473-4333
Chief Economist:
Thomas Marks 518-402-2670
Deputy Comptroller:
Christine Rutigliano 518-486-7982

Payroll & Revenue Services Div
Deputy Comptroller:
Daniel Berry 518-408-4149
Director, Unclaimed Funds:
Lawrence Schantz. 518-473-6438
Director, State Payroll Services:
Robin R Rabii 518-474-3400

Offices and agencies appear in alphabetical order.

Pension Investment & Public Finance

Deputy Comptroller:
David Loglisci 518-474-4003
Asst Comptroller:
Thad McTigue 518-408-3156
Asst Comptroller:
William Barrett 518-473-6396
Real Estate Investment:
Marjorie Tsang 212-383-1508
Director, Private Equity:
Nick Smirensky 212-678-4019
Director, Corporate Governance:
Julie Gresham 212-681-4480
Director, Domestic Equities & Fixed Income Investment:
Robert J Limage 518-474-6035

Press Office

Director, Communications:
David Neustadt 518-474-4015/fax: 518-473-8940
e-mail: dneustadt@osc.state.ny.us
Press Secretary:
Jeffrey Gordon 518-474-4015
e-mail: jgordon@osc.state.ny.us

Retirement Services

Deputy Comptroller:
Laura Anglin 518-474-2600
Asst Comptroller:
Nancy Burton 518-474-4600

Accounting Bureau
Director:
Daniel Burns 518-474-3670

Actuarial Bureau
Actuary:
Teri Landin 518-474-4537

Administration Services & Quality Performance
Director:
Melanie MacPherson 518-408-4193

Advisory Counsel Affairs
Director:
George S King 518-474-3592

Benefit Calculations & Disbursements
Director:
Veronica D'Alauro 518-473-0983

Benefit Information Services
Director:
Keith Zeto 518-474-5728

Disability Processing/Hearing Administration
Director:
Kathy Nowak 518-473-1347

Matrimonial & Hearing Review
Director:
Carolyn D'Agostino 518-474-1253

Member & Employee Services
Director:
Ginger Dame 518-474-1101

Retirement Communications
Director:
Paul Kentoffio 518-474-7096

State Deputy Comptroller for New York City

59 Maiden Lane, 29th Fl, New York, NY 10038

Deputy Comptroller:
Kenneth Bleiwas 212-383-3900

Agency Analysis Bureau
Director:
Michael Solomon 212-383-3870

Bureau of Economic Development & Policy Analysis
Director:
Adam Freed 212-383-3930

Bureau of Tax & Economic Analysis
Director:
Michael Brisson 212-383-3921

Infrastructure & Citywide Expenditure Analysis
Director:
Christopher Wieda 212-383-3936

State Department

41 State St
Albany, NY 12231
518-474-0050 Fax: 518-474-4765
Web site: www.dos.state.ny.us

123 William St
New York, NY 10038
212-417-5801
Fax: 212-417-5805

Secretary of State:
Randy A Daniels 518-474-0050
First Deputy Secretary of State:
Frank P Milano 518-474-0050
Deputy Secretary of State, Public Affairs:
Eamon Moynihan 212-417-5800
Counsel:
Glen Bruening 518-474-6740/fax: 518-473-9211
Asst Secretary of State for Communications:
Lawrence Sombke 518-474-4752/fax: 518-474-4597
e-mail: info@dos.state.ny.us

Business & Licensing Services Division

Deputy Secretary of State:
Keith W Stack 518-474-4429/fax: 518-473-6648
e-mail: licensing @dos.state.ny.us

Administrative Rules Division
Director:
Deborah Ritzko 518-474-6957/fax: 518-473-9055
e-mail: adminrules@dos.state.ny.us

Cemeteries Division
Director:
Richard D Fishman . . . . 518-474-6226 or 212-417-5713
fax: 518-473-0876
e-mail: cemeteries@dos.state.ny.us

Corporations, State Records & UCC Division
Director:
Daniel E Shapiro 518-473-2494/fax: 518-474-5173
e-mail: corporations@dos.state.ny.us

Ethics Commission

39 Columbia St, Albany, NY 12207-2717
Executive Director:
Karl J Sleight 518-432-8207/fax: 518-432-8255
e-mail: ethics@dos.state.ny.us

Offices and agencies appear in alphabetical order.

Chair:
    Paul Shechtman 518-432-8207

Local Government & Community Services

Deputy Secretary of State:
    Matthew Andrus 518-486-9888/fax: 518-474-6572

Coastal Resources & Waterfront Revitalization Division

Director:
    George Stafford. 518-474-6000/fax: 518-473-2464
    e-mail: coastal@dos.state.ny.us

Code Enforcement & Administration Division

Director:
    Ronald E Piester 518-474-4073/fax: 518-486-4487
    e-mail: codes@dos.state.ny.us

Community Services Division

Director:
    Evelyn M Harris 518-474-5741/fax: 518-486-4663
    e-mail: commserv@dos.state.ny.us

Fire Prevention & Control Office

State Fire Administrator:
    James A Burns. 518-474-6746/fax: 518-474-3240
    e-mail: fire@dos.state.ny.us
    New York State Academy of Fire Science
    600 College Ave, Montour Falls, NY 14865-9634
    Director:
        Richard Nagle. 607-535-7136/fax: 607-535-4841

Local Government Services Division

Director:
    Barbara Murphy 518-473-3355/fax: 518-474-6572
    e-mail: localgov@dos.state.ny.us

Open Government Committee

Director:
    Robert J Freeman. 518-474-2518/fax: 518-474-1927
    e-mail: opengov@dos.state.ny.us

Operations

Director, Administration & Management:
    Judith E Kenny 518-474-4751/fax: 518-474-4765

Administrative Support Services

Director:
    Rebecca Sabesta 518-473-8221/fax: 518-473-7182

Affirmative Action. . . . . fax: 518-473-3294

Affirmative Action Officer:
    Antonio Cortez. 518-474-2752

Fiscal Management

Director:
    Kym Landry 518-474-2754/fax: 518-474-4777

Human Resources Management

Director:
    Debra L Frisch. 518-474-2752/fax: 518-473-3294

Internal Audit

Director:
    Ralph Bizarro. 518-474-3772

Systems Management Bureau

Director:
    Steven S Lovelett 518-474-8512/fax: 518-474-6239

Regional Affairs Division

Director:
    John Rogers. 518-486-9896/fax: 518-473-0073

Regional Offices

Albany

Ofc of Local Gov't & Reg Affairs St C, Exec Chamber Rm 236,
    Albany, NY 12224
Regional Representative:
    John Rogers 518-486-9896/fax: 518-473-0073

Binghamton

State Office Bldg Annex, 44 Hawley St, 16TH FL ROOM 1605,
    Binghamton, NY 13901
Regional Representative:
    Donald Leonard 607-721-8751/fax: 607-721-8755

Buffalo

65 Court St, Buffalo, NY 14202
Upstate Regional Director:
    Jennifer McNamara. 716-847-7110
Regional Representative:
    Richard Solecky 716-847-7110/fax: 716-847-7969

Hicksville

303 Old Country Road, Hicksville, NY 11802
Regional Representative:
    Heidi Callahan 516-934-8572/fax: 516-934-8001

Olean

Municipal Bldg, PO Box 624, 101 East State St, Olean, NY 14760
Regional Representative:
    William Heaney 716-376-5706/fax: 716-376-5700

Peekskill

41 North Division St, 3rd Fl, Peekskill, NY 10566
Regional Representative:
    Cheryl Murray 914-788-3450/fax: 914-788-3452

Plattsburgh

22 US Oval, Bldg 426, Ste 1210, Plattsburgh, NY 12903
Regional Representative:
    Candace Luck. 518-562-3640/fax: 518-562-3645

Poughkeepsie

State Ofc Bldg, 4 Burnett Blvd, Poughkeepsie, NY 12603-2553
Regional Representative:
    John Bellucci 845-437-5140/fax: 845-437-5142

Rochester

1530 Jefferson Rd, Rochester, NY 14623
Regional Representative:
    Kelli O'Conner 585-424-9927/fax: 585-424-3658

Suffolk

State Office Bldg, 250 Veterans Memorial Hwy, Hauppauge, NY
    11788
Regional Representative:
    Steven Halsey. 631-952-6583/fax: 631-952-7910

Syracuse

St Ofc Bldg, 333 E Washington St, Rm 514, Syracuse, NY 13202
Regional Representative:
    Bebette Yunis. 315-428-4337/fax: 315-428-4261

Utica

State Office Bldg, 207 Genesee St, Utica, NY 13501
Regional Representative:
    Carole Kelly 315-793-2535/fax: 315-793-2635

Watertown

State Office Bldg, 317 Washington St, 4th Fl, Watertown, NY 13601
Regional Representative:
    Joanne Dicob 315-785-2561/fax: 315-785-2563

State Athletic Commission

123 William St, 20TH FL, New York, NY 10038
Chair:
    Ron Scott Stevens 212-417-5700/fax: 212-417-4987
    e-mail: athletic@dos.state.ny.us

Offices and agencies appear in alphabetical order.

Welfare Inspector General, Office of NYS

22 Cortlandt St
11th Fl
New York, NY 10007
212-417-5822 Fax: 212-417-5849

40 No Pearl St
Section 10B
Albany, NY 12224
518-474-9636
Fax: 518-486-6148

Inspector General:
Paul Balukas 212-417-5840
Deputy Inspector General:
Pasqualino Russo 212-417-5860
Counsel:
Andrew J Weiss 212-417-2395
Chief Investigator:
Joseph R Bucci 212-417-2026
Special Asst Attorney General:
Joseph Burruano 212-417-2051
Administrative Asst to Inspector General:
Wanda Hernandez 212-417-5822

CORPORATIONS, AUTHORITIES AND COMMISSIONS

Legislative Bill Drafting Commission

Capitol
Rm 308
Albany, NY 12224
518-455-7500 Fax: 518-455-7598

Commissioner:
Ronald H Backer 518-455-7501
e-mail: backer@lbdc.state.ny.us
Commissioner:
Randall G Bluth 518-455-7506
e-mail: bluth@lbdc.state.ny.us
Deputy Counsel:
Jamie-Lynne Elacqua 518-455-7538
e-mail: elaqua@lbdc.state.ny.us

Legislative Retrieval System . . . . fax: 518-455-7679
55 Elk St, Albany, NY 12210
800-356-6566 Fax: 518-455-7679
Director:
Barbara Lett 518-455-7673
e-mail: lett@lbdc.state.ny.us

New York State Athletic Commission

123 William St
20th Fl
New York, NY 10038-3804
212-417-5700 Fax: 212-417-4987
e-mail: athletic@dos.state.ny.us
Web site: www.dos.state.ny.us/athletic.html

Chair:
Ron Scott Stevens 212-417-5700

Secretary:
Robert Limerick 212-417-5700

New York State Commission on the Restoration of the Capitol

Corning Tower, 40th Fl
Empire State Plaza
Albany, NY 12242
518-473-0341 Fax: 518-486-5720

Executive Director:
Andrea J Lazarski 518-473-0341
e-mail: andrea.lazarski@ogs.state.ny.us

New York State Disaster Preparedness Commission

Building 22, Suite 101
1220 Washington Ave
Albany, NY 12226-2251
518-457-2222 Fax: 518-457-9930
Web site: www.nysemo.state.ny.us

Chairman:
James W McMahon 518-402-2227

New York State Dormitory Authority

515 Broadway
Albany, NY 12207-2964
518-257-3000 Fax: 518-257-3100
Web site: www.dasny.org

One Penn Plaza, 52nd Fl
New York, NY 12207-2964
212-273-5000
Fax: 212-273-5121

539 Franklin St
Buffalo, NY 14202-1109
716-884-9780
Fax: 716-884-9787

Chair:
Gail H Gordon 518-257-3180/fax: 518-257-3183
Executive Director:
Maryanne Gridley 518-257-3180/fax: 518-257-3183
Deputy Executive Director:
Michael T Corrigan 518-257-3192/fax: 518-257-3183
CFO:
John G Pasicznyk 518-257-3630/fax: 518-257-3100
e-mail: jpasiczn@dasny.org
General Counsel:
Jeffrey M Pohl 518-257-3120/fax: 518-257-3101
e-mail: jpohl@dasny.org
Managing Director, Construction:
Douglas M Van Vleck 518-257-3200/fax: 518-257-3100
e-mail: dvanvlec@dasny.org
Managing Director, Policy & Program Development:
Lora K Lefebvre 518-257-3163/fax: 518-257-3387
e-mail: llefebvr@dasny.org

Policy Areas

Offices and agencies appear in alphabetical order.

Managing Director, Public Finance:
Cheryl Ishmael. 518-257-3362/fax: 518-257-3100
e-mail: cishmael@dasny.org
Director, Communications & Marketing:
Paul Burgdorf .518-257-3380/fax: 518-257-3387
e-mail: pburgdor@dasny.org
Press Officer:
Claudia Hutton. 518-257-3382/fax: 518-257-3387
e-mail: chutton@dasny.org

New York State Ethics Commission
39 Columbia Street
4th FL
Albany, NY 12207-2717
518-432-8207 Fax: 518-432-8255
e-mail: ethics@dos.state.ny.us
Web site: www.dos.state.ny.us/ethc/ethics.html

Chair:
Paul Shechtman 518-432-8208
Commissioner:
Robert J Giuffra, Jr. 518-432-8208
Executive Director:
Karl J Sleight 518-432-8208
Counsel:
Bruce A Androphy 518-432-8250
Public Information Officer:
Walter C Ayres 518-432-8210
e-mail: wayres@dos.state.ny.us

New York State Financial Control Board
123 William St
23rd Fl
New York, NY 10038-3804
212-417-5046 Fax: 212-417-5055
e-mail: nysfcb@fcb.state.ny.us
Web site: www.fcb.state.ny.us

Acting Exec Director:
Jeffrey Sommer 212-417-5066
Deputy Director, Expenditure Analysis:
Dennis DeLisle. 212-417-5069
Acting Deputy Director, Economic & Revenue Analysis:
Martin Fischman. 212-417-5068
Assoc Director:
Mattie W Taylor 212-417-5053

New York State Law Reporting Bureau
One Commerce Plaza
Suite 1750
Albany, NY 12210
518-474-8211 Fax: 518-463-6869
Web site: www.courts.state.ny.us/reporter

State Reporter:
Gary D Spivey 518-474-8211
Deputy State Reporter:
Charles A Ashe. 518-474-8211
e-mail: cashe@courts.state.ny.us

New York State Temporary Commission of Investigation
59 Maiden Lane, 31st Fl
New York, NY 10038
212-344-6660 Fax: 212-344-6868
Web site: www.sic.state.ny.us

Chair:
Dineen A Riviezzo 212-344-6660
Chief Investigator:
Anthony Hellmer 212-344-6660
Deputy Commissioner/Chief Counsel:
Anthony T Cartusciello 212-344-6670

New York State Temporary Commission on Lobbying
2 Empire State Plaza
Ste 1701
Albany, NY 12223-1254
518-474-7126 Fax: 518-473-6492
e-mail: lobcom@emi.com
Web site: www.nylobby.state.ny.us

Commissioner:
Joseph Dunn 518-474-7126
Chair:
Bartley Livolsi 518-474-7126
Commissioner:
Andrew Cecci. 518-474-7126
Commissioner:
Peter Moschetti. 518-474-7126
Commissioner:
Kenneth Baer 518-474-7126
Vice Chair:
Patrick Bulgaro. 518-474-7126
Executive Director:
David M Grandeau. 518-474-7126
Director, Program & Finance Admin:
Jeannine M Clemente. 518-474-7126
Public Information Officer:
Kris Thompson 518-474-7126

Uniform State Laws Commission
c/o Coughlin & Gerhart LLP, 20 Hawley St
East Tower
Binghamton, NY 13902-2039
607-584-4193 Fax: 607-723-1530

Chair:
Richard B Long 607-584-4193
e-mail: rlong@cglawllp.com
Member:
Sandra Stern 212-207-8150
e-mail: ssternlaw@aol.com
Member:
Justin L Vigdor. 585-232-5300
e-mail: jvigdor@boylanbrown.com
Member:
Norman L Greene. 212-661-5030
e-mail: normlg510@aol.com

United Nations Development Corporation

2 United Nations Plaza
27th Fl
New York, NY 10017-4403
212-888-1618 Fax: 212-588-0758
Web site: www.undc.org

Chair, Board of Directors:
George Klein 212-888-1618
President & CEO:
Roy M Goodman 212-888-1618
Executive VP & Director of Development:
Jeffrey Feldman 212-888-1618
Senior VP, Operations:
Robert M Preissner 212-888-1618
Senior VP, Controller:
Rudy C Montenegro 212-888-1618

NEW YORK STATE LEGISLATURE

See Legislative Branch in Section 1 for additional Standing Committee and Subcommittee information.

Assembly Standing Committees

Consumer Affairs & Protection
Chair:
Audrey I Pheffer (D) 518-455-4292
Ranking Minority Member:
David G McDonough (R). 518-455-4633

Corporations, Authorities & Commissions
Chair:
Richard L Brodsky (D). 518-455-5753
Ranking Minority Member:
James G Bacalles (R) 518-455-5791

Ethics & Guidance
Chair:
Kevin A Cahill (D). 518-455-4436
Ranking Minority Member:
Robert Oaks (R) 518-455-5655

Governmental Operations
Chair:
RoAnn M Destito (D). 518-455-5454
Ranking Minority Member:
Louis Mosiello (R) 518-455-4505

Oversight, Analysis & Investigation
Chair:
James Brennan (D). 518-455-5377
Ranking Minority Member:
Donna Ferrara (R). 518-455-4684

Rules
Chair:
Sheldon Silver (D) 518-455-3791
Ranking Minority Member:
Charles H Nesbitt (R). 518-455-3751

Ways & Means
Chair:
Herman D Farrell, Jr (D) 518-455-5491
Ranking Minority Member:
Thomas F Barraga (R) 518-455-4611

Assembly Task Forces & Caucus

State-Local Relations, Legislative Commission on
Assembly Chair:
Darrel Aubertine. 518-455-5035
Program Manager:
William Kraus 518-455-5035/fax: 518-455-5396

Senate Select Committees

Interstate Cooperation, Select Committee on
Chair:
Hugh T Farley (R) 518-455-2181
Director:
Robert W Geddis. 518-455-2181/fax: 518-455-2271

Senate Standing Committees

Civil Service & Pensions
Chair:
Joseph E Robach (R) 518-455-2909
Ranking Minority Member:
Carl Andrews (D). 518-455-2431

Consumer Protection
Chair:
Charles J Fuschillo, Jr (R) 518-455-3341
Ranking Minority Member:
Jeffrey D Klein. 518-455-3595

Corporations, Authorities & Commissions
Chair:
Vincent L Leibell, III (R). 518-455-3111
Ranking Minority Member:
Ada L Smith (D). 518-455-3531

Ethics
Chair:
George H Winner, Jr (R) 518-455-2091
Ranking Minority Member:
William T Stachowski (D) 518-455-2426

Finance
Chair:
Owen H Johnson (R) 518-455-3411
Ranking Minority Member:
Neil D Breslin (D) 518-455-2225

Investigations & Government Operations
Chair:
Nicholas A Spano (R). 518-455-2231
Ranking Minority Member:
William T Stachowski (D) 518-455-2426

Rules
Chair:
Joseph L Bruno (R) 518-455-3191
Ranking Minority Member:
David A Paterson (D). 518-455-2701

Senate/Assembly Legislative Commissions

Ethics Committee, Legislative
Senate Co-Chair:
John J Flanagan (R) 518-455-2071
Assembly Co-Chair:
Mark Weprin (D) 518-455-5806

Offices and agencies appear in alphabetical order.

Policy Areas

Program Manager/Counsel:
  Melissa Ryan 518-455-2142/fax: 518-426-6850

Government Administration, Legislative Commission on
Assembly Chair:
  Joan Millman (D) 518-455-5426

Senate Vice Chair:
  Owen H Johnson (R) 518-455-3411
Program Manager:
  Philip Johnson 518-455-3632/fax: 518-455-4574

U.S. Government

EXECUTIVE DEPARTMENTS AND RELATED AGENCIES

Peace Corps
Web site: www.peacecorps.gov

New York Regional Office . . . . fax: 212-352-5441
  201 Varick St, Ste 1025, New York, NY 10014
Regional Manager:
  Edwin Jorge 212-352-5440
  e-mail: nyinfo@peacecorps.gov
Public Affairs Specialist:
  Bartel Kendrick 212-352-5446
  e-mail: bkendrick@peacecorps.gov

US Department of Homeland Security (DHS)
Web site: www.dhs.gov

Bureau of Immigration & Customs Enforcement (ICE)
  Web site: www.ice.gov

New York District Office
  601 W 26th St, Ste 820, New York, NY 10001
Special Agent-in-Charge:
  Martin Ficke 646-230-3200
  Albany Sub Office
  1086 Troy-Schenectady Rd, Latham, NY 12110
  Group Supervisor:
    LeRoy Tario 518-220-2100
  Resident Agent-in-Charge:
    Jack McQuade 518-220-2100

Customs & Border Protection (CBP)
  Web site: www.cbp.gov

Agriculture Inspections (AI)
  Brooklyn, Port of
  6405 7th Ave, 3rd Fl, Brooklyn, NY 11220
  Supervising Ag Specialist:
    Willie J Martin 718-340-5225
  Buffalo, Port of
  1 Peace Bridge Plaza, Room 316, Buffalo, NY 14213
  Agriculture Specialist:
    Samra Boukadida 716-884-5701/fax: 716-884-5679
  Champlain, Port of
  234 West Service Rd, Suite 2, Champlain, NY 12919
  Ag Specialist:
    Vacant 518-298-4332/fax: 518-298-4486
  JFK International Airport Area Office
  JFK Int'l Airport, Bldg #77, 2nd Fl, Jamaica, NY 11430
  Port Director:
    Camille Polimeni 718-487-5164

Buffalo Field Office
  4455 Genesee St, Buffalo, NY 14225
Director:
  Michael D'Ambrosio 716-626-0400 x201/fax: 716-626-9281

Albany, Port of
  445 Broadway, Room 216, Albany, NY 12207
  Port Director:
    Drew Wescott 518-431-0200/fax: 518-431-0203
Buffalo, Port of
  111 W Huron St, Buffalo, NY 14202
  Area Port Director:
    Joseph Wilson 716-646-3400/fax: 716-551-5011
Champlain, Port of
  198 W Service Rd, Champlain, NY 12919
  Area Port Director:
    Christopher Perry 518-298-8347/fax: 518-298-8314
Ogdensburg, Port of
  104 Bridge Approach Rd, Ogdensburg, NY 13669
  Port Director:
    John Korcz 315-393-1390/fax: 315-393-7472

New York Field Office
  1 Penn Plaza, 11th Fl, New York, NY 10119
Director, Field Operations:
  Susan T Mitchell 646-733-3100
Field Public Affairs Officer:
  Janet Rapaport 212-514-8324/fax: 212-344-3755
  Field Counsel - New York
  Associate Chief Counsel:
    Judith Altman 646-733-3200
  Laboratory Division
  Director:
    Tom Governo 973-368-1901

Environmental Measurements Laboratory
  201 Varick St, 5th Fl, New York, NY 10014-7447
  Web site: www.eml.doe.gov
Director:
  Mitchell D Erickson 212-620-3619/fax: 212-620-3651
  e-mail: erickson@eml.doe.gov
Deputy Director:
  Catherine S Klusek 212-620-3231
  e-mail: klusek@eml.doe.gov

Administration
Director:
  Joseph J Caroli 212-620-3604/fax: 212-620-3600
  e-mail: jcaroli@eml.doe.gov

Engineering & Computer Sciences Division
Director:
  Merrill Heit 212-620-3623/fax: 212-620-3600

Environmental Science
Director:
  Kevin M Miller 212-620-3572/fax: 212-620-3600
  e-mail: kmiller@eml.doe.gov

Quality Assurance/Metrology
Director:
  Richard J Larsen 212-620-3524/fax: 212-620-3600

Federal Emergency Management Agency (FEMA)
  Web site: www.fema.gov

Offices and agencies appear in alphabetical order.

National Disaster Medical System . . . . fax: 212-680-3608
26 Federal Plz, Rm 3835, New York, NY 10278
Coordinator:
Captain Bonita Pyler, USPHS 212-680-8542
e-mail: pyler@dhs.gov

New York Regional Office . . . . fax: 212-680-3681
26 Federal Plz, Ste 1311, New York, NY 10278
Acting Regional Director:
Joseph F Picciano 212-680-3612

Federal Protective Service (The)
26 Federal Plaza, Rm 17-130, New York, NY 10278
Director:
John A Ulianko 212-264-4255/fax: 212-264-9803

Plum Island Animal Disease Center
PO Box 848, Greenport, NY 11944
Director:
Beth Lautner 631-323-3202/fax: 631-323-3295

Transportation Security Administration (TSA)
201 Varick St, Rm 603, New York, NY 10014
Regional Spokesperson:
Mark Hatfield 212-337-2260/fax: 212-337-2261
e-mail: mark.hatfield@dhs.gov

US Citizenship & Immigration Services (USCIS)
Web site: www.uscis.gov

Buffalo District Office . . . . fax: 716-551-3131
Federal Center, 130 Delaware Ave, Buffalo, NY 14202
District Director:
M Frances Holmes 716-551-4741 x6000
Albany Sub Office
1086 Troy-Schenectady Rd, Latham, NY 12110
Officer-in-Charge:
Gary Hale 518-220-2100

CIS Asylum Offices
New York Asylum Office . . . . fax: 718-723-1121
One Cross Island Plaza, 3rd Fl, Rosedale, NY 11422
Director:
Patricia A Jackson 718-723-5954
Deputy Director:
Mick Dedvukaj 718-723-5954
Newark Asylum Office-Including NYS not served by New York City . . . . fax: 201-531-1877
1200 Wall St, West 4th Fl, Lindhurst, NJ 7071
Director:
Susan Raufer 201-531-0555
Deputy Director:
Aster Zeleke 201-531-0555

New York City District Office
26 Federal Plaza, New York, NY 10278
District Director:
Mary Ann Gantner 212-264-3972
Garden City Satellite Office
711 Stewart Ave, Garden City, NY 11530
Officer-in-Charge:
Linda Pritchett . . . . 516-228-9242 or 516-288-9243

US General Services Administration
Web site: www.gsa.gov

Region 2—New York
26 Federal Plaza, Rm 18-102, New York, NY 10278
Regional Administrator:
Eileen Long-Chelales 212-264-2600/fax: 212-264-3998

Deputy Regional Administrator:
Steve Ruggiero 212-264-2600/fax: 212-264-3998
Regional Counsel:
Lionel Bately, Jr 212-264-8306/fax: 212-264-1987
Regional Counsel:
Carol Latterman 212-264-8306/fax: 212-264-1987

Administration
Director, Program Support & Human Resources:
Joseph J Giorgianni 212-264-0780/fax: 212-264-6798

Federal Supply Service
Asst Regional Administrator:
Charles B Weill 212-264-3590/fax: 212-264-9759

Federal Technology Service
Asst Regional Administrator:
Kerry J Blette 212-264-1257/fax: 212-264-3631

Inspector General's Office
Asst Regional Inspector, Investigations:
Daniel Walsh 212-264-7300/fax: 212-264-7154
Regional Director, Audit:
Joseph Mastropietro 212-264-8620

Public Buildings Service
Asst Regional Administrator:
John Scorcia 212-264-4285/fax: 212-264-2232
Deputy Asst Regional Administrator:
Vacant 212-264-4285

Director, Property Management:
David Segermeister 212-264-4273/fax: 212-264-2746
Director, Realty Services:
Donald W Eigendorff 212-264-4210/fax: 212-264-9400

US Government Printing Office
Web site: www.gpo.gov

Region 2-I (New York)

Printing Procurement Office . . . . fax: 212-337-1346
201 Varick St, Rm 709, New York, NY 10014
Manager, NYC & Philadelphia Ofcs:
Ira Fishkin 212-620-3321/fax: 212-620-3378

US Postal Service
Web site: www.usps.gov

NORTHEAST AREA (Includes part of New York State) . . . . fax: 860-285-1253
6 Griffin Rd North, Windsor, CT 06006-7010
Vice President, Area Operations:
Megan Brennan 860-285-7040

New York Metro Area . . . . fax: 718-321-7150
142-02 20th Ave, Rm 318, Flushing, NY 11351-0001
Vice President, Area Operations:
David L Solomon 718-321-5823

US State Department
Web site: www.state.gov

Bureau of Educational & Cultural Affairs-NY Pgm Branch . . . . fax: 212-399-5783
666 Fifth Ave, Ste 603, New York, NY 10103
Fax: 212-399-5783
Web site: exchanges.state.gov

Offices and agencies appear in alphabetical order.

Policy Areas

Director:
Donna Shirreffs 212-399-5750

US Mission To the United Nations
140 East 45th St., New York, NY 10017
US Representative to the United Nations:
Acting Ambassador Ann Patterson 212-415-4404
Deputy US Representative to the United Nations:
Ambassador Ann Patterson 212-415-4410
US Representative for UN Management & Reform:
Ambassador Patrick Kennedy 212-415-4032
US Representative to ECOSOC:
Ambassador Sichan Siv 212-415-4278
Chief of Staff:
Thomas A Schweich 212-415-4481
Counselor for Host Country:
Russell F Graham 212-415-4131
Counselor for International Legal Affairs:
Charles Nicholas Rostow 212-415-4220
Counselor for Political Affairs:
William J Brencick 212-415-4363
Director, Communications, Spokesman:
Richard Grenell 212-415-4058
Military Staff Committee:
Col John B O'Dowd 212-415-4147

U.S. CONGRESS

See U.S. Congress Chapter for additional Standing Committee and Subcommittee information.

House of Representatives Standing Committees

Government Reform
Chair:
Thomas M Davis (R-VA) 202-225-1492
Ranking Minority Member:
Henry A Waxman (D-CA) 202-225-3976
New York Delegate:
Brian M Higgins (D) 202-225-3306
New York Delegate:
Carolyn B Maloney (D) 202-225-7944
New York Delegate:
John M McHugh (R) 202-225-4611
New York Delegate:
Major R Owens (D) 202-225-6231
New York Delegate:
Edolphus Towns (D) 202-225-5936

Homeland Security, Select Committee on
Chair:
Christopher Cox (R-CA) 202-225-5611
Ranking Minority Member:
Bennie G Thompson (D-MS) 202-225-5876
New York Delegate:
Peter T King (R) 202-225-7896
New York Delegate:
Nita M Lowey (D) 202-225-6506

Subcommittees
Economic Security, Infrastructure Protection & Cyebrsecurity
Chair:
Dan Lundgren (R-CA) 202-225-5716
Ranking Minority Member:
Loretta Sanchez (D-CA) 202-225-2965

Emergency Preparedness, Science & Technology
Chair:
Peter T King (R-NY) 202-225-7896
Ranking Minority Member:
Bill Pascrell, Jr (D-NJ) 202-225-5751
New York Delegate:
Nita M Lowey (D) 202-225-6506
Intelligence Information Sharing & Terrorism Risk Assessment
Chair:
Robert R Simmons (R-CT) 202-225-2076
Ranking Minority Member:
Zoe Lofgren (D-CA) 202-225-3072
New York Delegate:
Peter T King (R) 202-225-7896
New York Delegate:
Nita M Lowey (D) 202-225-6506
Management Integration & Oversight
Chair:
Mike Rogers (R-AL) 202-225-3261
Ranking Minority Member:
Kendrick B Meek (D-FL) 202-225-4506
Prevention of Nuclear & Biological Attack
Chair:
John Linder (R-GA) 202-225-4272
Ranking Minority Member:
James R Langevin (D-RI) 202-225-2735

Intelligence, Permanent Select Committee on
Chair:
Peter Hoekstra (R-MI) 202-225-4401
Ranking Minority Member:
Jane Harman (D-CA) 202-225-8820

Subcommittee
Technical & Tactical Intelligence
Chair:
Heather A Wilson (R-NM) 202-225-6316
Ranking Minority Member:
Anna G Eshoo (D-CA) 202-225-4801

Standards of Official Conduct
Chair:
Doc Hastings (R-WA) 202-225-5816
Ranking Minority Member:
Alan B Mollohan (D-WV) 202-225-4172

Senate Standing Committees

Ethics, Select Committee on
Chair:
George V Voinovich (R-OH) 202-224-3353
Vice Chair:
Tim Johnson (D-SD) 202-224-5842

Homeland Security & Governmental Affairs
Chair:
Susan Collins (R-ME) 202-224-2523
Ranking Minority Member:
Joseph I Lieberman (D-CT) 202-224-4041

Indian Affairs
Chair:
John McCain (R-AZ) 202-224-2235
Vice Chair:
Byron L Dorgan (D-ND) 202-224-2551

Intelligence, Select Committee on
Chair:
Pat Roberts (R-KS) 202-224-4774

Offices and agencies appear in alphabetical order.

Vice Chair:
   John D Rockefeller, IV (D-WV) 202-224-6472

Judiciary
Chair:
   Arlen Specter (R-PA) 202-224-4254
Ranking Minority Member:
   Patrick J Leahy (D-VT) 202-224-4242
New York Delegate:
   Charles E Schumer (D). 202-224-6542

   Subcommittees
    Immigration, Border Security & Citizenship
     Chair:
      John Cornyn (R-TX) 202-224-2934

Ranking Minority Mbr:
   Edward M Kennedy (D-MA) 202-224-4543
New York Delegate:
   Charles E Schumer (D) 202-224-6542
Terrorism, Technology & Homeland Security
   Chair:
    Jon Kyl (R-AZ) 202-224-4521
   Ranking Minority Member:
    Dianne Feinstein (D-CA) 202-224-3841

Private Sector

Academy of Political Science
475 Riverside Drive, Ste 1274, New York, NY 10115-1274
212-870-2500 Fax: 212-870-2202
e-mail: aps@psqonline.org
Web site: www.psqonline.org
Demetrios James Caraley, President
Analysis of government, economic & social issues

Albany Law School, Government Law Center
80 New Scotland Ave, Albany, NY 12208
518-445-2311 Fax: 518-445-2303
e-mail: glc@mail.als.edu
Web site: www.als.edu
Patricia Salkin, Associate Dean & Director, Governmental Law
Legal aspects of public policy reform

Association of Government Accountants, NY Capital Chapter
PO Box 1923, Albany, NY 12201
518-427-4765 or 212-872-5733
e-mail: lvacarro@kpmg.com
Web site: www.aganycap.org
Lori Vaccaro, Chapter President
Education for the government financial management community

Business Council of New York State Inc
152 Washington Ave, Albany, NY 12210
518-465-7511 x204 Fax: 518-465-4389
e-mail: elliott.shaw@bcnys.org
Web site: www.bcnys.org
Elliott A Shaw, Jr, Director, Government Affairs
Resources for business

Cayuga Nation
PO Box 11, Versailles, NY 14168
716-532-4847 Fax: 716-532-5417
e-mail: cayuga@sixnations.org
Web site: www.sixnations.org
Clint Halftown, Representative
Tribal government

Center for Governmental Research Inc (CGR)
1 South Washington St, Ste 400, Rochester, NY 14614-1125
585-325-6360 Fax: 585-325-2612
e-mail: pmalgieri@cgr.org
Web site: www.cgr.org
Stephen Acquario, Executive Director
Nonprofit, nonpartisan institution devoted to analyzing public policies to ensure that they benefit the community at large

Citizens Union of the City of New York
299 Broadway, Rm 700, New York, NY 10007-1978
212-227-0342 Fax: 212-227-0345
e-mail: citizens@citizensunion.org
Web site: www.citizensunion.org
Dick Dadey, Executive Director
Citizen watchdog organization; city & state public policy issues

Coalition of Fathers & Families NY, PAC
PO Box 782, Clifton Park, NY 12065
518-383-8202 Fax: 518-383-8202
e-mail: dadlobby@localnet.com
Web site: www.fafny.org/fafnypac.htm
James Hays, Treasurer
Political Action for fathers and families in New York

Columbia University, Exec Graduate Pgm in Public Policy & Administration
420 W 118th St, Rm 1314, New York, NY 10027
212-854-4445 Fax: 212-854-5765
e-mail: sc32@columbia.edu
Web site: www.columbia.edu/~sc32
Steven Cohen, Director
Urban & environmental policy; public management

Common Cause/NY
155 Ave of the Americas, 4th Fl, New York, NY 10013
212-691-6506 Fax: 212-807-1809
e-mail: cocauseny@aol.com
Web site: www.commoncause.org/ny
Rachel Leon, Executive Director
Campaign finance reform, ballot access, political gift disclosure & public interest lobbying

Offices and agencies appear in alphabetical order.

NYS Bar Assn, Task Force to Review Terrorism Legislation Cmte
Connors & Vilardo
1020 Liberty Bldg, 420 Main St, Buffalo, NY 14202-3510
716-852-5533 Fax: 716-852-5649
e-mail: ved@connors-vilardo.com
Vincent E Doyle, III, Chair

Council of State Governments, Eastern Conference
40 Broad St, Ste 2050, New York, NY 10004-2317
212-482-2320 Fax: 212-482-2344
e-mail: alan@csgeast.org
Web site: www.csgeast.org
Alan V Sokolow, Regional Director
Training, research & information sharing for state government officials

Crane, Parente, Cherubin & Murray
90 State Street, Ste 1515A, Albany, NY 12207
518-432-8000 Fax: 518-432-0086
e-mail: jcrane@cpcmlaw.com
James B Crane, II, Managing Partner
Governmental relations, banking & financial services, corporate law, construction law, energy, utilities, communications, land use, environmental & wireless telecommunications law

DeGraff, Foy, Kunz & Devine, LLP
90 State St, Albany, NY 12207
518-462-5300 Fax: 518-436-0210
e-mail: firm@degraff-foy.com
Web site: www.degraff-foy.com
David Kunz, Managing Partner
Government relations, administrative law & tax exempt/municipal financing, education, energy, transportation, public authorities & the environment

Fiscal Policy Institute
1 Lear Jet Lane, Latham, NY 12110
518-786-3156
e-mail: mauro@fiscalpolicy.org
Web site: www.fiscalpolicy.org
Frank Mauro, Executive Director
Nonpartisan research & education; tax, budget, economic & related public policy issues that affect quality of life & economic well-being

Fordham University, Department of Political Science
113 W 60th Street, New York, NY 10023
212-636-6334 Fax: 212-636-7153
e-mail: sbeck@fordham.edu
Susan Beck, Associate Professor of Political Science
Women in public office; importance of gender in understanding modes of governance

Geto & deMilly Inc
130 E 40th St, New York, NY 10016
212-686-4551 Fax: 212-213-6850
e-mail: pr@getodmilly.com
Ethan Geto, President
Public & government relations

NYS Bar Assn, Legislative Policy Cmte
Greenberg Traurig, LLP
54 State St, Albany, NY 12207-2505
518-689-1414 Fax: 518-689-1499
e-mail: greenbergh@gtlaw.com
Henry M Greenberg, Chair

Institute of Public Administration (The)
411 Lafayette St, Suite 303, New York, NY 10003
212-992-9898 Fax: 212-995-4876
e-mail: info@theipa.org
Web site: www.theipa.org
David Mammen, President
Non-profit research, consulting & educational institute

KPMG LLP
515 Broadway, Albany, NY 12207-2974
518-427-4600 Fax: 518-427-4620
e-mail: rhannmann@kpmg.com
Web site: www.kpmg.com
John R Miller, Vice Chair, Health Care & Public Sector
State & local government audit & advisory service

League of Women Voters of New York State
35 Maiden Lane, Albany, NY 12207-2712
518-465-4162 Fax: 518-465-0812
e-mail: rob@lwvny.org
Web site: www.lwvny.org
Rob Marchiony, Executive Director
Public policy issues forum; good government advocacy

Manhattan Institute (The)
52 Vanderbilt Ave, 2nd Fl, New York, NY 10017
212-599-7000 Fax: 212-599-3494
Web site: www.manhattan-institute.org
Lawrence J Mone, President
Research on public policy issues including taxes, welfare, crime, the legal system, urban life, race & education

Manhattan Institute for Policy Research
52 Vanderbilt Avenue, 2nd Floor, New York, NY 10017
212-599-7000 x315 Fax: 212-599-3494
e-mail: communications@manhattan-institute.org
Web site: www.manhattan-institute.org
Lindsay M Young, Executive Director, Communications
Think tank promoting the development & dissemination of new ideas that foster greater economic choice & individual responsibility

NYS Bar Assn, Court Structure & Judicial Selection Cmte
McMahon & Grow
301 N Washington St, PO Box 4350, Rome, NY 13442-4350
315-336-4700 Fax: 315-336-5851
e-mail: mgglaw@dreamscape.com
Hon Richard D Simons, Chair

Offices and agencies appear in alphabetical order.

NYS Bar Assn, Federal Constitution & Legislation Cmte
Mulholland & Knapp, LLP
641 Lexington Avenue, New York, NY 10022-4503
212-702-9027 Fax: 212-702-9092
e-mail: robknapp@mklex.com
Web site: www.mklex.com
Robert Knapp, Chair

NY Coalition of 100 Black Women - Not For Profit
PO Box 2555, Grand Central Station, New York, NY 10163
212-517-5700 Fax: 212-772-8771
Natalia Griffith, President
Leadership by example; women as advocates & agents for change in their communities in education, health, employment & community services

NY StateWatch Inc
100 State St, Ste 440, Albany, NY 12207
518-449-7425 Fax: 518-449-7431
e-mail: rob@statewatch.com
Web site: www.statewatch.com
Robert Dusablon, Executive Director
Legislative news/bill tracking service

NYS Association of Counties
111 Pine Street, Albany, NY 12207
518-465-1473 Fax: 518-465-0506
e-mail: sacquario@nysac.org
Web site: www.nysac.org
Stephen J Acquario, Executive Director
Lobbying, research & training services

NYS Bar Assn, Mass Disaster Response Committee
NYS Grievance Committee
Renaissance Plz, 335 Adams St, Ste 2400, Brooklyn, NY 11201
718-923-6300 Fax: 718-624-2978
e-mail: rsaltzma@courts.state.ny.us
Robert J Saltzman, Chair

NYS Bar Assn, Law Youth & Citizenship Committee
NYS Supreme Court
92 Franklin Street, 2ND Floor, Buffalo, NY 14202
716-845-9327 Fax: 716-858-4829
e-mail: oyoung@courts.state.ny.us
Oliver C Young, Chair

Nelson A Rockefeller Institute of Government
411 State St, Albany, NY 12203-1003
518-443-5522 Fax: 518-443-5788
e-mail: nathanr@rockinst.org
Web site: www.rockinst.org
Richard P Nathan, Director
Management & finance of welfare, health & employment of state & local governments nationally & especially in NY

New York Public Interest Research Group
9 Murray St, 3rd Fl, New York, NY 10007
212-349-6460 Fax: 212-349-1366
e-mail: nypirg@nypirg.org
Web site: www.nypirg.org
Christopher Meyer, Executive Director
Environmental preservation, public health, consumer protection & government reform

New York State Directory
185 Millerton Road, Po Box 860, Millerton, NY 12546
518-789-8700 or 800-562-2139 Fax: 518-789-0556
e-mail: customerservice@greyhouse.com
Web site: www.greyhouse.com
Leslie Mackenzie, Publisher
State government public policy directory

Oneida Indian Nation
Turning Stone Resort & Casino, Executive Offices, Patrick Road, Vernon, NY 13478
315-361-7633 Fax: 315-361-7721
Web site: www.oneida-nation.org
Ray Halbritter, Nation Repesentative & Chief Eexecutive Officer, Nation Enterprises
Tribal government

Onondaga Nation
Box 319-B, RR #1, Nedrow, NY 13120
315-492-4210 Fax: 315-469-1725
Web site: www.onondaganation.org
Irving Powless, Jr, Chief
Tribal government

Community Bankers Assn of NY State, Government Relations Cmte
Pioneer Savings Bank
21 Second St, Troy, NY 12180
518-274-4800 Fax: 518-274-3560
Web site: www.pioneersb.com
John M Scarchilli, Co-Chair

PricewaterhouseCoopers LLP
State St Ctr, 80 State St, Albany, NY 12207
518-462-2030 Fax: 518-427-4499
Web site: www.pwc.com
Rich Grant, Managing Partner

NYS Bar Assn, Civil Rights/Spec Cmte on Collateral Consequence of Criminal Proceedings
Proskauer Rose LLP
1585 Broadway, New York, NY 10036-8299
212-969-3261 Fax: 212-969-2900
e-mail: psherwin@proskauer.com
Web site: www.proskauer.com
Peter J W Sherwin, Chair

Policy Areas

Offices and agencies appear in alphabetical order.

Public Agenda
6 East 39th St, 9th Fl, New York, NY 10016
212-686-6610 Fax: 212-889-3461
e-mail: info@publicagenda.org
Web site: www.publicagenda.org
Claudia Feurey, Vice President, Communications & External
    Relations
*Nonpartisan, nonprofit organization dedicated to conducting
unbiased public opinion research & producing fair-minded citizen
education materials*

SUNY at Albany, Center for Technology in Government
187 Wolf Rd, Ste 301, Albany, NY 12205-1138
518-442-3892 Fax: 518-442-3886
e-mail: sdawes@ctg.albany.edu
Web site: www.ctg.albany.edu
Sharon S Dawes, Director
Government information management strategies

**SUNY at Albany, Center for Women in Government & Civil
Society**
135 Western Ave, Draper Hall, Rm 302, Albany, NY 12222
518-442-3900 Fax: 518-442-3877
e-mail: cwig@albany.edu
Web site: www.cwig.albany.edu
Judith R Saidel, Executive Director
*Through research, teaching, leadership development, networking &
public education, the center works to strengthen women's public
policy leadership, broaden access to policy knowledge, skills &
influence; advance equity, enhance nonprofit mgmnt*

**SUNY at Albany, Nelson A Rockefeller College of Public
Affairs & Policy**
135 Western Ave, Albany, NY 12222
518-442-5244 Fax: 518-442-5298
e-mail: thompson@albany.edu
Web site: www.albany.edu/rockefeller
Frank J Thompson, Dean
*Health policy, policy implementation, public personnel policy,
administrative politics*

SUNY at Albany, Rockefeller College
135 Western Ave, Albany, NY 12222
518-442-5378 Fax: 518-442-5298
Joseph F Zimmerman, Professor
*Intergovernmental relations; NY state & local government; ethics in
government; election systems & voting*

SUNY at New Paltz, College of Liberal Arts & Sciences
614 Faculty Tower, New Paltz, NY 12561-2499
845-257-3520 Fax: 845-257-3517
e-mail: benjamig@newpaltz.edu
Web site: www.newpaltz.edu
Gerald Benjamin, Dean & Professor of Political Science
*Local & state government process & structure; regionalism; politics
& election law*

SUNY at New Paltz, Department of History
75 South Manheim Blvd, New Paltz, NY 12561
845-257-3523 Fax: 845-257-2735
Laurence Hauptman, Professor of History
American Indian policies

Seneca Nation of Indians
G R Plummer Bldg, PO Box 231, Salamanca, NY 14779
716-945-1790 Fax: 716-945-1565
e-mail: sni@localnet.com
Web site: www.sni.org
Barry Snyder, President
Tribal government

Shinnecock Indian Nation
PO Box 5006, Southampton, NY 11969-5006
631-283-6143 Fax: 631-283-0751
e-mail: sination@optionline.net
Web site: www.shinnecocknation.com
Randy King, Chairman, Tribal Trustees
Tribal government

St Regis Mohawk Tribe
412 State Route 37, Hogansburg, NY 13655
518-358-2272 Fax: 518-358-4519
Web site: www.stregismohawktribe.com
Barbara Lazori, Chief
Tribal government

**Syracuse University, Maxwell School of Citizenship & Public
Affairs**
426 Eggers Hall, Syracuse, NY 13244-1020
315-443-3114 Fax: 315-443-1081
e-mail: ctrpol@syr.edu
Web site: www.maxwell.syr.edu
Timothy Smeeding, Professor of Public Policy; Director
Social welfare, income distribution & comparative social policies

Unkechaug Nation
Poospatuck Reservation, Box 86, Mastic, NY 11950
631-281-6464 Fax: 631-281-5859
e-mail: hwal1@aol.com
Harry Wallace, Chief
Tribal government

Offices and agencies appear in alphabetical order.

HEALTH

New York State

GOVERNOR'S OFFICE

Governor's Office
Executive Chamber
State Capitol
Albany, NY 12224
518-474-8390 Fax: 518-474-1513
Web site: www.state.ny.us

Governor:
George E Pataki 518-474-8390
Executive Director:
Kara Lanspery 518-474-8390
Secretary to the Governor:
John P Cahill. 518-474-4246
Deputy Secretary to the Governor for Health & Human Services:
Mark Kissinger. 518-408-2500
Senior Policy Advisor to the Governor:
Jeffrey Lovell 518-486-9671
Counsel to the Governor-Attorney General, Budget:
Richard Platkin. 518-474-8343
Asst Counsel to the Governor-Health, OMRDD, OASAS, Advocate for
Persons with Disabilities, Comsn on Quality of Care, Aging, Mental
Health:
Mark Ustin 518-474-8494
Director, Health Programs:
Megan Kearney 518-408-2500
Director, Communications:
David Catalfamo. 518-474-8418

EXECUTIVE DEPARTMENTS AND RELATED AGENCIES

Alcoholism & Substance Abuse Services, Office of
1450 Western Ave
Albany, NY 12203
518-473-3460 Fax: 518-457-5474
Web site: www.oasas.state.ny.us

501 7th Ave
8th Fl
New York, NY 10018
646-728-4533

Acting Commissioner:
Shari Noonan 518-457-2061
Executive Deputy Commissioner:
Vacant 518-457-1758
Counsel:
Henry F Zwack. 518-485-2312
Director, Communications:
Jennifer Farrell. 518-485-1768/fax: 518-485-6014
e-mail: jenniferfarrell@oasas.state.ny.us

Director, Human Resources Management:
Thomas M Torino. 518-457-2963
Director, Internal Audit:
Richard Kaplan. 518-485-2039
Director, Management & Information Services:
David Gardam 518-485-2351
Affirmative Action Officer:
Henry Gonzalez 518-457-2963
Public Information Officer:
Joseph Morrissey 518-485-1768
e-mail: josephmorrissey@oasas.state.ny.us

Administration Division
Assoc Commissioner:
Michael Lawler. 518-457-5312
e-mail: michaellawler@oasas.state.ny.us

Budget Management
Director:
Jay Runkel 518-485-2193

Capital Management
Director:
Laurie Felter. 518-457-2545

Federal Relations & Policy Analysis
Director:
Reba Architzel 518-485-1366

Fiscal Administration & Support Services
Director:
Vito Manzella. 518-457-4742

Health Care Financing & 3rd Party Reimbursement
Director:
Nicholas Colamaria 518-485-2207

Human Resources Management
Director:
Thomas Torino. 518-457-2963

Management & Information Services
Director:
David Gardam 518-485-2351

Prevention Services Division
Associate Commissioner:
Frances M Harding. 518-485-6022

Field Operations
Director:
Edward Freeman 518-485-1660

Program Design, System Development & Implementation
Director:
Frederick Meservey 518-485-2123

Science/Technology Transfer & Planning
Director:
John Ernst. 518-485-2132

Special Populations & Other Addictions
Director:
William Barnette 518-457-6206

Policy Areas

Offices and agencies appear in alphabetical order.

Standards & Quality Assurance Division
Associate Commissioner:
Neil Grogin 518-485-2257
Client Advocacy:
Michael Yorio 800-553-5790

Certification
Manager:
Elliott Lefkowitz 518-485-2251

Quality Assurance
Director:
Douglas Rosenberry 518-485-2260

Technical Assistance
Manager:
Joseph Burke 646-485-2249

Workforce Development
Manager:
William Lachanski 518-485-2033

Treatment Services Division
Acting Associate Commissioner:
Timothy P Williams 518-485-2322

Addiction Planning & Grants Development
Director:
Robert Ball 518-457-5989

Addiction Treatment
Director:
Thomas Nightingale 518-457-7077

Evaluation & Practice Improvement
Director:
Alan Kott 518-485-7189

Education Department
State Education Bldg
89 Washington Ave
Albany, NY 12234
518-474-3852 Fax: 518-486-5631
Web site: www.nysed.gov

Commissioner, University President:
Richard P Mills 518-474-5844
e-mail: rmills@mail.nysed.gov
Assistant to the Commissioner:
Peggy Rivers 518-474-5845
e-mail: privers@mail.nysed.gov
Counsel & Deputy Commissioner, Legal Affairs:
Kathy A Ahearn 518-474-6400
e-mail: kahearn@mail.nysed.gov

Office of the Professions . . . . fax: 518-473-2056
89 Washington Ave, EB, 2nd Fl, West Mezz, Albany, NY 12234
Fax: 518-473-2056
Web site: www.op.nysed.gov
Deputy Commissioner:
Johanna Duncan-Poitier 518-474-3817 x470
e-mail: opdepcom@mail.nysed.gov
Coordinator, Customer Service:
Tony Lofrumento 518-474-3817 x570
e-mail: op4info@mail.nysed.gov

Office of Professional Responsibility
Executive Director:
Frank Munoz 518-474-3817 x440
e-mail: opexdir@mail.nysed.gov

Professional Education Program Review
Supervisor:
Gail Rosettie 518-474-3817 x360
e-mail: opprogs@mail.nysed.gov

Professional Licensing Services
Director:
Robert G Bentley 518-474-3817 x340
e-mail: opdpls@mail.nysed.gov

State Boards for the Professions
Accupuncture, Occupational Therapy, Speech-Language Pathology & Audiology
Executive Secretary:
Vacant 518-474-3817 x100
Chiropractic
Executive Secretary:
Cynthia T Laks 518-474-3817 x190
Dentistry & Optometry
Executive Secretary:
Milton Lawney 518-474-3817 x550
Medicine, Dietetics-Nutrition, Athletic Training, Medical Physics & Veterinary Medicine
Executive Secretary:
Thomas J Monahan 518-474-3817 x560
Nursing & Respiratory Therapy
Executive Secretary:
Barbara Zittel 518-474-3817 x120
Pharmacy & Midwifery
Executive Secretary:
Lawrence H Mokhiber 518-474-3817 x130
Psychology & Massage Therapy
Executive Secretary:
Kathleen M Doyle 518-474-3817 x150
Social Work & Mental Health Practitioners
Executive Secretary:
David Hamilton 518-474-3817 x450

Health Department
Corning Tower
Empire State Plaza
Albany, NY 12237
518-474-7354
Web site: www.health.state.ny.us

Commissioner:
Antonia C Novello 518-474-2011
Executive Deputy Commissioner:
Dennis P Whalen 518-473-0458
Deputy Commissioner, Operations:
William Van Slyke 518-474-3384

AIDS Institute
Director:
Guthrie S Birkhead 518-473-7542/fax: 518-486-1455
Executive Deputy Director:
Barbara DeVore 518-473-2542
Assoc Director:
Sue Klein 518-473-7542
Director, Systems Development:
Vida Chernoff 518-402-6790
Director, Special Projects:
Andrea Small 518-473-2903
Director, Program Evaluation & Research:
James Tesoriero 518-402-6814
Medical Director:
Bruce D Agins 212-268-6142

Offices and agencies appear in alphabetical order.

HIV Health Care & Community Services
Director:
Humberto Cruz.................................518-474-7781

HIV Prevention
Director:
Daniel O'Connell............................518-473-2300
Associate Director:
Bethasbet Justiniano........................518-473-2300

Administration & Public Affairs
Deputy Commissioner:
William Van Slyke..........................518-474-3384

Fiscal Management Group
Director:
Robert W Reed...............................518-474-8565

Center for Community Health
Director:
Guthrie S Birkhead 518-474-5073/fax: 518-486-1455
Associate Director:
Ellen Anderson...............................518-474-5073

Chronic Disease Prevention & Adult Health
Director:
Mark S Baptiste.................518-474-0512/fax: 518-473-2853
Associate Director:
Thomas Blake 518-473-4438/fax: 518-473-2853

Epidemiology Division
Director:
Perry F Smith 518-474-1055/fax: 518-473-2301
Associate Director:
Karen Savicki................................518-474-4394

Family Health Division
Director:
Vacant 518-473-7922/fax: 518-473-2015
Associate Director:
Dennis P Murphy............................518-473-4441
Pediatric Director:
Christopher A Kus...........................518-474-6968

Minority Health
Director:
Wilma Waithe 518-474-2180

Nutrition Division
Director:
Patricia Hess...................518-402-7090/fax: 518-458-5508
Associate Director:
Mary Warr Cowans...........................518-402-7090

Center for Environmental Health...........fax: 518-402-7509
547 River St, Troy, NY 12180
Director:
Ronald Tramontano 518-402-7500

Division of Environmental Health Investigation
Associate Director:
G Anders Carlson............................518-402-7501

Environmental Health Assessment Division
Director:
Nancy Kim...................................518-402-7511
Assoc Director:
John Wilson 518-402-7511

Environmental Protection
Director:
Allison Wakeman.............................518-402-7510

Executive Offices

Executive & Advisory Council Operations
Director:
Karen Westervelt 518-474-8009
Assistant Director:
Donna Peterson 518-474-8009

Governmental Affairs
Assistant Commissioner:
Martha G McHugh 518-473-1124/fax: 518-473-9674
Legislative Counsel:
Kelly Seebold...............................518-473-1124

Health Research Inc
One University Place, Rensselaer, NY 12144
Web site: www.hrinet.org
Executive Director:
Michael Nazarko 518-431-1204

Managed Care Office
Director:
Kathleen Shure 518-474-1590/fax: 518-474-5738
Deputy Director:
Donna J Frescatore..........................518-474-5737
Medical Director:
Foster Gesten 518-486-6865

Medicaid Management Office
Deputy Commissioner:
Kathryn Kuhmerker 518-474-3018/fax: 518-486-6852
Deputy Director:
Vacant.....................................518-474-8646
Medical Director:
Harvey R Bernard 518-473-5876
Consumer & Local District Relations
Director:
Betty Rice 518-474-9138
Finance & Insurance
Director:
Stuart Feuerstein 518-478-1020
NYS Partnership for Long Term Care
Web site: www.nyspltc.org
Director:
Adrianna Takada.........................518-474-0662
Provider Relations
Director:
Joan Johnson 518-473-7735

School of Public Health, SUNY at Albany ....fax: 518-402-0414
One University Pl, Rensselaer, NY 12144
518-402-0283 Fax: 518-402-0414
Dean:
Peter J Levin 518-402-0281/fax: 518-402-0329

Task Force On Life & The Law
5 Penn Plaza, New York, NY 10001
Executive Director:
Tia Powell 212-268-6709
Counsel:
John Renehan...............................212-268-6714
Policy Analyst:
Kelly Pike.................................212-268-6714

Health Facilities Management
Acting Director:
Val S Gray.....................518-474-2772/fax: 518-474-0611

Helen Hayes Hospital
Rte 9W, West Haverstraw, NY 10993-1195

Policy Areas

Offices and agencies appear in alphabetical order.

845-786-4000
Web site: www.helenhayeshospital.org
Director:
Magdalena Ramirez 845-786-4202/fax: 845-947-0036
Deputy Director:
Edmund Zybert. 845-786-4201

New York State Veterans' Home at Batavia
220 Richmond Ave, Batavia, NY 14020
585-345-2049
Administrator:
Joanne I Hernick 585-345-2069/fax: 585-345-9030
Director, Nursing:
Barbara Bates 585-345-2000 x2041

New York State Veterans' Home at Montrose . . . . . . fax: 914-788-6100
2090 Albany Post Rd, Montrose, NY 10548
Administrator:
Oscar Carter 914-788-6000
Medical Director:
Cheryl Ziemba 914-788-6000

New York State Veterans' Home at Oxford
4211 State Highway 220, Oxford, NY 13830
607-843-3121
Administrator:
Vathsala Venugopalan 607-843-3129/fax: 607-843-3199
Medical Director:
Philip Dzwonczyk 607-843-3140

New York State Veterans' Home at St Albans
178-50 Linden Blvd, Jamaica, NY 11434-1467
718-990-0353
Administrator:
Neville Goldson 718-990-0329
Director, Nursing:
Elaine Boy-Brown 718-990-0316

Health Systems Management Office
Director:
David Wollner 518-474-7028

Health Care Financing
Assistant Director:
Mark Van Guysling. 518-474-6350/fax: 518-486-1346
Continuing Care Office
Director, Bureau of Surveillance & Quality Assurance:
Kristin Armstrong-Ross 518-408-1282/fax: 518-408-1287

Health Care Standards & Surveillance Division
Assistant Director:
Lisa McMurdo. 518-402-1040/fax: 518-402-1042

Health Facility Planning Division
Assistant Director:
Neil Benjamin 518-402-0967/fax: 518-402-0971

Professional Medical Conduct
Director:
Dennis Graziano. 518-402-0855

Review & Analysis
Director:
Thomas M Jung 518-402-0904

Human Resources & Operations
Director:
Darcy Williams. 518-486-4976

Human Resources Management Group
Director:
John R Conroy. 518-473-3394/fax: 518-486-7374

Operations Management Group
Director:
Colleen Driscoll 518-474-6936/fax: 518-474-8163

Information Systems & Health Statistics Group
Director:
Brian Y Scott. 518-474-8373/fax: 518-474-2288

Administrative Operations - Broadway
Director:
Peter Carucci 518-474-5245

Administrative Operations - Tower
Director:
Michael Ellrott 518-474-1301

HEALTHCOM Services
Director:
Janet Carmack 518-473-2902

Legal Affairs
General Counsel:
Donald P Berens, Jr. 518-474-7553/fax: 518-473-2802
Deputy Counsel:
James Dering 518-473-3818

Professional Medical Conduct
Chief Counsel:
Brian M Murphy 518-473-4282

Regulatory Reform
Director:
Margaret Buhrmaster 518-473-7488/fax: 518-486-4834

Planning, Policy & Resource Development Division
Deputy Commissioner:
Judith Arnold. 518-474-0180/fax: 518-474-3295
Associate Director:
Linda B Stackman 518-473-7541

Council on Graduate Medical Education
Executive Director:
Thomas F Burke 518-473-3513/fax: 518-473-8434

Regional/Area Offices

Capital District Regional Office
Frear Bldg, One Fulton St, Troy, NY 12180-3281
518-408-5300
Regional Co-Director:
Bruce Fage 518-408-5277
Regional Co-Director:
Geraldine Bunn 518-408-5277

Central New York Regional Office
217 So Salina St, Syracuse, NY 13202-1380
315-477-8100
Assoc Director:
Ronald Heerkens 315-477-8484
Assoc Director:
Pauline Frazier 315-477-8485

Metropolitan Area/Regional Office
5 Penn Plaza, New York, NY 10001-1803
212-268-6880
Regional Director:
Celeste M Johnson 212-268-7185
Deputy Regional Director:
Elizabeth C Tomson. 212-268-7215

Western Regional Office
584 Delaware Ave, Buffalo, NY 14202-1295
716-847-4500

Offices and agencies appear in alphabetical order.

Assoc Commissioner:
 Salvatore W Page 716-847-4302
Assistant Regional Director:
 Michael Linse 716-423-8041

Roswell Park Cancer Institute Corporation
Elm & Carlton Streets, Buffalo, NY 14263-0999
716-845-2300
Web site: www.roswellpark.org
President, CEO:
 David C Hohn 716-845-5770/fax: 716-845-8261
Executive VP:
 Virginia Oppiare 716-845-3385
Medical Director:
 Judy Smith 716-845-7724
Senior VP, Scientific Admin:
 Youcef Rustum 716-845-2389
Legal Counsel:
 Michael Sexton 716-845-5770
Executive Director, Government Affairs:
 Lisa Damiani 716-845-3079
 e-mail: lisa.damiani@roswellpark.org

Wadsworth Center
Director:
 Lawrence S Sturman 518-474-7592/fax: 518-474-3439
Deputy Director:
 David Martin 518-474-3157
Director, Education:
 Kathy Zdeb 518-474-6713/fax: 518-474-5049
Director, Extramural Funding:
 Martin Sorin 518-486-3882/fax: 518-474-3439
Director, Policy & Planning:
 Ann Willey 518-486-2523/fax: 518-474-3439
Director, Quality Assurance:
 Richard Jenny 518-474-2133/fax: 518-474-3439
Director, Research:
 Robert Trimble 518-474-5511/fax: 518-402-5540

Environmental Disease Prevention
Director:
 George Eadon 518-474-4170/fax: 518-486-1505
Deputy Director:
 Laurence Kaminsky 518-474-4920

Genetic Disorders
Director:
 Marlene Belfort 518-473-3345/fax: 518-474-3181
Deputy Director:
 Kenneth Pass 518-473-1993/fax: 518-486-2095

Herbert W Dickerman Library
Director:
 Thomas Flynn 518-474-6172/fax: 518-474-3933

Infectious Disease
Director:
 Harry Taber 518-474-8660/fax: 518-473-1326
Deputy Director:
 Ron Limberger 518-474-4177/fax: 518-486-7971

Laboratory Operations
Director:
 William J Kerr 518-474-1152/fax: 518-474-3439

Molecular Medicine
Director:
 Carmen Mannella 518-474-2462/fax: 518-402-5381
Deputy Director:
 Thomas Ryan 518-474-6193

Insurance Department
25 Beaver St
New York, NY 10004
212-480-6400
Web site: www.ins.state.ny.us

One Commerce Plaza
Albany, NY 12257
518-474-4567
Fax: 518-473-4600

Acting Superintendent:
 Howard Mills 518-474-4567

Health Bureau
Co-Chief, NYC:
 Charles Rapacciulo 212-480-5120/fax: 212-480-5216
Chief, Accident & Health Rating:
 James M Gutterman 518-474-5394

Life Bureau
Chief Examiner:
 Jeffrey Angelo 212-480-5026

Public Affairs & Research Bureau
Director:
 Michael Barry 212-480-5262/fax: 212-480-6077
 e-mail: public-affairs@ins.state.ny.us

Labor Department
Building 12
Room 500, State Campus
Albany, NY 12240
518-457-2741 Fax: 518-457-6908
e-mail: nysdol@labor.state.ny.us
Web site: www.labor.state.ny.us

345 Hudson St, Ste 8301
Box 662, Mail Stop 01
New York, NY 10014-0662
212-352-6000
Fax: 212-352-6824

Commissioner:
 Linda Angello 518-457-2746
Director, Communications:
 Robert Lillpopp 518-457-5519/fax: 518-485-1126

Worker Protection
Deputy Commissioner, Workforce Protection, Standards & Licensing:
 Connie Varcasia 518-457-4317

Safety & Health Division
Director:
 Anthony Germano 518-457-3518/fax: 518-457-1519
 Asbestos Control Bureau
 Program Manager:
  Wallace Renfrew 518-457-1255/fax: 518-485-8054
 Industry Inspection Unit
 Program Manager:
  David Ruppert 518-457-1327/fax: 518-485-8054
 On-Site Consultation Unit
 Program Manager:
  James Rush 518-457-2238/fax: 518-457-3454

Offices and agencies appear in alphabetical order.

Policy Areas

Public Employees Safety & Health (PESH) Unit
Program Manager:
Maureen Cox 518-457-1263/fax: 518-457-5545
Radiological Health Unit
Principal Radiophysicist:
Clayton Bradt 518-457-1202/fax: 518-485-7406

Law Department
State Capitol
Albany, NY 12224-0341
518-474-7330 Fax: 518-402-2472
Web site: www.oag.state.ny.us

120 Broadway
New York, NY 10271-0332
212-416-8000
Fax: 212-416-8942

Attorney General:
Eliot Spitzer 518-474-7330
First Deputy Attorney General:
Michele Hirshman 212-416-8050
Director, Public Information & Correspondence:
Peter A Drago 518-474-7330/fax: 518-402-2472

Criminal Division
Deputy Attorney General:
Peter B Pope 212-416-8058/fax: 212-416-8026
Assistant Deputy Attorney General:
Karen Lupuloff 212-416-8090/fax: 212-416-8026

Medicaid Fraud Control Unit
120 Broadway, 13th Fl, New York, NY 10271-0007
Deputy Attorney General-in-Charge:
William J Comisky 212-417-5250/fax: 212-417-5274
First Asst Dep Attny General:
Peter M Bloch 212-417-5261/fax: 212-417-5274
Assistant Deputy Attorney General:
George Quinlan 716-853-8584
Regional Director, Albany:
Steve Krantz 518-474-3032/fax: 518-474-4519
Deputy Regional Director, Buffalo:
Gary A Baldauf 716-853-8507/fax: 716-853-8525
Regional Director, Long Island:
Alan Buonpastore 631-952-6400/fax: 631-952-6382
Regional Dir, NYC:
Richard Harrow 212-417-5391/fax: 212-417-4725
Regional Director, Rochester:
Jerry Solomon 716-262-2860/fax: 716-262-2866
Regional Director, Syracuse:
Ralph Tortora, III 315-423-1121/fax: 315-423-1120
Deputy Regional Director, Westchester/Rockland:
Anne Jardine 845-732-7500/fax: 845-732-7555
Regional Director for Special Projects Unit:
Pat Lupinetti 845-732-7550/fax: 845-732-7557

Public Advocacy Division
Acting Deputy Attorney General:
Terryl Brown Clemons 212-416-8041/fax: 212-416-8068
Special Counsel:
Mary Ellen Burns 212-416-6155

Healthcare Bureau
Bureau Chief:
Joseph R Baker, III 212-416-8521/fax: 212-416-8034

State Counsel Division
Deputy Attorney General:
Richard Rifkin 518-473-7190

Claims Bureau
Bureau Chief:
Susan Pogoda 212-416-8516/fax: 212-416-8946

Litigation Bureau
Bureau Chief, Albany:
Bruce D Feldman 518-473-8238/fax: 518-473-1572
Bureau Chief, NYC:
James B Henley 212-416-8523/fax: 212-416-6075

CORPORATIONS, AUTHORITIES AND COMMISSIONS

New York State Dormitory Authority
515 Broadway
Albany, NY 12207-2964
518-257-3000 Fax: 518-257-3100
e-mail: dabonds@dasny.org
Web site: www.dasny.org

539 Franklin St
Buffalo, NY 14202-1109
716-884-9780
Fax: 716-884-9787

One Penn Plaza
52nd Fl
New York, NY 10119-0098
212-273-5000
Fax: 212-273-5121

Chair:
Gail H Gordon 518-257-3180/fax: 518-257-3183
Executive Director:
Maryanne Gridley 518-257-3180/fax: 518-257-3183
Deputy Executive Director:
Michael T Corrigan 518-257-3192/fax: 518-257-3183
CFO:
John G Pasicznyk 518-257-3630/fax: 518-257-3100
e-mail: jpasiczn@dasny.org
General Counsel:
Jeffrey M Pohl 518-257-3120/fax: 518-257-3101
e-mail: jpohl@dasny.org
Managing Director, Construction:
Douglas M VanVleck 518-257-3200/fax: 518-257-3100
e-mail: dvanvlec@dasny.org
Managing Director, Policy & Program Development:
Lora K Lefebvre 518-257-3163/fax: 518-257-3387
e-mail: llefebvr@dasny.org
Managing Director, Public Finance:
Cheryl Ishmael 518-257-3362/fax: 518-257-3100
e-mail: cishmael@dasny.org
Director, Communications & Marketing:
Paul Burgdorf 518-257-3380/fax: 518-257-3387
e-mail: pburgdor@dasny.org
Press Officer:
Claudia Hutton 518-257-3382/fax: 518-257-3387
e-mail: chutton@dasny.org

NEW YORK STATE LEGISLATURE

See Legislative Branch in Section 1 for additional Standing Committee and Subcommittee information.

Assembly Standing Committees

Aging
Chair:
Steven C Englebright (D) 518-455-4804
Ranking Minority Member:
Andrew P Raia (R) 518-455-5952

Alcoholism & Drug Abuse
Chair:
Jeffrey Dinowitz (D) 518-455-5965
Ranking Minority Member:
Jack Quinn 518-455-4462

Children & Families
Chair:
William Scarborough 518-455-4451
Ranking Minority Member:
Joseph A Errigo (R) 518-455-5662

Consumer Affairs & Protection
Chair:
Audrey I Pheffer (D) 518-455-4292
Ranking Minority Member:
David G McDonough (R) 518-455-4633

Health
Chair:
Richard N Gottfried (D) 518-455-4941
Ranking Minority Member:
Maureen C O'Connell (R) 518-455-5341

Senate Standing Committees

Aging
Chair:
Martin J Golden (R) 518-455-2730
Ranking Minority Member:
Carl Kruger (D) 518-455-2460

Alcoholism & Drug Abuse
Chair:
Vacant 518-455-3563
Ranking Minority Member:
Ruben Diaz, Sr (D) 518-455-2511

Children & Families
Chair:
Mary Lou Rath (R) 518-455-3161
Ranking Minority Member:
Velmanette Montgomery (D) 518-455-3451

Consumer Protection
Chair:
Charles J Fuschillo, Jr (R) 518-455-3341
Ranking Minority Member:
Jeffrey D Klein (D) 518-455-3595

Health
Chair:
Kemp Hannon (R) 518-455-2200
Ranking Minority Member:
John L Sampson (D) 518-455-2788

Senate/Assembly Legislative Commissions

Health Care Financing, Council on
Senate Chair:
Joseph L Bruno (R) 518-455-3191
Assembly Vice Chair:
Alexander B Grannis (D) 518-455-5676
Executive Director:
Al Cardillo 518-455-2067/fax: 518-426-6925

Toxic Substances & Hazardous Wastes, Legislative Commission on
Senate Chair:
Vacant 518-455-0000
Assembly Vice Chair:
David R Koon (D) 518-455-5784
Program Manager:
Richard D Morse, Jr 518-455-3711/fax: 518-455-3837

U.S. Government

EXECUTIVE DEPARTMENTS AND RELATED AGENCIES

US Department of Agriculture
Web site: www.usda.gov

Food & Nutrition Service

Albany Field Office
O'Brien Federal Bldg, Rm 752, Clinton Ave & N Pearl St, Albany, NY 12207
Officer in Charge:
Claudia Ortiz 518-431-4274/fax: 518-431-4271
e-mail: claudia.ortiz@FNS.usda.gov

New York City Field Office . . . . fax: 212-620-6948
201 Varick St, Rm 609, New York, NY 10014

Assistant Director:
Angela Mackey 212-620-7360

Rochester Field Office
Federal Bldg, 100 State St, Rm 318, Rochester, NY 14614
Officer in Chg:
Claudia Ortiz 585-263-6748/fax: 585-263-5807
e-mail: claudia.ortiz@FNS.usda.gov

Food Safety & Inspection Service
Web site: www.fsis.usda.gov

Field Operations-Albany District Office . . . . fax: 518-452-3118
230 Washington Ave Ext, Albany, NY 12203-5388
District Manager:
Louis C Leny 518-452-6870

Offices and agencies appear in alphabetical order.

US Department of Health & Human Services
Web site: www.os.dhhs.gov; www.hhs.gov/region2/

Administration for Children & Families .... fax: 212-264-4881
26 Federal Plaza, Rm 4114, New York, NY 10278
Fax: 212-264-4881
Web site: www.acf.hhs.gov
Regional Administrator:
MaryAnn Higgins 212-264-2890 x103
e-mail: mhiggins@acf.hhs.gov

Administration on Aging . . . . fax: 212-264-0114
26 Federal Plaza, Rm 38-102, New York, NY 10278
Fax: 212-264-0114
Web site: www.aoa.gov
Regional Administrator:
Robert F O'Connell 212-264-2976
e-mail: robert.oconnell@aoa.gov

Centers for Disease Control & Prevention
Web site: www.cdc.gov

Agency for Toxic Substances & Disease Registry (ATSDR)-EPA Region 2
290 Broadway, 28th Fl, New York, NY 10007
Web site: www.atsdr.cdc.gov
Senior Regional Representative:
Arthur Block 212-637-4305/fax: 212-637-3253

New York Quarantine Station
Terminal 4E, Rm 219 016, JFK Airport, Jamaica, NY 11430-1081
Officer-in-Charge:
Margaret A Becker 718-553-1685/fax: 718-553-1524

Centers for Medicare & Medicaid Services
26 Federal Plaza, Rm 3811, New York, NY 10278
Web site: www.cms.hhs.gov
Regional Administrator:
James T Kerr 212-616-2205/fax: 212-264-6189
e-mail: jkerr@cms.hhs.gov
Deputy Regional Administrator:
Gilbert Kunken 212-616-2205/fax: 212-264-6189
e-mail: gkunken@cms.hhs.gov

Medicaid and Children's Health (DMCH)
Associate Regional Administrator:
Sue Kelly 212-616-2428/fax: 212-264-6814
e-mail: skelly@cms.hhs.gov

Medicare Financial Management (DMFM)
Associate Regional Administrator:
Peter Reisman 212-616-2505/fax: 212-264-2790
e-mail: preisman@cms.hhs.gov

Medicare Operations Division (DMO)
Associate Regional Administrator:
Jose Mirabal 212-616-2333/fax: 212-264-2665
e-mail: jmirabal@cms.hhs.gov

Food & Drug Administration
Web site: www.fda.gov

Northeast Region
158-15 Liberty Ave, Jamaica, NY 11433
Regional Director:
Diana Kolaitis 718-662-5416/fax: 718-662-5434
New York District Office
District Director:
Jerome Woyshner 718-662-5447/fax: 718-662-5665
Northeast Regional Laboratory
158-15 Liberty Ave, Queens, NY 11433

Director:
Vacant 718-662-5450/fax: 718-662-5439

Health Resources & Svcs Admin Office of Performance Review . . . . fax: 212-264-2673
26 Federal Bldg, Rm 3337, New York, NY 10278
Regional Division Director:
Ron Moss 212-264-2664
e-mail: robert.moss@hrsa.hhs.gov
Operations Director:
Margaret Lee 212-264-2571
e-mail: margaret.lee@hrsa.hhs.gov
Director, Office of Engineering Services:
Emilio Pucillo. 212-264-3600
e-mail: emilio.pucillo@hrsa.hhs.gov

Indian Health Services-Area Office . . . . fax: 615-467-1501
711 Stewarts Ferry Pike, Nashville, TN 37214-2634
Director:
Richie Grinnell 615-467-1500

Office of Secretary's Regional Representative-Region 2-NY . . . . fax: 212-264-3620
26 Federal Plaza, Rm 3835, New York, NY 10278
Regional Director:
Deborah Konopko 212-264-4600
e-mail: deborah.konopko@hhs.gov
Senior Intergovernmental Affairs Specialist:
Joel S Truman. 212-264-4600
e-mail: joel.truman@hhs.gov
Intergovernmental Affairs Specialist:
Katherine Williams. 212-264-4600
e-mail: katherine.williams@hhs.gov

Office for Civil Rights. . . . . fax: 212-264-3039
26 Federal Plaza, Rm 3312, New York, NY 10278
Fax: 212-264-3039
Web site: www.hhs.gov/ocr
Regional Manager:
Michael Carter. 212-264-3313/fax: 212-264-3039
Deputy Regional Manager:
Linda Colon 212-264-3313

Office of General Counsel
26 Federal Plaza, Rm 3908, New York, NY 10278
Chief Counsel:
Annette H Blum 212-264-6373
e-mail: annette.blum@hhs.gov

Office of Inspector General
Regional Inspector General, Audit:
Timothy Horgan. 212-264-4620
e-mail: t.horgan@oig.hhs.gov
Regional Inspector General & Regional Coordinator, Investigations:
Brian Smith 212-264-1691
e-mail: b.smith@oig.hhs.gov
Regional Inspector General, Evaluations & Inspections:
Linda Ragone 212-264-1998
e-mail: lragone@oig.hhs.gov

Office of Public Health & Science
26 Federal Plaza, Rm 3835, New York, NY 10278
Regional Health Administrator:
Robert Amler 212-264-2560
e-mail: ramler@osophs.dhhs.gov
Deputy Regional Health Administrator:
Robert L Davidson 212-264-2560
Regional Family Planning Consultant:
Robin Lane. 212-264-3935
e-mail: rlane@osophs.hhs.gov

Offices and agencies appear in alphabetical order.

Regional Minority Health Consultant:
Claude Colimon 212-264-2560
Regional Women's Health Coordinator:
Sandra Estepa. 212-264-2560

US Department of Homeland Security (DHS)
Web site: www.dhs.gov

Federal Emergency Management Agency (FEMA)

National Disaster Medical System . . . . fax: 212-680-3608
26 Federal Plz, Rm 3835, New York, NY 10278
Coordinator:
Captain Bonita Pyler, USPHS 212-680-8542
e-mail: pyler@dhs.gov

New York Regional Office . . . . fax: 212-680-3681
26 Federal Plz, Ste 1311, New York, NY 10278
Acting Regional Director:
Joseph F Picciano. 212-680-3612

US Labor Department
Web site: www.dol.gov

Occupational Safety & Health Adminstration (OSHA)
201 Varick St, Rm 670, New York, NY 10014
212-337-2378
Web site: www.osha.gov
Regional Administrator:
Patricia K Clark. 212-337-2378/fax: 212-337-2371
Acting Deputy Reg Administrator:
Louis Ricca. 212-337-2326

Albany Area Office
401 New Karner Rd, Ste 300, Albany, NY 12205-3809
Area Director:
John M Tomich 518-464-4338/fax: 518-464-4337

Bayside Area Office
42-40 Bell Blvd, 5th Fl, Bayside, NY 11361
Area Director:
Harvey Shapiro 718-279-9060/fax: 718-279-9057

Buffalo Area Office
5360 Genesee St, Browmansville, NY 14026
Area Director:
Art Dube 716-684-3891/fax: 716-684-3896

Manhattan Area Office
201 Varick St, Rm 908, New York, NY 10014
Area Director:
Richard Mendelson 212-620-3200/fax: 212-620-4121

Syracuse Area Office
3300 Vickery Rd, North Syracuse, NY 13212
Area Director:
Christopher Adams 315-451-0808/fax: 315-451-1351

Tarrytown Area Office
660 White Plains Rd, Tarrytown, NY 10591
Area Director:
Diana Cortez 914-524-7510/fax: 914-524-7515

U.S. CONGRESS

See U.S. Congress Chapter for additional Standing Committee and Subcommittee information.

House of Representatives Standing Committees

Agriculture
Chair:
Robert Goodlatte (R-VA). 202-225-2171
Ranking Minority Member:
Collin C Peterson (D-MN) 202-225-2165

Subcommittee
Department Operations, Oversight, Nutrition & Forestry
Chair:
Gil Gutknecht (R-MN) 202-225-2472
Ranking Minority Member:
Joe Baca (D-CA) 202-225-6161

Energy & Commerce
Chair:
Joe Barton (R-TX) 202-225-6673
Ranking Minority Member:
John D Dingell (D-MI). 202-225-4071
New York Delegate:
Eliot L Engel (D) 202-225-2464
New York Delegate:
Vito Fossella (R). 202-225-3371
New York Delegate:
Edolphus Towns (D). 202-225-5936

Subcommittee
Health
Chair:
Nathan Deal (R-GA) 202-225-5211
Ranking Minority Member:
Sherrod Brown (D-OH). 202-225-3401
New York Delegate:
Eliot L Engel (D) 202-225-2464

Ways & Means
Chair:
William M Thomas (R-CA) 202-225-2915
Ranking Minority Member:
Charles B Rangel (D-NY) 202-225-4365
New York Delegate:
Michael R McNulty (D) 202-225-5076
New York Delegate:
Thomas M Reynolds (R) 202-225-5265

Subcommittee
Health
Chair:
Nancy L Johnson (R-CT) 202-225-4476
Ranking Minority Mbr:
Fortney Pete Stark (D-CA) 202-225-5065

Senate Standing Committees

Aging, Special Committee on
Chair:
Gordon Smith (R-OR) 202-224-3753
Ranking Minority Member:
Herb Kohl (D-WI) 202-224-5653

Agriculture, Nutrition & Forestry
Chair:
C Saxby Chambliss (R-GA). 202-224-3521
Ranking Minority Member:
Tom Harkin (D-IA) 202-224-3254

Health, Education, Labor & Pensions

Chair:
Michael Enzi (R-WY) 202-224-3324
Ranking Minority Member:
Edward M Kennedy (D-MA) 202-224-4543
New York Delegate:
Hillary Rodham Clinton (D). 202-224-4451

Subcommittees

Bioterrorism Preparedness & Public Health
Chair:
Michael Devine (R-OH) 202-224-2315

Ranking Minority Member:
Edward M Kennedy (D-MA) 202-224-4543
Retirement Security & Aging
Chair:
Michael Devine (R-OH) 202-224-2315
Ranking Minority Member:
Barbara A Mikulski (D-MD). 202-224-4654
New York Delegate:
Hillary Rodham Clinton (D) 202-224-4451

Private Sector

AIDS Council of Northeastern New York

927 Broadway, Albany, NY 12207-1306
518-434-4686 Fax: 518-427-8184
e-mail: info@aidscouncil.org
Web site: www.aidscouncil.org
Michele McClave, Executive Director
Provide HIV/AIDS education & outreach to at-risk individuals & the public; offer direct assistance & service coordination; serve as public advocates

Adelphi NY Statewide Breast Cancer Hotline & Support Program

School of Social Work, Adelphi University, Garden City, NY 11530
800-877-8077 or 516-877-4320 Fax: 516-877-4336
Web site: www.adelphi.edu/nysbreastcancer
Hillary Rutter, Director
Breast cancer information & referral hotline; community education, support groups, counseling & advocacy

Alzheimer's Association, Northeastern NY

85 Watervliet Ave, Albany, NY 12206
518-438-2217 Fax: 518-438-2219
e-mail: marvin.leroy@alz.org
Web site: www.alzneny.org
Monika Boekmann, President & Chief Executive Officer

American Cancer Society-Eastern Division

19 Dove St, Ste 103, Albany, NY 12210
518-449-5438 Fax: 518-449-7283
e-mail: michael.bopp@cancer.org
Web site: www.cancer.org
Michael Bopp, Director, Advocacy for NY State

American College of Nurse-Midwives, NYC Chapter

450 Clarkson Ave, Box 1227, Brooklyn, NY 11203-2098
718-270-7759 Fax: 718-270-7634
e-mail: gholmes@downstate.edu
Web site: www.nysmidwives.org; www.nyc.org
Grace Holmes, Chair
Midwifery/women's health

American College of Obstetricians & Gynecologists/NYS

152 Washington Ave, Albany, NY 12210
518-436-3461 Fax: 518-426-4728
e-mail: info@ny.acog.org
Web site: www.acog.org/goto/nys
Donna Montalto Williams, Executive Director
Women's health care & physician education

American College of Physicians, New York Chapter

100 State St, Ste 700, Albany, NY 12207
518-427-0366 Fax: 518-427-1991
Web site: www.acponline.org/chapters/ny
Linda Lambert, Executive Director
Develops & advocates policies on health issues

American Heart Association Northeast Affiliate

PO Box 3049, Syracuse, NY 13220-3049
Fax: 315-641-1098
e-mail: csugrue@heart.org
Web site: www.americanheart.org
William J Sugrue, Jr, Executive Vice President
Research, education & community service to reduce disability & death from heart disease & stroke

American Infertility Association

666 Fifth Ave, Ste 278, New York, NY 10103
888-917-3777 or 718-621-5083 Fax: 718-601-7722
e-mail: info@americaninfertility.org
Web site: www.americaninfertility.org
Pamela Madsen, Executive Director
Infertility, reproductive disorders, adoption; education, research, advocacy, support & referral

American Liver Foundation, Western NY Chapter

25 Canterbury Rd, Ste 316, Rochester, NY 14607
585-271-2859 Fax: 585-271-8642
e-mail: livrlady@aol.com
Web site: www.liverfoundation.org
Nancy Koris, Executive Director
Disease research, public education & patient support

Offices and agencies appear in alphabetical order.

American Lung Association of NYS Inc
3 Winners Circle, Ste 300, Albany, NY 12205-1187
518-453-0172 x308 Fax: 518-489-5864
e-mail: tnichols@alanys.org
Web site: www.alanys.org
Timothy Nichols, Director, Government Affairs
To prevent lung disease & promote lung health

Associated Medical Schools of New York
10 Rockefeller Plaza, Suite 1120, New York, NY 10020
212-218-4610 Fax: 212-218-5644
e-mail: jo.wiederhorn@amsny.org
Web site: www.amsny.org
Jo Wiederhorn, Executive Director
AMS is a consortium of the fourteen public and private medical schools in New York state. Our mission is to support quality health care in NYS through the continual strengthening of medical education, medical care, and medical research.

Association of Military Surgeons of the US (AMSUS), NY Chapter
105 Franklin Ave, Malverne, NY 11565-1926
516-542-0025 Fax: 516-593-3114
e-mail: amsusny@aol.com
Col John J Hassett, USAR, President NY Chapter
Improve federal healthcare service; support & represent military & other health care professionals

Bausch & Lomb Inc
One Bausch & Lomb Place, Rochester, NY 14604-2701
585-338-6000 Fax: 585-338-6007
Web site: www.bausch.com
Meg Graham, Vice President, Corporate Communication
Development, manufacture & marketing of contact lenses & lens care products, opthalmic surgical & pharmaceutical products

Bellevue Hospital Center, Emergency Care Institute
1st Ave & 27th St, Rm A-345, New York, NY 10016
212-562-3346 Fax: 212-562-3001
e-mail: goldfl03@popmail.med.nyu.edu
Lewis Goldfrank, Director, Emergency Medicine
Emergency medicine; medical toxicology

Brain Injury Association of NYS (BIANYS)
10 Colvin Ave, Albany, NY 12206
518-459-7911 Fax: 518-482-5285
e-mail: info@bianys.org
Web site: www.bianys.org
Judith I Avner, Executive Director
Public education & advocacy for brain injury persons & their families

Bristol-Myers Squibb Co
PO Box 4755, Syracuse, NY 13221-4755
315-432-2709 Fax: 315-432-2619
Web site: www.bms.com
Pamela M Brunet, Manager of Community Affairs
Develops & markets pharmaceuticals

Bronx-Lebanon Hospital Center
1276 Fulton Ave, Bronx, NY 10456
718-901-8595 Fax: 718-299-5447
Web site: www.bronxcare.org
Errol Schneer, Vice President-Planning, Marketing & Public Relations

Capital District Physicians' Health Plan Inc
Patroon Creek Corp Ctr, 1223 Washington Ave, Albany, NY 12206
518-641-5561 Fax: 518-641-5506
e-mail: info@cdphp.com
Web site: www.cdphp.com
Stephen R Sloan, Senior Vice President, Legal Affairs & Chief Counsel
Health insurance

Cerebral Palsy Association of New York State
90 State St, Ste 929, Albany, NY 12207-1709
518-436-0178 Fax: 518-436-8619
e-mail: malvaro@cpofnys.org
Web site: www.cpofnys.org
Michael Alvaro, Associate Executive Director
Advocate & provide direct services with & for individuals with cerebral palsy & other significant disabilities, & their families

Coalition of Fathers & Families NY
PO Box 782, Clifton Park, NY 12065
518-383-8202 Fax: 518-383-8202
e-mail: dadlobby@localnet.com
Web site: www.fafny.org/fafnypac.htm
James Hays, President
Working to keep fathers and families together

Columbia University, Mailman School of Public Health
Heilbrunn Dept of Population & Family He, 60 Haven Ave, B-2, New York, NY 10032
212-304-5281 Fax: 212-305-7024
e-mail: lpf1@columbia.edu
Web site: cpmcnet.columbia.edu/dept/sph/popfam
Lynn P Freedman, Associate Professor & Director
Theory, analysis & development of policy & programs supporting public health & human rights

Columbia University, Mailman School of Public Health, Center for Public Health
722 W 168th St, Ste 522, New York, NY 10032
212-342-1290 Fax: 212-543-8793
e-mail: eng9@columbia.edu
Web site: www.cpmcnet.columbia.edu/dept/sph
Eric N Gebbie, Project Coordinator

Commissioned Officers Assn of the US Public Health Svc Inc (COA)
8201 Corporate Dr, Ste 200, Landover, MD 20785
301-731-9080 Fax: 301-731-9084
e-mail: gfarrell@coausphs.org
Web site: www.coausphs.org
Jerry Farrell, Executive Director
Committed to improving the public health of the US; supports corps officers & advocates for their interests through leadership, education & communication

Offices and agencies appear in alphabetical order.

Policy Areas

Committee of Methadone Program Administrators Inc of NYS (COMPA)
1 Columbia Place, 4th Fl, Albany, NY 12207
518-689-0457 Fax: 518-426-1046
e-mail: compahb@hotmail.com
Web site: www.compa-ny.org
Henry Bartlett, Executive Director
Methadone treatment & substance abuse coalition building; advocacy, community education, standards & regulatory review & policy development

Commonwealth Fund
One E 75th St, New York, NY 10021-2692
212-603-3800 Fax: 212-606-3500
e-mail: cmwf@cmwf.org
Web site: www.cmwf.org
Karen Davis, President
Supports independent research on health access, coverage & quality issues affecting minorities, women, elderly & low income

Community Health Care Association of NYS
254 West 31st Street, 9th Fl, New York, NY 10001
212-279-9686 Fax: 212-279-3851
e-mail: skee@chcanys.org
Web site: www.chcanys.org
Sheila K Kee, Chief Executive Officer
Advocacy, education & services for the medically underserved throughout NYS

Continuum Health Partners Inc
555 West 57th, 18th Fl, New York, NY 10019
212-523-7772 Fax: 212-523-7885
e-mail: jmandler@bethisraelny.org
Web site: wehealnewyork.org
Jim Mandler, Corporate Director of Public Affairs

Cornell Cooperative Extension, College of Human Ecology, Nutrition, Health
185 MVR Hall, Cornell University, Ithaca, NY 14853-4401
607-255-2247 Fax: 607-255-3794
e-mail: jas56@cornell.edu
Web site: www.cce.cornell.edu
Josephine Swanson, Associate Director, Assistant Dean
Promoting nutritional well-being; safe preparation & storage of food; reducing food insecurity; improving access to health services

County Nursing Facilities of New York Inc
c/o NYSAC, 111 Pine Street, Albany, NY 12207
518-465-1473 Fax: 518-465-0506
e-mail: rmaloney@nysac.org
Richard J Maloney, Executive Director

Dental Hygienists' Association of the State of New York Inc
706 Quaker Lane, Delanson, NY 12053
518-895-2836 Fax: 518-895-2329
e-mail: dhasny@aol.com
Web site: www.dhasny.org
Mary Ellen Yankosky, Executive Director
Professional association representing registered dental hygienists; working to improve the oral health of New Yorkers

Doctors Without Borders USA
333 7th Ave, Fl 2, New York, NY 10001-5004
212-679-6800 Fax: 212-679-7016
e-mail: doctors@newyork.msf.org
Web site: www.doctorswithoutborders.org
Nicolas de Torrente, Executive Director
International medical assistance for victims of natural or man-made disasters & armed conflict

Empire Blue Cross & Blue Shield
11 West 42nd St, 18th Fl, New York, NY 10036
212-476-1000 Fax: 212-476-1281
e-mail: deborah.bohren@empireblue.com
Web site: www.empireblue.com
Deborah Bohren, Senior Vice President, Communications
Health insurance

Empire State Association of Adult Homes & Assisted Living Facilities
646 Plank Rd, Ste 207, Clifton Park, NY 12065
518-371-2573 Fax: 518-371-3774
e-mail: nyasstliv@aol.com
Web site: www.ny-assisted-living.org
Lisa Newcomb, Executive Director
Trade association representing NYS assisted living providers

Epilepsy Coalition of New York State Inc
111 Washington Ave, Albany, NY 12210
518-434-4360 Fax: 518-434-4542
e-mail: ecnys@epilepsyny.org
Web site: www.epilepsyny.org
Janice W Gay, President
Promotes awareness of epilepsy & its consequences

Eye-Bank for Sight Restoration Inc (The)
120 Wall St, New York, NY 10005-3902
212-742-9000 Fax: 212-269-3139
e-mail: info@ebsr.org
Web site: www.eyedonation.org
Patricia Dahl, Executive Director/Chief Executive Officer
Cornea & scleral transplants

Family Planning Advocates of New York State
17 Elk St, Albany, NY 12207-1002
518-436-8408 Fax: 518-436-0004
e-mail: smitj@fpaofnys.org
Web site: www.fpaofnys.org
JoAnn M Smith, President/Chief Executive Officer
Reproductive rights

Friends & Relatives of Institutionalized Aged Inc
18 John St, Suite 905, New York, NY 10038
212-732-5667 or 212-732-5935 Fax: 212-732-6945
e-mail: fria@fria.org
Web site: www.fria.org
Amy Paul, Executive Director
Nursing home & other long-term care placement & complaints

Offices and agencies appear in alphabetical order.

Generic Pharmaceutical Association
2300 Clarendon Blvd, Ste 400, Arlington, VA 22201-3367
703-647-2480 Fax: 703-647-2481
e-mail: info@gphaonline.org
Web site: www.gphaonline.org
Kathleen Jaeger, President & Chief Executive Officer
Education & consumer information on the quality & effectiveness of generic drugs; generic drug issues

Gertrude H Sergievsky Center (The)
630 West 168th St, New York, NY 10032
212-305-2391 Fax: 212-305-2518
e-mail: rpm2@columbia.edu
Richard Mayeux, Director
Neurological disease research correlating epidemiological techniques with genetic analysis & clinical investigation

Greater New York Hospital Association
555 W 57th St, New York, NY 10019
212-246-7100 Fax: 212-262-6350
e-mail: raske@gnyha.org
Web site: www.gnyha.org
Kenneth E Raske, President
Trade association representing more than 250 not-for-profit hospitals

Group Health Inc
441 9th Ave, New York, NY 10001
212-615-0891 Fax: 212-563-8561
e-mail: jgoodwin@ghi.com
Jeffrey Goodwin, Director, Governmental Relations
Affordable, quality health insurance for working individuals & families

Healthcare Association of New York State
1 Empire Dr, Rensselaer, NY 12144
518-431-7600 Fax: 518-431-7915
e-mail: skroll@hanys.org
Web site: www.hanys.org
Steven Kroll, Vice President, Governmental Affairs & External
    Relations
Representing New York's not-for-profit hospitals, health systems & continuing care providers

Home Care Association of New York State Inc
194 Washington Ave, 4th Fl, Albany, NY 12210-2314
518-426-8764 x214 Fax: 518-426-8788
e-mail: crodat@hcanys.org
Web site: www.hcanys.org
Carol A Rodat, President
Advocacy for home health care & related health services

Hospice & Palliative Care Association of NYS Inc
21 Aviation Rd, Ste 9, Albany, NY 12205
518-446-1483 Fax: 518-446-1484
e-mail: info@hpcanys.org
Web site: www.hpcanys.org
Kathy A McMahon, President & Chief Executive Officer
Hospice & palliative care information & referral service; educational programs; clinical, psychosocial & bereavement issues

INFORM Inc
120 Wall Street, 14th Flr, New York, NY 10005-4001
212-361-2400 Fax: 212-361-2412
e-mail: inform@informinc.org
Web site: www.informinc.org
Joanna D Underwood, President
Advocacy, research & education on practical methods to protect natural resources & public health

Institute for Urban Family Health (The)
16 East 16th St, New York, NY 10003
212-633-0800 x255 Fax: 212-691-4610
e-mail: ncalman@institute2000.org
Web site: www.institute2000.org
Neil S Calman, President, Chief Executive Officer
Family practice healthcare for NYC's underserved; health professions training; research & advocacy

Iroquois Healthcare Alliance
17 Halfmoon Executive Park Dr, Clifton Park, NY 12065
518-383-5060 Fax: 518-383-2616
e-mail: gfitzgerald@iroquois.org
Web site: www.iroquois.org
Gary Fitzgerald, President
Represents healthcare providers in upstate New York

Jewish Home & Hospital (The)
120 West 106 St, New York, NY 10025
212-870-4600 Fax: 212-870-4895
e-mail: aweiner@jhha.org
Web site: www.jewishhome.org
Audrey Weiner, President & Chief Executive Officer
Long term care & rehabilitation

League for the Hard of Hearing
50 Broadway, Fl 5, New York, NY 10004-1607
917-305-7700 or TTY: 917-305-7999 Fax: 917-305-7888
e-mail: postmaster@lhh.org
Web site: www.lhh.org
Laurie Hanin, Co-Executive Director
Rehabilitation & other services for the deaf & hard of hearing

Lighthouse International
111 East 59th St, New York, NY 10022
212-821-9550 Fax: 212-821-9702
e-mail: ffreedman@lighthouse.org
Web site: www.lighthouse.org
Fran Freedman, Senior Vice President, Public Affairs &
    Communications
Vision rehabilitation, research, education & awareness

Marion S Whelan School of Practical Nursing
Geneva General Hospital, 196 North St, Geneva, NY 14456
315-787-4005 Fax: 315-787-4770
e-mail: VictoriaRecord@flhealth.org
Web site: www.flhealth.org - Services & Programs
Victoria Record MS RPRN, Director
Health education/diabetes education

Offices and agencies appear in alphabetical order.

Medical Society of the State of NY, Governmental Affairs Division
One Commerce Plaza, Ste 1103, Albany, NY 12210
518-465-8085 Fax: 518-465-0976
e-mail: gconway@mssny
Web site: www.mssny.org
Gerard L Conway, Director
Healthcare legislation & advocacy

Memorial Sloan-Kettering Cancer Center
1275 York Ave, New York, NY 10021
212-639-3627 Fax: 212-639-3576
Web site: www.mskcc.org
Christine Hickey, Director, Communications
Nat'l Cancer Institute designated comprehensive cancer center

Mount Sinai Medical Center
One Gustave L Levy Plaza, New York, NY 10029-6514
212-659-9011 Fax: 212-410-6111
e-mail: brad.beckstrom@mssm.edu
Web site: www.mountsinaihospital.org
Brad Beckstrom, Director, Government Affairs

NY Health Information Management Association Inc
19 Aviation Rd, Albany, NY 12205
518-435-0422 Fax: 518-435-0457
e-mail: bdolph@nyhima.org
Web site: www.nyhima.org
Bonnie Dolph, Executive Director

NY Physical Therapy Association
5 Palisades Dr, Ste 330, Albany, NY 12205-1443
518-459-4499 Fax: 518-459-8953
e-mail: lesliew@nypta.org
Web site: www.nypta.org
Leslie Wood, Executive Director

NY State Society of Physician Assistants
251 New Karner Rd, Ste 10A, Albany, NY 12205
877-769-7722 Fax: 856-423-3420
e-mail: info@nysspa.org
Web site: www.nysspa.org
Kenneth Cleveland, Executive Director

NYS Academy of Family Physicians
260 Osborne Rd, Loudonville, NY 12211-1822
518-489-8945 Fax: 518-489-8961
e-mail: fp@nysafp.org
Web site: www.nysafp.org
Vito Grasso, CAE, Executive Vice President

NYS Association of County Health Officials
One United Way, Pine West Plaza, Albany, NY 12205
518-456-7905 Fax: 518-452-5435
e-mail: jab@nysacho.org
Web site: www.nysacho.org
JoAnn Bennison, Executive Director

NYS Association of Health Care Providers
99 Troy Road, Ste 200, East Greenbush, NY 12061
518-463-1118 Fax: 518-463-1606
e-mail: johnston@nyshcp.org
Web site: www.nyshcp.org
Christy Johnston, Executive Vice President, Government Affairs
Home health care; health care services for the aging

NYS Association of Nurse Anesthetists (NYSANA)
PO Box 8867, Albany, NY 12208-0867
585-682-3473 Fax: 585-682-3473
e-mail: mbrown@rochester.rr.com
Margy Brown, Chair, Government Relations Committee

NYS Dental Association
121 State St, Albany, NY 12207
518-465-0044 Fax: 518-427-0461
Web site: www.nysdental.org
Roy E Lasky, Executive Director

NYS Federation of Physicians & Dentists
521 5th Ave, Ste 1700, New York, NY 10175-0003
212-986-3859 Fax: 212-606-0838
Larry Nathan, Executive Director

NYS Optometric Association Inc
119 Washington Avenue, Albany, NY 12210
518-449-7300 Fax: 518-432-5902
e-mail: nysoa2020@aol.com
Web site: www.nysoa.org
Jan Dorman, Executive Director

NYS Public Health Association
150 State St, 4th Fl, Albany, NY 12207
518-427-5835 Fax: 518-427-5835
e-mail: nyspha@aol.com
Web site: www.timesunion.com/communities/nyspha
Damon Vasilakis, Coordinator
Reviewing & advocating for stronger legislation/regulation to protect public health in NYS

National Amputation Foundation Inc
40 Church St, Malverne, NY 11565
516-887-3600 Fax: 516-887-3667
e-mail: amps76@aol.com
Web site: www.nationalamputation.org
Paul Bernacchio, President
Programs & services geared to help the amputee & other disabled people; donated medical equipment give-away program

National League for Nursing (NLN)
61 Broadway, New York, NY 10006
212-363-5555 Fax: 212-812-0392
e-mail: rcorcor@nln.org
Web site: www.nln.org
Ruth Corcoran, Chief Executive Officer
Advances quality nursing education that prepares the nursing workforce to meet the needs of diverse populations in an ever-changing healthcare environment

National Marfan Foundation
22 Manhasset Ave, Port Washington, NY 11050
516-883-8712 Fax: 516-883-8040
e-mail: staff@marfan.org
Web site: www.marfan.org
Carolyn Levering, President & Chief Executive Officer
Marfan syndrome research, education & support

New School University, Milano Graduate School of Mgmt & Urban Policy, Healt
72 Fifth Ave, 6th Fl, New York, NY 10011
212-229-5337 x1516 Fax: 212-229-5335
e-mail: fahsm@newschool.edu
Web site: www.newschool.edu
Marianne C Fahs, Director

New York AIDS Coalition
231 W 29th St, New York, NY 10001
212-629-3075 Fax: 212-629-8403
Web site: www.nyaidscoalition.org
Joe Pressley, Executive Director
HIV/AIDS-related public policy & education

New York Association of Homes & Services for the Aging
150 State St, Ste 301, Albany, NY 12207-1698
518-449-2707 Fax: 518-455-8908
e-mail: cyoung@nyahsa.org
Web site: www.nyahsa.org
Carl Young, President
Long-term care

New York Business Group on Health Inc
386 Park Ave South, Ste 703, New York, NY 10016
212-252-7440 Fax: 212-252-7448
e-mail: laurel@nybgh.org
Web site: www.nybgh.org
Laurel Pickering, Executive Director
Business employers addressing healthcare cost & quality

New York Counties Registered Nurses Association
70 W 36th St, Rm 601, New York, NY 10018-1262
212-673-7110 Fax: 212-673-7762
e-mail: nycrna@aol.com
Web site: www.nysna.org/districts/13.htm
Marlene S Gerber, Executive Director

New York Health Plan Association
90 State St, Ste 825, Albany, NY 12207-1717
518-462-2293 Fax: 518-462-2150
e-mail: lmarks@nyhpa.org
Web site: www.nyhpa.org
Lee Marks, Director, Government Affairs
Promotes the development of managed healthcare plans

New York Medical College
Basic Science Bldg, Valhalla, NY 10595
914-594-4110 Fax: 914-594-4944
e-mail: francis_belloni@nymc.edu
Web site: www.nymc.edu
Francis L Belloni, Dean, Graduate School of Basic Medical Sciences
Cardiovascular physiology, graduate education

New York Medical College, Department of Community & Preventive Medicine
Munger Pavilion, Valhalla, NY 10595
914-594-4254 Fax: 914-594-4576
e-mail: joseph_cimino@nymc.edu
Web site: www.nymc.edu
Joseph A Cimino, Professor & Chairman
Health policy & public health

New York Medical College, Department of Medicine
Munger Pavilion, Valhalla, NY 10595
914-594-4415 Fax: 914-493-4432
e-mail: lerner@nymc.edu
Web site: www.nymc.edu
Robert G Lerner, Professor, Vice Chair-Department of Medicine
Hematology, oncology, research of coagulation & clotting

New York Medical College, School of Public Health
School of Public Health, Valhalla, NY 10595
914-594-4531 Fax: 914-594-4292
e-mail: james_obrien@nymc.edu
Web site: www.nymc.edu
James J O'Brien, Dean & Acting Vice President
Graduate education for public health & the health sciences

New York Presbyterian Hospital
Public Affairs Ofc, 525 East 68th St, Box 144, New York, NY 10021
212-821-0560 Fax: 212-821-0576
e-mail: krobinso@med.cornell.edu
Web site: www.med.cornell.edu; www.nyp.org
Kathleen Robinson, Director, Media Relations

New York State Association of Ambulatory Surgery Centers
c/o Harrison Center Outpatient Surgery I, 550 Harrison St, Suite 230, Syracuse, NY 13202
315-472-7315 Fax: 315-475-8056
e-mail: palteri@harrisonsurgery.com
Margaret M Alteri, President
Ambulatory surgery

New York State Health Facilities Association Inc
33 Elk St, Ste 300, Albany, NY 12207-1010
518-462-4800 Fax: 518-426-4051
e-mail: rmurphy@nyshfa.org
Web site: www.nyshfa.org
Robert J Murphy, CAE, Executive Vice President, Governmental Affairs
Short-term, long-term & continuing health care

New York State Health Facilities Association Inc
33 Elk St, Ste 300, Albany, NY 12207-1010
518-462-4800 x10 Fax: 518-426-4051
e-mail: rherrick@nyshfa.org
Web site: www.nyshfa.org
Richard J Herrick, President & Chief Executive Officer
Nursing homes & continuing care services

Policy Areas

New York State Nurses Association
11 Cornell Rd, Latham, NY 12110
518-782-9400 x279 Fax: 518-783-5207
e-mail: lola.fehr@nysna.org
Web site: www.nysna.org
Lola M Fehr, Executive Director
Labor union & professional association for registered nurses

New York State Ophthalmological Society
10 Colvin Ave, Albany, NY 12206
518-438-2020 Fax: 518-438-3008
e-mail: nysos2020@aol.com
Web site: www.nysos.com
Robin M Pellegrino, Executive Director

New York State Osteopathic Medical Society
18585 Broadway, New York, NY 10023
212-261-1784 Fax: 212-261-1786
e-mail: nysoms@nysoms.org
Web site: www.nysoms.org
Martin Diamond, Executive Director
*Advance the art & science of the osteopathic medical philosophy &
practice through continuing medical education programs*

New York State Podiatric Medical Association
1255 Fifth Ave, New York, NY 10029
212-996-4400 Fax: 646-672-9344
e-mail: nypod@aol.com
Web site: www.nyspma.org
Hiram Chirel, Executive Director

New York State Radiological Society Inc
9 E 40th St, New York, NY 10016
212-448-1866 Fax: 212-448-1863
e-mail: nysrad@aol.com
Richard Schiffer, Executive Director

New York University, Graduate School of Public Service
295 Lafayette St, 2nd Fl, New York, NY 10012
212-998-7455 or 212-998-7440 Fax: 212-995-4166
e-mail: john.billings@nyu.edu
Web site: www.nyu.edu/wagner
John Billings, Director, Center for Health & Public Service Research
Health care reform

New York University, Robert F Wagner Graduate School of Public Service
40 West 4th St, Rm 600, New York, NY 10012
212-998-7410 Fax: 212-995-4162
e-mail: jo.boufford@nyu.edu
Web site: www.nyu.edu/wagner
Jo Ivey Boufford, Dean & Professor of Public Administration
Health policy & management

Next Wave Inc
24 Madison Ave Ext, Albany, NY 12203
518-452-3351 Fax: 518-452-3358
e-mail: contact@nextwave.info
Web site: www.nextwave.info
John Shaw, President
Health services research, management consulting & evaluation

**NYS Bar Assn, Food, Drug & Cosmetic Law Section
North Shore-Long Island Jewish Health System**
Office of Legal Affairs, 150 Community Dr, Great Neck, NY 11021
516-465-8379 Fax: 516-465-8105
e-mail: cmcgowan2@nshs.edu
Coreen McGowan, Esquire

Nurse Practitioners Assn of NYS (The)
12 Corporate Dr, Clifton Park, NY 12065
518-348-0719 Fax: 518-348-0720
e-mail: info@thenpa.org
Web site: www.thenpa.org
Seth Gordon, President/Chief Executive Officer
Representation, communication & advocacy

OSI Pharmaceuticals
58 So Service Rd, Melville, NY 11747
631-962-2000 Fax: 631-962-2023
Web site: www.osip.com
Christine Boisclair, Director, Reguatory Affairs
Discovery & development of pharmaceutical products

Pharmacists Society of the State of New York
210 Washington Ave Extenstion, Albany, NY 12203
518-869-6595 Fax: 518-464-0618
e-mail: craigb@pssny.org
Web site: www.pssny.org
Craig Burridge, Executive Director
Continuing education, public information, health advocacy

Procter & Gamble Pharmaceuticals
PO Box 191, Norwich, NY 13815
607-335-2111 Fax: 607-335-2700
Web site: www.pg.com
Pamela Traister, Manager, Public Affairs
Research & development of prescription pharmaceuticals

Professional Standards Review Council of America Inc (PSRC)
200 Madison Ave, Suite 2108, New York, NY 10016
212-686-9147 Fax: 212-779-9307
e-mail: cwielk@psrc-of-america.org
Web site: www.psrc-of-america.org
Carol A Wielk, Executive Director
Health care QA/UR management; credentialing

Radon Testing Corp of America Inc
2 Hayes St, Elmsford, NY 10523
914-345-3380 or 800-457-2366 Fax: 914-345-8546
e-mail: rtca97@att.net
Web site: www.rtca.com
Nancy Bredhoff, President
*Radon detection services for health departments, municipalities,
homeowners; manufacture canister detectors*

Offices and agencies appear in alphabetical order.

Regeneron Pharmaceuticals Inc
777 Old Saw Mill River Rd, Tarrytown, NY 10591-6707
914-345-7400 Fax: 914-345-7688
e-mail: info@regeneron.com
Web site: www.regeneron.com
Stephen L Holst, Vice President, Quality Assurance & Regulatory
    Affairs
*Discovers, develops & intends to commercialize therapeutic drugs
for serious medical conditions, including rheumatoid arthritis,
cancer, asthma & obesity*

Robert P Borsody, PC
909 Third Ave, 17th Fl, New York, NY 10022
212-453-2727 Fax: 212-644-7485
e-mail: rborsody@fbwhlaw.com
Web site: www.borsodyhealthlaw.com
Robert P Borsody, Attorney
Health care law

**SUNY at Albany, School of Public Health, Center for Public
Health Preparedness**
One University Pl, Rensselaer, NY 12144-3456
518-486-7920 Fax: 518-402-1137
e-mail: mwatson@albany.edu
Web site: www.ualbanycphp.org
Margaret R Watson, Project Coordinator

Southern New York Association Inc
39 Broadway, Ste 1710, New York, NY 10006
212-425-5050 Fax: 212-968-7710
Web site: www.snya.org
Neil Heyman, President
Nursing home industry advocacy, training & resources

The Bachmann-Strauss Dystonia & Parkinson Foundation
Mount Sinai Medical Center, One Gustave L Levy Place, Box 1490,
New York, NY 10029
212-241-5614 Fax: 212-987-0662
e-mail: bachmann.strauss@mssm.edu
Web site: www.dystonia-parkinsons.org
Deborah Eger, Special Events Manager
*Funds research & creates public awareness of dystonia, Parkinson's
disease*

True, Walsh & Miller LLP
202 E State St, Ste 700, Ithaca, NY 14850
607-273-4200 Fax: 607-272-6694
e-mail: stt@twmlaw.com
Web site: www.twmlaw.com
Sally T True, Partner
Health care & corporate law

United Hospital Fund of New York
Empire State Building, 350 Fifth Ave, 23rd Fl, New York, NY
10118-2399
212-494-0777 Fax: 212-494-0830
e-mail: jtallon@uhfnyc.org
Web site: www.uhfnyc.org
James R Tallon, Jr, President
Health services, research & philanthropic organization

United New York Ambulance Network (UNYAN)
160 Homer Ave, Cortland, NY 13045
607-756-8389 Fax: 607-756-5199
e-mail: tmh@odyssey.net
Web site: unyan.net
Mark Zeek, Chairman
Ambulance trade association

We Move
204 W 84th St, New York, NY 10024
800-437-6682 Fax: 212-875-8389
e-mail: wemove@wemove.org
Web site: www.wemove.org
Susan B Bressman, President
*Education & information about movement disorders for both
healthcare providers & patients*

NYS Bar Assn, Health Law Section
Wilson Elser Moskowitz Edelman & Dicker
One Steuben Pl, Albany, NY 12207
518-449-8893 Fax: 518-449-4292
e-mail: rosenbergp@wemed.com
Philip Rosenberg, Chair

Winthrop University Hospital
286 Old Country Road, Mineola, NY 11501
516-663-2706 Fax: 516-663-2713
e-mail: jbroder@winthrop.org
Web site: www.winthrop.org
John P Broder, Vice President, External Affairs & Development

**Yeshiva University, A Einstein Clg of Med, OB/GYN &
Wmn's Health**
1300 Morris Park Ave, Ste B-502, Bronx, NY 10461
718-430-4192 Fax: 718-430-8813
e-mail: chairobgyn@aol.com
Web site: www.yu.edu
Irwin R Merkatz, Chair

Offices and agencies appear in alphabetical order.

HOUSING & COMMUNITY DEVELOPMENT

New York State

GOVERNOR'S OFFICE

Governor's Office
Executive Chamber
State Capitol
Albany, NY 12224
518-474-8390 Fax: 518-474-1513
Web site: www.state.ny.us

Governor:
  George E Pataki 518-474-8390
Executive Director:
  Kara Lanspery 518-474-8390
Secretary to the Governor:
  John P Cahill. 518-474-4246
Senior Policy Advisor to the Governor:
  Jeffrey Lovell 518-486-9671
Counsel to the Governor-Attorney General, Budget:
  Richard Platkin. 518-474-8343
Director, Communications:
  David Catalfamo. 518-474-8418
Deputy Secretary to the Governor for Public Authorities, Finance & Housing:
  Adam Barsky 518-473-2610
Asst Counsel to the Gov-Battery Pk, Child/Family Svcs, Child/Family
  Council, Family, Housing, Human Rts, Roosevelt Is, Temp/Disabl,
  Women, HFA/MBBA/SONYMA:
  Carolyn Betz Kerr. 518-474-1310

EXECUTIVE DEPARTMENTS AND RELATED AGENCIES

Housing & Community Renewal, Division of
Hampton Plaza
38-40 State Street
Albany, NY 12207
866-275-3427
Web site: www.dhcr.state.ny.us

25 Beaver Street
New York, NY 10004-2319
866-275-3427

Commissioner:
  Judith A Calogero 518-473-8384/fax: 518-473-9462
First Dep Commissioner:
  Donald A Clarey. 518-473-0632
Executive Assistant:
  Ellen DeVane 518-473-0632
Director, Communications:
  Jennifer Farina. 518-473-2526/fax: 518-474-5752

Administration
Deputy Commissioner:
  Mary Beth Labate 518-486-3370/fax: 518-473-9462

Housing Information Systems
Director:
  Robert G Kelly 518-473-5681/fax: 518-486-5056

Internal Audit

Office of Financial Administration
Director:
  Catherine Johnson. 518-486-3400/fax: 518-473-3260

Office of Training & Professional Development
Director:
  Richard Washburn. 518-486-5021/fax: 518-486-5027

Personnel
Director:
  Gerald Burke. 518-473-6977/fax: 518-486-5007

Support Services/Processing Services Unit
Director:
  Theodore T Minissale 518-486-6166/fax: 518-486-3366

Community Development
Deputy Commissioner:
  Joan F Hoover 212-480-6446/fax: 212-480-7450
Asst Commissioner, Operations:
  Vacant. 518-486-6399/fax: 518-474-7292
Asst Commissioner, Program Management:
  Vacant. 518-473-8536/fax: 518-474-7292
Asst Commissioner, Underwriting & Design Services:
  Ellen M Coyle 518-473-3890/fax: 518-473-7357
Asst Director, Community Development:
  Robert Shields 518-486-3305/fax: 518-486-3410

Community Service Bureau/Technical Assistance Unit
Director:
  Pat Doyle. 518-473-3247/fax: 518-486-5186

Energy Services Bureau/Weatherization
Director:
  Thom Carey. 518-474-5700/fax: 518-474-9907

Environmental Analysis Unit
Director:
  Barbara Wigzell 518-473-0457

Housing Trust Fund Program
Program Manager:
  Thomas Koenig. 518-486-7682/fax: 518-486-3410

Regional Offices
  Buffalo
    Statler Towers, 107 Delaware Ave, Ste 600, Buffalo, NY 14202
    Reg Director:
      Thomas H VanNortwick. 716-842-2244/fax: 716-842-2724
  Capital District
    Hampton Plaza, 38-40 State St, 9th Fl, Albany, NY 12207

Offices and agencies appear in alphabetical order.

Regional Director:
Debra Devine 518-486-5012/fax: 518-474-5752
New York City
25 Beaver St, New York, NY 10004
Regional Director:
Deborah Boatright 212-480-4543
Syracuse
800 South Wilbur Ave, Syracuse, NY 13204
Regional Director:
Vernita King 315-473-6930/fax: 315-473-6937

Fair Housing & Equal Opportunity
Asst Commissioner:
Providence Baker 518-474-6157/fax: 518-473-3173

Housing Operations
Deputy Commissioner:
David Cabrera 212-480-6440/fax: 212-480-7169
Asst Commissioner, Section 8:
Alan Smith 518-473-6183/fax: 518-474-5752
Asst Commissioner, Housing Operations:
Richmond McCurnin 212-480-6444/fax: 212-480-7169

Architecture & Engineering Bureau
Director:
Robert Damico 212-480-6266/fax: 212-480-6268

Housing Audits & Accounts Bureau
Director:
Vincent Giammarino 212-480-7224/fax: 212-480-7042

Housing Management Bureau
Director:
Jane Berrie 212-480-7252/fax: 212-480-7270
Mobile Home Unit
Director:
Dominic Cardillo 800-432-4210/fax: 518-486-3366
Subsidy Services
Director:
Linda Kedzierski 212-480-6482/fax: 212-480-6481

Legal Affairs
General Counsel:
Marcia P Hirsch 212-480-6709/fax: 212-480-6711

Albany Unit
Managing Attorney:
Brian Lawlor 518-486-6337/fax: 518-473-8206
Closing Coordinator:
Lawrence Gambino 518-486-6337/fax: 518-473-8206

General Law
Managing Attorney:
Sheldon Melnitsky 212-480-6789/fax: 212-480-7416
Senior Supervising Attorney:
Cullen McVoy 212-480-6787/fax: 212-480-7416
Litigation Unit Managing Attorney:
Sheldon Melnitsky 212-480-6789/fax: 212-480-7416

Policy & Intergovernmental Relations
Deputy Commissioner:
Lorrie Pizzola 518-474-9553/fax: 518-473-9462
Legislative Liaison:
Curtis Tucker 518-473-2519/fax: 518-474-5752

Rent Administration
92-31 Union Hall St, Jamaica, NY 11433
Deputy Commissioner:
Paul Roldan 718-262-4822/fax: 718-262-4008

Luxury Decontrol/Overcharge
Bureau Chief:
Gerald Garfinkle 718-262-4725/fax: 718-262-7932

Owner Multiple Applications
Bureau Chief:
Paul Fuller 718-262-4768/fax: 718-262-7938

Rent Control/ETPA
Bureau Chief:
Michael Rosenblatt 718-262-4713/fax: 718-262-4008

Rent Information & Mediation
Bureau Chief:
Edward Blanco 718-262-4816/fax: 718-262-4008

Services Compliance Owner Restoration Enforcement/SCORE
Bureau Chief:
Patrick Siconolfi 718-262-4765/fax: 718-262-4008

Law Department
120 Broadway
New York, NY 10271-0332
212-416-8000 Fax: 212-416-8942

State Capitol
Albany, NY 12224-0341
518-474-7330
Fax: 518-402-2472

Attorney General:
Eliot Spitzer 518-474-7330
First Deputy Attorney General:
Michele Hirshman 212-416-8050
Director, Public Information & Correspondence:
Peter A Drago 518-474-7330/fax: 518-402-2472

Public Advocacy Division
Acting Deputy Attorney General:
Terryl Brown Clemons 212-416-8041/fax: 212-416-8068
Special Counsel:
Mary Ellen Burns 212-416-6155

Civil Rights Bureau
Bureau Chief:
Dennis Parker 212-416-8250/fax: 212-416-8074

Consumer Fraud & Protection Bureau
Bureau Chief:
Thomas G Conway 518-474-2374/fax: 518-474-3618

State Counsel Division
Deputy Attorney General:
Richard Rifkin 518-473-7190
Assistant Deputy Attorney General:
Patricia Martinelli 518-473-0648/fax: 518-486-9777
Assistant Deputy Attorney General:
Susan L Watson 212-416-8579/fax: 212-416-6001

Litigation Bureau
Bureau Chief, Albany:
Bruce D Feldman 518-473-8328/fax: 518-473-1572
Bureau Chief, NYC:
James B Henley 212-416-8523/fax: 212-416-6075

Real Property Bureau
Asst Attorney General in Charge:
Henry A DeCotis 518-474-7151/fax: 518-473-5106

Offices and agencies appear in alphabetical order.

Policy Areas

Small Cities, Governor's Office for
Agency Building 4, 6th Fl
Empire State Plaza
Albany, NY 12223
518-474-2057 Fax: 518-474-5247
Web site: www.nysmallcities.com

Director:
  Glen King 518-474-2057
Executive Assistant to the Director:
  Patricia Longstaff 518-474-2057
First Deputy Director:
  Albert P Jurczynski 518-474-2057
Deputy Director:
  Kenneth J Flood 518-474-2057
Associate Counsel:
  Brian McCartney 518-474-2057
Public Information Officer:
  Tracey McNerney 518-474-2057
  e-mail: tmcnerney@nysmallcities.com

CORPORATIONS, AUTHORITIES AND COMMISSIONS

Capital District Regional Planning Commission
One Park Place
Suite 102
Albany, NY 12205-1606
518-453-0850 Fax: 518-453-0856
e-mail: cdrpc@cdrpc.org
Web site: www.cdrpc.org

Executive Director:
  Rocco Ferraro 518-453-0850

Development Authority of the North Country
Dulles State Office Bldg, 4th Fl
317 Washington St
Watertown, NY 13601
315-785-2593 Fax: 315-785-2591
Web site: www.danc.org

Chair:
  Douglas L Murray 315-785-2593
Executive Director:
  Robert S Juravich 315-785-2593
  e-mail: juravich@danc.org
Engineer:
  Carrie M Tuttle 315-785-8661
  e-mail: ctuttle@danc.org
Deputy Exec Director:
  Thomas R Sauter 315-785-2593
  e-mail: tsauter@danc.org
Fiscal Officer:
  John D Donaghy 315-785-2593
  e-mail: jdonaghy@danc.org
Solid Waste Mgmt Facilities General Manager:
  E William Seifried 315-232-3236
Director, Project Development:
  Kevin J Jordan 315-785-2593
  e-mail: kjordan@danc.org

Technical Services Supervisor:
  John J Condino 315-232-3236

Empire State Development Corporation
30 South Pearl St
Albany, NY 12245
518-292-5100 or 800-782-8369

633 Third Ave
New York, NY 10017-6706
212-803-3100
Fax: 212-803-3735

Chair & CEO:
  Charles A Gargano 212-803-3700
Executive VP & COO:
  Eileen Mildenberger 212-803-3730
Executive VP:
  Michael Wilton 518-292-5100/fax: 212-803-3735
Communications Director:
  Ron Jury 212-803-3740/fax: 212-803-3735
  e-mail: rjury@empire.state.ny.us
Senior VP, General Counsel:
  Anita W Laremont 212-803-3750
Senior VP, Chief Administrative Officer:
  Joseph J LaCivita 518-292-5102
Senior VP, Policy & Research:
  John Bacheller 518-292-5115
Senior VP, Marketing, Tourism, Advertising, International:
  Neville Bugwadia 212-803-2244

New York City Housing Development Corp
110 William St
10th Fl
New York, NY 10038
212-227-5500 Fax: 212-227-6865
e-mail: info@nychdc.com
Web site: www.nychdc.com

Chairman:
  Shaun Donovan 212-863-6100
President:
  Emily Youssouf 212-227-3600
Executive VP & Chief of Staff:
  John Crotty 212-227-9807
Senior VP & General Counsel:
  Richard Froehlich 212-227-7435
Senior VP, Portfolio Mgt:
  Teresa Gigliello 212-227-9133
Senior VP, Asset Mgmt:
  Randi E Gordon 212-227-8580
Senior VP & CFO:
  Carol Kostik 212-227-7494/fax: 212-227-6757
Chief Credit Officer:
  Urmas Naeris 212-227-9724
Vice President, Development:
  Rachel Grossman 212-227-9373
Director, Marketing & Public Affairs:
  Tracy Paurowski 212-227-9496/fax: 212-227-6846

New York City Residential Mortgage Insurance Corporation
Chair:
  Shaun Donovan 212-863-6100

Offices and agencies appear in alphabetical order.

President:
 Emily Youssouf 212-227-3600

New York State Housing Finance Agency (HFA)

641 Lexington Ave
New York, NY 10022
212-688-4000 Fax: 212-872-0678
Web site: www.nyhomes.org

Chair:
 Jerome M Becker 212-688-4000
President & CEO:
 Stephen J Hunt 212-688-4000
Senior VP & Special Asst to Pres/CEO for Policy Dev & Programs:
 James P Angley 212-688-4000
Senior VP, COO & CFO:
 Ralph J Madalena 212-688-4000
Senior VP & Counsel:
 Justin Driscoll 212-688-4000
Senior VP, Debt Issuance:
 Bernard Abramowitz 212-688-4000 x530
Vice President, Director of Development:
 Jonathan Cortrell 212-688-4000 x688
Vice President, Policy & Planning:
 Tracy A Oats 212-688-4000 x678
Vice President, Intergovernmental Relations:
 Michael Houseknecht 518-434-2118/fax: 518-434-7158

Affordable Housing Corporation
Senior VP & Special Asst to Pres/CEO for Policy Dev & Programs:
 James P Angley 212-688-4000

New York State Mortgage Loan Enforcement & Administration Corporation

633 Third Ave
35th Fl
New York, NY 10017-6754
212-803-3530 Fax: 212-803-3535
Web site: www.empire.state.ny.us

President & CEO:
 Garry P Ryan 212-803-3530
General Counsel:
 Anita W Laremont 212-803-3750
Chief Financial Officer:
 Frances Walton 212-803-3510
Public Affairs Officer:
 Deborah Wetzel 212-803-3740/fax: 212-803-3735
 e-mail: dwetzel@empire.state.ny.us

New York State Project Finance Agency

641 Lexington Ave
New York, NY 10022
212-688-4000 Fax: 212-872-0678

Chair:
 Jerome M Becker 212-688-4000
President & CEO:
 Stephen J Hunt 212-688-4000
Senior VP, COO & CFO:
 Ralph J Madalena 212-688-4000
Senior VP & Counsel:
 Justin Driscoll 212-688-4000

Senior VP, Debt Issuance:
 Bernard Abramowitz 212-688-4000 x530
Vice President, Director of Development:
 Jonathan Cortrell 212-688-4000 x688
Vice President, Policy & Planning:
 Tracy A Oats 212-688-4000 x678

Roosevelt Island Operating Corporation (RIOC)

591 Main St
Roosevelt Island, NY 10044
212-832-4540 Fax: 212-832-4582
e-mail: info@roosevelt-island.ny.us
Web site: www.rioc.com

President:
 Herbert E Berman 212-832-4540
Vice President, Operations:
 Sari Halper Dickson 212-832-4540
Chairperson, Board of Directors (ex officio):
 Judith A Calogero 518-473-8384/fax: 518-473-9462
Commissioner's Designate to Board of Directors:
 Mary Beth Labate 518-486-3370
General Counsel:
 Kenneth A Leitner 212-832-4540 x311
Chief Financial Officer:
 Vacant 212-832-4540
Public Information Officer:
 John Melia 212-832-4540

State of New York Mortgage Agency (SONYMA)

641 Lexington Ave
New York, NY 10022
212-688-4000 Fax: 212-872-0678
Web site: www.nyhomes.org

Chair:
 Joseph Strasburg 212-688-4000
President & CEO:
 Stephen J Hunt 212-688-4000
Senior VP & Special Asst to Pres/CEO for Policy Dev & Programs:
 James P Angley 212-688-4000
Senior VP, COO & CFO:
 Ralph J Madalena 212-688-4000
Senior VP & General Counsel:
 Justin Driscoll 212-688-4000
Senior VP, Single Family Programs & Financing:
 Charles Rosenwald 212-688-4000 x531
Vice President, Director, SONYMA Mortgage Insurance Fund:
 Michael Friedman 212-688-4000 x714
Vice President, Policy & Planning:
 Tracy A Oats 212-688-4000 x678
Vice President, Intergovernmental Relations:
 Michael Houseknecht 518-434-2118/fax: 518-434-7158

NEW YORK STATE LEGISLATURE

See Legislative Branch in Section 1 for additional Standing Committee and Subcommittee information.

Policy Areas

Offices and agencies appear in alphabetical order.

Assembly Standing Committees

Housing
Chair:
Vito J Lopez (D). 518-455-5537
Ranking Minority Member:
Catharine M Young (R) 518-455-5241

Local Government
Chair:
Robert K Sweeney (D). 518-455-5787
Ranking Minority Member:
Ann G Rabbitt (R) 518-455-5991

Senate Standing Committees

Housing, Construction & Community Development
Chair:
John J Bonacic (R) 518-455-3181
Ranking Minority Member:
Liz Krueger (D) 518-455-2297

Local Government
Chair:
Elizabeth Little (R). 518-455-2811
Ranking Minority Member:
Martin Connor (D) 518-455-2625

U.S. Government

EXECUTIVE DEPARTMENTS AND RELATED AGENCIES

US Department of Agriculture

Rural Development
Web site: www.rurdev.usda.gov/ny

New York State Office
The Galleries of Syracuse, 441 S Salina St, 5th Fl, Ste 357, Syracuse, NY 13202-2425
TDD: 315-477-6447
State Director:
Patrick H Brennan. 315-477-6400/fax: 315-477-6438
Special Projects Representative:
Joel Weirick 315-477-6433/fax: 315-477-6438
Program Director, Rural Business-Cooperative Service:
Walter D Schermerhorn 315-477-6425
e-mail: walter.schermerhorn@ny.usda.gov
Program Director, Rural Utilities Service:
David Miller 315-477-6427/fax: 315-477-6448
e-mail: david.miller@ny.usda.gov
Program Director, Rural Housing Service:
George Von Pless 315-477-6419/fax: 315-477-6468
e-mail: george.vonpless@ny.usda.gov
Human Resources Manager:
Ora Giles. 315-477-6405/fax: 315-477-6440
e-mail: ora.giles@ny.usda.gov

US Housing & Urban Development Department
Web site: www.hud.gov

New York State Office
26 Federal Plaza, 35th Fl, Rm 3541, New York, NY 10278-0068
Regional Director:
Marisel Morales. 212-264-1161/fax: 212-264-9377
Deputy Regional Director:
Carmen McCulloch 212-264-8000 x3173
Public Affairs Officer:
Adam Glantz 212-264-8000 x3158

Administration (Admin Service Center 1)
Deputy Director:
Lisa Surplus. 212-264-8000 x3331

Community Planning & Development
Director:
Robert Cardillo 212-264-2885 x3401

Fair Housing & Equal Opportunity Office
Director:
Stanley Seidenfeld. 212-264-1290 x3501

Field Offices
Albany Area Office & Financial Operations Center fax: 518-464-4300
52 Corporate Circle, Albany, NY 12203-5121
Director Financial Operations Center:
Lester J West 518-464-4200
Field Office Director:
Robert Scofield 518-464-4201
Buffalo Area Office . . . . fax: 716-551-5752
465 Main St, Lafayette Court, 2nd Fl, Buffalo, NY 14203
Field Office Director:
Stephen T Banko, III. 716-551-5755
e-mail: stephen_t._banko@hud.gov

General Counsel
Asst General Counsel:
Henry Czauski. 212-264-8000 x3201

Housing
Director:
Deborah VanAmerongen 212-264-0777 x3701

Inspector General
Special Agent-in-Charge, Investigation:
Ruth A Ritzema 212-264-8062
District Inspector General, Audit:
Alexander C Malloy 212-264-8000 x3976

Public Housing
Director:
Mirza Negron Morales 212-264-0903 x3601

U.S. CONGRESS

See U.S. Congress Chapter for additional Standing Committee and Subcommittee information.

House of Representatives Standing Committees

Financial Services
Chair:
Michael G Oxley (R-OH). 202-225-2676
Ranking Minority Member:
Barney Frank (D-MA) 202-225-5931
New York Delegate:
Gary L Ackerman (D) 202-225-2601

Offices and agencies appear in alphabetical order.

New York Delegate:
Joseph Crowley (D) 202-225-3965
New York Delegate:
Vito Fossella (R). 202-225-3371
New York Delegate:
Steve Israel (D). 202-225-3335
New York Delegate:
Sue W Kelly (R). 202-225-5441
New York Delegate:
Peter T King (R). 202-225-7896
New York Delegate:
Carolyn B Maloney (D) 202-225-7944
New York Delegate:
Carolyn McCarthy (D) 202-225-5516
New York Delegate:
Gregory W Meeks (D) 202-225-3461
New York Delegate:
Nydia M Velazquez (D) 202-225-2361

Subcommittee
Housing & Community Opportunity
Chair:
Robert W Ney (R-OH) 202-225-6265
Ranking Minority Member:
Maxine Waters (D-CA). 202-225-2201
New York Delegate:
Peter T King (R) 202-225-7896
New York Delegate:
Nydia M Velazquez (D) 202-225-2361

Transportation & Infrastructure
Chair:
Don Young (R-AK) 202-225-5765
Ranking Minority Member:
James L Oberstar (D-MN) 202-225-6211

New York Delegate:
Timothy H Bishop (D) 202-225-3826
New York Delegate:
Sherwood L Boehlert (R) 202-225-3665
New York Delegate:
Brian M Higgins (D) 202-225-3306
New York Delegate:
Sue W Kelly (R) 202-225-5441
New York Delegate:
John R (Randy) Kuhl (R) 202-225-3161
New York Delegate:
Jerrold Nadler (D). 202-225-5635
New York Delegate:
Anthony Weiner (D). 202-225-6616

Subcommittee
Economic Development, Public Buildings & Emergency Management
Chair:
Bill Schuster (R-PA) 202-225-2431
Ranking Minority Member:
Eleanor Holmes Norton (D-DC) 202-225-8050

Senate Standing Committees

Banking, Housing & Urban Affairs
Chair:
Richard C Shelby (R-AL). 202-224-5744
Ranking Minority Member:
Paul S Sarbanes (D-MD) 202-224-4524
New York Delegate:
Charles E Schumer (D). 202-224-6542

Private Sector

Albany County Rural Housing Alliance Inc
PO Box 407, 24 Martin Road, Voorheesville, NY 12186
518-765-2425 Fax: 518-765-9014
e-mail: acrha1@aol.com
Web site: www.timesunion.com/communities/acrha
Judith A Eisgruber, Executive Director
Development & management of low income housing; home repair programs; housing counseling & education

American Institute of Architects (AIA) New York State Inc
235 Lark St, Albany, NY 12210
518-449-3334 Fax: 518-426-8176
e-mail: aianys@aianys.org
Web site: www.aianys.org
Barbara J Rodriguez, Executive Vice President/Chief Executive
Officer
Architectural regulations & state policy

Association for Community Living
99 Pine Street, Suite 202JR, Albany, NY 12207
518-426-3635 Fax: 518-426-0504
e-mail: aclnys@webramp.info
Web site: www.aclnys.org
Antonio M Lasicki, Executive Director

Association for Neighborhood & Housing Development
50 Broad St, Suite 1125, New York, NY 10004-2376
212-747-1117 Fax: 212-747-1114
e-mail: irene.b@anhd.org
Web site: www.anhd.org
Irene Baldwin, Executive Director
Umbrella organization providing assistance to NYC nonprofits advocating for affordable housing & neighborhood preservation

Association for a Better New York
355 Lexington Ave, 11th Fl, New York, NY 10017
212-370-5800 Fax: 212-661-5877
e-mail: info@abny.org
Web site: www.abny.org
Michelle Adams, Executive Director
Business recruitment & retention, NYC public policy issues forums & committees

Offices and agencies appear in alphabetical order.

Brooklyn Housing & Family Services Inc
415 Albemarle Rd, Brooklyn, NY 11218
718-435-7585 Fax: 718-435-7605
e-mail: ljayson@brooklynhousing.org; carol@brooklynhousing.org
Web site: www.brooklynhousing.org
Larry Jayson, Executive Director
*Homelessness prevention, landlord/tenant dispute resolution &
advocacy, immigration services*

**CUNY Hunter College, Urban Affairs & Planning
Department**
695 Park Ave, New York, NY 10021
212-772-5515 Fax: 212-772-5593
e-mail: smoses@hunter.cuny.edu
Web site: www.hunter.cuny.edu
Stanley Moses, Chair
History of planning, employment & education

Center for an Urban Future
120 Wall St, 20th Fl, New York, NY 10005
212-479-3353 Fax: 212-344-6457
e-mail: cuf@nycfuture.org
Web site: www.nycfuture.org
Neil Scott Kleiman, Director
*Policy institute dedicated to aggressively pursuing solutions to
critical problems facing cities*

Citizens Housing & Planning Council of New York
50 East 42nd St, Ste 407, New York, NY 10017
212-286-9211 Fax: 212-286-9214
e-mail: info@chpcny.org
Web site: www.chpcny.org
Frank P Braconi, Executive Director

Community Housing Improvement Program (CHIP)
545 Madison Ave, New York, NY 10022
212-838-7442 Fax: 212-838-7456
e-mail: webmaster@chipnyc.org
Web site: www.chipnyc.org
Patrick J Siconolfi, Executive Director
Representing NYC apartment building owners

Community Preservation Corporation (The)
28 East 28th Street, 9th Floor, New York, NY 10016-7943
212-869-5300 x511 Fax: 212-683-0694
e-mail: mlappin@communityp.com
Web site: www.communityp.com
Michael D Lappin, President & Chief Executive Officer
*Multifamily housing rehabilitation financing for NYC & NJ
neighborhoods*

Community Service Society of New York
105 E 22nd St, New York, NY 10010
212-614-5492 Fax: 212-614-9441
e-mail: vbach@cssny.org
Web site: www.cssny.org
Victor Bach, Senior Housing Policy Analyst
*Research & advocacy for public policies & programs that improve
housing conditions & opportunities for low-income NYC residents &
communities*

**Cornell Cooperative Extension, Community & Economic
Vitality Program, Community**
41 Warren Hall, Cornell University, Ithaca, NY 14853
607-255-9510 Fax: 607-255-2231
e-mail: rlh13@cornell.edu
Web site: www.cce.cornell.edu; www.cardi.cornell.edu
Rod Howe, Assistant Director
*Work with community leaders, extension educators & elected
officials to strengthen the vitality of New York's communities*

**Council on the Environment of NYC, Open Space Greening
Program**
51 Chambers St, Rm 228, New York, NY 10007
212-788-7900 or 212-788-7928 Fax: 212-788-7913
e-mail: conyc@cenyc.orgm
Web site: www.cenyc.org
Gerard Lordahl, Director
*Material & technical assistance for housing groups to create &
maintain open community gardens & other public open spaces in
NYC*

Federal Home Loan Bank of New York
101 Park Ave, New York, NY 10178-0599
212-441-6813 Fax: 212-949-2126
e-mail: wolff@fhlbny.com
Web site: www.fhlbny.com
Donald J Wolff, Senior Vice President, Community Investment

Hofstra University, School of Law
121 Hofstra University, Hempstead, NY 11549
212-864-6092
William R Ginsberg, Emeritus Professor of Law
Land use & environmental law

Homes for the Homeless/Institute for Children & Families
36 Cooper Square, 6th Fl, New York, NY 10003
212-529-5252 Fax: 212-529-7698
e-mail: info@homesforthehomeless.com
Web site: www.homesforthehomeless.com
Karina Kwok, Media Contact
*Private non-profit providing education, social services &
transitional housing for homeless children & families in NYC*

Housing Action Council Inc - Not For Profit
55 S Broadway, Tarrytown, NY 10591
914-332-4144 Fax: 914-332-4147
e-mail: rnoonan@affordablehomes.org
Rosemarie Noonan, Executive Director
Financial feasibility, land use & zoning & affordable housing

Housing Works Inc
247 Lark St, 1st Fl, Albany, NY 12210
518-449-4207 Fax: 518-449-4219
Web site: www.housingworks.org
Michael Kink, Statewide Advocacy Coordinator & Legislative
  Counsel
*Housing, health care, advocacy, job training & support services for
homeless NY residents with HIV or AIDS*

Offices and agencies appear in alphabetical order.

Local Initiative Support Corporation
501 7th Ave, Fl 7, New York, NY 10018
212-455-9800 Fax: 212-682-5929
Web site: www.liscnet.org
Norman R Bobins, President & Chief Executive Officer
Support the development of local leadership & the creation of affordable housing, commercial, industrial & community facilities, businesses & jobs

Mid-Hudson Pattern for Progress
6 Albany Post Rd, Newburgh, NY 12550-1439
845-565-4900 Fax: 845-565-4918
e-mail: mditullo@pfprogress.org
Web site: www.pattern-for-progress.org
Michael J DiTullo, President & Chief Executive Officer
Regional planning, research & policy development

NY Manufactured Housing Association Inc
35 Commerce Ave, Albany, NY 12206
518-435-9858 Fax: 518-435-9839
e-mail: info@nymha.org
Web site: www.nymha.org
Nancy Geer, Executive Director
Manufactured, factory built, modular & mobile housing

NYS Tenants & Neighbors Coalition
236 West 27th St, 4th Fl, New York, NY 10001
212-608-4320 x302 Fax: 212-619-7476
e-mail: nystnc@aol.com
Web site: www.tandn.org
Jumaane D Williams, Executive Director
Advocacy for tenant protection legislation & affordable housing; tenant education & empowerment

National Trust for Historic Preservation
NE Office, 7 Faneuil Hall Marketplace, 4th Fl, Boston, MA 2109
617-523-0885 Fax: 617-523-1199
e-mail: wendy_nicholas@nthp.org
Web site: www.nthp.org
Wendy Nicholas, Director
Advocacy, education, technical assistance & funding for preservation & community revitalization

Neighborhood Preservation Coalition of NYS Inc
40 Colvin Ave, Ste 102, Albany, NY 12206-1104
518-432-6757 Fax: 518-432-6758
e-mail: agostine@npcnys.org
Web site: www.npcnys.org
Joseph A Agostine, Jr, Executive Director
Community organizations united to preserve & revitalize neighborhoods

Nelson A Rockefeller Inst of Govt, Urban & Metro Studies
411 State St, Albany, NY 12203-1003
518-443-5014 Fax: 518-443-5705
e-mail: wrightd@rockinst.org
Web site: www.rockinst.org
David J Wright, Director
Research on community capacity building, impacts of welfare reform on community development corporations, empowerment zone/enterprise communities & neighborhood preservation

New School University, Milano Graduate School of Management & Urban Policy
72 Fifth Ave, New York, NY 10011
212-229-5311 Fax: 212-229-5904
e-mail: melendeE@newschool.edu
Web site: www.newschool.edu
Edwin Melendez, Professor/Director
Research, policy analysis & evaluation on community development & urban poverty

New York Building Congress
44 W 28th St, 12th Fl, New York, NY 10001-4212
212-481-9230 Fax: 212-447-6037
e-mail: rtanders55@aol.com
Web site: www.buildingcongress.com
Richard T Anderson, President
Coalition of design, construction & real estate organizations

New York Community Bank
One Jericho Plz, PO Box 9005, Jericho, NY 11753
516-942-6994 Fax: 516-942-6995
e-mail: d.coniglio@mynycb.com
Donna Coniglio, Chair

New York Landmarks Conservancy
141 5th Ave, New York, NY 10010
212-995-5260 Fax: 212-995-5268
e-mail: nylandmarks@nylandmarks.org
Web site: www.nylandmarks.org
Peg Breen, President
Technical & financial assistance for preservation & reuse of landmark buildings

New York Lawyers for the Public Interest
151 W 30th Street, 11th Floor, New York, NY 10001
212-244-4664 Fax: 212-244-4570
e-mail: mar@nylpi.org
Web site: www.nylpi.org
Michael Rothenberg, Executive Director
Disability rights law; access to health care; pro bono clearingouse; environmental justice and community development

New York State Community Action Association
2 Charles Blvd, Guilderland, NY 12084
518-690-0491 Fax: 518-690-0498
e-mail: dan@nyscaaonline.org
Web site: www.nyscaaonline.org
Daniel Maskin, Chief Executive Officer
Dedicated to the growth & education of community action agencies in NYS to sustain their efforts in advocating & improving the lives of low-income New Yorkers

New York State Rural Advocates
PO Box 104, Blue Mountain Lake, NY 12812
518-352-7787
Nancy Berkowitz, Coordinator
Advocacy & education for affordable housing for rural New Yorkers

Policy Areas

Offices and agencies appear in alphabetical order.

New York State Rural Development Council
c/o NYS Dept of State, 41 State St, Ste 900, Albany, NY 12231
518-474-1967 Fax: 518-474-6572
e-mail: gedwards@dos.state.ny.us
Gayle Edwards, Executive Director
Identifies, discusses & takes action on issues important to rural NY, especially economic development & availability of community services

New York State Rural Housing Coalition Inc
879 Madison Ave, 2nd Fl, Albany, NY 12208
518-458-8696 Fax: 518-458-8896
e-mail: rhc@ruralhousing.org
Web site: www.ruralhousing.org
Blair W Sebastian, Executive Director
Rural & small city housing; community & economic development

New York University, Wagner Graduate School
295 Lafayette Street, 2ND Floor, New York, NY 10012
212-998-7400 Fax: 212-995-4162
e-mail: mitchell.moss@nyu.edu
Web site: www.nyu.edu/wagner
Mitchell Moss, Professor of Urban Policy & Planning
Research on urban planning & development, with special emphasis on technology & the future of cities

Park Resident Homeowners' Association Inc
PO Box 68, Ontario, NY 14519
315-524-6703 Fax: 315-524-7621
e-mail: info@prho.com
Web site: www.prho.com
George R Miles, President
Protecting the rights of homeowners living in mobile/manufactured park communities in NYS

Parodneck Foundation (The)
121 6th Ave, Suite 501, New York, NY 10013
212-431-9700 Fax: 212-431-9783
e-mail: info@parodneckfoundation.org
Harold DeRienzo, President
Resident-controlled housing; community development

Pratt Institute, Center for Community & Environmental Development
379 Dekalb Ave, 2nd Fl, Brooklyn, NY 11205
718-636-3486 Fax: 718-636-3709
e-mail: picced@picced.org
Web site: www.picced.org
Brad Lander, Director
Training & technical assistance in community economic development & housing

Project for Public Spaces
700 Broadway, 4th Fl, New York, NY 10003
212-620-5660 Fax: 212-620-3821
e-mail: pps@pps.org
Web site: www.pps.org
Fred I Kent, President
Nonprofit organization providing community planning, design & development services

Regional Plan Association
4 Irving Place, 7th Fl, New York, NY 10003
212-253-2727 Fax: 212-253-5666
e-mail: yaro@rpa.org
Web site: www.rpa.org
Robert D Yaro, President
Develops & implements land-use, transportation, open space preservation, economic development & social equity proposals

Rent Stabilization Assn of NYC Inc
123 William St, New York, NY 10038
212-214-9200 x222 Fax: 212-732-0617
Web site: www.rsanyc.org
Joseph Strasburg, President
NYC landlord organization

Rural Housing Action Corporation
400 East Ave, Rochester, NY 14607-1910
585-340-3366 Fax: 585-340-3309
e-mail: lbeaulac@ruralinc.org
Web site: www.ruralinc.org
Lee Beaulac, President
Rental, first-time homebuyer, property management & home improvement programs for farmworkers, seniors & the rural poor

Settlement Housing Fund Inc
1780 Broadway, 6th Fl, New York, NY 10019
212-265-6530 Fax: 212-757-0571
Web site: www.settlementhousingfund.org
Carol Lamberg, Executive Director
Low & moderate income housing development, leasing, community development

Turner/Geneslaw Inc
2 Executive Blvd, Suite 401, Suffern, NY 10901
845-368-1785 Fax: 845-368-1572
e-mail: tginc@msn.com
Robert Geneslaw, Consultant
Community planning & zoning

Urban Homesteading Assistance Board
120 Wall St, 20th Fl, New York, NY 10005
212-479-3300 Fax: 212-344-6457
e-mail: info@uhab.org
Web site: www.uhab.org
Andrew Reicher, Executive Director
Training, technical assistance & services for development & preservation of low income cooperative housing

Women's Housing & Economic Development Corporation (WHEDCO)
50 E 168th St, Bronx, NY 10452
718-839-1103 Fax: 718-839-1170
e-mail: nbiberman@whedco.org
Web site: www.whedco.org
Nancy Biberman, President
Non-profit organization dedicated to the economic advancement of low-income women & their families

Offices and agencies appear in alphabetical order.

HUMAN RIGHTS

New York State

GOVERNOR'S OFFICE

Governor's Office
Executive Chamber
State Capitol
Albany, NY 12224
518-474-8390 Fax: 518-474-1513
Web site: www.state.ny.us

Governor:
George E Pataki 518-474-8390
Executive Director:
Kara Lanspery 518-474-8390
Secretary to the Governor:
John P Cahill. 518-474-4246
Senior Policy Advisor to the Governor:
Jeffrey Lovell 518-486-9671
Counsel to the Governor-Attorney General, Budget:
Richard Platkin. 518-474-8343
Senior Dep Secretary to the Governor for Health & Human Services:
Mark Kissinger. 518-408-2500
Asst Counsel to the Governor-Battery Pk, Child/Family Svcs, Child/Family
Council, Family, Housing, Human Rts, Roosevelt Is, Temp/Disabl,
Women, HFA/MBBA/SONYMA:
Carolyn Betz Kerr. 518-474-1310
Senior Advisor to the Governor for Women's Issues:
Lynn Rollins. 212-681-4580
Director, Communications:
Lisa Dewald Stoll. 518-474-8418

EXECUTIVE DEPARTMENTS AND RELATED AGENCIES

Advocate for Persons with Disabilities, Office of
One Empire State Plaza
Ste 1001
Albany, NY 12223-1150
518-473-4538 Fax: 518-473-6005
Web site: www.oapwd.org

State Advocate:
Richard Warrender. 518-473-4129
Deputy Advocate & Counsel, Public Info Officer:
Gregory Jones. 518-473-4609
e-mail: oapwdinfo@oapwd.org

Civil Service Department
State Campus
Bldg 1
Albany, NY 12239
518-457-2487 Fax: 518-457-7547
Web site: www.cs.state.ny.us

Commissioner:
Daniel E Wall. 518-457-3701
Executive Deputy Commissioner:
John F Barr. 518-457-6212
Deputy Commissioner:
Regina M DuBois. 518-485-7515
Director, Public Information:
Marc E Carey. 518-457-9375/fax: 518-457-6654
e-mail: mec1@cs.state.ny.us
Public Records Access Officer:
Jane Prus 518-457-6875/fax: 518-457-6654

Classification & Compensation Division
Director:
Nicholas J Vagianelis 518-457-6226/fax: 518-457-8081
Asst Director:
Vacant 518-457-6226

Diversity, Planning & Management Division
Director:
Frank E Abrams. 518-457-4146/fax: 518-457-0399
Coordinator, Community Outreach:
George Swiers 518-457-7661/fax: 518-457-0399

Developmental Disabilities Planning Council
155 Washington Ave
2nd Fl
Albany, NY 12210
518-486-7505 or 800-395-DDPC Fax: 518-402-3505
Web site: www.ddpc.state.ny.us

Chair:
George E Fertal Sr 518-486-7505
Executive Director:
Sheila M Carey. 518-486-7505
Public Information Officer:
Thomas F Lee. 518-486-7505

Human Rights, State Division of
1 Fordham Plaza
4th Fl
Bronx, NY 10458-5871
718-741-8400 Fax: 718-741-3214
Web site: www.nysdhr.com

Commissioner:
Michelle Cheney Donaldson 718-741-8326
Executive Assistant to the Commissioner:
Tammy Collins. 718-741-8328
Executive Deputy Commissioner:
Edward A Friedland 718-741-8330
Deputy Commissioner, Federal Programs:
Edward A Watkins 718-741-8440
Deputy Commissioner, Public Affairs:
Denise L Ellison 718-741-8459
e-mail: dellison@dhr.state.ny.us

Policy Areas

Offices and agencies appear in alphabetical order.

Deputy Commissioner, Administration:
  Martha B Furlong 718-741-8358
General Counsel:
  Gina M Lopez-Summa 718-741-8398
Chief Administrative Law Judge:
  Migdalia Pares 718-741-8255
Acting Chief Information Officer:
  Stephen Lopez 718-741-8379
Acting Director, Affirmative Action:
  Ali Jafri 718-741-8357
Director, Training:
  Wyletta Barbee 718-741-8443

AIDS Discrimination Issues Office
20 Exchange Pl, 2nd Fl, New York, NY 10005
Regional Director:
  Stephen Lopez 212-480-2493/fax: 212-480-0143

Case Review & Special Projects Office
One Fordham Plaza, 4th Fl, Bronx, NY 10458
Director:
  Sallie Clark 718-741-8514/fax: 718-741-3214

Central Case Resolution Office
163 West 125th St, Rm 415, New York, NY 10027
Regional Director:
  Stephen Lopez 212-961-8616/fax: 212-961-5690

Regional Offices
Deputy Commissioner, Regional Affairs:
  Michele Heitzner 718-741-8332

Albany
Agency Bldg 2, 18th Fl, Empire State Plaza, Albany, NY 12220
Regional Director:
  Rey F Torres 518-474-2705/fax: 518-473-3422

Binghamton
44 Hawley St, Rm 603, Binghamton, NY 13901-4465
Regional Director:
  Rey Torres 607-721-8467/fax: 607-721-8470

Brooklyn/Staten Island
55 Hanson Place, Rm 304, Brooklyn, NY 11217
Regional Director:
  Joseph Kaufman 718-722-2856/fax: 718-722-2869

Buffalo
W J Mahoney State Ofc Bldg, 65 Court St, Ste 506, Buffalo, NY 14202
Regional Director:
  William Marks 716-847-7632/fax: 716-847-7625

Manhattan (Lower)
20 Exchange Place, 2nd Fl, New York, NY 10005
Regional Director:
  Leon Dimaya 212-480-2522/fax: 212-480-0143

Manhattan (Upper)
A C Powell State Ofc Bldg, 163 W 125th St, 4th Fl, New York, NY 10027
Regional Director:
  Wilson Ortiz 212-961-8650/fax: 212-961-4425

Nassau County
175 Fulton Ave, Ste 211, Hempstead, NY 11550
Regional Director:
  Angel M Rivera 516-538-1310/fax: 516-483-6589

Peekskill
8 John Walsh Blvd, Ste 204, Peekskill, NY 10566
Regional Director:
  Margaret Gormley King 914-788-8050/fax: 914-788-8059

Rochester
One Monroe Sq, 259 Monroe Ave, 3rd Fl, Rochester, NY 14607
Regional Director:
  Forrest Cummings, Jr 585-238-8250/fax: 585-238-8259

Suffolk County
State Ofc Bldg, Rm 3A-15, Veterans Memorial Hwy, Hauppauge, NY 11787
Regional Director:
  Angel M Rivera 631-952-6434/fax: 631-952-6436

Syracuse
333 E Washington St, Rm 443, Syracuse, NY 13202
Regional Director:
  Forrest Cummings, Jr 315-428-4633/fax: 315-428-4638

Sexual Harassment Issues Office
55 Hanson Pl, Rm 900, Brooklyn, NY 11217
Regional Director:
  Joyce Yearwood-Drury 718-722-2060/fax: 718-722-4525

Law Department
120 Broadway
New York, NY 10271-0332
212-416-8000 Fax: 212-416-8942

State Capitol
Albany, NY 12224-0341
518-474-7330
Fax: 518-402-2472

Attorney General:
  Eliot Spitzer 518-474-7330/fax: 518-402-2472
First Deputy Attorney General:
  Michele Hirshman 212-416-8050
Director, Public Information & Correspondence:
  Peter A Drago 518-474-7330/fax: 518-402-2472

Public Advocacy Division
Acting Deputy Attorney General:
  Terryl Brown Clemons 212-416-8041/fax: 212-416-8068
Special Counsel:
  Mary Ellen Burns 212-416-6155

Civil Rights Bureau
Bureau Chief:
  Dennis Parker 212-416-8250/fax: 212-416-8074

Temporary & Disability Assistance, Office of
40 N Pearl St
Albany, NY 12243
518-474-9003 or 800-342-3004 Fax: 518-474-7870
Web site: www.otda.state.ny.us

Commissioner:
  Robert Doar 518-474-4152/fax: 518-486-6255
  e-mail: robert.doar@dfa.state.ny.us
Director, Office of Intergovernmental & External Affairs:
  Lisa Irving 518-474-7420
Asst Commissioner, Public Information:
  John B Madden 518-474-9516/fax: 518-486-6935
  e-mail: nyspio@dfa.state.ny.us

Program Support & Quality Improvement
Deputy Commissioner:
  Mary Meister 518-473-3912

Offices and agencies appear in alphabetical order.

Asst Director:
Susan Faulkner 518-474-9715

Temporary Assistance Division
Deputy Commissioner:
Russell Sykes 518-474-9222

NEW YORK STATE LEGISLATURE

See Legislative Branch in Section 1 for additional Standing Committee and Subcommittee information.

Assembly Standing Committees

Aging
Chair:
Steven C Englebright (D) 518-455-4804
Ranking Minority Member:
Andrew P Raia (R) 518-455-5952

Correction
Chair:
Jeffrion L Aubry (D) 518-455-4561
Ranking Minority Member:
Thomas O'Mara (R) 518-455-4538

Labor
Chair:
Susan V John (D) 518-455-4527
Ranking Minority Member:
Patricia L Acampora (R) 518-455-5294

Mental Health
Chair:
Peter M Rivera (D) 518-455-5102
Ranking Minority Member:
Matthew Mirones (R) 518-455-5716

Assembly Task Forces

Puerto Rican/Hispanic Task Force
Chair:
Peter Rivera (D) 518-455-5102
Co-Chair:
Vito J Lopez 518-455-5537

Women's Issues, Task Force on
Chair:
Joan L Millman (D) 518-455-5426
Coordinator:
Jean Emery 518-455-3632/fax: 518-455-4574

Senate Standing Committees

Aging
Chair:
Martin J Golden (R) 518-455-2730
Ranking Minority Member:
Carl Kruger (D) 518-455-2460

Crime Victims, Crime & Correction
Chair:
Michael F Nozzolio (R) 518-455-2366
Ranking Minority Member:
Thomas K Duane (D) 518-455-2451

Labor
Chair:
George Maziarz (R) 518-455-2024
Ranking Minority Member:
Dianne J Savino (D) 518-455-2437

Mental Health & Developmental Disabilities
Chair:
Thomas P Morahan (R) 518-455-3261
Ranking Minority Member:
Ruben Diaz (D) 518-455-2511

U.S. Government

EXECUTIVE DEPARTMENTS AND RELATED AGENCIES

Equal Employment Opportunity Commission
Web site: www.eeoc.gov

New York District
33 Whitehall St, 5th Fl, New York, NY 10004
District Director:
Spencer H Lewis, Jr. 212-336-3620/fax: 212-336-3625

Buffalo Local
6 Fountain Plaza, Ste 350, Buffalo, NY 14202
Director:
Elizabeth Cadle 716-551-4441/fax: 716-551-4387

US Commerce Department
Web site: www.doc.gov

Minority Business Development Agency
Web site: www.mbda.gov

New York Region
26 Federal Plaza, Rm 3720, New York, NY 10278
Regional Director:
Heyward B Davenport. 212-264-3262/fax: 212-264-0725

US Commission on Civil Rights
Web site: www.usccr.gov

EASTERN REGION (includes New York State)
624 9th St NW, Rm 500, Washington, DC 20425
Acting Regional Director:
Ivy Davis 202-376-7533/fax: 202-376-7548

US Department of Health & Human Services
Web site: www.os.dhhs.gov; www.hhs.gov/region2/

Office of Secretary's Regional Representative-Region 2-NY . . . . fax: 212-264-3620
26 Federal Plaza, Rm 3835, New York, NY 10278

Offices and agencies appear in alphabetical order.

Regional Director:
Deborah Konopko 212-264-4600
e-mail: deborah.konopko@hhs.gov
Senior Intergovernmental Affairs Specialist:
Joel S Truman. 212-264-4600
e-mail: joel.truman@hhs.gov
Intergovernmental Affairs Specialist:
Katherine Williams. 212-264-4600
e-mail: katherine.williams@hhs.gov

Office for Civil Rights . . . . fax: 212-264-3039
26 Federal Plaza, Rm 3312, New York, NY 10278
Fax: 212-264-3039
Web site: www.hhs.gov/ocr
Regional Manager:
Michael Carter. 212-264-3313/fax: 212-264-3039
Deputy Regional Manager:
Linda Colon 212-264-3313

US Department of Homeland Security (DHS)
Web site: www.dhs.gov

US Citizenship & Immigration Services (USCIS)
Web site: www.uscis.gov

Buffalo District Office . . . . fax: 716-551-3131
Federal Center, 130 Delaware Ave, Buffalo, NY 14202
District Director:
M Frances Holmes 716-551-4741 x6000
Albany Sub Office
1086 Troy-Schenectady Rd, Latham, NY 12110
Officer-in-Charge:
Gary Hale. 518-220-2100

CIS Asylum Offices
New York Asylum Office . . . . fax: 718-723-1121
One Cross Island Plaza, 3rd Fl, Rosedale, NY 11422
Director:
Patricia A Jackson 718-723-5954
Deputy Director:
Mick Dedvukaj 718-723-5954
Newark Asylum Office-Including NYS not served by New York City . . . . fax: 201-531-1877
1200 Wall St, West 4th Fl, Lindhurst, NJ 7071
Director:
Susan Raufer 201-531-0555
Deputy Director:
Aster Zeleke. 201-531-0555

New York City District Office
26 Federal Plaza, New York, NY 10278
District Director:
Mary Ann Gantner 212-264-3972
Garden City Satellite Office
711 Stewart Ave, Garden City, NY 11530
Officer-in-Charge:
Linda Pritchett . . . . 516-228-9242 or 516-288-9243

See U.S. Congress Chapter for additional Standing Committee and Subcommittee information.

House of Representatives Standing Committees
Education & the Workforce
Chair:
John A Boehner (R-OH). 202-225-6205
Ranking Minority Member:
George Miller (D-CA) 202-225-2095
New York Delegate:
Timothy H Bishop (D) 202-225-3826
New York Delegate:
Carolyn McCarthy (D) 202-225-5516
New York Delegate:
Major R Owens (D) 202-225-6231

International Relations
Chair:
Henry J Hyde (R-IL) 202-225-4561
Ranking Minority Member:
Tom Lantos (D-CA) 202-225-3531
New York Delegate:
Gary L Ackerman (D) 202-225-2601
New York Delegate:
Joseph Crowley (D) 202-225-3965
New York Delegate:
Eliot L Engel (D) 202-225-2464
New York Delegate:
Amory Houghton (R) 202-225-3161
New York Delegate:
Peter T King (R) 202-225-7896
New York Delegate:
Gregory W Meeks (D) 202-225-3461

Subcommittee
International Terrorism, Nonproliferation & Human Rights
Chair:
Edward R Royce (R-CA). 202-225-4111
Ranking Minority Member:
Brad Sherman (D-CA). 202-225-5911
New York Delegate:
Joseph Crowley (D). 202-225-3965
New York Delegate:
Peter T King (R) 202-225-7896

Senate Standing Committees
Indian Affairs
Chair:
Ben Nighthorse Campbell (R-CO). 202-224-5852
Vice Chair:
Daniel K Inouye (D-HI). 202-224-3934

Offices and agencies appear in alphabetical order.

Private Sector

American Jewish Committee
165 E 56th St, New York, NY 10022-2709
212-751-4000 Fax: 212-891-1450
e-mail: pr@ajc.org
Web site: www.ajc.org
David Harris, Executive Director
Promoting tolerance, mutual respect & understanding among diverse ethnic, racial & religious groups

Amnesty International USA
5 Penn Plaza, 14th Floor, New York, NY 10001
212-807-8400 Fax: 212-627-1451
e-mail: aimember@aiusa.org
Web site: www.amnestyusa.org
William F Schulz, Executive Director
Worldwide campaigning movement working to promote internationally recognized human rights

Anti-Defamation League
823 United Nations Plz, New York, NY 10017
212-885-7707 Fax: 212-697-0109
e-mail: afoxman@adl.org
Web site: www.adl.org
Abraham H Foxman, National Director
Fighting anti-Semitism worldwide

Asian American Legal Defense & Education Fund Inc
99 Hudson St, 12th Fl, New York, NY 10013-2815
212-966-5932 Fax: 212-966-4303
e-mail: info@aaldef.org
Web site: www.aaldef.org
Margaret Fung, Executive Director
Defend civil rights of Asian Americans through litigation, legal advocacy & community education

NYS Bar Assn, Gender Equity Task Force Cmte
Bond Schoeneck & King PLLC
One Lincoln Ctr, Syracuse, NY 13202-1355
315-218-8230 Fax: 315-218-8100
e-mail: crichardson@bsk.com
M Catherine Richardson, Co-Chair

Cardozo School of Law
55 Fifth Ave, New York, NY 10003
212-790-0234 Fax: 212-790-0205
e-mail: mrosnfld@ymail.yu.edu
Web site: www.cardozo.yu.edu
Michel Rosenfeld, Justice Sidney L Robins Professor of Human Rights
Law & theory of human rights

Center for Constitutional Rights
666 Broadway, 7th Fl, New York, NY 10012
212-614-6464 x427 Fax: 212-614-6499
e-mail: fogelesq@ccr-ny.org
Web site: www.ccr-ny.org
Jeffrey Fogel, Legal Director
Dedicated to advancing & protecting rights guaranteed by the US Constitution & the Universal Declaration of Human Rights

Center for Independence of the Disabled in NY (CIDNY)
841 Broadway, Ste 301, New York, NY 10003
212-674-2300 or TTY: 212-674-5619 Fax: 212-254-5953
Web site: www.cidny.org
Susan Dooha, Executive Director
Rights & advocacy for the disabled

Center for Migration Studies of New York Inc
209 Flagg Pl, Staten Island, NY 10304-1199
718-351-8800 Fax: 718-667-4598
e-mail: cms@cmsny.org
Web site: www.cmsny.org
Rev Joseph Fugolo, Executive Director
Facilitate the study of sociodemographic, historical, economic, political, legislative & pastoral aspects of human migration & refugee movements

Children's Rights Inc
404 Park Ave South, 11th Floor, New York, NY 10016
212-683-2210 Fax: 212-683-4015
e-mail: info@childrensrights.org
Web site: www.childrensrights.org
Marcia Robinson Lowry, Executive Director
Advocacy & litigation on behalf of abused & neglected children

Citizens' Committee for Children of New York Inc
105 E 22nd St, New York, NY 10010
212-673-1800 x25 Fax: 212-979-5063
e-mail: info@kidsfirstnewyork.org
Web site: www.kidsfirstnewyork.org
Gail B Nayowith, Executive Director
Public policy advocacy; children's rights & services

Columbia University, Mailman School of Public Health
Heilbrunn Dept of Population & Family He, 60 Haven Ave, B-2, New York, NY 10032
212-304-5281 Fax: 212-305-7024
e-mail: lpf1@columbia.edu
Web site: cpmcnet.columbia.edu/dept/sph/popfam
Lynn P Freedman, Associate Professor & Director
Theory, analysis & development of policy & programs supporting public health & human rights

Offices and agencies appear in alphabetical order.

Cornell University, School of Industrial & Labor Relations
Ives Hall, Ithaca, NY 14853-3901
607-255-4381 Fax: 607-255-4496
e-mail: fdb4@cornell.edu
Web site: www.ilr.cornell.edu
Francine Blau, Professor
Inequality, discrimination & sexual harassment; occupational segregation

Cornell University, School of Industrial & Labor Relations
331 Ives, Ithaca, NY 14853-3901
607-255-9536 Fax: 607-255-2763
e-mail: smb23@cornell.edu
Web site: www.ilr.cornell.edu/ped
Susanne M Bruyere, Director, Program Employment & Disability
Americans with Disabilities Act (ADA)

Drum Major Institute for Public Policy - Not For Profit
1110 East 59th St, 28th Fl, New York, NY 10022
212-909-9663 Fax: 212-909-9493
e-mail: dmi@drummajorinstitute.org
Web site: www.drummajorinstitute.org
Andrea Batista Schlesinger, Executive Director
Progressive think tank sponsoring frank dialogue on social problems & developing public policy to promote social & economic justice & equity

Family Planning Advocates of New York State
17 Elk St, Albany, NY 12207-1002
518-436-8408 Fax: 518-436-0004
e-mail: smitj@fpaofnys.org
Web site: www.fpaofnys.org
JoAnn M Smith, President/Chief Executive Officer
Reproductive rights

Filipino American Human Services Inc
185-14 Hillside Ave, Jamaica, NY 11432
718-883-1295 Fax: 718-523-9606
e-mail: fahsi@fahsi.org
Web site: www.fahsi.org
Sherry Lynn Peralta, Executive Director
Youth program, family counseling referral, community education/advocacy & citizenship assistance services

Hispanic Outreach Services
40 North Main Ave, Albany, NY 12203
518-453-6655 Fax: 518-453-6792
e-mail: anne.tranelli@rcda.org
Web site: www.hispanicoutreachservices.org
Sister Anne Tranelli, Executive Director
Social service, youth guidance, language translation & immigration assistance programs

Human Rights First
333 Seventh Ave, 13th Fl, New York, NY 10001
212-845-5200 Fax: 212-845-5299
e-mail: nyc@humanrightsfirst.org
Web site: www.humanrightsfirst.org
Michael Posner, Executive Director
Advocacy for the promotion & protection of fundamental human rights worldwide

Human Rights Watch
350 Fifth Ave, 34th Fl, New York, NY 10118-3299
212-290-4700 Fax: 212-736-1300
e-mail: hrwnyc@hrw.org
Web site: www.hrw.org
Kenneth Roth, Executive Director
Working with victims & activists to prevent discrimination, uphold political freedom, protect people from inhumane conduct in wartime & to bring offenders to justice

International Institute of Buffalo, NY, Inc
864 Delaware Ave, Buffalo, NY 14209
716-883-1900 Fax: 716-883-9529
e-mail: hboot@iibuff.org
Web site: www.iibuff.org
Hinke T Boot, Executive Director
Assist newly arrived refugees & immigrants to find work, learn English; legal immigration service, translations & interpreting school advocacy

Jewish Community Relations Council of NY Inc
70 W 36th Street, Ste 700, New York, NY 10018
212-983-4800 Fax: 212-983-4084
e-mail: millerm@jcrcny.org
Web site: www.jcrcny.org
Michael Miller, Executive Vice President
Human rights, intergroup relations

Lambda Legal Defense & Education Fund Inc
120 Wall St, Ste 1500, New York, NY 10005-3904
212-809-8585 Fax: 212-809-0055
e-mail: lambda@lambdalegal.org
Web site: www.lambdalegal.org
Kevin M Cathcart, Executive Director
Gay rights & AIDS issues

Lesbian, Gay, Bisexual & Transgender Community Ctr - Not For Profit
208 West 13th Street, New York, NY 10011-7702
212-620-7310 Fax: 212-924-2657
e-mail: info@gaycenter.org
Web site: www.gaycenter.org
Miriam Yeung, Director, Public Policy
Mental health counseling, youth guidance, HIV/AIDS services, advocacy & programs

NYS Bar Assn, Issues Affecting People with Disabilities Cmte
NYS Education Department
Education Bldg, Rm 148, 89 Washington Ave, Albany, NY 12234
518-473-4921 Fax: 518-473-2925
e-mail: ksurgall@mail.nysed.gov
Melinda Saran, Chair

National Council of Jewish Women
53 W 23rd St, 6th Fl, New York, NY 10010
212-645-4048 Fax: 212-645-7466
e-mail: action@ncjw.org
Web site: www.ncjw.org
Phyllis Snyder, President
Human rights & social service advocacy & education

Offices and agencies appear in alphabetical order.

National Organization for Women, NYS
1500 Central Avenue, Albany, NY 12205
518-452-3944 Fax: 518-452-3861
e-mail: newyorkstatenow@aol.com
Web site: www.nownys.com
Marcia Pappas, President
Legislative lobbying on issues affecting women

New School University, Department of Political Science
65 Fifth Ave, New York, NY 10003
212-229-5722 Fax: 212-807-1669
e-mail: pollis@newschool.edu
Adamantia Pollis, Professor Emeritus, Political Science
Comparative politics, human rights, nationalism & ethnicity

New School University, Intl Center for Migration, Ethnicity & Citizenship
65 Fifth Ave, New York, NY 10003
212-229-5475 Fax: 212-989-0504
e-mail: arizol@newschool.edu
Web site: www.newschool.edu/icmec
Aristide R Zolberg, Director
International migrations, refugees

New York Civil Liberties Union
90 State St, Albany, NY 12207
518-436-8598 Fax: 518-426-9341
Web site: www.nyclu.org
Robert Perry, Legislative Director
Constitutional & civil rights

New York Civil Rights Coalition
3 W 35th Street, Penthouse, New York, NY 10001-2204
212-563-5636 Fax: 212-563-9757
e-mail: nycrc@aol.com
Web site: www.nycivilrights.org
Michael Meyers, Executive Director
Advocacy of racial equality & multiracial cooperation in advancing social progress through the protection & enforcement of civil rights & the unlearning of stereotypes

New York Immigration Coalition (The)
275 Seventh Ave, 9th Fl, New York, NY 10001
212-627-2227 x221 Fax: 212-627-9314
e-mail: aguerrero@thenyic.org
Web site: www.thenyic.org
Margie McHugh, Executive Director
Nonprofit umbrella advocacy organization for groups assisting immigrants

New York Lawyers for the Public Interest
151 W 30th Street, 11th Floor, New York, NY 10001
212-244-4664 Fax: 212-244-4570
e-mail: mar@nylpi.org
Web site: www.nylpi.org
Michael Rothenberg, Executive Director
Disability rights law; access to health care; pro bono clearinghouse; environmental justice and community development

New York State Council of Churches
18 Computer Dr West, Suite 107, Albany, NY 12205
518-436-9319 x14 Fax: 518-427-6705
e-mail: nyscoc@aol.com
Web site: www.nyscommunityofchurches.org
Mary Lu Bowen, Executive Director

NYS Bar Assn, Minorities in the Profession Cmte
Office of the Attorney General
120 Broadway, New York, NY 10271
212-416-6303 Fax: 212-416-8539
e-mail: lila.kirton@oag.state.ny.us
Lila E Kirton, Chair

Open Society Institute
400 West 59th St, New York, NY 10019
212-548-0600 Fax: 212-548-4600
Web site: www.soros.org
Stewart Paperin, Executive Vice President
Promotes open societies by shaping government policy & supporting education, media, public health, human & women's rights, as well as social, legal & economic reform

Puerto Rican Legal Defense & Education Fund Inc (PRLDEF)
99 Hudson St, 14th Fl, New York, NY 10013-2815
212-219-3360 or 800-328-2322 Fax: 212-431-4276
e-mail: info@prldef.org
Web site: www.prldef.org
Cesar Perales, President & General Counsel
Secure, promote & protect the civil & human rights of the Puerto Rican & wider Latino community through litigation, policy analysis & education

Resource Center for Independent Living (RCIL)
401-409 Columbia St, PO Box 210, Utica, NY 13503-0210
315-797-4642 or TTY 315-797-5837 Fax: 315-797-4747
e-mail: rcil@rcil.com
Web site: www.rcil.com
Burt Danovitz, Executive Director
Services & advocacy for the disabled & their families; public information & community education

SUNY Buffalo Human Rights Center
SUNY Buffalo, School of Law, 523 O'Brian Hall, Buffalo, NY 14260-1100
716-645-6184 Fax: 716-645-2064
e-mail: bhrc@buffalo.edu
Web site: wings.buffalo.edu/law/bhrlc
Makau Mutua, Professor & Director
Fostering scholarship, coursework, research & internships in international & human rights law

Self Advocacy Association of NYS
500 Balltown Rd, Bldg #5, Schenectady, NY 12304
518-382-1454 Fax: 518-382-1594
e-mail: sholmes@earthlink.net
Web site: www.sanys.org
Steve Holmes, Administrative Coordinator
Advocacy for & by persons with developmental disabilities to ensure civil rights & opportunities

Offices and agencies appear in alphabetical order.

Simon Wiesenthal Center, NY Tolerance Center
50 E 42nd St, Ste 1600, New York, NY 10017-5405
212-370-0320 Fax: 212-883-0895
e-mail: swcny@swcny.org
Web site: www.wiesenthal.com
Rhonda Barad, Eastern Director
*Preserve the memory of the Holocaust by fostering tolerance &
understanding through community involvement, educational
outreach & social action*

Tanenbaum Center for Interreligious Understanding
350 Fifth Ave, Ste 3502, New York, NY 10118
212-967-7707 Fax: 212-967-9001
e-mail: info@tanenbaum.org
Web site: www.tanenbaum.org
Joyce S Dubensky, Executive Director
*Puts interreligious understanding into practice; defuse the verbal &
physical violence done in the name of religion*

NYS Bar Assn, Gender Equity Task Force Cmte
The Legal Aid Society
65 W Broad St, Ste 400, Rochester, NY 14614
585-232-4090 Fax: 585-232-2352
e-mail: cpalumbo@lasroc.org
Carla M Palumbo, Chair

NYS Bar Assn, Issues Affecting Same Sex Couples
Whiteman Osterman & Hanna LLP
One Commerce Plz, Ste 1900, Albany, NY 12260-2015
518-487-7600 Fax: 518-487-7777
e-mail: mw@woh.com
Michael Whiteman, Chair

Women's Commission for Refugee Women & Children
122 East 42nd St, New York, NY 10168-1289
212-551-3000 Fax: 212-551-3180
e-mail: wcrwc@womenscommission.org
Web site: www.womenscommission.org
Carolyn Makinson, Executive Director
Advocacy on behalf of refugee women & children world-wide

Offices and agencies appear in alphabetical order.

INSURANCE

New York State

GOVERNOR'S OFFICE

Governor's Office
Executive Chamber
State Capitol
Albany, NY 12224
518-474-8390 Fax: 518-474-1513
Web site: www.state.ny.us

Governor:
  George E Pataki 518-474-8390
Executive Director:
  Kara Lanspery 518-474-8390
Secretary to the Governor:
  John P Cahill. 518-474-4246
Senior Policy Advisor to the Governor:
  Jeffrey Lovell 518-486-9671
Counsel to the Governor-Attorney General, Budget:
  Richard Platkin. 518-474-8343
Senior Asst Counsel to the Governor-Banking, Insurance, State Insurance
  Fund, Tort Reform, Uniform Laws, Workers' Compensation Board:
  Christopher McCarthy 518-474-2294
Director, Communications:
  David Catalfamo. 518-474-8418

EXECUTIVE DEPARTMENTS AND RELATED AGENCIES

Insurance Department
25 Beaver St
New York, NY 10004
212-480-6400 Fax: 518-473-4600
Web site: www.ins.state.ny.us

One Commerce Plaza
Albany, NY 12257
518-474-4567
Fax: 518-473-4600

Acting Superintendent:
  Howard Mills 518-474-4567
First Deputy Superintendent, Consumer Services, Fraud & Licensing:
  Louis W Pietroluongo. 212-480-2306
Senior Deputy Superintendent:
  Peter J Molinaro 518-474-4567
Deputy Superintendent, Property:
  Joseph A DeMauro. 212-480-2296

Administration & Operations
Director:
  Joseph J Burns. 518-474-6848/fax: 518-486-6600

Licensing Services Unit
Director:
  Salvatore Castiglione 518-474-7159/fax: 518-474-5048

Taxes & Accounts Unit
Director:
  Lori Fraser 518-474-8567

Consumer Services Bureau
Chief:
  Salvatore Castiglione 518-474-6600
  e-mail: scastigl@ins.state.ny.us
Asst Chief:
  Mitchel Gennaovi 212-480-4697/fax: 212-480-4735

Health Bureau
Co-Chief, Albany:
  Tom Zyra. 518-474-6272/fax: 518-473-4600
Chief, Accident & Health Rating:
  James M Gutterman 518-474-5394

Information Systems & Technology Bureau
Deputy Superintendent:
  Ronald Minafri. 212-480-2332

Insurance Frauds Bureau
Director:
  Charles Bardong. 212-480-6074

Life Bureau
Chief Examiner:
  Jeffrey Angelo 212-480-5026

Liquidation Bureau
123 William St, New York, NY 10038
Special Deputy Superintendent:
  James P O'Connor 212-341-6400

Office of General Counsel
Deputy Superintendent & General Counsel:
  Audrey M Samers. 212-480-5259

Property Bureau
Asst Deputy Superintendent & Bureau Chief:
  Mark Presser. 212-480-5565

Public Affairs & Research Bureau
Director:
  Michael Barry 212-480-5262/fax: 212-480-6077
  e-mail: public-affairs@ins.state.ny.us

Insurance Fund (NYS)
1 Watervliet Avenue Ext
Albany, NY 12206
888-875-5790
Web site: www.nysif.com

199 Church St
New York, NY 10007
888-875-5790

Executive Director/CEO:
  Kenneth J Ross. 212-312-7001

Offices and agencies appear in alphabetical order.

Policy Areas

Chief Fiscal Officer & Actuary:
Susan D Sharp 518-437-6168
General Attorney:
Douglas J Hayden. 212-312-7093
Deputy Executive Director & Marketing Director:
Ann F Formel 518-437-1879
Deputy Executive Director:
Christopher Barclay 518-437-5220
Deputy Executive Director:
Stephen D Nelson. 518-437-6196
Special Counsel:
Jacob H Weintraub 212-312-7872
Asst Deputy Director:
Jane Burgdorf 518-437-6151
Special Asst to the Exec Dir:
Kurt Rumpler 518-437-5209
Chief Information Officer:
Robert Sammons 518-437-5285
Public Information Officer:
Robert Lawson. 518-437-3504/fax: 518-437-1849

Administration
Director:
Albert K DiMeglio 212-312-7020

Claims & Medical Operations
Director:
Edward Hiller 212-312-7056

Field Services
Director:
Armin Holdorf 212-312-9591

Information Technology Service
Director, ITS:
Laurie Endries 518-437-3130

Insurance Fund Board of Commissioners
Chair:
Terence L Morris 212-312-7001
Vice Chair:
Robert H Hurlbut 212-312-7001
Secretary to the Board:
Christopher Barclay 518-437-5220
Asst Secretary to the Board:
Albert K DiMeglio 212-312-7020
Member (ex-officio)/Commissioner, NYS Dept of Labor:
Linda Angello. 212-312-7020
Member:
John F Carpenter. 212-312-7001
Member:
C Scott Bowen 212-312-7001
Member:
Donald T DeCarlo 212-312-7001
Member:
Jane A Halbritter. 212-312-7001
Member:
Charles L Loiodice 212-312-7001
Member:
Eugene Mazzola 212-312-7001

Investments
Director:
Bing Garrido. 212-312-9710

NYSIF District Offices
Albany . . . . fax: 518-437-5260
15 Computer Drive West, Albany, NY 12205

Business Manager:
Edward Obertubbesing. 518-437-6401
Buffalo . . . . fax: 716-851-2106
225 Oak St, Buffalo, NY 14203
Business Manager:
Ronald Reed. 716-851-2004

Endicott
Glendale Technology Park, 2001 E Perimeter Rd, Endicott, NY 13760
Business Manager:
James Fehrer 607-741-6100/fax: 607-741-5029

Nassau County, Long Island . . . . fax: 631-756-4242
8 Corporate Center Dr, 2nd Fl, Melville, NY 11747
Business Manager:
Cliff Meister. 631-756-4003

Rochester . . . . fax: 585-258-2065
100 Chestnut St, Ste 1000, Rochester, NY 14604
Business Manager:
Lisa Ellsworth 585-258-2100

Suffolk County, Long Island . . . . fax: 631-756-4260
8 Corporate Center Dr, 3rd Fl, Melville, NY 11747
Business Manager:
Eileen Wojnar. 631-756-4330

Syracuse . . . . fax: 315-453-8313
1045 Seventh North St, Liverpool, NY 13088
Business Manager:
Kathleen Campbell. 315-453-8300

White Plains . . . . fax: 914-701-2181
105 Corporate Park Dr, Ste 200, White Plains, NY 10604
Business Manager:
Carl Heitner 914-701-6292

Policyholder Services
Director:
Dennis Incitti 212-587-3600

Premium Audit
Director:
Glenn Cunningham. 212-587-7470

Safety Group Operations
Director:
John Massetti 212-312-9933

Underwriting
Director:
Vincent Troianiello. 212-312-7012

Labor Department
Building 12, Room 500
State Campus
Albany, NY 12240
518-457-2741 Fax: 518-457-6908
e-mail: nysdol@labor.state.ny.us
Web site: www.labor.state.ny.us

345 Hudson St, Ste 8301
Box 662, Mail Stop 01
New York, NY 10114-0662
212-352-6000
Fax: 212-352-6824

Offices and agencies appear in alphabetical order.

Commissioner:
Linda Angello.....................................518-457-2746
Executive Deputy Commissioner:
Dennis Ryan.....................................518-457-4318
Director, Communications:
Robert Lillpopp...................518-457-5519/fax: 518-485-1126

Employment & Unemployment Insurance Advisory Council

Employment Relations Board
Chair:
Anthony C Imbarrato............................212-564-2441

Industrial Board of Appeals
Chair:
Evelyn Heady...................................518-474-4789

Unemployment Insurance Appeal Board
Chair:
Richard M Rosenbaum.........................518-402-0205
Executive Director:
Joseph P Kearney..............................518-402-0205

Unemployment Insurance Division
Director:
Robert Davison.................518-457-2878/fax: 518-485-8604

Law Department
120 Broadway
New York, NY 10271-0332
212-416-8000 Fax: 212-416-8942

State Capitol
Albany, NY 12224-0341
518-474-7330
Fax: 518-402-2472

Attorney General:
Eliot Spitzer.....................................518-474-7330
First Deputy Attorney General:
Michele Hirshman...............................212-416-8050
Director, Public Information & Correspondence:
Peter A Drago....................518-474-7330/fax: 518-402-2472

State Counsel Division
Deputy Attorney General:
Richard Rifkin....................................518-473-7190
Asst Deputy Attorney General:
Patricia Martinelli.................518-473-0648/fax: 518-486-9777
Asst Deputy Attorney General:
Susan L Watson...................212-416-8579/fax: 212-416-6009

Civil Recoveries Bureau
Asst Attorney General in Charge:
Mary E House..................518-474-7131/fax: 518-474-1635

Claims Bureau
Bureau Chief:
Susan Pogoda..................212-416-8516/fax: 212-416-8946

Labor Bureau
Bureau Chief:
M Patricia Smith................................212-416-8710

Litigation Bureau
Bureau Chief, NYC:
James B Henley.................212-416-8523/fax: 212-416-6075

Real Property Bureau
Asst Attorney General in Charge:
Henry A DeCotis...............518-474-7151/fax: 518-473-5106

Workers' Compensation Board
20 Park Street
Albany, NY 12207
518-474-6670 Fax: 518-473-1415
Web site: www.wcb.state.ny.us

Chair:
David Wehner....................................518-474-6670
Vice Chair:
Jeffrey R Sweet..................................518-474-6670
Executive Director:
Richard A Bell...................................518-474-6670
General Counsel:
Vacant........................518-486-9564/fax: 518-473-2233
Director, Division of Appeals:
Carl Copps.....................518-402-0160/fax: 518-473-2233
Director, Internal Audit:
Albert Blackman.................518-473-6447/fax: 518-473-4761
Director, Public Information:
Jon A Sullivan...................518-474-6670/fax: 518-473-1415
Fraud Inspector General:
John Burgher....................888-363-6001/fax: 518-402-1059
Advocate for Business:
David Austin....................................518-486-3331
Advocate for Injured Workers:
Edwin Ruff.....................800-580-6665/fax: 518-486-7510

Administration
Deputy Executive Director:
Glenn Warren...................518-473-8900/fax: 518-486-6411
Director, Administrative Services:
Cathy King......................................518-486-3334
Director, Security:
Joseph V Smith.................518-402-0172/fax: 518-402-1059
Director, Finance & Policy:
Kathleen Griffin.................................518-486-9596
Director, Human Resources Management:
Lisa Sunkef.....................718-802-6612/fax: 718-834-2123
Affirmative Action Officer:
Jaime Benitez...................518-486-5128/fax: 518-486-6364

Operations
Deputy Executive Director:
Marsha Orndorff.................518-486-7143/fax: 518-474-9367
Director, Operations:
David M Donohue................518-486-3345/fax: 518-486-6411
Director, Disability Benefits:
Nicholas Dogias.................718-802-6947/fax: 718-802-6971
Director, WC Compliance & Regulatory Services:
Brian Collins...................518-474-2686/fax: 518-402-0701

District Offices
Albany
100 Broadway-Menands, Albany, NY 12241
District Administrator:
Linda Spano................866-750-5157/fax: 518-473-9166
Pat Wright
Binghamton
State Office Bldg, 44 Hawley St, Binghamton, NY 13901
District Admin:
Anthony Capozzi............866-802-3604/fax: 607-721-8464
David Wiktorek
Brooklyn
111 Livingston St, Brooklyn, NY 11201

Offices and agencies appear in alphabetical order.

District Administrator:
Edward Joyce 800-877-1373/fax: 718-802-6642
Tom Agostino
Buffalo
Statler Towers, 3rd Fl, 107 Delaware Ave, Buffalo, NY 14202-2898
District Administrator:
Jeffrey Quinn 866-211-0645/fax: 716-842-2171
Barbara Townsend
Hauppauge
220 Rabro Drive, Ste 100, Hauppauge, NY 11788-4230
District Admin:
Scott Firestone 866-681-5354/fax: 631-952-7966
Robert F Williams
Hempstead
175 Fulton Ave, Hempstead, NY 11550
District Administrator:
Alan Landman 866-805-3630/fax: 516-560-7799
Alan Gotlinaky
Manhattan
215 W 125th St, New York, NY 10027
District Admin:
Frank Vernuccio, Jr 800-877-1373/fax: 212-932-1488
Peekskill
41 N Division St, Peekskill, NY 10566
District Administrator:
Alida Carey. 866-746-0552/fax: 914-788-5793
Luis A Torres
Queens
168-46 91st Ave, Jamaica, NY 11432
District Administrator:
Wayne Allen. 800-877-1373/fax: 718-291-7248
Carl Gabbidon
Rochester
130 Main St West, Rochester, NY 14614
District Admin:
George A Park, Jr 866-211-0644/fax: 585-238-8351
MaryBeth Goodsell
Syracuse
935 James Street, Syracuse, NY 13203
District Administrator:
Janet Burman 866-802-3730/fax: 315-423-2938
Marc Johnson

Systems Modernization
Deputy Executive Director:
Nancy Mulholland. 518-486-7143/fax: 518-474-9367
Director, Management Information Systems:
Thomas Wegener. 518-486-5143/fax: 518-473-6379

Workers' Compensation Board of Commissioners
Chair:
David Wehner. 518-474-6670
Vice Chair:
Jeffrey R Sweet. 518-474-6670
Commissioner:
Mona Bargnesi 518-474-6670

Commissioner:
Michael T Berns. 518-486-9529
Commissioner:
Leslie J Botta 518-402-1071
Commissioner:
Candace K Finnegan. 518-402-6137
Commissioner:
Scott Firestone 518-402-1071
Commissioner:
Agatha Edel Groski 518-402-6135
Commissioner:
Karl A Henry 518-402-6136
Commissioner:
Frances Libous 518-474-6670
Commissioner:
Ellen O Paprocki. 518-474-6670
Commissioner:
Robert Zinck. 518-474-6670
Secretary to the Board:
Susan M Olson 518-402-6071

NEW YORK STATE LEGISLATURE

See Legislative Branch in Section 1 for additional Standing Committee and Subcommittee information.

Assembly Standing Committees

Insurance
Chair:
Alexander B Grannis (D) 518-455-5676
Ranking Minority Member:
William Barclay (R). 518-455-5481

Labor
Chair:
Susan V John (D) 518-455-4527
Ranking Minority Member:
Patricia L Acampora (R) 518-455-5294

Senate Standing Committees

Insurance
Chair:
James L Seward (R) 518-455-3131
Ranking Minority Member:
George Onorato (D) 518-455-3486

Labor
Chair:
George Maziarz (R) 518-455-2024
Ranking Minority Member:
Dianne J Savino (D). 518-455-2437

U.S. Government

U.S. CONGRESS

See U.S. Congress Chapter for additional Standing Committee and Subcommittee information.

House of Representatives Standing Committees

Financial Services
Chair:
Michael G Oxley (R-OH). 202-225-2676
Ranking Minority Member:
Barney Frank (D-MA) 202-225-5931

Offices and agencies appear in alphabetical order.

New York Delegate:
   Gary L Ackerman (D) 202-225-2601
New York Delegate:
   Joseph Crowley (D) 202-225-3965
New York Delegate:
   Vito Fossella (R). 202-225-3371
New York Delegate:
   Steve Israel (D). 202-225-3335
New York Delegate:
   Sue W Kelly (R). 202-225-5441
New York Delegate:
   Peter T King (R). 202-225-7896
New York Delegate:
   Carolyn B Maloney (D) 202-225-7944
New York Delegate:
   Carolyn McCarthy (D) 202-225-5516
New York Delegate:
   Gregory W Meeks (D) 202-225-3461
New York Delegate:
   Nydia M Velazquez (D) 202-225-2361

Subcommittee
Capital Markets, Insurance & Government Sponsored Enterprises
   Chair:
      Richard H Baker (R-LA). 202-225-3901
   Ranking Minority Member:
      Paul E Kanjorski (D-PA). 202-225-6511
   New York Delegate:
      Gary L Ackerman (D) 202-225-2601
   New York Delegate:
      Joseph Crowley (D). 202-225-3965
   New York Delegate:
      Vito Fossella (R) 202-225-3371

New York Delegate:
   Steve Israel (D) 202-225-3335
New York Delegate:
   Sue W Kelly (R) 202-225-5441
New York Delegate:
   Peter T King (R) 202-225-7896
New York Delegate:
   Carolyn McCarthy (D) 202-225-5516
New York Delegate:
   Gregory W Meeks (D). 202-225-3461
New York Delegate:
   Nydia M Velazquez (D) 202-225-2361

Senate Standing Committees

Finance
Chair:
   Charles E Grassley (R-IA) 202-224-3744
Ranking Minority Member:
   Max Baucus (D-MT) 202-224-2651

Subcommittees
Healthcare
   Chair:
      Orrin Hatch (R-UT). 202-224-5251
   Ranking Minority Mbr:
      John D Rockefeller, IV (D-WV) 202-224-6472
Social Security & Family Policy
   Chair:
      Rick Santorum (R-PA) 202-224-6324
   Ranking Minority Member:
      Kent Conrad (D-ND). 202-224-2043

Private Sector

Alliance of American Insurers
450 7th Ave, Ste 1600, New York, NY 10123
212-971-0879 Fax: 212-947-5772
e-mail: jcucci@allianceai.org
Web site: www.allianceai.org
E John Cucci, Vice President, Northeast Region

American International Group Inc
70 Pine St, 36th Fl, New York, NY 10270
212-770-6114 Fax: 212-785-4214
e-mail: ned.cloonan@aig.com
Web site: www.aig.com
Edward T Cloonan, Vice President International & Corporate Affairs
International business, government & financial services

Aon Group Inc
55 East 52nd St, 32nd Fl, New York, NY 10055
212-441-1150 Fax: 212-441-1929
e-mail: ellen_perle@ars.aon.com
Web site: www.aon.com
Ellen Perle, Associate General Counsel
Insurance brokerage, risk management & financing

Associated Risk Managers of New York Inc
4 Airline Drive, Suite 205, Albany, NY 12205
518-690-2072 or 800-735-5441 Fax: 518-690-2074
e-mail: arm@armnortheast.com
Web site: www.armnortheast.com
John McLaughlin, Executive Director

Capital District Physicians' Health Plan Inc
Patroon Creek Corp Ctr, 1223 Washington Ave, Albany, NY 12206
518-641-5561 Fax: 518-641-5506
e-mail: info@cdphp.com
Web site: www.cdphp.com
Stephen R Sloan, Senior Vice President, Legal Affairs & Chief
   Counsel
Health insurance

NYS Bar Assn, Torts, Insurance & Compensation Law Section
Connors & Corcoran LLP
Times Square Bldg, 45 Exchange St, Ste 250, Rochester, NY 14614
585-232-5885 Fax: 585-546-3631
e-mail: buholtz@frontiernet.net
Web site: www.connorscorcoran.com
Eileen E Buholtz, Chair

Offices and agencies appear in alphabetical order.

Dupee, Dupee & Monroe, PC
30 Matthews St, Box 470, Goshen, NY 10924
845-294-8900 Fax: 845-294-3619
e-mail: law@dupeelaw.com
Web site: www.dupeelaw.com
Jon C Dupee, Jr, Managing Partner
Litigation, personal injury law, medical malpractice, product liability, civil rights, discrimination, sexual harassment

Empire Blue Cross & Blue Shield
11 West 42nd St, 18th Fl, New York, NY 10036
212-476-1000 Fax: 212-476-1281
e-mail: deborah.bohren@empireblue.com
Web site: www.empireblue.com
Deborah Bohren, Senior Vice President, Communications
Health insurance

Equitable Life Assurance Society of the US
1290 Ave of the Americas, New York, NY 10104
212-314-3828 Fax: 212-707-1890
e-mail: wendy.cooper@axa.financial.com
Web site: www.axa-financial.com
Wendy E Cooper, Senior Vice President & Associate General
    Counsel, Government Relations
Life insurance regulation

Excess Line Association of New York
One Exchange Plz, 55 Broadway, 29th Fl, New York, NY 10006
646-292-5555 Fax: 626-292-5505
e-mail: dmaher@elany.org
Web site: www.elany.org
Daniel F Maher, Executive Director
Industry advisory association; facilitate & encourage compliance with the excess line law

Group Health Inc
441 9th Ave, 8th Fl, New York, NY 10001
212-615-0891 Fax: 212-563-8561
e-mail: jgoodwin@ghi.com
Jeffrey Goodwin, Director, Governmental Relations
Affordable, quality health insurance for working individuals & families

Insurance Brokers' Association of the State of New York
25 Chamberlain St, Glenmont, NY 12077
212-962-7771 Fax: 877-644-0422
e-mail: ibany@ibany.org
Web site: www.ibany.org
Susan Phillips, Executive Director

Levene, Gouldin & Thompson LLP
PO Box F-1706, Binghamton, NY 13902
607-584-5706 Fax: 607-763-9212
e-mail: dgouldin@binghamtonlaw.com
Web site: www.binghamtonlaw.com
David M Gouldin, Partner
Professional liability insurance

Life Insurance Council of New York Inc
551 Fifth Ave, 29th Floor, New York, NY 10176
212-986-6181 Fax: 212-986-6549
e-mail: tworkman@licony.org
Web site: www.licony.org
Thomas E Workman, President & Chief Executive Officer
Promote a legislative, regulatory & judicial environment that encourages members to conduct & grow their business

Marsh & McLennan Companies
1166 6th Ave, New York, NY 10036-2774
212-345-5000 Fax: 212-345-4838
e-mail: barbara.perlmutter@mmc.com
Web site: www.mmc.com
Barbara S Perlmutter, Senior Vice President, Public Affairs
Risk & insurance services; investment management; consulting

Medical Society of the State of New York, Division of Socio-Medical Economi
420 Lakeville Rd, PO Box 5404, Lake Success, NY 11042
516-488-6100 x332 Fax: 516-488-6136
e-mail: rmcnally@mssny.org
Web site: www.mssny.org
William Abrams, Executive Vice President
Workers compensations; health insurance programs

MetLife
27-01 Queens Plaza North, Long Island City, NY 11101
212-578-3603 Fax: 212-578-9890
e-mail: mzarcone@metlife.com
Web site: www.metlife.com
Michael A Zarcone, Seior Vice President, Government & Industry
    Relations

NY Life Insurance Co
51 Madison Ave, Suite 3200, New York, NY 10010
212-576-7000 Fax: 212-576-4473
e-mail: gayle_yeomans@newyorklife.com
Web site: www.newyorklife.com
Gayle A Yeomans, Vice President Government Affairs
Insurance products & financial services

NY Property Insurance Underwriting Association
100 William St, New York, NY 10038
212-208-9700 Fax: 212-344-9879
Web site: www.nypiua.com
Joseph Calvo, President

NYMAGIC Inc
919 3rd Ave, New York, NY 10022-3919
212-551-0600 Fax: 212-986-1310
e-mail: info@mmo.com
Web site: www.nymagic.com
George R Trumbull, Chairman & Chief Executive Officer
Marine insurance & excess & surplus lines

Offices and agencies appear in alphabetical order.

New York Insurance Association Inc
130 Washington Ave, Albany, NY 12210
518-432-4227 Fax: 518-432-4220
e-mail: bbourdeau@nyia.org
Web site: www.nyia.org
Bernard N Bourdeau, President
Property & casualty insurance

New York Long-Term Care Brokers Ltd
11 Halfmoon Executive Park, Clifton Park, NY 12065
518-371-5522 x116 Fax: 518-371-6131
e-mail: k_johnson@nyltcb.com
Web site: www.nyltcb.com
Kevin Johnson, President
*Long-term care, life & disability insurance; consulting & sales to
individual consumers & financial service industry professionals*

New York Municipal Insurance Reciprocal (NYMIR)
24 Aviation Rd, Ste 206, Albany, NY 12205
518-437-1171 Fax: 518-437-1182
Web site: www.nymir.org
Gale M Hatch, President
Insurance services for municipalities

New York Schools Insurance Reciprocal (NYSIR)
333 Earle Ovington Blvd, Uniondale, NY 11553
516-227-3355 x1468 or 1-800-476-9747 Fax: 516-227-2352
e-mail: jgoncalves@wrightrisk.com
Web site: www.nysir.org
Joseph Goncalves, Executive Director
Insurance & risk management services for public school districts

**New York State Association of Insurance & Financial
Advisors Inc**
38 Sheridan Ave, Albany, NY 12210
518-462-5567 Fax: 518-462-5569
e-mail: nysaifamail@aol.com
Web site: www.nysaifa.com
Mark L Yavornitzki, Executive Vice President & Chief
   Administrative Officer
*Association of individuals engaged in the sale of life, health &
property/casualty insurance & related financial services*

Professional Insurance Agents of New York State
25 Chamberlain St, PO Box 997, Glenmont, NY 12077-0997
800-424-4244 Fax: 888-225-6935
e-mail: kenb@piaonline.org
Web site: www.piany.org
Ken Bessette, President/Chief Executive Officer

SBLI USA Mutual Life Insurance Company Inc
460 W 34th St, Suite 800, New York, NY 10001-2320
212-356-0327 Fax: 212-624-0700
e-mail: dklugman@sbliusa.com
Web site: www.sbliusa.com
Vikki Pryor, President & Chief Executive Officer
Corporate insurance regulatory law & government affairs

**St John's University-Peter J Tobin College of Business,
School of Risk Mana**
101 Murray St, New York, NY 10007
212-815-9217 Fax: 212-815-9284
Web site: www.stjohns.edu
Ellen Thrower, Executive Director

Stroock & Stroock & Lavan LLP
180 Maiden Lane, New York, NY 10038-4982
212-806-5541 Fax: 212-806-2541
e-mail: dgabay@stroock.com
Donald D Gabay, Attorney
Insurance, reinsurance, corporate & regulatory law

Support Services Alliance Inc
107 Prospect St, PO Box 130, Schoharie, NY 12157
800-322-3920 or 518-295-7966 Fax: 518-295-8556
e-mail: info@ssamembers.com
Web site: www.smallbizgrowth.com
Steven Cole, President
Small business support services & insurance

Travelers Insurance Co
90 Merrick Ave, 4th Fl, East Meadow, NY 11554
516-296-2109 Fax: 516-296-2221
e-mail: tjmcdona@travelers.com
Tom McDonald, Regional Vice President
Property & casualty insurance

Unity Mutual Life Insurance Co
507 Plum St, PO Box 5000, Syracuse, NY 13250-5000
315-448-7000 Fax: 315-448-7100
e-mail: jwason@unity-life.com
Web site: www.unity-life.com
Jay Wason, Jr, General Counsel

Utica Mutual Insurance Co
PO Box 530, Utica, NY 13503-0530
1-800-274-1914 Fax: 315-734-2662
Web site: www.uticanational.com
Richard Creedon, Senior Vice President, Claims & General Counsel
Property, casualty, life insurance & related services

Policy Areas

Offices and agencies appear in alphabetical order.

JUDICIAL SYSTEM & LEGAL SYSTEM

New York State

GOVERNOR'S OFFICE

Governor's Office
Executive Chamber
State Capitol
Albany, NY 12224
518-474-8390 Fax: 518-474-1513
Web site: www.state.ny.us

Governor:
George E Pataki 518-474-8390
Executive Director:
Kara Lanspery 518-474-8390
Secretary to the Governor:
John P Cahill. 518-474-4246
Senior Policy Advisor to the Governor:
Jeffrey Lovell 518-486-9671
Counsel to the Governor-Attorney General, Budget:
Richard Platkin 518-474-8343
Director, Communications:
David Catalfamo. 518-474-8418
Senior Asst Counsel to the Governor-Criminal Justice, Inspector General,
Public Security, Special Prosecutors, State Investigation:
Roger McDonough 518-474-1291
Asst Counsel to the Governor-Econ Development, Empire State Dev Corp,
Jacob Javits Convention Ctr, NYSTAR, Olympic Regional Dev Auth,
Tourism:
Robert Ryan 518-474-2266
Asst Counsel to the Governor-Clemency, Crime Vics, Correcs, Correc Svcs,
Disaster, Extrads, Military/Naval/SEMO, Parole, Domestic Viol,
Probatn/Correc Alts, Veterans:
Gerald Connolly 518-474-8494

EXECUTIVE DEPARTMENTS AND RELATED AGENCIES

Criminal Justice Services, Division of
Four Tower Place
Albany, NY 12203-3764
518-457-1260 Fax: 518-457-3089
Web site: www.criminaljustice.state.ny.us

Commissioner & Director:
Chauncey G Parker. 518-457-1260
Executive Deputy Commissioner:
Martin Cirincione 518-457-6091
Affirmative Action Officer:
G Bernett Marion 518-457-6110
Director, Communications:
Lynn Rasic 518-485-0857
Public Information Officer:
Lyle Hartog 518-485-2465/fax: 518-485-2467

Administration Office
Director, Administration:
Paula Steigman 518-457-6100

Administrative Operations
Director:
Phyllis M Foster 518-457-1696

Human Resources Management
Director:
Alyce Ashe 518-457-6110

State Finance & Budget
Acting Director, Financial Administration:
Kimberly J Szady. 518-457-6105
Director, Internal Audit & Compliance:
William Gritsavage 518-457-1417

Advisory Groups

Juvenile Justice Advisory Group
15 Van Dyke Ave, Amsterdam, NY 12010
Acting Chair:
Michael Elmendorf. 518-474-7516

NYS Motor Vehicle & Insurance Fraud Prevention Board
Chair/Commissioner & Director:
Chauncey G Parker 518-457-1260

Legal Services & Forensic Services Office
Deputy Commissioner & Counsel:
Kimberly O'Conner 518-457-4181

Missing & Exploited Children Clearinghouse
Director:
Kenneth R Buniak 518-485-7632

Office of Forensic Services
Director:
John Hicks 518-457-7287

Sex Offender Registry
Director:
Jeanne Sample 518-457-7985

Office of Criminal Justice Operations
Deputy Commissioner:
Daniel Foro. 518-485-2995
Executive Director:
James Shea 518-457-8724

Information Technology Development Group
Director:
Thomas Meyer 518-457-9716

Information Technology Services Group
Director:
Alex Roberts. 518-457-3743

Office of Operations
Director:
William J Sillery 518-457-6050
Assistant Bureau Director:
Michael Tymeson. 518-457-6050

Offices and agencies appear in alphabetical order.

Chief, Records Management Bureau:
James Stanco 518-457-6051
Chief, Civil Identification Bureau:
Ann Sammons 518-485-5763

Office of Public Safety
Deputy Commissioner:
James DeLapp 518-457-6101
Director:
Mark R Lindsay 518-457-2667
Asst Director:
John R Digman 518-485-1414
Chief of Administrative Services:
David H Mahany 518-457-4135
Chief of Program Services:
Dennis W McCarty 518-485-1410

Advisory Groups
Law Enforcement Accreditation Council
518-457-6101
Deputy Commissioner:
James DeLapp 518-457-6101
Municipal Police Training Council
518-457-6101
Security Guard Advisory Council
518-457-6101
Chief, Administrative Services:
David H Mahany 518-457-6101
State Cmte for Coordination of Police Services for the Elderly (TRIAD)
518-457-6101
Deputy Commissioner:
James DeLapp 518-457-6101
Statewide Law Enforcement Telecommunications Cmte
518-457-6101
Deputy Commissioner:
James DeLapp 518-457-6101

Office of Strategic Planning
Deputy Commissioner:
Roger Jeffries 518-485-7433

Bureau of Justice Research & Innovation
Director:
Donna Hall 518-457-7301
Crime Reductions Strategies Unit
Chief:
Thomas Mitchell 518-457-7301
Justice Statistics & Performance Unit
Chief:
Susan Jacobsen 518-457-8381
Justice Systems Analysis Unit
Chief:
David vanAlstyne 518-457-7301
Offender Management Analysis Unit
Chief:
Bruce Frederick 518-457-3724

Funding & Program Assistance Office
Director:
AnneMarie Strano 518-457-8462

Law Department
120 Broadway
New York, NY 10271-0332
212-416-8000 Fax: 212-416-8942
Web site: www.oag.state.ny.us

State Capitol
Albany, NY 12224-0341
518-474-7330
Fax: 518-402-2472

Attorney General:
Eliot Spitzer 518-474-7330

Administration
Agency Bldg 4, Empire State Plaza, Albany, NY 12224-0341
Executive Director:
Sylvia Hamer 518-473-7900/fax: 518-474-0680
Asst Director:
Jean M Woodard 518-473-7969/fax: 518-474-0680

Administrative Services
Director:
George J Owad 518-474-6765/fax: 518-473-8224

Budget & Fiscal Management
Director:
Cynthia Izzo 518-474-7699/fax: 518-474-0714

Human Resources
Director:
Eric Schwenzfeier 518-474-4848/fax: 518-474-3578

Legal Technology & Systems Management
Director:
Robert J Vitello 518-474-7333/fax: 518-474-6588

Training & Staff Development
Manager:
Michael Kopcza 518-486-3994/fax: 518-486-5936

Appeals & Opinions Division
Solicitor General:
Caitlin J Halligan 212-416-8016/fax: 212-416-8942
Deputy Solicitor General:
Wayne L Benjamin 518-474-7138/fax: 518-473-8963
Deputy Solicitor General:
Daniel Smirlock 518-473-0903/fax: 518-486-3176
Deputy Solicitor General:
Michael Belohlavek 212-416-8028/fax: 212-416-8962
Deputy Solicitor General:
Michelle Aronowitz 212-416-8027/fax: 212-416-8962
Legal Records:
Cynthia Bogardus 518-474-5241

Law Library
Chief, Library Services:
Sarah Brown 518-474-3840/fax: 518-402-2271
Senior Librarian, New York City Office:
Franette Sheinwald 212-416-8012/fax: 212-416-6130

Criminal Division
Deputy Attorney General:
Peter B Pope 212-416-8058/fax: 212-416-8026
Asst Deputy Attorney General:
Karen Lupuloff 212-416-8090/fax: 212-416-8026

Criminal Prosecutions Bureau
Chief:
Janet Cohn 518-474-4096/fax: 518-474-3364
Deputy Bureau Chief, New York City:
Zachary Weiss 212-416-6095/fax: 212-416-8026
Deputy Bureau Chief, Albany:
Viola Abbitt 518-474-4096/fax: 518-474-3364

Policy Areas

Offices and agencies appear in alphabetical order.

Investigations Bureau
Chief Investigator:
    William M Casey . . . . 212-416-6328 or 518-486-4540

Medicaid Fraud Control Unit
120 Broadway, 13th Fl, New York, NY 10271-0007
Deputy Attorney General in Charge:
    William J Comiskey 212-417-5250/fax: 212-417-5274
First Asst Deputy Attorney General:
    Peter M Bloch 212-417-5261/fax: 212-417-5274
Asst Deputy Attorney General:
    George Quinlan 716-853-8584
Regional Director, Albany:
    Steve Krantz 518-474-3032/fax: 518-474-4519
Deputy Regional Director, Buffalo:
    Gary A Baldauf 716-853-8507/fax: 716-853-8525
Regional Director, Long Island:
    Alan Buonpastore 631-952-6400/fax: 631-952-6382
Regional Director, NYC:
    Richard Harrow 212-417-5391/fax: 212-417-4725
Regional Director, Rochester:
    Jerry Solomon 716-262-2860/fax: 716-262-2866
Regional Director, Syracuse:
    Ralph Tortora, III 315-423-1121/fax: 315-423-1120
Deputy Regional Director, Westchester/Rockland:
    Anne Jardine 845-732-7500/fax: 845-732-7555
Regional Director for Special Projects Unit:
    Pat Lupinetti 845-732-7550/fax: 845-732-7557

Organized Crime Task Force
Deputy Attorney General-in-Charge:
    J Christopher Prather 914-422-8714/fax: 914-422-8835

Intergovernmental Relations
Director:
    Lila Kirton 212-416-6044/fax: 212-416-8738
Deputy Director:
    Galen Kirkland 212-416-6342/fax: 212-416-8738
Director, Policy Resources:
    Mindy Bockenstein 212-416-8147/fax: 212-416-8738

Office of the Attorney General
First Deputy Attorney General:
    Michele Hirshman 212-416-8050
Asst First Deputy Attorney General:
    Francine James 212-416-8050
Chief of Staff:
    Richard Baum 212-416-8050
Counsel to Attorney General:
    David Nocenti 212-416-8050
Deputy Counsel to Attorney General:
    Avi Schick 212-416-8050
Deputy Attorney General for Operations:
    Kermit Brooks 212-416-8050
Deputy Attorney General:
    Beth L Golden 212-416-8050
Deputy Attorney General:
    Debra L W Cohn 212-416-8054
Asst Deputy Attorney General, Program Development:
    Daniel Feldman 212-416-8167
Asst Attorney General, Legal Education:
    Rachel Kretser 518-473-5582
Asst Attorney General, Legal Recruitment:
    Camille Chin-Kee-Fatt 212-416-8080
Asst Attorney General, Legislative Bureau:
    Kathy Bennett 518-486-3000
Director, Public Information & Correspondence:
    Peter A Drago 518-474-7330/fax: 518-402-2472

Scheduler:
    Marlene Turner 212-416-8050
Deputy Chief of Staff:
    Joseph Palozzola 212-416-8050

Press Office
Director, Communications:
    Darren Dopp 212-416-8060/fax: 212-416-6005
Press Secretary:
    Juanita Scarlett 212-416-8060
Press Officer:
    Maritere Arce 212-416-8065

Public Advocacy Division
Acting Deputy Attorney General:
    Terryl Brown Clemons 212-416-8041/fax: 212-416-8068
Special Counsel:
    Mary Ellen Burns 212-416-6155

Antitrust Bureau
Bureau Chief:
    Jay L Himes 212-416-8282/fax: 212-416-6015

Charities Bureau
Bureau Chief:
    William Josephson 212-416-8401/fax: 212-416-8393

Civil Rights Bureau
Bureau Chief:
    Dennis Parker 212-416-8250/fax: 212-416-8074

Consumer Fraud & Protection Bureau
Bureau Chief:
    Thomas G Conway 518-474-2374/fax: 518-474-3618

Environmental Protection Bureau
Bureau Chief:
    Peter Lehner 212-416-8450/fax: 212-416-6007

Healthcare Bureau
Bureau Chief:
    Joseph R Baker, III 212-416-8521/fax: 212-416-8034

Internet Bureau
Bureau Chief:
    Kenneth Dreifach 212-416-8433/fax: 212-416-8369

Investment Protection Bureau
Bureau Chief:
    David Brown 212-416-8198/fax: 212-416-8816

Telecommunications & Energy Bureau
Bureau Chief:
    Susanna M Zwerling 212-416-8333/fax: 212-416-8877

Regional Offices Division
Deputy Attorney General for Regional Offices:
    Martin Mack 315-448-4880/fax: 315-448-4899
Asst Deputy Attorney General for Regional Offices:
    Christopher Walsh 518-402-2184/fax: 518-473-8153

Binghamton
State Office Bldg, 17th Fl, 44 Hawley St, Binghamton, NY 13901-4433
Asst Attorney General in Charge:
    Dennis McCabe 607-721-8771/fax: 607-721-8789

Brooklyn
55 Hanson Place, Brooklyn, NY 11217-1523
Asst Attorney General in Charge:
    Lois Booker Williams 718-722-3949/fax: 718-722-3951

Buffalo
Statler Towers, 107 Delaware Ave, 4th Fl, Buffalo, NY 14202-3473

Offices and agencies appear in alphabetical order.

Asst Attorney General in Charge:
Kenneth Schoetz 716-853-6271/fax: 716-853-8571

Harlem
163 West 125th St, New York, NY 10027-8201
Asst Attorney General in Charge:
Guy H Mitchell 212-961-4475/fax: 212-961-4003

Nassau
200 Old Country Rd, Ste 460, Mineola, NY 11501-4241
Asst Attorney General in Charge:
Juan Merchan 516-248-3322/fax: 516-747-6432

Plattsburgh
70 Clinton St, Plattsburgh, NY 12901-2818
Asst Attorney General in Charge:
Robert Glennon 518-562-3282/fax: 518-562-3294

Poughkeepsie
235 Main St, 3RD FL, Poughkeepsie, NY 12601-3194
Asst Attorney General in Charge:
Mary Kavaney 845-485-3900/fax: 845-452-3303

Rochester
144 Exchange Blvd, 2nd Fl, Rochester, NY 14614-2176
Asst Attorney General in Charge:
Robert Colon 585-546-7430/fax: 585-546-7514

Suffolk
300 Motor Pkwy, Ste 205, Hauppauge, NY 11788-5127
Asst Attorney General in Charge:
Denis McElligott 631-231-2424/fax: 631-435-4757

Syracuse
615 Erie Blvd West, Suite 102, Syracuse, NY 13210-2339
Asst Attorney General in Charge:
Winthrop Thurlow 315-448-4800/fax: 315-448-4853

Utica
207 Genesee St, Room 504, Utica, NY 13501-2812
Asst Attorney General in Charge:
Joel L Marmelstein 315-793-2225/fax: 315-793-2228

Watertown
Dulles St Ofc Bldg, 317 Washington St, Watertown, NY 13601-3744
Asst Attorney General in Charge:
John Sullivan 315-785-2444/fax: 315-785-2294

Westchester
101 East Post Rd, White Plains, NY 10601-5008
Asst Attorney General in Charge:
Gary Brown 914-422-8755/fax: 914-422-8706

State Counsel Division
Deputy Attorney General:
Richard Rifkin 518-473-7190
Asst Deputy Attorney General:
Patricia Martinelli 518-473-0648/fax: 518-486-9777
Asst Deputy Attorney General:
Susan L Watson 212-416-8579/fax: 212-416-6001

Civil Recoveries Bureau
Asst Attorney General in Charge:
Mary E House 518-474-7131/fax: 518-473-1635

Claims Bureau
Bureau Chief:
Susan Pogoda 212-416-8516/fax: 212-416-8946

Labor Bureau
Bureau Chief:
M Patricia Smith 212-416-8710

Litigation Bureau
Bureau Chief, Albany:
Bruce D Feldman 518-473-8328/fax: 518-473-1572
Bureau Chief, NYC:
James B Henley 212-416-8523/fax: 212-416-6075

Real Property Bureau
Asst Attorney General in Charge:
Henry A DeCotis 518-474-7151/fax: 518-473-5106

JUDICIAL SYSTEM AND RELATED AGENCIES

Attorney Grievance Committee

1st Judicial Dept, Judicial Dist 1, 12
61 Broadway, 2nd Fl, New York, NY 10006
Chief Counsel:
Thomas J Cahill 212-401-0800/fax: 212-401-0810

2nd Judicial Dept, Judicial Dist 2, 9, 10, 11

Judicial Dist 2, 11
Renaissance Plz, 335 Adams St, Ste 2400, Brooklyn, NY 11201-3745
Chief Counsel:
Diana Masfield Kearse 718-923-6300/fax: 718-624-2978

Judicial Dist 9
399 Knollwood Rd, Ste 200, White Plains, NY 10603
Web site: www.nylawfund.org/gc9/instruct.htm
Chief Counsel:
Gary L Casella 914-949-4540

Judicial Dist 10
150 Motor Pkwy, Ste 102, Hauppauge, NY 11758
Chief Counsel:
Robert P Guido 631-231-3775/fax: 631-364-7355

3rd Judicial Dept, Judicial Dist 3, 4, 6
40 Stuben St, Ste 502, Albany, NY 12207-2109
Web site: www.courts.state.ny.us/ad3
Chief Counsel:
Mark S Ochs 518-474-8816/fax: 518-474-0389

4th Judicial Dept, Dist 5, 7, 8
Web site: www.courts.stte.ny.us/ad4

Judicial Dist 5 .... fax: 315-479-0123
224 Harrison St, Ste 408, Syracuse, NY 13202-3066
Chief Counsel:
David L Edmunds, Jr 315-471-1835
Principal Counsel:
Anthony J Gigliotti 315-471-1835

Judicial Dist 7 .... fax: 585-530-3191
50 East Ave, Ste 404, Rochester, NY 14604-2206
Chief Counsel:
David L Edmunds, Jr 585-530-3180
Principal Counsel:
Daniel A Drake 585-530-3180

Judicial Dist 8 .... fax: 716-856-2701
Ellicott Sq Bldg, 295 Main St, Ste 1036, Buffalo, NY 14203-2560
Chief Counsel:
David L Edmunds, Jr 716-858-1190
Deputy Chief Counsel:
Vincent L Scarsella 716-858-1190
Principal Counsel:
Margaret C Callanan 716-858-1190

Offices and agencies appear in alphabetical order.

Law Guardian Program

1st Judicial Dept
41 Madison Ave, 39th Fl, New York, NY 10010
Director:
Jane Schreiber 212-340-0502/fax: 212-340-0550

2nd Judicial Dept
335 Adams St, Ste 2400, Brooklyn, NY 11201
Director:
Harriet Weinberger 718-923-6350/fax: 718-624-5603
e-mail: hweinber@courts.state.ny.us

3rd Judicial Dept . . . . fax: 518-402-2530
PO Box 7288, Capital Station, Albany, NY 12224-0288
Fax: 518-402-2530
Web site: www.courts.state.ny.us/ad3/lg
Director:
John E Carter, Jr 518-486-4567
e-mail: lgp3d@courts.state.ny.us
Assistant Director:
Betsey R Ruslander 518-486-4567

4th Judicial Dept
50 East Ave, Ste 304, Rochester, NY 14604
Director:
Tracy M Hamilton 585-530-3170/fax: 585-530-3175

Mental Hygiene Legal Service

1st Judicial Dept . . . . fax: 212-779-1894
60 Madison Ave, 2nd Fl, New York, NY 10010
Director:
Marvin Bernstein 212-779-1734
Deputy Director:
Stephan Harkavy 212-779-1734

2nd Judicial Dept
170 Old Country Rd, Rm 500, Mineola, NY 11501
Director:
Sidney Hirschfeld 516-746-4545
Deputy Director:
Lesley De Lia 516-746-4545

3rd Judicial Dept
40 Steuben St, Ste 501, Albany, NY 12207-2109
Director:
Bruce S Dix 518-474-4453/fax: 518-473-5849
Deputy Director:
David M LeVine 607-721-8440/fax: 607-721-8447

4th Judicial Dept
50 East Ave, Ste 402, Rochester, NY 14604
Director:
Emmett J Creahan 585-530-3050
Deputy Director:
Neil J Rowe 585-530-3050/fax: 585-530-3079

Unified Court System
25 Beaver St
New York, NY 10004
212-428-2700 Fax: 212-428-2508
Web site: www.nycourts.gov

Agency Bldg 4, 20th Fl
Empire State Plaza
Albany, NY 12223

518-474-7469
Fax: 518-473-9909

Administrative Board of the Courts

Appellate Division
1st Judicial Department
Courthouse, 27 Madison Ave, New York, NY 10010
Presiding Justice:
John T Buckley 212-340-0400
2nd Judicial Department
45 Monroe Place, Brooklyn, NY 11201
Presiding Justice:
A Gail Prudenti 718-875-1300
3rd Judicial Department
Justice Bldg, 5th Fl, Empire State Plaza, Albany, NY 12207
Presiding Justice:
Anthony V Cardona 518-487-5170
4th Judicial Department
50 East Ave, Rochester, NY 14604
Presiding Justice:
Eugene F Piggott, Jr 716-845-2101

Court of Appeals
230 Park Ave, Suite 826, New York, NY 10169
Chief Judge:
Judith S Kaye 212-661-6787/fax: 212-682-2778

Court Administration
Chief Administrative Judge:
Jonathan Lippman 212-428-2100
Administrative Director, Office of Court Admin:
Lawrence K Marks 212-428-2884
First Deputy Chief Administrative Judge, Management Support:
Ann T Pfau 212-428-2120/fax: 212-428-2190
Deputy Chief Administrative Judge, Courts in NYC:
Joan B Carey 212-374-8540
Deputy Chief Administrative Judge, Courts outside NYC:
Jan Plumadore 518-474-3828
Deputy Chief Admin Judge, Justice Initiatives/Admin Judge NYC Criminal:
Juanita Bing Newton 212-374-4515/fax: 212-428-2192
Deputy Chief Admin Judge, Court Operations & Planning:
Judy Harris Kluger 212-428-2700
Administrative Judge, Matrimonial Matters:
Jacqueline W Silbermann 212-428-2140/fax: 212-428-2197
Executive Assistant to Deputy Chief Admin Judge, Courts in NYC:
Maria Logus 212-428-2133
Executive Assistant to Deputy Chief Admin Judge, Courts outside NYC:
David Sullivan 518-473-5517
Chief of Staff:
Paul Lewis 212-428-2148
Chief of Operations:
Ron Younkins 212-428-2126

Administrative Judge to the Court of Claims (NYS) . fax: 518-432-3410
Justice Bldg, Capitol Station, PO Box 7433, Albany, NY 12224
Presiding Judge:
Richard E Sise 518-432-3438

Administrative Judges to the Courts in New York City
1st Judicial District (Judicial Department 1)
Administrative Judge, Civil Term:
Jacqueline W Silbermann 212-374-4726
Administrative Judge, Criminal Term:
Micki A Scherer 212-374-4972/fax: 212-374-3003
2nd Judicial District (Judicial Department 2)
360 Adams St, Brooklyn, NY 11201
Administrative Judge:
Neil Firetog 718-643-7086/fax: 718-643-2095

Offices and agencies appear in alphabetical order.

Civil Court
111 Centre St, New York, NY 10013
Administrative Judge:
Fern Fisher-Brandveen 212-374-8082/fax: 212-374-5709
Criminal Court
100 Centre St, Rm 539, New York, NY 10013
Administrative Judge:
Juanita Bing Newton 212-374-3200/fax: 212-374-3004
Family Court
60 Lafayette St, 11th Floor, New York, NY 10013
Administrative Judge:
Joseph M Lauria 212-374-3711/fax: 212-374-2127

Administrative Judges to the Courts outside New York City
3rd Judicial District (Judicial Department 3)
125 State St, Albany, NY 12207
Administrative Judge:
George Ceresia 518-445-7867/fax: 518-447-7473
4th Judicial District (Judicial Department 3)
Lincoln Baths Bldg, PO Box 4370, Saratoga Springs, NY 12866
Administrative Judge:
Vito Caruso 518-587-3019/fax: 518-587-3179
5th Judicial District (Judicial Department 4)
Onondaga County Court House, Syracuse, NY 13202
Administrative Judge:
James C Tormey, III 315-671-1100/fax: 315-671-1183
6th Judicial District (Judicial Department 3)
203 Lake St, Hazlett Bldg, PO Box 588, Elmira, NY 14902-0588
Administrative Judge:
Judith F O'Shea 607-737-3560/fax: 607-737-3562
7th Judicial District (Judicial Department 4)
Hall of Justice, Civic Center Plz, Rochester, NY 14614
Administrative Judge:
Thomas M Van Strydonck 585-428-2885/fax: 585-428-2105
8th Judicial District (Judicial Department 4)
Erie County Hall, 92 Franklin St, Buffalo, NY 14202
Administrative Judge:
Sharon Townsend 716-851-3273/fax: 716-855-1611
9th Judicial District (Judicial Department 2)
County Court House, 111 Grove St, White Plains, NY 10601
Administrative Judge:
Francis A Nicolai 914-285-4100/fax: 914-285-4111
10th Judicial District (Judicial Department 2)
Administrative Judge, Nassau County:
Anthony F Marano 516-571-2684/fax: 516-571-3713
Administrative Judge, Suffolk County:
H Patrick Leis, III 631-853-5368/fax: 631-853-7741
11th Judicial District (Judicial Department 2)
88-11 Sutphin Blvd, Jamaica, NY 11435
Administrative Judge:
Leslie Leach 718-520-3763/fax: 718-520-4689
12th Judicial District (Judicial Department 1)
851 Grand Concourse, Bronx, NY 10451
Administrative Judge (Civil):
Gerald V Esposito 718-590-3942/fax: 718-590-8899

Counsel's Office
Counsel:
Michael Colodner 212-428-2160/fax: 212-428-2155

Management Support
First Deputy Chief Administrative Judge:
Ann T Pfau 212-428-2120/fax: 212-428-2190
Administrative Services Office
Director:
Laura Weigley Ross 212-428-2860/fax: 212-428-2819
Deputy Director:
Vacant 212-428-2812/fax: 212-428-2819

Court Operations
Director:
Nancy M Mangold 212-428-2761/fax: 518-428-2768
Coordinator, Alternative Dispute Resolution Program:
Daniel M Weitz 212-428-2863/fax: 212-428-2819
e-mail: dweitz@courts.state.ny.us
Director, Court Research & Technology:
Chester Mount 212-428-2990/fax: 212-428-2987
Chief of Court Security Services:
Matthew O'Reilly 212-428-2766/fax: 212-428-2768
Director, Internal Controls Office:
Dennis Donnelly 518-238-2064/fax: 518-238-2086
Special Inspector General, Bias Complaints:
Kay-Ann Porter . . . . 646-386-3507 or 212-457-2669
fax: 212-428-2190
Chief Law Librarian, Legal Info & Records Mgmt:
Ellen Robinson 518-473-1196/fax: 518-473-6860
Records Management Chief:
Richard Hogan 518-428-2875
Financial Management & Audit Services
Empire State Plaza, Ste 2001, Albany, NY 12223-1450
Director:
Joseph M deChants 518-474-4971/fax: 518-474-3218
Human Resources & Employee Relations
Director:
Lauren DeSole 212-428-2515/fax: 212-428-2513
Deputy Director, Career Services:
Juanita Norman 646-386-5640/fax: 212-406-4534
Deputy Director, Equal Employment Opportunity Division:
Alice Chapman-Minutello 212-428-2540/fax: 212-428-2545
Administrator, Judicial Benefits Division:
Brigid Gambella 212-428-2550/fax: 212-428-2555
Dean, Judicial Institute of Education & Training:
Robert G M Keating 914-682-3222/fax: 914-997-8964
Deputy Director, Payroll Division:
Terri A Collins 212-428-2625/fax: 212-428-2620
Deputy Director, Personnel Division:
Michael S Miller 212-428-2600/fax: 212-428-2606
Public Affairs Office
Director:
Gregory Murray 212-428-2116/fax: 212-428-2117
Director, Communications:
David Bookstaver 212-428-2500/fax: 212-428-2507
Communications Specialist:
Arelene Hackel 212-428-2116
Public Information Officer:
Tony Walters 212-428-2116

CORPORATIONS, AUTHORITIES AND COMMISSIONS

Capital Defender Office
217 Broadway
9th Fl
New York, NY 10007
212-608-3352 Fax: 212-608-4558
Web site: www.nycdo.org

Capital Defender:
Kevin Doyle 212-608-3352 x208
First Deputy Capital Defender, Albany Office:
Mark Harris 518-473-9521
First Deputy Capital Defender, New York City Office:
Susan Salomon 212-608-3352 x206

Offices and agencies appear in alphabetical order.

First Deputy Capital Defender, Rochester Office:
  William Easton 716-232-5480
Counsel to Board of Directors:
  Peter Sistrom 212-608-3352 x209

Interest on Lawyer Account (IOLA) Fund of the State of NY

11 East 44th St
Ste 1406
New York, NY 10017-0055
646-865-1541 Fax: 646-865-1545
e-mail: iolaf@iola.org
Web site: www.iola.org

Chair:
  William R Nojay 646-865-1541
Executive Director:
  Lorna Blake 646-865-1541
  e-mail: lblake@iola.org
General Counsel:
  Stephen Brooks 646-865-1541
  e-mail: sbrooks@iola.org
Asst Director & Director of Administration:
  Odette M McNeil 646-865-1541
  e-mail: omcneil@iola.org

Lawyers' Fund for Client Protection

119 Washington Ave
Albany, NY 12210
518-434-1935 Fax: 518-434-5641
e-mail: info@nylawfund.org
Web site: www.nylawfund.org

Chair:
  Eleanor Breitel Alter 518-434-1935
Vice Chair:
  Bernard F Ashe 518-434-1935
Executive Director & Counsel:
  Timothy O'Sullivan 518-434-1935
Deputy Counsel:
  Michael J Knight 518-434-1935

New York State Board of Law Examiners

Corporate Plaza - Bldg 3
254 Washington Ave Extension
Albany, NY 12203-5195
518-452-8700 Fax: 518-452-0175
Web site: www.nybarexam.org

Chair:
  Diane F Bosse 518-452-8700
Executive Director:
  John J McAlary 518-452-8700

New York State Commission on Judicial Nomination

c/o Phillips, Nizer LLP
666 Fifth Ave, 28th Fl
New York, NY 10103-0084
212-841-0715 Fax: 212-262-5152

Chair:
  John F O'Mara 607-733-4635
Counsel:
  Stuart A Summit 212-977-9700
  e-mail: ssummit@phillipsnizer.com
Asst Counsel:
  Frederick B Warder, III 212-336-2121
Asst Counsel:
  Stephen P Younger 212-336-2000

New York State Judicial Conduct Commission

61 Broadway
12th FL
New York, NY 10006
212-809-0566 Fax: 212-949-8864
e-mail: webmaster@scjc.state.ny.us
Web site: www.scjc.state.ny.us

Henry T Berger
Robert H Tembeckjian
Chief Attorney, Albany Office:
  Cathleen Cenci 518-474-5617
John J Postel
Jean M Savanyu

New York State Law Reporting Bureau

One Commerce Plaza
Ste 1750
Albany, NY 12210
518-474-8211 Fax: 518-463-6869
Web site: www.courts.state.ny.us/reporter

State Reporter:
  Gary D Spivey 518-474-8211
Deputy State Reporter:
  Charles A Ashe 518-474-8211
  e-mail: cashe@courts.state.ny.us

New York State Law Revision Commission

80 New Scotland Rd
Albany, NY 12208
518-472-5858 Fax: 518-445-2303
Web site: www.lawrevision.state.ny.us

Chairman:
  Robert M Pitler 518-472-5858
Executive Director:
  Rose Mary Bailly 518-472-5858

Uniform State Laws Commission

c/o Coughlin & Gerhart LLP
20 Hawley St, East Tower
Binghamton, NY 13902-2039
607-584-4193 Fax: 607-723-1530

Chair:
  Richard B Long 607-584-4193
  e-mail: rlong@cglawllp.com
Member:
  Norman L Greene 212-661-5030
Member:
  Sandra Stern 212-207-8150

Offices and agencies appear in alphabetical order.

Member:
   Justin L Vigdor 585-232-5300

NEW YORK STATE LEGISLATURE

See Legislative Branch in Section 1 for additional Standing Committee and Subcommittee information.

Assembly Standing Committees

Codes
Chair:
   Joseph R Lentol (D) 518-455-4477
Ranking Minority Member:
   Dierdre Scozzafava (R) 518-455-5797

Judiciary
Chair:
   Helene E Weinstein (D) 518-455-5462

Ranking Minority Member:
   Thomas Alfano (R) 518-455-4627

Senate Standing Committees

Codes
Chair:
   Dale M Volker (R) 518-455-3471
Ranking Minority Member:
   Thomas K Duane (D) 518-455-2451

Judiciary
Chair:
   John A DeFrancisco (R) 518-455-3511
Ranking Minority Member:
   Malcolm A Smith (D) 518-455-2195

U.S. Government

EXECUTIVE DEPARTMENTS AND FEDERAL COURTS

US Federal Courts

US Bankruptcy Court - New York

Eastern District
Web site: www.nyeb.uscourts.gov
Chief Bankruptcy Judge:
   Conrad B Duberstein 718-330-2188
Clerk of the Court:
   Joseph P Hurley 718-330-2188/fax: 718-330-2833

Northern District
Web site: www.nynb.uscourts.gov
Chief Bankruptcy Judge:
   Stephen D Gerling 315-266-1122
Clerk of the Court:
   Richard G Zeh, Sr 518-257-1661

Southern District
Alexander Hamilton Custom House, 1 Bowling Green, New York, NY
   10004-1408
Web site: www.nysb.uscourts.gov
Chief Judge:
   Stuart M Bernstein 212-668-2304
Clerk of the Court:
   Kathleen Farrell-Willoughby 212-668-2870

Western District
Web site: www.nywb.uscourts.gov
Chief Bankruptcy Judge:
   John C Ninfo, II 585-613-4200
Clerk of the Court:
   Paul R Warren 585-613-4200
   e-mail: pwarren@nywb.uscourts.gov

US Court of Appeals for the Second Circuit
Circuit Executive:
   Karen Milton 212-857-8700/fax: 212-857-8680
Clerk of the Court:
   Roseann B MacKechnie 212-857-8500

US Court of International Trade . . . . fax: 212-264-1085
One Federal Plaza, New York, NY 10278
212-264-2800 Fax: 212-264-1085
Web site: www.cit.uscourts.gov
Chief Judge:
   Jane A Restani 212-264-3668
Clerk of the Court:
   Leo M Gordon 212-264-2814

US DISTRICT COURT - NEW YORK (part of the Second Circuit)
Web site: www.nyed.uscourts.gov

Eastern District
Chief District Judge:
   Edward R Korman 718-260-2470
Chief Magistrate Judge:
   Joan M Azrack 718-260-2530
District Executive:
   James E Ward 718-260-2260
Clerk of the Court:
   Robert C Heinemann 718-260-2600
Chief Probation Off:
   Tony Garoppolo 347-534-3400/fax: 347-534-3509

Northern District
Web site: www.nynd.uscourts.gov
Chief District Judge:
   Frederick J Scullin, Jr. 315-234-8560
Chief Magistrate Judge:
   Gustave J DiBianco 315-234-8600
Clerk of the Court:
   Lawrence K Baerman 315-234-8500
Chief Probation Officer:
   Paul DeFelice 315-234-8700/fax: 315-234-8701

Southern District
US Courthouse, 40 Centre St, New York, NY 10007-1581
212-805-0136
Web site: www.nysd.uscourts.gov
Chief District Judge:
   Michael B Mukasey 212-805-0234

Offices and agencies appear in alphabetical order.

Chief Magistrate:
    Andrew J Peck 212-805-0036
District Executive:
    Clifford P Kirsch 212-805-0500
Clerk of the Court:
    J Michael McMahon 212-805-0136
Chief Probation Officer:
    Chris J Stanton 212-805-0040/fax: 212-805-0045

Western District
 Web site: www.nywd.uscourts.gov
Chief District Judge:
    Richard J Arcara 716-332-7810/fax: 716-551-4850
Clerk of the Court:
    Rodney C Early 716-332-1700
Chief Probation Off:
    Joseph A Giacobbe 716-551-4241/fax: 716-551-4988

US Tax Court
Chief Judge:
    Thomas B Wells 202-606-8700
Clerk of the Court:
    Charles S Casazza 202-606-8754

US Justice Department
Web site: www.usdoj.gov

Antitrust Division—New York Field Office
26 Federal Plaza, Rm 3630, New York, NY 10278-0096
Chief:
    Ralph T Giordano 212-264-0391/fax: 212-264-7453
    e-mail: ralph.giordano@usdoj.gov
Asst Chief:
    Philip F Cody 212-264-0394/fax: 212-264-7453

Civil Division - Commercial Litigation Branch
26 Federal Plz, Rm 346, New York, NY 10278

Community Relations Service - Northeast & Caribbean Region
26 Federal Plaza, Suite 36-118, New York, NY 10278
Regional Director:
    Reinaldo Rivera, Jr 212-264-0700/fax: 212-264-2143

OFFICE OF INSPECTOR GENERAL (including New York State)

Audit Division
701 Market St, Ste 201, Philadelphia, PA 19106
Regional Manager:
    Ferris B Polk 215-580-2111/fax: 215-597-1348

Investigations Division
JFK Airport, N Boundary Rd, Bldg 77, Penthouse 2, Jamaica, NY 11430
Spl-Agent-in-Chg:
    James E Tomlinson 718-553-7520/fax: 718-553-7533

US Attorney's Office - New York

Eastern District
147 Pierrepont St, Brooklyn, NY 11201
718-254-7000
US Attorney:
    Roslynn R Mauskopf 718-254-6260/fax: 718-254-6319
Chief Asst US Atty:
    Andrew C Hruska 718-254-6210/fax: 718-254-6300
Executive Asst US Attorney:
    William J Muller 718-254-6258/fax: 718-254-6329
Administrative Asst US Attorney:
    John Lenior 718-254-6255

Chief Asst US Attorney, Criminal Division:
    Daniel Alonso 718-254-6238/fax: 718-254-6150
Chief Asst US Attorney, Civil Division:
    Susan Riley 718-254-6037/fax: 718-254-7483
Chief Asst US Attorney, Appeals Division:
    Peter Norling 718-254-6280
Deputy Admin Officer:
    Peter Kurtin 718-254-6587/fax: 718-254-6550

Northern District
Albany
    James T Foley US Courthouse, #218, 445 Broadway, Albany, NY 12207
    Supervising Asst US Attorney:
        Grant C Jaquith 518-431-0247/fax: 518-431-0249
Binghamton
    US Courthouse, Ste 304, 15 Henry St, Binghamton, NY 13901
    Supervising Asst US Attorney:
        Thomas P Walsh 607-773-2887/fax: 607-773-2901
Syracuse
    J F Hanley Fed Bldg, 100 S Clinton St, Rm 900, Syracuse, NY 13261
    US Attorney:
        Glenn Suddaby 315-448-0672
    First Asst US Attny:
        Joseph A Pavone 315-448-0672
    Asst US Attorney, Chief Criminal Division:
        Andrew T Baxter 315-448-0672
    Asst US Attorney, Chief Civil Division:
        William H Pease 315-448-0672
    Administrative Officer:
        Martha Stratton 315-448-0672/fax: 315-448-0689

Southern District
New York City
    US Attorney:
        David N Kelley 212-637-2573
    Associate US Attorney:
        John M McEnany 212-637-2571
    Chief US Appellate Attorney:
        Gary Stein 212-637-1065
    Chief, Civil Division:
        James Cott 212-637-2695
    Chief, Criminal Division:
        Karen Patten Seymour 212-637-2508
    Administrative Officer:
        Edward Tyrrell 212-637-2269/fax: 212-637-0084
White Plains . . . . fax: 914-682-3392
    300 Quarropas St, 3rd Fl, White Plains, NY 10601
914-993-1900 Fax: 914-682-3392
    Chief Asst US Attorney:
        Maria A Barton 914-993-1909

Western District
Buffalo . . . . fax: 716-551-3052
    138 Delaware Ave, Buffalo, NY 14202
716-843-5700 Fax: 716-551-3052
    US Attorney:
        Michael A Battle 716-843-5814
    First Asst US Attorney:
        Kathleen M Mehltretter 716-843-5817
    Asst US Attorney, Civil Division Chief:
        Mary Pat Fleming 716-843-5867
    Asst US Attorney, Narcotics & Violent Crime Division Chief:
        Joseph M Guerra, III 716-843-5824
    Asst US Attorney, Strike Force Division Chief:
        Anthony M Bruce 716-843-5886
    Asst US Attorney, White Collar & General Crimes Division Chief:
        Paul J Campana 716-843-5819
    Administrative Officer:
        Barbara A Sweitzer 716-843-5826/fax: 716-551-3170

Offices and agencies appear in alphabetical order.

Rochester . . . . fax: 585-263-6226
   620 Federal Bldg, 100 State St, Rochester, NY 14614
585-263-6760 Fax: 585-263-6226
   Asst US Attorney-in-Charge:
      Bradley E Tyler 585-263-5717

US Marshals' Service - New York

Eastern District
225 Cadman Plaza East, Ste G-80, Brooklyn, NY 11201
718-254-6700
US Marshal:
   Eugene J Corcoran 718-254-6701/fax: 718-254-6720

Northern District
Albany
   US Courthouse, 2nd Fl, Rm 206, 445 Broadway, Albany, NY 12207
   US Marshal:
      James J Parmley 518-431-0101/fax: 518-431-0100
Syracuse
   Federal Bldg, 100 S Clinton St, 10th Fl, PO Box 7260, Syracuse, NY 13261
   US Marshal:
      James J Parmley 315-448-0341/fax: 315-448-0343

Southern District
500 Pearl St, Ste 400, New York, NY 10007
US Marshal:
   Joseph R Guccione 212-331-7100/fax: 212-637-6130

Western District
Buffalo
   Courthouse Bldg, Rm 129, 68 Court St, Buffalo, NY 14202
   US Marshal:
      Peter Lawrence 716-551-4851/fax: 716-551-5505
Rochester
   US Courthouse, Rm 284, 100 State St, Rochester, NY 14614
   US Marshal:
      Peter A Lawrence 585-263-5787/fax: 585-263-6741

US Trustee - Bankruptcy, Region 2
33 Whitehall St, 21st Fl, New York, NY 10004-2112

US Trustee:
   Deidre A Martini 212-510-0500/fax: 212-668-2255

U.S. CONGRESS

See U.S. Congress Chapter for additional Standing Committee and Subcommittee information.

House of Representatives Standing Committees

Judiciary
Chair:
   F James Sensenbrenner, Jr (R-WI) 202-225-5101
Ranking Minority Member:
   John Conyers, Jr (D-MI) 202-225-5126
New York Delegate:
   Jerrold Nadler (D) 202-225-5635
New York Delegate:
   Anthony D Weiner (D) 202-225-6616

   Subcommittee
   The Constitution
      Chair:
         Steve Chabot (R-OH) 202-225-2216
      Ranking Minority Member:
         Jerrold Nadler (D-NY) 202-225-5635

Senate Standing Committees

Judiciary
Chair:
   Orrin G Hatch (R-UT) 202-224-5251
Ranking Minority Member:
   Patrick J Leahy (D-VT) 202-224-4242
New York Delegate:
   Charles E Schumer (D) 202-224-6542

Private Sector

NYS Bar Assn, Judicial Independence Cmte
714 East 241st St, Bronx, NY 10470-1302
718-325-5000 Fax: 718-324-0333
e-mail: mspfeifer@aol.com
Maxwell S Pfeifer, Chair

ADR Associates LLC
1350 Broadway, Ste 2200, New York, NY 10018
212-594-4454 Fax: 212-594-4474
e-mail: mshaw@adrassociates.com
Web site: www.adrassociates.com
Margaret L Shaw, Principal
Mediation of civil, commercial & employment disputes; training & systems design

NYS Bar Assn, International Law & Practice Section
Alston & Bird LLP
90 Park Ave, 15th Fl, New York, NY 10016-1387
212-210-9540 Fax: 212-210-9444
e-mail: pmfrank@alston.com
Paul M Frank, Chair

NYS Bar Assn, Lawyer Referral Service Cmte
Amdursky Pelky Fennell & Wallen
26 E Oneida St, Oswego, NY 13126-2695
315-343-6363 Fax: 315-343-0134
e-mail: apfwlaw@twcny.rr.com
Web site: http://apfwlaw.com
Timothy J Fennell, Chair

NYS Bar Assn, Women in the Law Cmte
American Red Cross in Greater NY
150 Amsterdam Ave, New York, NY 10023
212-875-3023 Fax: 212-875-2309
e-mail: petrucellid@arcgny.org
Donna M Petrucelli, Chair

Offices and agencies appear in alphabetical order.

Policy Areas

Asian American Legal Defense & Education Fund Inc
99 Hudson St, 12th Fl, New York, NY 10013-2815
212-966-5932 Fax: 212-966-4303
e-mail: info@aaldef.org
Web site: www.aaldef.org
Margaret Fung, Executive Director
Defend civil rights of Asian Americans through litigation, legal advocacy & community education

Association of the Bar of the City of New York
42 W 44th St, New York, NY 10036-6689
212-382-6655 Fax: 212-382-6760
e-mail: jbigelsen@abcny.org
Web site: www.abcny.org
Jayne Bigelsen, Director, Communications

NYS Bar Assn, Review the Code of Judicial Conduct Cmte
Bond Market Association (The)
360 Madison Ave, 18th Fl, New York, NY 10017-7111
646-637-9200 Fax: 646-637-9126
e-mail: mgross@bondmarkets.com
Web site: www.bondmarkets.com
Herbert H McDade III, Chair

NYS Bar Assn, President's Cmte on Access to Justice
Boylan Brown
2400 Chase Sq, Rochester, NY 14604
585-232-5300 x256 Fax: 585-232-3528
e-mail: info@boylanbrown.com
Web site: www.boylanbrown.com
C Bruce Lawrence, Co-Chair

NYS Bar Assn, Tort System Cmte
Bracken Margolin & Gouvis LLP
1 Suffolk Sq, Ste 300, Islandia, NY 11749
631-234-8585 Fax: 631-234-8702
e-mail: jbracken@bracken-margolin.com
Web site: www.bracken-margolin.com
John P Bracken, Co-Chair

Brooklyn Law School
250 Joralemon St, Brooklyn, NY 11201
718-780-7900 Fax: 718-780-0393
e-mail: joan.wexler@brooklaw.edu
Web site: www.brooklaw.edu
Joan G Wexler, Dean

NYS Bar Assn, Cyberspace Law Cmte
Brown Raysman et al
900 Third Ave, 36th Floor, New York, NY 10022
212-895-2320 Fax: 212-895-2900
e-mail: jneuburger@brownraysman.com
Jeffrey D Neuburger, Chair

CASA - Advocates for Children of NYS
99 Pine St, Ste C102, Albany, NY 12207-2776
518-426-5354 Fax: 518-426-5348
e-mail: mail@casanys.org
Web site: www.casanys.org
Darlene Ward, Executive Director
Volunteer advocates appointed by family court judges to represent abused & neglected children in court

CPR Institute for Dispute Resolution
366 Madison Ave, 14th Floor, New York, NY 10017-3122
212-949-6490 Fax: 212-949-8859
e-mail: info@cpradr.org
Web site: www.cpradr.org
Thomas J Stipanowich, President & Chief Executive Officer
Alternative dispute resolution

Center for Court Innovation
520 8th Ave, New York, NY 10018
212-397-3050 Fax: 212-397-0985
e-mail: info@courtinnovation.org
Web site: www.courtinnovation.org
Greg Berman, Director
Foster innovation within NYS courts addressing quality-of-life crime, substance abuse, child neglect, domestic violence & landlord-tenant disputes

Center for Judicial Accountability Inc
PO Box 69, Gedney Station, White Plains, NY 10605-0069
914-421-1200 Fax: 914-428-4994
e-mail: judgewatch@aol.com
Web site: www.judgewatch.org
Doris L Sassower, Director
Nonpartisan citizens' organization documenting politicization & corruption of the judicial selection & discipline processes

Center for Law & Justice
Pine West Plaza, Bldg 2, Washington Ave Ext, Albany, NY 12205
518-427-8361 Fax: 518-427-8362
e-mail: cflj@knick.net
Web site: www.timesunion.com/communities/cflj
Alice P Green, Executive Director
Advocacy for fair treatment of poor people & communities of color by the justice system; referral, workshops, community lawyering & education

Coalition of Fathers & Families NY, PAC
PO Box 782, Clifton Park, NY 12065
518-383-8202 Fax: 518-383-8202
e-mail: dadlobby@localnet.com
Web site: www.fafny.org/fafnypac.htm
James Hays, Treasurer
Political Action for fathers and families in New York

NYS Bar Assn, Trial Lawyers Section
Connors & Connors, PC
766 Castleton Ave, Staten Island, NY 10310
718-442-1700 Fax: 718-442-1717
e-mail: jpc@connorslaw.com
Web site: www.connorslaw.com
John P Connors, Chair

Offices and agencies appear in alphabetical order.

NYS Bar Assn, Torts, Insurance & Compensation Law Section
Connors & Corcoran LLP
Times Square Bldg, 45 Exchange St, Ste 250, Rochester, NY 14614
585-232-5885 Fax: 585-546-3631
e-mail: buholtz@frontiernet.net
Web site: www.connorscorcoran.com
Eileen E Buholtz, Chair

Cornell Law School, Legal Information Institute
Myron Taylor Hall, Ithaca, NY 14853
607-255-1221 Fax: 607-255-7193
e-mail: lii@lii.law.cornell.edu
Web site: www.law.cornell.edu
Thomas R Bruce, Director
Distributes legal documents via the web & electronic mail

NYS Bar Assn, Judicial Section
Court of Claims
140 Grand St, Ste 507, White Plains, NY 10601
914-289-2310 Fax: 914-289-2313
e-mail: truderma@courts.state.ny.us
Hon Terry Jane Ruderman, Chair

NYS Bar Assn, Real Property Law Section
D H Ferguson, Attorney, PLLC
1115 Midtown Tower, Rochester, NY 14604
585-325-3620 Fax: 585-325-3635
e-mail: dhferguson@frontiernet.net
Dorothy H Ferguson, Chair

NYS Bar Assn, Trusts & Estates Law Section
Day, Berry & Howard LLP
875 Third Avenue, New York, NY 10022
212-829-3602 Fax: 212-829-3601
e-mail: gwwhitaker@dbh.com
Web site: www.dbh.com
G Warren Whitaker, Chair

NYS Bar Assn, Public Trust & Confidence in the Legal System
Debevoise & Plimpton LLP
919 Third Ave, New York, NY 10022
212-909-6096 Fax: 212-909-6836
e-mail: elieberman@debevoise.com
Web site: www.debcoise.com
Ellen Lieberman, Chair

NYS Bar Assn, Alternative Dispute Resolution Cmte
Elayne E Greenberg, Esq
4 Mirrielees Cir, Great Neck, NY 11021
516-829-5521 Fax: 516-466-8130
e-mail: elayneegreenberg@juno.com
Elayne E Greenberg, Chair

NYS Bar Assn, Review Judicial Nominations Cmte
Englert Coffey & McHugh
224 State St, PO Box 1092, Schenectady, NY 12305
518-370-4645 Fax: 518-370-4979
e-mail: pcoffey@ecmlaw.com
Web site: www.englertcoffeymchugh.com
Peter V Coffey, Chair

NYS Bar Assn, Cmte on the Jury System
FitzGerald Morris et al
One Broad St Plz, PO Box 2017, Glens Falls, NY 12801-4360
518-745-1400 Fax: 518-745-1576
e-mail: pdf@fmbf-law.com
Peter D FitzGerald, Chair

Fund for Modern Courts (The)
351 W 54th St, New York, NY 10019
212-541-6741 Fax: 212-541-7301
e-mail: justice@moderncourts.org
Web site: www.moderncourts.org
Kenneth Jockers, Executive Director
Improve the administration & quality of justice in NYS courts

NYS Bar Assn, Court Operations Cmte
Getnick, Livingston, Atkinson, Gigliotti & Priore LLP
258 Genesee St, Ste 401, Utica, NY 13502-4642
315-797-9261 Fax: 315-732-0755
e-mail: mgetnick@glagplawfirm.com
Michael E Getnick, Chair

NYS Bar Assn, Labor & Employment Law Section
Goodman & Zuchlewski LLP
500 5th Ave, Ste 5100, New York, NY 10110-5197
212-869-1940 Fax: 212-768-3020
e-mail: pz@goodznyc.com
Pearl Zuchlewski, Chair

Greater Upstate Law Project Inc
119 Washington Ave, Albany, NY 12210
518-462-6831 Fax: 518-462-6687
e-mail: nkrupski@wnylc.com
Web site: www.gulpny.org
Anne Erickson, President & Chief Executive Officer
No fee legal services in civil matters to low-income residents

NYS Bar Assn, Review Attorney Fee Regulation Cmte
Harris Beach LLP
99 Garnsey Rd, Pittsford, NY 14534
585-419-8800 Fax: 585-419-8801
e-mail: vbuzard@harrisbeach.com
Web site: www.nysba.org
A Vincent Buzard, Co-Chair/Bar President Elect

NYS Bar Assn, Intellectual Property Law Section
Hartman & Winnicki, PC
115 W Century Rd, Paramus, NJ 7654
201-967-8040 Fax: 201-967-0590
e-mail: rick@ravin.com
Web site: www.hartmanwinnicki.com
Richard L Ravin, Chair

Policy Areas

Offices and agencies appear in alphabetical order.

NYS Bar Assn, Procedures for Judicial Discipline Cmte
Hollyer Brady et al
551 Fifth Ave, 27th Fl, New York, NY 10176-0001
212-818-1110 Fax: 212-818-0494
e-mail: arh-esq@worldnet.att.net
A Rene Hollyer, Chair

NYS Bar Assn, Children & the Law Committee
Law Office of Anne Reynolds Copps
126 State St, 6th Fl, Albany, NY 12207
518-436-4170 Fax: 518-436-1456
e-mail: arcopps@nycap.rr.com
Anne Reynolds Copps, Chair

NYS Bar Assn, General Practice Section
Law Offices of D'Angelo & Begley
999 Franklin Ave, Ste 100, Garden City, NY 11530-2909
516-742-7601 Fax: 516-742-6070
e-mail: fgdangeloesq@aol.com
Frank G D'Angelo, Chair

Legal Action Center Inc
153 Waverly Place, New York, NY 10014
212-243-1313 Fax: 212-675-0286
e-mail: lacinfo@lac.org
Web site: www.lac.org
Paul N Samuels, President & Director
Legal & policy issues, alcohol/drug abuse, AIDS & criminal justice

Legal Aid Society
199 Water Street, New York, NY 10038
212-577-3300 Fax: 212-509-8432
Web site: www.legal-aid.org
Peter v Z Cobb, President
Civil & criminal defense, appeals, juvenile rights, federal defenders, civil legal services

Legal Aid Society, Community Law Offices
199 Water Street, New York, NY 10038
212-577-3300 Fax: 212-569-8763
e-mail: dwweschler@legal-aid.org
Web site: www.legal-aid.org
David W Weschler, Attorney-in-Charge, Volunteer Director
Public interest law, housing & economic development, AIDS, elder law, domestic relations, landlord-tenant, low-income taxpayer clinic

NYS Bar Assn, Legal Aid Cmte/Funding for Civil Legal Svcs Cmte
Legal Services of the Hudson Valley
4 Cromwell Pl, White Plains, NY 10601-5006
914-949-1305 x136 Fax: 914-949-6213
e-mail: bfinkelstein@lshv.org
Web site: www.lshv.org
Barbara D Finkelstein, Executive Director

NYS Bar Assn, Tort System Cmte
Levene, Gouldin & Thompson LLP
450 Plaza Dr, Binghamton, NY 13902-0106
607-763-9200 Fax: 607-763-9212
e-mail: dgouldin@binghamtonlaw.com
Web site: www.binghamtonlaw.com
David M Gouldin, Co-Chair

NYS Bar Assn, Elder Law Section
Littman Krooks LLP
81 Main St, White Plains, NY 10601
lkllp.lawinfo.com Fax: 914-684-9865
e-mail: hkrooks@lkllp.com
Web site: www.lkrlaw.com
Harold S Krooks, Chair

NYS Bar Assn, Unlawful Practice of Law Cmte
LoPinto Schlather Solomon & Salk
200 E Buffalo St, PO Box 353, Ithaca, NY 14850
607-273-2202 Fax: 607-273-4436
e-mail: mjs@lsss-law.com
Mark J Solomon, Chair

NYS Bar Assn, Court Structure & Judicial Selection Cmte
McMahon & Grow
301 N Washington St, PO Box 4350, Rome, NY 13442-4350
315-336-4700 Fax: 315-336-5851
e-mail: mgglaw@dreamscape.com
Web site: www.mgglaw.com
Hon Richard D Simons, Chair

NYS Bar Assn, Resolutions Committee
Meyer Suozzi English & Klein, PC
1505 Kellum Pl, PO Box 803, Mineola, NY 11501-4842
516-592-5704 Fax: 516-741-6706
e-mail: atlevin@nysbar.com
A Thomas Levin, Chair

NYS Bar Assn, Criminal Justice Section
Michael T Kelly, Esq
1217 Delaware Ave, Apt 1003, Buffalo, NY 14209
716-886-1922 Fax: 716-886-1922
e-mail: mkelly1005@aol.com
Michael T Kelly, Chair

NYS Bar Assn, Commercial & Federal Litigation Section
Montclare & Wachtler
110 Wall St, New York, NY 10005
212-509-3900 Fax: 212-509-7239
e-mail: ljwachtler@montclarewachtler.com
Lauren J Wachtler, Chair

NY County Lawyers' Association
14 Vessey St, New York, NY 10007
212-267-6646 Fax: 212-406-9252
e-mail: mflood@nycla.org
Web site: www.nycla.org
Marilyn J Flood, Counsel

Offices and agencies appear in alphabetical order.

NYS Association of Criminal Defense Lawyers
245 Fifth Ave, 19th Fl, New York, NY 10016
212-532-4434 Fax: 212-532-4468
e-mail: nysacdl@aol.com
Web site: www.nysacdl.org
Patricia Marcus, Executive Director
Criminal law

NYS Bar Assoc, President's Cmte on Access to Justice
1 Elk St, Albany, NY 12207
518-487-5555 or 212-351-4670 Fax: 212-878-8641
e-mail: kstandard@ebglaw.com
Kenneth G Standard, Bar President

NYS Council of Probation Administrators
Box 2 272 Broadway, Albany, NY 12204
518-434-9194 Fax: 518-434-0392
e-mail: president@nyscopa.org
Web site: www.nyscopa.org
Robert A Sudlow, President
Provide supervision & investigation services to courts

NYS Court Clerks Association
170 Duane St, New York, NY 10013
212-941-5700 Fax: 212-941-5705
Kevin E Scanlon, Sr, President

NYS Defenders Association
194 Washington Ave, Ste 500, Albany, NY 12210-2314
518-465-3524 Fax: 518-465-3249
e-mail: info@nysda.org
Web site: www.nysda.org
Jonathan E Gradess, Executive Director
Criminal defense

NYS Dispute Resolution Association
255 River St, #4, Troy, NY 12180
518-687-2240 Fax: 518-687-2245
e-mail: nysdra@nysdra.org
Web site: www.nysdra.org
Lisa U Hicks, Executive Director
Dispute resolution-mediation, arbitration, facilitation

NYS Magistrates Association
267 Delaware Ave, Delmar, NY 12054-1124
518-439-1087 Fax: 518-439-1204
e-mail: nysma@juno.com
Web site: www.nysmagassoc.homestead.com
Thomas W Baldwin, Executive Director
Association of town & village justices

NYS Bar Assn, Civil Practice Law & Rules Committee
NYS Supreme Court
50 Delaware Ave, Buffalo, NY 14202
716-845-9478 Fax: 716-851-3265
e-mail: sgerstma@courts.state.ny.us
Sharon Stern Gerstman, Chair

National Academy of Forensic Engineers
174 Brady Ave, Hawthorne, NY 10532
914-741-0633 Fax: 914-747-2988
e-mail: nafe@nafe.org
Web site: www.nafe.org
Marvin M Specter, Executive Director
Engineering consultants to legal professionals & expert witnesses in court, arbitration & administrative adjudication proceedings

NYS Bar Assn, Public Utility Law Committee
National Fuel Gas Distribution
Legal Department, 6363 Main Street, Buffalo, NY 14221
716-857-7313
Michael W Reville, Chair

NYS Bar Assn, Municipal Law Section
New York State Court of Claims
500 Court Exchange Bldg, 144 Exchange Blvd, Rochester, NY 14614
585-262-2320 Fax: 585-262-3019
e-mail: rminarik@courts.state.ny.us
Hon Renee Forgensi Minarik, Chair

New York State Supreme Court Officers Association
299 Broadway, Suite 1100, New York, NY 10007-1921
212-406-4292 or 212-406-4276 Fax: 212-791-8420
e-mail: lbroderick@nysscoa.org
Web site: www.nysscoa.org
John P McKillop, President
Supreme Court officers union

New York State Trial Lawyers
132 Nassau St, New York, NY 10038-2486
212-349-5890 Fax: 212-608-2310
e-mail: ecoleman@nystla.org
Web site: www.nystla.org
Elizabeth Coleman, Executive Director

New York University School of Law
40 Washington Square South, Rm 413, New York, NY 10012-1099
212-998-6217 Fax: 212-995-4881
e-mail: chase@juris.law.nyu.edu
Web site: www.law.nyu.edu/institutes/judicial
Alison Kinney, Program Coordinator-Inst of Judicial Administration
Judicial education & research

New York University, Law School
40 Washington Square South, New York, NY 10012-1012
212-998-6264 Fax: 212-995-4658
e-mail: stephen.gillers@nyu.edu
Stephen Gillers, Vice Dean & Professor of Law
Legal ethics

NYS Bar Assn, Media Law Committee
New Yorker
4 Times Square, 20th Fl, New York, NY 10036
212-286-5857 Fax: 212-286-5025
e-mail: edward_klaris@newyorker.com
Web site: www.newyorker.com
Edward Klaris, Chair

Offices and agencies appear in alphabetical order.

NYS Bar Assn, Courts of Appellate Jurisdiction Cmte
Norman A Olch, Esq
233 Broadway, New York, NY 10279
212-964-6171 Fax: 212-964-7634
e-mail: nao5@columbia.edu
Norman A Olch, Chair

NYS Bar Assn, Judicial Campaign Monitoring Cmte
Ostertag O'Leary & Barrett
17 Collegeview Ave, Poughkeepsie, NY 12603
845-486-4300 Fax: 845-486-4080
Web site: http://rlodmo.lawoffice.com
Robert L Ostertag, Chair

Pace University, School of Law, John Jay Legal Services Inc
80 N Broadway, White Plains, NY 10603-3711
914-422-4333 Fax: 914-422-4391
e-mail: vmerton@law.pace.edu
Web site: www.law.pace.edu
Vanessa Merton, Associate Dean for Clinical Education & Executive
    Director for John Jay Legal Svcs, Inc
Health law, poverty law, elder law, securities arbitration,
immigration

NYS Bar Assn, Federal Constitution & Legislation Cmte
Pitney Hardin et al
PO Box 1945, Morristown, NJ 07962-1945
973-966-8180 Fax: 973-966-1550
e-mail: jmaloney@pitneyhardin.com
Web site: www.pitneyhardin.com
John C Maloney, Jr, Chair

Prisoners' Legal Services of New York
114 Prospect St, Ithaca, NY 14850-5616
607-273-2283 Fax: 607-272-9122
e-mail: tterrizzi@plsny.org
Jerry Wein, Executive Director

Pro Bono Net
151 West 30th St, 10th Fl, New York, NY 10001
212-760-2554 Fax: 212-760-2557
e-mail: info@probono.net
Web site: www.probono.net
Michael Hertz, Executive Director
Connects & organizes the public interest legal community in an
online environment; a lawyer-to-lawyer network

NYS Bar Assn, Multi-jurisdictional Practice Cmte
Proskauer Rose LLP
1585 Broadway, New York, NY 10036-8299
212-969-3000 Fax: 212-969-2900
e-mail: keppler@proskauer.com
Web site: www.proskauer.com
Klaus Eppler, Chair

NYS Bar Assn, Fiduciary Appointments Cmte
Pruzansky & Besunder LLP
One Suffolk Sq, Ste 315, Islandia, NY 11749
631-234-9240 Fax: 631-234-9278
e-mail: jmp@prubeslaw.com
Joshua M Pruzansky, Chair

Puerto Rican Legal Defense & Education Fund Inc
(PRLDEF)
99 Hudson St, 14th Fl, New York, NY 10013-2815
212-219-3360 Fax: 212-431-4276
e-mail: info@prldef.org
Web site: www.prldef.org
Cesar A Perales, President & General Counsel
Secure, promote & protect the civil & human rights of the Puerto
Rican & wider Latino community through litigation, policy analysis
& education

NYS Bar Assn, Judicial Campaign Conduct Cmte
Supreme Court
401 Montgomery St, Rm 401, Syracuse, NY 13202-2127
315-671-1100 Fax: 315-671-1183
e-mail: maklein@courts.state.ny.us
Michael A Klein, Chair

Vera Institute of Justice
233 Broadway, 12th Fl, New York, NY 10279-1299
212-334-1300 Fax: 212-941-9407
e-mail: info@vera.org
Web site: www.vera.org
Michael Jacobson, Director
Research, design & implementation of demonstration projects in
criminal justice & social equity in partnership with government &
nonprofit organizations

NYS Bar Assn, Family Law Section
Vincent F Stempel, Jr Esq
1205 Franklin Ave, Ste 280, Garden City, NY 11530
516-742-8620 Fax: 516-742-6859
e-mail: vstempel@yahoo.com
Vincent F Stempel, Jr, Chair

Volunteers of Legal Service Inc
54 Greene St, New York, NY 10013
212-966-4400 Fax: 212-219-8943
e-mail: wdean@volsprobono.org
William J Dean, Executive Director
Providing pro bono legal services to disadvantaged individuals in
New York City

NYS Bar Assn, Diversity & Leadership Development Cmte
Whiteman Osterman & Hanna LLP
One Commerce Plz, Albany, NY 12260
518-487-7730 Fax: 518-487-7777
e-mail: lptharp@woh.com
Web site: www.woh.com
Lorraine Power Tharp, Chair

NYS Bar Assn, Health Law Section
Wilson Elser Moskowitz Edelman & Dicker
One Steuben Pl, Albany, NY 12207
518-449-8893 Fax: 518-449-4292
e-mail: rosenbergp@wemed.com
Philip Rosenberg, Chair

Offices and agencies appear in alphabetical order.

Women's Bar Association of the State of New York
PO Box 936, Planetarium Station, New York, NY 10024-0546
212-362-4445 Fax: 212-721-1620
e-mail: info@wbasny.org
Web site: www.wbasny.org
Mindy R Ziotogura, President

Policy Areas

Offices and agencies appear in alphabetical order.

LABOR & EMPLOYMENT PRACTICES

New York State

GOVERNOR'S OFFICE

Governor's Office
Executive Chamber
State Capitol
Albany, NY 12224
518-474-8390 Fax: 518-474-1513
Web site: www.state.ny.us

Governor:
George E Pataki 518-474-8390
Executive Director:
Kara Lanspery 518-474-8390
Secretary to the Governor:
John P Cahill. 518-474-4246
Senior Policy Advisor to the Governor:
Jeffrey Lovell 518-486-9671
Counsel to the Governor-Attorney General, Budget:
Richard Platkin. 518-474-8343
Senior Asst Counsel to the Governor-Banking, Insurance, State Insurance
Fund, Tort Reform, Uniform Laws, Workers' Compensation Board:
Chrisopher McCarthy. 518-474-2294
Asst Counsel to the Governor-Civil Svc, Elections, Empl Relations, Labor,
Motor Veh, Niagara Fr, Port Auth, Retirement/Pensions, Transp, Thruway,
Waterfr, MTA, PERB:
Christopher Staszak 518-474-1310
Director, Communications:
David Catalfamo. 518-474-8418

EXECUTIVE DEPARTMENTS AND RELATED AGENCIES

Insurance Fund (NYS)
199 Church St
New York, NY 10007
888-875-5790
Web site: www.nysif.com

Executive Director/CEO:
Kenneth J Ross. 212-312-7001
Chief Fiscal Officer & Actuary:
Susan D Sharp 518-437-6168
General Attorney:
Douglas J Hayden. 212-312-7093
Deputy Exec Director & Marketing Director:
Ann F Formel 518-437-1879
Deputy Exec Director:
Christopher Barclay 518-437-5220
Deputy Executive Director:
Stephen D Nelson. 518-437-6196
Special Counsel:
Jacob H Weintraub. 212-312-7872
Asst Deputy Director:
Jane Burgdorf. 518-437-6151

Special Asst to the Exec Director:
Kurt Rumpler 518-437-5209
Chief Information Officer:
Robert Sammons 518-437-5285
Public Information Officer:
Robert Lawson. 518-437-3504/fax: 518-437-1849

Administration
Director:
Albert K DiMeglio 212-312-7020

Claims & Medical Operations
Director:
Edward Hiller. 212-312-7056

Field Services
Director:
Armin Holdorf 212-312-9591

Information Technology Service
Director, ITS:
Laurie Endries 518-437-3130

Insurance Fund Board of Commissioners
Chair:
Terence L Morris 212-312-7001
Vice Chair:
Robert H Hurlbut 212-312-7001
Secretary to the Board:
Christopher Barclay 518-437-5220
Asst Secretary to the Board:
Albert K DiMeglio 212-312-7020
Member(ex-offico)/Commissioner, NYS Dept of Labor:
Linda Angello. 212-312-7001
Member:
John F Carpenter. 212-312-7001
Member:
C Scott Bowen 212-312-7001
Member:
Donald T DeCarlo 212-312-7001
Member:
Jane A Halbritter. 212-312-7001
Member:
Charles L Loiodice 212-312-7001
Member:
Eugene Mazzola 212-312-7001

Investments
Director:
Bing Garrido. 212-312-9710

NYSIF District Offices

Albany . . . . fax: 518-437-5260
15 Computer Drive West, Albany, NY 12205
Business Manager:
Edward Obertubbesing. 518-437-6401

Buffalo . . . . fax: 716-851-2106
225 Oak St, Buffalo, NY 14203

Offices and agencies appear in alphabetical order.

Business Manager:
Ronald Reed.................................. 716-851-2004

Endicott
Glendale Technology Park, 2001 E Perimeter Rd, Endicott, NY 13760
Business Manager:
James Fehrer.................. 607-741-6100/fax: 607-741-5029

Nassau County, Long Island .... fax: 631-756-4242
8 Corporate Center Dr, 2nd Fl, Melville, NY 11747
Business Manager:
Cliff Meister.................................. 631-756-4003

Rochester .... fax: 585-258-2065
100 Chestnut St, Ste 1000, Rochester, NY 14604
Business Manager:
Lisa Ellsworth 585-258-2100

Suffolk County, Long Island .... fax: 631-756-4260
8 Corporate Center Dr, 3rd Fl, Melville, NY 11747
Business Manager:
Eileen Wojnar................................. 631-756-4330

Syracuse .... fax: 315-453-8313
1045 Seventh North St, Liverpool, NY 13088
Business Manager:
Kathleen Campbell............................ 315-453-8300

White Plains................................. fax: 914-701-2181
105 Corporate Park Dr, Ste 200, White Plains, NY 10604
Business Manager:
Carl Heitner 914-701-6292

Policyholder Services
Director:
Dennis Incitti 212-587-3600

Premium Audit
Director:
Glenn Cunningham............................. 212-587-7470

Safety Group Operations
Director:
John Massetti 212-312-9933

Underwriting
Director:
Vincent Troianiello............................ 212-312-7012

Labor Department
Building 12, Room 500
State Campus
Albany, NY 12240
518-457-2741 Fax: 518-457-6908
e-mail: nysdol@labor.state.ny.us
Web site: www.labor.state.ny.us

345 Hudson St, Ste 8301
Box 662, Mail Stop 01
New York, NY 10014-0662
212-352-6000
Fax: 212-352-6824

Commissioner:
Linda Angello.................................. 518-457-2746
Executive Deputy Commissioner:
Dennis Ryan................................... 518-457-4318

Employment & Unemployment Insurance Advisory Council
Chair:
Vacant 518-457-2878

Employment Relations Board
Chair:
Anthony C Imbarrato........................... 212-564-2441

Industrial Board of Appeals
Chair:
Evelyn Heady................................. 518-474-4789

Unemployment Insurance Appeal Board
Chair:
Richard M Rosenbaum.......................... 518-402-0205
Executive Director:
Joseph P Kearney.............................. 518-402-0205

Administration & Public Affairs
Deputy Commissioner, Admin & Public Affairs:
Mary L Hines 518-457-3905
Associate Commissioner, Human Resources:
James W Leary................................ 518-457-9570
Director, Administrative Finance Bureau:
Roger Bailie 518-457-2647
Director, Communications:
Robert Lillpopp 518-457-5519/fax: 518-485-1126
Director, Personnel:
Debora O'Brien-Jordan 518-457-6651
Director, Staff & Organization Development:
Michael Cunningham 518-457-1168
Affirmative Action Administrator:
Andrew Adams................................ 518-457-1984

Counsel's Office
Counsel:
Jerome A Tracy 518-457-7069
Deputy Counsel:
Joan Connell.................................. 518-457-7069
Legislative Counsel:
Kevin Kerwin 518-457-4380

Inspector General's Office
Inspector General:
Brian Sanvidge................................ 518-457-7012
Director, Internal Audit:
Karen Stackrow 518-457-9016

Labor Planning & Technology
Chief Information Officer:
Celia Hamblin................................. 518-457-7994

Research & Statistics Division
Deputy Director:
David J Trzaskos 518-457-6369
Chief of Labor Market Information:
Norman Steele 518-457-6638
Statewide Labor Market Analyst:
Kevin Jack 518-457-2919

Veterans & Services
Deputy Commissioner, Veterans Affairs:
Ronald Tocci 518-457-1843

Employment Services Division
Director:
Karen Papandrea 518-457-3584
Assist Director:
Russell Oliver................................. 518-457-3584

Employer Services
Director:
Timothy O'Keefe. 518-457-6821
Rural Labor Services:
Delos Whitman 518-457-6799
Veterans Employment Service
Program Coordinator:
Earl Wallace 518-457-1343

Regional Offices
Central/Mohawk Valley. fax: 315-793-2342
207 Genesee St, Ste 712, Utica, NY 13501
Regional Administrator:
Kelli Owens. 315-793-2716
Finger Lakes Region . . . . fax: 585-258-8859
130 West Main St, Rochester, NY 14614
Regional Administrator:
Peter Pecor. 585-258-8858
Greater Capital District . . . . fax: 518-462-2777
175 Central Ave, Albany, NY 12206-2902
Regional Administrator:
David Wallingford. 518-462-7600
Hudson Valley . . . . fax: 914-287-2058
120 Bloomingdale Rd, White Plains, NY 10605
Acting Regional Administrator:
Frank Surdey 914-997-8711
Long Island Region . . . . fax: 516-934-8553
303 W Old County Rd, Hicksville, NY 11801
Regional Administrator:
Steve Salhaus. 516-934-8547
New York City. . . . . fax: 212-621-0730
247 West 54th St, New York, NY 10019
Regional Administrator:
John Harloff. 212-621-9349
Southern Tier . . . . fax: 607-741-4516
2001 Perimeter Rd East, Ste 3, Endicott, NY 13760
Regional Administrator:
John Flynn 607-741-4519
Western Region . . . . fax: 716-851-2792
290 Main St, Buffalo, NY 14202
Regional Administrator:
Samuel J Drago 716-851-2752

Unemployment Insurance Division
Director:
Robert Davison 518-457-2878/fax: 518-485-8604

Workforce Development & Training Division
Director:
Margaret Moree. 518-457-0380/fax: 518-457-9526
Employability Development/Apprentice Training
Director:
Christine Timber 518-457-6820

Worker Protection
Deputy Commissioner, Workforce Protection, Standards & Licensing:
Connie Varcasia 518-457-4317

Labor Standards Division
Director:
Richard Cucolo. 518-457-2460

Public Work Bureau
Director:
Chris Alund 518-457-5589

Safety & Health Division
Director:
Anthony Germano. 518-457-3518/fax: 518-457-1519

Asbestos Control Bureau
Program Manager:
Vacant 518-457-1255/fax: 518-485-8054
Industry Inspection Unit
Program Manager:
David Ruppert 518-457-1327/fax: 518-485-8054
On-site Consultation Unit
Program Manager:
James Rush. 518-457-2238/fax: 518-457-3454
Public Employees Safety & Health (PESH) Unit
Program Manager:
Maureen Cox 518-457-1263/fax: 518-457-5545
Radiological Health Unit
Principal Radiophysicist:
Clayton Bradt 518-457-1202/fax: 518-485-7406

Law Department
State Capitol
Albany, NY 12224-0341
518-474-7330 Fax: 518-402-2472
Web site: www.oag.state.ny.us

120 Broadway
New York, NY 12224-0341
212-416-8000
Fax: 212-416-8942

Attorney General:
Eliot Spitzer 518-474-7330
First Deputy Attorney General:
Michele Hirshman 212-416-8050
Director, Public Information & Correspondence:
Peter A Drago 518-474-7330/fax: 518-402-2472

Public Advocacy Division
Acting Deputy Attorney General:
Terryl Brown Clemons 212-416-8041/fax: 212-416-8068
Special Counsel:
Mary Ellen Burns 212-416-6155

Civil Rights Bureau
Bureau Chief:
Dennis Parker 212-416-8250/fax: 212-416-8074

State Counsel Division
Deputy Attorney General:
Richard Rifkin 518-473-7190
Assistant Deputy Attorney General:
Patricia Martinelli 518-473-0648/fax: 518-486-9777
Assistant Deputy Attorney General:
Susan L Watson 212-416-8579/fax: 212-416-6001

Labor Bureau
Bureau Chief:
M Patricia Smith 212-416-8710

Workers' Compensation Board
20 Park Street
Albany, NY 12207
518-474-6670 Fax: 518-473-1415
Web site: www.wcb.state.ny.us

Chair:
David Wehner. 518-474-6670
Vice Chair:
Jeffrey R Sweet. 518-474-6670

Offices and agencies appear in alphabetical order.

Executive Director:
Richard A Bell 518-474-6670
General Counsel:
Vacant. 518-486-9564/fax: 518-473-2233
Director, Division of Appeals:
Carl Copps. 518-402-0160/fax: 518-473-2233
Director, Internal Audit:
Albert Blackman 518-473-6447/fax: 518-473-4761
Director, Public Information:
Jon A Sullivan. 518-474-6670/fax: 518-473-1415
Fraud Inspector General:
John Burgher 888-363-6001/fax: 518-402-1059
Advocate for Business:
David Austin. 518-486-3331
Advocate for Injured Workers:
Edwin Ruff 800-580-6665/fax: 518-486-7510

Administration

Deputy Executive Director:
Glenn Warren 518-473-8900/fax: 518-486-6411
Director, Administrative Services:
Cathy King 518-486-3334
Director, Security:
Joseph V Smith 518-402-0172/fax: 518-402-1059
Director, Finance & Policy:
Kathleen Griffin 518-486-9596
Director, Human Resources Management:
Lisa Sunkef 718-802-6612/fax: 718-834-2123
Affirmative Action Officer:
Jaime Benitez. 518-486-5128/fax: 518-486-6364

Operations

Deputy Exec Director:
Marsha Orndorff 518-486-7143/fax: 518-474-9367
Director, Operations:
David M Donohue. 518-486-3345/fax: 518-486-6411
Director, Disability Benefits:
Nicholas Dogias. 718-802-6947/fax: 718-802-6971
Director, WC Compliance & Regulatory Services:
Brian Collins 518-474-2686/fax: 518-402-0701

District Offices

Albany
100 Broadway-Menands, Albany, NY 12241
District Administrator:
Linda Spano 866-750-5157/fax: 518-473-9166
District Manager:
Pat Wright. 866-750-5157/fax: 518-473-9166
Binghamton
State Office Bldg, 44 Hawley St, Binghamton, NY 13901
District Administrator:
Anthony Capozzi 866-802-3604/fax: 607-721-8464
District Manager:
David Wiktorek 866-802-3604/fax: 607-721-8464
Brooklyn
111 Livingston St, Brooklyn, NY 11201
District Administrator:
Edward Joyce 800-877-1373/fax: 718-802-6642
District Manager:
Tom Agostino. 800-877-1373/fax: 718-802-6642
Buffalo
Statler Towers, 3rd Fl, 107 Delaware Ave, Buffalo, NY 14202-2898
District Administrator:
Jeffrey Quinn 866-211-0645/fax: 716-842-2171
District Manager:
Barbara Townsend 866-211-0645/fax: 716-842-2171
Hauppauge
220 Rabro Drive, Ste 100, Hauppauge, NY 11788-4230

District Administrator:
Scott Firestone 866-681-5354/fax: 631-952-7966
District Manager:
Robert F Williams 866-681-5354/fax: 631-952-7966
Hempstead
175 Fulton Ave, Hempstead, NY 11550
District Administrator:
Alan Landman 866-805-3630/fax: 516-560-7807
District Manager:
Alan Gotlinsky 866-805-3630/fax: 516-560-7807
Manhattan
215 W 125th St, New York, NY 10027
District Administrator:
Frank Vernuccio, Jr 800-877-1373/fax: 212-932-1488
Peekskill
41 N Division St, Peekskill, NY 10566
District Administrator:
Alida Carey. 866-746-0552/fax: 914-788-5793
District Manager:
Luis A Torres 866-746-0552/fax: 914-788-5793
Queens
168-46 91st Ave, Jamaica, NY 11432
District Administrator:
Wayne Allen. 800-877-1373/fax: 718-291-7248
District Administrator:
Carl Gabbidon 800-877-1373/fax: 718-291-7248
Rochester
130 Main St West, Rochester, NY 14614
District Administrator:
George A Park, Jr 866-211-0644/fax: 585-238-8351
District Manager:
MaryBeth Goodsell 866-211-0644/fax: 585-238-8351
Syracuse
935 James Street, Syracuse, NY 13203
District Administrator:
Janet Burman 866-802-3730/fax: 315-423-2938
District Manager:
Marc Johnson 866-802-3730/fax: 315-423-2938

Systems Modernization

Deputy Exec Director:
Nancy Mulholland. 518-486-7143/fax: 518-474-9367
Director, Management Information Systems:
Thomas Wegener. 518-486-5143/fax: 518-473-6379

Workers' Compensation Board of Commissioners

Chair:
David P Wehner. 518-474-6670
Vice Chair:
Jeffrey R Sweet. 518-474-6670
Commissioner:
Mona Bargnesi 518-474-6670
Commissioner:
Michael T Berns 518-486-9529
Commissioner:
Leslie J Botta 518-402-1071
Commissioner:
Candace K Finnegan. 518-402-6137
Commissioner:
Scott C Firestone 518-402-1071
Commissioner:
Agatha Edel Groski 518-402-6135
Commissioner:
Karl A Henry 518-402-6136
Commissioner:
Frances Libous 518-474-6670
Commissioner:
Ellen O Paprocki. 518-474-6670

Offices and agencies appear in alphabetical order.

Commissioner:
Robert Zinck 518-474-6670
Secretary to the Board:
Susan M Olson 518-402-6071

CORPORATIONS, AUTHORITIES AND COMMISSIONS

Waterfront Commission of New York Harbor

39 Broadway
4th Fl
New York, NY 10006
212-742-9280 Fax: 212-480-0587
Web site: www.wcnyh.org

Commissioner, NY:
Michael C Axelrod 212-742-9280
Commissioner, NJ:
Michael J Madonna 212-742-9280
Executive Director:
Thomas De Maria 212-742-9280

NEW YORK STATE LEGISLATURE

See Legislative Branch in Section 1 for additional Standing Committee and Subcommittee information.

Assembly Standing Committees

Labor
Chair:
Susan V John (D) 518-455-4527

Ranking Minority Member:
Patricia L Acampora (R) 518-455-5294

Assembly Task Forces

Puerto Rican/Hispanic Task Force
Chair:
Peter Rivera (D) 518-455-5102
Co-Chair:
Vito J Lopez 518-455-5537

Skills Development & Career Education, Legislative Commission on
Assembly Chair:
Joan K Christensen (D) 518-455-5283
Program Manager:
Brenda Carter 518-455-4865

Women's Issues, Task Force on
Chair:
Joan L Millman (D) 518-455-5426
Coordinator:
Jean Emery 518-455-3632/fax: 518-455-4574

Senate Standing Committees

Labor
Chair:
George Maziarz (R) 518-455-2024
Ranking Minority Member:
Dianne J Savino (D) 518-455-2437

U.S. Government

EXECUTIVE DEPARTMENTS AND RELATED AGENCIES

Equal Employment Opportunity Commission
Web site: www.eeoc.gov

New York District . . . . fax: 212-620-0070
33 Whitehall St, 5th Fl, New York, NY 10004
District Director:
Spencer H Lewis, Jr . . . . 212-336-3620 or 212-336-3625

Buffalo Local
6 Fountain Plaza, Ste 350, Buffalo, NY 14202
Director:
Elizabeth Cadle 716-551-4441/fax: 716-551-4387

Federal Labor Relations Authority
Web site: www.flra.gov

Boston Regional Office
99 Summer St, Ste 1500, Boston, MA 2110
Regional Director:
Richard D Zaiger 617-424-5730/fax: 617-424-5743

Federal Mediation & Conciliation Service
Web site: www.fmcs.gov

Northeastern Region . . . . fax: 732-726-3124
517 US Hwy 1 So, Ste 3020, Iselin, NJ 8830
Regional Director:
John F Buettner 732-726-3120
Director, Mediation Services:
John E Sweeney 732-726-3120

National Labor Relations Board
Web site: www.nlrb.gov

Region 2 - New York City Metro Area
26 Federal Plaza, Rm 3614, New York, NY 10278-0104
Regional Director:
Celeste J Mattina 212-264-0330/fax: 212-264-2450

Region 29 - Brooklyn Area
One MetroTech Center North, 10th Fl, Brooklyn, NY 11201-4201
Regional Director:
Alvin P Blyer 718-330-7700/fax: 718-330-7579

Region 3 - New York Except Metro Area
Federal Bldg, Rm 901, 111 W Huron St, Buffalo, NY 14202-2387

Offices and agencies appear in alphabetical order.

Regional Dir:
Helen Marsh 716-551-4931/fax: 716-551-4972

Albany Resident Office
O'Brien Fed Bldg, Rm 342, Clinton Ave at N Pearl St, Albany, NY 12207
Resident Officer:
Jon Mackle 518-431-4156/fax: 518-431-4157

US Labor Department
Web site: www.dol.gov

Bureau of Labor Statistics (BLS)
201 Varick St, Rm 808, New York, NY 10014
Web site: www.bls.gov
Regional Commissioner (NY & Boston):
Dennis McSweeney . . . . .212-334-2451 or 617-565-2411
Reg Comm (NY):
Michael L Dolfman 212-337-2500/fax: 212-337-2411

Employee Benefits Security Administration (EBSA)
33 Whitehall St, Ste 1200, New York, NY 10004
Reg Administrator:
Francis C Clisham 212-607-8600/fax: 212-607-8681

Employment & Training Administration (ETA)
JFK Federal Bldg, RmE/350, Boston, MA 2203
Regional Administrator:
Joseph S Stoltz. 617-788-0170/fax: 617-788-0125

Employment Standards Administration

Federal Contract Compliance Programs Office (OFCCP)
201 Varick St, Rm 750, New York, NY 10014
Acting Regional Dir:
Harold M Busch 646-264-3170/fax: 646-264-3009

Labor-Management Standards Office (OLMS)
Web site: www.olms.dol.gov
Buffalo District Office
111 W Huron St, Rm 1310, Buffalo, NY 14202
District Director:
Joseph Wasik 716-551-4976/fax: 716-551-4978
New York District Office
201 Varick St, Rm 878, New York, NY 10014
District Director:
Ralph Gerchak 646-264-3190/fax: 646-264-3191

Wage-Hour Division (WHD)-Northeast Regional Office
170 So Independence Mall, Ste 850 West, Philadelphia, PA 19106
Regional Admin:
Corlis L Sellers 215-861-5800/fax: 215-861-5840
Albany District Office
Leo W O'Brien Fed Bldg, Rm 822, Albany, NY 12207
District Director:
Christopher Martin 518-431-4278/fax: 518-431-4281
Long Island District Office
1400 Old Country Rd, Ste 410, Westbury, NY 11590
District Director:
Irv Miljoner 516-338-1890/fax: 516-338-1895
New York City District Office
26 Federal Plz, Rm 3700, New York, NY 10278
District Director:
Philip Jacobson. 212-264-8185/fax: 212-264-9548

Workers' Compensation Programs (OWCP)
201 Varick St, Rm 740, New York, NY 10014
Regional Director:
Nancy Ricker. 646-264-3000/fax: 646-264-3006

Inspector General

Inspector General's Office for Audit (OIG-A)
201 Varick St, Rm 871, New York, NY 10014
Regional Inspector General, Audit:
Richard H Brooks 646-264-3510/fax: 646-264-3501

Inspector General's Office for Investigations (OIG-I)
201 Varick St, Rm 849, New York, NY 10014
Regional Inspector General, Investigations:
John R McGlynn. 646-264-3551/fax: 646-264-3502

Occupational Safety & Health Administration (OSHA)
201 Varick St, Rm 670, New York, NY 10014
212-337-2378
Web site: www.osha.gov
Regional Administrator:
Patricia K Clark. 212-337-2378/fax: 212-337-2371
Acting Dep Regional Administrator:
Louis Ricca. 212-337-2326

Albany Area Office
401 New Karner Rd, Ste 300, Albany, NY 12205-3809
Area Director:
John M Tomich 518-464-4338/fax: 518-464-4337

Bayside Area Office
42-40 Bell Blvd, 5th Fl, Bayside, NY 11361
Area Director:
Harvey Shapiro 718-279-9060/fax: 718-279-9057

Buffalo Area Office
5360 Genesee St, Bowmansville, NY 14026
Area Director:
Art Dube 716-684-3891/fax: 716-684-3896

Manhattan Area Office
201 Varick St, Rm 908, New York, NY 10014
Area Director:
Richard Mendelson 212-620-3200/fax: 212-620-4121

Syracuse Area Office
3300 Vickery Rd, North Syracuse, NY 13212
Area Director:
Christopher Adams 315-451-0808/fax: 315-451-1351

Tarrytown Area Office
660 White Plains Rd, Tarrytown, NY 10591
Area Director:
Diana Cortez. 914-524-7510/fax: 914-524-7515

Office of Asst Secretary for Administration & Mgmt (OASAM)
201 Varick St, Rm 815, New York, NY 10014
Regional Administrator (NY & Boston):
Debbra Williams. . . . . .212-337-2215 or 617-565-1990
fax: 212-337-2631

Office of the Solicitor
201 Varick St, Rm 983, New York, NY 10014
Reg Solicitor:
Patricia M Rodenhausen 212-337-2078/fax: 212-337-2112

Region 2 - New York Office of Secretary's Representative
201 Varick St, Rm 605-B, New York, NY 10014
Secretary's Regional Representative (SRR):
Angelica Tang. 212-337-2387/fax: 212-337-2386

Bureau of Apprenticeship & Training (BAT)
201 Varick St, Rm 602, New York, NY 10014
Regional Director:
Albert Hudanish 212-337-2313/fax: 212-337-2317

Offices and agencies appear in alphabetical order.

Policy Areas

Jobs Corps (JC)
201 Varick St, Rm 897, New York, NY 10014
Regional Director:
Joseph A Semansky 212-337-2282/fax: 212-620-6259

Office of Public Affairs (OPA) (serving New York State)
JFK Federal Bldg, Rm E120, Boston, MA 2203
Regional Director, Public Affairs:
John Chavez 617-565-2072/fax: 617-565-2076

Region 2 New York - Women's Bureau (WB)
201 Varick St, Rm 708, New York, NY 10014
Regional Admin:
Mary C Murphree 212-337-2389/fax: 212-337-2394
e-mail: murphree.mary@dol.gov

US Merit Systems Protection Board
Web site: www.mspb.gov

New York Field Office
26 Federal Plaza, Ste 3137A, New York, NY 10278-0022
Chief Administrative Judge:
Arthur Joseph 212-264-9372/fax: 212-264-1417

US Office of Personnel Management
Web site: www.usajobs.opm.gov

PHILADELPHIA SERVICE CENTER (serving New York)
William J Green Fed Bldg, Rm 3400, 600 Arch St, Philadelphia, PA 19106
Director:
Joseph D Stix 215-861-3031/fax: 215-861-3030
e-mail: philadelphia@opm.gov

US Railroad Retirement Board
Web site: www.rrb.gov

New York District Offices

Albany
O'Brien Fed Bldg, Rm 264, Clinton Ave & N Pearl St, Albany, NY 12201
District Manager:
Daniel M Layton, Jr 518-431-4004/fax: 518-431-4000
e-mail: albany@rrb.gov

Buffalo
111 W Huron St, Rm 1106, Buffalo, NY 14202
District Manager:
Philip C Dissek 716-551-4181/fax: 716-551-3802
e-mail: buffalo@rrb.gov

New York
26 Federal Plaza, Rm 3404, New York, NY 10278
District Manager:
Rose I Jonas 212-264-9820/fax: 212-264-1687
e-mail: newyork@rrb.gov

Westbury
1400 Old Country Rd, Ste 202, Westbury, NY 11590
District Manager:
Marie Baran 516-334-5940/fax: 516-334-4763

U.S. CONGRESS

See U.S. Congress Chapter for additional Standing Committee and Subcommittee information.

House of Representatives Standing Committees

Education & the Workforce
Chair:
John A Boehner (R-OH) 202-225-6205
Ranking Minority Member:
George Miller (D-CA) 202-225-2095
New York Delegate:
Timothy H Bishop (D) 202-225-3826
New York Delegate:
Carolyn McCarthy (D) 202-225-5516
New York Delegate:
Major R Owens (D) 202-225-6231

Small Business
Chair:
Donald A Manzullo (R-IL) 202-225-5676
Ranking Minority Member:
Nydia M Velazquez (D-NY) 202-225-2361
New York Delegate:
Sue W Kelly (R) 202-225-5441

Subcommittees
Regulatory Reform & Oversight
Chair:
Todd Akin (R-MO) 202-225-2561
Ranking Minority Member:
Madeleine Bordallo (D-GU) 202-225-1188
New York Delegate:
Sue W Kelly (R) 202-225-5441
Rural Enterprise, Agriculture & Technology
Chair:
Sam Graves (R-MO) 202-225-7041
Ranking Minority Member:
John Barrow (D-GA) 202-225-2823
Workforce, Empowerment & Government Programs
Chair:
Marilyn Musgrave (R-CO) 202-225-4676
Ranking Minority Member:
Dan Lipinski (D-IL) 202-225-5701

Senate Standing Committees

Health, Education, Labor & Pensions
Chair:
Michael Enzi (R-WY) 202-224-3424
Ranking Minority Member:
Edward M Kennedy (D-MA) 202-224-4543
New York Delegate:
Hillary Rodham Clinton (D) 202-224-4451

Small Business & Entrepreneurship
Chair:
Olympia J Snowe (R-ME) 202-224-5344
Ranking Minority Member:
John F Kerry (D-MA) 202-224-2742

Offices and agencies appear in alphabetical order.

Private Sector

ADR Associates LLC
1350 Broadway, Ste 2200, New York, NY 10018
212-594-4454 Fax: 212-594-4474
e-mail: mshaw@adrassociates.com
Web site: www.jamsadr.com
Carol Wittenberg, Arbitrator/Mediator
Mediation of civil, commercial & employment disputes: training & systems design

Abilities Inc, National Center for Disability Services
201 IU Willets Rd, Albertson, NY 11507-1599
516-465-1400 or 516-747-5355 (TTY) Fax: 516-465-3757
e-mail: ftishman@abilitiesinc.org
Web site: www.abilitiesinc.org
Charles W Hunt, Executive Director
Provides comprehensive services to help individuals with disabilities reach their employment goals; provides support services & technical assistance to employers who hire persons with disabilities

NYS Bar Assn, Pension Simplification Cmte
Alvin D Lurie Esq
145 Huguenot St, Rm 130, New Rochelle, NY 10801
914-235-6575 Fax: 914-235-6760
e-mail: allurie@worldnet.att.net
Alvin D Lurie, Chair

American Federation of Teachers
555 New Jersey Ave NW, Washington, DC 20001
800-238-1133 Fax: 202-393-7479
e-mail: emcelroy@aft.org
Web site: www.aft.org
Edward J McElroy, President

Associated Builders & Contractors, Construction Training Center of NYS
6369 Collamer Drive, East Syracuse, NY 13057-1115
315-463-7539 or 800-477-7743 Fax: 315-463-7621
e-mail: info@abc.org
Web site: www.abc.org/newyork
Thomas Schlueter, Vice President of Education Programs
Merit shop construction trades apprenticeship program

Blitman & King LLP
443 N Franklin St, Ste 300, Syracuse, NY 13204
315-422-7111 Fax: 315-471-2623
e-mail: btking@bklawyers.com
Web site: www.bklawyers.com
Bernard T King, Attorney/Senior Partner
Labor & employee benefits

Center for an Urban Future
120 Wall St, 20th Fl, New York, NY 10005
212-479-3353 Fax: 212-344-6457
e-mail: cuf@nycfuture.org
Web site: www.nycfuture.org
Neil Scott Kleiman, Director
Policy institute dedicated to aggressively pursuing solutions to critical problems facing cities

Civil Service Employees Union (CSEA), Local 1000, AFSCME, AFL-CIO
143 Washington Ave, Capitol Station Box 7125, Albany, NY 12224-0125
518-257-1000 or 800-342-4146 Fax: 518-462-3639
Web site: www.csealocal1000.org
Danny Donohue, President
Public/private employees union

Communications Workers of America, District 1
80 Pine St, 37th Floor, New York, NY 10005
212-344-2515 Fax: 212-425-2947
Web site: www.cwa-union.org
Christopher Shelton, Vice President

Cornell University, Institute on Conflict Resolution
621 Ives Hall, Ithaca, NY 14853-3901
607-255-5378 Fax: 607-255-6974
e-mail: dbl4@cornell.edu
Web site: www.ilr.cornell.edu
David Lipsky, Professor Collective Bargaining & Director
Collective bargaining; dispute resolution, negotiation

Cornell University, Sch of Industr & Labor Relations Inst for Women
16 E 34th Street, 4th Fl, New York, NY 10016
212-340-2850 Fax: 212-340-2893
e-mail: sb22@cornell.edu
Web site: www.ilr.cornell.edu/iws
Samuel B Bacharach, McKelvey-Grant Professor & Director
Substance abuse in the workplace; power & bargaining in organizations

Cornell University, School of Industrial & Labor Relations
Ives Hall, Ithaca, NY 14853-3901
607-255-4375 or 607-255-2223 Fax: 607-255-1836
e-mail: vmb2@cornell.edu
Web site: www.ilr.cornell.edu
Vernon Briggs, Professor
Immigration policy; labor market trends & analysis

Cornell University, School of Industrial & Labor Relations
356 ILR Research Bldg, Ithaca, NY 14853-3901
607-255-7581 Fax: 607-255-0245
e-mail: klb23@cornell.edu
Web site: www.ilr.cornell.edu
Kate Bronfenbrenner, Director, Labor Education Research
Public sector organizations; leadership; temporary & contract workers; union organizing; & collective bargaining

Cornell University, School of Industrial & Labor Relations
340 ILR Research Bldg, Ithaca, NY 14853-3901
607-255-2765 Fax: 607-255-2513
e-mail: rwh8@cornell.edu
Web site: www.ilr.cornell.edu
Richard Hurd, Professor Industrial & Labor Relations
Trade union administration & strategy

Offices and agencies appear in alphabetical order.

Cullen & Dykman
100 Quentin Roosevelt Blvd, Garden City Ctr, Garden City, NY 11530-4850
516-357-3703 Fax: 516-296-9155
e-mail: gfishberg@cullenanddykman.com
Web site: www.cullenanddykman.com
Gerard Fishberg, Partner
Municipal & labor law

Empire State Regional Council of Carpenters
27 Warehouse Rd, Albany, NY 12205
518-459-7182 Fax: 518-459-7798
e-mail: kevinrhicks@usa.com
Kevin R Hicks, Political & Legislative Director & Region 3 Director

Kaye Scholer LLP
425 Park Ave, 8th Fl, New York, NY 10022
212-836-8558 Fax: 212-836-6458
e-mail: jwaks@kayescholer.com
Web site: www.kayescholer.com
Jay W Waks, Partner
Chair, Labor & Employment Law Group (representing employers)

Lancer Insurance Co/Lancer Compliance Services
370 West Park Ave, Long Beach, NY 11561-3245
516-432-5000 Fax: 516-431-0926
e-mail: bcrescenzo@lancer-ins.com
Bob Crescenzo, Vice President
Substance abuse management & testing services for the transportation industry

MDRC
16 East 34th St, 19th Floor, New York, NY 10016-5936
212-532-3200 Fax: 212-684-0832
e-mail: information@mdrc.org
Web site: www.mdrc.org
Gordon Berlin, President
Nonprofit research & field testing of education & employment programs for disadvantaged adults & youth

Manhattan-Bronx Minority Business Development Center
350 5th Ave, Ste 2202, New York, NY 10118
212-947-5351 Fax: 212-947-1506
e-mail: mbmbdc@manhattan-bronx-mbdc.com
Web site: www.manhattan-bronx-mbdc.com
Lorraine Kelsey, Executive Director
Information & advocacy for local employment & business & contract opportunities

NY Association of Training & Employment Professionals (NYATEP)
111 Pine St, Albany, NY 12207
518-465-1473 Fax: 518-432-2417
e-mail: jtwomey@nyatep.org
Web site: www.nyatep.org
John Twomey, Executive Director
Represent local workforce development partnerships

NYS Building & Construction Trades Council
71 West 23 St, New York, NY 10010
212-647-0700 Fax: 212-647-0705
Edward J Malloy, President

NYS Council of Machinists
197 Stone St, Watertown, NY 13601
315-788-8292 Fax: 315-786-8013
e-mail: rockymaxson@msn.com
Rocky Maxon, Legislative Director

NYS Industries for the Disabled (NYSID) Inc
155 Washington Ave, Ste 400, Albany, NY 12210-2329
518-463-9706 or 800-221-5994 Fax: 518-463-9708
e-mail: admin@nysid.org
Web site: www.nysid.org
Lawrence L Barker, Jr, President & Chief Executive Officer
Business development through

National Federation of Independent Business
1 Commerce Plaza, Ste 1119, Albany, NY 12260-1000
518-434-1262 Fax: 518-426-8799
e-mail: matthew.guilbault@NFIB.org
Web site: www.nfib.com
Matthew Guilbault, Assistant State Director
Advocacy for small business

National Federation of Independent Business
1 Commerce Plaza, Ste 1119, Albany, NY 12260-1000
518-434-1262 Fax: 518-426-8799
e-mail: mark.alesse@nfib.org
Web site: www.nfib.org
Mark Alesse, State Director
Small business advocacy; supporting pro-small business candidates at the state & federal levels

National Writers Union
113 University Pl, 6th Fl, New York, NY 10003
212-254-0279 Fax: 212-254-0673
e-mail: nwu@nwu.org
Web site: www.nwu.org
Gerard Colby, President

New York Committee for Occupational Safety & Health
275 7th Ave, 8th Fl, New York, NY 10001
212-627-3900 Fax: 212-627-9812
e-mail: nycosh@nycosh.org
Web site: www.nycosh.org
Joel Shufro, Executive Director
Provide occupational safety & health training & technical assistance

New York State Nurses Association
11 Cornell Rd, Latham, NY 12110
518-782-9400 x279 Fax: 518-783-5207
e-mail: lola.fehr@nysna.org
Web site: www.nysna.org
Lola M Fehr, Executive Director
Labor union & professional association for registered nurses

Offices and agencies appear in alphabetical order.

New York University, Graduate School of Journalism
Arthur Carter Hall, 10 Washington Place, New York, NY 10003
212-998-7980 Fax: 212-995-4148
Web site: www.nyu.edu/gsas/dept/journal
Bill Serrin, Director, Graduate Studies
Labor issues & reporting

Osborne Association/South Forty
3631 38th St, Long Island City, NY 11101-1621
718-707-2600 Fax: 718-707-3105
e-mail: amclaughlin@osborneny.org
Web site: www.osborneny.org
Anne McLaughlin, Senior Director of Employment & Training
Career/educational counseling, job referrals & training for recently released prisoners

Public/Private Ventures
The Chanin Building, 122 East 42nd St, 42nd Fl, New York, NY 10168
212-822-2400 Fax: 212-949-0439
e-mail: melliott@ppv.org
Web site: www.ppv.org
Mark Elliott, Executive Vice President
Action-based research, public policy & program development organization

Realty Advisory Board on Labor Relations
292 Madison Ave, New York, NY 10017
212-889-4100 Fax: 212-889-4105
e-mail: jberg@rabolr.com
Web site: www.rabolr.com
James Berg, President
Labor negotiations for realtors & realty firms

Service Employees International Union (SEIU), Local 1199
310 W 43rd St, New York, NY 10036
212-261-2222 Fax: 212-956-5140
Web site: www.1199seiuonline.org
Dennis Rivera, President
Representing New York State healthcare workers

Transport Workers Union of America, AFL-CIO
1700 Broadway, 2nd Fl, New York, NY 10019
212-259-4900 Fax: 212-265-4537
Web site: www.twu.com
Michael O'Brien, International President
Bus, train, railroad & airline workers' union

Union of Needletrade, Textile & Industrial Employees (UNITE!)
275 7th Ave, Fl 11, New York, NY 10001-6708
212-265-7000 Fax: 212-265-3415
Web site: www.uniteunion.org
Bruce Raynor, President

United Food & Commercial Workers Local 1
106 Memorial Parkway, Utica, NY 13501
315-797-9600 Fax: 315-793-1182
e-mail: organize@ufcwone.org
Web site: www.ufcwone.org
Frank C DeRiso, President

Vedder Price Kaufman & Kammholz PC
805 3rd Ave, 23rd Floor, New York, NY 10022
212-407-7750 Fax: 212-407-7799
e-mail: akoral@vedderprice.com
Web site: www.vedderprice.com
Alan M Koral, Shareholder
Employment law

Vladeck, Waldman, Elias & Engelhard PC
1501 Broadway, Suite 800, New York, NY 10036
212-403-7300 Fax: 212-221-3172
e-mail: jvladeck@vladeck.com
Judith Vladeck, Senior Law Partner
Employment law, including discrimination cases

NYS Bar Assn, Labor & Employment Law Section Zuchlewski LLP
275 7th Avenue, Ste 2300, New York, NY 10001
212-869-1940 Fax: 212-768-3020
e-mail: pz@goodznyc.com
Pearl Zuchlewski, Chair

Policy Areas

Offices and agencies appear in alphabetical order.

MENTAL HYGIENE

New York State

GOVERNOR'S OFFICE

Governor's Office
Executive Chamber
State Capitol
Albany, NY 12224
518-474-8390 Fax: 518-474-1513
Web site: www.state.ny.us

Governor:
  George E Pataki 518-474-8390
Executive Director:
  Kara Lanspery 518-474-8390
Secretary to the Governor:
  John P Cahill. 518-474-4246
Senior Policy Advisor to the Governor:
  Jeffrey Lovell 518-486-9671
Counsel to the Governor-Attorney General, Budget:
  Richard Platkin. 518-474-8343
Asst Counsel to the Governor-Aging, Advocate for Persons with Disabilities,
  Commision on Quality of Care, Health, Mental Health, OASAS, OMRDD:
  Mark Ustin 518-474-8494
Director, Communications:
  David Catalfamo. 518-474-8418

EXECUTIVE DEPARTMENTS AND RELATED AGENCIES

Advocate for Persons with Disabilities, Office of
One Empire State Plz
Ste 1001
Albany, NY 12223-1150
518-473-4538 Fax: 518-473-6005
Web site: www.oapwd.org

State Advocate:
  Richard Warrender 518-473-4129
Deputy Advocate & Counsel, Public Info Officer:
  Gregory Jones. 518-473-4609
  e-mail: oapwdinfo@oapwd.org

Alcoholism & Substance Abuse Services, Office of
501 Seventh Ave
8th Fl
New York, NY 10018
646-728-4534

1450 Western Ave
Albany, NY 12203
518-473-3460
Fax: 518-457-5474

Acting Commissioner:
  Shari Noonan 518-457-2061
Executive Deputy Commissioner:
  Vacant 518-457-1758
Counsel:
  Henry F Zwack. 518-485-2312
Director, Communications:
  Jennifer Farrell 518-485-1768
  e-mail: jenniferfarrell@oasas.state.ny.us
Director, Human Resources Management:
  Thomas M Torino. 518-457-2963
Director, Internal Audit:
  Richard Kaplan. 518-485-2039
Director, Management & Information Services:
  David Gardam 518-485-2351
Affirmative Action Officer:
  Henry Gonzalez 518-457-2963
Public Information Officer:
  Joseph Morrissey 518-485-1768
  e-mail: josephmorrissey@oasas.state.ny.us

Administration Division
Assoc Commissioner:
  Michael Lawler. 518-457-5312

Budget Management
Director:
  Jay Runkel 518-485-2193

Capital Management
Director:
  Laurie Felter. 518-457-2545

Federal Relations & Policy Analysis
Director:
  Reba Architzel 518-485-1366

Fiscal Administration & Support Services
Director:
  Vito Manzella. 518-457-4742

Health Care Financing & 3rd Party Reimbursement
Director:
  Nicholas Colamaria 518-485-2207

Human Resources Management
Director:
  Thomas Torino. 518-457-2963

Management & Information Services
Director:
  David Gardam 518-485-2351

Prevention Services Division
Associate Commissioner:
  Frances M Harding. 518-485-6022

Field Operations
Director:
  Edward Freeman 518-485-1660

Offices and agencies appear in alphabetical order.

Program Design, System Development & Implementation
Director:
  Frederick Meservey 518-485-2123

Science/Technology Transfer & Planning
Director:
  John Ernst. 518-485-2132

Special Populations & Other Addictions
Director:
  William Barnette 518-457-6206

Standards & Quality Assurance Division
Associate Commissioner:
  Neil Grogin. 518-485-2257
Client Advocacy:
  Michael Yorio. 800-553-5790

Certification
Manager:
  Elliott Lefkowitz 518-485-2251

Quality Assurance
Director:
  Douglas Rosenberry. 518-485-2260

Technical Assistance
Manager:
  Joseph Burke 646-485-2249

Workforce Development
Manager:
  William Lachanski. 518-485-2033

Treatment Services Division
Acting Associate Commissioner:
  Timothy P Williams 518-485-2322

Addiction Planning & Grants Development
Director:
  Robert Ball. 518-457-5989

Addiction Treatment
Director:
  Thomas Nightingale. 518-457-7077

Evaluation & Practice Improvement
Director:
  Alan Kott 518-485-7189

Developmental Disabilities Planning Council
155 Washington Ave
2nd Fl
Albany, NY 12210
518-486-7505 or 800-395-DDPC Fax: 518-402-3505
Web site: www.ddpc.state.ny.us

Executive Director:
  Sheila M Carey. 518-486-7505
Deputy Exec Director:
  Anna Lobosco. 518-486-7505
Secretary to Exec Director:
  Lois M Goodwill 518-486-7505
Public Information Officer:
  Thomas F Lee. 518-486-7505

Education Department
State Education Bldg
89 Washington Ave
Albany, NY 12234
518-474-3852 Fax: 518-486-5631
Web site: www.nysed.gov

Commissioner, University President:
  Richard P Mills. 518-474-5844
  e-mail: rmills@mail.nysed.gov
Asst to the Commissioner:
  Peggy Rivers. 518-474-5845
  e-mail: privers@mail.nysed.gov
Counsel & Deputy Commissioner, Legal Affairs:
  Kathy A Ahearn 518-474-6400
  e-mail: kahearn@mail.nysed.gov

Office of the Professions .fax: 518-473-2056
89 Washington Ave, EB, 2nd Fl, West Mezz, Albany, NY 12234
Fax: 518-473-2056
Web site: www.op.nysed.gov
Deputy Commissioner:
  Johanna Duncan-Poitier. .518-474-3817 x470
  e-mail: opdepcom@mail.nysed.gov
Coordinator, Customer Service:
  Tony Lofrumento. 518-474-3817 x570
  e-mail: op4info@mail.nysed.gov

Office of Professional Responsibility
Executive Director:
  Frank Munoz. 518-474-3817 x440
  e-mail: opexdir@mail.nysed.gov

Professional Education Program Review
Supervisor:
  Gail Rosettie 518-474-3817 x360
  e-mail: opprogs@mail.nysed.gov

Professional Licensing Services
Director:
  Robert G Bentley. 518-474-3817 x340
  e-mail: opdpls@mail.nysed.gov

Vocational & Educational Services for Individuals with Disabilities Office (Vesid) . . . . .fax: 518-474-8802
One Commerce Plz, Rm 1606, Albany, NY 12234
Fax: 518-474-8802
Web site: www.vesid.nysed.gov
Deputy Commissioner:
  Rebecca Cort 518-474-2714
  e-mail: rcortl@mail.nysed.gov
Asst Commissioner:
  Edward Placke 518-473-4818

Fiscal & Administrative Services
Coordinator:
  Rosemary Ellis Johnson. 518-486-4038

Program Development & Support Svcs / Special Ed Policy & Partnerships
Coordinator:
  Fredric DeMay. 518-486-7462

Quality Assurance - Statewide Special Education
Acting Statewide Coordinator:
  Daniel Johnson. 518-486-6221

State School for the Blind at Batavia
2A Richmond Ave, Batavia, NY 14020

Offices and agencies appear in alphabetical order.

Superintendent:
Jennifer Spas Ervin 716-343-5384

Vocational Rehabilitation Operations
Acting Director, District Ofc Administration:
Debora Brown-Grant 518-473-1626
e-mail: dbrowngr@mail.nysed.gov
Asst Director, District Ofc Administration:
William Deschenes. 518-473-1626
e-mail: wdeschen@mail.nysed.gov

Mental Health, Office of
44 Holland Ave
Albany, NY 12229
518-474-4403 Fax: 518-474-2149
Web site: www.omh.state.ny.us

Commissioner:
Sharon E Carpinello 518-474-4403
Executive Deputy Commissioner:
Barbara Cohn 518-474-7056
Chief Medical Officer, Interim Director:
Lewis Opler 518-476-4327
Deputy Commissioner & Counsel:
John V Tauriello. 518-474-1331
Investigation & Audit:
Michael Dufresne 518-473-5940

Division of Adult Services

Division of Children and Family Services
Deputy Commissioner:
David Woodlock. 518-473-6328
Senior Deputy Commissioner:
Robert Myers 518-486-4327
Senior Associate Commissioner:
Al Holmes. 518-474-4447

Center for Human Resource Management
Director:
Robert Cafarelli 518-474-7952

Center for Information Technology & Evaluation Research
Senior Deputy Commissioner:
Chip J Felton. 518-474-7359

Division of Forensic Services
Associate Commissioner, Interim Director:
Richard Miraglia. 518-474-7219

Facilities

Bronx Children's Psychiatric Center
1000 Waters Place, Bronx, NY 10461-2799
Executive Director:
Mark Bienstock. 718-239-3600/fax: 718-239-3669

Bronx Psychiatric Center
1500 Waters Place, Bronx, NY 10461-2796
Executive Director:
LeRoy Carmichael 718-862-3300/fax: 718-826-4858

Brooklyn Children's Center
1819 Bergen St, Brooklyn, NY 11233
Acting Exec Director:
Diane Aman 718-221-4500/fax: 718-221-4581

Buffalo Psychiatric Center
400 Forest Ave, Buffalo, NY 14213-1298

Executive Director:
Thomas Dodson 716-816-2001/fax: 716-885-0710

Capital District Psychiatric Center
75 New Scotland Ave, Albany, NY 12208-3474
Acting Exec Director:
Lew Campbell. 518-447-9611/fax: 518-434-0041

Central New York Psychiatric Center
PO Box 300, Marcy, NY 13404-0300
Executive Director:
Hal Smith 315-736-8271/fax: 315-768-7210

Creedmoor Psychiatric Center
80-45 Winchester Blvd, Queens Village, NY 11427-2199
Executive Director:
Charlotte Seltzer 718-464-7500/fax: 718-264-3636

Elmira Psychiatric Center
100 Washington St, Elmira, NY 14902-1527
Executive Director:
William L Benedict. 607-737-4711/fax: 607-737-9080

Greater Binghamton Health Center
425 Robinson St, Binghamton, NY 13901-4199
Executive Director:
Margaret Dugan 607-724-1391/fax: 607-773-4387

Hudson River Psychiatric Center
10 Ross Cir, Poughkeepsie, NY 12601-1197
CEO:
Jean L Wolfersteig 845-452-8000/fax: 845-452-8040

Hutchings Psychiatric Center
620 Madison St, Syracuse, NY 13210-2319
Executive Director:
Colleen Zackoski. 315-473-4980/fax: 315-473-4984

Kingsboro Psychiatric Center
681 Clarkson Ave, Brooklyn, NY 11203-2199
Acting Exec Director:
Martin Darcy. 718-221-7700/fax: 718-221-7206

Kirby Forensic Psychiatric Center
600 East 125th St, Wards Island, NY 10035
Acting Exec Director:
Eileen Consilvio 646-672-5800/fax: 646-672-6893

Manhattan Psychiatric Center
600 East 125th St, Wards Island, NY 10035-6098
Executive Director:
Eileen Consilvio 646-672-6000/fax: 646-672-6446

Mid-Hudson Forensic Psychiatric Center
Box 158, Route 17-M, New Hampton, NY 10958-0158
Executive Director:
Howard Holanchock 845-374-3171/fax: 845-374-3961

Middletown Psychiatric Center
122 Dorothea Dix Dr, Middletown, NY 10940-6198
Executive Director:
James Bopp. 845-342-5511/fax: 845-342-4975

Mohawk Valley Psychiatric Center
1400 Noyes St, Utica, NY 13502-3082
Executive Director:
Maureen Ruben. 315-797-6800/fax: 315-738-4414

Nathan S Kline Institute for Psychiatric Research
140 Old Orangeburg Rd, Orangeburg, NY 10952-1197
Executive Director:
Robert Cancro 845-398-5500/fax: 845-398-5510

Offices and agencies appear in alphabetical order.

New York State Psychiatric Institute
1051 Riverside Dr, New York, NY 10032-2695
Director:
    Jeffrey A Lieberman, MD 212-543-5000/fax: 212-543-6012

Pilgrim Psychiatric Center
998 Crooked Hill Rd, West Brentwood, NY 11717-1087
Acting Exec Director:
    Dean Weinstock 631-761-3500/fax: 631-761-2600

Queens Children's Psychiatric Center
74-03 Commonwealth Blvd, Bellerose, NY 11426-1890
Acting Director:
    Keith Little 718-264-4500/fax: 718-740-0968

Rochester Psychiatric Center
1111 Elmwood Ave, Rochester, NY 14620-3972
Executive Director:
    Michael P Zuber, PhD 585-241-1200/fax: 585-241-1424

Rockland Children's Psychiatric Center
599 Convent Rd, Orangeburg, NY 10962-1199
Acting Exec Director:
    Barry Kutok 845-359-7400/fax: 845-359-7461

Rockland Psychiatric Center
140 Old Orangeburg Rd, Orangeburg, NY 10962-1196
Executive Director:
    James Bopp 845-359-1000/fax: 845-359-1744

Sagamore Children's Psychiatric Center
197 Half Hollow Rd, Dix Hills, NY 11746
Director:
    Dennis Dubey 631-673-7700/fax: 631-673-7770

South Beach Psychiatric Center
777 Seaview Ave, Staten Island, NY 10305-3499
Executive Director:
    William F Henri 718-667-2300/fax: 718-667-2344

St Lawrence Psychiatric Center
1 Chimney Point Dr, Ogdensburg, NY 13669-2291
Executive Director:
    James Spooner 315-541-2001/fax: 315-541-2041

Western New York Children's Psychiatric Center
1010 East & West Rd, West Seneca, NY 14224-3699
Acting Exec Director:
    David Heffler 716-674-9730/fax: 716-675-6455

Office of Consumer Affairs
Family Liaison:
    Rami Kaminski 518-474-4888
Director, Recipient Affairs:
    John Allen 518-474-6539
Coordinator, Cultural Competence:
    Cathy Cave 518-408-2026

Office of Financial Management
Deputy Commissioner:
    Martha J Schaefer Hayes 518-474-3631

Office of Public Affairs and Planning
Deputy Commissioner:
    Keith E Simons 518-474-6567

Office of Quality Management
Division Director:
    Jayne Van Bramer 518-474-6587

Mental Retardation & Developmental Disabilities, Office of
44 Holland Ave
Albany, NY 12229
518-474-6601 or TDD: 518-474-3964 Fax: 518-474-1335
Web site: www.omr.state.ny.us

Commissioner:
    Thomas A Maul 518-473-1997
Special Asst to the Commissioner:
    Tracy Durfee 518-473-1997
Executive Deputy Commissioner:
    Helene DeSanto 518-474-8115
General Counsel:
    Paul R Kietzman 518-474-7700
Deputy Commissioner, Admin & Revenue Support:
    James F Moran 518-473-2747
Deputy Commissioner, Quality Assurance:
    Jan Abelseth 518-474-3625
Associate Commissioner, Upstate Support:
    Peter F Pezzolla 518-474-9897
Affirmative Action Administrator:
    Dolores Lark 518-473-8084
Director, Internal Affairs:
    Daniel Reardon 518-474-4376
Director, Planning & Individualized Initiatives:
    Gary R Lind 518-473-9697
Director, Public Affairs:
    Deborah Sturm Rausch 518-474-6601

Developmental Disabilities Services Offices

Bernard Fineson Developmental Center
Hillside Complex, 80-45 Winchester Bl, Bldg 12, Queens Village, NY 11427
Interim Director:
    Frank Parisi 718-217-4242/fax: 718-217-4724

Brooklyn Developmental Center
888 Fountain Ave, Brooklyn, NY 11208
Director:
    Peter Uschakow 718-642-6000/fax: 718-642-6282

Broome Developmental Center & Developmental Disabilities Services Office
249 Glenwood Rd, Binghamton, NY 13905
Director:
    Patricia McDonnell 607-770-0211/fax: 607-770-8037

Capital District Developmental Disabilities Services Office
Balltown & Consaul Rds, Schenectady, NY 12304
Director:
    Roger Monthie 518-370-7370/fax: 518-370-7401

Central New York Developmental Disabilities Services Office
101 W Liberty St, Box 550, Rome, NY 13442
Director:
    Stephen M Smits 315-336-2300/fax: 315-339-5456

Finger Lakes Developmental Disabilities Services Office
620 Westfall Rd, Rochester, NY 14620
Director:
    James Whitehead 585-461-8500/fax: 585-461-0618

Hudson Valley Developmental Disabilities Services Office
Admin Bldg, 2 Ridge Rd, PO Box 470, Thiells, NY 10984
Director:
    Janet Wheeler 845-947-6000/fax: 845-947-6004

Policy Areas

Offices and agencies appear in alphabetical order.

Long Island Developmental Disabilities Services Office
45 Mall Dr, Ste 1, Commack, NY 11725
Interim Director:
Irene McGinn 631-493-1704/fax: 631-493-1803

Metro New York Developmental Disabilities Services Office
75 Morton St, New York, NY 10014
Director:
Hugh D Tarpley. 212-229-3000/fax: 212-924-0580

Staten Island Developmental Disabilities Services Office
1150 Forest Hill Rd, Staten Island, NY 10314
Director:
David Booth 718-983-5200/fax: 718-983-9768

Sunmount Developmental Ctr & Developmental Disabilities Service Office
2445 State Rte 30, Tupper Lake, NY 12986-2502
Director:
Joseph Colarusso. 518-359-3311/fax: 518-359-2276

Taconic Developmental Disabilities Services Office
26 Center Cir, Wassaic, NY 12592
Director:
John Mizerak. 845-877-6821/fax: 845-877-9177

Western New York Developmental Disabilities Services Office
1200 East & West Rd, West Seneca, NY 14224
Director:
Bruce Korotkin 716-674-6300/fax: 716-674-7488

Information Support Services
Balltown & Consaul Roads, Schenectady, NY 12304
Director:
Robert Vasko 518-381-2110

Institute for Basic Research in Developmental Disabilities
1050 Forest Hill Rd, Staten Island, NY 10314
Director:
W. Ted Brown. 718-494-0600/fax: 718-698-3803

New York City Regional Office
75 Morton St, New York, NY 10014
Assoc Comm:
Kathleen M Broderick. 212-229-3231/fax: 212-229-3234

JUDICIAL SYSTEM AND RELATED AGENCIES

Mental Hygiene Legal Service

First Judicial Dept. . . . . fax: 212-779-1894
60 Madison Ave, 2nd Fl, New York, NY 10010
Director:
Marvin Bernstein 212-779-1734
Deputy Director:
Stephan Harkavy 212-779-1734

Fourth Judicial Dept
50 East Ave, Ste 402, Rochester, NY 14604
Director:
Emmett J Creahan. 585-530-3050
Deputy Director:
Neil J Rowe. 585-530-3050/fax: 585-530-3079

Second Judicial Dept
170 Old Country Rd, Rm 500, Mineola, NY 11501
Director:
Sidney Hirschfeld. 516-746-4545

Deputy Director:
Lesley De Lia 516-746-4545

Third Judicial Dept
40 Steuben St, Ste 501, Albany, NY 12207-2109
Director:
Bruce S Dix 518-474-4453
Associate Attorney:
Richard Wenig. 607-721-8440/fax: 607-721-8447

CORPORATIONS, AUTHORITIES AND COMMISSIONS

New York State Commission on Quality of Care for the Mentally Disabled
401 State St
Schenectady, NY 12305-2397
518-388-2888 Fax: 518-388-2800
Web site: www.cqc.state.ny.us

Chair:
Gary D O'Brien 518-388-1281
Commissioner:
Elizabeth W Stack 518-388-2888
Executive Assistant:
Mindy Becker. 518-388-1281
Press Officer:
Gary W Masline 518-388-1270/fax: 518-388-1275

Administrative Services Bureau
Director:
Richard H Schaefer. 518-388-2804

Advisory Council
Chair:
Vacant 518-388-1277
Secretary:
Darlene Stefani. 518-388-1281

Advocacy Services Bureau
Director:
Marcel Chaine 518-388-2892

Counsel/Policy Analysis/Fiscal Investigations
Counsel/Director:
Robert J Bochlert 518-388-2835

Medical Review Board
Executive Secretary:
Thomas Harmon. 518-388-1281

Quality Assurance
Director:
Mark Keegan 518-388-2888

Surrogate Decision-Making Committees Program
Program Director:
Thomas Fisher 518-388-2820

NEW YORK STATE LEGISLATURE

See Legislative Branch in Section 1 for additional Standing Committee and Subcommittee information.

Offices and agencies appear in alphabetical order.

Assembly Standing Committees

Alcoholism & Drug Abuse
Chair:
Jeffrey Dinowitz (D). 518-455-5965
Ranking Minority Member:
William Reilich (R) 518-455-4664

Mental Health
Chair:
Peter M Rivera (D). 518-455-5102
Ranking Minority Member:
Matthew Mirones (R). 518-455-5716

Senate Standing Committees

Alcoholism & Drug Abuse
Chair:
Vacant 518-455-3563

Ranking Minority Member:
Ruben Diaz, Sr (D). 518-455-2511

Mental Health & Developmental Disabilities
Chair:
Thomas W Libous (R) 518-455-2677
Ranking Minority Member:
Velmanette Montgomery (D). 518-455-3451

Senate/Assembly Legislative Commissions

Health Care Financing, Council on
Senate Chair:
Joseph L Bruno (R) 518-455-3191
Assembly Vice Chair:
Alexander B Grannis (D) 518-455-5676
Executive Director:
Al Cardillo. 518-455-2067/fax: 518-426-6925

Private Sector

AIM Services Inc
3257 Route 9, Saratoga Springs, NY 12866
518-587-3208 Fax: 518-587-7236
e-mail: aimservices@aimservicesinc.org
Web site: www.aimservicesinc.org
Charlene Endal, Executive Director
Residential & home-based services for individuals with developmental disabilities & traumatic brain injuries

AMAC, Association for Metroarea Autistic Children
25 W 17th St, New York, NY 10011
212-645-5005 Fax: 212-645-0170
e-mail: rica@amac.org
Web site: www.amac.org
Frederica Blausten, Executive Director
Providing lifelong services to austistic & special needs children & adults; specializing in applied behavior analysis (ABA) methodology; serving ages 2 years to adults, schools, camps, group homes

Association for Addiction Professionals of New York
PO Box 1481, Lake Grove, NY 11755
877-862-2769 Fax: 585-394-1111
e-mail: info@appnycounselor.com
Web site: www.aapnycounselor.com
Edward Olsen, President
Alcohol & chemical dependency counselor organization

Association for Community Living
99 Pine Street, Suite 202JR, Albany, NY 12207
518-426-3635 Fax: 518-426-0504
e-mail: aclnys@webramp.info
Web site: www.aclnys.org
Antonia M Lasicki, Director
Membership organization for agencies that provide housing & rehab services to individuals diagnosed with serious mental illness

Association for Eating Disorders - Capital Region
1653 Central Ave, Albany, NY 12205
518-464-9043
Web site: www.geocities.com/craedny
William Friske, Treasurer
Support & referral services, wellness programs & education for recovering individuals, parents & health professionals

Association for the Help of Retarded Children
200 Park Ave S, New York, NY 10003
212-780-2500 Fax: 212-777-5893
e-mail: ahrcnyc@ahrcnyc.org
Web site: www.ahrcnyc.org
Michael Goldfarb, Executive Director
Social services, advocacy & public information on developmental disabilities

Brain Injury Association of NYS (BIANYS)
10 Colvin Ave, Albany, NY 12206
518-459-7911 Fax: 518-482-5285
e-mail: info@bianys.org
Web site: www.bianys.org
Judith I Avner, Executive Director
Public education & advocacy for persons with brain injury & their families

Cerebral Palsy Association of New York State
90 State Street, Suite 929, Albany, NY 12207
518-436-0178 Fax: 518-436-8619
e-mail: malvaro@cpofnys.org
Web site: www.cpofnys.org
Michael Alvaro, Associate Executive Director
Advocate and provide direct services with and for individuals with cerebral palsy and other significant disabilities and their families

Offices and agencies appear in alphabetical order.

Children's Village (The)
Echo Hills, Dobbs Ferry, NY 10522
914-693-0600 x1201 Fax: 914-674-9208
e-mail: jkohomban@childrensvillage.org
Web site: www.childrensvillage.org
Jeremy Kohomban, President & Chief Executive Officer
Residential school, located 20 mins outside NYC. Treatment & prevention of behavioral problems for youth; residential & community-based services, mental health, education, employment & runaway shelter services

Coalition of Voluntary Mental Health Agencies Inc (The)
90 Broad St, New York, NY 10004-2205
212-742-1600 x115 Fax: 212-742-2080
e-mail: psaperia@cvmha.org
Web site: www.cvmha.org
Phillip Saperia, Executive Director
Advocacy organization representing over 100 nonprofit, community-based mental health agencies in NYC

Committee of Methadone Program Administrators Inc of NYS (COMPA)
1 Columbia Place, 4th Fl, Albany, NY 12207
518-689-0457 Fax: 518-426-1046
e-mail: compahb@hotmail.com
Web site: www.compa-ny.org
Henry Bartlett, Executive Director
Methadone treatment & substance abuse coalition building; advocacy, community education, standards & regulatory review & policy development

Families Together in NYS Inc
15 Elk St, Albany, NY 12207
518-432-0333 x20 or 888-326-8644 (referr Fax: 518-434-6478
e-mail: info@ftnys.org
Web site: www.ftnys.org
Paige Macdonald, Executive Director
Advocacy for families with children having special social, emotional & behavioral needs; working to improve services & support for children & families

Federation Employment & Guidance Service (FEGS) Inc
315 Hudson St, 9th Fl, New York, NY 10013
212-366-8400 Fax: 212-366-8441
e-mail: info@fegs.org
Web site: www.fegs.org
Alfred P Miller, Chief Executive Officer
Diversified health & human services system to help individuals achieve their potential at work, at home & in the community

Federation of Organizations Inc
One Farmingdale Road, Route 109, West Babylon, NY 11704-6207
631-669-5355 Fax: 631-669-1114
e-mail: bfaron@fedoforg.org
Web site: www.fedoforg.org
Barbara Faron, Executive Director
Social welfare agency with programs in mental health & aging

InterAgency Council of Mental Retardatn & Developmental Disabilities
275 7th Ave, New York, NY 10001
212-645-6360 Fax: 212-627-8847
e-mail: mames@iacny.org
Web site: www.iacny.org
Margery E Ames, Executive Director

Jewish Board of Family & Children's Services
120 W 57th St, New York, NY 10019
212-582-9100 Fax: 212-956-5676
e-mail: asiskind@jbfcs.org
Web site: www.jbfcs.org
Alan B Siskind, Executive Vice President & Chief Executive Officer
Mental health services/human services

Lesbian, Gay, Bisexual & Transgender Community Ctr - Not For Profit
208 W 13th St, New York, NY 10011-7702
212-620-7310 Fax: 212-924-2657
e-mail: enealy@gaycenter.org
Web site: www.gaycenter.org
Miriam Yeung, Director, Public Policy
Mental health counseling, youth guidance, HIV/AIDS services, advocacy & programs

Lifespire
350 5th Ave, Ste 301, New York, NY 10118-0301
212-741-0100 Fax: 212-242-0696
e-mail: info@lifespire.org
Web site: www.lifespire.org
Mark Vanvoorst, Executive Director
Services for adults with developmental disabilites throughout the five boroughs of New York City

Little Flower Children & Family Services
186 Joralemon St, Brooklyn, NY 11201
718-875-3500 or 631-929-6200 Fax: 718-260-8863
e-mail: stupph@lfchild.org
Web site: www.littleflowerny.org
Herbert W Stupp, Chief Executive Officer
Foster care, adoption, child welfare, residential treatment services and residences for the developmentally disabled & day care; union free school district

Mental Health Association of NYC Inc
666 Broadway, Ste 200, New York, NY 10012
212-254-0333 x307 Fax: 212-529-1959
Giselle Stolper, Executive Director
Advocacy, public education, community-based services

Mental Health Association of NYS Inc
194 Washington Ave, Ste 415, Albany, NY 12210
518-434-0439 x20 Fax: 518-427-8676
e-mail: info@mhanys.org
Web site: www.mhanys.org
Glen Liebman, Chief Executive Officer
Technical assistance, advocacy, training & resource clearinghouse

Offices and agencies appear in alphabetical order.

NAMI-NYS
260 Washington Ave, Albany, NY 12210
518-462-2000 Fax: 518-462-3811
e-mail: naminys@naminys.org
Web site: www.naminys.org
J David Seay, Executive Director
Family advocates for the mentally ill

NY Council on Problem Gambling
119 Washington Ave, Albany, NY 12210
518-427-1622 Fax: 518-427-6181
e-mail: jmaney@nyproblemgambling.org
Web site: www.nyproblemgambling.org
James Maney, Executive Director
Statewide helpline, public information, referral svcs, advocacy for treatment & support svcs, in-service training & workshops

NY Counseling Association Inc
PO Box 12636, Albany, NY 12212-2636
518-235-2026 Fax: 518-235-0910
e-mail: nycaoffice@nycounseling.org
Web site: www.nycounseling.org
Donald Newell, Executive Manager
Counseling professionals in education, mental health, career, employment, rehabilitation & adult development

NYS Association of Community & Residential Agencies
99 Pine St, Ste C-110, Albany, NY 12207
518-449-7551 Fax: 518-449-1509
e-mail: nysacra@nysacra.org
Web site: www.nysacra.org
Ann M Hardiman, Executive Director
Advocating for agencies that serve individuals with developmental disabilities

NYS Conference of Local Mental Hygiene Directors
99 Pine Street, Ste C100, Albany, NY 12207
518-462-9422 Fax: 518-465-2695
e-mail: garyw@clmhd.org
Web site: www.clmhd.org
Gary Weiskopf, Executive Director

NYS Council for Community Behavioral Healthcare
155 Washington Ave, 2nd Flr, Albany, NY 12210-2329
518-445-2642 Fax: 518-445-2642
e-mail: nyscouncil@nycap.rr.com
Laurie Cole, Executive Director
Statewide membership organization representing community mental health centers

NYS Psychological Association
6 Executive Park Dr, Albany, NY 12203
800-732-3933 Fax: 518-437-0177
e-mail: nyspa@nyspa.org
Web site: www.nyspa.org
Gayle Everitt, Executive Director
Promote & advance profession of psychology; referral service

NYSARC Inc
393 Delaware Ave, Delmar, NY 12054
518-439-8311 Fax: 518-439-1893
e-mail: info@nysarc.org
Web site: www.nysarc.org
Marc N Brandt, Executive Director
Mental retardation & developmental disabilities programs, services & advocacy

New York Association of Psychiatric Rehabilitation Services (NYAPRS)
1 Columbia Place, 2nd Floor, Albany, NY 12207
518-436-0008 Fax: 518-436-0044
e-mail: nyaprs@aol.com
Web site: www.nyaprs.org
Harvey Rosenthal, Executive Director
Promoting the recovery, rehabilitation & rights of New Yorkers with psychiatric disabilities

New York Presbyterian Hospital, Department of Psychiatry
180 Fort Washington Ave, Room 270, New York, NY 10032
212-305-9249 Fax: 212-305-4724
e-mail: hjs1@columbia.edu
Herbert J Schlesinger, PhD, Director, Division of Clinical Psychology
Psychotherapy & public policy

New York State Rehabilitation Association
155 Washington Ave, Suite 410, Albany, NY 12210
518-449-2976 Fax: 518-426-4329
e-mail: nysra@nyrehab.org
Web site: www.nyrehab.org
Patricia Dowse, Vice President
Political advocacy, education, communications, networking & referral services for people with disabilities

Postgrad Center for Mental Health, Child, Adolescent & Family-Couples
138 E 26th St, Fl 4, New York, NY 10010-1843
212-576-4190 Fax: 212-576-4129
Diana Daimwood, Director
Psychotherapy & assessment services for children, adolescents & families

Postgraduate Center for Mental Health
344 W 36th St, New York, NY 10018
212-560-6757 Fax: 212-244-2034
e-mail: mholman@pgcmh.org
Web site: www.pgcmh-institute.org
Marcia Holman, CSW/Vice President, Clinical Services
Community-based rehabilitation & employment services for adults with mental illness

Research Foundation for Mental Hygiene Inc
44 Holland Ave, 6th Fl, Albany, NY 12229
518-474-5661 Fax: 518-474-6995
Robert E Burke, Managing Director
Not-for-profit responsible for administering grants & sponsored research contracts for the NYS Department of Mental Health & its agencies

Offices and agencies appear in alphabetical order.

SUNY at Albany, Professional Development Program, NE States Addiction
Rockefeller College, 135 Western Ave, RI 301, Albany, NY 12222
518-442-5700 Fax: 518-442-5768
e-mail: lparsons@pdp.albany.edu
Web site: www.pdp.albany.edu
Eugene J Monaco, Director
Dissemination of current research & best clinical practice information; coursework & programs for professionals in the field of addictions

SUNY at Buffalo, Research Institute on Addictions
1021 Main St, Buffalo, NY 14203-1016
716-887-2566 Fax: 716-887-2252
e-mail: connors@ria.buffalo.edu
Web site: www.ria.buffalo.edu
Gerard Connors, Director
Alcohol & substance abuse prevention, treatment & policy research

Samaritan Village Inc
138-02 Queens Blvd, Briarwood, NY 11435
718-206-2000 Fax: 718-206-4055
Web site: www.samaritanvillage.org
Ron Solarz, Executive Director
Substance abuse treatment; residential & outpatient therapeutic community

Schuyler Center for Analysis & Advocacy (SCAA)
150 State St, 4th Fl, Albany, NY 12207
518-463-1896 Fax: 518-463-3364
e-mail: drobinson@scaany.org
Web site: www.scaany.org
Davin Robinson, Senior Policy Associate
Advocacy, analysis & forums on mental health issues

Schuyler Center for Analysis & Advocacy (SCAA)
150 State St, 4th Fl, Albany, NY 12207
518-463-1896 x29 Fax: 518-463-3364
e-mail: bwalsh@scaany.org
Web site: www.scaany.org
Davin Robinson, Senior Policy Associate
Advocacy, analysis & forums on mental health issues

Self Advocacy Association of NYS
Capital District DSO, 500 Balltown Rd, Bldg #5, Schenectady, NY 12304
518-382-1454 Fax: 518-382-1594
e-mail: sholmes@earthlink.net
Web site: www.sanys.org
Steve Holmes, Executive Director
Advocacy for & by persons with developmental disabilities to ensure civil rights & opportunities

St Joseph's Rehabilitation Center Inc
PO Box 470, Saranac Lake, NY 12983
518-891-3950 Fax: 518-891-5507
e-mail: stjoes@sjrcrehab.org
Web site: www.sjrcrehab.org
Karl Kabza, Chief Executive Officer
Inpatient & outpatient alcohol & substance abuse treatment

Statewide Black & Puerto Rican/Latino Substance Abuse Task Force
2730 Atlantic Ave, Brooklyn, NY 11207-2820
718-647-8275 Fax: 718-647-7889
e-mail: info@nytaskforce.org; nystaskforce@ad.com
Web site: www.nytaskforce.org
Ralph Gonzalez, Executive Director
Substance abuse, HIV/AIDS & HepC prevention & treatment

Upstate Homes for Children & Adults Inc
2705 State Hwy 28, Oneonta, NY 13820
607-286-7171 Fax: 607-286-7166
e-mail: kennedyp@upstatehome.org
Web site: www.upstatehome.org
Patricia E Kennedy, Executive Director
Education/mental hygiene

William T Grant Foundation
570 Lexington Ave, 18th Fl, New York, NY 10022-6837
212-752-0071 Fax: 212-752-1398
e-mail: info@wtgrantfdn.org
Web site: www.wtgrantfoundation.org
Bob Granger, President
Funding for youth development programs & research

YAI/National Institute for People with Disabilities
460 W 34th St, New York, NY 10001-2382
212-273-6110 or 866-2-YAI-LINK Fax: 212-947-7524
e-mail: jmlcares@yai.org
Web site: www.yai.org
Joel M Levy, Chief Executive Officer
Programs, services & advocacy for people with autism, mental retardation & other developmental disabilities as well as learning disabilities of all ages & their families; special education & early learning programs

Yeshiva University, A Einstein Clg of Med, Div of Subs Abuse
1500 Waters Place, Bronx, NY 10461
718-409-9450 x312 Fax: 718-892-7115
e-mail: marion@aecom.yu.edu
Web site: www.aecom.yu.edu
Ira J Marion, Executive Director
Screening, assessment, diagnosis, treatment, support services, research & teaching & training related to chemical dependency & substance abuse

Offices and agencies appear in alphabetical order.

MUNICIPAL & LOCAL GOVERNMENTS

New York State

GOVERNOR'S OFFICE

Governor's Office
Executive Chamber
State Capitol
Albany, NY 12224
518-474-8390 Fax: 518-474-1513
Web site: www.state.ny.us

Governor:
  George E Pataki 518-474-8390
Executive Director:
  Kara Lanspery 518-474-8390
Secretary to the Governor:
  John P Cahill. 518-474-4246
Senior Policy Advisor to the Governor:
  Jeffrey Lovell 518-486-9671
Counsel to the Governor-Attorney General, Budget:
  Richard Platkin. 518-474-8343
Deputy Secretary to the Governor for Appointments & Intergovernmental
  Affairs:
  Robert Bulman 518-474-0491
Director, Communications:
  David Catalfamo. 518-474-8418
Director, State & Local Government Affairs:
  John Haggerty. 518-486-9896
Director, Intergovernmental Affairs:
  Michael Elmendorf. 518-474-8390
Asst Counsel to the Governor-Adirondack Pk Agency, Agric & Markets,
  Bond Act Coord, Consumer Protection Bd, Environ Facilities Corp, Parks
  & Recreation, State & Local Govt, OGS:
  James Walsh. 518-474-8327

New York City Office
633 Third Ave, 38th Fl, New York, NY 10017
Director:
  Ann McConnachie 212-681-4580
Director, Community Affairs:
  James Barcia. 212-681-4580
Director, Legislative Affairs-NYC:
  James Harding 212-681-4580

EXECUTIVE DEPARTMENTS AND RELATED AGENCIES

Budget, Division of the
State Capitol
Albany, NY 12224
518-473-3885
e-mail: dobinfo@budget.state.ny.us
Web site: www.budget.state.ny.us

Director:
  John F Cape 518-474-2300

Deputy Director:
  Ron Rock 518-474-6323
Deputy Director:
  Al Kaplan 518-474-6300
Administrative Officer:
  Karen Bodnar 518-474-6324
Director, Communications:
  Michael Marr 518-473-3885
Press Officer:
  Peter Constantakes 518-473-3885
Press Officer:
  Scott Reif 518-473-3885
Legislative Liaison:
  Christina Kidera. 518-474-7953/fax: 518-473-7243

Civil Service Department
State Campus
Bldg 1
Albany, NY 12239
518-457-2487 Fax: 518-457-7547
Web site: www.cs.state.ny.us

Commissioner:
  Daniel E Wall 518-457-3701
Executive Deputy Commissioner:
  John F Barr 518-457-6212
Deputy Commissioner:
  Regina M DuBois. 518-485-7515
Director, Civil Svc Ops & Admin:
  Patricia Hite 518-485-0340
Special Counsel:
  Thomas F Brennan 518-485-7278
Counsel:
  Brian S Reichenbach 518-457-3177
Director, Workforce & Occupational Planning:
  Nancy B Kiyonaga 518-485-9274
Director, Internal Audit:
  Vacant 518-457-7355
Director, Public Information:
  Marc E Carey. 518-457-9375/fax: 518-457-6654
  e-mail: mec5@cs.state.ny.us
Public Records Access Officer:
  Jane Prus 518-457-6875/fax: 518-457-6654

Administration

Administrative Services Unit
Director, Financial Administration:
  Michael Bosanko. 518-457-6490/fax: 518-457-5116

Classification & Compensation Division
Director:
  Nicholas J Vagianelis 518-457-6226/fax: 518-457-8081

Commission Operations
Director:
  Stella Chen Harding 518-457-2575

Offices and agencies appear in alphabetical order.

Policy Areas

Diversity, Planning & Management Division
Director:
 Frank E Abrams 518-457-4146/fax: 518-457-0399
Coordinator, Community Outreach:
 George Swiers. 518-457-7661/fax: 518-457-0399

Employee Benefits Division
Director:
 Robert DuBois. 518-457-9391/fax: 518-485-8952
Director, Employee Insurance Programs:
 Mary B Frye 518-457-1771/fax: 518-457-1311
Asst Director, Financial Management & Accounting:
 David Boland 518-457-5159/fax: 518-457-1311

Employee Health Services Division
Administrator, EHS:
 Maria C Steinbach. 518-457-6142/fax: 518-485-1995
Director, Health Services Nursing:
 Mary M McSweeney 518-457-2616

Information Resource Management
Director:
 Frank Slade 518-457-1775/fax: 518-485-5752
 e-mail: fhs1@cs.state.ny.us

Municipal Services Division
Director:
 Raymond C Greene. 518-457-9553/fax: 518-485-8244
Local Examinations:
 Will Martin. 518-457-4487

Personnel
Director:
 Susan China. 518-457-1077/fax: 518-457-6875

Planning Division
Director:
 Frank R Santora 518-457-5507

Staffing Services Division
Director:
 Terry Jordan 518-457-5781/fax: 518-457-4239
Asst Director:
 Crystal Hamelink. 518-457-5445
Attendance & Leave Unit:
 Margaret Harrigan 518-457-2295

Testing Services Division
Director:
 Paul Kaiser 518-457-9499/fax: 518-457-4239
Asst Director:
 Ray Mullin. 518-457-5465

Civil Service Commission
President:
 Daniel E Wall. 518-457-3701
Commissioner:
 Margaret Dadd 518-457-3504
Commissioner:
 Leo J Kesselring. 518-457-5444

Criminal Justice Services, Division of
Four Tower Place
Albany, NY 12203-3764
518-457-1260 Fax: 518-457-3089
Web site: www.criminaljustice.state.ny.us

Commissioner & Director:
 Chauncey G Parker. 518-457-1260

Executive Deputy Commissioner:
 Martin Cirincione. 518-457-6091
Affirmative Action Officer:
 G Bernett Marion 518-457-6110
Director, Communications:
 Lynn Rasic 518-485-0857
Public Information Officer:
 Lyle Hartog 518-485-2465/fax: 518-485-2467

Administration Office
Director, Administration:
 Paula Steigman. 518-457-6100

Administrative Operations
Director:
 Phyllis M Foster. 518-457-1696

Human Resources Management
Director:
 Alyce Ashe. 518-457-6110

State Finance & Budget
Acting Director, Financial Administration:
 Kimberly J Szady. 518-457-6105
Director, Internal Audit & Compliance:
 William Gritsavage 518-457-1417

Advisory Groups

Juvenile Justice Advisory Group
 15 Van Dyke Ave, Amsterdam, NY 12010
Acting Chair:
 Michael Elmendorf. 518-474-7516

NYS Motor Vehicle & Insurance Fraud Prevention Board
Chair/Commissioner & Director:
 Chauncey G Parker 518-457-1260

Legal Services & Forensic Services Office
Deputy Commissioner & Counsel:
 Kimberly O'Conner 518-457-4181

Missing & Exploited Children Clearinghouse
Director:
 Kenneth R Buniak 518-485-7632

Office of Forensic Services
Director:
 John Hicks. 518-457-7287

Sex Offender Registry
Director:
 Jeanne Sample 518-457-7985

Office of Criminal Justice Operations
Deputy Commissioner:
 Daniel Foro. 518-485-2995
Executive Director:
 James Shea. 518-457-8724

Information Technology Development Group
Director:
 Thomas Meyer 518-457-9716

Information Technology Services Group
Director:
 Alex Roberts. 518-457-3743

Office of Operations
Director:
 William J Sillery 518-457-6050
Assistant Bureau Director:
 Michael Tymeson. 518-457-6050

Offices and agencies appear in alphabetical order.

Chief, Records Management Bureau:
James Stanco 518-457-6051
Chief, Civil Identification Bureau:
Ann Sammons 518-485-5763

Office of Public Safety
Deputy Commissioner:
James DeLapp 518-457-6101
Director:
Mark R Lindsay 518-457-2667
Asst Director:
John R Digman 518-485-1414
Chief of Administrative Services:
David H Mahany 518-457-4135
Chief of Program Services:
Dennis W McCarty 518-485-1410

Advisory Groups
Law Enforcement Accreditation Council
518-457-6101
Deputy Commissioner:
James DeLapp 518-457-6101
Municipal Police Training Council
518-457-6101
Deputy Commissioner:
James DeLapp 518-457-6101
Security Guard Advisory Council
518-457-6101
Chief, Administrative Services:
David H Mahany 518-457-6101
State Cmte for Coordination of Police Services for the Elderly (TRIAD)
518-457-6101
Deputy Commissioner:
James DeLapp 518-457-6101
Statewide Law Enforcement Telecommunications Cmte
518-457-6101
Deputy Commissioner:
James DeLapp 518-457-6101

Office of Strategic Planning
Deputy Commissioner:
Roger Jeffries 518-485-7433

Bureau of Justice Research & Innovation
Director:
Donna Hall 518-457-7301
Crime Reductions Strategies Unit
Chief:
Thomas Mitchell 518-457-7301
Justice Statistics & Performance Unit
Chief:
Susan Jacobsen 518-457-8381
Justice Systems Analysis Unit
Chief:
David vanAlstyne 518-457-7301
Offender Management Analysis Unit
Chief:
Bruce Frederick 518-457-3724

Funding & Program Assistance Office
Director:
AnneMarie Strano 518-457-8462

Emergency Management Office, NYS (SEMO)
1220 Washington Ave
Bldg 22, Ste 101
Albany, NY 12226-2251

518-457-8900
Web site: www.nysemo.state.ny.us

Director:
James W Tuffey 518-457-2222
First Deputy Director:
Andrew X Feeney 518-457-9996
Deputy Director, Support Services:
Tom Rinaldi 518-457-8130
Deputy Director, Operations:
Thomas Fargione 518-457-9982
Counsel:
Lai Sun Yee 518-457-8901
Program Asst:
Judy Williams 518-457-2222/fax: 518-457-9995

Administration
Chief Budget Analyst:
Susan Mutch 518-457-9994
Manager, Recovery Section:
Les Radford 518-457-5285

Community Affairs
Asst Director:
Dennis J Michalski 518-485-5666
Public Information Officer:
Donald L Maurer 518-485-6011/fax: 518-457-4923
e-mail: donald.maurer@semo.state.ny.us

Operations
Chief, Operations:
Kevin Neary 518-457-9933

Preparedness
Chief Special Operations:
Robert Olazagasti 518-457-8916
Chief Training/Exercises:
William Campbell 518-457-8917
Chief Planning:
Radeph Anderson 518-457-9981

Technology
Chief, Communications:
Vacant 518-457-9935
Chief, Information Technology Services:
Vacant 518-485-0194
Chief, Logistics:
Robert Olazagasti 518-457-9927
Communications Officer:
Kenneth Goetz 518-457-9938
Network Administrator:
Ulrike Pohlig 518-457-9928

Real Property Services, Office of
16 Sheridan Ave
Albany, NY 12210-2714
518-486-5446 Fax: 518-474-9276
Web site: www.orps.state.ny.us

Executive Director:
Thomas G Griffen 518-474-5711
e-mail: thomas.griffen@orps.state.ny.us
Executive Deputy Director:
Thomas Bellard 518-473-6914
e-mail: tom.bellard@orps.state.ny.us

Offices and agencies appear in alphabetical order.

Policy Areas

Chief Appraiser:
Jeff Jordan 518-474-2854
e-mail: jeff.jordan@orps.state.ny.us
Counsel:
Richard J Sinnott 518-474-6753
e-mail: richard.sinnott@orps.state.ny.us
Chief Information Officer:
Bruce Sauter 518-474-8829
e-mail: bruce.sauter@orps.state.ny.us
Strategic Information Officer:
JoAnn Whalen 518-474-6742
e-mail: joann.whalen@orps.state.ny.us
Director, Budget/Fiscal Services:
Steve King 518-474-5762
e-mail: steve.king@orps.state.ny.us
Director, Public Information:
Geoffrey T Gloak 518-486-5446
e-mail: geoffrey.gloak@orps.state.ny.us

Central Support Services
Director:
Robert Zandri 518-474-5666
e-mail: robert.zandri@orps.state.ny.us

Information Technology Services
Director:
Dennis Jersey 518-474-6758
e-mail: dennis.jersey@orps.state.ny.us

Regional Customer Service Delivery
Director:
David Williams. 518-473-7574
e-mail: dave.williams@orps.state.ny.us

Albany (Northern Region) . . . . fax: 518-486-7752
16 Sheridan Ave, Albany, NY 12210
Regional Director:
Jeffrey Green 518-486-4403
e-mail: internet.northern@orps.state.ny.us

Batavia (Western Region)
Genesee County Bldg 2, 3837 W Main Rd, Batavia, NY 14020
Regional Director:
Joe Muscarella. 585-343-7456/fax: 585-343-9740
e-mail: internet.western@orps.state.ny.us

Melville Satellite Office. . . . . fax: 631-777-1859
560 Broadhollow Rd, Melville, NY 11474
Manager:
Susan Rosenblum. 631-777-1785
e-mail: internet.metro@orps.state.ny.us

Newburgh (Southern Region) . . . . fax: 845-567-2690
263 Route 17K, Ste 2001, Newburgh, NY 12550-8310
Regional Director:
John Wolham 845-567-2648
e-mail: internet.southern@orps.state.ny.us

Saranac Lake Satellite Office. . . . . fax: 518-891-2639
43 Broadway, Saranac Lake, NY 12983
Office Manager:
Dan Lancor. 518-891-1780
e-mail: internet.saranac@orps.state.ny.us

Syracuse (Central Region) . . . . fax: 315-471-3634
401 South Salina St, Syracuse, NY 13202-2415
Regional Director:
Robert Gawrelski 315-471-4816
e-mail: internet.central@orps.state.ny.us

Research, Information & Policy Development
Director:
James Dunne. 518-473-4532
e-mail: jim.dunne@orps.state.ny.us

State Board of Real Property Services
Chair:
Ifigenia Brown 518-474-5711
Member:
John M Bacheller 518-474-5711
Executive Secretary:
Thomas G Griffen. 518-474-5711
Asst to the Board:
Darlene A Maloney 518-474-3793/fax: 518-474-9276

State Valuation Services
Director:
Donald Card. 518-474-1071/fax: 518-486-7755
e-mail: don.card@orps.state.ny.us

Small Cities, Governor's Office for
Agency Building 4, 6th Fl
Empire State Plaza
Albany, NY 12223
518-474-2057 Fax: 518-474-5247
Web site: www.nysmallcities.com

Director:
Glen King 518-474-2057
Executive Assistant to the Director:
Patricia Longstaff 518-474-2057
First Deputy Director:
Albert P Jurczynski. 518-474-2057
Deputy Director:
Kenneth J Flood 518-474-2057
Associate Counsel:
Brian McCartney 518-474-2057
Public Information Officer:
Tracey McNerney. 518-474-2057
e-mail: tmcnerney@nysmallcities.com

State Comptroller, Office of the
633 Third Ave
31st Fl
New York, NY 10017-6754
212-681-4491 Fax: 212-681-4468

110 State St
15th Fl
Albany, NY 12236-0001
518-474-4040
Fax: 518-473-3004

State Comptroller:
Alan G Hevesi . . . . 518-474-4040 or 212-681-4491

Administration
Deputy Comptroller:
Harris Lirtzman 518-402-4884

Financial Administration
Director:
Larry Appel 518-474-7574

Offices and agencies appear in alphabetical order.

Information Technology Services
Director:
  Richard Green 518-474-7476

Management Services
Director:
  Paul Capobianco. 518-473-0675

Oil Spill Fund Office
Executive Director:
  Anne Hohenstein 518-474-6657

Division of Intergovernmental Affairs & Community Relations
Deputy Comptroller:
  Myrna Santiago 212-383-2662
Director, Intergovernmental Affairs:
  Douglas Forand 518-473-2449
Director, Community Relations & Constituent Services:
  Nicholas Acquafredda 212-417-5487
Director, Intergovernmental Affairs, Upstate & Long Island Rural Liais:
  Victor Mallison. 518-473-2449
Director, Intergovernmental Affairs, NYC, Brooklyn & Staten Island:
  Samuel Nicolas. 212-383-2672

Division of Investigations
Deputy Comptroller:
  Robert Brackman . . . . 212-681-4474 or 518-402-4926
Asst Comptroller for Internal Audit & Division Operations:
  Stephen R Hillerman 518-286-2622 x105
Chief Investigative Counsel:
  Samantha Biletsky . . . . 212-681-4475 or 518-486-3501
Director, Internal Audit:
  Robert Kosky. 518-286-2622 x110

Division of Local Govt Services & Economic Development
Deputy Comptroller:
  Mark P Pattison. 518-474-4037/fax: 518-486-6479
Asst Comptroller:
  Steve Hancox 518-474-4037
Asst Comptroller:
  John Clarkson. 518-474-4037
  Albany Area
  22 Computer Dr West, Albany, NY 12205
    Chief Examiner:
      Thomas J Kelly. 518-438-0093/fax: 518-438-0367
  Binghamton Area
  44 Hawley St, Rm 1701, Binghamton, NY 13901-4455
    Chief Examiner:
      Patrick Carbone 607-721-8306/fax: 607-721-8313
  Buffalo Area
  Ellicott Sq Bldg, Rm 1050, 295 Main St, Buffalo, NY 14203
    Chief Examiner:
      Robert Meller 716-847-3647/fax: 716-847-3643
  Glens Falls Area
  One Broad Street Plaza, Glens Falls, NY 12801
    Chief Examiner:
      Karl Smoczynski 518-793-0057/fax: 518-793-5797
  Hauppauge Area
  State Ofc Bldg, #3A10, Veterans Mem Hwy, Hauppauge, NY 11788-5533
    Chief Examiner:
      Richard Rennard. 631-952-6534/fax: 631-952-6530
  Rochester Area
  Powers Bldg, 16 West Main St, Ste 522, Rochester, NY 14614
    Chief Examiner:
      Edward Grant 585-454-2460/fax: 585-454-3545
  Syracuse Area
  State Office Bldg, 333 E Washington St, Syracuse, NY 13202-1440

    Chief Examiner:
      Debora Wagner. 315-428-4192/fax: 315-426-2119

Division of State Services
Deputy Comptroller:
  Lynn Canton. 518-474-5598

State Audit Group
Asst Comptroller:
  Lynn Canton. 518-474-5598
Director, Administration:
  Bob Blot. 518-474-3271
Director, Audit:
  Steve Sossei 518-474-3271
Director, Audit:
  David R Hancox. 518-474-3271

State Financial Services Group
Asst Controller:
  Joan Sullivan 518-402-4103
Director, Accounting Operations Bureau:
  Tom Mahoney 518-474-4017
Director, Accounting Systems Bureau:
  Bob Campano. 518-474-8657

Executive Office
Chief of Staff:
  Jack Chartier. 212-681-4498
First Deputy:
  Thomas Sanzillo 518-474-2909
Executive Deputy:
  Diana Jones Ritter. 518-474-3610
Deputy Chief of Staff:
  Dalia Schapiro 212-681-4540
Director, Correspondence Unit:
  Ellen J Evans 518-473-1323
Chief Information Officer:
  Jeffrey Grunfield 518-473-3004

Office of Budget & Policy Analysis
Deputy Comptroller:
  Kim Fine 518-473-4333
Chief Economist:
  Thomas Marks 518-402-3117
Deputy Comptroller:
  Christine Rutigliano 518-474-4541

Press Office
Director, Communications:
  David Neustadt 518-474-4015/fax: 518-473-8940
  e-mail: dneustadt@osc.state.ny.us
Press Secretary:
  Jeffrey Gordon 518-474-4015
  e-mail: jgordon@osc.state.ny.us

State Department
41 State St
Albany, NY 12231
518-474-0050 Fax: 518-474-4765
Web site: www.dos.state.ny.us

123 William St
New York, NY 10038
212-417-5801
Fax: 212-417-5805

Secretary of State:
  Randy A Daniels. 518-474-0050

Offices and agencies appear in alphabetical order.

First Deputy Secretary of State:
 Frank P Milano.........................518-474-0050
Deputy Secretary of State, Public Affairs:
 Eamon Moynihan.......................212-417-5800
Counsel:
 Glen Bruening..............518-474-6740/fax: 518-473-9211
Asst Dep Sec of State for Communications:
 Lawrence Sombke............518-474-4752/fax: 518-474-4597
 e-mail: info@dos.state.ny.us

Ethics Commission
39 Columbia St, Albany, NY 12207-2717
Executive Director:
 Karl J Sleight............518-432-8207/fax: 518-432-8255
 e-mail: ethics@dos.state.ny.us
Chair:
 Paul Shechtman.......................518-432-8207

Local Government & Community Services
Deputy Secretary of State:
 Matthew Andrus...........518-486-9888/fax: 518-474-6572

Coastal Resources & Waterfront Revitalization Division
Director:
 George Stafford..........518-474-6000/fax: 518-473-2464
 e-mail: coastal@dos.state.ny.us

Code Enforcement & Administration Division
Director:
 Ronald E Piester...........518-474-4073/fax: 518-486-4487
 e-mail: codes@dos.state.ny.us

Community Services Division
Director:
 Evelyn M Harris...........518-474-5741/fax: 518-486-4663
 e-mail: commserv@dos.state.ny.us

Fire Prevention & Control Office
State Fire Administrator:
 James A Burns............518-474-6746/fax: 518-474-3240
 e-mail: fire@dos.state.ny.us

Local Government Services Division
Director:
 Barbara Murphy...........518-473-3355/fax: 518-474-6572
 e-mail: localgov@dos.state.ny.us

New York State Academy of Fire Science
600 College Ave, Montour Falls, NY 14865-9643
Director:
 Richard Nagle.............607-535-7136/fax: 607-535-4841

Open Government Committee
Director:
 Robert J Freeman.........518-474-2518/fax: 518-474-1927
 e-mail: opengov@dos.state.ny.us

CORPORATIONS, AUTHORITIES AND COMMISSIONS

Municipal Assistance Corporation for the City of New York
420 Lexington Avenue
Room 1756
New York, NY 10170
212-840-8255 Fax: 212-840-8570
e-mail: macnyc@earthlink.net

Chairman:
 Jonathan A Ballan............212-840-8255 or 212-692-6772
Executive Director:
 Nancy H Henze.......................212-840-8255

New York State Assn of Fire Districts
PO Box 99
Mastic, NY 11950
800-520-9594 or 631-281-4577 Fax: 631-399-0873
Web site: www.firedistnys.com

President:
 Frank A Nocerino..........516-799-8575/fax: 516-799-2516
First VP:
 Kenneth Hoffarth.........916-946-2599/fax: 914-682-5208
Second VP:
 Randall Rider............716-875-0183/fax: 716-876-9566
Secretary & Treasurer:
 John F Dolezal...........800-520-9594/fax: 631-399-0873
Counsel:
 William N Young..........800-349-2904/fax: 518-869-5142

New York State Disaster Preparedness Commission
Building 22, Suite 101
1220 Washington Ave
Albany, NY 12226-2251
518-457-2222 Fax: 518-457-9930
Web site: www.nysemo.state.ny.us

Chairman:
 James W McMahon.......................518-402-2227
Chief of Ops, NYSEMO:
 Robert Olazagasti........518-457-9981/fax: 518-457-9930

State of New York Municipal Bond Bank Agency (MBBA)
641 Lexington Ave
New York, NY 10022
212-688-4000 Fax: 212-872-0678
Web site: www.nymbba.org

Senior VP & Special Asst to Pres/CEO for Policy Dev & Programs:
 James P Angley.......................212-688-4000
Chair:
 Jerome M Becker.....................212-688-4000
President & CEO:
 Stephen J Hunt......................212-688-4000
Senior VP, CFO & COO:
 Ralph J Madalena....................212-688-4000
Senior VP & Counsel:
 Robert M Drillings..................212-688-4000
Senior VP, Debt Issuance:
 Bernard Abramowitz...............212-688-4000 x530
Vice President, Policy & Planning:
 Tracy A Oats....................212-688-4000 x678

NEW YORK STATE LEGISLATURE

See Legislative Branch in Section 1 for additional Standing Committee and Subcommittee information.

Offices and agencies appear in alphabetical order.

Assembly Legislative Commissions

State-Local Relations, Legislative Commission on
Assembly Chair:
Vacant 518-455-5425
Program Manager:
William Kraus 518-455-5035/fax: 518-455-5396

Assembly Standing Committees

Cities
Chair:
Scott M Stringer (D). 518-455-5802
Ranking Minority Member:
Thomas J Kirwan (R) 518-455-5762

Economic Development, Job Creation, Commerce & Industry
Chair:
Robin L Schimminger (D) .518-455-4767
Ranking Minority Member:
Robert G Prentiss (R). 518-455-5931

Housing
Chair:
Vito J Lopez (D). 518-455-5537
Ranking Minority Member:
Catharine M Young (R) 518-455-5241

Local Government
Chair:
Robert K Sweeney (D). 518-455-5787
Ranking Minority Member:
Roy J McDonald (R) 518-455-5404

Transportation
Chair:
David F Gantt (D). 518-455-5606
Ranking Minority Member:
Dierdre K Scozzafava (R) .518-455-5797

Ways & Means
Chair:
Herman D Farrell, Jr (D) 518-455-5491

Ranking Minority Member:
Thomas F Barraga (R) 518-455-4611

Senate Standing Committees

Cities
Chair:
Serphin R Maltese (R) 518-455-3281
Ranking Minority Member:
Byron W Brown (D). 518-455-3371

Commerce, Economic Development & Small Business
Chair:
James S Alesi (R) 518-455-2015
Ranking Minority Member:
Efrain Gonzalez, Jr (D). 518-455-3395

Finance
Chair:
Owen H Johnson (R) 518-455-3411
Ranking Minority Member:
Neil D Breslin (D) 518-455-2225

Housing, Construction & Community Development
Chair:
John J Bonacic (R) 518-455-3181
Ranking Minority Member:
Liz Krueger (D) 518-455-2297

Local Government
Chair:
Elizabeth O'Connor Little (R) 518-455-2811
Ranking Minority Member:
Martin Connor (D) 518-455-2625

Transportation
Chair:
John R Kuhl, Jr (R). 518-455-2091
Ranking Minority Member:
Seymour P Lachman (D) 518-455-2437

Private Sector

Association of Fire Districts of the State of NY Inc
948 North Bay Avenue, North Massapequa, NY 11758-2581
516-799-8575 or 800-520-9594 Fax: 516-799-2516
e-mail: FNOC@aol.com
Web site: www.firedistnys.com
Frank A Nocerino, Secretary-Treasurer
Obtain greater economy in the administration of fire district affairs

Association of Towns of the State of New York
146 State St, Albany, NY 12207
518-465-7933 Fax: 518-465-0724
e-mail: jhaber@nytowns.org
Web site: www.nytowns.org
G Jeffrey Haber, Executive Director
Advocacy, education for local government

Citizens Budget Commision
11 Penn Plaza, Ste 900, New York, NY 10001
212-279-2605 Fax: 212-868-4745
e-mail: cmb2@is2.nyu.edu
Web site: www.cbcny.org
Charles Brecher, Executive VP & Director of Research
Studies & recommendations on funding of civic services

Citizens Union of the City of New York
299 Broadway, Rm 700, New York, NY 10007-1978
212-227-0342 Fax: 212-227-0345
e-mail: citizens@citizensunion.org
Web site: www.citizensunion.org
Dick Dadey, Executive Director
Citizen watchdog organization; city & state public policy issues

Offices and agencies appear in alphabetical order.

Columbia Law School, Legislative Drafting Research Fund
435 W 116th St, New York, NY 10027-7297
212-854-2640 Fax: 212-854-7946
e-mail: rb34@columbia.edu
Web site: www.law.columbia.edu
Richard Briffault, Vice Dean & Executive Director
State & local government law, property law & election law

Cornell Cooperative Extension, Local Government Program
43 Warren Hall, Cornell University, Ithaca, NY 14853
607-255-1593 Fax: 607-255-2231
e-mail: mrh3@cornell.edu
Web site: www.clgp.cornell.edu
Mike Hattery, Senior Extension Associate
Improve both governance, administrative capability & service delivery of local governments; assist in developing community level solutions to environmental protection

Council of State Governments, Eastern Conference
40 Broad St, Ste 2050, New York, NY 10004-2317
212-482-2320 Fax: 212-482-2344
e-mail: alan@csgeast.org
Web site: www.csgeast.org
Alan V Sokolow, Regional Director
Training, research & information sharing for state government officials

Cullen & Dykman
100 Quentin Roosevelt Blvd, Garden City Ctr, Garden City, NY 11530-4850
516-357-3703 Fax: 516-396-9155
e-mail: gfishberg@cullenanddykman.com
Web site: www.cullenanddykman.com
Gerard Fishberg, Partner
Municipal & labor law

Fordham University, Department of Political Science
441 E Fordham Road, Bronx, NY 10458
718-817-3960 Fax: 718-817-3972
e-mail: kantor@fordham.edu
Paul Kantor, Professor of Political Science
Urban politics & the social condition of American cities

Fund for the City of New York
121 Ave of the Americas, 6th Fl, New York, NY 10013
212-925-6675 Fax: 212-925-5675
e-mail: mmccormick@fcny.org
Web site: www.fcny.org
Mary McCormick, President
Innovations in policy, programs, practice & technology to advance the functioning of government & nonprofit organizations in NYC & beyond

Genesee Transportation Council
50 West Main Street, Suite 8112, Rochester, NY 14614-1227
585-232-6240 Fax: 585-262-3106
e-mail: rperrin@gtcmpo.org
Web site: www.gtcmpo.org
Richard Perrin, Acting Executive Director
Nine-county metropolitan planning organization

Hawkins Delafield & Wood LLP
67 Wall St, 11th Fl, New York, NY 10005
212-820-9470 Fax: 212-820-9615
e-mail: srkramer@hdw.com
Web site: www.hawkins.com
Stanley R Kramer, Attorney
Transportation, municipal & local government law

Housing Action Council Inc - Not For Profit
55 S Broadway, Tarrytown, NY 10591
914-332-4144 Fax: 914-332-4147
e-mail: rnoonan@affordablehomes.org
Rosemarie Noonan, Executive Director
Financial feasibility, land use & zoning & affordable housing

Institute of Public Administration (The)
411 Lafayette St, Suite 303, New York, NY 10003
212-992-9898 Fax: 212-995-4876
e-mail: info@theipa.org
Web site: www.theipa.org
David Mammen, President
Non-profit research, consulting & educational institute

KPMG LLP
345 Park Ave, Rm 4095, New York, NY 10154
212-872-5833 Fax: 212-872-3447
e-mail: jrmiller@kpmg.com
Michael D.V. Rake, Chairman, International & Senior Partner
Accounting

League of Women Voters of New York State
35 Maiden Lane, Albany, NY 12207-2712
518-465-4162 Fax: 518-465-0812
e-mail: lwvny@lwvny.org
Web site: www.lwvny.org
Rob Marchiony, Executive Director
Public policy issues forum; good government advocacy

MBIA Insurance Corporation
113 King St, Armonk, NY 10504
914-273-4545 Fax: 914-765-3555
e-mail: ethel.geisinger@mbia.com
Web site: www.mbia.com
Ethel Z Geisinger, Vice President, Government Relations
Insure municipal bonds & structured transactions

Manhattan Institute, Center for Civic Innovation
52 Vanderbilt Ave, 2nd Fl, New York, NY 10017
212-599-7000 Fax: 212-599-3494
Web site: www.manhattan-institute.org
Lindsay Young, Executive Director, Communications
Urban policy, reinventing government, civil society

Moody's Investors Service, Public Finance Group
99 Church St, New York, NY 10007
212-553-7780 Fax: 212-298-7113
e-mail: dennis.farrell@moodys.com
Web site: www.moodys.com
Dennis M Farrell, Group Managing Director
Municipal debt ratings & analysis

Offices and agencies appear in alphabetical order.

NY Association of Local Government Records Officers
PO Box 208, Buffalo, NY 14201
315-785-5149 Fax: 315-785-5145
e-mail: benc@co.jefferson.ny.us
Web site: www.nyalgro.org
Ben Cobb, President
Education advisory network for the development of sound records & information management programs

NY State Association of Town Superintendents of Highways Inc
PO Box 427, Belfast, NY 14711-0427
585-365-9380 Fax: 585-365-9382
e-mail: nysaotsoh@yahoo.com
William A Nichols, Executive Secretary & Treasurer

NYS Association of Counties
111 Pine Street, Albany, NY 12207
518-465-1473 Fax: 518-465-0506
e-mail: sacquario@nysac.org
Web site: www.nysac.org
Stephen J Acquario, Executive Director
Lobbying, research & training services

NYS Conference of Mayors & Municipal Officials
119 Washington Ave, Albany, NY 12210
518-463-1185 Fax: 518-463-1190
e-mail: info@nycom.org
Web site: www.nycom.org
Richard Bucci, President
Legislative advocacy for NYS cities & villages

NYS Magistrates Association
267 Delaware Ave, Delmar, NY 12054-1124
518-439-1087 Fax: 518-439-1204
e-mail: nysma@juno.com
Web site: www.nysmagassoc.homestead.com
Thomas W Baldwin, Executive Director
Association of town & village justices

New York Municipal Insurance Reciprocal (NYMIR)
24 Aviation Rd, Ste 206, Albany, NY 12205
518-437-1171 Fax: 518-437-1182
Web site: www.nymir.org
Gale M Hatch, President
Insurance services for municipalities

NYS Bar Assn, Municipal Law Section
New York State Court of Claims
500 Court Exchange Bldg, 144 Exchange Blvd, Rochester, NY 14614
585-262-2320 Fax: 585-262-3019
e-mail: rminarik@courts.state.ny.us
Hon Renee Forgensi Minarik, Chair

New York State Government Finance Officers Association Inc
7 Elk St, #2, Albany, NY 12207
518-465-1512 Fax: 518-434-4640
e-mail: info@nysgfoa.org
Web site: www.nysgfoa.org
Ann Marie Berg, President
Membership organization dedicated to the professional management of governmental resources

New York State Society of Municipal Finance Officers
Village of Speculator, PO Box 396, Speculator, NY 12164
518-548-7354 Fax: 518-54827742
Web site: www.nysmunicipalfinanceofficers.org
Bonnie J Page, President
Improve municipal financial & accounting operations & procedures in NYS

New York University, Wagner Graduate School
295 Lafayette Street, 2ND Floor, New York, NY 10012
212-998-7400 Fax: 212-995-4162
e-mail: mitchell.moss@nyu.edu
Web site: www.nyu.edu/wagner
Mitchell Moss, Professor of Urban Policy & Planning
Research on urban planning & development, with special emphasis on technology & the future of cities

Syracuse University, Maxwell School of Citizenship & Public Affairs
215 Eggers Hall, Syracuse, NY 13244-1090
315-443-5848 Fax: 315-443-9721
e-mail: bjump@maxwell.syr.edu
Bernard Jump, Jr, Professor of Public Administration
Capital financing & debt management; public employee pensions; financial management

Urbanomics
115 Fifth Ave, 3rd Fl, New York, NY 10003
212-353-7463 Fax: 212-353-7462
e-mail: d-sundell@peapc.com
Web site: www.urbanomics.org
David Sundell, Researcher
Economic development planning studies, market studies, tax policy analyses, program evaluations & economic & demographic forecasts

Whiteman Osterman & Hanna LLP
One Commerce Plaza, Albany, NY 12260
518-487-7619 Fax: 518-487-7777
e-mail: druzow@woh.com
Web site: www.woh.com
Daniel A Ruzow, Senior Partner
Environmental & zoning law

Offices and agencies appear in alphabetical order.

PUBLIC EMPLOYEES

New York State

GOVERNOR'S OFFICE

Governor's Office

Executive Chamber
State Capitol
Albany, NY 12224
518-474-8390 Fax: 518-474-1513
Web site: www.state.ny.us

Governor:
George E Pataki 518-474-8390
Executive Director:
Kara Lanspery 518-474-8390
Secretary to the Governor:
John P Cahill. 518-474-4246
Senior Policy Advisor to the Governor:
Jeffrey Lovell 518-486-9671
Counsel to the Governor-Attorney General, Budget:
Richard Platkin. 518-474-8343
Director, Communications:
David Catalfamo. 518-474-8418
Director, State & Local Government Affairs:
John Haggerty. 518-486-9896
Asst Counsel to the Governor-Civil Svc, Elections, Empl Relations, Labor, Motor Veh, Niagara Fr, Port Auth, Retirement/Pensions, Transp, Thruway, Waterfr, MTA, PERB:
Christopher Staszak 518-474-1310

EXECUTIVE DEPARTMENTS AND RELATED AGENCIES

Civil Service Department

State Campus
Bldg 1
Albany, NY 12239
518-457-2487 Fax: 518-457-7547
Web site: www.cs.state.ny.us

Commissioner:
Daniel E Wall. 518-457-3701
Executive Deputy Commissioner:
John F Barr. 518-457-6212
Deputy Commissioner:
Regina M DuBois. 518-485-7515
Director, Civil Svc Ops & Admin:
Patricia Hite 518-485-0340
Special Counsel:
Thomas F Brennan 518-485-7278
Counsel:
Brian S Reichenbach 518-457-3177
Director, Workforce & Occupational Planning:
Nancy B Kiyonaga 518-485-9274
Director, Internal Audit:
Vacant 518-457-7355

Director, Public Information:
Marc E Carey. 518-457-9375/fax: 518-457-6654
e-mail: mec5@cs.state.ny.us
Public Records Access Officer:
Jane Prus 518-457-6875/fax: 518-457-6654

Administration

Administrative Services Unit
Director, Financial Administration:
Michael Bosanko. 518-457-6490/fax: 518-457-5116

Classification & Compensation Division
Director:
Nicholas J Vagianelis 518-457-6226/fax: 518-457-8081

Commission Operations
Director:
Stella Chen Harding. 518-457-2575

Diversity, Planning & Management Division
Director:
Frank E Abrams 518-457-4146/fax: 518-457-0399
Coordinator, Community Outreach:
George Swiers. 518-457-7661/fax: 518-457-0399

Employee Benefits Division
Director:
Robert DuBois. 518-457-9391/fax: 518-485-8952
Director, Employee Insurance Programs:
Mary B Frye 518-457-1771/fax: 518-457-1311
Asst Director, Financial Management & Accounting:
David Boland 518-457-5159/fax: 518-457-1311

Employee Health Services Division
Administrator, EHS:
Maria C Steinbach. 518-457-6142/fax: 518-485-1995
Director, Health Services Nursing:
Mary M McSweeney 518-457-2616

Information Resource Management
Director:
Frank Slade 518-457-1775/fax: 518-485-5752
e-mail: fhs1@cs.state.ny.us

Municipal Services Division
Director:
Raymond C Greene. 518-457-9553/fax: 518-485-8244
Local Examinations:
Will Martin. 518-457-4487

Personnel
Director:
Susan China. 518-457-1077/fax: 518-457-6875

Planning & Training Division
Director:
Frank R Santora 518-457-5507

Staffing Services Division
Director:
Terry Jordan 518-457-5781/fax: 518-457-4239
Asst Director:
Crystal Hamelink 518-457-5445

Offices and agencies appear in alphabetical order.

Attendance & Leave Unit:
Margaret Harrigan 518-457-2295

Testing Services Division
Director:
Paul Kaiser 518-457-9499/fax: 518-457-4239
Asst Director:
Ray Mullin 518-457-5465

Civil Service Commission
President:
Daniel E Wall 518-457-3701
Commissioner:
Margaret Dadd 518-457-3504
Commissioner:
Leo J Kesselring 518-457-5444

Employee Relations, Governor's Office of
Two Empire State Plaza
Ste 1201
Albany, NY 12223
518-474-6988 Fax: 518-473-6795
e-mail: info@goer.state.ny.us
Web site: www.goer.state.ny.us

Director:
George Madison 518-474-6988/fax: 518-486-7304
Executive Deputy Director:
John Currier 518-474-6988/fax: 518-486-7304
General Counsel:
Walter J Pellegrini 518-474-4090
Director, Administration:
Paul Shatsoff 518-473-3467/fax: 518-473-6725
e-mail: pshatsoff@goer.state.ny.us
Director, Employee Benefits Unit:
Priscilla Feinberg 518-473-6211/fax: 518-423-6294
Director, Information Management Unit:
Debi Orton 518-473-6202/fax: 518-473-6725
Director, Research Unit:
Richard Martin 518-473-7233/fax: 518-486-5602
Co-Director, Workforce Training & Development Unit:
Onnolee Smith 518-474-6772/fax: 518-474-8587
Public Information Officer:
Michelle McDonald 518-474-4800/fax: 518-486-7304
e-mail: mgmcdonald@goer.state.ny.us

Labor/Management Committees

Family Benefits Committee
55 Elk St, Rm 301C, Albany, NY 12210-2331
Staff Director:
Deborah Long Miller 518-473-8091/fax: 518-473-3581

NYS/CSEA Discipline Unit . . . . fax: 518-486-9737
55 Elk St, Rm 301D, Albany, NY 12210-2333
Arbitration Panel Coordinator:
Linda Ronda 518-473-6070

NYS/CSEA Partnership for Education & Training . . fax: 518-473-0056
240 Washington Ave Extension, Ste 502, Albany, NY 12203
800-253-4532 Fax: 518-473-0056
Co-Director:
Deb Berg 518-473-8991

NYS/SSU Joint Labor-Management Committee . . . . fax: 518-457-9445
55 Elk St, Rm 301-B, Albany, NY 12210
Employee Program Assistant:
Patricia Merola 518-457-9420

NYS/UUP Labor-Management Committee . . . . fax: 518-457-9445
55 Elk St, Rm 301-B, Albany, NY 12210

Statewide Employee Assistance Programs . . . . fax: 518-486-9796
55 Elk St, Rm 301A, Albany, NY 12210-2316
Asst Director:
Michael Brace 518-486-9769

Public Employment Relations Board
80 Wolf Rd
Albany, NY 12205
518-457-2854 Fax: 518-457-2664
Web site: www.perb.state.ny.us

Chair:
Michael R Cuevas 518-457-2578
Member:
John T Mitchell 518-457-2578
Executive Director:
James R Edgar 518-457-2676
Deputy Chair & Counsel:
Robert A DePaula 518-457-2614
Asst Counsel to the Board:
Deborah A Sabin 518-457-2614
Secretary to the Board:
Sheila Talavera 518-457-2578

Administration Section
Administrative Officer:
Vacant 518-457-2922

Conciliation Section
Director:
Richard A Curreri 518-457-2690
Asst Director:
Vacant 518-457-2690

District Offices

Buffalo . . . . fax: 716-847-3690
125 Main St, Buffalo, NY 14203
Regional Director:
Vacant 716-847-3449

New York City . . . . fax: 718-722-4550
55 Hanson Pl, Ste 700, Brooklyn, NY 11217
Regional Director:
Philip Maier 718-722-4545

Employment Practices & Representation Section
Director:
Monte Klein 518-457-6410
Asst Director:
Vacant 518-457-6410

Legal Section
Associate Counsel:
William Busler 518-457-2678
Asst Counsel for Litigation:
Sandra Nathan 518-457-2678

State Comptroller, Office of the
110 State St, 15th Fl
Albany, NY 12236-0001
518-474-4040 Fax: 518-473-3004
Web site: www.osc.state.ny.us

Offices and agencies appear in alphabetical order.

Policy Areas

633 Third Ave
31st Fl
New York, NY 10017-6754
212-681-4491
Fax: 212-681-4468

State Comptroller:
  Alan G Hevesi . . . . 518-474-4040 or 212-681-4491

Division of State Services
Deputy Comptroller:
  Lynn Canton 518-474-5598

Payroll & Revenue Services Division
Deputy Comptroller:
  Daniel Berry 518-408-4149
Director, Unclaimed Funds:
  Lawrence Schantz 518-473-6438
Director, State Payroll Services:
  Robin R Rabii 518-474-3400

Executive Office
Chief of Staff:
  Jack Chartier 212-681-4498
First Deputy:
  Thomas Sanzillo 518-474-2909
Executive Deputy:
  Diana Jones Ritter 518-474-3610
Deputy Chief of Staff:
  Dalia Schapiro 212-681-4540
Chief Information Officer:
  Jeffrey Grunfeld 518-473-3004
Director, Correspondence Unit:
  Ellen J Evans 518-473-1323
Chief Information Officer:
  Jeffrey Grunfeld 518-473-3004
Internal Control Officer:
  Raymond H Harris 518-473-6017

Retirement Services
Deputy Comptroller:
  Laura Anglin 518-474-2600
Asst Comptroller:
  Nancy Burton 518-474-4600

Accounting Bureau
Director:
  Daniel Burns 518-474-3670

Actuarial Bureau
Actuary:
  Teri Landin 518-474-4537

Benefit Calculations & Disbursements
Director:
  Veronica D'Alauro 518-474-5556

Disability Processing/Hearing Administration
Director:
  Kathy Nowak 518-473-1347

Member & Employee Services
Director:
  Ginger Dame 518-474-1101

Retirement Communications
Director:
  Paul Kentoffio 518-474-7096

CORPORATIONS, AUTHORITIES AND COMMISSIONS

New York State Teachers' Retirement System
10 Corporate Woods Dr
Albany, NY 12211-2395
518-447-2666 Fax: 518-447-2695
Web site: www.nystrs.albany.ny.us

Executive Director:
  George M Philip 518-447-2666
  e-mail: execdir@nystrs.state.ny.us
General Counsel:
  Wayne Schneider 518-447-2722
Actuary:
  Lawrence A Johansen 518-447-2611
Director, Administration:
  William S O'Brien 518-447-2730
Director, Member Relations, Public Relations:
  David Daly 518-447-2910/fax: 518-447-2875
Real Estate Investment Officer:
  James D Campbell 518-447-2752
Securities Investment Officer:
  Joseph N Vet 518-447-2921

New York State Temporary Commission of Investigation
59 Maiden Lane, 31st Fl
New York, NY 10038
212-344-6660 Fax: 212-344-6868
Web site: www.sic.state.ny.us

Chair:
  Dineen AL Riviezzo 212-344-6660
Chief Investigator:
  Anthony Hellmer 212-344-6660
Deputy Commissioner/Chief Counsel:
  Anthony T Cartusciello 212-344-6670

NEW YORK STATE LEGISLATURE

See Legislative Branch in Section 1 for additional Standing Committee and Subcommittee information.

Assembly Standing Committees

Governmental Employees
Chair:
  Peter J Abbate, Jr (D) 518-455-3053
Ranking Minority Member:
  Joseph S Saladino (R) 518-455-5305

Labor
Chair:
  Susan V John (D) 518-455-4527
Ranking Minority Member:
  Patricia L Acampora (R) 518-455-5294

Offices and agencies appear in alphabetical order.

Senate Standing Committees

Civil Service & Pensions
Chair:
Joseph E Robach (R) 518-455-2909
Ranking Minority Member:
Carl Andrews (D) 518-455-2431

Labor
Chair:
George Maziarz (R) 518-455-2024
Ranking Minority Member:
Dianne J Savino (D) 518-455-2437

Senate/Assembly Legislative Commissions

Government Administration, Legislative Commission on
Assembly Chair:
David R Koon (D) 518-455-5784
Senate Vice Chair:
Owen H Johnson (R) 518-455-3411
Program Manager:
Philip Johnson 518-455-3632/fax: 518-455-4574

U.S. Government

EXECUTIVE DEPARTMENTS AND RELATED AGENCIES

US Merit Systems Protection Board
Web site: www.mspb.gov

New York Field Office
26 Federal Plaza, Room 3137A, New York, NY 10278-0022
Chief Administrative Judge:
Arthur Joseph 212-264-9372/fax: 212-264-1417

US Office of Personnel Management
Web site: www.usajobs.opm.gov

PHILADELPHIA SERVICE CENTER (serving New York)
William J Green Fed Bldg, Rm 3400, 600 Arch St, Philadelphia, PA 19106
e-mail: philadelphia@opm.gov
Director:
Joseph D Stix 215-861-3031/fax: 215-861-3030

U.S. CONGRESS

See U.S. Congress Chapter for additional Standing Committee and Subcommittee information.

House of Representatives Standing Committees

Government Reform
Chair:
Thomas M Davis (R-VA) 202-225-1492
Ranking Minority Member:
Henry A Waxman (D-CA) 202-225-3976
New York Delegate:
Carolyn B Maloney (D) 202-225-7944
New York Delegate:
John M McHugh (R) 202-225-4611
New York Delegate:
Major R Owens (D) 202-225-6231
New York Delegate:
Edolphus Towns (D) 202-225-5936

Subcommittee
Federal Workforce & Agency Organization
Chair:
Jon Potter (R-NV) 202-225-3252
Ranking Minority Member:
Danny K Davis (D-IL) 202-225-5006
New York Delegate:
Major R Owens (D) 202-225-6231

Senate Standing Committees

Governmental Affairs
Chair:
Susan Collins (R-ME) 202-224-2523
Ranking Minority Member:
Joseph I Lieberman (D-CT) 202-224-4041

Private Sector

AFSCME District Council 37
150 State St, Albany, NY 12207
518-436-0665 or 212-815-1550 Fax: 518-436-1066
Wanda Williams, Director
NYC employees union

AFSCME, New York
212 Great Oaks Blvd, Albany, NY 12203
518-869-2245 Fax: 518-869-8649
e-mail: bmcdonnell@organize.afscme.org
Web site: www.afscme.org
Brian McDonnell, Legislative Political Director
Union representing public service & healthcare workers; American Federation of State, County & Municipal Employees

Offices and agencies appear in alphabetical order.

Civil Service Employees Assn of NY (CSEA), Local 1000, AFSCME, AFL-CIO
143 Washington Ave, Albany, NY 12224-0125
518-257-1000 Fax: 518-462-3639
Web site: www.csealocal1000.org
Danny Donohue, President
Public/private employees union

Cornell University, School of Industrial & Labor Relations
356 ILR Research Bldg, Ithaca, NY 14853-3901
607-255-7581 Fax: 607-255-0245
e-mail: klb23@cornell.edu
Web site: www.ilr.cornell.edu
Kate Bronfenbrenner, Director, Labor Education Research
Public sector organizations; leadership; temporary & contract workers; union organizing; & collective bargaining

District Council 37, AFSCME, AFL-CIO
125 Barclay St, New York, NY 10007
212-815-1470 Fax: 212-815-1402
e-mail: dsullivan@dc37.net
Web site: www.dc37.net
Dennis Sullivan, Director, Research & Negotiations
NYC employees union

NYC Board of Education Employees, Local 372/AFSCME, AFL-CIO
125 Barclay Street, 6th Floor, New York, NY 10007
212-815-1372 Fax: 212-815-1347
Web site: www.local372.com
Veronica Montgomery-Costa, President - District Council 37/372

NYS Association of Chiefs of Police Inc
2697 Hamburg Street, Schenectady, NY 12303-3783
518-355-3371 Fax: 518-356-5767
e-mail: nysacop@nycap.rr.com
Web site: www.nychiefs.org
Joseph S Dominelli, Executive Director

NYS Association of Fire Chiefs
1670 Columbia Turnpike, Box 328, East Schodack, NY 12063-0328
518-477-2631 Fax: 518-477-4430
e-mail: tlabelle@nysfirechiefs.com
Web site: www.nysfirechiefs.com
Thomas LaBelle, Executive Director

NYS Correctional Officers & Police Benevolent Association Inc
102 Hackett Blvd, Albany, NY 12209
518-427-1551 Fax: 518-426-1635
Web site: www.nyscopba.org
Richard Harcrow, President

NYS Court Clerks Association
170 Duane St, New York, NY 10013
212-941-5700 Fax: 212-941-5705
Kevin E Scanlon, Sr, President

NYS Deputies Association Inc
61 Laredo Dr, Rochester, NY 14624
585-247-9322 Fax: 585-247-6661
e-mail: tross1@rochester.rr.com
Web site: www.nysdeputy.org
Thomas H Ross, Executive Director

NYS Bar Assn, Attorneys in Public Service Cmte
NYS Health Department
433 River St, 5th Fl, Ste 330, Troy, NY 12180-2299
518-402-0748 Fax: 518-402-0751
e-mail: jfh01@health.state.ny.us
Hon James F Horan, Chair
Advancing the interests of NY governmental & not-for-profit attorneys

NYS Law Enforcement Officers Union, Council 82, AFSCME, AFL-CIO
Hollis V Chase Bldg, 63 Colvin Ave, Albany, NY 12206
518-489-8424 Fax: 518-489-8430
e-mail: c82@council82.org
Web site: www.council82.org
Kathy B McCormack, Legislative Director

NYS Parole Officers Association
PO Box 5821, Albany, NY 12205-0821
518-393-6541 Fax: 518-393-6541
e-mail: hsj195@aol.com
Web site: www.nyspoa.org
H Susan Jeffords, President
Professional association representing NYS parole affairs

NYS Sheriffs' Association
27 Elk St, Albany, NY 12207-1002
518-434-9091 Fax: 518-434-9093
e-mail: pkehoe@nysheriffs.org
Web site: www.nysheriffs.org
Peter R Kehoe, Counsel & Executive Director

National Education Association of New York
217 Lark St, Albany, NY 12210
518-462-6451 Fax: 518-462-1731
e-mail: dbutler@neany.org
Web site: www.neany.org
Denis M Butler, Legislative & Educational Policy Coordinator
Public school employees union

New York State Public Employees Federation (PEF)
1168-70 Troy-Schenectady Rd, PO Box 12414, Albany, NY 12212
518-785-1900 x211 Fax: 518-783-1117
Web site: www.nyspef.org
Roger E Benson, President
Professional, scientific & technical employees union

New York State Supreme Court Officers Association
299 Broadway, Suite 1100, New York, NY 10007-1921
212-406-4292 or 212-406-4276 Fax: 212-791-8420
e-mail: lbroderick@nysscoa.org
Web site: www.nysscoa.org
John P McKillop, President
Supreme Court Officers Union

Offices and agencies appear in alphabetical order.

New York State United Teachers/AFT, AFL-CIO
800 Troy-Schenectady Road, Latham, NY 12110-2455
518-213-6000 or 800-342-9810
Web site: www.nysut.org
Richard Iannuzzi, President

Organization of NYS Management Confidential Employees
3 Washington Square, Albany, NY 12205
518-456-5241 or 800-828-6623 Fax: 518-456-3838
e-mail: omce@aol.com
Web site: www.nysomce.org
Barbara Zaron, President
Professional organization of state management & confidential employees

Patrolmen's Benevolent Association
40 Fulton St, 17th Fl, New York, NY 10038
212-233-5531 Fax: 212-233-3952
e-mail: union@nycpba.org
Web site: www.nycpba.org
Patrick Lynch, President
NYC patrolmen's union

Police Conference of NY Inc (PCNY)
112 State St, Ste 1120, Albany, NY 12207
518-463-3283 Fax: 518-463-2488
Web site: www.pcny.org
Edward W Guzdek, President
Advocacy for law enforcement officers

Professional Fire Fighters Association Inc (NYS)
111 Washington Ave, Suite 207, Albany, NY 12210-6511
518-436-8827 Fax: 518-436-8830
e-mail: nyspffapres@aol.com
Web site: www.nyspffa.org
Charles Morello, President
Union representing city, village & town firefighters

Retired Public Employees Association
435 New Karner Road, Albany, NY 12205-3833
518-869-2542 or 518-265-9284 Fax: 518-869-0631
e-mail: mail@rpea.org
Web site: www.rpea.org
Donald Hirshorn, Legislative Liaison & Counsel
Advocacy for retired public employees & their families

State Employees Federal Credit Union
1239 Washington Avenue, Albany, NY 12206-1067
518-452-8234 Fax: 518-464-5227
Web site: www.sefcu.com
John Gallagher, Director, Internal Audit

Syracuse University, Maxwell School of Citizenship & Public Affairs
215 Eggers Hall, Syracuse, NY 13244-1090
315-443-5848 Fax: 315-443-9721
e-mail: bjump@maxwell.syr.edu
Bernard Jump, Jr, Professor of Public Administration
Capital financing & debt management; public employee pensions; financial management

Trooper Foundation-State of New York Inc
3 Airport Park Blvd, Latham, NY 12110-1441
518-785-1002 Fax: 518-785-1003
e-mail: rmincher@nystf.org
Web site: www.nystrooperfoundation.org
Rachael L Mincher, Foundation Administrator
Supports programs & services of the NYS Police

Uniformed Fire Officers Association
225 Broadway, Suite 401, New York, NY 10007
212-293-9300 Fax: 212-292-1560
Web site: www.ufoa.org
Peter L Gorman, President
NYC fire officers' union

United Transportation Union
35 Fuller Rd, Suite 205, Albany, NY 12205
518-438-8403 Fax: 518-438-8404
e-mail: sjnasca@aol.com
Web site: www.utu.org
Samuel Nasca, Legislative Director
Federal government railroad, bus & airline employees; public employees

United University Professions
PO Box 15143, Albany, NY 12212-5143
518-640-6600 Fax: 518-640-6698
e-mail: feedback@uupmail.org
Web site: www.uupinfo.org
William E Scheuerman, President
SUNY labor union of academic & other professional faculty

Policy Areas

Offices and agencies appear in alphabetical order.

REAL PROPERTY

New York State

GOVERNOR'S OFFICE

Governor's Office
Executive Chamber
State Capitol
Albany, NY 12224
518-474-8390 Fax: 518-474-1513
Web site: www.state.ny.us

Governor:
  George E Pataki 518-474-8390
Executive Director:
  Kara Lanspery 518-474-8390
Secretary to the Governor:
  John P Cahill. 518-474-4246
Senior Policy Advisor to the Governor:
  Jeffrey Lovell 518-486-9671
Counsel to Governor-Attorney General, Budget:
  Richard Platkin. 518-474-8343
Asst Counsel to the Gov-Battery Pk, Child/Family Svcs, Child/Family
  Council, Family, Housing, Human Rts, Roosevelt Is, Temp/Disabl,
  Women, HFA/MBBA/SONYMA:
  Carolyn Betz Kerr. 518-474-1310
Director, Communications:
  David Catalfamo. 518-474-8418
Director, State & Local Government Affairs:
  John Haggerty. 518-486-9896

EXECUTIVE DEPARTMENTS AND RELATED AGENCIES

General Services, Office of
633 Third Ave
New York, NY 10017
212-681-4580 Fax: 212-681-4558

Corning Tower, 41st Fl
Empire State Plaza
Albany, NY 12242
518-474-3899
Fax: 518-474-1546

Commissioner:
  Daniel D Hogan 518-474-5991
  e-mail: daniel.hogan@ogs.state.ny.us
First Deputy Commissioner:
  Robert J Fleury. 518-473-6953
  e-mail: robert.fleury@ogs.state.ny.us
Asst Commissioner, Public Affairs:
  Jennifer Morris 518-474-5987/fax: 518-474-3187
  e-mail: jennifer.morris@ogs.state.ny.us

Real Estate Planning & Development Group
Deputy Commissioner:
  Bart Bush 518-473-8550
  e-mail: bart.bush@ogs.state.ny.us
Director, Real Estate Planning & Development:
  Joseph F Stellato. 518-474-4944
Asst Director, Real Estate Planning & Development:
  Amy Chevalier 518-474-4944
Bureau Chief, Land Management:
  Lee C Kiernan. 518-474-2195
Bureau Chief, Space Planning & Lease Construction & Compliance:
  Anne M Carr. 518-473-9887
Bureau Chief, Space Planning & Lease Construction & Compliance:
  John T Culliton. 518-473-9887
Bureau Chief, Real Estate Planning - Upstate:
  Joseph V Luvera. 518-486-1484
Bureau Chief, Real Estate Planning - Upstate:
  Timothy J Leonard 518-473-9887
Bureau Chief, Real Estate Planning - Downstate:
  Robert W Lazarou 518-486-7963

Real Property Management Group
Deputy Commissioner:
  Bart Bush. 518-473-8550/fax: 518-474-1523
  e-mail: bart.bush@ogs.state.ny.us
Director:
  Martin J Gilroy 518-474-6057/fax: 518-474-1523
Manager, Capital Planning:
  Richard Stock 518-473-3927/fax: 518-474-1523
Director, Construction Management:
  Thomas Tedisco. 518-402-5279/fax: 518-474-1312
Director, Downstate Regional Buildings:
  Glenn P Winski 212-681-4556/fax: 212-681-4558
Director, Empire State Plaza & Downtown Buildings:
  Thomas E Casey 518-474-8894/fax: 518-474-4182
Director, Upstate Harriman State Office Campus:
  James Lynch 518-457-2290/fax: 518-457-8297
Director, Utilities Management:
  Robert Lobdell. 518-474-3249/fax: 518-402-5682

Law Department
State Capitol
Albany, NY 12224-0341
518-474-7330 Fax: 518-402-2472
Web site: www.oag.state.ny.us

120 Broadway
New York, NY 10271-0332
212-416-8000
Fax: 212-416-8942

Attorney General:
  Eliot Spitzer 518-474-7330

Public Advocacy Division
Acting Deputy Attorney General:
  Terryl Brown Clemons 212-416-8041/fax: 212-416-8068

Offices and agencies appear in alphabetical order.

Special Counsel:
  Mary Ellen Burns 212-416-6155

Civil Rights Bureau
Bureau Chief:
  Dennis Parker 212-416-8250/fax: 212-416-8074

Investment Protection Bureau
Bureau Chief:
  David Brown 212-416-8198/fax: 212-416-6377

State Counsel Division
Deputy Attorney General:
  Richard Rifkin 518-473-7190
Assistant Deputy Attorney General:
  Patricia Martinelli 518-473-0648/fax: 518-486-9777
Assistant Deputy Attorney General:
  Susan L Watson 212-416-8579/fax: 212-416-6001

Claims Bureau
Bureau Chief:
  Susan Pogoda 212-416-8516/fax: 212-416-8946

Real Property Bureau
Asst Attorney General in Charge:
  Henry A DeCotis 518-474-7151/fax: 518-473-5106

Real Property Services, Office of
16 Sheridan Ave
Albany, NY 12210-2714
518-486-5446 Fax: 518-474-9276
Web site: www.orps.state.ny.us

Executive Director:
  Thomas G Griffen 518-474-5711
  e-mail: thomas.griffen@orps.state.ny.us
Executive Deputy Director:
  Thomas Bellard 518-473-6914
  e-mail: tom.bellard@orps.state.ny.us
Chief Appraiser:
  Jeff Jordan 518-474-2854
  e-mail: jeff.jordan@orps.state.ny.us
Counsel:
  Richard J Sinnott 518-474-6753
  e-mail: richard.sinnott@orps.state.ny.us
Chief Information Officer:
  Bruce Sauter 518-474-8829
  e-mail: bruce.sauter@orps.state.ny.us
Strategic Information Officer:
  JoAnn Whalen 518-474-6742
  e-mail: joann.whalen@orps.state.ny.us
Director, Budget/Fiscal Services:
  Steve King 518-474-5762
  e-mail: steve.king@orps.state.ny.us
Director, Public Information:
  Geoffrey T Gloak 518-486-5446
  e-mail: geoffrey.gloak@orps.state.ny.us

Central Support Services
Director:
  Robert Zandri 518-474-5666
  e-mail: robert.zandri@orps.state.ny.us

Information Technology Services
Director:
  Dennis Jersey 518-474-6758
  e-mail: dennis.jersey@orps.state.ny.us

Regional Customer Service Delivery
Director:
  David Williams 518-473-7574
  e-mail: dave.williams@orps.state.ny.us

Albany (Northern Region) . . . . fax: 518-486-7752
 16 Sheridan Ave, Albany, NY 12210
Regional Director:
  Jeffrey Green 518-486-4403
  e-mail: internet.northern@orps.state.ny.us

Batavia (Western Region)
 Genesee County Bldg 2, 3837 W Main Rd, Batavia, NY 14020
Regional Director:
  Joe Muscarella 585-343-7456/fax: 585-343-9740
  e-mail: internet.western@orps.state.ny.us

Melville Satellite Office . . . . fax: 631-777-1859
 560 Broadhollow Rd, Melville, NY 11474
Manager:
  Susan Rosenblum 631-777-1785
  e-mail: internet.metro@orps.state.ny.us

Newburgh (Southern Region) . . . . fax: 845-567-2690
 263 Route 17K, Ste 2001, Newburgh, NY 12550-8310
Regional Director:
  John Wolham 845-567-2648
  e-mail: internet.southern@orps.state.ny.us

Saranac Lake Satellite Office . . . . fax: 518-891-2639
 43 Broadway, Saranac Lake, NY 12983
Office Manager:
  Dan Lancor 518-891-1780
  e-mail: internet.saranac@orps.state.ny.us

Syracuse (Central Region) . . . . fax: 315-471-3634
 401 South Salina St, Syracuse, NY 13202
Regional Director:
  Robert Gawrelski 315-471-2347
  e-mail: internet.central@orps.state.ny.us

Research, Information & Policy Development
Director:
  James Dunne 518-473-4532
  e-mail: jim.dunne@orps.state.ny.us

State Board of Real Property Services
Chair:
  Ifigenia Brown 518-474-5711
Member:
  John M Bacheller 518-474-5711
Executive Secretary:
  Thomas G Griffen 518-474-5711
Asst to the Board:
  Darlene A Maloney 518-474-3793/fax: 518-474-9276

State Valuation Services
Director:
  Donald Card 518-474-1071/fax: 518-486-7755
  e-mail: don.card@orps.state.ny.us

Transportation Department
1220 Washington Ave
Albany, NY 12232
518-457-5100 Fax: 518-457-5583
Web site: www.dot.state.ny.us

Commissioner:
  Joseph H Boardman 518-457-4422
  e-mail: jboardman@dot.state.ny.us

Offices and agencies appear in alphabetical order.

First Deputy Commissioner:
Brian O Rowback 518-457-4422

Engineering Office
Deputy Commissioner & Chief Engineer:
Paul T Wells 518-457-4430
Director, Environmental Analysis Bureau:
Mary E Ivey 518-457-5672

Real Estate Division
Director:
Francis Mengel 518-457-2430
Acquisitions Management Bureau
Director:
Anne Flowers 518-457-1702
Appraisal Management Bureau
Director:
John Dessena 518-457-0553
Property Management Bureau
Director:
Anne Flowers 518-457-2760

NEW YORK STATE LEGISLATURE

See Legislative Branch in Section 1 for additional Standing Committee and Subcommittee information.

Assembly Standing Committees

Economic Development, Job Creation, Commerce & Industry
Chair:
Robin L Schimminger (D) 518-455-4767

Ranking Minority Member:
Marc Butler (R) 518-455-5393

Housing
Chair:
Vito J Lopez (D) 518-455-5537
Ranking Minority Member:
Catharine M Young (R) 518-455-5241

Real Property Taxation
Chair:
Brian M McLaughlin (D) 518-455-5172
Ranking Minority Mbr:
Sandra Lee Wirth (R) 518-455-4601

Senate Standing Committees

Commerce, Economic Development & Small Business
Chair:
James S Alesi (R) 518-455-2015
Ranking Minority Member:
Efrain Gonzalez, Jr (D) 518-455-3395

Housing Construction & Community Development
Chair:
John J Bonacic (R) 518-455-3181
Ranking Minority Member:
Liz Krueger (D) 518-455-2297

U.S. Government

EXECUTIVE DEPARTMENTS AND RELATED AGENCIES

US Department of Agriculture

Rural Development
Web site: www.rurdev.usda.gov/ny

New York State Office
The Galleries of Syracuse, 441 S Salina St, Ste 357, 5th Fl, Syracuse, NY 13202-2425
TDD: 315-477-6447
State Director:
Patrick H Brennan 315-477-6400/fax: 315-477-6438
Special Projects Representative:
Joel Weirick 315-477-6433/fax: 315-477-6438

US General Services Administration
Web site: www.gsa.gov

Region 2—New York
26 Federal Plaza, Rm 18-102, New York, NY 10278
Regional Administrator:
Eileen Long-Chelales 212-264-2600/fax: 212-264-3998
Deputy Regional Administrator:
Steve Ruggiero 212-264-2600/fax: 212-264-3998

Administration
Director, Program Support & Human Resources:
Joseph J Giorgianni 212-264-0780/fax: 212-264-6798

Federal Supply Service
Acting Asst Regional Administrator:
Charles B Weill 212-264-3590/fax: 212-264-9759

Federal Technology Service
Asst Regional Administrator:
Kerry J Blette 212-264-1257/fax: 212-264-3631

Inspector General's Office
Asst Regional Inspector, Investigations:
Daniel Walsh 212-264-7300/fax: 212-264-7154
Regional Director, Audit:
Joseph Mastropietro 212-264-8620

Public Buildings Service
Asst Regional Administrator:
John Scorcia 212-264-4285/fax: 212-264-2232
Deputy Asst Regional Administrator:
Vacant 212-264-4285
Director, Property Management:
David Segermeister 212-264-4273/fax: 212-264-2746
Director, Realty Services:
Donald W Eigendorff 212-264-4210/fax: 212-264-9400

Offices and agencies appear in alphabetical order.

Private Sector

Appraisal Education Network School & Merrell Institute
1461 Lakeland Ave, Bohemia, NY 11716
631-563-7720 Fax: 631-563-7719
e-mail: bcm@doctor.com
Web site: www.merrellinstitute.com
Bill C Merrell, Director
Real estate sales, broker, appraiser, mortgage & property management education courses, paralegal, continuing education, home inspection

Brookfield Properties Corporation
One Liberty Plaza, 6th Fl, New York, NY 10006
212-417-7000 Fax: 212-417-7195
e-mail: kkane@brookfieldproperties.com
Kathleen G Kane, General Counsel
Commercial real estate

Building & Realty Institute
80 Business Park Dr, Armonk, NY 10504
914-273-0730 Fax: 914-273-7051
e-mail: aaaa@buildersinstitute.org
Web site: www.buildersinstitute.org
Albert A Annunziata, Executive Director
Building, realty & construction industry membership organization

Colliers ABR Inc
40 E 52nd St, New York, NY 10022
212-758-0800 Fax: 212-758-6190
Web site: www.colliersabr.com
Mark P Boisi, Chairman
Commercial real estate & property management

NYS Bar Assn, Real Property Law Section
D H Ferguson, Attorney, PLLC
1115 Midtown Tower, Rochester, NY 14604
585-325-3635 Fax: 585-325-3620
e-mail: dhferguson@frontiernet.net
Dorothy H Ferguson, Chair

Ernst & Young
5 Times Square, New York, NY 10036-6350
212-773-4500 Fax: 212-773-4986
e-mail: dale.reiss@ey.com
Web site: www.ey.com
Dale Anne Reiss, Global & Americas Director-Real Estate,
    Hospitality & Construction

Fisher Brothers
299 Park Ave, New York, NY 10171
212-752-5000 Fax: 212-940-6879
Arnold Fisher, Partner
Real estate investment & development

GVA Williams
380 Madison Ave, 3RD Floor, New York, NY 10017
212-716-3500 Fax: 212-716-3566
e-mail: mtcohen@gvawilliams.com
Web site: www.gvawilliams.com
Michael T Cohen, President & Chief Executive Officer
Real estate brokerage, ownership, sales, leasing, management & consulting

Glenwood Management Corporation
1200 Union Turnpike, New Hyde Park, NY 11040
718-343-6400 Fax: 718-343-0009
Web site: www.glenwoodmanagement.com
Leonard Litwin, President
Property management

Greater Rochester Association of Realtors Inc
930 East Avenue, Rochester, NY 14607
585-292-5000 Fax: 585-292-5008
e-mail: karenw@grar.net
Web site: www.homesteadnet.com
Karen Wingender, Chief Executive Officer

Greater Syracuse Association of Realtors Inc
1020 Seventh North St, Ste 140, Liverpool, NY 13088
315-457-5979 Fax: 315-457-5884
e-mail: fetyko@cnyrealtor.com
Web site: www.cnyrealtor.com
Lynnore Fetyko, Chief Executive Officer

H J Kalikow & Co LLC
101 Park Ave, 25th Fl, New York, NY 10178
212-808-7000 Fax: 212-573-6380
Web site: www.hjkalikow.com
Peter S Kalikow, President
Real estate development

J J Higgins Properties Inc
20 North Main St, Pittsford, NY 14534
585-381-6030 Fax: 585-381-0571
e-mail: jjhigginsproperties@frontiernet.net
Web site: www.jjhigginsproperties.com
John J Higgins, President
Residental properties, relocation, commercial properties, home sales & listings, buyer agency

Landauer Realty Group Inc
55 East 59th Street, 4th Fl, New York, NY 10022
212-326-4880 Fax: 212-375-6811
e-mail: djackson@landauer.com
Web site: www.landauer.com
Deborah A Jackson, Executive Managing Director
Commercial real estate appraisers, analysts & transaction consultants

Policy Areas

Offices and agencies appear in alphabetical order.

MJ Peterson Corporation
501 Audubon Pkwy, Amherst, NY 14228
716-688-1234 Fax: 716-688-5463
e-mail: corporate@mjpeterson.com
Web site: www.mjpeterson.com
Victor L Peterson, Jr, President
Residential, commercial, property management, development

Mancuso Business Development Group
56 Harvester Ave, Batavia, NY 14020
585-343-2800 Fax: 585-343-7096
e-mail: tom@mancusogroup.com
Web site: www.mancusogroup.com
Tom Mancuso, President
Business development services; industrial & office properties

Metro/Colvin Realty Inc
2211 Sheridan Dr, Kenmore, NY 14223
716-874-0110 Fax: 716-874-9015
e-mail: metrocolvin1@aol.com
John Riordan, President
Residential & commercial property

Metro/Horohoe-Leimbach
3199 Delaware Ave, Kenmore, NY 14217
716-873-5404 Fax: 716-873-8901
e-mail: whorohoe@aol.com
Web site: metrohorohoe.com
William Horohoe, Vice President
Residential real estate

NY Commercial Association of Realtors
130 Washington Ave, Albany, NY 12210
518-463-5315 Fax: 518-462-5474
e-mail: nyscar@att.net
Web site: www.nyscarxchange.com
Steven Perfit, President
Commercial real estate

NYS Association of Realtors
130 Washington Ave, Albany, NY 12210-2298
518-463-0300 Fax: 518-462-5474
e-mail: admin@nysar.com
Web site: www.nysar.com
Charles M Staro, Chief Executive Officer

NYS Land Title Association
2 Rector St, Ste 901, New York, NY 10006-1819
212-964-3701 Fax: 212-964-7185
e-mail: nyslta@aol.com
Web site: www.nyslta.org
Sharon Sabol, Executive Vice President
Trade association for title insurance industry

NYS Society of Real Estate Appraisers
130 Washington Ave, Albany, NY 12210-2298
518-463-0300 Fax: 518-462-5474
e-mail: nyssrea@nysar.com
Web site: www.nyrealestateappraisers.com
Domenic Zagaroli, President
Real estate appraisal

Community Bankers Assn of NY State, Mortgages & Real Estate Cmte
New York Community Bank
615 Merrick Ave, Westbury, NY 11590
516-683-4100 Fax: 516-683-8344
Web site: www.mynycb.com
James O'Donovan, Chair

New York Landmarks Conservancy
141 5th Ave, New York, NY 10010
212-995-5260 Fax: 212-995-5268
e-mail: nylandmarks@nylandmarks.org
Web site: www.nylandmarks.org
Peg Breen, President
Technical & financial assistance for preservation & reuse of landmark buildings

New York State Assessors' Association
PO Box 888, Middletown, NY 10940
845-344-0292 Fax: 845-343-8238
e-mail: nysaa@warwick.net
Web site: www.nyassessor.com
Thomas Frey, Executive Secretary
Real property tax issues

Pomeroy Appraisal Associates Inc
Pomeroy Pl, 225 W Jefferson St, Syracuse, NY 13202
315-422-7106 Fax: 315-476-1011
e-mail: dfisher@pomeroyappraisal.com
Web site: pomeroyappraisal.com
Donald A Fisher, MAI, ARA
Real estate appraisal & consultation

R W Bronstein Corporation
3666 Main St, Buffalo, NY 14226
716-835-7400 Fax: 716-835-7419
e-mail: value@bronstein.net
Web site: www.bronstein.net
Richard W Bronstein, President
Real estate, appraisals & auctions; valuation & marketing of all types of realty and chattels

Real Estate Board of New York Inc
570 Lexington Ave, New York, NY 10022
212-532-3120 Fax: 212-481-0122
e-mail: stevenspinola@rebny.com
Web site: www.rebny.com
Steven Spinola, President
Representing real estate professionals & firms in New York City

Realty Advisory Board on Labor Relations
292 Madison Ave, New York, NY 10017
212-889-4100 Fax: 212-889-4105
e-mail: jberg@rabolr.com
Web site: www.rabolr.com
James Berg, President
Labor negotiations for realtors & realty firms

Offices and agencies appear in alphabetical order.

Realty USA
6505 E Quaker Rd, Orchard Park, NY 14127
716-662-2000 Fax: 716-662-3385
e-mail: mwhitehead@realtyusa.com
Web site: www.realtyusa.com
Merle Whitehead, President & Chief Executive Officer
Residential real estate

Red Barn Properties
Six Schoen Pl, Pittsford, NY 14534
585-381-2222 x11 Fax: 585-381-1854
e-mail: estelle@redbarnproperties.com
Web site: www.redbarnproperties.com
Estelle O'Connell, Relocation Director
Specializing in local, national & global residential relocation

Related Companies LP
60 Columbus Circle, 19th Fl, New York, NY 10023
212-421-5333 Fax: 212-801-1036
e-mail: bbeal@related.com
Web site: www.related.com
Bruce A Beal, Jr, Executive Vice President, NY Development Group
Residential & commercial real estate

Robert Schalkenbach Foundation
149 Madison Ave, Ste 601, New York, NY 10016
212-683-6424 Fax: 212-683-6454
e-mail: msullivan@schalkenbach.org
Web site: www.schalkenbach.org
Mark A Sullivan, Acting Executive Director
Land value taxation, real property & economic publications

Roohan Realty
519 Broadway, Saratoga Springs, NY 12866-2208
518-587-4500 Fax: 518-587-4509
e-mail: troohan@roohanrealty.com
Web site: www.roohanrealty.com
J Thomas Roohan, President
Commercial & residential property

Rose Associates Inc
200 Madison Ave, 5th Fl, New York, NY 10016-3998
212-210-6666 Fax: 212-210-6672
e-mail: er@rosenyc.com
Web site: www.rosenyc.com
Adam Rose, President
Commercial & residential real estate development & management

Silverstein Properties Inc
530 Fifth Ave, New York, NY 10036
212-490-0666 Fax: 212-687-0067
Larry A Silverstein, President, Chief Executive Officer
NYC commercial real estate

Sonnenblick-Goldman Company
712 Fifth Ave, New York, NY 10019
212-841-9200 Fax: 212-262-4224
e-mail: asonnenblick@sonngold.com
Web site: www.sonngold.com
Arthur I Sonnenblick, Senior Managing Director
Real estate investment banking

Tishman Speyer Properties
520 Madison Ave, New York, NY 10022
212-715-0300 Fax: 212-319-1745
e-mail: jspeyer@tishmanspeyer.com
Web site: www.tishmanspeyer.com
Jerry I Speyer, President
Owners/builders

United Jewish Appeal-Federation of Jewish Philanthropies
130 E 59th St, New York, NY 10022
212-836-1652 Fax: 212-836-1653
e-mail: flynnc@ujafedny.org
Web site: www.ujafedny.org
John S Ruskay, Executive Vice President & Chief Executive Officer
Real property portfolio management

Offices and agencies appear in alphabetical order.

SOCIAL SERVICES

New York State

GOVERNOR'S OFFICE

Governor's Office

Executive Chamber
State Capitol
Albany, NY 12224
518-474-8390 Fax: 518-474-1513
Web site: www.state.ny.us

Governor:
 George E Pataki 518-474-8390
Executive Director:
 Kara Lanspery 518-474-8390
Secretary to the Governor:
 John P Cahill. 518-474-4246
Deputy Secretary to the Governor for Health & Human Services:
 Mark Kissinger. 518-408-2500
Senior Policy Advisor to the Governor:
 Jeffrey Lovell 518-486-9671
Senior Advisor to the Governor for Women's Issues:
 Lynn Rollins. 212-681-4580
Counsel to the Governor-Attorney General, Budget:
 Richard Platkin. 518-474-8343
Asst Counsel to the Governor-Aging, Advocate for Persons with Disabilities,
 Commn of Quality of Care, Health, Mental Health, OASAS, OMRDD:
 Mark Ustin 518-474-8494
Asst Counsel to the Gov-Battery Pk, Child/Family Svcs, Child/Family
 Council, Family, Housing, Human Rts, Roosevelt Is, Temp/Disabl,
 Women, HFA/MBBA/SONYMA:
 Carolyn Betz Kerr. 518-474-1310
Director, Social Services Programs:
 Renee Rider 518-486-4079
Director, Communications:
 David Catalfamo. 518-474-8418

EXECUTIVE DEPARTMENTS AND RELATED AGENCIES

Aging, Office for the

Two Empire State Plaza
5th Floor
Albany, NY 12223-1251
518-474-5731 Fax: 518-474-0608
Web site: www.aging.state.ny.us

Acting Director:
 Neal Lane. 518-474-4425/fax: 518-474-1398
Deputy Director, Exec Division:
 Laurie Pferr. 518-473-4275
Secretary to Acting Director:
 Christine E Reilly. 518-474-7012
Counsel:
 Vacant 518-473-5796

Public Information Officer:
 Thomas Gallagher 518-474-7158/fax: 518-473-6565
 e-mail: tom.gallagher@ofa.state.ny.us

Advisory Groups

Aging Services Advisory Committee
Constituency Liaison:
 Elaine Richter 518-474-7012/fax: 518-474-1398

Governor's Advisory Committee
Constituency Liaison:
 Elaine Richter 518-474-7012/fax: 518-474-1398

Federal Relations
Staff Liaison:
 Sandra Longworth 518-474-5041/fax: 518-474-1398

Finance & Administration Division
Deputy Director:
 Robert A Bush. 518-474-2631/fax: 518-474-0608
Asst Director:
 James Foy. 518-473-4808
Director, Personnel:
 Mildred Hoghe 518-474-3545
Director, Information Technology Systems:
 Rebecca Stegman 518-474-8896

Local Program Operations
Deputy Director:
 Franklin DeMarinis 518-473-5705/fax: 518-474-0608

Targeting Services & Equal Opportunity Programs
Director:
 Carmen V Cunningham 518-474-5041

Agriculture & Markets Department

10B Airline Dr
Albany, NY 12235
518-457-3880 Fax: 518-457-3087
e-mail: info@agmkt.state.ny.us
Web site: www.agmkt.state.ny.us

Commissioner:
 Nathan Rudgers 518-457-8876
First Deputy Commissioner:
 Ruth A Moore. 518-457-2771
Public Information Officer:
 Jessica Chittenden 518-457-3136
 e-mail: jessica.chittenden@agmkt.state.ny.us

Agricultural Child Care
Program Administrator:
 Steven Greenberg. 518-457-7076

Offices and agencies appear in alphabetical order.

Alcoholism & Substance Abuse Services, Office of

501 7th Ave
8th Fl
New York, NY 10018
646-728-4533

1450 Western Ave
Albany, NY 12203
518-473-3460
Fax: 518-457-5474

Acting Commissioner:
  Shari Noonan 518-457-2061
Executive Deputy Commissioner:
  Vacant 518-457-1758
Counsel:
  Henry F Zwack 518-485-2312
Director, Communications:
  Jennifer Farrell 518-485-1768/fax: 518-485-6014
  e-mail: jenniferfarrell@oasas.state.ny.us
Director, Human Resources Management:
  Thomas M Torino 518-457-2963
Director, Internal Audit:
  Richard Kaplan 518-485-2039
Director, Management & Information Services:
  David Gardam 518-485-2351
Affirmative Action Officer:
  Henry Gonzalez 518-457-2963
Public Information Officer:
  Joseph Morrissey 518-485-1768
  e-mail: josephmorrissey@oasas.state.ny.us

Administration Division

Assoc Commissioner:
  Michael Lawler 518-457-5312

Budget Management
Director:
  Jay Runkel 518-485-2193

Capital Management
Director:
  Laurie Felter 518-457-2545

Federal Relations & Policy Analysis
Director:
  Reba Architzel 518-485-1366

Fiscal Administration & Support Services
Director:
  Vito Manzella 518-457-4742

Health Care Financing & 3rd Party Reimbursement
Director:
  Nicholas Colamaria 518-485-2207

Human Resources Management
Director:
  Thomas Torino 518-457-2963

Management & Information Services
Director:
  David Gardam 518-485-2351

Prevention Services Division

Associate Commissioner:
  Frances M Harding 518-485-6022

Field Operations
Director:
  Edward Freeman 518-485-1660

Program Design, System Development & Implementation
Director:
  Frederick Meservey 518-485-2123

Science/Technology Transfer & Planning
Director:
  John Ernst 518-485-2132

Special Populations & Other Addictions
Director:
  William Barnette 518-457-6206

Standards & Quality Assurance Division

Associate Commissioner:
  Neil Grogin 518-485-2257
Client Advocacy:
  Michael Yorio 800-553-5790

Certification
Manager:
  Elliott Lefkowitz 518-485-2251

Quality Assurance
Director:
  Douglas Rosenberry 518-485-2260

Technical Assistance
Manager:
  Joseph Burke 646-485-2249

Workforce Development
Manager:
  William Lachanski 518-485-2033

Treatment Services Division

Acting Associate Commissioner:
  Timothy P Williams 518-485-2322

Addiction Planning & Grants Development
Director:
  Robert Ball 518-457-5989

Addiction Treatment
Director:
  Thomas Nightingale 518-457-7077

Evaluation & Practice Improvement
Director:
  Alan Kott 518-485-7189

Children & Family Services, Office of

52 Washington St
Rensselaer, NY 12144
518-473-7793 Fax: 518-486-7550
Web site: www.ocfs.state.ny.us

Commissioner:
  John A Johnson 518-473-8437
Executive Deputy Commissioner:
  Roger Biagi 518-474-7768
Assist Commissioner, Public Affairs:
  Sandra A Brown 518-402-3130
  e-mail: cfspio@dfa.state.ny.us
Acting Director, Strategic Planning & Policy Development:
  Nancy Martinez 518-473-1776
Director, Equal Opportunity & Diversity Development:
  Mikki Ward-Harper 518-474-3715

Offices and agencies appear in alphabetical order.

Deputy Commissioner, Information Technology:
William Travis 518-402-3194

Administration Division
Deputy Commissioner:
Susan A Costello 518-486-7218

Audit & Quality Control
Director, Audit & Quality Control:
David Dorpfeld. 518-402-3985
External, Contract & Fiscal Audits:
Don Nicklas 518-486-1118
Internal Audits:
Lynn Dobriko. 518-473-2439
Director, Contract Management:
Karen Lopiccolo. 518-486-7224
Asst Director, Contract Management:
Harry Ritter 518-473-6001

Financial Management
Associate Commissioner:
Edna Mae Reilly. 518-486-1110
Director, Budget:
Deborah Hanor. 518-474-1361
Director, Financial Operations:
John Murray. 518-402-3380
Director, Grants Management:
Susan Kemp 518-473-1085
Director, Revenue & Rates Development:
Daniel Zeidman 518-474-9572

Human Resources
Associate Commissioner:
Nicole McCulloch 518-473-8453
Director, Training:
Peter Miraglia. 518-474-9645
Director, Human Resources:
John Monteiro 518-402-3211
Director, Labor Relations:
Walter Greenberg. 518-486-4240
Director, Personnel:
Charles Breiner. 518-474-5207

Management & Support Division
Assoc Commissioner:
Stephanie Donato. 518-402-3208
Director, Capital Services:
Raymond Beaudoin 518-473-0487
Director, Management Services:
Pamela Relyea 518-402-3926
Director, Security & Emergency Preparedness:
Joseph Impicciatore 518-402-3984

Commission for the Blind & Visually Handicapped
Associate Commissioner:
Thomas Robertson 518-473-1801
Deputy Director:
Brian Daniels 518-474-7299
Director, Program Evaluation, Support & Business Svcs:
Kenneth Galarneau. 518-474-7812
Director, Field Operations:
Priscilla Wrobel 518-473-9685
Director, Business Enterprise Program:
Debra Lomma. 518-474-5198

Albany
155 Washington Ave, 2nd Fl, Albany, NY 12210-2329
Manager:
Dale Keenan 518-473-1675

Buffalo
295 Main St, Room 590, Buffalo, NY 14203

Manager:
Barbara Kellerman. 716-847-3516
Supervisor:
Deborah Jauch 716-847-3518

Hempstead
50 Clinton St, Suite 208, Hempstead, NY 11550
Manager:
Anthony D'Angelo 516-564-4311

New York City
20 Exchange Pl, 2nd Fl, New York, NY 10005
Regional Coordinator:
Daniel Callahan. 212-825-5721
Supervisor:
Joanne Jack 212-383-1740
Manager:
Robin Gilman 212-825-5721
Elderly Services:
Vacant. 212-961-4440

Rensselaer
52 Washington St, South 201, Rensselaer, NY 12144
Supervisor:
Alan Gatoff 518-474-7198

Rochester Outstation
259 Monroe Ave, Room 303, Rochester, NY 14607
Manager:
Vacant. 585-238-8110

Syracuse
The Atrium, 2 Clinton Square, Syracuse, NY 13202
Manager:
Dennis Donahue 315-423-5417

White Plains
445 Hamilton Ave, Room 503, White Plains, NY 10601
Manager:
William Kane. 914-992-5370

Development & Prevention Services Division
Deputy Commissioner:
Larry Brown. 518-402-3108

Bureau of Early Childhood Services
Director:
Suzanne Sennett. 518-474-9454

Central Services
Associate Commissioner:
Christine Heywood. 518-402-3213

Adult Protective Services
Assistant Commissioner:
Susan Somers. 518-473-6446

State Adoption Services
Director:
Lee Lounsbury. 518-474-9406
Albany Regional Director:
William McLaughlin 518-486-7078
Buffalo Regional Director:
Linda Brown 716-847-3145
Metropolitan Regional Director:
Fred Levitan. 212-383-1788
Rochester Regional Director:
Linda Kurtz 585-238-8201
Syracuse Regional Director:
Jack Klump 315-423-1200
Yonkers Regional Director:
Patricia Sheehy 914-377-2080

State Central Registry
Director:
David Peters. 518-474-9607

Offices and agencies appear in alphabetical order.

Field Operations
Associate Commissioner:
  Christine Heywood 518-474-9465
Institute Abuse
  Director:
    Shelley Murphy 518-402-6546
Native American Services
  Director:
    Kim Thomas 716-847-3123

Program Support (Training, Local Planning, Monitoring & Compliance)
Associate Commissioner:
  Richard Nells 518-474-9431

Legal Affairs Division
Deputy Commissioner & General Counsel:
  Gail Gordon 518-473-8418
Deputy Counsel:
  John Ouimet 518-473-8418
Administrative Hearings:
  Steven Connolly 212-383-1671
Hearings & Litigation Appeals:
  Diane Deacon 518-473-8411
House Counsel:
  Charles Carson 518-474-9752
Legislation & Special Projects:
  Kathleen DeCataldo 518-473-9551
Ombudsman:
  Robert Dodig 518-473-8411

Office of Youth Development
Asst Commissioner:
  Sally Herrick 518-473-8455

Advantage AfterSchool Program
Director:
  Carole Miller 518-473-4463

Bureau of Compliance
Director:
  Matt Murell 518-402-3830

Office of National & Community Service / Americorps
Director:
  Matt Murell 518-473-8882

Youth Development Field Operations
Director & Regional Coordinator, Plattsburgh:
  Larry Pasti 518-561-8740
Regional Coordinator, Albany:
  Steve Conti 518-473-5294
Regional Coordinator, Buffalo:
  Andrew Johnson 716-847-3323
Regional Coordinator, New York City:
  Madra Spizer 212-383-4703
Regional Coordinator, Hempstead:
  Joseph R Marano 516-564-4430
Regional Coordinator, Syracuse:
  Denise Dyer 315-423-5486

Rehabilitative Services
Deputy Commissioner:
  Ed Ausborn 518-473-1786/fax: 518-486-7196

Facilities
Facility Coordinator:
  Ruth Noriega 212-961-4121
Facility Coordinator:
  Edgardo Lopez 315-479-8356

Facility Coordinator:
  Tony Hough 845-561-5620
ACA Accreditation Coordinator:
  Nelson Lopes 518-473-7279
Supervisor, Facilities Fire Safety:
  Kevin Duncan 518-473-4488
Adirondack Residential Center
  518 Norrisville Rd, Schuyler Falls, NY 12985
  Director:
    Todd Johnson 518-643-9444/fax: 518-643-9581
Adirondack Wilderness Challenge
  516 Norrisville Rd, Schuyler Falls, NY 12985
  Director:
    Sandra Strother 518-643-7188/fax: 518-643-0349
Allen Residential Center
  Rt 10, South Kortright, NY 13842
  Director:
    Ruben Reyes 607-538-9121/fax: 607-538-9509
Annsville Residential Center
  10011 Taberg-Florence Rd, Taberg, NY 13471
  Director:
    Richard Hogeboom 315-245-1720/fax: 315-245-2331
Auburn Residential Center
  6734 Pine Ridge Rd, Auburn, NY 13021
  Director:
    Pamela Klemme 315-253-2789/fax: 315-252-3858
Brace Residential Center
  10699 State Highway 8, Masonville, NY 13804
  Director:
    Larry Bleck 607-265-3291/fax: 607-265-3483
Brentwood Residential Center
  1230 Commack Rd, Dix Hills, NY 11746
  Director:
    Charlotte Morales 631-667-1188/fax: 631-667-1213
Brooklyn Residential Center
  1125 Carroll St, Brooklyn, NY 11225
  Director:
    Janice Pressley 718-773-2041/fax: 718-604-4648
Brookwood Secure Center
  PO Box 265, Claverack, NY 12513
  Director:
    E Patrick Sullivan 518-851-3211/fax: 518-851-2685
Cass Residential Center
  16 Camp Cass Road, Rensselaerville, NY 12147
  Director:
    Douglas Cannistra 518-797-3781/fax: 518-797-5133
Cattaraugus Residential Center
  575 Spittler Lane, Limestone, NY 14753
  Director:
    Geoffrey Holt 716-925-7051/fax: 716-925-7055
Ella McQueen Residential Center
  41 Howard Ave, Brooklyn, NY 11221
  Director:
    Cheryle Means 718-574-2911/fax: 718-574-2930
Goshen Residential Center
  97 Cross Road, Goshen, NY 10924
  Director:
    Roger Rascoe 845-615-3000/fax: 845-615-3016
Great Valley Residential Center
  6619 Mutton Hollow Rd, Great Valley, NY 14741
  Director:
    Richard Emke 716-945-3420/fax: 716-945-4293
Harlem Valley Secure Center
  PO Box 320, Wingdale, NY 12594-0320
  Director:
    Anthony Hough 845-832-6480/fax: 845-832-3210
Harriet Tubman Residential Center
  6706 Pine Ridge Rd, Auburn, NY 13021

Policy Areas

Offices and agencies appear in alphabetical order.

Director:
    Marilyn Riley 315-255-3481/fax: 315-255-3485
Highland Residential Center
629 N Chodikee Lake Rd, Highland, NY 12528
Director:
    A Farooq Mallick 845-691-6006/fax: 845-691-6570
Industry Limited Secure/Secure School
375 Rush-Scottsville Rd, Rush, NY 14543
Director:
    Gary Almond 585-533-2600/fax: 585-533-2822
Lansing Residential Center
270 Auburn Rd, Lansing, NY 14882
Director:
    Theresa Rodgers 607-533-4262/fax: 607-533-7309
Louis Gossett Jr Residential Center
250 Auburn Rd, Lansing, NY 14882
Director:
    Joseph Impicciatore 607-533-5000/fax: 607-533-5012
MacCormick Secure Center
300 South Rd, Brooktondale, NY 14817
Director:
    Alvin Lollie 607-539-7121/fax: 607-539-6588
Middletown Residential Center
393 County Rd 78, Middletown, NY 10940
Director:
    Maria Galarza 845-342-3936/fax: 845-342-1468
Pyramid Reception Center
470 East 161st St, Bronx, NY 10451
Director:
    Patricia Moses 718-993-5350/fax: 718-993-7831
Red Hook Residential Center
531 Turkey Hill Rd, Red Hook, NY 12571
Director:
    Edward Figueroa 845-758-4151/fax: 845-758-4508
Sgt Henry Johnson Youth Leadership Academy
PO Box 132, South Kortright, NY 13842-0132
Director:
    Ruben Reyes 607-538-1401/fax: 607-538-1403
Southern New York Residential Center
170 East 210th St, Bronx, NY 10467
Director:
    Joseph Dennison 718-798-6660/fax: 718-882-2430
Staten Island Residential Center
1133 Forest Hill Rd, Staten Island, NY 10314
Director:
    Maureen Downs 718-761-6033/fax: 718-698-6620
Taberg Residential Center
10011 Taberg-Florence Rd, Taberg, NY 13471
Director:
    Aaron Gregory 315-245-0084/fax: 315-245-0088
Tryon Girls Center . . . . fax: 518-762-2689
881 County Hwy 107, Johnstown, NY 12095
Director:
    Merle Brandwene 518-762-2331 x212
Tryon Residential Center
881 County Highway 107, Johnstown, NY 12095
Director:
    Lee Wynn 518-762-4681 x324/fax: 518-762-7209

Program Services
Associate Commissioner:
    Inez Nieves-Evans 518-486-6766
Bureau of Behavioral Health Services
Director:
    Edward R Shaw 518-402-7653
Bureau of Counseling Services
Acting Dir, Counseling Projects:
    Thomas Hoeg 518-486-7098

Bureau of Education & Employment Services
Director:
    Marilyn Watkins 518-473-7489
Bureau of Health Services
Director:
    Michael D Cohen 518-474-9560
Bureau of Ministerial Services
Director:
    Father Kofi Amissah 518-474-9400
Bureau of Priority Initiatives
Director:
    Leta Smith 518-402-7653
Program Support & Community Partnerships
Associate Commissioner:
    Michael Rose 518-473-4411
Aftercare Services
Director:
    Georgette Furey 518-474-1308
Upstate Aftercare Operations:
    Daniel Maxwell 518-486-5513
Downstate Aftercare Operations:
    Cheryl Collins-Rashid 212-961-4116
Classification & Movement Bureau
Director:
    Robert Pollack 518-473-8985
Management & Program Support
Director:
    Suzanne Norsby-Ovenshire 518-473-5325

Council on Children & Families
5 Empire State Plaza
Ste 2810
Albany, NY 12223
518-473-3652 Fax: 518-473-2570
e-mail: council@ccf.state.ny.us
Web site: www.ccf.state.ny.us

Executive Director:
    Alana M Sweeny 518-474-5522
    e-mail: alana.sweeny@ccf.state.ny.us
Counsel:
    Beth O'Connor 518-473-3652
Public Information/Personnel & Admin Assistant:
    Donna Ned 518-474-5522/fax: 518-473-7568
    e-mail: donna.ned@ccf.state.ny.us

Bureau of Policy, Research & Planning
Director:
    Deborah Benson 518-473-3652

Inter-Agency Coordination & Case Resolution Bureau
Director:
    Janet Sapio-Mayta 518-473-3652

Crime Victims Board
845 Central Ave
Rm 107
Albany, NY 12206-1504
518-457-8727 or 800-247-8035 Fax: 518-457-8658
e-mail: cvbinfo@cvb.state.ny.us
Web site: www.cvb.state.ny.us

55 Hanson Place
10th Fl

Offices and agencies appear in alphabetical order.

Brooklyn, NY 11217
718-923-4325
Fax: 718-923-4352

65 Court St
Rm 308
Buffalo, NY 14202
716-847-7992
Fax: 716-847-7995

Chairwoman:
  Joan A Cusack 718-923-4331
Commissioner:
  Christina Hernandez 518-485-5719
Commissioner:
  Charles F Marotta 718-923-4336
Commissioner:
  Jacqueline C Mattina 716-847-7948
Commissioner:
  Benedict J Monachino 718-923-4400
General Counsel:
  Everett Mayhew, Jr. 518-457-8066
Executive Director:
  Virginia A Miller 518-457-9320
Director, MIS:
  David Loomis 518-457-8050
Contract Supervisor:
  Ron Dickens 518-485-2763

Developmental Disabilities Planning Council

155 Washington Ave
2nd Fl
Albany, NY 12210
518-486-7505 or 800-395-DDPC Fax: 518-402-3505
Web site: www.ddpc.state.ny.us

Executive Director:
  Sheila M Carey 518-486-7505
Deputy Executive Director:
  Anna Lobosco 518-486-7505
Secretary to Exec Director:
  Lois M Goodwill 518-486-7505
Public Information Officer:
  Thomas F Lee 518-486-7505

Education Department

State Education Building
89 Washington Ave
Albany, NY 12234
518-474-3852 Fax: 518-486-5631
Web site: www.nysed.gov

Commissioner, University President:
  Richard P Mills 518-474-5844
  e-mail: rmills@mail.nysed.gov
Asst to the Commissioner:
  Peggy Rivers 518-474-5845
  e-mail: privers@mail.nysed.gov
Counsel & Deputy Commissioner, Legal Affairs:
  Kathy A Ahearn 518-474-6400
  e-mail: kahearn@mail.nysed.gov

Office of the Professions . . . . fax: 518-473-2056
  89 Washington Ave, EB, 2nd Fl, West Mezz, Albany, NY 12234

Fax: 518-473-2056
  Web site: www.op.nysed.gov
Deputy Commissioner:
  Johanna Duncan-Poitier 518-474-3817 x470
  e-mail: opdepcom@mail.nysed.gov
Coordinator, Customer Service:
  Tony Lofrumento 518-474-3817 x570
  e-mail: op4info@mail.nysed.gov

Office of Professional Responsibility
Executive Director:
  Frank Munoz 518-474-3817 x440
  e-mail: opexdir@mail.nysed.gov

Professional Education Program Review
Supervisor:
  Gail Rosettie 518-474-3817 x360
  e-mail: opprogs@mail.nysed.gov

Professional Licensing Services
Director:
  Robert G Bentley 518-474-3817 x340
  e-mail: opdpls@mail.nysed.gov

Vocational & Educational Services for Individuals with Disabilities Office (Vesid) . . . . fax: 518-474-8802

One Commerce Plaza, Rm 1606, Albany, NY 12234
Fax: 518-474-8802
Web site: www.vesid.nysed.gov
Deputy Commissioner:
  Rebecca Cort 518-474-2714
  e-mail: rcort@mail.nysed.gov
Asst Commissioner:
  Edward Placke 518-473-4818

Fiscal & Administrative Services
Coordinator:
  Rosemary Ellis Johnson 518-486-4038

Program Development & Support Svcs / Special Ed Policy & Partnerships
Coordinator:
  Fredric DeMay 518-486-7462
  Deaf & Hard of Hearing Services
    Manager:
      Dorothy Steele 518-474-2925
  Lifelong Services
    Supervisor:
      Daniel J Ryan 518-486-7462
  Special Education Policy & Partnerships
    Supervisor:
      Candace Shyer 518-473-2878

Quality Assurance - Statewide Special Education
Acting Statewide Coordinator:
  Daniel Johnson 518-486-6221

State School for the Blind at Batavia
  2A Richmond Ave, Batavia, NY 14020
Superintendent:
  Jennifer Spas Ervin 716-343-5384

Vocational Rehabilitation Operations
Acting Director, District Ofc Administration:
  Debora Brown-Grant 518-473-1626
  e-mail: dbrowngr@mail.nysed.gov
Asst Director, District Ofc Administration:
  William Deschenes 518-486-1626
  e-mail: wdeschen@mail.nysed.gov

Offices and agencies appear in alphabetical order.

Policy Areas

Labor Department

Building 12, Room 500
State Campus
Albany, NY 12240
518-457-2741 Fax: 518-457-6908
e-mail: nysdol@labor.state.ny.us
Web site: www.labor.state.ny.us

345 Hudson St, Ste 8301
Box 662, Mail Stop 01
New York, NY 10014-0662
212-352-6000
Fax: 212-352-6824

Commissioner:
   Linda Angello.....................................518-457-2746
Executive Deputy Commissioner:
   Dennis Ryan......................................518-457-4318
Counsel:
   Jerome A Tracy....................................518-457-7069
Inspector General:
   Brian Sanvidge....................................518-457-7012
Director for Communications:
   Robert Lillpopp..................518-457-5519/fax: 518-485-1126

Employment Services Division
Director:
   Karen Papandrea...............................518-457-3584
   Employer Services
   Director:
      Timothy O'Keefe.........................518-457-6821
   Veterans Employment Service
   Program Coordinator:
      Earl Wallace............................518-457-1343

Unemployment Insurance Division
Director:
   Robert Davison.................518-457-2878/fax: 518-485-8604

Workforce Development & Training Division
Director:
   Margaret Moree................518-457-0380/fax: 518-457-9526

Workforce Protection, Standards & Licensing

Deputy Commissioner:
   Connie Varcasia..................................518-457-4317

Labor Standards Division
Director:
   Richard Cucolo...................................518-457-2460

Safety & Health Division
Director:
   Anthony Germano...............518-457-3518/fax: 518-457-1519

Prevention of Domestic Violence, Office for the

80 Wolf Rd
Ste 406
Albany, NY 12205
518-457-5800 Fax: 518-457-5810
Web site: www.opdv.state.ny.us

Executive Director:
   Sherry Frohman...................................518-457-5800
General Counsel & Agency Affairs:
   Wendy Juracka-Maher.............................518-457-5800

Director, Training & Policy Development Unit:
   Gwen Wright.....................................518-457-5916
New York City Program:
   Sujata Warrier...................................212-417-4477
Administrative Officer:
   Linda Cassidy....................................518-457-7995
Public Information Officer:
   Suzanne Cecala...................................518-457-5744
   e-mail: scecala@opdv.state.ny.us

Temporary & Disability Assistance, Office of

40 N Pearl St
Albany, NY 12243
518-474-9003 or 800-342-3004 Fax: 518-474-7870
e-mail: nyspio@dfa.state.ny.us
Web site: www.otda.state.ny.us

Commissioner:
   Robert Doar....................518-474-4152/fax: 518-486-6255
   e-mail: robert.doar@dfa.state.ny.us
Executive Deputy:
   Sandra Pettinato.................................518-474-9475
Director, Office of Intergovernmental & External Affairs:
   Lisa Irving......................................518-474-7420

Budget Management & Finance
Director:
   Michael Normile..................................518-474-0183

Child Support Enforcement Division
Deputy Commissioner:
   Margot Bean.....................................518-474-9081

Disability Determinations Division
Deputy Commissioner:
   David Avenius....................................518-473-0070

Information Technology Services
Director:
   Robert Mastro....................................518-473-7858

Legal Affairs Division
Legal/Acting General Counsel:
   John Bailly......................................518-474-9502

Program Support & Quality Improvement
Deputy Commissioner:
   Mary Meister.....................................518-473-3912

Public Information
Asst Commissioner:
   John B Madden...................518-474-9516/fax: 518-486-6935
   e-mail: nyspio@dfa.state.ny.us

Temporary Assistance Division
Deputy Commissioner:
   Russell Sykes....................518-474-9222/fax: 518-474-5281

Welfare Inspector General, Office of NYS

22 Cortlandt St
11th Fl
New York, NY 10007
212-417-5822 Fax: 212-417-5849

40 North Pearl St
Section 10B

Offices and agencies appear in alphabetical order.

Albany, NY 12224
518-474-9636
Fax: 518-486-6148

Inspector General:
   Paul Balukas....................................212-417-5840
Deputy Inspector General:
   Pasqualino Russo 212-417-5860
Counsel:
   Andrew J Weiss 212-417-2395
Chief Investigator:
   Joseph R Bucci..................................212-417-2026
Special Asst Attorney General:
   Joseph Burruano.................................212-417-2051
Administrative Asst to Inspector General:
   Wanda Hernandez 212-417-5822

NEW YORK STATE LEGISLATURE

See Legislative Branch in Section 1 for additional Standing Committee and Subcommittee information.

Assembly Standing Committees

Aging
Chair:
   Steven C Englebright (D)...........................518-455-4804
Ranking Minority Mbr:
   Andrew P Raia (R)................................518-455-5952

Alcoholism & Drug Abuse
Chair:
   Jeffrey Dinowitz (D)..............................518-455-5965
Ranking Minority Member:
   Jack Quinn (R) 518-455-4462

Children & Families
Chair:
   William Scarborough (D)...........................518-455-4451
Ranking Minority Member:
   Joseph A Errigo (R) 518-455-5662

Social Services
Chair:
   Deborah J Glick (D)...............................518-455-4841

Ranking Minority Member:
   Vincent Ignizio (R)...............................518-455-4495

Assembly Task Forces

Puerto Rican/Hispanic Task Force
Chair:
   Peter M Rivera (D)...............................518-455-5102
Co-Chair:
   Vito J Lopez....................................518-455-5537

Women's Issues, Task Force on
Chair:
   Joan L Millman (D) 518-455-5426
Coordinator:
   Jean Emery 518-455-3632/fax: 518-455-4574

Senate Standing Committees

Aging
Chair:
   Martin J Golden (R) 518-455-2730
Ranking Minority Member:
   Carl Kruger (D) 518-455-2460

Alcoholism & Drug Abuse
Chair:
   Vacant 518-455-3563
Ranking Minority Member:
   Ruben Diaz, Sr (D)...............................518-455-2511

Children & Families
Chair:
   Mary Lou Rath (R)...............................518-455-3161
Ranking Minority Member:
   Velmanette Montgomery (D)......................518-455-3451

Social Services
Chair:
   Raymond A Meier (R) 518-455-3334
Ranking Minority Member:
   Velmanette Montgomery (D)......................518-455-3451

U.S. Government

EXECUTIVE DEPARTMENTS AND RELATED AGENCIES

Corporation for National & Community Service
Web site: www.cns.gov

New York Program Office
   Federal Bldg, 1 Clinton Sq, Ste 900, Albany, NY 12207
State Director:
   Donna M Smith...................518-431-4150/fax: 518-431-4154
   e-mail: ny@cns.gov

Social Security Administration
Web site: www.socialsecurity.gov

Region 2—New York ....fax: 212-264-1444
   26 Federal Plz, Rm 40-120, New York, NY 10278
Regional Commissioner:
   Beatrice M Disman..............................212-264-3915
Deputy Regional Commissioner:
   Paul M Doersam.................................212-264-3915
Asst Regional Commissioner, Management & Operations Support:
   Julio Infiesta 212-264-2507
Asst Regional Commissioner, Processing Center Operations:
   Anne Jacobosky 718-557-5000

Offices and agencies appear in alphabetical order.

Office of Hearings & Appeals
Regional Chief Administrative Law Judge:
  G Stephen Wright 212-264-4036

Office of Quality Assurance
Director:
  Susan Pike 212-264-2827

Office of the General Counsel
Chief Counsel:
  Barbara Spivak 212-264-3650

Program Operations Center
Director:
  Dennis Moss. 212-264-4004

Public Affairs
Regional Communications Director:
  John E Shallman 212-264-2500/fax: 212-264-1444

US Department of Health & Human Services
Web site: www.os.dhhs.gov; www.hhs.gov/region2/

Administration for Children & Families . . . . fax: 212-264-4881
26 Federal Plaza, Rm 4114, New York, NY 10278
Fax: 212-264-4881
Web site: www.acf.hhs.gov
Regional Administrator:
  MaryAnn Higgins 212-264-2890 x103
  e-mail: mhiggins@acf.hhs.gov

Administration on Aging . . . . fax: 212-264-0114
26 Federal Plaza, Rm 38-102, New York, NY 10278
212-264-2976 Fax: 212-264-0114
Web site: www.aoa.gov
Vacant

Centers for Disease Control & Prevention
Web site: www.cdc.gov

Agency for Toxic Substances & Disease Registry (ATSDR)-EPA Region 2
290 Broadway, 28th Fl, New York, NY 10007
Web site: www.atsdr.cdc.gov
Senior Regional Representative:
  Arthur Block 212-637-4305/fax: 212-637-4942

New York Quarantine Station
Terminal 4E, Rm 219 016, JFK Airport, Jamaica, NY 11430-1081
Officer-in-Charge:
  Margaret A Becker 718-553-1685/fax: 718-553-1524

Centers for Medicare & Medicaid Services
26 Federal Plaza, Rm 3811, New York, NY 10278
Web site: www.cms.hhs.gov
Regional Administrator:
  James T Kerr 212-616-2205/fax: 212-264-6189
  e-mail: jkerr@cms.hhs.gov
Deputy Regional Administrator:
  Gilbert Kunken 212-616-2205/fax: 212-264-6189
  e-mail: gkunken@cms.hhs.gov

Medicaid and Children's Health (DMCH)
Associate Regional Administrator:
  Sue Kelly. 212-616-2428/fax: 212-264-6814
  e-mail: skelly@cms.hhs.gov

Medicare Financial Management (DMFM)
Associate Regional Administrator:
  Peter Reisman 212-616-2505/fax: 212-264-2790
  e-mail: preisman@cms.hhs.gov

Medicare Operations Division (DMO)
Associate Regional Administrator:
  Jose Mirabal 212-616-2333/fax: 212-264-2665
  e-mail: jmirabal@cms.hhs.gov

Food & Drug Administration
Web site: www.fda.gov

Northeast Region
158-15 Liberty Ave, Jamaica, NY 11433
Regional Director:
  Diana Kolaitis 718-662-5416/fax: 718-662-5434
  New York District Office
  District Director:
    Jerome Woyshner 718-662-5447/fax: 718-662-5665
  Northeast Regional Laboratory
  158-15 Liberty Ave, Queens, NY 11433
  Director:
    Vacant 718-662-5450/fax: 718-662-5439

Health Resources & Svcs Admin Office of Performance Review . . . . fax: 212-264-2673
26 Federal Plaza, Rm 3337, New York, NY 10278
Regional Division Director:
  Ron Moss 212-264-2664
  e-mail: robert.moss@hrsa.hhs.gov
Operations Director:
  Margaret Lee 212-264-2571
  e-mail: margaret.lee@hrsa.hhs.gov
Director, Ofc of Engineering Services:
  Emilio Pucillo 212-264-3600
  e-mail: emilio.pucillo@hrsa.hhs.gov

Indian Health Services-Area Office . . . . fax: 615-467-1501
711 Stewarts Ferry Pike, Nashville, TN 37214-2634
Director:
  Richie Grinnell 615-467-1500

Office of Secretary's Regional Representative-Region 2-NY . . . . fax: 212-264-3620
26 Federal Plaza, Rm 3835, New York, NY 10278
Regional Director:
  Deborah Konopko 212-264-4600
  e-mail: deborah.konopko@hhs.gov
Sr Intergovernmental Affairs Specialist:
  Dennis Gonzalez. 212-264-4600
  e-mail: dennis.gonzalez@hhs.gov
Intergovernmental Affairs Specialist:
  Katherine Williams. 212-264-4600
  e-mail: katherine.williams@hhs.gov

Office for Civil Rights. . . . . fax: 212-264-3039
26 Federal Plaza, Rm 3312, New York, NY 10278
Fax: 212-264-3039
Web site: www.hhs.gov/ocr
Regional Manager:
  Michael Carter. 212-264-3313/fax: 212-264-3039
Deputy Regional Manager:
  Linda Colon 212-264-3313

Office of General Counsel
26 Federal Plaza, Rm 3908, New York, NY 10278
Chief Counsel:
  Annette H Blum 212-264-6373
  e-mail: annette.blum@hhs.gov

Office of Inspector General
Regional Inspector General, Audit:
  Timothy Horgan 212-264-4620
  e-mail: t.horgan@oig.hhs.gov

Offices and agencies appear in alphabetical order.

Regional Inspector General & Regional Coordinator, Investigations:
Brian Smith 212-264-1691
e-mail: b.smith@oig.hhs.gov
Acting Regional Inspector General, Evaluations & Inspections:
Jodi Nudelman 212-264-1998
e-mail: lragone@oig.hhs.gov

Office of Public Health & Science
26 Federal Plaza, Rm 3835, New York, NY 10278
Acting Regional Health Administrator:
Robert Davidson. 212-264-2560
e-mail: rdavidson@osophs.dhhs.gov
Deputy Regional Health Administrator:
Robert L Davidson 212-264-2560
e-mail: rdavidson@osophs.dhhs.gov
Regional Family Planning Consultant:
Robin Lane. 212-264-3935
e-mail: rlane@osophs.hhs.gov
Regional Minority Health Consultant:
Claude Colimon 212-264-2560
Regional Women's Health Coordinator:
Sandra Estepa. 212-264-2560

U.S. CONGRESS

See U.S. Congress Chapter for additional Standing Committee and Subcommittee information.

House of Representatives Standing Committees

Ways & Means
Chair:
William M Thomas (R-CA) 202-225-2915

Ranking Minority Member:
Charles B Rangel (D-NY) 202-225-4365
New York Delegate:
Michael R McNulty (D). 202-225-5076
New York Delegate:
Thomas M Reynolds (R) 202-225-5265

Subcommittee
Social Security
Chair:
Jim McCrery (R-LA). 202-225-2777
Ranking Minority Member:
Sander M Levin (D-MI) 202-225-4961

Senate Standing Committees

Health, Education, Labor & Pensions
Chair:
Michael Enzi (R-WY) 202-224-3424
Ranking Minority Member:
Edward M Kennedy (D-MA) 202-224-4543
New York Delegate:
Hillary Rodham Clinton (D-NY) 202-224-4451

Special Committee on Aging
Chair:
Larry E Craig (R-ID) 202-224-2752
Ranking Minority Member:
Daniel Akaka (D-HI) 202-224-6361

Private Sector

AARP
780 3rd Ave, Fl 33, New York, NY 10017-2024
866-227-7442 Fax: 212-644-6390
Web site: www.aarp.org
Lois Aronstein, NY State Director
AARP

Abilities Inc, National Center for Disability Services
201 IU Willets Rd, Albertson, NY 11507-1599
516-465-1400 or 516-747-5355 (TTY) Fax: 516-465-3757
e-mail: ftishman@abilitiesinc.org
Web site: www.abilitiesinc.org
Charles W Harles, Executive Director
Provides comprehensive services to help individuals with disabilities reach their employment goals; provides support services & technical assistance to employers who hire persons with disabilities

Action for a Better Community Inc
550 E Main St, Rochester, NY 14604
585-325-5116 or 585-295-1726 Fax: 585-325-9108
e-mail: fcaldwell@abcinfo.org
Web site: www.abcinfo.org
Freddie Caldwell, Deputy Director
Advocacy for programs enabling the low-income to become self-sufficient; social services for the needy

Agenda for Children Tomorrow
c/o Administration for Children's Servic, 2 Washington St, 20th Fl, New York, NY 10004
212-487-8284 or 212-487-8285 Fax: 212-487-8581
e-mail: actnet1@earthlink.net
Web site: www.actnyc.org
Eric B Brettschneider, Executive Director
Public, private & community collaboration to identify, plan for & deliver social & community services to families

Alliance - Catholic Charities
1654 W Onondaga St, Syracuse, NY 13204
315-424-1880 Fax: 315-424-1052
Mark Clary, Director, Child Abuse Prevention Program
Coordinate services for cases where child abuse has occurred or is likely to occur

American Red Cross in Greater NY
150 Amsterdam Ave, New York, NY 10023
212-875-2021 Fax: 212-875-2309
e-mail: saundersr@arcgny.org
Web site: www.nyredcross.org
Rowena Saunders, Executive Director

Offices and agencies appear in alphabetical order.

American Red Cross in NYS
33 Everett Rd, Albany, NY 12205-1437
518-458-8111 x3021 Fax: 518-459-8262
e-mail: striar@redcrossneny.org
Gary Striar, Director, State Relations

Asian American Federation of New York
120 Wall St, 3rd Fl, New York, NY 10005
212-344-5878 Fax: 212-344-5636
e-mail: info@aafny.org
Web site: www.aafny.org
Cao K. O, Executive Director
Nonprofit leadership organization for member health & human services agencies serving the Asian American community

Asian Americans for Equality
277 Grand St, 3rd FL, New York, NY 10002
212-680-1374 Fax: 212-680-1815
e-mail: info@aafe.org
Web site: www.aafe.org
Christopher Kui, Executive Director
Equal opportunities for minorities; affordable housing development, homeownership counseling, immigration services, housing rights

Berkshire Farm Center & Services for Youth
13640 Route 22, Canaan, NY 12029
518-781-4567 Fax: 518-781-4577
e-mail: jdecker@berkshirefarm.org
Web site: www.berkshirefarm.org
Rose W Washington, Executive Director
Multi-function agency for troubled youth & families

Big Brothers Big Sisters of NYC
223 East 30th St, New York, NY 10016
212-686-2042 Fax: 212-779-1221
e-mail: help@bigsnyc.org
Web site: www.bigsnyc.org
Allan Luks, Executive Director
Providing disadvantaged youth with one-to-one, long-term relationships with a trained volunteer

CASA - Advocates for Children of NYS
99 Pine St, C102, Albany, NY 12207-2776
518-426-5354 Fax: 518-426-5348
e-mail: mail@casanys.org
Web site: www.casanys.org
Darlene Ward, Executive Director
Volunteer advocates appointed by family court judges to represent abused & neglected children in court

Camp Venture Inc
100 Convent Rd, Box 402, Nanuet, NY 10954
845-624-3862 Fax: 845-624-7064
Web site: www.campventure.org
Daniel Lukens, Executive Director
Services for the developmentally disabled

Catholic Charities
1654 W Onondaga St, Syracuse, NY 13204
315-424-1810 Fax: 315-424-6839
Eleanor Carr, Director, Elder Abuse Prevention Program

Center for Anti-Violence Education Inc
421 5th Ave, Brooklyn, NY 11215-3315
718-788-1775 Fax: 718-499-2284
e-mail: cae@cae-bklyn.org
Web site: www.cae-bklyn.org
Annie Ellman, Executive Director
Self-defense & violence prevention education for children, youth & women

Center for Family & Youth (The)
Administrative Ofc, 135 Ontario St, PO Box 6240, Albany, NY 12206
518-462-4745 or 518-462-4630 Fax: 518-427-1464
e-mail: dbosworth@ctrfamyouth.com
David A Bosworth, Executive Director
Child welfare services, Project STRIVE

Center for Independence of the Disabled in NY (CIDNY)
841 Broadway, Ste 301, New York, NY 10003
212-674-2300 or TTY: 212-674-5619 Fax: 212-254-5953
Web site: www.cidny.org
Susan Dooha, Executive Director
Rights & advocacy for the disabled

Center for Urban Community Services
120 Wall St, 25th Fl, New York, NY 10005
212-801-3300 Fax: 212-801-3325
e-mail: cucsinfo@cucs.org
Web site: www.cucs.org
Anthony Hannigan, Executive Director
Services to the homeless & low-income individuals, training & technical assistance to not-for-profit organizations

Center for the Disabled
314 S Manning Blvd, Albany, NY 12208
518-437-5700 Fax: 518-437-5705
e-mail: krafchin@cftd.org
Web site: www.centercares.org
Alan Krafchin, President & Chief Executive Officer
Medical & dental services; education, adult & residential services & service coordination

Cerebral Palsy Association of New York State
90 State Street, Suite 929, Albany, NY 12207
518-436-0178 Fax: 518-436-8619
e-mail: malvaro@cpofnys.org
Web site: www.cpofnys.org
Michael Alvaro, Associate Executive Director
Advocate and provide direct services with and for individuals with cerebral palsy and other significant disabilities and their families

Children's Aid Society (The)
105 E 22nd St, New York, NY 10010
212-949-4918 Fax: 212-460-5941
e-mail: pcoltoff@childrensaidsociety.org
Web site: www.childrensaidsociety.org
Philip Coltoff, Chief Executive Officer
Child welfare, health, foster care/adoption, preventive services, community centers & public schools, camps

Offices and agencies appear in alphabetical order.

Children's Rights Inc
404 Park Ave South, New York, NY 10016
212-683-2210 Fax: 212-683-4015
e-mail: info@childrensrights.org
Web site: www.childrensrights.org
Marcia Robinson Lowry, Executive Director
Advocacy & class action lawsuits on behalf of abused & neglected children

Children's Village (The)
Echo Hills, Dobbs Ferry, NY 10522
914-693-0600 x1201 Fax: 914-674-9208
e-mail: jkohomban@childrensvillage.org
Web site: www.childrensvillage.org
Jeremy Kohomban, President & Chief Executive Officer
Residential school located twenty minutes outside of NYC. Treatment & prevention of behavioral problems for youth; residential & community-based services; employment & runaway shelter services

Citizens Committee for Children of New York Inc
105 E 22nd St, New York, NY 10010
212-673-1800 Fax: 212-979-5063
e-mail: info@kfny.org
Web site: www.kfny.org
Rose Anello, Associate Executive Director for Public Affairs
Advocacy & public education promoting improved quality of life for NYC children & families in need

Coalition Against Domestic Violence, NYS
350 New Scotland Ave, Albany, NY 12208
518-482-5465 Fax: 518-482-3807
e-mail: newell@nyscadv.org
Web site: www.nyscadv.org
Patti Jo Newell, Director, Public Policy

Coalition for Asian American Children & Families
50 Broad St, Rm 1701, New York, NY 10004
212-809-4675 Fax: 212-785-4601
e-mail: cacf@cacf.org
Web site: www.cacf.org
Wayne H Ho, Executive Director
Advocacy for programs & policies supporting Asian American children & families; training & resources for service providers

Coalition for the Homeless
129 Fulton St, 1st Flr, New York, NY 10038
212-776-2000 Fax: 212-964-1303
e-mail: info@cfthomeless.org
Web site: www.coalitionforthehomeless.org
Mary Brosnahan Sullivan, Executive Director
Food, shelter, clothing assistance program, services for homeless New Yorkers

Coalition of Animal Care Societies (The)
437 Old Albany Post Rd, Garrison, NY 10524
845-788-5070 Fax: 845-788-5071
e-mail: tzaleski@sprynet.com
Terence M Zaleski, Special Counsel
Association of humane societies & animal welfare groups in NYS

Coalition of Fathers & Families NY
PO Box 782, Clifton Park, NY 12065
518-383-8202 Fax: 518-383-8202
e-mail: dadlobby@localnet.com
Web site: www.fafny.org/fafnypac.htm
James Hays, President
Working to keep fathers & families together

Commission on Economic Opportunity for the Greater Capital Region
2331 Fifth Ave, Troy, NY 12180
518-272-6012 Fax: 518-272-0658
e-mail: dsuto@ceo-cap.org
Web site: www.ceo-cap.org
Karen E Gordon, Executive Director
Preserve & advance the self-sufficiency, well-being & growth of individuals & families through education, guidance & resources

Community Healthcare Network
79 Madison Avenue, Fl 6, New York, NY 10016-7802
212-366-4500 Fax: 646-312-0481
e-mail: cabate@chnnyc.org
Web site: www.chnnyc.org
Catherine Abate, President & Chief Executive Officer
Health & social services for low-income, ethnically diverse, medically underserved neighborhoods of NYC

Cornell Cooperative Extension, College of Human Ecology
365 Roberts Hall, Cornell University, Ithaca, NY 14853-5905
607-255-2247 Fax: 607-255-3794
e-mail: jas56@cornell.edu
Web site: www.cce.cornell.edu
Josephine Swanson, Associate Director, Assistant Dean
Children, youth & family economic & social well-being

Council of Community Services of NYS Inc
272 Broadway, Albany, NY 12204
518-434-9194 x103 Fax: 518-434-0392
e-mail: info@ccsnys.org
Web site: www.ccsnys.org
Doug Sauer, Executive Director
Build healthy, caring communities & human care delivery systems through a strong charitable nonprofit sector & quality community-based planning

Council of Family & Child Caring Agencies
19 West 21st St, Ste 501, New York, NY 10010
212-929-2626 Fax: 212-929-0870
e-mail: cofcca@cofcca.org
Web site: www.cofcca.org
James F Purcell, Executive Director
Child welfare services membership organization

EPIC-Every Person Influences Children Inc
1000 Main St, Buffalo, NY 14202
716-332-4100 Fax: 716-332-4101
Web site: www.epicforchildren.org
Linda Croglia, Executive Director
Uniting parents, teachers & community members to prevent child abuse & neglect, school dropout, juvenile crime, substance abuse & teenage pregnancy

Offices and agencies appear in alphabetical order.

Policy Areas

Education & Assistance Corp Inc
50 Clinton St, Ste 107, Hempstead, NY 11550
516-539-0150 Fax: 516-539-0160
e-mail: lelder@eacinc.org
Web site: www.eacinc.org
Lance W Elder, President & Chief Executive Officer
Rehabilitation for nonviolent offenders; advocacy, education &
counseling programs for youth, elderly & families

Family Planning Advocates of New York State
17 Elk St, Albany, NY 12207
518-436-8408 Fax: 518-436-0004
e-mail: info@fpaofnys.org
Web site: www.fpaofnys.org
JoAnn M Smith, President/Chief Executive Officer
Reproductive rights

Federation Employment & Guidance Service (FEGS) Inc
315 Hudson St, 9th Fl, New York, NY 10013
212-366-8400 Fax: 212-366-8441
e-mail: info@fegs.org
Web site: www.fegs.org
Alfred P Miller, Chief Executive Officer
Diversified health & human services system to help individuals
achieve their potential at work, at home & in the community

Federation of Protestant Welfare Agencies Inc
281 Park Ave South, New York, NY 10010
212-777-4800 x322 Fax: 212-673-4085
e-mail: fgoldman@fpwa.org
Web site: www.fpwa.org
Fatima Goldman, Executive Director
Childcare & child welfare, HIV/AIDS, elderly, income security

Filipino American Human Services Inc
185-14 Hillside Ave, Jamaica, NY 11432
718-883-1295 Fax: 718-523-9606
e-mail: fahsi@fahsi.org
Web site: www.fahsi.org
Sherry Lynn Peralta, Executive Director
Youth program, family counseling referral, community
education/advocacy & citizenship assistance services

Fordham University, Graduate School of Social Service
113 West 60th Street, Lincoln Center, New York, NY 10023
212-636-6616 Fax: 212-636-7876
e-mail: vaughan@fordham.edu
Web site: www.fordham.edu
Peter B Vaughan, Dean
Social work education, clinical social work, administration, client
centered management

Friends & Relatives of Institutionalized Aged Inc
18 John St, Suite 905, New York, NY 10038
212-732-5667 or 212-732-5935 Fax: 212-732-6945
e-mail: fria@fria.org
Web site: www.fria.org
Amy Paul, Executive Director
Nursing home & other long-term care placement & complaints

Greater Upstate Law Project Inc
119 Washington Ave, Albany, NY 12210
518-462-6831 Fax: 518-462-6687
e-mail: nkrupski@wnylc.com
Web site: www.gulpny.org
Anne Erickson, President & Chief Executive Officer
Rights of poor & low income residents

Green Chimneys School-Green Chimneys Children's
Services Inc
400 Doansburg Rd, Box 719, Brewster, NY 10509
845-279-2995 x119 Fax: 845-279-3077
Web site: www.greenchimneys.org
Joseph A Whalen, Executive Director
Residential treatment programs for emotionally troubled children &
youths; therapeutic/educational Farm & Wildlife Conservation
Center programs; therapeutic day school program

Guide Dog Foundation for the Blind Inc
371 East Jericho Turnpike, Smithtown, NY 11787-2976
631-930-9000 or 800-548-4337 Fax: 631-930-9009
e-mail: info@guidedog.org
Web site: www.guidedog.org
Wells B Jones, Chief Executive Officer
Provide guide dogs without charge to sight-impaired persons
seeking enhanced mobility & independence

HeartShare Human Services of New York, Roman Catholic
Diocese of Brooklyn
191 Joralemon St, Brooklyn, NY 11201
718-422-HEART Fax: 718-522-4506
e-mail: info@heartshare.org
Web site: www.heartshare.org
William R Guarinello, President & Chief Executive Officer
Service for the developmentally disabled children & family services
& programs for people with HIV/AIDS

Helen Keller Services for the Blind
57 Willoughby Street, Brooklyn, NY 11201
718-522-2122 Fax: 718-935-9463
e-mail: info@helenkeller.org
Web site: www.helenkeller.org
John P Lynch, Executive Director
Preschool, rehabilitation, employment & senior services, low vision
& braille library services

Hispanic Federation
130 William Street, 9th Floor, New York, NY 10038
212-233-8955 Fax: 212-233-8996
Web site: www.hispanicfederation.org
Lorraine Cortes-Vazquez, President
Technical assistance, capacity building, grantmaking & advocacy
for Latino nonprofit service providers

Hispanic Outreach Services
40 North Main Ave, Albany, NY 12203
518-453-6655 Fax: 518-453-6792
e-mail: anne.tranelli@rcda.org
Web site: www.hispanicoutreachservices.org
Sister Anne Tranelli, Executive Director
Social service, youth guidance, language translation & immigration assistance programs

Homes for the Homeless/Institute for Children & Families
36 Cooper Square, 6th Fl, New York, NY 10003
212-529-5252 Fax: 212-529-7698
e-mail: info@homesforthehomeless.com
Web site: www.homesforthehomeless.com
Karina Kwok, Media Contact
Private non-profit providing education, social services & transitional housing for homeless children & families in NYC

Hospice & Palliative Care Association of NYS Inc
21 Aviation Rd, Ste 9, Albany, NY 12205
518-446-1483 Fax: 518-446-1484
e-mail: info@hpcanys.org
Web site: www.hpcanys.org
Kathy A McMahon, President & Chief Executive Officer
Hospice & palliative care information & referral service; educational programs; clinical, psychosocial & bereavement issues

Housing Works Inc
247 Lark St, 1st Fl, Albany, NY 12210
518-449-4207 Fax: 518-449-4219
Web site: www.housingworks.org
Michael Kink, Statewide Advocacy Coordinator & Legislative
   Counsel
Housing, health care, advocacy, job training & support services for homeless NY residents with HIV or AIDS

Humane Society of the United States, Mid Atlantic Regional Office
Bartley Square, 270 Route 206, Flanders, NJ 07836
973-927-5611 Fax: 973-927-5617
e-mail: maro@hsus.org
Web site: www.hsus.org
Nina Austenberg, Regional Director
Humane treatment of animals;

Hunger Action Network of NYS (HANNYS)
275 State St, Albany, NY 12210
518-434-7371 Fax: 518-434-7390
e-mail: bhpham@hungeractionnys.org
Web site: www.hungeractionnys.org
Bich Ha Pham, Executive Director
Developing unified efforts to address the root causes of hunger & promote social justice

Hunter College, Brookdale Center on Aging
425 E 25th St, New York, NY 10010
212-481-3780 Fax: 212-481-3791
e-mail: info@brookdale.org
Web site: www.brookdale.org
Dennis Kodner, Executive Director
Policy research & development, training, publications & resources for institutions & community agencies

Institute for Socio-Economic Studies
10 New King St, White Plains, NY 10604
914-686-7112 Fax: 914-686-0581
e-mail: info@socioeconomic.org
Web site: www.socioeconomic.org
Leonard M Greene, President
Welfare reform, socioeconomic incentives, tax & healthcare reform

Japanese American Social Services Inc
275 Seventh Ave, 12th Fl, New York, NY 10001
212-255-1881 Fax: 212-255-3281
e-mail: info@jassi.org
Web site: www.jassi.org
Margaret Fung, Executive Director
Bilingual/bicultural programs; assistance with government benefits, housing, immigration & legal rights

Korean Community Services of Metropolitan NY
149 West 24th St, 6th Fl, New York, NY 10011
212-727-8745 Fax: 212-463-8347
e-mail: employment@kcsny.org
Web site: www.kcsny.org
Shin Son, Executive Director
Develop & deliver social services to support & assist members of the Korean & neighboring communities

NYS Bar Assn, Children & the Law Committee
Law Office of Anne Reynolds Copps
126 State St, 6th Fl, Albany, NY 12207
518-436-4170 Fax: 518-436-1456
e-mail: arcopps@nycap.rr.com
Anne Reynolds Copps, Chair

Lesbian, Gay, Bisexual & Transgender Community Ctr - Not For Profit
208 W 13th Street, New York, NY 10011-7702
212-620-7310 Fax: 212-924-2657
e-mail: info@gaycenter.org
Web site: www.gaycenter.org
Miriam Yeung, Director, Public Policy
Mental health counseling, youth guidance, HIV/AIDS services, advocacy & programs, alcohol & drug abuse intervention & prevention

Policy Areas

Little Flower Children & Family Services
186 Joralemon St, Brooklyn, NY 11201
718-875-3500 or 631-929-6200 Fax: 718-260-8863
e-mail: stupph@lfchild.org
Web site: www.littleflowerny.org
Herbert W Stupp, Chief Executive Officer
Foster care, adoption, child welfare, residential treatment services and residences for the developmentally disabled & day care; union free school district

Littman Krooks LLP
655 Third Ave, New York, NY 10017
212-490-2020 Fax: 212-490-2990
e-mail: bkrooks@lkllp.com
Web site: www.elderlawnewyork.com
Bernard A Krooks, Partner
Elder law

March of Dimes Birth Defects Foundation
1275 Mamaroneck Ave, White Plains, NY 10605
914-997-4641 Fax: 914-997-4585
e-mail: dstaples@marchofdimes.com
Web site: www.marchofdimes.com
Douglas Staples, Senior Vice President Strategic Marketing and Communications

NY Association for New Americans Inc
17 Battery Pl, New York, NY 10004-1102
212-425-2900 Fax: 212-344-1621
e-mail: mhandelm@nyana.org
Web site: www.nyana.org
Jose Valencia, President & Chief Executive Officer
Social service referrals for immigrants

NY Counseling Association Inc
PO Box 12636, Albany, NY 12212-2636
518-235-2026 Fax: 518-235-0910
e-mail: nycaoffice@nycounseling.org
Web site: www.nycounseling.org
Donald Newell, Executive Manager
Counseling professionals in education, mental health, career, employment, rehabilitation & adult development

NY Foundation for Senior Citizens Inc
11 Park Place, 14th FL, New York, NY 10007-2801
212-962-7559 Fax: 212-227-2952
e-mail: nyfscinc@aol.com
Web site: www.nyfsc.org
Linda Hoffman, President
Social services for seniors in New York City

NYC Coalition Against Hunger
16 Beaver St, 3rd Fl, New York, NY 10004
212-825-0028 Fax: 212-825-0267
Web site: www.nyccah.org
Joel Berg, Executive Director

NYS Association of Area Agencies on Aging
272 Broadway, Albany, NY 12204-2717
518-449-7080 Fax: 518-449-7055
e-mail: nysaaaa@aol.com
Web site: www.nysaaaa.org
Laura A Cameron, Executive Director
Agencies working to enhance effectiveness of programs for older persons

NYS Child Care Coordinating Council
230 Washington Ave Ext, Albany, NY 12203-5390
518-690-4217 Fax: 518-690-2887
e-mail: csaginaw@nyscccc.org
Web site: www.nyscccc.org
Carol Saginaw, Executive Director
Advocacy & education for the development of accessible or affordable, quality child care services

NYS Corps Collaboration
One Pine West Plaza, Ste 105, Albany, NY 12205-5531
518-464-2676 Fax: 518-464-2677
e-mail: info@nyscc.net
Web site: www.nyscc.net
Linda J Cohen, Executive Director
Statewide youth service & conservation corps addressing society's unmet needs & buiding self-esteem, a sense of civic responsibility & leadership skills

NYS Industries for the Disabled (NYSID) Inc
155 Washington Ave, Ste 400, Albany, NY 12210
518-463-9706 Fax: 518-463-9708
e-mail: admin@nysid.org
Web site: www.nysid.org
Lawrence L Barker, Jr, President & Chief Executive Officer
Business development through

National Association of Social Workers, NYS Chapter
188 Washington Ave, Albany, NY 12210-2304
518-463-4741 or 800-724-6279 Fax: 518-463-6446
e-mail: info@naswnys.org
Web site: www.naswnys.org
Thea Griffin, Interim Executive Director
Professional development & specialized training for professional social workers; standards for social work practice; advocacy for policies, services & programs that promote social justice

National Council of Jewish Women
53 W 23rd St, 6th Fl, New York, NY 10010
212-645-4048 Fax: 212-645-7466
e-mail: action@ncjw.org
Web site: www.ncjw.org
Phyllis Snyder, President
Human rights & social service advocacy & education

Offices and agencies appear in alphabetical order.

National Urban League Inc (The)
120 Wall St, New York, NY 10005
212-558-5300 Fax: 212-344-5189
e-mail: info@nul.org
Web site: www.nul.org
Michele M Moore, Senior Vice President Communications &
  Marketing
*Community-based movement devoted to empowering African
Americans to enter the economic & social mainstream*

Nelson A Rockefeller Inst of Govt, Federalism Research Grp
411 State St, Albany, NY 12203-1003
518-443-5522 Fax: 518-443-5788
e-mail: gaist@rockinst.org
Web site: www.rockinst.org
Thomas L Gais, Co-Director
State management systems for social service programs

New York Association of Homes & Services for the Aging
150 State St, Ste 301, Albany, NY 12207-1698
518-449-2707 Fax: 518-455-8908
e-mail: cyoung@nyahsa.org
Web site: www.nyahsa.org
Carl Young, President
Long term care

New York Community Trust (The)
909 Third Avenue, 22nd FL, New York, NY 10022
212-686-0010 Fax: 212-532-8528
e-mail: info@nycommunitytrust.org
Web site: www.nycommunitytrust.org
Lorie A Slutsky, President/Director
Administrators of philanthropic funds

New York Public Welfare Association
130 Washington Ave, Albany, NY 12210
518-465-9305 Fax: 518-465-5633
e-mail: nypwa@nycap.rr.com
Web site: www.nypwa.com
Sheila Harrigan, Executive Director
*Partnership of local social services districts dedicated to improve
the quality & effectiveness of social welfare policy*

New York Society for the Deaf
315 Hudson St, 4th Fl, New York, NY 10013
212-366-0066 Fax: 212-366-0051
Web site: www.nysd.org
Kathleen Cox, Executive Director
*Ensure full & equal access to appropriate, comprehensive clinical,
residential & support services for deaf & deaf-blind persons*

New York State Association of Family Services Agencies Inc
95 Columbia Street, Albany, NY 12210
518-465-5340 Fax: 518-465-6023
e-mail: info@albanygov.com
Web site: www.nysafsa.org
Michael Barrett, Governmental Affairs Representative
Social & human services assistance & advocacy

New York State Catholic Conference
465 State St, Albany, NY 12203-1004
518-434-6195 Fax: 518-434-9796
e-mail: info@nyscatholic.org
Web site: www.nyscatholic.org
Richard E Barnes, Executive Director
*Identify, formulate & implement public policy objectives of the NYS
Bishops in health, education, welfare, human & civil rights*

New York State Citizens' Coalition for Children Inc
410 East Upland Road, Ithaca, NY 14850-2551
607-272-0034 Fax: 607-272-0035
e-mail: office@nysccc.org
Web site: www.nysccc.org
Judith Ashton, Executive Director
Adoption & foster care advocacy

New York State Community Action Association
2 Charles Blvd, Guilderland, NY 12084
518-690-0491 Fax: 518-690-0498
e-mail: dan@nyscaaonline.org
Web site: www.nyscaaonline.org
Daniel Maskin, Chief Executive Officer
*Dedicated to the growth & education of community action agencies
in NYS to sustain their efforts in advocating & improving the lives of
low-income New Yorkers*

New York State Rehabilitation Association
155 Washington Ave, Suite 410, Albany, NY 12210
518-449-2976 Fax: 518-426-4329
e-mail: nysra@nyrehab.org
Web site: www.nyrehab.org
Patricia Dowse, Vice President
*Political advocacy, education, communications, networking &
referral services for people with disabilities*

New York Urban League
204 W 136th St, New York, NY 10030
212-926-8000 Fax: 212-283-2736
Web site: www.nyul.org
Darwin M Davis, President & Chief Executive Officer
Social services, job training, education & advocacy

Nonprofit Coordinating Committee of New York
1350 Broadway, Rm 1801, New York, NY 10018-7802
212-502-4191 Fax: 212-502-4189
e-mail: mclark@npccny.org
Web site: www.npccny.org
Michael Clark, Executive Director/President
Advocacy & government activities monitoring for NYC nonprofits

North Shore Animal League America
25 Lewyt Street, Port Washington, NY 11050
516-883-7900 x257 Fax: 516-944-5732
e-mail: webmaster@nsalamerica.org
Web site: www.nsalamerica.org
Perry Fina, Director, Marketing
Rescue, care & adoption services for orphaned companion animals

Offices and agencies appear in alphabetical order.

Planned Parenthood of NYC, Inc
26 Bleecker St, New York, NY 10012
212-274-7292 Fax: 212-274-7276
e-mail: carla.goldstein@ppnyc.org
Carla Goldstein, Vice President, Public Affairs

Prevent Child Abuse New York
134 S Swan St, Albany, NY 12210
518-445-1273 or 800-CHILDREN Fax: 518-445-1273
e-mail: info@preventchildabuseny.org
Web site: www.preventchildabuseny.org
Christine Deyss, Executive Director
Child abuse prevention advocacy, education, technical assistance

ProLiteracy Worldwide
1320 Jamesville Ave, Syracuse, NY 13210-4224
315-422-9121 Fax: 315-422-6369
e-mail: info@proliteracy.org
Web site: www.proliteracy.org
Rochelle A Cassella, Director, Corporate Communications
Sponsors educational programs & services to empower adults & families through the acquisition of literacy skills & practices

Public/Private Ventures
The Chanin Building, 122 East 42nd St, 42nd Fl, New York, NY 10168
212-822-2400 Fax: 212-949-0439
e-mail: melliott@ppv.org
Web site: www.ppv.org
Mark Elliott, Executive Vice President
Action-based research, public policy & program development organization

Resource Center for Independent Living (RCIL)
401-409 Columbia St, PO Box 210, Utica, NY 13503-0210
315-797-4642 or TTY 315-797-5837 Fax: 315-797-4747
e-mail: rcil@rcil.com
Web site: www.rcil.com
Burt Danovitz, Executive Director
Services & advocacy for the disabled & their families; public information & community education

Roman Catholic Diocese of Albany, Catholic Charities
40 N Main Ave, Albany, NY 12203
518-453-6650 Fax: 518-453-6792
Web site: www.ccrcda.org
Sister Maureen Joyce, Chief Executive Officer
Social & human services assistance: housing, shelters, day care, counseling, transportation, health & emergency

Rural & Migrant Ministry Inc
PO Box 4757, Poughkeepsie, NY 12602
845-485-8627 Fax: 845-485-1963
e-mail: hope@ruralmigrantministry.org
Web site: www.ruralmigrantministry.org
Richard Witt, Executive Director
Working to end poverty & increase self-determination, education & economic resources for migrant farmworkers & the rural poor

Rural Opportunities Inc
400 East Ave, Rochester, NY 14607
585-546-7180 Fax: 585-340-3335
e-mail: smitchell@ruralinc.org
Web site: www.ruralinc.org
Stuart J Mitchell, President & Chief Executive Officer
Advance self-sufficiency of farm workers, low-income & other disenfranchised people & communities through advocacy & programs including training & employment, child development, health & safety, & home ownership

Salvation Army, Empire State Division
PO Box 148, Syracuse, NY 13206-0148
315-434-1300 x310 Fax: 315-434-1399
Web site: www.salvationarmy.org
Norman E Wood, Divisional Commander

Sheltering Arms Children's Service
129 W 27th St, Fl 5, New York, NY 10001-6206
646-442-0301 Fax: 212-367-9124
e-mail: sacsnyc@aol.com
Web site: www.sacs-nyc.org
Wayne Mucci, Executive Director
Care, special education & programs for at-risk & economically disadvantaged children in NYC

Statewide Emergency Network for Social & Economic Security (SENSES)
275 State St, Albany, NY 12210
518-463-5576 Fax: 518-432-9073
e-mail: rdeutsch@sensesny.org
Web site: www.sensesny.org
Ron Deutsch, Executive Director
Poverty, welfare reform, tax policy, homelessness, community economic development

Syracuse University, Maxwell School of Citizenship & Public Affairs
426 Eggers Hall, Syracuse, NY 13244-1020
315-443-3114 Fax: 315-443-1081
e-mail: ctrpol@syr.edu
Web site: www.maxwell.syr.edu
Timothy Smeeding, Professor of Public Policy; Director
Social welfare, income distribution & comparative social policies

United Jewish Appeal-Federation of Jewish Philanthropies of NY
155 Washington Ave, Albany, NY 12210
518-436-1091 Fax: 518-463-1266
e-mail: solowayr@ujafedny.org
Web site: www.ujafedny.org
Ronald Soloway, Managing Director, Government & External Relations

Offices and agencies appear in alphabetical order.

United Neighborhood Houses - Not For Profit
70 W 36th St, 5th Fl, New York, NY 10018
212-967-0322 Fax: 212-967-0792
e-mail: nwackstein@unhny.org
Web site: www.unhny.org
Nancy Wackstein, Executive Director
*Federation of NYC settlement houses that provides issue advocacy &
management assistance for member agencies' social, educational &
cultural programs*

United Way of Central New York
518 James St, PO Box 2129, Syracuse, NY 13220-2227
315-428-2216 Fax: 315-428-2227
e-mail: ccollie@unitedway-cny.org
Web site: www.unitedway-cny.org
Craig E Collie, Vice President, Volunteer Community Resource
    Development
Fundraising & support to human & social services organizations

United Way of New York City
2 Park Ave, New York, NY 10016
212-251-2500 Fax: 212-696-1220
e-mail: lmandell@uwnyc.org
Web site: www.unitedwaynyc.org
Lawrence Mandell, President & Chief Executive Officer
*Works with partners from all sectors to create, support, & execute
strategic initiatives that seek to achieve measurable improvement in
the lives of the city's most valuable residents and communities*

Upstate Homes for Children & Adults Inc
2705 State Hwy 28, Oneonta, NY 13820
607-286-7171 Fax: 607-286-7166
e-mail: kennedyp@upstatehome.org
Web site: www.upstatehome.org
Patricia E Kennedy, Executive Director
Education/mental hygiene

Welfare Research Inc
112 State St, Rm 1020, Albany, NY 12207
518-432-2563 Fax: 518-432-2564
e-mail: administration@welfareresearch.org
Web site: www.welfareresearch.org
Virginia Hayes Sibbison, Executive Director
Contract research in social service & related policy areas

William T Grant Foundation
570 Lexington Ave, 18th Fl, New York, NY 10022-6837
212-752-0071 Fax: 212-752-1398
e-mail: info@wtgrantfdn.org
Web site: www.wtgrantfoundation.org
Robert Granger, President
Funding for youth development programs & research

World Hunger Year Inc
505 Eighth Ave, Suite 2100, New York, NY 10018-6582
212-629-8850 Fax: 212-465-9274
e-mail: why@worldhungeryear.org
Web site: www.worldhungeryear.org
Bill Ayres, Executive Director
*Addresses root causes of hunger & poverty by promoting effective &
innovative community-based solutions*

YAI/National Institute for People with Disabilities
460 W 34th St, New York, NY 10001-2382
212-273-6100 or 1-800-2-YAI-LINK Fax: 212-947-7524
e-mail: jmlcares@yai.org
Web site: www.yai.org
Joel M Levy, Chief Executive Officer
*Programs, services & advocacy for people with autism, mental
retardation & other developmental disabilities of all ages, and their
families; special education & early learning programs*

Policy Areas

Offices and agencies appear in alphabetical order.

TAXATION & REVENUE
New York State

GOVERNOR'S OFFICE

Governor's Office
Executive Chamber
State Capitol
Albany, NY 12224
518-474-8390 Fax: 518-474-1513
Web site: www.state.ny.us

Governor:
Geroge E Pataki 518-474-8390
Executive Director:
Kara Lanspery 518-474-8390
Secretary to the Governor:
John P Cahill. 518-474-4246
Deputy Secretary to the Governor for Administration:
Carolyn Ahl 518-408-2800
Deputy Secretary to the Governor for Appointments & Intergovernmental
Affairs:
Robert Bulman 518-474-0491
Senior Policy Advisor to the Governor:
Jeffrey Lovell 518-486-9671
Counsel to the Governor-Attorney General, Budget:
Richard Platkin. 518-474-8343
Senior Asst Counsel to the Governor-Indian Affairs, Lottery, Racing &
Wagering, State Liquor Auth:
Greg Allen 518-474-2266
Asst Counsel to the Governor-Econ Development, Empire State Dev Corp,
Jacob Javits Convention Ctr, NYSTAR, Olympic Regional Dev Auth:
Robert Ryan 518-474-2266
Director, Communications:
David Catalfamo. 518-474-8418

EXECUTIVE DEPARTMENTS AND RELATED AGENCIES

Alcoholic Beverage Control, Division of
84 Holland Ave
Albany, NY 12208
518-486-4767 Fax: 518-402-4015

105 W 125th St
4th Fl
New York, NY 12208
212-961-8385
Fax: 212-961-8299

Chair:
Edward F Kelly. . . . . 212-961-8347 or 518-473-6559
Commissioner:
Joseph Zarriello 518-474-0810
Counsel:
Thomas McKeon 212-961-8317

Administration
Deputy Commissioner, Administration & Public Affairs:
J Mark Anderson 518-486-4767
Director, Financial Administration:
Mark G Aldao. 518-474-0589
Director, Human Resources:
Dan Cunningham 518-473-5995

Licensing

Albany (Zone II)
84 Holland Ave, 2nd Fl, Albany, NY 12208
Director, Licensing:
Kerri O'Brien. 518-474-3114
Associate Counsel:
Leslie Trebby 518-474-6750
Asst Dir, ABC Compliance:
Richard Mann 518-473-2146/fax: 518-402-4015
Supervising Beverage Ctrl Investigator:
Thomas Pascucci. 518-474-0385/fax: 518-473-7527

Buffalo (Zone III)
Donovan State Office Bldg, 125 Main St, Buffalo, NY 14203
716-847-3035
Executive Officer:
Brandon Noyes. 716-847-3060
Associate Counsel:
Gerald Greenan 716-847-3057
Supervising Beverage Control Investigator:
Thomas Cocker 716-847-3039/fax: 716-847-5020

New York City (Zone I)
317 Lenox Avenue, New York, NY 10027
212-961-8385
Deputy Commissioner:
Fred Gioffre 212-961-8301
Supervising Attorney:
Stephen Kalinsky 212-961-8351
Asst Director, ABC Compliance:
Richard Mann 212-961-8376/fax: 212-961-8381

Budget, Division of the
State Capitol
Albany, NY 12224
518-473-3885
e-mail: dobinfo@budget.state.ny.us
Web site: www.budget.state.ny.us

Director:
John F Cape 518-474-2300
Deputy Director:
Ron Rock 518-474-6323
Deputy Director:
Al Kaplan 518-474-6300
Administrative Officer:
Karen Bodnar 518-474-6324
Director, Communications:
Michael Marr 518-473-3885

Offices and agencies appear in alphabetical order.

Press Officer:
Scott Reif 518-473-3885
Legislative Liaison:
Christina Kidera 518-474-7953/fax: 518-473-7243
Press Officer:
Peter Constantakes 518-473-3885

Law Department
120 Broadway
New York, NY 10271-0332
212-416-8000 Fax: 212-416-8942

State Capitol
Albany, NY 12224-0341
518-474-7330
Fax: 518-402-2472

Attorney General:
Eliot Spitzer 518-474-7330

Public Advocacy Division
Acting Deputy Attorney General:
Terryl Brown Clemons 212-416-8041/fax: 212-416-8068
Special Counsel:
Mary Ellen Burns 212-416-6155

Charities Bureau
Bureau Chief:
William Josephson 212-416-8401/fax: 212-416-8393

Internet Bureau
Bureau Chief:
Kenneth Dreifach 212-416-8433/fax: 212-416-8369

Investment Protection Bureau
Bureau Chief:
David Brown 212-416-8198/fax: 212-416-6377

State Counsel Division
Deputy Attorney General:
Richard Rifkin 518-473-7190
Assistant Deputy Attorney General:
Patricia Martinelli 518-473-0648/fax: 518-486-9777
Assistant Deputy Attorney General:
Susan L Watson 212-416-8579/fax: 212-416-6001

Civil Recoveries Bureau
Asst Attorney General in Charge:
Mary E House 518-474-7131/fax: 518-473-1635

Litigation Bureau
Bureau Chief, Albany:
Bruce D Feldman 518-473-8328/fax: 518-473-1572
Bureau Chief, NYC:
James B Henley 212-416-8523/fax: 212-416-6075

Lottery, Division of
One Broadway Center
PO Box 7500
Schenectady, NY 12301-7500
518-388-3300 Fax: 518-388-3403
Web site: www.nylottery.org

Director:
Nancy A Palumbo 518-388-3400
Executive Deputy Director:
Susan E Miller 518-388-3404

Director, Operations:
Joe Seeley 518-388-3411
Director, Financial Administration:
Gardner Gurney 518-388-3404
Director, Advertising:
Michael Flanagan 518-388-3430
e-mail: claverty@lottery.state.ny.us
Director, Administration:
Art DelSignore 518-388-3404
Director, Communications:
Jennifer Mauer 518-388-3415/fax: 518-388-3423
General Counsel:
Robert J McLaughlin 518-388-3408

Regional Offices

Adirondack-Capital District Region
One Broadway Center, Suite 700, Schenectady, NY 12305
Acting Regional Director:
Judy Drislane 518-388-5421

Central/Finger Lakes/Genesee Valley Regions
Rochester Office
First Federal Plaza Bldg, 28 E Main St, Rochester, NY 14604
Regional Director:
Bill Lonczak 877-358-3320
Syracuse Office
Deys Centennial Bldg, 401 S Salina St, Syracuse, NY 13202
Regional Director:
Bill Lonczak 315-448-4314

Hudson Valley Region
30 Westage Business Center, Ste 6, Fishkill, NY 12524
Regional Director:
Georgene Perlman 845-897-2412

Long Island Region
1000 Zeckendorf Blvd, Garden City, NY 11530
Regional Director:
Jim Benoit 516-222-8223

New York City Region
175 Varick St, 5th Fl, New York, NY 10014
Acting Regional Director:
Thomas Breig 646-486-6157

Western Region
Ellicott Sq Bldg, 295 Main St, Ste 120, Buffalo, NY 14203
Regional Director:
Len Lorenz 716-847-3786

Racing & Wagering Board
1 Watervliet Ave Ext
Ste 2
Albany, NY 12206-1668
518-453-8460 Fax: 518-453-8867
e-mail: info@racing.state.ny.us
Web site: www.racing.state.ny.us

Chair:
Michael J Hoblock, Jr 518-453-8460
Member:
Cheryl Ritchko-Buley 518-453-8460
Executive Director:
Edward J Martin 518-453-8460
Counsel:
Robert A Feuerstein 212-290-4401
Secretary to the Board:
Erin E Dahlmeyer 518-453-8460

Offices and agencies appear in alphabetical order.

Public Information Officer:
Stacy Clifford 518-453-8460 x3311/fax: 518-453-8867

Real Property Services, Office of
16 Sheridan Ave
Albany, NY 12210-2714
518-486-5446 Fax: 518-474-9276
Web site: www.orps.state.ny.us

Executive Director:
Thomas G Griffen. 518-474-5711
e-mail: thomas.griffen@orps.state.ny.us
Executive Deputy Director:
Thomas Bellard 518-473-6914
e-mail: tom.bellard@orps.state.ny.us
Chief Appraiser:
Jeff Jordan 518-474-2854
e-mail: jeff.jordan@orps.state.ny.us
Counsel:
Richard J Sinnott 518-474-6753
e-mail: richard.sinnott@orps.state.ny.us
Chief Information Officer:
Bruce Sauter 518-474-8829
e-mail: bruce.sauter@orps.state.ny.us
Strategic Information Officer:
JoAnn Whalen 518-474-6742
e-mail: joann.whalen@orps.state.ny.us
Director, Budget/Fiscal Services:
Steve King 518-474-5762
e-mail: steve.king@orps.state.ny.us
Director, Public Information:
Geoffrey T Gloak 518-486-5446
e-mail: geoffrey.gloak@orps.state.ny.us

Central Support Services
Director:
Robert Zandri 518-474-5666
e-mail: robert.zandri@orps.state.ny.us

Information Technology Services
Director:
Dennis Jersey 518-474-6758
e-mail: dennis.jersey@orps.state.ny.us

Regional Customer Service Delivery
Director:
David Williams. 518-473-8743
e-mail: dave.williams@orps.state.ny.us

Albany (Northern Region) . . . . fax: 518-486-7752
16 Sheridan Ave, Albany, NY 12210-2714
Regional Director:
Jeffrey Green 518-486-4403
e-mail: internet.northern@orps.state.ny.us

Batavia (Western Region)
Genesee County Bldg 2, 3837 W Main Rd, Batavia, NY 14020
Regional Director:
Vincent M Smith. 585-343-6329/fax: 585-343-9740
e-mail: internet.western@orps.state.ny.us

Melville Satellite Office. . . . . fax: 631-777-1859
560 Broadhollow Rd, Melville, NY 11474
Manager:
Paul N Petruzelli 631-777-1785
e-mail: internet.metro@orps.state.ny.us

Newburgh (Southern Region) . . . . fax: 845-567-2690
263 Route 17K, Ste 2001, Newburgh, NY 12550

Regional Director:
Charles Aviza. 845-567-2648
e-mail: internet.southern@orps.state.ny.us

Saranac Lake Satellite Office. . . . . fax: 518-891-2639
52 Broadway, Saranac Lake, NY 12983
Office Manager:
Dan Lancor. 518-891-1780
e-mail: internet.saranac@orps.state.ny.us

Syracuse (Central Region) . . . . fax: 315-471-3634
109 S Warren St, 2nd Fl, Syracuse, NY 13202
Regional Director:
Robert Gawrelski. 315-471-4816
e-mail: internet.central@orps.state.ny.us

Research, Information & Policy Development
Director:
James Dunne. 518-473-4532
e-mail: jim.dunne@orps.state.ny.us

State Board of Real Property Services
Chair:
Ifigenia Brown 518-474-5711
Member:
John M Bacheller 518-474-5711
Executive Secretary:
Thomas G Griffen. 518-474-5711
Asst to the Board:
Darlene A Maloney 518-474-3793/fax: 518-474-9276

State Valuation Services
Director:
Donald Card 518-474-1071
e-mail: don.card@orps.state.ny.us

Tax Appeals, Division of
Riverfront Professional Tower
500 Federal St, 5th Fl
Troy, NY 12180
518-266-3000 Fax: 518-271-0886
Web site: www.nysdta.org

Administrative Law Judges & Officers
Chief Administrative Law Judge:
Andrew Marchese. 518-266-3000
Asst Chief Administrative Law Judge:
Daniel Ranalli. 518-266-3000
Secretary & Administrative Officer:
Robert P Rivers. . . . . 518-266-3036 or 518-266-3062

Tax Appeals Tribunal
President:
Donald C Dewitt. 518-266-3050
Commissioner:
Caroll Jenkins. 518-266-3051
Commissioner:
Vacant 518-266-3051
Counsel:
Donna M Gardiner 518-266-3052

Taxation & Finance Department
State Campus
Bldg 9, Rm 227
Albany, NY 12227

Offices and agencies appear in alphabetical order.

518-457-4242 Fax: 518-457-2486
Web site: www.tax.state.ny.us

Commissioner:
Andrew S Eristoff................................518-457-2244
Executive Deputy Commissioner:
Barbara G Billet....................................518-457-7358
Deputy Commissioner & Counsel:
Christopher C O'Brien..............518-457-3746/fax: 518-457-8247
Special Asst to Commissioner for Business:
Holly Chamberlin....................................518-485-5080
Director, Conciliation & Mediation Services:
Barry M Bresler.....................................518-485-8063
Director, Executive Correspondence Control Unit:
Elizabeth Amodeo....................................518-457-8193
Director, Legislative Affairs:
John Evers...518-457-2398
Director, Communications:
Thomas Bergin.......................................518-457-4242

Enterprise Services Division
Director:
Brian Digman..518-457-4362

Office of Administration (OOA)
Deputy Commissioner:
Harry VanWormer.....................................518-457-4900

Human Resources Management
Director:
Deborah S Dammer....................................518-457-2786

Operations Support Bureau
Director:
Thomas Beckstein....................................518-485-7891

Office of Budget & Management Analysis
Chief Financial Officer:
Robert F Tangorre...................................518-457-1000

Bureau of Fiscal Services
Director:
Donald J Kohn.......................................518-457-8235

Planning & Management Analysis Bureau
Director:
Kiaran M Johnson....................................518-457-8660

Tax Enforcement, Office of
Deputy Commissioner:
Peter Farrell.......................................518-457-9693

Tax Operations, Office of
Deputy Commissioner:
Robert Gola...518-485-2863

Audit Division
Director, Tax Audits:
Nonie Manion..518-457-2750

Tax Compliance Division
Director:
Joseph F Gecewicz...................................518-457-1138

Tax Policy Analysis, Office of
Deputy Commissioner:
Michelle A Cummings.................................518-457-4357

Technical Services Division
Director:
Marilyn M Kaltenborn................................518-457-1153

Taxpayer Services & Revenue Division
Director:
Jamie Woodward......................................518-457-2261

Treasury Division
Deputy Commissioner & Treasurer:
Aida Brewer.....................518-474-4250/fax: 518-402-4118

e-MPIRE
Director:
Terry Atwater.......................................518-457-7934

CORPORATIONS, AUTHORITIES AND COMMISSIONS

New York State Financial Control Board
123 William St
23rd Fl
New York, NY 10038-3804
212-417-5046 Fax: 212-417-5055
e-mail: nysfcb@fcb.state.ny.us
Web site: www.fcb.state.ny.us

Acting Exec Director:
Jeffrey Sommer......................................212-417-5066
Deputy Director, Expenditure Analysis:
Dennis DeLisle......................................212-417-5069
Deputy Director, Economic & Revenue Analysis:
Martin Fischman.....................................212-417-5068
Assoc Director:
Mattie W Taylor.....................................212-417-5053

New York State Project Finance Agency
641 Lexington Ave
New York, NY 10022
212-688-4000 Fax: 212-872-0678

Chair:
Jerome M Becker.....................................212-688-4000
President & CEO:
Stephen J Hunt......................................212-688-4000
Senior VP, COO & CFO:
Ralph J Madalena....................................212-688-4000
Senior VP & General Counsel:
Justin Driscoll.....................................212-688-4000
Senior VP & Special Asst to Pres/CEO for Policy Dev & Programs:
James P Angley......................................212-688-4000
Senior VP, Debt Issuance:
Bernard Abramowitz.............................212-688-4000 x530
Vice President, Director of Development:
Jonathan Cortrell.............................212-688-4000 x688
Vice President, Policy & Planning:
Tracy A Oats..................................212-688-4000 x678

NEW YORK STATE LEGISLATURE

See Legislative Branch in Section 1 for additional Standing Committee and Subcommittee information.

Offices and agencies appear in alphabetical order.

Assembly Standing Committees

Racing & Wagering
Chair:
J. Gary Pretlow (D)..............................518-455-5291
Ranking Minority Member:
Robert Barra (R)................................518-455-4656

Real Property Taxation
Chair:
Brian M McLaughlin (D).........................518-455-5172
Ranking Minority Mbr:
Charles Nesbitt (R)..............................518-455-3751

Ways & Means
Chair:
Herman D Farrell, Jr (D) 518-455-5491

Ranking Minority Member:
Thomas F Barraga (R) 518-455-4611

Senate Standing Committees

Finance
Chair:
Owen H Johnson (R) 518-455-3411
Ranking Minority Member:
Neil D Breslin (D) 518-455-2225

Racing, Gaming & Wagering
Chair:
William J Larkin, Jr (R) 518-455-2770
Ranking Minority Member:
John D Sabini (D)...............................518-455-2529

U.S. Government

EXECUTIVE DEPARTMENTS AND RELATED AGENCIES

US Department of Homeland Security (DHS)
Web site: www.dhs.gov

Bureau of Immigration & Customs Enforcement (ICE)
Web site: www.ice.gov

New York District Office
601 W 26th St, Ste 820, New York, NY 10001
Special Agent-in-Charge:
Martin Ficke....................................646-230-3200
Albany Sub Office
1086 Troy-Schenectady Rd, Latham, NY 12110
Group Supervisor:
LeRoy Tario..............................518-220-2100
Resident Agent-in-Charge:
Jack McQuade...........................518-220-2100

Customs & Border Protection (CBP)
Web site: www.cbp.gov

Buffalo Field Office
4455 Genesee St, Buffalo, NY 14225
Director:
Michael D'Ambrosio 716-626-0400 x201/fax: 716-626-9281
Albany, Port of
445 Broadway, Room 216, Albany, NY 12207
Port Director:
Drew Wescott..............518-431-0200/fax: 518-431-0203
Buffalo, Port of
111 W Huron St, Buffalo, NY 14202
Area Port Director:
Joseph Wilson..............716-646-3400/fax: 716-551-5011
Champlain, Port of
198 W Service Rd, Champlain, NY 12919
Area Port Director:
Christopher Perry 518-298-8347/fax: 518-298-8314
Ogdensburg, Port of
104 Bridge Approach Rd, Ogdensburg, NY 13669
Port Director:
John Korcz 315-393-1390/fax: 315-393-7472

New York Field Office
1 Penn Plaza, 11th Fl, New York, NY 10119
Director, Field Operations:
Susan T Mitchell 646-733-3100
Field Public Affairs Officer:
Janet Rapaport.................212-514-8324/fax: 212-344-3755
Field Counsel - New York
Associate Chief Counsel:
Judith Altman 646-733-3200
Laboratory Division
Director:
Tom Governo...........................973-368-1901

US Justice Department
Web site: www.usdoj.gov

Bureau of Alcohol, Tobacco, Firearms & Explosives
Web site: www.atf.gov

New York Field Division.....................fax: 718-650-4001
241 37th St, Brooklyn, NY 11232
718-650-4000 Fax: 718-650-4001
Spec Agent-in-Chg:
William McMahon 718-650-4000/fax: 718-650-4071
Public Information Officer:
Joseph G Green 718-650-4000

US Treasury Department
Web site: www.ustreas.gov

Internal Revenue Service
Web site: www.irs.gov

Appeals Unit - Office of Directors
290 Broadway, 13th Fl, New York, NY 10007
Director, Appeals, Area 1 (Large Business & Specialty):
Richard Guevara 212-298-2270/fax: 212-298-2282
Director, Appeals, Area 1 (General):
Raymond Wolff.................212-298-2400/fax: 212-298-2648

Criminal Investigation Unit - New York Field Office
Spec Agent-in-Chg:
Michael J Thomas 212-436-1633/fax: 212-436-1957

Offices and agencies appear in alphabetical order.

Public Information Officer:
Joseph Foy.....................212-436-1032/fax: 212-436-1582

Large & Mid-Size Business Division (LMSB)
290 Broadway, 12th Fl, New York, NY 10007
Director, Financial Services:
Paul Denard...................212-298-2130/fax: 212-298-2124
Communications Manager:
Louise Kaminskyj 212-298-2220
e-mail: louise.kaminskyj@irs.gov
Office of Chief Counsel LMSB Area 1 ....fax: 917-421-3937
33 Maiden Ln, 12th Fl, New York, NY 10038
Area Counsel:
Roland Barral............................917-421-4667
Assoc Area Counsel:
Peter J Graziano..........................917-421-4632

Management Information Technology Services - Northeast Area
290 Broadway, 12th Fl, New York, NY 10007
Director, Information Technology:
Lauren Buschor.................212-298-2050/fax: 212-298-2595

Office of Chief Counsel
33 Maiden Ln, 14th Fl, New York, NY 10038
Area Counsel for SBSE & W & I:
Linda R Dettery.................917-421-4737/fax: 917-421-3944
Associate Area Counsel for SBSE & W & I:
Janet F Appel 917-421-4750

Small Business & Self-Employed Division (SBSE)
Web site: www.irs.gov/smallbiz/irssites.htm
New York SBSE Compliance Services
290 Broadway, 14th Fl, New York, NY 10007
Program Manager, Compliance Centers Document Matching
Programs:
Shirley Greene 212-298-2001/fax: 212-298-2062
SBSE-Compliance Area 2/New York
290 Broadway, 7th Fl, New York, NY 10007
Director, Compliance Area 2:
Michael Donovan 212-436-1886/fax: 212-436-1046
SBSE-Taxpayer Education & Communication (TEC)
10 Metro Tech Center, 625 Fulton St, 6th Fl, Brooklyn, NY 11201
Area Director:
Ellen Murphy 718-488-2000/fax: 718-488-2077

Tax Exempt & Government Entities Division (TEGE) - Northeast Area
10 Metro Tech Center, 625 Fulton St, Brooklyn, NY 11201
Area Manager, Employee Plans:
Robert Henn....................................718-488-2014
TEGE Area Counsel's Office
1600 Stewart Ave, Ste 601, Westbury, NY 11590
Area Counsel:
Laurence Ziegler............516-688-1701/fax: 516-688-1750

Taxpayer Advocate Service (TAS)
Andover Campus Service Center
310 Lowell St, Stop 120, Andover, MA 1812
Taxpayer Advocate for Upstate NY:
Vicki L Coss...............973-474-5549/fax: 978-691-6961
Brookhaven Campus Service Center
1040 Waverly Ave, Stop 102, Holtsville, NY 11742
Taxpayer Advocate for Downstate NY:
George Deller..............631-654-6686/fax: 631-447-4879
Brooklyn & Long Island Office
10 Metro Tech Center, 625 Fulton St, Brooklyn, NY 11201
Taxpayer Advocate:
Anita Kitson 718-488-2080/fax: 718-488-3100
Manhattan Office
290 Broadway, 7th Fl, New York, NY 10007

Taxpayer Advocate:
Peter L Gorga, Jr............212-436-1011/fax: 212-436-1900
Office of Director, Area 1 (New York State & New England)
290 Broadway, 14th Fl, New York, NY 10007
Area Director:
Mary Ann Silvaggio.........212-298-2015/fax: 212-298-2016
Upstate New York Office
Leo O'Brien Federal Bldg, Rm 154, 1 Clinton Sq, Albany, NY 12207
Taxpayer Advocate:
Georgeann Bailey...........518-427-5413/fax: 518-427-5494
Western New York State Office
201 Como Park Blvd, Buffalo, NY 14255-0219
Taxpayer Advocate:
William Wirth...............716-686-4850/fax: 716-686-4851

Wage & Investment Division (W & I) - Stakeholder Patnership Education & Communication (SPEC)
Albany Territory
1 Clinton Ave, Rm 600, Albany, NY 12207
Territory Manager:
Peter Stevens 518-427-4109/fax: 518-427-5421
Area 1 Director's Office
135 High St, Hartford, CT 6103
Area Director:
Sheldon Schwartz...........860-756-4666/fax: 860-756-4567
Buffalo Territory
201 Como Park Blvd, Cheektowaga, NY 14227
Territory Manager:
Thomas Kerr...............716-686-4800/fax: 716-686-4705
New York Territory
290 Broadway, 7th Fl, New York, NY 10007
Territory Mgr:
Michael McCormick.........212-436-1031/fax: 212-436-1629

US Mint..fax: 845-446-6258
Rte 218, PO Box 37, West Point, NY 10996
Fax: 845-446-6258
Web site: www.usmint.gov
Superintendent:
Ellen McCullom...................................845-446-6201
Chief, Mint Police:
Robert Beck 845-446-6234

U.S. CONGRESS

See U.S. Congress Chapter for additional Standing Committee and Subcommittee information.

House of Representatives Standing Committees

Appropriations
Chair:
Jerry Lewis (R-CA) 202-225-5861
Ranking Minority Member:
David R Obey (D-WI) 202-225-3365
New York Delegate:
Maurice D Hinchey (D) 202-225-6335
New York Delegate:
Nita M Lowey (D) 202-225-6506
New York Delegate:
Jose E Serrano (D) 202-225-4361
New York Delegate:
John E Sweeney (R).............................202-225-5614
New York Delegate:
James T Walsh (R)..............................202-225-3701

Offices and agencies appear in alphabetical order.

Policy Areas

Budget

Chair:
Jim Nussle (R-IA)................................. 202-225-2911
Ranking Minority Member:
John M Spratt, Jr (D-SC) 202-225-5501

Ways & Means

Chair:
William M Thomas (R-CA)........................ 202-225-2915
Ranking Minority Member:
Charles B Rangel (D-NY) 202-225-4365
New York Delegate:
Michael R McNulty (D)........................... 202-225-5076
New York Delegate:
Thomas M Reynolds (R) 202-225-5265

Joint Senate & House Standing Committees

Joint Committee on Taxation

Chair:
Rep William M Thomas (R-CA) 202-225-2915
Vice Chair:
Sen Charles E Grassley (D-IA) 202-224-3744
New York Delegate:
Rep Charles B Rangel (D) 202-225-4365

Senate Standing Committees

Appropriations

Chair:
Thad Cochran (R-MS) 202-224-5054

Ranking Minority Member:
Robert C Byrd (D-WV) 202-224-3954

Budget

Chair:
Judd Gregg (R-NH) 202-224-3324
Ranking Minority Member:
Kent Conrad (D-ND) 202-224-2043

Finance

Chair:
Charles E Grassley (R-IA) 202-224-3744
Ranking Minority Member:
Max Baucus (D-MT) 202-224-2651

Subcommittee
Taxation & IRS Oversight

Chair:
Jon Kyl (R-AZ) 202-224-4521
Ranking Minority Member:
James M Jeffords (I-VT) 202-224-5141

Homeland Security & Governmental Affairs

Chair:
Susan Collins (R-ME) 202-224-2523
Ranking Minority Member:
Joseph I Lieberman (D-CT) 202-224-4041

Private Sector

Association of Towns of the State of New York
146 State St, Albany, NY 12207
518-465-7933 Fax: 518-465-0724
e-mail: jhaber@nytowns.org
Web site: www.nytowns.org
G Jeffrey Haber, Executive Director
Advocacy, education for local government

Business Council of New York State Inc
152 Washington Ave, Albany, NY 12210
518-465-7511 x215 Fax: 518-465-4389
e-mail: rich.schwarz@bcnys.org
Web site: www.bcnys.org
Richard Schwarz, Director, Government & Fiscal Affairs & Tax
Counsel

Citizens Budget Commission
11 Penn Plaza, Ste 900, New York, NY 10001
212-279-2605 Fax: 212-868-4745
e-mail: cmb2@is2.nyu.edu
Web site: www.cbcny.org
Charles Brecher, Executive Vice President & Director of Research
Studies & recommendations on funding of civic services

Council of State Governments, Eastern Conference
40 Broad St, Ste 2050, New York, NY 10004-2317
212-482-2320 Fax: 212-482-2344
e-mail: alan@csgeast.org
Web site: www.csgeast.org
Alan V Sokolow, Regional Director
Economic & fiscal programs

NYS Bar Assn, Tax Section
Cravath, Swaine & Moore LLP
125 Broad Street, New York, NY 10004
212-558-4248 Fax: 212-558-3359
Web site: www.sullcrom.com
David P Hariton, Chair

NYS Bar Assn, Trusts & Estates Law Section
Day, Berry & Howard LLP
875 Third Avenue, New York, NY 10022
212-829-3602 Fax: 212-829-3601
e-mail: gwwhitaker@dbh.com
Web site: www.dbh.com
G Warren Whitaker, Chair

Offices and agencies appear in alphabetical order.

DeGraff, Foy, Kunz & Devine, LLP
90 State Street, Albany, NY 12207
518-462-5300 Fax: 518-436-0210
e-mail: firm@degraff-foy.com
Web site: www.degraff-foy.com
David Kunz, Managing Partner
Tax law & procedure, administrative law

Fiscal Policy Institute
1 Lear Jet Lane, Latham, NY 12110
518-786-3156
e-mail: mauro@fiscalpolicy.org
Web site: www.fiscalpolicy.org
Frank Mauro, Executive Director
Nonpartisan research & education; tax, budget, economic & related public policy issues

Community Bankers Assn of NY State, Accounting & Taxation Cmte
GreenPoint Bank
275 Broadhollow Road, Melville, NY 11747
631-844-1004
Web site: www.greenpoint.com
Aurelie Campbell, Co-Chair

Hawkins Delafield & Wood LLP
67 Wall St, 12th Fl, New York, NY 10005
212-820-9434 Fax: 212-820-9666
e-mail: jprogers@hdw.com
Web site: www.hawkins.com
Joseph P Rogers, Jr, Attorney
Tax law; public finance & municipal contracts

Manhattan Institute, Center for Civic Innovation
52 Vanderbilt Ave, 2nd Fl, New York, NY 10017
212-599-7000 Fax: 212-599-3494
Web site: www.manhattan-institute.org
Lindsay Young, Executive Director, Communications
NY city & state tax, fiscal policy

Moody's Investors Service, Public Finance Group
99 Church St, New York, NY 10007
212-553-7780 Fax: 212-298-7113
e-mail: dennis.farrell@moodys.com
Web site: www.moodys.com
Dennis M Farrell, Group Managing Director
Municipal debt ratings & analysis

NYS Conference of Mayors & Municipal Officials
119 Washington Ave, Albany, NY 12210
518-463-1185 Fax: 518-463-1190
e-mail: info@nycom.org
Web site: www.nycom.org
Richard Bucci, President
Legislative advocacy for NYS cities & villages

National Federation of Independent Business
1 Commerce Plaza, Ste 1119, Albany, NY 12260-1000
518-434-1262 Fax: 518-426-8799
e-mail: mark.alesse@nfib.org
Web site: www.nfib.org
Mark Alesse, State Director
Small business advocacy; supporting pro-small business candidates at the state & federal levels

Nelson A Rockefeller Institute of Government
411 State St, Albany, NY 12203-1003
518-443-5522 Fax: 518-443-5788
e-mail: nathanr@rockinst.org
Web site: www.rockinst.org
Richard P Nathan, Director
Management & finance of welfare, health & employment of state & local governments nationally & especially in NY

New York State Assessors' Association
PO Box 888, Middletown, NY 10940
845-344-0292 Fax: 845-343-8238
e-mail: nysaa@warwick.net
Web site: www.nyassessor.com
Thomas Frey, Executive Secretary
Real property tax issues

New York State Government Finance Officers Association Inc
7 Elk St, #2, Albany, NY 12207
518-465-1512 Fax: 518-434-4640
e-mail: info@nysgfoa.org
Web site: www.nysgfoa.org
Ann Marie Berg, President
Membership organization dedicated to the professional management of governmental resources

New York State Society of Certified Public Accountants
3 Park Avenue, 18TH Floor, New York, NY 10016-5991
212-719-8418 Fax: 212-719-3364
e-mail: doleary@nysscpa.org
Web site: www.nysscpa.org
Dennis O'Leary, Director, Government Relations

New York State Society of Municipal Finance Officers
Village of Speculator, PO Box 396, Speculator, NY 12164
518-548-7354 Fax: 518-548-2774
Web site: www.nysmunicipalfinanceofficers.org
Bonnie J Page, President
Improve municipal financial & accounting operations & procedures in NYS

New York State Society of Enrolled Agents
Office of David J Silverman
866 UN Plaza, #415, New York, NY 10017
212-752-6983 Fax: 212-758-5478
e-mail: taxproblm@aol.com
Web site: www.nyssea.org
David J Silverman, Chair, Legislative/Government Relations
    Committee

Offices and agencies appear in alphabetical order.

Robert Schalkenbach Foundation
149 Madison Ave, Ste 601, New York, NY 10016
212-683-6424 Fax: 212-683-6454
e-mail: msullivan@schalkenbach.org
Web site: www.schalkenbach.org
Mark A Sullivan, Acting Executive Director
Land value taxation, real property & economic publications

SCAA - Schuyler Center for Analysis & Advocacy
150 State St, 4th Fl, Albany, NY 12207-1626
518-463-1896 x24 Fax: 518-463-3364
e-mail: rsykes@scaany.org
Web site: www.scaany.org
Karen Schimke, President & Chief Executive Officer
Advocacy, analysis & forums on economic security, education, child care, child support, revenue & taxation issues

Urbanomics of New York
115 Fifth Ave, 3rd Fl, New York, NY 10003
212-353-7465 Fax: 212-353-7462
e-mail: r-armstrong@peapc.com
Web site: www.urbanomics.org
Regina B Armstrong, Principal
Economic development planning studies, market studies, tax policy analyses, program evaluations, economic & demographic forecasts

Wachtell, Lipton, Rosen & Katz
51 W 52nd St, New York, NY 10019
212-403-1241 Fax: 212-403-2241
e-mail: pccanellos@wlrk.com
Web site: www.wlrk.com
Peter C Canellos, Partner
Tax law

Offices and agencies appear in alphabetical order.

TOURISM, ARTS & SPORTS

New York State

GOVERNOR'S OFFICE

Governor's Office
Executive Chamber
State Capitol
Albany, NY 12224
518-474-8390 Fax: 518-474-1513
Web site: www.state.ny.us

Governor:
Ceorge E Pataki 518-474-8390
Executive Director:
Kara Lanspery 518-474-8390
Secretary to the Governor:
John P Cahill. 518-474-4246
Senior Policy Advisor to the Governor:
Jeffrey Lovell 518-486-9671
Counsel to the Governor-Attorney General, Budget:
Richard Platkin. 518-474-8343
Senior Asst Counsel to the Governor-Indian Affairs, Lottery, Racing &
  Wagering Board, State Liquor Auth:
Greg Allen 518-474-2266
Asst Counsel to the Gov-Battery Pk, Child/Family Svcs, Child/Family
  Council, Family, Housing, Human Rts, Roosevelt Is, Temp/Disabl,
  Women, HFA/MBBA/SONYMA:
Carolyn Betz Kerr. 518-474-1310
Asst Counsel to the Governor-Civil Svc, Elections, Empl Relations, Labor,
  Motor Veh, Niagara Fr, Port Auth, Retirement/Pensions, Transp, Thruway,
  Waterfr, MTA, PERB:
Christopher Staszak 518-474-1310
Asst Counsel to the Governor-Adirondack Pk Agency, Agric & Markets,
  Bond Act Coord, Consumer Protection Bd, Environ Facilities Corp, Parks
  & Recreation, State & Local Govt, OGS:
James Walsh. 518-474-8327
Director, Communications:
David Catalfamo. 518-474-8418

EXECUTIVE DEPARTMENTS AND RELATED AGENCIES

Council on the Arts
175 Varick St
3rd Fl
New York, NY 10014
212-627-4455 or TDD: 800-895-9838 Fax: 212-620-5911
Web site: www.nysca.org

Chair:
Richard J Schwartz. 212-627-4440
Vice Chair:
Debra R Black 212-627-4440
Acting Executive Director:
Richard J Schwartz. 212-627-8686
  e-mail: rschwartz@nysca.org

Deputy Director:
Al Berr 212-627-8444
  e-mail: aberr@nysca.org
Deputy Director:
Jack Lindahl 212-627-3338
  e-mail: glindahl@nysca.org
Deputy Director:
Debby Silverfine. 212-627-7778
  e-mail: dsilverfine@nysca.org
Assistant to Chair:
Susan Borozan 212-627-4440
  e-mail: sborozan@nysca.org

Administrative Services
Administrative Officer:
Tracy Hamilton-Thompson 212-627-3131
  e-mail: thamilton@nysca.org

Fiscal Management
Director:
Calvin Walker. 212-627-4884
  e-mail: cwalker@nysca.org

Information Services
Public Information Officer:
Margaret Keta. 212-627-5656
  e-mail: mketa@nysca.org

Program Staff

Architecture, Planning & Design/Capital Aid
Director:
Anne Van Ingen 212-741-7013
  e-mail: avaningen@nysca.org

Arts in Education
Director:
Amy Duggins Pender 212-741-5256
  e-mail: aduggins@nysca.org

Dance
Director:
Beverly D'Anne 212-741-3232
  e-mail: bd'anne@nysca.org

Electronic Media & Film
Director:
Karen Helmerson 212-741-3003
  e-mail: khelmerson@nysca.org

Folk Arts
Director:
Robert Baron 212-741-7755
  e-mail: rbaron@nysca.org

Individual Artists
Director:
Don Palmer. 212-741-6633
  e-mail: dpalmer@nysca.org

Offices and agencies appear in alphabetical order.

Policy Areas

Literature
Director:
Kathleen Masterson 212-741-2622
e-mail: kmasterson@nysca.org

Museum
Director:
Kristin Herron 212-741-7848
e-mail: kherron@nysca.org

Music
Director:
James Jordan 212-741-6562
e-mail: jjordan@nysca.org

Presenting
Director:
Bella Shalom 212-741-2221
e-mail: bshalom@nysca.org

Special Arts Services
Director:
Helen Cash Jackson 212-741-7148
e-mail: hcash@nysca.org

State & Local Partnerships/Decentralization
Director:
Megan White 212-741-7140
e-mail: mwhite@nysca.org

Theatre
Director:
Robert Zuckerman 212-741-7077
e-mail: rzuckerman@nysca.org

Visual Artists
Director:
Elizabeth Merena 212-741-5222
e-mail: emerena@nysca.org

Education Department
State Education Bldg
89 Washington Ave
Albany, NY 12234
518-474-3852 Fax: 518-486-5631
Web site: www.nysed.gov

Commissioner, University President:
Richard P Mills. 518-474-5844
e-mail: rmills@mail.nysed.gov
Asst to the Commissioner:
Peggy Rivers. 518-474-5845
e-mail: privers@mail.nysed.gov
Counsel & Deputy Commissioner, Legal Affairs:
Kathy A Ahearn 518-474-6400
e-mail: kahearn@mail.nysed.gov

Cultural Education Office
10A 33 Cultural Education Center, Madison Ave, Albany, NY 12230
Web site: www.oce.nysed.gov
Deputy Commissioner:
Carole F Huxley 518-474-5976/fax: 518-474-2718
e-mail: chuxley@mail.nysed.gov

State Museum Office
Asst Commissioner & Director:
Clifford A Siegfried 518-474-5812
e-mail: csiegfri@mail.nysed.gov

Exhibit Design, Division of Exhibits / Public & Educational Services
Director, Exhibits:
Mark Schaming 518-486-2031
Exhibit Production
Supervisor:
David LaPlante 518-402-5531
Floor Services
Director:
John Krumdieck. 518-474-0076
Museum Education - Public Programs & Visitor Services
Chief:
Jeanine Grinage 518-486-2003
Research & Collections
Director:
John Hart 518-474-5813
Acting State Geologist:
William Kelly 518-474-5816
Museum Services:
Vacant. 518-486-2037

Empire State Development
30 South Pearl St
Albany, NY 12245
518-292-5100
Web site: www.empire.state.ny.us

633 Third Ave
New York, NY 10017
212-803-3100

Commissioner:
Charles A Gargano 212-803-3700
Communications Director:
Ron Jury. 212-803-3740/fax: 212-803-3735
e-mail: rjury@empire.state.ny.us

Advertising, Marketing & Tourism
Web site: www.iloveny.state.ny.us
Senior VP & Sr Deputy Commissioner, Corporate Marketing:
Neville Bugwadia. 212-803-2244
Deputy Commissioner, Business Marketing, Advertising & Tourism:
Suzanne Morris. 518-292-5360

Governor's Office of Motion Picture & Television Development
Deputy Commissioner:
Patricia Kaufman. 212-803-2334/fax: 212-803-2339

General Services, Office of
Corning Tower, 41st Fl
Empire State Plaza
Albany, NY 12242
518-474-3899 Fax: 518-474-1546
Web site: www.ogs.state.ny.us

633 Third Ave
New York, NY 10017
212-681-4580
Fax: 212-681-4558

Commissioner:
Daniel D Hogan 518-474-5991
e-mail: daniel.hogan@ogs.state.ny.us

Offices and agencies appear in alphabetical order.

First Deputy Commissioner:
    Robert J Fleury 518-473-6953
    e-mail: robert.fleury@ogs.state.ny.us
Asst Commissioner, Public Affairs:
    Jennifer Morris 518-474-5987/fax: 518-474-3187
    e-mail: jennifer.morris@ogs.state.ny.us

Empire State's Convention & Cultural Events Office
Director:
    Heather Flynn 518-474-3195
Manager, Convention Center:
    Dick Hallocks 518-474-0558
Director, Marketing:
    Michael J Snyder 518-474-0538
Director, Curatorial & Tour Services:
    Dennis Anderson 518-473-7521
Curator, NYS Vietnam Memorial:
    Robert Allyn 518-473-5546/fax: 518-474-3465

Hudson River Valley Greenway
Capitol Building, Rm 254
Albany, NY 12224
518-473-3835 Fax: 518-473-4518
e-mail: hrvg@hudsongreenway.state.ny.us
Web site: www.hudsongreenway.state.ny.us

Greenway Conservancy for the Hudson River Valley
Board Chair:
    Kevin J Plunkett 518-473-3835
Executive Director:
    Carmella R Mantello 518-473-3835

Hudson River Valley Greenway Communities Council
Board Chair:
    Barnabas McHenry 518-473-3835
Executive Director:
    Carmella R Mantello 518-473-3835

Parks, Recreation & Historic Preservation, NYS Office of
Empire State Plaza
Bldg 1
Albany, NY 12238
518-486-1868 Fax: 518-486-2924
Web site: www.nysparks.com

Commissioner:
    Bernadette Castro 518-474-0443
Executive Deputy Commissioner:
    Christopher Pushkarsh 518-473-5385
Deputy Commissioner, Hudson Valley Operations:
    James F Moogan 518-474-0440
Deputy Commissioner, Business Marketing:
    Brian Akley 518-474-0430
Deputy Commissioner, Upstate Operations:
    Dominic Jacangelo 518-474-0402
Counsel:
    Paul Laudato 518-474-0430
Asst Commissioner, Public Affairs:
    Wendy Gibson 518-486-1868
Director, Natural Heritage Trust:
    Kevin Carey 518-474-2997
Director, Resource Management:
    Daniel S Kane 518-474-0414

Director, Natural Resources:
    Ralph Odell 845-889-4100
Chief, Park Police:
    Michael Daly 518-474-4029

Administration & Fiscal Affairs
Director:
    Christopher Pushkarsh 518-473-5385

Concession Management
Director:
    Harold Hagemann 518-486-2932

Empire State Games
Director:
    Frederick W Smith 518-474-8889

Fiscal Management
Director:
    Peter Finn 518-474-6949

Advisory Groups

State Board for Historic Preservation
Chairman:
    Robert MacKay 631-692-4664

State Council of Parks, Recreation & Historic Preservation
Chairman:
    Edward Cox 212-336-2029
Agency Contact:
    Bernadette Castro 518-486-1868

Historic Preservation
Counsel:
    Paul Laudato 518-486-0447

Field Services
 Peebles Island, Waterford, NY 12118
Director & Deputy State Historic Preservation Officer:
    Ruth Pierpont 518-237-8643

Historic Sites Bureau
 Peebles Island, Waterford, NY 12118
Director:
    James P Gold 518-237-8643

Marine & Recreational Vehicles
Director:
    Brian Kempf 518-474-0445

Regional Offices-Downstate District

New York City Region
 A C Powell State Ofc Bldg, 163 W 125th St, New York, NY 10027
Asst Deputy Commissioner:
    Mary Ellen Kris 212-866-2720

Taconic Region
 PO Box 308, Staatsburg, NY 12580
Regional Director:
    Vacant 845-889-4100

Regional Offices-Not Within Districts

Central Region
 Clark Reservation, 6105 E Seneca Turnpike, Jamesville, NY 13078-9516
Regional Director:
    Edward Heinrich 315-492-1756/fax: 315-492-3277

Finger Lakes Region
 2221 Taughannock Park Rd, Box 1055, Trumansburg, NY 14886
Regional Director:
    John C Clancy 607-387-7041/fax: 607-387-3390

Offices and agencies appear in alphabetical order.

Policy Areas

Long Island Region
Belmont Lake St Park, Box 247, Babylon, NY 11702-0247
Regional Director:
    John Norbeck 631-669-1000/fax: 631-667-2066

Palisades Interstate Park Commission
Administration Headquarters, Bear Mountain, NY 10911
Executive Director:
    Carol Ash 845-786-2701

Saratoga/Capital District Region
19 Roosevelt Drive, Saratoga Springs, NY 12866
Regional Director:
    Warren Holliday. 518-584-2000

Thousand Islands Region
Keewaydin State Park, Alexandria Bay, NY 13607
Regional Director:
    Kevin Kieff. 315-482-2593

Regional Offices-Western District

Allegany Region
Allegany State Park, Salamanca, NY 14779
Deputy Park Director:
    George Wyman 716-354-6575/fax: 716-354-2255

Genesee Region
One Letchworth State Park, Castile, NY 14427-1124
General Park Manager:
    Richard Parker. 585-493-3600/fax: 585-493-5272

Niagara Region & Western District Office . . . . fax: 716-278-1725
Niagara Frontier Park Region, Prospect P, PO Box 1132, Niagara Falls,
    NY 14303-0132
Asst Deputy Commissioner:
    Edward J Rutkowski 716-278-1702
Deputy General Mgr, Western District:
    Raymond Goll 716-278-1799

Resource Management

Environmental Management
Director:
    Thomas Lyons 518-474-0409

Planning & Development
Director:
    Robert W Reinhardt 518-474-0415

Racing & Wagering Board

1 Watervliet Ave Ext
Ste 2
Albany, NY 12206-1668
518-453-8460 Fax: 518-453-8867
e-mail: info@racing.state.ny.us
Web site: www.racing.state.ny.us

Chair:
    Michael J Hoblock, Jr. 518-453-8460
Member:
    Cheryl Ritchko-Buley. 518-453-8460
Executive Director:
    Edward J Martin 518-453-8460
Counsel:
    Robert A Feuerstein 212-290-4401
Secretary to the Board:
    Erin E Dahlmeyer. 518-453-8460
Public Information Officer:
    Stacy Clifford 518-453-8460 x3311/fax: 518-453-8867

CORPORATIONS, AUTHORITIES AND COMMISSIONS

Adirondack Park Agency
Route 86
PO Box 99
Ray Brook, NY 12977
518-891-4050 Fax: 518-891-3938
Web site: www.apa.state.ny.us

Chair:
    Ross Whaley. 518-891-4050
Executive Director:
    Daniel T Fitts 518-891-4050
    e-mail: dfitts@gw.dec.state.ny.us
Counsel:
    John S Banta. 518-891-4050
Associate Counsel:
    Barbara A Rottier 518-891-4050
Public Information Director:
    Keith McKeever 518-891-4050

Agriculture & NYS Horse Breeding Development Fund
90 State St
Albany, NY 12207
518-436-8713 Fax: 518-426-1490
Web site: www.nysirestakes.com

Executive Director:
    Peter Goold. 518-436-8713
Counsel:
    Steven Losquadro. 518-436-8713

Battery Park City Authority (Hugh L Carey)
One World Financial Center, 24th Fl
New York, NY 10281
212-417-2000 Fax: 212-417-2001
e-mail: info@bpcauthor.org
Web site: www.batteryparkcity.org

Chair:
    James F Gill 212-417-3192
Vice Chairman:
    Charles J Urstadt. 212-417-2000
President & CEO:
    Timothy S Carey 212-417-4205/fax: 212-417-4153
    e-mail: careyt@bpcauthor.org
Member:
    David B Cornstein 212-417-2000
Press Liaison:
    Leticia M Remauro 212-417-2276/fax: 212-417-2279
    e-mail: remaurol@bpcauthor.org

Capital District Regional Off-Track Betting Corporation
510 Smith St
Schenectady, NY 12305
518-344-5200 Fax: 518-370-5460
Web site: www.capitalotb.com

Offices and agencies appear in alphabetical order.

Chair:
Marcel Webb 518-344-5225
President & CEO:
Michael J Connery 518-344-5225
Vice President:
John F Signor 518-344-5224
Executive Asst to the President:
Tod Grenci 518-344-5408
Secretary:
G James Traub 518-482-5615
Chief Fiscal Officer:
Nancy Madrian 518-344-5233
General Counsel:
Robert Hemsworth 518-344-5298

Catskill Off-Track Betting Corporation
PO Box 3000
Pomona, NY 10970
845-362-0400 Fax: 845-362-0419
e-mail: otb@interbets.com
Web site: www.interbets.com

President:
Donald J Groth 845-362-0400

Nassau Regional Off-Track Betting Corporation
220 Fulton Ave
Hempstead, NY 11550
516-572-2800 Fax: 516-572-2840
e-mail: webmaster@nassauotb.com
Web site: www.nassauotb.com

President:
Lawrence Aaronson 516-572-2800
Executive Director of Operations:
Richard T Bennett, Jr. 516-572-2800 x155
Director, Public Affairs:
Joseph Galante 516-572-2800 x152
Comptroller:
Kevin R Conroy 516-572-2800 x141

New York City Off-Track Betting Corporation
1501 Broadway
New York, NY 10036-5572
212-221-5200 Fax: 212-221-8025
Web site: www.nycotb.com

President:
Raymond V Casey 212-704-5101
Executive VP & COO:
John Van Lindt 212-704-5108
Chief of Staff:
Denise DePrima 212-704-5107
Executive Vice President & CFO:
Peter Aranow 212-221-5200 x5214
Executive VP, General Counsel:
Ira H Block 212-221-5200 x5311
Executive Director, Legislative Affairs:
Daniel Wray 212-221-5200 x5230
Inspector General:
Robert E Unger 212-704-5642/fax: 212-221-8479
Senior VP, Marketing, Media & Communications:
Ron Ceisler 212-704-5152/fax: 212-704-5141

Senior VP, New Business, Real Estate, Facilities & Community Affairs:
Denis McManus 212-221-5200 x5583
Vacant

New York Convention Center Operating Corp
655 W 34th St
New York, NY 10001-1188
212-216-2000 Fax: 212-216-2588
e-mail: moreinfo@javitscenter.com
Web site: www.javitscenter.com

President & Chief Executive Officer:
Gerald T McQueen 212-216-2130
Vice President, Operations:
Myles McGrane 212-216-2211
Director, Public Affairs:
Michael Eisgrau 212-216-2176/fax: 212-216-2895

New York State Athletic Commission
123 William St
20th Fl
New York, NY 10038-3804
212-417-5700 Fax: 212-417-4987
e-mail: athletic@dos.state.ny.us
Web site: www.dos.state.ny.us/athletic.html

Chair:
Ron Scott Stevens 212-417-5700
Secretary:
Robert Limerick 212-417-5700

New York State Commission on the Restoration of the Capitol
Corning Tower, 40th Fl
Empire State Plaza
Albany, NY 12242
518-473-0341 Fax: 518-486-5720

Executive Director:
Andrea J Lazarski 518-473-0341
e-mail: andrea.lazarski@ogs.state.ny.us

New York State Olympic Regional Development Authority
Olympic Center
218 Main St
Lake Placid, NY 12946
518-523-1655 Fax: 518-523-9275
e-mail: info@orda.org
Web site: www.orda.org

Chair:
Charles A Gargano 212-803-3700
President & CEO:
Ted Blazer 518-523-1655 x201
Senior Vice President:
Jeffrey Byrne 518-523-1655 x203
Olympic Center Manager:
Denny Allen 518-523-1655 x222
Marketing Director:
Fran Sayers 518-523-1655 x209

Offices and agencies appear in alphabetical order.

Director, Events:
Jim Goff. 518-523-1655 x212
Director, Finance:
Kathy Bushy 518-523-1655 x208
Director, Communications:
Sandy Caligiore. 518-523-1655 x213
e-mail: sandyc@orda.org

New York State Thoroughbred Breeding & Development Fund

One Penn Plaza
Ste 725
New York, NY 10119
212-465-0660 Fax: 212-465-8205
Web site: www.nybreds.com

Chair:
William A Levin. 212-465-0660
Executive Director:
Martin G Kinsella. 212-465-0660

New York State Thruway Authority

200 Southern Blvd
Albany, NY 12209
518-436-2700 Fax: 518-436-2899
e-mail: publicinfo@thruway.state.ny.us
Web site: www.thruway.state.ny.us

Chair:
John L Buono 518-436-3000
Executive Director:
Michael R Fleischer 518-436-2900
General Counsel:
Sharon O'Conor 518-436-2840
Deputy Counsel:
Katherine McCartney. 518-436-3188
Director, Government Relations:
Pamela Davis. 518-436-2860/fax: 518-471-4340
Director, Public Information:
Dan Gilbert 518-436-2983/fax: 518-426-3995

New York State Canal Corporation
Web site: www.canals.state.ny.us
Acting Director:
Lawrence Frame. 518-436-3055

Northeastern Queens Nature & Historical Preserve Commission

Bldg 635 Bayside St, Box 5
Fort Totten, NY 11359-1012
718-229-8805 Fax: 718-229-6131
e-mail: sneq@aol.com
Web site: www.sneq.com

Chair:
Lucile Helfat. 718-229-8805
Vice Chair:
Bernard Haber 718-229-8805
Executive Director:
Joan M Vogt. 718-229-8805

Roosevelt Island Operating Corporation (RIOC)

591 Main St
Roosevelt Island, NY 10044
212-832-4540 Fax: 212-832-4582
e-mail: info@roosevelt-island.ny.us
Web site: www.rioc.com

President:
Herbert E Berman. 212-832-4540
Vice President, Operations:
Sari Halper Dickson 212-832-4540
Chairperson, Board of Directors (ex officio):
Judith A Calogero 518-473-8384/fax: 518-473-9462
Commissioner's Designate to Board of Directors:
Mary Beth Labate. 518-486-3370
General Counsel:
Kenneth A Leitner. 212-832-4540 x311
Chief Financial Officer:
Vacant 212-832-4540
Public Information Officer:
John Melia 212-832-4540

Suffolk Regional Off-Track Betting Corporation

5 Davids Dr
Hauppauge, NY 11788-2004
631-853-1000 Fax: 631-853-1086
e-mail: srotbc@suffolkotb.com
Web site: www.suffolkotb.com

President/CEO:
Anthony F Apollaro 631-853-1000
Vice President:
Jeffrey A Casale 631-853-1000
Assoc Counsel/Director, Executive Administration:
Neil H Tiger 631-853-1000
Pub Info:
DuWayne Gregory 631-853-1000 x3512/fax: 631-853-1086

Western Regional Off-Track Betting Corp

700 Ellicott St
Batavia, NY 14020
585-343-1423 Fax: 585-343-6873
Web site: www.westernotb.com

Chair:
Gregory L Davis. 585-343-1423
President & CEO:
Martin C Basinait. 585-343-1423
Executive Vice President:
Patrick T Murphy 585-343-1423
Vice President, Administration:
Michael Kane 585-343-1423
General Counsel & Secretary:
Timothy A McCarthy. 585-343-1423
Comptroller:
Nicholas A Noce. 585-343-1423

CONVENTION & VISITORS BUREAUS

Convention Centers & Visitors Bureaus

Albany County Convention & Visitors Bureau
25 Quackenbush Sq, Albany, NY 12207

Offices and agencies appear in alphabetical order.

800-258-3582
Web site: www.albany.org
President, CEO:
   Michele Vennard 518-434-1217/fax: 518-434-0887
   e-mail: accvb@albany.org

Binghamton/Broome County Convention & Visitors Bureau
29 Court St, PO Box 995, Binghamton, NY 13902
800-836-6740
Web site: www.steny.com
President & CEO:
   Alex S DePersis 607-772-8860 x312/fax: 607-722-4513
   e-mail: adepersis@broome-ny.com

Buffalo Niagara Convention & Visitors Bureau
617 Main St, Ste 200, Buffalo, NY 14203-1496
800-283-3256
Web site: www.visitbuffaloniagara.com
President & CEO:
   Richard Geiger 716-852-0511 x275/fax: 716-852-0131
   e-mail: geiger@buffalocvb.org

Chautauqua County Visitors Bureau
Chautauqua Institution Welcome Center, PO Box 1441, Route 394,
   Chautauqua, NY 14722
800-242-4569
Web site: www.tourchautauqua.com
Executive Director:
   R Andrew Nixon 716-357-4569/fax: 716-357-2284
   e-mail: nixon@tourchautauqua.com

Greater Rochester Visitors Assn
45 East Ave, Ste 400, Rochester, NY 14604-2294
800-677-7282
Web site: www.visitrochester.com
President/CEO:
   T Edward Hall 585-279-8316/fax: 585-232-4822
   e-mail: edh@visitrochester.com

Ithaca/Tompkins County Convention & Visitors Bureau
904 E Shore Dr, Ithaca, NY 14850
Web site: www.visitithaca.com
Director:
   Fred Bonn 607-272-1313/fax: 607-272-7617
   e-mail: fred@visitithaca.com

Lake Placid/Essex County Convention & Visitors Bureau
Olympic Center, 216 Main St, Lake Placid, NY 12946
800-447-5224
Web site: www.lakeplacid.com
President/CEO:
   James McKenna 518-523-2445/fax: 518-523-2605

Long Island Convention & Visitors Bureau & Sports Comission
330 Vanderbilt Motor Pkwy, Ste 203, Hauppauge, NY 11788
877-386-6654
Web site: www.funonli.com
President:
   Moke R McGowen 631-951-3900/fax: 631-951-3439
   e-mail: mmcgowen@funonli.com

NYC & Company/Convention & Visitors Bureau
810 Seventh Ave, New York, NY 10019
212-484-1200
Web site: www.nycvisit.com
Pres/CEO:
   Cristyne Lategano-Nicholas 212-484-1265/fax: 212-245-5943

Oneida County Convention & Visitors Bureau
PO Box 551, Utica, NY 13503-0551
800-426-3132
Web site: www.oneidacountycvb.com
President:
   Paul E Ziegler 315-724-7221/fax: 315-724-7335
   e-mail: paulzieg@dreamscape.com

Ontario County/Finger Lakes Visitor's Connection
25 Gorham St, Canandaigua, NY 14424
Web site: www.visitfingerlakes.com
President:
   Valerie Knoblauch 585-394-3915/fax: 585-394-4067

Saratoga Convention & Tourism Bureau
10 Railroad Pl, Ste 100, Saratoga Springs, NY 12866-3048
Web site: www.discoversaratoga.org
President:
   Gavin Landry 518-584-1531/fax: 518-584-2969
   e-mail: mail@discoversaratoga.org

Steuben County Conference & Visitors Bureau
1 West Market St, Ste 301, Corning, NY 14830
866-946-3386
Web site: www.corningfingerlakes.com
Executive Director:
   Peggy Coleman 607-936-6544/fax: 607-936-6575
   e-mail: sccvb@corningfingerlakes.com

Sullivan County Visitors Association . . . . fax: 845-794-1058
100 North Street, PO Box 5012, Monticello, NY 12701
800-882-2287 Fax: 845-794-1058
Web site: www.scva.net
President/CEO:
   Roberta Byron Lockwood 845-794-3000 x5010
   e-mail: sctoursim@scva.net

Syracuse Convention & Vistors Bureau
572 S Salina St, Syracuse, NY 13202
800-234-4797
Web site: www.visitsyracuse.org
President:
   Doug Small 315-470-1910/fax: 315-471-8545
   e-mail: cvb@visitsyracuse.org

Thousand Islands Int'l Tourism Council
Box 400, 43373 Collins Landing, Alexandria Bay, NY 13607
800-847-5263
Web site: www.visit1000islands.com
Director:
   Gary DeYoung 315-482-2520/fax: 315-482-5906
   e-mail: gary@visit1000islands.com

Westchester County Office of Tourism
222 Mamaroneck Ave, Ste 100, White Plains, NY 10605
800-833-9282
Web site: www.westchestertourism.com
Director:
   Margo Jones 914-995-8500/fax: 914-995-8505
   e-mail: tourism@westchestergov.com

NEW YORK STATE LEGISLATURE

See Legislative Branch in Section 1 for additional Standing Committee and Subcommittee information.

Offices and agencies appear in alphabetical order.

Assembly Standing Committees

Racing & Wagering
Chair:
J. Gary Pretlow (D) 518-455-5291
Ranking Minority Member:
Robert Barra (R) 518-455-4656

Tourism, Arts & Sports Development
Chair:
Joseph D Morelle (D) 518-455-5373
Ranking Minority Member:
Michael J Fitzpatrick (R) 518-455-5021

Senate Special Committees

Arts & Cultural Affairs, Special Committee on the
Chair:
Serphin R Maltese (R) 518-455-3281

Legislative Director:
Kristen Brown 518-455-3281

Senate Standing Committees

Racing, Gaming & Wagering
Chair:
William J Larkin, Jr (R) 518-455-2770
Ranking Minority Member:
John D Sabini (D) 518-455-2529

Tourism, Recreation & Sports Development
Chair:
Mary Lou Rath (R) 518-455-3161
Ranking Minority Member:
Jose Serrano (D) 518-455-2795

U.S. Government

EXECUTIVE DEPARTMENTS AND RELATED AGENCIES

National Archives & Records Administration

Franklin D Roosevelt Presidential Library & Museum
4079 Albany Post Rd, Hyde Park, NY 12538
Web site: www.fdrlibrary.marist.edu
Director:
Cynthia M Koch 845-486-7770/fax: 845-486-1147
e-mail: roosevelt.library@nara.gov

Smithsonian Institution

Cooper-Hewitt National Design Museum
2 East 91st St, New York, NY 10128
Web site: www.si.edu/ndm
Director:
Paul Thompson 212-849-8370/fax: 212-849-8367

National Museum of the American Indian-George Gustav Heye Center
US Custom House, One Bowling Green, New York, NY 10004
Web site: www.nmai.si.edu
GGHC Director:
John Haworth 212-514-3700/fax: 212-514-3800

US Department of the Interior
1849 C Street NW
Washington, DC 20240
202-208-3100
Web site: www.doi.gov

Fish & Wildlife Service-Northeast Region
300 Westgate Center Dr, Hadley, MA 01035-9589
Regional Director:
Marvin Moriarty 413-253-8200

National Park Service-Northeast Region
200 Chestnut St, US Custom House, Philadelphia, PA 19106

Web site: www.nps.gov
Acting Northeast Regional Director:
Mary A Bomar 215-597-7013/fax: 215-597-0815
Asst Regional Director, Communications & Tourism:
Edie Shean-Hammond 215-597-7989

Fire Island National Seashore
120 Laurel St, Patchogue, NY 11772
Web site: www.nps.gov/fiis/
Superintendent:
Michael T Reynolds 631-289-4810/fax: 631-289-4898

Fort Stanwix National Monument
112 E Park St, Rome, NY 13440
Web site: www.nps.gov/fost/
Superintendent:
James Perry 315-336-2090/fax: 315-334-5051

Gateway National Recreation Area
210 New York Ave, Staten Island, NY 10305
Web site: www.nps.gov/gate
General Superintendent:
Barry Sullivan 718-354-4665/fax: 718-354-4764
Jamaica Bay Unit
Deputy Superintendent:
Billy G Garrett 718-338-3605/fax: 718-338-3876
Sandy Hook Unit
Superintendent:
Richard Wells 732-872-5913/fax: 732-872-5915
Staten Island Unit
Superintendent:
Shirley McKinney 718-354-4640/fax: 718-354-4639

Manhattan Sites
26 Wall St, New York, NY 10005
Web site: www.nps.gov/masi
Superintendent:
Jim Pepper 212-825-6888/fax: 212-825-6874

Martin Van Buren National Historic Site
1013 Old Post Rd, Kinderhook, NY 12106
Web site: www.nps.gov/mava
Superintendent:
Daniel J Dattilio 518-758-9689/fax: 518-758-6986

Offices and agencies appear in alphabetical order.

Roosevelt-Vanderbilt National Historic Sites
4097 Albany Post Rd, Hyde Park, NY 12538
 Web site: www.nps.gov/vama
Superintendent:
 Sarah Olson 845-229-9115/fax: 845-229-0739

Sagamore Hill National Historic Site
20 Sagamore Hill Road, Oyster Bay, NY 11771-1809
 Web site: www.nps.gov/sahi
Superintendent:
 Gay Vietzke. 516-922-4788/fax: 516-922-4792

Saratoga National Historical Park
648 Rt 32, Stillwater, NY 12170
 Web site: www.nps.gov/sara
Superintendent:
 Frank Dean 518-664-9821/fax: 518-664-9830

Statue of Liberty National Monument & Ellis Island
Liberty Island, New York, NY 10004
 Web site: www.nps.gov/stli/
Superintendent:
 Cynthia Garrett 212-363-3206/fax: 212-363-8347

Theodore Roosevelt Inaugural National Historic Site
641 Delaware Ave, Buffalo, NY 14202
 Web site: www.nps.gov/thri/
Executive Director:
 Molly Quackenbush 716-884-0095/fax: 716-884-0330

Women's Rights National Historical Park
136 Fall St, Seneca Falls, NY 13148
 Web site: www.nps.gov/wori
Superintendent:
 Tina Orcutt 315-568-2991/fax: 315-568-2141

U.S. CONGRESS

See U.S. Congress Chapter for additional Standing Committee and Subcommittee information.

House of Representatives Standing Committees

Resources
Chair:
 Richard W Pombo (R-CA) 202-225-2761
Ranking Minority Member:
 Nick J Rahall, II (D-WV) 202-225-3452

 Subcommittee
 Forests & Forest Health
 Chair:
  Greg Walden (R-OR) 202-225-6730
 Ranking Minority Member:
  Tom Udall (D-NM) 202-225-6190
 National Parks, Recreation & Public Lands
 Chair:
  Devin Jones (R-CA) 202-225-2523
 Ranking Min Member:
  Donna M Christensen (D-VI) 202-225-1790

Senate Standing Committees

Energy & Natural Resources
Chair:
 Pete V Domenici (R-NM) 202-224-6621
Ranking Minority Member:
 Jeff Bingaman (D-NM) 202-224-5521
New York Delegate:
 Charles E Schumer (D) 202-224-6542

 Subcommittees
 National Parks
 Chair:
  Craig Thomas (R-WY) 202-224-6441
 Ranking Minority Member:
  Daniel K Akaka (D-HI) 202-224-6361
 Public Lands & Forests
 Chair:
  Larry E Craig (R-ID) 202-224-2752
 Ranking Minority Member:
  Ron Wyden (D-OR) 202-224-5244

Private Sector

AAA Northway
112 Railroad St, Schenectady, NY 12301
518-374-4575 Fax: 518-374-3140
Web site: www.aaanorthway.com
Eric Stigberg, Marketing, Public & Government Affairs Manager
Capital region membership, travel & touring sales & services

AAA Western & Central New York
100 International Dr, Buffalo, NY 14221
716-633-9860 Fax: 716-631-5925
e-mail: wsmith@nyaaa.com
Web site: www.aaa.com
Wallace Smith, Vice President

Adirondack Lakes Center for the Arts
Rte 28, PO Box 205, Blue Mountain Lake, NY 12812-0205
518-352-7715 Fax: 518-352-7333
e-mail: alca@telenet.net
Web site: www.adk-arts.org
Ellen C Butz, Executive Director
Multi/Arts Center

Adirondack Mountain Club Inc
301 Hamilton Street, Albany, NY 12210-1738
518-449-3870 Fax: 518-449-3875
e-mail: nwoodwor@nycap.rr.com
Web site: www.adk.org
Neil F Woodworth, Executive Director
Hiking, nonmotorized recreation, conservation & education

Offices and agencies appear in alphabetical order.

Adirondack/Pine Hill/NY Trailways
499 Hurley Ave, Hurley, NY 12443-5119
845-339-4230 Fax: 845-853-7035
Web site: www.trailwaysny.com
Eugene J Berardi, Jr, President
Tour & charter service

Alliance for the Arts
330 W 42nd St, Ste 1701, New York, NY 10036
212-947-6340 Fax: 212-947-6416
e-mail: info@allianceforarts.org
Web site: www.allianceforarts.org
Randall Bourscheidt, President
*Advocacy, promotion, research, information, referrals &
publications*

Alliance of NYS Arts Organizations
PO Box 96, Mattituck, NY 11952-0096
631-298-1234 Fax: 631-298-1101
e-mail: jkweiner@thealliancenys.org
Web site: www.thealliancenys.org
Judith Kaufman Weiner, Executive Director
Technical assistance, professional development & advocacy services

Alliance of Resident Theatres/New York (ART/New York)
575 Eighth Ave, Ste 17 South, New York, NY 10018
212-244-6667 Fax: 212-714-1918
Web site: www.offbroadwayonline.com
Virginia P Louloudes, Executive Director
*Services & advocacy for New York City's not-for-profit theatre
community*

American Federation of Musicians, Local 802
322 West 48th St, 5th Fl, New York, NY 10036
212-245-4802 Fax: 212-245-6255
Web site: www.local802afm.org
Heather Beaudoin, Director, Public Relations

American Museum of Natural History
Central Park West at 79th St, New York, NY 10024-5192
212-769-5100 Fax: 212-769-5018
e-mail: info@amnh.org
Web site: www.amnh.org
Ellen V Futter, President
Education, exhibition & scientific research

Art & Science Collaborations Inc
PO Box 358, Staten Island, NY 10301
941-955-5103
e-mail: asci@asci.org
Web site: www.asci.org
Cynthia Pannucci, Director
*Raising public awareness of art & artists using science & technology
to explore new forms of creative expression*

ArtsConnection Inc (The)
520 8th Ave, #321, New York, NY 10018
212-302-7433 Fax: 212-302-1132
e-mail: artsconnection@artsconnection.org
Web site: www.artsconnection.org
Steven Tennen, Executive Director
*Arts-in-education programming & training for children, teachers &
artists*

**Association of Independent Video & Filmmakers (AIVF),
(The)**
304 Hudson St, 6th Fl, New York, NY 10013
212-807-1400 Fax: 212-463-8519
e-mail: info@aivf.org
Web site: www.aivf.org
Beni Matias, Executive Director
*Membership service organization for independent producers &
filmmakers*

Automobile Club of New York
1415 Kellum Place, Garden City, NY 11530
516-873-2252 Fax: 516-873-2375
Web site: www.aaany.com
Dennis J Crossley, President

Brooklyn Botanic Garden
1000 Washington Ave, Brooklyn, NY 11225-1009
718-623-7200 Fax: 718-857-2430
Judith D Zuk, President
*Comprehensive study of plant biodiversity in metropolitan New
York; home gardener's resource center*

Brooklyn Museum of Art
200 Eastern Pkwy, Brooklyn, NY 11238
718-638-5000 Fax: 718-501-6136
Web site: www.brooklynmuseum.org
Schawannah Wright, Manager, Community Involvement

Buffalo Bills
One Bills Drive, Orchard Park, NY 14127
716-648-1800 x240 Fax: 716-648-3202
Web site: www.buffalobills.com
Scott Berchtold, Vice President-Communications

Buffalo Sabres
One Seymour H Knox III Plz, Buffalo, NY 14203
716-855-4100 x526 Fax: 716-855-4110
e-mail: michael.gilbert@sabres.com
Web site: www.sabres.com
Michael Gilbert, Director Public Relations

Buffalo Trotting Association Inc
5600 McKinley Parkway, PO Box 38, Hamburg, NY 14075
716-649-1280 Fax: 716-649-0033
e-mail: crawfords@buffaloraceway.com
Web site: www.buffaloraceway.com
Simon Crawford, General Manager
Harness horse racing

Offices and agencies appear in alphabetical order.

CUNY New York City College of Technology, Hospitality Mgmt
300 Jay St, Room 220, Brooklyn, NY 11201-2983
718-260-5630 Fax: 718-260-5997
Web site: www.nyct.cuny.edu
Jerry Van Loon, Professor & Chair
Hospitality & food service management; tourism

CUNY New York City College of Technology, Hospitality Mgmt
300 Jay St, Room 621, Brooklyn, NY 11201-2983
718-260-5637 Fax: 718-260-5995
e-mail: jjordan@citytech.cuny.edu
Web site: www.cuny.edu
Julia Jordan, NYC Advisory Board Member & Professor
Spoons Across America; American Institute of Wine & Food (The); James Beard Foundation (The)

Campground Owners of New York
PO Box 497, Dansville, NY 14437-0497
585-335-2710 Fax: 585-335-2710
e-mail: cony@frontiernet.net
Web site: www.nycampgrounds.com
Robert C Klos, Executive Director

Cendant Car Rental Group Inc
9 West 57TH Street, New York, NY 10019
973-428-9700
e-mail: elliot.bloom@cendant.com
Web site: www.cendant.com
Elliot Bloom, Senior Vice President, Corporate Communications
Travel & rental car services

Coalition of Living Museums
1000 Washington Ave, Brooklyn, NY 11225
718-623-7225 Fax: 718-857-2430
e-mail: loiscarswell@bbg.org
Web site: www.livingmuseums.org
Lois Carswell, Chair, Steering Committee
Advocacy organization for living museums (zoos, botanical gardens, aquaria, arboreta & nature centers) in NYS

Cold Spring Harbor Fish Hatchery & Aquarium
1660 Route 25A, Cold Spring Harbor, NY 11724
516-692-6768 Fax: 516-692-6769
e-mail: cshfha@optonline.net
Web site: www.cshfha.org
Norman Soule, Director
Largest living collection of NYS freshwater fish, amphibians & turtles

Columbia University, School of the Arts
305 Dodge Hall, 2960 Broadway, MC1808, New York, NY 10027
212-854-2876 Fax: 212-854-7733
e-mail: bwf3@columbia.edu
Web site: www.columbia.edu/cu/arts
Bruce W Ferguson, Dean

Culinary Institute of America
1946 Campus Dr, Hyde Park, NY 12538-1499
845-452-9430 Fax: 845-451-1052
e-mail: admissions@culinary.edu
Web site: www.ciachef.edu
Vance Peterson, Vice President Development
Four-year regionally accredited college offering Associate and Occupational Studies and Bachelor of Professional Studies in culinary and baking/pastry arts. Campuses in Hyde Park, New York, and St Helena, California.

Darien Lake Theme Park & Camping Resort
9993 Allegheny Rd, PO Box 91, Darien Center, NY 14040
585-599-4641 Fax: 585-599-4053
Bradley Paul, Vice President & General Manager

Egg (The), Center for the Performing Arts
Empire State Plaza, PO Box 2065, Albany, NY 12220
518-473-1061 Fax: 518-473-1848
e-mail: info@theegg.org
Web site: www.theegg.org
Peter Lesser, Executive Director
Dance, theatre, family entertainment, music, special events

NYS Bar Assn, Entertainment, Arts & Sports Law Section Elissa D Hecker, Esq
90 Quail Close, Irvington, NY 10533
914-478-0457
e-mail: eheckeresq@yahoo.com
Elissa D Hecker, Chair

Empire State Restaurant & Tavern Association Inc
40 Sheridan Ave, Albany, NY 12210
518-436-8121 Fax: 518-436-7287
e-mail: esrta@capital.net
Web site: www.esrta.org
Scott Wexler, Executive Director

Entertainment Software Association
317 Madison Ave, 22nd Fl, New York, NY 10017
917-522-3250 Fax: 917-522-3258
Web site: www.theesa.com
Gail Markels, Senior Vice President & General Counsel

Exhibition Alliance Inc (The)
Route 12B South, PO Box 345, Hamilton, NY 13346
315-824-2510 Fax: 315-824-1683
e-mail: donnao@exhibitionalliance.org
Web site: www.exhibitionalliance.org
Donna Ostraszewski Anderson, Executive Director
Exhibit-related services for museums in NYS & the surrounding region

Film/Video Arts
462 Broadway, Ste 520, New York, NY 10003
212-941-8787 Fax: 212-219-8924
e-mail: info@fva.com
Web site: www.fva.com
Chloe Kurabi, Programs Director, Fiscal Sponsorship and Filmmaker
Low cost training, postproduction suites, fiscal sponsorship, mentorship, internships

Policy Areas

Finger Lakes Racing Association
PO Box 25250, Farmington, NY 14425
585-924-3232 Fax: 585-924-3239
Web site: www.fingerlakesracetrack.com
Christian Riegle, General Manager
Horse racing & video lottery gaming

Finger Lakes Tourism Alliance
309 Lake St, Penn Yan, NY 14527
315-536-7488 Fax: 315-536-1237
e-mail: info@fingerlakes.org
Web site: www.fingerlakes.org
Alexa F Gifford, President
Regional tourism promotion

Gertrude Stein Repertory Theatre (The)
15 West 26th St, 2nd Fl, New York, NY 10010
212-725-0436 Fax: 212-725-7267
e-mail: info@gerstein.org
Web site: www.gertstein.org
Liz Dreyer, General Manager
Avant garde theater emphasizing international collaboration in experimental works incorporating new technologies

Great Escape Theme Park LLC (The)
PO Box 511, Lake George, NY 12845
518-792-3500 Fax: 518-792-3404
Web site: www.thegreatescape.com
John Collins, General Manager

Harvestworks
596 Broadway, Ste 602, New York, NY 10012
212-431-1130 Fax: 212-431-8473
e-mail: info@harvestworks.org
Web site: www.harvestworks.org
Carol Parkinson, Director
Nonprofit arts organization providing computer education & production studios for the digital media arts

Historic Hudson Valley
150 White Plains Rd, Tarrytown, NY 10591
914-631-8200 Fax: 914-631-0089
e-mail: mail@hudsonvalley.org
Web site: www.hudsonvalley.org
Waddell Stillman, President
Tourism promotion

Hotel Association of New York City Inc
320 Park Ave, 22nd Fl, New York, NY 10022-6838
212-754-6700 Fax: 212-688-2838
e-mail: jspinnato@hanyc.org
Web site: www.hanyc.org
Joseph E Spinnato, President

Hudson River Cruises
5 Field Court, Kingston, NY 12401-3605
845-340-4700 or 800-843-7472 Fax: 845-340-4702
e-mail: hudsonrivercruises@hvc.rr.com
Web site: www.hudsonrivercruises.com
Sandra Henne, Owner
Sightseeing, specialty & charter cruises

Hunter Mountain Ski Bowl
PO Box 295, Hunter, NY 12442
888-486-8376 or 518-263-4223 Fax: 518-263-3704
e-mail: info@huntermtn.com
Web site: www.huntermtn.com
Orville A Slutzky, General Manager
Skiing, snowshoeing, snowboarding & snowtubing; coaching & race camps; summer & fall festivals; Kaaterskill Hotel

Jewish Museum (The)
1109 Fifth Ave, New York, NY 10128-0117
212-423-3271 Fax: 212-423-3233
e-mail: ascher@thejm.org
Web site: www.thejewishmuseum.org
Anne Scher, Director, Communications
Museum of art and Jewish culture

Lincoln Center for the Performing Arts Inc
70 Lincoln Center Plaza, New York, NY 10023-6583
212-875-5370 or 212-875-5319 Fax: 212-875-5330
e-mail: visitorservices@lincolncenter.org
Web site: www.lincolncenter.org
Michael Wiertz, Director, Visitor Services
Guided tours of Lincoln Center; Meet-the-Artist programs;

Lower Manhattan Cultural Council
120 Broadway, 31ST Floor, New York, NY 10271
212-219-9401 Fax: 212-219-2058
e-mail: info@lmcc.net
Web site: www.lmcc.net
Mark Vevle, Director, Marketing & Communications
Supporting Manhattan arts organizations through funding assistance, support for creation & presentation of work & audience development

Madison Square Garden Corp
Two Penn Plaza, Madison Square Garden, New York, NY 10121
212-465-6000 Fax: 212-465-4423
Web site: www.thegarden.com
Barry Watkins, Senior Vice President, Communications
NY Knicks, NY Rangers, concerts, special events

Major League Baseball
245 Park Ave, New York, NY 10167
212-931-7800 Fax: 212-949-5654
Web site: www.mlb.com
Rich Levin, Senior Vice President, Public Relations

Metropolitan Museum of Art (The)
1000 Fifth Ave, New York, NY 10028
212-570-3902 Fax: 212-650-2102
Web site: www.metmuseum.org
Philippe de Montebello, Museum Director

Monticello Raceway
204 Rte 17-B, PO Box 5013, Monticello, NY 12701
845-794-4100 Fax: 845-791-1402
Web site: www.monticelloraceway.com
Clifford Ehrlich, President
Horse racing

Offices and agencies appear in alphabetical order.

Museum Association of New York
265 River St, Troy, NY 12180
518-273-3400 Fax: 518-273-3416
e-mail: info@manyonline.org
Web site: www.manyonline.org
Anne Ackerson, Director
Provides information, advocacy & training to strengthen the diverse museum community & enable museums to fulfill their missions

NY Film Academy
100 East 17th St, New York, NY 10003-2160
212-674-4300 Fax: 212-477-1414
e-mail: film@nyfa.com
Web site: www.nyfa.com
Jerry Sherlock, President & Founder
Film making

NY State Historical Association/The Farmers' Museum
PO Box 800, Cooperstown, NY 13326-0800
607-547-1400 Fax: 607-547-1404
e-mail: info@nysha.org
Web site: www.nysha.org; www.farmersmuseum.org
Eric Strauss, Acting Chief Executive Officer
Historical & cultural exhibition, preservation & education

NYC Arts Coalition
351-West 54th St, New York, NY 10019
212-246-3788 Fax: 212-246-3366
e-mail: info@nycityartscoalition.org
Web site: www.nycityartscoalition.org
Norma P Munn, Chair
Develops public policy analysis, provides reports on arts policy & funding issues & acts as an advocacy vehicle for a united voice for the nonprofit arts sector

NYS Alliance for Arts Education
PO Box 2217, Albany, NY 12220-0217
800-ARTS-N-ED or 518-473-0823 Fax: 518-486-7329
e-mail: info@nysaae.org
Web site: www.nysaae.org
Amy Williams, Executive Director
Advocacy, professional development, technical assistance & information for educators, organizations, artists, parents, policymakers

NYS Outdoor Guides Association
1936 Saranac Ave, Suite 2 PO Box 150, Lake Placid, NY 12946-1402
315-392-4592 Fax: 315-392-4592
e-mail: info@nysoga.org
Web site: www.nysoga.org
Alan R Woodruff, President
Provide NYS licensed guides with support services, representation & sense of community

NYS Passenger Vessel Association
PO Box 98, Brightwaters, NY 11718
866-321-9005 Fax: 631-589-7897
e-mail: info@cruisenewyork.com
Web site: www.cruisenewyork.com
Mike Eagan, Treasurer
Promote cruises on NYS's waterways

NYS Theatre Institute
37 First St, Troy, NY 12180
518-274-3200 Fax: 518-274-3815
e-mail: nysti@capital.net
Web site: www.nysti.org
Patricia Di Benedetto Snyder, Producing Artistic Director
Professional theater productions, training & education, internships, community/school outreach & cultural exchange programs

NYS Turfgrass Association
PO Box 612, 4 Youngs Place, Latham, NY 12110
518-783-1229 Fax: 518-783-1258
e-mail: nysta@nysta.org
Web site: www.nysta.org
Beth Seme, Executive Director
Grow & manage turf for golf courses, ball fields & landscape

National Basketball Association
645 5th Ave, New York, NY 10022
212-407-8000 Fax: 212-826-0579
Web site: www.nba.com
Brian McIntyre, Senior Vice President, Communications

National Football League
280 Park Ave, New York, NY 10017
212-450-2000 Fax: 212-681-7599
e-mail: aiellog@nfl.com
Web site: www.nfl.com
Greg Aiello, Vice President, Public Relations

National Hockey League
1251 Ave of the Americas, 47th Fl, New York, NY 10020
212-789-2000 Fax: 212-789-2020
e-mail: fbrown@nhl.com
Web site: www.nhl.com
Frank Brown, Vice President, Media Relations

National Women's Hall of Fame
PO Box 335, 76 Fall Street, Seneca Falls, NY 13148
315-568-8060 Fax: 315-568-2976
Web site: www.greatwomen.org
Billie Luisi-Potts, Executive Director
The hall celebrates outstanding American women & their achievements

New School University, Department of Sociology
65 Fifth Ave, New York, NY 10003
212-229-5782 or 212-229-5737 Fax: 212-229-5595
e-mail: zolbergv@newschool.edu
Web site: www.newschool/edu
Vera Zolberg, Professor, Sociology & Liberal Studies
Sociology of the arts; censorship; collective memory; outsider art

Policy Areas

Offices and agencies appear in alphabetical order.

New York Academy of Art Inc
111 Franklin St, New York, NY 10013-2911
212-966-0300 Fax: 212-966-3217
e-mail: info@nyaa.edu
Web site: www.nyaa.edu
Wayne A Linker, Executive Director

New York Aquarium
Surf Ave at West 8th St, Brooklyn, NY 11224
718-265-3428 or 718-265-3400 Fax: 718-265-3482
e-mail: fhackett@wcs.org
Web site: www.nyaquarium.com
Fran Hackett, Communications
Conservation, education & research

New York Artists Equity Associates Inc
498 Broome St, New York, NY 10013
212-941-0130 Fax: 212-941-0138
e-mail: regina@anny.org
Web site: www.anny.org
Regina Stewart, Executive Director
Web based advocacy for visual arts & cultural organizations

New York City Opera
20 Lincoln Center, New York, NY 10023
212-870-5633 Fax: 212-724-1120
Web site: www.nycopera.com
Susan Woelzl, Director, Press & Public Relations

New York Foundation for the Arts
155 Ave of the Americas, 14TH Floor, New York, NY 10013-1507
212-366-6900 Fax: 212-366-1778
e-mail: nyfainfo@nyfa.org
Web site: www.nyfa.org
Theodore S Berger, Executive Director
Advocacy, leadership, financial & resource support & collaborative relationships with those committed to the arts

New York Giants
Giants Stadium, East Rutherford, NJ 7073
201-935-8111 Fax: 201-935-8493
Web site: www.giants.com
Pat Hanlon, Vice President, Communications

New York Hall of Science
4701 111th Street, Queens, NY 11368
718-699-0005 x323 Fax: 718-699-1341
e-mail: wbrez@nyscience.org
Web site: www.nyscience.org
Wendy J Brez, Manager, Public Relations
Hands-on science exhibits & education program

New York Islanders
1535 Old Country Rd, Plainview, NY 11803
516-501-6700 Fax: 516-542-9348
Web site: www.newyorkislanders.com
Chris Botta, Vice President, Communications

New York Jets
1000 Fulton Ave, Hempstead, NY 11550
516-560-8100 Fax: 516-560-8197
e-mail: rcolangelo@jets.nfl.com
Web site: www.newyorkjets.com
Ron Colangelo, Vice President of Public Relations

New York Marine Trades Association
194 Park Ave, Suite B, Amityville, NY 11701
631-691-7050 Fax: 631-691-2724
e-mail: csqueri@nymta.com
Web site: www.nymta.com
Christopher Squeri, Executive Director
Promote & protect the marine & boating industry; own & operate three boat shows; monitor local, state & federal marine legislation

New York Mets
Shea Stadium, 123-01 Roosevelt Ave, Flushing, NY 11368
718-507-6387 Fax: 718-639-3619
Web site: www.mets.com
Fred Wilpon, Chairman & Chief Executive Officer

New York Racing Association
PO Box 90, Jamaica, NY 11417
718-641-4700 Fax: 718-843-7673
e-mail: nyra@nyraing.com
Web site: www.nyra.com
Glen Mathes, Director, Commications
Horse racing

New York State Hospitality & Tourism Association
80 Wolf Rd, Albany, NY 12205
800-642-5313 x13 or 518-465-2300 Fax: 518-465-4025
e-mail: dan@nyshta.org
Web site: www.nyshta.org
Daniel C Murphy, President
Hotels, motels, amusement parks & attractions

New York State Restaurant Association
409 New Karner Rd, Albany, NY 12205
518-452-4222 Fax: 518-452-4497
e-mail: ricks@nysra.org
Web site: www.nysra.org
Rick J Sampson, President & Chief Executive Officer

New York State School Music Association (NYSSMA)
718 The Plain Rd, Westbury, NY 11590-5931
888-697-7621 Fax: 516-997-1700
e-mail: nyssmaexec@nyssma.org
Web site: www.nyssma.org
Bert Nelson, Executive Administrator
Advocacy for a quality school music education for every student

New York State Snowmobile Association
PO Box 612, Long Lake, NY 12847
518-624-3849 Fax: 518-624-2441
e-mail: jimjennings@direcway.com
Web site: www.nyssnowassoc.org
Jim Jennings, Executive Director
Working to preserve & enhance snowmobiling & improve trails, facilities & services for participants

Offices and agencies appear in alphabetical order.

New York State Theatre Education Association
63 Hecla St, Buffalo, NY 14216
716-837-9434 Fax: 716-626-8207
e-mail: rogersouth@aol.com
Web site: www.nystea.org
Roger Paolini, President
Working to preserve & enhance drama & theater education & opportunities in NY schools & communities

New York State Travel & Vacation Association
PO Box 285, Akron, NY 14001
716-542-1586 or 888-698-2970 Fax: 716-542-1404
e-mail: info@nystva.org
Dawn L Borchert, Association Manager
The NYSTVA is the tourism industry's leader in communication, legislative awareness, professional development, and promotion.

New York University, Tisch School of the Arts
721 Broadway, 12th Fl, New York, NY 10003-6807
212-998-1800 Fax: 212-995-4064
e-mail: mary.campbell@nyu.edu
Web site: www.nyu.edu/tisch
Mary Schmidt Campbell, Dean
Arts Administration

New York Wine & Grape Foundation
350 Elm St, Penn Yan, NY 14527
315-536-7442 Fax: 315-536-0719
e-mail: info@newyorkwines.org
Web site: www.newyorkwines.org
James Trezise, President
Promotion of wine & grape products of New York; research for wine & grape related products & issues

New York Yankees
800 Ruppert Place, Bronx, NY 10451
718-293-4300 Fax: 718-293-8431
Web site: www.yankees.com
Randy Levine, President

Resources for Artists with Disabilities Inc
77 7th Ave, Suite PHH, New York, NY 10011-6644
212-691-5490 Fax: 212-691-5490
Lois Kaggen, President & Founder
Organizes & promotes exhibition opportunities for visual artists with physical disabilities

Saratoga Gaming & Raceway
PO Box 356, Saratoga Springs, NY 12866
518-584-2110 Fax: 518-583-0995
e-mail: info@saratogaraceway.com
Web site: www.saratogaraceway.com
George W Carlson, Vice President for Racing
Horse racing

Seaway Trail Inc
401 West Main Street, Ray & West Main Streets, PO Box 660, Sackets Harbor, NY 13685
315-646-1000 or 800-SEAWAY-T Fax: 315-646-1004
e-mail: info@seawaytrail.com
Web site: www.seawaytrail.com
Teresa Mitchell, Executive Director
Promotes coastal recreation, economic development, resource management & heritage, cultural, agricultural & culinary tourism along a 454 mile NYS highway system

Ski Areas of New York Inc
2144 Currie Rd, Tully, NY 13159
315-696-6550 Fax: 315-696-6567
e-mail: dirk@iskiny.com
Web site: www.iskiny.com
Dirk Gouwens, President
Promote skiing in NYS

Solomon R Guggenheim Foundation
1071 5th Ave, New York, NY 10128
212-423-3840 Fax: 212-966-0924
e-mail: publicaffairs@guggenheim.org
Web site: www.guggenheim.org
Thomas Krens, Director

Special Olympics New York
504 Balltown Road, Schenectady, NY 12304-2290
518-388-0790 Fax: 518-388-0795
Web site: www.nyso.org
Neal J Johnson, President & Chief Executive Officer
Not-for-profit organization provides year-round sports training & competition in Olympic-style sports for athletes with mental retardation

Sports & Arts in Schools Foundation
58-12 Queens Blvd, Suite 1 - 59th Entrance, Woodside, NY 11377
718-786-7110 Fax: 718-786-7635
e-mail: info@sasfny.org
Web site: www.sasfny.org
James R O'Neill, Executive Director
After-school, summer camps & clinics, winter-break festival

Staten Island Zoo
614 Broadway, Staten Island, NY 10310
718-442-3101 Fax: 718-981-8711
e-mail: sizoodir@aol.com
Web site: www.statenislandzoo.org
John C Caltabiano, Director

Tribeca Film Institute
375 Greenwich St, New York, NY 10013
212-941-2400 Fax: 212-941-3892
Web site: www.tribecafilminstitute.org
Madeyln Wils, President & Chief Executive Officer

Offices and agencies appear in alphabetical order.

USA Track & Field, Adirondack Association Inc
233 Fourth St, Troy, NY 12180
518-273-5552 Fax: 518-273-0647
e-mail: info@usatfadir.org
Web site: www.usatfadir.org
George Regan, President
*Leadership & opportunities for athletes pursuing excellence in
running, race walking & track & field*

Vernon Downs/Mid-State Raceway Inc
PO Box 860, Vernon Downs, NY 13476
315-829-2201 Fax: 315-829-4384
e-mail: vdowns@ny.tds.net
Web site: www.vernondowns.com
Justice Cheney, President
*Horse racing, concerts, motorcross, motorcycle, craft fairs & other
entertainment*

Willow Mixed Media Inc
PO Box 194, Glenford, NY 12433
845-657-2914
e-mail: video@hvc.rr.com
Web site: www.willowmixedmedia.org
Tobe Carey, President
*Not-for-profit specializing in documentary video & arts projects
addressing social concerns*

Yonkers Raceway
810 Central Park Ave, Yonkers, NY 10704
914-968-4200 Fax: 914-968-4479
Web site: www.yonkersraceway.com
Timothy Rooney, President
Horse racing

Offices and agencies appear in alphabetical order.

TRANSPORTATION

New York State

GOVERNOR'S OFFICE

Governor's Office
Executive Chamber
State Capitol
Albany, NY 12224
518-474-8390 Fax: 518-474-1513
Web site: www.state.ny.us

Governor:
  George E Pataki 518-474-8390
Executive Director:
  Kara Lanspery 518-474-8390
Secretary to the Governor:
  John P Cahill. 518-474-4246
Senior Policy Advisor to the Governor:
  Jeffrey Lovell 518-486-9671
Deputy Secretary to the Governor for Energy, Environment & Transportation:
  Charles Fox. 518-474-0411
Counsel to the Governor-Attorney General, Budget:
  Richard Platkin 518-474-8343
Asst Secretary to the Governor-Transportation:
  Thomas Madison 518-408-2552
Asst Counsel to the Gov-Battery Pk, Child/Family Svcs, Child/Family
  Council, Family, Housing, Human Rts, Roosevelt Is, Temp/Disabl,
  Women, HFA/MBBA/SONYMA:
  Carolyn Betz Kerr. 518-474-1310
Asst Counsel to the Governor-Civil Svc, Elections, Empl Relations, Labor,
  Motor Veh, Niagara Fr, Port Auth, Retirement/Pensions, Transp, Thruway,
  Waterfr, MTA, PERB:
  Christopher Staszak 518-474-1310
Director, State & Local Government Affairs:
  John Haggerty. 518-486-9896
Director, Communications:
  David Catalfamo. 518-474-8418

EXECUTIVE DEPARTMENTS AND RELATED AGENCIES

Motor Vehicles Department
Swan Street Building
6 Empire State Plaza
Room 411
Albany, NY 12228
518-474-0841 or 800-225-5368
Web site: www.nysdmv.com

Commissioner:
  Raymond P Martinez. 518-474-0841/fax: 518-474-0712
  e-mail: rpmart@dmv.state.ny.us
Executive Deputy Commissioner:
  Renato Donato. 518-474-0846/fax: 518-474-0712
Asst Commissioner, Transportation Safety:
  Robert M Dingman. 518-474-0972

Assoc Commissioner, Communications:
  Joe Picchi. 518-473-7000/fax: 518-473-1930
  e-mail: jpicc@dmv.state.ny.us
Director, Quality Development:
  Michael S Graziade 518-486-7402

Administration, Office for
Deputy Commissioner:
  Gregory J Kline 518-474-6876
Director, Audit Services:
  Edward Wade. 518-474-0881
Director, Fiscal & Human Services:
  David Goodall 518-474-0990
Director, Fiscal Management:
  Kathy Gilchrist 518-402-2538
Director, Human Resources Management:
  Mary Ellen Pugliano. 518-474-7602
Director, Information Technology:
  Linda Smith 518-474-0605
Director, Labor Relations:
  Robert Hoffmeister. 518-474-2902
Director, Program Analysis:
  Kenneth Rose 518-474-0686

Governor's Traffic Safety Committee
Web site: www.nysgtsc.state.ny.us/index.htm
Chairman:
  Raymond P Martinez 518-474-0841
Executive Director:
  Kenneth Carpenter. 518-474-5111/fax: 518-473-6946

Legal Affairs, Office for
Deputy Commissioner, Counsel:
  Jill A Dunn 518-474-1003
Legislative Counsel:
  Vacant 518-474-1352
Director, Legal:
  Neal W Schoen. 518-474-0871

Appeals Board
Chairman:
  George Christian 518-486-6636

Operations & Customer Service, Office for
Deputy Commissioner:
  John C Hilliard 518-473-5127
Asst Commissioner & Clerks Liaison:
  Brian Carso, Jr 518-473-1489
Director, Operations & Customer Service:
  John S Hope 518-402-2379
Director, Field Operations:
  Robert McDonough 518-474-0953
Director, Central Office Operations:
  Joseph Crisafulli. 518-473-7254
Director, Document Production & Mail Operations:
  Steve Berletic 518-474-2659

Safety, Consumer Protection & Clean Air, Office for
Deputy Commissioner:
  Donald F Savage. 518-402-4860

Offices and agencies appear in alphabetical order.

Policy Areas

Director, Consumer Protection & Auto Business Regulation:
Ernest J Kitchen, Jr. 518-473-3347
Director, Driver Program Regulation:
Barbara Askham 518-486-5572
Director, Driver Safety:
Vacant 518-474-2955
Director, Field Investigation:
Owen McShane 518-474-8805
Director, Motor Carrier & Driver Safety Services:
Kevin O'Brien 518-474-0855
Director, Vehicle Safety Services & Clean Air:
Michael Maher 518-474-0616

Transportation Department

50 Wolf Road
6th Floor
Albany, NY 12232
518-457-5100 Fax: 518-457-5583
Web site: www.dot.state.ny.us

Commissioner:
Joseph H Boardman 518-457-4422
e-mail: jboardman@dot.state.ny.us
First Deputy Commissioner:
Brian O Rowback 518-457-4422
Director, Public Affairs:
Jennifer Post 518-457-6400/fax: 518-457-6506
e-mail: jpost@dot.state.ny.us
Director, Planning & Strategy:
Timothy Gilchrist 518-452-6700
Director, Government Relations Division:
Steven Hewitt 518-457-2345
Director, Resource & Risk Management Bureau:
Richard D Albertin 518-485-8236

Budget & Finance Office

Assistant Commissioner:
Lawrence M Knapek 518-457-2226

Budgeting & Finance Division
Director:
Scott Wixson 518-457-2787
Accounting Bureau
Director:
Carlton N Boorn 518-457-2424
Budgeting Bureau
Director:
Scott A Wixson 518-457-2465
Business Services Bureau
Director:
Chip White. 518-457-6446

Program Management Division
Director:
Michael McCarthy 518-457-4056
Capitol Program Analysis Bureau
Director:
Michael F Soscia 518-457-6680
Project Operation Bureau
Director:
Jim Church. 518-457-9585

Engineering Office

Deputy Commissioner & Chief Engineer:
Paul T Wells. 518-457-4430
Director, Environmental Analysis Bureau:
Mary E Ivey 518-457-5672

Design Division
Director:
Philip J Clark 518-457-6452
Consultant Management Bureau
Acting Director:
Kevin Gregory. 518-457-3123
Design Quality Assurance Bureau
Director:
Dan D'Angelo 518-457-6467
Design Services Bureau
Director:
Richard Lee 518-457-5289
Landscape Architecture Bureau
Acting Director:
Charles Nagel 518-457-4460

Real Estate Division
Director:
Francis Mengel. 518-457-2430
Acquisitions Management Bureau
Director:
Anne Flowers. 518-457-1702
Appraisal Management Bureau
Director:
John Dessena 518-457-0553
Property Management Bureau
Director:
Anne Flowers. 518-457-2760

Structures Design & Construction Division
Acting Director:
George A Christian 518-457-6827
Bridge Program & Evaluation Services Bureau
Director:
Sreenivas Alampalli. 518-457-7412
Structural Engineering Services Bureau
Director:
Richard Marchione 518-457-4529
Structure Design Quality Assurance/Structure Design Bureau
Director:
Arthur Yannotti 518-457-4544

Technical Services Division
Deputy Chief Engineer, Director:
Robert L Sack. 518-457-4445
Geotechnical Engineering Bureau
Director:
Robert A Valenti 518-457-4710
Highway Data Services Bureau
Director:
Anthony Torre. 518-457-1965
Materials Bureau
Director:
John Rondinaro 518-457-3240
Transportation Research & Development Bureau
Director:
Gary Frederick. 518-457-5826

Traffic Engineering & Highway Safety Division
Director:
Bruce W Smith. 518-457-0271
Safety Program Management Bureau
Director:
David Clements. 518-457-3537
Traffic Operations Bureau
Director:
Russell B Vachon 518-457-7436

Offices and agencies appear in alphabetical order.

Equal Opportunity Development & Compliance Office
Director:
Garland Sweeney. 518-457-1134/fax: 518-457-1675

Human Resources Office
Asst Commissioner:
Lisa Wright. 518-457-6300

Employee Relations Bureau
Director:
Louis P DeSol 518-457-3543

Personnel Bureau
Director:
Carol Cross. 518-457-6460

Training Bureau
Director:
Greg Montague. 518-457-2942

Legal Affairs Office. . . . . fax: 518-457-4021
Acting Asst Commissioner & Chief Counsel:
Peter Loomis. 518-457-7097

Contract Management & Audit Division
Director:
Turk Albertin 518-457-2600

Internal Audit & Investigations Office
Director:
John Samaniuk. 518-457-4680

Legal Services Division
Director:
Peter S Loomis. 518-457-2411

Legislative Matters
Asst Counsel:
Thomas D Perreault 518-457-2411

Proceedings Division
Director:
David Nealon 518-457-1182

Operations Office
Asst Commissioner:
Clifford A Thomas 518-457-7475

Construction Division
Acting Director:
James F Tynan 518-457-6472

Equipment Management Division
Director:
Joseph L Darling 518-457-2875

Transportation Maintenance Division
Director:
Gary McVoy. 518-457-2779

Passenger & Freight Transportation Office
Asst Commissioner:
John F Guinan. 518-457-2320

Economic Development & Admin Bureau
Director:
G Mike Smith. 518-457-1046

Freight & Economic Development Division
Acting Director:
Stephen R Slavick 518-457-6774
Intermodal Pgm Evaluation & Service Development Bureau
Acting Director:
Paul E Pastecki 518-457-7332

Intermodal Project Development Bureau
Director:
Clarence W Scott. 518-457-5221

Passenger & Freight Safety Division
Director:
Dennison P Cottrell 518-457-6512
Motor Carrier Compliance
Director:
William Leonard 518-457-6236
Motor Carrier Safety Bureau
Director:
Joseph J Lee-Civalier 518-485-2448
Rail Safety Bureau
Director:
Gerald Shook. 518-457-6500
Safety Program & Evaluation Bureau
Director:
Donald A Baker. 518-457-4613

Passenger Transportation Division
Director:
Steven Lewis 518-457-7664
e-mail: slewis@dot.state.ny.us
Aviation Services Bureau
Director:
Seth Edelman. 518-457-2821
Passenger Policy & Program Evaluation Bureau
Director:
Ron Epstein 518-457-2100
Transit Services Bureau
Acting Director:
Ron Epstein 518-457-8343

Regional Offices

Region 1
328 State St, Schenectady, NY 12305
Director:
Thomas C Werner. 518-388-0388/fax: 518-388-0347

Region 10
State Ofc Bldg, 250 Veterans Memorial Hwy, Hauppauge, NY 11788
Director:
Subimal Chakraborti. 631-952-6632/fax: 631-952-6311

Region 11
Hunters Point Plaza, 47-40 21st St, Long Island City, NY 11101
Director:
Douglas Currey 718-482-4526/fax: 718-482-4525

Region 2
Utica State Ofc Bldg, 207 Genesee St, Utica, NY 13501
Acting Director:
Mark Silo. 315-793-2447/fax: 315-793-2719

Region 3
State Ofc Bldg, 333 E Washington St, Syracuse, NY 13202
Acting Director:
Carl F Ford 315-428-4351/fax: 315-428-8438

Region 4
1530 Jefferson Rd, Rochester, NY 14623
Director:
Charles E Moynihan 585-272-3310/fax: 585-427-8480

Region 5
Buffalo State Ofc Bldg, 125 Main St, Buffalo, NY 14203
Acting Director:
Alan E Taylor 716-847-3238/fax: 716-847-3961

Offices and agencies appear in alphabetical order.

Policy Areas

Region 6
107 Broadway, Hornell, NY 14843
Director:
  Peter E White 607-324-8404/fax: 607-324-0790

Region 7
Dulles State Ofc Bldg, 317 Washington St, Watertown, NY 13601
Director:
  R Carey Babyak 315-785-2333/fax: 315-785-2507

Region 8
Eleanor Roosevelt State Ofc Bldg, 4 Burnett Blvd, Poughkeepsie, NY 12603
Director:
  Robert A Dennison, III 845-431-5750/fax: 845-431-5703

Region 9
44 Hawley St, Binghamton, NY 13901
Director:
  Jack Williams 607-721-8116/fax: 607-721-8119

CORPORATIONS, AUTHORITIES AND COMMISSIONS

Albany County Airport Authority
Administration Bldg, 2nd Fl
Albany International Airport
Albany, NY 12211-1507
518-242-2222 x1 Fax: 518-242-2641
e-mail: info@albanyairport.com
Web site: www.albanyairport.com

CEO:
  John A O'Donnell 518-242-2222 x1
CFO:
  J Dwight Hadley 518-242-2222 x1
Director, Public Affairs:
  Doug Myers. 518-242-2222 x4
Counsel:
  Peter F Stuto 518-242-2222 x5
Airport Planner:
  Stephen A Iachetta. 518-242-2222 x3
Purchasing Agent:
  Mary Ann Mysliwiec. 518-242-2222 x2
Administrative Services Manager:
  Ginger Olthoff. 518-242-2222 x1

Albany Port District Commission
Administration Bldg
Port of Albany
Albany, NY 12202
518-463-8763 Fax: 518-463-8767
e-mail: portofalbany@portofalbany.com
Web site: www.portofalbany.com

Chair:
  Robert F Cross 518-463-8763
General Manager:
  Frank W Keane. 518-463-8763
Counsel:
  Thomas Owens. 518-463-1004

Buffalo & Fort Erie Public Bridge Authority (Peace Bridge Authority)
One Peace Bridge Plaza
Buffalo, NY 14213-2494
716-884-6744 Fax: 716-884-2089
Web site: www.peacebridge.com

Chair (American):
  Paul J Koessler 716-884-6744
Vice Chair (Canadian):
  John A Lopinski 716-884-6744
General Manager:
  Ron Rienas 716-884-6744

Capital District Transportation Authority
110 Watervliet Ave
Albany, NY 12206
518-482-1125 Fax: 518-689-3090
Web site: www.cdta.org

Chair:
  David M Stackrow 518-482-1125
Vice Chair:
  Donald C MacElroy 518-482-1125
Executive Director:
  Stephen G Bland. 518-482-1125
Deputy Executive Director, Development:
  Jack Reilly 518-482-4199
General Counsel:
  David Winans. 518-482-6359
CFO:
  Milt Pratt. 518-482-6258
Chief of Staff & Director, Marketing:
  Carm Basile. 518-482-3371/fax: 518-446-0675

Central New York Regional Transportation Authority
200 Cortland Ave
PO Box 820
Syracuse, NY 13205-0820
315-442-3300 Fax: 315-442-3337
Web site: www.centro.org

Chair, Board of Directors:
  Robert E Colucci 315-442-3300
Executive Director:
  Frank Kobliski 315-442-3360
  e-mail: fkoblisk@centro.org
Senior VP, Finance & Administration:
  Steven M Share. 315-442-3358
Senior VP, Corporation Operations:
  John Renock 315-442-3388

MTA Bridges & Tunnels
Triborough Station
PO Box 35
New York, NY 10035
646-252-7000 Fax: 646-252-7408
Web site: www.mta.info/bandt

Chairman & CEO:
  Peter S Kalikow 212-878-7200

Offices and agencies appear in alphabetical order.

President:
Michael C Ascher 212-360-3100
Vice President & Chief Engineer:
Stanley C Vonasek 212-360-3080
Vice President, Labor Relations:
Sharon Gallo-Kotcher 212-360-3015
Vice President, Operations:
Martha Walther 212-360-3060
Vice President, Procurement & Materials:
Roy Parks 646-252-7084
Vice President, Staff Services & Chief of Staff:
Catherine T Sweeney 646-252-7421
Chief Financial Officer:
David Moretti 646-252-7100
Chief Technology Officer:
Tariq Habib 646-252-7230
General Counsel:
Robert O'Brien 646-252-7617
Director, Public Affairs:
Frank Pascual 646-252-7416

MTA Long Island Bus
700 Commercial Ave
Garden City, NY 11530
516-542-0100 Fax: 516-542-1428
Web site: www.mta.info/libus

Chairman & CEO:
Peter S Kalikow 212-878-7200
President:
Neil S Yellin 516-542-0100 x4525
Senior VP, Operations:
William Norwich 516-542-0100 x4334
Vice President, Administration:
James R Campbell 516-542-0100 x4345
Vice President, Finance:
Joseph Pokorny 516-542-0100 x4439
General Counsel:
Cheryl Hartell 516-542-0100 x4429

MTA Long Island Rail Road
Jamaica Station
Jamaica, NY 11435
718-558-7400 Fax: 718-558-8212
Web site: www.mta.info/lirr

Chairman & CEO:
Peter S Kalikow 212-878-7200
President:
James J Dermody 718-558-8252
e-mail: jjdermo@lirr.org
Executive Vice President:
Albert Cosenza 718-558-7993
e-mail: accosen@lirr.org
Chief Information Officer:
Joseph M DeCarlo 718-588-8166
e-mail: jmdecar@lirr.org
Vice President & Chief Fiscal Officer:
Nicholas DiMola 718-558-7777
e-mail: ndimola@lirr.org
Vice President, General Counsel & Secretary:
Mary J Mahon 718-558-8264
e-mail: mmahon@lirr.org

Vice President, Labor Relations:
Jerry Moran 718-558-7405
e-mail: gmmoran@lirr.org
Vice President, Market Development & Public Affairs:
Brian P Dolan 718-558-7301
e-mail: bpdolan@lirr.org
Vice President, Service, Planning, Technology & Capital Program
Management:
John Coulter 718-558-7363
e-mail: jwcoult@lirr.org
Vice President, Safety System:
Jose R Fernandez 718-588-7711
e-mail: jrferna@lirr.org
Chief Fire Marshal:
Louis Scida 718-558-3007

MTA Metro-North Railroad
347 Madison Ave
New York, NY 10017
212-340-2677 Fax: 212-340-4995
Web site: www.mta.info/mnr

Chairman & CEO:
Peter S Kalikow 212-878-7200
President:
Peter A Cannito 212-340-2677
Executive Vice President:
Genevieve Firnhaber 212-340-2636
Vice President & General Counsel:
Richard Bernard 212-340-4933
Vice President, Human Resources & Diversity:
Gregory Bradley 212-340-2172
Vice President, Operations:
George Walker 212-499-4300
Vice President, Planning & Development:
Howard Permut 212-340-2500
Director, Corporate & Media Relations:
Donna Evans 212-672-1201/fax: 212-672-1220
Director, Government & Community Relations:
Mark Mannix 212-340-3024

MTA New York City Transit
370 Jay St
Brooklyn, NY 11201
718-330-3000 Fax: 718-596-2146
Web site: www.mta.info/nyct

Chairman & CEO:
Peter S Kalikow 212-878-7200
President:
Lawrence G Reuter 718-243-4321
Executive Vice President:
Barbara R Spencer 718-243-3052
Senior VP, Buses:
Millard Seay 718-243-4186
Senior VP, Capital Program Management:
Cosema Crawford 646-252-3034
Senior VP, Corp Communications:
Paul Fleuranges 718-243-8881
Senior VP, Subways:
Michael Lombardi 718-243-4567
Senior VP, System Safety:
Cheryl Kennedy 718-243-4780
Vice President & General Counsel:
Martin Schnabel 718-694-3900

Policy Areas

Offices and agencies appear in alphabetical order.

Vice President, Labor Relations:
    Ralph Agritelley 718-243-3218
Chief Officer, Staten Island Railway:
    John McCabe 718-876-8239

Metropolitan Transportation Authority

347 Madison Ave
New York, NY 10017
212-878-7000 Fax: 212-878-7030
Web site: www.mta.info

Chairman & CEO:
    Peter S Kalikow 212-878-7200
Executive Director & COO:
    Katherine N Lapp 212-878-7274
Deputy Exec Director, Director of Security:
    William Morange 212-878-7155
Deputy Executive Director, Corporate & Community Affairs:
    Christopher P Boylan 212-878-7160
Deputy Executive Dir, Policy/Special Advisor, Safety & Environmental
    Issues:
    Linda Kleinbaum 212-878-7206
Chief of Staff:
    Maureen E Boll 212-878-7420
Director, Labor Relations:
    Gary Dellaverson 212-878-7438
Director, Budgets & Financial Management:
    Gary Lanigan 212-878-7236
Director, Finance:
    Patrick McCoy 212-878-7278
Director, Human Resources:
    Margaret M Connor 212-878-7017
Director, Government Affairs:
    Michelle Goldstein 212-878-7313/fax: 212-878-7050
MTA Chief of Police:
    Thomas Lawless 212-878-1146
Press Secretary:
    Tom Kelly 212-878-7440

Metropolitan Transportation Authority, Office of the Inspector General

111 West 40th St
5th Fl
New York, NY 10018
212-878-0000 or 800-682-4448 (Compla Fax: 212-878-0003
Web site: www.mtaig.state.ny.us

Inspector General:
    Matthew D Sansverie 212-878-0007
    e-mail: msansver@mtaig.org
First Deputy Inspector General:
    Stephen M Spahr 212-878-0030
Deputy Inspector General, Intergovernmental & Public Affairs:
    James Bono 212-878-0000
    e-mail: jbono@mtaig.org
General Counsel:
    Carl Copertino 212-878-0074
    e-mail: copertino@mtaig.org

New York Metropolitan Transportation Council

45-46 21st St
Long Island City, NY 11101

718-472-3046 Fax: 718-482-7431
Web site: www.nymtc.org

Executive Director:
    Joel Ettinger 212-383-7363
Deputy Director, Admin Group:
    Alan Borenstein 212-383-7294
    e-mail: aborenstein@dot.state.ny.us
Asst Director, Planning Grp:
    Gerard J Bogacz 212-383-7260
Asst Director, Technical Grp:
    Kuo-Ann Chiao 212-383-7212

New York State Bridge Authority

Mid-Hudson Bridge Plaza
PO Box 1010
Highland, NY 12528
845-691-7245 Fax: 845-691-3560
Web site: www.nysba.net

Chair:
    Edmund A Fares 845-691-7245
Vice Chair:
    Morton Marshak 845-691-7245
Executive Director:
    George C Sinnott 845-691-7245
Deputy Executive Director:
    James J Bresnan 845-691-7245
    e-mail: jbresnan@nysba.state.ny.us
General Counsel:
    Carl Whitbeck 518-828-4107
Public Information Officer, Planning & Public Relations:
    Mark Sheedy 845-691-7245/fax: 845-691-3636
    e-mail: msheedy@nysba.state.ny.us

New York State Thruway Authority

200 Southern Blvd
Albany, NY 12209
518-436-2700 Fax: 518-436-2899
Web site: www.thruway.state.ny.us

Chair:
    John L Buono 518-436-3000
Executive Director:
    Michael R Fleischer 518-436-2900
General Counsel:
    Sharon O'Conor 518-436-2840
Deputy Counsel:
    Katherine McCartney 518-436-3188
Director, Government Relations:
    Pamela Davis 518-436-2860/fax: 518-471-4340
Director, Public Information:
    Dan Gilbert 518-436-2983/fax: 518-426-3995
    e-mail: publicinfo@thruway.state.ny.us

New York State Canal Corporation
    Web site: www.canals.state.ny.us
Acting Director:
    Lawrence Frame 518-436-3055

Niagara Falls Bridge Commission

PO Box 1031
Niagara Falls, NY 14302

Offices and agencies appear in alphabetical order.

716-285-6322 Fax: 716-282-3292
e-mail: general_inquiries@niagarafallsbridges.com
Web site: www.niagarafallsbridges.com

Chair:
Robert E Lewis.................................716-285-6322
Vice Chair:
Christine Whyte 716-285-6322
General Manager & Sec/Treas:
Thomas E Garlock 716-285-6322

Niagara Frontier Transportation Authority
181 Ellicott St
Buffalo, NY 14203
716-855-7300 Fax: 716-855-6655
e-mail: info@nfta.com
Web site: www.nfta.com

Chair:
Luiz F Kahl......................................716-855-7233
Executive Director:
Lawrence M Meckler 716-855-7369
e-mail: lawrence_meckler@nfta.com
Chief Financial Officer:
Deborah Leous 716-855-7250
General Counsel:
David M Gregory 716-855-7230
Director, Aviation:
William Vanecek 716-630-6030
Director, Employee Services:
Ruth McManus...................................716-855-7373
Director, Surface Transportation:
Walter D Zmuda.................................716-855-7252
General Manager, Engineering:
Harold Matuszak 716-855-7383
Director, Public Affairs:
C Douglas Hartmayer............................716-855-7420

Ogdensburg Bridge & Port Authority
One Bridge Plaza
Ogdensburg, NY 13669
315-393-4080 Fax: 315-393-7068
e-mail: obpa@ogdensport.com
Web site: www.ogdensport.com

Chair:
Connie G Augsbury 315-393-2636
Deputy Executive Director:
Joseph E Tracy 315-393-4080
e-mail: jtracy@ogdensport.com

Port Authority of New York & New Jersey
225 Park Ave South
18th Fl
New York, NY 10003
212-435-7000 Fax: 212-435-6543
Web site: www.panynj.gov

Chair, NJ:
Anthony R Coscia................................212-435-7000
Vice Chair, NY:
Charles A Gargano 212-435-7000

Executive Director:
Kenneth J Ringler...............................212-435-7271
Deputy Executive Director:
James P Fox 212-435-6667
Director Gov't & Community Relations:
Arthur Cifelli 212-435-6903
Chief of Staff:
Edmond Schorno 212-435-6688
General Counsel:
Darrell Buchbinder..............................212-435-3515
Chief Financial Officer:
A Paul Blanco....................................212-435-7738
Chief Admin Officer:
Louis J LaCapra 212-435-8140
Chief Operating Officer:
Ernesto Butcher 212-435-7887
Chief of Public & Government Affairs:
Michael A Petralia 212-435-6502
Chief Engineer:
Francis J Lombardi..............................212-435-7449
Director, Public Affairs:
Kayla M Bergeron 212-435-8041
Office of Secretary:
Karen E Eastman 212-435-6528

Port of Oswego Authority
1 East Second St
PO Box 387
Oswego, NY 13126
315-343-4503 Fax: 315-343-5498
e-mail: shipping@dreamscape.com
Web site: www.portoswego.com

Chair:
Steven Thomas 315-343-8095
Executive Director:
Thomas McAuslan 315-343-4503
Counsel:
Timothy Fennell.................................315-343-6363

Rochester-Genesee Regional Transportation Authority
1372 E Main St
PO Box 90629
Rochester, NY 14609
585-654-0200 Fax: 585-654-0224
Web site: www.rgrta.com

Chair:
John G Doyle 585-654-0200
Chief Executive Officer:
Mark R Aesch....................................585-654-0200
Chief Operating Officer:
Stephen W Hendershott 585-654-0200
Chief Financial Officer:
Robert W Frye 585-654-0200
Director, Transit Operations:
Bruce G Philpott.................................585-654-0200

Thousand Islands Bridge Authority
PO Box 428
Alexandria Bay, NY 13607

Offices and agencies appear in alphabetical order.

Policy Areas

315-482-2501 or 315-658-2281 Fax: 315-482-5925
Web site: www.tibridge.com

Chair:
  Donald J Grant 315-482-2501
Executive Director:
  Robert G Horr, III. 315-482-2501
  e-mail: roberthorr@tibridge.com
Legal Counsel:
  Anderson Wise 315-482-2501

Waterfront Commission of New York Harbor
39 Broadway
4th Fl
New York, NY 10006
212-742-9280 Fax: 212-480-0587
Web site: www.wcnyh.org

Commissioner, NY:
  Michael C Axelrod 212-742-9280
Commissioner, NJ:
  Michael J Madonna 212-742-9280
Executive Director:
  Thomas De Maria 212-742-9280

NEW YORK STATE LEGISLATURE

See Legislative Branch in Section 1 for additional Standing Committee and Subcommittee information.

Assembly Standing Committees

Corporations, Authorities & Commissions
Chair:
  Richard L Brodsky (D) 518-455-5753
Ranking Minority Member:
  James G Bacalles (R) 518-455-5791

Economic Development, Job Creation, Commerce & Industry
Chair:
  Robin L Schimminger (D) 518-455-4767

Ranking Minority Member:
  Marc Butler (R) 518-455-5393

Transportation
Chair:
  David F Gantt (D). 518-455-5606
Ranking Minority Member:
  Patrick Manning (R). 518-455-5177

Joint Legislative Commissions

Critical Transportation Choices, Legislative Commission on
Senate Chair:
  Thomas Libous (R). 518-455-2091
Assembly Vice Chair:
  Vacant 518-455-0000
Program Manager:
  Heidi Kromphardt. 518-455-4031

Senate Standing Committees

Commerce, Economic Development & Small Business
Chair:
  James S Alesi (R) 518-455-2015
Ranking Minority Member:
  Efrain Gonzalez, Jr (D). 518-455-3395

Corporations, Authorities & Commissions
Chair:
  Vincent L Leibell, III (R) 518-455-3111
Ranking Minority Member:
  Ada L Smith (D). 518-455-3531

Transportation
Chair:
  Thomas Libous (R). 518-455-2677
Ranking Minority Member:
  John Sabini (D). 518-455-2529

U.S. Government

EXECUTIVE DEPARTMENTS AND RELATED AGENCIES

Federal Maritime Commission
Web site: www.fmc.gov

New York Area Office
Bldg 75, Rm 205B, JFK Intl Airport, Jamaica, NY 11430
Area Rep:
  Emanuel J Mingione 718-553-2228/fax: 718-553-2229

National Transportation Safety Board
Web site: www.ntsb.gov

Aviation Division, Northeast Regional Office
2001 Route 46, Ste 504, Parsippany, NJ 07054-1315
Regional Director:
  Robert Pearce. 973-334-6531/fax: 973-334-6759

Office of Administrative Law Judges
490 L'Enfant Plaza, ESW, Washington, DC 20594
Chief Judge:
  William E Fowler, Jr 202-314-6151/fax: 202-314-6158

US Department of Homeland Security (DHS)
Web site: www.dhs.gov

Transportation Security Administration (TSA)
201 Varick St, Rm 603, New York, NY 10014

Offices and agencies appear in alphabetical order.

Regional Spokesperson:
Mark Hatfield 212-337-2260/fax: 212-337-2261
e-mail: mark.hatfield@dhs.gov

US Transportation Department
Web site: www.dot.gov

Federal Aviation Administration-Eastern Region . . . . . . fax: 718-995-5656
One Aviation Plaza, Jamaica, NY 11434
Fax: 718-995-5656
Web site: www.faa.gov
Regional Administrator:
Arlene B Feldman. 718-553-3000
Regional Executive Manager:
Manny Weiss 718-553-3001
Manager, Public Affairs:
Arlene Murry 718-553-3010

Accounting Division
Manager:
Fred Glassberg 718-553-4190

Aerospace Medicine Division
Regional Flight Surgeon:
Harriet Lester 718-553-3300

Air Traffic Division
Acting Area Director:
John G McCartney 718-553-4500

Airports Division
Manager:
William Flanagan 718-553-3331

Aviation Information & Services Division
Manager:
Alan Siperstein 718-553-3358

Engineering Services
Manager:
Selin Haber 718-553-3400

Flight Standards Division
Manager:
Lawrence Fields 718-553-3200

Human Resource Management Division
Manager:
Gloria Quay 718-553-3130

Logistics Division
Manager:
vacant 718-553-3050

Military Liaison Officers to the Federal Aviation Administration (Incl NYS)
12 New England Executive Park, Burlington, MA 1803
Air Force Regional Representatives
Representative:
Vacant 781-238-7901/fax: 781-238-7903
Transportation Specialist:
Cheryl W Carpenter. 781-238-7910
e-mail: cheryl.w.carpenter@faa.gov
Army Regional Representatives
Liaison Officer:
LTC Bill Walsh 781-238-7906
e-mail: bill.walsh@faa.gov
Liaison Officer:
MSGT Jason Williams 781-238-7905
e-mail: jason.williams@faa.gov

Navy Regional Representatives
Liaison Officer:
CDR Rick Perez 781-238-7907
e-mail: rick.perez@faa.gov
Liaison Officer:
ACCS Mark Moon 781-238-7908/fax: 781-238-7902
e-mail: mark.moon@faa.gov

Runway Safety Manager
Manager:
Bill DeGraaff 718-553-3326

Federal Highway Administration-New York Division . . fax: 518-431-4121
Leo W O'Brien Federal Bldg, Rm 719, Albany, NY 12207
Fax: 518-431-4121
Web site: www.fhwa.dot.gov
Division Administrator:
Robert Arnold. 518-431-4127
Asst Division Administrator:
Amy D Jackson-Grove 518-431-4131
Senior Attorney:
Kenneth Dymond. 518-431-4125 x224
Engineer Coordinator:
Thomas G Herritt, Jr 518-431-4125 x233

Federal Motor Carrier Safety Admin-New York Division . . . . fax: 518-431-4140
Leo O'Brien Federal Bldg, Rm 742, Albany, NY 12207
Fax: 518-431-4140
Web site: www.fmcsa.dot.gov
Division Administrator:
Brian Temperine 518-431-4145 x311
Field Office Supervisor, Upstate:
Pamela Noyes 518-431-4145 x316
State Program Specialist:
Andrew Choquette. 518-431-4145 x313
Manager, Intelligent Transportation Systems Commercial Vehicle Operati:
Carolyn Temperine 518-431-4145 x270

Federal Railroad Administration-Field Offices
Web site: www.fra.dot.gov

Hazardous Material
111 W Huron St, Rm 909B, Buffalo, NY 14202
Inspector:
Michael J Ziolkowski. 716-551-3955

Highway-Rail Grade Crossing
PO Box 2144, Ballston Spa, NY 12020
Program Manager:
Randall L Dickinson 518-899-5372/fax: 518-899-5372

Federal Transit Administration, Region II-New York
One Bowling Green, Rm 429, New York, NY 10004-1415
Web site: www.fta.dot.gov
Regional Admin:
Letitia Thompson. 212-668-2170/fax: 212-668-2136

Maritime Administration
Web site: www.marad.dot.gov

Great Lakes Region (includes part of New York State)
1701 E Woodfield Rd, Ste 203, Schaumburg, IL 60173-5127
Regional Director:
Doris J Bautch 847-995-0122/fax: 847-995-0133
e-mail: doris.bautch@marad.dot.gov

North Atlantic Region
One Bowling Green, Rm 418, New York, NY 10004-1415

Offices and agencies appear in alphabetical order.

Policy Areas

Regional Director:
Robert F McKeon 212-668-3330/fax: 212-668-3382
e-mail: robert.mckeon@marad.dot.gov

US Merchant Marine Academy . . . . fax: 516-773-5774
300 Steamboat Rd, Kings Point, NY 11024-1699
516-773-5000 Fax: 516-773-5774
Web site: www.usmma.edu
Superintendent:
VAdm Joseph D Stewart 516-773-5348/fax: 516-773-5347

National Highway Traffic Safety Administration, Reg II-NY
222 Mamaroneck Ave, Suite 204, White Plains, NY 10605
Web site: www.nhtsa.dot.gov
Reg Admin:
Thomas M Louizou 914-682-6162/fax: 914-682-6239

Office of Inspector General, Region II-New York . . . . . . fax: 212-264-9466
26 Federal Plaza, Rm 3134, New York, NY 10278
Fax: 212-264-9466
Web site: www.oig.dot.gov
Regional Audit Manager:
Michael E Goldstein 212-264-8701

Saint Lawrence Seaway Development Corporation
180 Andrews St, PO Box 520, Massena, NY 13662-0520
Web site: www.seaway.dot.gov; www.greatlakes-seaway.com
Assoc Administrator:
Salvatore Pisani 315-764-3209/fax: 315-764-3235
e-mail: sal.pisani@sls.dot.gov

U.S. CONGRESS

See U.S. Congress Chapter for additional Standing Committee and Subcommittee information.

House of Representatives Standing Committees

Transportation & Infrastructure
Chair:
Don Young (R-AK) 202-225-5765

Ranking Minority Member:
James L Oberstar (D-MN) 202-225-6211
New York Delegate:
Timothy H Bishop (D) 202-225-3826
New York Delegate:
Sherwood L Boehlert (R) 202-225-3665
New York Delegate:
Brian M Higgins (D) 202-225-3306
New York Delegate:
Sue W Kelly (R) 202-225-5441
New York Delegate:
John R (Randy) Kuhl (R) 202-225-3161
New York Delegate:
Jerrold Nadler (D) 202-225-5635
New York Delegate:
Anthony D Weiner (D) 202-225-6616

Senate Standing Committees

Commerce, Science & Transportation
Chair:
Ted Stevens (R-AK) 202-224-3004
Ranking Minority Member:
Daniel K Inouye (D-HI) 202-224-3934

Environment & Public Works
Chair:
James M Inhofe (R-OK) 202-224-4721
Ranking Minority Member:
James Jeffords (I-VT) 202-224-5141
New York Delegate:
Hillary Rodham Clinton (D) 202-224-4451

Subcommittee
Transportation & Infrastructure
Chair:
Christopher S Bond (R-MO) 202-224-5721
Ranking Minority Member:
Max Baucus (D-MT) 202-224-2651

Private Sector

ALSTOM Transportation Inc
1 Transit Dr, Hornell, NY 14843
607-281-2487 Fax: 607-324-2641
e-mail: chuck.wochele@transport.alstom.com
Web site: www.transport.alstom.com
Chuck Wochele, Vice President Business Development
High-speed trains, rapid transit vehicles, commuter cars, AC propulsion & signaling, passenger locomotives

Ammann & Whitney
96 Morton St, New York, NY 10014
212-462-8500 Fax: 212-929-5325
e-mail: nivanoff@ammann-whitney.com
Web site: www.ammann-whitney.com
Nick Ivanoff, President & Chief Executive Officer
Planning, engineering & construction mgmt for airport, transit, gov't, recreation & commercial facilities; highways; bridges

Automobile Club of New York
1415 Kellum Place, Garden City, NY 11530
516-873-2259 Fax: 516-873-2355
Web site: www.aaany.com
John Corlett, Director Government Affairs

Automotive Technology & Energy Group of Western NY
517 George Urban Blvd, Cheektowaga, NY 14225
716-894-1116 Fax: 716-894-1117
Robert Gliss, Executive Director
Garage & service station owners

Offices and agencies appear in alphabetical order.

British Airways PLC
75-20 Astoria Blvd, Jackson Heights, NY 11370
347-418-4729 Fax: 347-418-4204
e-mail: john.lampl@bausa.com
Web site: www.britishairways.com
John Lampl, Vice President, Communications-North America

CP Rail System
200 Clifton Corporate Parkway, PO Box 8002, Clifton Park, NY 12065
518-383-7200 Fax: 518-383-7222
Brent Szafron, Service Area Manager
Freight transport

DKI Engineering & Consulting USA, PC, Corporate World Headquarters
632 Plank Rd, Ste 208, Clifton Park, NY 12065
518-373-4999 Fax: 518-373-8989
e-mail: dki123@aol.com
Web site: www.dkitechnologies.com
D K Gupta, President & Chief Executive Officer
Design, engineering, planning, construction management & program management oversight for airports, bridges, highways, railroads, transit, tunnels, water & wastewater facilities

Empire State Passengers Association
PO Box 434, Syracuse, NY 13209
716-741-6384 Fax: 716-632-3044
e-mail: bbecker@westwoodcc.cc
Web site: www.trainweb.org/espa
Bruce Becker, President
Advocacy for improvement of rail passenger service

Ethan C Eldon Associates Inc
1350 Broadway, Ste 612, New York, NY 10018
212-967-5400 Fax: 212-967-2747
e-mail: eceaethan@aol.com
Ethan C Eldon, President
Environmental, EIS, traffic, hazardous & solid waste consulting

Gandhi Engineering Inc
111 John St, 3rd Fl, New York, NY 10038-3002
212-349-2900 Fax: 212-285-0205
e-mail: gandhi@gandhieng.com
Web site: www.gandhieng.com
Kirti Gandhi, President
Consulting architects & engineers; infrastructure projects & transportation facilities

General Contractors Association of NY
60 East 42nd St, Rm 3510, New York, NY 10165
212-687-3131 Fax: 212-986-4746
e-mail: ritas@mindspring.com
Rita Schwartz, Director, Government Relations
Heavy construction, transportation

Jacobs Engineering
260 Madison Ave, 12TH Floor, Suite 1200, New York, NY 10016
212-268-1500 Fax: 212-481-9484
Web site: www.jacobs.com
Vincent Mangieri, Vice President
Multi-modal surface transportation planning, design, engineering, construction & inspection services

Komanoff Energy Associates
636 Broadway, Rm 602, New York, NY 10012-2623
212-260-5237
e-mail: kea@igc.org
Charles Komanoff, Director
Energy, utilities & transportation consulting

Konheim & Ketcham Inc
175 Pacific St, Brooklyn, NY 11201
718-330-0550 Fax: 718-330-0582
e-mail: csk@konheimketcham.com
Web site: www.konheimketcham.com
Carolyn Konheim, President
Environmental impact analysis, traffic engineering, transportation planning & technical assistance to community groups

Kriss, Kriss, Brignola & Persing, LLP
350 Northern Blvd, Ste 306, Albany, NY 12204
518-449-2037 Fax: 518-449-7875
e-mail: mkriss@krisslaw.com
Web site: www.krisslaw.com
Mark C Kriss, Partner
Advocates for highway & auto safety

Long Island Rail Road Commuter's Council
347 Madison Ave, 8th Fl, New York, NY 10017
212-878-7087 Fax: 212-878-7461
e-mail: mail@pcac.org
Web site: www.pcac.org
James L McGovern, Chairman
Represent interest of LIRR riders

NY Airport Service
15 Second Ave, Brooklyn, NY 11215
718-875-8200 Fax: 718-875-7056
Web site: www.nyairportservice.com
Mark Marmurstein, Vice President
Airport shuttle bus services

NY Coalition For Transportation Safety
98 Cuttermill Road, Great Neck, NY 11021-3006
516-829-0099 Fax: 516-829-7315
e-mail: nycoalitio@aol.com
Web site: www.nycts.org
Cynthia Brown, Executive Director
Education & outreach for transportation safety & injury prevention for well & special needs populations

Policy Areas

NY State Association of Town Superintendents of Highways Inc
PO Box 427, Belfast, NY 14711-0427
585-365-9380 Fax: 585-365-9382
e-mail: nysaotsoh@yahoo.com
William A Nichols, Executive Secretary & Treasurer

NYS Association of Service Stations & Repair Shops
6 Walker Way, Albany, NY 12205-4946
518-452-4367 Fax: 518-452-1955
e-mail: nysassn@together.net
Web site: www.nysassrs.com
Ralph Bombardiere, Executive Director
Protect the interests of independent service stations & repair shops & the motoring public

NYS County Hwy Super Assn / NY Aviation Mgt Assn / NY Public Transit Assn
119 Washington Ave, Ste 100, Albany, NY 12210
518-465-1694 or 518-432-9973; 518-43 Fax: 518-465-1942; 5
e-mail: info@countyhwys.org; info@nyama.com; nypta@atdial.net
Web site: www.countyhwys.org; www.nyama.com; www.nytransit.org
Kathleen A Van De Loo, Communications Director
County highways & bridges in NYS; aviation industry in NYS; public transit industry in NYS

National Economic Research Associates
308 N Cayuga St, Ithaca, NY 14850
607-277-3007 Fax: 607-277-1581
e-mail: alfred.kahn@nera.com
Web site: www.nera.com
Alfred E Kahn, Professor Emeritus & Special Consultant
Utility & transportation regulation, deregulation & antitrust

New England Steamship Agents Inc
730 Downing St, Niskayuna, NY 12309
518-463-5749 Fax: 518-463-5751
e-mail: nesa0025@aol.com
Diane Delory, President
Domestic transportation, vessel agency/husbandry, customs brokerage & vessel brokerage

New York & Atlantic Railway (NYA)
68-01 Otto Rd, Glendale, NY 11385
718-497-3023 Fax: 718-497-3364
e-mail: fkrebs@anacostia.com
Web site: www.anacostia.com
Fred L Krebs, President
Freight transport

New York Public Interest Research Group Straphangers Campaign
9 Murray St, 3rd Fl, New York, NY 10007
212-349-6460 Fax: 212-349-1366
e-mail: grussian@nypirg.org
Web site: www.straphangers.org; www.nypirg.org
Gene Russianoff, Senior Staff Attorney
Mass transit & government reform

New York Roadway Improvement Coalition (NYRIC)
629 Old White Plains Road, Tarrytown, NY 10591
914-631-6070 Fax: 914-631-5172
e-mail: cicwhv@cicnys.org
Robert F Carlino, President
Heavy highway & bridge construction

New York Shipping Association Inc
100 Wood Ave South, Ste 304, Iselin, NJ 08830-2716
732-452-7800 Fax: 732-452-6312
e-mail: jcobb@nysanet.org
Web site: www.nysanet.org
James H Cobb, Jr, Director, Governmental Affairs
Maximizing the efficiency, cost competitiveness, safety & quality of marine cargo operations in the Port of New York & New Jersey

New York State Auto Dealers Association
37 Elk St, Albany, NY 12207
518-463-1148 x204 Fax: 518-432-1309
e-mail: bob@nysada.com
Web site: www.nysada.com
Robert Vancavage, President

New York State Motor Truck Association
828 Washington Ave, Albany, NY 12203-1622
518-458-9696 Fax: 518-458-2525
e-mail: nytrucks@aol.com
Web site: www.nytrucks.org
William G Joyce, Jr, President & Chief Executive Officer
Safety & regulatory compliance

New York State Transportation Engineering Alliance (NYSTEA)
99 Pine St, Ste 207, Albany, NY 12207
518-436-0786 Fax: 518-427-0452
e-mail: sdm@fcwc-law.com
Stephen D Morgan, Executive Director
Transportation & infrastructure

New York, Susquehanna & Western Railway
1 Railroad Ave, Cooperstown, NY 13326-1110
607-547-2555 Fax: 607-547-8676
e-mail: wrich@nysw.com
Web site: www.nysw.com
Walter G Rich, President & Chief Executive Officer
Subsidiaries operate freight & passenger railroad system

Parsons Brinckerhoff
One Penn Plaza, New York, NY 10119
212-465-5700 Fax: 212-465-5565
e-mail: bennett@pbworld.com
Web site: www.pbworld.com
Joel H Bennett, Senior Vice President
Engineering, planning, construction management & consulting for transit & transportation, power & telecom projects

Offices and agencies appear in alphabetical order.

Metro-North Railroad Commuter Council
Permanent Citizens Advisory Committee to the MTA
347 Madison Ave, New York, NY 10017
212-878-7087 Fax: 212-878-7461
e-mail: mail@pcac.org
Web site: www.pcac.org
Richard Cataggio, Chair
Represent interests of MNR riders

Regional Plan Association
4 Irving Place, 7th Fl, New York, NY 10003
212-253-2727 Fax: 212-253-5666
e-mail: jeff@rpa.org
Web site: www.rpa.org
Jeffrey M Zupan, Senior Fellow, Transportation
Regional transportation planning & development issues

Seneca Flight Operations
2262 Airport Dr, Penn Yan, NY 14527
315-536-4471 Fax: 315-536-4558
e-mail: flight@senecafoods.com
Web site: www.senecafoods.com
Richard Leppert, General Manager
Executive air transportation

Simmons-Boardman Publishing Corp
345 Hudson St, 12th Fl, New York, NY 10014-4590
212-620-7200 Fax: 212-633-1863
e-mail: sbrailgroup@sbpub.com
Web site: www.railwayage.com or www.rtands.com or
www.railjournal.com
Robert DeMarco, Publisher
*Publisher of: Railway Age, International Railway Journal & Rapid
Transit Review, Railway Track & Structures*

Systra Consulting Inc
470 Seventh Ave, 10th Floor, New York, NY 10018
212-494-9111 Fax: 212-494-9112
Web site: www.systraconsulting.com
Peter Allibone, Executive Vice President
*Engineering consultants specializing in urban rail & transit systems,
passenger & freight railroads & high speed rail*

Transport Workers Union of America, AFL-CIO
1700 Broadway, 2nd Fl, New York, NY 10019
212-259-4900 Fax: 212-265-4537
Web site: www.twu.com
Michael O'Brien, International President
Bus, train, railroad & airline workers' union

Transportation Alternatives
115 W 30th St, 12TH Floor, New York, NY 10001-4010
212-629-8080 Fax: 212-629-8334
e-mail: info@transalt.org
Web site: www.transalt.org
John Kaehny, Executive Director
NYC commute alternatives, traffic calming, pedestrian safety issues

Tri-State Transportation Campaign
350 W 31st St, Room 802, New York, NY 10001-2726
212-268-7474 Fax: 212-268-7333
e-mail: tstc@tstc.org
Web site: www.tstc.org
Jon Orcutt, Executive Director
*Public interest, transit advocacy, planning & environmental
organizations working to reform transportation policies*

United Transportation Union
35 Fuller Road, Suite 205, Albany, NY 12205
518-438-8403 Fax: 518-438-8404
e-mail: sjnasca@aol.com
Web site: www.utu.org
Samuel Nasca, Legislative Director
*Federal government railroad, bus & airline employees; public
employees*

Urbitran Group
71 West 23rd St, 11th Fl, New York, NY 10010
212-366-6200 Fax: 212-366-6214
e-mail: mhorodnicaenu@urbitran.com
Web site: www.urbitran.com
Michael Horodnicaenu, President & Chief Executive Officer
Engineering, architecture & planning

Policy Areas

VETERANS AND MILITARY

New York State

GOVERNOR'S OFFICE

Governor's Office
Executive Chamber
State Capitol
Albany, NY 12224
518-474-8390 Fax: 518-474-1513
Web site: www.state.ny.us

Governor:
  George E Pataki 518-474-8390
Executive Director:
  Kara Lanspery 518-474-8390
Secretary to the Governor:
  John P Cahill. 518-474-4246
Senior Policy Advisor to the Governor:
  Jeffrey Lovell 518-486-9671
Counsel to the Governor-Attorney General, Budget:
  Richard Platkin 518-474-8343
Asst Counsel to the Governor-Clemency, Crime Vics, Correcs, Correc Svcs,
  Disaster, Extrads, Military/Naval/SEMO, Parole, Domestic Viol,
  Probatn/Correc Alts, Veterans:
  Gerald Connolly 518-474-8494
Director, Communications:
  David Catalfamo. 518-474-8418
Director, State & Local Government Affairs:
  John Haggerty. 518-486-9896
Citizens Services:
  Linda Boyd 518-474-1041

EXECUTIVE DEPARTMENTS AND RELATED AGENCIES

Health Department
Corning Tower
Empire State Plaza
Albany, NY 12237
518-474-7354
Web site: www.health.state.ny.us

Health Facilities Management
Acting Director:
  Val S Gray 518-474-2772/fax: 518-474-0611

New York State Veterans' Home at Batavia
  220 Richmond Ave, Batavia, NY 14020
  585-345-2049
  Administrator:
    Joanne I Hernick 585-345-2069/fax: 585-345-9030

New York State Veterans' Home at Montrose
  2090 Albany Post Rd, Montrose, NY 10548
  914-788-6000
  Administrator:
    Oscar Carter 914-788-6003/fax: 914-788-6100

New York State Veterans' Home at Oxford
  4211 State Highway 220, Oxford, NY 13830-4305
  607-843-3121
  Administrator:
    Vathsala Venugopalan 607-843-3129/fax: 607-843-3199
  Medical Director:
    Philip Dzwonczyk 607-843-3140

New York State Veterans' Home at St Albans
  178-50 Linden Blvd, Jamaica, NY 11434-1467
  718-990-0353
  Administrator:
    Neville Goldson 718-990-0329
  Director, Nursing:
    Elaine Boy-Brown 718-990-0316

Labor Department
345 Hudson St, Ste 8301
Box 662, Mail Stop 01
New York, NY 10014-0662
212-352-6000 Fax: 212-352-6824

Building 12, Room 500
State Campus
Albany, NY 12240
518-457-2741
Fax: 518-457-6908

Commissioner:
  Linda Angello. 518-457-2746
Executive Deputy Commissioner:
  Dennis Ryan 518-457-4318
Deputy Commissioner, Veterans Affairs:
  Ronald Tocci 518-457-1343

  Employment Services Division
  Director:
    Karen Papandrea 518-457-3584
    Employer Services
    Director:
      Timothy O'Keefe. 518-457-6821
    Veterans Employment Service
    Program Coordinator:
      Earl Wallace 518-457-1343

Military & Naval Affairs, Division of
330 Old Niskayuna Rd
Latham, NY 12110-2224
518-786-4500 Fax: 518-786-4325
Web site: www.dmna.state.ny.us

Adjutant General:
  Maj Gen Thomas P Maguire, Jr 518-786-4502
Deputy Adjutant General:
  Col F David Sheppard 518-786-4502

Offices and agencies appear in alphabetical order.

Inspector General, Federal:
Col James D McDonough Jr 518-786-4426

Legal Counsel:
Robert G Conway, Jr 518-786-4541

Director, Resource Management:
Robert A Martin 518-786-4513

Director, Governmental Affairs:
Scott Hommel 518-786-4580

Director, Public Affairs:
Kent Kisselbrack 518-786-4581/fax: 518-786-4649
e-mail: kent.kisselbrack@ny.ngb.army.mil

Veterans' Affairs, Division of

5 Empire State Plaza
Ste 2836
Albany, NY 12223-1551
518-474-6114 Fax: 518-473-0379
Web site: www.veterans.state.ny.us

Director:
George P Basher 518-474-6114

Counsel:
William J Brennan 518-474-6114

Bureau of Veterans Education

Albany Office
5 Empire State Plaza, Ste 2836, Albany, NY 12223-1551
Supervisor:
Craig Farley 518-474-5322/fax: 518-474-5583

New York Office
116 W 32nd St, 14th Fl, New York, NY 10001
Chief:
James Bombard 212-564-8414

Counseling & Claims Service
Web site: www.veterans.state.ny.us/ofcs.htm

Eastern Region
VA Regional Ofc, 245 W Houston St, Rm 206, New York, NY 10014
Deputy Director:
Benjamin Weisbroth 212-807-3162/fax: 212-807-4021
Senior Counselor:
Steven Strandberg 845-831-2000 x5449
Senior Counselor:
L Ray Colow 212-807-3162

New York State Claims Offices
Buffalo VA Regional Office
307-06, 111 W Huron St, Buffalo, NY 14202-2638
Senior Counselor:
Gerald Grace 716-857-3330
Senior Counselor:
James Graziadei 716-857-3330
New York City VA Regional Office . . . . fax: 212-807-4021
245 W Houston St, Rm 206, New York, NY 10014
Senior Counselor:
Christopher Podgus 212-807-3162
Senior Counselor:
Joanne C Reich 212-807-3162

Western Region
Donovan State Office Bldg, 125 Main St, Buffalo, NY 14203-3042
Deputy Director:
Joseph Vogtli 716-847-3414/fax: 716-847-3410
Senior Counselor:
Bernie Dotterweich 716-847-3414

Senior Counselor:
Harry Rudy 716-847-3414

Public Information, Field Support, Budget, Finance, Personnel, Blind Annuity
Executive Deputy Director:
Harvey J McCagg 518-474-6784/fax: 518-473-0379
Training Coordinator:
Chris Stirling 518-486-3720

Veterans' Service Organizations

Albany Housing Coalition Inc . . . . fax: 518-465-6499
278 Clinton Ave, Albany, NY 12210
Executive Director:
Lynn Mack 518-465-5251
Director, Veterans Svcs:
Kevin Norfleet 518-465-5251

COPIN HOUSE (Homeless Veterans) . . . . fax: 716-283-5712
5622 Buffalo Ave, Niagara Falls, NY 14304
Executive Director:
Sharon McGrath 716-283-5622

Continuum of Care for Homeless Veterans in New York City

30th Street Shelter
400-430 East 30th St, New York, NY 10016
Director:
Yvonne Ballard 212-481-4730

Project TORCH, Veterans Health Care Center
40 Flatbush Ave Ext, 8th Fl, Brooklyn, NY 11201
Program Coordinator:
Julie Irwin 718-439-4345/fax: 718-439-4356

Hicksville Counseling Center, Veterans' Resource Center . . . . fax: 516-935-2717
385 West John St, Hicksville, NY 11801
Director, Substance Abuse Program & Veterans Resource Center:
Geryl Pecora 516-935-6858

Saratoga Cnty Rural Preservation Co (Homeless Veterans)
36 Church Ave, Ballston Spa, NY 12020
Executive Director:
Dottie Nixon 518-885-0091/fax: 518-885-0998
e-mail: rpc36@aol.com

Suffolk County United Veterans Halfway House Project Inc
PO Box 598, Patchogue, NY 11772
Executive Director:
John Lynch 631-924-8088/fax: 631-924-0160

Veterans House (The) . . . . fax: 518-465-6499
180 First St, Albany, NY 12210
House Manager:
John Jacobie 518-449-8430

Veterans Outreach Center Inc . . . . fax: 585-546-5234
459 South Ave, Rochester, NY 14620
Fax: 585-546-5234
Web site: www.eflagstore.com
President & Chief Executive Officer:
Thomas Cray 585-546-1081
e-mail: voc.frontiernet.net

Offices and agencies appear in alphabetical order.

Veterans Services Center of the Southern Tier .... fax:
607-771-9395
174 Clinton St, Binghamton, NY 13905
Executive Director:
Patricia Gaven 607-771-8387

Veterans' Coalition of the Hudson Valley ... fax: 845-471-6113
9 Vassar St, Poughkeepsie, NY 12601
845-471-6113 Fax: 845-471-6113
Administrator:
Marilyn Wickman................................ 845-471-6113
e-mail: vetcoal@aol.com

CORPORATIONS, AUTHORITIES AND COMMISSIONS

Brooklyn Navy Yard Development Corporation
63 Flushing Ave Unit 300
Bldg 292, 3rd Fl
Brooklyn, NY 11205-1054
718-907-5900 Fax: 718-643-9296
Web site: www.brooklynnavyyard.com

Chair:
Alan H Fishman 718-907-5900
President & Chief Executive Officer:
Eric Deutsch 718-907-5900

Senior Vice President, External Affairs:
Richard Drucker 718-907-5936
e-mail: rdrucker@brooklynnavyyard.org

NEW YORK STATE LEGISLATURE

See Legislative Branch in Section 1 for additional Standing Committee and Subcommittee information.

Assembly Standing Committees

Veterans Affairs
Chair:
Darryl C Towns (D) 518-455-5821
Ranking Minority Member:
Jeffrey Brown (R)................................. 518-455-4505

Senate Standing Committees

Veterans, Homeland Security & Military Affairs
Chair:
Michael A L Balboni (R) 202-224-2752
Ranking Minority Member:
Ruth Hassell-Thompson (D)...................... 202-224-2061

U.S. Government

EXECUTIVE DEPARTMENTS AND RELATED AGENCIES

US Defense Department

AIR FORCE-National Media Outreach ..... fax: 212-784-0149
805 Third Ave, 9th Fl, New York, NY 10022-7513
Director:
Lt Col Patrick Barnes 212-784-0147
e-mail: patrick.barnes@afnews.af.mil
Deputy Director:
Capt Jason Medina 212-784-0143
e-mail: jason.medina@afnews.af.mil

Air National Guard

Francis S Gabreski Airport, 106th Rescue Wing .... fax: 631-288-7619
150 Old Riverhead Rd, Westhampton Beach, NY 11978
Commander:
Col Michael F Canders........................... 631-723-7400
Public Affairs Officer:
Major Charles Killian............................. 631-723-7601

Hancock Field, 174th Fighter Wing
6001 E Molloy Rd, Syracuse, NY 13211-7099
315-454-6100
Commander:
Col Anthony Basile.............. 315-454-6599/fax: 315-454-6145

Army

Fort Drum .... fax: 315-772-5165
Bldg P-10000, Rm 121, Fort Drum, NY 13602-5028

Fax: 315-772-5165
Web site: www.drum.army.mil
Commander:
Maj Gen Lloyd J Austin III 315-772-5565
Public Affairs Officer:
Lt Col Paul Fitzpatrick........................... 315-772-5461

Fort Hamilton .... fax: 718-630-4709
Bldg 113, 2nd Flr, Brooklyn, NY 11252-5000
Commander:
Col Tracy E Nicholson........................... 718-630-4706

Fort Totten-77th Regional Support Command ..... fax: 718-352-5830
Headquarters, Bldg 200, Flushing, NY 11359-1016
Fax: 718-352-5830
Web site: www.usarc.army.mil/77thrsc
Commander:
Maj Gen Richard Colt 718-352-5077
Public Affairs Officer:
Maj Dana Minor................................. 718-352-5072
Community Relations Officer:
Chet Marcus 718-352-5226

Watervliet Arsenal
CO Bldg 10, Watervliet, NY 12189-4000
518-266-5111
Commander:
Col Donald C Olson.............................. 518-266-4294
Public Affairs Officer:
John E Swantek................. 518-266-5418/fax: 518-266-5859

Offices and agencies appear in alphabetical order.

Marine Corps

1st Marine Corps District . . . . fax: 516-228-5794
605 Stewart Ave, Garden City, NY 11530
Commander:
Col Warren J Foersch 516-228-5652
Public Affairs Officer:
Captain John Caldwell 516-228-5640

Public Affairs Office . . . . fax: 212-784-0169
805 Third Ave, 9th Fl, New York, NY 10022-7513
Director:
Maj David C Andersen 212-784-0160
Public Affairs Chief:
Gy Sgt John Jamison 212-784-0160

Navy

Saratoga Springs Naval Support Unit
19 JF King Dr, Saratoga Springs, NY 12866-9267
Officer-in-Charge & Public Affairs Officer:
Lt Cdr Sherry L Kirsche 518-886-0200/fax: 518-886-0120

US Department of Veterans Affairs
Web site: www.va.gov

National Cemetery Administration
Web site: www.cem.va.gov

Bath National Cemetery
San Juan Ave, Bath, NY 14810
Director:
Wesley R Jones 607-664-4853/fax: 607-664-4761

Calverton National Cemetery
210 Princeton Blvd, Calverton, NY 11933
Director:
Richard L.R. Boyd 631-727-5410 x31/fax: 631-369-4397

Cypress Hills National Cemetery
625 Jamaica Ave, Brooklyn, NY 11208
631-454-4949
Director:
Richard L.R. Boyd 631-454-4952/fax: 631-694-5422

Long Island National Cemetery
2040 Wellwood Ave, Farmingdale, NY 11735
631-454-4949
Director:
Richard L.R. Boyd 631-454-4952/fax: 631-694-5422

Saratoga National Cemetery
200 Duell Rd, Schuylerville, NY 12871-1721
Director:
Roseann Santore 518-581-9128/fax: 518-583-6975

Woodlawn National Cemetery
1825 Davis St, Elmira, NY 14901
Director:
Wesley R Jones 607-732-5411/fax: 607-732-1769

VA Regional Office of Public Affairs, Field Operations Svc
245 W Houston St, Ste 315B, New York, NY 10014
Regional Director:
Lawrence M Devine 212-807-3429/fax: 212-807-4030
Public Affairs Specialist:
James A Blue 212-807-3429
Public Affairs Specialist:
Leo Marinacci 212-807-3429

Veterans Benefits Administration

Buffalo Regional Office
Niagara Square Center, 130 South Elmwood, Buffalo, NY 14202
800-827-1000
Regional Director:
Donna Ferrell 716-857-3020/fax: 716-551-3072
Assistant Director:
Thomas D Brownell 800-827-1000
Veterans Service Center Manager:
James Rogers 800-827-1000
Regional Counsel:
Joseph Moreno 800-827-1000
Vocational Rehabilitation & Employment Division:
Joseph Senulis 800-827-1000
Chief, Education Division:
Robert Quall 800-827-1000

New York City Regional Office . . . . fax: 212-807-4024
245 West Houston St, New York, NY 10014
Director:
Patricia Amberg-Blyskal 212-807-3055
Adjudication Officer & Veterans Benefits & Services Officer:
Robert Dolan 212-807-3420
Vocational Rehabilitation & Counseling Division:
Bernard Finger 212-807-3030

Veterans Health Admin Integrated Svc Network (VISN)

VA Healthcare Network Upstate New York (VISN2)
113 Holland Ave, Bldg 7, Albany, NY 12208
Web site: www.va.gov/visns/visn02
Network Director:
William F Feeley 518-626-7317 x67317
e-mail: william.feeley@med.va.gov
Network Communications Manager:
Kathleen Hider 585-463-2642/fax: 585-463-2649
Albany VA Medical Center
113 Holland Ave, Albany, NY 12208
Director:
Mary-Ellen Piche 518-626-6731
e-mail: mary-ellen.piche@med.va.gov
Public Affairs Officer:
Linda Blumenstock 518-626-5522
Batavia VA Medical Center
222 Richmond Ave, Batavia, NY 14020
Director:
Michael Finnegan 716-862-8529
e-mail: michael.finnegan@med.va.gov
Public Affairs Liaison:
Kathleen Martin 585-344-3330
Bath VA Medical Center
76 Veterans Ave, Bath, NY 14810
Chief Operating Officer:
Linda Weiss 607-664-4722
e-mail: linda.weiss@med.va.gov
Public Affairs Officer:
Carl Haneline 607-664-4869
Buffalo VA Medical Center
3495 Bailey Ave, Buffalo, NY 14215
Director:
Michael Finnegan 716-862-8529
e-mail: michael.finnegan@med.va.gov
Public Affairs Officer:
Arlene Kelly 716-862-8751
Canandaigua VA Medical Center
400 Fort Hill Ave, Canandaigua, NY 14424
Director:
Dr Robert Ratliff 585-393-7208/fax: 585-393-8328
e-mail: w.david.smith@med.va.gov

Policy Areas

Offices and agencies appear in alphabetical order.

Chief of Staff:
Robert Babcock 585-393-7211
e-mail: robert.babcock2@med.va.gov

Syracuse VA Medical Center & Clinics
800 Irving Ave, Syracuse, NY 13210
Director:
James Cody 315-425-4892
e-mail: james.cody@med.va.gov
Public Affairs Officer:
Gordon Sclar 315-425-2422

VA NY/NJ Veterans Healthcare Network (VISN3)
Bldg 16, 130 W Kingsbridge Rd, Bronx, NY 10468
Web site: www.va.gov/visns/visn03
Network Director:
James J Farsetta 718-741-4143/fax: 718-741-4141
Deputy Network Director:
Gerald Culliton 718-741-4134

Bronx VA Medical Center
130 W Kingsbridge Rd, Bronx, NY 10468
Director:
MaryAnn Musumeci 718-584-9000 x6512
Chief of Staff:
Eric Langhoff 718-584-9000 x6522

Brooklyn Campus of the NY Harbor Healthcare System
800 Poly Pl, Brooklyn, NY 11209
Director:
John J Donnellan, Jr 718-630-3521
Associate Director:
Veronica J Foy 718-630-3524

Castle Point Campus of the VA Hudson Valley Healthcare System
PO Box 100, 100 Rte 9D, Castle Point, NY 12511
Executive Director:
Michael A Sabo 845-737-4400 x2460

Montrose Campus of the VA Hudson Valley Healthcare System
2094 Albany Post Rd, Rte 9A, Montrose, NY 10548
Director:
Michael A Sabo 914-737-4400 x2400
Public Affairs:
Nancy A Winter 914-737-4400 x2255

New York Campus of the NY Harbor Healthcare System
423 East 23rd St, New York, NY 10010
Executive Chief of Staff:
Michael S Simberkoff 212-951-3417
Associate Director:
Martina A Parauda 212-951-3240

Northport VA Medical Center
79 Middleville Rd, Northport, NY 11768
Director:
Robert Schuster 631-261-4400 x2747
Chief of Staff:
Edward Mack 631-261-4400 x2737

US Labor Department
Web site: www.dol.gov/dol/vets

New York State Field Offices
Albany
Harriman State Office Campus, Bldg 12, Rm 518, Albany, NY
12240-0099
Director:
J Frank Merges . . . . 518-435-0831 or 518-457-7465
e-mail: merges-frank@dol.gov
Veteran's Program Assistant:
Joan M Cramer 518-457-7465
e-mail: cramer-joan@dol.gov
Buffalo
290 Main St, Glass Rm, Buffalo, NY 14202

Assistant Director:
Vacant 716-851-2612/fax: 716-851-2638
New York City . . . . fax: 212-352-6185
345 Hudson St, Rm 8209, New York, NY 10014-0682
Assistant Director:
Alice F Jones 212-352-6183
e-mail: jones-alice@dol.gov
Veteran's Program Specialist:
Timothy D Hays 212-352-6547
e-mail: hays-timothy@dol.gov

US State Department
Web site: www.state.gov

US Mission To the United Nations
140 East 45th St, New York, NY 10022
US Representative to the United Nations:
Acting Ambassador Ann Patterson 212-415-4404
Director, Communications, Spokesman:
Richard Grenell 212-415-4058
Military Staff Committee:
Col John B O'Dowd 212-415-4147

U.S. CONGRESS

See U.S. Congress Chapter for additional Standing Committee and Subcommittee information.

House of Representatives Standing Committees

Armed Services
Chair:
Duncan Hunter (R-CA) 202-225-5672
Ranking Minority Member:
Ike Skelton (D-MO) 202-225-2876
New York Delegate:
John M McHugh (R) 202-225-4611
New York Delegate:
Steve Israel (D) 202-225-3335

Veterans' Affairs
Chair:
Christopher Smith (R-NJ) 202-225-3765
Ranking Minority Member:
Lane Evans (D-IL) 202-225-5905
New York Delegate:
Jack Quinn (R) 202-225-3306

Senate Standing Committees

Armed Services
Chair:
John W Warner (R-VA) 202-224-2023
Ranking Minority Member:
Carl Levin (D-MI) 202-224-6221
New York Delegate:
Hillary Rodham Clinton (D) 202-224-4451

Veterans' Affairs
Chair:
Larry Craig (R-ID) 202-224-2752
Ranking Minority Member:
Daniel Akaka (D-HI) 202-224-6361

Offices and agencies appear in alphabetical order.

Private Sector

369th Veterans Association Inc
PO Box 91, Lincolnton Station, New York, NY 10037
212-281-3308 Fax: 212-281-6308
e-mail: jamnat@earthlink.net
Nathaniel James, National President
Assistance & referrals for all veterans

Air Force Association (AFA)
1501 Lee Highway, Arlington, VA 22209-1198
703-247-5800 Fax: 703-247-5853
Web site: www.afa.org
Donald L Peterson, Executive Director
Support & advance the interest & recognition of the US Air Force

Air Force Sergeants Association (AFSA), Division 1
557 Sixth St, Dover, NH 3820
603-742-4844
e-mail: acaldwell557@comcast.net
Web site: www.afsahq.org
Alfred B Caldwell, President Division 1
Protect rights & benefits of enlisted personnel-active, retired, National Guard, reserve & their families

Air Force Women Officers Associated (AFWOA)
PO Box 780155, San Antonio, TX 78278
e-mail: patriciamurphy@afwoa.com
Web site: www.afwoa.org
Col Patricia M Murphy, USAF Retired, President
Represent interests of active duty, retired & former women officers of the Air Force; preserve the history & promote recognition of the role of military women

Albany Housing Coalition Inc
278 Clinton Ave, Albany, NY 12210
518-465-5251 Fax: 518-465-6499
e-mail: ahc@global2000.net
Web site: www.timesunion.com/communities/ahc
Kevin Norfleet, Director, Veterans Services
Providing a continuum of affordable housing for veterans & their families; rental housing referrals

American Legion, Department of New York
112 State St, Suite 400, Albany, NY 12207
518-463-2215 Fax: 518-427-8443
e-mail: info@nylegion.org
Web site: www.ny.legion.org
Richard M Pedro, New York State Adjutant
Advocate for veterans; entitlements for wartime veterans, their families & service to the community, children & youth of our nation

American Military Retirees Association Inc
5436 Peru St, Ste 1, Plattsburgh, NY 12901
800-424-2969 or 518-563-9479 Fax: 518-324-5204
e-mail: info@amra1973.org
Web site: www.amra1973.org
John E Campbell, Executive Director
Protecting the benefits of all military retirees & veterans

Army Aviation Association of America (AAAA)
755 Main St, Ste 4D, Monroe, CT 06468-2830
203-268-2450 Fax: 203-268-5870
William R Harris, Executive Director
Advance the cause & recognition of US Army aviation; benefit all personnel, current, retired, families & survivors

Army Aviation Association of America (AAAA), North Country Chapter
Bldg P10420, So Riva Ridge Dr, Fort Drum, NY 13602
315-772-8252 or 315-772-3177 Fax: 315-772-9093
Col Anthony Crutchfield, USA, Chapter President
Advance the cause & recognition of US Army aviation; benefit all Army aviation personnel, current, retired, families & survivors

Army Aviation Association of America (AAAA), Western NY Chapter
3 Glendale Dr, Clifton Park, NY 12065
518-786-4397 Fax: 518-786-4393
e-mail: nysaao@yahoo.com
LTC Mike Bobeck, NYARNG, Chapter President
Advance the cause & recognition of US Army aviation; benefit all Army aviation personnel, current, retired, families & survivors

Association of Military Surgeons of the US (AMSUS), NY Chapter
105 Franklin Ave, Malverne, NY 11565-1926
516-542-0025 Fax: 516-593-3114
e-mail: amsusny@aol.com
Col John J Hassett, USAR, President NY Chapter
Improve federal healthcare service; support & represent military & other health care professionals

Association of the US Army (AUSA)
2425 Wilson Blvd, Arlington, VA 22201
703-841-4300 x639 or 800-336-4570 Fax: 703-525-9039
e-mail: wloper@ausa.org
Web site: www.ausa.org
William Loper, Director Government Affairs
Champion the cause & objectives of the US Army by public relations, communications & legislative action

Black Veterans for Social Justice Inc
665 Willoughby Street, Brooklyn, NY 11221
718-852-6004 Fax: 718-852-4805
e-mail: admin@bvsj.org
Web site: www.bvsj.org
Job Mashariki, President & Chief Executive Officer
Assist all veterans in obtaining benefits, entitlements, employment & housing

Blinded Veterans Association New York Inc
245 W Houston St, 2nd Fl, Rm 208, New York, NY 10014
212-807-3173 Fax: 212-807-4022
Web site: www.bva.org
Jack Shapiro, Director

Catholic War Veterans of the United States of America

c/o James C Finkel, Sr Adjutant, 346 Broadway, Rm 812, New York, NY 10013
212-962-0988 Fax: 212-894-0517
e-mail: wyscwv@aol.com
Web site: www.nycatholicwarvets.org
Philip M Scola, State Commander
Veterans & auxiliary of the Roman Catholic faith; assisting all veterans & their families

Commissioned Officers Assn of the US Public Health Svc Inc (COA)

8201 Corporate Dr, Ste 200, Landover, MD 20785
301-731-9080 Fax: 301-731-9084
e-mail: gfarrell@coausphs.org
Web site: www.coausphs.org
Jerry Farrell, Executive Director
Committed to improving the public health of the US; supports corps officers & advocates for their interests through leadership, education & communication

Disabled American Veterans

PO Box 108, Baldwinsville, NY 13027
315-635-9289 Fax: 315-635-0026
George LePorte, Past State Commander, NYS

Disabled American Veterans, Department of New York

200 Atlantic Ave, Studio #1, Lynbrook, NY 11563-3597
516-887-7100 Fax: 516-887-7175
e-mail: davny@erols.com
Web site: www.davny.org
Sidney Siller, Adjutant
Service, support & enhance healthcare & benefits for wartime disabled veterans

Fleet Reserve Association (FRA)

125 North West St, Alexandria, VA 22314
703-683-1400 Fax: 703-549-6610
e-mail: news-fra@fra.org
Web site: www.fra.org
Joseph L Barnes, National Executive Secretary & Chief Lobbyist
Serving the interests of active duty, retired & reserve enlisted members of the US Navy, Marine Corps & Coast Guard

Fleet Reserve Association (FRA), NE Region (NJ, NY, PA)

1118 West Jefferson Street, Philadelphia, PA 19122-3442
215-235-7796 Fax: 215-765-2671
e-mail: charleserainey@post.com
Web site: www.fra.org
Charles Rainey, Regional President
Serving the interests of active duty, retired & reserve enlisted members of the US Navy, Marine Corps & Coast Guard

Gold Star Wives

763B Blackberry Lane, Yorktown, NY 10598
914-962-8083
Mary Dwyer, New York Contact
National nonprofit working to advance issues important to military service widows

Gold Star Wives of America Inc

5510 Columbia Pike, Ste 205, Arlington, VA 22204
888-479-9788
e-mail: gswives2@aol.com
Web site: www.goldstarwives.org
John Brennan, Government Relations Representative
Support for widows of American Servicemen

Jewish War Veterans of the USA

1811 R St NW, Washington, DC 20009
202-265-6280 Fax: 202-234-5662
e-mail: jwv@jwv.org
Web site: www.jwv.org
Louis Abramson, National Commander
Honoring & supporting all Jewish war veterans, their benefits & rights; fight bigotry & discrimination; patriotic voice of American Jewry

Jewish War Veterans of the USA, State of NY

346 Broadway, Rm 817, New York, NY 10013
212-349-6640 Fax: 212-577-2575
e-mail: deptny.jwv@juno.com
Web site: www.jwv.org
Saul Rosenberg, Department Commander
Honoring & supporting Jewish war veterans

Korean War Veterans

37 Rocklea Dr, Rochester, NY 14624-1350
585-426-1095
e-mail: andermoose@cs.com
Web site: www.kwva.org
Donald Anderson, President
Ensuring that Korean war vets are remembered

Marine Corps League

PO Box 505, White Plains, NY 10602
914-941-2118 Fax: 914-864-7173
e-mail: llc1@mclwestchester.com
Web site: www.mclwestchester.org
Alfonso Cavallo, Commandant
Marine Corps fraternal/veterans association

Marine Corps League (MCL)

PO Box 3070, Merrifield, VA 22116
703-207-9588 or 800-625-1775 Fax: 703-207-0047
e-mail: mcl@mcleague.org
Web site: www.mcleague.org
Michael Blum, Executive Director
Support & promote the interests, history & tradition of the Marine Corps & all Marines

Marine Corps League (MCL), Department of NY

46 Marine Corp Blvd, Staten Island, NY 10301
718-447-2306 Fax: 718-556-0590
Bob Powell, Commandant, Department of NY
Support & promote the interests, history & tradition of the Marine Corps & all Marines

Military Chaplains Association of the USA (MCA)
PO Box 7056, Arlington, VA 22207
703-276-2189 Fax: 703-276-2189
e-mail: chaplains@mca-usa.org
Web site: www.mca-usa-org
David White, Executive Director
Promotes the recognition & interests of military, Civil Air Patrol &
VA chaplains; develops & encourages candidates through national
institutes, scholarships & outreach

Military Officers Association of America
201 N Washington St, Alexandria, VA 22314-2539
703-549-2311 or 800-234-6622 Fax: 703-838-8173
Web site: www.moaa.org
Col Steve Strobridge, USAF Retired, Director Government Relations
Preserve earned entitlements of members of the uniformed services,
their families & survivors; support of strong national defense;
scholarship & support to members' families

Military Officers Association of America (MOAA), NYS Council
258 Randwood Dr, Williamsville, NY 14221
716-689-6295 Fax: 716-847-6405
e-mail: patc258@aol.com
Col Patrick Cunningham, USA Retired, President, NYS Council of
  Chapters
Benefit members of uniformed services, active & retired, family &
survivors; promote strong national defense

Military Order of the Purple Heart
Syracuse Veterans Administration Medical, 800 Irving Ave, Room
A176, Syracuse, NY 13210-2796
315-425-4685 Fax: 315-472-2356
e-mail: lois.reinhart-reyes@med.va.gov
Lois Reinhardt-Reyes, National Service Officer
Veterans' benefits & rehabilitation

Military Order of the Purple Heart (MOPH)
1945 MacArthur Dr, McLean, VA 22101
703-821-9629 Fax: 703-821-3254
e-mail: goberh@aol.com
Web site: www.purpleheart.org
Hershel Gober, National Legislative Director
Congressionally chartered organization representing the interests of
America's combat-wounded veterans

Montford Point Marine Association
346 Broadway St, New York, NY 10013
212-267-3318 Fax: 212-566-4903
Web site: www.montfordpointmarines.com
James Maillard, Financial Secretary

National Amputation Foundation Inc
40 Church St, Malverne, NY 11565
516-887-3600 Fax: 516-887-3667
Al Pennacchia, President
Programs & services geared to help the amputee & other disabled
people; donated medical equipment give-away program

National Guard Association of the US (NGAUS)
One Massachusetts Ave NW, Washington, DC 20001
202-789-0031 Fax: 202-682-9358
Web site: www.ngaus.org
Bill Goss, Director, Legislative Affairs
Promote the interests of the Army National Guard through
legislative action;

National Military Family Association (NMFA)
2500 North Van Dorn St, Ste 102, Alexandria, VA 22302-1601
703-931-6632 or 800-260-0218 Fax: 703-931-4600
e-mail: families@nmfa.org
Web site: www.nmfa.org
Joyce Raezer, Director Government Relations
Service to the families of active duty, retirees, reserve & National
Guard uniformed personnel

Naval Enlisted Reserve Association (NERA)
6703 Farragut Ave, Falls Church, VA 22042-2189
703-534-1329 or 800-776-9020 Fax: 703-534-3617
e-mail: members@nera.org
Web site: www.nera.org
Dave Davidson, Executive Director
Ensuring strong & well-trained Naval, Coast Guard & Marine
Corps Reserves; improving reserve equipment, promotion, pay &
retirement benefits through legislative action

Naval Reserve Association (NRA)
1619 King St, Alexandria, VA 22314-3647
703-548-5800 or 866-672-4968 Fax: 866-683-3647
e-mail: membership@navy-reserve.org
Web site: www.navy-reserve.org
Ike Puzon, USNR Retired, Director of Legislation
Premier education & professional organization for Naval Reserve
officers & the association voice of the Naval Reserve

Navy League of the US (NLUS)
2300 Wilson Blvd, Arlington, VA 22201-3308
703-528-1775 or 800-356-5760 Fax: 703-528-2333
e-mail: jfleet@navyleague.org
Web site: www.navyleague.org
John Fleet, Director for Legislative Affairs
Citizens in support of the Sea Services

Navy League of the US (NLUS), New York Council
c/o US Coast Guard, Battery Park Bldg, 1 South St, Rm 314, New
York, NY 10004
212-825-7333 Fax: 212-668-2138
e-mail: nlnyc1902@msn.com
Web site: www.nynavyleague.org
Dr Daniel Thys, President
Represent citizens in support of the Sea Services

New Era Veterans, Inc
1150 Commonwealth Ave, Bronx, NY 10472
718-904-7036 Fax: 718-904-7024
e-mail: neweravets@verizon.net
Web site: www.neweraveterans.org
John M Laguna, Chief Executive Officer
Post traumatic stress disorder

Offices and agencies appear in alphabetical order.

Policy Areas

New York State Air Force Association
PO Box 539, Merrick, NY 11566-0539
516-623-5714
e-mail: brave3@aaahawk.com
Web site: www.nysafa.org
Robert Braverman, Vice President Government Relations
Support & advance the interest & recognition of the US Air Force

North Country Vietnam Veterans Association, Post 1
PO Box 1161, Plattsburgh, NY 12901
518-563-3426 Fax: 518-563-3426
e-mail: kenhynes@charter.net; secretary@ncvva.org
Web site: www.ncvva.org
Ken Hynes, Contact
Peer counseling & referral

Reserve Officers Association (ROA)
One Constitution Ave, NE, Washington, DC 20002
202-646-7700 x710 or 800-809-9448 Fax: 202-646-7751
Web site: www.roa.org
Susan Lukas, Legislative Director
Advance the cause of reserve officers through legislative action; promote the interests & recognition of ROTC & military academy students

Reserve Officers Association (ROA), Department of NY
3 Wildwood Rd, Congers, NY 10920
845-638-5215 Fax: 845-638-5299
e-mail: generalwin@aol.com
Brig Gen Robert J Winzinger, USAR Retired President
Advance the cause of reserve officers of the US Armed Forces; promote the interests & recognition of ROTC & military academy students

United Spinal Association
75-20 Astoria Blvd, Jackson Heights, NY 11370
718-803-3782 Fax: 718-803-0414
e-mail: info@unitedspinal.org
Web site: www.unitedspinal.org
Linda Gutmann, Advocacy
Managed & long-term care, disability assistance & benefits, advocacy & legislation

Veterans of Foreign Wars
1044 Broadway, Albany, NY 12204
518-463-7427 Fax: 518-426-8904
Web site: www.vfwny.com
Art Koch III, State Adjutant

Veterans of Foreign Wars (VFW)
200 Maryland Ave, NE, Washington, DC 20002
202-543-2239 Fax: 202-543-0961
e-mail: dcullinan@vfwdc.org
Web site: www.vfwdc.org
Dennis Cullinan, Director National Legislative Affairs
Legislative action, community service & volunteerism in support of the nation's veterans, their families & survivors

Veterans of Foreign Wars Auxiliary
1044 Broadway, Albany, NY 12204
518-462-2668 Fax: 518-427-1994
e-mail: nylavfw@hotmail.com
Marna Szewczyk, Treasurer
Rights & benefits of veterans

Veterans' Widows International Network Inc (VWIN), New York
75-36 Bell Blvd, Flushing, NY 11364-3430
718-740-4797
e-mail: pumsmom@aol.com
Web site: www.vetsurvivors.com
Elsie Ryan, NY State Representative
Outreach to American veterans' survivors; assist with obtaining benefits; provide local contacts & support

Vietnam Veterans of America, NYS Council
82-42 Penelope Ave, Middle Village, NY 11379
718-326-4656 Fax: 718-894-0404
e-mail: vvanycs@aol.com
John Rowan, President

Women Marines Association
59 Sawyer Ave, Dorchester, MA 02125-2040
617-265-1572
e-mail: sgtkwm@aol.com
Web site: www.womenmarines.org
Catherine Carpenter, Area 1 Director

Women's Army Corps Veterans Association - Empire Chapter
121-16 Ocean Promenade, Unit 3H, Rockaway Park, NY 11694
718-634-0353
e-mail: adelewac@aol.com
Adele Brenner, President, WAC Chapter #89

Offices and agencies appear in alphabetical order.

Section 3:
STATE & LOCAL GOVERNMENT PUBLIC INFORMATION

PUBLIC INFORMATION OFFICES

This chapter includes state public information contacts with telephone and fax numbers as well as e-mail and Web site addresses, if available. For additional information, please refer to the related policy area or the indexes.

New York State

GOVERNOR'S OFFICE

Governor's Office
Web site: www.state.ny.us

Director, Communications:
David Catalfamo.................................518-474-8418
Press Secretary:
Kevin Quinn......................................518-474-8418
Deputy Press Secretary:
Todd Alhardt 518-474-8418
Press Officer:
Jennifer Meicht...................................518-474-8418
Press Officer:
Andrew Rush 518-474-8418
Director, Scheduling:
Audra Viscusi....................................518-474-4727
Director, Correspondence:
Tricia Curley......................................518-474-3612
Citizens Services:
Linda Boyd.......................................518-474-1041

New York City Office
NYC Press Secretary:
Lynn Rasic.......................212-681-4580/fax: 212-681-4608

New York State Office of Federal Affairs
Director & Counsel:
James Mazzarella 202-434-7100

Lieutenant Governor's Office
Acting Chief of Staff:
Karin Kennett 518-474-4623/fax: 518-486-4170
Executive Secretary:
Jane Burhans.....................................518-474-4623

EXECUTIVE & ADMINISTRATIVE DEPARTMENTS & AGENCIES

Advocate for Persons with Disabilities, Ofc of
One Empire State Plaza
Ste 101
Albany, NY 12223-1150
518-473-4538 Fax: 518-473-6005
Web site: www.advoc4disabled.state.ny.us

Deputy Advocate, Counsel & Public Info Officer:
Gregory Jones 518-473-4609/fax: 518-473-6005
e-mail: oapwdinfo@oapwd.org

Aging, Office for the
518-474-7158 Fax: 518-473-6565
Web site: www.aging.state.ny.us

Public Information Officer:
Thomas Gallagher 518-474-7158/fax: 518-473-6565
e-mail: tom.gallagher@ofa.state.ny.us

Agriculture & Markets Department
Web site: www.agmkt.state.ny.us

Public Information Officer:
Jessica Chittenden 518-457-3136/fax: 518-457-3087
e-mail: jessica.chittenden@agmkt.state.ny.us

Alcoholic Beverage Control, Division of
Web site: www.abc.state.ny.us

Deputy Commissioner, Administration & Public Affairs:
J Mark Anderson 518-486-4767/fax: 518-402-4015

Alcoholism & Substance Abuse Services, Office of
Web site: www.oasas.state.ny.us

Director, Communications:
Jennifer Farrell 518-485-1768
e-mail: jenniferfarrell@oasas.state.ny.us
Public Information Officer:
Joseph Morrissey 518-485-1768
e-mail: josephmorrissey@oasas.state.ny.us

Banking Department
Web site: www.banking.state.ny.us

Deputy Superintendent, Communications & Media Relations:
Catie Marshall 212-709-1691/fax: 212-709-1693
e-mail: catie.marshall@banking.state.ny.us

Budget, Division of the
Web site: www.state.ny.us/dob

Director, Communications:
Michael Marr 518-474-9041
Press Officer:
Peter Constantakes 518-473-3885
Press Officer:
Scott Reif 518-473-3885

Offices and agencies appear in alphabetical order.

CIO Office & Office for Technology

Web site: www.cio.state.ny.us

CIO Office
Web site: www.cio.state.ny.us
Chief Information Officer:
James T Dillon 518-474-3421/fax: 518-402-2976
e-mail: cio@cio.state.ny.us

Office for Technology
Web site: www.nyoft.state.ny.us
Director:
Michael McCormack 518-473-9450/fax: 518-402-2976
e-mail: nyoft@oft.state.ny.us

Children & Family Services, Office of

Web site: www.dfa.state.ny.us

Assistant Commissioner, Public Affairs:
Sandra A Brown 518-402-3130/fax: 518-486-7550
e-mail: cfspio@dfa.state.ny.us

Civil Service Department

Web site: www.cs.state.ny.us

Director, Public Information:
Marc E Carey 518-457-9375/fax: 518-457-6654
e-mail: mec5@cs.state.ny.us
Public Records Access Officer:
Jane Prus 518-457-6875/fax: 518-457-6654

Consumer Protection Board

Web site: www.consumer.state.ny.us

Director, Marketing & Public Relations:
Jon Sorensen 518-473-9472/fax: 518-474-2986

Correctional Services Department

Web site: www.docs.state.ny.us

Public Information Officer:
James Flateau 518-457-8182/fax: 518-457-7070

Council on Children & Families

Web site: www.ccf.state.ny.us

Public Information & Personnel:
Donna Ned 518-474-5522/fax: 518-473-7568
e-mail: donna.ned@dfa.state.ny.us

Council on the Arts

Web site: www.nysca.org

Public Information Officer:
Margaret Keta 212-627-5656/fax: 212-620-5911
e-mail: mketa@nysca.org

Crime Victims Board

Web site: www.cvb.state.ny.us

General Counsel:
Everett Mayhew, Jr 518-457-8066/fax: 518-457-8658

Criminal Justice Services, Division of

Web site: www.criminaljustice.state.ny.us

Director, Communications:
Lynn Rasic 518-485-0857/fax: 518-457-3089
Deputy Public Information Officer:
Lyle Hartog 518-485-2465/fax: 518-485-7715

Developmental Disabilities Planning Council

Web site: www.ddpc.state.ny.us

Public Information Officer:
Thomas F Lee 518-486-7505/fax: 518-402-3505

Education Department

Web site: www.nysed.gov

Director, Communications:
R Alan Ray 518-474-1200/fax: 518-473-2977
e-mail: aray@mail.nysed.gov
Secretary to the Board of Regents:
David Johnson 518-474-5889
e-mail: djohnson@mail.nysed.gov

State Library
Web site: www.nysl.nysed.gov
Assistant Commissioner & State Librarian:
Janet Welch 518-474-5930
e-mail: jwelch@mail.nysed.gov
Public Information Officer:
Valerie Chevrette 518-474-5961/fax: 518-486-2152
Coordinator, Statewide Library Services:
Carol Desch 518-474-7196
Interim Director, Research Library:
Mary Redmond 518-473-1189

Elections, State Board of

Web site: www.elections.state.ny.us

Director, Public Information:
Lee Daghlian 518-474-1953/fax: 518-473-8315
e-mail: ldaghlian@elections.state.ny.us

Emergency Management Office, NYS

Web site: www.nysemo.state.ny.us

Assistant Director, Community Affairs:
Dennis J Michalski 518-485-5666
Public Information Officer:
Donald L Mauer 518-485-6011/fax: 518-457-4923
e-mail: donald.maurer@semo.state.ny.us

Empire State Development

Web site: www.empire.state.ny.us

Communications Director:
Ron Jury 212-803-3740/fax: 212-803-3735
e-mail: rjury@empire.state.ny.us

Employee Relations, Governor's Office of

Web site: www.goer.state.ny.us

Offices and agencies appear in alphabetical order.

Public Information Officer:
Michelle McDonald 518-474-4800/fax: 518-486-7304
e-mail: mgmcdonald@goer.state.ny.us

Environmental Conservation Department
Web site: www.dec.state.ny.us

Assistant Commissioner of Media Relations:
Michael Fraser 518-402-8000/fax: 518-402-2209
Public Information Officer:
Maureen Wren 518-402-8000
Director, Public Affairs & Education Division:
Laurel Remus 518-402-8049/fax: 518-402-8050

Freshwater Wetlands Appeals Board
Counsel:
Michele M Stefanucci 518-402-0566/fax: 518-402-0588

General Services, Office of
Web site: www.ogs.state.ny.us

Assistant Commissioner, Public Affairs:
Jennifer Morris 518-474-5987/fax: 518-474-3187
e-mail: jennifer.morris@ogs.state.ny.us

Health Department
Web site: www.health.state.ny.us

Deputy Commissioner, Administration & Public Affairs:
William Van Slyke 518-474-3384/fax: 518-473-7071

Housing & Community Renewal, NYS Div of
Web site: www.dhcr.state.ny.us

Director, Communications:
Jennifer Farina 518-473-2526/fax: 518-474-5752
Press Secretary:
Peter Moses 212-480-6732/fax: 212-480-6737

Hudson River Valley Greenway
Web site: www.hudsongreenway.state.ny.us

Executive Director, Communities Council:
Carmella R Mantello 518-473-3835/fax: 518-473-4518
e-mail: carmella.mantello@hudsongreenway.state.ny.us
Executive Director, Greenway Conservancy:
Carmella R Mantello 518-473-3835/fax: 518-473-4518

Human Rights, State Division of
Web site: www.nysdhr.com

Deputy Commissioner, Public Affairs:
Denise L Ellison 718-741-8459/fax: 718-741-3214
e-mail: dellison@nysnet.net

Inspector General (NYS), Office of the
Web site: www.ig.state.ny.us

Direector, Communications:
Stephen Del Giacco 518-474-1010/fax: 518-486-3745
e-mail: steve.delgiacco@ig.state.ny.us

Insurance Department
Web site: www.ins.state.ny.us

Director, Public Affairs & Research Bureau:
Michael Barry 212-480-5262/fax: 212-480-6077
e-mail: public-affairs@ins.state.ny.us

Insurance Fund (NYS)
Web site: www.nysif.com

Chief Information Officer:
Robert Sammons 518-437-4640
Public Information Officer:
Robert Lawson 518-437-3504/fax: 518-437-1849

Labor Department
Web site: www.labor.state.ny.us

Deputy Commissioner, Administration & Public Affairs:
Mary L Hines 518-473-3905/fax: 518-485-6297
Director for Communications:
Robert Lillpopp 518-457-5519/fax: 518-485-1126

Law Department
Web site: www.oag.state.ny.us

Director, Public Information & Correspondence:
Peter A Drago 518-474-7330/fax: 518-402-2472
Director for Communications:
Darren Dopp 212-416-8060/fax: 212-416-6005
Press Secretary:
Juanita Scarlett 212-416-8060
Press Officer:
Maritere Arce 212-416-8065

APPEALS & OPINIONS DIVISION Law Library
Chief, Library Services:
Sarah Browne 518-474-3840/fax: 518-402-2271
Senior Librarian, New York City Office:
Fran Sheinwald 212-416-8012/fax: 212-416-6130

Lottery, Division of
Web site: www.nylottery.org

Director, Communications:
Carolyn M Hapeman 518-388-3415/fax: 518-388-3423
Director, Advertising:
Michael Flanagan 518-388-3430

Mental Health, Office of
Web site: www.omh.state.ny.us

Deputy Commissioner, Public Affairs & Planning:
Keith E Simons 518-474-6567

Mental Retardation & Developmental Disabilities, Office of
Web site: www.omr.state.ny.us

Director, Public Affairs:
Deborah Sturm Rausch 518-474-6601/fax: 518-474-1335

Offices and agencies appear in alphabetical order.

Military & Naval Affairs, Division of
Web site: www.dmna.state.ny.us

Director, Public Affairs:
Kent Kisselbrack 518-786-4581/fax: 518-786-4649
e-mail: kent.kisselbrack@ny.ngb.army.mil

Motor Vehicles Department
Web site: www.nydmv.state.ny.us

Associate Commissioner, Communications:
Joe Picchi 518-473-7000/fax: 518-473-1930
e-mail: jpicc@dmv.state.ny.us

Parks, Recreation & Historic Preservation, NYS Office of
Web site: www.nysparks.state.ny.us

Asst Commissioner, Public Affairs:
Wendy Gibson 518-486-1868/fax: 518-486-2924

Parole, Division of
Web site: parole.state.ny.us

Public Information Officer:
Scott E Steinhardt 518-486-4631/fax: 518-473-6037

Prevention of Domestic Violence, Office for the
Web site: www.opdv.state.ny.us

Public Information Off:
Suzanne Cecala 518-457-5744/fax: 518-457-5810
e-mail: scecala@opdv.state.ny.us

Probation & Correctional Alternatives, Div of
Web site: www.dpca.state.ny.us

General Counsel:
Linda Valenti 518-485-2394/fax: 518-485-5140

Public Employment Relations Board
Web site: www.perb.state.ny.us

Executive Director:
James R Edgar 518-457-2676/fax: 518-457-2664

Public Service Department
Web site: www.dps.state.ny.us

Director, Communications:
Robert H Mayer 518-474-1668/fax: 518-474-5616
Director, Public Affairs:
David C Flanagan 518-474-7080/fax: 518-473-2838

Racing & Wagering Board
Web site: www.racing.state.ny.us

Public Information Officer:
Stacy Clifford 518-453-8460 x3311/fax: 518-453-8867

Real Property Services, Office of
Web site: www.orps.state.ny.us

Director, Public Information:
Geoffrey T Gloak 518-486-5446/fax: 518-474-9276
e-mail: geoffrey.gloak@orps.state.ny.us

Regulatory Reform, Governor's Office of
Web site: www.gorr.state.ny.us

Public Information Officer:
David Pietrusza 518-486-3292/fax: 518-473-9342

Science, Technology & Academic Research, Office of
Web site: www.nystar.state.ny.us

Director, Public Information:
James A Denn 518-292-5700/fax: 518-292-5798
e-mail: jdenn@nystar.state.ny.us

Small Cities, Governor's Office for
Web site: www.nysmallcities.com

Public Information Officer:
Tracey McNerney 518-474-2057/fax: 518-474-5247
e-mail: tmcnerney@nysmallcities.com

State Comptroller, Office of the
Web site: www.osc.state.ny.us

Director, Communications:
David Neustadt 518-474-4015/fax: 518-473-8940
e-mail: dneustadt@osc.state.ny.us
Press Secretary:
Jeffrey Gordon 518-474-4015/fax: 518-473-8940
e-mail: jgordon@osc.state.ny.us

State Department
Web site: www.dos.state.ny.us

Assistant Secretary of State for Communications:
Lawrence Sombke 518-474-4752/fax: 518-474-4597
e-mail: info@dos.state.ny.us

State Police, Division of
Web site: www.troopers.state.ny.us

Director & Technical Lieutenant, Public Information:
Glenn R Miner 518-457-2180/fax: 518-485-7818
Crime Prevention Coordinator:
Sgt. Kern Fwoboda 518-457-2180/fax: 518-485-7818

Tax Appeals, Division of
Web site: www.nysdta.org

Secretary & Administrative Officer:
Robert P Rivers 518-266-3062/fax: 518-271-0886

Taxation & Finance Department
Web site: www.tax.state.ny.us

Offices and agencies appear in alphabetical order.

Director, Communications:
Thomas Bergin 518-457-4242/fax: 518-457-2486

Temporary & Disability Assistance, Office of
Web site: www.dfa.state.ny.us

Assistant Commissioner, Public Information:
John B Madden 518-474-9516/fax: 518-486-6935
e-mail: nyspio@dfa.state.ny.us

Transportation Department
Web site: www.dot.state.ny.us

Director, Public Affairs:
Jennifer Post 518-457-6400/fax: 518-457-6506
e-mail: jpost@gw.dot.state.ny.us

Veterans' Affairs, Division of
Web site: www.veterans.state.ny.us

Executive Deputy Director:
Harvey J McCagg 518-474-6784/fax: 518-473-0379

Welfare Inspector General, Office of NYS
Chief Investigator:
Joseph R Bucci 212-417-2026/fax: 212-417-5849

Workers' Compensation Board
Web site: www.wcb.state.ny.us

Director, Public Information:
Jon A Sullivan 518-474-6670/fax: 518-473-1415

JUDICIAL SYSTEM AND RELATED AGENCIES

Unified Court System
Web site: www.courts.state.ny.us

Director, Public Affairs:
Greg Murray 212-428-2116/fax: 212-428-2117
Director for Communications:
David Bookstaver 212-428-2500/fax: 212-428-2507
Chief Law Librarian:
Ellen Robinson 518-473-1196/fax: 518-473-6860

LEGISLATIVE BRANCH

Assembly
Press Secretary to the Speaker:
Charles Carrier. 518-455-3888/fax: 518-455-3858
Director, Minority Communications:
Kelliann Cummings. 518-455-3756/fax: 518-455-3750
Assembly Public Information Officer:
Sharon Walsh. 518-455-4218/fax: 518-455-5175
Director, Assembly Communication & Information Services:
John Longo 518-455-5767/fax: 518-455-4963

Legislative Library
Legislative Librarian:
Ellen Breslin 518-455-2468/fax: 518-426-6901
Legislative Librarian:
James Giliberto. 518-455-2468
Law Librarian:
Kate Balassie 518-455-2468

Senate
Director, Majority Communications:
John E McArdle. 518-455-2264/fax: 518-455-2260
Majority Press Secretary:
Marcia White. 518-455-3191/fax: 518-455-2448
Director, Minority Communications:
Valerie Berlin 518-455-2701/fax: 518-426-6933
Minority Press Secretary:
William Reynolds 518-455-2415/fax: 518-426-6955
Director, Student Programs Office:
James A Utermark 518-455-2611/fax: 518-432-5470

CORPORATIONS, AUTHORITIES AND COMMISSIONS

Adirondack Park Agency
Web site: www.apa.state.ny.us

Public Information Director:
Keith McKeever 518-891-4050/fax: 518-891-3938

Agriculture & NYS Horse Breeding Development Fund
Web site: www.nysirestakes.com

Executive Director:
Peter Goold 518-436-8713/fax: 518-426-1490

Albany County Airport Authority
Web site: www.albanyairport.com

Director, Public Affairs:
Doug Myers 518-242-2222 x4/fax: 518-242-2641
e-mail: info@albanyairport.com

Albany Port District Commission
Web site: www.portofalbany.com

General Manager:
Frank W Keane 518-463-8763/fax: 518-463-8767
e-mail: portofalbany@portofalbany.com

Atlantic States Marine Fisheries Commission
Web site: www.asmfc.org

Public Affairs & Resource Specialist:
Tina Berger 202-289-6400/fax: 202-289-6051
e-mail: tberger@asmfc.org

Battery Park City Authority (Hugh L Carey)
Web site: www.batteryparkcity.org

Offices and agencies appear in alphabetical order.

Press Liaison:
Leticia Remauro 212-417-2276/fax: 212-417-2279
e-mail: remaurol@pbcauthor.org

Brooklyn Navy Yard Development Corporation
63 Flushing Ave
Bldg 292, 3rd Fl
Unit 300
Brooklyn, NY 11205-1054
718-907-5900 Fax: 718-643-9296
Web site: www.brooklynnavyyard.org

Senior Vice President, External Affairs:
Richard Drucker 718-907-5936/fax: 718-643-9296
e-mail: rdrucker@brooklynnavyyard.org

Buffalo & Fort Erie Public Bridge Authority (Peace Bridge Authority)
Web site: www.peacebridge.com

General Manager:
Ron Rienas. 716-884-6744/fax: 716-884-2089

Capital Defender Office
Web site: www.nycdo.org

Capital District Regional Off-Track Betting Corporation
Web site: www.capitalotb.com

General Counsel:
Robert Hemsworth. 518-344-5298/fax: 518-370-5460

Capital District Regional Planning Commission
One Park Place, Ste 102
Albany, NY 12205
518-453-0850 Fax: 518-453-0856
e-mail: cdrpc@cdrpc.org
Web site: www.cdrpc.org

Executive Director:
Rocco Ferraro 518-453-0850/fax: 518-453-0856
e-mail: cdrpc@cdrpc.org

Capital District Transportation Authority
Web site: www.cdta.org

Chief of Staff & Director, Marketing:
Carm Basile. 518-482-3371/fax: 518-446-0675

Catskill Off-Track Betting Corporation
Web site: www.interbets.com

President:
Donald J Groth 845-362-0400/fax: 845-362-0419
e-mail: otb@interbets.com

Central New York Regional Market Authority
Executive Director:
Benjamin Vitale. 315-422-8647/fax: 315-442-6897
e-mail: cnyrma@aol.com

Central New York Regional Transportation Authority
Web site: www.centro.org

Executive Director:
Frank Kobliski. 315-442-3360/fax: 315-422-3337
e-mail: fkoblisk@centro.org

Central Pine Barrens Joint Planning & Policy Commission
Web site: www.pb.state.ny.us

Executive Director:
Ray Corwin. 631-224-2604

City University Construction Fund
Fiscal Coordinator:
Denise Phillips. 212-541-0190/fax: 212-541-0401
e-mail: denise.phillips@mail.cuny.edu

Delaware River Basin Commission
Web site: www.drbc.net

Communications Manager:
Clarke Rupert 609-883-9500 x260/fax: 609-883-9522

Development Authority of the North Country
Web site: www.danc.org

Executive Director:
Robert S Juravich 315-785-2593/fax: 315-785-2591
e-mail: juravich@danc.org

Empire State Development Corporation
Web site: www.empire.state.ny.us

Communications Director:
Ron Jury. 212-803-3740/fax: 212-803-3735
e-mail: rjury@empire.state.ny.us

Great Lakes Commission
Web site: www.glc.org

vacant
Program Manager, Communications & Internet Technology:
Christine Manninen 734-971-9135 x112/fax: 734-971-9150
e-mail: glc@great.lakes.net

Hudson River-Black River Regulating District
Web site: www.hrbrrd.com

Executive Director:
Richard Lefebvre. 518-465-3491/fax: 518-432-2485
e-mail: hrbrrd@choicemail.com

Offices and agencies appear in alphabetical order.

Interest on Lawyer Account (IOLA) Fund of the State of NY
Web site: www.iola.org

Executive Director:
Lorna Blake 646-865-1541/fax: 646-865-1545
e-mail: lblake@iola.org

Interstate Environmental Commission
Web site: www.iec-nynjct.org

Executive Director & Chief Engineer:
Howard Golub 212-582-0380/fax: 212-581-5719
e-mail: iecmail@iec-nynjct.org

Interstate Oil & Gas Compact Commission
Web site: www.iogcc.state.ok.us

Executive Director:
Christine Hansen 405-525-3556/fax: 405-525-3592
e-mail: iogcc@iogcc.state.ok.us
NYS Official Representative:
Bradley J Field 518-402-8076

Lake George Park Commission
Web site: www.lgpc.state.ny.us

Executive Director:
Michael P White 518-668-9347/fax: 518-668-5001
e-mail: info@lgpc.state.ny.us

Lawyers' Fund for Client Protection
Web site: www.nylawfund.org

Executive Director & Counsel:
Timothy O'Sullivan 518-434-1935/fax: 518-434-5641
e-mail: info@nylawfund.org

Legislative Bill Drafting Commission
Deputy Counsel:
Jamie-Lynne Elacqua 518-455-7538/fax: 518-455-7598
e-mail: elacqua@lbdc.state.ny.us

Long Island Power Authority
Web site: www.lipower.org

Vice President, Communications:
Bert Cunningham 516-222-7700/fax: 516-222-9137
e-mail: bcunningham@lipower.org

MTA Bridges & Tunnels
Web site: www.mta.info/bandt

Director, Public Affairs:
Frank Pascual 646-252-7416/fax: 646-252-7408

MTA Long Island Bus
Web site: www.mta.info/libus

Vice President, Administration:
James R Campbell 516-542-0100 x4345

MTA Long Island Rail Road
Web site: www.mta.info/lirr

Vice President, Market Development & Public Affairs:
Brian P Dolan 718-558-7301/fax: 718-558-8212
e-mail: bpdolan@lirr.org

MTA Metro-North Railroad
Web site: www.mta.info/mnr

Director, Corporate & Media Relations:
Donna Evans 212-672-1201/fax: 212-672-1220
Director, Government & Community Relations:
Mark Mannix 212-340-3024/fax: 212-340-4995

MTA New York City Transit
Web site: www.mta.info/nyct

Senior Vice President, Corporate Communications:
Paul Fleuranges 718-243-8881/fax: 718-596-2146

Metropolitan Transportation Authority
Web site: www.mta.info

Deputy Executive Director, Corporate & Community Affairs:
Christopher Boylan 212-878-7160/fax: 212-878-7030
Press Secretary:
Tom Kelly 212-878-7440/fax: 212-878-7030

Metropolitan Transportation Authority, Office of the Inspector General
Web site: www.mtaig.state.ny.us

Inspector General:
Matthew D Sansverie 212-878-0007/fax: 212-878-0003
e-mail: msansver@mtaig.org

Municipal Assistance Corporation for the City of New York
Executive Director:
Nancy H Henze 212-840-8255/fax: 212-840-8570
e-mail: macnyc@earthlink.net

Nassau Regional Off-Track Betting Corporation
Web site: www.nassauotb.com

Director, Public Affairs:
Joseph Galante 516-572-2800 x152/fax: 516-572-2840

New England Interstate Water Pollution Control Commission
Web site: www.neiwpcc.org

Deputy Director:
Susan Sullivan 978-323-7929/fax: 978-323-7919
e-mail: mail@neiwpcc.org
Acting Commissioner, New York State:
Denise M Sheehan 518-485-8940

Offices and agencies appear in alphabetical order.

New York City Housing Development Corp

110 Williams St, 10th Fl
New York, NY 10038
212-227-5500 Fax: 212-227-6865
e-mail: info@nychdc.com
Web site: www.nychdc.org

Director, Marketing & Public Affairs:
Tracy Paurowski 212-227-9496/fax: 212-227-6846
e-mail: info@nychdc.com

New York City Off-Track Betting Corp

1501 Broadway
New York, NY 10036-5572
212-221-5200 Fax: 212-221-8025
Web site: www.nycotb.com

Senior Vice President, Marketing, Media & Communications:
Ron Ceisler 212-704-5152/fax: 212-704-5141

New York City School Construction Authority

Web site: www.nycsca.org

Corporate Secretary:
Michael Szabaga 718-472-8302/fax: 718-472-8088

New York Convention Center Operating Corp

Web site: www.javitscenter.com

Director, Public Affairs:
Michael Eisgrau. 212-216-2176/fax: 212-216-2895
e-mail: moreinfo@javitscenter.com

New York Metropolitan Transportation Council

Web site: www.nymtc.org

Public Information Officer:
Vacant. 718-472-3046/fax: 718-482-7431

New York Power Authority

Web site: www.nypa.gov

Director, Public Relations:
Jack Murphy 914-390-8198/fax: 914-390-8190
e-mail: jack.murphy@nypa.gov

New York State Assn of Fire Districts

Web site: www.firedistnys.com

Counsel:
William N Young 800-349-2904/fax: 518-869-5142

New York State Athletic Commission

123 William St, 20th Fl
New York, NY 10038-3804
212-417-5700 Fax: 212-417-4987
e-mail: athleticdos.state.ny.us
Web site: www.dos.state.ny.us/athletic.html

Secretary:
Robert Limerick. 212-417-5700/fax: 212-417-4987
e-mail: athletic@dos.state.ny.us

New York State Board of Law Examiners

254 Washington Ave Ext
Bldg 3, Corp Plaza
Albany, NY 12203
518-452-8700 Fax: 518-452-0175
Web site: www.nybarexam.org

Executive Director:
John J McAlary 518-452-8700/fax: 518-452-5729

New York State Bridge Authority

Web site: www.nysba.state.ny.us

Public Information Officer, Public Relations & Planning:
Mark Sheedy 845-691-7245/fax: 845-691-3636
e-mail: msheedy@nysba.state.ny.us

New York State Commission of Correction

30 Wolfe Road, 4th Fl
Albany, NY 12205
518-485-2346 Fax: 518-485-2467
e-mail: infoscoc@scoc.state.ny.us
Web site: www.scoc.state.ny.us

Deputy Public Information Officer:
Lyle Hartog 518-485-2346/fax: 518-485-2467
e-mail: infoscoc@scoc.state.ny.us

New York State Commission on Judicial Nomination

Counsel:
Stuart A Summit 212-977-9700/fax: 212-262-5152
e-mail: ssummit@phillipsnizer.com

New York State Commission on Quality of Care for the Mentally Disabled

Web site: www.cqc.state.ny.us

Press Officer:
Gary W Masline 518-388-1270/fax: 518-388-1275

New York State Commission on the Restoration of the Capitol

Corning Tower, 40th Fl
Empire State Plaza
Albany, NY 12242
518-473-0341

Executive Director:
Andrea J Lazarski 518-473-0341/fax: 518-486-5720
e-mail: andrea.lazarski@ogs.state.ny.us

New York State Disaster Preparedness Commission

Web site: www.nysemo.state.ny.us

Offices and agencies appear in alphabetical order.

Chairman:
James W McMahon 518-402-2227

New York State Dormitory Authority
Web site: www.dasny.org

Director, Communications & Marketing:
Paul Burgdorf 518-257-3380/fax: 518-257-3387
e-mail: pburgdor@dasny.org
Press Officer:
Claudia Hutton. 518-257-3382/fax: 518-257-3387
e-mail: chutton@dasny.org

New York State Energy Research & Development Authority
Web site: www.nyserda.org

Director, Communications:
Thomas G Collins. 518-862-1090 x3250/fax: 518-464-8249
e-mail: tgc@nyserda.org

New York State Environmental Facilities Corp
Web site: www.nysefc.org

Director, Corporate Communications & Records Access Officer:
Susan Mayer 518-402-6957/fax: 518-486-9323

New York State Ethics Commission
Web site: www.dos.state.ny.us/ethc/ethics.html

Public Information Officer:
Walter C Ayres 518-432-8210/fax: 518-432-8255
e-mail: wayres@dos.state.ny.us

New York State Financial Control Board
Web site: www.fcb.state.ny.us

Acting Executive Director:
Jeffrey Sommer 212-417-5066/fax: 212-417-5055

New York State Higher Education Services Corp (NYSHESC)
Web site: www.hesc.org

Senior Vice President, Communications:
Ronald Kermani. 518-474-3349/fax: 518-474-2839
e-mail: rkermani@hesc.org

New York State Housing Finance Agency (HFA)
Web site: www.nyhomes.org

Vice President, Policy & Planning:
Tracy A Oats. 212-688-4000 x678/fax: 212-872-0678

New York State Judicial Conduct Commission
61 Broadway
12th Fl
New York, NY 10006

212-809-0566 Fax: 212-949-8864
e-mail: webmaster@scjc.state.ny.us
Web site: www.scjc.state.ny.us

Counsel:
Robert H Tembeckjian 212-949-8860 x231/fax: 212-949-8864
e-mail: scjcny@nysnet.net

New York State Law Reporting Bureau
Web site: www.courts.state.ny.us/reporter

State Reporter:
Gary D Spivey 518-474-8211
Deputy State Reporter:
Charles A Ashe 518-474-8211/fax: 518-463-6869
e-mail: cashe@courts.state.ny.us

New York State Law Revision Commission
Web site: www.lawrevision.state.ny.us

Executive Director:
Rose Mary Bailly. 518-472-5858/fax: 518-445-2303

New York State Liquor Authority
Web site: www.abc.state.ny.us

Public Information Officer:
Kimberly Morella. 212-961-8331

New York State Mortgage Loan Enforcement & Administration Corporation
Web site: www.empire.state.ny.us

Public Affairs Officer:
Deborah Wetzel. 212-803-3740/fax: 212-803-3735
e-mail: dwetzel@empire.state.ny.us

New York State Olympic Regional Development Authority
Web site: www.orda.org

Director, Communications:
Sandy Caligiore 518-523-1655 x213/fax: 518-523-9275
e-mail: sandyc@orda.org

New York State Project Finance Agency
Vice President, Policy & Planning:
Tracy Oats 212-688-4000 x678/fax: 212-872-0678

New York State Teachers' Retirement System
Web site: www.nystrs.albany.ny.us

Director, Member Relations, Public Relations:
David Daly. 518-447-2910/fax: 518-447-2875

New York State Temporary Commission of Investigation
Web site: www.sic.state.ny.us

State & Local Government Public Information

Offices and agencies appear in alphabetical order.

Deputy Commissioner/Chief Counsel:
Anthony T Cartusciello 212-344-6670/fax: 212-344-6868

New York State Temporary Commission on Lobbying
Web site: www.nylobby.state.ny.us

Public Information Officer:
Kris Thompson 518-474-7126/fax: 518-473-6492
e-mail: lobcom@attglobal.net

New York State Thoroughbred Breeding & Development Fund
Web site: www.nybreds.com

Executive Director:
Martin G Kinsella 212-465-0660/fax: 212-465-8205

New York State Thruway Authority
Web site: www.thruway.state.ny.us

Director, Public Information:
Dan Gilbert 518-436-2983/fax: 518-426-3995
e-mail: publicinfo@thruway.state.ny.us

New York State Tug Hill Commission
Web site: www.tughill.org

Executive Director:
John K Bartow 315-785-2380/fax: 315-785-2574
e-mail: john@tughill.org

Niagara Falls Bridge Commission
Web site: www.niagarafallsbridges.com

General Manager & Secretary/Treasurer:
Thomas E Garlock 716-285-6322/fax: 716-282-3292

Niagara Frontier Transportation Authority
Web site: www.nfta.com

Director, Public Affairs:
C Douglas Hartmayer 716-855-7420/fax: 716-855-6655
e-mail: info@nfta.com

Northeastern Forest Fire Protection Commission
Web site: www.nffpc.org

Executive Director:
Thomas G Parent 207-968-3782/fax: 207-968-3782
e-mail: necompact@pivot.net

Northeastern Queens Nature & Historical Preserve Commission
Web site: www.sneq.com

Executive Director:
Joan M Vogt 718-229-8805/fax: 718-229-6131
e-mail: sneq@aol.com

Ogdensburg Bridge & Port Authority
Web site: www.ogdensport.com

Executive Director:
Joseph E Tracy 315-393-4080/fax: 315-393-7068
e-mail: jtracy@ogdensport.com

Ohio River Valley Water Sanitation Commission
Web site: www.orsanco.org

Public Information Programs Manager:
Jeanne Ison 513-231-7719/fax: 513-231-7761
e-mail: jison@orsanco.org

Port Authority of New York & New Jersey
Web site: www.panynj.gov

Director, Public Affairs:
Kayla M Bergeron 212-435-8041/fax: 212-435-6543

Port of Oswego Authority
Web site: www.portoswego.com

Executive Director:
Thomas McAuslan 315-343-4503/fax: 315-343-5498
e-mail: shipping@dreamscape.com

Rochester-Genesee Regional Transportation Authority
Web site: www.rgrta.org

Chief Executive Officer:
Mark R Aesch 585-654-0200/fax: 585-654-0224

Roosevelt Island Operating Corporation (RIOC)
Web site: www.rioc.com

Public Information Officer:
John Melia 212-832-4540/fax: 212-832-4582
e-mail: info@roosevelt-island.ny.us

State University Construction Fund
Web site: www.sucf.suny.edu

Acting General Counsel:
William K Barczak 518-689-2514/fax: 518-689-2634

State of New York Mortgage Agency (SONYMA)
Web site: www.nyhomes.org

Vice President, Policy/Planning:
Tracy A Oats 212-688-4000 x678/fax: 212-872-0686

State of New York Municipal Bond Bank Agency (MBBA)
Vice President, Policy/Planning:
Tracy A Oats 212-688-4000 x678/fax: 212-872-0686

Offices and agencies appear in alphabetical order.

Suffolk Regional Off-Track Betting Corp
Web site: www.suffolkotb

Public Information Officer:
DuWayne Gregory 631-853-1000 x3512/fax: 631-853-1086
e-mail: srotbc@suffolkotb.com

Thousand Islands Bridge Authority
Web site: www.tibridge.com

Executive Director:
Robert G Horr, III 315-482-2501/fax: 315-482-5925
e-mail: roberthorr@tibridge.com

Uniform State Laws Commission
Chair:
Richard B Long 607-584-4193/fax: 607-723-1530
e-mail: rlong@cglawllp.com

United Nations Development Corporation
Web site: www.undc.org

Senior Vice President, Operations:
Robert M Preissner 212-888-1618/fax: 212-588-0758

Waterfront Commission of New York Harbor
Web site: www.wcnyh.org

Executive Director:
Thomas DeMaria 212-742-9280/fax: 212-480-0587

Western Regional Off-Track Betting Corp
Web site: www.westernotb.com

Director, Public Relations:
Vacant 585-343-1423/fax: 585-343-6873

Offices and agencies appear in alphabetical order.

U.S. CONGRESS

U.S. Senate: New York Delegation

Internet access, including e-mail addresses, is available at: www.senate.gov

Charles E Schumer (D) 202-224-6542/fax: 202-228-3027
313 Hart Senate Office Bldg, Washington, DC 20510
Committees: Banking, Housing and Urban Affairs; Energy and Natural
Resources; Judiciary; Rules and Administration

Hillary Rodham Clinton (D) . . . . . (202) 224-4451/fax: 202-228-0282
476 Russell Senate Office Bldg, Washington, DC 20510
Committees: Armed Services; Environment and Public Works; Health,
Education, Labor & Pensions

U.S. House of Representatives: New York Delegation

Internet access, including e-mail addresses, is available at: www.house.gov

Gary L Ackerman (D) 202-225-2601/fax: 202-225-1589
2243 Rayburn House Office Bldg, Washington, DC 20515-3205
Congressional District: 5
Committees: Financial Services; International Relations

Timothy H Bishop (D) 202-225-3826/fax: 202-225-3143
1133 Longworth House Office Bldg, Washington, DC 20515-3201
Congressional District: 1
Committees: Education and the Workforce; Transportation and Infrastructure

Sherwood L Boehlert (R) 202-225-3665/fax: 202-225-1891
2246 Rayburn House Office Bldg, Washington, DC 20515-3223
Congressional District: 24
Committees: Science; Transportation and Infrastructure

Joseph Crowley (D) 202-225-3965/fax: 202-225-1909
312 Cannon House Office Bldg, Washington, DC 20515-3207
Congressional District: 7
Committees: Financial Services; International Relations

Eliot L Engel (D) 202-225-2464/fax: 202-225-5513
2264 Rayburn House Office Bldg, Washington, DC 20515
Congressional District: 17
Committees: Energy and Commerce; International Relations

Vito J Fossella (R) 202-225-3371/fax: 202-226-1272
1239 Longworth House Office Bldg, Washington, DC 20515-0005
Congressional District: 13
Committees: Energy and Commerce; Financial Services

Brian Higgins (D) 202-225-3306/fax: 202-226-0347
41 Cannon House Office Bldg, Washington, DC 20515-3227
Congressional District: 27
Committees: Government Reform; Transportation & Infrastructure

Maurice D Hinchey (D) 202-225-6335/fax: 202-226-0774
2431 Rayburn House Office Bldg, Washington, DC 20515-3222
Congressional District: 22
Committees: Appropriations

Steve Israel (D) 202-225-3335/fax: 202-225-4669
429 Cannon House Office Bldg, Washington, DC 20515
Congressional District: 2
Committees: Armed Services; Financial Services

Sue W Kelly (R) 202-225-5441/fax: 202-225-3289
1127 Longworth House Office Bldg, Washington, DC 20515-3219
Congressional District: 19
Committees: Financial Services; Small Business; Transportation and
Infrastructure

Peter T King (R) 202-225-7896/fax: 202-226-2279
436 Cannon House Office Bldg, Washington, DC 20515
Congressional District: 3
Committees: Financial Services; International Relations; Homeland Security

John R (Randy) Kuhl (R) 202-225-3161/fax: 202-226-6599
1505 Longworth House Office Bldg, Washington, DC 20515-3229
Congressional District: 29
Committees: Agriculture; Education & Workforce; Transportation &
Infrastructure

Nita M Lowey (D) 202-225-6506/fax: 202-225-0546
2329 Rayburn House Office Bldg, Washington, DC 20515-3218
Congressional District: 18
Committees: Appropriations; Homeland Security

Carolyn B Maloney (D) 202-225-7944/fax: 202-225-4709
2331 Rayburn House Office Bldg, Washington, DC 20515-3214
Congressional District: 14
Committees: Financial Services; Government Reform

Carolyn McCarthy (D) 202-225-5516/fax: 202-225-5758
106 Cannon House Office Bldg, Washington, DC 20515-3204
Congressional District: 4
Committees: Education and the Workforce; Financial Services

Offices and agencies appear in alphabetical order.

John M McHugh (R).............202-225-4611/fax: 202-226-0621
2333 Rayburn House Office Bldg, Washington, DC 20515-3223
Congressional District: 23
Committees: Armed Services; Government Reform; Intelligence

Michael R McNulty (D)..........202-225-5076/fax: 202-225-5077
2210 Rayburn House Office Bldg, Washington, DC 20515-3221
Congressional District: 21
Committees: Ways and Means

Gregory W Meeks (D)...........202-225-3461/fax: 202-226-4169
1710 Longworth House Office Bldg, Washington, DC 20515-3206
Congressional District: 6
Committees: Financial Services; International Relations

Jerrold Nadler (D)...............202-225-5635/fax: 202-225-6923
2334 Rayburn House Office Bldg, Washington, DC 20515-3208
Congressional District: 8
Committees: Judiciary; Transportation and Infrastructure

Major R Owens (D)..............202-225-6231/fax: 202-226-0112
2309 Rayburn House Office Bldg, Washington, DC 20515-3211
Congressional District: 11
Committees: Education and the Workforce; Government Reform

Charles B Rangel (D).............202-225-4365/fax: 202-225-0816
2354 Rayburn House Office Bldg, Washington, DC 20515-3215
Congressional District: 15
Committees: Ways and Means

Thomas M Reynolds (R).........202-225-5265/fax: 202-225-5910
332 Cannon House Office Bldg, Washington, DC 20515-3226
Congressional District: 26
Committees: Administration; Rules

Jose E Serrano (D)...............202-225-4361/fax: 202-225-6001
2227 Rayburn House Office Bldg, Washington, DC 20515-3216
Congressional District: 16
Committees: Appropriations

Louise McIntosh Slaughter (D) ...202-225-3615/fax: 202-225-7822
2469 Rayburn House Office Bldg, Washington, DC 20515
Congressional District: 28
Committees: Rules

John E Sweeney (R)..............202-225-5614/fax: 202-225-6234
416 Cannon House Office Bldg, Washington, DC 20515-3220
Congressional District: 20
Committees: Appropriations

Edolphus Towns (D)..............202-225-5936/fax: 202-225-1018
2232 Rayburn House Office Bldg, Washington, DC 20515-3210
Congressional District: 10
Committees: Energy and Commerce; Government Reform

Nydia M Velazquez (D)..........202-225-2361/fax: 202-226-0327
2241 Rayburn House Office Bldg, Washington, DC 20515-2104
Congressional District: 12
Committees: Financial Services; Small Business

James T Walsh (R) 202-225-3701/fax: 202-225-4042
2369 Rayburn House Office Bldg, Washington, DC 20515
Congressional District: 25
Committees: Appropriations

Anthony D Weiner (D)...........202-225-6616/fax: 202-226-7253
1122 Longworth House Office Bldg, Washington, DC 20515
Congressional District: 9
Committees: Judiciary; Transportation & Infrastructure

U.S. Senate Standing Committees

Agriculture, Nutrition & Forestry
Chair:
    C Saxby Chambliss (R-GA).........................202-224-3521
Ranking Minority Member:
    Tom Harkin (D-IA) 202-224-3254

Subcommittees

Forestry, Conservation & Rural Revitalization
Chair:
    Michael D Crapo (R-ID) 202-224-6142
Ranking Minority Member:
    Blanche Lincoln (D-AR) 202-224-4843

Marketing, Inspection & Product Promotion
Chair:
    James M Talent (R-MO) 202-224-6154
Ranking Minority Member:
    Max Baucus (D-MT) 202-224-2651

Production & Price Competitiveness
Chair:
    Elizabeth Dole (R-NC).............................202-224-6342
Ranking Minority Member:
    Kent Conrad (D-ND) 202-224-2043

Research, Nutrition & General Legislation
Chair:
    Rick Santorium (R-PA) 202-224-6324
Ranking Minority Member:
    Patrick J Leahy (D-VT) 202-224-4242

Appropriations
Chair:
    Thad Cochran (R-MS) 202-224-5054
Ranking Minority Member:
    Robert C Byrd (D-WV) 202-224-3954

Subcommittees

Agriculture, Rural Development & Related Agencies
Chair:
    Robert Bennett (R-UT) 202-224-5444
Ranking Minority Member:
    Herbert Kohl (D-WI).............................202-224-5653

Commerce, Justice, State & Judiciary
Chair:
    Richard C Shelby (R-AL) 202-224-5744

Offices and agencies appear in alphabetical order.

Ranking Minority Member:
Barbara A Mikulski (D-MD) 202-224-4654

Defense
Chair:
Ted Stevens (R-AK) 202-224-3004
Ranking Minority Member:
Daniel K Inouye (D-HI) 202-224-3934

District of Colombia
Chair:
Mike DeWine (R-OH) 202-224-2315
Ranking Minority Member:
Mary L Landrieu (D-LA) 202-224-5824

Energy & Water Development
Chair:
Pete V Domenici (R-NM) 202-224-6621
Ranking Minority Member:
Harry Reid (D-NV) 202-224-3542

Foreign Operations & Related Programs
Chair:
Mitch McConnell (R-KY) 202-224-2541
Ranking Minority Member:
Patrick J Leahy (D-VT) 202-224-4242

Homeland Security
Chair:
Judd Gregg (R-NH) 202-224-3324
Ranking Minority Member:
Robert C Byrd (D-WV) 202-224-3954

Interior
Chair:
Conrad R Burns (R-MT) 202-224-2644
Ranking Minority Member:
Byron L Dorgan (D-ND) 202-224-2551

Labor, Health & Human Services, Education
Chair:
Arlen Specter (R-PA) 202-224-4254
Ranking Minority Member:
Tom Harkin (D-IA) 202-224-3254

Legislative Branch
Chair:
Sam Brownback (R-KS) 202-224-6521

Military Construction
Chair:
Kay Bailey Hutchison (R-TX) 202-224-5922
Ranking Minority Member:
Dianne Feinstein (D-CA) 202-224-3841

Transportation/Treasury/Judiciary/Housing/Urban Development
Chair:
Christopher S Bond (R-MO) 202-224-5721
Ranking Minority Member:
Patty Murray (D-WA) 202-224-2621

Armed Services
Chair:
John W Warner (R-VA) 202-224-2023
Ranking Minority Member:
Carl Levin (D-MI) 202-224-6221
New York Delegate:
Hillary Rodham Clinton (D) 202-224-4451

Subcommittees

Airland
Chair:
John McCain (R-AZ) 202-224-2235
Ranking Minority Member:
Joseph I Lieberman (D-CT) 202-224-4041
New York Delegate:
Hillary Rodham Clinton (D-NY) 202-224-4041

Emerging Threats & Capabilities
Chair:
John Cornyn (R-TX) 202-224-2934
Ranking Minority Member:
Jack Reed (D-RI) 202-224-4642

Personnel
Chair:
Lindsey Graham (R-SC) 202-224-5972
Ranking Minority Member:
Ben Nelson (D-NE) 202-224-6551

Readiness & Management Support
Chair:
John Ensign (R-NV) 202-224-6244
Ranking Minority Member:
Daniel K Akaka (D-HI) 202-224-6361
New York Delegate:
Hillary Rodham Clinton (D-NY) 202-224-4451

SeaPower
Chair:
James M Talent (R-MO) 202-224-6154
Ranking Minority Member:
Edward M Kennedy (D-MA) 202-224-4543

Strategic Forces
Chair:
Jeff Sessions (R-AL) 202-224-4124
Ranking Minority Member:
Bill Nelson (D-FL) 202-224-5274

Banking, Housing & Urban Affairs
Chair:
Richard C Shelby (R-AL) 202-224-5744
Ranking Minority Member:
Paul S Sarbanes (D-MD) 202-224-4524
New York Delegate:
Charles E Schumer (D) 202-224-6542

Subcommittees

Economic Policy
Chair:
Jim Bunning (R-KY) 202-224-4343
Ranking Minority Member:
Charles E Schumer (D-NY) 202-224-6542

Financial Institutions
Chair:
Robert F Bennett (R-UT) 202-224-5444
Ranking Minority Member:
Tim Johnson (D-SD) 202-224-5842

Housing & Transportation
Chair:
Wayne Allard (R-CO) 202-224-5941
Ranking Minority Member:
Jack Reed (D-RI) 202-224-4642
New York Delegate:
Charles E Schumer (D) 202-224-6542

Offices and agencies appear in alphabetical order.

International Trade & Finance
Chair:
    Michael D Crapo (R-ID) 202-224-6142
Ranking Minority Member:
    Evan Bayh (D-IN) 202-224-5623

Securities & Investment
Chair:
    Charles E Hagel (R-NE) 202-224-4224
Ranking Minority Member:
    Christopher J Dodd (D-CT) 202-224-2823
New York Delegate:
    Charles E Schumer (D) 202-224-6542

Budget
Chair:
    Judd Gregg (R-NH) 202-224-3324
Ranking Minority Member:
    Kent Conrad (D-ND) 202-224-2043

Commerce, Science & Transportation
Chair:
    Ted Stevens (R-AK) 202-224-3004
Ranking Minority Member:
    Daniel K Inouye (D-HI) 202-224-3934

Subcommittees

Aviation
Chair:
    Conrad R Burns (R-MT) 202-224-2644
Ranking Minority Mbr:
    John D Rockefeller, IV (D-WV) 202-224-6472

Consumer Affairs, Product Safety & Insurance
Chair:
    George Allen (R-VA) 202-224-4024
Ranking Minority Member:
    Mark Pryor (D-AR) 202-224-2353

Disaster Prevention & Prediction
Chair:
    James DeMint (R-SC) 202-224-6121
Ranking Minority Member:
    Bill Nelson (D-NE) 202-224-6551

Fisheries & Coast Guard
Chair:
    Olympia J Snowe (R-ME) 202-224-5344
Ranking Minority Member:
    Maria Cantwell (D-WA) 202-224-3441

Global Climate Change
Chair:
    David Vitter (R-LA) 202-224-4623
Ranking Minority Member:
    Frank Lautenberg (D-NJ) 202-224-3224

National Ocean Policy Study
Chair:
    John Sununu (R-NH) 202-224-2841
Ranking Minority Member:
    Barbara Boxer (D-CA) 202-224-3553

Science & Space
Chair:
    Kay Bailey Hutchison (R-TX) 202-224-5922
Ranking Minority Member:
    Bill Nelson (D-FL) 202-224-5274

Surface Transportation & Merchant Marine
Chair:
    Trent Lott (R-MS) 202-224-6253
Ranking Minority Member:
    Daniel K Inouye (D-HI) 202-224-3934

Technology Innovation & Competitiveness
Chair:
    John Ensign (R-NV) 202-224-6244
Ranking Minority Member:
    John F Kerry (D-MA) 202-224-2742

Trade, Tourism & Economic Development
Chair:
    Gordon Smith (R-OR) 202-224-3753
Ranking Minority Member:
    Byron L Dorgan 202-224-2551

Energy & Natural Resources
Chair:
    Pete V Domenici (R-NM) 202-224-6621
Ranking Minority Member:
    Jeff Bingaman (D-NM) 202-224-5521

Subcommittees

Energy
Chair:
    Lamar Alexander (R-TN) 202-224-4944
Ranking Minority Member:
    Byron L Dorgan (D-ND) 202-224-2551

National Parks
Chair:
    Craig Thomas (R-WY) 202-224-6441
Ranking Minority Member:
    Daniel K Akaka (D-HI) 202-224-6361

Public Lands & Forests
Chair:
    Larry E Craig (R-ID) 202-224-2752
Ranking Minority Member:
    Ron Wyden (D-OR) 202-224-5244

Water & Power
Chair:
    Lisa Murkowski (R-AK) 202-224-6665
Ranking Minority Member:
    Tim Johnson (D-SD) 202-224-5842

Environment & Public Works
Chair:
    James M Inhofe (R-OK) 202-224-4721
Ranking Minority Member:
    James Jeffords (I-VT) 202-224-5141
New York Delegate:
    Hillary Rodham Clinton (D) 202-224-4451

Subcommittees

Clean Air, Climate Change & Nuclear Safety
Chair:
    George V Voinovich (R-OH) 202-224-3353
Ranking Minority Member:
    Thomas R Carper (D-DE) 202-224-2441

Fisheries, Wildlife & Water
Chair:
    Lincoln D Chafee (R-RI) 202-224-2921

State & Local
Government
Public Information

Offices and agencies appear in alphabetical order.

Ranking Minority Member:
Hillary Rodham Clinton (D-NY) 202-224-4451

Superfund & Waste Management
Chair:
John R Thune (R-SD) 202-224-2321
Ranking Minority Member:
Barbara Boxer (D-CA) 202-224-3553

Transportation & Infrastructure
Chair:
Christopher S Bond (R-MO) 202-224-5721
Ranking Minority Member:
Max Baucus (D-MT) 202-224-2651

Finance
Chair:
Charles E Grassley (R-IA) 202-224-3744
Ranking Minority Member:
Max Baucus (D-MT) 202-224-2651

Subcommittees

Health Care
Chair:
Orrin G Hatch (R-UT) 202-224-5251
Ranking Minority Mbr:
John D Rockefeller, IV (D-WV) 202-224-6472

International Trade
Chair:
Craig Thomas (R-WY) 202-224-6441
Ranking Minority Member:
Jeff Bingaman (D-NM) 202-224-5521

Long-Term Growth Debt & Deficit Reduction
Chair:
Gordon Smith (R-OR) 202-224-3753
Ranking Minority Member:
John Kerry (D-MA) 202-224-2742

Social Security & Family Policy
Chair:
Rick Santorum (R-PA) 202-224-6324
Ranking Minority Member:
Kent Conrad (D-ND) 202-224-2043

Taxation & IRS Oversight
Chair:
Jon Kyl (R-AZ) 202-224-4521
Ranking Minority Member:
James M Jeffords (I-VT) 202-224-5141

Foreign Relations
Chair:
Richard G Lugar (R-IN) 202-224-4814
Ranking Minority Member:
Joseph R Biden, Jr (D-DE) 202-224-5042

Subcommittees

African Affairs
Chair:
Mel Martinez (R-FL) 202-224-3041
Ranking Minority Member:
Russell D Feingold (D-WI) 202-224-5323

East Asian & Pacific Affairs
Chair:
Lisa Murkowski (R-AK) 202-224-6665

Ranking Minority Member:
John F Kerry (D-MA) 202-224-2742

European Affairs
Chair:
George Allen (R-VA) 202-224-4024
Ranking Minority Member:
Joseph R Biden, Jr (D-DE) 202-224-5042

International Economic Policy, Export & Trade Promotion
Chair:
Charles E Hagel (R-NE) 202-224-4224
Ranking Minority Member:
Paul S Sarbanes (D-MD) 202-224-4524

International Operations & Terrorism
Chair:
John Sununu (R-NH) 202-224-2841
Ranking Minority Member:
Bill Nelson (D-FL) 202-224-5274

Near Eastern & South Asian Affairs
Chair:
Lincoln D Chafee (R-RI) 202-224-2921
Ranking Minority Member:
Barbara Boxer (D-CA) 202-224-3553

Western Hemisphere, Peace Corps & Narcotics Affairs
Chair:
Norm Coleman (R-MN) 202-224-5641
Ranking Minority Member:
Christopher J Dodd (D-CT) 202-224-2823

Health, Education, Labor & Pensions
Chair:
Michael Enzi (R-WY) 202-224-3424
Ranking Minority Member:
Edward M Kennedy (D-MA) 202-224-4543
New York Delegate:
Hillary Rodham Clinton (D) 202-224-4451

Subcommittees

Bioterrorism Preparedness & Public Health
Chair:
Richard Burr (R-NC) 202-224-3154
Ranking Minority Member:
Edward M Kennedy (D-MA) 202-224-4543

Education & Early Childhood Development
Chair:
Lamar Alexander (R-TN) 202-224-4944
Ranking Minority Member:
Christopher J Dodd (D-CT) 202-224-2823
New York Delegate:
Hillary Rodham Clinton (D) 202-224-4451

Employment & Workplace Safety
Chair:
Johnny Isakson (R-GA) 202-224-3643
Ranking Minority Member:
Patty Murray (D-WA) 202-224-2621

Retirement Security & Aging
Chair:
Michael Devine (R-OH) 202-224-2315
Ranking Minority Member:
Barbara A Mikulski (D-MD) 202-224-4654
New York Delegate:
Hillary Rodham Clinton (D) 202-224-4451

Offices and agencies appear in alphabetical order.

Homeland Security & Governmental Affairs
Chair:
　Susan Collins (R-ME) 202-224-2523
Ranking Minority Member:
　Joseph I Lieberman (D-CT) 202-224-4041

Subcommittees

Financial Management, Government Information & International Security
Chair:
　Tom Coburn (R-OK) 202-224-5754
Ranking Minority Member:
　Thomas R Carper (D-DE) 202-224-2441

Oversight of Government Management, the Federal Workforce & the District of Columbia
Chair:
　George V Voinovich (R-OH). 202-224-3353
Ranking Minority Member:
　Daniel K Akaka (D-HI) 202-224-6361

Permanent Subcommittee on Investigations
Chair:
　Norm Coleman (R-MN). 202-224-5641
Ranking Minority Member:
　Carl Levin (D-MI) 202-224-6221

Judiciary
Chair:
　Arlen Specter (R-PA). 202-224-4254
Ranking Minority Member:
　Patrick J Leahy (D-VT) 202-224-4242
New York Delegate:
　Charles E Schumer (D). 202-224-6542

Subcommittees

Administrative Oversight & the Courts
Chair:
　Jeff Sessions (R-AL) 202-224-4124
Ranking Minority Member:
　Charles E Schumer (D-NY) 202-224-6542

Antitrust, Competition Policy & Consumer Rights
Chair:
　Michael DeWine (R-OH). 202-224-2315
Ranking Minority Member:
　Herbert Kohl (D-WI) 202-224-5653

Constitution, Civil Rights & Property Rights
Chair:
　Sam Brownback (R-KS) 202-224-6521
Ranking Minority Member:
　Russell D Feingard (D-WI) 202-224-5323

Corrections & Rehabilitations
Chair:
　Tom Coburn (R-OK) 202-224-5754

Crime & Drugs
Chair:
　Lindsey O Graham (R-SC). 202-224-5972
Ranking Minority Member:
　Joseph R Biden, Jr (D-DE). 202-224-5042

Immigration, Border Security & Citizenship
Chair:
　John Cornyn (R-TX) 202-224-2934

Ranking Minority Member:
　Edward M Kennedy (D-MA). 202-224-4543
New York Delegate:
　Charles E Schumer (D) 202-224-6542

Terrorism, Technology & Homeland Security
Chair:
　Jon Kyl (R-AZ) 202-224-4521
Ranking Minority Member:
　Dianne Feinstein (D-CA). 202-224-3841

Rules & Administration
Chair:
　Trent Lott (R-MS) 202-224-6253
Ranking Minority Member:
　Christopher J Dodd (D-CT) 202-224-2823
New York Delegate:
　Charles E Schumer (D). 202-224-6542

Small Business & Entrepreneurship
Chair:
　Olympia J Snowe (R-ME) 202-224-5344
Ranking Minority Member:
　John F Kerry (D-MA). 202-224-2742

Veterans' Affairs
Chair:
　Larry E Craig (R-ID) 202-224-2752
Ranking Minority Member:
　Daniel Akaka (D-HI) 202-224-6361

OTHER, SELECT & SPECIAL COMMITTEES

Aging, Special Committee on
Chair:
　Gordon Smith (R-OR) 202-224-3753
Ranking Minority Member:
　Herbert Kohl (D-WY) 202-224-5653

Ethics, Select Committee on
Chair:
　George V Voinovich (R-OH). 202-224-3353
Vice Chair:
　Tim Johnson (D-SD) 202-224-5842

Indian Affairs, Committee on
Chair:
　John McCain (R-AZ) 202-224-2235
Vice Chair:
　Byron L Dorgan (D-ND) 202-224-2551

Intelligence, Select Committee on
Chair:
　Pat Roberts (R-KS). 202-224-4774
Vice Chair:
　John D Rockefeller, IV (D-WV) 202-224-6472

Offices and agencies appear in alphabetical order.

389

U.S. House of Representatives Standing Committees

Chair:
    F James Sensenbrenner, Jr (R-WI) 202-225-5101
Ranking Minority Member:
    John Conyers, Jr (D-MI) 202-225-5126

Agriculture
Chair:
    Robert Goodlatte (R-VA) 202-225-2171
Ranking Minority Member:
    Collin C Peterson (D-MN) 202-225-2165

Subcommittees

Conservation, Credit, Rural Development & Research
Chair:
    Frank D Lucas (R-OK) 202-225-5565
Ranking Minority Member:
    Tim Holden (D-PA) 202-225-5546

Department Operations, Oversight, Nutrition & Forestry
Chair:
    Gil Gutknecht (R-MN) 202-225-2472
Ranking Minority Member:
    Joe Baca (D-CA) 202-225-6161

General Farm Commodities & Risk Management
Chair:
    Jerry Moran (R-KS) 202-225-2715
Ranking Minority Member:
    Bob Etheridge (D-NC) 202-225-4531

Livestock & Horticulture
Chair:
    Robert (Robin) Hayes (R-NC) 202-225-3715
Ranking Minority Member:
    Ed Case (D-HI) 202-225-4906

Specialty Crops & Foreign Agriculture Programs
Chair:
    William Jenkins (R-TN) 202-225-6356
Ranking Minority Member:
    Mike McIntyre (D-NC) 202-225-2731

Appropriations
Chair:
    Jerry Lewis (R-CA) 202-225-5861
Ranking Minority Member:
    David R Obey (D-WI) 202-225-3365
New York Delegate:
    Maurice D Hinchey (D) 202-225-6335
New York Delegate:
    Nita M Lowey (D) 202-225-6506
New York Delegate:
    Jose E Serrano (D) 202-225-4361
New York Delegate:
    John E Sweeney (R) 202-225-5614
New York Delegate:
    James T Walsh (R) 202-225-3701

Subcommittees

Agriculture, Rural Development, Food & Drug Administraton & Related Agencies
Chair:
    Henry Bonilla (R-TX) 202-225-4511

Ranking Minority Member:
    Rosa L DeLauro (D-CT) 202-225-3661
New York Delegate:
    Maurice D Hinchey (D) 202-225-6335

Defense
Chair:
    C W (Bill) Young (R-FL) 202-225-5961
Ranking Minority Member:
    John P Murtha (D-PA) 202-225-2065

Energy & Water Development & Related Agencies
Chair:
    David L Hobson (R-OH) 202-225-4324
Ranking Minority Member:
    Peter J Visclosky (D-IN) 202-225-2461

Foreign Operations, Export Financing & Related Programs
Chair:
    Jim Kolbe (R-AZ) 202-225-2542
Ranking Minority Member:
    Nita M Lowey (D-NY) 202-225-6506

Homeland Security
Chair:
    Harold Rogers (R-KY) 202-225-4601
Ranking Minority Member:
    Martin O Sabo (D-MN) 202-225-4755
New York Delegate:
    Jose E Serrano (D) 202-225-5614
New York Delegate:
    John E Sweeney (R) 202-225-5614

Interior, Environment & Related Agencies
Chair:
    Charles H Taylor (R-NC) 202-225-6401
Ranking Minority Member:
    Norman D Dicks (D-WA) 202-225-5916
New York Delegate:
    Maurice D Hinchey (D) 202-225-6335

Labor, Health & Human Services, Education & Related Agencies
Chair:
    Ralph Regula (R-OH) 202-225-3876
Ranking Minority Member:
    David R Obey (D-WI) 202-225-3365
New York Delegate:
    Nita M Lowey (D) 202-225-6506

Military Quality of Life, Veterans Affairs & Related Agencies
Chair:
    James T Walsh (R-NY) 202-225-3701
Ranking Minority Member:
    Chet Edwards (D-TX) 202-225-6105

Science, State, Justice & Commerce & Related Agencies
Chair:
    Frank R Wolf (R-VA) 202-225-5136
Ranking Minority Member:
    Alan B Mollohan (D-WV) 202-225-4172
New York Delegate:
    Jose E Serrano (D-NY) 202-225-4361

Transportation, Treasury, Housing, Urban Development, Judiciary & District of Columbia
Chair:
    Joe Knollenberg (R-MI) 202-225-5802

Offices and agencies appear in alphabetical order.

Ranking Minority Member:
John W Olver (D-MA)......................202-225-5335
New York Delegate:
John E Sweeney (R).......................202-225-5614

Armed Services
Chair:
Duncan Hunter (R-CA)...................202-225-5672
Ranking Minority Member:
Ike Skelton (D-MO)......................202-225-2876
New York Delegate:
Steve Israel (D).........................202-225-3335
New York Delegate:
John M McHugh (R).......................202-225-4611

Subcommittees

Personnel
Chair:
John M McHugh (R-NY)...................202-225-4611
Ranking Minority Member:
Vic Snyder (D-AR).......................202-225-2506

Projection Forces
Chair:
Roscoe G Bartlett (R-MO)...............202-225-2721
Ranking Minority Member:
Gene Taylor (D-MS)......................202-225-5772
New York Delegate:
Steve Israel (D)........................202-225-3461

Readiness
Chair:
Joel Hefley (R-CO)......................202-225-4422
Ranking Minority Member:
Solomon P Ortiz (D-TX).................202-225-7742
New York Delegate:
John M McHugh (R).......................202-225-4611

Strategic Forces
Chair:
Terry Everett (R-AL)....................202-225-2901
Ranking Minority Member:
Silvestre Reyes (D-TX).................202-225-4831

Tactical Air & Land Forces
Chair:
Curt Weldon (R-PA)......................202-225-2011
Ranking Minority Member:
Neil Abercrombie (D-HI)................202-225-2726
New York Delegate:
Steve Israel (D)........................202-225-3335

Terrorism, Unconventional Threats & Capabilities
Chair:
Jim Saxton (R-NJ).......................202-225-4765
Ranking Minority Member:
Martin T Meehan (D-MA).................202-225-3411

Budget
Chair:
Jim Nussle (R-IA).......................202-225-2911
Ranking Minority Member:
John M Spratt, Jr (D-SC)...............202-225-5501

Education & The Workforce
Chair:
John A Boehner (R-OH)..................202-225-6205

Ranking Minority Member:
George Miller (D-CA)...................202-225-2095
New York Delegate:
Timothy H Bishop (D)...................202-225-3826
New York Delegate:
Carolyn McCarthy (D)...................202-225-5516
New York Delegate:
Major R Owens (D).......................202-225-6231

Subcommittees

21st Century Competitiveness
Chair:
Howard P (Buck) McKeon (R-CA)..........202-225-1956
Ranking Minority Member:
Dale Kildee (D-MI)......................202-225-3611
New York Delegate:
Carolyn McCarthy (D)...................202-225-5516
New York Delegate:
Major R Owens (D).......................202-225-6231

Education Reform
Chair:
Michael N Castle (R-DE)................202-225-4165
Ranking Minority Member:
Lynn Woolsey (D-CA)....................202-225-5161
New York Delegate:
John R (Randy) Kuhl (R)................202-225-3161

Employer-Employee Relations
Chair:
Sam Johnson (R-TX)......................202-225-4201
Ranking Minority Member:
Robert E Andrews (D-NJ)................202-225-6501
New York Delegate:
Carolyn McCarthy (D)...................202-225-5516

Select Education
Chair:
Patrick J Tiberi (R-OH)................202-225-5355
Ranking Minority Member:
Ruben Hinojosa (D-TX)..................202-225-2531

Workforce Protections
Chair:
Charlie Norwood (R-GA).................202-225-4101
Ranking Minority Member:
Major R Owens (D-NY)...................202-225-6231
New York Delegate:
Timothy H Bishop (D)...................202-225-3826

Energy & Commerce
Chair:
Joe Barton (R-TX).......................202-225-2002
Ranking Minority Member:
John D Dingell (D-MI)..................202-225-4071
New York Delegate:
Eliot L Engel (D).......................202-225-2464
New York Delegate:
Vito Fossella (R).......................202-225-3371
New York Delegate:
Edolphus Towns (D)......................202-225-5936

Subcommittees

Commerce, Trade & Consumer Protection
Chair:
Cliff Stearns (R-FL)...................202-225-5744
Ranking Minority Member:
Jan Schakowsky (D-IL)..................202-225-2111

Offices and agencies appear in alphabetical order.

State & Local Government Public Information

New York Delegate:
Edolphus Towns (D-NY)..........................202-225-5936

Energy & Air Quality
Chair:
Ralph M Hall (R-TX)..........................202-225-6673
Ranking Minority Member:
Rick Boucher (D-VA)..........................202-225-3861
New York Delegate:
Eliot L Engel (D)..........................202-225-2464
New York Delegate:
Vito Fossella (R)..........................202-225-3371

Environment & Hazardous Materials
Chair:
Paul E Gillmor (R-OH)..........................202-225-6405
Ranking Minority Member:
Hilda L Solis (D-CA)..........................202-225-5464
New York Delegate:
Vito Fossella (R)..........................202-225-3371

Health
Chair:
Nathan Deal (R-GA)..........................202-225-5211
Ranking Minority Member:
Sherrod Brown (D-OH)..........................202-225-3401
New York Delegate:
Edolphus Towns (D)..........................202-225-5936

Oversight & Investigations
Chair:
Ed Whitfield (R-KY)..........................202-225-3115
Ranking Minority Member:
Bart Stupak (D-MI)..........................202-225-2927

Telecommunications & the Internet
Chair:
Fred Upton (R-MI)..........................202-225-3761
Ranking Minority Member:
Edward J Markey (D-MA)..........................202-225-2836
New York Delegate:
Edolphus Towns (D-NY)..........................202-225-5936
New York Delegate:
Vito Fossella (R)..........................202-225-3371

Financial Services

Chair:
Michael G Oxley (R-OH)..........................202-225-2676
Ranking Minority Member:
Barney Frank (D-MA)..........................202-225-5931
New York Delegate:
Gary L Ackerman (D)..........................202-225-2601
New York Delegate:
Joseph Crowley (D)..........................202-225-3965
New York Delegate:
Vito Fossella (R)..........................202-225-3371
New York Delegate:
Steve Israel (D)..........................202-225-3335
New York Delegate:
Sue W Kelly (R)..........................202-225-5441
New York Delegate:
Peter T King (R)..........................202-225-7896
New York Delegate:
Carolyn B Maloney (D)..........................202-225-7944
New York Delegate:
Carolyn McCarthy (D)..........................202-225-5516
New York Delegate:
Gregory W Meeks (D)..........................202-225-3461

New York Delegate:
Nydia M Velazquez (D)..........................202-225-2361

Subcommittees

Capital Markets, Insurance & Government Sponsored Enterprises
Chair:
Richard H Baker (R-LA)..........................202-225-3901
Ranking Minority Member:
Paul E Kanjorski (D-PA)..........................202-225-6511
New York Delegate:
Gary L Ackerman (D)..........................202-225-2601
New York Delegate:
Joseph Crowley (D)..........................202-225-3965
New York Delegate:
Vito Fossella (R)..........................202-225-3371
New York Delegate:
Steve Israel (D)..........................202-225-3335
New York Delegate:
Sue W Kelly (R)..........................202-225-5441
New York Delegate:
Peter T King (R)..........................202-225-7896
New York Delegate:
Carolyn McCarthy (R)..........................202-225-5516
New York Delegate:
Gregory W Meeks (D)..........................202-225-3461
New York Delegate:
Nydia M Velasquez (D)..........................202-225-2361

Domestic & International Monetary Policy, Trade & Technology
Chair:
Deborah Pryce (R-OH)..........................202-225-2015
Ranking Minority Member:
Carolyn B Maloney (D-NY)..........................202-225-7944
New York Delegate:
Joseph Crowley (D)..........................202-225-3965

Financial Institutions & Consumer Credit
Chair:
Spencer Bachus, III (R-AL)..........................202-225-4921
Ranking Minority Member:
Bernard Sanders (D-VT)..........................202-225-4115
New York Delegate:
Gary L Ackerman (D)..........................202-225-2601
New York Delegate:
Joseph Crowley (D)..........................202-225-3965
New York Delegate:
Vito Fossella (R)..........................202-225-3371
New York Delegate:
Sue W Kelly (R)..........................202-225-5441
New York Delegate:
Carolyn B Maloney (D)..........................202-225-7944
New York Delegate:
Carolyn McCarthy (D)..........................202-225-5516
New York Delegate:
Gregory W Meeks (D)..........................202-225-3461

Housing & Community Opportunity
Chair:
Robert W Ney (R-OH)..........................202-225-6265
Ranking Minority Member:
Maxine Waters (D-CA)..........................202-225-2201
New York Delegate:
Peter T King (R)..........................202-225-7896
New York Delegate:
Nydia M Velazquez (D)..........................202-225-2361

Oversight & Investigations
Chair:
Sue W Kelly (R-NY)..........................202-225-5441

Offices and agencies appear in alphabetical order.

Ranking Minority Member:
  Luis V Gutierrez (D-IL) 202-225-8203
New York Delegate:
  Carolyn B Maloney (D) 202-225-7944

Government Reform

Chair:
  Thomas M Davis, III (R-VA) 202-225-1492
Ranking Minority Member:
  Henry A Waxman (D-CA) 202-225-3976
New York Delegate:
  Brian M Higgins (D) 202-225-3306
New York Delegate:
  Carolyn B Maloney (D) 202-225-7944
New York Delegate:
  John M McHugh (R) 202-225-4611
New York Delegate:
  Major R Owens (D) 202-225-6231
New York Delegate:
  Edolphus Towns (D) 202-225-5936

Subcommittees

Criminal Justice, Drug Policy & Human Resources

Chair:
  Mark Edward Souder (R-IN) 202-225-4436
Ranking Minority Member:
  Elijah E Cummings (D-MD) 202-225-4741
New York Delegate:
  Carolyn B Maloney (D) 202-225-7944
New York Delegate:
  Major R Owens (D) 202-225-6231

Energy & Resources

Chair:
  Darrell Issa (R-CA) 202-225-3906
Ranking Minority Member:
  Diane E Watson (D-CA) 202-225-7084
New York Delegate:
  Major R Owens (D) 202-225-6231

Federal Workforce & Agency Organization

Chair:
  Jon Potter (R-NV) 202-225-3252
Ranking Minority Member:
  Danny Davis (D-IL) 202-225-5006
New York Delegate:
  Major R Owens (D) 202-225-6231

Federalism & the Census

Chair:
  Mike Turner (R-OH) 202-225-6465
Ranking Minority Mbr:
  William Lacy Clay, Jr (D-MO) 202-225-2406

Government Management Finance & Accountability

Chair:
  Todd R Platts (R-PA) 202-225-5836
Ranking Minority Member:
  Edolphus Towns (D-NY) 202-225-5936
New York Delegate:
  Major R Owens (D) 202-225-4611
New York Delegate:
  Carolyn B Maloney (D) 202-225-7944

National Security, Emerging Threats & International Relations

Chair:
  Christopher Shays (R-CT) 202-225-5541
Ranking Minority Member:
  Dennis J Kucinich (D-OH) 202-225-5871

New York Delegate:
  Brian M Higgins (D) 202-225-3306
New York Delegate:
  Carolyn B Maloney (D) 202-225-7944
New York Delegate:
  John M McHugh (R) 202-225-4611

Regulatory Affairs

Chair:
  Candice Miller (R-MI) 202-225-2106
Ranking Minority Member:
  Stephen Lynch (D-MA) 202-225-8273
New York Delegate:
  Nita M Lowey (D) 202-225-6506
Chair:
  Dan Lundgren (R-CA) 202-225-5716
New York Delegate:
  Nita M Lowey (D) 202-225-6506

House Administration

Chair:
  Robert W Ney (R-OH) 202-225-6265
Ranking Minority Member:
  John B Larson (D-CT) 202-225-2265
New York Delegate:
  Thomas M Reynolds (R) 202-225-5265

International Relations

Chair:
  Henry J Hyde (R-IL) 202-225-4561
Ranking Minority Member:
  Tom Lantos (D-CA) 202-225-3531
New York Delegate:
  Gary L Ackerman (D) 202-225-2601
New York Delegate:
  Joseph Crowley (D) 202-225-3965
New York Delegate:
  Eliot L Engel (D) 202-225-2464
New York Delegate:
  Amory Houghton (R) 202-225-3161
New York Delegate:
  Peter T King (R) 202-225-7896
New York Delegate:
  Gregory W Meeks (D) 202-225-3461

Subcommittees

Africa, Global Human Rights & International Operations

Chair:
  Christopher H Smith (R-NJ) 202-225-3765
Ranking Minority Member:
  Donald M Payne (D-NJ) 202-225-3436
New York Delegate:
  Gregory W Meeks (D) 202-225-3461

Asia & the Pacific

Chair:
  James A Leach (R-IA) 202-225-6576
Ranking Minority Member:
  Eni F H Faleomavaega (D-AS) 202-225-8577
New York Delegate:
  Gary L Ackerman (D) 202-225-2601

Europe

Chair:
  Elton Gallegly (R-CA) 202-225-5811
Ranking Minority Member:
  Robert Wexler (D-FL) 202-225-3001

Offices and agencies appear in alphabetical order.

New York Delegate:
Eliot L Engel (D) 202-225-2464
New York Delegate:
Peter T King (R) 202-225-7896

International Terrorism, Nonproliferation & Human Rights
Chair:
Edward R Royce (R-CA) 202-225-4111
Ranking Minority Member:
Brad Sherman (D-CA) 202-225-5911
New York Delegate:
Joseph Crowley (D) 202-225-3965
New York Delegate:
Peter T King (R) 202-225-7896

Middle East & Central Asia
Chair:
Ileana Ros-Lehtinen (R-FL) 202-225-3931
Ranking Minority Member:
Gary L Ackerman (D-NY) 202-225-2601
New York Delegate:
John M McHugh (R) 202-225-4611
New York Delegate:
Eliot L Engel (D) 202-225-2464
New York Delegate:
Joseph Crowley (D) 202-225-3965

Oversight & Investigations
Chair:
Dana Rohrabacher 202-225-2415

The Western Hemisphere
Chair:
Dan Burton (R-IN) 202-225-0016
Ranking Minority Member:
Robert Menendez (D-NJ) 202-225-7919
New York Delegate:
Gregory W Meeks (D) 202-225-3461

Judiciary
Chair:
F James Sensenbrenner, Jr (R-WI) 202-225-5101
Ranking Minority Member:
John Conyers, Jr (D-MI) 202-225-5126
New York Delegate:
Jerrold Nadler (D) 202-225-5635
New York Delegate:
Anthony D Weiner (D) 202-225-6616

Subcommittees

Commercial & Administrative Law
Chair:
Chris Cannon (R-UT) 202-225-7751
Ranking Minority Member:
Melvin L Watt (D-NC) 202-225-1510
New York Delegate:
Jerrold Nadler (D) 202-225-5635
New York Delegate:
Anthony D Weiner (D) 202-225-6616

Courts, the Internet & Intellectual Property
Chair:
Lamar S Smith (R-TX) 202-225-5741
Ranking Minority Member:
Howard L Berman (D-CA) 202-225-4695
New York Delegate:
Anthony D Weiner (D) 202-225-6616

Crime, Terrorism & Homeland Security
Chair:
Howard Coble (R-NC) 202-225-3926
Ranking Minority Member:
Robert C Scott (D-VA) 202-225-8351

Immigration, Border Security & Claims
Chair:
John N Hostettler (R-IN) 202-225-4346
Ranking Minority Member:
Sheila Jackson-Lee (D-TX) 202-225-3816

Task Force on Antitrust
Chair:
F James Sensenbrenner, Jr (R-WI) 202-225-5101
Ranking Minority Member:
John Conyers, Jr (D-MI) 202-225-5126

The Constitution
Chair:
Steve Chabot (R-OH) 202-225-2216
Ranking Minority Member:
Jerrold Nadler (D-NY) 202-225-5635

Resources
Chair:
Richard W Pombo (R-CA) 202-225-2761
Ranking Minority Member:
Nick J Rahall, II (D-WV) 202-225-3452

Subcommittees

Energy & Mineral Resources
Chair:
Jim Gibbons (R-NV) 202-225-6155
Ranking Minority Member:
Raul Grisalva (D-AZ) 202-225-2435

Fisheries Conservation, Wildlife & Oceans
Chair:
Wayne Gilchrest (R-MD) 202-225-5311
Ranking Minority Member:
Frank Pallone, Jr (D-NJ) 202-225-4671

Forests & Forest Health
Chair:
Greg Walden (R-OR) 202-225-6730
Ranking Minority Member:
Tom Udall (D-NM) 202-225-6190

National Parks, Recreation & Public Lands
Chair:
Devin Jones (R-CA) 202-225-2523
Ranking Minority Member:
Donna M Christensen (D-VI) 202-225-1790

Native American & Insular Affairs
Chair:
Richard W Pombo (R-CA) 202-225-1947
Ranking Minority Member:
Nick J Rahall (D-WY) 202-225-3452

Water & Power
Chair:
George Radanovich (R-CA) 202-225-4540
Ranking Minority Member:
Grace Napolitano (D-CA) 202-225-5256

Offices and agencies appear in alphabetical order.

Rules

Chair:
    David Dreier (R-CA) 202-225-2305
Ranking Minority Member:
    Martin Frost (D-TX) 202-225-3605
New York Delegate:
    Thomas M Reynolds (R) 202-225-5265
New York Delegate:
    Louise McIntosh Slaughter (D) 202-225-3615

Subcommittees

Legislative & Budget Process
Chair:
    Lincoln Diaz-Balart (R-FL) 202-225-4211
Ranking Minority Member:
    Alcee Hastings (D-FL) 202-225-1313

Rules & Organization of the House
Chair:
    Doc Hastings (R-WA) 202-225-5816
Ranking Minority Member:
    James P McGovern (D-MA) 202-225-6101

Science

Chair:
    Sherwood L Boehlert (R-NY) 202-225-3665
Ranking Minority Member:
    Bart Gordon (D-TN) 202-225-4231

Subcommittees

Energy
Chair:
    Judy Biggert (R-IL) 202-225-3515
Ranking Minority Member:
    Mike Honda (D-CA) 202-225-2631

Environment, Technology & Standards
Chair:
    Vernon J Ehlers (R-MI) 202-225-3831
Ranking Minority Member:
    David Wu (D-OR) 202-225-0855

Research
Chair:
    Bob Inglis (R-SC) 202-225-6030
Ranking Minority Member:
    Darlene Hooley (D-OR) 202-225-5711

Space & Aeronautics
Chair:
    Ken Calvert (R-CA) 202-225-1986
Ranking Minority Member:
    Mark Udall (D-CO) 202-225-2161

Small Business

Chair:
    Donald A Manzullo (R-IL) 202-225-5676
Ranking Minority Member:
    Nydia M Velazquez (D-NY) 202-225-2361
New York Delegate:
    Sue W Kelly (R) 202-225-5441

Subcommittees

Regulatory Reform & Oversight
Chair:
    Todd Akin (R-MO) 202-225-2561

Ranking Minority Member:
    Madeleine Bordallo (D-GU) 202-225-1188
New York Delegate:
    Sue W Kelly (R) 202-225-5441

Rural Enterprises, Agriculture & Technology
Chair:
    Sam Graves (R-MO) 202-225-7041
Ranking Minority Member:
    John Barrow (D-GA) 202-225-2823

Tax, Finance & Exports
Chair:
    Jeb Bradley (R-NH) 202-225-5456
Ranking Minority Member:
    Juanita Millendar-McDonald (D-CA) 202-225-7924

Workforce, Empowerment & Government Programs
Chair:
    Marilyn Musgrave (R-CO) 202-225-4676
Ranking Minority Member:
    Dan Lipinski (D-IL) 202-225-5701

Standards of Official Conduct

Chair:
    Doc Hastings (R-WA) 202-225-5816
Ranking Minority Member:
    Alan B Mollohan (D-WV) 202-225-4172

Transportation & Infrastructure

Chair:
    Don Young (R-AK) 202-225-5765
Ranking Minority Member:
    James L Oberstar (D-MN) 202-225-6211
New York Delegate:
    Timothy H Bishop (D) 202-225-3826
New York Delegate:
    Sherwood L Boehlert (R) 202-225-3665
New York Delegate:
    Brian M Higgins (D) 202-225-3306
New York Delegate:
    Sue W Kelly (R) 202-225-5441
New York Delegate:
    John R (Randy) Kuhl (R) 202-225-3161
New York Delegate:
    Jerrold Nadler (D) 202-225-5635
New York Delegate:
    Anthony D Weiner (D) 202-225-6616

Subcommittees

Aviation
Chair:
    John L Mica (R-FL) 202-225-4035
Ranking Minority Member:
    Jerry F Costello (D-IL) 202-225-5661
New York Delegate:
    Sue W Kelly (R) 202-225-5441
New York Delegate:
    John R (Randy) Kuhl (R) 202-225-3161
New York Delegate:
    Anthony D Weiner (D) 202-225-6616

Coast Guard & Maritime Transportation
Chair:
    Frank A LoBiondo (R-NJ) 202-225-6572
Ranking Minority Member:
    Bob Filner (D-CA) 202-225-8045

Offices and agencies appear in alphabetical order.

Economic Development, Public Buildings & Emergency Management
Chair:
    Bill Shuster (R-PA) 202-225-2431
Ranking Minority Member:
    Eleanor Holmes Norton (D-DC) 202-225-8050

Highways, Transit & Pipelines
Chair:
    Thomas E Petri (R-WI) 202-225-2476
Ranking Minority Member:
    Peter A DeFazio (D-OR) 202-225-6416
New York Delegate:
    Timothy H Bishop (D) 202-225-3826
New York Delegate:
    Sue W Kelly (R). 202-225-5441
New York Delegate:
    Jerrold Nadler (D) 202-225-5635
New York Delegate:
    Anthony D Weiner (D). 202-225-6616

Railroads
Chair:
    Steven C La Tourette (R-OH) 202-225-5731
Ranking Minority Member:
    Corrine Brown (D-FL). 202-225-0123
New York Delegate:
    Sherwood L Boehlert (R). 202-225-3665
New York Delegate:
    Jerrold Nadler (D) 202-225-5635

Water Resources & Environment
Chair:
    John J Duncan, Jr (R-TN) 202-225-5435
Ranking Minority Member:
    Eddie Bernice Johnson (D-TX) 202-225-8885
New York Delegate:
    Timothy H Bishop (D) 202-225-3826
New York Delegate:
    Sherwood L Boehlert (R) 202-225-3665
New York Delegate:
    Brian M Higgins (D) 202-225-3306
New York Delegate:
    Sue W Kelly (R). 202-225-5441

Veterans' Affairs

Chair:
    Stephen E Buyer (R-IN). 202-225-5037
Ranking Minority Member:
    Lane Evans (D-IL) 202-225-5905

Subcommittees

Disability Assistance
Chair:
    Jeff Miller (R-FL) 202-225-4136
Ranking Minority Member:
    Shelley Berkley (D-NV) 202-225-5965

Economic Opportunity
Chair:
    John Boozman (R-AR). 202-225-4301
Ranking Minority Member:
    Stephanie Herseth (D-SD) 202-225-2801

Health
Chair:
    Henry Brown (R-SC) 202-225-3176
Ranking Minority Member:
    Michael Michaud (D-ME) 202-225-6306

Oversight & Investigations
Chair:
    Mike Billirakis (R-FL). 202-225-5755
Ranking Minority Member:
    Ted Strickland (D-OH) 202-225-5705

Ways & Means

Chair:
    William M Thomas (R-CA). 202-225-2915
Ranking Minority Member:
    Charles B Rangel (D-NY) 202-225-4365
New York Delegate:
    Thomas M Reynolds (R) 202-225-5265
New York Delegate:
    Michael R McNulty (D). 202-225-5076

Subcommittees

Health
Chair:
    Nancy L Johnson (R-CT). 202-225-4476
Ranking Minority Member:
    Fortney Pete Stark (D-CA). 202-225-5065

Human Resources
Chair:
    Wally Herger (R-CA). 202-225-3076
Ranking Minority Member:
    Jim McDermott (D-WA) 202-225-3106

Oversight
Chair:
    Jim Ramstad (R-MN). 202-225-2871
Ranking Minority Member:
    John Lewis (D-GA) 202-225-3801
New York Delegate:
    Michael R McNulty (D). 202-225-5076
New York Delegate:
    Charles B Rangel (D). 202-225-4365
New York Delegate:
    Thomas M Reynolds (R) 202-225-5265

Select Revenue Measures
Chair:
    Dave Camp (R-MI) 202-225-3561
Ranking Minority Member:
    Michael R McNulty (D-NY) 202-225-5076
Ranking Minority Member:
    Thomas M Reynolds (R) 202-225-5265

Social Security
Chair:
    Jim McCrery (R-LA) 202-225-2777
Ranking Minority Member:
    Sander M Levin (D-MI). 202-225-4961

Trade
Chair:
    E Clay Shaw, Jr (R-FL) 202-225-3026
Ranking Minority Member:
    Benjamin L Cardin (D-MD). 202-225-4016

OTHER, SELECT & SPECIAL COMMITTEES

Homeland Security, Select Committee on
Chair:
    Christopher Cox (R-CA) 202-225-5611

Offices and agencies appear in alphabetical order.

Ranking Minority Member:
    Bennie G Thompson (D-MS) 202-225-5876
New York Delegate:
    Peter T King (R) 202-225-7896

Subcommittees

Economic Security, Infrastructure Protection and Cybersecurity
Ranking Minority Member:
    Loretta Sanchez (D-CA) 202-225-2965

Emergency Preparedness, Science & Technology
Chair:
    Peter T King (R-NY) 202-225-7896
Ranking Minority Member:
    Bill Pascrell, Jr (D-NJ) 202-225-5751
New York Delegate:
    Nita M Lowey (D) 202-225-6506

Intelligence Information Sharing & Terrorism Risk Assessment
Chair:
    Robert R Simmons (R-CT) 202-225-2076
Ranking Minority Member:
    Zoe Lofgren (D-CA) 202-225-3072

Management Integration & Oversight
Chair:
    Mike Rogers (R-AL) 202-225-3261
Ranking Minority Member:
    Kendrick B Meek (D-FL) 202-225-4506

Prevention of Nuclear & Biological Attack
Chair:
    John Linder (R-GA) 202-225-4272
Ranking Minority Member:
    James R Langevin (D-RI) 202-225-2735

Intelligence, House Permanent Select Committee on
Chair:
    Peter Hoekstra (R-MI) 202-225-4401
Ranking Minority Member:
    Jane Harman (D-CA) 202-225-8820

Subcommittees

Human Intelligence, Analysis & Counterintelligence
Chair:
    Randy Cunningham (R-CA) 202-225-5452
Ranking Minority Member:
    Leonard L Boswell (D-IA) 202-225-3806
Ranking Minority Member:
    Leonard L Boswell (D-IA) 202-225-3806

Intelligence Policy & National Security
Chair:
    Jo Ann S Davis (R-VA) 202-225-4261
Ranking Minority Member:
    Rush Holt (D-NJ) 202-225-5801

Oversight
Chair:
    William M Thornberry (R-TX) 202-225-3706
Ranking Minority Member:
    Robert E Cramer (D-AL) 202-225-4801

Technical & Tactical Intelligence
Chair:
    Heather A Wilson (R-NM) 202-225-6316
Ranking Minority Member:
    Anna G Eshoo (D-CA) 202-225-8104
Ranking Minority Member:
    Robert E (Bud) Cramer (D-AL) 202-225-4801

Joint Senate and House Committees

Economic Committee, Joint
Vice Chair:
    Sen Robert Bennett (R-UT) 202-224-5444
Chair:
    Rep Jim Saxton (R-NJ) 202-225-4765
Ranking Minority Member:
    Jack Reed (R-RI) 202-224-4642
New York Delegate:
    Maurice D Hinchey (D) 202-225-6335
New York Delegate:
    Carolyn Maloney 202-225-7944

Library, Joint Committee on the
Chair:
    Sen Ted Stevens (R-AK) 202-224-3004
Vice Chair:
    Sen Vernon J Ehlers (R-MI) 202-224-3831
New York Delegate:
    Charles Schumer (D) 202-224-6542

Printing, Joint Committee on
Chair:
    Vacant 202-225-6265
Vice Chair:
    Sen John T Doolittle (R-CA) 202-224-2511
Vice Chair:
    Thomas M Reynolds (R) 202-224-5265

Taxation, Joint Committee on
Vice Chair:
    Rep William M Thomas (R-CA) 202-225-2915
Vice Chair:
    Sen Charles E Grassley (D-IA) 202-224-3744
New York Delegate:
    Rep Charles B Rangel (D) 202-225-4365

Offices and agencies appear in alphabetical order.

State & Local
Government
Public Information

COUNTY GOVERNMENT

This section identifies senior government officials in all New York counties.

Albany County

112 State St, Rm 200
Albany, NY 12207
518-447-7040 Fax: 518-447-5589
e-mail: countyexec@albanycounty.com
Web site: www.albanycounty.com

Chairman, County Legislature (D):
  Charles E Houghtaling, Jr. 518-447-7117
Majority Leader (D):
  Frank J Commisso 518-447-7117
Minority Leader (R):
  Christine M Benedict 518-447-7164
Counsel to the Majority:
  William J Conboy, II 518-447-7117
Clerk, Legislature:
  Paul T Devane 518-447-7168
County Executive:
  Michael G Breslin 518-447-7040/fax: 518-447-5589
County Clerk:
  Thomas G Clingan. 518-487-5100/fax: 518-487-5099
  e-mail: countyclerk@albanycounty.com
Deputy Clerk of the County Legislature:
  Gloria Dilella 518-447-7168
District Attorney:
  P David Soares 518-487-5460/fax: 518-487-5093
Sheriff:
  James L Campbell 518-487-5400/fax: 518-487-5037
Comptroller:
  Michael F Conners, II 518-447-7130/fax: 518-433-1554
Commissioner of Management & Budget:
  David R Polan 518-447-5525/fax: 518-447-5589

Allegany County

County Office Bldg, 7 Court St
Belmont, NY 14813
585-268-9222 Fax: 585-268-9446
Web site: www.alleganyco.com

Chairman, Board of Legislators (R):
  James G Palmer 585-268-9222
Majority Leader (R):
  Curtis Crandall 585-268-9222
Clerk, Board of Legislators:
  Brenda A Rigby. 585-268-9222/fax: 585-268-9446
County Administrator:
  John E Margeson 585-268-9217
County Clerk:
  Robert L Christman 585-268-9270
District Attorney:
  Terrance M Parker 585-268-9225
Public Defender:
  Beth Farwell 585-593-7111
Sheriff:
  Randal J Belmont 585-268-9200/fax: 585-268-9475
Treasurer:
  Terri L Ross 585-268-9289

County Attorney:
  Daniel J Guiney 585-268-9410
Director, Development/IDA:
  John E Foels 585-268-7472/fax: 585-268-7473
Director, Emergency Services:
  John C Tucker. 585-268-7658
Director, Information Technology:
  Deborah M Button. 585-268-9288/fax: 585-268-9473
Superintendent, Public Works:
  David Roeske 585-268-9230
Social Services Commissioner:
  Patricia A Schmelzer 585-268-9622
County Historian:
  Craig R Braack 585-268-9293

Bronx County (NYC Borough of the Bronx)

851 Grand Concourse
Bronx, NY 10451
718-590-3500 Fax: 718-590-3537
Web site: www.bronxcountyclerksoffice.com

Borough President:
  Adolfo Carrion, Jr 718-590-3557/fax: 718-590-3537
Deputy Borough President:
  Earl D Brown 718-590-3565
County Clerk:
  Hector L Diaz 718-590-3648/fax: 718-590-8122
  e-mail: hdiaz@courts.state.ny.us
District Attorney:
  Robert T Johnson 718-590-2000
Public Administrator:
  Esther Rodriguez 718-293-7660

Broome County

Edwin L Crawford County Office Bldg
PO Box 1766
Binghamton, NY 13902-1766
607-778-2131 Fax: 607-778-8869
Web site: www.gobroomecounty.com

Chairman, County Legislature (R):
  Daniel A Schofield 607-778-2131
Ranking Majority Member (R):
  Arthur Schafer 607-778-2131
Ranking Minority Member (D):
  Brian Brunza. 607-778-2131
Clerk, Legislature:
  Louis Augostini 607-778-2131
  e-mail: laugostini@co.broome.ny.us
County Executive:
  Barbara J Fiala 607-778-2109/fax: 607-778-2044
  e-mail: bfiala@co.broome.ny.us
County Clerk:
  Richard Blythe. 607-778-2451/fax: 607-778-2243

Offices and agencies appear in alphabetical order.

County Attorney:
Joseph Sluzar 607-778-2117/fax: 607-778-6122
e-mail: bclaw@co.broome.ny.us
District Attorney:
Gerald F Mollen 607-778-2423/fax: 607-778-8870
Public Defender:
Jay L Wilber 607-778-2403/fax: 607-778-2432
Sheriff (R):
David E Harder 607-778-2492/fax: 607-778-2100
Comptroller:
Alex McLaughlin. 607-778-2178/fax: 607-778-2236
Finance Cmnsr:
Jerome Z Kniebel 607-778-2161/fax: 607-778-2176
Commissioner, Public Works:
Henry Weissmann 607-778-2909/fax: 607-778-6051

Cattaraugus County
County Center
303 Court St
Little Valley, NY 14755
716-938-9111 Fax: 716-938-9306
Web site: www.cattco.org

Chairman, County Legislature (R):
Gerard J Fitzpatrick. 716-938-9111 x2385
Vice Chairperson (R):
Crystal Abers. 716-938-9111 x2396
Minority Leader (D):
Vergilio L Giardini Jr 716-938-9111 x2397
Jon K Baker
County Administrator & Clerk, Legislature:
John R Searles 716-938-9111
e-mail: jrsearles@cattco.org
County Clerk:
James Griffith 716-938-9111 x2293
County Attorney:
Dennis Tobolski 716-938-9111 x2391/fax: 716-938-9438
District Attorney:
Edward M Sharkey 716-938-9111 x2222
Acting Sheriff:
Dennis B John 716-938-9191/fax: 716-938-6420
Treasurer:
Joseph Keller 716-938-9111 x2286/fax: 716-938-6897
Public Defender:
Mark S Williams 716-373-6004/fax: 716-373-3462
e-mail: pubdef@ccpd.cattco.org

Cayuga County
160 Genesee St
Auburn, NY 13021
315-253-1308 Fax: 315-253-1586
Web site: www.co.cayuga.ny.us

Chairman, County Legislature (R):
Herbert D Marshall, Jr. 315-253-1273/fax: 315-776-4771
e-mail: district3@cayugacounty.us
Majority Leader (R):
Ann Petruf 315-253-1273
Minority Leader (D):
William Catto 315-253-1273
Clerk, Legislature:
Lee Brew 315-253-1308
e-mail: lclerk@co.cayuga.ny.us

County Clerk:
Susan M Dwyer 315-253-1271/fax: 315-253-1006
e-mail: sdwyer@co.cayuga.ny.us
County Attorney:
Fredrick Westphal 315-253-1274/fax: 315-253-1098
e-mail: coatty@cayugacounty.us
District Attorney:
James B Varagson 315-253-1391/fax: 315-253-1521
e-mail: cayugada@cayugacounty.us
Director, Planning & Development:
David C Miller 315-253-1276
e-mail: planning@cayugacounty.us
Sheriff:
C Robert Outhouse, Jr 315-253-1222/fax: 315-253-3022
e-mail: sheriff@co.broome.ny.us
Treasurer:
David A Farrell 315-253-1211/fax: 315-253-1369
e-mail: treasurer@cayugacounty.us
County Historian:
Sheila Tucker 315-253-1300
e-mail: history@co.cayuga.ny.us

Chautauqua County
3 N Erie St
Mayville, NY 14757-1007
716-753-4000 Fax: 716-753-4277
Web site: www.co.chautauqua.ny.us

Chairman, County Legislature (D):
Keith D Ahlstrom 716-753-4215
e-mail: kda@netsync.net
Majority Caucus Leader (D):
Robert Anderson. 716-753-4215
e-mail: anderr@netsync.net
Minority Caucus Leader (R):
James Caflisch 716-753-4215
e-mail: jkjmcreek@madbbs.com
Clerk, Legislature:
Chuck Cornell. 716-753-4215
e-mail: cornellc@chautauqua.ny.us
County Executive:
Mark Thomas 716-753-4211
e-mail: thomasm@co.chautauqua.ny.us
County Clerk:
Sandra K Sopak 716-753-4331/fax: 716-753-4293
e-mail: travis@co.chautauqua.ny.us
County Attorney:
Fredrick Larson 716-753-4247
District Attorney:
James P Subjack 716-753-4241
e-mail: subjackj@co.chautauqua.ny.us
Public Defender:
William Coughlin 716-753-4376
Sheriff:
Joseph A Gerace 716-753-4231
Comptroller:
Dennis Goggin 716-753-4433
e-mail: goggind@co.chautauqua.ny.us
Finance Director:
Jean Blackmore 716-753-4223

Chemung County
John H Hazlett Bldg, 203 Lake St
PO Box 588
Elmira, NY 14902

Offices and agencies appear in alphabetical order.

607-737-2912 Fax: 607-737-0351
e-mail: info@chemungcounty.com
Web site: www.chemungcounty.com

Chairman, County Legislature (R):
   Cornelius J Milliken 607-737-2066/fax: 607-737-2851
Majority Leader (R):
   Donna L Draxler. 607-737-2066
Minority Leader (D):
   Theodore A Bennett 607-737-2066
Clerk, Legislature:
   Linda D Palmer. 607-737-2066
County Executive:
   Thomas J Santulli 607-737-2912
County Clerk:
   Catherine K Hughes 607-737-2920
   e-mail: chughes@co.chemung.ny.us
County Attorney:
   Weeden Wetmore 607-737-2982
District Attorney:
   John R Trice 607-737-2944/fax: 607-737-2965
Public Defender:
   Paul Corradini. 607-737-2969
Sheriff:
   John A Brinthaupt. 607-737-2932
   e-mail: jbrinthaupt@co.chemung.ny.us
Treasurer:
   Joseph E Sartori, III. 607-737-2927/fax: 607-737-2846
   e-mail: jsartori@co.chemung.ny.us

Chenango County
County Office Bldg
5 Court St
Norwich, NY 13815
607-337-1430 Fax: 607-337-1435
Web site: www.co.chenango.ny.us

Chairman, Board of Supervisors (R):
   Richard B Decker. 607-337-1401
Clerk, Board of Supervisors:
   Thomas M Whittaker 607-337-1430
County Clerk:
   Mary C Weidman 607-337-1450
County Attorney:
   Richard W Breslin 607-337-1405
District Attorney:
   Joseph A McBride 607-337-1745
Public Defender:
   Alan E Gordon 607-843-8955
Sheriff:
   Thomas Loughren. 607-334-2000
Treasurer:
   William E Evans. 607-337-1414
County Historian:
   Dale Storms 607-337-1845

Clinton County
County Government Ctr
137 Margaret St, Ste 208
Plattsburgh, NY 12901
518-565-4600 Fax: 518-565-4616
e-mail: legislature@co.clinton.ny.us
Web site: www.clintoncountygov.com

Chairman (R):
   James R Langley, Jr 518-643-9052
   e-mail: langleyins@charter.net
Majority Leader (R):
   Samuel J Trombley 518-594-7109/fax: 518-594-7742
Minority Leader (D):
   Keith M Defayette 518-565-4600
   e-mail: keith@primelink1.net
Clerk, Board of Legislators & County Administrator:
   Michael E Zurlo 518-565-4600
County Clerk:
   John H Zurlo 518-565-4700/fax: 518-565-4718
County Attorney:
   Dennis D Curtin. 518-561-4400/fax: 518-561-4848
District Attorney:
   Richard E Cantwell 518-565-4770/fax: 518-565-4777
   e-mail: da@co.clinton.ny.us
Sheriff:
   David N Favro 518-565-4300/fax: 518-565-4333
   e-mail: sheriff@co.clinton.ny.us
Treasurer:
   Janet L Duprey 518-565-4730/fax: 518-565-4516
   e-mail: treasurer@co.clinton.ny.us
County Historian:
   Addie L Shields 518-565-4749/fax: 518-565-4616
   e-mail: historian@co.clinton.ny.us

Columbia County
401 State St
Hudson, NY 12534
518-828-1527 Fax: 518-822-0684
e-mail: dicosmo@govt.co.columbia.ny.us
Web site: www.columbiacountyny.com

Chairman, Board of Supervisors (R):
   Gerald Simons 518-828-1527
Majority Leader (R):
   Elizabeth Young. 518-828-1527
Minority Leader (D):
   Douglas McGivney. 518-758-6385
Clerk, Board of Supervisors:
   Gladys Goesch 518-828-1527
County Clerk:
   Holly C Tanner 518-828-3339/fax: 518-828-5299
   e-mail: htanner@govt.co.columbia.ny.us
County Attorney:
   Daniel Tuczinski 518-828-3303/fax: 518-828-9535
District Attorney:
   Beth G Cozzolino 518-828-3414
Public Defender:
   Charles E Inman 518-828-3410/fax: 518-828-4076
Director, Planning:
   Roland Vosburgh. 518-828-3375/fax: 518-828-2825
   e-mail: vosburgh@govt.co.columbia.ny.us
Sheriff:
   Walter Shook . . . . 518-828-0601 or 518-828-3344
   fax: 518-828-9088
Treasurer:
   Kenneth H Wilber 518-828-0513/fax: 518-828-1110
County Historian:
   Mary Howell 518-828-3442/fax: 518-828-2969
   e-mail: mhowell@govt.co.columbia.ny.us

Offices and agencies appear in alphabetical order.

Cortland County
County Office Bldg, 60 Central Ave
Cortland, NY 13045-2746
607-753-5048 Fax: 607-756-3492
Web site: www.cortland-co.org

Chairman, County Legislature (R):
  Scott E Steve. 607-753-5049
  e-mail: ssteve@cortland-co.org
Majority Leader (R):
  Paul DiGiovanni 607-753-5049
  e-mail: pdigiovanni@cortland-co.org
Minority Leader (D):
  Marilyn Brown 607-753-5049
  e-mail: mbrown@cortland-co.org
County Administrator:
  Scott Schrader. 607-753-5048
  e-mail: sschrader@cortland-co.org
Clerk, Legislature:
  Carletta Edwards 607-753-5095/fax: 607-756-3492
  e-mail: cedwards@cortland-co.org
County Clerk:
  Elizabeth Larkin 607-753-5021/fax: 607-753-5378
  e-mail: elarkin@cortland-co.org
County Attorney:
  John Bardsley 607-753-5095
  e-mail: jbardsley@cortland-co.org
District Attorney:
  David S Hartnett 607-753-5008/fax: 607-756-3477
  e-mail: districtattorney@cortland-co.org
Public Defender:
  Keith Dayton 607-753-5046/fax: 607-753-0781
  e-mail: kdayton@cortland-co.org
Sheriff:
  Lee A Price 607-753-5006
  e-mail: lprice@cortland-co.org
Treasurer:
  Donald F Ferris 607-753-5070/fax: 607-758-5512
  e-mail: dferris@cortland-co.org
County Historian:
  Cathy Barber. 607-753-5360
  e-mail: cbarber@cortland-co.org

Delaware County
Senator Charles D Cook Co Ofc Bldg
111 Main St
Delhi, NY 13753
607-746-2603 Fax: 607-746-7012
Web site: www.co.delaware.ny.us

Chairman, Board of Supervisors (R):
  James E Eisel, Sr 607-746-6691
Vice Chairman, Board of Supervisors (R):
  Tina Mole 607-746-2603
Clerk, Board of Supervisors:
  Christa M Schafer. 607-746-2603
  e-mail: cob@co.delaware.ny.us
County Clerk:
  Gary L Cady 607-746-2123/fax: 607-746-6924
  e-mail: clerk@co.delaware.ny.us
County Attorney:
  Richard B Spinney 607-652-3443
District Attorney:
  Richard D Northrup, Jr 607-746-3557/fax: 607-746-2297

Sheriff:
  Thomas E Mills 607-746-2336/fax: 607-746-2632
  e-mail: shrf@co.delaware.ny.us
Treasurer:
  Beverly J Shields. 607-746-2121/fax: 607-746-7433
  e-mail: treas@co.delaware.ny.us
County Historian:
  Patrick H Grimes 845-676-3790
  e-mail: hist@co.delaware.ny.us

Dutchess County
County Office Bldg
22 Market St, 6th Fl
Poughkeepsie, NY 12601
845-486-2100 Fax: 845-486-2113
e-mail: countylegislature@co.dutchess.ny.us
Web site: www.dutchessny.gov

Chairman, County Legislature (R):
  Bradford Kendall 845-486-2103
Majority Leader (R):
  Noreen H Reilly. 845-229-0042/fax: 845-229-7086
  e-mail: repcon35@aol.com
Minority Leader (D):
  Roger Higgins 845-298-5110/fax: 845-486-2113
  e-mail: rogerhig@optonline.com
County Executive:
  William R Steinhaus 845-486-2000/fax: 845-486-2021
  e-mail: countyexec@co.dutchess.ny.us
Clerk, Legislature:
  Patricia J Hohmann. 845-486-2100
County Clerk:
  Colette Lafuente 845-486-2120/fax: 845-486-2138
  e-mail: clafuente@co.dutchess.ny.us
County Attorney:
  Ian MacDonald 845-486-2110/fax: 845-486-2002
  e-mail: countyattorney@co.dutchess.ny.us
District Attorney:
  William V Grady. 845-486-2300/fax: 845-486-2324
Public Defender:
  David Goodman . . . . 845-486-2280 or 800-660-8818
  fax: 845-486-2266
  e-mail: publicdefender@co.dutchess.ny.us
Sheriff:
  Adrian H Anderson. 845-486-3800
  e-mail: sheriff@co.dutchess.ny.us
Comptroller:
  Richard Noel 845-486-2050/fax: 845-486-2055
  e-mail: comptroller@co.dutchess.ny.us
Finance Commissioner:
  Rita A Brannen 845-486-2025/fax: 845-486-2198
  e-mail: rptaxfinance@co.dutchess.ny.us
Records Management/History:
  Donald Miller 845-486-3677

Erie County
95 Franklin Street
Buffalo, NY 14202-3903
716-858-6000 Fax: 716-858-8072
Web site: www.erie.gov

Chairman, County Legislature (D):
  George A Holt, Jr 716-842-0490/fax: 716-854-5722
  e-mail: holt@erie.gov

Offices and agencies appear in alphabetical order.

Majority Leader, County Legislature (D):
   Lynn M Marinelli 716-832-0493/fax: 716-832-0494
   e-mail: lynnm@buffnet.net
Minority Leader, County Legislature (R):
   Michael H Ranzenhofer. 716-631-8695/fax: 716-634-4321
   e-mail: ranzenhofer@erie.gov
Clerk, Legislature:
   Kevin M Kelly. 716-858-7045/fax: 716-858-8895
County Executive (R):
   Joel A Giambra. 716-858-8500
County Clerk (D):
   David J Swarts. 716-858-8865/fax: 716-858-6550
   e-mail: swartsd@erie.gov
County Attorney:
   Frederick A Wolf 716-858-2200
District Attorney (D):
   Frank J Clark 716-858-2424/fax: 716-858-7425
Sheriff (R):
   Patrick M Gallivan 716-858-7608/fax: 716-662-5554
Comptroller (R):
   Nancy A Naples. 716-858-8400/fax: 716-858-8507

Essex County
County Government Ctr
7551 Court St
PO Box 217
Elizabethtown, NY 12932
518-873-3350 Fax: 518-873-3356
Web site: www.co.essex.ny.us

Chairman, Board of Supervisors (R):
   George H Canon. 518-873-3353
   e-mail: adksupv@aol.com
Vice Chairman, Board of Supervisors (R):
   Noel H Merrihew III. 518-873-3353
Clerk, Board of Supervisors:
   Deborah L Palmer 518-873-3353/fax: 518-873-3356
   e-mail: dpalmer@co.essex.ny.us
County Manager:
   Vacant 518-873-3333
County Clerk:
   Joseph A Provoncha. 518-873-3601
   e-mail: jprovon@co.essex.ny.us
County Attorney:
   Richard Meyer 518-873-3381
District Attorney (R):
   Ronald J Briggs 518-873-3335
   e-mail: dabriggs1@aol.com
Sheriff (R):
   Henry H Hommes. . . . . 518-873-3346 or 518-873-6321
   e-mail: hhommes@ co.essex.ny.us
Treasurer (R):
   Michael G Diskin 518-873-3317/fax: 518-873-3310
   e-mail: mdiskin@co.essex.ny.us

Franklin County
Courthouse
355 W Main St
Malone, NY 12953
518-481-1640 Fax: 518-481-1693
Web site: www.franklincony.org

Chairman, County Legislature (D):
   Earl J Lavoie. 518-481-1640

Vice Chairman, County Legislature (D):
   Guy Smith. 518-481-1640
Clerk, Legislature:
   Gloria Valone 518-481-1640/fax: 518-481-1639
County Manager:
   James N Feeley 518-481-1693/fax: 518-483-0141
   e-mail: jfeeley@co.franklin.ny.us
County Clerk:
   Wanda D Murtagh 518-481-1684
   e-mail: murtaghw@nyslgti.gen.ny.us
County Attorney:
   Jonathan J Miller 518-483-8400
District Attorney:
   Derek P Champagne 518-481-1544/fax: 518-481-1545
Chief Public Defender-North:
   Alexander Lesyk 518-481-1624/fax: 518-483-4690
Public Defender-South:
   Virginia Morrow. 518-891-7003
Public Defender-Family Court:
   Steve Alteri. 518-481-1624
Sheriff:
   Jack Pelkey 518-483-3304/fax: 518-483-3205
Treasurer:
   Byron A Varin 518-481-1515

Fulton County
223 W Main St
Johnstown, NY 12095
518-736-5540 Fax: 518-762-0224
e-mail: fultbos@superior.net
Web site: www.fulton.ny.us

Chairman, Board of Supervisors (R):
   Pasquale O'Lucci 518-736-5540
Administrative Officer/Clerk of Board:
   Jon R Stead. 518-736-5540
County Clerk:
   William E Eschler 518-736-5555/fax: 518-762-3839
County Attorney:
   Arthur Carl Spring. 518-736-5083/fax: 518-762-4504
District Attorney:
   Louise Kauffman-Sira 518-736-5511/fax: 518-762-2042
Public Defender:
   J Gerard McAuliffe, Jr. 518-736-5820/fax: 518-762-0122
Sheriff:
   Thomas Lorey 518-736-2100/fax: 518-736-2126
Treasurer:
   Bruce Ellsworth. 518-736-5580/fax: 518-762-0224
County Historian:
   William Loveday Jr 518-736-5667
   e-mail: lov270@superior.net

Genesee County
Old Courthouse, 7 Main Street
Batavia, NY 14020
585-344-2550 x2202 Fax: 585-344-8582
e-mail: legis@co.genesee.ny.us
Web site: www.co.genesee.ny.us

Chairman, County Legislature (R):
   Mary Pat Hancock 585-343-1011
Vice Chairman, County Legislature (R):
   Richard Rudolph. 585-542-2169
Minority Leader (D):
   Michael Welsh. 585-344-2550 x2202

Offices and agencies appear in alphabetical order.

County Manager:
Jay Gsell 585-344-2550 x2204/fax: 585-344-8582
e-mail: comanager@co.genesee.ny.us
Clerk, Legislature:
Carolyn Pratt 585-344-2550 x2202
County Clerk:
Don Read 585-344-2550 x2242
e-mail: coclerk@co.genesee.ny.us
County Attorney:
John L Rizzo 585-344-2550 x2205
District Attorney:
Larry Friedman 585-344-2550 x2250/fax: 585-344-8544
Public Defender:
Gary Horton 585-344-2550 x2280
e-mail: publicdefender@co.genesee.ny.us
Sheriff:
Gary Maha 585-345-3000 x239/fax: 585-343-9129
e-mail: sheriff@co.genesee.ny.us
Treasurer:
Scott German 585-344-2550 x2210
e-mail: treas@co.genesee.ny.us

Greene County
411 Main St, 4th Fl
PO Box 467
Catskill, NY 12414
518-719-3270 Fax: 518-719-3793
e-mail: government@discovergreene.com
Web site: www.discovergreene.com

Chairman, County Legislature (R):
Frank Stabile, Jr 518-943-3080
Majority Leader (R):
Dorothy Prest 518-943-3080
Minority Leader (D):
James VanSlyke 518-943-3080
Acting Clerk, Legislature:
Tammy Barbato 518-943-3080
County Administrator:
Douglas J Brewer 518-943-3080
County Clerk:
Mary Ann Kordich 518-943-2050
County Attorney:
Carol Stevens 518-719-3540
District Attorney:
Terry J Wilhelm 518-943-3450
Public Defender:
Dominic Cornelius 518-943-3277
Sheriff:
Richard H Hussey 518-943-3300
Treasurer:
Willis Vermilyea 518-943-4152

Hamilton County
County Courthouse, Rte 8
PO Box 205
Lake Pleasant, NY 12108
518-548-6651 Fax: 518-548-7608
e-mail: hamcosup@klink.net

Chairman, Board of Supervisors (R):
William G Farber . . . . 518-548-6385 or 518-548-6651
Vice Chairman, Board of Supervisors (R):
Brian Towers . . . . 518-548-6651 or 518-942-7912

Clerk, Board of Supervisors:
Suzanne A Blanchard 518-548-6651
County Clerk:
Jane Zarecki 518-548-7111
County Attorney:
Charles Getty Jr 315-336-3900
District Attorney:
James T Curry 518-648-5113
Sheriff:
Douglas A Parker 518-548-3113
Treasurer:
Beth A Hunt 518-548-7911

Herkimer County
109 Mary St, Ste 1310
Herkimer, NY 13350
315-867-1108 or 315-867-1112 Fax: 315-867-1109
e-mail: herkimercounty@herkimercounty.org
Web site: www.herkimercounty.org

Chairman, County Legislature (R):
Leonard R Hendrix 315-867-1108
Majority Leader (R):
Patrick E Russell 315-867-1108
Minority Leader (D):
Claudine F Grande 315-867-1108
Clerk, Legislature:
Carole L LaLonde 315-867-1108
County Administrator:
James W Wallace, Jr 315-867-1112
County Clerk:
Sylvia M Rowan 315-867-1129/fax: 315-866-4396
County Attorney:
Robert J Malone 315-867-1123
District Attorney:
John Crandall 315-867-1155/fax: 315-867-1348
Sheriff:
A Sam Jess 315-867-1167/fax: 315-867-1354
Treasurer:
Jennifer J Haggerty 315-867-1145/fax: 315-867-1315
Administrator Public Defender Program:
Keith Bowers 315-866-0006
County Historian:
James M Greiner 315-866-1398

Jefferson County
County Office Bldg
175 Arsenal St
Watertown, NY 13601
315-785-3075 Fax: 315-785-5070
Web site: www.co.jefferson.ny.us

Chairman, Board of Legislators (R):
Robert J Thomas 315-785-3075
Vice Chairman, Board of Legislators (R):
Robert A Boice 315-785-3075
County Administrator/Budget Officer & Clerk, Board:
Robert F Hagemann, III 315-785-3075
e-mail: roberth@co.jefferson.ny.us
County Clerk:
Jo Ann M Wilder 315-785-3081/fax: 315-785-5145
County Attorney:
John V Hartzell 315-785-3088/fax: 315-785-5178
District Attorney:
Cindy Intschert 315-785-3053/fax: 315-785-3371

Offices and agencies appear in alphabetical order.

403

Public Defender:
   Julie Hutchins 315-785-3152/fax: 315-785-5058
   e-mail: joannem@co.jefferson.ny.us
Sheriff:
   John P Burns 315-786-2700/fax: 315-786-2775
Treasurer:
   Nancy Brown 315-785-3055

Kings County (NYC Borough of Brooklyn)

209 Joralemon St
Brooklyn, NY 11201
718-802-3900 Fax: 718-802-3778
Web site: www.brooklyn-usa.org

Borough President (D):
   Marty Markowitz 718-802-3700
   e-mail: askmarty@brooklynbp.nyc.gov
Deputy Borough President:
   Yvonne J Graham 718-802-3842
   e-mail: ygraham@brooklynbp.nyc.gov
County Clerk:
   Wilbur A Levin 718-643-7037
District Attorney:
   Charles J Hynes 718-802-2000
Director, Public Information:
   Jerry Schmetterer 718-250-2000
   e-mail: schmetj@brooklynda.org

Lewis County

Courthouse
7660 N State St
Lowville, NY 13367
315-376-5356 Fax: 315-376-5445
Web site: www.lewiscountyny.org

Chairman, Legislative Board (D):
   Bruce R Krug 315-397-2523
   e-mail: b.krug@lewiscountyny.org
Clerk, Board of Legislature:
   Teresa L Kenealy 315-376-5356
County Clerk:
   Douglas Hanno 315-376-5333/fax: 315-376-3768
   e-mail: clerk@lewiscountyny.org
County Attorney:
   Richard Graham 315-376-5282/fax: 315-376-3857
   e-mail: rgraham@lewiscountyny.org
District Attorney:
   Michael F Young 315-376-5390
Public Defender:
   Daniel King 315-376-6565/fax: 315-376-8418
Sheriff:
   L Michael Tabolt 315-376-3511/fax: 315-376-5232
   e-mail: LCSD@lewiscountyny.org
Treasurer:
   Vickie Roy 315-376-5325/fax: 315-376-3768
   e-mail: treasurer@lewiscountyny.org
County Manager/Budget Officer:
   Sharon Cihocki 315-376-5354/fax: 315-376-5445
   e-mail: county.manager@lewiscountyny.org
County Historian:
   Lisa Becker 315-376-2825

Livingston County

Livingston County Government Ctr
6 Court St
Geneseo, NY 14454
585-243-7030 Fax: 585-243-7045
e-mail: info@co.livingston.ny.us
Web site: www.co.livingston.state.ny.us

Chairman, Board of Supervisors (R):
   James C Merrick 585-243-7030
Vice Chairman, Board of Supervisors (R):
   Gary D Moore 585-243-7030
Clerk, Board of Supervisors:
   Virginia O Amico 585-243-7030
   e-mail: vamico@co.livingston.ny.us
County Administrator:
   Dominic F Mazza 585-243-7040/fax: 585-243-7045
   e-mail: dmazza@co.livingston.ny.us
County Clerk:
   James A Culbertson 585-243-7010/fax: 585-243-7928
   e-mail: jculbertson@co.livingston.ny.us
County Attorney:
   David J Morris . . . . 585-243-7033 or 585-468-2770
   e-mail: dmorris@co.livingston.ny.us
District Attorney:
   Thomas E Moran 585-243-7020/fax: 585-243-7199
   e-mail: tmoran@co.livingston.ny.us
Public Defender:
   Marcea A Clark 585-243-7028/fax: 585-243-7193
   e-mail: maclark@co.livingston.ny.us
Sheriff:
   John M York 585-243-7120/fax: 585-243-7926
   e-mail: sheriffyork@co.livingston.ny.us
Treasurer:
   Carolyn D Taylor 585-243-7050/fax: 585-243-7597
   e-mail: ctaylor@co.livingston.ny.us
Historian:
   Annie Alden 585-243-2311/fax: 585-243-3874
   e-mail: historian@co.livingston.ny.us

Madison County

County Office Bldg
138 N Court St
PO Box 635
Wampsville, NY 13163
315-366-2201 Fax: 315-366-2502
e-mail: supervisors@co.madison.ny.us
Web site: www.madisoncounty.org

Chairman, Board of Supervisors (R):
   Rocco J DiVeronica 315-366-2201
   e-mail: rocco.diveronica@co.madison.ny.us
Clerk, Board of Supervisors:
   Cindy Urtz 315-366-2201
County Clerk:
   O Perry Tooker, III 315-366-2261
County Attorney:
   S John Campanie 315-366-2203/fax: 315-366-2502
District Attorney:
   Donald F Cerio, Jr 315-366-2236/fax: 315-366-2503
Public Defender Director:
   Paul H Hadley 315-366-2585/fax: 315-366-2583
Sheriff:
   Ronald Cary 315-366-2318/fax: 315-366-2286

Offices and agencies appear in alphabetical order.

Treasurer:
    Harold C Landers 315-366-2371/fax: 315-366-2705
Public Information Officer:
    Sharon A Driscoll. 315-366-2788
County Historian:
    Deborah Harmon. 315-366-2453/fax: 315-366-2742

Monroe County
110 County Office Bldg
39 W Main St
Rochester, NY 14614
585-428-5350 Fax: 585-428-2032
Web site: www.monroecounty.gov

President, County Legislature (R):
    Wayne E Zyra. 585-428-5255
    e-mail: monroe2@monroecounty.gov
Majority Leader (R):
    Bill Smith 585-428-5622
    e-mail: bill@billsmith.org
Minority Leader (D):
    Stephanie Polowe Aldersley. 585-428-2040
    e-mail: srpnc4@rit.edu
Clerk, Legislature:
    Joanne B Zelazny 585-428-5350
County Executive:
    Maggie Brooks. 585-428-5301
County Clerk:
    Cheryl Dinolfo. 585-428-5177/fax: 585-428-5447
County Attorney:
    Daniel M DeLaus, Jr. . . . . 585-428-3182 or 585-428-5280
    fax: 585-428-2031
District Attorney:
    Michael C Green 585-428-2334/fax: 585-428-4224
Sheriff:
    Patrick M O'Flynn. 585-428-5780/fax: 585-428-5851
    e-mail: sheriff@monroecountysheriff.info
Public Defender:
    Edward J Nowak 585-428-5210/fax: 585-428-2234
Chief Fiscal Officer:
    Stephen W Gleason 585-428-5257/fax: 585-428-5133
Treasury(Tax Collection):
    Josette Palmiere. 585-428-5290/fax: 585-428-3227
Public Information Officer:
    Larry Staub 585-428-2380/fax: 585-428-3268
County Historian:
    Carolyn Vacca. 585-428-8352/fax: 585-428-8353

Montgomery County
County Annex Bldg 20 Park St
PO Box 1500
Fonda, NY 12068-1500
518-853-4304 Fax: 518-853-8220
Web site: www.co.montgomery.ny.us

Chairman, Board of Supervisors:
    William E Strevy 518-853-4304
    Vacant
County Clerk:
    Helen A Bartone. 518-853-8111
County Attorney:
    Douglas E Landon 518-829-5067
District Attorney:
    James E Conboy. 518-853-8250

Public Defender:
    William Martuscello. 518-853-8305
Sheriff:
    Michael J Amato. . . . . 518-853-5500 or 518-853-4312
    fax: 518-853-4096
Treasurer:
    Shawn J Bowerman. 518-853-8175/fax: 518-853-8344
County Historian:
    Kelly A Farquhar. 518-853-8187/fax: 518-853-8392
    e-mail: histarch@superior.net

Nassau County
One West St
Mineola, NY 11501
516-571-3000 Fax: 516-739-2636
Web site: www.nassaucountyny.gov

Presiding Officer of the Legislature (D):
    Judith A Jacobs 516-571-6216/fax: 516-571-6636
Deputy Presiding Officer of the Legislature (D):
    Roger Corbin 516-571-6202
Peter J Schmitt
Clerk, Legislature:
    William P Geier 516-571-4252
County Executive:
    Thomas R Suozzi 516-571-3131
    e-mail: thomas.suozzi@mail.co.nassau.ny.us
County Clerk:
    Karen V Murphy. 516-571-2663
County Attorney:
    Lorna Goodman 516-571-3056
District Attorney:
    Denis Dillon. 516-571-2994/fax: 516-248-9479
    e-mail: denis.dillon@nassauda.org
Director, Legislative Affairs:
    Marilyn Gottlieb 516-571-4397
Sheriff:
    Edward Reilly. 516-572-4100
James H Lawrence
Comptroller:
    Howard S Weitzman. 516-571-2386
    e-mail: nccomptroller@nassaucountyny.gov
Treasurer:
    Henry M Dachowitz. 516-571-2090
    e-mail: nctreasurer@nassaucountyny.gov

New York County (NYC Borough of Manhattan)
Municipal Bldg
One Centre St, 19th Fl S
New York, NY 10007
212-669-8300 Fax: 212-669-4305
Web site: www.manhattanbp.org

Borough President:
    C Virginia Fields 212-669-8155
    e-mail: bp@manhattanbp.org
County Clerk:
    Norman Goodman 646-386-5956
Chief Deputy County Clerk:
    James A Rossetti. 646-386-5956
District Attorney:
    Robert M Morgenthau 212-335-9000
Public Administrator:
    Ethel J Griffin. 212-788-8433

Offices and agencies appear in alphabetical order.

Niagara County

Courthouse
Lockport, NY 14094-2740
716-439-7000 Fax: 716-439-7124
Web site: www.niagaracounty.com

Chairman, County Legislature (C):
 William L Ross. 716-439-7003
Majority Leader (R):
 Malcolm A Needler 716-694-8332
Minority Leader (D):
 Dennis F Virtuoso. 716-285-1582
Clerk, Legislature:
 Michael P Carney 716-439-7177/fax: 716-439-7124
County Clerk:
 Wayne F Jagow 716-439-7022/fax: 716-439-7035
County Manager:
 Gregory Lewis. 716-439-7006/fax: 716-439-7212
 e-mail: greg.lewis@niagaracounty.com
County Attorney:
 Claude A Joerg 716-439-7105/fax: 716-439-7114
 e-mail: claude.joerg@niagaracounty.com
District Attorney:
 Matthew J Murphy, III 716-439-7085/fax: 716-439-7102
Public Defender:
 Michael J Violante 716-439-7071
Sheriff:
 Thomas A Beilein 716-438-3370/fax: 716-438-3357
Treasurer:
 David S Broderick. 716-439-7018/fax: 716-439-7021
Historian:
 David Dickinson. 716-439-7324

Oneida County

County Office Bldg
800 Park Ave
Utica, NY 13501
315-798-5900 Fax: 315-798-5924
e-mail: bol@co.oneida.ny.us or bol@ocgov.net
Web site: www.co.oneida.ny.us or www.ocgov.net

Chairman, County Legislature (R):
 Gerald J Fiorini. 315-798-5900
Majority Leader (R):
 James M D'Onofrio 315-798-5901
Minority Leader (D):
 Harry A Hertline. 315-798-5049
Clerk, Legislature:
 Susan L Crabtree 315-798-5404
County Executive:
 Joseph A Griffo. 315-798-5800/fax: 315-798-2390
 e-mail: ce@ocgov.net
County Clerk:
 Richard D Allen 315-798-5794
 e-mail: countyclerk@ocgov.net
County Attorney:
 Randal B Caldwell. 315-798-5910/fax: 315-798-5603
 e-mail: coatty@ocgov.net
District Attorney:
 Michael A Arcuri. 315-798-5766/fax: 315-798-5582
 e-mail: distatty@ocgov.net
Public Defender-Criminal Division:
 Frank J Nebush Jr 315-798-5870/fax: 315-798-0364
 e-mail: pubdef@ocgov.net

Public Defender-Civil Division:
 Frank J Furno. 315-266-6100/fax: 315-266-6105
 e-mail: pdcivil@ocgov.net
Sheriff:
 Daniel G Middaugh . . . . 315-738-7804 or 315-765-2222
Comptroller:
 Joseph A Timpano 315-798-5780
Finance Commissioner:
 Anthony R Carvelli. 315-798-5750
 e-mail: finance@ocgov.net

Onondaga County

407 Courthouse
Syracuse, NY 13202
315-435-2070 Fax: 315-435-8434
Web site: www.ongov.net

Chairman, County Legislature (R):
 Dale A Sweetland. 315-435-2070
 e-mail: dalesweetland@ongov.net
Majority Leader (R):
 Bernard Kraft 315-435-2070
 e-mail: berniekraft@msn.com
Minority Leader (D):
 Edward F Ryan. 315-435-2070
County Executive:
 Nicholas J Pirro. 315-435-3516/fax: 315-435-8582
Clerk, Legislature:
 Deborah Fichera 315-435-2070
 e-mail: debbiefichera@ongov.net
County Clerk:
 Ann M Ciarpelli 315-435-2226
County Attorney:
 Anthony P Rivizzigno 315-435-2170
 e-mail: lwdrobb@nysnet.net
District Attorney:
 William J Fitzpatrick 315-435-2470
 e-mail: daweb@ongov.net
Sheriff:
 Kevin E Walsh 315-435-3044
Comptroller:
 Donald F Colon 315-435-2130/fax: 315-435-2250
Chief Fiscal Officer:
 Joe C Mareane. 315-435-3346/fax: 315-435-3439

Ontario County

Ontario Co Municipal Bldg
20 Ontario St
Canandaigua, NY 14424
585-396-4447 Fax: 585-396-8818
e-mail: bos@co.ontario.ny.us
Web site: www.co.ontario.ny.us

Chairman, Board of Supervisors (R):
 Carmen Orlando 585-396-4447/fax: 585-396-8818
Vice Chairman, Board of Supervisors (R):
 Wayne F Houseman 585-396-4447
Clerk, Board of Supervisors:
 Karen R DeMay 585-396-4447
 e-mail: karen.demay@co.ontario.ny.us
County Administrator:
 Geoffrey C Astles. 585-396-4400
 e-mail: geoff.astles@co.ontario.ny.us
Deputy County Administrator:
 Darlys McDonough 585-396-4401

Offices and agencies appear in alphabetical order.

County Clerk:
Jack Cooley 585-396-4200
County Attorney:
John W Park 585-396-4411/fax: 585-396-4481
District Attorney:
R Michael Tantillo. 585-396-4010/fax: 585-396-4860
Treasurer:
Joyce A. Keeney. 585-396-4432
Sheriff:
Philip C Povero. 585-394-4560
e-mail: sheriffinfo@co.ontario.ny.us
Historian:
Preston Pierce. 716-396-4034
e-mail: pep646@frontiernet.net

Orange County
County Government Center
255 Main St
Goshen, NY 10924
845-291-4800 Fax: 845-291-4809
e-mail: legislature@co.orange.ny.us
Web site: www.co.orange.ny.us

Chairman, County Legislature (R):
A Alan Seidman 845-291-4800
Majority Leader (R):
M William Lahey. 845-291-4800
Minority Leader (D):
Anthony R Marino 845-291-4800
County Administrative Officer:
Catherine M Bartlett. 845-291-2700
Clerk, Legislature:
Gail Sicina 845-291-4800
County Executive:
Edward A Diana 845-291-2700/fax: 845-291-2724
e-mail: ceoffice@co.orange.ny.us
County Clerk:
Donna L Benson 845-291-2690/fax: 845-291-2691
Acting County Attorney:
David Darwin. 845-291-3150
District Attorney:
Francis D Phillips, II. 845-291-2050
Sheriff:
Carl E DuBois 845-291-4033/fax: 845-294-1590
Finance Commissioner:
Joel Kleiman 845-291-2485/fax: 845-291-2516

Orleans County
Courthouse Sq
3 South Main St
Albion, NY 14411-1495
585-589-7053 Fax: 585-589-1618
Web site: www.orleansny.com

Chairman, County Legislature (R):
Marcia B Tuohey . . . . 585-589-7053 or 585-798-0118
Vice Chairman (R):
Kenneth E Rush . . . . 585-589-7053 or 585-682-5546
Majority Leader (R):
David B Callard 585-589-7053
Minority Leader (D):
Richard Bennett 585-589-7053
Clerk, Legislature:
Kathleen M Ahlberg. 585-589-7053
e-mail: kahlberg@orleansny.com

Chief Administrative Officer:
Stanley J Dudek 585-589-7053
e-mail: sdudek@orleansny.com
County Clerk:
Carol R Lonnen 585-589-5334
e-mail: clonnen@orleansny.com
County Attorney:
David C Schubel 585-798-2250/fax: 585-798-0776
e-mail: occoa@eznet.net
District Attorney:
Joseph V Cardone 585-590-4127/fax: 585-590-4129
e-mail: da@orleansny.com
Public Defender:
Sanford A Church 585-589-7335/fax: 585-589-2592
e-mail: publicdefender@eznet.net
Sheriff:
Scott D Hess 585-590-4142/fax: 585-590-4178
e-mail: ocsher1@orleansny.com
Treasurer:
Susan M Heard 585-589-5353/fax: 585-589-9220
e-mail: sheard@orleansny.com
County Historian:
C.W. Lattin. 585-589-4174

Oswego County
46 E Bridge St
Oswego, NY 13126
315-349-8230 Fax: 315-349-8237
Web site: www.co.oswego.ny.us

Chairman, County Legislature (R):
Russ W Johnson 315-349-8230
Majority Leader (R):
Barry Leemann. 315-349-8230
Minority Leader (D):
Mike Kunzwiler 315-349-8230
Clerk, Legislature:
Theodore I Jerrett 315-349-8230
e-mail: tjerrett@oswegocounty.com
County Administrator:
Stephen P Lyman. 315-349-8235/fax: 315-349-8237
e-mail: pchurch@oswegocounty.com
County Clerk:
George J Williams 315-349-8385
e-mail: williamsg@oswegocounty.com
County Attorney:
Richard C Mitchell. 315-349-8296
District Attorney/Coroner:
Donald H Dodd 315-349-3200/fax: 315-349-3212
e-mail: teaston@oswegocounty.com
Treasurer:
John Kruk 315-349-8393/fax: 315-349-8255
e-mail: marthas@oswegocounty.com
Sheriff:
Reuel A Todd 315-349-3302/fax: 315-349-3303
e-mail: sheriff@oswegocounty.com

Otsego County
County Office Bldg
197 Main St
Cooperstown, NY 13326-1129
607-547-4202 Fax: 607-547-4260
e-mail: childl@otsegocounty.com
Web site: www.otsegocounty.com

Offices and agencies appear in alphabetical order.

Chairman, Board of Representatives (R):
Carl F Higgins 607-547-4202
e-mail: carmarhiq@usadatanet.net
Vice Chairman, Board of Representatives:
Eugene E Wells 607-547-4202
e-mail: ewellssr@stny.rr.com
Clerk, Board of Representatives:
Laura A Child. 607-547-4202
e-mail: childl@otsegocounty.com
County Clerk:
Kathleen Sinnott Gardner 607-547-4276/fax: 607-547-7544
e-mail: gardnerk@otsegocounty.com
County Attorney:
James E Konstanty 607-547-4208/fax: 607-547-7572
e-mail: mis_director@co.otsego.ny.us
District Attorney:
John M Muehl 607-547-4249/fax: 607-547-4373
e-mail: distatty@otsegocounty.com
Public Defender:
Richard A Rothermel. 607-432-7410/fax: 607-433-2168
Sheriff:
Donald R Mundy Sr 607-547-4271
Treasurer:
Theodora Moore 607-547-4235/fax: 607-547-7579
e-mail: mooret@otsegocounty.com
County Historian:
Nancy S Milavec 607-397-9705

Putnam County

40 Gleneida Avenue
Carmel, NY 10512
845-225-8690 Fax: 845-225-0715
e-mail: putcoleg@putnamcountyny.com
Web site: www.putnamcountyny.com

Chairman, County Legislature (R):
Robert McGuigan, Jr 845-225-8690
Deputy Chairman, County Legislature (R):
Terry Intrary 845-225-8690
Acting Clerk, Legislature:
M Chris Marrone 845-225-8690
County Executive:
Robert J Bondi 845-225-3641 x200/fax: 845-225-0294
County Clerk:
Dennis J Sant. 845-225-3641 x260
County Attorney:
Carl F Lodes 845-225-3641 x251
District Attorney:
Kevin Wright. 845-225-3641 x277
Sheriff:
Donald Blaine Smith 845-225-4300/fax: 845-225-4399
Finance Commissioner:
William J Carlin, Jr . . . . 845-225-3641 x321 or 845-225-3848
fax: 845-225-8290
County Historian:
Allan J Warnecke 845-278-7209/fax: 845-278-4865
e-mail: putpast@bestweb.net

Queens County (NYC Borough of Queens)

120-55 Queens Blvd
Kew Gardens, NY 11424
718-286-3000 Fax: 718-286-2876
e-mail: info@queensbp.org
Web site: www.queensbp.org

Borough President:
Helen M Marshall. 718-286-3000
Deputy Borough President:
Karen Koslowitz. 718-286-2900
Public Information Officer:
Daniel Andrews 718-286-2640
County Clerk:
Gloria D'Amico 718-298-0600
District Attorney:
Richard Brown 718-286-6000
Public Administrator:
Lois M Rosenblatt . . . . 718-526-5037 or 718-520-3710
fax: 718-526-5043
Susan B Brown
Gerard J Sweeney

Rensselaer County

County Office Bldg
1600 Seventh Ave
Troy, NY 12180
518-270-2880 Fax: 518-270-2983
Web site: www.rensco.com or www.rensselaercounty.org

Chairperson, County Legislature (R):
Neil J Kelleher 518-270-2880
Vice Chairman (R):
Martin T Reid. 518-270-2880
Vice Chairman-Finance (R):
Margaret H VanDeusen 518-270-2880
Majority Leader (C):
Robert Mirch 518-270-2880
Minority Leader (D):
William L Dedrick 518-270-2890
Clerk, Legislature:
Jenet N Allard. 518-270-2880
County Executive:
Kathleen M Jimino 518-270-2900/fax: 518-270-2961
County Clerk:
Frank Merola 518-270-4080
County Attorney:
Robert A Smith 518-270-2952/fax: 518-270-2954
District Attorney:
Patricia A DeAngelis 518-270-4040
Public Defender:
Jerome K Frost 518-270-4030
Sheriff:
Jack Mahar 518-270-5448
Chief Fiscal Officer:
Michael J Slawson 518-270-2750

Richmond County (NYC Borough of Staten Island)

Public Admin Office
130 Stuyvesant Pl, Ste 402
Staten Island, NY 10301
718-876-7228 Fax: 718-876-8377
e-mail: gdgpa@msn.com
Web site: www.statenislandusa.com

Borough President:
James P Molinaro. 718-816-2200
County Clerk:
Stephen J Fiala 718-390-5396

Offices and agencies appear in alphabetical order.

District Attorney:
Daniel M Donovan 718-556-7050/fax: 718-556-7054
Public Administrator:
Gary D Gotlin 718-876-7228/fax: 718-876-8377

Rockland County
County Office Bldg
11 New Hempstead Rd
New City, NY 10956
845-638-5100 Fax: 845-638-5675
Web site: www.co.rockland.ny.us

Chairwoman, County Legislature (D):
Harriet D Cornell 845-638-5100
Majority Leader (D):
William L Darden. 845-638-5100
Minority Leader (R):
Douglas J Jobson 845-638-5100
Clerk, Legislature:
Laurence O Toole. 845-638-5100
e-mail: legclerk@co.rockland.ny.us
County Executive:
C Scott Vanderhoef 845-638-5122
County Clerk:
Ed Gorman. 845-638-5070/fax: 845-638-5647
e-mail: rocklandcountyclerk@co.rockland.ny.us
County Attorney:
Patricia Zugibe 845-638-5180
District Attorney:
Michael E Bongiorno 845-638-5001
Public Defender:
James D Licata 845-638-5660
e-mail: licataj@co.rockland.ny.us
Sheriff:
James F Kralik . . . . 845-638-5464 or 845-638-5400
fax: 845-638-5035
Finance Commissioner:
Robert E Bergman, Jr. 845-638-5131

Saratoga County
County Municipal Center
40 McMaster St
Ballston Spa, NY 12020
518-885-5381 Fax: 518-884-4771
e-mail: sarckbd1@govt.co.saratoga.ny.us
Web site: www.co.saratoga.ny.us

Chairman, Board of Supervisors (R):
Mary Ann Johnson 518-885-2240
e-mail: ma.johnson@adelphia.net
Vice Chairman, Board of Supervisors (R):
Harry Gutheil 518-885-2240
e-mail: gutheilh@govt.co.saratoga.ny.us
County Administrator:
David A Wickerham. 518-884-4742
Clerk, Board of Supervisors:
Barbara J Plummer 518-885-2240
County Clerk:
Kathleen A Marchione 518-885-2213/fax: 518-884-4726
e-mail: marchiok@govt.co.saratoga.ny.us
County Attorney:
Mark Rider 518-884-4770
e-mail: saracaty@govt.co.saratoga.ny.us
District Attorney:
James A Murphy, III 518-884-8627/fax: 518-884-4766

Public Defender:
John Ciulla 518-884-4795
Sheriff:
James Bowen 518-885-6761
County Treasurer:
J Christopher Callaghan 518-884-4724
e-mail: sartreas@govt.co.saratoga.ny.us

Schenectady County
County Legislature
620 State St
Schenectady, NY 12305
518-388-4280 Fax: 518-388-4591
e-mail: legislative@countyofschenectady.com
Web site: www.schenectadycounty.com

Chairperson, County Legislature (D):
Susan E Savage. 518-388-4280
Majority Leader (D):
Kent W Gray. 518-388-4280
Minority Leader (R):
Robert T Farley. 518-388-4280
Clerk, Legislature:
Brian L Quail . . . . , ... 518-388-4280
County Manager:
Kevin D DeFebbo. 518-388-4355
County Clerk:
John J Woodward 518-388-4220/fax: 518-388-4224
e-mail: john.woodward@schenectadycounty.com
County Attorney:
Christopher H Gardner 518-388-4276/fax: 518-388-4493
District Attorney:
Robert M Carney. 518-388-4364/fax: 518-388-4569
e-mail: districtattorney@schenectadycounty.com
Public Defender:
Mark J Caruso. 518-386-2266
Sheriff:
Harry C Buffardi 518-388-4300/fax: 518-388-4593
Finance Commissioner:
George Davidson 518-388-4266

Schoharie County
284 Main St
PO Box 429
Schoharie, NY 12157
518-295-8421 Fax: 518-295-8482
e-mail: www.schohariecounty-ny.gov

Chairman, Board of Supervisors (R):
Earl VanWormer, III 518-875-6109
Majority Leader (R):
Charles D Buck. 607-652-2926
Minority Leader (D):
Philip Skowfoe 518-827-4896
Clerk, Board of Supervisors:
Karen Miller 518-295-8421/fax: 518-295-8482
e-mail: millerk@co.schoharie.ny.us
County Clerk:
Peter D Lopez. . . . . 518-295-8316 or 518-295-8317
fax: 518-295-8338
e-mail: peterlopez@co.schoharie.ny.us
County Attorney:
Michael West. 518-296-8844/fax: 518-296-8855
District Attorney:
James L Sacket 518-295-8257/fax: 518-295-8266

Offices and agencies appear in alphabetical order.

Sheriff:
  John S Bates, Jr 518-295-7066/fax: 518-295-7094
Treasurer:
  William E Cherry . . . . 518-295-8386 or 518-295-8348
  fax: 518-295-8364
Administrator Legal Defense:
  Raynor B Duncombe 518-295-7515/fax: 518-295-7519

Schuyler County
County Bldg
105 Ninth St, Unit 6
Watkins Glen, NY 14891
607-535-8100 Fax: 607-535-8109
e-mail: legislature@co.schuyler.ny.us
Web site: www.schuylercounty.us

Chairman, County Legislature (R):
  Thomas M Gifford 607-535-8100
  e-mail: t5141@aol.com
Clerk, Legislature:
  Gail M Hughey 607-535-8100
County Clerk:
  Linda M Compton 607-535-8133
County Administrator/Budget Officer:
  Timothy M O'Hearn 607-535-8106
County Attorney:
  James P Coleman 607-535-8121
District Attorney:
  Joseph G Fazzary 607-535-8383
Public Defender:
  Connie Fern Miller 607-535-9354
Sheriff:
  Michael J Maloney 607-535-8222
  e-mail: mmaloney@co.schuyler.ny.us
Treasurer:
  Margaret Starbuck 607-535-8181
County Historian:
  Barbara Bell 607-535-4577

Seneca County
1 DiPronio Dr
Waterloo, NY 13165
315-539-1800 Fax: 315-539-0207
Web site: www.co.seneca.ny.us

Chairman, Board of Supervisors (R):
  Robert Shipley, Jr 315-539-1700/fax: 315-539-0207
  e-mail: rshipley@rochester.rr.com
Minority Leader (D):
  Peter W Same 315-539-1700
Majority Leader (R):
  David Kaiser 315-539-1700
Clerk, Board of Supervisors:
  Margaret E Li 315-539-0207
  e-mail: mli@co.seneca.ny.us
County Clerk:
  Christina L Lotz 315-539-1771/fax: 315-539-3789
  e-mail: clotz@co.seneca.ny.us
Deputy (Acting) County Manager:
  Sharon L Secor 315-539-1701
County Attorney:
  Steven J Getman 315-539-1833/fax: 315-539-1657
  e-mail: sgetman@co.seneca.ny.us

District Attorney:
  Richard E Swinehart 315-539-1300/fax: 315-539-9531
  e-mail: rswinehart@co.seneca.ny.us
Sheriff:
  Leo T Connolly . . . . 315-539-9241 or 315-539-9244
  fax: 315-539-0121
  e-mail: lconnolly@co.seneca.ny.us
Public Defender:
  Michael Mirras 315-568-4975
Treasurer:
  Nicholas A Sciotti 315-539-1735/fax: 315-539-1731
  e-mail: nsciotti@co.seneca.ny.us
County Historian:
  Walt Gable 315-539-1785
  e-mail: wgable@co.seneca.ny.us

St Lawrence County
County Courthouse
48 Court St
Canton, NY 13617-1169
315-379-2276 Fax: 315-379-2333
Web site: www.co.st-lawrence.ny.us

Chair, Board of Legislators (R):
  Thomas A Nichols 315-379-2276
Vice Chair, Board of Legislators (R):
  Thomas R Grow 315-379-2276
County Administrator & Clerk, Board of Legislature:
  Donald R Brining 315-379-2276
  e-mail: dbrining@co.st-lawrence.ny.us
County Clerk:
  Patricia Ritchie 315-379-2237
Deputy Clerk of the Board:
  Chandra L Pharoah 315-379-2276
Deputy Clerk of the Board:
  Ruth A E Doyle 315-379-2276
County Attorney:
  William F Maginn 315-379-2269
Acting District Attorney:
  Gary Miles 315-379-2225
Sheriff:
  Gary Jarvis 315-379-2365
Treasurer:
  Robert O McNeil 315-379-2234

Steuben County
County Office Bldg
3 East Pulteney Square
Bath, NY 14810
607-776-9631 Fax: 607-776-6926
Web site: www.steubencony.org

Chairman, County Legislature (R):
  Philip J Roche 607-776-9631
Vice Chair, County Legislature & Majority Leader (R):
  Gary D Swackhamer 607-776-9631
Minority Leader (D):
  Richard A Argentieri 607-776-9631
Clerk, County Legislature:
  Christine Kane 607-776-9631 ext2247
  e-mail: chris@co.steuben.ny.us
County Administrator:
  Mark R Alger 607-776-9631 ext2245
County Clerk:
  Judith M Hunter 607-776-9631 ext3203

Offices and agencies appear in alphabetical order.

County Attorney:
   Frederick H Ahrens, Jr 607-776-9631 ext2355
District Attorney:
   John C Tunney 607-776-9631 ext2270
Public Defender:
   Byrum W Cooper Jr. 607-776-9631 ext2413
Sheriff:
   Richard C Tweddell . . . . 607-776-7009 or 800-724-7777
Treasurer:
   Lawrence P Crossett 607-776-9631 ext2488

Suffolk County

William H Rogers Legislature Bldg
725 Veterans Memorial Hwy
Smithtown, NY 11787
631-853-4070 Fax: 631-853-4899
Web site: www.co.suffolk.ny.us

Presiding Officer, County Legislature (R):
   Joseph Caracappa 631-854-2700/fax: 631-854-2703
   e-mail: joseph.caracappa@suffolkcountyny.gov
Deputy Presiding Officer, County Legislature (R):
   Angie Carpenter. 631-854-4100/fax: 631-854-4103
   e-mail: angie.carpenter@suffolkcountyny.gov
Minority Leader (D):
   William J Lindsay 631-854-9611/fax: 631-854-9687
   e-mail: william.lindsay@suffolkcountyny.gov
Majority Leader (R):
   Peter O'Leary 631-852-1300/fax: 631-852-1303
   e-mail: peter.o'leary@suffolkcountyny.gov
Clerk, County Legislature:
   Henry L Barton, Jr. 631-853-4074/fax: 631-853-4899
   e-mail: henry.barton@co.suffolk.ny.us
County Executive:
   Steve Levy 631-853-4000
   e-mail: county.executive@suffolkcountyny.gov
Assistant Deputy County Exec, Intergovernmental Relations:
   Jeanine Dillon 631-853-5026/fax: 631-853-4086
County Clerk:
   Edward P Romaine 631-852-2000/fax: 631-852-2004
   e-mail: romainee@nyslgti.gen.ny.us
County Attorney:
   Christine Malafi. 631-853-4049/fax: 631-853-5169
District Attorney:
   Thomas J Spota. 631-853-4161
   e-mail: infoda@co.suffolk.ny.us
Sheriff:
   Alfred Tisch 631-852-2200
Treasurer:
   John C Cochrane. 631-852-1500

Sullivan County

County Gov't Center
100 North St
PO Box 5012
Monticello, NY 12701-5192
845-794-3000 x3300 Fax: 845-794-3459
e-mail: info@co.sullivan.ny.us
Web site: www.co.sullivan.ny.us

Chairman (D):
   Christopher A Cunningham 845-794-3000 x3300/fax: 845-794-0650
Vice-Chairman (D):
   Jonathan Rouis. 845-794-3000 x3300

Majority Leader (D):
   Kathleen LaBuda. 845-794-3000 x3300
Minority Leader (R):
   Rodney Gaebel 845-794-3000 x3300
Clerk, County Legislature:
   AnnMarie Martin. 845-794-3000 x3300
   e-mail: annmarie.martin@co.sullivan.ny.us
Deputy Clerk, County Legislature:
   Deniese A Harting. 845-794-3000 x3300
County Manager:
   Daniel L Briggs 845-794-3000 x3322/fax: 845-794-0230
County Clerk:
   George L Cooke, II. 845-794-3000 x5012/fax: 845-794-0230
   e-mail: george.cooke@co.sullivan.ny.us
County Attorney:
   Samuel S Yasgur 845-794-3000 x3565/fax: 845-794-4924
District Attorney:
   Stephen F Lungen 845-794-3344/fax: 845-794-3646
Sheriff:
   Daniel Hogue . . . . 845-794-7100 or 845-794-7102
   fax: 845-791-7979
Treasurer:
   Olga Parlow. 845-794-3000 x5016
County Historian:
   John Conway 845-557-3434

Tioga County

County Office Bldg
56 Main St
Owego, NY 13827
607-687-8200 Fax: 607-687-8232
Web site: www.tiogacountyny.com

Chair, County Legislature (R):
   Martin L Borko. 607-687-8240
Clerk, County Legislature:
   Maureen L Dougherty 607-687-8235
County Manager:
   John C Byrne. 607-687-8236/fax: 607-223-7018
   e-mail: byrnej@co.tioga.ny.us
County Clerk:
   Robert L Woodburn. 607-687-8660/fax: 607-687-4612
County Attorney:
   David Dutko 607-687-8253/fax: 607-223-7003
District Attorney:
   Gerald A Keene. 607-687-8647/fax: 607-687-1614
Public Defender:
   Robert L Miller. 607-565-2455
Sheriff:
   Gary Howard. 607-687-1010/fax: 607-687-6755
Treasurer:
   James P McFadden 607-687-8668/fax: 607-223-7035
   e-mail: mcfaddenj@co.tioga.ny.us

Tompkins County

125 E Court St
Ithaca, NY 14850
607-274-5434 Fax: 607-274-5430
Web site: www.tompkins-co.org

Chairman, Board of Representatives (D):
   Tim J Joseph. 607-274-5434
   e-mail: joseph@tompkins-co.org
Vice Chairman, Board of Representatives (D):
   Michael Lane 607-274-5434

Offices and agencies appear in alphabetical order.

Clerk, Board of Representatives:
  Catherine Covert. 607-274-5434
County Administrator:
  Stephen F Whicher 607-274-5551/fax: 607-274-5558
Deputy County Administrator:
  Edward C Marx 607-274-5560/fax: 607-274-5578
County Clerk:
  Aurora R Valenti 607-274-5431
  e-mail: avalenti@tompkins-co.org
County Attorney:
  Jonathan Wood 607-274-5546
  e-mail: countyattorney@tompkins-co.org
District Attorney:
  George M Dentes. 607-274-5461/fax: 607-274-5429
  e-mail: distatty@tompkins-co.org
Sheriff:
  Peter Meskill 607-257-1345/fax: 607-266-5436
  e-mail: pmeskill@tompkins-co.org
Comptroller:
  David Squires 607-274-5502
  e-mail: dsquires@tompkins-co.org

Ulster County
244 Fair St
PO Box 1800
Kingston, NY 12402-1800
845-340-3900 Fax: 845-340-3651
e-mail: egov@co.ulster.ny.us
Web site: www.co.ulster.ny.us

Chairman, County Legislature (R):
  Richard A Gerentine. 845-340-3699
Majority Leader (R):
  Michael L Stock 845-340-3900
Minority Leader (D):
  David Donaldson 845-340-3900
Clerk of the County Legislature:
  Ellen DiFalco 845-340-3666
County Administrator:
  Arthur J Smith III 845-340-3800/fax: 845-340-3651
County Clerk:
  Albert Spada 845-340-3288/fax: 845-340-3299
County Attorney:
  Francis T Murray. 845-340-3685/fax: 845-340-3691
District Attorney:
  Donald A Williams, Jr. 845-340-3280/fax: 845-340-3185
Public Defender:
  Paul L Gruner 845-340-3232/fax: 845-340-3744
  e-mail: mwol@co.ulster.ny.us
Sheriff:
  J Richard Bockelmann. 845-338-3640/fax: 845-330-3718
  e-mail: sheriff@co.ulster.ny.us
Treasurer:
  Lewis C Kirschner. 845-340-3460/fax: 845-340-3430
  e-mail: lkir@co.ulster.ny.us

Warren County
Municipal Center, 1340 State Rte 9
Lake George, NY 12845
518-761-6535 Fax: 518-761-7652
e-mail: boardofsupervisors@co.warren.ny.us
Web site: www.co.warren.ny.us

Chairman, Board of Supervisors (R):
  William H Thomas 518-761-6535

Vice Chairman, Board of Supervisors (R):
  Frederick Monroe 518-761-6535
Clerk, Board of Supervisors & County Administrator:
  Joan Parsons 518-761-6535
County Clerk:
  Pamela J Vogel 518-761-6427
County Attorney:
  Paul Dusek 518-761-6463
District Attorney:
  Kate Hogan. 518-761-6405
Sheriff:
  Larry Cleveland 518-743-2500
Treasurer:
  Frank O'Keefe 518-761-6375

Washington County
383 Broadway
Fort Edward, NY 12828
518-746-2100 Fax: 518-746-2108
e-mail: countyadmin@co.washington.ny.us
Web site: www.washco.net

Chairman, Board of Supervisors (R):
  Andrew J Williamson 518-746-2210
Vice Chairman (R):
  JoAnn Trinkle. 518-746-2210
Clerk, Board of Supervisors:
  Debra R Prehoda. 518-746-2210
County Administrator:
  Kevin G Hayes 518-746-2100
County Clerk:
  Deborah Beahan 518-746-2170
County Attorney:
  Roger A Wickes 518-746-2216
District Attorney:
  Robert Winn 518-746-2525
Public Defender:
  Joseph H Oswald 518-747-0609
Sheriff:
  Roger W Leclaire 518-854-7130
Treasurer:
  Phyllis Cooper 518-746-2220

Wayne County
Courthouse
26 Church St
Lyons, NY 14489
315-946-5400 Fax: 315-946-5407
Web site: www.co.wayne.ny.us

Chairman, Board of Supervisors (R):
  Marvin E Decker 315-946-5400
  e-mail: dliseno@co.wayne.ny.us
Majority Leader (R):
  Donna Chittenden. 315-483-4430
  e-mail: dchitt@rochester.rr.com
Minority Leader (D):
  Carmen Pascarella, Jr 315-587-4418
  e-mail: dennypat@rochester.rr.com
Clerk, Board of Supervisors:
  Sandra Sloan. 315-946-5403
County Administrator:
  Kim Park. 315-946-5400
  e-mail: kpark@co.wayne.ny.us

Offices and agencies appear in alphabetical order.

County Clerk:
Linda A Shaffer 315-946-7470/fax: 315-946-5978
e-mail: lshaffer@co.wayne.ny.us
County Attorney:
Daniel M Wyner 315-946-7442
e-mail: dwyner@co.wayne.ny.us
District Attorney:
Richard Healy 315-946-5905/fax: 315-946-5911
e-mail: rhealy@co.wayne.ny.us
Public Defender:
Ronald C Valentine 315-946-7472/fax: 315-946-7478
e-mail: rvalentine@co.wayne.ny.us
Sheriff:
Richard J Pisciotti 315-946-9711/fax: 315-946-5811
e-mail: rjpisciotti@co.wayne.ny.us
Treasurer:
Thomas A Warnick 315-946-7441/fax: 315-946-5949
e-mail: warnicktreasurer@co.wayne.ny.us
County Historian:
Peter Evans 315-946-5470
e-mail: historian@co.wayne.ny.us

Westchester County

Michaelian Bldg
148 Martine Ave
White Plains, NY 10601
914-995-2800 Fax: 914-995-3884
e-mail: pmol@westchestergov.com
Web site: www.westchestergov.com/bol

Chair, Board of Legislators (D):
Bill Ryan. 914-995-2827
e-mail: wjr1@westchestergov.com
Majority Leader (D):
Clinton I Young, Jr 914-995-2837
e-mail: cyy9@westchestergov.com
Minority Leader (R):
George Oros 914-995-2828
e-mail: goo6@westchestergov.com
Clerk, Board of Legislature & Chief of Staff:
Perry M Ochacher 914-995-2805
e-mail: pmo1@westchestergov.com
County Executive:
Andrew J Spano 914-995-2900
e-mail: ceo@westchestergov.com
Deputy County Executive:
Lawrence Schwartz 914-995-2900/fax: 914-995-3372
e-mail: iss8@westchestergov.com
Senior Assistant Deputy County Executive/Government Relations:
Karen Pasquale 914-995-2924/fax: 914-995-3372
County Clerk:
Leonard N Spano 914-995-3080/fax: 914-995-4030
e-mail: cclerk@westchestergov.com
County Attorney:
Charlene M Indelicato 914-995-2690
District Attorney:
Jeanine Pirro 914-995-3408
Sheriff/Public Safety Commissioner:
Thomas Belfiore 914-864-7700
e-mail: dmlz@westchestergov.com
Finance Commissioner:
Peter P Pucillo 914-995-2757
e-mail: dept-of-finance@westergov.com
Human Rights Commissioner:
Alison E Greene 914-995-7710

Wyoming County

Gov't Center, 143 N Main St
Warsaw, NY 14569
585-786-8800 Fax: 585-786-8802
Web site: www.wyomingco.net

Chairman, Board of Supervisors (R):
A Douglas Berwanger 585-786-8877
e-mail: adberwanger@wyomingco.net
Vice Chairman, Board of Supervisors (R):
Jerry Davis 585-786-8800
Clerk, Board of Supervisors:
Paula Parker 585-786-8800
e-mail: pparker@wyomingco.net
County Clerk:
Janet Coveny 585-786-8810/fax: 585-786-3703
e-mail: jcoveny@wyomingco.net
County Attorney:
Eric T Dadd 585-591-1724/fax: 585-591-1722
District Attorney:
Gerald L Stout 585-786-8822/fax: 585-786-8842
e-mail: gstout@wyomingco.net
Public Defender:
Norman P Effman 585-591-1600/fax: 585-591-1602
e-mail: attlegal@iinc.com
Sheriff:
Farris H Heimann 585-786-8989/fax: 585-786-8961
e-mail: fheimann@wyomingco.net
Treasurer:
John B Edwards 585-786-8812/fax: 585-786-0466
e-mail: jedwards@wyomingco.net
County Historian:
Bannister Doris 585-786-8818

Yates County

417 Liberty St
Penn Yan, NY 14527
315-536-5150 Fax: 315-536-5166
Web site: www.yatescounty.org

Chairman, County Legislature (R):
Robert N Multer 315-536-5150
e-mail: legislature@yatescounty.org
Vice Chairman, County Legislature (R):
Patrick H Flynn. 315-536-5150
County Administrator:
Sarah Purdy 315-536-5100/fax: 315-536-5118
e-mail: ycadministrator@yatescounty.org
Clerk, County Legislature:
Connie C Hayes 315-536-5150
e-mail: chayes@yatescounty.org
County Clerk:
Julie D Betts 315-536-5120/fax: 315-536-5545
e-mail: countyclerk@yatescounty.org
County Attorney:
Bernetta A Bourcy 315-531-3233
District Attorney:
Susan H Lindenmuth 315-536-5550/fax: 315-536-5556
Public Defender:
Edward J Brockman . . . . 315-374-6439 or 585-536-0352
Sheriff:
Ronald G Spike 315-536-4438/fax: 315-536-5191
e-mail: sheriff@yatescounty.org

State & Local
Government
Public Information

Offices and agencies appear in alphabetical order.

Treasurer:
    Bonnie L Percy 315-536-5192/fax: 315-536-5527
    e-mail: treasurer@yatescounty.org

MUNICIPAL GOVERNMENT

This section identifies senior public officials for cities, towns and villages in New York State with populations greater than 20,000. New York City departments are included in the city listing.

Albany, City of
City Hall
24 Eagle St, Rm 102
Albany, NY 12207
518-434-5100 Fax: 518-434-5013
Web site: www.albanyny.org

Mayor:
    Gerald D Jennings 518-434-5100/fax: 518-434-5013
Deputy Mayor:
    Philip F Calderone 518-434-5077/fax: 518-434-5074
Executive Asst to the Mayor:
    Joseph J Rabito 518-434-5100
President, Common Council:
    Helen R Desfosses 518-434-5087/fax: 518-434-5081
    e-mail: hdesfosses@aol.com
City Clerk:
    John Marsolais 518-434-5090/fax: 518-434-5081
Corporation Counsel:
    John Reilly 518-434-5050
City Comptroller:
    Thomas Nitido 518-434-5023/fax: 518-434-5098
City Treasurer:
    Betty Barnette 518-434-5036/fax: 518-434-5041
Commissioner, General Services:
    Willard Bruce . . . . 518-432-1144 or 518-434-2489
    fax: 518-427-7499
Commissioner, Taxation & Assessment:
    Keith McDonald 518-434-5155/fax: 518-434-5098
Police Chief:
    James E Turley 518-462-8014
Fire Chief:
    Michael P Dunn 518-447-7877
Director, Housing & Community Development:
    Joseph Montana 518-434-5240
Commissioner, Development & Planning:
    Lori Harris 518-434-2532/fax: 518-434-9846
Director, Building & Codes:
    Valerie Scott 518-434-5995

Amherst, Town of
5583 Main St
Williamsville, NY 14221
716-631-7000 Fax: 716-631-7146
Web site: www.amherstny.us

Town Supervisor:
    Susan J Grelick 716-631-7032
    e-mail: sgrelick@amherstny.com
Town Clerk:
    Susan K Jaros 716-631-7021
    e-mail: sjaros@amherst.ny.us
Town Attorney:
    E Thomas Jones 716-631-7030/fax: 716-631-7101
Comptroller:
    Maureen Eilano 716-631-7005

Police Chief:
    John J Moslow 716-689-1311/fax: 716-689-1310
    e-mail: jmoslow@apdny.org

Amsterdam, City of
61 Church St
Amsterdam, NY 12010
518-841-4311 Fax: 518-842-6802
Web site: www.amsterdamedz.com

Mayor:
    Joseph R Emanuele III 518-841-4311/fax: 518-842-9064
    e-mail: mayorje@choiceonemail.com
City Clerk:
    Jane DiCaprio 518-841-4305
Corporation Counsel:
    Robert Going 518-841-4364
Controller:
    Kim Brumley 518-841-4332
Zone Coordinator, Amsterdam Florida Glen Empire:
    Fred Quist 518-841-4369
Police Chief:
    Thomas Brownell 518-842-1100
    e-mail: chief.brownell@amsterdampd.com
Fire Chief:
    Richard Liberti 518-843-1312

Auburn, City of
Memorial City Hall
24 South Street
Auburn, NY 13021
315-255-4100 Fax: 315-255-4181
Web site: http://auburnny.virtualtownhall.net

Mayor:
    Timothy Lattimore 315-255-4104/fax: 315-253-8345
    e-mail: mayor@ci.auburn.ny.us
City Manager:
    John Salomone 315-255-4146/fax: 315-255-4735
    e-mail: citymanager@ci.auburn.ny.us
City Clerk:
    Debra A McCormick 315-255-4101/fax: 315-255-4181
    e-mail: dmccormick@ci.auburn.ny.us
Corporation Counsel:
    Thomas G Leone, Jr 315-255-4176/fax: 315-255-4735
    e-mail: tleone@ci.auburn.ny.us
Director, Planning & Economic Development:
    Steve Lynch 315-255-4115/fax: 315-253-0282
    e-mail: slynch@ci.auburn.ny.us
Treasurer:
    Marie Nellenback 315-255-4143/fax: 315-255-4727
    e-mail: mnellenback@ci.auburn.ny.us
Police Chief:
    Gary J Giannotta 315-253-3231/fax: 315-255-0022
    e-mail: ggiannotta@ci.auburn.ny.us

Offices and agencies appear in alphabetical order.

Babylon, Town of
200 E Sunrise Highway
Lindenhurst, NY 11757-2598
631-957-3000 Fax: 631-957-7440
e-mail: info@townofbabylon.com
Web site: www.townofbabylon.com

Town Supervisor:
  Steven Bellone 631-957-3072
Chief of Staff:
  Ronald Kluesner 631-957-3072
Town Clerk:
  Janice Tinsley-Colbert 631-957-3005
Town Attorney:
  Dennis Cohen 631-957-3029
Director, Finance:
  Victoria Marotta 631-957-3179
Commissioner, Public Works:
  John Miller 631-957-3161
Commissioner, General Services:
  Patricia Kaphan 631-957-3025

Bethlehem, Town of
445 Delaware Ave
Delmar, NY 12054-3098
518-439-4955 Fax: 518-439-1699
Web site: www.townofbethlehem.org

Town Supervisor:
  Theresa Egan 518-439-4955 x164
Town Clerk:
  Kathleen A Newkirk 518-439-4955 x183
  e-mail: knewkirk@townofbethlehem.org
Town Attorney:
  James Potter. 518-436-0751/fax: 518-436-4751
Comptroller:
  Judith E Kehoe 518-439-4955 x123
  e-mail: jkehoe@townofbethlehem.org
Police Chief:
  Louis G Corsi 518-439-9973 x206
  e-mail: lcorsi@cityofbethlehem.org
Commissioner, Public Works:
  Oliver Holmes 518-439-4955 x132
  e-mail: oholmes@cityofbethlehem.org

Binghamton, City of
City Hall
38 Hawley St
Binghamton, NY 13901
607-772-7005 Fax: 607-772-0508
Web site: www.cityofbinghamton.com

Mayor:
  Richard A Bucci 607-772-7001
Executive Assistant to the Mayor:
  Richard David. 607-772-7001
City Clerk:
  Eric Denk 607-772-7005
  e-mail: clerk@cityofbinghamton.com
Corporation Counsel:
  Gregory Poland. 607-772-7013
City Treasurer:
  Kathleen Bevelacqua 607-772-7027

City Assessor:
  Mark Minoia. 607-772-7002
Commissioner, Public Works:
  Lou Kelly 607-772-7021
Police Chief:
  John A Butler. 607-723-5321/fax: 607-772-7169
Administrator, Civil Service:
  Scott McNerney 607-772-7008
Director, Finance:
  Beverly J Palmer. 607-772-7011
  e-mail: finance@cityofbinghamton.com
Director, Planning/Housing/Community Development:
  John R Chanecka. 607-772-7028/fax: 607-772-7063
  e-mail: jrchanecka@cityofbinghamton.com
Director, Economic Development:
  Darcy Duguid 607-772-7161
  e-mail: ecodev@cityofbinghamton.com

Brighton, Town of
2300 Elmwood Ave
Rochester, NY 14618
585-784-5250 Fax: 585-784-5373
e-mail: brtown@rochester.rr.com
Web site: www.townofbrighton.org

Town Supervisor:
  Sandra L Frankel 585-784-5251
  e-mail: sfrankel@rochester.rr.com
Town Clerk:
  Susan Kramarsky . . . . 585-784-5247 or 585-784-5240
  e-mail: skramar@rochester.rr.com
Director, Finance:
  Kenneth Rohr 585-784-5210
Police Chief:
  Thomas Voelkl 585-784-5150
Town Attorney:
  William Moehle . . . . 585-271-3249 or 585-274-5258
  fax: 585-271-0847
Director, Communications:
  Stephen Dodd 585-784-5253

Brookhaven, Town of
One Independence Hill
Farmingville, NY 11738
631-451-6955 Fax: 631-451-6677
Web site: www.brookhaven.org

Town Supervisor:
  John Jay LaValle 631-451-6955
Deputy Town Clerk/Registrar:
  Lauri Murray 631-451-9101/fax: 631-451-9264
Town Attorney:
  Karen M Wilutis 631-451-6500/fax: 631-698-4489
Commissioner of Finance:
  Leonard Bernard. 631-451-6680
Commissioner, Public Safety:
  Richard Friscia. 631-451-6291/fax: 631-451-6908
Receiver of Taxes:
  George A Davis 631-451-9009/fax: 631-451-9008

Buffalo, City of
City Hall
65 Niagara Square
Buffalo, NY 14202

Offices and agencies appear in alphabetical order.

716-851-4200 Fax: 716-851-4360
Web site: www.ch.ci.buffalo.ny.us

Mayor:
Anthony M Masiello. 716-851-4841
e-mail: amasiello@city-buffalo.com
Executive Assistant to the Mayor:
Eva M Hassett. 716-851-4841
Council President:
David Franczyk 716-851-4138
e-mail: dfranczy@city-buffalo.com
City Clerk:
Gerald Chwalinski 716-851-5431
e-mail: gchwalinski@city-buffalo.com
Corporation Counsel:
Michael B Risman 716-851-4343
e-mail: mrisman@city-buffalo.com
Comptroller:
Andrew A San Filippo. 716-851-5255/fax: 716-851-4031
e-mail: asanfilippo@city-buffalo.com
Commissioner, Administration & Finance:
James B Milroy. 716-851-5722
e-mail: jmilroy@city-buffalo.com
Commissioner, Police:
Rocco J Diina 716-851-4571
Commissioner, Public Works:
Joseph N Giambra 716-851-5636
Commissioner, Human Resources:
Leonard A Matarese. 716-851-4095
e-mail: lmatarese@city-buffalo.com

Carmel, Town of
60 McAlpin Ave
Mahopac, NY 10541
845-628-1500 Fax: 845-628-7434
Web site: www.carmelny.org

Town Supervisor:
Robert Pozzi .845-628-1470/fax: 845-628-6836
Town Clerk:
Constance Munday. 845-628-1500
Town Counsel:
Servino, Santangelo & Randazzo LLP . . 845-328-5590/fax: 845-328-5591
Comptroller:
Tom Carey. 845-628-1500/fax: 845-628-7085
Police Chief:
Michael Johnson 845-628-1300/fax: 845-628-2597
e-mail: polcapt@bestweb.net

Cheektowaga, Town of
Town Hall
3301 Broadway
Cheektowaga, NY 14227
716-686-3465 Fax: 716-686-3551
Web site: www.tocny.org

Town Supervisor:
Dennis H Gabryszak. 716-686-3465
e-mail: dgabryszak@tocny.org
Town Clerk:
Mary F Holtz 716-686-3434
e-mail: mholtz@tocny.org
Town Attorney:
Michael J Stachowski 716-686-3457/fax: 716-686-3997
e-mail: mstachowski@tocny.org

Director, Administration & Finance:
Brian Krause. 716-686-3492
e-mail: bkrause@tocny.org
Police Chief:
Christine M Ziemba. 716-686-3500/fax: 716-686-3935
e-mail: cziemba@tocny.org

Chili, Town of
3333 Chili Avenue
Rochester, NY 14624
585-889-3550 Fax: 585-889-8710
e-mail: info@townofchili.org
Web site: www.townofchili.org

Town Supervisor:
Tracy L Logel 585-889-3550 x210
e-mail: tlogel@townofchili.org
Deputy Town Supervisor:
Richard J Brongo. 585-889-3550 x125
e-mail: rbrongo@townofchili.org
Comptroller:
Dianne O'Meara 585-889-3550 x120
Town Attorney:
Richard Stowe 585-352-1831/fax: 585-352-1387
Commissioner, Public Works:
Joe Carr. 585-889-2630

Cicero, Town of
8236 S Main St
PO Box 1517
Cicero, NY 13039
315-699-1414 Fax: 315-699-0039
Web site: www.ciceronewyork.net

Town Supervisor:
Chet Dudzinski. 315-699-1414
e-mail: supervisor@cynmail.com
Town Clerk:
Tracy M Cosilmon. 315-699-8109/fax: 315-699-0039
e-mail: clerk@cynmail.com
Comptroller:
Shirlie Stuart. 315-699-2759
Police Chief:
Joseph F Snell Jr 315-699-3677/fax: 315-699-8128

Clarkstown, Town of
10 Maple Ave
New City, NY 10956
845-639-2050 Fax: 845-639-2008
Web site: www.town.clarkstown.ny.us

Town Supervisor:
Alexander J Gromack. 845-639-2050
e-mail: a_gromack@town.clarkstown.ny.us
Deputy Supervisor:
John Maloney 845-639-2049
Town Clerk:
Patricia Sheridan. 845-639-2010
e-mail: p_sheridan@town.clarkstown.ny.us
Town Attorney:
John Costa 845-639-2060/fax: 845-639-2189

Offices and agencies appear in alphabetical order.

Comptroller:
Edward Duer...............................845-639-2020
e-mail: e_duer@town.clarkstown.ny.us
Police Chief:
Peter Noonan..............................845-639-5800
e-mail: cpd@town.clarkstown.ny.us

Clay, Town of
4401 State Route 31
Clay, NY 13041
315-652-3800 Fax: 315-622-7259
Web site: www.townofclay.org

Town Supervisor:
Mark J Rupprecht..............................315-652-3800
e-mail: supervisor@townofclay.org
Town Clerk:
Vivian I Mason..............................315-652-3800
e-mail: vmason@townofclay.org
Town Attorney:
Robert M Germain..............................315-652-3800
e-mail: legal@townofclay.org
Commissioner of Finance:
John Shehadi..............................315-652-3800
Commissioner, Public Safety:
Owen P Honors..............................315-652-3848
e-mail: police@townofclay.org

Clifton Park, Town of
1 Town Hall Plaza
Clifton Park, NY 12065
518-371-6651 Fax: 518-371-1136
Web site: www.cliftonpark.org

Town Supervisor:
Philip Barrett..............................518-371-6651x240
e-mail: pbarrett@cliftonpark.org
Town Administrator:
Michael Shahen..............................518-371-6651 ext243
e-mail: administrator@cliftonpark.org
Town Clerk:
Patricia O'Donnell.................518-371-6681/fax: 518-383-5088
e-mail: townclerk@cliftonpark.org
Town Attorney:
James Trainor.................518-371-6651/fax: 518-371-1136
Comptroller:
Mark Heggen.................518-371-6651/fax: 518-371-1136
e-mail: comptroller@cliftonpark.org

Cohoes, City of
97 Mohawk St
Cohoes, NY 12047
518-233-2121 Fax: 518-537-0072
e-mail: mail@ci.cohoes.ny.us
Web site: www.cohoes.com

Mayor:
John T McDonald, III..............................518-233-2119
City Clerk:
Lori A Yando..............................518-233-2141
e-mail: cityclerk@ci.cohoes.ny.us
Council President:
April A Kennedy..............................518-237-4475
e-mail: akennedy@ci.cohoes.ny.us

Corporation Counsel:
Darrin Derosia..............................518-233-2114
Comptroller:
Michael Durocher..............................518-233-2124
e-mail: comptroller@ci.cohoes.ny.us
Director, Community & Economic Development:
Edward Tremblay..............................518-233-2117
Police Chief:
Bill Heslin..............................518-237-5333
e-mail: wheslin@ci.cohoes.ny.us
Treasurer:
Adam Hotaling..............................518-233-2111
e-mail: ahotaling@ci.cohoes.ny.us

Colonie, Town of
Colonie Memorial Town Hall
534 Loudon Rd
Newtonville, NY 12128
518-783-2700 Fax: 518-782-2360
Web site: www.colonie.org

Town Supervisor:
Mary Brizzell..............................518-783-2728
e-mail: brizzellm@colonie.org
Town Clerk:
Elizabeth A DelTorto...............518-783-2734/fax: 518-786-6525
e-mail: deltortoe@colonie.org
Town Attorney:
Arnis Zilgme.................518-783-2704/fax: 518-786-7324
e-mail: attorney@colonie.org
Comptroller:
Ron Caponera.................518-783-2709/fax: 518-783-2877
Police Chief:
Steven H Heider.................518-783-2800/fax: 518-786-7326

Cortland, City of
City Hall
25 Court St
Cortland, NY 13045
607-753-0872 Fax: 607-753-0385
Web site: www.cortland.org

Mayor:
Tom Gallagher..............................607-753-0872
e-mail: mayor@cortland.org
City Clerk:
John O Reagan.................607-756-6521/fax: 607-756-4644
e-mail: cityclerk@cortland.org
City Attorney:
Lawrence Knickerbocker..............................607-753-0872
Director, Administration & Finance:
Andrew Damiano..............................607-756-7312
e-mail: finance@cortland.org
Chief of Police:
James C Nichols.................607-753-3001/fax: 607-758-3658
e-mail: jnichols@cortland.org

Cortlandt, Town of
1 Heady St
Cortlandt Manor, NY 10567-1224
914-734-1002 Fax: 914-734-1025
e-mail: townhall@peekskillcortlandt.com
Web site: www.townofcortlandt.com

Offices and agencies appear in alphabetical order.

Town Supervisor:
Linda D Puglisi 914-734-1002/fax: 914-734-1003
Town Clerk:
Jo-Ann Dyckman. 914-734-1020/fax: 914-734-1102
e-mail: joannd@townofcortlandt.com
Town Attorney:
Thomas Wood 914-736-0930/fax: 914-736-9082
Comptroller:
Glenn Cestaro 914-734-1071/fax: 914-734-1077
e-mail: glennc@townofcortlandt.com

DeWitt, Town of
5400 Butternut Drive
East Syracuse, NY 13057-8509
315-446-3428 Fax: 315-449-0620
Web site: www.townofdewitt.com

Town Supervisor:
James G DiStefano 315-446-3428/fax: 315-449-2065
e-mail: supervisor@townofdewitt.com
Town Clerk:
Barbara K Klim 315-446-3826/fax: 315-446-3912
e-mail: bklim@townofdewitt.com
Town Attorney:
Gregory Scicchitano 315-428-8344/fax: 315-475-8230
Police Chief:
Eugene J Conway 315-449-3640/fax: 315-449-3644
e-mail: police@townofdewitt.com
Comptroller:
John A Curulla. 315-446-3392/fax: 315-449-2065
e-mail: comptroller@townofdewitt.com

Eastchester, Town of
Town Hall
40 Mill Rd
Eastchester, NY 10709
914-771-3300 Fax: 914-771-3366
Web site: www.eastchester.org

Town Supervisor:
Anthony S Colavita 914-771-3304
e-mail: supervisor@eastchester.org
Town Clerk:
Linda Doherty 914-771-3351/fax: 914-771-3366
e-mail: townclerk@eastchester.org
Town Attorney:
John A Sarcone III. 914-771-3325/fax: 914-771-3367
e-mail: legal@eastchester.org
Comptroller:
Ann Marie Berg. 914-771-3330/fax: 914-771-9409
e-mail: comptroller@eastchester.org
Police Chief:
David Speidell 914-961-3464
e-mail: police@eastchester.org

Elmira, City of
City Hall
317 E Church St
Elmira, NY 14901
607-737-5644 Fax: 607-737-5824
e-mail: cityhall@ci.elmira.ny.us
Web site: www.ci.elmira.ny.us

Mayor:
Stephen M Hughes 607-737-5644
City Manager:
Samuel F Iraci, Jr 607-737-5644
City Clerk:
Angela J Williams 607-737-5673/fax: 607-737-5783
e-mail: cityclerk@ci.elmira.ny.us
Corporation Counsel:
John Ryan. 607-737-5674
Chamberlain:
Joy J Bates. 607-737-5661/fax: 607-737-5783
Police Chief:
W Scott Drake III 607-735-8600

Freeport, Village of
46 North Ocean Ave
Freeport, NY 11520
516-377-2200 Fax: 516-377-2323
e-mail: freeportmail1@freeportny.gov
Web site: www.freeportny.com

Village Mayor:
William F Glacken 516-377-2252
Village Clerk:
Anna Knoeller 516-377-2300
e-mail: aknoeller@vil.freeport.ny.us
Village Attorney:
Harrison J Edwards 516-377-2249/fax: 516-377-2366
Treasurer:
Vilma I Lancaster. 516-377-2260
Chief of Police:
Michael Woodward 516-378-0700

Garden City, Village of
351 Stewart Ave
Garden City, NY 11530
516-465-4000 Fax: 516-742-5223
Web site: www.gardencityny.net

Mayor:
Barbara K Miller. 516-465-4051
Administrator & Treasurer:
Robert L Schoelle, Jr 516-465-4000
Village Clerk:
Brian Ridgway 516-465-4053
e-mail: bridgeway@gardencityny.net
Police Commissioner:
Ernest J Cipullo 516-465-4100

Gates, Town of
1605 Buffalo Rd
Rochester, NY 14624
585-247-6100 Fax: 585-247-0017
Web site: www.townofgates.org

Town Supervisor:
Ralph J Esposito 585-247-6100
Town Clerk:
Richard A Warner. 585-247-6100
e-mail: rwarner@townofgates.org
Town Attorney:
John DiCaro 585-247-6100
Finance Director:
Christopher Russo 585-247-6100

State & Local
Government
Public Information

Offices and agencies appear in alphabetical order.

419

Police Chief:
Thomas J Roche 585-247-2262
Director, Building & Public Works:
John Lathrop 585-247-6100 ext241

Glen Cove, City of
9 Glen St
Glen Cove, NY 11542
516-676-2000 Fax: 516-676-0108
Web site: www.glencove-li.com

Mayor:
Mary Ann Holzkamp 516-676-2000
City Clerk:
Carolyn Willson 516-676-3345
e-mail: cwillson@cityofglencove.ny.org
City Attorney:
Dan Deegan 516-676-2000
Controller:
Joseph Gill 516-676-2000

Glens Falls, City of
42 Ridge St
Glens Falls, NY 12801
518-761-3800 Fax: 518-743-0663
Web site: www.cityofglensfalls.com

Mayor:
Robert A Regan 518-761-3804/fax: 518-761-0234
e-mail: gfmayor@cityofglensfalls.com
City Clerk:
Robert Curtis 518-761-3801
e-mail: gfclerk@cityofglensfalls.com
Controller:
Bruce Crouser 518-761-3809/fax: 518-761-3859
City Engineer:
G David Knowles 518-761-3834/fax: 518-761-3874
e-mail: engineer@cityofglensfalls.com
Fire Chief:
Ron Coteald 518-761-3822/fax: 518-761-3824
e-mail: gffire@capital.net
Chief of Police:
Richard P Carey 518-761-3840/fax: 518-798-4345
e-mail: rcarey@glensfallspd.com

Glenville, Town of
18 Glenridge Rd
Glenville, NY 12302
518-688-1200 Fax: 518-384-0140
Web site: www.townofglenville.org

Town Supervisor:
Clarence W Mosher 518-688-1201
e-mail: cmosher@townofglenville.org
Town Clerk:
Linda Neals 518-688-1200x402
e-mail: lneals@townofglenville.org
Town Attorney:
Arkley L Mastro 518-690-7000
Town Planner:
Kevin Corcoran 518-688-1200x407
e-mail: kcorcoran@townofglenville.org

Comptroller:
George W Phillips 518-688-1200/fax: 518-384-0140
e-mail: gphillips@townofglenville.org
Highway Superintendent & Commissioner, Public Works:
Andimo A Coppola 518-382-1406/fax: 518-382-3015
e-mail: acoppola@townofglenville.org
Director, Human Services:
Jamie MacFarland 518-688-1221
e-mail: jmacfarland@townofglenville.org
Police Chief:
Daniel B Boyle 518-384-3444/fax: 518-384-0141
e-mail: jpaparella@townofglenville.org

Greece, Town of
1 Vince Tofany Blvd
Greece, NY 14612-5016
585-225-2000 Fax: 585-723-2459
Web site: www.townofgreece.org

Town Supervisor:
John T Auberger 585-723-2311
Deputy Town Supervisor:
Vacant 585-581-6320
Director, Constituent Services:
Kathryn J Firkins 585-723-2361
Town Clerk:
Patricia Anthony 585-723-2341
e-mail: panthony@townofgreece.ny.gov
Town Attorney:
Ray DiRaddo 585-723-2331
Director, Finance:
Rick Pellegrino 585-723-2335
Police Chief:
Merritt Rahn 585-865-9200
Acting Town Assessor:
Mike Bonanza 585-723-2308

Greenburgh, Town of
Town Hall, 177 Hillside Avenue
Greenburgh, NY 10607
Web site: www.greenburghny.com

Town Supervisor:
Paul J Feiner 914-993-1540/fax: 914-993-1541
e-mail: pfeiner@greenburgh.com
Town Clerk:
Alfreda Williams 914-993-1500/fax: 914-993-1626
e-mail: townclk@greenburgh.com
Interim Town Attorney:
Timothy Lewis 914-993-1546/fax: 914-993-1656
e-mail: legal@greenburgh.com
Comptroller:
James Heslop 914-993-1528/fax: 914-993-1647
e-mail: finance@greenburgh.com
Comsnr, Public Works:
Albert S Regula 914-993-1573/fax: 914-993-1554
e-mail: dpw@greenburgh.com
Chief of Police:
John A Kapica 914-682-5340/fax: 914-682-5342
e-mail: jkapica@greenburgh.com

Offices and agencies appear in alphabetical order.

Guilderland, Town of

Town Hall, Rte 20
PO Box 339
Guilderland, NY 12084
518-356-1980 Fax: 518-356-3955
Web site: www.guilderland.org

Town Supervisor:
  Kenneth Runion 518-356-1980
Town Clerk:
  Rosemary Centi 518-356-1980
  e-mail: centir@townofguilderland.org
Town Attorney:
  Richard Sherwood 518-356-1980
Comptroller:
  Jean Sterling 518-356-1980
Police Chief:
  James Murley 518-356-1980

Hamburg, Town of

6100 South Park Ave
Hamburg, NY 14075
716-649-6111 Fax: 716-649-4087
Web site: www.townofhamburgny.com

Town Supervisor:
  Patrick H Hoak 716-649-6111 x380
Town Clerk:
  Catherine A Rybczynski 716-649-6111 x360
  e-mail: townclerk@townofhamburg.ny.com
Town Attorney:
  Vincent J Sorrentino 716-649-6111 x370
Director, Finance:
  James Spute 716-649-6111 x383
Police Chief:
  Joseph Coggins 716-649-6111 x501

Harrison, Town/Village of

Alfred Sulla Municipal Bldg
1 Heineman Pl
Harrison, NY 10528
914-670-3000 Fax: 914-835-8067
Web site: www.townharrison.org

Supervisor/Mayor:
  Stephen Malfitano 914-670-3000 x3004
Town Clerk:
  Joan B Walsh. 914-670-3031/fax: 914-835-2009
Town Attorney:
  Frank Allegretti 914-670-3090 x3093
Village Attorney:
  Fred Castiglia. 914-670-3000 x3091
Comptroller:
  Maureen Mackenzie 914-670-3084

Haverstraw, Town of

1 Rosman Rd
Garnerville, NY 10923
845-429-2200 Fax: 845-429-4701
Web site: www.townofhaverstraw.us

Town Supervisor:
  Howard T Phillips, Jr 845-429-2200
Town Clerk:
  Josephine E Carella 845-429-2200
Town Attorney:
  William Stein 845-429-2200
Finance Director:
  Michael J Gamboli 845-429-2200
Police Chief:
  Charles B Miller 845-354-7800

Hempstead, Town of

Town Hall Plaza
1 Washington St
Hempstead, NY 11550
516-489-5000 Fax: 516-538-2908
Web site: www.townofhempstead.org; www.toh.li

Town Supervisor:
  Kate Murray 516-489-5000
Town Clerk:
  Mark A Bonilla. 516-489-5000
  e-mail: markbon@tohmail.org
Town Attorney:
  Joseph J Ra 516-489-5000
Comptroller:
  John Mastromarino. 516-489-5000
Director, Communications:
  Michael J Deery. 516-812-3310/fax: 516-481-3183

Hempstead, Village of

Village Hall, 99 Nichols Court
PO Box 32
Hempstead, NY 11550
516-489-3400 Fax: 516-489-4285
Web site: www.villageofhempstead.org

Mayor:
  James A Garner 516-489-3400
Village Clerk:
  Tanya L Ford. 516-489-3400 x201
  e-mail: clerk@villageofhempstead.org
Village Attorney:
  W Charles Robinson 212-286-0423/fax: 212-286-0450
Deputy Village Attorney:
  Donna Green 516-489-3400 x429
Chief of Police:
  James Russo 516-489-3400

Henrietta, Town of

475 Calkins Rd
PO Box 999
Henrietta, NY 14467
585-334-7700 Fax: 585-334-9667
Web site: www.townofhenrietta.org

Town Supervisor:
  James R Breese. 585-359-7001
Town Clerk:
  Patricia Shaffer. 585-359-7035
  e-mail: pshaffer@townofhenrietta.org
Town Attorney:
  Daniel J Mastrella. 585-232-8810

Offices and agencies appear in alphabetical order.

Director, Finance:
Paul Liess, Jr. 585-359-7020

Huntington, Town of
100 Main St
Huntington, NY 11743
631-351-3014 Fax: 631-424-7856
Web site: www.townhuntington.ny.us

Town Supervisor:
Frank P Petrone 631-351-3305
Town Clerk:
Jo-Ann Raia 631-351-3206/fax: 631-351-3205
e-mail: jraia@town.huntington.ny.us
Town Attorney:
John J Leo 631-351-3043/fax: 631-351-3032
Comptroller:
Kathleen Cannon 631-351-3038
Deputy Comptroller:
Joseph Ludwig 631-351-3318

Hyde Park, Town of
4383 Albany Post Rd
Hyde Park, NY 12538
845-229-5111
Web site: www.hydeparkny.us

Town Supervisor:
Yancy F McArthur 845-229-5111x7/fax: 845-229-0831
Town Clerk:
Carole A Clearwater 845-229-2511x5/fax: 845-229-7583
Town Attorney:
Scott Volkman 845-454-3250

Irondequoit, Town of
1280 Titus Ave
Rochester, NY 14617
585-467-8840 Fax: 585-467-2862
Web site: www.irondequoit.org

Town Supervisor:
David W Schantz 585-467-8840
Town Clerk:
Andrea Sevio 585-467-8840
e-mail: townclerk@irondequoit.org
Town Attorney:
Stacey Romeo 585-336-6053
Comptroller:
John Bovenzi 585-467-8840
Police Chief:
Richard Boyan 585-336-6000 x306

Islip, Town of
Town Hall
655 Main St
Islip, NY 11751
631-224-5500 Fax: 631-581-8424

Town Supervisor:
Pete McGowan 631-224-5500
Town Clerk:
Joan B Johnson 631-224-5490

Town Attorney:
Vincent Messina 631-224-5550/fax: 631-224-5573
Comptroller:
Douglas Celiberti 631-224-5575
Commissioner, Public Works:
John Petito 631-224-5611
Public Information:
Michele Remsen 631-224-5485/fax: 631-581-8424
Public Safety:
Martin Raber 631-224-5300
Director, Economic Development:
William G Mannix 631-224-5512

Ithaca, City of
City Hall
108 E Green St
Ithaca, NY 14850
607-274-6570 Fax: 607-272-7348
Web site: www.cityofithaca.org

Mayor:
Carolyn K Peterson 607-274-6501/fax: 607-274-6526
e-mail: asherman@cityofithaca.org
City Clerk:
Julie Conley Holcomb 607-274-6570/fax: 607-272-7348
e-mail: julieh@cityofithaca.org
City Attorney:
Martin A Luster 607-274-6504/fax: 607-274-6507
e-mail: dawnt@cityofithaca.org
Controller:
Steven P Thayer 607-274-6576
e-mail: carols@cityofithaca.org
Chief of Police:
Lauren E Signer 607-272-9973
e-mail: laurens@cityofithaca.org

Jamestown, City of
Municipal Bldg
200 E Third St
Jamestown, NY 14701
716-483-7612 Fax: 716-483-7771

Mayor:
Samuel Teresi 716-483-7600
City Clerk:
Shirley A Sanfilippo 716-483-7612
e-mail: clerk@cityofjamestownny.com
Corporation Counsel/Attorney:
Marilyn Fiore-Nieves 716-483-7540
Comptroller:
Joseph A Bellitto 716-483-7775
Treasurer:
James N Olson 716-483-7581
Police Chief:
William R Maclaughlin 716-483-7530

Kingston, City of
420 Broadway
Kingston, NY 12401
845-331-0080 Fax: 845-334-3904
e-mail: mayor@ci.kingston.ny.us
Web site: www.ci.kingston.ny.us

Offices and agencies appear in alphabetical order.

Mayor:
James M Sottile 845-331-0080
City Clerk:
Kathy Janeczek 845-334-3915/fax: 845-334-3918
e-mail: cityclerk@ci.kingston.ny.us
Corporation Counsel:
Daniel Heppner 845-334-3947/fax: 845-334-3959
e-mail: corpcounsel@ci.kingston.ny.us
Comptroller:
Penny M Radel 845-334-3935/fax: 845-334-3944
e-mail: comptroller@ci.kingston.ny.us
Chief of Police:
Gerald Keller . . . . 845-331-1671 or 845-331-2061
e-mail: police@ci.kingston.ny.us

Lackawanna, City of
714 Ridge Rd
Lackawanna, NY 14218
716-827-6464 Fax: 716-827-6665
Web site: www.ci.lackawanna.ny.us

Mayor:
Norman L Polanski, Jr. 716-827-6464/fax: 716-827-6678
e-mail: mayor@ci.lackawanna.ny.us
City Clerk:
Jacqueline A Caferro 716-827-6452/fax: 716-827-6453
e-mail: cityclerk@ci.lackawanna.ny.us
City Attorney:
Richard S Juda 716-827-6479/fax: 716-827-6480
e-mail: cityattorney@ci.lackawanna.ny.us
Director Administration/Finance:
Robert C Marciniak 716-827-6481/fax: 716-827-6482
e-mail: adminfin@ci.lackawanna.ny.us
Director Public Safety:
Richard Startek 716-827-6418
e-mail: publicsafety@ci.lackawanna.ny.us
Treasurer:
Joyce M Warthling 716-827-6471/fax: 716-827-6434
e-mail: citytreasurer@ci.lackawanna.ny.us

Lancaster, Town of
21 Central Ave
Lancaster, NY 14086
716-683-1610 Fax: 716-683-0512
e-mail: lookatus@lancasterny.com
Web site: www.erie.gov/lancaster/depts;
www.lancasterny.com

Town Supervisor:
Robert H Giza 716-683-1610
Town Clerk:
Johanna M Coleman . . . . 716-683-9028 or 716-683-1328
fax: 716-683-2094
e-mail: jcoleman@lancaster.ny.com
Town Attorney:
Richard J Sherwood 716-684-3342/fax: 716-681-7475
e-mail: townattorney@lancasterny.com
Director, Administration & Finance:
David J Brown 716-683-1610
Police Chief:
Gary Stoldt Jr. 716-683-2800/fax: 716-681-2352
Town Assessor:
Christine A Fusco 716-683-1311/fax: 716-681-7054

Lindenhurst, Village of
430 S Wellwood Ave
Lindenhurst, NY 11757
631-957-7500 Fax: 631-957-4605
e-mail: info@villageoflindenhurst.com
Web site: www.villageoflindenhurst.com

Village Mayor:
Thomas A Brennan 631-957-7500
Administrator/Clerk/Treasurer:
Shawn Cullinane 631-957-7504
Village Attorney:
Gerard Glass 631-321-1400/fax: 631-321-1491

Lockport, City of
Lockport Municipal Building
One Locks Plaza
Lockport, NY 14094
716-439-6665 Fax: 716-439-6668
Web site: www.elockport.com

Mayor:
Michael W Tucker 716-439-6665
City Clerk/Budget Director:
Richard P Mullaney 716-439-6676/fax: 716-439-6684
e-mail: cityclerk@clockport.com
Corporation Counsel:
John J Ottaviano 716-438-0488
Treasurer:
James W Ashcraft, Jr. 716-439-6744/fax: 716-439-6617
Police Chief:
Neil B Merritt 716-433-7700

Long Beach, City of
City Hall
1 West Chester St
Long Beach, NY 11561
516-431-1000 x201 Fax: 516-431-1389
e-mail: info@longbeachny.org
Web site: www.longbeachny.org

City Manager:
Charles T Theofan 516-431-1000 x201
Council President:
James P Hennessy 516-431-1000 x264
City Clerk:
Marcia Markowitz 516-431-1000 x314
City Attorney:
Carolyn Cairns Olson 516-431-1000 x255/fax: 516-431-1016
Comptroller:
Alice Schildkraut 516-431-1000 x298
Police Commissioner:
Thomas R Sofield, Sr 516-431-1800/fax: 516-431-1459
e-mail: lbpd@longbeachny.org

Mamaroneck, Town of
Town Center
740 W Boston Post Rd
Mamaroneck, NY 10543

Offices and agencies appear in alphabetical order.

914-381-7805 Fax: 914-381-7809
e-mail: townclerk@townofmamaroneck.org
Web site: www.townofmamaroneck.org

Town Supervisor:
Valerie Moore O'Keeffe............................914-381-7805
e-mail: townsupervisor@townofmamaroneck.org
Town Administrator:
Stephen Altieri.....................................914-381-7810
Town Clerk:
Patricia A DiCioccio 914-381-7870/fax: 914-381-7813
Comptroller:
Carmine DeLuca.....................................914-381-7850
Police Chief:
Richard Rivera.....................914-381-6100/fax: 914-381-7897
Town Counsel:
William Maker Jr 914-381-7815

Manlius, Town of
301 Brooklea Dr
Fayetteville, NY 13066
315-637-3521 Fax: 315-637-0713
e-mail: supervisor@townofmanlius.org
Web site: www.townofmanlius.org

Town Supervisor:
Henry Chapman....................315-637-3414/fax: 315-637-0713
Town Clerk:
Terry Sloan.......................................315-637-3521
e-mail: tcsloan@townofmanlius.org
Town Attorney:
Timothy A Frateschi 315-637-1465/fax: 315-637-9807
Police Chief:
Francis Marlowe...................................315-682-2212

Middletown, City of
City Hall
16 James St
Middletown, NY 10940
845-346-4100 Fax: 845-343-7439

Mayor:
Joseph M DeStefano................................845-346-4100
e-mail: jdestef@warwick.net
Common Council President:
Robert Moson......................................845-346-4166
Common Council Clerk/Registrar:
Charles Mitchell 845-346-4166/fax: 845-344-5428
City Attorney:
Alex Smith.......................845-346-4140/fax: 845-346-4146
Treasurer:
Michael Amodio 845-346-4150/fax: 845-343-1101
Comissioner, Public Works:
Jacob Tawil 845-343-3169/fax: 845-343-4104
Chief of Police:
Matthew Byrne 845-343-3151/fax: 845-343-2660
Fire Chief:
Ralph Parenti 845-343-4169

Monroe, Town of
11 Stage Road
Monroe, NY 10950

845-783-1900 Fax: 845-782-5597
Web site: www.monroeny.org

Town Supervisor:
Sandy Leonard.................................845-783-1900 x227
Town Clerk & Registrar:
Judith L Dise..................................845-783-1900 x221
e-mail: townclerk@monroeny.org
Town Attorney:
Kevin Dowd.......................................845-778-5442
Chief of Police:
Dominic Giudice Jr.................................845-782-8644
Tax Collector:
William Bollenbach.................................845-782-4459

Mount Pleasant, Town of
One Town Hall Plaza
Valhalla, NY 10595
914-742-2300 Fax: 914-769-3155
Web site: www.mtpleasant.americantowns.com

Town Supervisor:
Robert F Meehan 914-742-2300
e-mail: rmeehan@mtpleasantny.com
Town Clerk:
Patricia June Scova................................914-742-2312
e-mail: pscova@mtpleasantny.com
Town Attorney:
David C Dempsey.....................................914-742-2357
e-mail: ddempsey@mtpleasantny.com
Comptroller:
Tina Peretti.....................914-742-2360 or 914-742-2359
e-mail: tperetti@mtpleasantny.com
Police Chief:
Louis Alagno ....914-769-1998 or 914-769-1941
fax: 914-769-7199
e-mail: lalagno@mtpleasantny.com

Mount Vernon, City of
City Hall
1 Roosevelt Square
Mount Vernon, NY 10550
914-665-2300 Fax: 914-665-2496
Web site: www.ci.mount-vernon.ny.us

Mayor:
Ernest D Davis...................................914-665-2360/2361
e-mail: mayor@cmvny.com
Council President:
Karen Watts......................................914-665-2352
City Clerk:
Lisa A Copeland 914-665-2348/fax: 914-668-6044
Corporation Counsel:
Helen M Blackwood 914-665-2366/fax: 914-665-9142
Comptroller:
Maureen Walker....................................914-665-2312
Public Safety/Police Commissioner:
Bernice Kennedy 914-665-2500
Public Works Commissioner:
James Finch.......................................914-665-2334
Civil Defense, Director:
Peter W Sherrill 914-665-2390

Offices and agencies appear in alphabetical order.

New Rochelle, City of

City Hall
515 North Ave
New Rochelle, NY 10801
914-654-2000 Fax: 914-654-2174
Web site: www.newrochelleny.com

Mayor:
    Timothy C Idoni 914-654-2150/fax: 914-654-2357
    e-mail: tidoni@ci.new-rochelle.ny.us
City Manager:
    Charles B Strome III. 914-654-2145
    e-mail: cstrome@ci.new-rochelle.ny.us
City Clerk:
    Dorothy Allen. 914-654-2159
Corporation Counsel:
    Bernis Shapiro 914-654-2125
    e-mail: bshapiro@ci.new-rochelle.ny.us
Finance/Administrative Services Commissioner:
    Howard Rattner 914-654-2063
    e-mail: hrattner@ci.new-rochelle.ny.us
Public Works Commissioner:
    James W Maxwell 914-654-2129
    e-mail: jmaxwell@ci.new-rochelle.ny.us
Police Commissioner:
    Patrick J Carroll 914-654-2300
Fire Commissioner:
    Raymond Kiernan. 914-654-2211
    e-mail: rkiernan@ci.new-rochelle.ny.us

New Windsor, Town of

555 Union Avenue
New Windsor, NY 12553
845-565-8800 Fax: 845-563-4693
Web site: http://town.new-windsor.ny.us

Town Supervisor/Chief Fiscal Officer:
    George J Meyers. 845-563-4610
    e-mail: gmeyers@town.new-windsor.ny.us
Town Clerk:
    Deborah Green. 845-563-4611/fax: 845-563-4670
    e-mail: dgreen@town.new-windsor.ny.us
Town Attorney:
    Philip A Crotty 845-563-4630/fax: 845-563-4692
    e-mail: pcrotty@town.new-windsor.ny.us
Comptroller:
    Lawrence Reis 845-563-4626
Police Chief:
    Michael C Biasotti. 845-565-7000/fax: 845-563-4694

New York City

City Hall
New York, NY 10007
212-788-3000 Fax: 212-788-3247
Web site: www.nyc.gov; www.ci.nyc.ny.us

Mayor:
    Michael R Bloomberg . . . . 212-788-3000 or Fax: 212-788-2460
    fax: 212-791-9628
Deputy Mayor, Economic Development & Rebuilding:
    Daniel L Doctoroff. 212-788-3000
Deputy Mayor, Administration:
    Patricia E Harris 212-788-3000

Deputy Mayor, Legal Affairs:
    Carol A Robles-Roman 212-788-3000
Deputy Mayor, Operations:
    Marc V Shaw 212-788-3000
Deputy Mayor, Policy:
    Dennis M Walcott. 212-788-3000
Director, Communications:
    William T Cunningham 212-788-3000
Special Advisor, Governance & Strategic Planning:
    Ester Fuchs. 212-788-3000
Senior Advisor to Mayor:
    Shea Fink 212-788-3000
Chief of Staff:
    Peter J Madonia . . . . 212-788-2728 or 212-788-3000
    fax: 212-788-2460
Special Advisor to Mayor/Campaign Mgr:
    Kevin Sheekey 212-788-3000
Press Secretary:
    Edward Skyler 212-788-2958
City Clerk:
    Victor L Robles 212-669-8898

Aging, Dept for the, NYC . . . . fax: 212-442-1095 or

2 Lafayette St, 7th Fl, New York, NY 10007
212-442-1322 Fax: 212-442-1095 or
Web site: www.nyc.gov/aging

Commissioner:
    Edwin Mendez-Santiago 212-442-1100
    e-mail: emendez@aging.nyc.gov
First Deputy Commiss/General Counsel:
    Sally Renfro 212-442-1104
    e-mail: srenfro@aging.nyc.gov
Assistant Commissioner, Bureau of Emergency Planning, Health Promotions:
    Linda Whitaker 212-442-1099/fax: 212-442-1286
    e-mail: lwhitaker@aging.nyc.gov
Director, Public Affairs:
    Christopher Miller. 212-442-1111/fax: 212-676-0685
    e-mail: cmiller@aging.nyc.gov

Art Commission, NYC. . . . . fax: 212-788-3086

City Hall, 3rd Fl, New York, NY 10007
212-788-3071 Fax: 212-788-3086
Web site: www.nyc.gov/artcommission

Executive Director:
    Jackie Snyder 212-788-3071
    e-mail: jsnyder@cityhall.nyc.gov
Project Manager:
    Sara Lev 212-788-3071
Sculptor:
    Alice Aycock 212-788-3071
Painter:
    Byron Kim 212-788-3071
Mayor's Representative/VP:
    Nancy Rosen. 212-788-3071
Architect:
    LeAnn Shelton 212-788-3071
Director, Tour Programs:
    Joan H Bright 212-788-3071

Buildings, Department of, NYC . . . . fax: 212-566-3784

280 Broadway, 7th Fl, New York, NY 10007-1801
212-566-5000 or TTY: 212-566-4769 Fax: 212-566-3784
Web site: www.nyc.gov/buildings

Commissioner:
    Patricia J Lancaster 212-566-3111/fax: 212-566-3784
Deputy Commissioner, Admin/Technology:
    Mark Topping 212-566-3489/fax: 212-566-3865
Deputy Commissioner, Operations:
    Robert LiMandri 212-566-3103/fax: 212-566-3785

State & Local Government Public Information

Offices and agencies appear in alphabetical order.

Acting Dep Commissioner, Technical Affairs:
Fatma Amer. 212-566-3188/fax: 212-566-3796
General Counsel:
Phyllis Arnold 212-566-3291/fax: 212-566-3843
Executive Director, Investigations/Audits:
Leslie Torres. 212-442-2000/fax: 212-442-2072
Assistant Commissioner, Citywide Inspections:
Robert Iulo. 212-566-3364/fax: 212-566-3848

Campaign Finance Board, NYC. . . . . fax: 212-306-7143
40 Rector St, 7th Fl, New York, NY 10006
212-306-7100 Fax: 212-306-7143
e-mail: info@nyccfb.info
Web site: www.nyccfb.info
Chair:
Frederick A O Schwarz, Jr. 212-306-7100
Executive Director:
Nicole A Gordon 212-306-7110
Press Secretary:
Tanya Domi 212-306-7150

City Council, NYC. . . . . fax: 212-788-7207
City Hall, New York, NY 10007
212-788-7210 Fax: 212-788-7207
Web site: www.nyccouncil.info
Speaker:
Gifford Miller. 212-788-7210
e-mail: miller@council.nyc.ny.us
Majority Leader:
Joel Rivera 212-788-7069
Deputy Majority Leader:
Bill Perkins 212-788-7396
Minority Leader:
James S Oddo. 212-788-7158
Majority Whip:
Leroy G Comrie 212-788-7084

City Planning, Department of, NYC. . . . . fax: 212-720-3219
22 Reade St, Rm 2W, New York, NY 10007-1216
212-720-3300 Fax: 212-720-3219
Web site: www.ci.nyc.ny.us/html/dcp
Chair, Planning Commission & Director, Dept of City Planning:
Amanda M Burden 212-720-3200
Executive Director:
Richard Barth 212-720-3500
Director, Public Affairs:
Rachaele Raynoff. 212-720-3471
General Counsel:
David Karnovsky 212-720-3400

Citywide Administrative Services, Department of, NYC . . . . fax: 212-669-8992
Municipal Bldg, One Centre St, 17th Fl S, New York, NY 10007
212-669-7000 Fax: 212-669-8992
Web site: www.nyc.gov/dcas
Commissioner:
Martha K Hirst 212-669-7111
First Dep Commissioner/General Counsel:
Lewis S Finkelman 212-669-7771/fax: 212-669-7898
Communication Director:
Mark Daly 212-669-7140/fax: 212-669-4664
e-mail: mdaly@dcas.nyc.gov

Civil Service Commission, NYC. . . . . fax: 212-669-2727
One Centre St, Rm 2300 N, New York, NY 10007
212-669-2609 Fax: 212-669-2727
e-mail: commission@nyc.csc.nyc.gov
Web site: www.nyc.gov/html/csc

Chair:
Stanley K Schlein 212-669-2608
Director & General Counsel:
Norma Lopez 212-669-2608
Office Manager:
Evelyn Horowitz. 212-669-2608

Collective Bargaining, Office of, NYC. . . . . . . fax: 212-306-7167
40 Rector St, 7th Fl, New York, NY 10006
212-306-7160 Fax: 212-306-7167
e-mail: nyc-ocb@ocb.nyc.gov
Web site: www.ocb-nyc.org
Chair:
Marlene A Gold 212-306-7170
Deputy Chair, Disputes:
Susan Panepento 212-306-7190
General Counsel:
Steven C DeCosta. 212-306-7180
Director, Information:
Vacant 212-306-7179

Comptroller, NYC. . . . . fax: 212-669-8878
Municipal Bldg, One Centre St, Rm 530, New York, NY 10007
212-669-3500 Fax: 212-669-8878
Web site: www.comptroller.nyc.gov
Comptroller:
William C Thompson, Jr 212-669-3500
First Deputy Comptroller:
Gayle Horwitz 212-669-2357
Deputy Comptroller:
Greg Brooks 212-669-8493
Deputy Comptroller, External Relations:
Eduardo Castell 212-669-3858
Director, Intergovernmental Relations:
Fong Chan 212-669-8977/fax: 212-669-3192
Press Secretary:
Jeff Simmons 212-669-2636

Conflicts of Interest Board, NYC. . . . . fax: 212-442-1407
2 Lafayette St, Ste 1010, New York, NY 10007
212-442-1400 Fax: 212-442-1407
Web site: nyc.gov/html/conflicts
Executive Director:
Mark Davies 212-442-1400
e-mail: davies@coib.nyc.gov
Deputy Exec Director/Chief of Enforcement:
Joan R Salzman 212-442-1400
e-mail: salzman@coib.nyc.gov
General Counsel:
Wayne G Hawley 212-442-1400
e-mail: hawley@coib.nyc.gov
Director Management Info Systems:
Christopher Lall 212-442-3500
Director, Training/Education Unit:
Joel Rogers 212-442-3500

Consumer Affairs, Department of, NYC . . fax: 212-487-4197 or
42 Broadway, New York, NY 10004
212-487-4401 Fax: 212-487-4197 or
Web site: www.nyc.gov/html/dca
Commissioner:
Gretchen Dykstra 212-487-4401
Press Secretary:
Dina Improta. 212-487-4283

Correction, Board of, NYC . . . . fax: 212-788-7860
51 Chambers St, Room 923, New York, NY 10007
212-788-7840 Fax: 212-788-7860

Offices and agencies appear in alphabetical order.

Chair:
Hildy Simmons. 212-788-7840
e-mail: nycboc@earthlink.net
Executive Director:
Richard T Wolf. 212-788-7845

Correction, Department of, NYC. . . . . fax: 646-248-1219
60 Hudson St, 6th Fl, New York, NY 10013-4393
212-266-1000 Fax: 646-248-1219
Web site: www.nyc.gov/boldest
Commissioner:
Martin F Horn. 212-266-1212
Chief of Department:
Robert N Davoren. 212-266-1590
Senior Dep Commissioner:
John J Antonelli 212-266-1271
Deputy Commissioner, Public Information:
Thomas Antenen 212-266-1414/fax: 212-266-1597

Cultural Affairs, Department of, NYC . . . . . . fax: 212-643-7780
330 West 42nd St, 14th Fl, New York, NY 10036
212-643-7770 Fax: 212-643-7780
Web site: www.ci.nyc.ny.us/html/dcla
Commissioner:
Kate D Levin . . . . 212-643-2101 or 212-643-2102
Deputy Commissioner:
Margaret Morton 212-643-3924
Executive Secretary (Scheduling):
Doris Littlejohn 212-643-2106

Design & Construction, Dept of, NYC . . . . . . fax: 718-391-1608
30-30 Thomson Avenue, Long Island City, NY 11101
718-391-1000 Fax: 718-391-1608
Web site: www.nyc.gov/html/ddc
Commissioner:
David J Burney. 718-391-1000
Chief of Staff:
Rachel Laiserin. 718-391-1877
Assistant Commissioner, Public Affairs:
Matthew Monahan. 718-391-1640/fax: 718-391-1892
General Counsel:
David Varoli. 718-391-1721

Disabilities, Mayor's Office, for People with fax: 212-341-9843
100 Gold Street, 2nd Floor, New York, NY 10038
212-788-2830 or 212-788-2838 TTY Fax: 212-341-9843
Web site: www.nyc.gov/html/mopd
Executive Director:
Matthew P Sapolin 212-788-2830
Executive Assistant:
Asma Quddus. 212-788-2830

Economic Development Corp, NYC
110 William Street, New York, NY 10038
212-312-3600 or 888-692-0100
Web site: www.nycedc.com
President:
Andrew M Alper. 212-312-3500
Executive Assistant:
Justine Sullivan. 212-312-3500
Public Information Officer:
Michael Sherman 212-312-3804

Education, Dept of, NYC . . . . fax: 212-374-5588
52 Chambers St, New York, NY 10007
212-374-5110 Fax: 212-374-5588
Web site: www.nycenet.edu
Chancellor:
Joel I Klein 212-374-5110

Deputy Chancellor, Finance/Admin:
Kathleen Grimm 212-374-0209/fax: 212-374-5588
Deputy Chancellor, Operations/Planning:
Laverne Evans Srinivasan 212-374-5070
e-mail: lsrinivasan@nycboe.net
Deputy Chancellor, Teaching/Learning:
Carmen Farina 212-374-5115
Chief of Staff:
Maureen Hayes. 212-374-6467
Senior Counselor Education Policy/Youth Devel:
Michele Cahill 212-374-0210
Senior Superintendent, School Programs/Support Svcs:
Rose Albanese-DePinto. 212-374-5090/fax: 212-374-5598
e-mail: ralbane@nycboe.net
Chief Executive for Strategic Partnerships:
Caroline Kennedy 212-374-2874/fax: 212-374-5571
e-mail: ckenned@nycboe.net
General Counsel & Ofc of Legal Svcs:
Judy Nathan . . . . 212-374-2993 or 212-374-3439
fax: 212-374-5596
e-mail: jnathan@nycboe.net
Executive Director, Intergovernmental Affairs:
Stephen Allinger. . . . . 212-374-4946 or 518-449-2013
fax: 518-449-4937
e-mail: salling@nycboe.net
Communications & Media Relations:
Jerry Russo 212-374-5141/fax: 212-374-5584
e-mail: jrusso@nycboe.net

Educational Construction Fund, NYC . . . . . . fax: 718-752-8285
30-30 Thomson Ave, Rm 4012, Long Island City, NY 11101
718-472-8287 Fax: 718-752-8285
Web site: www.nycenet.edu/offices/ecf
Chair:
Joel I Klein. 212-374-0200
Executive Director:
Jamie A Smarr 212-374-5026
e-mail: jsmarr@nycboe.net
General Counsel to Chair:
Michael Best 212-374-0220/fax: 212-374-5588
e-mail: mbest2@nycboe.net
General Counsel:
James P Cullen 212-278-1565/fax: 212-278-1733
e-mail: jcullen@andersonkill.com
Director, Finance:
Juanita Rosillo 718-472-8285
e-mail: jrosillo@nycsca.org

Elections, Board of, NYC. . . . . fax: 212-487-5349
32 Broadway, 7th Fl, New York, NY 10004-1609
212-487-5300 or TDD 212-487-5496 Fax: 212-487-5349
Web site: www.vote.nyc.ny.us
President, Commissioners:
Frederic M Umane. 212-487-5300
e-mail: fumane@boe.nyc.ny.us
Executive Director:
John Ravitz. 212-487-5412
e-mail: webmail_ravitzj@boe.nyc.ny.us
Deputy Executive Director:
George Gonzalez 212-487-5403
e-mail: webmail_gonzalezg@boe.nyc.ny.us
Administrative Manager:
Pamela Perkins 212-487-5406
e-mail: webmail_perkinsp@boe.nyc.ny.us
Director, Public Affairs/Communications:
Christopher Riley 212-487-5404
e-mail: webmail_rileyc@boe.nyc.ny.us

Offices and agencies appear in alphabetical order.

Environmental Protection, Department of, NYC .... fax: 718-595-3525
59-17 Junction Blvd, 10th Fl, Flushing, NY 11373
718-595-6565 Fax: 718-595-3525
Web site: www.nyc.gov/html/dep
Commissioner:
Emily Lloyd 718-595-6565
e-mail: cward@dep.nyc.gov
First Dep Commissioner:
David Tweedy 718-595-6576
Chief of Staff:
Shauna Grob...................................... 718-595-3480
Director, Intergovernmental Relations:
Mark Lanaghan.................................. 718-595-3519

Equal Employment Practices Commission, NYC .... fax: 212-788-8652
40 Rector St, 14th Fl, New York, NY 10006
212-788-8646 Fax: 212-788-8652
Executive Director:
Abraham May, Jr 212-788-8646
e-mail: amay@eepc.nyc.gov
Deputy Director:
Eric Matusewitch 212-788-8573
e-mail: ematusewitch@eepc.nyc.gov
General Counsel:
Lisa Badner...................................... 212-788-8644

Film, Theatre & Broadcasting, Mayor's Office of, NYC fax: 212-307-6237
1697 Broadway, Ste 602, New York, NY 10019
212-489-6710 Fax: 212-307-6237
e-mail: info@film.nyc.gov
Web site: www.nyc.gov/html/film
Commissioner:
Katherine Oliver................................. 212-489-6710
Executive Assistant:
Vivian Cannon.............................. 212-489-6710 x214

Finance, Department of, NYC .... fax: 212-669-2275
One Centre St, Rm 500, 5th Fl, New York, NY 10007
212-669-4855 Fax: 212-669-2275
e-mail: starkm@finance.nyc.gov
Web site: www.nyc.gov/finance
Commissioner:
Martha E Stark 212-669-4855
First Deputy Commissioner:
Rochelle Patricof 212-669-2525
Assistant Commissioner, Communications/Customer Service:
Sam Miller..................... 212-669-4763/fax: 212-669-3945
Budget Director:
Pat Mattera-Russell 212-669-4472
Treasury Deputy Commissioner:
Robert Lee 212-669-4472

Fire Department, NYC .... fax: 718-999-1031
9 Metrotech Center, 8th Fl, Brooklyn, NY 11201
718-999-2000 Fax: 718-999-1031
Web site: www.nyc.gov/html/fdny
Commissioner:
Nicholas Scoppetta............................. 718-999-2004
First Deputy Commissioner:
Frank Cruthers................... 718-999-2000/fax: 718-999-2582
Chief of NYC Fire Department:
Peter E Hayden.................................. 718-999-2010
Deputy Commissioner, Administration:
Douglas White 718-999-2007
Deputy Commissioner, Technology & Support Services:
Milton Fischberger.............................. 718-999-2062

Deputy Commissioner, Intergovernmental Affairs:
Daniel Shacknai 718-999-2013
Deputy Commissioner, Legal:
Mylan Denerstein 718-999-2016
Deputy Commissioner, Office of Public Information:
Francis X Gribbon 718-999-2025
Chief of Operations:
Salvatore J Cassano 718-999-2000

Health & Hospitals Corporation, NYC...... fax: 212-788-3673
125 Worth St, Rm 514, New York, NY 10013
212-788-3339 Fax: 212-788-3673
Web site: www.nyc.gov/hhc
Acting President & CEO:
Alan D Aviles 212-788-3321
Senior VP, Corporate Planning/Community Health/Intergvt Relations:
LaRay Brown 212-788-3448
Senior VP, Operations:
Frank J Cirillo.................................. 212-788-3669
Senior VP, Medical & Professional Affairs:
Van Dunn 212-788-3648
Senior VP, Finance:
Marlene Zurach 212-788-3494
Acting General Counsel:
Richard A Levy 212-788-3300
Corporate Communications Director:
Kate McGrath.................................... 212-788-3386
e-mail: kate.mcgrath@nychhc.org

Health & Mental Hygiene, Dept of, NYC.... fax: 212-964-0472
125 Worth St, New York, NY 10013
212-788-5261 or 212-219-5520 Fax: 212-964-0472
Web site: www.nyc.gov/html/doh
Commissioner:
Thomas R Frieden 212-219-5400
Executive Deputy Commissioner, Mental Hygiene:
Lloyd Sederer................................... 212-219-5520
Special Assistant to the Commissioner:
Christina Chang 212-788-5259
e-mail: cchang@health,nyc.gov
Public Information Officer:
Sandra Mullin................................... 212-788-5290
e-mail: smullin@health.nyc.gov
Deputy Commissioner, Administrative Services:
Scottie Owings-Leaks............................ 212-788-5265
e-mail: swings-leaks@health.nyc.gov
Deputy Commissioner, Disease Control:
Isaac Weisfuse 212-788-4711
e-mail: iweisfuse@health.nyc.gov
Deputy Commissioner, Health Care Access/Improvement:
James L Capoziello.............................. 212-788-5354
e-mail: jcapoziello@health.nyc.gov
Deputy Commissioner, Epidemiology:
Lorna Thorpe 212-788-4478
Deputy Commissioner, Environmental Health:
Gregory Carmichael 212-788-4641
Deputy Commissioner, Health Promotion/Disease Prevention:
Mary Bassett.................................... 212-788-5318
Deputy Commissioner, Financial & Strategic Management:
Andrew Rein.................................... 212-788-5347
General Counsel, Health:
Wilfredo Lopez.................................. 212-788-5025
General Counsel, Mental Hygiene:
William Martin.................................. 212-788-4285

Homeless Services, Department of, NYC.... fax: 212-361-7950
33 Beaver St, 17th Fl, New York, NY 10004
212-361-8000 Fax: 212-361-7950
Web site: www.nyc.gov/dhs

Offices and agencies appear in alphabetical order.

Commissioner:
Linda Gibbs 212-361-8000
Chief of Staff:
Angeles Pai....................................... 212-361-8000
First Deputy Commissioner:
Fran Winter.. 212-361-8000
Associate Commissioner, Communication/External Affairs:
Jim Anderson 212-361-8000
Assistant Commissioner, Community Relations:
Robert Mascali 212-361-7900
General Counsel:
Clarke Bruno 212-361-8000
Deputy Commissioner, Prevention:
Carine Barometre 212-361-8000
Deputy Commissioner, Adult Services:
Mark Hurwitz...................................... 212-361-8000
Deputy Commissioner, Family Services:
Roger Newman 212-361-8000
Deputy Commissioner, Facility Maint/Development:
Robert Skallerup.................................. 212-361-8000

Housing Authority, NYC .... fax: 212-306-8888
250 Broadway, 12th Fl, New York, NY 10007
212-306-3000 Fax: 212-306-8888
Web site: www.nyc.gov/nycha
Chair:
Tino Hernandez 212-306-3434
General Manager:
Douglas Apple 212-306-3416
General Counsel:
Ricardo Morales................................... 212-776-5151
Chief of Staff:
Y. Stacey Cumberbatch 212-306-3423
Deputy General Mgr/Chief Information Officer:
Avi Duvdevani 212-306-8833
Deputy General Mgr, Capital Projects & Development:
Joseph Farro 212-306-8685
Deputy General Mgr, Finance:
Felix Lam 212-306-3770
Deputy General Mgr, Operations:
Robert Podmore 212-306-8874
Deputy General Mgr, Administration:
Natalie Y Rivers.................................. 212-306-8786
Deputy General Mgr, Policy Planning/Management:
Sherry Schuh 212-306-3302
Deputy General Mgr, Community Operations:
Hugh Spence....................................... 212-306-7038

Housing Preservation & Development, Dept of, NYC .. fax:
212-863-6302
100 Gold St, 5th Fl, New York, NY 10038
212-863-6100 Fax: 212-863-6302
Web site: www.nyc.gov/html/hpd
Commissioner:
Shaun Donovan 212-863-6100
Deputy Commissioner/General Counsel:
Matthew Shafit.................................... 212-863-8686
Deputy Commissioner, Ofc of Intergovernmental Affairs & Planning Svcs:
Joseph Rosenberg................................. 212-863-5241
Deputy Commissioner, Housing Operations:
Laurie LoPrimo 212-863-8570
Deputy Commissioner, Preservation Services:
Luiz Aragon 212-863-7001
Deputy Commissioner, Administration:
Bernard Schwarz 212-863-6610
Deputy Commissioner, Development:
Rafael Cestero 212-863-6400
Deputy Commissioner, Community Partnerships:
Kimberly D Hardy 212-863-5128

Assistant Commissioner, Public Affairs:
Carol Abrams...................... 212-863-5176/fax: 212-863-8071
Chief of Staff:
Laurel Blatchford 212-863-7982

Human Resources Administration, Dept of, NYC ...... fax:
212-331-6214
180 Water St, 17th Fl, New York, NY 10038
212-331-6000 Fax: 212-331-6214
Web site: www.nyc.gov/html/hra
Administrator/Commissioner:
Verna Eggleston.................................. 212-331-6000
e-mail: egglestonv@hra.nyc.gov
First Dep Commissioner:
Patricia M Smith.................................. 212-331-6230
Executive Deputy Commissioner, Medical Insurance/Commun Svcs
Administration:
Iris Jimenez-Hernandez 212-273-0001
Executive Deputy Commissioner, Finance Office:
Frank Donno....................................... 212-331-3980
Executive Deputy Commissioner, Policy & Program Development:
Jane Corbett 212-331-5500
Executive Deputy Commissioner, Agency Chief Contractor Officer:
Sandra Glaves-Morgan............................ 212-331-3434
Executive Deputy Commissioner, Family Independence Admin:
Seth Diamond..................................... 212-331-6180
Executive Deputy Commissioner, Program Reporting Analysis &
Accountability:
Swati Desai....................................... 212-331-6075
Executive Deputy Commissioner, Office of Staff Resources:
Jean Matthews 212-331-3333
Executive Deputy Commissioner, Customized Assistance Services:
Frank R Lipton.................................... 212-242-7245
Executive Deputy Commissioner, Audit Services/Organizational Analysis:
Holly E Brown 212-331-3978
Senior Exec Dep Commissioner, Operations & Administration:
Peter Peta 212-331-6170
Deputy Commissioner, HIV AIDS Services Administration:
Elsie del Campo 212-620-4644
Deputy Commissioner, General Support Services:
Ralph Permahos 212-274-5200
Deputy Commissioner, Office of Constituency & Community Affairs:
Burton Blaustein................... 212-331-4640 or 212-331-4641
Deputy Commissioner, Office of Domestic Violence & Emergency Intervent:
Cecile Noel....................................... 212-331-4500
Deputy Commissioner, Office of Revenue & Investigation:
Peter Jenik 212-274-4740
Deputy Commissioner, Management Information Systems:
Richard Siemer................... 718-510-8614 or 718-510-0614
General Counsel, Office of Legal Affairs:
Richard O'Halloran 212-331-6167
Acting Inspector General:
Benjamin Defibaugh............................... 212-331-3030
Chief of Staff:
David Hansell..................................... 212-331-6225
Press Secretary, Office of Marketing/Communications:
Bob McHugh 212-331-6200

Human Rights Commission on, NYC .... fax: 212-306-7595
40 Rector St, 10th Fl, New York, NY 10006
212-306-7450 Fax: 212-306-7595
Web site: www.nyc.gov/html/cchr
Chair & Commissioner:
Patricia L Gatling 212-306-7550
Deputy Commissioner, General Counsel:
Cliff Mulqueen 212-306-7741
Deputy Commissioner, Law Enforcement:
Avery S Mehlman.................................. 212-306-7764

Offices and agencies appear in alphabetical order.

State & Local Government Public Information

Deputy Commissioner, Public Affairs:
Lee Hudson. 212-306-7773
Director, Public Information:
Betsy Herzog 212-306-7530
Managing Attorney:
Lanny R Alexander. 212-306-7423

Information Technology & Telecommunications, Dept of, NYC . . . . fax: 212-788-8130
75 Park Place, 9th Fl, New York, NY 10007
212-788-6600 Fax: 212-788-8130
Web site: www.nyc.gov/html/doitt
Commissioner, Chief Information Officer:
Gino P Menchini. 212-788-6633
First Dep Commissioner, Strategic Technology Development:
Larry Knafo 212-788-6624
Deputy Commissioner, Data/Networking:
Peter Tighe 718-403-8301
General Counsel & Dep Commissioner, Legal/Franchise/PPT:
Agostino Cangemi. 212-788-6600/fax: 212-788-6528
Deputy Commissioner, Finance/Admin:
Margery Brown 212-788-6616

Intergovernmental Affairs Ofc, NYC Mayor's . . . . fax: 212-788-9711
City Hall, 2nd Fl, New York, NY 10007
212-788-2162 Fax: 212-788-9711
Director:
Haeda B Mihaltses 212-788-2162

Investigation, Department of, NYC . . . . fax: 212-825-2505
80 Maiden Lane, 18th Fl, New York, NY 10038
212-825-5900 Fax: 212-825-2505
Web site: www.nyc.gov/html/doi
Commissioner:
Rose Gill Hearn 212-825-5913
e-mail: rghearn@doi.nyc.gov
First Dep Commissioner:
Walter Arsenault. 212-825-5910
Deputy Commissioner, Investigations:
Daniel D Brownell 212-825-2147
Deputy Commissioner, Mgmt & Budget:
Jan English 212-825-5899
General Counsel:
Marjorie Landa. 212-825-2403
Public Information Officer:
Emily Gest 212-825-5931

Juvenile Justice, Department of, NYC . . . . . . fax: 212-431-4874
365 Broadway, 4th Fl, New York, NY 10013
212-925-7779 or TTY/TDD: 212-334-687 Fax: 212-431-4874
e-mail: nycdjj@djj.nyc.gov
Web site: www.nyc.gov/html/djj
Commissioner:
Neil Hernandez 212-925-7779 x254
Chief of Staff:
Andrew Miller. 212-925-7779 x253
Deputy Commissioner, Operations & Detention:
Thomas Tsotsoros 212-925-7779 x202
Deputy Commissioner, Administration & Policy:
Andrew A Gonzalez 212-925-7779 x294
General Counsel:
Herman Dawson. 212-925-7779 x211/fax: 646-274-7160
Director, Public Affairs:
Scott Trent. 212-925-7779 x205

Labor Relations, Office of, NYC . . . . fax: 212-306-7202
40 Rector St, 4th Fl, New York, NY 10006

212-306-7200 Fax: 212-306-7202
Web site: www.nyc.gov/html/olr
Commissioner:
James F Hanley 212-306-7210/fax: 212-306-7732
First Dep Commissioner:
Pamela S Silverblatt 212-306-7220/fax: 212-306-7202
General Counsel:
Deborah M Gaines. 212-306-7230/fax: 212-306-7223
Director, Employee Benefits Program:
Dorothy A Wolfe 212-306-7200
Director, Citywide Programs/Pre-Tax Benefits:
Georgette Gestely 212-306-7200/fax: 212-306-7376

Landmarks Preservation Commission, NYC fax: 212-669-7960
One Centre Street, 9th Fl North, New York, NY 10007
212-669-7700 Fax: 212-669-7960
Web site: www.nyc.gov/html/lpc/home.html
Chair:
Robert B Tierney 212-669-7700
e-mail: rtierney@lpc.nyc.gov
Public Information Officer/ 311 Liaison:
Doris Hernandez 212-669-7817/fax: 212-669-7818
e-mail: dhernandez@lpc.nyc.gov
Press Secretary:
Diane Jackier 212-669-7923

Law, Department of, NYC. . . . . fax: 212-788-0367
100 Church St, New York, NY 10007-2601
212-788-0303 Fax: 212-788-0367
Web site: www.nyc.gov/html/law
Corporation Counsel:
Michael A Cardozo. 212-788-0303
e-mail: mcardozo@law.nyc.gov
Managing Attorney:
G Foster Mills 212-788-0300/fax: 212-732-3097
e-mail: gmills@law.nyc.gov
Inspector General:
Clive I Morrick. . . . . .212-825-2409 or 212-825-2177
e-mail: cmorrick@doi.nyc.gov
Communications Director:
Kathleen O'Brien Ahlers. 212-788-0400/fax: 212-788-8716
e-mail: kahlers@law.nyc.gov

Legislative Affairs Office, NYC Mayor's City . . . . fax: 212-788-2647
253 Broadway, 14th Fl, New York, NY 10007
212-788-3678 Fax: 212-788-2647
e-mail: citylegislativeaffairs@cityhall.nyc.gov
Web site: www.ci.nyc.ny.us
Director:
Karen E Meara 212-788-3678

Legislative Affairs Office, NYC Mayor's State. . . . . fax: 518-462-5870
119 Washington Ave, Albany, NY 12210
518-447-5200 Fax: 518-462-5870
Director:
Anthony P Piscitelli 518-447-5200

Library, Brooklyn Public. . . . . .fax: 718-398-1595
Grand Army Plaza, Brooklyn, NY 11238
718-230-2100 Fax: 718-398-1595
Web site: www.brooklynpubliclibrary.org
Executive Director:
Ginnie Cooper 718-230-2403
e-mail: g.cooper@brooklynpubliclibrary.org
Deputy Exec Director:
Siobhan Reardon 718-230-2162
e-mail: s.reardon@brooklynpubliclibrary.org

Offices and agencies appear in alphabetical order.

Deputy Dir, Business/Admin:
  John Vitali 718-230-2407
  e-mail: j.vitali@brooklynpubliclibrary.org
President, BPL Foundation:
  Cindy Freidmutter 718-230-2158
  e-mail: c.freidmutter@brooklynpubliclibrary.org
Assistant Director, Public Service:
  Janet Kinney 718-230-2408
  e-mail: j.kinney@brooklynpubliclibrary.org
Director, Government Affairs:
  Steven Schechter 718-230-2091
  e-mail: s.schechter@brooklynpubliclibrary.org

Library, New York Public . . . . fax: 212-930-9299
  5th Ave & 42nd St, New York, NY 10018
  212-930-0051 Fax: 212-930-9299
  Web site: www.nypl.org
President & CEO:
  Paul LeClerc 212-930-0736
Senior VP, External Affairs:
  Catherine Carver Dunn 212-930-0611
Senior VP/Chief Administrative Officer:
  David Offensend 212-930-0600
Vice President, Development:
  Heather Lubov 212-930-0692
  e-mail: hlubov@nypl.org
Vice President & General Counsel:
  Robert J Vanni 212-930-0744
Vice President, Budget & Planning:
  Jeffrey Roth 212-592-7400
Manager Public Relations:
  Caroline Oyama 212-704-8643
Director, Government & Community Affairs:
  Catherine Dente 212-930-0051
Volunteer Coordinator:
  Maura Muller 212-930-0502

Library, Queens Borough Public . . . . fax: 718-291-8936
  89-11 Merrick Blvd, Jamaica, NY 11432
  718-990-0700 or TTY 718-990-0809 Fax: 718-291-8936
  Web site: www.queenslibrary.org
Interim Director:
  Thomas W Galante 718-990-0794
  e-mail: thomas.w.galante@queenslibrary.org
Deputy Director, Customer Services:
  Vacant 718-990-8677
Deputy Director, Planning/Organizational Development:
  Carol L Sheffer 718-990-0818
Director, Public Affairs & Communications:
  Joseph Catrambone 718-990-0830/fax: 718-291-2695

Loft Board, NYC . . . . fax: 212-788-7501
  100 Gold St, 2nd Fl, New York, NY 10007
  212-788-7610 Fax: 212-788-7501
  Web site: www.nyc.gov/loft
Chairperson:
  Marc Rauch 212-788-7610
Executive Director:
  Dianne E Dixon 212-788-7610

Management & Budget, Mayor's Office of, NYC . . . . fax: 212-788-6300
  75 Park Place, 8th Fl, New York, NY 10007
  212-788-5900 Fax: 212-788-6300
  Web site: www.nyc.gov/html/omb
Director:
  Mark Page 212-788-5900
First Deputy Director:
  Stuart Klein 212-788-5904

General Counsel:
  Marjorie Henning 212-788-5880
Deputy Director:
  P.V. Anatharam 212-788-5900
Deputy Director:
  Michael Dardia 212-788-5891

Medical Examiner, Office of Chief, NYC . . . fax: 212-447-2744
  520 First Ave, New York, NY 10016
  212-447-2030 Fax: 212-447-2744
  Web site: www.nyc.gov
Chief Medical Examiner:
  Charles S Hirsch 212-447-2034
Deputy Commissioner, Administration:
  Thomas Brondolo 212-447-2087
Director, Medicolegal Investigations:
  Barbara Butcher 212-447-2036
Director, Public Affairs:
  Ellen Borakove 212-447-2041/fax: 212-447-2755
General Counsel:
  Jody Lipton 212-447-8757

Parks & Recreation, Department of, NYC . . fax: 212-360-1345
  The Arsenal, Central Park, 830 Fifth Ave, New York, NY 10021
  212-360-1305 Fax: 212-360-1345
  e-mail: commissioner@parks.nyc.gov
  Web site: www.nyc.gov/parks
Commissioner:
  Adrian Benepe 212-360-1305
First Deputy Commissioner, Operations:
  Liam Kavanagh 212-360-1307
Deputy Commissioner, Capital Projects:
  Amy Freitag 718-760-6602
Deputy Commissioner, Public Programs:
  Kevin Jeffrey 212-360-1382
Deputy Commissioner, Management/Budget:
  Robert L Garafola 212-360-1302
Director, Public Information:
  Warner Johnston 212-360-1311/fax: 212-360-1333

Police Department, NYC . . . . fax: 646-610-5865
  One Police Plaza, New York, NY 10038
  646-610-5400 Fax: 646-610-5865
  Web site: www.nyc.gov/nypd
Police Commissioner:
  Raymond W Kelly 646-610-5410
Chief of Staff:
  Joseph P Wuensch 646-610-8534
First Dep Commissioner:
  George A Grasso 646-610-5420
Chief of Department:
  Joseph J Esposito 646-610-6710
Deputy Chief, Ofc of Dep Commissioner, Community Affairs:
  Joyce A Stephens 646-610-5323
Deputy Commissioner, Administration:
  Charles D DeRienzo 646-610-8541
Deputy Commissioner, Strategic Initiatives:
  Michael J Farrell 646-610-8534
Deputy Commissioner, Counter Terrorism:
  Michael Sheehan 646-610-6169
Deputy Commissioner, Intelligence:
  David Cohen 718-765-4305
Deputy Commissioner, Equal Employment Opportunity:
  Neldra M Zeigler 646-610-5330
Deputy Commissioner, Labor Relations:
  John P Beirne 646-610-5060
Deputy Commissioner, Trials:
  Simon P Gourdine 646-610-5424

Offices and agencies appear in alphabetical order.

Deputy Commissioner, Training:
James J Fyfe 212-477-9767
Deputy Commissioner, Legal Matters:
S Andrew Schaffer 646-610-5336
Deputy Commissioner, Management & Budget:
Edward J Allocco 646-610-6670
Deputy Commissioner, Operations:
Garry F McCarthy 646-610-6100
Deputy Commissioner, Technological Development:
V James Onalfo 646-610-6873
Deputy Commissioner, Public Information:
Paul J Browne 646-610-6700

Probation, Department of, NYC . . . . fax: 212-361-0686
33 Beaver St, New York, NY 10004
888-226-5395 or 212-232-0684 Fax: 212-361-0686
Web site: www.nyc.gov/probation
Commissioner:
Martin F Horn 212-361-8977
e-mail: mhorn@probation.nyc.gov
1st Deputy Commissioner:
Richard Levy 212-361-8970
e-mail: rlevy@probation.nyc.gov
Director, Public Info/Records Access:
Jack Ryan 212-232-0684
e-mail: jryan@probation.nyc.gov
Chief of Staff:
Judith LaPook 212-361-8973
General Counsel:
Florence Hutner 212-232-0700
Deputy Commissioner, Admin/Planning/Operations:
Frank Marchiano 212-361-8965
Deputy Commissioner, Family Court Services:
Patricia Brennan 212-232-0486
Deputy Commissioner/Chief Information Officer:
Kael S Goodman 212-361-8801

Public Advocate, Office of the . . . . fax: 212-669-4701
Municipal Bldg, One Centre St, 15th Fl North, New York, NY 10007
212-669-7200 Fax: 212-669-4701
Web site: www.pubadvocate.nyc.gov
Public Advocate:
Betsy Gotbaum 212-669-4102
e-mail: bgotbaum@pubadvocate.nyc.gov
Counsel:
Mary Mastropaolo 212-669-7200
Chief of Staff:
Scott Coccaro 212-669-7200
Director, Administration:
Elba Feliciano 212-669-7200
Ombudsman:
Jessica Burgos 212-669-7250
Executive Assistant:
Yoni Appelblum 212-669-4258

Records & Information Services, Dept of, NYC . . . . fax:
212-788-8614
31 Chambers St, Rm 305, New York, NY 10007
212-639-9675 or TTY: 212-788-8615 Fax: 212-788-8614
Web site: www.nyc.gov/html/records
Commissioner:
Brian G Andersson 212-788-8607
e-mail: bgandersson@records.nyc.gov
Deputy Commissioner:
Eileen M Flannelly 212-788-8610
Director, Administration:
Vickie Moore 212-788-8622
Director, Municipal Archives:
Leonora Gidlund 212-788-8585

Director, Municipal Records Management Division:
Pearl L Boatswain 212-788-8550
Director, City Hall Library:
Paul C Perkus 212-788-8596

Rent Guidelines Board, NYC . . . . fax: 212-385-2554
51 Chambers St, Ste 202, New York, NY 10007
212-385-2934 Fax: 212-385-2554
e-mail: ask@housingnyc.com
Web site: www.housingnyc.com
Chair:
Marvin Markus 212-385-2934
Executive Director:
Andrew McLaughlin 212-385-2934 x12
Public Information Officer:
Charmaine Frank 212-385-2934
Senior Research Associate:
Brian Hoberman 212-385-2934

Sanitation, Department of, NYC
125 Worth St, New York, NY 10013
e-mail: comroffc@dsny.nyc.gov
Web site: www.nyc.gov/sanitation
Commissioner:
John J Doherty 646-885-5020
Deputy Commissioner, of Public Info & Community Affairs:
Vito A Turso 646-885-5020/fax: 212-791-3386

Small Business Services, Department of, NYC . . . . fax:
212-618-8991 or
110 William St, 3rd Fl, New York, NY 10038
212-513-6300 Fax: 212-618-8991 or
Web site: www.nyc.gov/html/sbs
Commissioner:
Robert W Walsh 212-513-6350
First Deputy Commissioner:
Andrew Schwartz 212-513-6428
Deputy Commissioner, Div of Business Assistance:
Vacant 212-618-8840
Deputy Commissioner, Div of Neighborhood Development:
Mark Newhouse 212-618-8802
Deputy Commissioner, Workforce Development:
David Margalit 212-442-2249
General Counsel:
David Farber 212-442-2249
Chief of Staff, Special Counsel for Intergovernmental Affairs:
Carl Hum 212-618-8746
Assistant Commissioner, External Affairs & Community Relations:
Michael C Smith 212-513-6368
Assistant Commissioner, Finance & Administration:
Shaz Ali 212-618-8735
Assistant Commissioner, One Stop System:
Scott Zucker 212-442-2352
Assistant Commissioner, Workforce Development Policy:
Maria Buck 212-442-2160
Assistant Commissioner, Economic & Financial Opportunity:
Vacant 212-513-6437
Assistant Commissioner, Public-Private Partnerships:
Lisa Laudico 212-442-2210
Assistant Commissioner, Neighborhood Development:
George Glatter 212-513-6442
Assistant Commissioner, Contract Adminstration:
Jean Seltzer 212-442-2459

Sports Commission, NYC . . . . fax: 212-788-7514
2 Washington Street, 15th Floor, New York, NY 10004
877-692-7767 or 212-487-7120 Fax: 212-788-7514
Web site: www.nyc.gov/sports

Offices and agencies appear in alphabetical order.

Commissioner:
Kenneth J Podziba 212-487-5676
e-mail: kpodziba@cityhall.nyc.gov
Deputy Commissioner:
Andy Gould 212-487-5665

Standards & Appeals, Board of, NYC . . . . fax: 212-788-8769
40 Rector Street, 9th Floor, New York, NY 10006-1705
212-788-8500 Fax: 212-788-8769
e-mail: ppacific@dcas.nyc.gov
Web site: www.nyc.gov/html/bsa
Chair/Commissioner:
Meenakshi Srinivasan. 212-788-8547
Vice Chair:
Satish K Babbar 212-788-8454
Commissioner:
James Chin 212-788-8788
Commissioner:
Vacant 212-788-8603
Commissioner:
Joel A Miele 212-788-8661
Executive Director:
Pasquale Pacifico 212-788-8805
Deputy Director:
Roy E Starrin 212-788-8797
Counsel:
John Reisinger 212-788-0296
Application Desk Supervisor:
Alice Boone 212-788-8762
Senior Examiner:
Jed Weiss 212-788-8781

Tax Commission, NYC
Municipal Building, 1 Centre St, Rm 936, New York, NY 10007
212-669-4410
Web site: www.nyc.gov/html/taxcomm
President:
Glenn Newman. 212-669-4401
Director, Operations:
Myrna Hall. 212-669-4420/fax: 212-669-2003
Director, Information Technology:
Iftikhar Ahmad 212-669-2954
Director, Appraisal & Hearings:
Carlo Silvestri 212-669-4402
General Counsel:
Reed Schneider. 212-669-4407

Taxi & Limousine Commission, NYC . . . . fax: 212-676-1100
40 Rector St, New York, NY 10006
212-639-9675 Fax: 212-676-1100
Web site: www.nyc.gov/taxi
Commissioner/Chair:
Matthew W Daus 212-676-1003
Chief of Staff:
Ira Goldstein 212-676-1017/fax: 212-676-2002
Deputy Commissioner, Legal Affairs:
Charles Fraser. 212-676-1117
Deputy Commissioner, Licensing:
Barbara Schechter. . . . . 718-391-5667 or 718-391-5666
First Deputy Commissioner:
Andrew Salkin . . . . 212-676-1147 or 212-676-1148
Deputy Commissioner, Public Affairs:
Allan J Fromberg. 212-676-1013/fax: 212-676-1101
Deputy Commissioner of Financial Management & Administration:
Louis Tazzi. 212-676-1035

Transportation, Department of, NYC . . . . fax: 212-442-7007
40 Worth St, New York, NY 10013

212-676-0868 Fax: 212-442-7007
Web site: www.nyc.gov/dot
Commissioner:
Iris Weinshall. 212-676-0868/fax: 212-442-7007
General Counsel:
Phillip Damashek. 212-442-7739/fax: 212-442-7733
First Deputy Commissioner:
Judith Bergtraum 212-442-7042/fax: 212-442-5296

Veterans' Affairs, Mayor's Office of, NYC . . fax: 212-442-4170
346 Broadway, Rm 819, New York, NY 10013
212-442-4171 Fax: 212-442-4170
Web site: www.nyc.gov/veterans
Executive Director:
Clarice Joynes. 212-442-4171
Deputy Director:
Jim Fuchs 212-442-4171
Executive Asst:
Rashad Pitts 212-442-4171

Voter Assistance Commission (VAC), NYC . fax: 212-788-3298
100 Gold Street, 2nd Floor, New York, NY 10038-1605
212-788-8384 Fax: 212-788-3298
e-mail: access via web site
Web site: www.nyc.gov.html/vac
Chairman:
Jeffrey F Kraus 212-788-8384
Vice Chair:
Jane Kalmus 212-788-8384
Executive Director/Coordinator:
Onida Coward Mayers 212-788-8384
Office Manager:
Bibi N Yusuf. 212-788-8384

Water Finance Authority, Municipal, NYC . fax: 212-788-9197
75 Park Place, 6th Fl, New York, NY 10007
212-788-5889 Fax: 212-788-9197
Web site: www.nyc.gov/nyw
Executive Director:
Alan L Anders 212-788-5889
Director, Investor Relations:
Raymond J Orlando 212-788-5875

Youth & Community Development, Department of, NYC . . . . fax: 212-442-5998
156 William St, New York, NY 10038
212-442-5900 Fax: 212-442-5998
Web site: www.nyc.gov/dycd
Commissioner:
Jeanne B Mullgrav 212-442-6006
General Counsel:
Everett Hughes 212-442-5980
Chief of Staff:
Michael Ognibene 212-442-5989
Deputy Commissioner, Administration:
Regina Miller 212-442-8573
Deputy Commissioner, Community Development:
Suzanne M Lynn. 212-442-6015
Deputy Commissioner, Program Operations:
Janice Molnar 212-676-8216

New York City Boroughs

Bronx (Bronx County). fax: 718-590-3537
Executive Division, 851 Grand Concourse, Rm 301, Bronx, NY 10451
718-590-3500 Fax: 718-590-3537
e-mail: webmail@bronxbp.nyc.gov
Web site: http://bronxboropres.nyc.gov

Offices and agencies appear in alphabetical order.

Borough President:
    Adolfo Carrion, Jr 718-590-3557/fax: 718-590-3537
Deputy Borough President/Chief of Staff:
    Earl D Brown 718-590-3565
President of BOEDC:
    Rafael Salaberrios. 718-590-3549
Director, Communications:
    Eldin L Villafane 718-590-3508
Press Secretary:
    Anne Fenton 718-590-3543
General Counsel:
    Lee Llambelis 718-590-8555

Brooklyn (Kings County) . . . . fax: 718-802-3778
Borough Hall, 209 Joralemon St, Brooklyn, NY 11201
718-802-3900 Fax: 718-802-3778
Web site: www.brooklyn-usa.org
Borough President:
    Marty Markowitz 718-802-3700
    e-mail: askmarty@brooklynbp.nyc.gov
Deputy Borough President:
    Yvonne J Graham. 718-802-3842
Chief of Staff:
    Greg Atkins 718-802-3862
General Counsel:
    Fred Ariaga. 718-802-3757
Director, Communications:
    Vacant 718-802-3832

Manhattan (New York County) . . . . fax: 212-669-4900
Municipal Bldg, One Centre St, 19th Fl South, New York, NY 10007
212-669-8300 Fax: 212-669-4900
Web site: www.cvfieldsmbp.org
Borough President:
    C Virginia Fields 212-669-8155
    e-mail: bp@manhattanbp.org
Deputy Borough President:
    Barbara Baer. 212-669-8137
Chief of Staff:
    Luther A Smith 212-669-2527
Senior Exec Assistant:
    Maggie Peyton 212-669-2728
General Counsel:
    Denise A Outram 212-669-8157
Director, Communications:
    Daniel Willson 212-669-8139

Queens (Queens County) . . . . fax: 718-286-2876
Executive Division, 120-55 Queens Blvd, Kew Gardens, NY 11424
718-286-3000 or TTY: 718-286-2656 Fax: 718-286-2876
e-mail: info@queensbp.org
Web site: www.queensbp.org
Borough President:
    Helen M Marshall. 718-286-3000
Deputy Borough President:
    Karen Koslowitz. 718-286-2900
Chief of Staff:
    Alexandra Rosa 718-286-2970
General Counsel:
    Hugh Weinberg 718-286-2880
Public Information Officer:
    Daniel Andrews 718-286-2640

Staten Island (Richmond County) . . . . fax: 718-816-2026
Borough Hall, 10 Richmond Terrace, Staten Island, NY 10301
718-816-2000 Fax: 718-816-2026
Web site: www.statenislandusa.com
Borough President:
    James P Molinaro. 718-816-2200

Vacant
Executive Assistant:
    Edward Burke. 718-816-2231
Legal Counsel:
    John Zaccone 718-816-2056
Borough Commissioner:
    John Giaccio. 718-816-2387

Newburgh, City of
83 Broadway
Newburgh, NY 12550
845-569-7301 Fax: 845-569-7370
e-mail: info@mail.cityofnewburgh-ny.gov
Web site: www.newburgh-ny.com

Mayor:
    Nicholas J Valentine. 845-569-7301
Executive Director:
    Robert McKenna 845-569-9400/fax: 845-569-9700
City Clerk:
    Lorene Vitek 845-569-7311/fax: 845-569-7314
Corporation Counsel:
    Geoffrey Chanin 845-569-7335/fax: 845-569-7338
Comptroller:
    Dawn Gobeo 845-569-7320/fax: 845-569-7490
Chief of Police:
    Eric Paolilli 845-561-3131/fax: 845-565-5662

Newburgh, Town of
1496 Rte 300
Newburgh, NY 12550
845-564-4552 Fax: 845-566-1432
Web site: www.townofnewburgh-ny.gov

Town Supervisor:
    Wayne C Booth 845-564-4552
Town Clerk:
    Andrew J Zarutskie. 845-564-4554
    e-mail: ncityclerk@hvc.rr.com
Town Attorney:
    Mark Taylor. 845-562-9100/fax: 845-565-1999
Accountant:
    Jacqueline Calarco 845-564-5220
Police Chief:
    Charles Kehoe 845-565-1100

Niagara Falls, City of
City Hall, 745 Main St
PO Box 69
Niagara Falls, NY 14302-0069
716-286-4310 Fax: 716-286-4349
Web site: www.niagarafallsusa.org

Mayor:
    Vincenzo V Anello. 716-286-4310
City Administrator:
    Daniel S Bristol 716-286-4320
City Clerk:
    Carol Antonucci 716-286-4393
    e-mail: cantonucci@falls.niagara.ny.us
Corporate Counsel:
    Ronald D Anton. 716-286-4420/fax: 716-286-4424

Offices and agencies appear in alphabetical order.

Controller:
  Maria C Brown 716-286-4338

North Hempstead, Town of
220 Plandome Rd
PO Box 3000
Manhasset, NY 11030
516-627-0590 Fax: 516-627-4204
Web site: www.northhempstead.com

Town Supervisor:
  Jon Kaiman 516-869-7700
Town Clerk:
  Michelle Schimel 516-869-7646
  e-mail: schimelm@northhempstead.com
Town Attorney:
  Richard S Finkel 516-869-7600
Director, Operations:
  Chris Senior 516-869-7714
Commissioner, Public Works & Solid Waste Management Authority:
  Gil Anderson 516-739-6711
Commissioner, Finance:
  Helene Raps-Beckerman 516-869-7741
Commissioner, Community Services:
  Madge Kaplan 516-869-7715

North Tonawanda, City of
City Hall
216 Payne Ave
North Tonawanda, NY 14120
716-695-8000 Fax: 716-695-8557
Web site: www.northtonawanda.org

Mayor:
  David J Burgio 716-695-8540/fax: 716-695-8541
Common Council President:
  Brett M Sommer 716-692-4798
City Clerk:
  Thomas M Jaccarino 716-695-8555
  e-mail: cityclerk@northtonawanda.org
City Attorney:
  Shawn P Nickerson 716-695-8590/fax: 716-695-8592
City Engineer:
  Dale W Marshall 716-695-8565/fax: 716-695-8568
Treasurer:
  Leslie J Stolzenfels 716-695-8575
Police Chief:
  Randy D Szukala 716-692-4111
Fire Chief:
  Gregory R Frank 716-693-2201

Olean, City of
Olean Municipal Bldg, 101 E State St
PO Box 668
Olean, NY 14760
716-376-5604 Fax: 716-376-4906
Web site: www.cityofolean.com

Mayor:
  William J Quinlan 716-376-5615
City Clerk/Treasurer:
  Stephen Piechota 716-376-5604
  e-mail: spiechota@cityofolean.org

Chief Fiscal Officer/Auditor:
  Steven Pachla 716-376-5613
Superintendent of Public Works:
  Robert Ring 716-376-5650
Fire Chief:
  Robert Bell 716-376-5687
Chief of Police:
  Brian Donnelly 716-376-5677
City Attorney:
  M Mark Howden 716-376-5682

Orangetown, Town of
26 Orangeburg Rd
Orangeburg, NY 10962
845-359-5100 Fax: 845-359-5126
Web site: www.orangetown.com

Town Supervisor:
  Thom Kleiner 845-359-5100
Town Clerk:
  Charlotte E Madigan 845-359-5100 x263
Town Attorney:
  Teresa Kenny 845-359-5100/fax: 845-359-2715
Director, Finance:
  Charles Richardson 845-359-5100
Police Chief:
  Kevin A Nulty 845-359-3700

Orchard Park, Town of
4295 S Buffalo St
Orchard Park, NY 14127
716-662-6410 Fax: 716-662-6413
e-mail: cdarussoj@orchardparkny.org
Web site: www.orchardparkny.org

Town Supervisor:
  Toni M Cudney 716-662-6400
  e-mail: opsupervisor@orchardparkny.org
Town Clerk:
  Janis A Colarusso 716-662-6410
  e-mail: colarussoj@orchardpark.ny.org
Town Attorney:
  Leonard Berkowitz 716-662-9808/fax: 716-662-9546
Town Auditor:
  Thomas Malecki 716-843-7200
Police Chief:
  Samuel McCune 716-662-6470

Ossining, Town of
16 Croton Ave
Ossining, NY 10562
914-762-6000 Fax: 914-762-7710
Web site: www.townofossining.com

Town Supervisor:
  John Chervokas 914-762-6000
Town Clerk:
  Mary Ann Roberts 914-762-8428
  e-mail: townclerk@townofossining.com
Deputy Town Attorney:
  Joseph Milano 914-923-3255/fax: 914-923-3221
Auditor:
  Bennett Kileson 914-421-5600

Offices and agencies appear in alphabetical order.

Police Chief:
Kenneth Donato 914-762-6007

Oswego, City of
13 W Oneida St
Oswego, NY 13126
315-342-8116 Fax: 315-342-8100
Web site: www.oswegony.org

Mayor:
John J Gosek 315-342-8136
City Clerk:
Jeanne Berlin 315-342-8116
e-mail: jberlin@oswegony.org
City Attorney:
Edward Izyk 315-342-0162
City Chamberlain:
Bruce Manwaring 315-342-8105
Director, Tourism:
Frederick Crisafulli 315-342-7245

Oyster Bay, Town of
Town Hall East
54 Audrey Ave
Oyster Bay, NY 11771
516-624-6498 Fax: 516-624-6387
Web site: www.oysterbaytown.com

Town Supervisor:
John Venditto 516-624-6350
Town Clerk:
Steven L Labriola 516-624-6333
Attorney:
Gregory J Giammalvo 516-624-6150
Comptroller:
Thomas D Galasso 516-624-6440

Penfield, Town of
3100 Atlantic Ave
Penfield, NY 14526
585-340-8600 Fax: 585-340-8667
Web site: www.penfield.org

Town Supervisor:
George C Wiedemer 585-340-8630
e-mail: supervisor@penfield.org
Town Clerk:
Cassie Williams 585-340-8629
e-mail: clerk@penfield.org
Town Attorney:
Richard Horwitz 585-264-0590
Town Comptroller:
Robert Beedon 585-340-8621

Perinton, Town of
1350 Turk Hill Rd
Fairport, NY 14450
585-223-0770 Fax: 585-223-3629
Web site: www.perinton.org

Town Supervisor:
James E Smith 585-223-0770
e-mail: jsmith@perinton.org
Town Clerk:
Susan Roberts 585-223-0770
e-mail: sroberts@perinton.org
Town Attorney:
Robert Place 585-425-1060/fax: 585-223-3252
Director, Finance:
Kevin Spacher 585-223-0770
e-mail: kspacher@perinton.org

Pittsford, Town of
11 S Main St
Pittsford, NY 14534
585-248-6200 Fax: 585-248-6247
Web site: www.townofpittsford.com

Town Supervisor:
William A Carpenter 585-248-6220
Town Clerk:
Patricia E Chuhta 585-248-6210
e-mail: pchuhta@townofpittford.com
Town Attorney:
Jared C Lusk 585-248-6216
Director, Finance:
Gregory J Duane 585-248-6225

Plattsburgh, City of
41 City Hall Place
Plattsburgh, NY 12901
518-563-7701 Fax: 518-561-7367
Web site: www.cityofplattsburgh.com

Mayor:
Daniel L Stewart 518-563-7701
City Clerk:
Keith A Herkalo 518-563-7702
City Chamberlain:
James Buran 518-563-7704
Director of Public Works:
Kevin Murphy 518-563-6841
Fire Chief:
James Squires 518-561-5965
Chief of Police:
Desmond Racicot 518-563-3416
City Attorney:
Lori Cantwell 518-563-4884

Port Chester, Village of
10 Pearl Street
Port Chester, NY 10573
914-939-5200 Fax: 914-937-3169
Web site: www.portchesterny.com

Mayor:
Gerald Logan 914-939-2200
Village Manager:
Richard A Falanka 914-939-2200
Village Clerk:
Anthony S Siligato 914-939-5202
Village Attorney:
Anthony M Cerreto 914-939-5208

Offices and agencies appear in alphabetical order.

Village Treasurer:
Anthony S Siligato 914-939-5205

Poughkeepsie, City of
Municipal Building
PO Box 300
Poughkeepsie, NY 12602
845-451-4200 Fax: 845-451-4239
Web site: www.cityofpoughkeepsie.com

Mayor:
Nancy Cozean. 845-451-4076
City Administrator:
James Marquette. 845-451-4072
City Chamberlain:
Felicia M Santos 845-451-4225/fax: 845-451-4239
e-mail: fsantos@cityofpoughkeepsie.com
Police Chief:
Ronald Knapp. 845-451-4132
City Attorney:
Stephen Wing 845-451-4065/fax: 914-451-4070

Poughkeepsie, Town of
One Overocker Rd
Poughkeepsie, NY 12603
845-485-3603 Fax: 845-485-8583
Web site: www.townofpoughkeepsie.com

Town Supervisor:
Joseph E Davis 845-485-3607
Town Clerk:
Susan Miller. 845-485-3620/fax: 845-485-8583
e-mail: smiller@townofpoughkeepsie.ny.gov
Town Attorney:
Thomas D Mahar, Jr 845-485-3633/fax: 845-486-7878
Comptroller:
Charles Emberger. 845-485-3610
Police Chief:
Peter Wilkinson 845-485-3660

Ramapo, Town of
Town Hall, 237 Route 59
Suffern, NY 10901
845-357-5100 Fax: 845-357-3877
e-mail: supervisor@ramapo.org
Web site: www.ramapo.org

Town Supervisor:
Christopher P St Lawrence. 845-357-5100
Town Clerk:
Christian G Sampson 845-357-5100 x263/fax: 845-357-8513
e-mail: townclerk@ramapo.org
Town Attorney:
Michael Klein 845-357-5100/fax: 845-357-2936
Director, Finance:
Ilan Schoenberger. 845-357-5100
Director, Public Works:
Ted Dzurinko 845-357-0591
Police Chief:
Edward Dolan. 845-357-2400

Rochester, City of
City Hall
30 Church St
Rochester, NY 14614
585-428-7000 Fax: 585-428-6059
Web site: www.ci.rochester.ny.us

Mayor:
William A Johnson, Jr 585-428-7045
Deputy Mayor:
Jeffrey Carlson 585-428-7163
Assistant to Mayor, Intergovernmental Affairs:
Richard Hannon. 585-428-7407/fax: 585-428-6651
City Clerk:
Carolee A Conklin 585-428-7431
e-mail: conklinc@cityofrochester.gov
Corporation Counsel:
Linda Kingsley 585-428-6986
City Treasurer:
Charles A Benincasa. 585-428-6705
City Assessor:
Thomas Huonker 585-428-6983
Commissioner, Community Development:
Linda Stango. 585-428-6550
Commissioner, Economic Development:
R Fashun Ku 585-428-6808
Commissioner, Environmental Services:
Edward J Doherty 585-428-6855
Commissioner, Parks, Recreation & Human Services:
Loretta Scott 585-428-6749
Police Chief:
Robert J Duffy 585-428-7033
Fire Chief:
Floyd A Madison 585-428-7485
Director, Emergency Communications:
John M Merklinger. 585-528-2222
Director, Finance:
Vincent Carfagna 585-428-7151
Director, Neighborhood Empowerment Team:
Rodrick Cox-Cooper 585-428-6524
Director, Zoning:
Margaret A Wuerstle 585-428-7435
Director, Public Information:
Bridgette Burch 585-428-7405

Rockville Centre, Village of
1 College Place
PO Box 950
Rockville Centre, NY 11571
516-678-9300 Fax: 516-678-9225
e-mail: rvc@li.net
Web site: www.ci.rockville-centre.ny.us

Village Mayor:
Eugene J Murray. 516-678-9260
Village Administrator:
Ron Wasson 516-678-9212
Village Clerk:
Carol Kramer 516-678-9263
Village Attorney:
Martha Krisel 516-678-9206

Offices and agencies appear in alphabetical order.

Rome, City of

City Hall
Liberty Plaza
Rome, NY 13440
315-336-6000 Fax: 315-339-7788
Web site: www.romenewyork.com

Mayor:
  James F Brown 315-339-7677
  e-mail: mayor@romecitygov.com
Common Council President:
  John J Mazzaferro 315-339-7659
City Clerk:
  Louse Glasso 315-339-7659
  e-mail: jreid@romecitygov.com
Corporation Counsel:
  Jame Rizzo 315-339-7670
Treasurer:
  John Nash 315-339-7678
Chief of Police:
  Otto Panara 315-339-7705

Rotterdam, Town of

1100 Sunrise Blvd
Rotterdam, NY 12306
518-355-7820 Fax: 518-355-7837
Web site: www.rotterdamny.org

Town Supervisor:
  John J Paolino 518-355-7575
Town Clerk:
  Eunice O Esposito 518-355-7820
Town Attorney:
  Andrew Brick 518-374-8494/fax: 518-374-5906
Comptroller:
  Patrick Aragosa 518-355-7575
Police Chief:
  James Hamilton 518-355-7739

Rye, Town of

10 Pearl St
Port Chester, NY 10573
914-939-3075 Fax: 914-939-0786
e-mail: ryetown@nysnet.net
Web site: www.townofryeny.com

Town Supervisor:
  Robert A Morabito 914-939-3075
Town Clerk:
  Frances C Nugent 914-939-3570
Town Attorney:
  Monroe Y Mann 914-939-3098
Comptroller:
  Joseph M Granchelli 914-939-3585

Salina, Town of

201 School Rd
Liverpool, NY 13088
315-457-6661 Fax: 315-457-4317
Web site: www.salina.ny.us

Town Supervisor:
  Mary Ann Schadt 315-457-6661
Town Clerk:
  Christopher J Shepherd 315-457-2710
  e-mail: cshepherd@salina.ny.us
Town Attorney:
  Steven Primo 315-452-2440/fax: 315-671-1550
Comptroller:
  Daniel Nolan 315-451-4210

Saratoga Springs, City of

City Hall
474 Broadway
Saratoga Springs, NY 12866
518-587-3550 Fax: 518-587-1688
Web site: www.saratoga-springs.org

Mayor:
  Michael Lenz 518-587-3550
City Clerk & Comsr of Accounts:
  Stephen E Towne 518-587-3550/fax: 518-587-6512
  e-mail: stephen.towne@saratogasprings.org
City Attorney:
  Matthew Dorsey 518-587-3550
Comsr, Finance:
  Matthew McCabe 518-587-3550/fax: 518-580-0781
Comsr, Public Safety:
  Thomas Curley 518-587-3550/fax: 518-587-1068
Comsr, Public Works:
  Thomas McTygue 518-587-3550/fax: 518-587-2417
Director, Community Development:
  Brad Birge 518-587-3550
  e-mail: bbirge@saratoga-springs.org
Chief of Police:
  Edward Moore 518-584-1800

Schenectady, City of

City Hall
105 Jay St
Schenectady, NY 12305
518-382-5000 Fax: 518-382-5272
Web site: www.cityofschenectady.com

Mayor:
  Brian U Stratton 518-382-5199 x5420
City Council President:
  Mark W Blanchfield 518-382-5089
City Clerk:
  Carolyn Friello 518-382-5199 x5302
  e-mail: cityclk1@nycap.rr.com
Corporation Counsel:
  Alfred L Goldberger 518-382-5073/fax: 518-382-5074
Finance Commissioner:
  John Paolino 518-382-5010
Director, Public Works:
  Vacant 518-382-5093
Chief of Police:
  Michael N Geraci Sr 518-382-5205

Smithtown, Town of

99 W Main St
PO Box 575
Smithtown, NY 11787

631-360-7600 Fax: 631-360-7668
Web site: www.smithtowninfo.com

Town Supervisor:
   Patrick R Vecchio. 631-360-7600
Town Clerk:
   Donna M Hill. 631-360-7620/fax: 631-360-7692
Town Attorney:
   Yvonne Lieffrig. 631-360-7570/fax: 631-360-7719
Comptroller:
   Anthony Minerva. 631-360-7530/fax: 631-360-7625

Southampton, Town of
116 Hampton Rd
Southampton, NY 11968
631-283-6000 Fax: 631-283-5606
Web site: www.town.southamptonny.us

Town Supervisor:
   Patrick (Skip) Heaney. 631-283-6055
Town Clerk:
   Marietta Seaman. 631-287-5740
   e-mail: mseanman@town.southhampton.ny.us
Town Attorney:
   Eileen Powers. 631-287-3065
Comptroller:
   Charlene Kagel. 631-283-6094
Highway Superintendent:
   William H Masterson. 631-728-3600
Police Chief:
   James Overton. 631-728-5000

Syracuse, City of
203 City Hall
233 East Washington St
Syracuse, NY 13202
315-448-8005 Fax: 315-448-8067
e-mail: mayor@ci.syracuse.ny.us
Web site: www.syracuse.ny.us

Mayor:
   Matthew J Driscoll. 315-448-8005
Common Cncl Pres:
   Beathaida Gonzalez. 315-448-8466/fax: 315-448-8423
City Clerk:
   John P Copanas. 315-448-8216/fax: 315-448-8489
   e-mail: jcopanas@ci.syracuse.ny.us
Corporation Counsel:
   Terri Bright. 315-448-8400/fax: 315-448-8381
Commissioner, Assessment:
   John Gamage. 315-448-8280/fax: 315-448-8190
Commissioner, Community Development:
   Fernando Ortiz, Jr. 315-448-8620/fax: 315-448-8659
Commissioner, Finance:
   Brian Roulin. 315-448-8310/fax: 315-448-8424
Commissioner, Public Works:
   James R Collins. 315-448-8515/fax: 315-448-8531
Director, Administration:
   Ken Mokrzycki. 315-448-8005
Director, Operations:
   Vacant. 315-448-8700/fax: 315-448-8036
Director, Research:
   Joann Coria. 315-448-8061
Director, Government & Community Affairs:
   Christine Fix. 315-448-8005

Director, Budget:
   Vacant. 315-448-8252
Police Chief:
   Steve P Thompson. 315-442-5250/fax: 315-442-5198
Press Secretary:
   Sherri Owens. 315-448-8005

Tonawanda, Town of
2919 Delaware Ave
Kenmore, NY 14217
716-877-8800 Fax: 716-877-0578
Web site: www.tonawanda.ny.us

Town Supervisor:
   Ronald H Moline. 716-877-8804
Town Clerk:
   Cal Champlin. 716-877-8800
   e-mail: cchamplin@tonawanda.ny.us
Town Attorney:
   Craig Johnson. 716-875-9947
Comptroller:
   Edward Mongold. 716-877-8810
Police Chief:
   Samuel Palmiere. 716-879-6607

Troy, City of
City Hall
One Monument Square
Troy, NY 12180
518-270-4401 Fax: 518-270-4609
Web site: www.troyny.org

Mayor:
   Harry J Tutunjian. 518-270-4401
Deputy Mayor:
   James Walsh. 518-270-4403
President, City Council:
   Marjorie Mahar DerGurahian. 518-270-4493
City Clerk:
   Flora O'Malley. 518-270-4541
   e-mail: teri.kippen@troyny.org
Corporation Counsel:
   Dave Mitchell. 518-270-4606
Comptroller:
   Debbie Witkowski. 518-270-4631
Chief of Police:
   Nicholas Kaiser. 518-270-4441

Union, Town of
3111 E Main St
Endwell, NY 13760
607-786-2900 Fax: 607-786-2998
Web site: www.townofunion.com

Town Supervisor:
   John M Bernardo. 607-786-2995
Town Clerk:
   Gail L Springer. 607-786-2915
   e-mail: townclerk@townofunion.com
Town Attorney:
   Alan J Pope. 607-584-4900/fax: 607-584-4901
Comptroller:
   Gary E Leighton. 607-786-2930

Offices and agencies appear in alphabetical order.

Utica, City of
City Hall
One Kennedy Plz
Utica, NY 13502
315-792-0100 Fax: 315-734-9250
Web site: www.cityofutica.com

Mayor:
  Timothy J Julian 315-792-0100
Common Council President:
  Patrick J Donovan. 315-792-0113
City Clerk:
  Joan M Brenon 315-792-0113
  e-mail: jbrenon@cityofutica.com
Corporation Counsel:
  Linda Fatata. 315-792-0171/fax: 315-792-0175
  e-mail: ulaw@cityofutica.com
Comptroller:
  Joan Scalise 315-792-0133
City Assessor:
  David Williams. 315-792-1025
Commissioner, Parks:
  David Short. 315-738-0172
Commissioner, Urban & Economic Development:
  Mark Mojave 315-792-0181
Commissioner, Public Works:
  Michael Cerminaro. 315-738-0172
City Engineer:
  Mike Mahoney 315-792-0100
Police Chief:
  Al Pylman. 315-735-3302
Fire Chief:
  Russell Brooks 315-724-5151

Valley Stream, Village of
123 S Central Ave
Valley Stream, NY 11580
516-825-4200 Fax: 516-825-8316
e-mail: vsitdept@valleystream.govoffice.com
Web site: www.valleystreamvillage.org

Mayor:
  Edward W Cahill 516-825-4200
Village Clerk/Administrator:
  Vincent W Ang. 516-825-4200
  e-mail: vsclerk@valleystream.govoffice.com
Village Attorney:
  Michael McKenna 516-825-4200
Treasurer:
  Jerome Leonardi. 516-825-4200

Vestal, Town of
605 Vestal Parkway East
Vestal, NY 13850-1495
607-748-1514 Fax: 607-786-3631
Web site: www.vestalny.com

Town Supervisor:
  Anndrea Starzak. 607-748-1514
  e-mail: astarzak@vestalny.com
Town Clerk:
  Constance Lightner. 607-748-1514

Town Attorney:
  Daniel Gorman 607-748-1514
  e-mail: dgorman@vestalny.com
Comptroller:
  Laura McKane 607-748-1514
  e-mail: lmckane@vestalny.com

Watertown, City of
245 Washington St, Rm 302
Watertown, NY 13601
315-785-7720 Fax: 315-785-7796
Web site: www.citywatertown.org

Mayor:
  Jeffrey E Graham 315-785-7720
City Manager:
  Mary M Corriveau 315-785-7720
City Clerk:
  Donna M Dutton. 315-785-7780
  e-mail: ddutton@watertown-ny.com
City Attorney:
  Robert J Slye .315-786-0266/fax: 315-786-3488
Comptroller:
  James Mills. 315-785-7754
Chief of Police:
  Robert Piche 315-782-2233

Webster, Town of
1000 Ridge Rd
Webster, NY 14580
585-872-1000 Fax: 585-872-1352
Web site: www.ci.webster.ny.us

Supervisor:
  Cathryn Thomas. 585-872-7068
Town Clerk:
  Barbara Ottenschot. 585-872-7060
  e-mail: townclerk@ci.webster.ny.us
Town Attorney:
  Charles Genese. 585-872-1000
Director, Finance:
  Kathy Tanea 585-872-7067

West Seneca, Town of
1250 Union Rd
West Seneca, NY 14224
716-674-5600 Fax: 716-677-4330
Web site: www.westseneca.net

Town Supervisor:
  Paul T Clark 716-558-3203
Town Clerk:
  Patricia C Wisniewski 716-558-3215
  e-mail: wisniewp@nysnet.net
Town Attorney:
  Timothy Greenan 716-558-3240
Comptroller:
  Charles Koller. 716-558-3205
Police Chief:
  Edward Gehen 716-674-2943

Offices and agencies appear in alphabetical order.

White Plains, City of

City Hall
255 Main St
White Plains, NY 10601
914-422-1411 Fax: 914-422-1395
Web site: www.cityofwhiteplains.com

Mayor:
  Joseph M Delfino 914-422-1411
    e-mail: jdelfino@ci.white-plains.ny.us
City Clerk:
  Janice Mineri 914-422-1227
    e-mail: jmineri@ci.whiteplains.ny.us
Corporation Counsel:
  Edward Dunphy. 914-422-1241/fax: 914-422-1231
Commissioner, Finance:
  Gina Cuneo-Harwood. 914-422-1233
Commissioner, Public Works:
  Joseph Nicoletti 914-422-1200
Chief of Police:
  James Bradley. 914-422-6230

Yonkers, City of

City Hall
40 S Broadway
Yonkers, NY 10701
914-377-6000 Fax: 914-377-6048
Web site: www.cityofyonkers.com

Mayor:
  Philip A Amicone. 914-377-6300
President, City Council:
  Richard J Martinelli 914-377-6060
City Clerk:
  Joan C Deierlen 914-377-6020
    e-mail: joan.deierlen@cityofyonkers.com
Corporation Counsel:
  Frank J Rubino 914-377-6240/fax: 914-964-0563
City Assessor:
  Mark Russell. 914-377-6200
Commissioner, Affordable Housing:
  Greg Arcaro 914-377-6693
Commissioner, Finance & Mgmt Services:
  James LaPerche 914-377-6100
Commissioner, Parks, Recreation & Conservation:
  Mitch Tutoni 914-377-6425
Commissioner, Public Works:
  John Liszewski. 914-377-6270
Commissioner, Planning & Development:
  Stephen Whetstone. 914-377-6650
Director, Public Affairs & Community Relations:
  Richard Halevy. 914-377-6053
Superintendent, Water:
  John Speight 914-377-6737
Police Commissioner:
  Robert Taggart 914-377-7200
Fire Commissioner:
  Anthony Pagano 914-377-7500

State & Local
Government
Public Information

Offices and agencies appear in alphabetical order.

NEW YORK POLITICAL PARTIES

New York Conservative Party

New York State Conservative Party
486 78th St
Brooklyn, NY 11209
718-921-2158 Fax: 718-921-5268

Albany Office
325 Parkview Dr
Schenectady, NY 12303
518-356-7882
Fax: 518-356-3773

Statewide Party Officials
State Chairman:
Michael R Long 718-921-2158
486 78th St, Brooklyn, NY 11209
Executive Committee Member:
Carol Birkholz 518-623-9151
1 Pucker St, Warrensburg, NY 12885
State Exec Vice Chairman:
James P Molinaro 718-442-3676
85 Lyman Ave, Staten Island, NY 10305
State Vice Chairman:
Pasquale J Curcio 631-789-2788
10 Hampden Rd, Copiague, NY 11726
State Executive Director:
Shaun Marie Levine 518-356-7882
325 Parkview Dr, Schenectady, NY 12303
Regional Vice Chairman:
Daniel F Fitzgerald 315-853-8816
118 Sanford Ave, Clinton, NY 13323
Secretary:
Howard Lim, Jr. 914-939-7180
83 Valley Terrance, Rye Brook, NY 10573
Treasurer:
James M Gay 718-633-9552
4012 7th Ave, Brooklyn, NY 11232
Law Chairman:
Thomas A Bolan 212-682-8184
521 5th Avenue, New York, NY 10175
National Affairs Chair:
Allen Roth 516-776-2784
43 Lehigh Court, Rockville Centre, NY 11570
Deputy Counsel:
Michael V Ajello 718-258-9804
1970 Flatbush Ave, Brooklyn, NY 11234

County Chairs

Albany
Richard Stack 518-463-8679
53 Nicholas Dr, Colonie, NY 12205

Allegany
Glen Hall 585-593-5259
472 Alma Hill Rd, Wellsville, NY 14895

Bronx
William Newmark 718-328-5616
1325 Bronx River Ave, Bronx, NY 10472

Broome
James M Thomas 607-648-5308
25 Woodland Rd, Binghamton, NY 13901

Cattaraugus
Warren G Schmidt 716-492-3812
1244 Eagle St, Arcade, NY 14009

Cayuga
Gregory S Rigby 315-253-0736
124 Oswasco St, Auburn, NY 13021

Chautauqua
Jan R Van Stee-Potter 716-595-2479
PO Box 101, Stockton, NY 14784

Chemung
Louis F DeCiccio 607-796-5129
4905 Hillview Rd, Millport, NY 14864

Clinton
Robert Church 518-846-8944
22 Ladd Dr, Chazy, NY 12921

Columbia
Matthew G Torrey 518-392-9610
91 Nelson Avenue, Ghent, NY 12075

Cortland
Kurt Van Hamlin 607-756-6870
227 Port Watson St, Cortland, NY 13045

Delaware
John Bjorkander 845-676-4604
PO Box 180, Andes, NY 13731

Dutchess
Patricia K Killian 845-454-2697
20 Hillview Dr, Poughkeepsie, NY 12603

Erie
Ralph C Lorigo 716-675-8611
75 Rolling Woods, West Seneca, NY 14224

Essex
Aaron Turetsky 518-834-9678
1682 Front St, Keeseville, NY 12944

Fulton
Wayne Brooks 518-725-1270
274 N Main St, Gloversville, NY 12078

Genesee
Arthur Munger 716-762-9323
2753 Pearl St Rd, Batavia, NY 14020

Greene
Nicholas J Passero 518-622-9407
Caryl Day Lane, Round Top, NY 12473

Herkimer
Daniel Pollak 315-866-0936
RD#1, Box 71, Folts Road, Herkimer, NY 13350

Offices and agencies appear in alphabetical order.

Jefferson
Raymond C Carpenter 315-286-1247
PO Box 61, Adams, NY 13605

Kings
Gerard Kassar 718-748-9010
7521 10th Ave, Brooklyn, NY 11228

Lewis
James H Koch 315-688-4131
RR #1, Box 88, Copaigue, NY 13626

Madison
Kurt J Ryan 315-363-3311
422 W Railroad St, Oneida, NY 13421

Monroe
Thomas Cook 716-385-4039
29 Washington Ave, Pittsford, NY 14534

Montgomery
Robert Mead 518-842-4345
1 Northhampton Road, Amsterdam, NY 12010

Nassau
Roger Bogsted 516-796-3155
105 Bobolink Lane, Levittown, NY 11756

New York
Jim M Kerr 212-426-0024
200 East 90th St 7B, New York, NY 10128

Niagara
Dean L Walker 716-772-5137
4816 Gasport Road, Gasport, NY 14067

Oneida
David D Eaton 315-735-3526
5518 Maynard Park Drive, Marcy, NY 13403

Onondaga
Clay D Smith 315-677-3243
3100 Eager Road, Lafayette, NY 13084

Ontario
Alan L Hagerman 585-394-3308
5460 Wells Curtice Rd, Canandaigua, NY 14424

Orange
John P DeLessio 845-562-4963
7 Hill Street, Newburgh, NY 12550

Orleans
Karen L McAllister 716-589-5843
105 McClelland Street, Albion, NY 14411

Oswego
Oswego:
H Leonard Schick 315-593-0770
26 North Pollard, Fulton, NY 13069

Otsego
Stan Konopka 607-287-1045
PO Box 566, Cooperstown, NY 13326

Putnam
James Maxwell 845-628-7716
117 Vista Terrace, Mahopac, NY 10541

Queens
Thomas M Long 718-474-3826
6 Beach 219th St, Rockaway Pt, NY 11697

Richmond
Carmine F Ragucci 718-818-8888
67 Commodore Dr, Staten Island, NY 10309

Rockland
Mary G Loeffler 845-634-6715
15 Oak Rd, New City, NY 10956

Saratoga
Robert D Roe 518-581-1941
PO Box 1326, Saratoga Springs, NY 12866

Schenectady
Paul F Brown 518-356-7917
1336 Evergreen Ave, Schenectady, NY 12306

Schuyler
Linda D Moore 607-535-7591
2485 Irelandville Rd, Watkins Glen, NY 14891

Seneca
William R White 315-539-2534
19 Brookside Dr, Waterloo, NY 13165

St Lawrence
Henry Ford 315-262-2824
113 Stowe Bay Rd, Colton, NY 13625

Steuben
Donald E Gwinner 607-583-2246
5582 Mail Route Rd, Savona, NY 14879

Suffolk
Pasquale J Curcio 631-789-2788
10 Hampden Rd, Copiague, NY 11726

Sullivan
William Higgins 845-292-8710
365 Breezy Hill Rd, Parksville, NY 12768

Tompkins
Thomas Straight 607-838-3426
45 McLean Rd, Cortland, NY 13045

Ulster
Debra L Hewitt 845-339-3074
PO Box 668, Adorn Lane, Port Ewen, NY 12466

Warren
Carol Birkholz 518-623-9151
1 Pucker St, Warrensburg, NY 12885

Washington
Louis Imhof 518-692-7251
217 Kenyon Rd, Greenwich, NY 12834

Wayne
James F Quinn, Jr 315-483-2240
8239 Lake St, Sodus Point, NY 14555

Westchester
Gail M Burns 914-965-7273
510 Midland Avenue, Yonkers, NY 10710

Wyoming
Laurence E Buehler 518-462-2601
158 S Main St #2, Perry, NY 14530

Yates
R Michael Briggs 315-536-8085/fax: 315-536-5957
PO Box 127, Penn Yan, NY 14527

Offices and agencies appear in alphabetical order.

New York State Democratic Party

New York State Democratic Committee

60 Madison Ave
Ste 1201
New York, NY 10010
212-725-8825 or 518-463-1663 Fax: 212-725-8867
Web site: www.nydems.org

Statewide Party Officials

State Chair:
Herman D Farrell, Jr 212-725-8825/fax: 212-725-8867
60 Madison Ave, Ste 1201, New York, NY 10010
Executive Director:
Rodney Capel 212-725-8825/fax: 212-725-8867
60 Madison Ave, Ste 1201, New York, NY 10010
Young Democrats:
Evan Lederman 212-725-8825/fax: 212-725-8867
60 Madison Avenue, Ste 1201, New York, NY 10010
Executive Committee Chair:
Denise King 518-392-1560 x2139/fax: 518-392-3978
12 Mill Street, Chatham, NY 12037
First Vice Chair:
Inez Dickens 212-749-2580/fax: 212-283-1151
2153 Adam Clayton Powell Jr Blvd, New York, NY 10027
Vice Chair:
Betty Barnette. 518-438-5150
3 Oxford Rd, Albany, NY 12203
Secretary:
Peter Stein 807-255-4843/fax: 807-255-9412
315 Day Hall, Ithaca, NY 14850
Treasurer:
David A Alpert 914-946-8300/fax: 914-946-8090
170 East Post Rd, White Plains, NY 10601
Sergeant-at-Arms:
Michael Reich 718-631-0694/fax: 718-729-0871
46-12 Queens Blvd, Ste 205, Sunnyside, NY 11104
Counsel & Law Chair:
Gerard Harper 212-373-3263/fax: 212-379-2769
1285 Ave of the Americas, New York, NY 10019
Policy Cmte Chair:
Mike Schell. 315-782-0004
316 Sherman St, Watertown, NY 13601
Labor Task Force:
Suzy Ballantyne. 518-436-8516/fax: 518-463-6901
100 S Swan St, Albany, NY 12210

County Chairs

Albany
Betty J Barnette 518-438-8282/fax: 518-438-8375
3 Oxford Rd, Albany, NY 12203

Allegany
Joan Lester. 607-587-9382/fax: 607-587-2348
52 High St, Alfred, NY 14802

Bronx
Jose Rivera. 718-931-5200/fax: 718-792-3882
135 Westchester Sq, Bronx, NY 10461

Broome
Michael A Najarian 607-773-8369/fax: 607-772-0183
97 Beethoven St, Binghamton, NY 13905

Cattaraugus
Daniel W McCandless 716-676-5716
8003 Rogers Rd, Franklinville, NY 14737

Cayuga
Laurie A Michelman. 315-252-1774
PO Box 547, Auburn, NY 13021

Chautauqua
Norman P Green. 716-753-4250
635 Fairmount Ave, Jamestown, NY 14701

Chemung
Cynthia Emmer 607-733-2844/fax: 607-734-6330
858 Davis St, Elmira, NY 14901

Chenango
Robert B Decker. 607-337-1700
5 Court Street, Norwich, NY 13815

Clinton
John Gallagher. 518-561-0484/fax: 518-561-1486
41 Draper Ave, Plattsburgh, NY 12901

Columbia
Denise King 518-828-6778
12 Mill Street, Chatham, NY 12037

Cortland
Bill Wood 607-756-6537
26 Madison St, Cortland, NY 13045

Delaware
Leonard Sienko. 607-632-5400
12 East Main St, PO Box 579, Hancock, NY 13783

Dutchess
Joseph Ruggiero 845-485-1934/fax: 845-485-3398
2 LaGrange Ave, Ste 201, Poughkeepsie, NY 12603

Erie
Leonard R Lenihan 716-853-2511/fax: 716-853-2448
Ellicott Square Bldg, Ste 115, Buffalo, NY 14203

Essex
Stuart Brody. 518-963-7479/fax: 518-963-7099
Po Box 127, Essex, NY 12736

Franklin
Joseph Pickreign. 518-891-1174
Rt 86 RFD 1, Box 322A, Saranac Lake, NY 12983

Fulton
Albert Hays, Sr 518-762-7598/fax: 518-762-7598
2470 State Highway 29, Johnstown, NY 12095

Genesee
Raymond E Yacuzzo 716-768-8377/fax: 716-768-8377
4 East Ave, LeRoy, NY 14482

Greene
Barbara Van Kuren. 518-943-4191
120 Kings Rd, Coxsackie, NY 12051

Hamilton
Linda M Mitchell 518-731-8397
PO Box 163, Indian Lake, NY 12842

Offices and agencies appear in alphabetical order.

Herkimer
Toni Scalise 315-866-9663
PO Box 216, Mohawk, NY 13407

Jefferson
Mark Pacilio 315-646-2426
PO Box 303, Sackets Harbor, NY 13655

Kings
Clarence Norman, Jr 718-875-5870/fax: 718-596-4013
16 Court St, Brooklyn, NY 11241

Lewis
Ed Murphy 315-286-1900
5510 Jackson St, Lowville, NY 13367

Livingston
Virginia Kanada 585-588-2581
PO Box 172, York, NY 14592

Madison
Dorothy U Betz 315-691-9960/fax: 315-691-4513
1394 Rte 12, Earlville, NY 13332

Monroe
Rick Dollinger 585-232-2410/fax: 585-232-1223
121 East Ave, Rochester, NY 14604

Montgomery
Debbie Marek 518-842-4902/fax: 518-842-6671
134 Pawling St, Hagaman, NY 12086

Nassau
Jay Jacobs .516-294-3366/fax: 516-873-0810
300 Garden City Plaza, Ste 240, Garden City, NY 11530

New York
Herman D Farrell, Jr 212-725-8825/fax: 212-725-8867
60 Madison Ave Ste 1201, New York, NY 10010

Niagara
Charles J Naughton 716-873-8833
PO Box 26, Niagara Falls, NY 14304

Oneida
William Morris 315-732-4171 x203/fax: 315-732-4190
PO Box 505, New Hartford, NY 13413

Onondaga
Bob Smith .315-471-2020/fax: 315-471-2033
375 West Onondaga St, Ste 24, Syracuse, NY 13202

Ontario
Charles Evangelista 585-394-7500
60 North Main St, Geneva, NY 14456

Orange
Jonathan G Jacobson 845-567-6778/fax: 845-567-7721
25 Pierces Rd, Newburgh, NY 12550

Orleans
Jeanne Crane 585-798-2197
709 West Ave, Medina, NY 14103

Oswego
William W Scriber 315-342-8261
147 West 5th St, Oswego, NY 13126

Otsego
Henry J Nicols 607-547-4675/fax: 607-547-4616
2515 State Highway 28, Oneonta, NY 13820

Putnam
Susan Spear 845-628-0432
36 Astor Dr, Mahopac, NY 10541

Queens
Thomas Manton 718-268-5100/fax: 718-268-7363
95-25 Queens Blvd, Flushing, NY 11375

Rensselaer
M Lynne Mahoney 518-273-2797
PO Box 846, Troy, NY 12181

Richmond
John Lavelle .718-983-5009/fax: 718-983-5541
274 Watchogue Rd, Staten Island, NY 10314

Rockland
Vincent Monte 845-398-1309/fax: 845-210-9333
PO Box 266, New City, NY 10956

Saratoga
Larry Bulman 518-792-0321/fax: 518-792-4876
13 Moreau Dr, South Glens Falls, NY 12803

Schenectady
Chris Gardner 518-393-2813/fax: 518-489-8430
46 Warwick Way, Niskayuna, NY 12309

Schoharie
Cliff Hay 518-234-7165
RR3 Box 261, Cobleskill, NY 12043

Schuyler
Ruth Young 607-535-9566
1580 Sugar Hill Rd, Watkins Glen, NY 14891

Seneca
Theodore Young 315-539-9614/fax: 561-423-0783
32 West Wright Ave, Waterloo, NY 13165

St Lawrence
June O'Neill 315-386-3882
2262 County Rte 14, Canton, NY 13617

Steuben
Shawn Hogan 607-324-7421/fax: 607-324-3156
12 Mays Ave, Hornell, NY 14843

Suffolk
Richard H Schaffer 631-439-0400/fax: 631-439-0404
4250 Veterans Mem Hwy, Holbrook, NY 11741

Sullivan
Christopher Cunningham 845-794-3000/fax: 845-794-3459
100 North St, P O Box 5012, Monticello, NY 12701

Tioga
Gloria L Whitmore 607-687-1476
3058 Valley Rd, Owego, NY 13827

Tompkins
Irene W Stein 607-266-7579/fax: 607-266-7571
PO Box 6798, Ithaca, NY 14850

Ulster
Arthur J Smith, III 845-340-3800/fax: 845-340-3651
County Offc Bldg, 244 Fair St, Kingston, NY 12401

Warren
William Montfort 518-251-3138
PO Box 9, Johnsburg, NY 12843

Washington
Sheila Comar 518-642-9566
29 Depot St, Middle Granville, NY 12849

Wayne
Carmen Pascarella 315-587-9333
4868 South Main St, North Rose, NY 14516

Offices and agencies appear in alphabetical order.

Westchester
Reginald A LaFayette 914-946-8300/fax: 914-946-8090
170 East Post Rd, Ste 210, White Plains, NY 10601

Wyoming
Anne R Weidman 585-786-2782
PO Box 39, Wyoming, NY 14591

Yates
Barbara Steinwachs 315-536-7895/fax: 315-536-7895
1128 E Bluff Dr, Penn Yan, NY 14527

New York State Republican Party

New York State Republican Party
315 State St
Albany, NY 12210
518-462-2601 Fax: 518-449-7443
Web site: www.nygop.org

Statewide Party Officials
Vice Chair:
Robert Davis 716-856-8700/fax: 716-856-8703
107 Delaware Ave, Buffalo, NY 14202
Chairman:
Sandy Treadwell 518-462-2601
315 State St, Albany, NY 12210
Vice Chair:
John F Nolan 518-584-7900/fax: 518-581-0748
77 Van Dam St, Saratoga Springs, NY 12866
Vice Chair:
Peter Savago 914-338-6245/fax: 914-338-7098
PO Box 34313, Kingston, NY 12402
Executive Vice Chair:
Rita DiMartino 518-462-2601
315 State Street, Albany, NY 12210
Treasurer:
Mike Avella 518-462-2601
315 State St, Albany, NY 12210
Secretary:
Marty Smith 315-866-2056
402 Prospect St, Herkimer, NY 13350
National Committeeman:
Joseph Mondello 516-334-5800/fax: 516-334-4406
164 Post Ave, Westbury, NY 11590
Counsel:
Jeffrey T Buley 518-462-2601/fax: 518-449-7443
315 State St, Albany, NY 12210
Executive Director:
William McGahay 518-462-2601/fax: 518-449-7443
315 State St, Albany, NY 12210

County Officials

Albany
Peter Kermani 518-626-0720/fax: 518-626-0300
915 Broadway, Albany, NY 12207

Allegany
Tom Hayden 585-593-0678/fax: 814-260-3715
426 South Main Street, Wellsville, NY 14895

Bronx
Victor Tosi 718-792-5800/fax: 718-863-2301
2113 Williamsbridge Rd, Bronx, NY 10461-1606

Broome
Anthony J Capozzi 607-723-8201/fax: 607-723-3036
59-61 Court St, Ste 707, Binghamton, NY 13901

Cattaraugus
Jeremiah J Moriarty, III 716-676-5524/fax: 716-676-3541
PO Box 126, Franklinville, NY 14737-0126

Cayuga
Cherl Heary 315-364-8632/fax: 315-364-8173
PO Box 420, King Ferry, NY 13081

Chautauqua
John A Glenzer 716-679-1243/fax: 716-679-7074
183 Water St, Fredonia, NY 14063

Chemung
G Thomas Tranter 607-974-7818/fax: 607-974-4050
116 Kennedy Dr, Horseheads, NY 14845

Chenango
Thomas L Morrone 607-334-3234/fax: 607-334-4625
213 Randall Ave, Norwich, NY 13815-1613

Clinton
William Favreau 518-562-0600
206 West Bay Plaza, Plattsburgh, NY 12901

Columbia
Tod Grenci 518-799-6801/fax: 518-799-6801
Box 58, Stuyvesant Falls, NY 12174

Cortland
Shirley Fish 607-753-6381/fax: 607-758-9007
4356 Miller St Ext, Cortland, NY 13045

Delaware
Martin Donnelly 845-676-3114/fax: 845-676-4796
Main St, P O Box 525, Andes, NY 13731

Dutchess
Elizabeth Brilliant 845-897-4291/fax: 845-897-4792
61 West Redoubt Rd, Fishkill, NY 12524

Erie
Robert Davis 716-856-8700/fax: 716-856-8703
107 Delaware Ave, Ste 17, Buffalo, NY 14202

Essex
Joyce W Morency 518-891-3189/fax: 518-891-6092
PO Box 135, Bloomingdale, NY 12913

Franklin
James Ellis 518-359-2580/fax: 518-359-2289
58 Broad St, Tupper Lake, NY 12986-2122

Fulton
Anne Jung 518-835-3970
130 Jung Road, Caroga Lake, NY 12032

Genesee
Richard E Siebert 585-343-5925/fax: 585-344-8521
8585 Seven Springs Rd, Batavia, NY 14020

Offices and agencies appear in alphabetical order.

Greene
Brent E Bogardus 518-369-6098
7 Molly White Drive, Coxsackie, NY 12051

Hamilton
William Farber. 315-826-7744/fax: 315-826-3215
Mountain Home Rd, Hoffmeister, NY 13353

Herkimer
Marty Smith. 315-866-2056/fax: 315-866-2056
402 Prospect St, Herkimer, NY 13350

Jefferson
Paul Warnick 315-788-4120/fax: 315-786-1387
161 Clinton St, Ste 204, Watertown, NY 13601

Kings
Hy Singer. 718-582-9454/fax: 718-339-4170
26 Court St, Ste 2305, Brooklyn, NY 11235

Lewis
Pat Mahar. 315-376-2112/fax: 315-688-4311
PO Box 203, Copenhagen, NY 13626

Livingston
Lowell G Conrad 716-243-2665/fax: 716-243-2711
123 Main St, Geneseo, NY 14454-1113

Madison
Michael St Leger 315-655-4522/fax: 315-363-4195
5880 Fieldstone Dr, Cazenovia, NY 13035-9625

Monroe
Stephen Minarik, III 585-546-8040/fax: 585-546-8519
301 Exchange Blvd, Rochester, NY 14608

Montgomery
Lore Koppel. 518-993-3233/fax: 518-993-4216
16 West St, P O Box 390, Fort Plain, NY 13339

Nassau
Joseph Mondello 516-334-5800/fax: 516-333-4406
164 Post Ave, Westbury, NY 11590-3170

New York
James Ortenzio 212-517-8444/fax: 212-517-3142
122 East 83rd Street, New York, NY 10028

Niagara
Henry F Wojtaszek 716-693-5517/fax: 716-694-0506
150 Payne Ave, North Tonowanda, NY 14120

Oneida
Mark Scheidleman. 315-724-5714/fax: 315-732-7427
1750 Genesee St, Utica, NY 13501

Onondaga
Robert Smith 315-471-2020/fax: 315-471-2033
375 West Onondaga St, Syracuse, NY 13202-3207

Ontario
Jay Dutcher 585-415-9803/fax: 585-394-8830
493 S Main St, Ste 11, Canandaigua, NY 14424

Orange
William L DeProspo 845-469-5200/fax: 845-469-5211
One Winkler Place, Chester, NY 10918

Orleans
Bruce Schmidt 716-837-1515
3100 Gaines Rd, Albion, NY 14411

Oswego
George Williams 315-342-0840/fax: 315-342-2143
102 W Utica St, Oswego, NY 13126

Otsego
Charlotte P Koniuto. 607-286-7522/fax: 607-286-7522
3650 Hwy 28, Milford, NY 13807

Putnam
Anthony Scannapieco 914-225-2002/fax: 914-225-2002
PO Box 203, Carmel, NY 10512-0203

Queens
Serphin Maltese. 718-628-9522/fax: 718-381-4807
71-20 Myrtle Ave, Glendale, NY 11385

Rensselear
John T Casey 518-272-2111/fax: 518-272-7522
PO Box 686, Troy, NY 12181

Richmond
Robert Helbock 718-667-4600/fax: 718-816-0718
58 New Dorp Plaza, Staten Island, NY 10306

Rockland
Vincent Reda 845-634-7100/fax: 845-634-2423
172 S Main St, New City, NY 10956

Saratoga
John Nolan. 518-584-7900/fax: 518-581-0748
77 Van Dam St, Saratoga Springs, NY 12866-2023

Schenectady
Armando Tebano. 518-377-2469/fax: 518-377-2716
1093 Maryland Avenue, Schenectady, NY 12309

Schoharie
Lewis Wilson. 518-234-2534/fax: 518-234-3422
826 E Main St, Cobleskill, NY 12043-0039

Schuyler
Philip C Barnes. 607-535-4600
203 Lakeview Avenue, Watkins Glen, NY 14891

Seneca
Angelo Bianchi 315-539-9301/fax: 315-539-9725
PO Box 504, Waterloo, NY 13165-0504

St Lawrence
Joseph Gray 315-764-0133/fax: 315-769-5084
PO Box 5243, Massena, NY 13662

Steuben
William O Hatch 607-698-2100/fax: 607-698-2355
6550 Hughes Rd, Canisteo, NY 14823

Suffolk
Patricia Acampora 631-580-1482/fax: 631-580-1490
3340 Veterans Memorial Hwy, Bohemia, NY 11716

Sullivan
Gregory Goldstein 845-434-7755/fax: 845-434-8763
489 State Rt 52, Woodburn, NY 12788

Tioga
Don Leonard 607-589-4501/fax: 607-723-3246
PO Box 361, Spencer, NY 14883

Tompkins
Elizabeth Cree 607-257-4068/fax: 607-272-4038
9 Fairwinds Way, Ithaca, NY 14850

Ulster
Peter Savago 845-338-6245/fax: 845-255-4792
PO Box 3413, Kingston, NY 12402

Warren
Michael O'Connor. 518-792-8728/fax: 518-792-6972
19 West Notre Dame Rd, Glen Falls, NY 12801

Offices and agencies appear in alphabetical order.

Washington
John Aspland 518-792-6554/fax: 518-746-1864
10544 State Rt 149, Fort Ann, NY 12827

Wayne
Daniel Olson 315-946-4937/fax: 315-946-4937
12 William St, PO Box 200, Lyons, NY 14489

Westchester
RoseMarie Panio 914-949-3020/fax: 914-949-2275
214 Mamaroneck Ave, White Plains, NY 10601

Wyoming
Gordon Brown 716-675-8620/fax: 716-675-1619
PO Box 191, Warsaw, NY 14569

Yates
R Michael Briggs 315-536-8085/fax: 315-536-8085
PO Box 127, Penn Yan, NY 14527

Political Parties,
Lobbyists & PACs

Offices and agencies appear in alphabetical order.

LOBBYISTS

Each entry includes the name of the registered principal lobbyist, then lists names of additional lobbyists as well as all clients.

1199/SEIU GNYHA Healthcare Education Project
330 W 42nd St, Rm 739
New York, NY 10036
212-603-1741 Fax: 212-603-1764
e-mail: debra@healtheducation.org
Web site: www.healtheducationproject.org

Clients:
1199/SEIU & GNYHA Healthcare Education Project

Lobbyists:
Debra Pucci

1199/SEIU New York's Health & Human Service Union
310 West 43rd St
New York, NY 10036
212-582-1890 Fax: 212-956-5140
Web site: www.1199seiuonline.org

Clients:
1199/SEIU New York's Health & Human Service Union

Lobbyists:
Lillie Carino
Derek Carr
Jennifer Cunningham
Patrick Gaspard
Jennifer Hibit
Michael Keane
Pat Lipold
Dennis Rivera
Erin Sheldon

215 Argyle Inc
277 West 10th St, Ste 2E
New York, NY 10014
212-929-8528 Fax: 501-421-3233

Clients:
Times Square Alliance

Lobbyists:
Robert Hammond

AAA Western & Central NY
100 International Dr
Amherst, NY 14221
716-626-3225 Fax: 716-631-5925
e-mail: wsmith@nyaaa.com

Clients:
AAA Western & Central New York

Lobbyists:
Diana Dibble
Wallace D Smith
James Yoerg

AIDS Coalition (NY)
231 West 29th St, Ste 1002
New York, NY 10001
212-629-3075 Fax: 212-629-8403
e-mail: ckazanas@nyaidsc.org
Web site: www.nyaidscoalition.org

Clients:
AIDS Coalition (NY)

Lobbyists:
Christina Kazanas
Joe Pressley

AMDeC Foundation
10 Rockefeller Plaza, Ste 1120
New York, NY 10020
212-218-5640 Fax: 212-218-5644
e-mail: info@amdec.org
Web site: www.amdec.org

Clients:
AMDeC Foundation Inc

Lobbyists:
Maria K Mitchell

ANHD Inc
50 Broad St, Ste 1125
New York, NY 10004
212-747-1117

Clients:
ANHD Inc

Lobbyists:
Benjamin Dulchin
David Greenberg
David Hunter
David Schuffler Jr

Action for a Better Community Inc
550 E Main St
Rochester, NY 14604
585-325-5116 Fax: 585-3252266

Clients:
Action for a Better Community Inc

Offices and agencies appear in alphabetical order.

450

Lobbyists:
James H Norman

Adams, Daniel J Associates
47 Sweetbrier Dr
Ballston Lake, NY 12019
518-877-8225 Fax: 518-877-8225

Clients:
Coors Brewing Co
Illinois Tool Works Inc
Matt Brewing Co (The)

Lobbyists:
Daniel J Adams

Adirondack Council Inc (The)
103 Hand Ave, PO Box D2
Elizabethtown, NY 12932
518-873-2240 or 518-432-6757 Fax: 518-873-6675
e-mail: info@adirondackcouncil.org
Web site: www.adirondackcouncil.org

Clients:
Adirondack Council (The)

Lobbyists:
Brian L Houseal
Scott Lorey
Jessica Ottney

Adirondack Mountain Club Inc
301 Hamilton St
Albany, NY 12210-1738
518-449-3870 Fax: 518-449-3875
e-mail: nwoodwor@nycap.rr.com
Web site: www.adk.org

Clients:
Adirondack Mountain Club Inc
Catskill Center for Conservation & Development

Lobbyists:
Marisa Iannacito
Neil F Woodworth

Adolf, Jay
350 Broadway, Ste 900
New York, NY 10007
212-897-5848

Clients:
Big Apple Circus

Advance Group Inc (The)
481 Eighth Ave, Ste 1760
New York, NY 10001
212-239-7323

Clients:
American Red Cross in Greater NY

Fleishman-Hillard Inc
Hotel Trades Council (NYC)

Lobbyists:
Scott Levenson

Affinity Health Plan
2500 Halsey St
Bronx, NY 10461
718-794-5744 Fax: 718-794-7800

Clients:
Affinity Health Plan

Lobbyists:
Abenaa Abboa-Offei
Maura Bluestone

After-School Corporation (The)
925 Ninth Ave
New York, NY 10019
212-547-6950 Fax: 212-548-4657

Clients:
After-School Corporation (The)

Lobbyists:
John Albert
Lucy Friedman
Shari Gruber

Agostine Jr, Joseph A
Nghbhd Preserv Coalition of NYS
40 Colvin Ave
Albany, NY 12206
518-432-6757 Fax: 518-432-6758
e-mail: agostine@npcnys.org
Web site: www.npcnys.org

Clients:
Neighborhood Preservation Coalition of NYS Inc

Ahern, Barbara J
One Commerce Plaza, Ste 400
Albany, NY 12210-2822
518-463-0723 Fax: 518-463-7809
e-mail: bjahern@albany.net

Clients:
Croplife America
First Data Corporation & Subsidiaries
Group Self Insurance Assn of NY Inc (GSIANY)
Hearing Healthcare Alliance of NY Inc (HHCANY)
National Marine Manufacturers Assn
Personal Watercraft Industry Assn
Responsible Industry for a Sound Environment (RISE)

Alesse, Mark
One Commerce Plaza, Ste 1119
Albany, NY 12260

Offices and agencies appear in alphabetical order.

518-434-1262 Fax: 518-426-8799
e-mail: mark.alesse@nfib.org
Web site: www.nfib.com

Clients:
National Federation of Independent Business

Lobbyists:
Mark Alesse
Matthew Guilbault

Allegue, Raul R
St Paul Travelers Companies
1 Tower Sq-8MS
Hartford, CT 6183
860-277-4738 Fax: 860-277-4563

Clients:
St Paul Travelers Companies Inc (The)

Lobbyists:
John D Miletti

Alliance Against Sexual Assault (NYC)
411 W 114th St, Ste 6D
New York, NY 10025
212-523-4344

Clients:
Alliance Against Sexual Assault (NYC), Intervention & Prevention

Allocco, Carol
13 Sky Hollow Dr
Menands, NY 12204
518-432-8636 Fax: 518-432-8637
e-mail: callocco@corus.jnj.com

Clients:
Johnson & Johnson

Alteri, Richard
Cable Telecom Assn of NY
80 State St
Albany, NY 12207
518-463-6676 Fax: 518-463-0574
e-mail: rfa@nycap.rr.com

Clients:
Cable Telecommunications Assn of NY Inc

Lobbyists:
Christopher Duryea

Altman, Robert S
Szold & Brandwen, PC
14 Wall St, 28th Fl
New York, NY 10005
212-732-0606 Fax: 212-766-0229

Clients:
Building Industry Assn of NY Inc

Queens & Bronx Building Assn

Altria Corporate Services
120 Park Ave
New York, NY 10017
917-663-3406 Fax: 917-663-5716

Clients:
Altria Corporate Services, Inc (ALCS)

Lobbyists:
Tod I Gimbel
Armando Mejia-Gallardo

Amalgamated Transit Union
5025 Wisconsin Ave NW
Washington, DC 20016
202-537-1645

Clients:
Amalgamated Transit Union

Lobbyists:
Luis Alzate
Antoine Breaux
Lawrence Hanley
Dannek Miller

AmeriChoice of NY
284 State St, 2nd Fl
Albany, NY 12210-2194
518-432-0893 Fax: 518-432-0895
e-mail: vgrey@americhoice.com

Clients:
AmeriChoice of NY Inc (Affiliate of United Healthcare Svcs Inc)

Lobbyists:
Valerie Grey

American Academy of Pediatrics District II (NYS)
420 Lakeville Rd, Rm 244
Lake Success, NY 11042
516-326-0310

Clients:
American Academy of Pediatrics, District II (NYS)

Lobbyists:
George Dunkel

American Academy of Sleep Medicine
One Westbrook Corporate Ctr
Ste 920
Westchester, IL 60154
708-492-0930

Clients:
American Academy of Sleep Medicine

Offices and agencies appear in alphabetical order.

Lobbyists:
David Barrett
Jerome Barrett
Lawrence J Epstein MD
Michael J Sateia MD
Michael White

American College of Ob & Gyn, District II/NY

152 Washington Ave
Albany, NY 12210-2203
518-436-3461 Fax: 518-426-4728
e-mail: info@ny.acog.org
Web site: www.acog.org/goto/nys

Clients:
American College of Obstetricians & Gynecologists, District II/NY

Lobbyists:
Stacey Montalto
Christa Nyman
Donna M Williams

American Continental Group

2099 Pennsylvania Ave, NW
Ste 850
Washington, DC 20006
202-419-2500 Fax: 202-419-2510
Web site: www.acgrep.com

Clients:
American Standard Companies Inc

Lobbyists:
David A Metzner
Shawn Smeallie

American Heart Assn/American Stroke Assn

440 New Karner Rd
Albany, NY 12205
518-869-4040 Fax: 518-869-8180
e-mail: paul.hartman@heart.org
Web site: www.americanheart.org;
www.strokeassociation.org

Clients:
American Heart Assn/American Stroke Assn

Lobbyists:
Tamiko Byrd
Amit Chitre
Jeff Foley
Paul Hartman
Nicole Higgins
June Holloman
Mark Hurley
Ryan Lafferty
John Romano
George Rosales
Kelvin Sapp
Leisha Smallwood
Roseanne Stephan
Merrilee Sweet
Trina Tardone-Steinhart

Duncan Ververs
Simon Vukelj

American Insurance Assn

95 Columbia St
Albany, NY 12210-2707
518-462-1695 Fax: 518-465-6023
e-mail: ghenning@aiadc.org
Web site: www.aiadc.org

Clients:
American Insurance Assn

Lobbyists:
Gary Henning
Laura Kersey
Michael Moran
Paul Moran

American Lung Assn of the City of New York

432 Park Ave S, 8th Fl
New York, NY 10016
212-889-3370 Fax: 212-889-3375

Clients:
American Lung Assn of the City of NY

Lobbyists:
Irwin Berlin
Peter Iwanowicz
Timothy Nichols
Robert Roth
Neil Schacter
Neil Sohluger
Louise A Vetter

American Museum of Natural History

79th St & Central Park W
New York, NY 10024-5192
212-769-5333 Fax: 212-313-7990
Web site: www.amnh.org

Clients:

Lobbyists:
Lisa Guggenheim
Barbara Gunn

Ames, Margery E

Interagency Cncl Mental Retard/Dev Disab
275 7th Ave, 19th Fl
New York, NY 10001
212-645-6360

Clients:
Interagency Cncl of Mental Retardation & Dev Disabilities

Lobbyists:
Margery E Ames
Charles Archer

Offices and agencies appear in alphabetical order.

Anderson, David
23 Hunters Run Blvd
Cohoes, NY 12407
518-785-4589 Fax: 518-785-0883
e-mail: david.anderson@astrazeneca.com

Clients:
Astrazeneca Pharmaceuticals

Andrew, Ralph
Eye & Ear Infirmary (NY)
310 East 14th St
New York, NY 10003
212-979-4578 Fax: 212-353-5779

Clients:
Eye & Ear Infirmary (NY)

Andrews Kurth, LLP
450 Lexington Ave
15th Fl
New York, NY 10017
212-850-2883

Clients:
Darien Lake Theme Park & Camping Resort Inc

Lobbyists:
Andrew Feiner
Daniel Schoenberg

Animal Welfare Advocacy
PO Box 737
Mamaroneck, NY 10543
914-381-6177

Clients:
Animal Welfare Advocacy

Lobbyists:
Lydia Antoncic
Brad Goldberg
Kelley Wind

Anson, Joseph L
Bayer
10 Applewood Dr
Rexford, NY 12148-1601
518-371-0393 Fax: 518-371-5070

Clients:
BayerCorp Pharmaceutical Div, Bayer Healthcare LLC

Apple Assn Inc (NY)
7645 Main St, PO Box 350
Fishers, NY 14453-0350
585-924-2171 Fax: 585-924-1629
e-mail: jimallen@nyapplecountry.com
Web site: www.nyapplecountry.com

Clients:
Apple Assn Inc (NY)

Lobbyists:
James Allen
David McClurg

Apple Computer, Inc
1 Infinite Loop, MS81-2CF
Cupertino, CA 95014
408-974-2367
e-mail: shughes@apple.com
Web site: www.apple.com

Clients:
Apple Computer, Inc

Lobbyists:
Scott Hughes

Arthur J Finkelstein & Associates Inc
16 North Astor St
Irvington, NY 10533
914-591-8142

Clients:
Madison Square Garden

Lobbyists:
Arthur Finkelstein

Arts Coalition (NYC)
351-A West 54 St
New York, NY 10019
212-246-3788

Clients:
Arts Coalition (NYC)

Lobbyists:
Norma Munn

Arzt, George Communications Inc
123 William St, 22nd Fl
New York, NY 10038
212-608-0333 Fax: 212-608-0458
e-mail: chief@arztcomm.com

Clients:
62 Imlay Street Real Estate, LLC
Abax Incorporated
Bovis Lend Lease
Christodora House (The)
Clear Channel Adshel Inc
Coalition of Concerned Whitney Neighbors
Crossroads Ventures, LLC
Homecrest Community Services Inc
Hunts Point Terminal Produce Cooperative Assn Inc
Inside Broadway
Madison Avenue Leasehold LLC
New School University
New Yorkers Against the Death Penalty
Prestige Properties & Development Co Inc

Offices and agencies appear in alphabetical order.

St Barnabas Hospital
Sterling & Seventh, LLC

Lobbyists:
George Arzt
Jane Crotty
Brian Krapf
Bob Liff
Fred Winters

Asciutto, Georgia M
Conf Big 5 Sch Dist
1 Steuben Pl, 5th Fl Loft
Albany, NY 12207
518-465-4274 Fax: 518-465-0638
e-mail: big5schools@mindspring.com
Web site: big5schools.home.mindspring.com

Clients:
Conference of Big 5 School Districts

Assn for Community Living
99 Pine St, Ste 202JR
Albany, NY 12207
518-426-3635 Fax: 518-425-0504
e-mail: aclnys@webramp.info
Web site: www.aclnys.org

Clients:
Assn for Community Living

Lobbyists:
Antonia M Lasicki

Assn of Community & Residential Agencies (NYS)
99 Pine St, Ste C110
Albany, NY 12207
518-449-7551 Fax: 518-449-1509
Web site: www.nysacra.org

Clients:
Assn of Community & Residential Agencies (NYS)

Lobbyists:
Forest Cotten
Ann Hardiman
James Kosakoski

Assn of Counties & Its Affiliated Organizations (NYS)
111 Pine St
Albany, NY 12207
518-465-1473 Fax: 518-465-0506
Web site: www.nysac.org

Clients:
Assn of Counties & Its Affiliated Organizations (NYS)

Lobbyists:
Stephen Acquario

Adriano Bongiorno
Kenneth Crannell
Jeffrey Osinski
Gay Petri
Peter Savage

Assn of PBAS, Inc (NYS)
111 Washington Ave
Albany, NY 11210-2207
518-465-1141 Fax: 518-465-3048

Clients:
Assn of PBAS, Inc (NYS)

Lobbyists:
Gus Danese
Gary Dela Raba
William Diebold
Jeff Frayler
Ray Gimmler
Patrick Hall
Chris Heimgartner
Floyd Holloway
James Hughes
Lionel Markee
Lou Matarazzo
Tim Morris
Michael O'Meara
Peter B Paterson
Frederick A Sales
Gordon Warnock
Thomas Willdigg

Assn of School Business Officials (NYS)
7 Elk St
Albany, NY 12207-1002
518-434-2281 Fax: 518-434-1303
e-mail: asbomail@nysasbo.org
Web site: www.nysasbo.org

Clients:
Assn of School Business Officials (NYS)

Lobbyists:
Gregory Beal
Margaret Boice
Joan Colvin
Carl Fraser
Dick Lasselle
Richard Longhurst
Mary Beth Lovejoy
George A Perry
Terry Schruers
Michael Sheperd
Steven Van Hoesen
Susan Villiers
Bruce Watkins

Assn of Towns of the State of NY
146 State St
Albany, NY 12207
518-465-7933 Fax: 518-465-0724

Offices and agencies appear in alphabetical order.

Clients:
Assn of Towns of the State of NY

Lobbyists:
Thomas Bodden
Kevin A Crawford
Jeffrey G Haber
Mike Kenneally
Lori Mithen

Association of Chiefs of Police-NYS
2697 Hamburg St
Schenectady, NY 12303
518-355-3371

Clients:
Association of Chiefs of Police-NYS

Auto Collision Technician's Assn Inc (NYS)
PO Box 482
Centereach, NY 11720
631-941-9647 Fax: 631-941-9647

Clients:
Auto Collision Technician's Assn Inc (NYS)

Lobbyists:
Edward Kizenberger

Automobile Dealers Assn (NYS)
37 Elk St, PO Box 7347
Albany, NY 12224-0347
518-463-1148 Fax: 518-432-1309
Web site: www.nysada.com

Clients:
Automobile Dealers Assn (NYS)

Lobbyists:
Robert E Vancavage

Ayers, Deborah
Delphi Corp
200 Upper Mountain Rd, Bldg 6
Lockport, NY 14094
716-439-3245

Clients:
Delphi Corporation

BP America Inc
1 W Pennsylvania Ave, Ste 440
Towson, MD 21204-5000
410-825-4173
e-mail: shutega@bp.com

Clients:
BP America Inc

Lobbyists:
Bruce C Johnson

Badillo, Herman
115 Broadway
New York, NY 10006
646-285-3544

Clients:
Imagine Schools Inc

Baker & Hostetler, LLP
1050 Connecticut Ave NW
Ste 1100
Washington, DC 20036
202-861-1500

Clients:
National Paint & Coatings Assn

Lobbyists:
Tom McDonald

Baldwin, Kristina
14 Norwood St
Albany, NY 12203
518-446-1105

Clients:
Property Casualty Insurers Assn of America (PCIAA)

Balinsky, John
Catholic Charities, 1150 Buffalo Rd
Rochester, NY 14624-1890
585-328-3210 Fax: 585-594-9534

Clients:
Catholic Charities of the Diocese of Rochester

Lobbyists:
Jann Armantrout
Anthony Barbaro
Domenic Carisetti
Joseph Dimino
Kathy Dubel
Scarlett Emerson
George Ferrari
Rick Fowler
Paul Hesler
Bridget Hurley
Janet Korn
Loretta Kruger
Marvin Mich
Laura Opelt
Paul Pickering
Carolyn Portanova
Ruth Putnam
Edie Reagen
Bridget Steed
Judy Taylor
Joseph Weider

Offices and agencies appear in alphabetical order.

Banks, Steven

Legal Aid Society (The)
199 Water St
New York, NY 10038
212-577-3277 Fax: 212-809-1574
e-mail: sbanks@legal-aid.org

Clients:
Legal Aid Society (The)

Barba, James J

Albany Medical Ctr
43 New Scotland Ave
Albany, NY 12208-3478
518-262-3830

Clients:
Albany Medical Center

Lobbyists:
Richard Cook

Barnes, Richard E

NYS Catholic Conference
465 State St
Albany, NY 12203-1004
518-434-6195 Fax: 518-434-9796
Web site: www.nyscatholic.org

Clients:
Catholic Conference (NYS)

Lobbyists:
Lani Candelora
James Cultrara
S Earl Eichelberger
Kathleen M Gallagher
Ronald Guglielmo
Jason Kramer
Dennis Poust

Barnett, Claire L

Healthy Schools Network, Inc
733 Madison Ave
Albany, NY 12208
518-462-0632 Fax: 518-462-0433
e-mail: info@healthyschools.org
Web site: www.healthyschools.org

Clients:
Healthy Schools Network Inc

Lobbyists:
Stephen Boese

Barrett Associates

95 Columbia St
Albany, NY 12210-2707
518-465-5340 Fax: 518-465-6023

Clients:
Acadia Insurance Company
America's Health Insurance Plans
Assn of Family Service Agencies (NYS)
Automobile Insurance Plan (NY)
Central Mutual Fire Insurance Co (NY)
Construction Contractors Assn of the Hudson Valley Inc
IAAC Inc
Independent Insurance Agents & Brokers of NY
Insurance Brokers Assn of NYS
Jefferson-Lewis et al School Employees Healthcare Plan
Property Insurance Underwriting Assn (NY)

Lobbyists:
Michael V Barrett
Todd Gold
Gregory Sehr

Bauer, Peter

Residents Cmte Protect Adirondack
PO Box 27
North Creek, NY 12853
518-251-4257 Fax: 518-251-5068

Clients:
Residents Committee to Protect the Adirondacks

Bedford Stuyvesant Family Health Center, Inc

1413 Fulton St
Brooklyn, MD 11216
718-636-4500

Clients:
Bedford Stuyvesant Family Health Center, Inc

Behan Communications Inc

13 Locust St, PO Box 922
Glens Falls, NY 12801
518-792-3856

Clients:
Finch, Pruyn & Co Inc

Lobbyists:
Mark Behan
John Brodt
Robert Dingman
Peter Lanahan

Bennett Firm, LLC (The)

100 State St, Ste 700
Albany, NY 12207-1805
518-432-6600 Fax: 518-432-7498

Clients:
American College of Surgeons Inc (NYS Chapter)
Lancaster Bingo Co Inc
Long Island Ophthalmological Society
Society of Orthopaedic Surgeons (NYS)

Lobbyists:
Heather Bennett
Amy Clinton

Offices and agencies appear in alphabetical order.

Bennett, Michael
33 South Clinton Ave
Hastings-on-Hudson, NY 10706-3602
914-478-0056

Clients:
Assn of Electrical Contractors, Inc (NYS)
Council of NECA Chapters (NYS)

Bergin, Robert J
Rochester Gas & Electric Corp
89 East Ave
Rochester, NY 14649
585-771-2294 Fax: 585-724-8668
e-mail: robert_bergin@rge.com
Web site: www.rge.com

Clients:
Rochester Gas & Electric Corp

Berry, Sally
Loretto Management Corp
700 E Brighton Ave
Syracuse, NY 13205
315-469-5570 Fax: 315-469-6558

Clients:
Loretto Management Corporation

Bigelsen, Jayne
Assn Bar of City NY
42 W 44th St
New York, NY 10036
212-382-6655

Clients:
Assn of the Bar of the City of NY

Biggerstaff Law Firm, LLP (The)(FKA Degraff Foy Holt-Harris Kunz & Devine, LLP)
Main Sq, 318 Delaware Ave
Delmar, NY 12054
518-475-9500

Clients:
Association of Small City School Districts (NYS)
Coalition of 853 Schools Inc (NYS)
National Paint & Coatings Assn
Siemens Building Technologies, Bau Division

Lobbyists:
Elizabeth Biggerstaff
Laura Biggerstaff
Robert E Biggerstaff

Billig, Jacob
140 Pinetree Dr
Glen Wild, NY 12738
845-434-4780

Clients:
Trading Cove NY, LLC

Bloom, Marc, LLP
35 Worth St, 4th Fl
New York, NY 10013
212-966-2680 Fax: 212-226-7554
e-mail: mbloom519@msn.com

Clients:
City of Yonkers
Pipetrades Assn (NYS)
Richmond UNI Home Care Inc

Lobbyists:
Marc Bloom

Blumenthal, Karen
Student Advocacy
3 West Main St, Ste 212
Elmsford, NY 10523-2414
914-347-7039

Clients:
Student Advocacy

Bogdan Lasky & Kopley, LLC
111 Washington Ave, Ste 750
Albany, NY 12210-2213
518-434-9000 Fax: 518-434-2510
e-mail: mnisengard@blklobby.com
Web site: www.blklobby.com

Clients:
AES New York, LLC
Academic Health Center Consortium
Alfred University
American Chemistry Council
Anheuser-Busch Companies Inc
Assn of Nurse Anesthetists Inc (NYS)
AstraZeneca Pharmaceuticals, LP
Bellevue Womans Hospital
Car Wash Association (NYS)
Casella Waste Systems Inc
Cendant Corporation
Comprehensive Care Management Corp
Constellation Energy Group
eBay
Entertainment Software Assn
Girl Scout Legislative Network (NYS)
Graduate College of Union University
HLR Service Corporation (Roche)
High Falls Film Festival
Industrial Uniform & Linen Supply Assn (NYS)
International Council of Shopping Centers
Jackson Hewitt Tax Service Inc
Local 1457 New York City Juvenile Ctr Employees
McLane Company Inc
Merrill Lynch & Co Inc
Motion Picture Assn of America Inc
National Assn of Theatre Owners of NYS (NATO)
Proctor & Gamble Company (The)
Rochester Business Alliance

Sergeants Benevolent Assn
Sprint Corporation
St Paul Travelers
Thoroughbred Breeders Inc (NY)
University of Rochester
US Interactive Inc
Wine Institute

Lobbyists:
Edward A Bogdan, III
Peter V Carr, Jr
Diane E Frazier
Mary K Kopley
James A Lasky
Denise Murphy McGraw
Erica Tricomi

Bolton St Johns Inc
146 State St
Albany, NY 12207
518-462-4620 Fax: 518-426-1631
e-mail: mail@boltonstjohns.com
Web site: www.boltonstjohns.com

Clients:
AMDEC Foundation Inc
Adult Day Health Care Council (ADHCC)
Agencies for Children's Therapy Services
Continuing Care Leadership Coalition
Berkshire Farm Ctr & Services for Youth
Capital District Regional Off-Track Betting Corp
County of Erie
Catskill Off-Track Corporation
Citigroup
City Ctr of Music & Drama Inc
Committee for Taxi Safety
Lower Manhattan Cultural Council
County Nursing Facilities of New York
Mutual Redevelopment Houses Inc
Nassau Regional Off-Track Betting Corporation
Express Scripts Inc
PMSI (Multistate Associates Inc)
Fuel Cell Energy Inc
Gay Men's Health Crisis Inc
Rochester Rhinos Stadium, LLC
Greater New York Hospital Assn
Health Insurance Plan of Greater NY (HIP)
Hebrew Academy for Special Children
Strong Museum
Hoffend & Sons Inc
Interior Designers for Legislation in NY (IDLNY)
International Union of Operating Engineers, Local 891
Island Peer Review Organization Inc
Keyspan Energy
Kingsbrook Jewish Medical Ctr
Taxi Club Management Inc
Local 32-BJ
Third Party Solutions
Moms Pharmacy
Monroe County
Monroe County Airport Authority
Trustees of Columbia University in the City of NY (The)
Village Care of New York
New School University
Pencil
Phelps Dodge Refining Corporation

Pipe Trades Assn
Professional Staff Congress (The)
Recording Industry Assn of America Inc
Shawanga Lodge, LLC
Working Rx
Somethingdigital.com, LLC
Suffolk County Assn of Municipal Employees PAC Inc
Sysco Food Services of Albany, LLC
Unity Health System
University of Phoenix (Apollo Group Inc)
Utica College
Value Options Inc
Verizon Wireless
Visy Paper (NY)
YMCA of New York State
Yum! Brands Inc
X-Ray Optical Systems Inc
Vytra Health Plans

Lobbyists:
Norman M Adler
Jay Adolf
Tom Connolly
Georgio DeRosa
Edward Draves
Emily Giske
Bill McCarthy
Melvin Miller

Boltz, John J Consulting
14 Linden Ct
Clifton Park, NY 12065
518-371-2790 Fax: 518-373-1536

Clients:
Altria Corporate Services
Building & Realty Institute
Miller Brewing Company
National Assn of Marine Manufacturers (Ahern, Barbara J)
Personal Watercraft Industry Association

Lobbyists:
John J Boltz

Bombardiere, Ralph
NYSASSRS
6 Walker Way
Albany, NY 12205-4946
518-452-1979 Fax: 518-452-1955
e-mail: nysassn@together.net
Web site: www.nysassrs.com

Clients:
Assn of Service Stations & Repair Shops Inc (NYS)

Bonagura, David (FKA Hoops, Jeffrey)
Ernst & Young LLP
395 N Service Rd
Melville, NY 11747
631-752-6125

Clients:
Ernst & Young LLP

Political Parties, Lobbyists & PACs

Lobbyists:
Paul Bader
Robert Michael Duffey
Michael R Press

Bond, Schoeneck & King, PLLC
111 Washington Ave
Albany, NY 12210-2211
518-533-3036 Fax: 518-462-7441

Clients:
Associated Credit Bureaus of NYS Inc
Automobile Dealers Assn (NYS)
Climax Manufacturing Co
Collectors Assn Inc (NYS)
Dairylea Cooperative Inc
First Cardinal Corporation
H & R Block Eastern Enterprises
Financial Service Centers of NY Inc
Ski Areas of NY Inc
Bally Total Fitness Corp
Utica Mutual Insurance Co

Lobbyists:
Frank Breselor
Hermes Fernandez
Richard L Smith

Bookman, Robert S
Newsstand Operators
325 Broadway, Ste 501
New York, NY 10007
212-513-1988 Fax: 212-385-0564

Clients:
Newsstand Operators Assn (NYC)
Nightlife Association (NY)

Bopp, Michael F
American Cancer Society
19 Dove St, Ste 103
Albany, NY 12210
518-449-5438 Fax: 518-449-7283
e-mail: michael.bopp@cancer.org
Web site: www.cancer.org

Clients:
American Cancer Society, Eastern Division Inc

Lobbyists:
Hillary Clarke
Lillian Jones
Russell Sciandra
Peter Slocum
Angela Smith
William Stoner
Sherry Tomasky

Botanical Garden (The) (NY)
200th St & Kazimiroff Blvd
Bronx, NY 10458
718-817-8962

Clients:
Botanical Garden (The)

Lobbyists:
J V Cossaboom
Rosemary Ginty
Gregory Long

Bourdeau, Bernard N
NY Insurance Assn, Inc
130 Washington Ave
Albany, NY 12210-2219
518-432-4227 Fax: 518-432-4220
e-mail: emelch@nyia.org
Web site: www.nyia.org

Clients:
Insurance Assn Inc (NY)

Lobbyists:
Ellen Melchionni

Boykin-Towns, Karen
Pfizer, Inc
235 East 42nd St, 12th Fl
New York, NY 10017
212-573-7627 Fax: 212-808-8880
e-mail: karen.boykin-towns@phizer.com
Web site: www.pfizer.com

Clients:
Pfizer, Inc

Brennan Center for Justice
161 Ave of the Americas, 12th Fl
New York, NY 10013
212-998-6730

Clients:
Brennan Center for Justice

Lobbyists:
Laura Abel
Patricia Allard
Jessie Allen
Monifa Bandele
Annette Bernhardt
Jeremy Creelan
Deborah Goldberg
Aziz Huq
Natalia Kennedy
Mary Lapas
Kirsten Levingston
Adam Morse
Nathan Newman
Rashad Robinson
Scott Schell
Paul Sonn
David Udell
Jennifer Weiser
Wendy Weiser
Catherine Weiss

Offices and agencies appear in alphabetical order.

Brescia, Richard
321 Loudon Rd
Loudonville, NY 12211
518-436-6733

Clients:
New York Propane Gas Assn

Brody, Gary
Community Bankers Assn NYS
655 3rd Ave, Ste 816
New York, NY 10017
212-573-5500

Clients:
Community Bankers Assn of NYS

Bronx Health Reach
16 East 16th St
New York, NY 10003
212-633-0800

Clients:
Bronx Health Reach

Lobbyists:
Neil Calman
Maxine Golub
Lorraine Gonzalez
Charmaine Ruddock

Brower, Michael R
SUNY College of Environ Science & Forest
1 Forestry Dr
Syracuse, NY 13210-2778
315-470-6639 Fax: 315-470-6977

Clients:
SUNY College of Environmental Science & Forestry

Brown McMahon & Weinraub, LLC
79 Columbia St
Albany, NY 12210
518-427-7350 Fax: 518-427-7792

Clients:
American Forest & Paper Assn Inc
Assn of Alcoholism & Substance Abuse Providers Inc (NY)
Assn of the Bar of the City of NY (The)
Building Congress of New York
Blue Chip Farms, LLC
Boymelgreen
Brooklyn Center for an Urban Environment
Court Officers Benevolent Assn of Nassau Cnty Inc
Entergy Nuclear Operations
Goldman Sachs
Hispanic Federation
Hispanic Information Technology Network
Hospice & Palliative Care Assn of NYS
Interfaith Medical Center
Brooklyn Economic Development Corporation
Center for Employment Opportunities (The)

Church Avenue Merchants Block Assn
Fund for Modern Courts
Indra (Global USA Inc)
Employment & Training Coalition (NYC)
Women's Bar Assn of the State of NY
Sprint
PSCH-Professional Svc Ctrs for the Handicapped
PhRMA-Pharmaceutical Research & Manufacturers Assn of America
Northrop Grumman Corporation
Real Estate Tax Review Bar Assn
Snapple Beverage Corp, Dr Pepper/Seven U Inc & Motts, LLP
Time Inc
Trading Cove New York, LLC

Lobbyists:
Patrick Brown
James McMahon
Thomas McMahon
Sandra Rivera
David Weinraub

Browne, Brian
St John's University
8000 Utopia Pkwy
Jamaica, NY 11439
718-990-2762 Fax: 718-990-2518
Web site: www.stjohns.edu

Clients:
St John's University

Bryan Cave, LLP
1290 Avenue of the Americas
New York, NY 10104
212-541-2386

Clients:
Viacom Outdoor Inc

Lobbyists:
Robert Davis
Judith Gallent
Margery Perlmutter

Buchanan Ingersoll
One Chase Manhattan Plaza
35th Fl
New York, NY 10005
212-440-4400 Fax: 212-440-4401

Clients:
Marijuana Policy Project (Public Strategies)

Lobbyists:
James Maisano

Buffalo Niagara Assn of Realtors, Inc
100 Sylvan Pkwy
Amherst, NY 14228
716-636-9000

Clients:
Buffalo Niagara Assn of Realtors, Inc

Offices and agencies appear in alphabetical order.

Lobbyists:
Charlene Zoratti

Buffalo State College
Institute Advancement
1300 Elmwood Ave, GC 516
Buffalo, NY 14222
716-878-4324 Fax: 716-878-5300

Clients:
Buffalo State College

Lobbyists:
Carmine Grande
Muriel Howard

Build PAC (NY)
One Commerce Plaza, Ste 704
Albany, NY 12210
518-465-2492 Fax: 518-465-0635
e-mail: info@nysba.com
Web site: www.nysba.com

Clients:
New York State Builders Assn
Build PAC (NY)

Lobbyists:
Philip La Rocque

Buley Public Affairs, LLC
27 Elk St
Albany, NY 12207
518-432-9563 Fax: 518-434-9093

Clients:
Care Plus
AMDEC Policy Group Inc
HealthNow New York Inc
Sequoia Voting Systems Inc
MCIC Vermont
Supreme Court Officers Assn (NYS)

Lobbyists:
Jeffrey T Buley
Albert J Pirro Jr

Buley, Jeffrey T
27 Elk St
Albany, NY 12207
518-432-9563

Clients:
Empire Resorts Inc
Jets, LLC (NY)
Lorillard Tobacco Company
North America Elder Law Attorneys - NY Chapter

Lobbyists:
Jeffrey T Buley

Burns, Miriam P
Selfhelp Community Svcs Inc
520 8th Ave
New York, NY 10018
212-971-7610 Fax: 212-967-1723

Clients:
Selfhelp Community Services, Inc

Business Council of NYS Inc
152 Washington Ave
Albany, NY 12210-2289
518-465-7511 Fax: 518-465-4389

Clients:
Business Council of NYS Inc (The)

Lobbyists:
Nicholas Dubray
Kerry Kirwan
Margarita Mayo
Thomas Minnick
Kenneth Pokalsky
Edward Reinfurt
Richard Schwarz
Elliott Shaw
Anne Van Buren
Daniel Walsh
Robert Ward

Business Development Group
PO Box 1013
Schenectady, NY 12301
518-377-2040

Clients:
Capital Living & Rehabilitation Centres

Butler, Denis M
Nat'l Education Assn of NY
217 Lark St
Albany, NY 12210-1192
518-462-6451 Fax: 518-462-1731

Clients:
National Education Assn of NY

Lobbyists:
Matt Jacobs
William Ninness
Maryellen Quinn
Robin Rapaport
Rosa Soria
Paul Webster

CNA
CNA Plaza
43rd Fl
Chicago, IL 60685
312-822-1739 Fax: 312-822-1186

Offices and agencies appear in alphabetical order.

Clients:
CNA

Lobbyists:
Andrew Bordon
Heather Davis

COFCCA Inc
19 West 21st St, Ste 501
New York, NY 10010
212-929-2626

Clients:
COFCCA Inc

Lobbyists:
Mary Jane Dessables
Dianne Heggie
William Pryylucki
James Purcell

CSC Holdings, Inc
1111 Stewart Ave
Bethpage, NY 11714
516-803-2387 Fax: 516-803-2667

Clients:
CSC Holdings, Inc

Lobbyists:
Lorraine Cortes-Vasquez
Joan Gilroy
Joan Hendricks
Elilzabeth Losinski
John McElhinney
Timothy Rooney
Lisa Rosenblum
Lee Schroeder
Dodie Tschirch

CTIA - The Wireless Assn
CTIA The Wireless Assn
1400 16th St NW, Ste 600
Washington, DC 20036
202-785-0081

Clients:
CTIA - The Wireless Assn

Caccese, Albert E
Audubon Nat'l Society
200 Trillium Lane
Albany, NY 12203
518-869-9731 Fax: 518-869-0737
e-mail: acaccese@audubon.org
Web site: www.ny.audubon.org

Clients:
Audubon National Society

Lobbyists:
Graham Cox
Sean Mahar

Calabrese, Joseph
United Way Greater Rochester
75 College Ave
Rochester, NY 14607-1009
585-242-6400 Fax: 585-242-6500

Clients:
United Way of Greater Rochester

Lobbyists:
Kathy Lewis
William McCullough
Nissa Youngren

Calvin, James S
Assn of Convenience Stores
130 Washington Ave, Ste 300
Albany, NY 12210
518-432-1400 Fax: 518-432-7400
e-mail: jim@nyacs.org
Web site: www.nyacs.org

Clients:
Assn of Convenience Stores (NY)

Campaign for Fiscal Equity, Inc
35 Maiden Ln
Albany, NY 12207
518-810-0031 Fax: 518-810-0108
Web site: www.cfequity.org

Clients:
Campaign for Fiscal Equity, Inc

Lobbyists:
Samira Ahmed
Michael Rebell

Capalino, James F & Associates Inc
850 Third Ave, 19th Floor
New York, NY 10022-6222
212-822-2285
e-mail: james@capalino.com
Web site: www.capalino.com

Clients:
All Stars Project Inc (The)
Alliance for the Arts
Literacy Assistance Center
M & H Realty, LLC
Rockrose Development Corp
Starrett Corporation
Two Trees Management Inc
Viacom Outdoor Inc

Lobbyists:
James Capalino
Travis Terry
Mark Thompson

Political Parties,
Lobbyists & PACs

Offices and agencies appear in alphabetical order.

Capital District Physicians' Health Plan Inc

1223 Washington Ave
Albany, NY 12206-1057
518-641-5211 Fax: 518-641-5205
Web site: www.cdphp.com

Clients:
Capital District Physicians' Health Plan Inc

Lobbyists:
William J Cromie

Capital Public Affairs

111 Washington Ave, Rm 104
Albany, NY 12210
518-465-8760 Fax: 518-427-6931

Clients:
Aetna Inc
Amgen
ING America Insurance Holdings
Medical Liability Mutual Insurance Co (MLMIC)
Pharmacists Society of the State of NY
Podiatric Medical Assn (NYS)
Schering-Plough External Affairs Inc
Sepracor Inc (Multistate Associates Inc)
Ticketmaster
Wyeth

Lobbyists:
Elizabeth M Lasky
Roy E Lasky

Capitol Consultants Inc (NY)

120 Washington Ave
Albany, NY 12210
518-449-3333 Fax: 518-427-6781
e-mail: judith@nycapcon.com

Clients:
American Council of Engineering Companies of NY
American Lawyer Media
Astoria Energy
BP America Inc
Bus Distributors Assn Inc (NYS)
Independent Automobile Dealers Assn Inc (NY)
Rein Corp
Self Storage Assn Inc (NY)
Sunoco Inc
Unions for Jobs & the Environment
Monroe County Deputy Sheriff's Association Inc

Lobbyists:
M Joe Landry
Christopher G McGrath

Capitol Group, LLC

29 Elk St
Albany, NY 12207-1002
518-463-4841 Fax: 518-463-5301
e-mail: nick@capitolgroupllc.com; tim@capitolgroupllc.com
Web site: www.capitolgroupllc.com

Clients:
ARC Inc (NYC Chapter)
Accupuncture Society of NY Inc
American Safety Institute Inc
Citrix Systems
Consumer Healthcare Products Assn
ECOR Solutions Inc
Empire State Marine Trades Assn
Grocery Manufacturers of America
City Media Concepts Inc
Long Island Forum for Technology
Rent-A-Center (Stateside Associates)
Rite Aid Corporation
Aramark Sports & Entertainment Services Inc
Snowmobile Assn (NYS)
Oak Point Properties, LLC
Turner Construction Co
Waste Management of NY, LLC
National Assn of Professional Employer Organizations

Lobbyists:
Nicholas Barrella
Timothy Sheridan

Capitol Hill Management Services Inc

90 State St, Ste 1009
Albany, NY 12207
518-463-8644 Fax: 518-463-8656
e-mail: chms@caphill.com
Web site: www.caphill.com

Clients:
Higher Education Opportunity Program - Professional Org
Outdoor Advertising Council of NY Inc
Poultry Assn Inc (NY)
Public Adjusters Assn (NY)
Society of Opticians Inc (NYS)
Epilepsy Foundation of Northeastern NY Inc

Lobbyists:
Molly Conners
Fred Field
John A Graziano, Jr
Douglas Mercado
Matthew Morgan

Capitol Strategies Group, LLC

113 State St
Albany, NY 12207
518-432-3676

Clients:
Map Info Corporation

Lobbyists:
Christopher Cotrona
Louis Cotrona
Joseph Magno

Cappelli, Allen

148 Kissel Ave
Staten Island, NY 10310
917-355-2720

Offices and agencies appear in alphabetical order.

Clients:
Building Industry Assn of NYC, Inc
R Randy Lee
Senior Housing Resource Corp
Melbar Development Company LLC
Staten Island Chamber of Commerce

Lobbyists:
Corey Bearak
Allen Cappelli
Robert Olivari

Carpenters Labor-Management Council, NYS
27 Warehouse Row
Albany, NY 12205
518-459-7182 Fax: 518-459-7798
e-mail: kevinhicks@usa.com

Clients:
Carpenters Labor-Management Council, NYS

Lobbyists:
Kevin Hicks

Carr Public Affairs Inc
388 Broadway, 4th Floor
Albany, NY 12207-2941
518-434-8830 Fax: 518-434-0072
e-mail: john@carrpublicaffairs.com
Web site: www.carrpublicaffairs.com

Clients:
4201 Schools Assn
American Forest & Paper Assn
Barr Laboratories Inc
Association of American Publishers
Coalition of Special Act School Districts
Federation of School Administrators (NYS)
Healthcare Distribution Management Assn (HDMA)
Home Care Council of New York City
Internet Security Systems Inc
Joint Council for Mental Health Svcs-Legislative Coalition
Literacy Volunteers of America-NYS Inc
NYS Assn of Supts of School Buildings & Grounds
Toyota Motor Sales, USA

Lobbyists:
James J Carr
John C Carr
Jean M Cox
Heather Evans
Vincent G Graber
Eugene K Tyksinski

Carr, Bernard
Assn for Affordable Housing
5925 Broadway
Bronx, NY 10463
718-432-2100 Fax: 718-432-2400
Web site: www.nysafah.org

Clients:
Assn for Affordable Housing (NYS)

Carroll, Sandra A
NYS Coalition for the Aging
244 Hudson Ave
Albany, NY 12210
518-465-0641

Clients:
Coalition for the Aging Inc (NYS)

Carson, Martin
105 Fiddlers Elbow Rd
PO Box 63
Middle Falls, NY 12848-0063
518-692-3162 Fax: 518-692-3164

Clients:
Lorillard Tobacco Co

Caruso, David A
Golub Corporation
501 Duanesburg Rd
Schenectady, NY 12306
518-379-1391 Fax: 518-379-3536

Clients:
Golub Corporation (The)

Lobbyists:
Lewis Golub
Neil M Golub

Casey, Kinsey
403 West 40th St
New York, NY 10018
212-967-1644

Clients:
Clinton Housing Development Corporation

Lobbyists:
Joe Restuccia

Castelbuono, A J
10 Airline Dr, Ste 203
Albany, NY 12205-1025
518-456-1134 Fax: 518-456-1198
e-mail: ajcastel@agcnys.org
Web site: www.agcnys.org

Clients:
Associated Gen'l Contractors of America Inc (NYS)
Crisis Program (The)

Lobbyists:
Steven Stallmer

Center for Independence of the Disabled in NY
841 Broadway, Ste 301
New York, NY 10003
212-674-2300

Offices and agencies appear in alphabetical order.

Clients:
Ctr for Independence of the Disabled, NY

Lobbyists:
Susan M Dooha
Michael Fuller
Julie Hyman
Lunetha Lancaster
Ramon Santos
Sharon Shapiro
Margi Trapani
Paula Wolff

Centro Independiente de Trabajadores Agricolas (CITA)
PO Box 109
Albion, NY 14411
585-589-7460 Fax: 585-589-7460

Clients:
Centro Independiente de Trabajadores Agricolas (CITA)

Lobbyists:
Aspacio Alcantara
Rosa Rivera
Francisco Rosario
Salvador Solis

Chadwick, Cindy
NYSEG
18 Link Dr, PO Box 5224
Binghamton, NY 13902-5224
607-762-7310 Fax: 607-762-8751
e-mail: ctchadwick@nyseg.com
Web site: www.nyseg.com

Clients:
Electric & Gas Corp (NYS)
Rochester Gas & Electric Corp

Chaifetz, Jill
Advocates for Children of NY
151 W 30th St, 5th Fl
New York, NY 10001
212-947-9779

Clients:
Advocates for Children of NY Inc

Lobbyists:
Elisa Hyman
Sonal Patel

Charter Schools Assn (NY)
One Commerce Plaza
99 Washington Ave, Ste 402
Albany, NY 12210
518-694-3110 Fax: 518-465-3383

Clients:
Charter Schools Assn (NY)

Lobbyists:
William A Phillips
Veria Samaroo

Child Care Coordinating Council (NYS)
230 Washington Ave Ext
Albany, NY 12203
518-690-4217 Fax: 518-427-6603

Clients:
Child Care Coordinating Council (NYS)

Lobbyists:
Jan Barbieri
Jane Brown
James Campbell
Rhonda Carloss-Smith
Karen Carpenter-Palumbo
Mon Cochran
Valerie Cooley
Dana Friedman
Celeste Frye
Susan Gibbons
Sue Dale Hall
Lottie Harris
Carla Hibbard
Lynn Kohrs
Sue Kowaleski
Peggy Liuzzi
Barbara-Ann Mattle
Dianne Meckler
Howard Milbert
Stephanie Mumford-Brown
Sandra Murrin
Patricia Myers
Carol Saginaw
James Sonneborn
Lori Van Auken
Jeanne Wagner
Janet Walerstein
Lynda Weismantel
Claudia Whitmire

Child Care Inc
322 Eighth Ave
New York, NY 10001
212-929-7604 x3010 Fax: 212-929-5785
e-mail: info@childcareinc.org
Web site: www.childcareinc.org

Clients:
Child Care Inc

Lobbyists:
Shannon Farrell
Betty Holcomb
Nancy Kolben
Charles Paprocki
Rhonda Smith

Children's Health Fund (The)
317 E 64th St
New York, NY 10021
212-535-9400

Offices and agencies appear in alphabetical order.

Clients:
Children's Health Fund (The)

Lobbyists:
Dennis Johnson
Violet Moss

Ciaravino, Anthony S
20480 Vernier Rd
Harper Woods, MI 48225
313-882-3700 Fax: 313-882-7630

Clients:
Wine Institute

Ciccone, Stephen J
1250 H St NW, Ste 800
Washington, DC 20005
202-857-3474 Fax: 202-857-3401
e-mail: stephen.ciccone@kodak.com
Web site: www.kodak.com

Clients:
Eastman Kodak Co

Lobbyists:
Jasprit Deol
Richard Jarman
John Richardson

Citizens Budget Commission
11 Penn Plaza, Ste 900
New York, NY 10001
212-279-2605

Clients:
Citizens Budget Commission

Lobbyists:
Charles Brecher
Jo Brill
Diana Fortuna
Elizabeth Lynam

Citizens Campaign for the Environment
225A Main St
Farmingdale, NY 11735
516-390-7150 Fax: 516-390-7160
e-mail: ccefli@citizenscampaign.org
Web site: www.citizenscampaign.org

Clients:
Citizens Campaign for the Environment

Lobbyists:
William Cooke
Maureen Dolan
Adrienne Esposito
Dereth Glance
Brendan Mahoney
Emmett Pepper
Brian Smith

Citizens' Committee for Children of New York Inc
105 East 22nd St, 7th Fl
New York, NY 10010-5413
212-673-1800 Fax: 212-979-5063
Web site: www.kfny.org

Clients:
Citizens' Committee for Children of New York Inc

Lobbyists:
Rose Anello
Jennifer March-Joly
Danielle Marchione
Gail Nayowith

City University of New York (CUNY)
111 Washington Ave, Ste 605
Albany, NY 12210
518-463-2177 Fax: 518-463-2170
Web site: www.cuny.edu

Clients:
City University of New York (CUNY)

Lobbyists:
Nasser Abdellatif
Anthony Allicino
Angelo Aponte
Fred Beaufait
Debra Bick-Duggan
Carole Birdsall
Jerome Blue
Leonard Ciaccio
Mary Coleman
Roger Witherspoon
Frances Degen Horowitz
Terry Rosen Deutsch
Allan Dobrin
Dolores M Fernandez
Ricardo R Fernandez
John Flateau
Maria Fosco
Adolphus C Frazier
Anna Garcia Reyes
Lia Gartner
Kristin Booth Glen
Eileen Goldmann
Matthew Goldstein
Steve Gorelick
Robert Hampton
Carlos Hargraves
Terrance Harris
Paulette Henriquez
Jay Hershenson
Otis Hill
Robert Holden
Audrey Hoover
Russell Hotzler
Bonnie Impagliazzo
Carol Jackson
Edison O Jackson
Brian Kell
MaryKaye Kellogg
Christoph M Kimmich

Offices and agencies appear in alphabetical order.

Oliver Klapper
John Kotowski
Miok Lee
Regina Linder
Emma Macari
Patrick S Madama
Fred Malamet
Ernesto Malave
Rosemarie Maldonado
Brenda Malone
James Malone
Ruby Malone
Eduardo Marti
Byron M McClenney
Matthew McGee
Gail Mellow
Nicholas Michelli
Virginia Mishkin
Meghan Moore Wilk
Meaghan Moore Wilke
Cynthia Murphy
James Muyskens
Jhony Nelson
Ivan Nunez
Dale Nussbaum
Gbubemi Okatieuro
Jose Orengo
Hector Ortiz
Sandra Palleja
Angelo Pappagallo
Antonio Perez
Nilda Perez
Regina Peruggi
Joanna Pestka
Robert Pignatello
Frederick Price
Jennifer J Raab
Eneida Rivas
Augustus Rivera
Felix Matos Rodriguez
A William Rogers
Chris Rosa
Deborah Rose
Chris Ross
Mary Rothlein
Tracey Rudnick
Sandra Ruiz
Angela Sales
Milton Santiago
Joseph Scelsa
Frederick Schaffer
Maureen Shields
Mary Ellen Smolka
Marlene Springer
Arthur Taylor
David Taylor
Doris Torres
Jeremy Travis
Carlos Vargas
Margaret Venditti

Civil Service Employees Assn, Inc

143 Washington Ave
Albany, NY 12210
518-257-1319 Fax: 518-465-2382

Clients:
Civil Service Employees Assn, Inc

Lobbyists:
George Boncoraglio
Danny Donohue
Kathy Garrison
Diane Hewitt
Nicholas Lamorte
Maureen Malone
James Moore
Barbara Reeves
Mary Sullivan
Florence Tripi

Clark, Frank A

Adirndk Landowner's Assn
608 State Tower Bldg
Syracuse, NY 13202-1704
315-471-3027 Fax: 315-472-3530

Clients:
Adirondack Landowners Assn Inc

Clarke, Donald

Exxon Mobile
1400 Old Country Rd, Ste 203
Westbury, NY 11590
516-333-3177 Fax: 516-333-3428

Clients:
Exxon Mobile Corp

Clarkson University

Govt Relations
8 Clarkson Ave
Potsdam, NY 13699-5537
315-268-6474 Fax: 315-268-6515

Clients:
Clarkson University

Lobbyists:
Robert H Wood, Jr

Cleary, Kevin Government Relations, LLC

39 N Pearl St, 3rd Fl
Albany, NY 12207
518-463-2399 Fax: 518-463-2397
e-mail: kevin@albanyinsider.com
Web site: www.albanyinsider.com

Clients:
AIDS Service Network, NYC
AIM Healthcare Services Inc
Assn of Psychiatric Rehabilitation Svcs (NY)
Caremark Rx
Camphill Village USA Inc
City of Rochester, NY
Fountain House
Institute for Community Living Inc
Medical Equipment Providers Assn (NY)

Offices and agencies appear in alphabetical order.

United Healthcare Services Inc
University of Rochester

Lobbyists:
Kevin J Cleary

Coalition Against Domestic Violence (NYS)
350 New Scotland Ave
Albany, NY 12208
518-482-5465 Fax: 518-482-3807

Clients:
Coalition Against Domestic Violence (NYS)

Lobbyists:
Sherry Frohman
Patti Jo Newell
Sherri Salvione

Coalition Against Hunger (NYC)
16 Beaver St, 3rd Fl
New York, NY 10004
212-825-0028

Clients:
Coalition Against Hunger (NYC)

Lobbyists:
Joel Berg

Coalition for Children's Mental Health Services (NYS)
PO Box 7124
Albany, NY 12224-0124
518-436-8715

Clients:
Coalition for Children's Mental Health Services (NYS)

Lobbyists:
Andrea Smyth

Coalition for Education Reform & Accountability
4 Chelsea Pl
Clifton Park, NY 12065
518-383-2598 Fax: 518-383-2841

Clients:
Coalition for Education Reform & Accountability

Lobbyists:
Brian D Backstrom
Maureen Blum
Thomas W Carroll

Coalition for the Homeless
25 Elk St, Lower Level
Albany, NY 12207-1002
518-436-5612 Fax: 518-436-5615

Clients:
Coalition for the Homeless

Lobbyists:
Mary Brosnahan-Sullivan
Lindsey Davis
Patrick Markee
Ann Nortz
Diana Olaizola
Duayne Sorrell
Dan Tietz
Jeff Wise

Coalition of Voluntary Mental Health Agencies, Inc
90 Broad St, 8th Fl
New York, NY 10004
212-742-1600 Fax: 212-742-2080

Clients:
Coalition of Voluntary Mental Health Agencies, Inc

Lobbyists:
Meggan Christman
Patricia Gallo Goldstein
Michael Polenberg
Phillip Saperia

Cobb Jr, James H
Shipping Assn, Inc (NY)
100 Wood Ave, Ste 304
Iselin, NJ 08830-2716
732-452-7808

Clients:
Shipping Association, Inc (NY)

Cohen, Marsha A
Reinsurance Assn of America
1301 Pennsylvania Ave, NW, Ste 900
Washington, DC 20004-1701
202-683-3690 Fax: 202-638-0936
e-mail: cohen@reinsurance.org
Web site: www.reinsurance.org

Clients:
Reinsurance Assn of America

Coleman, Elizabeth
Trial Lawyers' Assn (NYS)
132 Nassau St
New York, NY 10038
212-349-5890 Fax: 212-608-2310
e-mail: ecoleman@nystla.org
Web site: www.nystla.org

Clients:
Trial Lawyers' Assn (NY)

Lobbyists:
Christopher Goeken

Offices and agencies appear in alphabetical order.

Brenda Morrow
Lawrence Park
Glenn Von Nostitz
Val Washington

Committee for an Independent Public Defense Commission

One Commerce Plaza, Ste 1900
Albany, NY 12260
518-487-7738 Fax: 518-487-7777

Clients:
Committee for an Independent Public Defense Commission

Lobbyists:
Michael Whiteman

Community Advocacy & Advisory Services

247 Lark St, 1st Fl
Albany, NY 12210
518-449-2772 Fax: 518-449-2710
e-mail: kmk@communityadvocacy.com
Web site: www.communityadvocacy.com

Clients:
AIDS Day Services Assn Advocacy Committee
Prevent Child Abuse New York

Lobbyists:
Christine Deyss
Charles King
Michael Kink

Community Bankers Association of NYS

655 Third Ave, Ste 816
New York, NY 10017
212-573-5500 Fax: 212-573-5509
e-mail: gbrody@cbanys.org
Web site: www.cbanys.org

Clients:
Community Bankers Assn of NYS

Lobbyists:
Mariel Donath

Community Health Care Association of NYS

254 West 31st St, 9th Fl
New York, NY 10001
212-279-9686
e-mail: kbreslin@chcanys.org
Web site: www.chcanys.org

Clients:
Community Health Care Assn of NYS

Lobbyists:
Katherine Breslin
John Corwin

Community Healthcare Network

79 Madison Ave, 6th Fl
New York, NY 10016
212-366-4500 Fax: 212-366-4616
Web site: www.chnnyc.org

Clients:
Community Healthcare Network

Lobbyists:
Catherine Abate
Phuong Tran

Community Preservation Corporation (The)

28 East 28th St, 9th Fl
New York, NY 10016-7943
212-869-5300 x511 Fax: 212-683-0694
e-mail: mlappin@communityp.com
Web site: www.communityp.com

Clients:
Community Preservation Corporation (The)

Lobbyists:
Kathleen Dunn
Richard A Kumro
Michael D. Lappin
John M McCarthy
Brenda Ratliff

Community Service Society of NY

105 E 22nd St
New York, NY 10010-5413
212-254-8900 Fax: 212-614-9441
e-mail: vbach@cssny.org
Web site: www.cssny.org

Clients:
Community Service Society of NY

Lobbyists:
Victor Bach
Debra Berman
Jacqueline Burger
David Campbell
Juan Cartagena
Walter Fields
Janeene Freeman
Donald Friedman
Aviva Goldstein
David R Jones
Steven Krause
Mark Levitan
Christine Molnar
Nancy Rankin
Sabine Salandy
Denise Soffel
Robin Willig

Community Voices Heard

170 East 116th St, Ste 1E
New York, NY 10029
212-860-6001 Fax: 212-996-9481

Offices and agencies appear in alphabetical order.

Clients:

Community Voices Heard

Lobbyists:

Gail Aska
Paul Getsos
Jeremy Saunders
Henry Serrano
Sondra Youdelman

Compensation Action Network (NY)

5784 Widewaters Pkwy, 1st Fl
Dewitt, NY 13214
800-962-7950

Clients:

Compensation Action Network (NY)

Lobbyists:

Lawrence Gilroy
Richard Poppa

Conference of Mayors & Municipal Officials (NYS)

119 Washington Ave
Albany, NY 12210
518-463-1185

Clients:

Conference of Mayors & Municipal Officials (NYS)

Lobbyists:

Peter Baynes
Wade Beltramo
Mary Carmel
Edward C Farrell
Lynn Flansburg
John H Galligan
Donna M C Giliberto
Riele Morgiewicz
Jennifer Purcell
Deanna Walker

Connelly & McLaughlin

64 Fulton St
New York, NY 10038
212-437-7373

Clients:

Alexandria Real Estate Equities, Inc
BFC Construction Corp
Building Trades Employers Assn
Chip-Community Housing Improvement Program, Inc
Edison Properties
Edward J Minskoff Equities, Inc
Entertainment Software Association
General Contractors Assn of NY, Inc (The)
Gilbane Building Company
GP Eleventh Corp
Hunter College
Independence Plaza Associates LLC
International Code Council
Metropolitan Taxicab Board of Trade
Museum of Modern Art (The)

Northside Waterfront Improvement Group
Oil Heating Assn (NY)
Seventh Regiment Armory Conservancy
Trillium USA, Inc
Vsleray Real Estate Company, Inc
Wooster, LLC-RJH Development Corp

Lobbyists:

Maureen Connelly
Kathy Cudahy
Martin McLaughlin
Michael Woloz

Connelly Communications, Inc

64 Fulton St
New York, NY 10038
212-437-7373

Clients:

Doctors Council

Lobbyists:

Maureen Connelly
Michael Woloz

Constantinople Consulting

123 William St, 22nd Fl
New York, NY 10038
212-393-6500 Fax: 212-393-6501
e-mail: constantinople@worldnet.att.net

Clients:

Commerce Bank
Deep-Water Port Corp (NY)
Tan International Group
Ecoglo, Ltd
Grace Asphalt Inc
Hunts Point Terminal Produce Cooperative Assn
Junior Tennis League (NY)
Migdol Realty LLC
Sports & Arts in Schools Foundation
Waste Management

Lobbyists:

Anthony J Constantinople III
Anthony J Constantinople, Jr
Robert Fonti
Raymond Frier
Anthony Riccio
Paul Vallone
Peter F Vallone, Sr

Conway, Gerard L, Jr

Plug Power, Inc
968 Albany Shaker Rd
Latham, NY 12110
518-782-7700 Fax: 518-690-4446
e-mail: gerard.conway@plugpower.com
Web site: www.plugpower.com

Clients:

Plug Power Inc

Lobbyists:
John Elter
Roger Saillant
Mark Sperry

Coppola Ryan McHugh Riddell

119 Washington Avenue, 2nd Fl
Albany, NY 12210
518-434-7400 Fax: 518-434-0558
e-mail: crmlobby@aol.com
Web site: www.nylobbyist.com

Clients:
Time Warner Inc
Assn of Convenience Stores (NY)
Assn of Mortgage Brokers (NY)
Western Regional Off-Track Betting Corp
Assn of Surrogate's & Supreme Court Reporters
Brookhaven Energy Ltd Partnership by ANP Brookhaven Energy Co Gen
Building Trades Employer's Assn
C&S Engineers Inc
BJK Inc/dba Chem Rx
Children's Vision Coalition
Assn of Naturopathic Physicians (NY)
Contractors Assn of Greater NY
NRG Energy Inc
Supreme Court Officers Assn (NYS)
Exxon Mobil Corporation
Group for Equitable Tax Practices
Law School Admission Council
M/A-Com Inc
Mastercard International Inc
McDonald's Corporation
Metropolitan Transportation Authority
Norfolk Southern Corporation
Optometric Assn (NYS)
Pfizer Inc
Reckitt Benckiser Inc
Trustees of Columbia University (The)
Verizon
Williams Companies (The)
Children's Institute
Catskill Region Off-Track Betting Corp
Building & Realty Institute of Westchester & the Mid-Hudson Regio

Lobbyists:
Charles Coppola
Veronica M Coppola
Diana Georgia
Patrick J McHugh
Glenn T Riddell

Coppola, John J

ASAPNYS
1 Columbia St
Albany, NY 12207
518-426-3122 Fax: 518-426-1046
e-mail: jcoppola@asapnys.org
Web site: www.asapnys.org

Clients:
Assn of Alcoholism & Substance Abuse Providers Inc (NY)

Cordeau, David P

Greater Syracuse Chamber of Commerce
572 S Salina St
Syracuse, NY 13202-3320
315-470-1800 Fax: 315-471-8545
e-mail: dcordeau@syracusechamber.com
Web site: www.syracusechamber.com

Clients:
Greater Syracuse Chamber of Commerce

Lobbyists:
Doug Small
Deborah Warner

Cordo, John

99 Pine St
Albany, NY 12207
518-436-0786

Clients:
Cigar Assn of America Inc

Corning Place Consulting, LLC

121 State St
Albany, NY 12207-0693
518-689-7286

Clients:
NYSCOP Inc

Lobbyists:
Mark Amodeo

Couch White, LLP

540 Broadway
PO Box 22222
Albany, NY 12201
518-426-4600 Fax: 518-426-0376
e-mail: bbrenner@couchwhite.com
Web site: www.couchwhite.com

Clients:
MCI
Industrial Energy Consumers Coalition
Mirant New York Inc
Power for Economic Prosperity Group

Lobbyists:
Barbara S Brenner
Maureen Helmer
Robert Loughney
Lawrence Malone
Algird White

Council for Community Behavioral Healthcare (NYS)

155 Washington Ave, 2nd Fl
Albany, NY 12210
518-445-2642 Fax: 518-445-2642

Offices and agencies appear in alphabetical order.

Clients:
Council for Community Behavioral Healthcare (NYS)

Lobbyists:
Lauri Cole

Council of Community Services of NYS Inc
272 Broadway
Albany, NY 12204-2717
518-434-9194 x110 Fax: 518-434-0392
e-mail: dsauer@ccsnys.org
Web site: www.ccsnys.org

Clients:
Council of Community Services of NYS Inc

Lobbyists:
Krista Clark
Jill Farnam
Denise Harlow
Katherine Markey
Douglas McCuen
Alisha Russo
William Sauer

Council of Senior Ctrs & Services of NYC, Inc
49 W 45th St, 7th Fl
New York, NY 10036
212-398-6565 Fax: 212-398-8395

Clients:
Council of Senior Ctrs & Services of NYC, Inc

Lobbyists:
Bobbie Sackman

Council of the City of New York
111 Washington Ave, Ste 410
Albany, NY 12210-2208
518-462-5461 Fax: 518-462-1398
Web site: www.council.nyc.ny.us

Clients:
Council of the City of NY (The)

Lobbyists:
Natasha Kerry
Angelo Larian
Gloria Mullen
Michael D Nieves

Council on Homeless Policies & Services
70 West 36th St, Ste 1404
New York, NY 10018
646-827-2270

Clients:
Council on Homeless Policies & Services

Lobbyists:
Lauren Bholai-Pareti

Crane & Vacco, LLC
90 State St, Ste 1507
Albany, NY 12207
518-426-0606 Fax: 518-432-0086

Clients:
Southern Tier Acquisition LLC
Brain Trauma Foundation
Cable Telecommunications Assn of NY, Inc (The)
Stub Hub, Inc
United NY Ambulance Network (UNYAN)
Crown Castle Atlantic, Inc
Delaware North Companies, Inc
Duane Reade, Inc
United NY Ambulance Network

Lobbyists:
Constance Crane
James B Crane
Andrea Kosier
Dennis Vacco

Credit Union League Inc & Affiliates (NYS)
19 British American Blvd
Latham, NY 12110
518-437-8122 Fax: 518-782-4212

Clients:
Empire Corporate Federal Credit Union

Lobbyists:
Joseph Herbst
Amy Hines-Kramer
Christina G Hyland
Michael Lanotte
William Mellin
Dirck VanDeusen

Crosier, Barbara V
United Cerebral Palsy Assn
90 State St, Ste 929
Albany, NY 12207
518-436-0178 Fax: 518-436-8619
e-mail: bcrosier@cerebralpalsynys.org
Web site: www.cerebralpalsynys.org

Clients:
United Cerebral Palsy Assns of NYS Inc

Lobbyists:
Michael Alvaro
Susan Constantino
Joanne Genovese

Crossett, Susan M
300 Erie Blvd W
Syracuse, NY 13202
315-428-5430 Fax: 315-428-3406
e-mail: susan.crossett@us.ngrid.com
Web site: www.niagaramohawk.com

Clients:
Niagara Mohawk - A National Grid Company

Offices and agencies appear in alphabetical order.

Niagara Mohawk Holdings Inc

Lobbyists:
William Flynn

Curran, Brian F
Public Employee Federation
100 State St, Ste 1070
Albany, NY 12207-1806
518-432-4003 Fax: 518-432-7739
e-mail: bcurran@pef.org

Clients:
Public Employees Federation (NYS)

Lobbyists:
Helen Brooks
John Murphy
Mark Streb

D & O Consultants
101 Park Ave, Ste 2506
New York, NY 10178
212-883-5608 Fax: 212-883-5643

Clients:
Destiny USA Inc

Lobbyists:
Alfonse D'Amato
John O'Mara

D'Ambrosio, John A
Orange County Chamber of Commerce
11 Racquet Rd
Newburgh, NY 12550
845-567-6229

Clients:
Orange County Chamber of Commerce

Lobbyists:
Debra Bogdanski

D'Onofrio, Paul
67 Chestnut St
Albany, NY 12210
518-432-7393

Clients:
Assn of Electrical Workers (NYS)
Council of Sheet Metal Workers Int'l Assn (NYS)
Monticello Raceway Management Inc

Dadey, Dick
299 Broadway, Ste 700
New York, NY 10007
212-227-0342 Fax: 212-227-0345

Clients:
Citizens Union of the City of New York

Lobbyists:
Doug Israel

Dahill, Kevin
1383 Veterans Memorial Hwy, Ste 26
Hauppauge, NY 11788
631-435-3000 Fax: 631-435-2343
Web site: www.nshc.org

Clients:
Nassau-Suffolk Hospital Council Inc

Lobbyists:

Dames, Reid, LLC
1285 6th Ave, 35th Fl
New York, NY 10019
212-554-4244 Fax: 212-554-4245

Clients:
Arthritis Foundation (NY Chapter)
Citizens Committee for Children of NY Inc
Coalition of Voluntary Mental Health Agencies Inc
Safe Horizon
Empire State Pride Agenda
Human Services Council of NYC Inc
National Assn of Social Workers (NYC Chapter)
Therapeutic Communities Assn of NY Inc
Women in Need Inc
Foundation to Cure Paralysis
Jewish Board of Family & Children's Services Inc
Alzheimer's Assn, NYC Chapter

Lobbyists:
Cynthia Dames
Lisa Reid

Dan Klores Communications Inc
386 Park Ave South, 10th Fl
New York, NY 10016
212-685-4300

Clients:
Motorola, Inc

Darien Lake Theme Park & Camping Resort
9933 Allegheny Rd
PO Box 91
Darien Center, NY 14040
585-599-4641

Clients:
Darien Lake Theme Park & Camping Resort, Inc

Lobbyists:
Bradley Paul

Darwak, Stephanie
3 Independence Row
Stillwater, NY 12170
518-664-5880

Offices and agencies appear in alphabetical order.

Clients:
Pfizer, Inc

Davenport, Nancy
American Council of Life Insurers
19 Lounsbury Court
Kingston, NY 12401
845-339-1511 Fax: 845-339-1611
e-mail: nancydavenport@acli.com
Web site: www.acli.com

Clients:
American Council of Life Insurers

Davidoff, Malito & Hutcher, LLP
150 State St, 4th Fl
Albany, NY 12207
518-465-8230 Fax: 518-465-8230

Clients:
Abbott Laboratories
Adelphi University
Altria Corporate Services Inc
American Society for Dermatological Surgery
Cybershift Inc
Heartwood 88, LLC
Life Settlements International
Clear Channel Outdoor
Concert Connection, Ltd (The)
Nassau County Village Officials Assn
Council of School Supervisors & Administrators
State Court Reporters Assn Inc (NY)
Docking Pilots of NJ/NY
National Center for Disability Services
Election Systems & Software Inc
Epilepsy Foundation of Long Island
National Electrical Manufacturers Assn
National Foundation for Teaching Entreprenership
Greater NY Hospital Assn
Helen Keller Services for the Blind
Construction Materials Association (NY)
St Vincent Catholic Medical Centers
Nestle Waters North America Holdings Inc
North Shore Child & Family Guidance Assn
Palladia Inc (Formerly Project Return Foundation Inc)
Project Renewal
Queens Borough Public Library
Rainbow Chimes Inc, Child Care Ctr
Staffing Assn (NY)
Taxicab Service Assn
Uniformed Firefighters Assn
Westchester County Health Care Corp
Wildcat Services Corporation
YAI/National Institute for People with Disabilities
Incorporated Village of Freeport (The)
Tax Ease, LP
Westbury Property Investment Co

Lobbyists:
Jeff Citron
Peter R Crouse
Sid Davidoff
Arthur Goldstein
John B Kiernan
Robert J Malito

Stephen A Malito
Juan Reyes
Keith Serwick
Howard Weiss

Davis, Michael J
6790 Lainhart Rd
Altamont, NY 12009
518-356-1508
e-mail: mdavis10@rdg.boehringer-ingelheim.com

Clients:
Boehringer Ingelheim Pharmaceuticals, Inc

Delio, Vincent J
University at Albany
1400 Washington Ave, UAB 429
Albany, NY 12222
518-437-4901

Clients:
University at Albany

Lobbyists:
Vincent Delio
Michael Fancher
Kermit Hall
James Sammons
Stephanie Wacholder

Demos:A Network for Ideas & Action
220 Fifth Ave, 5th Fl
New York, NY 10001
212-633-1405

Clients:
Demos:A Network for Ideas & Action

Lobbyists:
Steven Carbo
Joseph Hayden
Blain Ludovic
Miles Rapoport
Sarah Tobias
Meron Wondwosen

Deutsch, Ronald
Senses
275 State St
Albany, NY 12210-2101
518-463-5576

Clients:
Senses

Devorsetz Stinziano Gilberti Heintz & Smith, PC
555 E Genesee St
Syracuse, NY 13202-2159
518-476-2001

Offices and agencies appear in alphabetical order.

Clients:
Catskill Off-Track Betting Corp
Center for Jewish History (The)
Country Club Condominiums

Lobbyists:
Tarky Lombardi, Jr
Carol Philippi

Dewey Ballantine LLP
1301 Avenue of the Americas
New York, NY 10019-6022
212-259-8000

Clients:
New York Racing Assn Inc (The)

Lobbyists:
Mary Deluca
Michael Hefter
Eamon O'Kelly
Bradford Race

DiPalermo, Christian
NY'ers for Parks
457 Madison Ave, 6th Fl
New York, NY 10022
212-838-9410 Fax: 212-371-6048

Clients:
New Yorkers for Parks

Lobbyists:
Mark Caserta
Allison Farina
Anna Maria Jones

Diamond Asphalt Corp
91 Paidge Ave
Brooklyn, NY 11222
718-383-4198

Clients:
Diamond Asphalt Corp

Lobbyists:
John Labozza

Dierks, John W
591 Upper Grassy Hill Rd
Woodbury, CT 06798
203-263-2878

Clients:
Roche Diagnostics Corp

Digiovanni, Joseph
Liberty Mutual
175 Berkeley St
Boston, MA 2117
617-357-9500 Fax: 617-574-5783
Web site: www.libertymutual.com

Clients:
Liberty Mutual Group

Diorio, L Todd
451A Little Britian Rd
Newburgh, NY 12550
845-565-2737

Clients:
Hudson Valley Building & Construction Trades Council
Laborers Int'l Union of North America AFL-CIO, Local 17

District Council 37, AFSCME
125 Barclay St
New York, NY 10007
212-815-1500 Fax: 212-815-1516
Web site: www.district37.net

Clients:
District Council 37, AFSCME

Lobbyists:
Leonard Allen
Susan Graham
Oliver Gray
Wanda Williams

Doherty, C R & Co
29 Grant Hill Court
Clifton Park, NY 12065-7704
518-383-8513 Fax: 518-383-9414
e-mail: cd1136@aol.com

Clients:
District Attorneys Investigators of Westchester County Inc
Service Station Dealers of Greater NY Inc
Vehicle Rental Assn (NY)
Westchester Co Correction Superior Officers Assn
Westchester Co Dept of Public Safety Services, PBA

Lobbyists:
Charles Robert Doherty

Donnellan, James
Metropolitan Life Ins Co
27-01 Queens Plaza N, Area 4
Long Island City, NY 11101-4015
212-578-3968

Clients:
Metropolitan Life Insurance Co

Lobbyists:
Robert Benmoschie
Ellie Jurado-Nieves
James L Lipscomb
Joseph Reali
Timothy Ring
Michael Zarcone

Offices and agencies appear in alphabetical order.

Donnelly, Edwin

AFL-CIO (NYS)
100 S Swan St
Albany, NY 12210
518-436-8516 Fax: 516-436-8470
e-mail: edonnelly@nysaflcio.org
Web site: www.nysaflcio.org

Clients:
AFL-CIO (NYS)

Lobbyists:
Denis Hughes
Arthur Wilcox

Donohue, Gavin J

Independent Power Prod of NY
19 Dove St, Ste 302
Albany, NY 12210
518-436-3749 Fax: 518-436-0369
e-mail: gavin@ippny.org
Web site: www.ippny.org

Clients:
Independent Power Producers of NY Inc

Lobbyists:
Carolyn Brown
Glenn Haake
Radmila Miletich

Doyle, Michael R

NYS Petroleum Council
150 State St
Albany, NY 12207-1675
518-465-3563 Fax: 518-465-4022
e-mail: doylem@api.org
Web site: www.api.org

Clients:
American Petroleum Institute

Lobbyists:
Cathy A Kenny

Dryfoos Group

444 Park Ave South, Ste 1202
New York, NY 10016
646-742-3715 Fax: 718-786-7633
e-mail: bob@thedryfoosgroup.com

Clients:
American Folk Art Museum
Creative Arts Team/CUNY
Ctr for Educational Innovation-Public Education Assn
Ensemble/Studio Theatre
Institute for Student Achievement
Junior Tennis League (NY)
Shareing & Careing Inc
Sports & Arts in School Foundation
Young Women's Leadership Foundation
Performance Space Izz

Big Brothers Big Sisters of NYC
Italian American Museum
Small & Family Business Foundation Inc
South Street Seaport Museum
Metropolitan Athletics Congress Inc
Midori and Friends

Lobbyists:
Robert J Dryfoos
Paul E Greenfield
Laura Jean Hawkins
Alexandria Jones
Suzanne Towns

Dudley Associates

57 Lodge St
Albany, NY 12207-1518
518-463-2203 Fax: 518-449-4941
e-mail: dudleyassoc@worldnet.att.net

Clients:
Albany College of Pharmacy
American Standard Company
Outokumpu American Brass Inc
Trial Lawyers' Assn (NYS)

Lobbyists:
David R Dudley
Kathleen M Haggerty

Duncan, Craig A

127 Eastern Union Tpk
Averill Park, NY 12018
518-674-5261

Clients:
Northeast Health & Affiliates

Dunne, Richard C

15 Trues Dr
West Islip, NY 11795
631-422-1320

Clients:
Northrop Grumman Corporation

E-3 Communications

43 Court St, Ste 910
Buffalo, NY 14202
716-854-8182 Fax: 716-852-6985
Web site: www.e3communications.com

Clients:
NOCO Energy Corp
Niagara Tourism & Convention Corp
Park Associates (The)
Power for Economic Prosperity Group
Independent Oil & Gas Assn of NY

Lobbyists:
Margaret Duffy
Earl V Wells, III

Offices and agencies appear in alphabetical order.

Economic Development Council Inc (NYS)

19 Dove St, Ste 101
Albany, NY 12210
518-426-4058 Fax: 518-426-4059
e-mail: mcmahon@nysedc.org
Web site: www.nysedc.org

Clients:
Economic Development Council Inc (NYS)

Lobbyists:
Brian T McMahon

Educational Conference Board (NYS)

NYS Assn of School Business Officials
7 Elk St
Albany, NY 12207-1002
518-434-2281 Fax: 518-434-1303

Clients:
Educational Conference Board (NYS)

Lobbyists:
Timothy Kremer
Penny Leask
Alan Lubin
Edward McCormick
George A Perry

Educational Priorities Panel

225 Broadway, 39th Fl
New York, NY 10007-3001
212-964-7347

Clients:
Educational Priorities Panel

Lobbyists:
Martine Guerrier

Elinski, Karen

TIAA/CREF
730 Third Ave
New York, NY 10017-3206
212-916-6476 Fax: 212-916-5952
e-mail: kelinski@tiaa-creff.org
Web site: www.tiaa-cref.org

Clients:
College Retirement Equities Fund
Teachers Ins & Annuity Assn

Lobbyists:
Malcolm O Campbell

Empire State College, State University of NY

1 Union Ave
Saratoga Springs, NY 12866
518-587-2100 Fax: 518-587-2886
e-mail: marycaroline.powers@esc.edu
Web site: www.esc.edu

Clients:
Empire State College, State University of NY

Lobbyists:
Joseph B Moore
Mary Caroline Powers

Empire State Forest Products

828 Washington Ave
Albany, NY 12203
518-463-1297 Fax: 518-426-9502
Web site: www.esfpa.org

Clients:
Empire State Forest Products Assn

Lobbyists:
Kevin King

Empire State Water Well Drillers' Assn Inc

354 Stonechurch Rd
Ballston Spa, NY 12020
518-885-7952 Fax: 518-885-8973

Clients:
Empire State Water Well Drillers' Assn Inc

Lobbyists:
Janice Hawk-Baldwin

Employer Alliance for Affordable Health Care

PO Box 1412
Albany, NY 12201-1412
518-462-2296 Fax: 518-462-2150
Web site: employeralliance.com

Clients:
Employer Alliance for Affordable Health Care

Lobbyists:
Jeffrey Leeland

Energy Assn of NYS (The)

111 Washington Ave, Ste 601
Albany, NY 12210-2276
518-449-3440 Fax: 518-449-3446

Clients:
Energy Assn of NYS (The)

Lobbyists:
Patrick Curran
Sharon Foley
Stephen Hanse
Michael Rynasko
Howard Shapiro
Stuart Silbertgleit

Entergy Nuclear Operations, Inc

440 Hamilton Ave
White Plains, NY 10601
914-272-3350

Offices and agencies appear in alphabetical order.

Clients:

Entergy Nuclear Operations, Inc

Lobbyists:

Debbie Fay
Michael Kansler
Michael Slobodien
Jim Steets
Kenneth Theobalds

Enterprise Rent-A-Car

1550 Route 23 North
Wayne, NJ 7470
973-709-2499 Fax: 973-709-2455

Clients:

Enterprise Rent-A-Car

Lobbyists:

Thomas Cantilli

Environmental Advocates of NY

353 Hamilton St
Albany, NY 12210
518-462-5526

Clients:

Environmental Advocates of NY

Lobbyists:

Laura Dibetta
David Higby
Jeff Jones
Robert Moore
Anne Reynolds
Tim Sweeney
Christine Vanderlan

Environmental Business Assn of NYS Inc

126 State St, 3rd Fl
Albany, NY 12207-1637
518-432-6400 Fax: 518-432-1383
e-mail: info@eba-nys.org
Web site: www.eba-nys.org

Clients:

Environmental Business Assn of NYS Inc

Lobbyists:

Kelly Bennett
Ira Rubenstein

Equinox Inc

95 Central Ave
Albany, NY 12206
518-434-6135 Fax: 518-432-5607
e-mail: mseeley@equinoxinc.org
Web site: www.equinoxinc.org

Clients:

Equinox Inc

Lobbyists:

Wendy Ball
Alicia Borns
Melissa Dandeneau
Danyelle Gipson
Glenda Gustafson
Maribel Jerominek
Kathy Magee
Liliian McCarthy
Mitchell Patterson
Ramona Ramos
Christine Rodriguez
Mary Seeley
James Steed
Jackie Wall

Ewashko, John J

111 Washington Ave, Ste 700
Albany, NY 12210
518-434-8435 Fax: 518-434-8462

Clients:

Eli Lilly & Co

Facer & Stamoulas, PC

1025 Connecticut Ave NW
Ste 610
Washington, DC 20036
202-464-0400

Clients:

Oneida Indian Nation

Lobbyists:

Maria Stamoulas

Fahey, William C

3 Gannett Dr
Ste 400
White Plains, NY 10604
914-323-7000 Fax: 914-323-7001

Clients:

School Bus Contractors Assn (NY)

Faist Government Affairs Group, LLC

54 Willett St
Albany, NY 12210-1104
518-432-0599 Fax: 518-449-2294
e-mail: tfaist@aol.com

Clients:

Guardian Life Insurance Co of America
Life Insurance Council of NY, Inc
Chlorine Chemistry Council of American Chemistry Cncl, Inc
Combined Life Insurance Co of NY
Council of Life Insurance Brokers of Greater NY, Inc
Chemical Alliance (NYS)
National Assn of Health Underwriters

Lobbyists:

Thomas W Faist

Offices and agencies appear in alphabetical order.

Families Together in NYS Inc

15 Elk St
Albany, NY 12207-1002
518-432-0333 Fax: 518-434-6478
Web site: www.ftnys.org

Clients:
Families Together in NYS Inc

Lobbyists:
Ruth Foster
Paige MacDonald

Family Policy Council, Inc (NY)

3 E-Comm Square
Albany, NY 12207
518-694-4660

Clients:
Family Policy Council, Inc (NY)

Lobbyists:
Steven J Kidder

Farrell, Pamela

30 Rockefeller Plaza
New York, NY 10112
212-664-2823

Clients:
General Electric Co

Lobbyists:
Brian O'Leary
Scott Roberti

Fashion Institute of Technology

Seventh Ave @ 27th St
New York, NY 10001-5992
212-217-7637 Fax: 212-217-7639
Web site: www.fitnyc.edu

Clients:
Fashion Institute of Technology

Lobbyists:
Joyce F Brown
Herbert Cohen
Dario Cortes
Edwin A Goodman
Loretta Lawrence Keane
Judith Kornberg
Frank Sirianai
Harvey Spector
Lisa Wagner

Fassler, Michael S

Beth Abraham Family Health Svcs
612 Allerton Ave
Bronx, NY 10467-7404
718-519-4001

Clients:
Beth Abraham Family of Health Services

Lobbyists:
Susan Aldrich

Featherstonhaugh Wiley Clyne & Cordo, LLP

99 Pine St
Albany, NY 12207
518-436-0786 Fax: 518-427-0452

Clients:
AAA New York State Inc
Industrial Retention Network (NY)
Institute for Integrative Nutrition
Assn of Cemeteries (NYS)
Bottlers Assn (NYS)
Liberty Election Systems
Cigar Assn of America Inc
City of Buffalo
Consortium for Worker Education (The)
Construction Ind Cncl of Westchester & Hudson Valley Inc
District Council of Carpenter's PAC (NYC)
Dormitory Authority of the State of NY
Empire State Mortgage Bankers Assn
Entergy Nuclear Operations Inc
Erie County
Goldman Sachs & Co
Gtech Corporation
NYC & Company
Public Library (NY), Astor, Lenox & Tilden Foundations
Long Island Contractor's Assn
Medco Health Solutions Inc
Metropolitan Life Insurance Co
Roadway Improvement Coalition (NY)
1199/SEIU & GNYHA Healthcare Education Project
Sesame Inc
Shea's Performing Arts Ctr
Saint Regis Mohawk Tribe (Caesars Entertainment Inc)
Society of Physician Assistants (NYS)
Thoroughbred Horsemen's Assn Inc (NY)
Transportation Engineering Alliance (NYS)
Visiting Nurse Service of NY
1199/SEIU NY's Health & Human Service Union
Saratoga Harness Racing Inc
Tracfone Wireless Inc
Unite Here

Lobbyists:
Elizabeth K Clyne
John Cordo
Mary Dwyer
Victor Farley
James D Featherstonhaugh
David F Fleming, Jr
John L Hardy
Daniel Long
Stephen D Morgan
Scott Wigger

Federation of Protestant Welfare Agencies Inc

281 Park Ave South
New York, NY 10010

212-777-4800 x322 Fax: 212-673-4085
e-mail: fgoldman@fpwa.org
Web site: www.fpwa.org

Clients:
Federation of Protestant Welfare Agencies Inc

Lobbyists:
Rachel Barranca
Gregory Campbell
Christina Di Meo
Kathleen Fitzgibbons
Fatima Goldman
Terri Jackson
Kimberleigh Smith
Jillynn Stevens

Feld Entertainment
8607 Westwood Center Dr
Vienna, VA 22182
703-749-5570

Clients:
Feld Entertainment, Inc

Lobbyists:
Thomas Albert
Cassie Folk
Jerome Mayer

Ferris, William E
AARP
One Commerce Plaza, Ste 706
Albany, NY 12260
518-434-4194 Fax: 518-434-6949
e-mail: wferris@aarp.org
Web site: www.aarp.org

Clients:
AARP

Lobbyists:
Patricia Angona
Joan Anson
Curtis Ashby
Julia Ashby
Carl Backus
Stella Baker
Barbara Barr
Gene Barrett
Sheila Bellen
Linda Waddington
John Wolfe
Arlene Bolton
Irene Borowski
Mary Buske
Wilhelmina Carney
Josephine Collins
Judith Cotsovites
Doris Cotto
John Cushman
Carol Decker
Marjorie Defazio
Vivian Devens
Winifred Deyo

Donald Drew
Constance Dunn
Kay Emerick
Ronald Fairbank
Leonard Feder
Rosalyn Feder
Jo Freedman
Brian Fuller
Tuulia Fuller
Gloria Gatti
Joanne Gillen
Olive Glascow
Judith Gleason
David Golden
Victoria Goldfarb
Natalie Gordon
Samuel Gross
William Hall
Charles Hallenbeck
Eileen Hallenbeck
Annette Harrison
Josephine Hennessy-Cardimone
Fay Hill
Edward Himpler
Maryanne Himpler
David Hodgkins
Joan Jenkins
Lew Jenkins
Doris Johnson
Dorothy Kerins
Adele Klenk
Richard Kuhn
Kenneth Larsen
Janet Long
Rubin Martin
Jean McBride
Daisy McCain
William McCarthy
Rosa May McCormick
Meola McDonald
David McNally
David McNally
Patrick McNally
Shirley McNally
Mary Ann Milkalski
John Mills
Shirley Mills
Dolores Moffett
MaryAlice Morgan
Jeffrey Neal
Carolyn Normile
Mary Alice O'Brien
Robert O'Connor
Claude O'Dell
Helen O'Dell
Barbara Olum
Gerard Petite
Lavarne Pound
Joan Powell
Joan Powell
Irene Regni-Sheptak
Gwendolyn Richardson
Ollie Ross
Ralph Schlesinger
Rosemary Schlesinger
Irene Sikora
Leonard Sikora
Gillard Sinoba

Offices and agencies appear in alphabetical order.

Anita Sohn
Harold Sohn
Jane Springler
Richard Stack
Jane Stanley
Andrew Stegemoeller
Leon Taylor
Zula Taylor

Fight Crime:Invest in Kids NY
146 Washington Ave, Ste 100
Albany, NY 12210
518-465-5462

Clients:
Fight Crime:Invest in Kids NY

Lobbyists:
Meredith Wiley

Fioramonti, Frank R
305 Madison Ave, Ste 1442
New York, NY 10165-0006
212-867-3680 Fax: 212-867-3684
e-mail: frfwine@aol.com

Clients:
Vision Rehabilitation Assn (NY)

Lobbyists:

Fisher Development Strategies
21 Choir Lane
Westbury, NY 11590
516-997-5258

Clients:
Nassau Community College
Chamber Players International

Lobbyists:
Daniel M Fisher, Jr

Fitzgerald, Gary J
Iroq Healthcare Alliance
17 Halfmoon Exec Park Dr
Clifton Park, NY 12065
518-383-5060 Fax: 518-383-2616
e-mail: gfitzgerald@iroquois.org
Web site: www.iroquois.org

Clients:
Iroquois Healthcare Alliance
Upstate Health Care Coalition

Fitzpatrick, Christine M
Adult Day Hlth Care Cncl
150 State St, Ste 301
Albany, NY 12207-1698

518-449-2707 x130 Fax: 518-449-8210
e-mail: cfitzpatrick@nyahsa.org
Web site: www.nyahsa.org

Clients:
Adult Day Health Care Council (ADHCC)

Lobbyists:
Kellie Peters

Focus Media Group Inc
198 Bridgeville Rd
Monticello, NY 12701
845-796-3342

Clients:
Catskill Casino Coalition

Lobbyists:
Joshua Cohen

Foley, Patrick J
569 North Country Club Dr
Atlantis, FL 33462-1020
321-302-6363

Clients:
American International Group

Food Industry Alliance of NYS Inc
130 Washington Ave
Albany, NY 12210
518-434-1900 Fax: 518-434-9962

Clients:
Food Industry Alliance of NYS Inc

Lobbyists:
Patricia Brodhagen
James T Rogers
Michael E Rosen

Francis J Sanzillo & Associates
One N Lexington Ave, 15th Fl
White Plains, NY 10601
914-448-0199 Fax: 914-448-0267

Clients:
Dairyfoods Inc (NYS)
Ford Motor Co
Institute for Student Achievement
Rent-A-Ctr (Stateside Associates)
United Parcel Service

Lobbyists:
Francis Sanzillo

Franco, William A
8 Towline Lane
Clifton Park, NY 12065
518-373-1818 Fax: 518-373-1963

Offices and agencies appear in alphabetical order.

Clients:
Merck & Co Inc

Frank, Robin
Healthcare Assn of NYS
One Empire Dr
Rensselaer, NY 12144
518-431-7600

Clients:
Healthcare Association of NYS

Lobbyists:
Renee Bernard
Karen Bonilla
Ju-Ming Chang
Kathleen Ciccone
Kristie Coppernoll
Matthew Cox
Jeannie Cross
Joanne Cunningham
Rose Duhan
Jeffrey Gold
Stephen Harwell
Walter Koshykar
Steven Kroll
Debora Lebarron
Cindy Levernois
Monica Mahaffey
Edward McGill
Robert McLeod
Molly Poleto
Karen Roach
Lee Santos
Daniel Sisto
Raymond Sweeney
Mary Therriault
Shelby Wafer
Sue Ellen Wagner
Christopher Wilkes
Mary Jane Wurth

Freeman, Bruce
8313 Johnson Mill Rd
Bahama, NC 27503-9236
919-471-6784

Clients:
Procter & Gamble Pharmaceuticals

Fried Frank Harris Shriver & Jacobson, LLP
One New York Plaza
New York, NY 10004
212-859-8780

Clients:
Dermot Company (The)
Park Tower Group
Pulte Homes of NY Inc

Lobbyists:
Jonathan Ball
Stephen Lefkowitz
Melanie Meyers

Friedman, John P
USAA
325 Columbia Tpk
Florham Park, NJ 7932
973-377-6662 Fax: 973-377-6607
e-mail: john.friedman@usaa.com

Clients:
United Services Automobile Assn (USAA)

Friedman, Michael B
12 Old Mamaroneck Rd
White Plains, NY 10605
914-686-2886 Fax: 914-948-4956
e-mail: mbfriedman@aol.com

Clients:
Mental Health Association of NYC, Inc
Mental Health Assn of Westchester Co, Inc

Friends of NY Racing Inc
40 East 52nd St
New York, NY 10021
212-521-5304

Clients:
Friends of NY Racing Inc

Lobbyists:
Timothy G Smith

Funeral Directors Assn Inc (NYS)
426 New Karner Rd
Albany, NY 12205
518-452-8230 Fax: 518-452-8667
e-mail: info@nysfda.org
Web site: www.nysfda.org

Clients:
Funeral Directors Assn Inc (NYS)

Lobbyists:
Bonnie L McCullough
Randy L McCullough

Gaines, John
420 Lexington Ave, Ste 215
New York, NY 10017
212-599-5856

Clients:
Assn of Commuter Rail Employees

Gallo, Richard J
142 State St
Albany, NY 12207-1678
518-465-3545 Fax: 518-465-3584
e-mail: rjgallo@msn.com

Offices and agencies appear in alphabetical order.

Clients:

Psychiatric Assn Inc (NYS)

Lobbyists:

Karin Moran

Gangi, Robert

Correctional Assn of NY
135 East 15th St
New York, NY 10003-3534
212-254-5700 Fax: 212-473-2807
e-mail: rgangi@correctionalassociation.org
Web site: www.correctionalassociation.org

Clients:

Correctional Assn of NY Inc (The)

Lobbyists:

John Beck
Ashrufa Faruquer
Tamar Kraft-Stoler
Margaret Loftus
Jennifer Wym

Garigliano Law Offices, LLP

449 Broadway
Monticello, NY 12701
845-796-1010 Fax: 845-796-1040

Clients:

Caesars Entertainment, Inc

Lobbyists:

Barbara Garigliano
Walter Garigliano

Garner Associates LLC

64 Meech Ave
Buffalo, NY 14208
716-886-1699

Clients:

United Food & Commercial Workers Dist Council NY & N NJ

Lobbyists:

Maurice Garner
Joyce Nixon

Gay Men's Health Crisis Inc

119 W 24th St
New York, NY 10011-1995
212-367-1250 Fax: 212-367-1247
e-mail: ronaldj@gmhc.org
Web site: www.gmhc.org

Clients:

Gay Men's Health Crisis Inc

Lobbyists:

Michele Bonan
Laura Caruso
Thomas Cornell
Ronald Johnson

Darryl Ng
Ana Oliveira

Gaylord, Joan

c/o Christian Science Cmte
51 E 42nd St, Ste 600
New York, NY 10017
212-661-3838

Clients:

Christian Science Cmte on Publication for NYS

Geer, Nancy P

Mfg Housing Assn
35 Commerce Ave
Albany, NY 12206-2081
518-435-9858 Fax: 518-435-9839
e-mail: info@nymha.org
Web site: www.nymha.org

Clients:

Manufactured Housing Assn Inc (NY)

Geiger, Bruce W & Associates

29 Elk St, Ste 100
Albany, NY 12207
518-432-1607 Fax: 518-463-5301

Clients:

Alliance of Automobile Manufacturers Inc
Empire State Marine Trades Assn
Long Island Gasoline Retailers Assn Inc
Nurse Practitioners Assn of NYS (The)
Homebridge Mortgage Bankers
Pinelawn Cemetery
Snowmobile Assn (NYS)

Lobbyists:

Bruce W Geiger

General Motors Corporation

MC 482-C27-D21
PO Box 300
Detroit, MI 48265-3000
313-665-2979

Clients:

General Motors Corporation

Lobbyists:

Edward Donovan
Bryan Roosa

Genovese, Marta

AAA NYS
1415 Kellum Place
Garden City, NY 11530-1690
516-873-2259 Fax: 516-873-2355
e-mail: mgenovese@aaany.com
Web site: www.aaanys.com

Offices and agencies appear in alphabetical order.

Clients:
AAA New York State Inc
Automobile Club of New York Inc

Lobbyists:
John A Corlett
Antoanela Vaccaro
Edward Welsh

Gergela III, Joseph
Long Island Farm Bureau
104 Edwards Ave
Calverton, NY 11933
631-727-3777

Clients:
Long Island Farm Bureau

Lobbyists:
Julie Debold

Gerrard, Michael B
Arnold & Porter LLP
399 Park Ave
New York, NY 10022-4690
212-715-1190

Clients:
Madison Square Garden LP

Geto & deMilly Inc
130 East 40th St, 16th Fl
New York, NY 10016-1726
212-686-4551 Fax: 212-213-6850
e-mail: pr@getodemilly.com
Web site: www.getodemilly.com

Clients:
AMDeC Foundation Inc
Callen-Lorde Community Health Ctr
Ctr Against Domestic Violence
Common Ground Community Inc
Eldridge Street Project
Ford Models Inc
In-Sink Erator
Forest City Ratner Companies
Plumbing Foundation of the City of NY
IMG Models
W2001Z/15CPW Holdings LLC

Lobbyists:
Joyce Baumgarten
Elaine Bennett
Kendall Christiansen
Ethan Geto
Michele deMilly

Gibson Dunn & Crutcher, LLP
200 Park Ave
New York, NY 10166

212-351-4000 Fax: 212-351-4035
e-mail: alance@gibsondunn.com
Web site: www.gibsondunn.com

1050 Connecticut Ave NW
Washington, DC 20036
202-955-8613

Clients:
Madison Square Garden LP
Sergeants Benevolent Assn

Lobbyists:
Andrew Lance
Randy Mastro

Gilligan, Donald
610 Mountain St
Sharon, MA 2067
781-793-0250 Fax: 781-793-0600
e-mail: donaldg@ma.ultranet.com

Clients:
Nat'l Assn of Energy Service Companies

Glover Park Group, Inc (The)
3299 K St NW, Ste 500
Washington, DC 20007
202-337-0808

Clients:
Madison Square Garden

Lobbyists:
Gigi Georges
Laura Walters

Glusko, John P
Central Hudson Gas & Elec
284 South Ave
Poughkeepsie, NY 12601
845-486-5218 Fax: 845-486-5544
e-mail: jglusko@cenhud.com
Web site: www.cenhud.com

Clients:
Central Hudson Gas & Electric Corp

Lobbyists:
Steven Lant
Denise VanBuren

Goggin, David
31 1/2 Englewood Ave #2
Brookline, MA 02445
805-313-9930

Clients:
Amgen

Offices and agencies appear in alphabetical order.

Goldberg, Edward

Macy's East, Inc
151 West 34th St
New York, NY 10001
212-494-5568 Fax: 212-494-1857
e-mail: egoldberg@fds.com

Clients:
Macy's East Inc

Golden, Ben

Arc, Inc (NYS)
393 Delaware Ave
Delmar, NY 12054-3094
518-439-8311

Clients:
Arc Inc (NYS)

Goldman, Gerald

10 East 40th St, Ste 1308
New York, NY 10016
212-268-1911 Fax: 201-487-3954

Clients:
Financial Service Centers of NY, Inc

Lobbyists:
Richard Smith

Goldstein, Carla (FKA Browne, Christopher)

Planned Parenthood of NYC
26 Bleecker St
New York, NY 10012
212-274-7290

Clients:
Planned Parenthood of NYC

Lobbyists:
Laurie Beck
Alice Berger
Vicki Breitbart
Dana Czuczka
Linda Freeman
Anne Keenan
Joan Malin
Haydee Morales
Maria Pimienta
Roger Rathman
Sabrina Shulman

Goldstein, Eric A

Natural Resources Def Cncl
40 W 20th St
New York, NY 10011
212-727-2700 Fax: 212-727-1773

Clients:
Natural Resources Defense Council Inc

Lobbyists:
John Adams
Rita Barol
Dale Bryk
Sarah Chasis
Nathaniel Greene
Ashok Gupta
Mark A Izeman
Richard Kassel
Katherine Kennedy
Robert Kennedy
Robin Marx
Theodore Spencer

Goodwin, Jeffrey

Group Health Incorporated
441 9th Ave
New York, NY 10001-1681
212-615-0891 Fax: 212-563-8561
e-mail: jgoodwin@ghi.com

Clients:
Group Health Incorporated

Lobbyists:
Frank J Branchini
Donna Lynne
Ilene Margolin
William Mastro

Gordinier, Timothy

Inst Humanist Studies
18 Corp Woods Blvd
Albany, NY 12211
518-432-7820 Fax: 518-432-7821
e-mail: tim@humaniststudies.org
Web site: www.humaniststudies.org

Clients:
Institute for Humanist Studies

Greater NY Auto Dealers' Assn Inc

18-10 Whitestone Expwy
Whitestone, NY 11357-3067
718-746-5900 Fax: 718-746-5557
Web site: www.gnyada.com

Clients:
Greater NY Automobile Dealers' Assn Inc

Lobbyists:
Robert Fusco
Louis Giordano Jr
Stuart Rosenthal
Mark Schienberg
Marvin Suskin

Greater Upstate Law Project Inc

119 Washington Ave
Albany, NY 12210
518-462-6831

Clients:

Greater Upstate Law Project Inc

Lobbyists:

Susan Antos
Kristin Brown
Kate Callery
Trilby Dejung
Anne Erickson
Mike Hanley
Bryan Hetherington
Kristen Hughes
Kirsten Keefe
Ruhi Maker
Amy Schwartz
Louise Tarantino
Barbara Van Kerkhove
Barbara Weiner
Anzala Wilson

Green & Seifter Attorneys, PLLC

900 One Lincoln Ctr
110 W Fayette St
Syracuse, NY 13202
315-422-1391

Clients:

Cayuga Nation of NY

Lobbyists:

Daniel French
Kimberly Zimmer

Greenberg Traurig, LLP

54 State St, 6th Fl
Albany, NY 12207
518-689-1400 Fax: 518-689-3499
Web site: www.gtlaw.com

Clients:

Affinity Health Plan
Alliance for Child with Special Needs-School Age (NYS)
Assn General Contractors of America, Inc (NYS Chapter)
Bailey House, Inc
Assn for Marriage & Family Therapy, Inc (NYD)
Assn of Health Information Outsourcing Services
Assn of Licensed Midwives (NYS)
Assn of School Psychologists (NY)
Auto Collision Technician's Assn, Inc (NYS)
CNA
Canadian Pacific Railway
Capital Region Council for Children with Special Needs
Children's Day Treatment Coalition
Cingular Wireless
Coalition for Children with Special Needs (NYC)
Conocophillips
Credit Union League, Inc (NYS)
Crisis Program (The)
Bar Association (NYS)
CPS 1 Realty LP
Enterprise Rent-A-Car
Empire State Water Well Drillers' Assn, Inc
General Builders Contractors of NYS, Inc
Health Plan Assn (NY)
Honda North America, Inc

Hudson Alliance for Children with Special Needs
Four Seasons Nursing & Rehabilitation Center
Just Kids Early Childhood Learning Ctr
Liberty Mutual
Long Island Coalition for Children with Special Needs
Long Term Care Pharmacy Alliance
Manufactured Housing Assn, Inc (NY)
Microsoft Corporation
Motorola, Inc
God's Love We Deliver
Servicemaster Co (The)
Stop DWI Coordinators Assn (NYS)
North County Alliance for Children with Special Needs
Tomra
JCDecaux North America
Wellcare Health Plans, Inc
Western NY Alliance for Children with Special Needs
Jets (NY)
World Wrestling Entertainment, Inc
Zurich North America
Just Kids Diagnostic & Treatment Center
Kidde US, Residential & Commercial (National Strategies Inc)
Life Insurance Council of New York, Inc
March of Dimes Birth Defects Foundation
Coalition for Modular Reform (NYS)
Shakespeare Project (The)
Health & Hospitals Corporation (NYC)
Thrivent Financial for Lutherans
Union College

Lobbyists:

Tricia Asaro
Stephen Buhr
Deidre Carson
Christopher Cernik
Mark Glaser
Robert Harding
Harold Iselin
Pamela Madeiros
John Mascialino
Jake Menges
Lance Michaels
Michael Murphy
Elizabeth Sacco
Jay Segal
Elizabeth Shields
Adam Varley
Edward Wallace

Griffin Plummer & Associates, LLC

61 Columbia St, Ste 403
Albany, NY 12210-2736
518-463-5949 Fax: 518-463-5991

Clients:

Genworth Financial
General Electric Co
Hunter Mountain Ski Bowl
Nat'l Electric Manufacturers Assoc
Railroads of NY, (RONY)

Lobbyists:

John Griffin
Daniel Plummer
Norman Schneider

Offices and agencies appear in alphabetical order.

Griffin, Mary A
Citigroup Mgmt Corp
95 Columbia St
Albany, NY 12210
518-432-1286 Fax: 518-465-6023

Clients:
Citigroup Management Corp

Grossman Strategies
630 Johnson Ave, Ste 105
Bohemia, NY 11716-2628
631-563-4400 Fax: 631-563-4422
e-mail: mail@grossman.net
Web site: www.grossman.net

Clients:
Pinelawn Cemetery

Lobbyists:
Mark J Grossman

Haberman, Michael C
24 W 4th St, 5th Fl
New York, NY 10012
212-998-2402 Fax: 212-995-4822

Clients:
New York University

Lobbyists:
Karen Acker
Michael Alfano
Robert Berne
Lynne Brown
Gilda Ventresca Ecroyd
Marcia Maxwell
John Sexton
Diane Yu

Hager, Susan
UWNYS
155 Washington Ave, 2nd Fl
Albany, NY 12210-2323
518-463-2522 Fax: 518-463-2534
e-mail: hagers@uwnys.org
Web site: www.uwnys.org

Clients:
United Way of NYS

Hancock Public Affairs, LLC
201 W Genesse St, Box 101
Fayetteville, NY 13066
315-447-6057

Clients:
Northeast Biofuels

Lobbyists:
Stewart Hancock III

Hanna Paquin Associates
7166 Overlook Dr
PO Box 157
Sodus Point, NY 14555-0157
315-483-0116 Fax: 315-483-0117
e-mail: hannapaq@aol.com

Clients:
Chicago Title Insurance Co
Commonwealth Land Title Insurance Co
Conestoga Title Insurance Co
Fidelity National Title Insurance Co
Lawyers Title Insurance Corp
Monroe Title Insurance Corp
Old Republic National Title Insurance Co
Stewart Title Insurance Co
United General Title Insurance Co
Washington Title Insurance Co

Lobbyists:
Nancy A Hanna-Paquin
Guy Paquin

Hannan, K T Public Affairs Inc
107 Washington Ave, 2nd floor
Albany, NY 12210-2200
518-465-6550 Fax: 518-465-6557
e-mail: khannan401@aol.com
Web site: www.kthpa.com

Clients:
Assurant Solutions
Conpor Conference of Private Organizations (NYS)
Consumer Finance Assn (NYS)
Firemen's Assn of the State of NY
National Safety Council
Davita Inc
Hannaford Bros Co
National Traffic Safety Administration
Northeastern NY Safety & Health Council Inc
Symantec Corp (Albers & Co)
Usinpac (Albers & Co)

Lobbyists:
Kirby T Hannan
Ross Hannan
Jan VanDeCarr

Harris, Kevin
10 W Market St, Ste 1190
Indianapolis, IN 46204
317-464-8199

Clients:
National Conference of Insurance Guaranty Funds

Harris, O Lewis
108-25 62nd Dr
Forest Hills, NY 11375
718-592-5757 Fax: 718-592-2933

Clients:
Forest Hills Community House, Inc (The)

Offices and agencies appear in alphabetical order.

Lobbyists:
Mary Abbate
Susan Matloff
Irma Rodriguez
Christine Roland
Kathryn-Celia Williams

Harter Secrest & Emery, LLP

1600 Bausch & Lomb Place
Rochester, NY 14604-2711
585-232-6500 Fax: 585-232-2152
e-mail: admin@hselaw.com
Web site: www.hartersecrest.com

Clients:
Alliance for Fine Wine Wholesalers, Ltd (NY)
Assn of Safety Group Managers
Biotechnology Assn Inc (NY)
Buffalo & Pittsburgh Railroad Inc
Chiropractic Assn Inc (NYS)
Clinical Laboratory Assn Inc (NYS)
Cold Spring Harbor Laboratory
DaimlerChrysler Corp
Delta Air Lines Inc
Emerging Industries Alliance of NYS
Empire State Petroleum Assn Inc
Finger Lakes Horsemen's Benv & Protective Assn Inc
Genesee & Wyoming Railroad Inc
GlaxoSmithKline, PLC
Amalgamated Transit Union
Hall of Science (NY)
Movers' & Warehousemen's Assn Inc (NYS)
OSI Pharmaceuticals Inc
Restaurant Assn (NYS)
Rochester & Southern Railroad Inc
Telecommunications Assn Inc (NYS)
Upstate Farms Cooperative Inc
Rochester Tooling & Machine Assn Inc

Lobbyists:
Amy Kellogg
Ross Lanzafame
Donald S Mazzulo
Richard E Scanlan

Hartford Financial Svcs Group Inc

Hartford Plaza HO 1-11
690 Asylum Ave
Hartford, CT 06115
860-547-2944

Clients:
Hartford Financial Services Group Inc

Lobbyists:
Carol Clapp

Hastings, Jamie

4 Sylvan Way
Parsippany, NJ 7054
973-292-8919

Clients:
T-Mobile USA Inc

Hawayek, Jonathan F

728 Main St
East Aurora, NY 14052
716-652-2038

Clients:
Allergan, Inc

Hayes, Thomas J & Associates Inc

45 Sutton Pl S, Ste 9D
New York, NY 10022
212-838-5221
e-mail: tomhayes@thayesconsulting.com

Clients:
Sound Shore Health System

Lobbyists:
Thomas J Hayes

Health Insurance Plan of Greater NY

111 Washington Ave, Ste 411
Albany, NY 12210
518-462-5611

Clients:
Health Insurance Plan of Greater NY

Lobbyists:
Kerry DeWitt
Michael Fullwood
Daniel McGowan
Leslie Strassberg
Anthony Watson

Health Plan Assn Inc (NY)

90 State St, Ste 825
Albany, NY 12207-1717
518-462-2293 Fax: 518-462-2150
e-mail: info@nyhpa.org
Web site: www.nyhpa.org

Clients:
Health Plan Assn Inc (NY)

Lobbyists:
Arlene Halpert
Sheila Humiston
Kim Kelly
Paul F Macielak
Lee R Marks
Leslie S Moran
Elizabeth Mulvey

Healthcare Tort Reform Coalition (NY)

Combined Coor Council
14 Penn Plaza, Ste 720
New York, NY 10122
212-643-8100

Clients:
Healthcare Tort Reform Coalition (NY)

Offices and agencies appear in alphabetical order.

Lobbyists:
Lisa Kramer
Ronald B Milch
Christopher Smith

Heimgartner, Christian
34 Chestnut Lane
PO Box 296
Oakdale, NY 11769-0296
631-567-3783

Clients:
Lieutenants Benevolent Assn

Heyman, Neil
Southern NY Association
39 Broadway, Ste 1710
New York, NY 10006
212-425-5050 Fax: 212-968-7710
e-mail: njheyman@snya.com
Web site: www.snya.org

Clients:
Southern NY Assn

Higgins Roberts Beyerl & Coan, PC
1430 Balltown Rd
Niskayuna, NY 12309
518-374-3399 Fax: 518-374-9416

Clients:
Society of Anesthesiologists, Inc (NYS)

Lobbyists:
Charles J Assini Jr

Hightower, A Dirk
Chldren's Institute
274 N Goodman St, Ste D103
Rochester, NY 14607-1154
585-295-1000 Fax: 585-295-1090

Clients:
Children's Institute, Inc

Lobbyists:
Dirk Hightower

Hill & Gosdeck
One Commerce Plaza
99 Washington Ave, Ste 400
Albany, NY 12210
518-463-5449 Fax: 518-463-0947
e-mail: nylobbyists@aol.com

Clients:
AT&T Corp
Alliance of Automobile Manufacturers
Altria Corporate Services Inc
Consumer Data Industry Assoc

Cosmetic Toiletry & Fragrance Assn (The)
Group Self-Insurance Assn of NY (GSIANY)
International Business Machines Corp
Lexmark International Inc
Miller Brewing Co
Monsanto Co
Program Risk Mgmt Inc
SGS Testcom
Soap & Detergent Assoc
Veterinary Medical Society (NYS)

Lobbyists:
Thomas J Gosdeck
Jeffrey L Hill

Hiller, Elise L
Cable TV & Telecommunications Assn of NY
80 State St
Albany, NY 12207
518-463-6676 Fax: 518-463-0574
e-mail: elh@nycap.rr.com
Web site: www.cabletvny.com

Clients:
Cable Telecommunications Assn of NY

Hines-Kramer, Amy
Credit Union League
19 British American Blvd
Latham, NY 12110
518-437-8122 Fax: 518-782-4212
Web site: www.nycreditunions.org

Clients:
Credit Union League Inc (NYS)

Lobbyists:
Cheryl Halter
Michael Lanotte
William Mellin

Hinman Straub, PC
121 State St
Albany, NY 12207-1693
518-436-0751 Fax: 518-436-4751
e-mail: reception@hspm.com
Web site: www.hspm.com

Clients:
1199/SEIU New York's Health & Human Service Union
Academic Dental Centers (NYS)
Boys & Girls Clubs Inc (NYS Alliance)
Business Development Corporation (NY)
Assn of Proprietary Colleges
Associated Medical Schools of NY
Charmer Industries Inc
Charter Schools Assn (NY)
Children's Aid Society (The)
Cigna Companies
Consolidated Edison Co of NY Inc
Consumer Specialty Products Assn
Community Preservation Corporation (The)
Education & Research Network Inc (NYS)

Offices and agencies appear in alphabetical order.

Electronic Data Systems Corporation (EDS)
Contractors Agents & Brokers Association Inc
Empire State Assn of Adult Homes/Assisted Living Facilities
Estee Lauder Inc
Excellus Health Plan Inc
Federation of Mental Health Ctrs Inc (The)
Conversent Communications, LLC
Hillside Family of Agencies
Institute for Special Education (NY)
Medical & Health Research Assn of NYC Inc
Medical College (NY)
3C Communities
American Insurance Association
National Heritage Academies
Assn of Service Stations & Repair Shops Inc (NYS)
BOC Gases
Opthalmological Society (NYS)
Organization of NYS Management Confidential Employees Inc
Park Police Benevolent Assn Inc (NYS)
Parker Jewish Institute for Health Care & Rehab
Pet Industry Joint Advisory Council
Pharmaceutical Research & Manufacturers of America
Builders Association (NYS)
Stonehenge Capital Corporation
Stony Brook University
Supreme Court Justices' Assn of the City of NY Inc
University of Rochester
Dell Inc
Foundling Hospital (NY) (The)
Independent Bankers Association of NYS
Life Settlement Institute (The)
Nightlife Association (NY)
Pearson Education Inc
Professional Firefighters Association Inc (NYS)
Racing Association Inc (NY) (The)
Rent Stabilization Assn of NYC Inc
Research Foundation of NY University at Buffalo
Retirees for Tier 1
SLE Foundation (The)
School Administrators Association of NYS
School of Visual Arts
Sheriff's Employees Association of Rensselaer County
Superpower Inc
Support Services Alliance Inc
Technical Assistance Centers' Assn for Transferring Success
TransCanada Pipelines Ltd
Wellchoice Inc

Lobbyists:
John Black
Stephen M Cleary
James Clyne
Bartley J Costello, III
William Y Crowell III
Terri Crowley
Sean M Doolan
John Federman
Bruce N Gyory
Keith R Jacques
John J Lynch
Kevin P Quinn
Janet Silver

Hirshorn, Donald P
860 Hereford Way
Niskayuna, NY 12309-4904

518-372-3479 Fax: 518-869-0631
e-mail: mail@rpea.org
Web site: www.rpea.org

Clients:
Retired Public Employees Association

Hodes Associates
284 State St
Albany, NY 12210
518-465-8303 Fax: 518-465-8320
e-mail: nhodes@hodesassoc.org

Clients:
Albany Institute of History & Art (AIHA)
Education & Work Consortium (The)
Home Care Assn
Independent Health Assn Inc
Instructional Systems Inc
Sunrise Senior Living
Visiting Nurse Regional Health Care System
Metropolitan College of NY
Alterra Healthcare Corporation
Assisted Living Federation of America (ALFA)

Lobbyists:
Nancy L Hodes
Virginia Lynch-Landy
Michele O'Connor

Hodgson Russ, LLP
One M&T Plaza, Ste 2000
Buffalo, NY 14203-2391
716-856-4000 Fax: 716-849-0349
Web site: www.hodgsonruss.com

Clients:
Group Health Incorporated
Kaleida Health
Society of Certified Public Accountants, NYS
M&T Bank

Lobbyists:
Paul Comeau
Christopher Doyle
Frederick J Jacobs

Holch, Neils
400 N Capitol St NW, Ste 585
Washington, DC 20001
202-783-5300

Clients:
Oneida Indian Nation

Lobbyists:

Hollander, Ellen
1259 Central Ave
Albany, NY 12205

Offices and agencies appear in alphabetical order.

518-437-1802 Fax: 518-437-1048
e-mail: apc@apc-colleges.org
Web site: www.apc-colleges.org

Clients:
Assn of Proprietary Colleges

Holloway, Jr, Floyd
State Farm Insurance Co
225 Wilmington W Chester Park
Ste 300
Chadds Ford, PA 19317-9039
610-361-4150 Fax: 610-361-4110
e-mail: floyd.holloway.clxm@statefarm.com

Clients:
State Farm Insurance Companies

Holloway, Sr, Floyd
260 Leaf Ave
Central Islip, NY 11722-3541
631-582-9882 Fax: 631-582-8544
e-mail: floholl@optonline.net

Clients:
Assoc of PBA'S, Inc (NYS)
Correction Captain's Assoc, Dept of Corrections, City of NY, Inc
Correction Officer's Benevolent Assoc, City of NY, Inc
Deputies Assoc, Inc (NYS)
Sanitation Officer's Assoc (NYC)

Lobbyists:
Floyd Holloway, Sr

Home Care Assn of NYS Inc
194 Washington Ave, Ste 400
Albany, NY 12210
518-426-8764 Fax: 518-426-8788
e-mail: info@hcanys.org
Web site: www.hcanys.org

Clients:
Home Care Assn of NYS Inc

Lobbyists:
Patrick Conole
Andrew Koski
Carol Rodat

Honda North America Inc
1001 G St NW, Ste 950
Washington, DC 20001
202-661-4400

Clients:
Honda North America Inc

Lobbyists:
Edward Cohen
Kent Dellinger
Don Francy
Benjamin Knight

Ember A Rosenberg

Hood, William L
American Airlines
9525 W Bryn Mawr Ave, #800
Rosemont, IL 60018
847-928-5437 Fax: 847-928-5695
e-mail: bill.hood@aa.com
Web site: www.aa.com

Clients:
American Airlines

Horner, H Blair
NYPIRG
107 Washington Ave, 2nd Fl
Albany, NY 12210-2270
518-436-0876 Fax: 518-432-6178
Web site: www.nypirg.org

Clients:
Public Interest Research Group (NY)

Lobbyists:
Farouk Abdallah
Christine Agic
Okenfe Aigbe
Roseberte Auguste
Jason Babbie
Rhonda Belluso
Dan Botting
Cathleen Breen
Charity Carbine
Robyn Citizen
Fran Clark
Catherine Contino
Kate Evanciew
Aisha Fraites
Diana Fryda
Alanna Gothard
Michael Grenetz
Laura Haight
Russ Haven
Darren Hearn
Michael Hernandez
Joel Kelsey
Miriam Kramer
Timothy Marvin
Melissa Morahan
Charlotte Nunes
Neysa Prenger
Melissa Reburniano
Camille Rivera
Neal Rosenstein
Gene Russianoff
Tracy Shelton
Melinda Sobin
Joseph Stelling
Carla Sterling
Kaytrue Ting
Erin Treacy
Josh Turner
Rebecca Weber
Laurie Wheelock

Offices and agencies appear in alphabetical order.

Housing Conservation Coordinators

500 W 52nd St, 4th Fl
New York, NY 10019
212-541-5996

Clients:
Housing Conservation Coordinators

Lobbyists:
Sarah Desmond
Harvey Epstein
John Raskin

Housing Works, Albany Advocacy Ctr

247 Lark St, 1st Fl
Albany, NY 12210
518-449-4207 Fax: 518-449-4219
e-mail: kink@housingworks.org; hayes@housingworks.org
Web site: www.housingworks.org

Clients:
Housing Works Inc

Lobbyists:
Mark Hayes
Michael Kink
Terri Smith-Caronia

Hudacs, John

61 Paxwood Rd
Delmar, NY 12054
518-439-7570

Clients:
College of Staten Island (Research Foundation of CUNY)

Human Services Council of NYC

130 East 59th St
New York, NY 10022
212-836-1230

Clients:
Human Services Council of NY

Lobbyists:
Allison Sesso
Michael Stoller

Hunger Action Network of NYS

275 State St
Albany, NY 12210
518-431-7371 Fax: 518-434-7390

Clients:
Hunger Action Network of NYS

Lobbyists:
Mark Dunlea
Kim Gilliland
Bich Ha Pham

Hurley, John R

Guardian Life Ins Co
7 Hanover Sq H23E
New York, NY 10004-2616
212-598-8854 Fax: 212-919-2693

Clients:
Guardian Life Insurance Co of America (The)

Lobbyists:
Armand Depalo
Sanford Herman
Ulysses Lee

Ianniello, Anderson & Reilly, PC

Drugrisk Solutions, LLC
805 Route 146
Clifton Park, NY 12065
518-371-8888 Fax: 518-371-1755

Clients:
American Psychoanalytic Assn

Lobbyists:
David S Carroll

Immigration Coalition, Inc (NY)

275 77th Ave, 9th Fl
New York, NY 10001
212-627-2227

Clients:
Immigration Coalition (The) (NY)

Lobbyists:
Ana Maria Bazan
Jose Davila
Norman Eng
Adam Gurvitch
Chung-Wha Hung
Margaret McHugh
Barbara Michalska
Avideh Moussavian
Minerva Moya
Randolph Quezada
Benjamin Ross
Dan Smulian
Jacqueline Vimo
Jackie Wong
Su Yon Yi

Ingham Communications, Inc

4500 9th Ave, NE, Ste 300
Seattle, WA 98105
206-547-6100 Fax: 206-633-6049

Clients:
Wireless Access Coalition (NY) (T-Mobile)

Lobbyists:
Ann Barre

*Political Parties,
Lobbyists & PACs*

Offices and agencies appear in alphabetical order.

Island Public Affairs

34 E Main St, Ste 359
Smithtown, NY 11787
631-724-0017

Clients:
Adelante of Suffolk County, Inc
Lake Grove Treatment Centers, Inc
Literacy Suffolk, Inc
St Catherine of Siena Medical Ctr
Suffolk Coalition of Mental Health Service Providers
Hands Across Long Island, Inc
Human Resources Research & Management Group, Inc
Mental Health Assn in Suffolk Co (The)

Lobbyists:
Steven Moll

Island Strategies, Inc

190 EAB Plazas
East Tower, 15th Fl
Uniondale, NY 11556-0190
516-663-6688

Clients:
Bowling Proprietor's Assn (NYS)
Correction Officers & Police Benevolent Assn, Inc (NYS)
General Motors Corp

Lobbyists:
Keith Fink
Arthur Kremer

J Adams Consulting, LLC

14 Wall St, 20th Fl
New York, NY 10005
212-618-1500 Fax: 212-618-1510

Clients:
Continental Airlines, Inc

Lobbyists:
Catherine Giuliani

JLW Consulting, LLC

19 Book Hill Rd
Essex, CT 06426-1318
860-767-2814

Clients:
Newspaper Publishers Assn (NY)

Lobbyists:
Jerome Wilson

Janeway, William C

The Nature Conservancy
415 River St, 4th Fl
Troy, NY 12180
518-273-9408 Fax: 518-273-5022

Clients:
Nature Conservancy (The)

Lobbyists:
Tim Abbot
Andrew C Beers
Scott Cullen
Neil Gifford
Wayne Grothe
Chris Hawver
Jim Howe
Nancy Kelley
Fran Lawler
Cara Lee
Stuart Lowrie
Alpa Panda
William Patterson
Kerri Pogue
Paul Rabinovitch
Henry Tepper
Doug Thompson
Tony Wilkinson
Kristin M Williams

Jenkins, Joanne E

NY Life Ins
111 Washington Ave, 3rd Fl
Albany, NY 12210
518-463-6649 Fax: 518-436-0226

Clients:
Life Insurance Co (NY)

Lobbyists:
David Bangs
Scott Berlin
Martin Claire
Melvin Feinberg
Jodi Krantz
Carol Mayer
Michael Oleske
Lee Parkin
Anne Pollack
Robert Rock
Janis Rubin
Richard Schwartz
Fred Sievert
Irwin Silber
Joel Steinberg
Seymour Sternberg
Gil Valdes
Michael Watson
Paul Whitman
Lori Whittaker
Gayle Yeomans
Richard Zuccaro

Jets, LLC (NY)

50 W 57th St, 2nd Fl
New York, NY 10019
212-969-1800

Clients:
Jets, LLC (NY)

Lobbyists:
Larry Scott Blackmon
Jay L Cross
Matt Higgins
Robert Johnson
William Senn
Thad Sheeley
Marissa Shorenstein

Jockers, Ken
351 West 54th St
New York, NY 10019
212-541-6741

Clients:
Fund for Modern Courts

Lobbyists:
Anne Marie Couser

Johnson, Mario
Builders Assn Hudson Valley
338 Meadow Ave
Newburgh, NY 12550
845-562-0002

Clients:
Builders Assn of the Hudson Valley

Lobbyists:
Jean Rowe

Johnson, Stephen Philip
Cornell University
114 Day Hall
Ithaca, NY 14853-2801
607-255-8307 Fax: 607-255-5396
e-mail: spj2@cornell.edu
Web site: www.cornell.edu

Clients:
Cornell University

Lobbyists:
Charles J Kruzansky
Vanda B McMurtry
Jacqueline K Powers
Stanley W Telega
Paula A Willsie

Kantor Davidoff Wolfe Mandelker & Kass, PC
51 East 42nd St
Ste 1700
New York, NY 10017-5497
212-682-8383 Fax: 212-949-5206

Clients:
American International Group Inc
Assn for Affordable Housing (NYS)
Land Title Assn - Agents Section (NYS)
Metropolitan Retail Assn, LLC (NY)
Metropolitan Taxicab Board of Trade Inc

National Cleaners Assn
Ecumenical Community Development Organization
Institute for the Study of Infection Control Inc (The)

Lobbyists:
Donald M Halperin
Lawrence A Mandelker

Kaplan, Randy L
LI Bd of Realtors
300 Sunrise Hwy
West Babylon, NY 11704
631-661-4800 Fax: 631-661-5202
e-mail: rkaplan@mlslirealtor.com

Clients:
Long Island Board of Realtors

Karp, Esther
274 N Goodman St, Ste D103
Rochester, NY 14607
585-295-1000 Fax: 585-295-1090

Clients:
Childrens Institute, Inc

Lobbyists:
Brian Sampson

Kase, Jean
Rochester Business Alliance
150 State St
Rochester, NY 14614
585-244-3667 Fax: 585-244-4864
e-mail: jean.kase@rballiance.com
Web site: www.rochesterbusinessalliance.com

Clients:
Builders Exchange Inc-Rochester
Rochester Business Alliance

Lobbyists:
Brian Sampson

Kasirer Consulting
321 Broadway, Ste 201
New York, NY 10007
212-285-1800 Fax: 212-285-1818
e-mail: skasirer@kasirerconsulting.com

Clients:
92-94 Greene Street, LLC
92nd Street Y
ATCO Properties & Management Inc
AFA Protective Systems
American Cancer Society, Eastern Division Inc
Bedford Stuyvesant Family Health Ctr
Care Plus
Cemusa Inc
Citymeals-on-Wheels
American Society for the Prevention of Cruelty to Animals (ASPCA)
Elad Properties, LLC

Offices and agencies appear in alphabetical order.

Escape Rescue Systems
Kingsborough Community College (Research Foundation of CUNY)
Museum of Arts & Design
Nontraditional Employment for Women
Northside Center for Child Development
Port Parties, Ltd
Project Renewal
Restoration Project (NY)
S&R Medallion Corporation
Safe Horizon Inc
Silverman Foundation (Marty & Dorothy) (The)
T-Mobile
Wall Street Rising
GDC Properties Inc
Hamilton, Rabinovitz & Alschuler Inc
Intell Management
JC Studios, LLC
Lower Manhattan Cultural Council
McCarren Manor LLC
Historical Society (NY)
Noble Communications/CGBP
Silverite Construction
Dynamic Group (The)
Plaza/CPS 1 (The)
Urban Health Plan
Volunteers of America

Lobbyists:
Julie Greenberg
Sara Kasirer
Nick Vagelatos

Katz, Arthur H
Wholesale Marketers & Distributors
211 E 43rd St
New York, NY 10017-4707
212-682-3576 Fax: 212-867-7844

Clients:
Assn of Wholesale Marketers & Distributors (NYS)

Keycorp & Subsidiaries
127 Public Square
Cleveland, OH 44114
518-257-9820

Clients:
Keycorp & Subsidiaries

Lobbyists:
Christopher Pugliese

King, Barbara
555 W 57th St, 5th Fl
New York, NY 10019
212-523-5367 Fax: 212-523-2617
e-mail: bking@chpnet.org
Web site: www.wehealnewyork.org

Clients:
Beth Israel Medical Ctr
Long Island College Hospital
St Luke's-Roosevelt Hospital Ctr

Lobbyists:
Bradley Korn

Kirsch, Richard
Citizen Action of NY
94 Central Ave
Albany, NY 12206
518-465-4600 Fax: 518-465-2890
Web site: www.citizenactionny.org

Clients:
Citizen Action of NY

Lobbyists:
Mary Clark
Robert Cohen
Gaddy Collington Davia
Daphne Gathers
Shanna Goldman
Ricardo Gotla
Joyce E Gould
Michele Maglione
Ceylane Meyers
Katie Pepe
Sam Radford
Karen Scharff

Klein, Mitchell
65 W Red Oak Ln
White Plains, NY 10604
914-697-5361

Clients:
Alpha Marketing, Inc

Knighton, Ethel V
15811 Glacier Ct
North Potomac, MD 20878
301-840-9161

Clients:
Medco Health Solutions, Inc

Kramer Levin Naftalis & Frankel, LLP
919 Third Ave
New York, NY 10022
212-715-7835 or 212-715-9100 Fax: 212-715-7850
Web site: www.kramerlevin.com

Clients:
601 Eighth Ave, LLC
611 Eighth Ave, LLC
East River Realty Company, LLC
Edison Properties, LLC
Gracie Point Community Council
Northside Waterfront Improvement Group, LLC
Silverstein Development Corp
Solow Management Corp
Trustees of Columbia University in the City of NY (The)
Valeray Real Estate Co Inc

Offices and agencies appear in alphabetical order.

Lobbyists:
Robert E Flahive
Albert Fredericks
Richard G Leland
Samuel H Lindenbaum
James P Powers
Michael T Sillerman
Gary R Tarnoff
Rachel Winard

Kriss, Kriss, Brignola & Persing, LLP

350 Northern Blvd, Ste 306
Albany, NY 12204
518-449-2037 Fax: 518-449-7875

Clients:
Chickering Group (The)
Collateral Loanbrokers Assn of NY
Society of Professional Engineers Inc (NYS)

Lobbyists:
Mark C Kriss

Kruly, Kenneth

2001 Main St, LY 206
Buffalo, NY 14208-1098
716-888-3755 Fax: 716-888-3102
e-mail: krulyk@canisius.edu
Web site: www.canisius.edu

Clients:
Canisius College

Lobbyists:
Vincent M Cooke SJ
Patrick J Greenwald
John J Hurley
Kenneth C Kruly

Krupke, Bruce W

Dairy Foods
201 S Main St, # 302
North Syracuse, NY 13212-2166
315-452-6455
e-mail: info@nysdfi.org
Web site: www.nysdfi.org

Clients:
Dairy Foods Inc (NYS)

Kutsher Country Club

Kutsher Rd
Monticello, NY 12701
845-794-6000 Fax: 845-794-0157
e-mail: kutshers@warwick.net
Web site: www.kutshers.com

Clients:
Kutsher Country Club

Lobbyists:
Harriet Brahms

Mark Kutsher

La Fuente, A Tri State Worker & Community Fund Inc

101 Ave of the Americas, 23rd Fl
New York, NY 10013
212-388-3208

Clients:
La Fuente, A Tri State Worker & Community Fund

Lobbyists:
Zahida Pirani
Blanca Ramirez
Gouri Sadhwani
Angel Vera

Labor-Religion Coaltion, Inc (NYS)

800 Troy-Schenectady Rd
Latham, NY 12110-2455
518-213-6000 x6294 Fax: 518-213-6414
e-mail: info@labor-religion.org
Web site: www.labor-religion.org

Clients:
Labor-Religion Coalition, Inc (NYS)

Lobbyists:
Ed Felton
Luisa Linares
Joan Malone
Elisa Meredith
Brian O'Shaughnessy
Candice Wetherell

Lambert, Linda A

Am College of Physicians
100 State St, Ste 700
Albany, NY 12207-1817
518-427-0366 Fax: 518-427-1991

Clients:
American College of Physicians Svcs Inc (NY Chapter)

Lamishaw, Hilary

c/o Troy Rehab & Improvement Program
415 River St
Troy, NY 12180-2834
518-272-8289 Fax: 518-272-1950
e-mail: hilary@triponline.org

Clients:
Troy Rehabilitation & Improvement Program, Inc

Lanahan, Kevin

Con Edison, Inc
4 Irving Place, Rm 1650-S
New York, NY 10003
518-434-1193
Web site: www.coned.com

Offices and agencies appear in alphabetical order.

Clients:
Consolidated Edison Co of NY, Inc & its subsidiaries

Lobbyists:
John Banks
Dan Brown
Larry Carbone
Andrew Chin
Eric Dessen
Joan Freilich
Martin Heslin
Robert Hoglund
Stephen Ianello
Kenneth Reinhart
William Talbot
Joseph Tringali

Land Trust Alliance Northeast Program
110 Spring St
PO Box 792
Saratoga Springs, NY 12866
518-587-0774 Fax: 518-587-6467
e-mail: newyork@lta.org
Web site: www.lta.org

Clients:
Land Trust Alliance Northeast Program

Lobbyists:
Henrietta Jordan
Ezra Milchman

Landau-Painter, Cathy
KPMG, LLP
2001 M St NW
Washington, DC 20036
202-533-4018 Fax: 202-533-8516

Clients:
KPMG, LLP

Lobbyists:
Robert Arning
Terrill Menzel

Landry, M Joe
120 Washington Ave
Albany, NY 12210
518-449-3333

Clients:
Empire State Passengers Assn

Landsman, David
12 Welwyn Rd, Ste C
Great Neck, NY 11021
516-829-2742

Clients:
National Money Transmitters Assn

Langdon, David
491 State St, 3A
Albany, NY 12203-1019
518-432-5440

Clients:
Niagara Mohawk Power Corp

Lapidus, Marc
New Yorkers for Fiscal Fairness
75 Varick St, Ste 1404
New York, NY 10013
212-219-0022 Fax: 917-237-0509

Clients:
New Yorkers for Fiscal Fairness

Larowe, Mary (FKA Pike, William D)
Western NY Healthcare Assn
1876 Niagara Falls Blvd
Tonawanda, NY 14150-6439
716-695-0843

Clients:
Western NY Healthcare Assn

Lobbyists:
Paul Sweet

Lasky, Roy E
NYS Dental Assn
121 State St, 4th Fl
Albany, NY 12207-1622
518-465-0044 Fax: 518-427-0461
e-mail: rlasky@nysdental.org
Web site: www.nysdental.org

Clients:
NYS Dental Assn

Lobbyists:
Laura Leon

Lawyers for the Public Interest (NY)
151 W 30th St, 11th Fl
New York, NY 10001-4007
212-244-4664 Fax: 212-244-4570

Clients:
Communities United for Responsible Energy (CURE)
Lawyers for the Public Interest (NY)
Organization of Waterfront Neighborhoods (OWN)

Lobbyists:
Sarah Alvarez
Eddie Bautista
Marnie Berk
Dennis Boyd
Anthony Feliciano
John Gresham
Yesenia Guiterrez

Offices and agencies appear in alphabetical order.

Chris Johnson
Gavin Kearney
Marianne Lado
Amanda Masters
Roberta Mueller
Jaclyn Okin
Rebecca Price
Michael Rothenberg
Michael Scherz
Michael Silverman
Kim Sweet
Larry Tilley
Paola Urrea
Janette Wipper
Pauline Yoo

LeBoeuf Lamb Greene & MacRae, LLP
99 Washington Ave, Ste 2020
Albany, NY 12210
518-626-9000 Fax: 518-626-9010

125 W 55th St
New York, NY 10019
212-424-8000

Clients:
AFLAC NY
Assn of Financial Guaranty Insurors
Excess Line Assn of NY
International Underwriting Assn of London
Lloyds of London
Medical Liability Mutual Insurance Co
Mortgage Insurance Companies of America
State Farm Insurance Companies
Columbia Natural Resources LLC
Cooper Union for the Advancement of Science & Art (The)

Lobbyists:
Gordon J Davis (NY Office)
Thomas Dawson
Jay B Martin
John Mulhern
Edmond Valente
Thomas West

League of Women Voters of New York State
35 Maiden Ln
Albany, NY 12207
518-465-4162

Clients:
League of Women Voters of New York State

Lobbyists:
Aimee Allaud
Heather Baker-Sullivan
Lenore Banks
Barbara Bartoletti
Paula Blum
Marian Bott
Hillary Brizell-Delise
Jane Chase
Jeanette Conners
Gail Davenport
Lois Haignere

Joan Johnson
Martha Kennedy
Ellen Kotlow
Marcia Merrins
Jacki Moriarty
Anne Riordan
Sally Robinson
Carol Saginaw
Charlotte Shapiro
Evelyn Stock
Betsey Swan
Katherine Tarbell
Dare Thompson
Lyle Toohey
Edna Vincente
Elsie Wager
Mildred Whalen
Roberta Wiernak

Learning Disabilities Assn of NYS Inc
1202 Troy-Schenectady Rd
Bldg 1, Rm 225
Latham, NY 12110
518-608-8992

Clients:
Learning Disabilities Assn of NYS Inc

Lobbyists:
Heather Loukmas

Lefebvre, Glenn
Bar Assn (NYS)
One Elk St
Albany, NY 12207
518-487-5652

Clients:
Bar Assn (NYS)

Lobbyists:
Kathleen R Baxter
Patricia K Bucklin
A Vincent Buzard
Ronald F Kennedy
Kenneth G Standard

Legal Action Ctr of the City of NY Inc
153 Waverly Place, 8th Fl
New York, NY 10014-3897
212-243-1313 Fax: 212-675-0286
e-mail: tgardner@lac.org
Web site: www.lac.org

Clients:
Legal Action Ctr of the City of NY Inc

Lobbyists:
Tracie M Gardner
Anita R Marton
Debbie Mukamal
Paul N Samuels

Offices and agencies appear in alphabetical order.

Legal Services of the Hudson Valley

4 Cromwell Pl
White Plains, NY 10601
914-949-1305

Clients:
Legal Services of the Hudson Valley

Lobbyists:
Jill Bradshaw-Soto
Paul Callagy
Rosalie Cicogna
Lewis G Creekmore
Mary Grace Ferone
Barbara Finkelstein
William Flynn
Peter M Frank
Jacqueline R Frost
Erin Guven
Kathleen Healey
Ursula Inghem
Kathleen Jones
Nancy Marrone
Aida Ramirez
Barbara Shealy
Judy Studebaker
Eileen Swan
Mary Jo Wheatley
David Wright

Lehrer, Sander

Scarola Reavis & Parent LLP
888 Seventh Ave, 45th Fl
New York, NY 10106
212-757-0007

Clients:
United Nations Development Corp

Lemery Greisler, LLC

10 Railroad Pl
Saratoga Springs, NY 12866
518-581-8800

Clients:
Great Escape Theme Park LLC (The)

Lobbyists:
John Lemery

Leon, Rachel

Common Cause (NY)
155 Ave of the Americas
New York, NY 10013
212-691-6421

Clients:
Common Cause (NY)

Lobbyists:
Joanna Erenberg
Megan Quattlebaum

Levi, Ross D

Empire State Pride Agenda, 1 Commerce Pl
99 Washington Ave, Ste 805
Albany, NY 12260
518-472-3330 Fax: 518-472-3334
e-mail: rlevi@prideagenda.org
Web site: www.prideagenda.org

Clients:
Empire State Pride Agenda

Lobbyists:
Alan Van Capelle
Carmen Vazquez

Levine, Laurence J

BTOBA
1140 Bay St, Ste A & B
Staten Island, NY 10305
718-727-7613 Fax: 718-727-7619
e-mail: btoba@inetmail.att.net
Web site: www.btoba.org

Clients:
Bridge & Tunnel Officers Benevolent Assn

Levine, Paul

Jewish Board of Family & Children Svcs
120 W 57th St
New York, NY 10019
212-632-4614

Clients:
Jewish Board of Family & Children's Services Inc

Levy, Norman PC

575 Madison Ave, Ste 1006
New York, NY 10022
212-605-0313 Fax: 212-333-8720

Clients:
Abbey Gardy, LLP
College of Technology (Research Foundation of CUNY)
Living Independently Inc
Polytechnic University
Met-Tel Corporation
United Neighborhood Houses
Viacom Outdoor Inc

Lobbyists:
Norman Levy

Lewinter Associates, Murray

120 Washington Ave
Albany, NY 12210
518-449-3333 Fax: 518-427-6781

Clients:
Cingular Wireless
National Promotions & Advertising

Offices and agencies appear in alphabetical order.

Lobbyists:
Murray Lewinter

Lewis, Mark
124 Burnett Rd
Saugerties, NY 12477
845-246-8881

Clients:
Immigration Coalition (NY)

Liantonio, John J
AT&T Wireless Services
15 E Midland Ave
Paramus, NJ 7652
201-576-5083 Fax: 201-576-7881
e-mail: john.liantonio@attws.com

Clients:
Cingular Wireless

Library Assn (NY)
252 Hudson Ave
Albany, NY 12210-1802
518-432-6952 Fax: 518-427-1697
e-mail: nyladirector@pobox.com
Web site: www.nyla.org

Clients:
Library Assn (NY)

Lobbyists:
Michael J Borges

Lieberman, Geoff
Coalition of Institlzd Aged & Disabled
425 East 25th St
New York, NY 10010
212-481-7572 Fax: 212-481-5149

Clients:
Coalition of Institutionalized Aged & Disabled

Lobbyists:
Tanya Kessler

Lieberman, Mark L
900 Merchants Concourse, Ste 214
Westbury, NY 11590
516-228-4226 Fax: 516-228-6569

Clients:
American Lawyer Media
Brunswick Hospital Ctr Inc
Court Clerks Assn (NYS)
EAC Inc
Forestcitydaly Housing
Nassau Regional Off-Track Betting Corporation
Sanitary District No 6
Town of Hempstead

Lincoln Ctr for the Performing Arts Inc
70 Lincoln Center Plaza
New York, NY 10023-6583
212-875-5000 Fax: 212-875-5122
e-mail: efinkelstein@lincolncenter.org
Web site: www.lincolncenter.org

Clients:
Lincoln Ctr for the Performing Arts Inc

Lobbyists:
Rosemarie Gaipoli
Scott Noppe-Brandon
Levy Reynold
Melissa Thornton
Evelyn Tsimis

Lipman & Biltekoff, LLP
333 International Dr, Ste B-4
Williamsville, NY 14221
716-633-3200

Clients:
Rural Energy Development Corp

Lobbyists:
Michael Joy

Lipsky, Richard Associates Inc
11 Patricia Dr
New City, NY 10956
914-572-2865 Fax: 845-639-0687

Clients:
Babylon Paper Stock
Neighborhood Retail Alliance
Red Apple Group
United Food & Commercial Workers Union, Dist Council of Region 1
Forest City Ratner Companies
All Med Medical & Rehabilitation Centers

Lobbyists:
Richard Lipsky

Liske, Anne
Coalition Against Sexual Assault
63 Colvin Ave
Albany, NY 12206
518-482-4222 Fax: 518-482-4278
e-mail: aliske@nyscasa.org
Web site: www.nyscasa.org

Clients:
Coalition Against Sexual Assault (NYS)

Lobbyists:
Jacqui C Williams

LoCicero & Tan Inc
123 William St, 22nd Fl
New York, NY 10038
212-608-0888 Fax: 212-608-0458

Offices and agencies appear in alphabetical order.

Clients:

Bluestone Organization (The)
American Ref-Fuel Co
Care Plus
Cherit Group, LLC (The)
Community Preservation Corporation (The)
Council of Senior Ctrs & Services of NYC Inc
Claremont Square, LLC
Fashion Institute of Technology
Forest City Ratner Companies
Hospital for Special Surgery
Consumer Information & Dispute Resolution Inc
Parkchester Preservation Co, LP
SL Green Realty Corp
Flushing Commons
TDC Development & Construction Corp
Towers at Spring Creek
Village Care of NY Inc
Yonkers Contracting Co Inc
JBI International
Martin Motor Sales Inc

Lobbyists:

John LoCicero
Eva Tan

Logan, Ernest

Council of School Supervs/Administrators
16 Court St
Brooklyn, NY 11241-1254
718-852-3000

Clients:

Council of School Supervisors & Administrators

Lobbyists:

Barbara Jaccoma
Jill Levy
Richard Relkin

Long Island Association

80 Hauppauge Rd
Commack, NY 11725-4495
631-493-3002 Fax: 631-499-2194

Clients:

Long Island Association

Lobbyists:

Matthew Crosson
Matthew Groneman
Mitchell H Pally

Long Term Care Community Coalition

242 West 30th St, Ste 306
New York, NY 10001
212-385-0355 Fax: 212-732-6945
e-mail: crnhcc@aol.com
Web site: www.nhccnys.org

Clients:

Long Term Care Community Coalition

Lobbyists:

Richard Mollot
Cynthia Rudder

Long, Margaret

822 Salem Dr
Ballston Spa, NY 12020-2336
518-885-8415 Fax: 518-884-8045

Clients:

Novartis Pharmaceuticals Corp

Losquadro, Steven E

701D Route 25A
Rocky Point, NY 11778
631-744-9070

Clients:

Caithness Energy, LLC

Louloudes, Virginia

575 Eighth Ave, Ste 1720
New York, NY 10018-3011
212-244-6667 Fax: 212-714-1918
e-mail: questions@art-newyork.org
Web site: www.offbroadwayonline.com

Clients:

Alliance of Resident Theatres/New York (ART)

Lowry, Robert

Council of School Superintendents
7 Elk St, 3rd Fl
Albany, NY 12207-1002
518-449-1063

Clients:

Council of School Superintendents (NYS)

Lobbyists:

Douglas Gerhardt
Thomas Rogers

Luria, Robert S

GlaxoSmithKline
12 Spruce Run
East Greenbush, NY 12061-9611
518-477-2581 Fax: 800-561-5825
e-mail: robert.s.luria@gsk.com

Clients:

GlaxoSmithKline, PLC

Lustig, Esther Public Affairs

86-29 155th Ave, Ste 6L
Howard Beach, NY 11414
718-845-2855 Fax: 718-845-0282
e-mail: lustigpa@aol.com

Offices and agencies appear in alphabetical order.

Clients:

Federation Employment & Guidance Service Inc (FEGS)
Folksbiene Yiddish Theatre
JCC of Mid-Westchester
Jamaica Chamber of Commerce
Lexington School for the Deaf/Ctr for the Deaf Inc
Mosholu Montefiore Community Ctr
Partnership with Children
YMS Management

Lobbyists:

Esther Lustig

Luthin Associates, Inc

15 Walling Pl
Avon by the Sea, NJ 07717
732-774-0005

Clients:

Consumer Power Advocates

Lobbyists:

Catherine Luthin

Lynch, Bill Associates, LLC

41 Hamilton Terr
New York, NY 10031
212-283-7515

Clients:

Jets, LLC (NY)

Lobbyists:

William Lynch

Lynch, Patricia Associates

111 Washington Ave, Ste 606
Albany, NY 12210
518-432-9220 Fax: 518-432-9186
e-mail: plynch@plynchassociates.com

Clients:

Accenture
Albany Law School
Albany Port District Commission
Alliance for Downtown New York Inc
Baldwin-Grand Canal & Baldwin-West-End Canal Improvement District
Buffalo Niagara Partnership
Cendant Car Rental Group Inc
ABC Inc
Coca-Cola Bottling Co of NY (The)
Concerned Home Care Providers
Continental Industrial Capital, LLC
Destiny USA
EW Enterprises
Eastern Paramedics Inc
Educational Broadcasting Corporation Thirteen/WNET
Electric & Gas Corporation (NYS)
Empire State Distributors & Wholesalers Assn Inc
Forest City Ratner Companies
Foundation for Accounting Practitioners
General Motors Corp
Hetrick-Martin Institute, Home of Harvey Milk HS (The)
King Ferry Winery

Long Island Power Authority
LP Ciminelli Inc
Lower East Side Tenement Museum
American Waterways Operators
Madison Square Garden LP
Magna Entertainment Corp
Automotive Recyclers Association (NY)
Maritime Assn
Mohawk Ambulance Service
Motor Truck Assn (NYS)
Nurse Practitioners Assn of NYS (The)
Oneida Indian Nation
BBL Construction Services Inc
Park Avenue Health Care Management
Pharmaceutical Research & Mfrs of America (PHRMA)
Precision Jet Management Inc
Pyramid Managing Group Inc
Rochester Gas & Electric Corp
SCI of New York Inc
Bersin Properties, LLC
Seneca Niagara Falls Gaming Corp
Syracuse City School District
Tech Valley Communications Inc
Vector Group Limited
Venetian Casino Resort, LLC
Walt Disney Corp (The)
Westchester County
Western Regional Off-Track Betting
Cablevision (CSC Holdings Inc)
Caramoor
CH2M Hill
Criterion Strategies Inc (FKA First Responder Inc)
Golden Technology Management, LLC
Hudson Valley Fois Gras (HVFG, LLC)
Kidspeace
Lifespan
Lilac Corporation
Mark IV IVHS Inc
Metrocare Ambulance
Norvest Financial Services Inc
NVR Inc
Professional Insurance Agents of NYS Inc
Radiant Energy Corporation
Rochester-Genesee Regional Transportation Authority c/o Renaissan
Spring Valley Homes
Suffolk County Executive
Legal Aid Society (The)
Witkoff Group (The)
Tyco international (USA) Inc
Viacom Inc
Wal-Mart
Waste Management of NY, LLC

Lobbyists:

Christopher Bombardier
Gerald R DeLuca
Christopher Grimaldi
Gerald J Jennings
Allison Lee
Patricia Lynch
Patrick McCarthy
Samir S NeJame

M & R Strategic Services

80 Broad St, 16th Fl
New York, NY 10004
212-764-3878

Offices and agencies appear in alphabetical order.

Clients:
AIDS Service Center of NYC
Naral Pro-Choice NY
Pharmacist Society (NYC)
Pratt Institute Center for Community & Environmental Development

Lobbyists:
Arthur Malkin
Michael O'Loughlin
Donald Ross

MCI (FKA Worldcom)
99 Washington Ave, 17th Fl
Albany, NY 12210
518-433-4003
Web site: www.mci.com

Clients:
MCI

Lobbyists:
Richard Fipphen
Laura Gallo
Charles Williams

MRH & Company, Inc
570 Lexington Ave
New York, NY 10022
212-750-0103

Clients:
Electric Sign Board of NY, Inc

Lobbyists:
Mary Hardin

MacKenzie, Duncan R
NYS Assn of Realtors
130 Washington Ave
Albany, NY 12210-2220
518-463-0300 Fax: 518-462-5474
e-mail: govt@nysar.com
Web site: www.nysar.com

Clients:
Assn of Realtors (NYS)

Lobbyists:
Michael J Kelly
Charles M Staro

Mackin, Robert E
Association of Financial Guaranty Ins
139 Lancaster St
Albany, NY 12210-1903
518-449-4698 Fax: 518-432-5651
e-mail: bmackin@mackinco.com

Clients:
Assn of Financial Guaranty Insurors

Lobbyists:
Teresa Casey

Madison Square Garden LP
2 Penn Plaza
New York, NY 10121
212-465-4176

Clients:
Madison Square Garden LP

Lobbyists:
Andrew Lynn

Maher, Daniel F, Jr
Excess Line Assn of NY
55 Broadway, 1 Exchange Plz, 29th Fl
New York, NY 10006-3728
646-292-5555 Fax: 646-292-5500
e-mail: dmaher@elany.org
Web site: www.elany.org

Clients:
Excess Line Assn of NY

Maier, Ronald S
E P Olmsted Medical Center
1170 Main St
Buffalo, NY 14209
716-882-1025 Fax: 716-882-5577

Clients:
Elizabeth Pierce Olmsted MD Ctr for the Visually Impaired

Make the Road by Walking Inc
301 Grove St
Brooklyn, NY 11237
718-418-7690

Clients:
Make the Road by Walking Inc

Lobbyists:
Manuel Castro
Oona Chatterjee
Andrew Friedman
Nieves Padilla
David Perez
Placida Rodriguez
Yorelis Vidal

Malkin & Ross
100 State St, Ste 400
Albany, NY 12207-1801
518-449-3359 Fax: 518-449-5788
e-mail: amalkin@malkinross.com
Web site: www.malkinross.com

Clients:
Advocates for Adult Day Services
Alliance for Quality Education
American Jewish Committee
American Wind Energy Assoc
Ascension Health

Offices and agencies appear in alphabetical order.

Aseptic Packaging Council
Assc of Perioperative Registered Nurses
Business Outreach Ctr Network
Camp Directors Assn (NYS)
Coalition for the Homeless
Coalition of NYS Alzheimer's Assn Chapters
Center for Justice & Democracy
Center for Constitutional Rights
Center for the Independence of the Disabled in NY Inc
Defenders Assn (NYS)
Direct Marketing Assoc Inc (Dehart & Darr Assoc Inc)
Family Decisions Coalition (Open Society Policy Ctr)
Food Industry Alliance of NYS Inc
Friends of Hudson River Park
Gay Men's Health Crisis (GMHC)
Forgotten Victims of Attica
Land Trust Alliance
Lesbian Gay Bisexual & Transgender Community Ctr (The)
Naral Pro Choice New York
Bedford Stuyvesant Family Health Center Inc
Natural Resource Defense Council
Center for Policy Reform
New Yorkers for Accessible Health Coverage
Nurses Assn (NYS)
Pharmaceutical Research & Manufacturers of America
Regional Community Service Pgms (NYS)
School Food Service Assn (NYS)
New Yorkers Against the Death Penalty (The Justice Project)
Regional Food Bank of Northeastern NY
Trial Lawyers' Assn (NYS)
VIP Community Services
AIDS Service Center of NY

Lobbyists:
John Cochran
Gene DeSantis
Arthur N Malkin
Josh Oppenheimer
Terry Pratt
Donald K Ross
Jessica Schrafroth
Christine Tramontano
Tracy Tress

Maloney, Richard
County Nursing Facilities of NY
111 Pine St
Albany, NY 12207
518-465-1473 Fax: 518-465-0506
e-mail: rmaloney@nysac.org

Clients:
County Nursing Facilities of NY, Inc

Manatt, Phelps & Phillips, LLP
121 State St, 3rd Fl
Albany, NY 12207
518-432-5990 Fax: 518-432-5996

Clients:
83-30 Austin Street LLC
Assn of Public Broadcasting Stations of NY
American Council of Public Broadcasting Stations of NY
Community Health Care Assoc of NYS
Corporation for Supportive Housing

Coalition of Voluntary Safety Net Hospitals (NYS)
Federation of Protestant Welfare Agencies Inc
Glimmerglass Coalition
Group Health Incorporated
Health & Hospitals Corp (NYC)
Independent Care System (ICS)
Sephardic Bikur Holim
Memorial Sloan-Kettering Cancer Center
Montefiore Medical Ctr
Structural Biology Center (NY)
Coalition of Prepaid Health Svcs Plans (NYS)
NYS Council of Health-System Pharmacists
National Multiple Sclerosis Society, NY MS Coalition Action Netwo
Primary Care Development Corporation
Visiting Nurse Service of NY

Lobbyists:
Marcia Alazraki
Deborah Bachrach
Robert Belfort
Patti Boozang
Melinda Dutton
John Faso (Executive On
Karen Lipson
James Lytle
Shelley Mayer
Helen Pfister
Carol Rosenthal
Vanessa Wisnienski

Mandelker, Lawrence A
51 East 42nd St, 17th Fl
New York, NY 10017
212-682-8383 Fax: 212-949-5206

Clients:
NY Junior Tennis League
Sports & Arts in Schools Foundation Inc

Manhattan Chamber of Commerce Inc
1375 Broadway, 3rd Fl
New York, NY 10018
212-473-7875

Clients:
Manhattan Chamber of Commerce, Inc

Lobbyists:
Ronald Paltrowitz
Nancy Ploeger

Maniscalco, John D
Oil Heating Association
14 Penn Plz, Ste 1102
New York, NY 10122
212-695-1380 Fax: 212-594-6583
e-mail: nyoilheating@nyoha.org
Web site: www.nyoha.org

Clients:
New York Oil Heating Assoc, Inc

Offices and agencies appear in alphabetical order.

Mannella, Peter F
266 Hudson Ave
Albany, NY 12210
518-463-4937

Clients:
Assn for Pupil Transportation (NY)

Mannis, David
140 E 45th St
New York, NY 10017-3144
646-658-7128

Clients:
Cigna Corporation

Manufacturers Assn of Central NY Inc
One Webster's Landing, 5th Fl
Syracuse, NY 13202-1044
315-474-4201

Clients:
Manufacturers Assn of Central NY Inc

Lobbyists:
Karen DeJarnette
Kristen Heath
Randall Wolken

Marcus Attorneys
13 Greene Ave
Brooklyn, NY 11238
718-643-6555 Fax: 718-643-9111
e-mail: law@marcusattorneys.com
Web site: www.marcusattorneys.com

Clients:
Ballet Hispanico of NY Inc
Bam-Local Development Corporation
Manhattan Theatre Club Inc
United Talmudical Academy
Haim Marcovici

Lobbyists:
Kenya Jui
Philip Lavender
Jed S Marcus
Andrew Weltchek

Margiotta, Joseph M
99 Quentin Roosevelt Blvd
Ste 201
Garden City, NY 11530
516-486-6600 Fax: 516-794-9034

Clients:
Institute of Technology (NY)
Physicians' Reciprocal Insurers

Maritato, Anna Maria
Pfizer Inc
284 State St, 2nd Fl
Albany, NY 12210
518-463-9133 Fax: 518-463-9136

Clients:
Pfizer Inc

Lobbyists:
Aimee Falchuk
Neal Masia

Marsh & Associates, PC
111 Washington Ave, Ste 405
Albany, NY 12210
518-436-6000 Fax: 518-436-6009
e-mail: marshpc@attglobal.net

Clients:
Assn of Independent Schools (NYS)
Canadian National Railway
Care Plus Health Plan
Council of Licensed Physiotherapists of NYS Inc
Education & Work Consortium (The)
Greater NY Health Care Facilities Assoc
Maximus Inc
Mentoring Partnership Coalition
Olympus America Inc
Preservation League of New York State
Saratoga Performing Arts Ctr
Town Clerks Assn Inc (NYS)
UST Public Affairs Inc
Cardtronics LP
Friends of NY Racing Inc
Chief Executives Network for Manufacturing
Greene International Golf Assn
Metropolitan College of NY

Lobbyists:
Thomas C Barletta
Kerry D Marsh

Martens, Joseph J
Open Space Institute
1350 Broadway, Rm 201
New York, NY 10018
212-629-3981 Fax: 212-344-2441
Web site: www.osiny.org

Clients:
Open Space Institute Inc

Lobbyists:
Jennifer Grosman

Maskin, Daniel
2 Charles Blvd
Guilderland, NY 12084
518-690-0491
e-mail: dmaskin@nycap.rr.com
Web site: www.nyscaaonline.org

Offices and agencies appear in alphabetical order.

Clients:
Community Action Assn (NYS)

Massiah, Lesley A
Fordham University
441 E Fordham Rd, Admin Bldg, Room 220
Bronx, NY 10458-9993
718-817-3023 Fax: 718-817-5722
e-mail: massiah@fordham.edu
Web site: www.fordham.edu

Clients:
Fordham University

Lobbyists:
Brian J Byrne
Rev. Joseph M McShane
Michael A Molina
Joseph P Muriana

Master, Robert
CWA, District 1
80 Pine St, 37th Fl
New York, NY 10005
212-344-2515 Fax: 212-425-2947

Clients:
Communications Workers of America, District 1

Lobbyists:
Kenneth Peres

Matarazzo, Louis
36 Muirfield Rd
Rockville Centre, NY 11570
516-764-0117 Fax: 516-766-1534

Clients:
Captains Endowment Assn, NYC Police Department

McCann, Michael
Prudential Financial
2358 S County Trl, Ste 4
East Greenwich, RI 2818
401-541-9170

Clients:
Prudential Financial Inc

McCulley & Associates Inc
150 State St, 4th Fl
Albany, NY 12207
518-432-3300 Fax: 518-432-4007

Clients:
Ambulette Coalition Inc (NY)
Assn of Home Inspectors Inc (NYS)
Associated Builders & Contractors Inc (Empire St)
Fortuna Energy Inc
International Health, Raquet & Sportsclub Assn
Concerned Citizens of Southampton

Mothers Against Drunk Driving-NYS Office
Rehabilitation Assn Inc (NYS)

Lobbyists:
James McCulley

McDevitt, William L
Metro Pkg Store Assn
6 Xavier Dr, Ste 315
Yonkers, NY 10704-1392
914-423-4500 Fax: 914-423-4508

Clients:
Metropolitan Package Store Assn Inc

McEvoy, Frank
99 Washington Ave, Ste 400
Albany, NY 12210
518-427-9071

Clients:
USA Trading Company, Inc

McGuire, Michael J
Mason Tenders DC
266 W 37th St #1150
New York, NY 10018
212-452-9501 Fax: 212-452-9552

Clients:
Mason Tenders District Council Greater NY & Long Island PAC

Lobbyists:
Robert Asaro-Angelo
Kris Kohler

McInnis, Stephen C
395 Hudson St, 9th Fl
New York, NY 10014
212-366-3388

Clients:
District Council of Carpenters, PAC (NYC)

Lobbyists:
Marina Vranich

McLaughlin, Martin J Communications
64 Fulton St, Ste 1105
New York, NY 10038
212-437-7373 Fax: 212-437-7378

Clients:
HJ Kalikow & Co, LLC
Manhattan Theatre Club, Inc
S & M Enterprises

Lobbyists:
Kathy Cudahy
Martin J McLaughlin
Michael Woloz

Offices and agencies appear in alphabetical order.

McNamee Lochner Titus & Williams, PC

677 Broadway
Albany, NY 12207
518-447-3200 Fax: 518-447-3368
e-mail: quinones@mltw.com
Web site: www.mltw.com

Clients:
Council of Prof Geologists (NYS)

Lobbyists:
William A Hurst
Michael L Kinum
John J Privitera

McSpedon, William J

100 South Swan St
Albany, NY 12210-1939
518-463-7551 Fax: 518-463-7556

Clients:
Conf of the Int'l Union of Operating Engineers (NYS)

Meara, Brian R, Public Relations Inc

321 Broadway, Ste 600
New York, NY 10007
518-465-8760

Clients:
Altria Corporate Services Inc (ALCS)
American Lawyer Media Co
Black Car Operators' Injury Compensation Fund (NY)
Delaware North Companies Gaming & Entertainment Inc
Bus Association of NYS Inc
Court Officers Assn (NYS)
EAC Inc
Empire State Assn of Adult Homes & Assist Living Facilities
Finger Lakes Racing Association
Glenwood Management Corporation
Insurance Premium Finance Assn Inc
Ref-Fuel Company
Reliant Resources Inc
Parker Jewish Inst for Health Care & Rehab
Physicians' Reciprocal Insurers
Retailers Alliance (The)
Solow Management Company
Simon Weisenthal Ctr Museum of Tolerance
Southern Tier Acquisition, LLC
Suffolk County Court Employees
Transit Alliance
Verizon
University Medical Ctr Dept of Psyciatry (NY)
Wilmorite Holdings, LP
Yankees Partnership (NY)
Educational Housing Services (Regional Programs Inc)
Empire Resorts Inc
Guardian Life Insurance Company of America (The)
Lincoln Center for the Performing Arts Inc
New York Medical Staff Leadership Council
NYC & Company
NYC 2012

Lobbyists:
Brian R Meara

Meister, Seelig & Fein, LLP

140 E 145th St, 19th Fl
New York, NY 10017
212-655-3500 Fax: 212-655-3535

Clients:
Independence Plaza Associates, LP

Lobbyists:
Stacey Ashby
Thomas Friedman
Stephen Meister

Melchionni, William, III

Nationwide Insurance
125 State St
Albany, NY 12207
518-455-8930 Fax: 518-426-5891
e-mail: melchib@nationwide.com

Clients:
Nationwide Insurance

Mele, Don

One Battery Park Plz, 4th Fl
New York, NY 10004-1479
212-493-7400 Fax: 212-493-7778
e-mail: dmele@nycp.org
Web site: www.nycp.org

Clients:
Partnership for New York City

Lobbyists:
Maria Gotsch
Philip Lentz
Clara Rainis
Alberto Robaina
MarySol Rodriguez
Michael Simas
Kathryn Wylde

Melewski & Greenwood, LLP

32 Fryer Ln
Altamont, NY 12009
518-861-6477

Clients:
Adirondack Council (The)
Citizens Campaign for the Environment
Sagamore Institute of the Adirondacks

Lobbyists:
David Greenwood
Bernard Melewski

Mental Health Assn of Westchester Co Inc

2269 Saw Mill River Rd, Bldg 1A
Elmsford, NY 10523-3832

Offices and agencies appear in alphabetical order.

914-345-5900 Fax: 914-347-8859
e-mail: hedlundc@mhawestchester.org
Web site: mhawestchester.org

Clients:
Mental Health Assn of Westchester Co Inc

Lobbyists:
Michael Friedman
Carolyn S Hedlund

Mental Health Association of NYC Inc
194 Washington Ave, Ste 415
Albany, NY 12210-2314
518-434-0439 Fax: 518-427-8676
e-mail: mhapres@mhanys.org
Web site: www.mhanys.org

Clients:
Mental Health Association of NYC Inc

Lobbyists:
Glenn Liebman
Micheal Seereiter

Mercury Public Affairs
137 5th Ave, 3rd Fl
New York, NY 10010-7147
212-681-1380 Fax: 212-681-1381
Web site: www.mercurypublicaffairs.com

Clients:
AT&T Corp
Bodega Assoc of the US Inc (The)
American Red Cross in Greater NY
Distilled Spirits Council of the US
Federation of Taxi Drivers Inc (NYS)
Liberty Lines Express Inc
Jets, LLC (NY)
Mercy College
Empire Resorts Inc
Buffalo Niagara Partnership
Greater NY Health Care Facilities Assn
Western Regional Off-Track Betting Corporation
Natural Resources Defense Council
Niagara Falls Memorial Medical Arts Center
Pfizer Inc
Police Benevolent Assn of the NYS Troopers Inc
Shinnecock Nation Gaming Authority

Lobbyists:
Peter Barden
Thomas Doherty
John Lonergan
Kieran Mahoney
Michael McKeon
Mike Relyea
Kevin Schuler
Greg Strimple

Mesick, Edie
Nutrition Consortium of NYS
235 Lark St
Albany, NY 12210
518-436-8757 Fax: 518-427-7992

Clients:
Nutrition Consortium of NYS Inc

Lobbyists:
Lisa Allison
Christine Barberio
Gail Cooney
Mark Denley
Lisa Frank
Yvette James
Misha Marvel
Colleen Pawling
Catherine Roberts

Meyer Suozzi English & Klein, PC
One Commerce Plaza, Ste 1102
Albany, NY 12260
518-465-5551 Fax: 518-465-2033

Clients:
1199/SEIU New York's Health & Human Services Union
Actors Fund of America (The)
Brooklyn Public Library
Committee for Occupational Safety & Health (NY)
Committee for Workers' Compensation Reform
Conservation Service Group
Council for Unity
Consortium for Workers Education
Int'l Brotherhood of Teamsters, AFL-CIO (Local 237)
Laborers' Political Action Committee (NYS)
Garment Industry Development Corporation
Local 1180, CWA, AFL-CIO
Mount Sinai Medical Center
MFY Legal Services
Screen Actors Guild (National & Hollywood Offices)
Suffolk County Correction Officers Assn
Susquehanna & Western Railway Corp (NY)
Production Alliance (NY)
Unite Here
Utility Workers Union, Local 1-2, AFL-CIO
SEIU Local 200 United
Working Today
SEIU, Local 300
City Works Foundation, (The)
Traffipax Inc

Lobbyists:
Thomas Hartnett
Julie Ruttan
Lawrence Scherer
Richard D Winsten

Mid-Hudson Catskill Rural & Migrant Ministry Inc
360 Noxon Rd
PO Box 4757
Poughkeepsie, NY 12602

Offices and agencies appear in alphabetical order.

845-485-8627 Fax: 845-485-1963
e-mail: hope@ruralmigrantministry.org
Web site: www.ruralmigrantministry.org

Clients:
Mid-Hudson Catskill Rural & Migrant Ministry Inc

Lobbyists:
William Abom
Richard Witt, Jr

Midtown Consultants, Inc
345 W 44th St
New York, NY 10036
212-265-2494

Clients:
GVA Williams, Inc-Hudson Telegraph Associates

Lobbyists:
Bernie Cohen
James McManus

Miller, Monica
4691 Route 66
PO Box 118
Malden Bridge, NY 12115
518-766-0322

Clients:
Foundation for the Advancement of Innovative Medicine
Health Freedom NY

Mills, Josephine
Avon Products, Inc
1345 Ave of the Americas
New York, NY 10105-0196
212-282-5609 Fax: 212-282-6086
e-mail: josephine.mills@avon.com

Clients:
Avon Products Inc

Mirant New York Inc
140 Samsondale Ave
West Haverstraw, NY 10993
845-786-8111
e-mail: louis.friscoe@mirant.com

Clients:
Mirant New York Inc

Lobbyists:
Louis Friscoe
Mark Lynch

Mirram Global, LLC
895 Broadway, 5th Fl
New York, NY 10003
212-505-6633/212-260 Fax: 212-505-0845/21
e-mail: mirramglobal@aol.com

Clients:
Healthplex Inc
New York First
Coalition for the Homeless
Center Care Inc
Morris Heights Health Ctr
New Visions for Public Schools
Vote Here, Inc

Lobbyists:
Luis A Miranda Jr
Roberto Ramirez Jr
Roberto Ramirez Sr
Kim Ramos
Jon Silvan

Mirram Group, LLC (The)
895 Broadway, 5th Fl
New York, NY 10003
212-505-6633 Fax: 212-505-0845
e-mail: mirramgroup@aol.com

Clients:
Transport Workers Union, Local 100

Lobbyists:
Luis A Miranda Jr
Roberto Ramirez Sr
Kim Ramos

Mohawk Valley Chamber of Commerce, Inc
520 Seneca St
Utica, NY 13502
315-724-3151 Fax: 315-724-3177

Clients:
Mohawk Valley Chamber of Commerce, Inc

Lobbyists:
William Nicholson

Montalbano Initiatives Inc
64 Fulton St, Ste 603
New York, NY 10038
212-587-0587 Fax: 212-587-0667
Web site: www.nyclobbyist.com

Clients:
Historic District Council
Legal Services for NYC Inc
Teamsters Local 237
Social Service Employees Union, Local 371

Lobbyists:
Vincent Montalbano

Morano, Regina G
Preferred Care
259 Monroe Ave
Rochester, NY 14607
585-327-2413

Offices and agencies appear in alphabetical order.

Clients:
Preferred Care

Morello, Charles J
NYS PFFA
111 Washington Ave, Ste 207
Albany, NY 12210
518-436-8827 Fax: 518-436-8830
e-mail: nyspffapres@aol.com
Web site: www.nyspffa.org

Clients:
Professional Fire Fighters Assn Inc (NYS)

Lobbyists:
Michael McManus

Morgan Associates
12 North Main St
Homer, NY 13077
518-463-8644 Fax: 518-463-8656

Clients:
Park Outdoor Advertising of NY Inc

Lobbyists:
Matthew A Morgan

Morgante, Samuel
700 12th St NW, Ste 710
Washington, DC 20005
202-662-2577

Clients:
Genworth Financial

Lobbyists:
Sandra Jones

Morris & McVeigh LLP
19 Dove St
Albany, NY 12210
518-426-8111 Fax: 518-426-5111
e-mail: rjm@mormc.com

Clients:
80/90 Maiden Lane, LLC
Albany Institute of History & Art (AIHA)
Botanical Garden (NY) (The)
Collegiate Church Corp
McGraw-Hill Education
Opera (NYC)
Preservation League of NYS
Cogito LLC
Greenwich House, Inc
Oxford LLC

Lobbyists:
Richard J Miller Jr

Morris, Mark
Hanys Insurance Co
217 Great Oaks Blvd
Albany, NY 12203-5964
518-862-0676

Clients:
Hanys Insurane Company, Inc

Morse, Alan
Jewish Guild for the Blind (The)
15 W 65th St
New York, NY 10023
212-769-6215 Fax: 212-595-4907
e-mail: armorse@jgb.org
Web site: www.jgb.org

Clients:
Jewish Guild for the Blind (The)

Lobbyists:
Annemarie O'Hearn

Motley, Duane R
PO Box 107
Spencerport, NY 14559-0107
585-225-2340 Fax: 585-225-2810
e-mail: family@nyfrf.org
Web site: www.nyfrf.org

Clients:
New Yorkers for Constitutional Freedoms, Ltd

Mount Sinai Medical Center
One Gustave L Levy Pl
Box 1499
New York, NY 10029-6574
212-659-9011

Clients:
Mount Sinai Medical Center

Lobbyists:
Brad Beckstrom

Muhs, Robert E
Cendant Car Rental Group, Inc
6 Sylvan Way
Parsippany, NJ 7054
973-496-3532 Fax: 973-496-3444
e-mail: rmuhs@avis.com

Clients:
Cendant Car Rental Group Inc & Subsidiaries

Mullane, Robert A
MEUA
445 Electronics Pkwy, Ste 207
Liverpool, NY 13080-6001

Offices and agencies appear in alphabetical order.

315-453-7851 Fax: 315-473-7849
e-mail: info@meua.org
Web site: www.meua.org

Clients:
Municipal Electric Utilities Assn of NYS (MEUA)

Municipal Art Society
457 Madison Ave
New York, NY 10022
212-935-3960 Fax: 212-753-1816

Clients:
Municipal Art Society

Lobbyists:
Eve Baron
Kent Barwick
Lisanne Beretta
Micaela Birmingham
Carter Craft
Alan Gentile
Jasper Goldman
Vanessa Gruen
Amanda Hiller
Lisa Kersavage
Kimberly Miller
Ann Peter Gaines
Frank Sanchis
Philip Schneider
Loren Talbot

Murphy, Daniel C
NY Hosp & Tourism Assn
80 Wolf Rd
Albany, NY 12205
518-465-2300 Fax: 518-465-4025
e-mail: dan@nyshta.org
Web site: nyshta.org

Clients:
Hospitality & Tourism Assn (NYS)

Murphy, Robert J
Health Facilities Assn
33 Elk St, Ste 300
Albany, NY 12207-1010
518-462-4800 Fax: 518-426-4051
e-mail: rmurphy@nyshfa.org

Clients:
Health Facilities Assn (NYS)

Lobbyists:
Carl Dembrosky
Edwin Graham
Richard Herrick
Nancy Leveille
Karen Morris

Murphy, Thomas V
United Federation of Teachers
52 Broadway
New York, NY 10004
212-777-7500 Fax: 212-260-6393
Web site: www.uft.org

Clients:
United Federation of Teachers

Lobbyists:
Carol L Gerstl
Ann Kessler
Sandra March
Thomas V Murphy
Amina Rachman
Briget Rein
Burton Sacks
Nina Tribble

Murray, Claire
1501 Twelfth Ave
Watervliet, NJ 12189-2402
518-273-1525

Clients:
New York Organization of Nurse Executives Inc

NAMI-NYS
260 Washington Ave
Albany, NY 12210
518-462-2000 Fax: 518-462-3811

Clients:
NAMI-NYS

Lobbyists:
J David Seay

NARAL Pro-Choice, New York
427 Broadway, 3rd Fl
New York, NY 10013
212-343-0114 Fax: 212-343-0119
e-mail: info@prochoiceny.org
Web site: www.prochoiceny.org

Clients:
NARAL Pro-Choice, NY

Lobbyists:
Kelli Conlin
Robert Jaffe
Destiny Lopez
Cristina Page
Andrew Stern
Sara Weinstein

NYC & Company, Inc
810 Seventh Ave, 3rd Fl
New York, NY 10019
212-484-1280

Offices and agencies appear in alphabetical order.

Clients:
NYC & Company, Inc

Lobbyists:
Mai Hariu
James Whelan

NYC 2012
1 Liberty Plz, 34th Fl
New York, NY 10006
646-587-5406

Clients:
NYC 2012

Lobbyists:
Andrew Kimball
Jay L Kriegel
Brenda Levin

Nasca, Samuel J
United Transp Union
35 Fuller Rd, Ste 205
Albany, NY 12205
518-438-8403 Fax: 518-438-8404
e-mail: sjnasca@aol.com

Clients:
United Transportation Union

National Alliance for the Mentally Ill of NYC, Inc
805 Eighth Ave, Ste 1103
New York, NY 10018
212-684-3365

Clients:
National Alliance for the Mentally Ill of NYC, Inc

Lobbyists:
Wendy Brennan
Alison Burke
Evelyn Roberts
Jessica Whalen

National Assn of Chain Drug Stores
477 Congress St, 5th Fl
Portland, ME 04101
207-773-3942
Web site: www.nacds.org

Clients:
National Assn of Chain Drug Stores

Lobbyists:
Michael Sargent

National Assn of Social Workers (NYS Chapter)
188 Washington Ave
Albany, NY 12210

518-463-4741 Fax: 518-463-6446
e-mail: karin_moran@naswnys.org

Clients:
National Assn of Social Workers (NYS Chapter)

Lobbyists:
Denise Dipace
Thea Griffin

Nelson, Debra
United Teachers
800 Troy Schenectady Rd
Latham, NY 12110-2455
518-213-6000 Fax: 518-213-6488

Clients:
United Teachers (NYS)
Professional Staff Congress (The)

Lobbyists:
Christopher J Black
Floyd Cameron
John Costello
Joseph Garba
John Green
Alan B Lubin
Patrick Lyons
Maria Neira
Cassie Prugh
Charles Santelli

New York First
5784 Widewaters Pkwy, 1st Fl
Dewitt, NY 13214
800-962-7950

Clients:
New York First

Lobbyists:
Richard Poppa

New York State Nurses Association
Nurses Assn (NYS)
11 Cornell Rd
Latham, NY 12110-1499
518-782-9400

Clients:
Nurses Association (NYS)

Lobbyists:
Ellen Brickman
Lola Fehr
Shaun Flynn
Tina Gerardi
Janet Haebler
Ann Purchase
Alithia Rolon

New Yorkers Against the Death Penalty
40 N Main Ave
Albany, NY 12203
518-453-6797

Clients:
New Yorkers Against the Death Penalty

Lobbyists:
David Kaczynski
Laura Porter

New Yorkers for Accessible Health Coverage
841 Broadway, Ste 301
New York, NY 10003
646-442-4184

Clients:
New Yorkers for Accesible Health Coverage

Lobbyists:
David Wunsch

New Yorkers for Civil Justice Reform
One Commerce Plaza
Ste 1119
Albany, NY 12260
518-434-1262 Fax: 518-426-8799
Web site: www.nycjr.org

Clients:
New Yorkers for Civil Justice Reform

Lobbyists:
Mark P Alesse

Newcomb, Lisa
Empire St Assn Adult Homes
646 Plank Rd, Ste 207
Clifton Park, NY 12065
518-371-2573 Fax: 518-371-3774

Clients:
Empire State Assn of Adult Homes & Assisted Living Facilities

Newman-Limata, Nancy
PricewaterhouseCoopers LLP
300 Madison Ave
New York, NY 10017
646-471-0514

Clients:
PricewaterhouseCoopers

Lobbyists:
Robert Moritz

Newspaper Publishers Assn (NY)
120 Washington Ave
Albany, NY 12210
518-449-1667 Fax: 518-449-5053

Clients:
Newspaper Publishers Assn (NY)

Lobbyists:
Diane Kennedy

Nixon Peabody, LLP
Omni Plaza
30 S Pearl St, 9th Fl
Albany, NY 12207
518-427-2650 Fax: 518-427-2666

Clients:
A Peek in the Pod LLC
Assn of Laser Hair Removal Specialists, Inc (NYS)

Lobbyists:
Peter Millock

Nolan & Heller, LLP
39 North Pearl St
3rd Fl
Albany, NY 12207
518-449-3300
e-mail: tburke@nolanandheller.com

Clients:
Empire State Subcontractors Assn

Lobbyists:
Terence Burke

Norat, Cecilia E
American Int'l Group, Inc
70 Pine St, 6th Fl
New York, NY 10270
212-770-5235

Clients:
American International Group, Inc

Lobbyists:
Paul S Brown
Maurice R Greenberg

Norris Jr, Robert C
George W Long
4600 Culver Rd
Rochester, NY 14622
585-323-1900

Clients:
George W Long, Inc

Norris, Kelly K
Society of Professional Engineers, Inc (
RPI Technology Park, 385 Jordan Rd
Troy, NY 12180-7620
518-283-7490
Web site: www.nysspe.org

Offices and agencies appear in alphabetical order.

Clients:
Society of Professional Engineers, Inc (NYS)

Northeast Health Inc
2212 Burdett Ave
Troy, NY 12180
518-271-5000 Fax: 518-271-5088
Web site: www.nehealth.com

Clients:
Northeast Health & Affiliates

Lobbyists:
Jo-Ann Costantino
Norman E Dascher Jr

Northern Metropolitan Hospital Assn
400 Stony Brook Court
Newburgh, NY 12550-5162
845-562-7520 Fax: 845-562-0187
e-mail: awein@normet.org

Clients:
Northern Metropolitan Hospital Assn

Lobbyists:
Neil Abitabilo
Arthur E Weintraub

Nurse Practitioners Assn of NYS (The)
12 Corporate Dr
Clifton Park, NY 12065-8603
518-348-0719 Fax: 518-348-0720
e-mail: info@thenpa.org
Web site: www.thenpa.org

Clients:
Nurse Practitioners Assn of NYS (The)

Lobbyists:
Seth Gordon

O'Brien, Stewart
Plumbing Foundation
44 West 28th St, 12th Fl
New York, NY 10001
212-481-9740 Fax: 212-481-7185

Clients:
Plumbing Foundation City of NY Inc

O'Connell, Peter B
130 Washington Ave
Albany, NY 12210-2219
518-436-7202 Fax: 518-436-7203

Clients:
Automatic Vending Assn (NYS)
Empire State Towing & Recovery Assn
Pest Management Assn
Western Regional Off-Track Betting Corp

Capital District Physicians' Health Plan Inc
Campground Owners of NY Inc

O'Connor, John
12 Sheridan Ave
Albany, NY 12207
518-449-5370 Fax: 518-449-5413

Clients:
Pharmaceutical Research & Manufacturers of America

O'Dwyer & Bernstien
52 Duane St
New York, NY 10007
212-571-7100

Clients:
Sequoia Voting Systems, Inc

Lobbyists:
Michael Carroll
Brian O'Dwyer

O'Mara, John P
84 Oak Hill
Horseheads, NY 14624
585-349-7700

Clients:
Eber Bros Wine & Liquor Corp

Ocean Conservancy (The)
1725 Desales St NW, Ste 600
Washington, DC 20036
202-429-5609

Clients:
Ocean Conservancy (The)

Lobbyists:
Dennis Heinemann

Ohrenstein & Brown, LLP
One Penn Plaza, 46th Fl
New York, NY 10119
212-682-4500 Fax: 212-947-8180

Clients:
Greenburgh Eleven UFSD
Metropolitan Transportation Authority (NYS)

Lobbyists:
Manfred Ohrenstein

Omnibuzz Associates
38 Little Plains Rd
Southampton, NY 11968
631-283-0300 Fax: 631-283-0515
e-mail: info@omnibuzz.net
Web site: www.omnibuzz.net

Political Parties,
Lobbyists & PACs

Offices and agencies appear in alphabetical order.

Clients:
Nurse Practitioners Assn of NYS (The)

Lobbyists:
Edwin M Schwenk

Organization of NYS Management/Confidential Employees Inc

3 Washington Square
Albany, NY 12205-5523
518-456-5241 Fax: 518-456-3838
e-mail: omce@aol.com
Web site: www.nysomce.org

Clients:
Org of NYS Mgmt/Confidential Employees, Inc

Lobbyists:
Joseph Sano
Barbara Zaron

Ostroff, Hiffa & Associates Inc

12 Sheridan Ave
Albany, NY 12207
518-436-6202 Fax: 518-436-1956
e-mail: ostroff_associates@msn.com
Web site: www.ostroff-hiffa.com

Clients:
Adirondack Pine Hill NY Trailways
Amerada Hess Corporation
Assn of Town Superintendents of Highways Inc (NYS)
CATS VLT, LLC (Canadian American Transportation Systems)
Cemetery Employer Assn of Greater NY
Cephalon Inc
Courtroom Television Network
Creative Coalition (The)
Crisis Program (The)
Dreyfus Corporation (The)
Empire State Restaurant & Tavern Assn
Fahs-Rolston Paving Corp
Central NY Railroad
Greater NY Health Care Facilities Assn
Cross Harbor Railroad (NY)
International Imaging Technology Council (I-ITC)
Liquid Asphalt Distributors Assoc Inc of NY
Monument Builders Assn (NYS)
Cumberland Packing Corporation
Public Library (NY), Astor, Lenox & Tilden Foundations
Electric & Gas Corporation (NYS)
Eponymous Associates LLC (FKA Steiner Studios)
Pratt Institute
Riverside South Planning Corp
Rochester Gas & Electric Corp
Suit-Kote Corp
UST Public Affairs Inc
United Health Services
Washington Cemetery

Lobbyists:
James Cantwell
Frederick T Hiffa
Richard L Ostroff
Erin T Waterhouse

Pappas, Marcia

1500 Central Ave
Albany, NY 12205
518-482-3944

Clients:
National Organization for Women (NYS)

Lobbyists:
Lori Gardner
Barbara Kirkpatrick

Park Strategies, LLC

101 Park Ave, Ste 2506
New York, NY 10178
212-883-5608 Fax: 212-883-5643

Clients:
Concerned Home Care Providers
Aetna Inc
Manhattan Theatre Club
Canadian American Transportation Systems, LLC
Vector Group, Ltd
Lilac Capital LLC
Madison Square Garden LP
Magna Entertainment Corp
Subway Surface Supervisors Assn

Lobbyists:
Alfonse M D'Amato
Christopher P D'Amato
David Poleto
John Zagame

Parkside Group, LLC

132 Nassau St, Ste 619
New York, NY 10038
212-571-7717 Fax: 212-571-7757
Web site: www.theparksidegroup.com

Clients:
AAFE Managment Co
American Museum of the Moving Image Inc
Assn for the Advancement of Blind & Retarded Inc
Business Outreach Center Network Inc
Central Labor Council (NYC)
Coastal Communications Services Inc
Communication Workers of America, Local 1182
Danaher Controls Inc
Flushing Council on Culture & the Arts Inc
Fresh Direct, LLC
Assn for Neurologically Impaired Brain Injured Children Inc
Jamaica Ctr for Arts & Learning Inc
Church Avenue Merchants Block Association Inc
Metropolitan Life Insurance Co
Mulvihill ICS Inc
New York Cares Inc
Plaza College
Queens Chamber of Commerce
Queens Child Guidance Center Inc
Queens Economic Development Corp
Queens Centers for Progress Inc
Queens Theatre in the Park
Queensborough Comm College Auxiliary Enterprise Assn Inc
Service Employees International Union, Local 300

Offices and agencies appear in alphabetical order.

South Queens Boys & Girls Club Inc
Supershuttle NY Inc
Telebeam Telecommunications Corp
United Food & Commercial Workers Dist Cncl of NY & Northern NJ
Community Financial Services Association of America
Crystal Window & Door Systems, Ltd
Educational Assistance Corporation
Entergy Nuclear Operations Inc
Gaucho LLC
Gowanus Village 1 Inc
Jets (NY)
National Council to Prevent Delinquency Inc
Nextel Operations Inc
NYC & Company
Pratt Institute for Community & Environment Development
Queens College Foundation-Research of CUNY
Rockefeller Group International Inc (The)

Lobbyists:
William Driscoll
Harry Giannoulis
Barry Grodenchik
Tiffany Raspberry
Evan Stavisky

Pastel & Rosen, LLP

130 Washington Ave
Albany, NY 12210
518-462-4715 Fax: 518-462-4756

Clients:
Carco Group Inc
Chubb & Son (Division of Federal Insurance Co)
Coalition for Mold Reform (State Farm Insurance Cos)
Fireman's Fund Insurance Co
Insurance Assn Inc (NY)
Professional Insurance Wholesalers Assoc of NYS Inc
Progressive Insurance Companies
Robert Plan Corporation (The)

Lobbyists:
Robert S Pastel
Michael E Rosen

Patterson & McLaughlin

64 Fulton St
New York, NY 10038
212-437-7373

Clients:
Verizon Corporate Services Corp

Lobbyists:
Cathy Cudahy
Martin McLaughlin

Pelosi, Andrew

NY Against Gun Violence
3 W 29th St, Ste 1007
New York, NY 10001
212-679-2345 Fax: 212-679-2485
e-mail: nyagv@nyagv.org
Web site: www.nyagv.org

Clients:
New Yorkers Against Gun Violence

Lobbyists:
Barbara Hohlt
Jacqueline Kuhls

Pepe, Ross J

CIC
629 Old White Plains Rd
Tarrytown, NY 10591-5100
914-631-6070 Fax: 914-631-5172

Clients:
Construction Industry Cncl of Westchester & Hudson Valley Inc

Perkins, Janice C

One Far Mill Crossing
PO Box 904
Shelton, CT 06484
203-225-8630

Clients:
Health Net of the Northeast

Perlee, Jeffrey

International Game Tech
170 Maple Ave, PO Box 475
Altamont, NY 12009
518-221-5373 Fax: 518-861-7442

Clients:
International Game Technology

Perry, Robert

CLU-NY
125 Broad St, 17th Fl
New York, NY 10004
212-344-3005 Fax: 212-344-3318

Clients:
Civil Liberties Union (NY)

Lobbyists:
Elizabeth Benjamin
Linda Berns
Barbara Bernstein
Christopher Dunn
Arthur Eisenberg
Jared Feuer
Barrie Gewanter
Yanilda Gonzalez
Beth Haroules
Lee Che Leong
Donna Lieberman
Jeanne-Noel Mahoney
Udi Ofer
Anna Schissel
Christian Smith-Socaris
Irum Tagi
Melanie Trimble
Barbara Williams Deleeuw

Offices and agencies appear in alphabetical order.

Peters, Jeffrey R
212 N Third St, Ste 101
Harrisburg, PA 17101
717-232-5634 Fax: 717-232-0691

Clients:
SUNOCO Inc

Petraitis, Brian J
College Board (The)
122 South Swan St
Albany, NY 12210-1716
518-472-1515 Fax: 518-472-1516
e-mail: bpetraitis@collegeboard.org
Web site: www.collegeboard.com

Clients:
College Board (The)

Phillips & Associates, PLLC
50 Beaver St
Albany, NY 12207-2830
518-432-6857 Fax: 518-445-9143

Clients:
National Assn of Social Workers (NYS Chapter)
Occupational Therapy Assn (NYS)
Dynegy Inc

Lobbyists:
Frank Bifera
Catherine M Hedgeman
Lois R Phillips

Phillips Nizer, LLP
666 Fifth Ave
New York, NY 10103-0084
212-841-0743

Clients:
CSC Holdings, Inc
Madison Square Garden

Lobbyists:
Kevin McGrath

Pinsky & Pinsky, PC
5790 Widewaters Pkwy
PO Box 250
Syracuse, NY 13214-0250
315-446-2384 Fax: 315-446-3016

Clients:
Radiological Society Inc (NYS)

Lobbyists:
Philip C Pinsky

Pinsky & Skandalis
5790 Widewaters Pkwy
PO Box 250
Syracuse, NY 13214-0250
315-446-2384 Fax: 315-446-3016
e-mail: pinskyskan@aol.com

Clients:
7-Eleven Inc
Adirondack League Club
Assn for Community Living
City of Yonkers
Board of Commissioners of Pilots of the State of NY
Cable Telecommunications Assn of NY Inc
Calpine Corporation
City of White Plains (The)
Graduate Mgmt Admission Council
Health Insurance Plan of Greater NY
Industries for the Disabled Inc (NYS)
Jets (NY)
Land Title Assn (NYS)
North Shore-Long Island Jewish Health System Inc
Phoenix House Foundation Inc
Plug Power Inc
Randi Weingarten, MLC Chair & UFT President
Westchester County Health Care Corporation
Society of Certified Public Accountants (NYS)
Xerox Corp

Lobbyists:
Philip C Pinsky

Pirro-Buley & Associates
27 Elk St
Albany, NY 12207
518-432-9563

Clients:
Concord Associates LP
Elevator Industries Assn, Inc
LC Main, LLC

Lobbyists:
Jeffrey T Buley
Albert J Pirro

Plunkett & Jaffe, PC
111 Washington Ave
Albany, NY 12210
518-462-1800 Fax: 518-462-4875

Clients:
Apple Computer Inc
Catskill Gaming Project
Rochester Electric & Gas Corp
Louis P Ciminelli Construction Companies
PSEG Power LLC
Wellchoice Inc
CUNY (Research Foundation)

Lobbyists:
John Harris
Kelly Lamendola
William Mooney
Kathleen O'Connor

Offices and agencies appear in alphabetical order.

Poklemba, John J
358 Broadway, Ste 307
Saratoga Springs, NY 12866
518-581-9797 Fax: 518-581-9590

Clients:
Deputy Sheriff's Assn (NYC)
Patrolmen's Benevolent Assn (NYC)

Lobbyists:
Steve Watts

Police Benevolent Assn of the NYS Troopers Inc
112 State St
Albany, NY 12207
518-462-7448 Fax: 518-462-0790
e-mail: nystpba@capital.net
Web site: www.nystpba.org

Clients:
Police Benevolent Assn of the NYS Troopers Inc

Lobbyists:
Daniel DeFedericis
Gordon Warnock

Potenza, Anthony F
Pipe Trades Assn (NYS)
308 Wolf Rd
Latham, NY 12110
518-785-9808 Fax: 518-785-9855

Clients:
Pipe Trades Assn (NYS)

Lobbyists:
James Hart

Powers & Company
90 State St, Ste 1422
Albany, NY 12207
518-431-0720 Fax: 518-431-0721
Web site: www.powerscompany.com

Clients:
Alternative Risk Concepts Inc
American Bio Medica
Bank of America
BBL Enterprises
Bearing Point
Boulevard ALP Associates
Broadcasters Assn (NYS)
Brookdale University Hospital & Medical Center
Building Contractors Assn Inc
Building Trades Employees' Association
Colony Liquor & Wine Distributors, LLC
Computer Associates
Edison Properties
Empire Liquor Store Assoc
Federal Home Loan Mortgage Corp
Funding Source (The)
HMS Host
Kasselman Electric

Law Enforcement Officers Union, Distr Cncl 82 (NYS)
Lincoln Center for the Performing Arts
Meadows Furnishing Solutions
Medical Society of the State of New York
Merrill Lynch Global Markets
Moinian Group (The)
New York State Laborers PAC
New York Yankees
NYU Downtown Hospital
Omni Asset Management
Power Plant Entertainment New York, LLC
Pro Tech Monitoring Inc
PSCH Inc
Public Financial Management
Quaker Valley Farms
Racing and Gaming Services Inc
Servidone Construction Corporation
Shaker Museum (The)
Siena College
Stratford Business Corp
Susan O'Dell Taylor School for Children
Trustco Bank
TVI Corporation
Verizon
Weatherguard Industries
WelchAllyn Inc
Wilmorite Holdings

Lobbyists:
Heather C Briccetti
John J Curry
Thomas J Murphy
Jason A Powers
Matthew D Powers
William D Powers
Paul W Zuber

Powers Global Strategies, LLC
152 West 57th St, 11th Fl
New York, NY 10019
212-582-0833 Fax: 212-582-0199

Clients:
ACS State & Local Solutions Inc
ADT Security Services Inc
American Continental Properties Inc
BearingPoint Inc
Beth Israel Medical Center
HNTB, New York
St Luke's-Roosevelt Hospital Centers
Long Island College Hospital (The)
United Parcel Service
World Trade Center Properties, LLC

Lobbyists:
Seth Kaye
Sylvia Ng
Peter Powers

Pozzi, Brian M
100 Motor Pkwy, Ste 140
Hauppauge, NY 11788
631-233-6050
Web site: www.allstate.com

Offices and agencies appear in alphabetical order.

Clients:

Allstate Insurance Co

Lobbyists:

Vincent Fusco
Maureen Sullivan

Presbyterian Hospital (NY)

Herbert Irving Pavillion
161 Ft Washington Ave
14th Fl, Rm 1428
New York, NY 10032
212-305-4223 Fax: 212-342-5265

Clients:

Presbyterian Hosptial (NY)

Lobbyists:

Julio Batista
David Liss
Helen Morik
Herbert Pardes
William A Polf

Pryor Cashman Sherman & Flynn LLP

111 Washington Ave
Albany, NY 12210
518-449-3320 Fax: 518-449-5812
e-mail: rbishop@pryorcashman.com
Web site: www.pryorcashman.com

Clients:

Advertising Alliance (NYS)
Broadcasters Assn (NYS)
Daytop Village Foundation Inc
Court Clerks Assn (NYS)
Hospital Queens (NY)
Hotel & Motel Trades Council, AFL-CIO (NY)
Hotel Employees & Restaurant Empl Int'l Union, AFL-CIO
Local 6, Hotel Restaurant & Club Empl Bartenders' Union, AFL-CIO
Metropolitan Transportation Authority
Sandy Hook Pilots Assn (NY & NJ)
Securities Industry Assn, NY District
Uniformed Sanitationmen's Assn
Local 30, Int'l Union Assn of Operating Engineers, AFL-CIO
Office of Professional Employees Int'l Union, Local 153
Professional Bull Riders Inc
American Lawyer Media Company
Board of Education Empl Union, AFSCME, AFL-CIO, Local 372 (NYC)

Lobbyists:

Robert Bishop
Theresa Cosgrove
Jon Del Giorno
Matthew Mataraso
Vincent Pitta
Bernard Ruggieri

Psychological Assn (NYS)

6 Executive Park Dr
Albany, NY 12203
518-437-1040 Fax: 518-437-0177

Clients:

Psychological Assn (NYS)

Lobbyists:

Christopher Black
Debra Nelson
Stephanie H Wacholder

Public Library, Astor, Lenox & Tilden Foundations (NY)

5th Ave & 42nd St
New York, NY 10018-2788
212-930-0745 Fax: 212-869-3567

Clients:

Public Library, Astor, Lenox & Tilden Fdns (NY) (The)

Lobbyists:

Anne Coriston
Catherine Dunn
Paul Leclerc

Public Strategies, LLC

247 Murray Ave
Larchmont, NY 10538
914-912-0526 Fax: 914-834-8397
e-mail: vmarrone@publicstrategiesllc.net
Web site: www.publicstrategiesllc.net

Clients:

AIDS Coalition (NY)
Beginning with Children Foundation
Center for Policy Reform
Cmte for Mentor Supervision Cert (Big Brothers Big Sisters of NYC
Compassion in Dying Federation
Gay & Lesbian Anti-Violence Project (NYC)
Harm Reduction Coalition
Legal Services for Working Poor New Yorkers Coalition
Marijuana Policy Project
Medicare Rights Center
Center for Charter School Excellence (NYC)
Positive Health Project

Lobbyists:

Vincent Marrone
John Wright

Public Utility Law Project of New York Inc

90 State St, Ste 601
Albany, NY 12207-1715
518-449-3375 Fax: 518-449-1769
e-mail: info@pulp.tc
Web site: www.pulp.tc

Clients:

Public Utility Law Project of New York Inc

Lobbyists:

Charles J Brennan
Gerald A Norlander
Ben Wiles

Offices and agencies appear in alphabetical order.

Public Welfare Assn (NY)
130 Washington Ave
Albany, NY 12210-2204
518-465-9305 Fax: 518-465-5633
e-mail: nypwa@nycap.rr.com
Web site: www.nypwa.com

Clients:
Public Welfare Assn (NY)

Lobbyists:
Sheila Harrigan
Jessica Morelli

Puckett, Robert R
Telecommunications Assn
100 State St, Ste 650
Albany, NY 12207
518-443-2700 Fax: 518-443-2810
e-mail: rpuckett@nysta.com
Web site: www.nysta.com

Clients:
Telecommunications Assn Inc (NYS)

Quirk, James S
Memorial Sloan-Kettering Cancer Ctr
1275 York Ave
New York, NY 10021
212-639-7533 Fax: 212-717-3080

Clients:
Memorial Sloan-Kettering Cancer Center

Lobbyists:
Elizabeth Vega

R J Reynolds Tobacco Co
401 North Main St
Winston-Salem, NC 27102-2959
336-741-6141 Fax: 336-741-7977
e-mail: powersd@rjrt.com
Web site: www.rjrt.com

Clients:
R J Reynolds Tobacco Co

Lobbyists:
David M Powers

Rad USA, Inc
58 Countryman Rd
Voorheesville, NY 12186
518-437-8630

Clients:
Jets, LLC (NY)

Lobbyists:
Louis Tomson

Rappleyea Lobbying Group, LLC
54 State St, 8th Floor
Albany, NY 12207
518-431-1004 Fax: 518-431-1007

Clients:
BFS Retail & Commercial Operations, LLC
Multimedia Games Inc
Erickson Retirement Communities
Media-Promotions Inc
Harrah's Operating Co Inc
HSBC-North America
Lyonsdale Biomass, LLC
Indoor Tanning Assoc
Lafarge North America Inc
Prism Health Networks
Seneca Nation of Indians
Linebarger Goggan Blair & Sampson, LLP

Lobbyists:
Clarence Rappleyea
Philip D Sprio
Patrick A Zlogar

Raustiala, Margaret
428 River Rd
Nissequogue, NY 11780
631-724-7767

Clients:
Alliance of Long Island Agencies

Raylman, Robert
133 Deer Ridge Dr
Staatsburg, NY 12580
845-889-4235

Clients:
American Ref-Fuel Co

Rea, Michelle
Press Assn (NY)
1681 Western Ave
Albany, NY 12203-4305
518-464-6483 Fax: 518-464-6489
e-mail: mkrea@nynewspapers.com
Web site: www.nynewspapers.com

Clients:
Press Assn (NY)

Real Estate Board of NY Inc
570 Lexington Ave
New York, NY 10022
212-532-3100 Fax: 212-481-0420
e-mail: jdoyle@rebny.com
Web site: www.rebny.com

Clients:
Real Estate Board of NY Inc

Political Parties, Lobbyists & PACs

Offices and agencies appear in alphabetical order.

Lobbyists:
Lisa Castrigno
John Cole
Marolyn Davenport
John Doyle
Sheila Horgan
Kristen Morriseau
Michael Slattery
Steven Spinola
Carol Trezza

Rehabilitation Assn Inc (NYS)

155 Washington Ave, Ste 410
Albany, NY 12210-2332
518-449-2976 Fax: 518-426-4329
e-mail: nysra@nyrehab.org
Web site: www.nyrehab.org

Clients:
Rehabilitation Assn Inc (NYS)

Lobbyists:
Patricia Dowse

Reiter/Begun Associates, LLC

233 Broadway, Ste 842
New York, NY 10279-0808
212-513-0080

Clients:
NYU School of Medicine

Lobbyists:
Martin Begun

Rensselaer Polytechnic Institute

110 Eighth St
Low Ctr 4119
Troy, NY 12180-3590
518-276-8682 Fax: 518-276-2732
Web site: www.rpi.edu

Clients:
Rensselaer Polytechnic Institute

Lobbyists:
Shirley Ann Jackson
John MacEnroe
Larry Snavley

Rent Stabilization Assn of NYC Inc

123 William St, 14th Fl
New York, NY 10038
212-214-9266 Fax: 212-732-0617

Clients:
Rent Stabilization Assn of NYC Inc

Lobbyists:
Jack Freund
Mitchell Posilkin
Frank P Ricci
Joseph Strasburg

Repas, Peter G

33 Elk St, Ste 200
Albany, NY 12207
518-462-1590 Fax: 518-462-1390
e-mail: apbs@wxxi.org

Clients:
Assn of Public Broadcasting Stations of NY

Retired Public Employees Association

435 New Karner Rd
Albany, NY 12205-3858
518-869-2542 Fax: 518-869-0631

Clients:
Retired Public Employees Association

Lobbyists:
Michael Fitzgerald
Scott Lundstedt
Kevin Murray

Rice & Justice

111 Washington Ave, Ste 700
Albany, NY 12210
518-434-8435 Fax: 518-434-8462

Clients:
Countrywide Home Loans Inc
Container Terminal Inc (NY)
Eli Lilly & Co
Industry Ad Hoc Committee on Pilotage
Lexmark International Inc
Air Transport Assn Inc
Business Council of NYS Inc (The)

Lobbyists:
Lawrence P Justice
Bradley F Rice
John Carter Rice

Rich Results, Inc

4796 E River Rd
Grand Island, NY 14072
716-909-9203

Clients:
Buffalo Niagara Partnership

Lobbyists:
Lewis Rich

Right to Life Committee Inc (NYS)

41 State St, Ste M-100
Albany, NY 12207
518-434-1293 Fax: 518-426-1200
e-mail: lhougens1@aol.com
Web site: www.nysrighttolife.org

Clients:
Right to Life Committee Inc (NYS)

Offices and agencies appear in alphabetical order.

Lobbyists:
Thomas Conway
Chris Fadden Fitch
Lori Kehoe

Riverkeeper, Inc
25 Wing & Wing
Garrison, NY 10524
845-422-4228 Fax: 845-424-4150
e-mail: info@riverkeeper.org
Web site: www.riverkeeper.org

Clients:
Riverkeeper, Inc

Lobbyists:
Sara Froikin
Leila Goldmark
Robert Kennedy
Alex Matthiessen
Basil Seggos
Reed Super
Victor Tafur
Lisa Van Suntum
Christopher Wilde
Marc Yaggi

Rochester Regional Healthcare Advocates
3445 Winton Place, Ste 222
Rochester, NY 14623
585-273-8180 Fax: 585-273-8189

Clients:
Rochester Regional Healthcare Advocates

Lobbyists:
Diane Ashley

Rodriguez, Barbara J
AIA New York State, Inc
235 Lark St
Albany, NY 12210-1108
518-449-3334 Fax: 518-426-8176
e-mail: aianys@aianys.org
Web site: www.aianys.org

Clients:
AIA New York State Inc

Roffe, Andrew S, PC
111 Washington Ave, Ste 409
Albany, NY 12210
518-432-7841 Fax: 518-432-4267
e-mail: aroffe@rc.com

Clients:
7-Eleven Inc
Adirondack League Club
Apple Computer Inc
Assn for Community Living
City of Yonkers
Board of Commissioners of Pilots of the State of NY

CSX Transportation Inc
Cable Telecommunications Assn of NY Inc
Calpine Corporation
Chiropractic Council (NY)
City of White Plains (The)
Graduate Management Admission Council
Health Insurance Plan of NY
Independent Living Services Inc
Industries for the Disabled Inc (NYS)
JP Morgan Chase & Co
Jets (NY)
Land Title Assn Inc (NYS)
Loretto Management Corp
Museum of Modern Art (The)
North Shore-Long Island Jewish Health System Inc
Phoenix House Foundation Inc
Plug Power Inc
Westchester County Health Care Corp
Randi Weingarten
Society of Certified Public Accountants (NYS)
Xerox Corp

Lobbyists:
Andrew S Roffe
Joelle Zullo

Roland Fogel Koblenz & Petroccione, LLP
One Columbia Place
Albany, NY 12207-1072
518-434-8112 Fax: 518-434-3232

Clients:
Empire State Petroleum Assn Inc
Industries for the Blind of NYS Inc

Lobbyists:
Emilio Petroccione

Rooney, Timothy J
Yonkers Raceway
Yonkers & Central Aves
Yonkers, NY 10704
914-968-4200

Clients:
Yonkers Raceway

Lobbyists:
Robert J Galtiero
Timothy J Rooney Jr

Roos, David E
AT&T Corp
111 Washington Ave, Ste 706
Albany, NY 12210-2213
518-463-3107 Fax: 518-463-5943
e-mail: droos@att.com

Clients:
AT&T Corp

Lobbyists:
Deborah Bierbaum

Political Parties,
Lobbyists & PACs

Offices and agencies appear in alphabetical order.

Ropes & Gray
45 Rockefeller Plaza
New York, NY 10111-0087
212-841-0681 Fax: 212-841-5725

Clients:
Pfizer, Inc

Lobbyists:
Stephen A Warnke

Rosario, Stephen M
Am Chemistry Cncl
99 Washington Ave, Ste 701
Albany, NY 12210
518-432-7835 Fax: 518-426-2276
e-mail: steve_rosario@americanchemistry.org
Web site: www.americanchemistry.org

Clients:
American Chemistry Council
American Plastics Council

Lobbyists:
Geoffrey Hall

Rose, Michael M
Nat'l Fuel Gas Co
6363 Main St
Williamsville, NY 14221-5887
716-857-7438

Clients:
National Fuel Gas Company & its subsidiaries

Lobbyists:
Patricia Paul

Rosenthal, Harvey
NYAPRS
1 Columbia Pl, 2nd Fl
Albany, NY 12207
518-436-0008 Fax: 518-436-0044
e-mail: nyaprs@aol.com
Web site: www.nyaprs.org

Clients:
Assn of Psychiatric Rehabilitation Services (NY)

Lobbyists:
Kevin Cleary

Rougeux, Elizabeth
Syracuse University
2-212 Center for Science & Technology
Syracuse, NY 13244-4100
315-443-3919

Clients:
Syracuse University

Lobbyists:
Nancy Cantor
Jessica Crawford
Eleanor Ware

Rouse, James
Praxair, Inc
39 Old Ridgebury Rd
Danbury, CT 06810-5113
203-837-2270

Clients:
Praxair, Inc

Lobbyists:
David Grant

Rubenstein Associates Inc
1345 Ave of the Americas
New York, NY 10105-0109
212-843-8000 Fax: 212-843-9300

Clients:
Park Tower Group
Path Medical
Millenium Hilton Hotel (The)
Gloria Wise Boys & Girls Club
Metropolitan TV Alliance
Tishman Speyer/Citigroup Alternative
Trinity Church

Lobbyists:
Howard Cannon
Howard J Rubenstein
Steven Rubenstein
Patrick Smith

Rubenstein Communications Inc
1345 Ave of the Americas
New York, NY 10105-0109
212-843-8000 Fax: 212-843-9200

Clients:
Collegiate Church Corp
Cooper Union for Advancement of Science & Art (The)
Duane Street Realty
Madame Tussaud's New York
Olnick Organization Inc (The)
Van Wagner Communications, LLC
Gracie Piont Community Council
Congregation Shearith Israel
Poets House
SEF Industries Inc

Lobbyists:
Amanita Duga-Carroll
Chris Fein
Suzanne Halpin
Donald Kaplan
Gerald McKelvey
Howard J Rubenstein
Steven Rubenstein
Patrick Smith
Robin Verges

Offices and agencies appear in alphabetical order.

Rubino, Cynthia A
78 Broadway
White Plains, NY 10603
914-422-4105

Clients:
Pace University

Lobbyists:
David A Caputo

Runes, Richard
3 Kirby Ln N
Rye, NY 10580
914-967-4900 Fax: 212-592-4900
e-mail: rrunes@amlaw.com

Clients:
American Lawyer Media

Rural Law Ctr of NY Inc
56 Cornelia St
Plattsburgh, NY 12901
518-561-5460 Fax: 518-561-5468
e-mail: rlc@capital.net
Web site: www.ruruallawcenter.org

Clients:
Rural Law Ctr of NY Inc

Lobbyists:
Susan L Patnode

Rutherford, Clyde E
Dairylea Co-op
5001 Brittonfield Pkwy, PO Box 4844
Syracuse, NY 13221-4844
315-433-0100 Fax: 315-433-2345
e-mail: clyde.rutherford@dairylea.com
Web site: www.dairylea.com

Clients:
Dairylea Cooperative Inc

Lobbyists:
Richard P Smith

Rutnik Law Firm (The)
80 State St, 9th Fl
Albany, NY 12207
518-436-9646 Fax: 518-436-9655

Clients:
ACS State & Local Solutions Inc
Altria Corporate Services Inc
Genentech Inc
Wilmorite Holdings, LP
American Lawyer Media Inc

Lobbyists:
Douglas P Rutnik

Ryan, Desmond M
150 Motor Pkwy, Ste LL60
Hauppauge, NY 11772
631-951-2410 Fax: 631-951-2412

Clients:
Alliance of Long Island Agencies
Shoreham-Wading-River School District
Stop & Shop Supermarket Co (The)

Ryan, Marc
8725 Henderson Rd
Tampa, FL 33634
813-290-6271

Clients:
Wellcare Health Plans, Inc

SEIU, Local 32BJ, AFL-CIO
101 Avenue of the Americas
New York, NY 10013
212-388-3800 or 212-388-3992 Fax: 212-388-3210

Clients:
SEIU, Local 32BJ, AFL-CIO

Lobbyists:
Trevor Bolden
Ericka Bozzi-Gomez
Peter Colavito
Hector Figueroa
Richard Harley
Ari Holtzblatt
Brian Honan
Saul Nieves

SUNY College at Brockport
350 New Campus Dr
Brockport, NY 14420
585-395-2451

Clients:
SUNY College at Brockport

Lobbyists:
John Clark
Ray Dipasquale

SUNY Upstate Medical University
750 East Adams St
Syracuse, NY 13210-1834
315-464-4832 Fax: 315-464-4519

Clients:
SUNY Upstate Medical University

Lobbyists:
Kenneth Barker
Steven C Brady
Gregory L Eastwood
Daniel N Hurley
Ben Moore III

Offices and agencies appear in alphabetical order.

Michael F Roizen
Steven Scheinman
Thomas Welch
William Williams
Ronald R Young

SUNY at Stony Brook

Administrative Bldg, Rm 328
Stony Brook, NY 11794-1212
631-632-6265 Fax: 631-632-6621

Clients:
State University of NY at Stony Brook

Lobbyists:
Bridget Baio
Tyrone Bennett
Helen Carrano
Marie Chandick
Lisa Clark
David Conover
Norman Edelman
Paul Edelson
Diane Fabel
James Fiore
Patricia Gilbert
Brian Gordon
Arthur Grollman
Gail Habicht
Gary Halada
Vanessa Herman
Susan Katz
Theresa Leonard
Richard Mann
Robert McGrath
Fred Preston
Janice Rohlf
Joseph Scaduto
Bruce Schroeffel
Fred Sganga
Yacov Shamash
Shirley Strum Kenny
Bruce Teifer

SUNY, System Administration

State University Plaza
Albany, NY 12246-0001
518-443-5355 Fax: 518-443-5360

Clients:
State University of NY, System Administration

Lobbyists:
James J Campbell
Stacey B Hengsterman
Robert L King
Martin Reid
Michael C Trunzo

Sabol, Sharon

Land Title Association
Two Rector St, Ste 901
New York, NY 10006-1819

212-964-3701 Fax: 212-964-7185
e-mail: nyslta@aol.com
Web site: www.nyslta.org

Clients:
Land Title Assn Inc (NYS)

Safe Horizon Inc

2 Lafayette St
New York, NY 10007
212-577-7738 Fax: 212-577-3039
Web site: www.safehorizon.org

Clients:
Safe Horizon Inc

Lobbyists:
Alix Allison
Alicia Alvarez
Louise Arbitol
Michelle Archer
Jane Barker
Melody Blass
Valencia Brewer-Shelton
Florrie Burke
Paula Calby
Gordon Campbell
Vicleri Courtney Carr
Hilda Castillo
Jackie Chall
Amy Coakley
Lydia Colon-Flores
Sherene Crawford
Casey Cullen
Maureen Curtis
Michelle Davilla
Olive Demetrius
Ernie Duff
Carrier Eberhardy
Patti Fallarca
Caridad Freyberg
Genoveva Garcia
Jose Gonzales
Eloisa Gordon
Julie Ana Grant
Bea Hanson
Beatrice Hanson
Richard Harris
Tisha Hillman
Sara Hodge
Rosie Howard
Kristen Illes
Vito Interrante
Ernesto Issac
Julie Jamison
Fernando Janer
Kerry Janey
Nicole Johnson
Brenda Jones
Selena Kaye
Caryn Ketteringham
Christa Larose
Danielle Latimer
Jennifer Lawrence
Catherine Lewis
Zorayda Lonzano

Offices and agencies appear in alphabetical order.

Felix Lopez
Michelle Maroney
Elizabeth McCarthy
Mary Jo McLean
Vickie Messina
Scott Millstein
Elizabeth Murano
David Nish
Tanaz Pardiwala
Jennifer Patrick
Allegra Perhaes
Tracy Perrizo
Tina Piniero
Carmen Plaja-Cordero
Karolyn Reddy
Kate Renolds
Esther Resto
Martha Reyes
Selena Rodgers
Tinnyn Rodriguez
Paula Rogowsky
Melissa Roman
Liz Roncal
Diana Rosato
Hilda Ruiz
Kyoko Sagara
Hema Sarangapani
Myra Shapiro
Debra Shime
Amy Siniscalchi
Alvina Smith
Mina Song
Julie Sriken
Jeffrey Stephens
Christa Stewart
Monica Thorton
Alexandra Tique
Christina Tobey
Vanessa Torres
Christine Vargo
Michelle Vigeant
Gabriella Villareal
Barbara Wood
Maya Zarate

Saiger, Molly

JASA
132 W 31st St, 15th Fl
New York, NY 10001
212-273-5261 Fax: 212-695-9070
e-mail: jpac@jasa.org
Web site: www.jasa.org

Clients:
Jewish Assn for Services for the Aged

Sampson, Rick J

Restaurant Association (NYS)
409 New Karner Rd
Albany, NY 12205
518-452-4222 Fax: 518-452-4497
e-mail: ricks@nysra.org
Web site: www.nysra.org

Clients:
Restaurant Assn (NYS)

Lobbyists:
Melissa Fleischut
E Charles Hunt

Sanjek, Lani

Statewide Senior Action Cncl
275 State St
Albany, NY 12210-2101
518-436-1006

Clients:
Statewide Senior Action Council, Inc (NY)

Lobbyists:
Michael Burgess

Saunders, Wendy E

NYAHSA
150 State St, Ste 301
Albany, NY 12207-1692
518-449-2707 Fax: 518-449-8210
e-mail: wsaunders@nyahsa.org
Web site: www.nyahsa.org

Clients:
Assn of Homes & Services for the Aging (NY)

Lobbyists:
Elizabeth Briand
Patrick Cucinelli
Ken Harris
Dan Heim
Darius Kirstein
John Richter
Nancy Tucker
Carl Young

Scenic Hudson Inc

One Civic Center Plaza
Ste 200
Poughkeepsie, NY 12601-3157
845-473-4440 Fax: 845-473-2648
e-mail: wreiss@scenichudson.org
Web site: www.scenichudson.org

Clients:
Scenic Hudson Inc

Lobbyists:
Jeff Anzevino
Andrew Bicking
James Burgess
Sarah Charlop-Powers
Joshua Clague
Richard Cook-Schiafo
Raymond Curran
Deborah Meyer Dewan
Alexandra Gerosa
Margery Groten
Jeanne Gural

Offices and agencies appear in alphabetical order.

Joseph Kiernan
Heather Lavarnway
Maryanne McGovern
Seth McKee
Warren Reiss
Steven Rosenberg
Molly Shubert
Edward O Sullivan
Cari Watkins-Bates

Schaum & Wiener

600 Old Country Rd #320
Garden City, NY 11530
516-228-8766 Fax: 516-228-3559
e-mail: craigschaum@msn.com

Clients:
Society of Physical Medicine & Rehabilitation (NY)
Osteopathic Medical Society (NYS)

Lobbyists:
Craig Schaum
Martin Schaum

Schillinger, Lawrence R

5 Palisades Dr, Ste 300
Albany, NY 12205-6433
518-459-0600

Clients:
Institute of Scrap Recycling Industries-Empire Chapter
Institute of Scrap Recycling Industries-NY Chapter

Schlein, Stanley

481 King Ave
Bronx, NY 10464
917-359-3186

Clients:
Jets, LLC (NY) (Greenberg Traurig LLP)

Schnell, William A & Associates Inc

143 E Main St
Smithtown, NY 11787
631-724-6569 Fax: 631-724-8427
e-mail: wmasainc@earthlink.net

Clients:
Amusement & Music Owners Assn of NY
UST Public Affairs Inc
Federation of Organizations Inc
S/S Vending Equipment Inc
Securitas
Suffolk County Ambulance Chiefs Assoc
Suffolk County Deputy Sheriff's Police Benevolent Assn
Long Island Gasoline Retailers Assn

Lobbyists:
William A Schnell

Schomberg, Dora

Fund for Animals Inc
PO Box 9029
Albany, NY 12209
518-478-9760 Fax: 518-478-9764

Clients:
HSUS Fund for Animals Inc (The)

School Administrators Association of NYS

8 Airport Park Blvd
Latham, NY 12110
518-782-0600 Fax: 518-782-9552

Clients:
School Administrators Association of NYS

Lobbyists:
Casey Kevin
Richard Thomas

School Boards Assn (NYS)

24 Century Hill Dr, Ste 200
Latham, NY 12210-2116
518-783-0200 Fax: 518-783-0211
e-mail: nyssba@nyssba.org
Web site: www.nyssba.org

Clients:
School Boards Assn (NYS)

Lobbyists:
Anne Byrne
Charles Dawson
David Ernst
Timothy G Kremer
David Little
Jenny Rizzo
Diane Ward
Jay Worona

Schuler, Kevin C

Buffalo Niagara Partnership
665 Main St #200
Buffalo, NY 14203
716-852-7100 Fax: 716-852-2761

Clients:
Buffalo Niagara Partnership

Lobbyists:
Bridget Corcoran

Schuyler Center for Analysis & Advocacy (SCAA)

150 State St, 4th Fl
Albany, NY 12208-1626
518-463-1896 Fax: 518-463-3364
e-mail: info@scaany.org
Web site: www.scaany.org

Offices and agencies appear in alphabetical order.

Clients:
Schuyler Ctr for Analysis & Advocacy (SCAA)

Lobbyists:
Davin Robinson
Karen Schimke
Bridget Walsh

Shanahan Group
4019 County Rte 21
Schodack Landing, NY 12156
518-732-3312 Fax: 518-732-2859
e-mail: tom@shanahangroup.com
Web site: www.shanahangroup.com

Clients:
Brookhaven Science Associates Inc
Guide Dog Foundation for the Blind Inc
Irrigation Assn of New York
Long Island Water Conference
Rural Water Assn (NY)
Suffolk County Water Authority

Lobbyists:
Thomas Shanahan

Shannon, Michael J
Lorillard Tobacco
714 Green Valley Rd
PO Box 10529
Greensboro, NC 27408
336-335-7711 Fax: 336-335-7752

Clients:
Lorillard Tobacco Co

Shaw, James M
ALCOA, Inc
27 County Rte 43
Massena, NY 13662-3130
315-769-2088 Fax: 315-764-4203
e-mail: james.shaw@alcoa.com

Clients:
Alcoa Inc

Shaw, Linda R
1125 Crossroads Bldg
2 State St
Rochester, NY 14614
585-546-8430 Fax: 585-546-4324

Clients:
Independent Petroleum Marketers of NY
Atlas Park, LLC
Dermot Company (The)

Sheinkopf, Ltd
152 Madison Ave
Ste 1603
New York, NY 10016
212-725-2378 Fax: 212-772-2334

Clients:
Bear Stearns & Co, Inc
Met-Tel Corporation
Empire Resorts, Inc
Four Seasons Nursing Home
Riverside Memorial Chapel

Lobbyists:
Elnatan Rudolph
Henry A Sheinkopf

Sherin, James R
Retail Council of NYS
258 State St, PO Box 1992
Albany, NY 12201-1992
518-465-3586 Fax: 518-465-7960

Clients:
Retail Council of New York State

Lobbyists:
Rebecca Marion
Edward A Potrikus

Sierra Club, Atlantic Chapter
353 Hamilton St
Albany, NY 12210-1709
518-426-9144 Fax: 518-426-3052

Clients:
Sierra Club Atlantic Chapter

Lobbyists:
Ken Baer
Christian Ballantyne
Mark Bettinger
Diane Buxbaum
Michael Cafaro
Don Carlson
Frank Eadie
Laurie Farber
Margaret Hayes-Young
Rhea Jezer
Elizabeth Kasubski
John Klotz
William Koebbeman
Sarah Kogel-Smucker
Charles Lamb
Susan Lawrence
Tullia Limarzi
Suzanne Mattei
James Mays
Hugh Mitchell
Robert Muldoon
Don Pachner
Frank Regan
Marion Rose
John Stouffer
Yvonne Trasker-Rothenberg

Offices and agencies appear in alphabetical order.

Anne Wilson
Carolyn Zolas

Sloane & Company, LLC
570 Lexington Ave
New York, NY 10022
212-446-1860

Clients:
Madison Square Garden, LP

Smith, Joann
17 Elk St
Albany, NY 12207
518-436-8408

Clients:
Family Planning Advocates of NYS, Inc

Lobbyists:
Carol Blowers
Susan Pedo

Smith, Michael P
NY Bankers Association
99 Park Ave, 4th Fl
New York, NY 10016-1502
212-297-1600 Fax: 212-297-1658
e-mail: msmith@nyba.com
Web site: www.nyba.com

Clients:
Bankers Assn (NY)

Lobbyists:
William J Bosies, Jr
Karen L Jannetty
Roberta Kotkin

Smith, Robert A
CoBank
PO Box 9061
Springfield, MA 1001
413-821-0212 Fax: 413-821-0250
e-mail: bsmith@cobank.com

Clients:
CoBank

Smyth, A Advocacy
17 Elk St, 5th Fl
Albany, NY 12207-1014
518-426-8354 Fax: 518-426-8355
e-mail: asmyth@capital.net

Clients:
AIDS Service Organizations (NYC)
Medical Equipment Providers Assn (NY)
Coalition for Natural Health
United Neighborhood Houses of NY Inc
Assn of NYS Youth Bureaus

Lobbyists:
Andrea Smyth

Solowan, Richard
One Geico Plaza
Washington, DC 20076-0001
301-986-3948 Fax: 301-718-5207
e-mail: rsolowan@geico.com

Clients:
Government Employees Insurance Co (GEICO)

Soloway, Ronald
United Jewish Appeal Federation
155 Washington Ave
Albany, NY 12210
518-436-1091 Fax: 518-463-1266
e-mail: solowayr@ujafedny.org
Web site: www.ujafedny.org

Clients:
United Jewish Appeal Federation - Jewish Philanthropies NY

Lobbyists:
Anita Altman
Elana Broitman
Daniel Rosenthal
John Ruskay
Elizabeth Seidel

Sommer, Judah
c/o Goldman Sachs & Co
101 Constitution Ave NW
Ste 1000E
Washington, DC 20001
202-637-3760 Fax: 202-637-3773

Clients:
Goldman Sachs & Co

Lobbyists:
Timur Galen
Jessica Healy
Mark Patterson

St Mary's Healthcare System for Children, Inc
29-01 216 St
Bayside, NY 11360
718-281-8800 Fax: 718-229-8968

Clients:
St Mary's Healthcare System for Children, Inc

Lobbyists:
Burton Grebin
Mark Hoffacker
Edwin Simpser

Statewide Corporate Strategies Inc

1111 Park Ave
Ste 10B
New York, NY 10128
212-987-4616 Fax: 212-987-4616
e-mail: suzan.kremer@verison.net
Web site: www.statewidestrat.com

Clients:
Altria Corporate Services Inc
Caesers Entertainment Inc

Lobbyists:
Arthur Kremer
Suzan R Kremer

Statewide Youth Advocacy Inc

17 Elk St, 5th Floor
Albany, NY 12207-1014
518-436-8525 Fax: 518-427-6576
e-mail: esw@syanys.org
Web site: www.syanys.org

Clients:
Statewide Youth Advocacy Inc

Lobbyists:
Elie Ward

Steadman, Martin J

11 Kingsbury Rd
Garden City, NY 11530
516-294-4723

Clients:
Catskill Region Off-Track Betting Corporation
Life Insurance Council of NY Inc
Uniformed Fire Officers Assn

Stegemann, Robert S

International Paper
99 Washington Ave, Ste 400
Albany, NY 12210
518-465-5600 Fax: 516-465-5618
e-mail: robert.stegemann@ipaper.com

Clients:
International Paper

Stegemoeller, Rudy

PO Box 359
Poestenkill, NY 12140
518-283-0933

Clients:
NY State Electric & Gas Corp
Plug Power, Inc
Rochester Gas & Electric Corp

Stendardi, Deborah M

Rochester Institute
30 Lomb Memorial Dr
Rochester, NY 14623-5604
585-475-5040 Fax: 585-475-2240
e-mail: dmsgrl@rit.edu

Clients:
Rochester Institute of Technology

Strategic Services, Inc

170 E Post Rd, Ste 207B
White Plains, NY 10601
914-946-8400

Clients:
City of Mount Vernon

Lobbyists:
Arnold Linhardt

Striar, Gary H

American Red Cross
33 Everett Rd
Albany, NY 12205-1437
518-458-8111 Fax: 518-459-8262
e-mail: striar@redcrossneny.org

Clients:
American Red Cross in Greater NY

Stryker, Patricia

International Brotherhood of Teamsters
216 W 14th St
New York, NY 10011
212-924-2000 Fax: 212-242-8772

Clients:
Local 237, Int'l Brotherhood of Teamsters

Stuart, John H

Occidental Chemical Corp
5005 LBJ Freeway
Dallas, TX 75244-6119
972-404-3260 Fax: 972-404-3995

Clients:
Occidental Chemical Corp

Lobbyists:
Tony Garfalo
Candace Jaunzemis
James Leinert

Stuto, Diane D

111 Washington Ave, Ste 300
Albany, NY 12210
518-436-8417 Fax: 518-436-0226
Web site: www.licony.org

Offices and agencies appear in alphabetical order.

Clients:
Life Insurance Council of NY Inc

Lobbyists:
Elizabeth J Byrne
Diana A Ehrlich
Raul Rivera
Thomas E Workman

Suffolk Community Council (FKA Pannullo, Judith)
180 Oser Ave, Ste 850
Hauppauge, NY 11788
631-434-9277

Clients:
Suffolk Community Council

Lobbyists:
Judith Pannullo

Sullivan County Chamber of Commerce & Industry, Inc
59 N Main St, Ste 300
Liberty, NY 12754
845-292-8500 Fax: 845-292-5366

Clients:
Sullivan County Chamber of Commerce & Industry, Inc

Lobbyists:
Jonathan Westergreen

Sullivan, Edward C
606 W 116th St, Ste 43
New York, NY 10027
212-678-6962

Clients:
Hello World Language Center
St Francis College

Sullivan, Veronica
Stock Exchange (NY)
11 Wall St
New York, NY 10005
212-656-3000

Clients:
Stock Exchange (NY)

Tallon Jr, James R
Empire State Building
350 5th Ave, 23rd Fl
New York, NY 10118-2399
212-494-0777 Fax: 212-494-0830

Clients:
United Hospital Fund

Lobbyists:
Kathryn Haslanger

Tenants & Neighbors Coalition (NYS)
236 W 27th St, 4th Fl
New York, NY 10001
212-608-4320 Fax: 212-619-7476
e-mail: nystnc@aol.com
Web site: www.tandu.org

Clients:
Tenants & Neighbors Coalition (NYS)

Lobbyists:
Andrea Foley Murphy
Margaretta Homsey
Michael McKee
Thomas Waters
Jumaane Williams

Thorpe, Vernon
Transport Workers Union
80 West End Ave
New York, NY 10023
212-873-6000 Fax: 212-579-3363

Clients:
Transport Workers Union, Local 100

Lobbyists:
Roger Toussaint
Ed Watt

Tourism Industry Coalition (TIC)
80 Wolf Rd
Albany, NY 12205
518-465-2300 Fax: 518-465-4025

Clients:
Tourism Industry Coalition

Lobbyists:
Daniel C Murphy

Trading Cove NY, LLC
914 Hartford Turnpike
Waterford, CT 06385
860-442-1202

Clients:
Trading Cove NY, LLC

Lobbyists:
Len Wolman

Tranter, G Thomas, Jr
Corning Incorporated
MP-BH-06
Corning, NY 14831

Offices and agencies appear in alphabetical order.

607-974-7818 Fax: 607-974-4050
e-mail: trantergt@corning.com
Web site: www.corning.com

Clients:
Corning Incorporated

Tribeca Film Institute
375 Greenwich St
New York, NY 10013
212-941-2400

Clients:
Tribeca Film Institute

Lobbyists:
Madelyn Wils

Trustees of Columbia University in the City of NY (The)
535 West 116th St
302 Low Library
New York, NY 10027
212-854-3394

Clients:
Trustees of Columbia Univ in the City of NY (The)

Lobbyists:
Lisa Anderson
Peter Awn
Matthew Bianco
Lee Bollinger
Alan Brinkley
David H Cohen
Jonathan Cole
Larry Dais
Ronald Feldman
Bruce Ferguson
Gerald Fischbach
Ross Frommer
Zvi Galil
Sandra Harris
David Hirsch
Robert Kasdin
Raphael Kasper
Ira Katznelson
Elizabeth Keefer
Ira Lamster
David W Leebron
Susan Long
Thomas Morris
Nicholas Moustakas
Mary Mundinger
Henry Pinkham
Austin Quigley
Allan Rosenfield
Jeffrey Sachs
Janet Schinderman
Ellen Smith
Jeanette Takamura
Vincent Tomaselli
Loretta Ucelli
Frank Wolf

Tully Abdo, Susan
AETNA
15 Columbia Circle
Albany, NY 12203
518-451-3019 Fax: 518-451-3604
e-mail: strohmengertc@aetna.com

Clients:
Aetna Inc

Lobbyists:
Susan Tully Abdo

Turner, Francine
CSEA-PAC
143 Washington Ave
Albany, NY 12210
518-436-8622 Fax: 518-427-1677
e-mail: turner@cseainc.org

Clients:
Civil Service Employees Political Action Fund

Lobbyists:
Adam Acquario
Joseph Brady
Dorothy Breen
Matthew D'Amico
Jason Haenel
Kathleen Lewis
Michael Neidl
Michael Ottaviano
Gretchen Penn
Robert Scholz
Kevin Younis

Twersky, Zippora
740 West End Ave
New York, NY 10025
212-662-2174

Clients:
Federation of Jewish Philanthropies of NY

Tyo, Keith
Plattsburgh State Univ of NY
101 Broad St
Plattsburgh, NY 12901-2697
518-564-3933

Clients:
Plattsburgh State University of NY

Lobbyists:
John Ettling
John Homburger
Susan Spissinger

Offices and agencies appear in alphabetical order.

Tyson, Lisa

Long Island Progressive Coalition
90 Pennsylvania Ave
Massapequa, NY 11758-4978
516-541-1006 Fax: 516-541-2113
e-mail: lisa@lipc.org
Web site: www.lipc.org

Clients:
Long Island Progressive Coalition

Ungar, Robert A Associates Inc

200 Garden City Plaza
Ste 201
Garden City, NY 11530
516-227-2400 Fax: 516-227-2406
e-mail: fireandems@aol.com

Clients:
Advanced Drainage Systems Inc
Assn of Plumbing Heating Cooling Contractors Inc (NYS)
Building & Construction Trades Council (NYS)
Building & Construction Trades Council of Graeter NY
Building Trades Employers' Assn
Civil Svc Technical Guild, Local 375 DC-37, AFSCME AFL-CIO
Constr Laborers, Hwy Reprs & Water Shed Maint, Local 376, DC-37,
Council of Administrators & Supervisors
IXP Corporation
Local 3, IBEW Communications Electricians
Local 246, SEIU
Motor Vehicle Operators Union, Local 983, DC-37, AFSCME
Nassau County PHCC
Oneida Tribe of Indians of Wisconsin (The)
Plumbing Contractors Assn of Long Island Inc
Plumbing Foundation City of NY Inc
Purvis Systems Inc
TBTA Maintenance Employees, Local 1931, DC-37, AFSCME
Uniformed EMS Officers Union, FDNY, Local 3621
Uniformed EMT's & Paramedics, Local 2507-FDNY
Uniformed Fire Alarm Dispatchers Benevolent Assn-FDNY

Lobbyists:
Robert A Ungar

United Healthcare Services, Inc (FKA Oxford LLC)

Oxford Health Plans LLC
48 Monroe Tpk
Trumbull, CT 06611
203-459-7271

Clients:
United Healthcare Services, Inc

Lobbyists:
Timothy Meyer

United Neighborhood Houses of NY

70 West 36th St, 5th Fl
New York, NY 10018-8007
212-967-0322 Fax: 212-967-0792

Clients:
United Neighborhood Houses of NY

Lobbyists:
Anthony Ng
Susan Stamler
Hilda Valdez
Nancy Wackstein
Jessica Walker

United Spinal Assn (FKA Eastern Paralyed Veterans Assn)

75-20 Astoria Blvd
Jackson Heights, NY 11370-1177
718-803-3782 Fax: 718-803-1089

Clients:
United Spinal Assn

Lobbyists:
Daniel Anderson
Linda Gutmann

United University Professions

PO Box 15143
Albany, NY 12212-5143
518-640-6600
e-mail: input@uupmail.org
Web site: www.uupinfo.org

Clients:
United University Professions

Lobbyists:
Christopher Black
Debra Nelson

University at Buffalo

520A Capen Hall
Buffalo, NY 14260-1629
716-645-7730 Fax: 716-645-5877
Web site: www.government.buffalo.edu

Clients:
University at Buffalo

Lobbyists:
Wayne Anderson
Dennis Black
Beth Delgenio
Robert Genko
William Greiner
Bruce Holm
Mark Karwan
Ryan McPherson
Norma Nowak
Margaret Paroski
Janet Penksa
Michael Pietkiewicz
John Simpson
Maurizio Trevisan
Satish Tripathi
James Willis

Offices and agencies appear in alphabetical order.

Upstate Consultants, Inc

121 College St
Buffalo, NY 14201
716-432-3602 Fax: 716-885-2415
e-mail: gregsehr@aol.com

Clients:
Catholic Health System

Lobbyists:
Gregory Sehr

Upstate Farms Cooperative Inc

25 Anderson Rd
Buffalo, NY 14225
716-892-3156 Fax: 716-892-3157

Clients:
Upstate Farms Cooperative Inc

Lobbyists:
Timothy R Harner
Kimberly Pickard-Dudley
Thomas J Rodak
William Young

Vacek, Harris & McCormack PC

90 South Swan St
Ste 4
Albany, NY 12210
518-436-4077 Fax: 518-436-4636

Clients:
Bankers Assn (NYS)
Beer Wholesalers Assn Inc (NYS)
Feld Entertainment Inc
Free Community Newspapers of NY
Funeral Directors (NYS)
Property Casualty Insurers Assn Inc
R J Reynolds Tobacco Co
Real Estate Board of New York Inc
Yonkers Raceway Corp

Lobbyists:
Steven W Harris
R Christopher McCormack
Michael E Vacek

Vandervort Group, LLC (The)

111 Washington Ave, Ste 703
Albany, NY 12210-2222
518-463-3202 Fax: 518-463-7952
e-mail: thevgroup@aol.com

Clients:
Alliance for Environmental Concerns (NY)
Alumni Assn - SUNY Maritime College
Bluestone Association (NYS)
CNA Surety/Western Surety Co
Covanta Energy Corp Inc
Hewlett-Packard Co
Merck & Co Inc
Moneygram International

Multi Housing Laundry Assn
Nextel Communications Inc
Northeastern Retail Lumber Assn
Recreation Vehicle Industry Assn
Reed Elsevier Inc
IMS Health Inc
US Fireworks Safety Commission Inc
Oxford, LLC (Morris & McVeigh, LLP)
Roche Diagnostics Corporation
Sanofi Aventis

Lobbyists:
Christopher J Revere
John W Vandervort
Todd H Vandervort

Ventresca-Ecroyd, Gilda

NYU Hospitals Center
3 Park Ave, 15th Fl
New York, NY 10016
212-404-4077 Fax: 212-404-4061
e-mail: gilda-ventresca-ecroyd@med.nyu.edu
Web site: www.med.nyu.edu

Clients:
NYU Hospitals Ctr

Lobbyists:
Karen Ann Acker

Verizon

1095 Avenue of the Americas
Rm 4143
New York, NY 10036
212-395-1078 Fax: 212-597-2560

Clients:
Verizon

Lobbyists:
William Allan
Paul Crotty
Thomas Dunne
Susan Hays
David Lamendola
Richard Windram

Vidal Group, LLC (The)

150 State St, 4th Fl
Albany, NY 12207
518-434-5856

Clients:
Building Trades Employers' Assn of the City of NY Inc
Hispanic Federation
Hispanic Information Telecommunications Network
Latino Commission on AIDS
Jets LLC (NY)
Novartis Pharmaceuticals Corp
Sheldrake Organization Inc

Lobbyists:
Alfredo Vidal

Offices and agencies appear in alphabetical order.

Visiting Nurse Service of NY
107 East 70th St
New York, NY 10021
212-609-1541 Fax: 212-794-6357

Clients:
Visiting Nurse Service of NY

Lobbyists:
Judith Duhl
Judith Farrell

Wacholder, Stephanie
42 Berkshire Dr
East Greenbush, NY 12061
518-479-3556

Clients:
United Teachers (NYS)

Wagner, Claudia Law Office of
277 Broadway
Ste 1300
New York, NY 10007
212-619-2052 Fax: 212-619-6351

Clients:
ART/New York
Alvin Ailey Dance Theater
American Museum of Natural History
Asphalt Green
BAM-Local Development Corp
Big Apple Circus
Brooklyn Academy of Music
City Parks Foundation
Common Cents NY
Cooper Union for the Advancement of Science & Art (The)
Council of NY Cooperatives Inc
Dance Theater Workshop
Danspace Project at St Marks Church
Jazz at Lincoln Ctr
Joyce Theater (The)
Lincoln Ctr for the Performing Arts Inc
Moving Image (The) (dba The Film Forum)
Museum for African Art
Npowerny
Repertorio Espanol
Roundabout Theatre Co
Second Stage Theatre
Snug Harbor Cultural Ctr
Socrates Sculpture Park Inc
Symphony Space
Wireless Access Coalition (NY) (Elliott Bay Group)
MCI
New Museum of Contemporary Art
Tribeca Film Institute
Whitney Museum (The)
Civic Builders
F A Bartlett Tree Expert Company
Barbizon Hotel Associates, LP

Lobbyists:
Elizabeth H Berger
William Floyd
Adam Rich

Claudia Wagner

Walsh, John B
Ecology & Environment, Inc
368 Pleasantview Dr
Lancaster, NY 14086
716-684-8060 Fax: 716-684-4832
e-mail: jbwalsh@ene.com

Clients:
Buffalo & Erie Cnty Naval & Military Park
Ecology & Environment Inc

Wang, Phyllis A
NYSHCP
99 Troy Rd
Ste 200
East Greenbush, NY 12061
518-463-1118 Fax: 518-463-1606
e-mail: hcp@nyshcp.org
Web site: www.nyshcp.org

Clients:
Assn of Health Care Providers Inc (NYS)

Lobbyists:
Nancy Erdoes
Christine L Johnston
Julia Tighe
Molly Williams

Wason, Jay W, Jr
Unity Mutual Life Insurance
507 Plum St
Syracuse, NY 13204
315-448-7136 or 315-448-7136 Fax: 315-448-7203
e-mail: jwason@unity-life.com

Clients:
Unity Mutual Life Insurance Co

Lobbyists:
Patrick A Mannion
Joseph Masella

Watkins, James
Wyeth
5 Giralda Farms
Madison, NJ 7940
973-660-5027 Fax: 973-660-8535
e-mail: watkinj2@wyeth.com

Clients:
Wyeth

Weaver, Gregory G
Deloitte & Touche
1633 Broadway
New York, NY 10019
212-492-3942

Offices and agencies appear in alphabetical order.

Clients:
Deloitte & Touche LLP

Lobbyists:
William Freda
Thomas Hogan
James Wetzler

Weekley, Daniel A
Dominion Resources
Rope Ferry Rd
Waterford, CT 6385
860-444-5271 Fax: 860-437-5813
e-mail: daniel_a_weekley@dom.com
Web site: www.dominion.com

Clients:
Dominion Resources

Weingarten, Reid & McNally, LLC
One Commerce Plaza
Ste 1103
Albany, NY 12210
518-465-7330 Fax: 518-465-0273
e-mail: bobr@lobbywr.com
Web site: www.lobbywr.com

Clients:
Academy of Family Physicians (NYS)
American Cancer Society, Eastern Division Inc
American College of Emergency Physicians (NY Chapter)
American Heart Assn/American Stroke Assn
Assn of Health Care Providers Inc (NYS)
Chain Pharmacy Assn of NYS
Community General Hospital
Wildlife Conservation Society Inc
Delphi Corp
Diageo, PLC
Elmhurst Dairy Group
Fidelity National Financial Inc
Prime Risk Management, Inc & PRM Claim Services Inc
Independent Petroleum Marketers of NY
Iroquois Healthcare Alliance
Life Insurance Co (NY)
NOCO Energy Co
Natural & Complementary Practices Project (NY) (FKA Natural Healt
New Yorkers for the Advancement of Medical Research
Northeast Health
Presbyterian Hosp/Coal for School-Based Primary Care (NY)
Public Transit Assn (NY)
Republican Majority for Choice (NY Chapter)
Securities Industry Assn
Society of Anesthesiologists Inc (NYS)
Speech, Language Hearing Assn Inc (NYS)
St Peter's Health Care Services
Interfit Health
Cerebral Palsy Assns of NYS Inc
Upstate Health Care Coalition (Iroquois Healthcare Alliance)
Willert Home Products
Wildwood Programs Inc
American Health Professionals Insurance Assn

Lobbyists:
Shauneen M McNally

Robert W Reid
Marcy Wamp
Steven B Weingarten

Weiskopf, Gary
CLMHD
99 Pine St
Albany, NY 12207
518-462-9422 Fax: 518-465-2695
e-mail: clmhd@clmhd.org
Web site: www.clmhd.org

Clients:
Conf of Local Mental Hygiene Directors (NYS)

Lobbyists:
Kathleen Mayo
Linda Tremblay

Wexler, Scott
Restaurant & Tavern Assn
40 Sheridan Ave
Albany, NY 12210
518-436-8121 Fax: 518-436-7287
e-mail: esrta@captial.net
Web site: www.esrta.org

Clients:
Empire State Restaurant & Tavern Assn Inc

Whitehead, David
65 Oak St
Rensselaer, NY 12144-9742
518-283-0946 Fax: 518-283-0171

Clients:
Bristol-Myers Squibb Co

Whiteman Osterman & Hanna LLP
One Commerce Plaza, 19th Fl
Albany, NY 12260
518-487-7741 Fax: 518-487-7777
Web site: www.woh.com

Clients:
Educational Testing Service
American Express Co
AIA New York State Inc
Assn of Homes & Services for the Aging (NY)
Aventis Pasteur Inc
Bristol-Myers Squibb Co
COFCCA Inc
Council of New York Cooperatives
Creosote Council III
Distilled Spirits Council of the US
Hertz Corporation (The)
Institute for Student Achievement
Johnson & Johnson
Long Island Life Sciences Initiative
MCI
Metropolitan Museum of Art (The)
Physical Therapy Assn (NY)

Offices and agencies appear in alphabetical order.

Presbyterian Hospital (NY)
Quest Diagnostics Inc
Reinsurance Assn of America
Roundabout Theatre Co
SC Johnson & Son Inc
Society for Respiratory Care Inc (NYS)
Advantage Capital Partners
Syracuse University
Teachers Insurance & Annuity Assn/College Retirement Equities Fun
Haverstraw-Stony Point Central School District
Managed Funds Association
MBIA Insurance Corporation
Natural Resources Defense Council Inc
St Elizabeth Medical Center
Scotts Company (The)

Lobbyists:
John R Dunne
Philip Gitten
Aggie Leahy
Richard E Leckerling
Brian J Lucey
Michael Whiteman

Wieboldt, Robert

Builders Institute
1757-8 Veterans Memorial Hwy
Islandia, NY 11749
631-232-2345 Fax: 631-232-2349
e-mail: evp@libi.org
Web site: libi.org

Clients:
Long Island Builders Institute

Wiener, Judith R

Lower Hudson Education Coalition
1102 Palmer Ave
Larchmont, NY 10538
914-833-0094 Fax: 914-833-0104

Clients:
Lower Hudson Education Coalition

Wildlife Conservation Society

2300 Southern Blvd
Bronx, NY 10460
718-220-7353 Fax: 718-220-6890
Web site: www.wcs.org

Clients:
Wildlife Conservation Society

Lobbyists:
John F Calvelli
Rosemary DeLuca
Sara S Marinello

Wiliams, Samuel G

Region 9 UAW
35 George Karl Blvd

Ste 100
Amherst, NY 14221
716-632-1540

Clients:
Region 9, UAW

Williams Esq, Christopher A

Long Island University
700 Northern Blvd
Brookville, NY 11548-1327
516-299-3834

Clients:
Long Island University

Lobbyists:
Richard W Gorman
David J Steinberg
Kim Williams

Williams, Carla

99 Troy Rd, Ste 200
East Greenbush, NY 12061
518-533-7878

Clients:
Alliance for Donation (NY)

Williams, Jacquelyn A

169 MacDonough St
Brooklyn, NY 11216
917-604-1304

Clients:
Jets LLC (NY)

Wilson Elser Moskowitz Edelman & Dicker

One Steuben Place, 2nd Fl
Albany, NY 12207
518-449-8893 Fax: 518-449-8927
Web site: www.wemed.com

Clients:
Albany Medical Ctr
Alice Hyde Medical Center
Alliance Capital Management
American Insurance Assn
American International Group Inc (AIG)
Alliance of Resident Theatres (NY)
Assc of Professional Land Surveyors Inc (NYS)
Assn of Realtors Inc (NYS)
Athletic Trainers' Assn (NYS)
National Medical Health Card Systems Inc (NMHCRX)
Bankers Assn (NY)
Blythedale Children's Hospital
Carnegie Hall
Cathedral Church of St John the Devine (The)
Combined Coordinating Council Inc
Community Hospital Network of NY Eductl & Rsch Fund Inc
Community Nursing Home of Potsdam
Community Service Society of NY

Offices and agencies appear in alphabetical order.

Consolidated Edison Co of NY Inc
Cortland Memorial Hospital
Crouse Hospital
Center for the Disabled
David B Kriser Dental Center of NY University
Daxor Corp
DeVry Incorporated
Deloitte & Touche, LLP
Elevator Industry Work Preservaton Fund
Elliott Management
Norwegian Cruise Line
Epilepsy Institute
Ernst & Young, LLP
Family Planning Advocates
Forest City Ratner Companies
United Hospital Fund
Glens Falls Hospital
Greater New York Automobile Dealers Assn
Groton Community Health Care Center
HANYS Insurance Co Inc
HANYS Member Hospitals Self-Insurance Trust
HANYS Services Inc
Trustees of Columbia University in the City of NY (The)
Harbar Motors, Ltd
Healthcare Assn of NYS
Hebrew Home for the Aged at Riverdale (The)
Henningson, Durham & Richardson Arch & Engr, PC
Henry Schein Inc
Hertz Corporation (The)
Highbridge-Woodycrest Center Inc
Hospitality & Tourism Assn (NYS)
Hotel Assn of NYC Inc
Intrepid Museum Foundation
KPMG, LLP
League of American Theatres & Producers Inc
Little Falls Hospital
Long Island Health Network
Long Island University
Tanglewood Manor
MCIC Vermont Inc
Magna Entertainment Corp
Marshals Assn (NYC)
Taconic IPA Inc
Metropolitan Parking Assn
Morgan Stanley
Niagara Mohawk Power Corp
North Country Healthcare Providers Eductl & Rsch Fund Inc
Oneida Tribe of Indians of Wisconsin (The)
Peerless Importers
Phelps Memorial Hospital Center
Planned Parenthood of NYC Inc
PricewaterhouseCoopers, LLP
Rochester Institute of Technology
School Bus Contractor's Coalition (NY)
Segway, LLC
Society for Clinical Social Work Inc (NYS)
St Luke's Cornwall Hospital
St Mary's Healthcare System for Children Inc
T-Mobile USA Inc
To Life
New York University (NYU)
University School of Medicine (NY) & Hospitals (NY)
Viahealth
University of Rochester & Affiliates
Yonkers Raceway
Presbyterian Hospital (NY)
Assn of Independent Commercial Producers Inc
Asurion Insurance Services Inc

Atlantic Imaging of NY, PC
AXA Equitable Life Insurance Company
CGI Group (FKA American Management Services)
City of Syracuse Industrial Development Agency
Dell Inc
Enhanced Care Initiatives (National Strategies Inc)
Hadassah the Women's Zionist Organization of America Inc
IMG Models
Infilco Degremont Inc (FKA Ondeo Degremont Inc)
Jewish Museum (The)
Lilac Capital, LLC
Lock/Line, LLC
Madison Square Garden

Lobbyists:
Nicholas Antenucci
Alexander L Betke
Kenneth R Bruno
Cecilia Capers
Douglas Clark
Donna Clyne
Laurie T Cohen
Victoria M Contino
Jerry S Hoffman
Darrell E Jeffers
Arnold Kideckel
Lisa M Marrello
Mary Ann Mclean
Paula O'Brien
Peter A Piscitelli
Jason M Poliner
Philip Rosenberg
Theresa Russo
Jill Sandhaas
Kenneth L Shapiro
Cynthia D Shenker
Lester Skulklapper
Mark Thomas

Wingender (Vanderiver), Karen M
Greater Rochester Assn of Realtors
930 East Ave
Rochester, NY 14607
585-341-2144 Fax: 585-292-5008
e-mail: karenv@grar.net

Clients:
Greater Rochester Assn of Realtors Inc

Wojnar, David E
Distilled Spirits Council
1250 I St NW, Ste 400
Washington, DC 20005-3998
202-682-8805 Fax: 202-682-8849

Clients:
Distilled Spirits Council of the US

Wolf, Block, Schorr & Solis-Cohen, LLP
250 Park Ave
New York, NY 10177

Offices and agencies appear in alphabetical order.

212-883-4923 Fax: 212-986-0604
e-mail: sshorenstein@wolfblock.com
Web site: www.wolfblock.com

Clients:
MGM Mirage

Lobbyists:
Stuart Shorenstein

Wolf, Stacy
PO Box 100
Cropseyville, NY 12052
518-465-2061

Clients:
American Society for the Prevention of Cruelty to Animals

Lobbyists:
Lisa Weisberg

Wood Rafalsky & Wood
62 William St, 2nd Fl
New York, NY 10005-1547
212-248-3001 Fax: 212-248-3008

Clients:
Clinical Laboratory Assoc, Inc (NYS)

Lobbyists:
Thomas R Rafalsky

Workers' Rights Law Ctr of NY Inc
101 Hurley Ave, Ste 5
Kingston, NY 12401
845-331-6615

Clients:
Workers' Rights Law Ctr of NY Inc

Lobbyists:
Patricia Kakalec
Daniel Werner

Working Assets Funding Service Inc
101 Market St, Ste 700
San Francisco, CA 94105
415-369-2000 Fax: 415-371-1048

Clients:
Working Assets Funding Service Inc

Lobbyists:
Sarah Clusen Buecher

YMCAS of NYS Inc
33 Elk St, Ste 200
Albany, NY 12207
518-462-8241 Fax: 518-462-8491

Clients:
YMCAs of NYS Inc

Lobbyists:
John Murray
Kyle Stewart

Yavornitzki, Mark L
NYSAIFA
38 Sheridan Ave
Albany, NY 12210-2714
518-462-5567 Fax: 518-462-5569
e-mail: nysaifa@aol.com
Web site: www.nysaifa.com

Clients:
Assn of Insurance & Financial Advisors (NYS)

Yoswein New York Inc
150 Broadway
Ste 1300
New York, NY 10038
212-233-5700 Fax: 212-233-5757
e-mail: info@yosweinnewyork.com
Web site: www.yosweinnewyork.com

Clients:
Academy of Medicine (NY)
Brooklyn Botanic Garden
Brooklyn Chamber of Commerce
Brooklyn Technical High School Alumni Assn
Brooklyn Philharmonic
General Cigar Company Inc
Glenwood Management Corp
New 42nd Street Inc (The)
Ikea Property Inc
Keyspan Energy
Park Tower Group
Metropolitan Funeral Directors Assoc
Mt Sinai Hospital of Queens
Outward Bound Center (NYC)
SUNY Downstate Medical Center
Maimonides Medical Center
St Francis College
Standardbred Owners Assn of NY

Lobbyists:
Rachel Gold
Cassaundra Manning
Jamie Van Bramer
Joni A Yoswein

Young Jr, William N
2400 Western Ave
Guilderland, NY 12084-0309
518-456-6767

Clients:
Assn of Fire Districts of the State of NY, Inc

Young Sommer Ward Ritzenberg Wooley Baker Moore, LLC
5 Palisades Dr
Albany, NY 12205

518-438-9907 Fax: 518-438-9914
e-mail: dwooley@youngsommer.com
Web site: www.youngsommer.com

Clients:
American Wind Energy Assn

Lobbyists:
Valerie Strauss
Douglas Ward
David Wooley

Zaleski, Terence M
437 Old Albany Post Rd
Garrison, NY 10524
845-788-5070 Fax: 845-788-5071
e-mail: tzaleski@sprynet.com

Clients:
Coalition of NYS Career Schools
Full Spectrum of New York, LLC
Green Chimneys Children's Services Inc
League for the Hard of Hearing
Putnam Associated Resource Ctrs
Institute for the Study of Infection Control Inc (The)

Zogg, Jeffrey
General Bldg Contractors
6 Airline Dr
Albany, NY 12205

518-869-2207 Fax: 518-869-0846
e-mail: joeh@gbcnys.agc.org
Web site: www.gbcnys.agc.org

Clients:
General Building Contractors of NYS Inc

Lobbyists:
Joseph Hogan
Brenda Manning

Zowader, Don
Takeda Pharma
3749 Chesapeake St NW
Washington, DC 20016
202-237-1522

Clients:
Takeda Pharmaceuticals America

Zwerdling, Hilary
1211 Chestnut St
Ste 400
Philadelphia, PA 19107
215-557-0406

Clients:
Advocacy Inc

Lobbyists:
Rob Stuart

Political Parties,
Lobbyists & PACs

Offices and agencies appear in alphabetical order.

POLITICAL ACTION COMMITTEES

1170 PEC
John P Pusloskie, Treasurer
1451 Lake Avenue, Rochester, NY 14615
585-647-1170

1199/SEIU New York State Political Action Fund
George Gresham, Treasurer
330 West 42nd Street, 7th Floor, New York, NY 10036
212-261-2342

21st Century Democrats
Michael Lux, Treasurer
1311 L St NW, #300, Washington, DC 20005
202-626-5620 Fax: 202-347-0956

500 Club
Edward L Barlow, Treasurer
C/O Judy Winslow, 70 Hamilton Avenue, Greenwich, CT 06830
203-869-6612

504 Democratic Club Campaign Committee
Marty Sesmer, Treasurer
332 E 29th St, Ste 5A, New York, NY 10002
212-684-6287

ABO Build PAC Inc
Nicholas LaPorte, Jr, Tresurer
Assoc Builders & Owners, 55 John St, 4th Fl, New York, NY 10038
212-385-4949 Fax: 212-385-1442
e-mail: associatedbuilders@yahoo.com
Web site: www.abogny.com

ACENY-PAC
Jay J Simson, Treasurer
1771 Van Antwerp Road, Niskayuna, NY 12309
518-372-4936

AES NYS PAC
Amy V Conley, Treasurer
7725 Lake Rd, Barker, NY 14012
716-795-9501 Fax: 716-795-3153
e-mail: aconley@aes.com

AFGI PAC
Robert E Mackin, Treasurer
139 Lancaster St, Albany, NY 12210-1903
518-449-4698 Fax: 518-432-5651
e-mail: bmackin@mackinco.com

ALPAC (ALCAS PAC)
Jack A Lorenz, Treasurer
418 Cherry St, Olean, NY 14760
716-373-1406
e-mail: jlorenz@alcas.com

ASAPPAC
David N Weinraub, Treasurer

Brown & Weinraub, LLC, 79 Columbia St, Albany, NY 12210
518-427-7350 Fax: 518-427-7792

ATPAM COPE State Fund
Gordon G Forbes, Treasurer
1560 Broadway, Ste 700, New York, NY 10036
212-719-3666 Fax: 212-302-1585
e-mail: gforbe@atpam.com
Web site: www.atpam.com

ATU-NY Cope Fund
Oscar Owens, President
5025 Wisconsin Ave NW, Washington, DC 20016
202-537-1645 Fax: 202-244-7824

Abate RRF Inc
Brian J Trafford, Treasurer
216 Lincoln St, Riverhead, NY 11901
516-369-0729

Action Fund for Good Government
David JG Chambers, Treasurer
164 Fruitwood Terrace, Williamsville, NY 14221
716-626-4893

Aetna Inc PAC
Jonathan M Topodas, Treasurer
1331 F Street, NW, Suite 450, Washington, DC 20004
202-463-4023 Fax: 202-223-4424
e-mail: jonathan.topodas@aetna.com

Affordable Housing PAC, LTD
Frank J Anelante Jr, Treasurer
c/o Lumley & Woolf, 5925 Broadway, Bronx, NY 10463
718-884-7676 x201

Allied Bldg Metal Industries Inc State PAC
Arthur Rubinstein, Treasurer
211 East 43rd St, Ste 804, New York, NY 10017
212-697-5551 Fax: 212-818-0976

Allstate Insurance Company PAC
James P Zils, Treasurer
3075 Sanders Road, Suite G2H, Northbrook, IL 60062
847-402-3074

American Express Company PAC (AXP PAC)
Robert B Thompson, III, Treasurer
801 Pennsylvania Ave, NW, Suite 650, Washington, DC 20004
202-434-0156

American Insurance Assn New York PAC
Leigh Ann Pusey, Treasurer

Offices and agencies appear in alphabetical order.

1130 Connecticut Ave NW, Ste 1000, Washington, DC 20036
202-828-7100 Fax: 202-293-1219
Web site: www.aiadc.org

American Motorcyclist Assn PAC
C Alexandar Ernst, Treasurer
PO Box 250, Clarksville, NY 12041
518-768-8191 Fax: 775-361-1342
e-mail: a.ernst@ernst.cc

American Resort Dev/Assn Resort Owners' Coalition PAC
Sandra Y Depoy, Treasurer
1201 15th St NW, Ste 400, Washington, DC 20005
202-371-6700 Fax: 202-289-8544
Web site: www.arda.org

American Telephone & Telegraph Co PAC NY
Frederick K Wallach, Treasurer
32 Avenue of the Americas, Room 2700, New York, NY 10013
212-387-5611

Arts PAC Non-Federal
Peggy Kaplan, Treasurer
c/o R Feldman Fine Arts, 31 Mercer St, New York, NY 10013
212-226-3232

Asbestos Workers Local 12 Political Action Committee
Matthew P Aracich, Treasurer
25-19 43rd Avenue, Long Island City, NY 11101-4208
718-784-3456

Assn for a Better Long Island - PAC (ABLI)
John V Klein, Treasurer
1505 Kellum Pl, Mineola, NY 11501
516-741-6565 Fax: 516-741-6706

Assn of Independent Commercial Producers Inc PAC
David L Gould, Treasurer
555 So Flower St, Ste 4210, Los Angeles, CA 90071-2300
213-489-4792 Fax: 213-489-4818

Association of Commuter Rail Employees PAC NY
John Gaines, Treasurer
1016 Summit Woods, New Windsor, NY 12553
845-656-2469

Association of New York State Young Republicans Inc
Daniel Butler, Treasurer
157 E 32nd St, Apt 19B, New York, NY 10016
212-689-0256

Astoria Financial Corp PAC
Daniel J Quirk, Treasurer
Astoria Fed S&L, 1 Astoria Fed Plz, Lake Success, NY 11042
516-327-7823 Fax: 516-328-2035

Automobile Dealers of New York PAC
Robert E Vancavage, Treasurer

PO Box 7347, Albany, NY 12224
518-463-1148 Fax: 518-432-1309
e-mail: bobv@nysada.com

BAC Local 2 PAC
John Buck, Treasurer
302 Centre Dr, Albany, NY 12203
518-456-5477 Fax: 518-456-7420
Web site: www.bac2.org

BBL PAC
Stephen J Obermayer, Treasurer
504 Victory Circle, Ballston Spa, NY 12020
518-884-8018

BCSA-PAC
Thomas F Vitale, Treasurer
2495 Main Street, OTC Suite 100, Buffalo, NY 14214
716-833-9145

BMW PAC
David N Weinraub, Treasurer
79 Columbia Street, Albany, NY 12210
518-427-7350

BRAB PAC, INC
Michael Laub, Treasurer
C/O Bronx Realty Advisory Board, 6 Xavier Drive, Suite 301, Yonkers, NY 10704
914-966-2000

BXNY PAC
John A Emrick, II, Treasurer
1469 East Ave, #2C, Bronx, NY 10462
718-829-5142

Bank of America NY PAC
Gregory E Swanson, Treasurer
600 Peachtree St, NE, 3rd Fl, Atlanta, GA 30308
404-607-5267
Web site: www.bankofamerica.com

Bear Stearns Political Campaign Committee
Michael J Abatemarco, Treasurer
1 Metrotech Center N, 9th Fl, Brooklyn, NY 11201
212-272-8750 Fax: 347-643-2524
e-mail: mabatemarco@bear.com

Bell Atlantic Corporation PAC
Sandra L Borders, Treasurer
1717 Arch Street, 47S, Philadelphia, PA 19103
215-963-6387

Bethpage Federal Credit Union PAC
Brian Clarke, Treasurer
899 South Oyster Bay Rd, Bethpage, NY 11714
516-349-6767 Fax: 516-349-6765
e-mail: bclarke@bethpagefcu.com

Better Health Care PAC
Jesse Ellman, Treasurer

Offices and agencies appear in alphabetical order.

POLITICAL ACTION COMMITTEES

18 Lexington Road, New City, NY 10956

Black Car PAC
Wayne I Baden, Treasurer
Fox Horan & Camerini, 825 3rd Ave, 11th Fl, New York, NY 10020
212-363-7020 Fax: 212-709-0248
e-mail: wibaden@foxlex.com

Bricklayers & Allied Craftsmen Local Union 1 PAC
Santo Lanzafame, Treasurer
4 Court Square, Long Island City, NY 11101
718-392-0525 Fax: 718-392-1068

Bricklayers & Allied Craftworkers Local 5 NY PAC
Tony Piacente, Treasurer
126 Innis Ave, Poughkeepsie, NY 12601
845-452-3689 Fax: 845-452-4711

Bricklayers Allied Craftworkers Local 3 Buffalo PAC
Daniel Rose, President
1807 Elmwood Avenue, Buffalo, NY 14207
716-873-1141

Bristol-Myers Squibb Co Employee PAC
Peter Cheng, Treasurer
345 Park Avenue, New York, NJ 10154
212-546-3243

Bronx Coalition for Good Government
Egidio Sementilli, Treasurer
1754 Hobart Avenue, Bronx, NY 10461
718-239-7700

Brooklyn Democrats
William H Boone, III, Treasurer
16 Court St, Ste 1115, Brooklyn, NY 11241
718-875-5870 Fax: 718-596-4013

Broome County Association of PHCC PAC
Rudolph W Gaspar, Treasurer
20 Meadow Street, Binghamton, NY 13905
Web site: www.nysphcc.org

Buffalo Niagara Builders' Assn Build PAC
Joseph W McIvor, Jr, Treasurer
90 Sylvan Pkwy, West Amherst, NY 14228
716-636-9655 Fax: 716-636-9658
e-mail: joe@bnba.org
Web site: www.bnba.org

Buffalo Professional Firefighters PAC
Daniel J O'Connor, Treasurer
255 Delaware Ave, Buffalo, NY 14202
716-856-4130 Fax: 716-854-1783
e-mail: buffalo.firefighters@verizon.net
Web site: www.local282iaff.com

Buffalo Teachers Federation PAC
Donna Stempniak, Treasurer

271 Porter Avenue, Buffalo, NY 14201
716-881-5400

Builders' PAC
Robert A Wieboldt, Treasurer
1757-8 Veterans Hwy, Islandia, NY 11749
631-232-2345 Fax: 631-232-2349
e-mail: evp@libi.org
Web site: www.libi.org

Building & Construction Trades Council PAC
Edward Malloy, Treasurer
71 W 23rd St, Ste 501-03, New York, NY 10010
212-647-0700 Fax: 212-647-0705

Building Contractors Assn Inc
Richard Harding, Treasurer
451 Park Ave S, 4th Fl, New York, NY 10016
212-683-8080 Fax: 212-683-0404
e-mail: nybca1@aol.com
Web site: ny-bca.com

Building Industry Association of New York City, Inc
Jessica Fortino, Executive Vice President
406 Forest Avenue, Staten Island, NY 10301
718-720-3070 Fax: 718-720-3088
e-mail: jfortino@webuildnyc.com

Business First PAC
Todd L Shimkus, Treasurer
PO Box 158, Glens Falls, NY 12801
518-798-1761 Fax: 518-792-4147

Business-Industry PAC of Central NY Inc
John F Osta, Treasurer
5161 Wagon Trails End, Syracuse, NY 13215
315-472-8371 Fax: 315-487-0802
e-mail: jfosta@gallinger.com

CAPE PAC
William Phillips, Treasurer
Hinman Straub, PC, 121 State Street, Albany, NY 12207
518-694-3110

CAS PAC
Luke Morgan, Treasurer
48 Mary Pitkin Path, PO Box 80, Shoreham, NY 11786
516-233-0476 Fax: 631-744-6078
e-mail: morgans48@hotmail.com

CIGNA Corporation Political Action Committee
David M Porcello, Treasurer
24 Magnolia Drive, Suffield, CT 06078

CNY Labor PAC
John Hutchings, Treasurer

404 Oak Street, Lower Level, Syracuse, NY 13203
315-422-3363

CWA SSF (NY)
Robert Master, Treasurer
80 Pine Street, 37th Floor, New York, NY 10005
212-344-2515

Cable PAC
Richard F Alteri, Treasurer
18 Olive Tree Lane, Albany, NY 12208
518-463-6676 Fax: 518-463-0574
e-mail: ralteri@nycap.rr.com

Cablevision Systems New York PAC
Sheila A Mahony, Treasurer
1111 Stewart Avenue, Bethpage, NY 11714
516-803-2387

Campaign for Democratic Victory
Socrates Solano, Treasurer
659 W 162nd St, Ste 67, New York, NY 10032
917-521-2556 Fax: 212-781-0707

Campaign for Renewable Energy
William Bastuk, Treasurer
125 Eastman Estates, Rochester, NY 14622
585-342-1375

Captain's Endowment Assn PAC
Francis Porcelli, Treasurer
Captain's Endowmt, 233 B Way, Ste 850, New York, NY 10027
212-964-7500 Fax: 212-406-3105

Carpenters Local No. 19 PAC
Kevin T Smith, Treasurer
52 Stone Castle Rd, Ste 3, Rock Tavern, NY 12575
845-567-6985

Carpenters' Local 747 PAC
Richard Waite, Treasurer
3247 Vickery Rd, North Syracuse, NY 13212
315-455-5797 Fax: 315-455-8326
e-mail: carpenters@local.747.com

Carpenters' Local Union 85 PAC
John Mattle, Treasurer
244 Paul Rd, Rochester, NY 14624
716-328-6251 Fax: 585-436-4231
e-mail: smcdade@rochestercarpenters.org

Cayuga Community College Faculty Assn PAC
Teresa R Hoercher, Treasurer
197 Franklin St, Auburn, NY 13021
315-255-1743 Fax: 315-255-2050

Cendant Corporation NY PAC
David Wyshner, Treasurer

1 Campus Way, Parsippany, NJ 7054
973-496-5040 Fax: 973-496-5080

Central Brooklyn Medical Group, PC
Martin Valdes MD, Treasurer
242 E 72nd St Apt 18, New York, NY 10021
212-737-3636

Central NY Labor PAC
John Hutchings, Treasurer
404 Oak St, Lower Level, Syracuse, NY 13203
315-422-3363 Fax: 315-422-2260

Central NY PAC Region 9 UAW
Samuel G Williams, Director
35 George Karl Blvd, Ste 100, Amherst, NY 14221
716-632-1540 Fax: 716-632-1797

Chain Pharmacy Assn PAC
Steven B Weingarten, Treasurer
1 Commerce Plaza, Ste 1103, Albany, NY 12210
518-465-7330 Fax: 518-465-0273
e-mail: stevew@lobbywr.com
Web site: www.lobbywr.com

Change WNY Now
Alexandra V Lawkowski, Treasurer
1588 Broadway, Buffalo, NY 14212

Charter PAC
Tracy Nagler, Treasurer
575 Lexington Ave, 33rd Fl, New York, NY 10022
212-750-9320 Fax: 212-753-5927
Web site: www.bncf.org

Cingular Wireless LLC EPAC
James Hoeberling, Treasurer
Comerica Bank, PAC Svcs, PO Box 75000, Detroit, MI 48275-2250
248-371-5562

Citigroup Inc PAC - Federal/State
Theresa A Russell, Treasurer
125 Broad St, 6th Fl, New York, NY 10004
212-291-2838
e-mail: PAC@citi.com

Citizen Action of NY Political Contribution Acct
Richard Kirsch, Executive Director
94 Central Ave, Albany, NY 12206
518-465-4600 Fax: 518-465-2890
e-mail: mail@citizenaction.org
Web site: www.citizenactionny.org

Citizens United for Ethical Government
Raymond Johnson, Treasurer
127 Quaker Hill Rd, Pawling, NY 12564
845-855-8043

Citizens for Public Broadcasting
Peter G Repas, Treasurer

Political Parties, Lobbyists & PACs

Offices and agencies appear in alphabetical order.

POLITICAL ACTION COMMITTEES

33 Elk St, Ste 200, Albany, NY 12207
518-462-1590

Citizens for Responsible Representation
Diane Hunt, Treasurer
PO Box 280202, Brooklyn, NY 11228-0202
212-816-3826

Citizens for Sports & Arts, Inc
Barbara Dillon, Treasurer
6601 Broadway, Bronx, NY 10471

Civil Service Employees' PAF
Maureen S Malone, Treasurer
143 Washington Ave, Albany, NY 12210
518-434-0191
Web site: www.csealocal1000.net

Civil Service Technical Guild PAC
Ronaldo Vega, Treasurer
32-34 34th St, Rm 600, Astoria, NY 11106
718-626-7620

Clean PAC Inc
Nora Nealis, Treasurer
252 W 29th St, New York, NY 10001
212-967-3002 Fax: 212-967-2240

Clear Channel Communications Inc PAC
Stu Olds, CEO
c/o Katz Media, 125 W 55th St, New York, NY 10019
212-424-6780 Fax: 212-424-6769
Web site: www.katz-media.com

Cmte for Action for a Responsible Electorate (CARE)
Robert J Murphy, Treasurer
c/o NYSHFA, 33 Elk St, Ste 300, Albany, NY 12207-1010
518-462-4800 Fax: 518-426-4051

Cmte for Medical Eye Care PAC
Hobart A Lerner, Treasurer
c/o 121 State St, Albany, NY 12207
716-271-7892

Cmte for Workers' Compensation Reform
Ronald Balter, Treasurer
132 Nassau St, Ste 1200, New York, NY 10038
212-732-8333 Fax: 212-962-5523

Cmte for a Proud Huntington
Irene J Midgett, Treasurer
39 Ontario St, Huntington, NY 11743
631-423-0655

Coalition of Fathers & Families NY
James Hays, Treasurer

PO Box 782, Clifton Park, NY 12065
518-383-8202

Columbus Circle Agency, Inc
Edmund J Bergassi, Treasurer
35 Portman Road, New Rochelle, NY 10801
914-637-8100

Committee for Economic Growth
Anita M Genovese, Treasurer
665 Main Street, Suite 200, Buffalo, NY 14203-1487
716-852-7100

Committee of Interns & Residents SEIU Loc 1957 Health Care Advocacy Fund (CARE)
Mark Levy, Treasurer
Cir, 520 Eighth Avenue, Suite 1200, New York, NY 10018
212-356-8100

Communication Workers of America, District 1 PAC
Robert Master, Political Coordinator
80 Pine St, 37th Fl, New York, NY 10005
212-344-2515 Fax: 212-425-2947
e-mail: rmaster@cwa-union.org

Community Mental Health PAC
Antonia M Lasicki, Treasurer
52 Dublin Dr, Niskayuna, NY 12309
518-783-9166 Fax: 518-426-0504
e-mail: toni@aclnys.org

Compac, NJ
Douglas J Pauls, Treasurer
1701 Route 70 East, Cherry Hill, NJ 08034
856-751-9000

Conservative Action Fund
Ross Brady, Treasurer
2064 84th Street, Brooklyn, NY 11214
718-265-3378

Consolidated Business Political Action Committee
Randy Mi Liu, Treasurer
3248 38th Street, #3, Astoria, NY 11103
718-956-3151

Consolidated Edison Co of NY Inc Employees' PAC
Edward J Rasmussen, Vice President & Controller
4 Irving Pl, Rm 506, New York, NY 10003
212-406-4202 Fax: 212-475-1809
e-mail: rasmussene@coned.com

Consolidated Edison, Inc. Employees' Political Action Committee (CEIPAC)
Edward J Rasmussen, Treasurer
4 Irving Place, Room 506, New York, NY 10003
212-460-4202

Construction Contractors Assn PAC
Richard O'Beirne, Treasurer

Offices and agencies appear in alphabetical order.

330 Meadow Ave, Newburgh, NY 12250
845-562-4280 Fax: 845-562-1448

Construction Industry Council - NYS PAC
Ross J Pepe, Treasurer
629 Old White Plains Rd, Tarrytown, NY 10591
914-631-6070 Fax: 914-631-5172

Consumer Advocacy PAC
Neil Reiff, Treasurer
50 E St SE, Ste 300, Washington, DC 20003
703-455-1327 Fax: 202-479-1115

Contractors, Agents, & Brokers PAC
Frank E O'Brien Jr, Treasurer
2 Valley View Drive, Albany, NY 12208
518-482-0686

Convenience PAC
James S Calvin, Treasurer
130 Washington Ave, Ste 300, Albany, NY 12210
518-432-1400 Fax: 518-432-7400
e-mail: jim@nyacs.org
Web site: www.nyacs.org

Cope 25
James Plant, Treasurer
269 Barn Swallow Road, Manorville, NY 11949
516-874-6131

Cope AFL-CIO
John J Kaczorowski, President
295 Main St, Rm 532, Buffalo, NY 14203
716-852-0375 Fax: 716-855-1802
e-mail: buffaloaflcio@aol.com

Corning Incorporated Employees PAC
Timothy J Regan, Treasurer
1300 I St NW, Ste 500, Washington, DC 20005
202-682-3200 Fax: 202-682-3130

Correction Captains Assn PAC
Peter Meringold, Treasurer
299 Broadway, Ste 1610, New York, NY 10007
212-227-4090 Fax: 212-962-4819

Correction Officers' Benevolent Assn PAC
Elias Husamudeen, Treasurer
335 Broadway, Rm 915, New York, NY 10013
212-274-8000 Fax: 212-274-8255
e-mail: cobanyc@aol.com
Web site: www.cobanyc.org

Couch White PAC
Barbara S Brenner, Treasurer

540 Broadway, PO Box 22222, Albany, NY 12201-2222
518-426-4600 Fax: 518-426-0533
e-mail: bbrenner@couchwhite.com

Council of School Supervisors & Admin, Local 1 AFSA AFL-CIO
Manfred Korman, Executive VP
16 Court St, 4th Floor, Brooklyn, NY 11241-1003
718-852-3000 Fax: 718-403-0278
e-mail: ernest@csa-nyc.org
Web site: www.csa-nyc.org

Council of Urban Investors
Taurus Richardson, Treasurer
666 Third Ave, 29th Fl, New York, NY 10017
212-455-9641 Fax: 212-455-9603

Credit Unions' PAC (CUPAC)
Eugene Gizzi, Coordinator
811 Croton St, Rome, NY 13440
315-336-7578 Fax: 315-336-7578
e-mail: governmentalaffairs@nyscul.org
Web site: www.nyscul.org

D&M P.A.C., LLC
Arthur Goldstein, Treasurer
Davidoff Malito & Hutcher LLP, 605 Third Avenue, New York, NY 10158
212-557-7200
e-mail: agg@dmlegal.com

D.R.I.V.E.-Democratic, Republican, Independent Voter Education
John C Keegel, Treasurer
25 Louisiana Avenue, NW, Washington, DC 20001
202-624-6905

DC 37 PAC
Oliver Gray, Treasurer
125 Barclay Street, Room 525, New York, NY 10007
212-815-1504 Fax: 212-815-1516
e-mail: ogray@dc37.net

Daimler Chrysler Corporation Political Support Committee-New York
Timothy P Dykstra, Treasurer
1000 Chrysler Drive, CIMS 485-09-82, Auburn Hills, MI 48326-2766
248-512-6130

Delois Brassell Political Action Committee
Robert Brassell Jr, Treasurer
PO Box 131, Greenlawn, NY 11740-0131
631-271-5028

Democracy for America-New York
Holly Webster, Treasurer

PO Box 8313, Burlington, VT 05402
802-651-3200

Democratic Governors' Assn - NY
Vacant, Treasurer
499 South Capitol St SW, Suite 422, Washington, DC 20003
202-772-5600 Fax: 202-772-5602
Web site: www.democraticgovernors.org

Democratic Rural Conference of New York State
Cynthia Emmer, Treasurer
858 Davis St, Elmira, NY 14901
607-733-2844

Detectives' Endowment COPE
Paul DiGiacomo, Treasurer
26 Thomas St, New York, NY 10007
212-587-1000 Fax: 212-732-4863
e-mail: info@nycdetectives.org
Web site: www.nycdetectives.org

Dewey Ballantine LLP Political Action Committee-New York
Andrew W Kentz, Treasurer
1775 Pennsylvania Avenue NW, Washington, DC 20006
202-862-1086

District Council 9 PAC
William O'Brien, Treasurer
45 West 14th St, New York, NY 10011
212-255-2950 Fax: 212-255-1151

Diverse New York PAC
Alfredo M Vidal, Treasurer
PO Box 7194, Albany, NY 12224-0194

Dominion PAC-NY
James W Hoeberling, Treasurer
Comerica Bank PAC Services, MC 2250, PO BOx 75000, Detroit, MI 48275-2250
248-371-7268

Drug Policy Alliance Network (SSF)
James F McCauley, Treasurer
70 West 36th Street, 16th Floor, New York, NY 10018
646-335-2262

Dynegy NY PAC
Martin W Daley, Treasurer
c/o Martin W Daley, 992 River Road, Newburgh, NY 12550
845-563-4903 Fax: 845-563-4992
e-mail: martin.w.daley@dynegy.com

EISPAC
Robert C Rosenberg, Treasurer
419 Park Ave South, Room 1403, New York, NY 10016
212-689-7744 Fax: 212-679-5576

ESMBA PAC MOR
Jonathan Pinaro, Treasurer

21 Gladstone Avenue, West Islip, NY 11725
631-661-6950

ESPAC
James R Buhrmaster, Treasurer
111 Washington Ave, Ste 203, Albany, NY 12210
518-449-0702 Fax: 518-449-0779
e-mail: info@espa.net
Web site: www.espa.net

ESSAA - PAC (Empire State Supervisors & Admin Assn)
Janet Mulvey, Treasurer
35 Park View Ave, Apt 5F, Bronxville, NY 10708
914-779-3806

EYP PAC NY
Timothy N Burditt, Treasurer
Einhorn Yaffee Prescott, PO BOx 617, Albany, NY 12201
518-431-3464

East Side Republican District Leaders Committee
Debra I Heitner, Treasurer
122 East 83rd Street, New York, NY 10028
212-517-8444

Eastman Kodak Co Employee PAC
M Celeste Amaral, Treasurer
343 State Street, Rochester, NY 14650-0914
585-724-9808
e-mail: m.celeste.amaral@kodak.com

Ecology & Environment NYS Committee for Responsible Government
Ronald L Frank, Treasurer
368 Pleasantview Drive, Lancaster, NY 14086
716-684-8060

Educational Leadership (EL) PAC
Richard J Thomas, Treasurer
8 Airport Park Blvd, Albany Airport Park, Latham, NY 12110
518-782-0600 Fax: 518-782-9552
e-mail: rthomas@saanys.org
Web site: www.saanys.org

Eleanor Roosevelt Legacy Cmte Inc
Margo Alexander, Treasurer
138 East 92nd St, New York, NY 10128
212-348-9179

Elevator Constructors Union Local No 1 Political Action Committee
Anthony J Carudo, Treasurer
47-24 27th Street, Long Island City, NY 11101
e-mail: acarudo@iueclocal1.com

Eli Lilly & Company PAC
James Davlin, Assistant Treasurer

Offices and agencies appear in alphabetical order.

Lilly Corp Ctr, Indianapolis, IN 46285
317-873-4845

Emigrant Savings Bank PAC
Daniel C Hickey, Treasurer
9 Ferris La, Bedford, NY 10506

Emily's List
Callie Fines, Treasurer
1120 Connecticut Ave NW, #1100, Washington, DC 20036
Fax: 202-326-1415
e-mail: cfines@emilyslist.org
Web site: www.emilyslist.org

Empire Dental PAC
Warren M Shaddock, DDS, Treasurer
59 Winding Creek Lane, Rochester, NY 14625-2175
716-586-3941

Empire Leadership Council
Albert Nocciolino, Treasurer
PO Box 2598, Albany, NY 12220

Empire Liquor Store Association
Steve M Glmuzina, Treasurer
54 Birchwood Drive, Williamsville, NY 14221
716-689-2569

Empire State ABC PAC
Rebecca A Meinking, Treasurer
118 Sylvan Way, Camillus, NY 13031
315-487-3266

Empire State Association of Adult Homes, Inc PAC
James Vitale, Treasurer
170 Murray Street, Auburn, NY 13021
315-253-2755

Empire State Leadership PAC
Patricia Krzesinski, Treasurer
11 Hunters Lane, Williamsville, NY 14221
716-632-4762

Empire State Pride Agenda PAC
Alan Van Capelle, Treasurer
16 West 22nd St, Second FL, New York, NY 10010
212-627-0305 Fax: 212-627-4136
e-mail: prideagenda@prideagenda.org
Web site: www.prideagenda.org

Empire State Regional Council of Carpenters Political Action Fund-NYS
Michael L Conroy, Treasurer
270 Motor Parkway, Hauppauge, NY 11788
631-952-0808

Energy Action Fund
Dennis J Bender, Treasurer

PO Box 5224, Binghamton, NY 13902-5224
607-762-4924 Fax: 607-762-8045
e-mail: djbender@nyseg.com

Energy for NY PAC
Patrick J Curran, III, Treasurer
111 Washington Ave, Ste 601, Albany, NY 12210
518-449-3440 Fax: 518-449-3446

Engineers PEF-Local 832
Ferne Fantauzzo, Treasurer
PO Box 93310, Rochester, NY 14692
716-272-9890

Engineers Voluntary Political Action Fund
Theron H Hogle, Treasurer
127 East Glen Avenue, Syracuse, NY 13205
315-492-1752

Entergy Corporation Political Committee NY (ENPAC-NY)
Darren Peters, Assistant Treasurer
425 W Capitol, Ste 40B, Little Rock, AR 72201
501-377-5820 Fax: 501-377-5822

Enterprise Rent-A-Car Company NY PAC
Raymond T Wagner, Jr, Vice President Government Affairs
600 Corporate Park Drive, St Louis, MO 63105
314-512-5000 Fax: 314-512-4897
Web site: www.enterprise.com
Rent, sell, lease vehicles

Erdman Anthony & Assoc Employees' PAC
Angelo Magagnoli, Treasurer
2165 Brighton Henrietta Rd, Rochester, NY 14623
585-427-8888 Fax: 585-427-8914

Ernst & Young Cmte for Good Government
David G Bonagura, Treasurer
Ernst & Young LLP, 395 N Service Rd, Ste 400, Melville, NY 11747
631-752-6125 Fax: 631-752-6118
e-mail: david.bonagura@ey.com
Web site: www.ey.com

Excelsior 2000
Leon Ilnitzki, Treasurer
PO BOx 2566, Syracuse, NY 13220
315-452-7825

FED PAC
Andrew Pardo, Treasurer
792 Columbus Ave, New York, NY 10025
212-866-3493

FUTURENY
Scott J Goodman, Treasurer
595 New Loudon Road, Box 263, Latham, NY 12110

Faculty Association PAC
Paul Waite, Treasurer

Offices and agencies appear in alphabetical order.

POLITICAL ACTION COMMITTEES

3111 Saunders Settlement Rd, Sanborn, NY 14132
716-614-6463
e-mail: waite@niagaracc.suny.edu

Fair PAC
John G Neidhart, Treasurer
3085 Southwestern Blvd, Orchard Park, NY 14127
716-674-5500 Fax: 716-674-5501

Family Physicians PAC
Vito F Grasso, Treasurer
260 Osborne Rd, Loudonville, NY 12211
518-489-8945 Fax: 518-489-8961
e-mail: ft@nyfafp.org
Web site: www.nyfafp.org

Federal Express New York State Political Action Committee
Robert T Molinet, Treasurer
942 South Shady Grove Road, Memphis, TN 38120
901-818-7159

Federations of Police PAC Fund
Paul D Hartman, Treasurer
PO Box 76, Briarcliff Manor, NY 10510-0076
914-941-4103 Fax: 914-941-4472

Finger Lakes Chapter NECA PAC Fund
Robert J Serafini, Treasurer
PO Box 222, 112 Pickard Dr East, Syracuse, NY 13211
315-451-4278 Fax: 315-451-1327
Web site: www.flneca.org

Finger Lakes PAC
Wilson E Mitchell, Treasurer
2729 Miller Road, Waterloo, NY 13165
315-539-8456

Fire Island Pines Property Owners Assn PAC
Jon Gilbert, Treasurer
114 W 76th St, New York, NY 10023
212-580-2024

First District Dental Society Political Action Committee
Robert B Raiber, Treasurer
6 East 43rd Street, 11th Floor, New York, NY 10017
e-mail: drrobertr@aol.com

Fleet Bank of New York PAC
Christian M Abeel, Treasurer
1125 US Route 22 West, Bridgewater, NJ 08807
908-253-4757

Ford Motor Company Civic Action Fund
James W Hoeberling, Treasurer
PO Box 75000, Detroit, MI 48275-2250
248-371-5562 Fax: 248-371-7272
e-mail: martha_k_denbaas@comerica.com

Fraternal Order of Police Empire State Lodge Inc
Ross Paternostro, Treasurer

911 Police Plaza, Hicksville, NY 11801
516-433-4455 Fax: 516-433-4473

Free PAC
Joseph J O'Hara, Treasurer
PO Box 1187, Albany, NY 12201-1187
518-445-3840

Freedom America
Douglas J Pauls, Treasurer
1701 Route 70 East, Cherry Hill, NJ 08034
856-751-9000

Friend of Cultural Institutions
Richard J Miller Jr, Treasurer
19 Dove St, Albany, NY 12210
518-426-8111 Fax: 518-426-5111

Friends of Lazio
Gerard Glass, Treasurer
72 East Main St, Babylon, NY 11702
631-321-1400 or 631-321-1400 Fax: 631-321-1491

Friends of New York Racing PAC
Timothy G Smith, Treasurer
211 East 70th Street, Apt 12B, New York, NY 10021
212-737-9098

Friends of Schumer
Steven D Goldenkranz, Treasurer
1551 East 23rd Street, Brooklyn, NY 11210-5105
718-338-8138

Friends of Upstate Labor
Kenneth L Warner, Treasurer
1163 East Ave, #6, Rochester, NY 14607
716-737-8420

Friends of the Volunteer Firefighter
Kirby Hannan, Treasurer
c/o KTHPA Inc, 107 Washington Ave, Albany, NY 12210
518-465-6550 Fax: 518-465-6557

Fund for Better Transportation PAC
James Ferrari, Treasurer
854 Livingston Avenue, Syracuse, NY 13210

GEICO NY PAC
Michael H Campbell, Treasurer
1303 Roosevelt St, Annapolis, MD 21403
410-268-3050
Automobile insurance

Gay and Lesbian Victory Fund
Brian A Johnson, Treasurer

Offices and agencies appear in alphabetical order.

1705 DeSales St NW, Ste 500, Washington, DC 20036
202-842-8679 Fax: 202-289-3863
Web site: www.victoryfund.org

General Building Contractors of NYS PAC
Jeffrey J Zogg, Treasurer
Six Airline Drive, Albany, NY 12205
518-869-2207 Fax: 518-869-0846
e-mail: jeffz@gbcnys.agc.org
Web site: www.gbcnys.agc.org

General Contractors Assn of NY PAC
Paul T Duffy, Treasurer
60 E 42nd St, Rm 3510, New York, NY 10165
212-687-3131 Fax: 212-808-5267

General Motors Corporation Political Action Committee-NY (GM PAC-NY)
Annette Guarisco, Treasurer
1660 L Street NW, Suite 400, Washington, DC 20036
202-775-5080

Glacier Creek PAC
Stephen J Siano, Treasurer
6723 Towpath Road, Box 66, Syracuse, NY 13214-0066
315-446-9120

Go PAC Dutchess
David T Warshaw, Treasurer
13 Bird Ln, Poughkeepsie, NY 12603-5001
845-462-3769

Golden Apple Business Action Committee, PAC
Marsha Gordon, Treasurer
235 Mamaroneck Ave, White Plains, NY 10605
914-948-2110 Fax: 914-948-0122
e-mail: mgordon@westchesterny.org
Web site: www.westchesterny.org

Goldman Sachs NY PAC
Judah C Sommer, Treasurer
101 Constitution Ave NW, Suite 1000 East, Washington, DC 20001
202-637-3760 Fax: 202-637-3773
e-mail: judah.sommer@gs.com
Web site: www.gs.com

Greater NY Auto Dealers' Assn Inc
Mark Schienberg, Treasurer
18-10 Whitestone Expwy, Whitestone, NY 11357
718-746-5900 Fax: 718-746-5557

Green Worlds Coalition Fund
Barbara W Bonfiglio, Treasurer
1155 21st St NW, Ste 300, Washington, DC 20036
202-659-8201 Fax: 202-659-5249

Greenberg, Traurig Political Action Committee
Clifford A Schulman, Treasurer

1221 Brickell Avenue, Miami, FL 33126
305-579-0500
Web site: www.gtlaw.com

Group Health Inc State PAC
Jeffrey L Goodwin, Treasurer
Group Health Inc, 441 Ninth Ave, New York, NY 10001
212-615-0891 Fax: 212-563-8561
e-mail: jgoodwin@ghi.com

Guardian Life PAC
John R Hurley, Treasurer
c/o Guardian Life Insurance, 7 Hanover Square, PO Box 300975, New York, NY 10004
212-598-8854
e-mail: jrhurley@glic.com

HBA of CNY Local Build PAC
Robert F Tomeny, Treasurer
3675 James Street, Syracuse, NY 13206
315-463-6261 Fax: 315-463-6263
e-mail: hba@hbaofcny.com
Web site: www.hbaofcny.com

HIC PAC
Mark D Morris, Treasurer
25 Pinecrest Dr, Niskayuna, NY 12309-1641
518-382-1581

HPA PAC
Leslie Moran, Treasurer
90 State Street, Suite 825, Albany, NY 12207-1719
518-462-2293

HSBC North America, Inc PAC (H-PAC)
Janet St Amand, Treasurer
1401 I St, NW, Ste 520, Washington, DC 20005
202-466-3561 Fax: 202-466-3583

HUBPAC Political Action Committee
Michael A Schiavone, Treasurer
130 Woodcrest Drive, Hopewll JCT, NY 12533
845-221-1653

Haitian-American Association for Political Action
Pierre M Michel, Treasurer
PO Box 300975, Brooklyn, NY 11230
718-915-7098

Harris Beach Political Committee
William H Kedley, Treasurer
99 Garnsey Road, Pittsford, NY 14534
585-419-8904

Hartford Advocates Fund (The)
Robert J Price, Treasurer

Offices and agencies appear in alphabetical order.

POLITICAL ACTION COMMITTEES

Hartford Plaza, Hartford, CT 6115
860-547-8495
e-mail: robert.price@thehartford.com

Health Access Affiliates Good Government Fund
David K Smith, Treasurer
8735 Henderson Road, Ren 2, Tampa, FL 33634
800-960-2530

Health Care Providers' PAC
James Dwyer, Treasurer
99 troy Rd, Ste 200, East Greenbush, NY 12061
518-463-1118 Fax: 518-463-1606
e-mail: hcp@nyshcp.org
Web site: www.nyshcp.org

Healthcare Assn of NYS PAC (HANYS PAC)
Steven Kroll, Treasurer
HANYS PAC, One Empire Drive, Rensselaer, NY 12144
518-431-7600 Fax: 518-431-7915
e-mail: skroll@hanys.org
Web site: www.hanys.org

Healthone PAC, Inc
Yves-Richard Blanc, Treasurer
210 Linden Blvd, 3rd Fl Ste, Brooklyn, NY 11226
718-282-3000 Fax: 718-282-8565
e-mail: info@healthonepac.com

Healthy Kids NY
Gina Cioffi, Treasurer
80 Broad Street, 17th Floor, New York, NY 10004
317-680-2938

Healthy New York
Kathleen M Dougan, Treasurer
C/O Healthy New York PAC, 360 W 31st Street, Suite 303, New York, NY 10001
212-871-0310

Hearing Healthcare Alliance of NY PAC
Barbara J Ahern, Treasurer
1 Commerce Plz, Ste 400, Albany, NY 12210-2823
518-463-0723

Hellenic American PAC - State
Hercules Argyriou, Treasurer
1217 83rd St, Brooklyn, NY 11228
718-759-1802
e-mail: jacny@aol.com

Hempstead PBA PAC
Francis McNamee, Treasurer
PO Box 41, Hempstead, NY 11551
516-483-6200
e-mail: hemppba@aol.com

High-Need Hospital PAC Inc
Barbara King, Treasurer

12 Stuyvesant Oval, Apt 9A, New York, NY 10009
212-674-6122

HillPAC-NY
Janice Enright, Treasurer
The Ickes & Enright Group, 1300 Connecticut Ave #600, Washington, DC 20036
202-887-6726 Fax: 202-223-0358

Holland & Knight Committee for Responsible Gov't (The)
James H Power, Treasurer
Holland & Knight, LLP, 195 Broadway, New York, NY 10007-3189
212-513-3494 Fax: 212-395-9010
e-mail: jhpower@hklaw.com
Web site: www.hklaw.com

Hotel Assn of NYC Inc PAC
Xavier S Lividini, Treasurer
320 Park Ave S, 22nd Fl, New York, NY 10022-6838
212-754-6700 Fax: 212-754-0243
Web site: www.hanyc.org

Hotel Employees Restaurant Int'l Union Tip Edu Fund
John W Wilhelm, Treasurer
1219 - 28th St NW, Washington, DC 20007
202-393-4373 Fax: 202-333-0468
e-mail: hereunion@hereunion.org

Hudson Valley Bank PAC
Stephen R Brown, Treasurer
51 Pondfield Road, Bronxville, NY 10708
914-771-3212 Fax: 914-961-7378

Hudson Valley Builders PAC
Michael Meyers, Treasurer
1161 Little Britain Road, New Windsor, NY 12553
845-567-6600 Fax: 845-562-1166

Hudson Valley Chapter, Nat'l Electrical Contractors Assn (NECA), PAC
Salvatore J DiFede, Treasurer
375 Route 32, Central Valley, NY 10917
845-928-3575 Fax: 845-928-3581
e-mail: hudneca@frontiernet.net
Web site: www.electricnewyork.org

Hudson Valley Citizens for Change
Cathleen Parise, Treasurer
9 Scott Lane, Lagrangeville, NY 12540
845-227-5049

Huntington Chamber Committee for Better Gov't
William R Bohn II, Treasurer
2 Sherwood Drive, Huntington, NY 11743
631-367-2255

Hunts Point Produce Market Redevelopment PAC
Jeffrey B Haas, Treasurer

Henry Haas, Inc, 464 New York City Terminal Market, Bronx, NY 10474
718-378-2550

I Love Good Government
Tarky Lombardi, III, Treasurer
5213 Hook Circle, Jamesville, NY 13078
315-466-0812

I.U.O.E. Local 15 PAC
Brian S Kelly, Treasurer
265 West 14th Street, Ste 505, New York, NY 10011
212-929-5327 Fax: 212-206-0357

IBEW Local Union #1249 PAC
Harry D Saville, Treasurer
6518 Fremont Rd, PO Box 277, East Syracuse, NY 13057
315-656-7253 Fax: 315-656-7579

IBEW Local Union #237 Community Action Program
Darren P Aderman, Treasurer
7821 Porter Rd, Niagara Falls, NY 14304
716-298-5762 Fax: 716-297-8471
e-mail: ibew237@yahoo.com

IBEW Local Union 363 PAC
Joseph N Maraia, Treasurer
9 Johnson Dr, New City, NY 10956
914-634-4601 Fax: 845-634-4924

ING America Insurance Holdings Inc PAC (ING NY PAC)
John R Obolchoz Jr, Treasurer
PO Box 105006, Powers Ferry Rd NW, Atlanta, GA 30348-5006
804-227-2276

IUOE Local 106 Voluntary PAF
Daniel J McGraw, II, Treasurer
1284 Central Ave, Albany, NY 12205
518-453-6518 Fax: 518-453-6549
e-mail: mail@iuoelocal106.org
Web site: www.iuoelocal106.org

IUOE Local 14-14B Voluntary PAC
Edloin L Christian, President
141-57 Northern Blvd, Flushing, NY 11354
718-939-0600 Fax: 718-939-3131

IUOE Local 17 PAC
Mark N Kirsch, Treasurer
150 North America Dr, West Seneca, NY 14224
716-627-2648 Fax: 716-627-2649
Web site: www.iuoe17.org

IUOE Local 463 State & Local PAC & PEF
Paul McCollum, Treasurer

3365 Ridge Rd, Ransomville, NY 14131
716-434-3327 Fax: 716-434-2160
e-mail: iuoe463diane@adlphia.net
Web site: www.iuoe463.org

IUOE Local 825 Political Action & Education Cmte
Joseph Whittles, Political Action Director
65 Springfield Ave, Springfield, NJ 7081
973-921-1900 Fax: 973-921-2918
e-mail: markl@iuoe825.org

Independent Agents PAC
Kathleen A Weinheimer, Treasurer
5784 Widewaters Pkwy, 1st Fl, Dewitt, NY 13214
800-962-7950
e-mail: kweinheimer@iiaany.org
Web site: www.iiaany.org

Independent Health Assn Inc Political Alliance
Sidney N Weiss, Treasurer
2495 Kensington Ave, Buffalo, NY 14226
716-839-2024 Fax: 716-839-3962

Independent Oil and Gas Association of NY, Inc Political Action Committee
R Stephan Gollaher, Treasurer
828 Four Mile Road, Gollaher Oil Bldg, Allegany, NY 14706
716-372-5354

Independent Petroleum Mktrs of NY PAC
Robert W Reid, Treasurer
41 Hawthorne Ave, Albany, NY 12203-2113
518-438-7104 Fax: 518-465-0273

Independent Power Producers of NY PAC
Roger Kelley, Treasurer
8159 Golden Oak Cir, Williamsville, NY 14221
716-689-6960 Fax: 716-436-1000
e-mail: rogerkk@aol.com
Web site: www.ippny.org

Insurance Brokers' Assn of NY PAC
Donald Privett, Treasurer
25 Chamberlain St, PO Box 997, Glenmont, NY 12077
212-962-7771 Fax: 877-644-0422
e-mail: ibany@global2000.net

Int'l Longshoremen's Assn AFL-CIO COPE
Robert E Gleason, Treasurer
17 Battery Place, New York, NY 10004
212-425-1200 Fax: 212-425-2928

Intercounty Health Facilities Assn PAC
Theresa M Santmann, Treasurer
66 Cedar Lane, Babylon, NY 11702
631-422-1330 Fax: 631-581-6018

Intermagnetics State PAC
Arthur P Kazanjian, Treasurer

Political Parties, Lobbyists & PACs

Offices and agencies appear in alphabetical order.

C/O Hinman Straub PC, 121 State Street, Albany, NY 12207
518-346-1414

International Paper Political Action Committee
John C Runyan, Treasurer
1101 Pennsylvania Avenue NW, Washington, DC 20004
202-628-1223

International Union of Painters and Allied Trades Legislative & Educational Committee
George Galis, Treasurer
1750 New York Avenue NW, Washington, DC 20006
202-637-0725

International Union of operating Engineers Local 891 PAC
Gary A Chiappetta, Treasurer
626 Bond Ct, North Merrick, NY 11566
516-538-6406

Iron Workers' Local 12 PAF
Gary M Simmons, Treasurer
900 Lark Drive, Albany, NY 12207
518-436-1294 Fax: 518-436-6781
e-mail: iron12@msn.com

Iron Workers' Local 40 Voluntary COPE
Edward W Walsh, Treasurer
451 Park Ave S, New York, NY 10016
212-889-1320 Fax: 212-779-3267

Iron Workers' Local 60 PAC
Gary E Robb, Treasurer
500 West Genesee St, Syracuse, NY 13204
315-471-3413 Fax: 315-478-2630
e-mail: iwl60@verizon.net

Ironworkers Political Action League
John Gans, Director
1750 New York Ave NW, Suite 400, Washington, DC 20006
202-383-4880 Fax: 202-347-3569
Web site: www.ironworkers.org

Issues Mobilization Fund - Greater Rochester
Robert Migioratti, Treasurer
930 East Avenue, Rochester, NY 14607
585-292-5000 Fax: 585-292-5008

J P Morgan Chase & Co State & Federal PAC
Bridget Lawless, Treasurer
270 Park Ave, 29th Fl, New York, NY 10017
212-270-0774 Fax: 646-534-2102
e-mail: bridget.lawless@jpmchase.com

JBDS NYS PAC
Margaret J O'Brien, Treasurer
633 Third Avenue, New York, NY 10017
212-850-0604

JOE-PAC NON-Federal
Scott G Kaufmann, Treasurer

84-54 Grand Avenue, Elmhurst, NY 11373

JY Trans PAC
William W Sherwood, Jr, Treasurer
201 Edgewater St, Staten Island, NY 10305
718-448-3900

Johnson & Johnson Employees' Good Gov't Fund PAC
Richard W Lloyd, Treasurer
1 Johnson & Johnson Plz, New Brunswick, NJ 8933
732-524-3726 Fax: 732-524-3005
e-mail: jsosa@corus.jnj.com

Keycorp PAC-NY
Erskine E Cade, Treasurer
127 Public Sq, Cleveland, OH 44114
216-689-4486 Fax: 216-689-8710
e-mail: erskine_cade@keybank.com

Keyspan Energy State PAC (KEYSPAC)
Edward A.T. Carr, Treasurer
175 E Old Country Road, Hicksville, NY 11801
516-545-4405 Fax: 516-545-5065
e-mail: ecarr@keyspanenergy.com

Keyspan Services PAC
Joseph Witt, Treasurer
Keyspan Service PAC, Riverfront Plaza, PO Box 200003, Newark, NJ 07102
732-560-9700

Kings County C-PAC
Harvey S Rossel, Treasurer
790 Carroll St, Brooklyn, NY 11215-1404
718-638-4626 Fax: 718-638-5036

KleinPAC
Dominick Calderon, Treasurer
744 Lydis Ave, Bronx, NY 10462
718-319-1400 Fax: 718-239-0716

LCR New York Political Action Committee
Robert A Arko, Treasurer
Radio City Station, PO Box 2321, New York, NY 10101
845-365-8752

Laborers' Int'l Union of North America Local 214 PAF
William F Shannon, Jr, Treasurer
23 Mitchell St, Oswego, NY 13126
315-343-7661

Laborers' Local 103 PAF Cmte
Donald Calabrese, Treasurer
PO Box 571, Geneva, NY 14456
315-539-4220 Fax: 315-539-4150

Laborers' Local 17 PAC
Joseph Libonati, Treasurer

Offices and agencies appear in alphabetical order.

PO Box 202, Marlboro, NY 12542
914-236-4747 Fax: 845-565-3099
e-mail: tdiorio555@aol.com

Laborers' Local Union 190 PAC
Anthony M Fresina, Treasurer
668 Wemple Rd, PO Box 339, Glenmont, NY 12077
518-465-1254 Fax: 518-465-1257

Land Surveyors PAC
John A Robinson, Treasurer
146 Washington Avenue, Albany, NY 12210
518-432-4046
e-mail: j24601@aol.com

Latina Political Action Committee
Alexandra Soriano-Tavera, Treasurer
692 Larch Avenue, Teaneck, NJ 07666
201-530-0879

Latino PAC
Saul A Maneiro, Treasurer
35 Conklin Ave, Rochester, NY 14609
585-482-1865
e-mail: latinopac@yahoogroups.com

Lawyers' PAC (LAWPAC)
Arthur M Luxenberg, Treasurer
180 Maiden Ln, New York, NY 10038
212-558-5613 Fax: 212-344-5465
Web site: www.weitzlux.com

LeBoeuf Lamb Greene & MacRae PAC
Christopher Tsakiris, Treasurer
125 W 55th St, New York, NY 10019
212-424-8187 Fax: 212-424-8500

Liberty Mutual Insurance Co PAC - NY
Paul Mattera, Secretary
175 Berkeley St, Boston, MA 02117
617-357-9500

Life Insurance Council of NY PAC (LICONY)
Diane D Stuto, Treasurer
111 Washington Ave, Suite 300, Albany, NY 12210
518-436-8417 Fax: 518-436-0226
e-mail: dstuto@licony.org
Web site: www.licony.org

Life of the Party
Philip Blitz, Treasurer
404 Oakland Ave, Staten Island, NY 10310
718-273-1935

Local #30 PAC
Leslie Fletcher, Treasurer
213 Ontario Pl, Liverpool, NY 13088
315-457-2304 Fax: 315-475-4042

Local #41 Int'l Brotherhood of Electrical Workers' PAC
John Pavlovic, Treasurer

S-3546 California Rd, Orchard Park, NY 14127
716-662-6111 Fax: 716-662-9644

Local 137 PEF
Salvatore Santamorena, Treasurer
50 Finnerty Place, Putnam Valley, NY 10579
845-762-1268 Fax: 845-762-0524

Local 138, 138A & 138B International Union of Operating Engineers
Kenneth Huber, Treasurer
C/O Local 138, 138A & 138B Intl Union, PO Box 206, Farmingdale, NY 11735-0206
631-694-2480

Local 147 PAF
Richard Fitzsimmons, Treasurer
32 Clarewood Drive, Hastings, NY 10706
914-478-4803

Local 1814 Intl Longshoremens Assn AFL-CIO PA & ED Fund
Anthony Graffino, Treasurer
70 - 20th St, Brooklyn, NY 11232
718-499-9600 Fax: 718-499-9626

Local 1814 Intl Longshoremens Assn AFL-CIO PA & ED Fund
Anthony Graffino, Treasurer
70 20th Street, Brooklyn, NY 11232
718-499-9600

Local 23-25, Unite State & Local Campaign Cmte
Kevin McCann, Treasurer
1 Chestnut Ct, Monroe Twp, NJ 8831
732-521-9251

Local 237 I.B.T. PAC
Gregory Floyd, Treasurer
216 West 14th Street, New York, NY 10011
212-924-2000

Local 30 IUOE PAC
John Ahern, Treasurer
115-06 Myrtle Ave, Richmond Hill, NY 11418
718-847-8484
Web site: www.iuoe30.org

Local 32BJ SEIU NY/NJ American Dream Fund
Hector J Figueroa, Treasurer
Local 32BJ SEIU, 101 Ave of Americas, New York, NY 10013
212-388-3851 Fax: 212-388-3210
e-mail: hfigueroa@seiu32bj.org

Local 420 Political Action Committee
Peter Da Leon, Treasurer
125 Barclay Street, New York, NY 10007
212-815-1227

Local 73 Plumbers and Steamfitters PAC Fund
DAvid J Decaire, Treasurer

Offices and agencies appear in alphabetical order.

555

PO Box 911, Oswego, NY 13126
315-343-4037

Local Union #373 UA Political Action Fund
Werner J Koby, Treasurer
PO Box 58, 76 Pleasant Hill Rd, Mountainville, NY 10953
845-534-1050 Fax: 845-534-1053

Log Cabin Republicans Hudson Valley PAC
Robert A Arko, Treasurer
Martine Station, PO Box 8263, White Plains, NY 10602
914-206-4059

Long Island Assn Action Cmte
Mitchell H Palley, Assistant Treasurer
300 Broadhollow Road, Melville, NY 11747
631-493-3002
e-mail: mpally@longislandassociation.org
Web site: www.longislandassociation.org

Long Island Chapter/American Institute of Architects LIC (AIA PAC)
Michael W Spinelli, Treasurer
AIA Long Island, 499 Sericato Trnpk, Suite 101, Mineola, NY 11051
516-294-0971 Fax: 516-294-0973

Long Island Contractors Assn PAC Inc
Robert Carlino, Treasurer
2805 Veterans Memorial Hwy, Ronkonkoma, NY 11779
631-467-4230 Fax: 631-467-4211

Long Island Federation of Labor AFL-CIO
Vacant, President
1111 Route 110, Ste 320, Farmingdale, NY 11735
631-396-1170 Fax: 631-396-1174
Web site: www.lilabor.org

Long Island Gasoline Retailers' Assn PAC
Robert Santasiero, Treasurer
270 Spagnoli Road, Melville, NY 11747
631-277-9490 Fax: 631-859-0145
e-mail: steve@sdautorepire.com

Lower Manhattan Alliance for Political Action
Arthur Z Schwartz, Treasurer
269 West 11th Street, New York, NY 10014
212-741-0866

Lynbrook P.B.A. PAC
Harold Comastri, Treasurer
PO BOx 509, Lynbrook, NY 11563
516-599-3300

MAC PAC
Barbara Zaron, President

NYS Mgmt Conf Empl, 3 Washington Sq, Albany, NY 12205-5523
518-456-5241 Fax: 518-456-3838
e-mail: omce@aol.com
Web site: www.nysomce.org

MLCA PAC
Kenneth Theobalds, Treasurer
909 Webster Ave, New Rochelle, NY 10804
914-654-0868

MLMICPAC
Stanley L Grossman, Treasurer
82 Susan Dr, Newburgh, NY 12550-1409
845-562-2067 Fax: 845-562-3870
e-mail: slgrossman@verizon.net

Maloney Committee NYS PAC
Andrew R Tulloch, Treasurer
C/O Lowenstein Sandler PC, 1251 Avenue of the Americas, 18th Floor, New York, NY 10020
646-414-6792

Manufactured Housing PAC
Nancy P Geer, Treasurer
35 Commerce Ave, Albany, NY 12206-2081
518-435-9858 or 800-721-4663 Fax: 518-435-9839
e-mail: info@nymha.com
Web site: www.nymha.org

Manufacturers & Traders Trust Company PAC
Marlene Tomaselli, Treasurer
One M&T Plaza, 19th Floor, Buffalo, NY 14203
716-842-5657

Marx PAC
David M Stackrow, Treasurer
314 Hoosick St, Troy, NY 12180
518-274-9081 Fax: 518-274-9085

Mason Tenders' District Council of Greater NY PAC
Kris Kohler, Administrative Director
c/o MTDCPAC, 266 West 37th St, 7th Fl, New York, NY 10018
212-452-9552 Fax: 212-452-9599
e-mail: mtdcpac@juno.com
Web site: www.masontenders.org

Medical Society of the State of New York PAC
Anthony A Clemendor, Treasurer
125 East 80th St, New York, NY 10021
212-628-1210 Fax: 212-861-1140
e-mail: aclemendor@aol.com

MetLife Ins Co Political Fund B
Michael J Sheridan, Treasurer
27-01 Queens Plaza North, 4th Floor, Long Island City, NY 11101
212-578-8005 Fax: 212-578-8869
e-mail: msheridan@metlife.com
Web site: www.metlife.com

Metalic Lathers Local 46 PAC
Robert A Ledwith, Treasurer

Offices and agencies appear in alphabetical order.

1322 Third Ave, New York, NY 10021
212-928-9141

Metlife Inc Emplyees' Political Participation Fund A
Timothy J Ring, Treasurer
27-01 Queens Plaza North, Area 4-D, Long Island City, NY 11101
212-578-2640

Metret PAC, Inc
Donald Halperin, Treasurer
Kantor Davidoff, 51 E. 42nd St, New York, NY 10017
212-682-8383 Fax: 212-949-5206
e-mail: halperin@kantorlawonline.com

Metropolitan Garage Owners Assn PAC
Joel Stahl, Treasurer
299 Broadway, New York, NY 10007
212-406-3590 Fax: 212-732-4981
e-mail: metpkg@rcn.com

Metropolitan Package Store, Inc Assoc PAF
William L McDevitt, Treasurer
6 Xavier Drive, Yonkers, NY 10704-1392
914-423-4500

Meyer, Suozzi, English & Klein, PC - Political Acct
Patricia Cairo, Treasurer
1505 Kellum Pl, Mineola, NY 11501
516-741-6565 Fax: 516-741-6706

Mid Island Democratic PAC (MIDPAC)
Kristy Cusick, Treasurer
937 Victory Blvd, Apt 4G, Staten Island, NY 10301
718-442-3219

Millenia Committee
Jackie D Burns, Treasurer
49 North Street, Marcellus, NY 13108
315-673-1932

Minority & Women Business Advocacy PAC
Cynthia Cruickshank, Treasurer
160 Broadway, Suite 905, New York, NY 10038
718-531-3599

Mirant Corporation State Political Action committee Inc-NY
Greg Weber, Treasurer
1155 Perimeter Center West, Atlanta, GA 30338-5416
678-579-6530

Mohawk Valley Chamber PAC
Margaret E Francis, Treasurer
Mohawk Valley Chamber of Commerce, 520 Seneca Street, Third Floor, Utica, NY 13502
315-724-3151

Monument Industry PAC
John S Wallenstein, Treasurer

220 Old Country Rd, Mineola, NY 11501
516-742-5600 Fax: 516-742-5040
e-mail: johnlawli@aol.com

Morris & McVeigh NYS PAC
Richard J Miller Jr, Treasurer
19 Dove Street, Albany, NY 12210
518-426-8111

Mountaintop Democratic Club
William Haltermann Jr, Treasurer
PO Box 494, 299 Nauvoo Road, Windham, NY 12496
518-734-5481

Movers & Warehousemen Political Action Committee
James Gomiela, Treasurer
757 Chenango Street, Binghamton, NY 13901
607-723-1023

NARAL/Pro/Choice Multicandidate PAC
Barbara Klar, Political Director
427 Broadway, 3rd Flr, New York, NY 10013
212-343-0114 Fax: 212-343-0119
e-mail: info@prochoiceny.org
Web site: www.prochoiceny.org

NASW-NYS Political Action Committee
Milagros Dueno, Treasurer
NASW-NYC, 188 Washington Avenue, Albany, NY 12210
518-463-4741

NATPAC 2000
Warren E O'Hearn, Treasurer
15602 Northgate Drive, Montclair, VA 22026-1832

NBT PAC State Fund
Brian J Page, Treasurer
52 South Broad St, Norwich, NY 13815
607-337-6258 Fax: 607-337-6294
e-mail: bpage@nbtbci.com

NEA of New York PAC
William R Ninness, Treasurer
217 Lark Street, Albany, NY 12210
518-462-6451 Fax: 716-835-2811

NIC-PAC
Steven A Lessmann, Treasurer
NIC Holding, 25 Melville Park Rd, POB 2937, Melville, NY 11747
631-753-4250

NLOA-PAC
Charles Castro, Treasurer
30-71 49th Street, Astoria, NY 11103
866-579-5809
Web site: www.nloaus.org

NOW Alliance PAC of Long Island, Inc
Gail Segui, Treasurer

Offices and agencies appear in alphabetical order.

2305 Nicole Drive, Port Jefferson, NY 11776
631-476-8154

NRA Political Victory Fund
Mary R Adkins, Treasurer
11250 Waples Mill Rd, Ste 5027, Fairfax, VA 22030
703-267-1152

NRG New York PAC
Jennifer A Gregson, Treasurer
3500 River Road, Tonawanda, NY 14150
716-879-3890 Fax: 716-879-3950

NY Anesthesiologists PAC
David S Bronheim, Treasurer
c/o NYSSA, 85 Fifth Ave, 8th Fl, New York, NY 10003
212-867-7140 Fax: 212-867-7153

NY Chiropractic PAC
Margaret H Savitzky, Treasurer
110-21 73 Rd, Apt 41, Forest Hills, NY 11375
718-261-3911

NY Coca Cola Enterprise EMP NonPartisan Cmte for Good Govt
Laura B Asman, Treasurer
PO Box 723040, Atlanta, GA 31139
770-989-3023

NY Film PAC
Thomas Igner, Jr, Treasurer
MPAA, 15503 Ventura Blvd, Encino, CA 91436
818-887-4440 Fax: 818-382-1795
e-mail: tom_igner@mpaa.org

NY Independent Bankers' PAC
William Y Crowell, Treasurer
NY Independent Bankers PAC, 125 State St, Albany, NY 12207-1622
518-436-4646 Fax: 518-436-4648

NY Insurance Assn Inc PAC
Bernard N Bourdeau, Treasurer
130 Washington Ave, Albany, NY 12210
518-237-5789 Fax: 518-432-4220
e-mail: bbourdeau@nyia.org
Web site: www.nyia.org

NY Physical Therapy PAC
Gregory S Hullstrung, Treasurer
5 Palisades Dr, Ste 330, Albany, NY 12205
518-459-4499

NY Podiatry PAC
Leonard Thaler, Treasurer

1255 Fifth Ave, New York, NY 10029
212-996-4400 Fax: 212-996-4389
e-mail: nyspma@nyspma.org
Web site: www.nyspma.org

NY Propane PAC
Thomas Heslop, Treasurer
c/o Amos Post Inc, PO Box 351, Catskill, NY 12414
518-943-3500 Fax: 518-943-7090

NY Region 9A UAW PAC Cmte
Robert Madore, Treasurer
111 South Rd, Farmington, CT 06032-2560
860-674-0143 Fax: 860-674-1164
e-mail: bmador@uaw.net

NY School Bus Operators for Effective Gov't
John J Corrado, Treasurer
10 Moffit Blvd, Bayshore, NY 11706
631-665-3210 Fax: 631-665-9128

NYAHSA PAC
Carl S Young, Treasurer
150 State Street, Suite 301, Albany, NY 12207
Web site: www.nyahsa.org

NYC Americans for Democratic Action
Stephen R Parker, Treasurer
275 7th Avenue, 15th Fl, New York, NY 10001-0001
212-367-8883 Fax: 212-367-8884
e-mail: nycada@earthlink.net
Web site: www.nycada.com

NYC Columbus Circle PAC
George D Skinner, Treasurer
35 Portman Road, New Rochelle, NY 10801
914-576-9300

NYC District Council of Carpenters' PAC
Peter Thomassen, President
395 Hudson Street, 9th Fl, New York, NY 10014
212-366-7500 Fax: 212-675-3118
Web site: www.nycdistrictcouncil.com

NYMTA Boat PAC
Walter Werner, Treasurer
194 B Park Avenue, Suite B, Amityville, NY 11701
631-691-7050
e-mail: dwall@nymta.com

NYNHP-PAC
Shauneen McNally, Treasurer
c/o Weingarten & Reid, 1 Commerce Plz, #1103, Albany, NY 12210
518-465-9273 Fax: 518-427-7792

NYPD Lieutenants Benevolent Association PAC
Peter Martin, Treasurer

Offices and agencies appear in alphabetical order.

30 Carman Avenue, East Rockaway, NY 11518
516-593-2275

NYPD Superior Officers Assn, Retired PAC
John J Coughlin, Treasurer
124 Wright Ave, Deer Park, NY 11729
631-667-1829

NYS AFL-CIO COPE
Paul F Cole, Treasurer
100 South Swan St, Albany, NY 12210
518-436-8516 Fax: 518-462-1824
e-mail: pcole@nysaflcio.org
Web site: www.nysaflcio.org

NYS Architects PAC
Barbara J Rodriguez, Treasurer
407 3rd St, Troy, NY 12180
518-449-3334 Fax: 518-426-8176
e-mail: aianys@aianys.org
Web site: www.aianys.org

NYS Assn of Tobacco & Candy Distributors Inc
Arthur H Katz, Treasurer
211 E 43rd Street, Ste 1101, New York, NY 10017
212-682-3576 Fax: 212-867-7844
e-mail: arthurkatz@covad.net

NYS Association of PBAs
Patrick Hall, Treasurer
23 Reynolds Rd, Glen Cove, NY 11542
516-609-2732 Fax: 516-676-3956

NYS Association of Service Stations & Repair Shops
Jordan Weine, Treasurer
12 Walker Way, Albany, NY 12205-4946
518-452-1979

NYS Automatic Vending Association PAC
Robert Desormeau, Treasurer
421 Old Niskayuna Road, Latham, NY 12110
518-785-4569

NYS BPW/PAC
Lucretia D Hunt, Treasurer
903 Bleecker St, Utica, NY 13501
315-732-1032 Fax: 315-738-7218

NYS Bowling Proprietors Assn PAC
Marvin Sontz, Treasurer
4 Bethlehem Ct, Elsmere, NY 12054
518-378-7148

NYS Broadcasters Association
Joseph A Reilly, Treasurer
1805 Western Avenue, Albany, NY 12203
518-456-8888

NYS Car Wash PAC
Michael A Benmosche, Treasurer

26 Valdepenas Lane, Clifton Park, NY 12065
518-371-6542
e-mail: mikebenmosche@manginsurance.com

NYS Cemeteries PAC
Frank Giglio, Treasurer
PO Box 780004, Maspeth, NY 11378
718-326-1280

NYS Chapter AGC PAC
A J Castelbuono, Treasurer
10 Airline Dr, Ste 203, Albany, NY 12205-1025
518-456-1134 Fax: 518-456-1198
e-mail: ajcastel@agcnys.org
Web site: www.agcnys.org

NYS Clinical Laboratory Assn PAC
Thomas R Rafalsky, Treasurer
62 William St, 2nd Fl, New York, NY 10005
212-664-7999 Fax: 212-248-3008
e-mail: info@nyscla.com
Web site: www.nyscla.com

NYS Committee for the Advancement of Mental Health Therapy
James J Carr, Treasurer
388 Broadway, 4th Fl, Albany, NY 12207
518-434-8830 Fax: 518-434-0072

NYS Conference of the IUOE Pol Action Acct
William J McSpedon, Treasurer
100 South Swan St, Albany, NY 12210
518-463-7551 Fax: 518-463-7556
e-mail: nysconiuoe@aol.com

NYS Council of Physiotherapists PAC
Allen Bistrong, Treasurer
142 Joralemm Street, Brooklyn, NY 11201
Web site: www.nycouncilpt.org

NYS Dairy Foods PAC
Bruce W Krupke, Treasurer
201 S Main St, Ste 302, North Syracuse, NY 13212-3105
315-452-6455 Fax: 315-452-1643
e-mail: bkrupke@nysdfi.org
Web site: www.nysdfi.org

NYS Food Industry PAC
James T Rogers, Treasurer
50 Edison Place, Niskayuna, NY 12309
518-372-1764 Fax: 518-434-9962
e-mail: jim@fiany.com
Web site: www.fiany.com

NYS Funeral Directors Association PAC
Bonie L Tippy, Treasurer

Offices and agencies appear in alphabetical order.

426 New Karner Road, Albany, NY 12205
518-452-8230 Fax: 518-452-8667
e-mail: info@nysfda.org
Web site: www.nysfda.org

NYS Hospitality & Tourism Assn PAC
Daniel C Murphy, Treasurer
80 Wolf Rd, Albany, NY 12205
518-465-2300 Fax: 518-465-4025
Web site: www.nyshta.org

NYS Laborers' PAC
Charles Coleman, Treasurer
215 Old Nyack Tpke, Chestnut Ridge, NY 10977
845-425-5073
e-mail: info@nysliuna
Web site: www.nysliuna.org

NYS Nurses Assn PAC
Audrey C Ludmer, Treasurer
NYS Nurses Assn - Attn: P Phillips, 11 Cornell Rd, Latham, NY
12110
518-782-9400 Fax: 518-782-9530
Web site: www.nysna.org

NYS Occupational Therapy PAC
Peggy A Lounsbury, Treasurer
119 Washington Avenue, Albany, NY 12210
518-583-8371

NYS Optometric Assn PAC
Jan S Dorman, Treasurer
119 Washington Ave, Albany, NY 12210
518-449-7300 Fax: 518-432-5902
e-mail: nysoa2020@aol.com
Web site: www.nysoa.org

NYS Pest Control Assn PAC
Charles Frommer, Treasurer
PO Box 405, Roslyn, NY 11576
516-487-4511 Fax: 516-626-9337

NYS Pest Management Association PAC
Charles Frommer, Treasurer
22 Roosevelt Avenue, Box 405, Roslyn, NY 11576
516-676-0149

NYS Plumbing, Heating & Cooling Contractors PAC
Mark Whalen, Treasurer
17 S Lynn St, Warwick, NY 10990
800-933-9040 Fax: 845-986-4050

NYS Psychiatric PAC Inc
Seeth Vivek, Treasurer
Psych Assn, 100 Quentin Roosevelt Blvd, Garden City, NY 11530
516-542-0077 Fax: 516-542-0094

NYS Public Employees' Federation PAC
Jane Hallum, Treasurer

PO Box 12414, Albany, NY 12212-2414
518-785-1900 Fax: 518-783-1117
e-mail: jhallum@pef.org
Web site: www.pef.org

NYS Radiologists PAC
Philip C Pinsky, Treasurer
c/o Pinsky & Pinsky, PC, 5790 Widewaters Pwky, PO Box 250,
Syracuse, NY 13214-0250
315-446-2384 Fax: 315-446-3016
e-mail: pinskyskan@aol.com

NYS Restaurant Assc PAC
Rick J Sampson, President
455 New Karner Rd, Albany, NY 12205
518-452-4222 Fax: 518-452-4497
e-mail: ricks@nysra.org
Web site: www.nysra.org

NYS Right to Life PAC
Thomas J Balch, Treasurer
41 State Street, M-100, Albany, NY 12207
518-434-1293

NYS Sheriffs' Good Government Fund
Charles J Gallo, Director
27 Elk St, Albany, NY 12207
518-434-9091 Fax: 518-434-9093
e-mail: cgallo@nysheriffs.org

NYS Society CPA PAC Inc
Louis Grumet, Treasurer
3 Park Ave, 18th Fl, New York, NY 10016-5991
212-719-8301 Fax: 212-719-3364

NYS Society for Clinical Social Workers PAC
Marsha Wineburgh, Treasurer
263 West end Ave, #1F, New York, NY 10023
212-595-6518

NYS Speech-Language-Hearing Assn Inc - COMPAC
Salvatore Gruttadauria, Executive Director
2 Northway Lane, Latham, NY 12110-4809
518-786-0947 Fax: 518-786-9126
e-mail: dan@nysslha.org
Web site: www.nysslha.org

NYS Telecommunications PAC
Richard W Moneymaker, Treasurer
c/o NY State Telephone Assn Inc, 100 State St, Albany, NY 12207
518-443-2700 Fax: 518-443-2810
e-mail: rmoneymaker@nysta.com

NYS Title Agents PAC
Donald M Halperin, Treasurer

Offices and agencies appear in alphabetical order.

51 East 42nd St, New York, NY 10017
212-682-8383 Fax: 212-949-5206
e-mail: halperin@kantorlawonline.com
Web site: halperin@kantorlawonline.com

NYS Transit & Tour Operators' PAC
Stanley Brettschneider, President
PO Box 12035, Albany, NY 12212
212-851-5540 Fax: 212-987-4616
e-mail: ajkremer@rmfpc.com

NYS Troopers PAC
Daniel M De Federicis, Treasurer
120 State Street, Albany, NY 12207
518-462-7448

NYS Veterinary PEC
Thomas J Gosdeck, Treasurer
99 Washington Ave, Ste 1950, Albany, NY 12210
518-463-5449 Fax: 518-463-0947
e-mail: tjgosdeck@aol.com

NYSAIFA-PAC
Mark L Yavornitzki, Treasurer
14 Bridle Place, East Greenbush, NY 12061
518-477-2278

NYSALM State PAC
Beth A Coleman, Treasurer
3188 Knapp Road, Vestal, NY 13850
607-797-5270

NYSCHP PAC
Debra B Feinberg, Treasurer
435 New Karner Road, Albany, NY 12205
518-456-8819

NYSCOPBA PAC
Richard Harcrow, President
c/o Hinman Straub, PC, 121 State St, Albany, NY 12207
518-427-1551
e-mail: nyscopba@nyscopba.org

NYSE State PAC
Cecile Srodes, Treasurer
801 Pennsylania Ave, NW, Ste 630, Washington, DC 20004
202-347-4300
e-mail: crussell@nyse.com
Web site: www.nyse.com

NYSFRW Women Power PAC
Jill W Jackson, Treasurer
265 Kissel Avenue, Staten Island, NY 10310
718-981-1849

NYSIA NY PAC
Thomas Flaherty, Treasurer

920 Broadway, Suite 902, New York, NY 10010
212-475-4503

NYYRC PAC
Dennis Cariello, Treasurer
63-28 84th Place, Middle Village, NY 11379
917-613-3235

Nassau County Detectives Association Inc
Nicholas L Ewen, Treasurer
777 Old Country Road, Suite 202, Plainview, NY 11803
516-681-8442

Nassau County PBA PAC
Edmund Farrell, Treasurer
5 Modell Ct, East Northport, NY 11731

Nat'l Assn of Social Workers - New York City Chapter
David Roth, Treasurer
1064 E 19th St, Brooklyn, NY 11230-4502
718-338-1395 Fax: 212-558-9991

Nat'l Federation of Independent Business/ NY Save America's Free Enterpri
Daniel Richardson, Treasurer
2100 Latta Rd, Rochester, NY 14612
585-225-0910

National Fuel Gas New York PAC
Jon T Gallinger, Treasurer
10 Lafayette Sq, Rm 900, Buffalo, NY 14203
716-857-7564 Fax: 716-857-7439

National Marine Manufacturers Association PAC (NAT PAC)
Monita W Fontaine, Treasurer
C/O Barbara Ahern, One Commerce Plaza, Suite 400, Albany, NY 12210
202-737-9750

National Organization for Women- NYS PAC
Amy Smith, Treasurer
120 77th St, Niagara Falls, NY 14304
716-283-8485

Nationwide NY Political Participation Fund
Carol L Dove, Treasurer
One Nationwide Plaza 1-32-06, Columbus, OH 43215
614-249-6963

Neighborhood Preservation PAF
Sandra K Paul, Treasurer
360 E 72nd St, A710, New York, NY 10021
212-472-1459

New York Anesthesiologists Political Action Committee
David S Bronheim MD, Treasurer

Offices and agencies appear in alphabetical order.

85th Fifth Avenue, 8th Floor, New York, NY 10003
212-867-7140

New York Association of Independent Lumber Dealers PAC (NAIL PAC)
John J Maiuri, Treasurer
PO Box 523, Catskill, NY 12414
518-943-7400

New York Association of Mortgage Brokers Political Action Committee
Patrick J McHugh, Treasurer
99 Pine Street, 4th Floor, Albany, NY 12207
518-434-7400

New York Association of Temporary Services State PAC
Edward A Lenz, Treasurer
277 S Washington, Suite 200, Alexandria, VA 22314
703-253-2020

New York Bankers Political Action Comittee
Karen L Jannetty, Treasurer
99 Park Avenue, 4th Floor, New York, NY 10016
212-297-1635

New York Build PAC
Philip A Laraque, Treasurer
One Commerce Plaza #704, Albany, NY 12210
518-465-2492

New York Building Congress PAF
Richard T Anderson, Treasurer
44 West 28th Street, 12th Floor, New York, NY 10001
212-481-9230

New York Check PAC
Henry F Shyne, Treasurer
10 East 40th Street, New York, NY 10016
212-268-1911

New York Children's Advocates Making Progress
Robert Wortman, Treasurer
484 South Wood Road, Rockville Centre, NY 11570
516-867-3895

New York Chiropratic Political Action Fund
Peter H Morgan DC, Treasurer
PO Box 756, Mamaroneck, NY 10543
914-698-6626

New York Choice PAC
Shelby White, Treasurer
1202 Lexington Ave, Box 246, New York, NY 10028
212-517-3522

New York City Central Labor Council Political Action Committee
Ted Jacobson, Treasurer

31 west 15th Street, Floor 3, New York, NY 10011
212-604-9552 Fax: 212-604-9550
e-mail: nycaflcio@aol.com
Web site: www.ycclc.org

New York City Deputy Sheriff's Assn, PAC
Thomas Doyle, President
36-22A Francis Lewis Blvd #208, Flushing, NY 11358
718-359-1913 Fax: 718-359-6950

New York City, Partnership for, PAC
Brad Hoylman, Treasurer
One Battery Park Plaza, New York, NY 10004
212-493-7484

New York Emergency Medicine PAC
Joan Tarantelli, Treasurer
1070 Sibley Tower, Rochester, NY 14604
585-546-7241 Fax: 585-546-5141
e-mail: nysacep@aol.com

New York Financial Services PAC
Kirby Hannan, Treasurer
107 Washington Avenue, Albany, NY 12210
518-465-6550

New York Good Hearing Political Education Committee
Albert Shrive, Treasurer
C/O PHI, 1020 W Lackawanna Avenue, Scranton, PA 18504
717-343-1414

New York Hotel & Motel Trades Council Committee on Political education
Michael Goodwin, Treasurer
707 Eighth Avenue, 4th Floor, New York, NY 10036
212-245-8100

New York Hygiene PAC
Lynda Lederer, Treasurer
42 Hilltop Acres, Yonkers, NY 10704
914-966-7205

New York Insurance Assn Inc Political Action Committee
Bernard N Bourdeau, Treasurer
130 Washington Avenue, Albany, NY 12210
518-237-5789

New York League of Conservation Voters Action Fund
John Ernst, Treasurer
NYLCV, 29 Broadway, Suite 1100, New York, NY 10006
212-361-6350

New York Life-New York State PAC
Jonathon Poane, Treasurer
51 Madison Ave, Rm 117M, New York, NY 10010
212-576-7842 Fax: 212-576-4473

New York Medical Equipment Providers PAC
Tom Ryan, Treasurer

Offices and agencies appear in alphabetical order.

27 Elk Street, Albany, NY 12207
631-752-0555

New York Mercantiles Exchange Political Action Committee, Inc
Kenneth Shifrin, Treasurer
One North End Avenue, 14th Floor, New York, NY 10282
212-299-2525

New York Pan Hel Political Action Committee
Leslie Wyche, Treasurer
1270 Fifth Avenue, New York, NY 10029
212-749-9120

New York Pepsi Cola PAC
Mark J Johnson, Treasurer
50-35 56th Rd, Maspeth, NY 11378
718-392-1018

New York Professional Engineers
Randolph W Rakaczynski, Treasurer
250 Ridgewood Drive, Snyder, NY 14226
716-633-5887

New York Retailers for Effective Government
James R Sherin, Treasurer
460 Orchard Street, Delmar, NY 12054
Web site: www.retailcouncilnys.com

New York State Beer Wholesalers
Larry Smith, Treasurer
90 South Swan Street, Suite 400, Albany, NY 12210
518-465-6115

New York State Dietetic Association
Susan Branning, Treasurer
935 S Pines Street, Endicott, NY 13760
607-786-9793

New York State Federation of School Administrators Political Action Committee
William Moore, Treasurer
622 Cardinal Road, Cortland, NY 10567
914-737-9276

New York State Park Police PBA PAC Inc
Kenneth Roseland, Treasurer
1214 Campbell Road, Wantagh, NY 11793

New York State Political Action Committee, Region 9, UAW
Samuel G Williams, Treasurer
35 George Karl Boulevard, Suite 100, Amherst, NY 14221
716-632-1540

New York State Society of Physician Assistants PAC
Todd Bruce, Treasurer

NYSSPA, 251 New Karner Road, Suite 10A, Albany, NY 12205
877-769-7722

New York Thoroughbred Horsemen's Assn, Inc Political Action Committee
Michael P Shanley, Treasurer
PO Box 170070, Jamaica, NY 11417
718-848-5045

New York Thoroughbred Racing Industry PAC
Barry K Schwartz, Treasurer
C/O Hinman Straub, PC, 121 State Street, Albany, NY 12207
718-641-4700

New York Truck PAC
William G Joyce, Treasurer
828 Washington Ave, Albany, NY 12203
518-458-9696 Fax: 518-458-2525
e-mail: bjoyce@nytrucks.org
Web site: www.nytrucks.org

New York's Tomorrow
Michael A Avella, Treasurer
19 Trumpeter Place, Slingerlands, NY 12159
518-478-9478 Fax: 413-832-2102

New Yorker for Action
Jenny P Jimenez, Treasurer
97-24 Linden Blvd, Ozone Park, NY 11417
718-529-5062

New Yorkers Against Gun Violence PAC
Barbara E Hohlt, Treasurer
40 East 10th Street - PHC, Ste 1007, New York, NY 10003
212-995-2297 Fax: 212-679-2484

New Yorkers for Better Libraries PAC
John Hammond, Treasurer
PO Box 795, Canton, NY 13617
315-212-0182

New Yorkers for Constitutional Freedom PAC
Gary Parrett, Treasurer
1909 Westside Dr, Rochester, NY 14559
585-594-1678

New Yorkers for Fairness
S.A. Anderson, Treasurer
163 Amsterdam Ave #143, New York, NY 10023
212-724-2284

Niagara Mohawk Holdings, Inc Corp Voluntary State PAC
Jeffrey Williams, Treasurer
Niagara Mohawk, 535 Washington St, 6th Fl, Buffalo, NY 14203
716-857-4295 Fax: 716-845-9748
e-mail: jeffrey.williams@US.ngrid.com

Ninth Decade Fund
Arthur A Zatz, Treasurer

Political Parties, Lobbyists & PACs

Offices and agencies appear in alphabetical order.

1650 Arch St, 22nd Fl, Philadelphia, PA 19103-2097
215-977-2274 Fax: 215-405-3874
e-mail: azatz@wolfblock.com

Nisource Inc PAC-NY
Vincent H Devito Jr, Treasurer
200 Civic Center Drive, Columbus, OH 43215
614-460-4207

North Hempstead Century Club
Salvatore Iannucci Jr, Treasurer
164 Post Avenue, Westbury, NY 11590
516-334-5800

Northeastern PAC
David Pardi, Treasurer
106 Memorial Pkwy, Utica, NY 13501
315-797-9600 Fax: 315-797-2820

Northeastern Subcontractors Assn, PAC
Lori E Mayott, Treasurer
7 Washington Square, Albany, NY 12205
518-456-6663 Fax: 518-456-3975

Nucor Corporation, PAC NY
Ron Colella, Treasurer
Nucor Steel - Auburn Inc, PO Box 2008, Auburn, NY 13021
315-258-4201 Fax: 315-258-4392

Nurse Anesthesia - CRNA - PAC Fund
Kathleen M O'Donnell, Treasurer
PO Box 8867, Albany, NY 12208
518-262-4303 Fax: 518-861-8876

Nurse Practitioners of NYS PAC
Alice Caton, Treasurer
12 Corporate Dr, Clifton Park, NY 12065-8603
518-348-0719 Fax: 518-348-0720

OILHEATPAC
John Maniscalco, Treasurer
14 Penn Plaza, Suite 1102, New York, NY 10122
212-695-1380 Fax: 212-594-6583
e-mail: info@nyoha.org
Web site: www.nyoha.org

OMMLLP PAC
Jose W Fernandez, Treasurer
7 Times Square, 27th FL, New York, NY 10036
212-326-2000 Fax: 212-326-2061
e-mail: jmarlin@omm.com

ONPAC
Charles M Iavarone, Treasurer
127 Circle Road, North Syracuse, NY 13212-4032
315-451-5617

OPEIU Local 153 (VOTE) Voice of the Electorate
Richard Lanigan, Treasurer

265 W 14th St, New York, NY 10011
212-741-8282 Fax: 212-463-9479

ORISKA PAC
James M Kernan, Treasurer
1310 Utica Street, Oriskany, NY 13424
315-736-8823

Oil Heat Institute PAC
Kevin M Rooney, Treasurer
601 Veterans Memorial Hwy, Suite 180, Hauppauge, NY 11788
631-360-0200 Fax: 631-360-0781
e-mail: info@ohili.org
Web site: www.ohili.org

Oilheat PAC, Inc
John Maniscalco, Treasurer
14 Penn Plaza, Suite 1102, New York, NY 10122
212-695-1380

Old Country PAC
Gerard A Sims, Treasurer
520 Old Country Rd, CS 1818, Hicksville, NY 11801-4112
516-681-0562 Fax: 516-942-0802

One Eleven PAC
Edward A Bogdan, Jr, Treasurer
111 Washington Ave, Ste 750, Albany, NY 12210
518-434-9000 Fax: 518-434-2510
e-mail: ebogdan@blklobby.com

Opticians PAC
Michael P Buenau, Vice President
c/o Buenau's Opticians Inc, 228 Delaware Ave, Delmar, NY 12054
518-439-7012 Fax: 518-439-8471
e-mail: elvisbue1@aol.com
Web site: www.buenausopticians.com

Organization of Staff Analysts PAC
Sheila Gorsky, Treasurer
220 East 23rd St, Ste 707, New York, NY 10010
212-686-1229 Fax: 212-686-1231
e-mail: osart@earthlink.net
Web site: www.osaunion.org

Ortho-PAC of New York
Edward A Toriello, Treasurer
78-15 Eliot Ave, Middle Village, NY 11379-1300
718-458-8944
Web site: www.nyssos.org

Outdoor Advertising NY PAC
Matthew Duddy, Treasurer
48 Howard St, Albany, NY 12207
518-783-7784 Fax: 518-783-7805

Oxford Health Plans Inc-NY Cmte for Quality Health Care
Robert Della Corte, Treasurer

Offices and agencies appear in alphabetical order.

Oxford Health Plans, 48 Monroe Tpke, Trumbull, CT 6611
203-459-7424 Fax: 203-452-4688
e-mail: rdellaco@oxhp.com

PAC Police Assoc City of Yonkers
Keith Olson, Treasurer
104 South Broadway, Yonkers, NY 10701
914-377-7938

PAC Port Washington PBA
Dennis F Gaynor Jr, Treasurer
88-15 69 Avenue, Forest Hills, NY 11375
718-263-5597

PAC of Nassau Police Conference
Jack B Grape, Treasurer
82 Garfield Avenue, Sayville, NY 11782
631-589-0239

PAC of the Assoc Building Contractors of the Triple Cities, Inc
Bradley P Walters, Treasurer
535 Vestal Parkway, Suite 1, Vestal, NY 13850
716-938-9912

PAC of the Patrolmen's Benevolent Association of the City of NY, Inc
Joseph A Alejandro, Treasurer
C/O PBA of the City of New York, Inc, 40 Fulton Street, New York, NY 10038
212-233-5531

PAC of the Rochester Business Alliance
Paul M Nasipak, Treasurer
150 State Street, Rochester, NY 14614
716-546-3747

PCI State Political Account I
June Holmes, Treasurer
2600 River Road, Des Plaines, IL 60018
847-297-7800

Peckham Industries Inc PAC
John R Peckham, Treasurer
20 Harlem Ave, White Plains, NY 10603
914-949-2000 Fax: 914-949-2075

Pepsi-Cola Bottlers' PAC
Peter G Wilcox, Treasurer
3195 Woodfield Court, Yorktown Heights, NY 10598
914-243-0358 Fax: 914-249-8203
e-mail: pwilcox@pepsi.com

Pfizer PAC - NY
Richard A Passov, Treasurer
235 East 42nd St, New York, NY 10017
212-573-7073 Fax: 212-338-1558

Pharmacy PAC of New York State
Selig Corman, Treasurer
53 Fleetwood Ave, Albany, NY 12208
518-438-9759 Fax: 518-464-0618
e-mail: seligc@pssny.org
Web site: www.pssny.org

Physicians Fund
Robert B Bergmann, Treasurer
1200 Stewart Ave, Garden City, NY 11530
516-541-7181 Fax: 516-832-2323

Pipe Trades Political Action PAC
Anthony F Potenza, Treasurer
308 Wolf Rd, Latham, NY 12110
518-785-4425 Fax: 518-785-9855

Piper Rudnick LLP New York State Political Action Committee
John A Merrigan, Treasurer
c/o 1251 Avenue of the Americas, Main Reception on 29th Floor, New York, NY 10020-1104
202-861-6455

Plumbers & Pipefitters Local No 13 Pol Fund
Robert Byer, Treasurer
1645 St Paul St, Rochester, NY 14621
585-338-2360 Fax: 585-544-0600

Plumbers & Pipefitters Local Union 112 PAC
James G Rounds, Jr., Treasurer
PO Box 670, Binghamton, NY 13902
607-723-9593 Fax: 607-723-9467

Plumbers & Steamfitters Local 267 Ithaca/Syracuse PAC
Frank R Ficarra, Jr, Secretary/Treasurer
150 Midler Park Dr, Syracuse, NY 13206
315-437-7397 Fax: 315-437-2951

Plumbers & Steamfitters Local Union 21
Robert Philp, Treasurer
1024 McKinley St, Peekskill, NY 10566
914-737-7220 Fax: 914-737-7299

Plumbers Local Union 200 PAF
Arthur Gipson, Treasurer
137 Willis Ave, Mineola, NY 11501
516-747-4910

Plumbing Contractors PAC of the City of NY Inc
John O'Donnell, Treasurer
44 West 28th Street, 12th Floor, New York, NY 10007
212-481-4260 Fax: 212-481-7185
e-mail: acpcny@aol.com
Web site: www.acpcny.org

Police Conference of New York Inc PAC
Edward W Guzdek, Treasurer

Offices and agencies appear in alphabetical order.

112 State St, Ste 1120, Albany, NY 12207
518-463-3283
Web site: www.pcny.org

Political Action Committee Buffalo PBA
William J Misztal, Treasurer
72 Woodgate Road, Tonawanda, NY 14150
716-832-3379

Political Action Committee of Council 82
Thomas J McGraw, Treasurer
63 Colvin Ave, Albany, NY 12206
518-489-8424 Fax: 518-435-1523
Web site: www.council82.org

Port Authority PBA, Inc State of New York PAC
Robert E Morris, Treasurer
611 Palisade Avenue, Englewood Cliff, NJ 07632
201-871-2100

Port Authority Sergeants Benevolent Assn PAC
Stephen Pruspero, Treasurer
220 Bridge Plaza S, Fort Lee, NJ 07024
201-592-6191 Fax: 201-592-5982

Praxair PAC NY
James B Rouse, Treasurer
PO Box 921, Tonawanda, NY 14151-0921
203-837-2270

Probation Political Action Committee (PROPAC)
Donna Vigilante, Treasurer
PO Box 35, Yaphank, NY 11980
631-852-4928

Professional Insurance Agents of New York Political Action Committee
Robert Franzese, Treasurer
34 Cloverfield Dr, Loudonville, NY 12211
518-437-1767

Professionals Political Action committee-NY
James Hoeberling, Treasurer
Comerica Bank, PAC Services, PO Box 75000, MC 2250, Detroit, MI 48275-2250
248-371-7268

Prudential New York Political Action Committee
Maureen E Madolf, Treasurer
751 Broad Street, 14th Floor, Newark, NJ 07102-3777
973-802-6504

Psychologists for Legislative Action in NY
Lester Schad, Treasurer
6 Executive Park Dr, Albany, NY 12203
518-437-1040

Public Telecommunications Alliance
Paul S Jason, Treasurer

417 Harwood Bldg, Scarsdale, NY 10583-4199
914-472-7287 Fax: 914-723-9137

Quest Diagnostics NY PAC
Robin M Sexton, Treasurer
2330 Putnam Ln, Crofton, MD 21114
301-858-1942

RC Build PAC of the Rockland County Builders Assn
Julie Weishaar, Treasurer
337 N Main St, Ste 14A, New City, NY 10956
845-634-3849 Fax: 845-634-3329
e-mail: rcba@rcba.org
Web site: www.rcba.org

RG & E Employees' NYS Pol Comm Inc
Richard J Marion, Treasurer
4430 St. Paul Blvd, Rochester, NY 14617
716-266-4042

RPA-PAC
Patrick W Brophy, Treasurer
504 E 84th St, #3W, New York, NY 10028
212-879-4059

RSA - PAC Inc
Sante Guatelli, Treasurer
123 William St, New York, NY 10038
212-214-9277

RWDSU, Local 338 PAC
John R Durso, Treasurer
Local 338, 97-45 Queens Blvd, Rego Park, NY 11374
718-997-7400

Rangel for Congress - NY State
Basil A Paterson, Treasurer
1505 Kellum Place, Mineola, NY 11501
516-741-6565 Fax: 516-741-6706
e-mail: bpaterson@msek.com

Real Estate Board PAC
Steven Spinola, President
570 Lexington Ave, New York, NY 10022
212-532-3100 Fax: 212-481-0122
Web site: www.rebny.com

Realtors PAC
Gregory J Connors, Director, Government Affairs
130 Washington Ave, Albany, NY 12210
518-463-0300 Fax: 518-462-5474
e-mail: govt@nysar.com
Web site: www.nysar.com

Rehabilitation Associates PAC
Walter W Stockton, Treasurer
PO Box 82, 2953 Quogue Rd, Quogue, NY 11959
631-653-6765

Renew NY PAC
Arthur W Jaspan, Treasurer

Offices and agencies appear in alphabetical order.

300 Garden City Plaza, 5th Fl, Garden City, NY 11530
516-393-8210

Repair Shop & Gasoline Dealers' PAC Fund
William J Adams, Treasurer
501 Main St, East Rochester, NY 14445
585-381-9110

Republican Main Stream Coalition of New York
Lawrence E Macdonald, Treasurer
155 Drake Dr, Rochester, NY 14617
585-338-7676

Republican Majority for Choice PAC
Susan B Walrich, Treasurer
57 West 57th Street, Suite 1101, New York, NY 10019
212-207-8266

Responsible Government Coalition
Nowell Denker, Treasurer
220-55 46th Ave, Bayside, NY 11361
718-281-3073

Retirees Association of DC 37 Political Action Committee
Robert S Pfefferman, Treasurer
125 Barclay Street, #980, New York, NY 10007
212-815-7585

Riverhead Police Benevolent Assn PAC Inc
Scott A Wicklund, Treasurer
210 Howell Ave, Riverhead, NY 11901
631-727-4500 Fax: 631-727-8630

Rochester Area Right to Life Cmte-PAC
Wilda Liana, Treasurer
675 Ling Rd, Ste 3, Rochester, NY 14612
585-621-4690 Fax: 585-621-6966

Rochester Build PAC
Bruce G Boncke, Treasurer
2024 West Henrietta Rd, Ste 5H, Rochester, NY 14623
585-377-7360 Fax: 585-272-8206

Rochester Health Alliance PAC
John Urban, Treasurer
c/o Preferred Care, 259 Monroe Ave, Rochester, NY 14607
585-327-2211 or 585-325-3920 Fax: 585-327-2578

Rochester Higher Education and Research PAC
Stephen B Mullen, Treasurer
PO Box 2046, New City, NY 10956
585-263-1573

Rochester Regional Joint Board State PAC
Christopher T Ferriter, Treasurer

c/o UNITE, 750 East Ave, Rochester, NY 14607
716-473-3284
Web site: www.uniterrjb.org

Rockland County Correction Officers Benevolent Association PAC
Katherine Bruso, Treasurer
PO Box 2046, New City, NY 10956
845-708-2349

Rockland County PBA Association PAC NY
Michael J Fennessey, Treasurer
PO Box 1024, Suffern, NY 10901
845-727-3960

Rockland County Sheriff's Deputy Assn, PAC
Thomas G Rapelye, Treasurer
55 New Hempstead Rd, New City, NY 10956
845-638-5400 Fax: 845-638-5035

Roofers' Pol Education & Legislative Fund of NY
Grace Felschow, Treasurer
2800 Clinton Street, West Seneca, NY 14224
716-828-0488 Fax: 716-828-0487

Rough Rider PAC
Michael Moriarty, Treasurer
C/O Windels Marx Lane & Mittendorf, 156 West 56th Street, New York, NY 10019
212-237-1132

Royal Indemnity Comapny Voluntary PAC (Royal & Sun Alliance PAC)
Jeffrey M Klein, Treasurer
9300 Arrowpoint Blvd, Charlotte, NC 28273
704-522-3141

Rural/Metro Emp Providing Health & Safety Solutions
Thaddeus Zientek Jr, Treasurer
481 William Gaites Pkwy, Buffalo, NY 14215
716-882-8400 Fax: 716-887-8379
e-mail: ted_zientek@rmetro.com
Web site: www.rmetro.com

SBA Political Action Committee
Robert W Johnson, Treasurer
C/O Sergeants Benevolent Assoc, 35 Worth Street, New York, NY 10013
212-226-2180

SEIU Local 200 United PAC
Robert Connolly, Treasurer
SEIU Local 200 United, PO Box 1540, Syracuse, NY 13201
315-424-1750 Fax: 315-479-9030

SEIU Local 704 PAC
Angelo Arena, President

Offices and agencies appear in alphabetical order.

945 North Broadway, Yonkers, NY 10701
914-377-6290 Fax: 914-377-6299
e-mail: seiulocal704@optonline.net

SEIU PEA State Fund
Anna Burger, Treasurer
1313 L Street, NW, Washington, DC 20005

SPEAKERPAC
Howard Lazar, Treasurer
C/O Sheldon Silver, 17th Floor, 180 Maiden Lane, New York, NY 10038
212-677-4451

SSL Political Action Cmte
James L Burns, Treasurer
47 Henry St, Brooklyn, NY 11201
718-403-0047
e-mail: jburns@stroock.com

Save American Jobs PAC
Matthew J Bova, Treasurer
PO Box 2005, 12600 Clarence Center Road, Akron, NY 14001
716-542-5200

Savings & Banking Political Action Committee
Thomas W Schettino, Treasurer
Community Bankers Assoc NYS, 655 Third Avenue, Suite 816, New York, NY 10017
212-573-5500

Securities Industry Assn PAC, NY District
Bernard Beal, Treasurer
120 Broadway, 35th Fl, New York, NY 10271
212-618-0594

Semper FI NY State PAC Inc
Peter J Johnson Jr, Treasurer
115 East 9th Street, New York, NY 10003

Sen Dem
Arnold J Ludwig, Treasurer
26 Court St, Brooklyn, NY 11242
201-303-4582

Service Station & Repair Shop Operators, Upstate NY Inc
Stewart D Hill, Treasurer
3650 James St, Ste 101, Syracuse, NY 13206
315-455-1301

Sheet Metal Workers Int'l Assn Local 137 PAL Fund
Richard Quaresima, Treasurer
21-42 44th Drive, Long Island City, NY 11101-4710
718-937-4514 Fax: 718-937-4113

Sheet Metal Workers LU 38 -PAC
Stephen M Quaranto, Treasurer

38 Starr Ridge Road, PO Box 119, Brewster, NY 10509
845-278-6868

Sheet Metal Workers' Intl Assoc Local 28 Political Action Committee
Michael Belluzzi, Treasurer
Sheet Metal Workers LU 28, 500 Greenwich Street, New York, NY 10013
212-941-7700

Sheet Metal Workers' Local 46 PAF
Alan G Taylor, Treasurer
40 Rutter St, Rochester, NY 14606
585-254-9151 Fax: 585-254-8584
e-mail: mjmorgan@frontiernet.net
Web site: www.smw46.com

Sheet Metal Workers' Local union 83 Political Action Committee
David B Mellon, Treasurer
C/O Sheet Metal Workers LU 83, 718 Third Avenue, Albany, NY 12206
518-489-1377

Soft Drink & Brewery Workers' PAC
Warren Marsh, Treasurer
11 Stillwell Ave, Yonkers, NY 10704
914-776-7834

Solidarity Task Force
Gary Steszewski, Treasurer
95 Cresthaven Dr, Buffalo, NY 14225
716-837-1158 Fax: 716-836-4599
e-mail: garski@adelphia.net

Southern Tier HB & REM Build-PAC
Gary Brownell, Treasurer
80 Rockwell Road, Vestal, NY 13850
607-772-0889

Southern tier Business PAC
James J Lewis, Treasurer
112 Wisconsin Drive, Binghamton, NY 13901
607-648-2523

Southhampton Town Young Republicans
Gary Bronat, Treasurer
9 Douglas Ct, PO Box 684, Hampton Bays, NY 11946
e-mail: info@southamptontownyrs.com
Web site: www.southamptontownyrs.com

Southold Town Police Benevolent Assn Tax PAC.COM
Jennifer Combs-Quanty, Treasurer
PO Box 185, 55 Depot Lane, Cutchogue, NY 11935
631-765-0065

Stars & Stripes PAC
Albert A Annunziata, Treasurer

Offices and agencies appear in alphabetical order.

80 Business Park Dr, Ste 309, Armonk, NY 10504
914-273-0730 Fax: 914-273-7051

State & Local Election Fund AFSCME Local 2054, DC 37
Kenneth Lieb, Treasurer
Local 2054, DC 37, 125 Barclay St, New York, NY 10007
212-815-1060

State & Local Election Fund Local 1070
Janice A Swift, Treasurer
Local 1070, 125 Barclay St, New York, NY 10007
718-590-3675 Fax: 718-590-8914

State Street Associates PAC
Sean M Doolan, Treasurer
121 State St, Albany, NY 12207
518-436-0751 Fax: 518-436-4751

Staten Island Political Action Committee
Lorraine A Witzak, Treasurer
32 Cunard Place, Staten Island, NY 10304
718-442-8713

Statewide Association of Minority Businesses PAC
Yuri C Martinez, Treasurer
133-54 41st Avenue, 4th Floor, Flushing, NY 11355
212-717-6846

Steamfitters' Union Local 638 PAC
Patrick E Dolan, Secretary/Treasurer
32-32 48th Ave, Long Island City, NY 11101
718-392-3420 Fax: 718-784-7285

Subcontractors Trade Assn Inc State PAC
Greg S Fricke, Jr, Vice President
570 Seventh Ave, Suite 1100, New York, NY 10018
212-244-8878 Fax: 212-398-6224
Web site: www.stanyc.com

Success PAC
Walter J Edwards, Treasurer
C/O Lynn M Zaleski, 437 Old Albany Post Road, Garrison, NY 10524
212-864-7410

Suffolk & Nassau Counties Plumbing & Heating Contractors Assoc PAC
Joseph L Kaufman, Treasurer
16 Lucinda Dr, Babylon, NY 11702
516-422-3945

Suffolk Co Detective Investigators PBA Inc PAC
Peter Tartaglia, Treasurer
868 Church Street, Bohemia, NY 11716
631-853-4150

Suffolk Co Police Dept Superior Officers Assoc Public Affairs Comm
Edmund M Erickson, Treasurer

39 Highland Court, Huntington, NY 11743-3234
516-421-5223

Suffolk County Assn of Municipal Employees' PAC Inc
Cheryl A Felice, President
30 Orville Dr, Bohemia, NY 11716
631-589-8400 Fax: 631-589-3860
e-mail: cherylfelice@scame.org
Web site: www.scame.org
Labor union representing support staff, both white and blue color, for Suffolk County government.

Suffolk County Chapter Nat'l Womens Political Caucus
Irene C Grasso, Treasurer
75 Wendy Dr, Farmingville, NY 11738
631-289-6741 Fax: 631-289-8139
Web site: www.nwpc.org

Suffolk County Correction Officers' Assn PAC
Gary Bennett, Treasurer
SCCOA, 400 West Main St, Ste 202, Riverhead, NY 11901
631-708-1301 Fax: 631-208-1333
e-mail: csclafani@sccoa.net
Web site: www.sccoa.net

Suffolk County Deputy Sheriffs Benevolent Assn Inc PAC
Bernard Cinquemani, Treasurer
2650 Rt 112, Medford, NY 11763
631-289-1768 Fax: 631-289-1813
e-mail: scdsba@optonline.net
Web site: www.scdsba.com

Suffolk County Police Benevolent Assn PAC
Patricia A O'Donnell, Treasurer
868 Church St, Bohemia, NY 11716
631-563-4200 Fax: 631-563-4204

Suffolk County Police Conference PAC
Kevin J Duchemin, Treasurer
12 Brandywine Dr, Sag Harbor, NY 11963
631-725-5652

Superior Officers Assoc-Nassau County Police
Brian J Hoesl, Treasurer
777 Old Country Road, Suite 201, Plainview, NY 11803
516-681-8624

Superior Officers' Benevolent Assn of the TBTA PAC
Matthew Cirelli, Treasurer
225 Jericho Trnpk, Floral Park, NY 11001
516-358-7097 Fax: 516-358-1258

Surgeon PAC
John D Nicholson, Treasurer
100 State St, Ste 405, Albany, NY 12207
518-433-0397

Syracuse Tomorrow
Michael J Lorenz, Treasurer

Offices and agencies appear in alphabetical order.

5109 Waterford Wood Way, Fayetteville, NY 13066
315-637-3965 Fax: 315-471-8545

TAP PAC-APC
John Crossley, Treasurer
c/o 121 State St, 2nd Fl, Albany, NY 12207
315-733-2446

TEAPAC
Anthony Puglisi, Treasurer
160 E 38th St, Apt 4E, New York, NY 10016
212-986-7528

THOROPAC - Thoroughbred Breeders' PAC
Jane Decoteau, Treasurer
57 Phila St, #2, Saratoga Springs, NY 12866
518-587-0777 Fax: 518-587-1551
e-mail: thoroughbred@acmenet.net
Web site: www.nybreds.com

TOW PAC
John H Beauman, Treasurer
175 Oakhurst Street, Lockport, NY 14094
716-433-6481

Teaching Hospital Education PAC
William A Polf, Treasurer
80 Central Park West, Apt 16E, New York, NY 10023
212-580-0452

Teamsters Local 317 PAC
Gary R Staring, Treasurer
566 Spencer St, Syracuse, NY 13204
315-471-4164 Fax: 315-471-4328
e-mail: cindy@twcny.rr.com

Teamsters Local 72 PAC
Terrance R Eldridge, Jr, Treasurer
Local 72 IBOFT, 265 West 14th St, New York, NY 10011
212-691-4228 Fax: 212-645-5026

Telecommunications Improvement Council
Keith J Roland, Treasurer
One Columbia Place, Albany, NY 12207
518-434-8112 Fax: 518-434-3232
e-mail: kroland@rfkplaw.com

Telecommunications Int'l Union
Sarah Willacy, Treasurer
71 Warwick Road, Bronxville, NY 10708
914-961-4929

Tempo 802
William R Dennison, Treasurer
183 Rockne Rd, Yonkers, NY 10701
914-968-9126 Fax: 212-489-6030
e-mail: eprice@local802.org

The Business Council PAC Inc
Kathleen Carlitz, Treasurer

152 Washington Avenue, Albany, NY 12210
518-465-7511

The Coca-Cola Bottling Company of New York, PAC
Christopher Grimaldi, Treasurer
111 Washington Avenue, Suite 606, Albany, NY 12210
518-432-9220

The Italian American Poltical Action Committee of New York
James C Lisa, Treasurer
48-08 111th Street, Corona, NY 11368
718-592-2196

The Nestle Waters North America, Inc Political Action Committee-New York
Lori L Brello, Treasurer
777 West Putnam Avenue, Greenwich, CT 06830
203-863-0307

The Next New York
Deni Frand, Treasurer
530 E 90th Street, New York, NY 10128

The Shaw Licitra PAC
George P Esernio, Treasurer
1475 Franklin Avenue, Garden City, NY 11530
516-742-0610

The Wine PAC
Leonard M Fogelman, Treasurer
305 Madison Avenue, New York, NY 10165
212-370-1530

The Young Democratic Rural Conference
John D Byrne, Treasurer
73 Buck Street, Canton, NY 13617
315-323-3848

Theatrical Protective Union Local No One Iatse NYS Stagehands PAC
Donald B Kleinschmidt, Treasurer
320 West 46th Street, New York, NY 10036
212-333-2500

Thoroughbred Horsemen of Western NY PAC
Jonathan Buckley, Treasurer
PO Box 25250, Farmington, NY 14425
585-924-3004 Fax: 585-924-1433
e-mail: flhbpa@frontiernet.net

Tile Layers Subordinate Union Loacal 7 of New York and New Jersey PAC
Charles Hill, Treasurer
45-34 Court Square, Long Island City, NY 11101
516-485-9289

Title Underwriters' PAC
Guy D Paquin, Treasurer

PO Box 157, Sodus Point, NY 14555
212-683-6400 Fax: 315-483-0117

Tourism Advocacy Coalition PAC
George Lence, Treasurer
810 Seventh Ave, 3rd Fl, New York, NY 10019
212-484-1259 Fax: 212-247-6193
e-mail: glence@nycvisit.com

Transit Supervisors Organization PAC
Vincent Modafferi, Treasurer
5768 Mosholu Ave, Bronx, NY 10471
718-601-5700 Fax: 718-601-6300
e-mail: sld139@aol.com

Transport Workers Union Local 100 Political Contributions Committee
Ed Watt, Treasurer
140B 126th Street, Rockaway, NY 11694
718-634-8747

U.S.W.A. Local 420A PAC
David G Rabideau, Treasurer
24 Woodlawn Avenue, Massena, NY 13662
315-764-0531

UA Plumbers & Pipefitters LU 773 Voluntary NYS PAC Fund
Lawrence J Gonnelly, Treasurer
Local 773, PO Box 1396, South Glens Falls, NY 12803
518-792-9157 Fax: 518-792-4876
Web site: www.lu773.org

UA Plumbers & Steamfitters Local 22 PAC Inc
Michael W McNally, Treasurer
3509 Human Rd, Sanborn, NY 14132
716-731-4683

UFCW Active Ballot Club
Anthony M Perrone, Treasurer
1775 K Street NW, Washington, DC 20006-1598
202-223-3111

UFT COPE Local
Melvyn Aaronson, COPE Director
52 Broadway, New York, NY 10004
212-598-9528 Fax: 212-475-2320
Web site: www.uft.org

UHAP PAC
Gary J Fitzgerald, Treasurer
Iroquois, 17 Halfmoon Exec Park Dr, Clifton Park, NY 12065
518-383-5060 Fax: 518-383-2616
e-mail: gfitzgerald@iroquois.org
Web site: www.upstatehealthcare.org

UNITE HERE and Local Election & Political Education Fund
Edgar Romney, Treasurer

275 Seventh Avenue, 7th Floor, New York, NY 10001
212-929-2600 Fax: 212-929-2946
Web site: www.unitehere.org

UNYAN PAC
Edna Moyer, UNYAN PAC Co-Chair
941 Pauline Ave, Pine City, NY 14871
607-734-8056

USB Fund for Good Government Inc
Harold J Peterson, Treasurer
Union State Bank, 100 Dutch Hill Road, Orangeburg, NY 10962
845-398-5812 Fax: 845-365-4672

USWA, SEIU, AFL-CIO, CLC-PAC
Edward L Byrne, Treasurer
138-50 Queens Blvd, Briarwood, NY 11435

UWUA Local 1-2 Non Federal PAC
Robert Conetta, Treasurer
5 W 37th St, New York, NY 10018
212-575-4400 Fax: 212-575-3852

Uniformed Fire Officers Association 527 Account
Arthur J Parrinello, Treasurer
225 Broadway, Suite 401, New York, NY 10007
212-293-9300 or .

Uniformed Firefighters Assoc State FirePAC Political Action Committee
Robert Straub, Treasurer
204 East 23rd Street, New York, NY 10010
212-545-6975

Union for a Better New York
Peter Ward, President
707 Eighth Ave, New York, NY 10036
212-245-8100 Fax: 212-977-5714

United Parcel Service Inc PAC NY
Clifford L Hinds, Treasurer
55 Glenlake Pkwy NE, Atlanta, GA 30328
404-828-6872

United Restaurant, Hotel & Tavern Association of NY Statewide PAC
John M Egan, Treasurer
40 Sheridan Avenue, Albany, NY 12210
518-436-8121 or 877-436-8121 Fax: 518-436-7287
e-mail: esrta@capital.net
Web site: www.esrta.org

United Steelworkers of America
James D English, Int'l Secretary/Treasurer
USWA-Five Gateway Center, Pittsburgh, PA 15222
412-562-2325 Fax: 412-562-2317
e-mail: jenglish@uswa.org

United Steelworkers of America, District 4 PAC
William J Pienta, Treasurer

Political Parties, Lobbyists & PACs

Offices and agencies appear in alphabetical order.

4285 Genesee St, Ste 110, Cheektowaga, NY 14225
716-565-1720 Fax: 716-565-1727

United Transportation Union Political Action Cmte (UTU PAC)
Daniel E Johnson III, Treasurer
14600 Detroit Avenue, Cleveland, OH 44107-4250
216-228-9400

United for Good Government
James E Dellarmi, Treasurer
21 Water Street, Eastchester, NY 10709
914-337-7451

Unity PAC
Joyce H Kopcik, Treasurer
PO Box 5000, Syracuse, NY 13250-5000
315-448-7000 Fax: 315-448-7100
e-mail: jkopcik@unity-life.com
Web site: www.unity-life.com

Verizon Communications Good Government Club New York PAC
Sandra L Borders, Treasurer
Verizon Communications, 1717 Arch Street 47S, Philadelphia, PA 19103
215-963-6387

Voice of Teachers for Educational/Comm on Political Education
Alan Lubin, Treasurer
NYSUT, 800 Troy-Schenectady Road, Latham, NY 12110
518-213-6000
Web site: www.nysut.org

WYETH Good Gov't Fund
Jack M O'Connor, Administrator
Five Giralda Farms, Madison, NJ 07940
973-660-5000 Fax: 973-660-6030

Wachovia New York Employees Good Government Fund
Ross E Jeffries Jr, Treasurer
301 South College Street, Charlotte, NC 28288-0630
704-374-3234

Weingarten, Reid & McNally, LLC
Robert Reid, Treasurer
1 Commerce Plaza, Suite 1103, Albany, NY 12210
518-465-7330

Wellchoice PAC
Michael Fedyna, Treasurer
Wellchoice, 11 W 42nd St, New York, NY 10036
212-476-3652 Fax: 212-476-2040

Westchester Coalition for Legal Abortion PAC
Judith S Lerman, Treasurer

237 Mamaroneck Avenue, White Plains, NY 10605
914-946-5363

Westchester County Conservative Party PAC
Joseph J Malara, Treasurer
185 Albemarle Rd, White Plains, NY 10605
914-428-4870

Westchester Republican Womens Club PAC
Lesley Cooper Richman, Vice President
125 Lake St, Apt 11 K-S, White Plains, NY 10604
914-686-4710

Westchester Right to Life PAC
Margaret Maroldy, Treasurer
45 Longue Vue Avenue, New Rochelle, NY 10804
914-632-9498

Westcons PAC
Nicholas Caputo, Treasurer
80 Ferris Place, Ossining, NY 10562
914-941-7983

Western NY Majority Leader PAC
Kathleen A Meyerhofer, Treasurer
37 Lucy Lane, Cheektowaga, NY 14225
716-683-3546

Western NY PAC Region 9 UAW
Samuel G Williams, Treasurer
35 George Karl Blvd, Ste100, Amherst, NY 14221
716-632-1540

Western NY Regional Council PAC Fund
David F Haines, Jr, Treasurer
23 Market St, Binghamton, NY 13905
607-798-6940 Fax: 607-729-2087

Western NY Safari Club PAC
Ann Boller, Treasurer
440 Winspar Rd, Elma, NY 14059-9110
716-685-8099 Fax: 718-683-6260

Western New Yorkers for Economic Growth
Robert J Fischer, Treasurer
400 Andrews Street, Suite 600, Rochester, NY 14604
585-325-0900

Wilson Elser Moskowitz Edelman & Dicker PAC
Cynthia D Shenker, Treasurer
One Steuben Place, Albany, NY 12207
518-449-8893 Fax: 518-449-4292
e-mail: shenkerc@wemed.com

Women PAC
Regina M Calcaterra, Treasurer
200 west 72nd Street, Suite 56, New York, NY 10023
646-672-2846

Women's TAP Fund
Alice Kryzan, Treasurer

Offices and agencies appear in alphabetical order.

7 Cloister Ct, Amherst, NY 14226
716-832-4617

Yonkers Council of School Administrators PAC
William J Moore, Treasurer

622 Cardinal Road, Cortlandt Manor, NY 10567
914-737-9276
e-mail: billmoore622@cs.com

CHAMBERS OF COMMERCE and ECONOMIC AND INDUSTRIAL DEVELOPMENT ORGANIZATIONS

Provides a combined listing of public and private organizations involved in regional economic development.

Adirondack Economic Dev Corp
Ernest S Hohmeyer, President
60 Main St, Ste 200, PO Box 747, Saranac Lake, NY 12983-0747
518-891-5523 Fax: 518-891-9820
e-mail: info@aedconline.com
Web site: www.aedconline.com

Adirondack Regional Chambers of Commerce
Todd L Shimkus, President/CEO
5 Warren St, Glens Falls, NY 12801
518-798-1761 Fax: 518-792-4147
e-mail: tshimkus@adirondackchamber.org
Web site: www.adirondackchamber.org

Adirondacks Speculator Region Chamber of Commerce
Mary Ann Ryan, Director, Tourism
PO Box 184, Rts 30 & 8, Speculator, NY 12164
518-548-4521 Fax: 518-548-4905
e-mail: adrkmts@frontiernet.net
Web site: www.adrkmts.com

African American Chamber of Commerce of Westchester & Rockland Counties
Robin L Douglas, President, CEO
100 Stevens Ave, Ste 202, Mount Vernon, NY 10550
914-699-9050 Fax: 914-699-6279
Web site: www.africanamericanchamberofcommercenys.org

Albany County Ind Dev Agency
Fowler J Riddick, Chairman
112 State St, Room 1116, Albany, NY 12207-2021
518-447-4841 Fax: 518-447-5695
Web site: www.albanycounty.com/IDA

Albany Ind Dev Agency (City of)
Lori Harris, Commissioner
21 Lodge St, Albany, NY 12207
518-434-2532 Fax: 518-434-9846
Web site: www.albanyny.org

Albany-Colonie Regional Chamber of Commerce
Lyn Taylor, President

107 Washington Ave, Albany, NY 12210
518-431-1400 Fax: 518-434-1339
e-mail: lyn@ac-chamber.org
Web site: www.ac-chamber.org

Alexandria Bay Chamber of Commerce
Thomas Weldon, Executive Director
7 Market St, PO Box 365, Alexandria Bay, NY 13607
315-482-9531 or 800-541-2110 Fax: 315-482-5434
e-mail: info@alexbay.org
Web site: www.alexbay.org

Allegany County Office of Development
John E Foels, Director, Development & IDA
Crossroads Commerce Conference Center, 6087 NYS Rte 19 North, Belmont, NY 14813
585-268-7472 or 800-893-9484 Fax: 585-268-7473
e-mail: development@alleganyco.com
Web site: www.alleganyco.com

Amherst Chamber of Commerce
Colleen DiPirro, CEO & President
325 Essjay Rd, Ste 200, Williamsville, NY 14221
716-632-6905 Fax: 716-632-0548
e-mail: cdipirro@amherst.org
Web site: www.amherst.org

Amherst Ind Dev Agency (Town of)
James Allen, Executive Director
130 John Muir Dr, Ste 300, Amherst, NY 14228-1148
716-688-9000 Fax: 716-688-0205
e-mail: jallen@amherstida.com
Web site: www.amherstida.com

Amsterdam Ind Dev Agency
Frank Valiante, Executive Director
City Hall, 61 Church St, Amsterdam, NY 12010
518-842-5011 Fax: 518-843-2862
Web site: www.amsterdamedz.com

Arcade Area Chamber of Commerce
Hugh Ely, Executive Director
278 Main St, Arcade, NY 14009
585-492-2114 Fax: 585-492-5103
Web site: www.arcadechamber.org

Babylon Ind Dev Agency
Robert Stricoff, Executive Director

Offices and agencies appear in alphabetical order.

47 West Main St, Babylon, NY 11702
631-587-3679 Fax: 631-226-3530
e-mail: info@babylonida.org
Web site: www.babylonida.org

Bainbridge Chamber of Commerce
Helen Hernandez, President
PO Box 2, Bainbridge, NY 13733
607-967-8700 Fax: 607-967-3207
Web site: www.bainbridgechamberny.org

Baldwin Chamber of Commerce
Doris Duffy, Co-President
PO Box 813, Baldwin, NY 11510
516-223-8080
Web site: www.baldwin.org

Baldwinsville Chamber of Commerce (Greater Baldwinsville)
Kevin Baker, President
50 Oswego St, Baldwinsville, NY 13027
315-638-0550
e-mail: bchamber@gisco.net
Web site: www.baldwinsvillechamber.com

Bath Area Chamber of Commerce (Greater Bath Area)
Josie Stratton, Director, Services
10 Pulteney Square W, Suite 101, Bath, NY 14810
607-776-7122 Fax: 607-776-7122
e-mail: bathchamber@infoblvd.net
Web site: www.bathnychamber.com

Bayshore Chamber of Commerce
Donna Periconi, President
77 East Main St, PO Box 5110, Bayshore, NY 11706
631-665-7003 Fax: 631-665-5204
Web site: www.bayshorecommerce.com

Bellmores, Chamber of Commerce of the
Dorothy Medico, Co-President; Virginia McClean, Co-President
PO Box 861, Bellmore, NY 11710
516-679-1875 Fax: 516-409-0544
e-mail: bellmorecc@aol.com
Web site: www.bellmorechamber.com

Bethlehem Chamber of Commerce
Marty DeLaney, President
318 Delaware Ave, Delmar, NY 12054-1911
518-439-0512 or 888-439-0512 Fax: 518-475-0910
e-mail: info@bethlehemchamber.com
Web site: www.bethlehemchamber.com

Bethlehem Ind Dev Agency (Town of)
Brian Hannafin, Executive Director
445 Delaware Ave, Delmar, NY 12054
518-439-4955 Fax: 518-439-1699
e-mail: bhannafin@townofbethlehem.org
Web site: www.bethlehemida.com

Binghamton Chamber of Commerce (Greater Binghamton)
Alex S DePersis, President & CEO

Metrocenter, 49 Court St, PO Box 995, Binghamton, NY 13902-0995
607-772-8860 Fax: 607-722-4513
e-mail: chamber@binghamtonchamber.com
Web site: www.binghamtonchamber.com

Black Lake Chamber of Commerce
William Dashnshaw, President
PO Box 12, Hammond, NY 13646
315-578-2895
e-mail: blcc@blacklake.org
Web site: www.blacklakeny.com

Blooming Grove Chamber of Commerce
Carole McCann, President
PO Box 454, Washingtonville, NY 10992
845-496-5449 Fax: 845-497-7718
e-mail: cmac@frontiernet.net

Blue Mountain Lake Assn
John Collins, President
PO Box 156, Blue Mountain Lake, NY 12812
518-352-7717 Fax: 518-352-7385
e-mail: jrc@telenet.net

Bolton Landing Chamber of Commerce
David R Stotler, President
PO Box 368, Bolton Landing, NY 12814-0368
518-644-3831 Fax: 518-644-5951
e-mail: boltoncc@capital.net
Web site: www.boltonchamber.com

Boonville Area Chamber of Commerce
Kathy Graver, Executive Coordinator
122 Main St, PO Box 163, Boonville, NY 13309
315-942-5112
e-mail: info@boonvillechamber.org
Web site: www.boonvillechamber.org

Brewster Chamber of Commerce
Linda A Klein, Executive Director
31 Main St, Brewster, NY 10509
845-279-2477 Fax: 845-278-8349
e-mail: brewster@computer.net
Web site: www.brewsterchamber.com

Brockport Chamber of Commerce (Greater Brockport)
Elaine Bader, President
PO Box 119, Brockport, NY 14420
585-637-8684 Fax: 585-637-7389

Bronxville Chamber of Commerce
Mary Liz Mulligan, Executive Director
81 Pondfield Rd, Bronxville, NY 10708
914-337-6040 Fax: 914-337-6322
e-mail: cocbville@aol.com
Web site: www.bronxvillechamber.com

Brookhaven Industrial Development Agency
Anthony J Aloisio, Executive Director

Offices and agencies appear in alphabetical order.

1 Independence Hill, Farmingville, NY 11738
631-451-6563 Fax: 631-451-6925
e-mail: taloisio@brookhaven.org
Web site: www.brookhaven.org

Brooklyn Chamber of Commerce
Kenneth Adams, President
25 Elm Place, Suite 200, Brooklyn, NY 11201
718-875-1000 Fax: 718-237-4274
e-mail: info@brooklynchamber.com
Web site: www.ibrooklyn.com

Brooklyn Economic Dev Corp
Joan G Bartolomeo, President
175 Remsen St, Ste 350, Brooklyn, NY 11201-4300
718-522-4600 Fax: 718-797-9286
e-mail: jgb@bedc.org
Web site: www.bedc.org

Broome County Ind Dev Agency
Richard D'Attilio, Executive Director
225 Water St, Garden Level, PO Box 1510, Binghamton, NY 13902-1510
607-584-9000 Fax: 607-584-9009
e-mail: info@bcida.com
Web site: www.bcida.com

Buffalo Economic Renaissance Corp
Michelle Barron, Vice President of Operation
65 Niagara Square, RM 920, Buffalo, NY 14202-3309
716-842-6923 Fax: 716-842-6942
e-mail: mbarron@berc.org
Web site: www.growbfo.org

Buffalo Niagara Partnership
Andrew J Rudnick, President/CEO
665 Main Street, Suite 200, Buffalo, NY 14203-1487
716-852-7100 or 800-241-0474 Fax: 716-852-2761
Web site: www.thepartnership.org

Canandaigua Area Chamber of Commerce
Elmer Adkins, Interim President/CEO
113 S Main St, Canandaigua, NY 14424
585-394-4400 Fax: 585-394-4546
e-mail: chamber@canadaigua.com
Web site: www.canandaigua.com

Canastota Chamber of Commerce
Rick & Penny Stevens, Co-Presidents
222 S Peterboro St, PO Box 206, Canastota, NY 13032
315-697-3677
Web site: www.canastota.org

Canisteo Chamber of Commerce
William Moogan, President
PO Box 34, Canisteo, NY 14823
607-324-1010 Fax: 607-324-2637
e-mail: wmoogan@fsbcanisteo.com

Canton Chamber of Commerce
Sally Roberson, Executive Director

PO Box 369, Canton, NY 13617
315-386-8255 Fax: 315-386-8255
e-mail: cantoncc@northnet.org
Web site: www.cantonnychamber.org

Cape Vincent Chamber of Commerce
Shelley Higgins, Executive Director
PO Box 482, Cape Vincent, NY 13618
315-654-2481 Fax: 315-654-4141
e-mail: thecape@tds.net
Web site: www.capevincent.org

Carthage Area Chamber of Commerce
Tammy R Trowbridge, Executive Secretary
313 State St, Carthage, NY 13619
315-493-3590 Fax: 315-493-3590
e-mail: carthage@gisco.net
Web site: www.carthageny.com

Cattaraugus Empire Zone Corp
John Sayegh, Chief Operating Officer
120 N Union St, Olean, NY 14760
716-373-9260 Fax: 716-372-7912
e-mail: jsayegh@oleanny.com
Web site: www.cattempirezone.org

Cayuga County Chamber of Commerce
Terri Bridenbecker, Executive Director
36 South Street, Auburn, NY 13021
315-252-7291 Fax: 315-255-3077
Web site: www.cayugacountychamber.com

Cazenovia Area Chamber of Commerce (Greater Cazenovia Area)
Paul C Brooks, Chairman
59 Albany St, Cazenovia, NY 13035
315-655-9243 or 888-218-6305 Fax: 315-655-9244
e-mail: cazchamber@alltel.net
Web site: www.cazenoviachamber.com

Central Adirondack Assn
Chip Kiefer, Publicity Director
PO Box 68, Old Forge, NY 13420
315-369-6983 Fax: 315-369-2676
Web site: www.oldforgeny.com

Champlain Ind Dev Agency & Local Dev Corp (Town of)
Rob Casey, Chairman
Rte 9, PO Box 3144, Champlain, NY 12919
518-298-3224 Fax: 518-298-8896

Chautauqua County Chamber of Commerce
Pamela S Lydic, President
101 W Fifth St, Jamestown, NY 14701
716-488-1101 or 716-366-6200 Fax: 716-487-0785
e-mail: paml@chautauquachamber.org
Web site: www.chautauquachamber.org

Chautauqua County Chamber of Commerce, Dunkirk Branch
Pamela S Lydic, President

Offices and agencies appear in alphabetical order.

10785 Bennett Road, Dunkirk, NY 14048
716-366-6200 Fax: 761-366-4276
e-mail: cccc@chautauquachamber.org
Web site: www.chautauquachamber.org

Chautauqua County Ind Dev Agency
Richard Alexander, Administrative Dir
200 Harrison St, Jamestown, NY 14701
716-664-3262 Fax: 716-664-4515
e-mail: ccida@ccida.com
Web site: www.co.chautauqua.ny.us/ccida

Cheektowaga Chamber of Commerce
Debra S Liegl, President
2875 Union Rd, #50, Cheektowaga, NY 14227
716-684-5838 Fax: 716-684-5571
e-mail: chamber@cheektowaga.org
Web site: www.cheektowaga.org

Chemung County Chamber of Commerce
Kevin D Keeley, CEO & President
400 E Church St, Elmira, NY 14901-2803
607-734-5137 Fax: 607-734-4490
e-mail: info@chemungchamber.org
Web site: www.chemungchamber.org

Chemung County Ind Dev Agency
George Miner, Director
PO Box 251, Elmira, NY 14902
607-733-6513 Fax: 607-734-2698
e-mail: gminer@steg.com
Web site: www.steg.com/ccida.html

Chenango County Chamber of Commerce
Tammy J Carnrike, CCE, President & CEO
19 Eaton Ave, Norwich, NY 13815
607-334-1400 Fax: 607-336-6963
e-mail: info@chenangony.org
Web site: www.chenangony.org

Clarence Chamber of Commerce
Rob Schofield, President
8975 Main St, Clarence, NY 14031
716-631-3888 Fax: 716-631-3946
e-mail: info@clarence.org
Web site: www.clarence.org

Clarence Ind Dev Agency (Town of)
Henry Bourg, Chairman
1 Town Place, Clarence, NY 14031
716-741-8930 Fax: 716-741-4715
Web site: clarence.ny.us

Clayton Chamber of Commerce
Karen Goetz, Executive Director

517 Riverside Dr, Clayton, NY 13624
315-686-3771 or 800-252-9806 Fax: 315-686-5564
e-mail: ccoc@gisco.net
Web site: www.1000islands-clayton.com

Clifton Springs Area Chamber of Commerce
Mike Ford, President
PO Box 86, Clifton Springs, NY 14432
315-462-6420 Fax: 315-548-6429
Web site: www.cliftonspringschamber.com

Clinton Chamber of Commerce Inc
David Forbes, Executive VP
PO Box 142, Clinton, NY 13323
315-853-1735 Fax: 315-853-1735
e-mail: ccc1@adelphia.net
Web site: www.clintonnychamber.org

Clinton County, The Development Corp
Adore F Kurtz, President
61 Area Development Dr, Plattsburgh, NY 12901
518-563-3100 Fax: 518-562-2232
e-mail: tdc@thedevelopcorp.com
Web site: www.thedevelopcorp.com

Clyde Industrial Dev Corp
Kenneth DiSanto, President
PO Box 92, Clyde, NY 14433
315-923-7998 Fax: 315-923-7855
e-mail: kdisanto@tds.net
Web site: www.clydeontheerie.com

Cohoes Chamber of Commerce
Michael J Brooks, Executive Director
PO Box 341, Cohoes, NY 12047
518-237-1766 Fax: 518-235-3086
e-mail: director@cohoeschamber.com
Web site: www.cohoeschamber.com

Cohoes Ind Dev Agency (City of)
John T McDonald, Chairman
97 Mohawk Street, Cohoes, NY 12047
518-233-2118 Fax: 518-233-2168
e-mail: jscavo@ci.cohoes.ny.us
Web site: www.ci.cohoes.ny.us

Columbia County Chamber of Commerce
David B Colby, President
507 Warren St, Hudson, NY 12534
518-828-4417 Fax: 518-822-9539
e-mail: mail@columbiachamber-ny.com
Web site: www.columbiachamber-ny.com

Columbia Hudson Partnership
James P Galvin, Executive Director

Offices and agencies appear in alphabetical order.

444 Warren St, Hudson, NY 12534
518-828-4718 Fax: 518-828-0901
e-mail: jgalvin@chpartnership.com
Web site: www.chpartnership.net

Coney Island Chamber of Commerce
Al O'Hagan, Chairman of the Board
1015 Surf Ave, Brooklyn, NY 11224
718-266-1234 Fax: 718-714-0379

Cooperstown Chamber of Commerce
Polly Renckens, Director
31 Chestnut St, Cooperstown, NY 13326
607-547-9983 Fax: 607-547-6006
e-mail: director@cooperstownchamber.org
Web site: www.cooperstownchamber.org

Corinth Ind Dev Agency (Town of)
Richard B Lucia, Chairman
600 Palmer Ave, Corinth, NY 12822
518-654-9232 Fax: 518-654-7751
Web site: www.townofcorinthny.com

Corning Area Chamber of Commerce
Coleen Fabriezi, Vice-President
1 West Market Street, Suite 302, 2nd Fl, Corning, NY 14830-2688
607-936-4686 Fax: 607-936-4685
e-mail: info@corningny.com
Web site: www.corningny.com

Cortland County Chamber of Commerce
Garry VanGorder, Executive Director
37 Church St, Cortland, NY 13045
607-756-2814 Fax: 607-756-4698
e-mail: crtchmbr@clarityconnect.com
Web site: www.cortlandchamber.com

Cutchogue-New Suffolk Chamber of Commerce
Jim Trentalange, President
PO Box 610, Cutchogue, NY 11935
631-734-2335
Web site: www.cutchoguenewsuffolk.org

Dansville Chamber of Commerce
Richard de Asis, President
126 Main St, PO Box 105, Dansville, NY 14437
585-335-6920 Fax: 585-335-5863
e-mail: dansvillechamber@hotmail.com
Web site: www.dansvilleny.net

Delaware County Chamber of Commerce
Mary Beth Silano, Executive Director
114 Main St, Delhi, NY 13753
607-746-2281 or 800-642-4443 Fax: 607-746-3571
e-mail: info@delawarecounty.org
Web site: www.delawarecounty.org

Delaware County Planning Department
Nicole Franzese, Director, Planning

PO Box 367, Delhi, NY 13753
607-746-2944 Fax: 607-746-8479
e-mail: pln.director@co.delaware.ny.us
Web site: www.co.delaware.ny.us

Deposit Chamber of Commerce
Rick Golding, President
PO Box 222, Deposit, NY 13754
607-467-2556
Web site: www.tds.net/depositchamber

Development Authority of the North Country
Robert S Juravich, Executive Director
317 Washington St, Watertown, NY 13601
315-785-2593 Fax: 315-785-2591
e-mail: juravich@danc.org
Web site: www.danc.org

Dover-Wingdale Chamber of Commerce
Melanie Ryder, President
PO Box 643, Dover Plains, NY 12522
845-877-9800

Downtown-Lower Manhattan Assn
Carl B Weisbrod, President
120 Broadway, Rm 3340, New York, NY 10271
212-406-9100 or 212-566-6700 Fax: 212-406-9103
e-mail: cweisbrod@dowtownny.com
Web site: downtownny.com

Dutchess County Economic Dev Corp
Anne N Conroy, Acting President & CEO
3 Neptune Rd, Poughkeepsie, NY 12601
845-463-5410 Fax: 845-463-5401
e-mail: rcoan@dcedc.com
Web site: www.dcedc.com

East Aurora Chamber of Commerce (Greater East Aurora)
Gary D Grote, Executive Director
431 Main Street, East Aurora, NY 14052-1783
716-652-8444 or 800-441-2881 Fax: 716-652-8384
e-mail: eanycc@choiceonemail.com
Web site: www.eanycc.com

East Hampton Chamber of Commerce
Marina Van, Executive Director
79-A Main St, East Hampton, NY 11937
631-324-0362 Fax: 631-329-1642
e-mail: info@easthamptonchamber.com
Web site: www.easthamptonchamber.com

East Islip Chamber of Commerce
Tony Fanni, President
PO Box 88, East Islip, NY 11730
631-859-5000
Web site: www.isliplife.com/eastislipchamber

East Meadow Chamber of Commerce
Brandon Bloom, President

Chambers of Commerce

Offices and agencies appear in alphabetical order.

CHAMBERS OF COMMERCE/ECONOMIC DEVELOPMENT ORGANIZATIONS

PO Box 77, East Meadow, NY 11554
516-794-3727
Web site: www.emchamber.com

Eastchester-Tuckahoe Chamber of Commerce
Carla Moccia Paribello, President
PO Box 66, Eastchester, NY 10709
914-779-7344
e-mail: cetcoc@aol.com

Ellenville/Wawarsing Chamber of Commerce
Janet Mcdonnell, Office Sec
PO Box 227, 5 Berme Rd, Ellenville, NY 12428
845-647-4620
Web site: www.wawarsing.net

Ellicottville Chamber of Commerce
Lisa Ives, Administrative Asst
9 W Washington St, PO Box 456, Ellicottville, NY 14731
716-699-5046 or 800-349-9099 Fax: 716-699-5637
e-mail: info@ellicottvilleny.com
Web site: www.ellicottvilleny.com

Erie County Ind Dev Agency
Charles E Webb, President
275 Oak St, Buffalo, NY 14203
716-856-6525 Fax: 716-856-6754
e-mail: cwebb@ecidany.com
Web site: www.ecidany.com

Erie County Planning & Economic Dev
Andrew M Eszak, Deputy Commissioner
95 Franklin St, Rm 1016, Buffalo, NY 14202
716-858-8390 Fax: 716-858-7248
e-mail: eszaka@erie.gov
Web site: www.erie.gov

Erwin Ind Dev Agency (Town of)
Jack Benjamin, President
Three Rivers Dev Corp Inc, 114 Pine St Suite 201, Corning, NY 14830
607-962-4693 Fax: 607-936-9132
e-mail: jebrivers@stny.rr.com
Web site: www.threeriversdevelopment.com

Essex County Ind Dev Agency
Carol Calabrese, Co-Executive Director
107 Hand Ave, Ste 1, PO Box 217, Elizabethtown, NY 12932
518-873-9114 Fax: 518-873-2011
e-mail: info@essexcountyida.com
Web site: www.essexcountyida.com

Fair Haven Area Chamber of Commerce
David M Holdridge, President
PO Box 13, Fair Haven, NY 13064
315-947-6037
e-mail: info@fairhavenny.com
Web site: www.fairhavenny.com

Farmington Chamber of Commerce
Rose M Kleman, President

1000 County Rd, #8, Farmington, NY 14425
315-986-8182 Fax: 315-986-4377

Farmingville/Holtsville Chamber of Commerce
Wayne Carrington, President
PO Box 66, Holtsville, NY 11742
631-758-0544 Fax: 631-758-0544
e-mail: fhcoc@fhcoc.com
Web site: www.fhcoc.com

Fort Brewerton/Greater Oneida Lake Chamber
Henry Gloude, President
PO Box 655, Brewerton, NY 13029
315-668-3408 Fax: 315-668-3408
Web site: www.oneidalakechamber.com

Fort Edward Chamber of Commerce
Pamela Brooks, President
PO Box 267, Fort Edward, NY 12828
518-747-3000 Fax: 518-747-0622
Web site: www.ftedward.com

Franklin County Ind Dev Agency
Brad W Jackson, Executive Director
10 Elm Street, Suite 2, Malone, NY 12953
518-483-9472 Fax: 518-483-2900
e-mail: frctyida@twcny.rr.com

Franklin Square Chamber of Commerce
Frank Cutolo, President
PO Box 11, Franklin Square, NY 11010
516-775-0001

Fredonia Chamber of Commerce
Mary Beth Fagan, Executive Director
5 East Main St, Fredonia, NY 14063
716-679-1565
e-mail: fredcham@netsync.net
Web site: www.fredoniachamber.org

French-American Chamber of Commerce
Martin Biscoff, Director
122 E 42ND St, Siute 2015, New York, NY 10168
212-867-0123 Fax: 212-867-9050

Fulton County Economic Dev Corp
Jeffrey Bray, Executive VP
55 East Main St, Ste 110, Johnstown, NY 12095
518-762-8700 Fax: 518-762-8702
e-mail: fcedc@sites4u.org
Web site: www.sites4u.org

Fulton County Ind Dev Agency
James Mraz, Secretary
One East Montgomery St, Johnstown, NY 12095
518-736-5660 Fax: 518-762-4597
e-mail: planning@co.fulton.ny.us

Fulton County Reg Chamber of Commerce & Ind
Wally Hart, President

Offices and agencies appear in alphabetical order.

2 N Main St, Gloversville, NY 12078
518-725-0641 Fax: 518-725-0643
e-mail: info@fultoncountyny.org
Web site: www.fultoncountyny.org

Garden City Chamber of Commerce

Althea Robinson, Executive Director
230 Seventh Street, Garden City, NY 11530
516-746-7724 Fax: 516-746-7725
Web site: www.gardencitychamber.org

Genesee County Chamber of Commerce

Lynn Freeman, President
210 E Main St, Batavia, NY 14020
585-343-7440 or 800-622-2686 Fax: 585-343-7487
e-mail: chamber@geneseeny.com
Web site: www.geneseeny.com

Genesee County Economic Development Center

Steven G Hyde, CEO
One Mill Street, Batavia, NY 14020
585-343-4866 or 888-7-GENESE Fax: 585-343-0848
e-mail: gcedc@gcedc.com
Web site: www.gcedc.com

Geneva Area Chamber of Commerce

Rob Gladden, Pres/ CEO
35 Lakefront Dr, PO Box 587, Geneva, NY 14456
315-789-1776 or 877-543-6382 Fax: 315-789-3993
e-mail: rgladden@genevany.com
Web site: www.genevany.com

Geneva Ind Dev Agency (City of)

Richard E Rising, City Manager
47 Castle St, Geneva, NY 14456
315-789-6104 Fax: 315-789-8373
e-mail: rrising@geneva.ny.us
Web site: www.geneva.ny.us

Glen Cove Chamber of Commerce

Michael Davidson, Executive Director
PO Box 721, Glen Cove, NY 11542
516-676-6666
e-mail: info@glencovechamber.org
Web site: www.glencovechamber.org

Gore Mountain Region Chamber of Commerce

Emily Stanton, President
Rte 28N Main St, PO Box 84, North Creek, NY 12853
518-251-2612 Fax: 518-251-5317
e-mail: goremtn@superior.net
Web site: www.goremtnregion.org

Goshen Chamber of Commerce

Pip Klein, Executive Director

44 Park Place, PO Box 506, Goshen, NY 10924
845-294-7741 Fax: 845-294-3998
e-mail: gcc1@frontiernet.net
Web site: www.goshennychamber.com

Gouverneur Chamber of Commerce

Donna Lawrence, Executive Director
214 East Main St, Gouverneur, NY 13642
315-287-0331 Fax: 315-287-3694
e-mail: info@governcurchamber.com
Web site: www.gouveneurchamber.net

Gowanda Area Chamber of Commerce

Rev Travis Grubbs, President
28 Jamestown St, PO Box 45, Gowanda, NY 14070
716-532-2834 Fax: 716-532-2834
e-mail: gowandausa@yahoo.com
Web site: www.gowandachamber.org

Grand Island Chamber of Commerce

Beverly Kinney, President
1980 Whitehaven Rd, Grand Island, NY 14072
716-773-3651 Fax: 716-773-3316
e-mail: info@gichamber.org
Web site: www.gichamber.org

Granville Chamber of Commerce

Dan Brown, President
One Main St, PO Box 13, Granville, NY 12832
518-642-2815 Fax: 518-642-2772
e-mail: info@granvillechamber.com
Web site: www.granvillechamber.com

Great Neck Chamber of Commerce

David L Lurie, Administrative Secretary
643 Middle Neck Rd, Great Neck, NY 11023
516-487-2000 Fax: 516-829-5472
Web site: www.greatneckchamber.org

Greece Chamber of Commerce

Carlos H Mercado Jr, President & CEO
2496 West Ridge Rd, Ste 201, Greece, NY 14626-3049
585-227-7272 Fax: 585-227-7275
e-mail: cmercado@greecechamber.org
Web site: www.greecechamber.org

Green Island Ind Dev Agency (Village of)

Sean E Ward, Chairman
20 Clinton St, Green Island, NY 12183
518-273-2201 Fax: 518-273-2235
e-mail: seanw@villageofgreenisland.com

Greene County Dept of Planning & Economic Development

Warren Hart, AICP, Director
411 Main Street, Catskill, NY 12414
518-719-3290 Fax: 518-719-3789
Web site: www.discovergreene.com

Greene County Tourism Promotion

Daniela Marino, Director

Offices and agencies appear in alphabetical order.

Rte 23B at NYS Thruway, Exit 21, PO #527, Catskill, NY 12414
518-943-3223 or 800-355-CATS Fax: 518-943-2296
e-mail: tourism@discovergreene.com
Web site: www.greenetourism.com

Greenport-Southold Chamber of Commerce
John Barnes, President
PO Box 1415, Southold, NY 11971
631-765-3161 Fax: 631-765-3161
Web site: www.greenportsoutholdchamber.org

Greenvale Chamber of Commerce (Greater Greenvale)
Michael Lucarelli, Executive Director
PO Box 123, Greenvale, NY 11548
516-621-2110 Fax: 516-484-7468
Web site: www.greenvalechamber.com

Greenville Area Chamber of Commerce
Debbie Magee, President & CEO
PO Box 385, Greenville, NY 12083
518-966-5050 Fax: 518-966-5050
e-mail: chamber@greenville-ny.com
Web site: www.greenville-ny.com

Greenwich Chamber of Commerce (Greater Greenwich)
Kathy Nichols Tomkins, Secretary
6 Academy St, Greenwich, NY 12834
518-692-7979 Fax: 518-692-7979
e-mail: info@greenwichchamber.org
Web site: www.greenwichchamber.org

Greenwich Village-Chelsea Chamber of Commerce
June Lee, Executive Director
80 Eighth Avenue, #412, New York, NY 10011
212-255-5811 Fax: 212-255-5058
e-mail: info@gvccc.com
Web site: www.gvccc.com

Greenwood Lake Chamber of Commerce
Ann Chaimowitz, Director
PO Box 36, Greenwood Lake, NY 10925
845-477-0112 Fax: 845-477-2577
e-mail: info@greenwoodlakeny.org
Web site: www.greenwoodlakeny.org

Guilderland Chamber of Commerce
Jane M Schramm, Executive Director
2021 Western Ave, Ste 105, Guilderland, NY 12203
518-456-6611 Fax: 518-456-6690
e-mail: info@guilderlandchamber.com
Web site: www.guilderlandchamber.com

Guilderland Ind Dev Agency (Town of)
James Shahda, Chairman
Town Hall, PO Box 339, Guilderland, NY 12084
518-456-0336 Fax: 518-356-5514
e-mail: stacia@guilderland.org
Web site: www.guilderland.org

Hamburg Chamber of Commerce
Betty Newell, President & CEO

8 South Buffalo St, Hamburg, NY 14075
716-649-7917 or 877-322-6890 Fax: 716-649-6362
e-mail: president@hamburg-chamber.org
Web site: www.hamburg-chamber.org

Hamburg Ind Dev Agency
Michael J Bartlett, Executive Director
S6100 South Park Avenue, Hamburg, NY 14075
716-648-6216 Fax: 716-648-0151
e-mail: hamburgida@townofhamburgny.com
Web site: www.townofhamburgny.com

Hampton Bays Chamber of Commerce
Stan Glinka, President
140 West Main St, Hampton Bays, NY 11946
631-728-2211 Fax: 631-728-0308
Web site: www.hamptonbayschamber.com

Hancock Area Chamber of Commerce
Christopher Gross, President
Box 525, Hancock, NY 13783
607-637-4756
e-mail: chamber@hancock.net
Web site: www.hancockareachamber.com

Harlem Chamber of Commerce (Greater Harlem)
Lloyd Williams, President & CEO
200 A West 136th St, New York, NY 10030
212-862-7200 Fax: 212-862-8745
e-mail: harlemchamber@hotmail.com
Web site: www.harlemdiscover.com

Hastings-on-Hudson Chamber of Commerce
Joseph R LoCascio, Jr, President
PO Box 405, Hastings-on-Hudson, NY 10706
914-478-0900 Fax: 914-478-1720
Web site: www.hastingsgov.org

Hempstead Ind Dev Agency (Town of)
Frederick Parola, Executive Director
350 Front St, Rm 240, Hempstead, NY 11550
516-489-5000 x4200 Fax: 516-489-3179
e-mail: idamail@hotmail.org
Web site: www.tohida.org

Herkimer County Chamber of Commerce
Matthew Stubley, Executive Director
PO Box 129, 28 W Main St, Mohawk, NY 13407-0129
315-866-7820 or 877-984-4636 Fax: 315-866-7833
e-mail: hccomm@ntcnet.com
Web site: www.herkimercountychamber.com

Herkimer County Ind Dev Agency
Mark Feane, Executive Director
301 N Washington St, PO Box 390, 4TH FL, Herkimer, NY 13350
315-867-1373 Fax: 315-867-1515
e-mail: ida@herkimercounty.org
Web site: www.herkimercountyida.com

Hicksville Chamber of Commerce
Judith K Lombardi, Executive Secretary

Offices and agencies appear in alphabetical order.

10 W Marie St, Hicksville, NY 11801
516-931-7170 Fax: 516-931-8546
e-mail: hicksvillechamber@earthlink.net
Web site: www.hicksvillechamber.com

Hornell Area Chamber of Commerce/ Hornell Ind Dev Agency (City of)
James W Griffin, President/Exec Director
40 Main St, Hornell, NY 14843
607-324-0310 Fax: 607-324-3776
e-mail: griff@hornellny.com
Web site: www.hornellny.com

Hudson Valley Gateway Chamber of Commerce
Bernard Molloy, President & CEO
One S Division St, Peekskill, NY 10566
914-737-3600 Fax: 914-737-0541
e-mail: bmolloy@hvgatewaychamber.com
Web site: www.hvgatewaychamber.com

Hunter Chamber of Commerce (Town of)
Michael McCrary, President
PO Box 177, Hunter, NY 12442
518-263-4900 Fax: 518-589-0117
e-mail: hunterch@mhonline.net
Web site: www.hunterchamber.org

Huntington Township Chamber of Commerce
Michael P Forbes, CEO/President
164 Main St, Huntington, NY 11743
631-423-6100 Fax: 631-351-8276
e-mail: dennis@huntingtonchamber.com
Web site: www.huntingtonchamber.com

Hyde Park Chamber of Commerce
Elizabeth Roger, President
PO Box 17, Hyde Park, NY 12538
845-229-8612 Fax: 845-229-8638
e-mail: hydepark@bestweb.net
Web site: www.hydeparkchamber.org

Indian Lake Chamber of Commerce
Brenda Lamphear, President
PO Box 724, Indian Lake, NY 12842
518-648-5112 or 800-328-5253 Fax: 518-648-5489
e-mail: ilcoc@telenet.net
Web site: www.indian-lake.com

Inlet Information Office
Adele Burnett, Director, Information & Tourism
Route 28, PO Box 266, Inlet, NY 13360
315-357-5501 or 866-GOINLET Fax: 315-357-3570
e-mail: inletny@telenet.net
Web site: www.inletny.com

Islip Chamber of Commerce
Harvey Allen, President

PO Box 112, Islip, NY 11751-0112
631-581-2720 or 631-581-2720
Web site: www.islipchamberofcommerce.com

Islip Economic Dev Div (Town of)
William G Mannix, Director
40 Nassau Ave, Islip, NY 11751
631-224-5512 Fax: 631-224-5532
e-mail: ecodev@isliptown.org
Web site: www.isliptown.org

Islip Ind Dev Agency (Town of)
Peter McGowan, Chairman
40 Nassau Ave, Islip, NY 11751
631-224-5512 Fax: 631-224-5517
e-mail: ecodev@isliptown.org
Web site: www.islip.org

Jamaica Chamber of Commerce
Robert M Richards, President
90-25 161st St, Ste 505, Jamaica, NY 11432
718-657-4800 Fax: 718-658-4642
e-mail: jamaicachamber@earthlink.net
Web site: www.jamaicachamberofcommerce.org

Jamaica Dev Corp (Greater Jamaica)
Helen Levine, Executive Vice President
90-04 161st Street, Jamaica, NY 11432
718-291-0282 x120 Fax: 718-658-1405
e-mail: hlevine@gjdc.org

Japanese Chamber of Commerce
Motoatsu Sakwrai, President
145 W 57th St, New York, NY 10019
212-246-8001 Fax: 212-246-8002
Web site: www.jcciny.org

Kenmore-Town of Tonawanda Chamber of Commerce
Daniel J Barufaldi, President
3411 Delaware Ave, Kenmore, NY 14217
716-874-1202 Fax: 716-874-3151
e-mail: info@ken-ton.org
Web site: www.ken-ton.org

Kings Park Chamber of Commerce
Charles Gardner, President
PO Box 322, Kings Park, NY 11754
631-269-7678 Fax: 631-269-5575
e-mail: kingsparkli.com
Web site: www.kingsparkli.com

Lackawanna Area Chamber of Commerce
Aimee Gomlack-Brace, President
638 Ridge Rd, Lackawanna, NY 14218
716-823-8841 or 1-800-747-8841 Fax: 716-823-8848
e-mail: sunnylany@aol.com
Web site: www.lackawannachamber.com

Lake George Regional Chamber of Commerce
Christine Molella, Office Manager

Offices and agencies appear in alphabetical order.

PO Box 272, Lake George, NY 12845-0272
518-668-5755 Fax: 518-668-4286
e-mail: info@lgchamber.org
Web site: www.lakegeorgechamber.com

Lake Luzerne Chamber of Commerce
George Beagle, President
PO Box 222, Lake Luzerne, NY 12846-0222
518-696-3500
e-mail: llcc@telenet.net
Web site: www.lakeluzernechamber.org

Lake Placid Chamber of Commerce
James McKenna, CEO
216 Main St, Lake Placid, NY 12946
518-523-2445 Fax: 518-523-2605
e-mail: info@lakeplacid.com
Web site: www.lakeplacid.com

Lancaster Area Chamber of Commerce
Kathy Konst, Executive Director
PO Box 284, 39 Central Ave, Lancaster, NY 14086
716-681-9755 Fax: 716-684-3385
e-mail: director@laccny.org; laccny@aol.com
Web site: www.laccny.org

Lancaster Ind Dev Agency (Town of)
Robert H Giza, Chairman
21 Central Avenue, Lancaster, NY 14086
716-683-1610 Fax: 716-683-0512
e-mail: lookatus@lancasterny.com
Web site: www.lancasterny.com

Latham Area Chamber of Commerce
Nancy A Kruegler, Executive Director
849 New Loudon Rd, Latham, NY 12110
518-785-6995 Fax: 518-785-7173
e-mail: info@lathamchamber.org
Web site: www.lathamchamber.org

Lewis County Chamber of Commerce
Gary Hamburg, Executive Director
7383-C Utica Blvd, Lowville, NY 13367
315-376-2213 or 800-724-0242 Fax: 315-376-0326
e-mail: lcchambr@northnet.org
Web site: www.lewiscountychamber.org

Lewis County Ind Dev Agency
Ned E Cole, Executive Director
7642 State St, PO Box 106, Lowville, NY 13367
315-376-3014 Fax: 315-376-7880
e-mail: lcida@northnet.org
Web site: www.lcida.org

Liverpool Chamber of Commerce (Greater Liverpool)
Mary F Price, Executive Director

314 Second St, PO Box 154, Liverpool, NY 13088
315-457-3895 Fax: 315-234-3226
e-mail: mary@liverpoolchamber.com
Web site: www.liverpoolchamber.com

Livingston County Chamber of Commerce
Cynthia Oswald, President
4560 Millennium Dr, Geneseo, NY 14454-1134
585-243-2222 or 800-538-7365 Fax: 585-243-4824
e-mail: coswald@livchamber.com
Web site: www.livchamber.com

Livingston County Economic Dev Office & Ind Dev Agency
Patrick J Rountree, Director
Livingston Cty Gov't Ctr, 6 Court St, #306, Geneseo, NY 14454-1043
585-243-7124 or 877-284-5343 Fax: 585-243-7126
e-mail: build-here@co.livingston.ny.us
Web site: www.build-here.com

Lockport Ind Dev Agency (Town of)
Lewis L Staley, Administrative Director
6560 Dysinger Rd, Lockport, NY 14094
716-439-9520 Fax: 719-439-0528
e-mail: town-lkptida@elockport.com
Web site: www.elockport.com

Long Beach Chamber of Commerce
Lawrence E Elovoch, President
350 National Blvd, Long Beach, NY 11561-3312
516-432-6000 Fax: 516-432-0273

Long Island Association
Matthew Crosson, President
80 Hauppauge Rd, Commack, NY 11725-4495
631-499-4400 Fax: 631-499-2194
e-mail: info@longislandassociation.org
Web site: www.longislandassociation.org

Long Island Council of Dedicated Merchants Chamber of Commerce
Maureen Schneider, President
PO Box 512, Miller Place, Long Island, NY 11764
631-821-1313 or 631-331-2833 Fax: 631-331-0027
e-mail: sch1999@aol.com
Web site: www.cdmlongisland.com

Long Island Dev Corp
Roslyn D Goldmacher, President & CEO
45 Seaman Ave, Bethpage, NY 11714-3701
516-433-5000 Fax: 516-433-5046
e-mail: roz-goldmacher@lidc.org
Web site: www.lidc.org

Madison County Ind Dev Agency
Peter L Cann, Director

Offices and agencies appear in alphabetical order.

Canastota Business Ctr, 11 Madison Blvd, Canastota, NY 13032
315-697-9817 Fax: 315-697-8169
e-mail: plcann@twcny.rr.com
Web site: www.madisoncountyny.com/mcida

Mahopacs, Chamber of Commerce, Inc
Kevin Bailey, Executive Director
953 South lake Blvd, PO Box 160, Mahopac, NY 10541-0160
845-628-5553 Fax: 845-628-5962
e-mail: mahopacchamber@computer.net
Web site: www.mahopacchamber.com

Malone Chamber of Commerce
Pat O'Donnell, Director
170 E Main St, Malone, NY 12953
518-483-3760 or 877-625-6631 Fax: 518-483-3172
e-mail: info@malonenychamber.com
Web site: www.malonenychamber.com

Mamaroneck Chamber of Commerce
Thomas DeRosa, President
430 Center Ave, Mamaroneck, NY 10543
914-698-4400
Web site: www.mamaroneckchamberofcommerce.org

Manhasset Chamber of Commerce
Diane Harragan, Co-President; Bernard Rolston, Co-President
62 Manhasset Ave, Manhasset, NY 11030
516-627-1098 Fax: 516-365-7644
Web site: www.manhasset.org

Manhattan Chamber of Commerce Inc
Nancy Ploeger, President
1375 Broadway, Third Floor, New York, NY 10018
212-479-7772 Fax: 212-473-8074
e-mail: info@manhattancc.org
Web site: www.manhattancc.org

Massapequa Chamber of Commerce
Joyce Hewston, President
674 Broadway, Massapequa, NY 11758
516-541-1443 Fax: 516-541-8625
e-mail: masscoc@aol.com
Web site: www..massapequachamber.com

Massena Chamber of Commerce
Paul A Haggett, Executive Director
50 Main St, Massena, NY 13662
315-769-3525 Fax: 315-7695-2955
e-mail: massena@gisco.net
Web site: www.massenany.com

Mastics/Shirley Chamber of Commerce
Pat Peluso, President
PO Box 4, Mastic, NY 11950
631-399-2228
e-mail: subwaybill@aol.com
Web site: www.chamberms.com

Mattituck Chamber of Commerce
Domenico Mautarelli, President

PO Box 1056, Mattituck, NY 11952
631-298-5757
Web site: www.mattituckchamber.org

Mayville/Chautauqua Chamber of Commerce
Deborah Marsala, Coordinator
PO Box 22, Mayville, NY 14757
716-753-3113 Fax: 716-753-3113
Web site: www.mayville-chautauquachamber.org

Mechanicville Area Chamber of Commerce
Sharon Zappola, President
312 N 3RD Ave, PO Box 205, Mechanicville, NY 12118
518-664-7791 Fax: 518-664-0826
e-mail: mechcham@msm.com

Mechanicville/Stillwater Ind Dev Agency
Sam A Carabis, Treasurer
City Hall, 36 North Main Street, Mechanicville, NY 12118
518-664-7303 Fax: 518-664-5362
Web site: www.mechanicville-stillwater-ida.org

Merrick Chamber of Commerce
Salvatore Vassallo, President
PO Box 53, Merrick, NY 11566
516-546-3077 Fax: 516-377-6063
e-mail: plussizegal11566@juno.com
Web site: www.merrickchamber.com

Mid-Hudson Pattern for Progress
Michael J DiTullo, President
Desmond Campus, 6 Albany Post Rd, Newburgh, NY 12550
845-565-4900 Fax: 845-565-4918
e-mail: mditullo@pfprogress.org
Web site: www.pattern-for-progress.org

Miller Place/Mt Sinai/Sound Beach/ Rocky Point Chamber of Commerce
Maureen Schneider, President
PO Box 512, Miller Place, NY 11764
631-821-1313
e-mail: sch1999@aol.com
Web site: www.cdmlongisland.com

Mineola Chamber of Commerce
Carmela Bernacchio, President
PO Box 62, Mineola, NY 11501
516-408-3554 Fax: 516-408-3554
Web site: www.mineolachamber.com

Mohawk Valley Chamber of Commerce
Bill Nicholson, Interim-President
520 Seneca St, Utica, NY 13502
315-724-3151 Fax: 315-724-3177
e-mail: info@mvchamber.org
Web site: www.mvchamber.org

Mohawk Valley Economic Dev District
Michael Reese, Executive Director

Offices and agencies appear in alphabetical order.

26 W Main St, PO Box 69, Mohawk, NY 13407-0106
315-866-4671 Fax: 315-866-9862
e-mail: mvedd@twcny.rr.com

Mohawk Valley Economic Dev Growth Enterprises
Shawna Papale, Vice President Economic & Marketing Manager
153 Brooks Rd, Rome, NY 13441
315-338-0393 or 800-765-4990 Fax: 315-338-5694
e-mail: jgkaram@mvedge.org
Web site: www.mvedge.org

Monroe County Ind Dev Agency (COMIDA)
T Slaybaugh, Executive Director
50 W Main St, Ste 8100, Rochester, NY 14614
585-428-5260 Fax: 585-428-5336
e-mail: rocco@growmonroe.com
Web site: www.growmonroe.org

Montgomery County Chamber of Commerce/ Montgomery County Partnership, In
Deborah Auspelmyer, President
366 Main, Amsterdam, NY 12010
518-842-8200 or 800-743-7337 Fax: 518-843-8327
e-mail: chamber@montgomerycountyny.com
Web site: www.montgomerycountyny.com

Moravia Chamber of Commerce
Mark Wood, President
PO Box 647, Moravia, NY 13118
315-497-1341 Fax: 315-497-9319
e-mail: jwellauer@scccinternet.com
Web site: www.cayuganet.org

Mount Kisco Chamber of Commerce
Anne Feldman, Executive Director
3 N Moger Ave, Mount Kisco, NY 10549
914-666-7525 Fax: 914-666-7663
e-mail: mtkiscochamber@aol.com
Web site: www.mtkisco.com

Mount Vernon Chamber of Commerce
Cloey Sepe, President
22 West First Street, Suite 210, Mount Vernon, NY 10550
914-667-7500 Fax: 914-699-0139
e-mail: mvny.coc@verizon.net
Web site: www.mvnycoc.org

Mount Vernon Ind Dev Agency (City of)
Constance (Gerrie) Post, Secretary
City Hall, Roosevelt Square, Mount Vernon, NY 10550
914-665-2300 Fax: 914-665-2496
e-mail: gerriepost@ci.mount-vernon.ny.us
Web site: www.cmvny.com

Nassau Council of Chambers
Richard M Bivone, President

308 East Meadow Ave, East Meadow, NY 11554
516-396-0200 Fax: 516-396-5097
e-mail: rmbivone@ncchambers,org
Web site: ncchambers.org

Nassau County Ind Dev Agency
Joseph Gioino, Executive Director
1100 Franklin Ave, Suite 300, Garden City, NY 11530
516-571-4160 Fax: 516-571-4161
e-mail: jgioino@nassauida.com
Web site: www.nassauida.com

New City Chamber of Commerce
Gillian Ballard, Executive Director
PO Box 2021, New City, NY 10956
845-638-1395 Fax: 845-638-1395
Web site: www.newcitychamberofcommerce.org

New Paltz Regional Chamber of Commerce
Joyce M Minard, President
124 Main St, New Paltz, NY 12561-1525
845-255-0243 Fax: 845-255-5189
e-mail: info@newpaltzchamber.org
Web site: www.newpaltzchamber.org

New Rochelle, Chamber of Commerce, Inc
Denise Lally, Executive Director
459 Main St, New Rochelle, NY 10801-6412
914-632-5700 or 914-632-7222 Fax: 914-632-0708
Web site: www.newrochellechamber.org

New York Chamber of Commerce (Greater New York)
Helana Natt, Executive Director
172 Madison Ave, 7th fl, New York, NY 10016
212-686-7220 Fax: 212-686-7232
e-mail: info@chamber.com
Web site: www.chamber.com

New York City, Partnership for
Kathryn S Wylde, President & CEO
One Battery Park Plaza, 5th Floor, New York, NY 10004-1405
212-493-7400 Fax: 212-493-7475
e-mail: info@pfnyc.org
Web site: www.pfnyc.org

New Yorktown Chamber of Commerce (The)
Michael Turton, Executive Director
Parkside Corner, PO Box 632, Suite 203, Yorktown Heights, NY 10598
914-245-4599 Fax: 914-734-7171
e-mail: staff@yorktownchamber.org
Web site: www.yorktownchamber.org

Newark Chamber of Commerce
Gloria Becker, Administrator

Offices and agencies appear in alphabetical order.

203 W Miller St, Newark, NY 14513
315-331-2705 Fax: 315-331-2705
e-mail: newarkcc@redsuspenders.com
Web site: www.newarknychamber.org

Niagara County Ind Dev Agency
Samuel M Ferraro, Executive Director
6311 Inducon Corporate Dr, Ste 1, Sanborn, NY 14132-9099
716-278-8750 Fax: 716-278-8757
e-mail: sam.ferraro@niagaracounty.com
Web site: www.ncida.org

Niagara USA Chamber of Commerce
Thomas Kraus, President
6311 Inducon Corporate Dr, Sanborn, NY 14132
716-433-3828 x24 Fax: 716-433-1154
e-mail: rlnewman@niagarachamber.org
Web site: www.niagarachamber.org

North Greenbush IDA
Paul Tazbir, Chairman
2 Douglas Street, Wynantskill, NY 12198-7561
518-283-5313 Fax: 518-283-5345
e-mail: tazbir@townofng.com

North Warren Chamber of Commerce
Greg Beckler, President
PO Box 490, Chestertown, NY 12817
518-494-2722 or 888-404-2722 Fax: 518-494-2722
e-mail: chamber@netheaven.com
Web site: www.adirondacklakesandrivers.com

Nyack Chamber of Commerce
Lorie Reynolds, Executive Director
PO Box 677, Nyack, NY 10960
845-353-2221 Fax: 845-353-4204
e-mail: coc@spyral.net
Web site: www.thenyacks.net

Oceanside Chamber of Commerce
Robert E Towers, President
PO Box 1, Oceanside, NY 11572
516-763-9177 Fax: 516-766-4575
Web site: www.oceansidechamber.org

Ogdensburg Chamber of Commerce (Greater Ogdensburg)
Laura Ashley, Executive Director
1020 Park Street, Ogdensburg, NY 13669
315-393-3620 Fax: 315-393-1380
e-mail: chamber@gisco.net
Web site: www.ogdensburgny.com

Olean Area Chamber of Commerce (Greater Olean)
John Sayegh, COO
120 N Union Street, Olean, NY 14760
716-372-4433 Fax: 716-372-7912
e-mail: jsayegh@oleanny.com
Web site: www.oleanny.com or www.oleaninfo.com

Oneida Chamber of Commerce (Greater Oneida Area)
Phyllis Montague Harris, Executive Director

136 Lenox Ave, Oneida, NY 13421
315-363-4300 Fax: 315-361-4558
e-mail: oneidach@dreamscape.com
Web site: www.oneidachamber.org

Oneida Ind Dev Agency (City of)
John Haskell, Chairman
Municipal Bldg, 109 N Main St, Oneida, NY 13421
315-363-4800 Fax: 315-363-9558

Onondaga County Ind Dev Agency
Donald Western, Assistant Secretary
421 Montgomery St, 14th Fl, Civic Ctr Bldg, Syracuse, NY 13202
315-435-3770 Fax: 315-435-3669
e-mail: donaldwestern@ongov.net
Web site: www.syracusecentral.com

Ontario Chamber of Commerce
Jim Switzer, Board of Directors
PO Box 100, Ontario, NY 14519-0100
315-524-5886 Fax: 315-524-9709
e-mail: jswitzer@eznet.net

Ontario County Ind Dev Agency & Econ Dev
Michael J Manikowski, Executive Director & Director
20 Ontario Street, Suite 106B, Canandaigua, NY 14424
585-396-4460 Fax: 585-396-4594
e-mail: golfbag@co.ontario.ny.us
Web site: www.ontariocountydev.org

Orange County Chamber of Commerce Inc
John A D'Ambrosio, President
11 Racquet Rd, Newburgh, NY 12550
845-567-6229 Fax: 845-567-6271
e-mail: drjohn@orangeny.com
Web site: www.orangeny.com

Orange County Partnership
Maureen Halahan, President/CEO
40 Matthews St, Suite 108, Goshen, NY 10924
845-294-2323 Fax: 845-294-8023
e-mail: info@ocpartnership.org
Web site: www.ocpartnership.org

Orchard Park Chamber of Commerce
Nancy L Conley, Executive Director
4211 N Buffalo St, Ste 14, Orchard Park, NY 14127-2401
716-662-3366 Fax: 716-662-5946
e-mail: opcc@orchardparkchamber.com
Web site: www.orchardparkchamber.com

Orleans County Chamber of Commerce
David Kelly, Executive Director
121 N Main St, #110, Albion, NY 14411
585-589-7727 Fax: 585-589-7326
e-mail: dkelly@orleanschamber.com
Web site: www.orleanschamber.com

Orleans Economic Development Agency (OEDA)
Donald F Kennedy, Executive Director

Offices and agencies appear in alphabetical order.

111 West Ave, Albion, NY 14411
585-589-7060 Fax: 585-589-5258
e-mail: dkennedy@orleansdevelopment.org
Web site: www.orleansdevelopment.org

Oswego Chamber of Commerce (Greater Oswego)
Jennifer B Hill, Executive Director
156 W Second St, Oswego, NY 13126
315-343-7681 Fax: 315-342-0831
e-mail: gocc@oswegochamber.com
Web site: www.oswegochamber.com

Oswego County Chamber of Commerce
Betsy Sherman Saunders, President
41 South Second St, PO Box 148, Fulton, NY 13069
315-598-4231 Fax: 315-592-9050
e-mail: bsaunders@twcny.rr.com
Web site: oswegocountychamber.com

Oswego County, Operation/Oswego County Ind Dev Agency
L Michael Treadwell, Executive Director
44 West Bridge St, Oswego, NY 13126
315-343-1545 Fax: 315-343-1546
e-mail: ooc@oswegocounty.org
Web site: www.oswegocounty.org

Otsego County Chamber (The)
Rob Robinson, President & CEO
12 Carbon St, Oneonta, NY 13820
607-432-4500 or 877-5-OTSEGO Fax: 607-432-4506
e-mail: tocc@otsegocountychamber.com
Web site: www.otsegocountychamber.com

Otsego County Economic Dev Dept & Ind Dev Agency
Lynn Bass, Economic Developer
242 Main St, Oneonta, NY 13820
607-432-8871 Fax: 607-432-5117
e-mail: bassl@otsegocounty.com
Web site: www.otsegoeconomicdevelopment.com

Oyster Bay Chamber of Commerce
Susan Manno, President
34 Audrey Ave, PO Box 21, Oyster Bay, NY 11771
516-922-6464 Fax: 516-624-8082
e-mail: tonij@oysterbay.org
Web site: www.oysterbay.org

Painted Post Area Board of Trade
Sheila Thomas, President
PO Box 128, Painted Post, NY 14870
607-962-5021 Fax: 607-937-4080
e-mail: crnny@stny.rr.com
Web site: www.paintedpostny.com

Patchogue Chamber of Commerce (Greater Patchogue)
Gail Hoag, Executive Director

15 N Ocean Ave, Patchogue, NY 11772
631-475-0121 Fax: 631-475-1599
e-mail: pagelinx1@cs.com
Web site: www.patchoguechamber.com

Peekskill Ind Dev Agency (City of)
Brian Havranek, Director, Planning, Development & Code Assist
840 Main Street, Room 31, Peekskill, NY 10566-2016
914-734-4210 Fax: 914-737-2688
Web site: www.cityofpeekskill.com

Perry Area Chamber of Commerce
Lorraine Sturm, Secretary
PO Box 35, Perry, NY 14530
585-237-5040
e-mail: perrchamberny@yahoo.com
Web site: www.perrychamber.com

Plattsburgh-North Country Chamber of Commerce
Garry Douglas, CEO & President
7061 Route 9, PO Box 310, Plattsburgh, NY 12901
518-563-1000 Fax: 516-563-1028
e-mail: chamber@westelcom.com
Web site: www.northcountrychamber.com

Port Chester-Rye Brook Chamber of Commerce
Peter Iasillo, Executive Director
110 Willett Ave, Port Chester, NY 10573
914-939-1900 Fax: 914-939-2733
e-mail: pcrbchamber@aol.com
Web site: www.portchesterryebrookchamber.com

Port Jefferson Chamber of Commerce (Greater Port Jefferson)
Joanne Cornell, President
118 W Broadway, Port Jefferson, NY 11777
631-473-1414 Fax: 631-474-4540
e-mail: info@portjeffchamber.com
Web site: www.portjeffchamber.com

Port Morris Local Development Corp
John Martin, Zone Coordinator
555 Bergen Ave, Bronx, NY 10455
718-292-3113 Fax: 718-292-3115
e-mail: dtaveras@sobro.org
Web site: www.sobro.org

Port Washington Chamber of Commerce
Warren Schein, President
329 Main St, PO Box 121, Port Washington, NY 11050
516-883-6566 Fax: 516-883-6591
e-mail: pwcoc@optonline.net
Web site: www.portwashington.org

Potsdam Chamber of Commerce
Abigail Lee, Executive Director

Offices and agencies appear in alphabetical order.

CHAMBERS OF COMMERCE/ECONOMIC DEVELOPMENT ORGANIZATIONS

PO Box 717, Potsdam, NY 13676
315-265-5440 Fax: 315-268-0330
e-mail: potsdam@slic.com
Web site: www.potsdam.ny.us

Poughkeepsie Area Chamber of Commerce
Charles S North, President
One Civic Center Plaza, Suite 400, Poughkeepsie, NY 12601
845-454-1700 Fax: 845-454-1702
e-mail: office@pokchamb.org
Web site: www.pokchamb.org

Pulaski-Eastern Shore Chamber of Commerce
Nancy Farrell, President
3044 State Route 13, PO Box 34, Pulaski, NY 13142-0034
315-298-2213
e-mail: pulaski@dreamscape.com
Web site: www.pulaskinychamber.com

Putnam County Econ Dev Corp
Ross M Weale, President
34 Gleneida Ave, Carmel, NY 10512
845-225-2300 Fax: 845-225-0311
e-mail: pedc@computer.net
Web site: www.putnamedc.org

Queens Chamber of Commerce (Borough of)
William R Egan, Executive VP
75-20 Astoria Blvd, #140, Jackson Heights, NY 11370-1131
718-898-8500 Fax: 718-898-8599
e-mail: queenschamber@worldnet.att.net
Web site: www.queenschamber.org

Red Hook Area Chamber of Commerce
Jeff Ackerly, President
PO Box 254, Red Hook, NY 12571-0254
845-758-0824 Fax: 845-758-1731
e-mail: info@redhookchamber.org
Web site: www.redhookchamber.org

Rensselaer County Regional Chamber of Commerce
Linda Hillman, President
255 River St, Troy, NY 12180
518-274-7020 Fax: 518-272-7729
e-mail: lhillman@renscochamber.com
Web site: www.renscochamber.com

Rhinebeck Chamber of Commerce
Susie Linn, Executive Director
PO Box 42, Rhinebeck, NY 12572
845-876-4778 or 845-876-5904 Fax: 845-876-8624
e-mail: info@rhinebeckchamber.com
Web site: www.rhinebeckchamber.com

Richfield Area Chamber of Commerce
E Lawrence Budro, Executive Director

PO Box 909, Richfield Springs, NY 13439-0909
315-858-2553
e-mail: elbudro@aol.com

Riverhead Chamber of Commerce
Barry Karlin, President
542 E Main St, Suite 2, Riverhead, NY 11901
631-727-7600 Fax: 631-727-7946
e-mail: info@riverheadchamber.com
Web site: www.riverheadchamber.com

Rochester Business Alliance Inc
Sandra Parker, CEO
150 State St, Rochester, NY 14614
585-244-1800 Fax: 585-263-3679
e-mail: t.mooney@rballiance.com
Web site: www.rochesterbusinessalliance.com

Rochester Downtown Development Corporation
Heidi N Zimmer-Meyer, President
183 E Main St, Suite 1300, Rochester, NY 14604
585-546-6920 Fax: 585-546-4784
e-mail: rddc@rddc.org
Web site: www.rochesterdowntown.com

Rochester Economic Dev Corp
R Fashun Ku, President
30 Church Street, Room 005A, Rochester, NY 14614
585-428-6808 Fax: 585-428-6042
e-mail: fashun@cityofrochester.gov
Web site: www.redco.net

Rockaway Dev & Revitalization Corp
Ivor A Quashie, Zone Coordinator
1920 Mott Ave, 2ND FL, Far Rockaway, NY 11691
718-327-5300 Fax: 718-327-4990
e-mail: rdrc1@netzero.net
Web site: www.rdrc.org

Rockaways, Chamber of Commerce, Inc
Joanie Omeste, Executive Director
253 Beach 116th St, Rockaway Park, NY 11694
718-634-1300 Fax: 718-634-9623
e-mail: rockawaychamber@aol.com
Web site: www.rockawaychamberofcommerce.com

Rockland Chamber of Commerce
Martin Bernstein, President
PO Box 2001, New City, NY 10956
845-634-5175 Fax: 845-634-6481
e-mail: martreal@aol.com

Rockland Economic Development Corp
Holly Freedman, President & CEO
1 Blue Hill Plaza, PO Box 1575, Pearl River, NY 10965-1575
845-735-7040 Fax: 845-735-5736
e-mail: info@redc.org
Web site: www.redc.org

Rockville Centre Chamber of Commerce
Michael Rechter, President

Offices and agencies appear in alphabetical order.

CHAMBERS OF COMMERCE/ECONOMIC DEVELOPMENT ORGANIZATIONS

PO Box 226, Rockville Centre, NY 11571-0226
516-766-0666
e-mail: info@rockvillecentrechamber.com
Web site: www.rockvillecentrechamber.com

Rome Area Chamber of Commerce
William K Guglielmo, President
139 West Dominick St, Rome, NY 13440-5809
315-337-1700 Fax: 315-337-1715
e-mail: info@romechamber.com
Web site: www.romechamber.com

Rome Industrial Dev Corp
Mark Kaucher, Executive Director
139 West Dominick St, Rome, NY 13440-5809
315-337-6360 Fax: 315-337-0918
e-mail: mkaucher@romeny.org
Web site: www.romeny.org

Ronkonkoma Chamber of Commerce
James Cotgreave, President
PO Box 2546, Ronkonkoma, NY 11779
631-584-4035 Fax: 631-584-3639
Web site: www.ronkonkomachamber.com

Sackets Harbor Chamber of Commerce
Michael Campbell, President
PO Box 17, Sackets Harbor, NY 13685
315-646-1700 Fax: 315-646-2066
e-mail: shvisit@gisco.net
Web site: www.sacketsharborny.com

Sag Harbor Chamber of Commerce
Robert Evjen, President
The Windmill, PO Box 2810, Sag Harbor, NY 11963
631-725-0011 Fax: 631-725-6663
e-mail: sagchamber@peconic.net
Web site: www.sagharborchamber.com

Salamanca Area Chamber of Commerce
Joelle Eddy, Chamber Administrator
26 Main St, Salamanca, NY 14779-1516
716-945-2034 Fax: 716-945-2034
e-mail: salcofc@localnet.com
Web site: salamancacofc.homstead.comm

Salamanca Ind Dev Agency
Janet Schmick, Officer Manager
225 Wildwood Ave, Salamanca, NY 14779-1547
716-945-3230 Fax: 716-945-8289
Web site: www.salmun.com

Saranac Lake Area Chamber of Commerce
Joseph Fiorile, President
39 Main St, Saranac Lake, NY 12983
518-891-1990 or 800-347-1992 Fax: 518-891-7042
e-mail: besttown@saranaclake.com
Web site: www.saranaclake.com

Saratoga County Chamber of Commerce
Joseph W Dalton, Jr, President

28 Clinton St, Saratoga Springs, NY 12866
518-584-3255 Fax: 518-587-0318
e-mail: info@saratoga.org
Web site: www.saratoga.org

Saratoga County Ind Dev Agency
Lawrence D Benton, Administrator
50 W High St, Ballston Spa, NY 12020
518-884-4705 Fax: 518-884-4780
e-mail: sarplan@govt.co.saratoga.ny.us
Web site: www.saratogacountyida.org

Saratoga Economic Dev Corp
Kenneth A Green, President
28 Clinton St, Saratoga Springs, NY 12866
518-587-0945 or 800-587-0945 Fax: 518-587-5855
e-mail: kgsaratoga@aol.com; kgreen@saratogaedc.com
Web site: www.saratogaedc.com

Sayville Chamber of Commerce (Greater Sayville)
Michael Furlinger, President
Lincoln Ave & Montauk Hwy, PO Box 235, Sayville, NY 11782-0235
631-567-5257 Fax: 631-218-0881
e-mail: sayvillechamber@aol.com
Web site: www.sayvillechamber.com

Schenectady County Chamber of Commerce
Charles P Steiner, President
306 State St, Schenectady, NY 12305-2302
518-372-5656 or 800-962-8007 Fax: 518-370-3217
e-mail: csteiner@schenectadychamber.org
Web site: www.schenectadychamber.org

Schenectady County Ind Dev Agency/ Economic Dev Corp
George Robertson, President
One Broadway Center, Suite 750, Schenectady, NY 12305
518-393-7252 Fax: 518-393-8687
e-mail: sedc12301@aol.com
Web site: sedc12301@aol.com

Schoharie County Chamber of Commerce
James Batsford, Executive Director
315-1 Main St, PO Box 400, Schoharie, NY 12157-0400
518-295-7033 or 800-41-VISIT Fax: 518-295-7453
e-mail: info@schohariechamber.com
Web site: www.schohariechamber.com

Schoharie County Ind Dev Agency
Ronald Filmer, Director
349 Mineral Springs Rd, Cobleskill, NY 12043
518-234-3751 Fax: 518-234-3951
e-mail: rfscrpc@midtel.net
Web site: www.schohariebiz.com

Schroon Lake Area Chamber of Commerce
DeeDee Cheviron, President

Offices and agencies appear in alphabetical order.

1075 US Rte 9, PO Box 726, Schroon Lake, NY 12870-0726
518-532-7675 or 888-SCHROON Fax: 518-532-7675
e-mail: schroon@capital.net; info@schroonlakechamber.com
Web site: www.schroonlakechamber.com

Schuyler County Chamber of Commerce
James Berg, President
100 N Franklin St, PO Box 268, Watkins Glen, NY 14891-0268
607-535-4300 or 800-607-4552 Fax: 607-535-6243
e-mail: info@schuylerny.com
Web site: www.schuylerny.com

Schuyler County Ind Dev Agency
Kelsey Jones, Executive Director
2 N Franklin St, Ste 330, Watkins Glen, NY 14891
607-535-4341 Fax: 607-535-7221
e-mail: scoped@lightlink.com
Web site: www.scoped.biz

Schuyler County Partnership for Econ Dev
J Kelsey Jones, Executive Director
2 N Franklin St, Ste 330, Watkins Glen, NY 14891
607-535-4341 Fax: 607-535-7221
e-mail: scoped@lightlink.com
Web site: www.scoped.biz

Seaford Chamber of Commerce
Seth Jay Sultan, President
PO Box 1634, Seaford, NY 11783
516-783-5544 Fax: 516-221-8683
e-mail: chamber@seaford.li
Web site: www.seaford.li

Seneca County Chamber of Commerce
Dominic R Christopher, Executive Director
2020 Rtes 5 & 20 West, PO Box 70, Seneca Falls, NY 13148-0070
315-568-2906 or 800-732-1848 Fax: 315-568-1730
e-mail: windmill@flare.net
Web site: www.senecachamber.org

Seneca County Ind Dev Agency
Glenn R Cooke, Executive Director
One Di Pronio Dr, Waterloo, NY 13165
315-539-1722 Fax: 315-539-4340
e-mail: gcooke@co.seneca.ny.us
Web site: www.scida.org

Sidney Chamber of Commerce
Doninic A Nuciforo, President
24 River St, PO Box 2295, Sidney, NY 13838
607-561-2642 Fax: 607-561-2644
e-mail: sidneychamber@mkl.com
Web site: www.sidneychamber.org

Skaneateles Chamber of Commerce
Susan Dove, Executive Director

PO Box 199, 22 Jordan St, Skaneateles, NY 13152
315-685-0552 Fax: 315-685-0552
e-mail: skaneateles-chamber@worldnet.att.net
Web site: www.skaneateles.com

Sleepy Hollow Chamber of Commerce
Anne Marie Basher, Executive Administrator
54 Main Street, Tarrytown, NY 10591-3660
914-631-1705 Fax: 914-366-4291
e-mail: katrina@bestweb.net
Web site: www.sleepyhollowchamber.com

Smithtown Chamber of Commerce
Judith Shivak, Executive Director
One W Main St, PO Box 1216, Smithtown, NY 11787
631-979-8069 Fax: 631-979-2206
e-mail: smithcoc@spec.net
Web site: www.smithtownchamber.com

South Jefferson Chamber of Commerce
Crystal Cobb, President
10924 US Rte 11, S.J. Plaza, Ste 2, Adams, NY 13605-3126
315-232-4215 Fax: 315-232-3967
e-mail: chamrep@northnet.org

Southampton Chamber of Commerce
Millie A Fellingham, Executive Director
76 Main St, Southampton, NY 11968
631-283-0402 Fax: 631-283-8707
e-mail: info@southamptonchamber.com
Web site: www.southamptonchamber.com

Southeastern New York, Council of Industry of
Harold King, Executive Vice President
6 Albany Post Rd, Newburgh, NY 12550
845-565-1355 Fax: 845-565-4918
e-mail: hking@councilofindustry.org
Web site: www.councilofindustry.org

Southern Dutchess Chamber of Commerce (Greater Southern Dutchess)
Ann Chambers Meagher, President & CEO
2582 South Ave, Wappingers Falls, NY 12590
845-296-0001 Fax: 845-296-0006
e-mail: bcoleman@gsdcc.org
Web site: www.gsdcc.org

Southern Saratoga County Chamber of Commerce
Peter L Aust, President/CEO
15 Park Ave, Ste 7B, PO Box 399, Clifton Park, NY 12065
518-371-7748 Fax: 518-371-5025
e-mail: info@ssccc.org
Web site: www.southernsaratogachamber.org

Southern Tier Economic Growth Inc
James C Johnson, Vice President

Offices and agencies appear in alphabetical order.

400 E Church St, PO Box 251, Elmira, NY 14902-0251
607-733-6513 Fax: 607-734-2698
e-mail: jjohnson@steg.com
Web site: www.steg.com

Southern Ulster County Chamber of Commerce
Ken Stewart, President
33 Main St, Highland, NY 12528
845-691-6070 Fax: 845-691-9194
e-mail: info@southernulsterchamber.org
Web site: www.southernulsterchamber.org

Springville Area Chamber of Commerce
Duane W Fischer, Executive Director
23 N Buffalo St, PO Box 310, Springville, NY 14141
716-592-4746 Fax: 716-592-4746
e-mail: dfish1063@aol.com
Web site: www.springvillechamber.com

St James Chamber of Commerce
Caren Anderson-Perez, President
PO Box 286, St James, NY 11780
631-584-8510
Web site: www.stjamesny.org

St Lawrence County Chamber of Commerce
Karen St Hilaire, Executive Director
101 Main Street, Canton, NY 13617-1248
315-386-4000 Fax: 315-379-0134
e-mail: slccoc@northnet.org
Web site: www.northcountryguide.com

St Lawrence County Ind Dev Agency
Raymond H Fountain, Administrative Director
80 State Highway 310, Ste 6, Canton, NY 13617-1496
315-379-9806 Fax: 315-386-2573
e-mail: rfountain@co.st-lawrence.ny.us
Web site: www.slcida.com

Staten Island Chamber of Commerce
Linda M Baran, President & CEO
130 Bay St, Staten Island, NY 10301
718-727-1900 Fax: 718-727-2295
e-mail: info@sichamber.com
Web site: www.sichamber.com

Staten Island Economic Dev Corp
Cesar J Claro, Executive Director
900 South Ave, Ste 402, Staten Island, NY 10314
718-477-1400 Fax: 718-477-0681
e-mail: siedc@si.rr.com
Web site: www.siedc.net

Steuben County Ind Dev Agency
James P Sherron, Executive Director

7234 Rte 54, PO Box 393, Bath, NY 14810-0390
607-776-3316 Fax: 607-776-5039
e-mail: scida@empacc.net
Web site: www.steubencountyida.com

Suffern Chamber of Commerce
Lenny Perles, President
PO Box 291, Suffern, NY 10901
845-357-8424
Web site: www.suffernchamberofcommerce.org

Sullivan County Chamber of Commerce
Jacquie Leventoff, President
59 N Main St, Ste 300, Liberty, NY 12754-1832
845-292-8500 Fax: 845-292-5366
e-mail: chamber@catskills.com
Web site: www.catskills.com

Sullivan County Ind Dev Agency
Jennifer C S Brylinski, Executive Director
1 Cablevision Ctr, Ferndale, NY 12734-5313
845-295-2603 Fax: 845-295-2604
e-mail: scida@hvc.rr.com

Syracuse & Central NY, Metropolitan Dev Assn of
Irwin L Davis, President
1900 State Tower Bldg, Syracuse, NY 13202
315-422-8284 Fax: 315-471-4503
e-mail: mda@mda-cny.com
Web site: www.mda-cny.com

Syracuse Chamber of Commerce (Greater Syracuse)
David P Cordeau, President
572 S Salina St, Syracuse, NY 13202-3320
315-470-1800 Fax: 315-471-8545
e-mail: dcordeau@syracusechamber.com
Web site: www.syracusechamber.com

Syracuse Economic Development
Marge Simcuski, Zone Coordinator
233 East Washington St, Room 312, City Hall, Syracuse, NY 13202
315-448-8100 Fax: 315-448-8036
e-mail: msimcuski@yahoo.com
Web site: www.syracuse.ny.us

Syracuse Ind Dev Agency
David Michel, Administrative Director
City Hall, 233 E Washington St, Syracuse, NY 13202
315-448-8100 Fax: 315-448-8036
e-mail: syrdev@emi.com; vsciscioli@edsyracuse.com
Web site: www.syracuse.ny.us/development/

Three Rivers Dev Foundation Inc
John E Benjamin, President
114 Pine St, Suite 201, Corning, NY 14830
607-962-4693 Fax: 607-936-9132
e-mail: jebrivers@stny.rr.com
Web site: www.threeriversdevelopment.com

Ticonderoga Area Chamber of Commerce
Debra Malaney, Executive Director

Offices and agencies appear in alphabetical order.

94 Montcalm Street, Suite 1, Ticonderoga, NY 12883
518-585-6619 Fax: 518-585-9184
e-mail: tacc@bluemoo.net
Web site: www.ticonderogany.com

Tioga County Chamber of Commerce
Martha Sauerbrey, President & CEO
188 Front St, Owego, NY 13827
607-687-2020 Fax: 607-687-9028
e-mail: business@tiogachamber.com
Web site: www.tiogachamber.com

Tioga County Ind Dev Agency
Aaron Gowan, Chairman
County Office Bldg, 56 Main Street, Owego, NY 13827
607-687-8255 or 607-687-8200 Fax: 607-687-1435
e-mail: tinneyl@co.tioga.ny.us
Web site: www.developtioga.com

Tompkins County Area Dev
Michael B Stamm, President
200 E Buffalo St, Ste 102A, Ithaca, NY 14850
607-273-0005 Fax: 607-273-8964
e-mail: tcad@lightlink.com
Web site: www.tcad.org

Tompkins County Chamber of Commerce
Jean McPheeters, President
904 E Shore Drive, Ithaca, NY 14850
607-273-7080 Fax: 607-272-7617
e-mail: jean@tompkinschamber.org
Web site: www.tompkinschamber.org

Tonawanda (Town Of) Dev Corp
Robert L Dimmig, Executive Director
169 Sheridan Parkside Dr, Tonawanda, NY 14150
716-871-8072 Fax: 716-871-8073
e-mail: ttdc@tonawanda.ny.us
Web site: www.tonawanda.com

Tonawandas, Chamber of Commerce of the
Kurt Alverson, Executive Director
15 Webster St, Suite 3, North Tonawanda, NY 14120
716-692-5120 Fax: 716-692-1867
e-mail: chamber@the-tonawandas.com
Web site: www.the-tonawandas.com

Tupper Lake Chamber of Commerce
Jon Kopp, Executive Director
60 Park St, Tupper Lake, NY 12986
518-359-3328 or 888-TUP-LAKE Fax: 518-359-2507
e-mail: tuppercc@adelphia.net
Web site: www.tupperlakeinfo.com

Ulster County Chamber of Commerce
Ward Todd, President & CEO

55 Albany Ave, Kingston, NY 12401
845-338-5100 Fax: 845-338-0968
e-mail: info@ulsterchamber.org
Web site: www.ulsterchamber.org

Ulster County Dev Corp/Ulster County Ind Dev Agency
Chester J Straub, Jr, President
5 Development Court, Kingston, NY 12401
845-338-8840 Fax: 845-338-0409
e-mail: cstraub@ulsterny.com
Web site: www.ulsterny.com

Union Local Dev Corp (Town of)
Joseph M Moody, Director, Economic Development
3111 E Main St, Endwell, NY 13760
607-786-2900 Fax: 607-786-2998
e-mail: economicdevelopment@townofunion.com
Web site: www.townofunion.com

Utica Ind Dev Agency (City of)
Joseph H Hobika Jr, Executive Director
One Kennedy Plz, Utica, NY 13501
315-792-0287 Fax: 315-792-9819
e-mail: jhobikajr@cityofutica.com
Web site: www.cityofutica.com

Valley Stream Chamber of Commerce
Boris Klerer, President
PO Box 1016, Valley Stream, NY 11580-1016
516-825-1741 Fax: 516-825-1741
Web site: www.vscc.org

Victor Chamber of Commerce
Susan Stehling, President
PO Box 86, Victor, NY 14564-0086
585-742-1476 Fax: 585-924-0523
e-mail: victorchamber@aol.com
Web site: www.victorchamber.com

Waddington Chamber of Commerce
Seryl Evans, President
PO Box 291, Waddington, NY 13694
315-388-5576
Web site: www.waddingtonny.us

Wantagh Chamber of Commerce
Marion F Romeo, President
PO Box 660, Wantagh, NY 11793
516-679-0100 or 516-781-6145
e-mail: wantaghchamber@wantaghmall.org
Web site: www.wantaghmall.org

Warren & Washington Ind Dev Agency
Susan Pruiksma, Office Administrator
5 Warren St, Suite 210, Glens Falls, NY 12801
518-792-1312 Fax: 518-792-4147
e-mail: wwida@localnet.com

Warren County Econ Dev Corp
Leonard Fosbrook, President

Offices and agencies appear in alphabetical order.

234 Glen Street, Glens Falls, NY 12801
518-761-6007 Fax: 518-761-9053
e-mail: info@warrencounty.org
Web site: www.warrencounty.org

Warrensburg Chamber of Commerce
Lynn Smith, President
3847 Main St, Warrensburg, NY 12885
518-623-2161 Fax: 518-623-2184
e-mail: info@warrensburgchamber.com
Web site: www.warrensburgchamber.com

Warsaw Chamber of Commerce (Greater Warsaw)
Christie Gerasimchik, President
PO Box 221, Warsaw, NY 14569
585-786-3730 Fax: 585-786-5159
e-mail: info@warsawchamber.com
Web site: warsawchamber.com

Warwick Valley Chamber of Commerce
Linda Glohs, Executive Director
South St, Caboose, PO Box 202, Warwick, NY 10990
845-986-2720 Fax: 914-986-6982
e-mail: info@warwickcc.org
Web site: www.warwickcc.org

Washington County Local Dev Corp
Mark Galough, Executive Director
County Office Bldg, 383 Broadway, Fort Edward, NY 12828
518-746-2292 Fax: 518-746-2293
e-mail: mgalough@co.washington.ny.us
Web site: www.wcldc.org

Watertown Empire Zone
R. Michael N'dolo, Zone Coodinator
PO Box 3367, Saratoga Springs, NY 12866
315-782-1167 Fax: 518-899-9642
e-mail: andrew@camoinassociates.com
Web site: www.watertownempirezone.com

Watertown-North County Chamber of Commerce (Greater Watertown)
Karen Delmonico, President & CEO
1241 Coffeen St, Watertown, NY 13601
315-788-4400 Fax: 315-788-3369
e-mail: chamber@watertownny.com
Web site: www.watertownny.com

Wayne County Ind Dev Agency & Econ Dev
Margaret Churchill, Director
16 William St, Lyons, NY 14489
315-946-5917 or 888-219-2963 Fax: 315-946-5918
e-mail: bharper@co.wayne.ny.us
Web site: www.wedcny.org

Webster Chamber of Commerce
Elizabeth Bernard, Administrator

26 E Main St, Webster, NY 14580-3280
585-265-3960 Fax: 585-265-3702
e-mail: bbernard@websterchamber.com
Web site: www.websterchamber.com

Wellsville Area Chamber of Commerce
Sarah Bray, Executive Director
114 N Main St, Wellsville, NY 14895
585-593-5080 Fax: 585-593-5088
e-mail: wlsvchamber@adelphia.com
Web site: www.wellsvilleny.com

West Seneca Chamber of Commerce
Carol J Dill, Administrative Director
950A Union Rd, Suite 5, West Seneca, NY 14224-3432
716-674-4900 Fax: 716-674-5846
e-mail: cdillchamber@westseneca.org
Web site: www.westseneca.org

West Side Chamber of Commerce
Andrew Albert, Executive Director
1841 Broadway, #701, New York, NY 10023
212-541-8880 Fax: 212-541-8883
e-mail: mail@westsidechamber.org
Web site: www.westsidechamber.org

Westchester County Association Inc (The)
William M Mooney, Jr, President
707 Westchester Ave, Suite 213, White Plains, NY 10604
914-948-6444 Fax: 914-948-6913
e-mail: wmooney@westchester.org
Web site: www.westchester.org

Westchester County Chamber of Commerce
Marsha Gordon, President & CEO
108 Corporate Park Dr, Ste 101, White Plains, NY 10604-3801
914-948-2110 Fax: 914-948-0122
Web site: www.westchesterny.org

Westchester County Ind Dev Agency
Theresa G Waivada, Executive Director
148 Martine Ave, Rm 903, White Plains, NY 10601
914-995-2916 Fax: 914-995-3044
e-mail: tgw1@westchestergov.com
Web site: www.westchestergov.com/ida

Westfield/Barcelona Chamber of Commerce
Kathy Grant, President
27 East Main St, Westfield, NY 14787-1319
716-326-4000 Fax: 716-326-2299
e-mail: chamber@cecomet.net

Westhampton Chamber of Commerce (Greater Westhampton)
Hank Beck, President

Offices and agencies appear in alphabetical order.

7 Glovers Lane, PO #1228, Westhampton Beach, NY 11978
631-288-3337 Fax: 631-288-3322
e-mail: info@whbcc.org
Web site: www.whbcc.org

Whiteface Mountain Regional Visitor's Bureau
Diane Buckley, Office Manager
PO Box 277, Whiteface-Wilmington, NY 12997
518-946-2255 or 888-944-8332 Fax: 518-946-2683
e-mail: info@whitefaceregion.com
Web site: www.whitefaceregion.com

Willistons, Chamber of Commerce, Inc
Evelyn Atanas, President
PO Box 207, Williston Park, NY 11596-0207
516-739-1943 Fax: 516-747-3742
e-mail: eatanas@aol.com
Web site: www.chamberofthewillistons.org

Woodstock Chamber of Commerce & Arts
Barry Samuels, President
PO Box 36, Woodstock, NY 12498
845-679-2205
e-mail: info@woodstockchamber.com
Web site: www.woodstockchamber.com

Wyoming County Chamber of Commerce
James M Pierce, Executive Director

6470 Route 20A, Suite 2, Perry, NY 14530-9798
585-237-0230 or 800-951-9774 Fax: 585-237-0231
e-mail: jpierce@wycochamber.org
Web site: www.wycochamber.org

Yates County Chamber of Commerce
Michael Linehan, President & CEO
2375 Rte 14A, Penn Yan, NY 14527
315-536-3111 Fax: 315-536-3791
e-mail: info@yatesny.com
Web site: www.yatesny.com

Yates County Ind Dev Agency
Steve Isaacs, Executive Director
One Keuka Business Park, Suite 104, Penn Yan, NY 14527
315-536-7328 Fax: 315-536-2389
e-mail: info@yatesida.com
Web site: www.yatesida.com

Yonkers Chamber of Commerce
Kevin T Cacace, President
20 S Broadway, Ste 1207, Yonkers, NY 10701
914-963-0332 Fax: 914-963-0455
e-mail: info@yonkerschamber.com
Web site: www.yonkerschamber.com

Yonkers Economic Dev/ Yonkers Ind Dev Agency (City of)
Edward A Sheeran, Executive Director
City Hall, 40 South Broadway, Rm 416, Yonkers, NY 10701
914-377-6797 Fax: 914-377-6003
e-mail: yonkersida@aol.com
Web site: www.cityofyonkersida.com

Chambers of
Commerce

Offices and agencies appear in alphabetical order.

NEWS MEDIA

This chapter identifies key journalists and editorial management for daily and weekly newspapers in New York State, major news services with reporters assigned to cover State government, radio stations with a news format and television stations with news staff.

Newspapers

Newspapers included in this chapter employ reporters who cover state and regional news. The newspapers are listed alphabetically by primary city served.

ALBANY

Legislative Gazette *Weekly Circulation: 15,500*

Legislative Gazette
ESP, Concourse Level Rm 106, PO Box 7329, Albany, NY 12224
518-486-6513 or 518-473-9739 Fax: 518-486-6609
e-mail: editor@legislativegazette.com
Web site: www.legislativegazette.com
Executive Publisher . . . . Alan Chartock
    e-mail: editor@legislativegazette.com
Editor/Instructor . . . . John W Bechtel
General Manager & Advertising Director . . . . Glenn S Vadney

Business Review (The) *Weekly Circulation: 10,500*

The Business Review
40 British American Blvd, Latham, NY 12210
518-640-6800 Fax: 518-640-6801
e-mail: albany@bizjournals.com
Web site: www.albany.bizjournals.com
Chairman . . . . Ray Shaw
    e-mail: albany@bizjournals.com
Publisher . . . . Carolyn M Jones
Editor . . . . Michael Hendricks
Managing Editor . . . . Neil Springer

Times Union *Weekday Circulation: 110,000*

Times Union
645 Albany Shaker Rd, Box 15000, Albany, NY 12212
518-454-5420 Fax: 518-454-5628 (n
e-mail: tucitydesk@timesunion.com
Web site: www.timesunion.com
Publisher . . . . David White
    e-mail: tucitydesk@timesunion.com
Editor . . . . Rex Smith
    e-mail: rsmith@timesunion.com
Managing Editor . . . . Mary Fran Gleason
Editor, Opinion Pages . . . . Joann Crupi
Assistant Managing Editor . . . . James Wright
State Editor . . . . Jay Jochnowitz
Legislative Correspondent . . . . Elizabeth Benjamin

AMSTERDAM

Recorder (The) *Weekday Circulation: 11,000*

Recorder (The)
One Venner Rd, PO Box 640, Amsterdam, NY 12010
518-843-1100 Fax: 518-843-6580 (n
e-mail: news@recordernews.com
Web site: www.recordernews.com
Publisher . . . . Richard Barker
    e-mail: news@recordernews.com
General Manager . . . . Kevin McClary
    e-mail: kevin@recordernews.com
Director, News Operations . . . . Geoff Dylong
    e-mail: geoff@recordernews.com
Executive Editor . . . . Kevin Mattison
    e-mail: mattison@recordernews.com

AUBURN

Citizen (The) *Weekday Circulation: 14,500*

Auburn Publishers Inc
25 Dill St, Auburn, NY 13021
315-253-5311 Fax: 315-253-6031
e-mail: citizennews@lee.net
Web site: www.auburnpub.com
Publisher . . . . Rick Emanuel
    e-mail: citizennews@lee.net
Editor . . . . Mikel LeFort
News Editor . . . . Jeremy Boyer

BATAVIA

Daily News (The) *Weekday Circulation: 13,280*

Batavia Newspapers Corp
2 Apollo Drive, PO Box 870, Batavia, NY 14020
585-343-8000 Fax: 585-343-2623 or
e-mail: news@batavianews.com
Publisher . . . . Thomas Turnbull
    e-mail: news@batavianews.com
Editorial Page Editor . . . . Sharon Larsen

Offices and agencies appear in alphabetical order.

News Media

Managing Editor. . . . . Mark Graczyk
News Editor . . . . Dirk Hoffman

BINGHAMTON

Press & Sun Bulletin *Weekday Circulation: 55,000*

Gannet Co Inc
PO Box 1270, Binghamton, NY 13902-1270
607-798-1234 Fax: 607-798-1113
Web site: www.pressconnects.com
Executive Editor. . . . . Vacant
Assistant Managing Editor - News. . . . . Al Vieira
Assistant Managing Editor - Online . . . . Stephen W Spero
Editorial Page Editor . . . . Frank Roessner

BRONXVILLE-EASTCHESTER

Review Press *Weekly Circulation: 4,965*

Journal News (The)/Gannett Co Inc
One Gannett Drive, White Plains, NY 10604
914-694-9300 Fax: 914-694-5018
e-mail: reviewpress@journalnews.com
Web site: www.thejournalnews.com
Editor/Vice President News . . . . Henry Freeman
   e-mail: reviewpress@journalnews.com
President/Publisher . . . . Gary F Sherlock
Executive Vice President . . . . Tom Donovan

BROOKLYN

Brooklyn Phoenix *Weekly Circulation: 13,000*

Brooklyn Eagle Publications
30 Henry St, Brooklyn, NY 11201
718-858-2300 Fax: 718-858-4483
e-mail: edit@brooklyneagle.net
Publisher. . . . . Dozier Hasty
   e-mail: edit@brooklyneagle.net

Brooklyn Daily Eagle *Weekly Circulation: 12,500*

Brooklyn Eagle Publications
30 Henry St, Brooklyn, NY 11201
718-858-2300 Fax: 718-858-4483
e-mail: edit@brooklyneagle.net
Publisher. . . . . Dozier Hasty
   e-mail: edit@brooklyneagle.net

Brooklyn Heights Press *Weekly Circulation: 12,500*

Brooklyn Eagle Publications
30 Henry St, Brooklyn, NY 11201
718-858-2300 Fax: 718-858-4483
e-mail: edit@brooklyneagle.net
Publisher. . . . . Dozier Hasty
   e-mail: edit@brooklyneagle.net
Managing Editor . . . . Raanan Geberer
Legal Editor . . . . Vacant

Daily Challenge *Weekday Circulation: 81,000*

Daily Challenge
1195 Atlantic Ave, Brooklyn, NY 11216
718-636-9500 Fax: 718-857-9115
e-mail: challengegroup@yahoo.com
Web site: www.challenge-group.com
Publisher . . . . Thomas H Watkins, Jr
   e-mail: challengegroup@yahoo.com
Managing Editor . . . . Gary Brown

BUFFALO

Buffalo News (The) *Weekday Circulation: 225,000*

Buffalo News (The)
One News Plaza 3rd Fl, PO Box 100, Buffalo, NY 14240
716-849-4444 Fax: 716-856-5150
Web site: www.buffalo.com
Editor . . . . Margaret M Sullivan
Albany Bureau Chief. . . . . Tom Precious
Managing Editor . . . . Edward L Cuddihy
Editorial Page Editor . . . . Gerald I Goldberg
Managing Editor. . . . . Stephen W Bell
News Editor. . . . . John Neville
Political Editor. . . . . Robert McCarthy

CANANDAIGUA

Daily Messenger (The) *Weekday Circulation: 14,000*

Messenger Post Newspapers
73 Buffalo St, Canandaigua, NY 14424
585-394-0770 Fax: 585-394-4160
e-mail: messengerpost@mpnewspapers.com
Web site: www.mpnewspaper.com
President & Publisher . . . . George M Ewing, Jr
   e-mail: messengerpost@mpnewspapers.com
Editor & Chairman. . . . . George M Ewing
Managing Editor . . . . Kevin Frisch
Editorial Page Editor. . . . . Dan Hall

CATSKILL

Daily Mail (The) *Weekday Circulation: 40,000*

Hudson Valley Newspapers Inc
414 Main St, PO Box 484, Catskill, NY 12414
518-943-2100 Fax: 518-943-2063
Web site: www.thedailymail.net
Publisher. . . . . Roger Coleman
Editor. . . . . Ray Pignone

Offices and agencies appear in alphabetical order.

CORNING

Leader (The) *Weekday Circulation: 14,000*

Liberty Group Publishing
34 W Pulteney St, Corning, NY 14830
607-936-4651 Fax: 607-936-9939
Web site: www.the-leader.com
Publisher . . . . Dennis Bruen
Managing Editor . . . . Joe Dunning
City Editor . . . . Charles Kraebel
Sports Editor . . . . Shawn Vargo

CORTLAND

Cortland Standard *Weekday Circulation: 11,000*

Cortland Standard Printing Co Inc
110 Main St, PO Box 5548, Cortland, NY 13045
607-756-5665 Fax: 607-756-5665
e-mail: news@cortlandstandard.net
Web site: www.cortland.org/news
Editor & Publisher . . . . Kevin R Howe
    e-mail: news@cortlandstandard.net
Managing Editor . . . . Kevin Conlon
News Editor . . . . Gary Pellesino
Opinion Page Editor . . . . Skip Chapman

DUNKIRK-FREDONIA

Observer *Weekday Circulation: 11,000*

Ogden Newspapers Inc
10 E 2nd St, Dunkirk, NY 14048
716-366-3000 Fax: 716-366-3005
e-mail: editorial@observertoday.com
Web site: www.observertoday.com
General Manager . . . . Karl T Davis
    e-mail: editorial@observertoday.com
Editor . . . . John D'Agostino
News Editor . . . . Bill Hammond
City Editor . . . . Doug Coy

Star-Gazette *Weekday Circulation: 27,804*

Gannett Co Inc
201 Baldwin St, PO Box 285, Elmira, NY 14901
607-734-5151 Fax: 607-733-4408
Web site: www.stargazette.com
Executive Editor . . . . Bill Church
Associate Editor . . . . David Kubissa
    e-mail: dkubissa@stargazette.com
Managing Editor . . . . Lois Wilson
    e-mail: lowilson@stargazette.com

GENEVA

Finger Lakes Times *Weekday Circulation: 16,836*

Finger Lakes Printing Co
218 Genesee St, Geneva, NY 14456
800-388-6652 Fax: 315-789-4077
e-mail: fltimes@fltimes.com
Web site: www.fltimes.com
Publisher . . . . Philip G Beckley
    e-mail: fltimes@fltimes.com
Managing Editor . . . . Anne Schuhle

GLENS FALLS

Post-Star (The) *Weekday Circulation: 33,123*

Lee Corporation
Lawrence & Cooper Sts, PO Box 2157, Glens Falls, NY 12801
518-792-3131 Fax: 518-761-1255
Web site: www.poststar.com
Publisher/Editor . . . . James G Marshall
Managing Editor . . . . Ken Tingley
    e-mail: tingley@poststar.com
Operations Director . . . . David E Guay
Advertising Director . . . . Judith H Goralski

GLOVERSVILLE-JOHNSTOWN

Leader-Herald (The) *Weekday Circulation: 11,500*

William B Collins Co
8 E Fulton St, Gloversville, NY 12078
518-725-8616 Fax: 518-725-7407
e-mail: publisher@leaderherald.com; editor@leaderherald.com
Web site: www.leaderherald.com
Publisher . . . . Patricia Beck
    e-mail: publisher@leaderherald.com; editor@leaderherald.com
Managing Editor . . . . Tim Fonda
Advertising Director . . . . Doug Hill
Circulation Director . . . . Toni Mosconi

HERKIMER

Evening Telegram (The) *Weekday Circulation: 7,000*

Liberty Group New York Holdings Inc
111 Green St, PO Box 551, Herkimer, NY 13350
315-866-2220 Fax: 315-866-5913
e-mail: news@herkimertelegram.com
Web site: www.herkimertelegram.com
Publisher . . . . Beth A Brewer
    e-mail: news@herkimertelegram.com
Managing Editor/Editorial Page Editor . . . . Richard A Petrillo

HORNELL

Evening Tribune (The) *Weekday Circulation: 7,900*

Liberty Group Publishing
85 Canisteo St, Hornell, NY 14843
607-324-1425 Fax: 607-324-2317
e-mail: news@eveningtribune.com
Web site: www.eveningtribune.com
Publisher . . . . Kelly Luvison
    e-mail: news@eveningtribune.com
General Manager . . . . John Frungillo
Managing Editor . . . . Andrew Thompson
    e-mail: athompson@infoblvd.com

HUDSON

Register-Star *Weekday Circulation: 45,000*

Johnson Newspaper Corporation
364 Warren St, PO Box 635, Hudson, NY 12534
800-836-4069 or 518-828-1616 Fax: 518-828-3870
e-mail: editorial@registerstar.com
Web site: www.registerstar.com
Publisher . . . . Roger F Coleman
    e-mail: editorial@registerstar.com
Editor . . . . Theresa Hyland
City Editor . . . . Joseph A Brill

ITHACA

Ithaca Journal (The) *Weekday Circulation: 20,000*

Gannett Co Inc
123-127 W State St, Ithaca, NY 14850
607-274-9231 Fax: 607-272-4248
Web site: www.theithacajournal.com
President/Publisher . . . . Jim Fogler
Managing Editor . . . . Bruce Estes
    e-mail: bestes@ithaca.gannett.com
Editorial Page Editor . . . . John Carberry
    e-mail: jcarberry@ithaca.gannett.com
Editorial Page Editor . . . . Joe Schwartz
    e-mail: jschwartz@ithaca.gannett.com

JAMESTOWN

Post-Journal *Weekday Circulation: 23,000*

Post-Journal
15 W Second St, PO Box 190, Jamestown, NY 14702-0190
716-487-1111 or 866-756-9600 Fax: 716-664-3119
e-mail: editorial@post-journal.com
Web site: www.post-journal.com
Publisher . . . . James Austin
    e-mail: editorial@post-journal.com
Editor . . . . Cristie L Herbst
City Editor . . . . Rodney Stebbins

KINGSTON

Daily Freeman *Weekday Circulation: 21,500*

Daily Freeman
79 Hurley Ave, Kingston, NY 12401-3449
845-331-5000 Fax: 845-331-3557 (n
e-mail: news@freemanonline.com
Web site: www.midhudsoncentral.com
Publisher . . . . Ira Fusfeld
    e-mail: news@freemanonline.com
Managing Editor . . . . Sam Daleo
    e-mail: sdaleo@freemanonline.com
Assistant Managing Editor . . . . Tony Adamis
City Editor . . . . Jeremy Schiffres
    e-mail: jschiffres@freemanonline.com
Political Editor . . . . Hugh Reynolds

LITTLE FALLS

Evening Times (The) *Weekday Circulation: 5,000*

Liberty Group Publishing
347 S 2nd St, Little Falls, NY 13365
315-823-3680 Fax: 315-823-4086
e-mail: lfet@twcny.rr.com
Web site: www.littlefallstimes.com
Publisher . . . . Don Paparella
    e-mail: lfet@twcny.rr.com
Editor . . . . Larry Neely

LOCKPORT

Lockport Union-Sun & Journal *Weekday Circulation: 16,000*

Greater Niagara Newspapers
170 East Ave, Lockport, NY 14094
716-439-9222 Fax: 716-439-9249
Web site: www.lockportjournal.com
Publisher . . . . Milton L Rogers
Interim Editor . . . . William Wolcott
Feature Editor . . . . Anne Calos

LONG ISLAND

Newsday *Weekday Circulation: 470,316*

Newsday Inc
235 Pinelawn Rd, Melville, NY 11747-4250
631-843-2020 Fax: 631-843-2953
Web site: www.newsday.com
Editor & Executive Vice President . . . . Howard Schneider
Publisher/President/Chief Executive Officer . . . . Timothy Knight
Vice President/Editorial Page Editor . . . . James Klurfeld
Managing Editor . . . . Richard Galant
Assistant Managing Editor - Long Island . . . . Debbie Henley
New York Editor . . . . Les Payne
Albany Bureau Chief . . . . Jordan Rau
    e-mail: jordon.rau@newsday.com

Offices and agencies appear in alphabetical order.

MALONE

Malone Telegram *Weekday Circulation: 6,000*

Johnson Newspaper Corp
469 E Main St, Ste 4, PO Box 69, Malone, NY 12953
518-483-4700 Fax: 518-483-8579
e-mail: news@mtelegram.com
Web site: www.mtelegram.com
Publisher . . . . Charles Kelly
    e-mail: news@mtelegram.com
Editor . . . . Joe Ricco

MASSENA

Daily Courier-Observer *Weekday Circulation: 7,800*

Johnson Newspaper Corporation
One Harrowgate Commons, PO Box 300, Massena, NY 13662
315-769-2451 Fax: 315-764-0337
Web site: www.mpcourier.com
Publisher & Editor . . . . Charles Kelly
Assistant General Manager . . . . Sean McNamara
Managing Editor-Massena/Pottsdam . . . . Ryne R Martin
Deputy Managing Editor-Massena/Potsdam . . . . Matt Akins

MEDINA

Journal-Register *Weekday Circulation: 4,500*

Greater Niagara Newspapers
409-413 Main St, Medina, NY 14103
585-798-1400 Fax: 585-798-0290
e-mail: thejournalregister@mail.com
Web site: www.journal-register.com
Group Publisher . . . . Wayne K Lowman
    e-mail: thejournalregister@mail.com

MIDDLETOWN

Times Herald-Record *Weekday Circulation: 200,000*

Orange County Publications
40 Mulberry St, PO Box 2046, Middletown, NY 10940
845-343-2181 Fax: 845-343-2170
Web site: www.recordonline.com
Publisher . . . . James A Moss
Executive Editor . . . . Mike Levine
Managing Editor . . . . Meg McGuire
City Editor . . . . Adrianne Reilly

MOUNT KISCO-NORTH SALEM

Patent Trader *Weekly Circulation: 30,323*

Journal News (The)/Gannett Co Inc
185 Kisco Ave, Mount Kisco, NY 10549
914-666-6156 Fax: 914-666-6013
e-mail: patenttrader@thejournalnews.com
Web site: www.thejournalnews.com
Executive Editor . . . . Caryn McBride
    e-mail: patenttrader@thejournalnews.com
Editor . . . . Tracey Princiotta
    e-mail: tprincio@gannett.com

NEW YORK CITY

New York Law Journal *Weekday Circulation: 16,000*

American Lawyer Media Inc
345 Park Ave, South, 8th Fl, New York, NY 10010
800-888-8300 Fax: 212-696-4287
Web site: www.law.com
Editor-in-Chief . . . . Kris Fischer
Managing Editor . . . . Michael Paquette
Legislative Correspondent . . . . John Caher
Senior Writer . . . . Daniel Wise

Journal of Commerce *Weekly Circulation: 10,000*

Commonwealth Business Media
33 Washington St, 13 Fl, Newark, NJ 07102-3107
973-848-7000 Fax: 973-837-7004
e-mail: editor@joc.com
Web site: www.joc.com
Editor-in-Chief . . . . Peter M Tirschwell
    e-mail: editor@joc.com
Deputy Editor . . . . Joseph Bonney
    e-mail: jbonney@joc.com
Editorial Operations Chief . . . . Barbara Wyker
    e-mail: bwyker@joc.com

Wall Street Journal (The) *Daily Circulation: 1,826,493*

Dow Jones & Company
200 Liberty St, New York, NY 10281
212-416-2000 Fax: 212-416-2255
Web site: www.wsj.com
Vice President & Managing Editor . . . . Paul Steiger
Editorial Page Editor . . . . Paul Gigot

People's Weekly World *Weekly Circulation: 25,000*

Long View Publishing Co
235 W 23rd St, New York, NY 10011
212-924-2523 Fax: 212-645-5436
e-mail: pww@pww.org
Web site: www.pww.org
Editor . . . . Terri Albano
    e-mail: pww@pww.org
Circulation Manager . . . . Jen Barnett

News Media

Offices and agencies appear in alphabetical order.

New York Post *Weekday Circulation: 686,207*

NYP Holdings Inc
1211 Ave of the Americas, 10th Fl, New York, NY 10036-8790
212-930-8000 Fax: 212-930-8540
Web site: www.nypost.com
Publisher . . . . Lachlan Murdoch
Editor-in-Chief. . . . . Col Allan
Associate Editor. . . . . Anne Aquilina
Managing Editor . . . . Colin Myler
Metropolitan Editor . . . . Jesse Angelo
Editorial Page Editor . . . . Robert McManus
Bureau Chief & State News Editor . . . . Frederic Dicker

New York Daily News *Weekday Circulation: 763,975*

New York Daily News
450 West 33rd St, 3rd Fl, New York, NY 10001
212-210-2100 Fax: 212-643-7831 or
e-mail: editors@edit.nydailynews.com
Web site: www.nydailynews.com
Publisher . . . . Mortimer Zuckerman
      e-mail: editors@edit.nydailynews.com
Deputy Publisher & Editorial Director . . . . Martin Dunn
Executive Editor . . . . Michael Goodwin
Senior Managing Editor . . . . Robert Sapio
Senior Editor . . . . Bill Boyle
Managing Editor . . . . Dick Belsky

New York Observer (The) *Weekday Circulation: 50,000*

The New York Observer
54 E 64th St, New York, NY 10021
212-755-2400 Fax: 212-688-4889
e-mail: editorial@observer.com
Web site: www.nyobserver.com
Publisher. . . . . Arthur L Carter
      e-mail: editorial@observer.com
Editor . . . . Peter W Kaplan
Managing Editor. . . . . Tom McGeveran
City Editor. . . . . Terry Golway

New York Times (The) *Weekday Circulation: 1,121,057*

The New York Times
229 W 43rd St, New York, NY 10036
212-556-1234 Fax: 212-556-3690 (n
e-mail: nytnews@nytimes.com; managing-editor@nytimes.com
Web site: www.nytimes.com
Chairman/Publisher . . . . Arthur Sulzberger, Jr
      e-mail: nytnews@nytimes.com; managing-editor@nytimes.com
Executive Editor. . . . . Bill Keller
Managing Editor . . . . Jill Abramson
Managing Editor . . . . John Geddes

Village Voice (The) *Weekly Circulation: 250,000*

Village Voice Media, Inc
36 Cooper Sq, New York, NY 10003
212-475-3300 Fax: 212-475-8944
Web site: www.villagevoice.com
Editor in Chief . . . . Donald H Forst
Managing Editor. . . . . Doug Simmons
Executive Editor. . . . . Laura Conaway

NIAGARA FALLS

Niagara Gazette *Weekday Circulation: 22,816*

Greater Niagara Newspapers
310 Niagara St, PO Box 549, Niagara Falls, NY 14302-0549
716-282-2311 Fax: 716-286-3895
Web site: www.niagara-gazette.com
Publisher . . . . Wayne Lowman
Managing Editor . . . . Teresa Martinez
Production Director. . . . . Les Rogers

NORWICH

Evening Sun *Weekday Circulation: 5,000*

Snyder Communications Corp
29 Lackawanna Ave, PO Box 151, Norwich, NY 13815
607-334-3276 Fax: 607-334-8273
e-mail: news@evesun.com
Web site: www.evesun.com
President/Publisher. . . . . Richard Snyder
      e-mail: news@evesun.com
Editor-in-Chief/Managing Editor . . . . Jeffrey Genung
      e-mail: jeff@evesun.com
Reporter . . . . Vince Keenan

OGDENSBURG

Ogdensburg Journal *Weekday Circulation: 5,200*

St Lawrence County Newspapers
308 Isabella St PO Box 409, Ogdensburg, NY 13669
315-393-1000 Fax: 315-393-5108
Web site: www.ogd.com
Editor . . . . Charles W Kelly
Managing Editor . . . . James E Reagen

OLEAN

Times Herald (The) *Weekday Circulation: 15,000*

Bradford Publications Inc
639 Norton Dr, Olean, NY 14760
716-372-3121 Fax: 716-373-6397
e-mail: news@oleantimesherald.com
Web site: www.oleantimesherald.com
Publisher/General Manager. . . . . Bill Fitzpatrick
      e-mail: news@oleantimesherald.com

Offices and agencies appear in alphabetical order.

Managing Editor . . . . Jim Eckstrom
News Editor . . . . Rick Jozwiak

ONEIDA

Oneida Daily Dispatch *Weekday Circulation: 7,252*

Journal Register Co
130 Broad St, PO Box 120, Oneida, NY 13421
315-363-5100 Fax: 315-363-9832
Web site: www.oneidadispatch.com
Publisher . . . . Phil Austin
Managing Editor . . . . Kurt W Wanfried
City Editor . . . . Jaques Picard

ONEONTA

Daily Star (The) *Weekday Circulation: 21,000*

Ottaway Newspapers Inc
102 Chestnut St, PO Box 250, Oneonta, NY 13820
607-432-1000 Fax: 607-432-5707
Web site: www.thedailystar.com
President & Publisher . . . . Daniel B Swift
Editor. . . . . Sam Pollak
    e-mail: spollak@thedailystar.com
Managing Editor . . . . Cary Brunswick
    e-mail: cary@thedailystar.com

OSWEGO-FULTON

Palladium-Times (The) *Weekday Circulation: 8,500*

The Palladium Times
140 W First St, Oswego, NY 13126
315-343-3800 Fax: 315-343-0273
Web site: www.pall-times.com
Publisher . . . . Paul R Scott
Managing Editor. . . . . Lou Sorendo
    e-mail: lsorendo@palltimes.com
Associate Editor. D Scott Allardice
City Editor . . . . Carrie Gayne

PLATTSBURGH

Press-Republican *Weekday Circulation: 20,210*

Ottaway Newspapers (The)
170 Margaret St, PO Box 459, Plattsburgh, NY 12901
518-561-2300 Fax: 518-561-3362
e-mail: news@pressrepublican.com
Web site: www.pressrepublican.com
Publisher. . . . . Robert Parks
    e-mail: news@pressrepublican.com
Editor . . . . James D Dynko
    e-mail: jdynko@pressrepublican.com
Managing Editor . . . . Bob Grady
    e-mail: bgrady@pressrepublican.com
News Editor . . . . Lois Clermont

Assistant News Editor . . . . Michael Dowd

POUGHKEEPSIE

Poughkeepsie Journal *Weekday Circulation: 40,202*

Gannett Co Inc
85 Civic Center Plz, Poughkeepsie, NY 12601
845-454-2000 Fax: 845-437-4921
e-mail: newsroom@poughkee.gannett.com
Web site: www.poughkeepsiejournal.com
President/Publisher. Barry Rothfield
    e-mail: newsroom@poughkee.gannett.com
Executive Editor . . . . Margaretta Downey
Managing Editor. . . . . Richard L Kleban
News Editor . . . . Jim Konrad
City Editor . . . . John Ferro

ROCHESTER

Daily Record (The) *Weekday Circulation: 15,000*

Dolan Media Co
11 Centre Park, Rochester, NY 14614
585-232-6920 Fax: 585-232-2740
Web site: www.nydailyrecord.com
Vice President & Publisher . . . . Peter L Mio
Editor. . . . . Kevin Momot
    e-mail: kevin.momot@nydailyrecord.com
Assistant Editor . . . . Jill Miller
    e-mail: jill.miller@nydailyrecord.com

Democrat and Chronicle *Weekday Circulation: 170,000*

Gannett Co Inc
55 Exchange Blvd, Rochester, NY 14614
585-258-2220 Fax: 585-258-2485
e-mail: feedback@democratandchronicle.com
Web site: www.democratandchronicle.com
Editor & Vice President, News . . . . Karen Magnuson
    e-mail: feedback@democratandchronicle.com
Vice President Communications. . . . . Thomas P Flynn
Managing Editor . . . . Jane Sutter
Assistant Managing Editor, Administration. . . . . Matt Dudek
Editoral Page Editor . . . . Jim Lawrence
Metro Editor . . . . Maria Hileman

ROME

Daily Sentinel *Weekday Circulation: 15,500*

Rome Sentinel Co
333 W Dominick St, PO Box 471, Rome, NY 13442-0471
315-337-4000 Fax: 315-337-4704
e-mail: sentinel@rny.com
Web site: www.rny.com
President. . . . . George B Waters
    e-mail: sentinel@rny.com
Managing Editor. . . . . David C Swanson
News Editor. . . . . Chip Haley

Offices and agencies appear in alphabetical order.

News Media

SALAMANCA

Salamanca Press *Weekday Circulation: 2,200*

Bradford Publishing Co
36 River St, PO Box 111, Salamanca, NY 14779
716-945-1644 Fax: 716-945-4285
e-mail: salpress@eznet.net
Web site: www.salamancapress.com
Publisher & Editor . . . . Kevin Burleson
    e-mail: salpress@eznet.net
News Editor . . . . Laura Howard

SARANAC LAKE

Adirondack Daily Enterprise *Weekday Circulation: 5,000*

Adirondack Publishing Co Inc
54 Broadway, PO Box 318, Saranac Lake, NY 12983
518-891-2600 Fax: 518-891-2756
e-mail: adenews@adirondackguide.com
Web site: www.adirondackguide.com
Publisher. . . . . Catherine Moore
    e-mail: adenews@adirondackguide.com
Editor . . . . Peter Crowley

SARATOGA SPRINGS

Saratogian (The) *Weekday Circulation: 10,400*

Journal Register Company
20 Lake Ave, Saratoga Springs, NY 12866
518-584-4242 Fax: 518-587-7750
e-mail: news@saratogian.com
Web site: www.saratogian.com
Publisher . . . . Michael O'Sullivan
    e-mail: news@saratogian.com
Managing Editor . . . . Barbara A Lombardo
News Editor. . . . . Beverly McKim
City Editor. . . . . Connie Jenkins

SCHENECTADY

Daily Gazette (The) *Weekday Circulation: 53,800*

Daily Gazette Co
2345 Maxon Rd Ext, PO Box 1090, Schenectady, NY 12301-1090
518-374-4141 Fax: 518-395-3089
e-mail: gazette@dailygazette.com
Web site: www.dailygazette.com
Editor & Publisher . . . . John E N Hume, III
    e-mail: gazette@dailygazette.com
Managing Editor . . . . Thomas L Woodman
City Editor . . . . George Walsh

STATEN ISLAND

Staten Island Advance *Weekday Circulation: 73,000*

Advance Publications Inc
950 Fingerboard Rd, Staten Island, NY 10305
718-981-1234 Fax: 718-981-5679
e-mail: newsroom@siadvance.com
Web site: www.silive.com
Publisher . . . . Caroline Harrison
    e-mail: newsroom@siadvance.com
Editor. . . . . Brian J Laline
Managing Editor . . . . William A Huus
City Editor . . . . Paul McPolin
Editorial Page Editor . . . . Mark Hanley
Political Reporter . . . . Thomas Wrobleski
Legislative Correspondent . . . . Robert Gavin

SYRACUSE

Post-Standard (The) *Weekday Circulation: 120,000*

Syracuse Newspapers Inc
1 Clinton Sq, PO Box 4915, Syracuse, NY 13221
315-470-0011 Fax: 315-470-3019
e-mail: letters@syracuse.com
Web site: www.syracuse.com
Executive Editor . . . . Michael J Connor
    e-mail: letters@syracuse.com
Deputy Executive Editor . . . . Timothy D Bunn
Senior Managing Editor. . . . . Stan Linhorst
Managing Editor/Systems . . . . Bart Pollock
Managing Editor (Day). . . . . Rosemary Robinson
Legislative Correspondent. Erik Kriss

TONAWANDA

Tonawanda News *Weekday Circulation: 11,000*

Greater Niagara Newspapers
435 River Rd, PO Box 668, North Tonawanda, NY 14120
716-693-1000 x154 Fax: 716-693-0124
Web site: www.tonawanda-news.com
Associate Publisher. . . . . Terry Shaw
Managing Editor . . . . Tim Schmitt

TROY

Record (The) *Weekday Circulation: 21,912*

Journal Register Co
501 Broadway, Troy, NY 12180
518-270-1200 Fax: 518-270-1202
e-mail: newsroom@troyrecord.com
Web site: www.troyrecord.com
Publisher. . . . . Frank McGivern Sr
    e-mail: newsroom@troyrecord.com
News Editor. . . . . Jan Shields
City Editor . . . . Nicholas A Cantiello
Editor . . . . Lisa Robert Lewis

Offices and agencies appear in alphabetical order.

UTICA

Observer-Dispatch *Weekday Circulation: 46,000*

Gannett Co Inc
221 Oriskany Plz, Utica, NY 13501
315-792-5000 Fax: 315-792-5033
e-mail: o-d@uticaod.com
Web site: www.uticaod.com
Editor . . . . John Broadbooks
      e-mail: o-d@uticaod.com
Managing Editor. . . . . Mike Kilian
Metro Editor . . . . Colleen Passalacqua
Opinion Editor . . . . Dave Dudajek

WATERTOWN

Watertown Daily Times *Weekday Circulation: 29,393*

Johnson Newspaper Corp
260 Washington St, Watertown, NY 13601
315-782-1000 Fax: 315-661-2523 (n
e-mail: news@wdt.net
Web site: www.wdt.net
Editor. . . . . John B Johnson, Jr
      e-mail: news@wdt.net

Executive Editor . . . . Bert Gault
Managing Editor. . . . . Robert Gorman
Legislative Correspondent. Chris Garifo
Washington Correspondent . . . . Marc Heller

WELLSVILLE

Wellsville Daily Reporter/Spectator *Weekday Circulation: 4,000*

Liberty Group Publishing
159 N Main St, Wellsville, NY 14895
585-593-5300 Fax: 585-593-5303
e-mail: editor@wellsvilledaily.com
Web site: www.wellsvilledaily.com
Publisher . . . . Oak Duke
      e-mail: editor@wellsvilledaily.com
Managing Editor . . . . John Anderson
Reporter . . . . Kathryn Ross
Reporter Page Editor . . . . Heather Matta

News Services/Magazines

ABC News (New York Bureau)
47 W 66th St, New York, NY 10023
212-456-7777 Fax: 212-456-2795
Web site: www.abc.com
Bureau Chief. . . . . Kris Sebastian

Associated Press (Albany/Upstate Bureau)
Capitol Newspapers Building, 645 Albany-Shaker Road, PO Box 11010, Albany, NY 12211
518-458-7821 Fax: 518-438-5891
e-mail: info@ap.org
Web site: www.ap.org
Bureau Chief. . . . . David Marcus
      e-mail: info@ap.org
News Editor . . . . Rik Stevens
Political Editor. . . . . Marc Humbert
Capitol Correspondent. . . . . Michael Gormley

Associated Press (New York/Metro Bureau)
450 West 33rd St, New York, NY 10001
212-621-1670 or 212-621-1676 Fax: 212-621-1679
e-mail: info@ap.org
Web site: www.ap.org
Bureau Chief . . . . Jocelyn Noveck
      e-mail: info@ap.org
News Editor . . . . Vacant
City Hall Reporter . . . . Timothy Williams

BNA (formerly Bureau of National Affairs)
PO Box 7169, Albany, NY 12224
518-399-8414 Fax: 518-399-8403
Web site: www.bna.com
NYS Correspondent . . . . Gerald Silverman

CBS News (New York Bureau)
524 West 57th St, New York, NY 10019
212-975-4321 Fax: 212-975-9387
Web site: www.cbsnews.com
Assignment Editor. . . . . Brian Lowder
Assignment Editor . . . . Andrew Friedman

City Journal (Manhattan Institute for Policy Research)
52 Vanderbilt Ave, New York, NY 10017
212-599-7000 Fax: 212-599-0371
e-mail: cj@city-journal.org
Web site: www.city-journal.org
Senior Editor. . . . . Brian C Anderson
      e-mail: cj@city-journal.org
Editor. . . . . Myron Magnet
Assistant Editor. Edward John Craig

Crain's New York Business
711 Third Ave, New York, NY 10017-4036
212-210-0277 Fax: 212-210-0799
Web site: www.crainsny.com
Publisher . . . . Alair Townsend
Editor . . . . Greg David
Managing Editor. . . . . Richard Barbieri

Offices and agencies appear in alphabetical order.

Deputy Managing Editor . . . . Erik Ipsen
Assistant Managing Editor . . . . Valerie Block
Senior Reporter, Politics, Government, Utilities, Environment . Anne Michaud

Cuyler News Service
PO Box 7205, State Capitol, Albany, NY 12224
518-465-2647 or 518-465-1745 Fax: 518-465-6849
e-mail: efmnews@aol.com
Bureau Chief . . . . Elizabeth G Flood
 e-mail: efmnews@aol.com
Legislative Correspondent . . . . Muriel Gibbons
Legislative Correspondent . . . . Carol Breen

Dow Jones Newswires (Dow Jones & Company)
Harborside Financial Ctr, 800 Plaza Two, Jersey City, NJ 07311
201-938-5400 Fax: 201-938-5600
e-mail: spotnews@priority.dowjones.com
Web site: www.djnewswires.com
President . . . . Paul J Ingrassia
 e-mail: spotnews@priority.dowjones.com
Vice President & Executive Editor . . . . Richard J Levine

Empire State Report (CINN Worldwide Inc)
25-35 Beechwood Ave, PO Box 9001, Mount Vernon, NY 10553-1314
914-699-2020 Fax: 914-699-2025
e-mail: empire@cinn.com
Web site: www.empirestatereport.com
Associate Vice President/Publisher/Executive Editor . . . . . . Stephen Acunto, Jr
 e-mail: empire@cinn.com

Gannett News Service
150 State St, 2nd Fl, Albany, NY 12207
518-436-9781 Fax: 518-436-0130
e-mail: gannett@albany.net
Web site: www.gannett.com
Bureau Chief . . . . Jay Gallagher
 e-mail: gannett@albany.net
Correspondent . . . . Yancey Roy
Correspondent . . . . Erika Rosenberg

ITAR-TASS News Agency
70080 Third Ave, 19th FL, New York, NY 10017
212-245-4250 Fax: 212-245-4258
e-mail: itar@aol.com
Web site: www.itar-tass.com
Bureau Chief . . . . Alex Berezhkov
 e-mail: itar@aol.com

Inside Albany Productions Inc
Capitol Station, PO Box 7328, Albany, NY 12224
518-426-3771 Fax: 518-426-5396
e-mail: mail@insidealbany.com
Web site: www.insidealbany.com
Producer . . . . Lise Bang-Jensen
 e-mail: mail@insidealbany.com
Producer . . . . David Hepp
Videographer . . . . Gary Glinski

Legislative Correspondents Association
PO Box 7340, State Capitol, 3rd Fl, Albany, NY 12224
518-455-2388
Press Room Supervisor . . . . Jean Gutbrodt

Mid-Hudson News Network
42 Marcy Lane, Middletown, NY 10941
845-537-1500 or 845-695-2923 Fax: 845-692-2921
e-mail: news@midhudsonnews.com/news@empirestatesnews.net
Web site: www.midhudsonnews.com; www.empirestatenews.net
Managing Director/Publisher . . . . Hank Gross
 e-mail: news@midhudsonnews.com/news@empirestatesnews.net

NBC News (New York Bureau)
30 Rockefeller Plaza, 300 West, New York, NY 10112
212-664-5900 Fax: 212-790-4711
Web site: www.nbc.com
Bureau Chief . . . . TBA
Desk Producer . . . . Frank Salamone

NY Capitolwire (Associated Press)
PO Box 7248, Albany, NY 12224
518-432-0710 Fax: 518-432-0275
Web site: www.capitolwire.com
New York Bureau Chief . . . . Kyle Hughes

New York Magazine (New York Metro LLC)
444 Madison Ave, New York, NY 10022-6999
212-508-0700 Fax: 212-583-7507
Web site: www.newyorkmetro.com
Editor-in-Chief . . . . Adam Moss
Executive Editor . . . . John Homans
Managing Editor . . . . Ann Clarke
Contributing Editor, 'The City Politic' . . . . Greg Sargent
Deputy Editor . . . . Jon Gluck

Newsweek Magazine (MSNBC, Microsoft Corp)
251 W 57th St, New York, NY 10019
212-445-4000 Fax: 212-445-4695
Web site: www.newsweek.msnbc.com
Chairman & Editor-in-Chief . . . . Richard M Smith
Editor . . . . Mark Whitaker
Director, Communications . . . . Ken Weine

Ottaway News Service (NYS only)
State Capitol, 3rd Fl, Albany, NY 12224
518-463-1157 Fax: 518-463-7486
Legislative Correspondent . . . . Paul Ertelt

Reuters (New York Bureau)
Three Times Square, New York, NY 10036
646-223-6280 Fax: 646-223-6289
Web site: www.reuters.com
Bureau Chief, Northeastern United States . . . . Mark Egan
Correspondent . . . . Ellen Wulfhorst
Correspondent . . . . Larry Fine
Correspondent . . . . Claudia Parsons
 e-mail: claudia.parsons@reuters.com

Offices and agencies appear in alphabetical order.

Scripps Howard News Service
1090 Vermont Ave NW, Ste 1000, Washington, DC 20005
202-408-1484 Fax: 202-408-5950
Web site: www.shns.com
General Manager/Editor . . . . Peter Copeland

Managing Editor . . . . Karen Timmons
Assistant Managing Editor/News . . . . Pamela Reeves
Department News Editor . . . . Tom Mentzer
    e-mail: mentzert@shns.com

Radio

Stations included in this chapter produce news and/or public affairs programming and are listed alphabetically by primary service area.

ALBANY

WAMC (90.3 FM)
318 Central Ave, Albany, NY 12206
518-465-5233 or 800-323-9262 Fax: 518-432-6974
e-mail: mail@wamc.org
Web site: www.wamc.org
Executive Director . . . . Alan Chartock
    e-mail: mail@wamc.org
Assistant Executive Director . . . . Selma Kaplan
Assistant Executive Director . . . . David Galletly
News Director . . . . Clarence Santo
Executive Producer, Host . . . . Alan Chartock
Producer, (Legislative Gazette) . . . . David Guistina

**WFLY (92.3 FM), WAJZ (96.3 FM), WROW (590 AM),
WYJB (95.5 FM), WZMR (104.9)**
6 Johnson Road, Latham, NY 12110
518-786-6600 or 518-786-6715 (news) Fax: 518-786-6610
Web site: www.albanyradio.net; www.pamal.com
President & General Manager . . . . Mr Morrell
News Director (WAJZ/WROW) . . . . Mike Carey
Program Director (WROW) . . . . Paul Vandenburgh
Program Director (WFLY) . . . . John Fox
Program Director (WAJZ) . . . . Ron Williams
Music Director (WYJB) . . . . Chad O'Hara
Community Affairs Director (WFLY/ WROW/ WYJB/ WAJZ) . Joe
    Condon

WGY (810 AM)
One Washington Square, Albany, NY 12205
518-452-4800 Fax: 518-452-4859
e-mail: news@wgy.com
Web site: www.wgy.com
News Director . . . . Chuck Custer
    e-mail: news@wgy.com
Program Manager . . . . Greg Foster
Vice President/General Manager . . . . Dennis Lamme
Sales Director . . . . Kristen Delaney

WPTR (1540 AM)
4243 Albany Street, Albany, NY 12205-4609
518-862-1540
e-mail: wptr@crawfordbroadcasting.com
Station Manager . . . . Robert Hammond
    e-mail: wptr@crawfordbroadcasting.com
PSA Director . . . . Kathy Leto

WPYX (106.5 FM), WRVE (99.5 FM)
One Washington Square, Albany, NY 12205
518-452-4800 or 800-476-1065 Fax: 518-452-4855
Web site: www.pyx106.com
Vice President, General Manager . . . . Dennis Lamme
WPYX Station Manager/Program Director . . . . John Cooper
WPYX Sales Director . . . . Kristen Delaney
WRVE Operations Manager/Program Director . . . . Randy McCarten
WRVE News Director . . . . Chuck Custer

BALDWINSVILLE

WSEN (92.1 FM)
8456 Smokey Hollow Road, Baldwinsville, NY 13027
315-635-3971 Fax: 315-635-3490
Web site: www.wsenfm.com
General Manager . . . . Doug Fleniken
Program Manager . . . . John Carucci
Program & Music Director . . . . Jim Tate
Sales Manager . . . . Judith Kelly

BATH

WCII (88.5 FM), WCOT (90.9 FM)
7634 Campbell Creek Rd, Bath, NY 14810-0506
607-776-4151 Fax: 607-776-6929
e-mail: mail@fln.org
Web site: www.fln.org
PSA Director . . . . Randy Snively
    e-mail: mail@fln.org
Program Director . . . . John Owens
Chief Executive Officer/President . . . . Rick Snively

BEACON

WSPK (104.7 FM)
715 Rte 52, Beacon, NY 12508
845-838-6000 Fax: 845-838-2109
Web site: www.k104online.com
General Manager . . . . Fred Bennett
Program Director . . . . Scotty Mac
News Director . . . . Rich Flaherty

News Media

Offices and agencies appear in alphabetical order.

BINGHAMTON

WMRV (105.7)
320 N Jensen Road, Vestal, NY 13850
607-584-5800 Fax: 607-584-5900
Web site: www.whrw.org
General Manager...............................Joanne Alloi
News Director...............................Dave Lozzi

**WNBF (1290 AM), WHWK (98.1FM), WYOS (1360 AM),
WAAL (99.1 FM), WWYL (104.1)**
59 Court St, Binghamton, NY 13901
607-772-8400 Fax: 607-772-3438
Web site: www.wnbf.com; www.991thewhale.com;
www.981thehawk.com
General Manager.......................Mary Beth Walsh
Program Director (WAAL) (WYOS).............Randy Horton
News Director..............................Bernard Fionti
News Director (WAAL)........................Kathy Whyte
Program Director (WNBF &WYOS)..............Roger Neel
Program Director (WHWK).....................Ed Walker
Program Director (WWYL).....................KJ Bryant

WSKG (89.3 FM), WSQX (91.5 FM)
601 Gates Road, Vestal, NY 13850
607-729-0100 or 800-424-9754 Fax: 607-729-7328
e-mail: wskg_@wskg.pbs.org
Web site: www.wskg.org
Program Director.........................David Paltrowitz
      e-mail: wskg_@wskg.pbs.org
Music Director.............................Bill Snyder

BRONX

WFUV (90.7 FM)
Fordham University, Bronx, NY 10458
718-817-4550 Fax: 718-365-9815
General Manager.........................Dr Ralph Jennings
News & Public Affairs Director.............Julianne Welby
Program Director.........................Chuck Singleton

BUFFALO

**WBFO (88.7 FM) WOLN (91.3 FM), WUBJ (88.7 FM)
NPR/PRI - SUNY at Buffalo**
205 Allen Hall, 3435 Main St, Buffalo, NY 14214-3003
716-829-6000 Fax: 716-829-2277
e-mail: mail@wbfo.org
Web site: www.wbfo.org
News Director...............................Mark Scott
      e-mail: mail@wbfo.org
Operation Manager & Host...................Mark Wozniak
News Producer.............................Eileen Buckley
Associate Vice President & General Manager...Carole Smith Petro
Program Director/Assistant General Manager.......David Benders

WBLK (93.7 FM), WJYE (96.1 FM)
14 Lafayette Sq, Ste 1300, Buffalo, NY 14203
716-852-9393 or 800-828-2191 Fax: 716-852-9390
Web site: www.wjye.com OR www.wblk.com
General Manager.............................Jeff Silver
Production & Program Director...............Chris Reynolds
Production Director.........................Frank Dawkins

WDCX (99.5 FM)
625 Delaware Avenue, Buffalo, NY 14202
716-883-3010 Fax: 716-883-3606
e-mail: info@wdcxfm.com
Web site: www.wdcxfm.com
General Manager.............................Nevin Larson
      e-mail: info@wdcxfm.com
Music Director.............................Rob Stoddard

WHTT (104.1 FM)
50 James E Casey, Buffalo, NY 14206
716-881-4555 Fax: 716-884-2931
e-mail: whtt@whtt.com
Web site: www.whtt.com
Program Manager...........................Stacy Berent
      e-mail: whtt@whtt.com
News Director.............................Gail Ann Hubert
Music Director.............................Joe Siragusa
Sales Manager.............................Paul Maurer

WNED (94.5 FM)
PO Box 1263, Buffalo, NY 14240-1263
716-845-7000 Fax: 716-845-7043
e-mail: classical@wned.org
Web site: www.wned.org
Broadcasting Vice President.................Richard Daly
      e-mail: classical@wned.org
Program/Music Director.....................Peter Goldsmith
Promotions Director.......................Mary Summers

WYRK (106.5 FM), WBUF (92.9 FM)
14 Lafayette Sq., Suite 1200, Buffalo, NY 14203
716-852-9292 Fax: 716-852-9290
General Manager.............................Jeff Silver
Program Director...........................John Paul
Assistant Program Director/Music Director...........Joe Russo
Sales Manager.........................Catherine McCracken

CHAMPLAIN

WCHP (760 AM)
PO Box 888, Champlain, NY 12919
518-298-2800 Fax: 518-298-2604
e-mail: info@wchp.com
Web site: www.wchp.com
General Manager...........................Teri L Billiter
      e-mail: info@wchp.com
Program Director...........................Brandi Lloyd
Public Service Director.....................Tonya Billiter

Offices and agencies appear in alphabetical order.

CORTLAND

WKRT (920 AM), WIII (99.9 or 100.3 FM)
277 Tompkins Street, Cortland, NY 13045
607-756-2828 x29 Fax: 607-756-2953
Web site: www.wiii.com; www.wkrt.com
News Director . . . . Todd Mallinson
Operations Manager . . . . Tony DeFranco
    e-mail: tony.defranco@citcomm.com

ELMIRA

WNKI (106.1 FM), WPGI (100.9 FM), WNGZ (104.9 FM), WWLZ (820 AM)
2205 College Avenue, Elmira, NY 14903
607-732-4400 Fax: 607-732-7774 (n
e-mail: sabrenews@onlineimage.com
Web site: www.wink106.com
General Manager. . . . . Kevin White
    e-mail: sabrenews@onlineimage.com
Promotions Director . . . . Caryl Sutterby
    e-mail: brandanmckay@wink106.com
Sales Manager. . . . . Scott Benjamin

HORNELL

WKPQ (105.3 FM)
1484 Beach Street, PO Box 726, Hornell, NY 14843
607-324-2000 or 800-258-1430 Fax: 607-324-2001
General Manager. . . . . Devin Storm
News Director . . . . Jonathon Mark
Music Director . . . . Buck Montana

HORSEHEADS

WMTT (94.7 FM)
734 Chemung Street, Horseheads, NY 14845
607-772-1005 Fax: 607-772-2945
e-mail: themetrocks@aol.com
General Manager. . . . . George Harris
    e-mail: themetrocks@aol.com
Program/News/Music Director . . . . Stephen Shimer

ITHACA

WHCU (870 AM), WTKO (1470 AM), WYXL (97.3 FM), WQNY (103.7 FM)
1751 Hanshaw Rd, Ithaca, NY 14850
607-257-6400 Fax: 607-257-6497
Web site: www.whcu870.com; www.lite97fm.com; www.qcountryfm.com
General Manager . . . . Ken Cowan
Operations Manager. . . . . Tom Joseph
News Director. . . . . Bob Steinkamp
    e-mail: news@radioeagle.com
Program Director . . . . Chris Alinger
Sales Manager . . . . Susan Johnson

JAMESTOWN

WKZA (106.9 FM)
106 West 3rd Street, Suite 106, Jamestown, NY 14701
716-487-1106 or 866-367-1069 Fax: 716-488-2169
Web site: www.1069kissfm.com
General Manager . . . . John Newman
Program/Public Affairs Director. . . . . JJ Michaels

LATHAM

WYJB (95.5 FM)
6 Johnson Road, Latham, NY 12110
518-786-6600 Fax: 518-786-6695
e-mail: comments@b95.com
Web site: www.b95.com
General Manager . . . . Stacy Rogers
    e-mail: comments@b95.com
Program Director . . . . Kevin Callahan
Music Director . . . . Chad O'Hara

MIDDLETOWN

WALL (1340 AM), WRRV (92.7 FM)
PO Box 416, Poughkeepsie, NY 12602-0416
845-471-1500 Fax: 845-454-1204
e-mail: wrrv@wrrv.com
Web site: www.wrrv.com
Program/News Director. . . . . Nick Robbins
    e-mail: wrrv@wrrv.com
Program Director (WRRV). . . . . Andrew Boris
    e-mail: boris@wrrv.com

NEW ROCHELLE

WVOX (1460 AM), WRTN (93.5 FM)
1 Broadcast Forum, New Rochelle, NY 10801
914-636-1460 or 914-235-3279 editor Fax: 914-636-2900
e-mail: info@wvox.com
Web site: www.wvox.com
Chairman & Editorial Director. . . . . William O'Shaughnessy
    e-mail: info@wvox.com
News Director . . . . Larry Goldstein
Senior Vice President, Operations & Programming . . . . Don Stevens
    e-mail: don@wvox.com
Public Affairs Director . . . . Nancy Curry O'Shaughnessy
General Manager. . . . . Cindy Hall Gallagher
    e-mail: cindy@wvox.com (traffic)
Chief Correspondent. . . . . Sally Pierson

NEW YORK CITY

WABC (770 AM)
2 Penn Plaza, New York, NY 10121
212-613-3800 Fax: 212-613-3823
e-mail: postmaster@wabcradio.com
Web site: www.wabcradio.com
President & General Manager . . . . Tim McCarthy
    e-mail: postmaster@wabcradio.com

Offices and agencies appear in alphabetical order.

News Media

Program Director . . . . Phil Boyce

WAXQ (104.3 FM)
1180 Avenue of the Americas, 6th Floor, New York, NY 10036
212-575-1043 Fax: 212-302-7814
Web site: www.q1043.com
General Manager . . . . Andrew Rosen
Program Director . . . . Bob Buchmann

WBBR (1130 AM) Bloomberg News
499 Park Ave, 15th Fl, New York, NY 10022
212-318-2350 Fax: 212-940-1994
Web site: www.bloomberg.com
General Manager . . . . Al Mayers
News Director . . . . John Meehan
Program Director . . . . Michael Lysak

WCBS (880 AM)
524 W 57th St, 8th Fl, New York, NY 10019
212-975-2127 (news) or 212-975-4321 Fax: 212-975-1907
e-mail: wcbs880@wcbs880.com
Web site: www.wcbs880.com
Vice President & General Manager . . . . Steve Swenson
    e-mail: wcbs880@wcbs880.com
Programming Director . . . . Crys Quinby
News Director . . . . Tim Scheld

WINS (1010 AM)
888 Seventh Ave, New York, NY 10106
212-315-7000 Fax: 212-489-7034
e-mail: info@1010winsmail.com
Web site: www.1010wins.com
News Director . . . . Ben Mevorach
    e-mail: info@1010winsmail.com
Executive Editor & Program Director . . . . Mark Mason
City Hall Reporter . . . . Stan Brooks

WLTW (106.7 FM)
1133 Avenue of the Americas, 34th FL, New York, NY 10036
212-603-4600 Fax: 212-603-4602
e-mail: contact@1067litefm.com
Web site: www.1067litefm.com
General Manager . . . . Andrew Rosen
    e-mail: contact@1067litefm.com
Program Coordinator . . . . Morgan Prue

WOR (710 AM)
111 Broadway, 3rd FL, New York, NY 10006
212-642-4467 Fax: 212-642-4533
e-mail: news@wor710.com
Web site: www.wor710.com
Executive Director . . . . Chris Thompson
    e-mail: news@wor710.com
Vice President/General Manager . . . . Bob Bruno

OLEAN

WPIG (95.7 FM), WHDL (1450 AM)
3163 NYS Route 417, Olean, NY 14760-1853
716-372-0161 or 800-877-9749 Fax: 716-372-0164
General Manager . . . . John J Morton

News Director . . . . Gary Nease

PEEKSKILL

WHUD (100.7 FM)
PO Box 188, Peekskill, NY 10566
845-838-6000 Fax: 845-838-2109
Web site: www.whud.com
Program Director . . . . Steve Petrone
Sales Manager . . . . Jason Finkleberg

POUGHKEEPSIE

WPDH (101.5 FM)
2 Pendell Rd, PO Box 416, Poughkeepsie, NY 12602
845-471-1500 Fax: 845-454-1204
Web site: www.wpdh.com
General Manager . . . . Chuck Benfer
Program Director . . . . Gary Lee

ROCHESTER

WHAM (1180 AM)
207 Midtown Plaza, Rochester, NY 14604-2016
585-454-4884 Fax: 585-454-5081
e-mail: wham@eznet.com
Web site: www.wham1180.com
General Manager/Program Director . . . . Jeff Howlett
    e-mail: wham@eznet.com
News Director . . . . Randy Gorbman

SCHENECTADY

WGNA (107.7 FM)
1241 Kings Road, Schenectady, NY 12303
518-881-1515 or 800-476-1077 Fax: 518-881-1516
e-mail: wgna@aol.com
Web site: www.wgna.com
General Manager . . . . Robert Ausfield
    e-mail: wgna@aol.com
Program Manager . . . . Buzz Brindle
Music Director . . . . Bill Earley

SYRACUSE

WNTQ (93.1 FM), WAQX (95.7 FM)
1064 James St, Syracuse, NY 13203
315-472-0200 Fax: 315-472-1146
Web site: www.93Q.com; www.95x.com
General Manager . . . . Reggie Jordan
Program Director (WNTQ) . . . . Tom Mitchell
Program Director (WAQX) . . . . Alexis Thang

WVDA (105.1 FM)
7095 Myers Road, East Syracuse, NY 13057-9748
315-656-2231 Fax: 315-656-2259
Sales/General Manager . . . . James Wall
Public Service Coordinator . . . . Susan Anderson
Music Director . . . . Allen Elson

Offices and agencies appear in alphabetical order.

WYYY (94.5 FM)
Y94FM Bridgewater Place, 500 Plum St, Suite 100, Syracuse, NY 13204
315-472-9797 Fax: 315-478-6455
e-mail: y94fm@clearchannel.com
Program Director . . . . Kathy Rowe
    e-mail: y94fm@clearchannel.com
Music Director . . . . John Smith

UTICA

WOUR (96.9 FM)
239 Genesee Street, Suite 500, Utica, NY 13501-3412
315-797-0803 Fax: 315-797-7813
General Manager . . . . Brian Delaney

News/Music Director . . . . Alison Ryan

WATERTOWN

WFRY (97.5 FM)
134 Mullin Street, Watertown, NY 13601
315-788-0790 Fax: 315-788-4379
General Manager . . . . Don Wagner
Program/Music Director . . . . Stan Sobelski

Television

Stations included in this chapter produce news and/or public affairs programming and are listed alphabetically by primary service area.

ALBANY

WMHT (17) Public Broadcasting-NY Capitol Region
PO Box 17, Schenectady, NY 12301
518-357-1700 Fax: 518-357-1709
e-mail: email@wmht.org
Web site: www.wmht.org
President & General Manager . . . . Deborah Onslow
    e-mail: email@wmht.org

WNYT (13)
Box 4035, 15 N Pearl St, Albany, NY 12204
518-436-4791 Fax: 518-426-9463
e-mail: comments@wnyt.com
Web site: www.wnyt.com
General Manager . . . . Steve Baboulis
    e-mail: comments@wnyt.com
News Director . . . . Paul Conti
Director, Public Affairs & Special Promotions . . . . . . Maryann Ryan

WRGB (6)
1400 Balltown Rd, Schenectady, NY 12309
518-346-6666 Fax: 518-346-6249
e-mail: news@wrgb.com
Web site: www.wrgb.com
General Manager . . . . Robert J Furlong
    e-mail: news@wrgb.com
News Director . . . . Beau Duffy
Production . . . . Margaret Holmes
Legislative Correspondent . . . . Judy Sanders

WTEN (10)
341 Northern Blvd, Albany, NY 12204
518-433-4290 Fax: 518-462-6065
e-mail: news@wten.com
Web site: www.wten.com
General Manager & Program Director . . . . Rene LaSpina
    e-mail: news@wten.com
News Director . . . . Rob Puglisi

WXXA (23)
28 Corporate Circle, Albany, NY 12203
518-862-2323 Fax: 518-862-0995
Web site: www.fox23news.com
General Manager . . . . Jeff Whitson
News Director . . . . Gene Ross
Program Director . . . . Paul Pelliccia

WYPX (55)
1 Charles Blvd, Guilderland, NY 12084
518-464-0143 Fax: 518-464-0633
Web site: www.paxalbany.tv
General Manager . . . . Charmaine Ushkow
Public Affairs Director . . . . Chris Iorio
    e-mail: chrisiorio@pax.net

BINGHAMTON

WBNG (12), WBXI (11)
560 Columbia Dr, #1, Johnson City, NY 13790
607-729-8812 Fax: 607-797-6211
e-mail: wbng@wbngtv.com
Web site: www.wbng.com
General Manager . . . . Joe McNamara
    e-mail: wbng@wbngtv.com
News Director . . . . Greg Catlin
    e-mail: catlin@wbngtv.com

Offices and agencies appear in alphabetical order.

WICZ (40)
4600 Vestal Pkwy E, Vestal, NY 13850
607-770-4040 Fax: 607-798-7950
e-mail: fox40@wicz.com
Web site: www.wicz.com
General Manager . . . . John Leet
    e-mail: fox40@wicz.com
News Director. . . . . Kent Garret
Program Director . . . . Vernon Rowlands

WIVT/WBGH (34)
203 Ingraham Hill Rd, Binghamton, NY 13903
607-771-3434 Fax: 607-723-6403
Web site: www.newschannel34.com
News Director . . . . Jim Ehmke
Program Director . . . . Chris Wurth

WSKG (46) Public Broadcasting
Box 3000, Binghamton, NY 13902
607-729-0100 Fax: 607-729-7328
e-mail: wskg_mail@wskg.pbs.org
Web site: www.wskg.com
President & Chief Executive Officer . . . . Gary Reinbolt
    e-mail: wskg_mail@wskg.pbs.org
Producer/Moderator . . . . William Jaker

BUFFALO

WGRZ (2)
259 Delaware Ave, Buffalo, NY 14202
716-849-2222 or 716-849-2200 (news) Fax: 716-849-7602
Web site: www.wgrz.com
News Director. . . . . Ellen Crooke
Assignment Editor . . . . Maria Sisti
Program Director . . . . Paulette Harris

WIVB (4), WNLO (23)
2077 Elmwood Ave, Buffalo, NY 14207
716-874-4410 Fax: 716-874-8173
e-mail: wivbweb@wivb.com
Web site: www.wivb.com
News Director. . . . . Joseph Schlaerth
    e-mail: wivbweb@wivb.com
Business Manager . . . . Nancy Kenney

WKBW (7)
7 Broadcast Plaza, Buffalo, NY 14202
716-845-6100 Fax: 716-856-8784
e-mail: news@wkbw.com
Web site: www.wkbw.com
News Director . . . . Bill Payer
    e-mail: news@wkbw.com
Head of Programming & Promotion . . . . John Disciullo
    e-mail: johndis@wkbw.com

WNED (17) Western NY Public Broadcasting
Horizons Plz, 140 Lower Terrace, Box 1263, Buffalo, NY
14240-1263
716-845-7000 Fax: 716-845-7036
e-mail: news@wned.org
Web site: www.wned.org
News Director. . . . . James Ranney
    e-mail: news@wned.org
Programming Director. . . . . Al Wallack

WETM (18)
101 E Water St, Elmira, NY 14901
607-733-5518 Fax: 607-733-4739
e-mail: news@wetmtv.com
Web site: www.wetmtv.com
General Manager . . . . Randy Reid
    e-mail: news@wetmtv.com
News Director . . . . Scott Nichols

HORSEHEADS

WENY (36)
474 Old Ithaca Rd, Horseheads, NY 14845
607-739-3636 Fax: 607-796-6171
e-mail: info@weny.com
Web site: www.weny.com
General Manager/Program Manager . . . . Jason Arnold
    e-mail: info@weny.com
News Director . . . . Jody Davis

KINGSTON

WRNN (62)
721 Broadway, Kingston, NY 12401-3449
845-339-6200 Fax: 845-339-6210
Web site: www.rnntv.com
General Manager. . . . . Richard French
Sports Director . . . . Kevin Connors

LONG ISLAND

WLIW (21) Public Broadcasting
Box 21, Channel 21 Dr, Plainview, NY 11803-0021
516-367-2100 Fax: 516-692-7629
e-mail: viewersvoice@wliw.org
Web site: www.wliw.org
General Manager. . . . . Terrel Cass
    e-mail: viewersvoice@wliw.org
Producer/ Local Production . . . . Theresa Statz-Smith

MELVILLE

WLNY (55)
Box 1355, 270 S Service Rd, Melville, NY 11747
631-622-9442 Fax: 631-420-4822
Web site: www.wlnytv.com
Chief Executive Officer . . . . Marvin Chauvin
News Director . . . . Richard Rose

Offices and agencies appear in alphabetical order.

NEW YORK CITY

Bloomberg Television
499 Park Ave, 15th Fl, New York, NY 10022
212-318-2319 Fax: 212-940-1757
Web site: www.bloomberg.com/tv
News Editor . . . . Marty Schenker

Fox News Channel
1211 Ave of the Americas, C-1, New York, NY 10036
212-301-3000 Fax: 212-301-8274
Web site: www.foxnews.com
Assignment Editor . . . . David Rhodes
Vice President/News Operations . . . . Sharri Berg

New York 1 News (1)
75 Ninth Avenue, New York, NY 10011
212-691-6397 Fax: 212-379-3575
e-mail: ny1news@ny1.com
Web site: www.ny1.com
Albany Reporter . . . . Rita Nissan
    e-mail: ny1news@ny1.com
Political Reporter, Anchor & Co-Host, ... Dominic Carter
Political Reporter, Anchor & Co-Host, ... Davidson Goldin
Politcal Reporter . . . . Sandra Endo

WABC (7)
7 Lincoln Sq, New York, NY 10023
212-456-1000 or 212-456-3100 Fax: 212-456-2381
e-mail: eyewitness.news@abc.com
Web site: www.7online.com
News Director. . . . . Ken Plotnik
    e-mail: eyewitness.news@abc.com
Program Director . . . . Art Moore

WCBS (2)
524 W 57th St, New York, NY 10019
212-975-5867 Fax: 212-975-9387
Web site: www.cbsnewyork.com
Vice President & News Director . . . . Dianne Doctor
Assistant News Director . . . . Philip O'Brien
Director, Communications . . . . Audry Pass
Director, Station Services & Community Affairs. . . . . . . Jean Hodge
Manager, Station Services & New Jersey Affairs. . . . . Rafael Rivera

WNBC (4)
30 Rockefeller Plaza, New York, NY 10112
212-664-4444 or 212-664-2731 (news) Fax: 212-664-2994
Web site: www.nbc.com
News Director . . . . Dan Forman
Program Director . . . . Adele Rifken
Vice President/Director of Press & Public Affairs . . Anna Carbonell

WNYW (5)
205 E 67th St, New York, NY 10021
212-452-5555 Fax: 212-717-5849
Web site: www.fox5ny.com
Vice President/General Manager . . . . James Clayton
Vice President/News Director . . . . Scott Matthews

WPIX (11)
220 East 42nd St, New York, NY 10017
212-949-1100 Fax: 212-210-2591
e-mail: wpix@tribune.com or wpix@aol.com
Web site: www.wb11.com
News Director. . . . . Karen Scott
    e-mail: wpix@tribune.com or wpix@aol.com
Program Director . . . . Julie O'Neill

WWOR (UPN 9)
9 Broadcast Plaza, Secaucus, NJ 7096
201-330-2223 Fax: 201-330-3844
e-mail: newsdesk@wwortv.com
Web site: www.upn9.tv
News Director . . . . Scott Matthews
    e-mail: newsdesk@wwortv.com
Assistant News Editor. . . . . Michael St Peter
Assignment Editor . . . . Kevin Schwab
Assignment Editor . . . . Kim Lowe
Planning Editor . . . . Adam Cousins

PLATTSBURGH

WPTZ (5) NBC
5 Television Dr, Plattsburgh, NY 12901
518-561-5555 Fax: 518-561-5940
e-mail: newstips@thechamplainchannel.com
Web site: www.thechamplainchannel.com
General Manager . . . . Paul Sands
    e-mail: newstips@thechamplainchannel.com
News Director . . . . Vacant
Assignment Editor. . . . . Matt Morin

ROCHESTER

WHEC (10)
191 East Ave, Rochester, NY 14604
585-546-5670 Fax: 585-546-5688
e-mail: news1@10nbc.com
Web site: www.10nbc.com
News Director. . . . . Adam Bradshaw
    e-mail: news1@10nbc.com
Program Director . . . . Terry Fauth

WOKR (13)
Box 20555, 4225 W Henrietta Rd, Rochester, NY 14623
585-334-8700 Fax: 585-334-8719
e-mail: news@wokr13.tv
Web site: www.wokr13.tv
News Director. . . . . Chuck Samuels
    e-mail: news@wokr13.tv
TV Community Affairs Director. . . . . Charlotte Clarke

WROC (8)
201 Humboldt St, Rochester, NY 14610
585-288-8888 Fax: 585-288-1505
e-mail: newsroom@wroctv.com
Web site: www.wroctv.com
News Director. . . . . Lee Eldridge
    e-mail: newsroom@wroctv.com

Offices and agencies appear in alphabetical order.

News Media

Vice President/General Manager . . . . Marc Jaromin
Business Manager/Human Resources . . . . Bonnie Alalmo

WUHF (31)
360 East Ave, Rochester, NY 14604
585-232-3700 Fax: 585-546-4774
e-mail: foxrochester@foxrochester.com
Web site: www.foxrochester.com
News Director . . . . Mike Sahrle
    e-mail: foxrochester@foxrochester.com

WXXI (21) Public Broadcasting
280 State St, Rochester, NY 14614
585-325-7500 Fax: 585-258-0335
e-mail: wxxinews@wxxi.org
Web site: www.wxxi.org
President/Chief Executive Officer . . . . Norm Silverstein
    e-mail: wxxinews@wxxi.org
Vice President, Television . . . . Gary Walker
    e-mail: gwalker@wxxi.org
Director, Television News & . . . . Michael Caputo

SYRACUSE

WCNY (24)
Box 2400, 506 Old Liverpool Rd, Syracuse, NY 13220-2400
315-453-2424 Fax: 315-451-8824
Web site: www.wcny.org
Program Manager . . . . Dale Wagner
Producer . . . . George Kilpatrick
Host . . . . Dan Cummings

WIXT (9)
5904 Bridge St, East Syracuse, NY 13057
315-446-9999 Fax: 315-446-9283
e-mail: newschannel9@wixt.com
Web site: www.wixt.com
News Director . . . . Jim Tortora
    e-mail: newschannel9@wixt.com
Program Director . . . . Vince Spicola

WSTM (3)
1030 James St, Syracuse, NY 13203
315-474-5000 Fax: 315-474-5122
e-mail: wstmnews@wstm.com
Web site: www.wstm.com
General Manager . . . . Jim Lutton
    e-mail: wstmnews@wstm.com
News Director . . . . Cathy Younkin

WSYT (68)
1000 James St, Syracuse, NY 13203
315-472-6800 Fax: 315-471-8889
Web site: www.wyst68.com
Group Manager . . . . Aaron Olander

WTVH (5)
980 James St, Syracuse, NY 13203
315-425-5555 Fax: 315-425-0129
e-mail: onyourside@whtv.com
Web site: www.wtvh.com
President/General Manager . . . . Les Vann
    e-mail: onyourside@whtv.com
News Director . . . . Frank Kracher
Program Manager . . . . Molly Herwood

UTICA

WKTV (2)
Box 2, Utica, NY 13503
315-733-0404 Fax: 315-793-3498
e-mail: newslink@wktv.com
Web site: www.wktv.com
Program Director . . . . Tom Coyne
    e-mail: newslink@wktv.com
News Director . . . . Steve McMurray
Vice President/General Manager . . . . Vic Vetters

WATERTOWN

WWNY (7)
120 Arcade St, Watertown, NY 13601
315-788-3800 Fax: 315-782-7468
e-mail: wwny@wwnytv.net
Web site: www.wwnytv.com
General Manager . . . . Cathy Pircsuk
    e-mail: wwny@wwnytv.net
News Director . . . . Scott Atkinson
Program Director . . . . Jim Corbin

WWTI (50)
Box 6250, 1222 Arsenal St, Watertown, NY 13601
315-785-8850 Fax: 315-785-0127
Web site: www.newswatch50.com
General Manager . . . . David J Males
News Director . . . . John Moore

Offices and agencies appear in alphabetical order.

COLLEGES AND UNIVERSITIES

State University of New York

SUNY Board of Trustees

State University of New York
State University Plz
Albany, NY 12246
518-443-5157 Fax: 518-443-5159
Web site: www.suny.edu

Chair:
Thomas F Egan (2006) 212-661-4431
Vice Chair:
Randy A Daniels (2004) 212-417-5804
Member:
Steven L Alfasi (2003) 718-293-7660
Member:
Aminy I Audi (2009) 315-682-5500
Member:
Christopher P Conners (2008) 518-786-6000
Member:
Edward F Cox (2006) 212-336-2000
Member:
Father John J Cremins (2007) 718-268-6143
Member:
Candace de Russy (2007) 914-779-9607
Member:
Gordon R Gross (2008) 716-854-4300
Member:
Stephanie Gross (2005) 518-321-4651
Member:
Lou Howard (2009) 631-264-3636
Member:
Pamela R Jacobs (2007) 716-875-4441
Member:
Celine R Paquette (2005) 518-298-2000
Member:
Ronald B Stafford (2008) 518-561-4400
Member:
Patricia Elliott Stevens (2006) 585-274-6298
Member:
Harvey F Wachsman (2004) 516-624-2999

SUNY System Administration & Executive Council

State University Plz
Albany, NY 12246
518-443-5555
Web site: www.suny.edu

Chancellor:
Robert L King 518-443-5355/fax: 518-443-5360
e-mail: kingro@sysadm.suny.edu
Vice Chancellor & Chief of Staff:
Elizabeth D Capaldi 518-443-5328/fax: 518-443-5369
e-mail: capaldi@sysadm.suny.edu
Vice Chancellor/Secretary of the University/President Research Foundation:
John J O'Connor 518-443-5157/fax: 518-443-5131
e-mail: oconnojj@sysadm.suny.edu

Provost & Vice Chancellor, Academic Affairs:
Peter D Salins 518-443-5152/fax: 518-443-5321
e-mail: salinspd@sysadm.suny.edu
Vice Chancellor & CFO:
Vacant 518-443-5150/fax: 518-443-5470
e-mail: richteda@sysadm.suny.edu
Vice Chancellor, Business & Industry Relations:
Vacant 518-443-5869/fax: 518-443-5603
e-mail: dieselwa@sysadm.suny.edu
Vice Chancellor for Community Colleges:
Carol W Eaton 518-443-5134/fax: 518-443-5250
Counsel:
Donald Andrew Edwards, Jr 518-443-5400/fax: 518-443-5409
e-mail: edwardda@sysadm.suny.edu
Senior Assoc Vice Chancellor for University Relations:
Michael C Trunzo 518-443-5148/fax: 518-443-5151
e-mail: trunzom@sysadm.suny.edu
Vice Chancellor, Enrollment & University Life:
Wayne A Locust 518-443-5565/fax: 518-443-5225
e-mail: locustwa@sysadm.suny.edu

New York African American Institute

41 State St, Rm 702, Albany, NY 12246
Director:
Anne Pope 518-443-5798/fax: 518-443-5803
e-mail: popean@spo.rf.suny.edu

New York Network

Empire State Plaza, S Concourse, Ste 146, PO Box 2058, Albany, NY 12223
Web site: www.nyn.suny.edu
Executive Director:
William F Snyder 518-443-5333/fax: 518-426-4198
e-mail: snyderwf@nyn.suny.edu
Director of Administration & Broadcast Svcs:
Roy T Saplin 518-443-5333
Director of Engineering:
Gary Talkiewicz 518-443-5333

Rockefeller Institute of Government . . . . fax: 518-443-5788

411 State St, Albany, NY 12203-1003
518-443-5522 Fax: 518-443-5788
Web site: www.rockinst.org
Co-Director:
Richard P Nathan 518-443-5522
e-mail: nathanr@rockinst.org
Co-Director:
Thomas L Gais 518-443-5522
e-mail: gaist@rockinst.org

SUNY Metropolitan Recruitment Center

420 Lexington Ave, Ste 1640, New York, NY 10017
212-818-1204
Web site: www.suny.edu
Director:
Randy H Miller 212-818-1204/fax: 212-818-9079
e-mail: millerra@sysadm.suny.edu

Small Business Development Center

SUNY, Administration Bldg, 41 State St, Ste 700, Albany, NY 12246

Offices and agencies appear in alphabetical order.

800-732-7232
Web site: www.nyssbdc.org
State Director:
James L King 518-443-5398/fax: 518-443-5275
e-mail: j.king@nyssbdc.org

State University Construction Fund
353 Broadway, Albany, NY 12246
518-689-2500
Web site: www.sucf.suny.edu
General Manager:
Philip W Wood 518-689-2501/fax: 518-689-2634
Acting General Counsel:
William K Barczak 518-689-2516

UNIVERSITY CENTERS

NYS College of Agriculture & Life Sciences at Cornell

260 Roberts Hall
Ithaca, NY 14853-5901
607-255-2241 Fax: 607-255-3803
Web site: www.cals.cornell.edu

Dean:
Susan A Henry 607-255-3803
e-mail: sah42@cornell.edu

NYS College of Ceramics at Alfred University

2 Pine St
Alfred, NY 14802-1205
607-871-2137 Fax: 607-871-2339
Web site: www.alfred.edu

Interim Provost:
William Hall 607-871-2137

NYS College of Human Ecology at Cornell University

N112 Van Rensselaer Hall
Ithaca, NY 14853-4401
607-255-2216 Fax: 607-255-3794
Web site: www.human.cornell.edu

Dean:
Patsy Brannon 607-255-2138

NYS College of Veterinary Medicine at Cornell University

Schurman Hall
Ithaca, NY 14853-6401
607-253-3771 Fax: 607-253-3701
Web site: www.vet.cornell.edu

Dean:
Donald F Smith 607-253-3771
e-mail: dfs6@cornell.edu

NYS School of Industrial & Labor Relations at Cornell University

187 Ives Hall
Ithaca, NY 14853-3901
607-255-1812 Fax: 607-255-7774
Web site: www.ilr.cornell.edu

Dean:
Edward J Lawler 607-255-2185
e-mail: ejl3@cornell.edu

State College of Optometry

33 West 42nd St
New York, NY 10036-8003
212-780-4900 Fax: 212-780-5094
Web site: www.sunyopt.edu

President:
Alden N Haffner 212-780-5050/fax: 212-780-4949
e-mail: anhaffner@sunyopt.edu

State University Health Science Center Upstate Medical University

750 E Adams St
Syracuse, NY 13210
315-464-5158 Fax: 315-464-4838
Web site: www.upstate.edu

President:
Gregory L Eastwood 315-464-4513/fax: 315-464-5275

State University of New York College of Environmental Science & Forestry

224 Bray Hall
One Forestry Dr
Syracuse, NY 13210
315-470-6500 or TDD: 315-470-6966 Fax: 315-470-6933
e-mail: esfinfo@esf.edu
Web site: www.esf.edu

President:
Cornelius B Murphy, Jr 315-470-6681/fax: 315-470-6977
e-mail: cbmurphy@esf.edu

State University of New York Downstate Medical Center

450 Clarkson Ave
Brooklyn, NY 11203
718-270-1000 or 718-270-3160 Fax: 718-270-4732
Web site: www.downstate.edu

President:
John C LaRosa 718-270-2611
e-mail: jclarosa@downstate.edu

Offices and agencies appear in alphabetical order.

State University of New York at Albany

1400 Washington Ave
UAB 430
Albany, NY 12222
518-442-3300 or TDD: 518-442-3366
Web site: www.albany.edu

President:
Kermit L Hall 518-437-4920/fax: 518-437-4927

State University of New York at Binghamton

PO Box 6000
Binghamton, NY 13902-6000
607-777-2000 Fax: 607-777-4000
Web site: www.binghamton.edu

President:
Lois B DeFleur 607-777-2131/fax: 607-777-2533
e-mail: ldefleur@binghamton.edu

State University of New York at Buffalo

501 Capen Hall
Buffalo, NY 14260-1600
716-645-2901 Fax: 716-645-3728
Web site: www.buffalo.edu

President:
John B Simpson 716-645-2901
e-mail: simpson@buffalo.edu

State University of New York at Stony Brook

310 Administration Bldg
Stony Brook, NY 11794-0701
631-632-6000
Web site: www.sunysb.edu

President:
Shirley Strum Kenny 631-632-6265/fax: 631-632-6621
e-mail: shirley.kenny@stonybrook.edu

UNIVERSITY COLLEGES

State University College at Brockport

350 New Campus Dr
Brockport, NY 14420-2916
585-395-2211 Fax: 585-395-2401
Web site: www.brockport.edu

Interim President:
John Clark 585-395-2361

State University College at Buffalo

1300 Elmwood Ave
Buffalo, NY 14222-1095
716-878-4000 or TTD 716-878-3182 Fax: 716-878-3039
e-mail: webadmin@buffalostate.edu
Web site: www.buffalostate.edu

President:
Muriel A Howard 716-878-4101/fax: 716-878-6527
e-mail: howardma@buffalostate.edu

State University College at Cortland

PO Box 2000
Cortland, NY 13045
607-753-2011 Fax: 607-753-5999
Web site: www.cortland.edu

President:
Erik J Bitterbaum 607-753-2201/fax: 607-753-5993
e-mail: bitterbaume@cortland.edu

State University College at Fredonia

280 Central Ave
Fredonia, NY 14063-1136
716-673-3111 Fax: 716-673-3156
Web site: www.fredonia.edu

President:
Dennis L Hefner 716-673-3456/fax: 716-673-3446
e-mail: dennis.hefner@fredonia.edu

State University College at Geneseo

1 College Cir
Geneseo, NY 14454-1450
585-245-5211 Fax: 585-245-5005
Web site: www.geneseo.edu

President:
Christopher C Dahl 585-245-5501/fax: 585-245-5555
e-mail: cdahl@geneseo.edu

State University College at New Paltz

75 South Manheim Blvd
New Paltz, NY 12561-2443
845-257-2121 Fax: 845-257-3009
Web site: www.newpaltz.edu

President:
Steven G Poskanzer 845-257-3288/fax: 845-257-3389
e-mail: poskanzer@newpaltz.edu

State University College at Old Westbury

Route 107
Old Westbury, NY 11568-0210
516-876-3000
Web site: www.oldwestbury.edu

President:
Calvin O Butts, III 516-876-3160/fax: 516-876-3347
e-mail: buttsc@oldwestbury.edu

State University College at Oneonta

Ravine Pkwy
Oneonta, NY 13820-4015
607-436-3500
Web site: www.oneonta.edu

Colleges,
Universities &
School Districts

President:
Alan B Donovan 607-436-2500/fax: 607-436-3089
e-mail: donovaab@oneonta.edu

State University College at Oswego

Culkin Hall
State Route 104
Oswego, NY 13126
315-312-2500 Fax: 315-312-5438
e-mail: admiss@oswego.edu
Web site: www.oswego.edu

President:
Deborah Flemma Stanley 315-312-2211
e-mail: stanley@oswego.edu

State University College at Plattsburgh

101 Broad St
Plattsburgh, NY 12901
518-564-2000 Fax: 518-564-2094
Web site: www.plattsburgh.edu

President:
John Ettling 518-564-2010/fax: 518-564-3932
e-mail: john.ettling@plattsburgh.edu

State University College at Potsdam

44 Pierrepont Ave
Potsdam, NY 13676-2294
315-267-2000 Fax: 315-267-2496
Web site: www.potsdam.edu

President:
John A Fallon, III 315-267-2100
e-mail: fallonja@potsdam.edu

State University College at Purchase

735 Anderson Hill Rd
Purchase, NY 10577-1400
914-251-6000
Web site: www.purchase.edu

President:
Thomas J Schwarz 914-251-6010/fax: 914-251-6014
e-mail: thomas.schwarz@purchase.edu

State University Empire State College

One Union Ave
Saratoga Springs, NY 12866-4391
518-587-2100 x250 Fax: 518-587-3033
e-mail: kirk.starczewski@esc.edu
Web site: www.esc.edu

President:
Joseph B Moore 518-587-2100 x260
e-mail: joseph.moore@esc.edu

COLLEGES OF TECHNOLOGY

Alfred State College of Technology

10 Upper College Dr
Alfred, NY 14802
607-587-4215 or 800-425-3733 Fax: 607-587-4299
e-mail: admissions@alfredstate.edu
Web site: www.alfredstate.edu

President:
Uma G Gupta 607-587-4211/fax: 607-587-4209

Cobleskill College of Agriculture & Technology

Route 7
Cobleskill, NY 12043
518-255-5011 or 800-295-8988 Fax: 518-255-5333
Web site: www.cobleskill.edu

President:
Thomas J Haas 518-255-5111/fax: 518-255-5888
e-mail: presoff@cobleskill.edu

Farmingdale State College of Technology

2350 Broadhollow Rd
Farmingdale, NY 11735-1021
631-420-2000
e-mail: webmaster@farmingdale.edu
Web site: www.farmingdale.edu

President:
Jonathan C Gibralter 631-420-2239/fax: 631-420-2753
e-mail: gibralter@farmingdale.edu

Morrisville State College

PO Box 901
Morrisville, NY 13408
315-684-6000 or 800-258-0111 Fax: 315-684-6116
Web site: www.morrisville.edu

President:
Raymond W Cross 315-684-6044/fax: 315-684-6109
e-mail: crossrw@morrisville.edu

State University College of Technology at Canton

34 Cornell Dr
Canton, NY 13617
315-386-7011 or 800-388-7123 Fax: 315-386-7929
Web site: www.canton.edu

President:
Joseph L Kennedy 315-386-7204/fax: 315-386-7934
e-mail: president@canton.edu

State University College of Technology at Delhi

2 Main St
Delhi, NY 13753-1190
800-963-3544
Web site: www.delhi.edu

Offices and agencies appear in alphabetical order.

President:
Candace S Vancko. 607-746-4090/fax: 607-746-4346

State University Institute of Technology

Horatio St
PO Box 3050
Utica, NY 13504-3050
315-792-7500 Fax: 315-792-7837
Web site: www.sunyit.edu

Interim President:
Peter A Spina. 315-792-7400/fax: 315-792-7407
e-mail: spinap@sunyit.edu

State University of New York Maritime College

6 Pennyfield Ave
Fort Schuyler
Throgs Neck, NY 10465
718-409-7200 or 800-642-1874 Fax: 718-409-7392
Web site: www.sunymaritime.edu

President:
VADM John R Ryan 718-409-7270
e-mail: jryan@sunymaritime.edu

COMMUNITY COLLEGES

Adirondack Community College

640 Bay Rd
Queensbury, NY 12804
518-743-2200 Fax: 518-745-1433
e-mail: info@sunyacc.edu
Web site: www.sunyacc.edu

President:
Marshall E Bishop. 518-743-2237/fax: 518-743-2262
e-mail: bishopm@acc.sunyacc.edu

Broome Community College

PO Box 1017
Upper Front St
Binghamton, NY 13902
607-778-5000 Fax: 607-778-5310
Web site: www.sunybroome.edu

President:
Laurence D Spraggs 607-778-5100
e-mail: president@sunybroome.edu

Cayuga County Community College

197 Franklin St
Auburn, NY 13021-3099
315-255-1743 Fax: 315-255-2117
Web site: www.cayuga-cc.edu

President:
Dennis Golladay 315-255-1743 x2208
e-mail: golladayd@cayuga-cc.edu

Clinton Community College

136 Clinton Point Dr
Plattsburgh, NY 12901
518-562-4200 Fax: 518-562-4158
Web site: www.clinton.edu

Interim President:
Agnes Pearl 518-562-4100/fax: 518-561-4890

Columbia-Greene Community College

4400 Route 23
Hudson, NY 12534-0327
518-828-4181 Fax: 518-828-8543
Web site: www.sunycgcc.edu

President:
James R Campion 518-828-4181x3325/fax: 518-822-2006

Corning Community College

1 Academic Dr
Corning, NY 14830
607-962-9222 Fax: 607-962-9456
Web site: www.corning-cc.edu

President:
Floyd Amann. 607-962-9232/fax: 607-962-9485
e-mail: amann@corning-cc.edu

Dutchess Community College

53 Pendell Rd
Poughkeepsie, NY 12601-1595
845-431-8000 Fax: 845-431-8955
Web site: www.sunydutchess.edu

President:
D David Conklin. 845-431-8980
e-mail: conklin@sunydutchess.edu

Erie Community College

121 Ellicott St
Buffalo, NY 14203-2698
716-851-1200 Fax: 716-851-1029
Web site: www.ecc.edu

President:
William J Mariani. 716-851-1200
e-mail: mariani@ecc.edu

Fashion Institute of Technology

7th Ave at 27th St
New York, NY 10001-5992
212-217-7999
Web site: www.fitnyc.edu

President:
Joyce F Brown. 212-217-7660/fax: 212-217-7639

Offices and agencies appear in alphabetical order.

Finger Lakes Community College

4355 Lakeshore Dr
Canandaigua, NY 14424
585-394-3500 Fax: 585-394-5017
e-mail: admissions@flcc.edu
Web site: www.fingerlakes.edu

President:
Daniel T Hayes 585-394-3500 x7201
e-mail: hayesdt@flcc.edu

Fulton-Montgomery Community College

2805 State Hwy 67
Johnstown, NY 12095-3790
518-762-4651 Fax: 518-762-4334
Web site: www.fmcc.suny.edu

President:
Barry M Weinberg. 518-762-4651 x8000
e-mail: bweinberg@fmcc.suny.edu

Genesee Community College

One College Rd
Batavia, NY 14020-9704
585-343-0055 Fax: 585-343-4541
Web site: www.genesee.edu

President:
Stuart Steiner 585-345-6812
e-mail: ssteiner@genesee.edu

Herkimer County Community College

100 Reservoir Rd
Herkimer, NY 13350-9987
315-866-0300 or 888-464-4222 Fax: 315-866-7253
Web site: www.hccc.suny.edu

President:
Ronald F Williams 315-866-0300 x261/fax: 315-866-5539
e-mail: williams@hccc.suny.edu

Hudson Valley Community College

80 Vandenburgh Ave
Troy, NY 12180
518-629-4822 or 877-325-4822 Fax: 518-629-7586
Web site: www.hvcc.edu

President:
Marco J Silvestri. 518-629-4530

Jamestown Community College

525 Falconer St
PO Box 20
Jamestown, NY 14702-0020
716-665-5220 Fax: 716-665-9110
Web site: www.sunyjcc.edu

President:
Gregory T DeCinque 716-665-5220 x2315/fax: 716-483-2726
e-mail: gregdecinque@mail.sunyjcc.edu

Jefferson Community College

1220 Coffeen St
Watertown, NY 13601
315-786-2200 Fax: 315-786-0158
Web site: www.sunyjefferson.edu

President:
Joseph B Olson. 315-786-2230
e-mail: jolson@sunyjefferson.edu

Mohawk Valley Community College

1101 Sherman Dr
Utica, NY 13501-5394
315-792-5400 Fax: 315-792-5666
Web site: www.mvcc.edu

President:
Michael I Schafer 315-792-5333/fax: 315-792-5678
e-mail: mschafer@mvcc.edu

Monroe Community College

1000 E Henrietta Rd
Rochester, NY 14623
585-292-2000 Fax: 585-292-3060
Web site: www.monroecc.edu

President:
R Thomas Flynn. 585-292-2100

Nassau Community College

1 Education Dr
Garden City, NY 11530-6793
516-572-7501 Fax: 516-572-8118
Web site: www.ncc.edu

President:
Sean A Fanelli 516-572-7205
e-mail: fanellis@ncc.edu

Niagara County Community College

3111 Saunders Settlement Rd
Sanborn, NY 14132
716-614-6222 Fax: 716-614-6700
Web site: www.niagara.cc.suny.edu

President:
James P Klyczek 716-614-5905/fax: 716-614-6824

North Country Community College

23 Santanoni Ave
PO Box 89
Saranac Lake, NY 12983-0089
518-891-2915 Fax: 518-891-5029
Web site: www.nccc.edu

President:
Gail Rogers Rice 518-891-2915 x201

Offices and agencies appear in alphabetical order.

Onondaga Community College

4941 Onondaga Rd
Syracuse, NY 13215
315-498-2622
Web site: www.sunyocc.edu

President:
Debbie L Sydow 315-498-2211/fax: 315-469-4475
e-mail: sydowd@sunyocc.edu

Orange County Community College

115 South St
Middletown, NY 10940
845-344-6222 Fax: 845-343-1228
Web site: orange.cc.ny.us

President:
William Richards. 845-341-4701/fax: 845-341-4998
e-mail: president@sunyorange.edu

Rockland Community College

145 College Rd
Suffern, NY 10901
845-574-4000
Web site: www.sunyrockland.edu

President:
Cliff L Wood 845-574-4214

Schenectady County Community College

78 Washington Ave
Schenectady, NY 12305
518-381-1200 Fax: 518-346-0379
Web site: www.sunysccc.edu

President:
Gabriel J Basil. 518-381-1304/fax: 518-346-8680
e-mail: basilgj@gw.sunysccc.edu

Suffolk County Community College

533 College Rd
Selden, NY 11784
631-451-4000 Fax: 631-451-4715
Web site: www.sunysuffolk.edu

President:
Shirley R Pippins 631-451-4950
e-mail: pippins@sunysuffolk.edu
Executive Dean:
John Pryputniewicz 631-451-4000

Sullivan County Community College

112 College Rd
Loch Sheldrake, NY 12759-5151
845-434-5750 or 800-577-5243 Fax: 845-434-4806
Web site: www.sullivan.suny.edu

President:
Mamie Howard Golladay 845-434-5750 x4261/fax: 845-434-9308
e-mail: mgollada@sullivan.suny.edu

Tompkins Cortland Community College

170 North St
PO Box 139
Dryden, NY 13053-0139
607-844-8211 or 888-567-8211 Fax: 607-844-9665
Web site: www.sunytccc.edu

President:
Carl E Haynes. 607-844-8211 x4368/fax: 607-844-6545
e-mail: haynesc@sunytccc.edu

Ulster County Community College

Cottekill Rd
Stone Ridge, NY 12484
845-687-5000 or 800-724-0833 Fax: 845-687-5083
Web site: www.sunyulster.edu

President:
Donald C Katt 845-687-5050/fax: 845-687-5292
e-mail: kattd@sunyulster.edu

Westchester Community College

75 Grasslands Rd
Valhalla, NY 10595-1693
914-785-6600 Fax: 914-785-6565
Web site: www.sunywcc.edu

President:
Joseph N Hankin 914-785-6707/fax: 914-785-6780
e-mail: joseph.hankin@sunywcc.edu

EDUCATIONAL OPPORTUNITY CENTERS

Bronx Educational Opportunity Center

1666 Bathgate Ave
Bronx, NY 10457
718-530-7000 Fax: 718-583-0783

Executive Director:
Wendell Joyner. 718-530-7045

Brooklyn Educational Opportunity Center

111 Livingston St
Brooklyn, NY 11201
718-802-3353 Fax: 718-802-3313
e-mail: henryd@bklyn.eoc.cuny.edu
Web site: www.bklyn.eoc.cuny.edu

Executive Director/Asst Dean:
Lois Blades-Rosado 718-246-2057
e-mail: rosadol@bklyn.eoc.cuny.edu

Buffalo Educational Opportunity Center

465 Washington St
Buffalo, NY 14203
716-849-6727 Fax: 716-849-6755

Offices and agencies appear in alphabetical order.

Director:
Sherryl D Weems 716-849-6727 x125
e-mail: weems@acsu.buffalo.edu

Capital District Educational Opportunity Center

145 Congress St
Troy, NY 12180
518-273-1900 Fax: 518-273-1919
Web site: www.alb.eoc.suny.edu

Executive Director:
Lucille A Marion 518-273-1900 x2212
e-mail: marioluc@hvcc.edu

Educational Opportunity Center of Westchester

26 S Broadway
Yonkers, NY 10701
914-606-7600 Fax: 914-606-7640

Associate Dean & Director:
Renee Guy 914-606-7612
e-mail: renee.guy@sunywcc.edu

Long Island Educational Opportunity Center

SUNY Farmingdale
Farmingdale, NY 11735
631-420-2280 Fax: 631-420-2510
Web site: www.farmingdale.edu/lieoc

Dean:
Veronica Henry 631-420-2507
e-mail: henryv@farmingdale.edu

Manhattan Educational Opportunity Center

163 W 125th St
New York, NY 10027
212-961-4320 Fax: 212-961-4343
Web site: www.nyc.eoc.suny.edu

Interim Director:
John Evans 212-961-4320

North Bronx Career Counseling & Outreach Center

3950 Laconia Ave
Bronx, NY 10466

718-547-1001 Fax: 718-547-1973
Web site: www.nbx.eoc.suny.edu

Director:
Reginald Marshall 718-547-1001

Queens Educational Opportunity Center

SUNY
158-29 Archer Ave
Jamaica, NY 11433
718-725-3300 Fax: 718-658-5604

Director:
Khayriyyah Ali 718-725-3300
e-mail: kali@qns.eoc.cuny.edu

Rochester Educational Opportunity Center

305 Andrews St
Rochester, NY 14604
585-232-2730 Fax: 585-546-7824
Web site: www.rch.eoc.suny.edu

Dean:
Melva L Brown 585-232-2730 x269/fax: 585-232-8154
e-mail: mebrown@brockport.edu

SUNY College & Career Counseling Center

120 Emmons St
Schenectady, NY 12304
518-370-2654 Fax: 518-370-2661
e-mail: sunyeccc@thebiz.net

Director:
Lois Tripp-Ferguson 518-370-2654

Syracuse Educational Opportunity Center

100 New St
Syracuse, NY 13202
315-472-0130 Fax: 315-472-1241
Web site: www.morrisville.edu/eoc

Dean:
Bill Harper 315-472-0130
e-mail: harperbg@morrisville.edu

The City University of New York

Borough of Manhattan Community College

199 Chambers St
New York, NY 10007
212-220-8000 Fax: 212-220-1244
Web site: www.bmcc.cuny.edu

President:
Antonio Perez 212-220-1230
e-mail: aperez@bmcc.cuny.edu

Bronx Community College

University Ave & West 181st St
Bronx, NY 10453

Offices and agencies appear in alphabetical order.

718-289-5100
Web site: www.bcc.cuny.edu

President:
Carolyn G Williams. 718-289-5151/fax: 718-289-6011

CUNY Bernard M Baruch College

One Bernard Baruch Way
New York, NY 10010
646-312-1400 Fax: 646-312-1363
Web site: www.baruch.cuny.edu

President:
Kathleen M Waldron. 646-312-3310/fax: 646-312-3311

CUNY Board of Trustees

535 E 80th St
New York, NY 10021
212-794-5450 Fax: 212-794-5678
Web site: www.cuny.edu

Chair:
Benno C Schmidt Jr (2006) 212-794-5555
Member:
Valerie Lancaster Beal (2009) 212-794-5450
Member:
Rev John S Bonnici (2008). 212-794-5450
Member:
John J Calandra (2005). 212-794-5450
Member:
Wellington Z Chen (2003) 212-794-5450
Member:
Kenneth E Cook (2004) 212-794-5450
Member:
Rita DiMartino (2010) 212-794-5450
Member:
Joseph J Lhota (2011). 212-794-5450
Member:
Randy M Mastro (2006). 212-794-5450
Member:
Hugo M Morales MD (2007) 212-794-5450
Member:
Kathleen M Pesile (2004). 212-794-5450
Member:
Carol A Robles-Roman (2008). 212-794-5450
Member:
Nilda Soto Ruiz (2002). 212-794-5450
Member:
Marc V Shaw (2007) 212-794-5450
Member:
Jeffrey Wiesenfeld (2006) 212-794-5450

CUNY Brooklyn College

2900 Bedford Ave
Brooklyn, NY 11210
718-951-5000
Web site: www.brooklyn.cuny.edu

President:
Christoph M Kimmich. 718-951-5671/fax: 718-951-4872

CUNY Central Administration

535 E 80th St
New York, NY 10021
212-794-5555
Web site: www.cuny.edu

Chancellor:
Matthew Goldstein 212-794-5311/fax: 212-794-5671
Senior Vice Chancellor/COO:
Allan H Dobrin. 212-794-5305
Deputy COO:
Ronald Spalter 212-794-5609
Vice Chancellor, Budget & Finance:
Ernesto Malave. 212-794-5403
Vice Chancellor, University Relations:
Jay Hershenson. 212-794-5317
Vice Chancellor, Facilities, Planning, Construction & Mgmt:
Emma Espino Macari. 212-794-5315
Vice Chancellor, Faculty & Staff Relations:
Brenda Richardson Malone 212-794-5353
Executive Vice Chancellor, Academic Affairs:
Selma Botman 212-794-5414
Vice Chancellor, Legal Affairs & General Counsel:
Frederick P Schaffer. 212-794-5506
Vice Chancellor for Student Development/Enrollment Management:
Otis O Hill 212-794-5775
Research Compliance Officer:
Gillian Small. 212-794-5417
Senior University Dean, Academic Affairs:
John Mogulescu 212-794-5429
University Dean, Executive Office:
Robert Ptachik 212-794-5509
University Dean, Instructional Technology & Info Services:
Michael Ribaudo 212-541-0370
Special Counsel to the Chancellor:
Dave Fields. 212-794-5313
Interim Vice Chancellor, Administration & Planning:
Michael J Zavelle 212-794-5326

City University Construction Fund. . . . . fax: 212-541-0401

555 W 57th St, 10th Fl, New York, NY 10019
212-541-0171 Fax: 212-541-0401
Chairman:
Harvey Auerbach 212-541-0171
Executive Director:
Emma Espino-Macari. 212-794-5315
e-mail: emma.macari@mail.cuny.edu
Counsel:
Frederick Schaffer 212-794-5506
Special Assistant:
Nancy Nichols 212-541-0171
e-mail: nancy.nichols@mail.cuny.edu
Chief Fiscal Officer:
Catherine Yang. 212-541-0458
e-mail: catherine.yang@mail.cuny.edu

CUNY College of Staten Island

2800 Victory Blvd
Staten Island, NY 10314
718-982-2000
Web site: www.csi.cuny.edu

President:
Marlene Springer. 718-982-2400/fax: 718-982-2404

Offices and agencies appear in alphabetical order.

CUNY Graduate Center

365 Fifth Ave
New York, NY 10016-4309
212-817-7000
Web site: www.gc.cuny.edu

President:
    Frances Degen Horowitz. 212-817-7100/fax: 212-817-1606
    e-mail: pres@gc.cuny.edu
School of Professional Svcs:
    John Mogulescu 212-817-7255

CUNY Herbert H Lehman College

250 Bedford Park Blvd West
Bronx, NY 10468-1589
718-960-8000 Fax: 718-960-8212
Web site: www.lehman.cuny.edu

President:
    Ricardo R Fernandez. 718-960-8111/fax: 718-584-1765

CUNY Hunter College

695 Park Ave
New York, NY 10021
212-772-4000
Web site: www.hunter.cuny.edu

President:
    Jennifer J Raab 212-772-4242/fax: 212-772-4724
    e-mail: jennifer.raab@hunter.cuny.edu

CUNY John Jay College of Criminal Justice

899 Tenth Ave
New York, NY 10019
212-237-8000 Fax: 212-237-8607
Web site: www.jjay.cuny.edu

President:
    Jeremy Travis 212-237-8600
Director Public Relations:
    Joe Calderone 212-237-8628/fax: 212-237-8610

CUNY Medgar Evers College

1650 Bedford Ave
Brooklyn, NY 11225
718-270-4900 Fax: 718-270-5126
Web site: www.mec.cuny.edu

President:
    Edison O Jackson 718-270-5000

CUNY New York City College of Technology

300 Jay St
Brooklyn, NY 11201
718-260-5500 Fax: 718-260-5406
e-mail: connect@citytech.cuny.edu
Web site: www.citytech.cuny.edu

President:
    Russell K Hotzler 718-260-5400

CUNY Queens College

65-30 Kissena Blvd
Flushing, NY 11367-1597
718-997-5000 or 718-997-5556
Web site: www.qc.edu

President:
    James L Muyskens 718-997-5550/fax: 718-793-8044

CUNY School of Law at Queens College

65-21 Main St
Flushing, NY 11367
718-340-4200 Fax: 718-340-4482
Web site: www.law.cuny.edu

Dean:
    Kristin Booth Glen 718-340-4201
    e-mail: glen@mail.law.cuny.edu

CUNY York College

94-20 Guy R Brewer Blvd
Jamaica, NY 11451
718-262-2000
Web site: www.york.cuny.edu

President:
    Marcia Keizs 718-262-2350/fax: 718-262-2352

City College of New York, The

Convent Ave & 138th St
New York, NY 10031
212-650-7285 Fax: 212-650-7680
Web site: www.ccny.cuny.edu

President:
    Gregory H Williams. 212-650-7286
    e-mail: gwilliams@ccny.cuny.edu
President/Sophie Davis Biomedical Education:
    Standford H Roman Jr 212-650-5275

Eugenio Maria De Hostos Community College

500 Grand Concourse
Bronx, NY 10451
718-518-4444 Fax: 718-518-4294
Web site: www.hostos.cuny.edu

President:
    Dolores M Fernandez. 718-518-4300
    e-mail: dfernandez@hostos.cuny.edu

Fiorello H LaGuardia Community College

31-10 Thomson Ave
Long Island City, NY 11101
718-482-5050 Fax: 718-609-2009
Web site: www.lagcc.cuny.edu

President:
    Gail O Mellow 718-482-5050
    e-mail: gmellow@lagcc.cuny.edu

Offices and agencies appear in alphabetical order.

Kingsborough Community College

2001 Oriental Blvd
Brooklyn, NY 11235
718-368-5000 Fax: 718-368-5003
e-mail: webmaster@kbcc.cuny.edu
Web site: www.kbcc.cuny.edu

President:
 Regina S Peruggi 718-368-5000

Queensborough Community College

222-05 56th Ave
Bayside, NY 11364-1497
718-631-6262
Web site: www.qcc.cuny.edu

President:
 Eduardo J Marti 718-631-6262/fax: 718-281-5588
 e-mail: emarti@qcc.cuny.edu

Independent Colleges & Universities

Adelphi University

1 South Ave
Garden City, NY 11530
516-877-3050 or 800-233-5744 Fax: 516-877-3845
Web site: www.adelphi.edu

President:
 Robert A Scott 516-877-3838/fax: 516-877-3845

Albany College of Pharmacy

106 New Scotland Ave
Albany, NY 12208-3492
518-445-7200 or 888-203-8010 Fax: 518-445-7202
e-mail: info@acp.edu
Web site: www.acp.edu

President:
 James J Gozzo 518-445-7255/fax: 518-445-7294
 e-mail: gozzoj@acp.edu

Albany Law School

80 New Scotland Ave
Albany, NY 12208-3494
518-445-2311 Fax: 518-445-2315
e-mail: info@mail.als.edu
Web site: www.als.edu

President/Dean:
 Thomas F Guernsey. 518-445-2380/fax: 518-472-5865

Albany Medical College

47 New Scotland Ave
Albany, NY 12208
518-262-6008 Fax: 518-262-6515
Web site: www.amc.edu/academic

Dean:
 Vincent P Verdile 518-262-6008
 e-mail: verdilv@mail.amc.edu

Alfred University

Saxon Dr
Alfred, NY 14802
800-541-9229 or 607-871-2115 Fax: 607-871-2198
Web site: www.alfred.edu

President:
 Charles M Edmondson 607-871-2101

American Academy McAllister Institute of Funeral Service

619 West 54th St, 6th Fl
New York, NY 10019
212-757-1190 Fax: 212-765-5923
e-mail: info.a-a-m-i.org
Web site: www.a-a-m-i.org

President/CEO:
 Meg Dunn. 212-757-1190

Bank Street College of Education

610 West 112th St
New York, NY 10025-1898
212-875-4400 Fax: 212-875-4759
e-mail: collegepubs@bankstreet.edu
Web site: www.bankstreet.edu

President:
 Augusta Souza Kappner 212-875-4595/fax: 212-875-4594
 e-mail: akappner@bankstreet.edu
Acting Dean, Institutional Advancement:
 Patricia Fisher 212-961-3322/fax: 212-961-3345
 e-mail: paddy@bankstreet.edu

Bard College

PO Box 5000
Annandale-on-Hudson, NY 12504-5000
845-758-6822 Fax: 845-758-5208
Web site: www.bard.edu

President:
 Leon Botstein 845-758-7423
 e-mail: president@bard.edu

Barnard College

3009 Broadway
New York, NY 10027
212-854-5262 Fax: 212-749-6531
Web site: www.barnard.edu

Offices and agencies appear in alphabetical order.

Colleges,
Universities &
School Districts

President:
Judith R Shapiro 212-854-2021
e-mail: jshapiro@barnard.edu

Boricua College

3755 Broadway
New York, NY 10032
212-694-1000 Fax: 212-694-1015
e-mail: acruz@boricuacollege.edu
Web site: www.boricuacollege.edu

President:
Victor G Alicea 212-694-1000
e-mail: valicea@boricuacollege.edu

Bramson ORT College

69-30 Austin St
Forest Hills, NY 11375-4239
718-261-5800 Fax: 718-575-5118
Web site: www.bramsonort.org

Director:
Ephraim Buhks 718-261-5800 x102
e-mail: ebuhks@ortopsusa.org

Brooklyn Law School

250 Joralemon St
Brooklyn, NY 11201-3798
718-625-2200 Fax: 718-780-0393
Web site: www.brooklaw.edu

Dean:
Joan G Wexler 718-780-7900
e-mail: joan.wexler@brooklaw.edu

Canisius College

2001 Main St
Buffalo, NY 14208-1098
716-883-7000 Fax: 716-888-2525
Web site: www.canisius.edu

President:
Rev Vincent M Cooke 716-888-2100/fax: 716-888-3220
e-mail: cookevm@canisius.edu

Cazenovia College

22 Sullivan St
Cazenovia, NY 13035
315-655-7000 or 800-654-3210 Fax: 315-655-4143
Web site: www.cazenovia.edu

President:
Mark John Tierno 315-655-7116

Christ the King Seminary

711 Knox Rd
East Aurora, NY 14052

716-652-8900 Fax: 716-652-8903
e-mail: cksacad@cks.edu
Web site: www.cks.edu

President/Rector:
Rev Richard W Siepka 716-652-8900
e-mail: rsiepka@cks.edu

Clarkson University

8 Clarkson Ave
Potsdam, NY 13699
315-268-6400 or 800-527-6577 Fax: 315-268-7993
Web site: www.clarkson.edu

President:
Anthony G Collins 315-268-6444
e-mail: tony.collins@clarkson.edu

Cochran School of Nursing

St John's Riverside Hospital
967 N Broadway
Yonkers, NY 10701
914-964-4282 Fax: 914-964-4266
e-mail: kvitola@riversidehealth.org
Web site: www.riversidehealth.org

President of Hospital:
James Foy 914-964-4221
e-mail: jfoy@riversidehealth.org
Vice President for Education/Director Nursing School:
Kathleen Dirschel 914-964-4282

Colgate Rochester Crozer Divinity School

1100 S Goodman St
Rochester, NY 14620
585-271-1320 Fax: 585-271-8013
Web site: www.crcds.edu

President:
Thomas Halbrooks 585-271-1320 x210
e-mail: thalbrooks@crcds.edu

Colgate University

13 Oak Dr
Hamilton, NY 13346
315-228-1000 Fax: 315-228-7798
Web site: www.colgate.edu

President:
Rebecca S Chopp 315-228-7444/fax: 315-228-6010
e-mail: rchopp@mail.colgate.edu

College of Mount Saint Vincent

6301 Riverdale Ave
Riverdale, NY 10471-1093
800-665-2678 or 718-405-3267 Fax: 718-549-7945
e-mail: admissns@mountsaintvincent.edu
Web site: www.mountsaintvincent.edu

Offices and agencies appear in alphabetical order.

President:
Charles L Flynn, Jr 718-405-3232

College of New Rochelle (The)
29 Castle Pl
New Rochelle, NY 10805-2339
800-211-7077 Fax: 914-654-5833
e-mail: info@cnr.edu
Web site: www.cnr.edu

President:
Stephen J Sweeny 914-654-5000 x5522/fax: 914-654-5980
e-mail: ssweeny@cnr.edu

College of Saint Rose (The)
432 Western Ave
Albany, NY 12203-1490
800-637-8556 or 518-454-5111 Fax: 518-454-2080
Web site: www.strose.edu

President:
R Mark Sullivan 518-454-5120
e-mail: sullivan@strose.edu

Columbia University
202 Low Memorial Library
New York, NY 10027
212-854-9970 Fax: 212-854-9973
Web site: www.columbia.edu

President:
Lee C Bollinger 212-854-9970
e-mail: bollinger@columbia.edu

Concordia College
171 White Plains Rd
Bronxville, NY 10708
914-337-9300 Fax: 914-395-4500
Web site: www.concordia-ny.edu

President:
Viji D George 914-337-9300 x2111
e-mail: vdg@concordia-ny.edu

Cooper Union for the Advancement of Science & Art
30 Cooper Sq
New York, NY 10003-7120
212-353-4000 Fax: 212-353-4244
Web site: www.cooper.edu

President:
George Campbell Jr 212-353-4240

Cornell University
300 Day Hall
Ithaca, NY 14853-2801

607-254-4636 Fax: 607-255-5396
e-mail: info@cornell.edu
Web site: www.cornell.edu

President:
Jeffrey S Lehman 607-255-5201/fax: 607-255-9924
e-mail: president@cornell.edu

Crouse Hospital School of Nursing
736 Irving Ave
Syracuse, NY 13210
315-470-7111 Fax: 315-470-7232
e-mail: crouseson@crouse.org
Web site: www.crouse.org/nursing

Director:
JoAnn Herne 315-470-7481

Culinary Institute of America
1946 Campus Dr
Hyde Park, NY 12538-1499
845-452-9430 or 800-285-4627 Fax: 845-451-1068
e-mail: personnel@culinary.edu
Web site: www.ciachef.edu

President:
Tim Ryan 845-451-1352

D'Youville College
320 Porter Ave
Buffalo, NY 14201
716-829-8000 or 800-777-3921 Fax: 716-881-7790
Web site: www.dyc.edu

President:
Sister Denise A Roche 716-881-7673/fax: 716-881-7780
e-mail: roche@dyc.edu

Daemen College
4380 Main St
Amherst, NY 14226
716-839-3600 Fax: 716-839-8516
Web site: www.daemen.edu

President:
Martin J Anisman 716-839-8210/fax: 716-839-8279
e-mail: manisman@daemen.edu

Davis College
400 Riverside Dr
Johnson City, NY 13790
607-729-1581 or 800-331-4137 Fax: 607-729-2962
e-mail: dc@davisny.edu
Web site: www.davisny.edu

President:
George D Miller, III 607-729-1581 x316/fax: 607-729-1581

Offices and agencies appear in alphabetical order.

Dominican College

470 Western Highway
Orangeburg, NY 10962
845-359-7800 Fax: 845-359-2313
Web site: www.dc.edu

President:
   Sister Mary Eileen O'Brien 845-359-7800/fax: 845-359-7988
   e-mail: mary.eileen.obrien@dc.edu

Dorothea Hopfer School of Nursing at Mount Vernon Hospital

53 Valentine St
Mount Vernon, NY 10550
914-664-8000 x3220 Fax: 914-665-7047
e-mail: hopferadmissions@sshsw.org
Web site: www.ssmc.org

CEO:
   John R Spicer 914-664-8000 x3100
Dean of Nursing Education:
   Joanna Scalabrini 914-664-8000 x3220

Dowling College

Idle Hour Blvd
Oakdale, NY 11769
631-244-3000 or 800-369-5464 Fax: 631-589-6644
Web site: www.dowling.edu

President:
   Albert E Donor 631-244-3200/fax: 631-589-7551
   e-mail: donor@dowling.edu

Ellis Hospital School of Nursing

1101 Nott St
Schenectady, NY 12308
518-243-4471 Fax: 518-243-4470
Web site: www.ehson.org

Director:
   Mary Lee Pollard 518-243-4471
   e-mail: pollardm@shine.org

Elmira College

One Park Pl
Elmira, NY 14901
607-735-1800 or 800-935-6472
Web site: www.elmira.edu

President:
   Thomas K Meier 607-735-1790
   e-mail: tmeier@elmira.edu

Excelsior College

7 Columbia Cir
Albany, NY 12203-5159
518-464-8500 or 888-647-2388 Fax: 518-464-8777
e-mail: info@excelsior.edu
Web site: www.excelsior.edu

President:
   C Wayne Williams 518-464-8524
   e-mail: wwilliams@excelsior.edu

Fordham University

Rose Hill
441 East Fordham Rd
Bronx, NY 10458
718-817-1000
Web site: www.fordham.edu

President:
   Joseph M McShane 718-817-3000/fax: 718-817-3005

Gamla College

1213 Elm Ave
Brooklyn, NY 11230
718-339-4747 Fax: 718-998-5766
e-mail: drsmt@gamlacollege.edu

President:
   Shlomo Teichman 718-339-4747

General Theological Seminary of the Episcopal Church

175 Ninth Ave
Chelsea Sq
New York, NY 10011-4977
212-243-5150 Fax: 212-727-3907
Web site: www.gts.edu

President/Dean:
   Rev Ward B Ewing 212-243-5150/fax: 212-647-0294
   e-mail: ewing@gts.edu

Hamilton College

198 College Hill Rd
Clinton, NY 13323
315-859-4421 or 800-843-2655 Fax: 315-859-4457
Web site: www.hamilton.edu

President:
   Joan Hinde Stewart 315-859-4105
   e-mail: jstewart@hamilton.edu

Hartwick College

One Hartwick Dr
Oneonta, NY 13820-4020
800-427-8942 or 607-431-4000 Fax: 607-431-4206
Web site: www.hartwick.edu

President:
   Richard P Miller, Jr 607-431-4990
   e-mail: president@hartwick.edu

Offices and agencies appear in alphabetical order.

Hebrew Union College - Jewish Institute of Religion

The Brookdale Center
One W 4th St
New York, NY 10012
212-674-5300 Fax: 212-388-1720
Web site: www.huc.edu

President:
David Ellenson 800-424-2201 x1336/fax: 212-979-0853
e-mail: presoff@huc.edu

Helene Fuld College of Nursing North General Hospital

1879 Madison Ave
New York, NY 10035
212-423-2700 Fax: 212-427-2453
e-mail: jessica.belalmy@helenefuld.edu
Web site: www.helenefuld.edu

President:
Margaret Wines 212-423-2750

Hilbert College

5200 South Park Ave
Hamburg, NY 14075
716-649-7900 Fax: 716-558-6380
Web site: www.hilbert.edu

President:
Sister Edmunette Paczesny 716-649-7900 x201
e-mail: edmunette@hilbert.edu

Hobart & William Smith Colleges

629 S Main St
Geneva, NY 14456-3397
315-781-3000
Web site: www.hws.edu

President:
Mark D Gearan 315-789-3309
e-mail: gearan@hws.edu

Hofstra University

1000 Fulton Ave
Hempstead, NY 11550
800-463-7872 or 516-463-6600 Fax: 516-463-4867
e-mail: pride@hofstra.edu
Web site: www.hofstra.edu

President:
Stuart Rabinowitz 516-463-6800/fax: 516-463-6096
e-mail: pres@hofstra.edu

Houghton College

1 Willard Ave
Houghton, NY 14744-0128
800-777-2556 Fax: 585-567-9572
Web site: www.houghton.edu

President:
Daniel R Chamberlain 585-567-9310
e-mail: daniel.chamberlain@houghton.edu

Institute of Design & Construction

141 Willoughby St
Brooklyn, NY 11201
718-855-3661 Fax: 718-852-5889
Web site: www.idc.edu

Director:
Vincent C Battista 718-855-3661
e-mail: vcbattista@idc.edu

Iona College

715 North Ave
New Rochelle, NY 10801
914-633-2000 or 800-231-4662 Fax: 914-633-2018
Web site: www.iona.edu

President:
Br James A Liguori 914-633-2203
e-mail: jliguori@iona.edu

Ithaca College

953 Danby Rd
Ithaca, NY 14850
607-274-3011 Fax: 607-274-1900
Web site: www.ithaca.edu

President:
Peggy R Williams 607-274-3111/fax: 607-274-1500
e-mail: president@ithaca.edu

Jewish Theological Seminary of America

3080 Broadway
New York, NY 10027-4649
212-678-8000 Fax: 212-678-8947
Web site: www.jtsa.edu

Chancellor/President of Faculties:
Ismar Schorsch 212-678-8071
e-mail: isschorsch@jtsa.edu

Juilliard School (The)

60 Lincoln Center Plz
New York, NY 10023-6588
212-799-5000 Fax: 212-724-0263
Web site: www.juilliard.edu

President:
Joseph W Polisi 212-799-5000
Dean:
Stephen Clapp 212-799-5000 x204

Keuka College

141 Central Ave
Keuka Park, NY 14478
315-279-5000 Fax: 315-279-5216
Web site: www.keuka.edu

Offices and agencies appear in alphabetical order.

President:
  Joseph Burke 315-279-5201/fax: 315-279-5335
  e-mail: president@mail.keuka.edu

King's College (The)
Empire State Bldg
350 Fifth Ave, Ste 1500
New York, NY 10118
888-969-7200 or 212-659-7200 Fax: 212-659-7210
e-mail: info@tkc.edu
Web site: www.tkc.edu

President:
  Jack Stanley Oakes, Jr 212-659-7200
  e-mail: kleedy@tkc.edu

Le Moyne College
1419 Salt Springs Rd
Syracuse, NY 13214-1301
315-445-4100 Fax: 315-445-4540
Web site: www.lemoyne.edu

President:
  Rev Charles J Beirne 315-445-4120/fax: 315-445-4691
  e-mail: beirnecj@lemoyne.edu

Long Island College Hospital School of Nursing
340 Court St
Brooklyn, NY 11231
718-780-1953 Fax: 718-780-1936

Dean:
  Janet MacKin 718-780-1998

Long Island University
University Center
700 Northern Blvd
Brookville, NY 11548-1327
516-299-2501 or 516-299-1926 Fax: 516-299-2072
Web site: www.liu.edu

President:
  David J Steinberg 516-299-2501
  e-mail: pres@liu.edu

Manhattan College
Manhattan College Pkwy
Riverdale, NY 10471
718-862-8000 or 800-622-9235
Web site: www.manhattan.edu

President:
  Brother Thomas J Scanlan 718-862-7301/fax: 718-862-8030
  e-mail: thomas.scanlan@manhattan.edu

Manhattan School of Music
120 Claremont Ave
New York, NY 10027

212-749-2802 Fax: 212-749-5471
Web site: www.msmnyc.edu

President:
  Marta C Istomin 914-493-4477
  e-mail: officeofthepresident@msmnyc.edu

Manhattanville College
2900 Purchase St
Purchase, NY 10577
914-694-2200 Fax: 914-694-2386
Web site: www.mville.edu

President:
  Richard A Berman 914-323-5230/fax: 914-694-6234
  e-mail: president@mville.edu

Maria College of Albany
700 New Scotland Ave
Albany, NY 12208
518-438-3111 Fax: 518-438-7170
Web site: www.mariacollege.edu

President:
  Sister Laureen A Fitzgerald 518-438-3111
  e-mail: lfitz@mariacollege.edu

Marist College
3399 North Rd
Poughkeepsie, NY 12601-1387
845-575-3000 Fax: 845-471-6213
e-mail: timmian.massie@marist.edu
Web site: www.marist.edu

President:
  Dennis J Murray 845-575-3600
  e-mail: dennis.murray@marist.edu

Marymount College of Fordham University
100 Marymount Ave
Tarrytown, NY 10591-3796
800-724-4312 or 914-631-3200 Fax: 914-332-7442
e-mail: mcenroll@fordham.edu
Web site: www.fordham.edu

Provost:
  Mary Ann Quaranta 914-332-8268

Marymount Manhattan College
221 East 71st St
New York, NY 10021
800-627-9668 or 212-517-0430 Fax: 212-517-0567
Web site: marymount.mmm.edu

President:
  Judson R Shaver 212-517-0560
  e-mail: jshaver@mmm.edu

Offices and agencies appear in alphabetical order.

Medaille College
18 Agassiz Cir
Buffalo, NY 14214-2695
716-884-3281 or 800-292-1582 Fax: 716-884-0291
Web site: www.medaille.edu

President:
  Joseph W Bascuas 716-884-3411 x201
  e-mail: jbascuas@medaille.edu

Memorial Hospital School of Nursing
600 Northern Blvd
Albany, NY 12204
518-471-3260 Fax: 518-447-3559
e-mail: dorseyp@nehealth.com
Web site: www.nehealth.com

Director:
  Mary Harknett-Martin 518-471-3260
  e-mail: martinm@nehealth.com

Mercy College
Main Campus
555 Broadway
Dobbs Ferry, NY 10522
800-637-2969 Fax: 914-674-7382
e-mail: admissions@mercy.edu
Web site: www.mercy.edu

President:
  Louise H Feroe 914-674-7369/fax: 914-674-5978

Metropolitan College of New York
75 Varick St
New York, NY 10013
212-343-1234 or 800-338-4465 Fax: 212-343-7399
Web site: www.metropolitan.edu

President:
  Stephen R Greenwald 212-343-1234 x3301/fax: 212-343-8560
  e-mail: sgreenwald@metropolitan.edu

Mid-America Baptist Theological Seminary Northeast Branch
2810 Curry Rd
Schenectady, NY 12303
518-355-4000 or 800-209-3447 Fax: 518-355-8298
e-mail: info@mabts.edu
Web site: www.mabts.edu

Director:
  David H Shepherd 518-355-4000
  e-mail: dshepherd@mabtsne.edu

Molloy College
1000 Hempstead Ave
PO Box 5002
Rockville Centre, NY 11571-5002

516-678-5000 or 888-466-5569 Fax: 516-256-2247
Web site: www.molloy.edu

President:
  Drew Bogner 516-678-5000 x6200/fax: 516-678-5321
  e-mail: dbogner@molloy.edu

Mount Saint Mary College
330 Powell Ave
Newburgh, NY 12550
845-561-0800 Fax: 845-562-6762
Web site: www.msmc.edu

President:
  Sister Ann Sakac 845-561-0800
  e-mail: sakac@msmc.edu

Mount Sinai School of Medicine
One Gustave L Levy Pl
New York, NY 10029-6574
212-241-6500
Web site: www.mssm.edu

President/CEO/Dean:
  Kenneth L Davis 212-659-8888/fax: 212-803-6772
  e-mail: kenneth.davis@mssm.edu

Nazareth College of Rochester
4245 East Ave
Rochester, NY 14618-7390
585-389-2525 Fax: 585-586-2452
Web site: www.naz.edu

President:
  Robert A Miller 585-389-2001/fax: 585-389-2015
  e-mail: rmiller6@naz.edu

New School University
66 West 12th St
New York, NY 10011
212-229-5600 Fax: 212-229-5937
e-mail: kerreyb@newschool.edu
Web site: www.newschool.edu

President:
  Robert Kerrey 212-229-5656

New York Academy of Art Inc
111 Franklin St
New York, NY 10013
212-966-0300 Fax: 212-966-3217
e-mail: info@nyaa.edu
Web site: www.nyaa.edu

Executive Director:
  Wayne A Linker 212-966-0300
Dean:
  Erica Ehrenberg 212-966-0300

Colleges, Universities & School Districts

Offices and agencies appear in alphabetical order.

New York Chiropractic College

2360 Route 89
Seneca Falls, NY 13148
315-568-3000 or 800-234-6922 Fax: 315-568-3012
Web site: www.nycc.edu

President:
Frank J Nicchi. 315-568-3100
e-mail: fnicchi@nycc.edu

New York College of Health Professions

6801 Jericho Tpke
Syosset, NY 11791-4413
516-364-0808 or 800-922-7337 Fax: 516-364-6645
Web site: www.nycollege.edu

President:
Lisa E Pamintuan 516-364-0808
e-mail: pamintuan@nycollege.edu

New York College of Podiatric Medicine

1800 Park Ave
New York, NY 10035-1940
212-410-8000 Fax: 212-722-4918
e-mail: admissions@nycpm.edu
Web site: www.nycpm.edu

President/CEO:
Louis L Levine 212-410-8023/fax: 212-876-7670
e-mail: llevine@nycpm.edu

New York Institute of Technology

Old Westbury Campus
PO Box 8000
Old Westbury, NY 11568-8000
516-686-7516 or 80-345-6948 Fax: 516-686-7613
Web site: www.nyit.edu

President:
Edward Guiliano. 516-686-7650
e-mail: president@nyit.edu

New York Law School

57 Worth St
New York, NY 10013
212-431-2872 or 212-431-2100 Fax: 212-406-0103
e-mail: alevat@nyls.edu
Web site: www.nyls.edu

President/Dean:
Richard A Matasar. 212-431-2840/fax: 212-219-3752
e-mail: rmatasar@nyls.edu

New York Medical College

Administration Bldg
100 Grasslands Rd
Valhalla, NY 10595
914-594-4000
Web site: www.nymc.edu

President/CEO:
Rev Msgr Harry C Barrett 914-594-4600

New York School of Interior Design

170 East 70th St
New York, NY 10021
212-472-1500 or 800-336-9743 Fax: 212-472-3800
e-mail: admissions@nysid.edu
Web site: www.nysid.edu

President:
Inge Heckel. 212-472-1500 x401/fax: 212-472-1952
Dean:
Scott M Ageloff 212-472-1500

New York Theological Seminary

475 Riverside Dr, Ste 500
New York, NY 10115-0083
212-870-1211 Fax: 212-870-1236
e-mail: online@nyts.edu
Web site: www.nyts.edu

President:
Hillary Gaston, Sr 212-870-1211/fax: 212-870-1235
e-mail: drhgaston@nyts.edu

New York University

70 Washington Square South
New York, NY 10012
212-998-1212
Web site: www.nyu.edu

President:
John Sexton 212-998-2345/fax: 212-995-4790

Niagara University

Lewsiton Rd
Niagara University, NY 14109
716-285-1212 or 800-778-3450 Fax: 716-286-8710
Web site: www.niagara.edu

President:
Rev Joseph L Levesque. 716-286-8350/fax: 716-286-8355
e-mail: president@niagara.edu

Nyack College

1 South Blvd
Nyack, NY 10960-3698
845-358-1710 Fax: 845-358-1751
e-mail: president@nyack.edu
Web site: www.nyackcollege.edu

President:
David E Schroeder 845-358-1710

Pace University

1 Pace Plz
New York, NY 10038

Offices and agencies appear in alphabetical order.

212-346-1200 Fax: 212-346-1933
Web site: www.pace.edu

President:
David A Caputo 212-346-1097/fax: 212-346-1384
e-mail: president@pace.edu

Paul Smith's College

Routes 86 & 30
PO Box 265
Paul Smiths, NY 12970-0265
518-327-6227 or 800-421-2605 Fax: 518-327-6016
Web site: www.paulsmiths.edu

President:
John W Mills 518-327-6223/fax: 518-327-6060
e-mail: millsj@paulsmiths.edu

Phillips Beth Israel School of Nursing

310 E 22nd St
New York, NY 10010
212-614-6110 Fax: 212-614-6109
Web site: www.futurenursebi.org

Dean:
Janet MacKin 212-614-6107
e-mail: jmackin@chpnet.org

Polytechnic University

Main Campus
6 Metrotech Ctr
Brooklyn, NY 11201-2999
718-260-3600 Fax: 718-260-3136
e-mail: inquiry@poly.edu
Web site: www.poly.edu

President:
David C Chang 718-260-3500
e-mail: chang@poly.edu

Pratt Institute

200 Willoughby Ave
Brooklyn, NY 11205
718-636-3600 Fax: 718-636-3785
Web site: www.pratt.edu

President:
Thomas F Schutte 718-636-3647
e-mail: tschutte@pratt.edu

Rensselaer Polytechnic Institute

110 8th St
Troy, NY 12180
518-276-6000
Web site: www.rpi.edu

President:
Shirley Ann Jackson 518-276-6211/fax: 518-276-8702

Roberts Wesleyan College

2301 Westside Dr
Rochester, NY 14624-1997
585-594-6000 or 800-777-4792 Fax: 585-594-6371
e-mail: admissions@roberts.edu
Web site: www.roberts.edu

President:
John A Martin 585-594-6100/fax: 585-594-6780
e-mail: presidentsoffice@roberts.edu

Rochester Institute of Technology

One Lomb Memorial Dr
7000 Eastman Bldg
Rochester, NY 14623-5603
585-475-2411 Fax: 585-475-5700
e-mail: webmaster@rit.edu
Web site: www.rit.edu

President:
Albert J Simone 585-475-2394
e-mail: ajspro@rit.edu

Rochester, University of

Wallis Hall
Administration
Rochester, NY 14627
585-275-2121 Fax: 585-275-0359
Web site: www.rochester.edu

President:
Thomas H Jackson 585-275-8356/fax: 585-256-2473
e-mail: tjackson@admin.rochester.edu

Rockefeller University

1230 York Ave
New York, NY 10021
212-327-8000 Fax: 212-327-7974
e-mail: pubinfo@rockefeller.edu
Web site: www.rockefeller.edu

President:
Sir Paul Nurse 212-327-8000
e-mail: nurse@rockefeller.edu

Sage Colleges (The)

45 Ferry St
Troy, NY 12180
518-244-2000 or 888-837-9724 Fax: 518-244-2470
Web site: www.sage.edu

President:
Jeanne H Neff 518-244-2214
e-mail: neffj@sage.edu

Samaritan Hospital School of Nursing

2215 Burdett Ave
Troy, NY 12180

518-271-3285 Fax: 518-271-3303
e-mail: access via website
Web site: www.nehealth.com

Director:
Mary Harknett-Martin 518-271-3285
e-mail: martinm@nehealth.com

Sarah Lawrence College
1 Mead Way
Bronxville, NY 10708-5999
914-337-0700 Fax: 914-395-2515
e-mail: slcadmit@slc.edu
Web site: www.slc.edu

President:
Michele Tolela Myers 914-395-2201/fax: 914-395-2668
Dean:
Barbara Kaplan 914-395-2303

Seminary of the Immaculate Conception
440 West Neck Rd
Huntington, NY 11743
631-423-0483 Fax: 631-423-2346
e-mail: info@icseminary.edu
Web site: www.icseminary.edu

Rector:
Rev Msgr Francis J Schneider 631-423-0483/fax: 631-421-6842
e-mail: fschneider@icseminary.edu

Siena College
515 Loudon Rd
Loudonville, NY 12211-1462
518-783-2300 Fax: 518-783-4293
Web site: www.siena.edu

President:
Fr Kevin E Mackin 518-783-2302
e-mail: mackin@siena.edu

Skidmore College
815 N Broadway
Saratoga Springs, NY 12866-1632
518-580-5000 Fax: 518-580-5699
e-mail: info@skidmore.edu
Web site: www.skidmore.edu

President:
Philip A Glotzbach 518-580-5700/fax: 518-580-5699
e-mail: pglotzba@skidmore.edu

St Bernard's School of Theology & Ministry
120 French Rd
Rochester, NY 14618
585-271-3657 Fax: 585-271-2045
Web site: www.stbernards.edu

President:
Patricia A Schoelles 585-271-3657
e-mail: pschoelles@stbernards.edu

St Bonaventure University
3261 W State Rd
St Bonaventure, NY 14778-2284
716-375-2000 or 800-462-5050
Web site: www.sbu.edu

President:
Sister Margaret Carney 716-375-2222

St Elizabeth College of Nursing
2215 Genesee St
Utica, NY 13501
315-798-8125 Fax: 315-798-8271
e-mail: conadmin@stemc.org
Web site: www.stemc.org

Dean:
Marianne Monahan 315-798-8125
e-mail: mmonahan@stemc.org

St Francis College
180 Remsen St
Brooklyn Heights, NY 11201
718-489-5200 or 718-522-2300 Fax: 718-237-8964
Web site: www.stfranciscollege.edu

President:
Frank J Macchiarola 718-489-5354
e-mail: fmacchia@stfranciscollege.edu

St John Fisher College
3690 East Ave
Rochester, NY 14618
585-385-8000 Fax: 585-385-8289
Web site: www.sjfc.edu

Interim President:
Donald E Bain 585-385-8010

St John's University
Queens Campus
8000 Utopia Pkwy
Jamaica, NY 11439
718-990-2000 or 888-978-5646 Fax: 718-990-5723
e-mail: admhelp@stjohns.edu
Web site: http://new.stjohns.edu

President:
Rev Donald J Harrington 718-990-6301
e-mail: pres@stjohns.edu

St Joseph's College
Main Campus
245 Clinton Ave
Brooklyn, NY 11205-3688

Offices and agencies appear in alphabetical order.

718-636-6800 Fax: 718-636-7242
Web site: www.sjcny.edu

President:
   Elizabeth A Hill 718-636-6800/fax: 718-636-6102

St Joseph's Seminary Institute of Religious Studies
201 Seminary Ave
Yonkers, NY 10704
914-476-1172 Fax: 914-966-1490
e-mail: sjsirs@aol.com
Web site: http://ny.archdiocese.org/education

Dean:
   Rev Msgr Michael J Wrenn 914-968-6200

St Lawrence University
23 Romoda Dr
Canton, NY 13617
315-229-5011 or 800-285-1856 Fax: 315-229-7422
Web site: www.stlawu.edu

President:
   Daniel F Sullivan 315-229-5892
   e-mail: dsullivan@stlawu.edu

St Thomas Aquinas College
125 Route 340
Sparkill, NY 10976-1050
845-398-4000
Web site: www.stac.edu

President/CEO:
   Margaret M Fitzpatrick 845-398-4012/fax: 845-359-8136
   e-mail: mfitzpat@stac.edu

St Vincent Catholic Medical Centers of New York
School of Nursing
175-05 Horace Harding Expy
Fresh Meadows, NY 11365
718-357-0500 Fax: 718-357-4683
Web site: www.svcmcny.org

Director:
   Genevieve M Jensen 718-357-0500 x127
   e-mail: gjensen@svcmcny.org

St Vladimir's Orthodox Theological Seminary
575 Scarsdale Rd
Crestwood, NY 10707-1699
914-961-8313 Fax: 914-961-4507
e-mail: info@svots.edu
Web site: www.svots.edu

Dean:
   John H Erickson 914-961-8313
   e-mail: jhe@svots.edu

Sunbridge College
285 Hungry Hollow Rd
Spring Valley, NY 10977
845-425-0055 Fax: 845-425-1413
e-mail: info@sunbridge.edu
Web site: www.sunbridge.edu

Administrator:
   John Greene 845-425-0055 x16
   e-mail: jgreene@sunbridge.edu

Syracuse University
300 Tolley Administration Bldg
Syracuse, NY 13244-1100
315-443-1870 Fax: 315-443-3503
Web site: www.syr.edu

Chancellor & President:
   Nancy Cantor 315-443-2235
   e-mail: chancellor@syr.edu

Teachers College, Columbia University
525 W 120th St
New York, NY 10027
212-678-3000
Web site: www.tc.columbia.edu

President:
   Arthur E Levine 212-678-3131/fax: 212-678-3205
   e-mail: levine@exchange.tc.columbia.edu

Touro College
27-33 W 23rd St
New York, NY 10010
212-463-0400 Fax: 212-627-9144
Web site: www.touro.edu

President:
   Bernard Lander 212-463-0400 x715/fax: 212-627-9049

Trocaire College
360 Choate Ave
Buffalo, NY 14220-2094
716-826-1200 Fax: 716-828-6109
e-mail: info@trocaire.edu
Web site: www.trocaire.edu

President:
   Paul B Hurley, Jr 716-826-1200
   e-mail: hurleyp@trocaire.edu

Unification Theological Seminary
30 Seminary Dr
Barrytown, NY 12507
845-752-3000 Fax: 845-752-3016
e-mail: admissions@uts.edu
Web site: www.uts.edu

Offices and agencies appear in alphabetical order.

President:
Tyler O Hendricks 845-752-3000
e-mail: th@uts.edu

Union College
807 Union St
Schenectady, NY 12308-3107
518-388-6000 Fax: 518-388-6006
Web site: www.union.edu

President:
Roger H Hull 518-388-6101
e-mail: hullr@union.edu

Union Theological Seminary
3041 Broadway at 121st St
New York, NY 10027
212-662-7100 Fax: 212-280-1416
e-mail: contactus@uts.columbia.edu
Web site: www.uts.columbia.edu

President:
Joseph C Hough, Jr. 212-280-1403

Utica College
1600 Burrstone Rd
Utica, NY 13502-5159
315-792-3006 Fax: 315-792-3003
Web site: www.utica.edu

President:
Todd S Hutton 315-792-3228/fax: 315-792-3292
e-mail: president@utica.edu

Vassar College
124 Raymond Ave
Poughkeepsie, NY 12604
845-437-7000 Fax: 845-437-7187
Web site: www.vassar.edu

President:
Frances Daly Fergusson 845-437-7200/fax: 845-437-7726

Vaughn College of Aeronautics & Technology
86-01 23rd Ave
Flushing, NY 11369
718-429-6600 or 866-682-8446 Fax: 718-779-2231
Web site: www.vaughn.edu

President:
John C Fitzpatrick. 718-429-6600 x104/fax: 718-429-4020
e-mail: fitzpatric@vaughn.edu

Villa Maria College of Buffalo
240 Pine Ridge Rd
Buffalo, NY 14225

716-896-0700 Fax: 716-896-0705
e-mail: info@villa.edu
Web site: www.villa.edu

President:
Sr Marcella Marie Garus 716-896-0700 x1868
e-mail: smgarus@villa.edu

Wagner College
1 Campus Rd
Staten Island, NY 10301
718-390-3100 or 800-221-1010 Fax: 718-390-3105
Web site: www.wagner.edu

President:
Richard Guarasci 718-390-3131/fax: 718-390-3170

Watson school of Biological Sciences at Cold spring Harbor Laboratory
One Bungtown Rd
Cold Spring Harbor, NY 11724
516-367-6890 Fax: 516-367-6919
e-mail: gradschool@cshl.edu
Web site: www.cshl.edu/gradschool

President/CEO:
Bruce Stillman 516-367-6890

Webb Institute
298 Crescent Beach Rd
Glen Cove, NY 11542-1398
516-671-2213 Fax: 516-674-9838
Web site: www.webb.institute.edu

President:
Ronald K Kiss. 516-671-2213
e-mail: rkiss@webb-institute.edu

Wells College
170 Main St
PO Box 500
Aurora, NY 13026-0500
315-364-3266
Web site: www.wells.edu

President:
Lisa Marsh Ryerson. 315-364-3265/fax: 315-364-3335
e-mail: president@wells.edu

Yeshiva University
500 W 185th St
New York, NY 10033-3201
212-960-5400
Web site: www.yu.edu

President:
Richard M Joel 212-960-5311

Offices and agencies appear in alphabetical order.

Proprietary Colleges

Art Institue of New York City (The)
75 Varick St, 16th Fl
New York, NY 10013
212-226-5500 Fax: 212-966-0706
Web site: www.ainyc.aii.edu

Interim President:
Joe Marzano 212-625-6003
e-mail: jmarzano@edmc.edu

Berkeley College, New York City Campus
3 East 43rd St
New York, NY 10017
212-986-4343 Fax: 212-986-8901
Web site: www.berkeleycollege.edu

President:
Mildred Garcia 212-986-4343 x4101
e-mail: president@berkeleycollege.edu

Berkeley College, Westchester Campus
99 Church St
White Plains, NY 10601
914-694-1122 Fax: 914-328-9470
Web site: www.berkeleycollege.edu

Senior VP/Operating Officer:
Michael J Smith 914-694-1122/fax: 914-328-9470
e-mail: mj@berkeleycollege.edu

Briarcliffe College-Bethpage
1055 Stewart Ave
Bethpage, NY 11714
516-918-3603 Fax: 516-470-6020
e-mail: info@bcl.edu
Web site: www.bcl.edu

Chancellor:
Neal A Raisman 516-918-3603
e-mail: nraisman@bcl.edu

Briarcliffe College-Patchogue
225 West Main St
Patchogue, NY 11772
631-730-2008 Fax: 631-730-1245
Web site: www.bepat.com

President:
David Schuchman 631-730-2008

Bryant & Stratton College
Executive Offices
2350 N Forest Rd, Ste 12A
Getzville, NY 14068
716-250-7500 Fax: 716-250-7510
Web site: www.bryantstratton.edu

Chairman of the Board:
Bryant H Prentice, III 716-250-7500
CEO/President:
John J Staschak 716-250-7500

Bryant & Stratton College-Albany Campus
1259 Central Ave
Albany, NY 12205
518-437-1802 Fax: 518-437-1048
Web site: www.bryantstratton.edu

Campus Director:
Michael Gutierrez 518-437-1802
e-mail: magutierrez@bryantstratton.edu

Bryant & Stratton College-Amherst Campus
40 Hazelwood Dr
Amherst, NY 14228
716-691-0012 Fax: 716-691-6716
Web site: www.bryantstratton.edu

Campus Director:
William Schatt 716-691-0012

Bryant & Stratton College-Buffalo Campus
465 Main St, Ste 400
Buffalo, NY 14203
716-884-9120 Fax: 716-884-0091
Web site: www.bryantstratton.edu

Director:
Jeffrey P Tredo 716-884-9120

Bryant & Stratton College-Greece Campus
150 Bellwood Dr
Rochester, NY 14606
585-720-0660 Fax: 585-720-9226
Web site: www.bryantstratton.edu

Campus Director:
Marc Ambrosi 585-720-0660

Bryant & Stratton College-Henrietta Campus
1225 Jefferson Rd
Rochester, NY 14623
585-292-5627 Fax: 585-292-6015
Web site: www.bryantstratton.edu

Director of Rochester Colleges:
Anne L Loria 585-292-5627

Bryant & Stratton College-North Campus
8687 Carling Rd
Liverpool, NY 13090

Offices and agencies appear in alphabetical order.

315-652-6500 Fax: 315-652-5500
Web site: www.bryantstratton.edu

Campus Director:
Susan Cumoletti 315-652-6500

Bryant & Stratton College-Southtown Campus
200 Red Tail
Orchard Park, NY 14127
716-677-9500 Fax: 716-677-9599
Web site: www.bryantstratton.edu

Campus Director:
Marvel Ross-Jones 716-677-9500

Bryant & Stratton College-Syracuse Campus
953 James St
Syracuse, NY 13203-2502
315-472-6603 Fax: 315-474-4383
Web site: www.bryantstratton.edu

Campus Director:
Michael Sattler 315-472-6603

Business Informatics Center
134 S Central Ave
Valley Stream, NY 11580
516-561-0050 Fax: 516-561-0074
Web site: www.thecollegeforbusiness.com

President:
Joseph Brown 516-561-0050

College of Westchester (The)
325 Central Ave
PO Box 710
White Plains, NY 10606
914-948-4442 Fax: 914-948-5441
e-mail: admissions@cw.edu
Web site: www.cw.edu

President:
Karen J Smith 914-948-4442

DeVry Institute of Technology, Long Island City Campus
3020 Thomson Ave
Long Island City, NY 11101
718-472-2728 Fax: 718-472-9856
Web site: www.ny.devry.edu

President:
John Ballheim 718-269-4201

Elmira Business Institute
303 N Main St
Elmira, NY 14901-2731

607-733-7177 Fax: 607-733-7178
e-mail: info@ebi-college.com
Web site: www.ebi-college.com

President:
Brad C Phillips 607-733-7177

Elmira Business Institute-Vestal
4100 Vestal Rd
Vestal, NY 14901
607-729-8915 Fax: 607-729-8916
Web site: www.ebi-college.com

Campus Director:
Diana Petrolawicz 607-729-8915

Five Towns College
305 N Service Rd
Dix Hills, NY 11746-5871
631-424-7000 Fax: 631-424-7008
e-mail: info@ftc.edu
Web site: www.ftc.edu

President:
Stanley G Cohen 631-424-7000

ITT Technical Institute
13 Airline Dr
Albany, NY 12205
518-452-9300 Fax: 518-452-9393
Web site: www.itt-tech.edu

Director:
Christopher Chang 518-452-9300
e-mail: cchang@itt-tech.edu

Interboro Institute
450 West 56th St
New York, NY 10019
212-399-0093 Fax: 212-765-5772
Web site: www.interboro.edu

President:
Stephen H Adolphus 212-399-0093
e-mail: sadolphus@interboro.edu

Island Drafting & Technical Institute
128 Broadway, Route 110
Amityville, NY 11701-2704
631-691-8733 Fax: 631-691-8738
e-mail: info@idti.edu
Web site: www.idti.edu

President:
James G DiLiberto 631-691-8733
e-mail: dilibertoj@idti.edu

Jamestown Business College

7 Fairmount Ave
Jamestown, NY 14702
716-664-5100 Fax: 716-664-3144
e-mail: admissions@jbcny.org
Web site: www.jbcny.org

President:
Tyler Swanson 716-664-5100

Katharine Gibbs School-Melville

Melville Campus
320 S Service Rd
Melville, NY 11747
631-370-3300 Fax: 631-293-0429
Web site: www.gibbsmelville.com

President:
Patricia A Martin 631-370-3300

Katherine Gibbs School-New York City

50 W 40th St
New York, NY 10018
646-218-2595 Fax: 646-218-2550
Web site: www.gibbsnewyork.com

President:
Lynn Salvage 646-218-2595

Laboratory Institute of Merchandising

12 East 53rd St
New York, NY 10022
212-752-1530 Fax: 212-750-3718
e-mail: info@limcollege.edu
Web site: www.limcollege.edu

President:
Elizabeth S Marcuse 212-752-1530

Long Island Business Institute-Commack

6500 Jericho Tpke
Commack, NY 11725
631-499-7100 Fax: 631-499-7114
e-mail: libiny@email.com
Web site: www.libi.edu

President:
Philip Stander 631-499-7100

Long Island Business Institute-Flushing

37-12 Prince St
Flushing, NY 11354
718-939-5100 Fax: 718-939-9235
Web site: www.libi.edu

Branch Director & Academic Dean:
Henry Moss 718-939-5100

Monroe College-Bronx

2501 Jerome Ave
Bronx, NY 10468
718-933-6700 Fax: 718-295-5861
Web site: www.monroecollege.edu

President:
Stephen J Jerome 718-933-6700

Monroe College-New Rochelle

434 Main St
New Rochelle, NY 10801
914-632-5400 Fax: 914-632-5457
Web site: www.monroecollege.edu

Executive VP:
Marc M Jerome 914-632-5400 x803

New York Career Institute

11 Park Row
New York, NY 10007
212-962-0002 Fax: 212-608-8210
e-mail: info@nyci.com
Web site: www.nyci.com

President:
David Reid. 212-962-0002 x102
CEO:
Ivan Londa 212-962-0002

Olean Business Institute

301 North Union St
Olean, NY 14760
716-372-7978 Fax: 716-372-2120
e-mail: admin@obi.edu
Web site: www.obi.edu

President:
Jennifer Madison 716-372-7978

Plaza College

74-09 37th Ave
Jackson Heights, NY 11372
718-779-1430 Fax: 718-779-7423
e-mail: plazainfo@plazacollege.edu
Web site: www.plazacollege.edu

President:
Charles E Callahan. 718-779-1430

Rochester Business Institute

1630 Portland Ave
Rochester, NY 14621-3007
585-266-0430 Fax: 585-266-8243
Web site: www.rochester-institute.com

President:
Carl A Silvio. 585-266-0430
e-mail: csilvio@cci.edu

Offices and agencies appear in alphabetical order.

Colleges, Universities & School Districts

School of Visual Arts
209 East 23rd St
New York, NY 10010
212-592-2100 or 212-592-2000 Fax: 212-260-7621
e-mail: admissions@sva.edu
Web site: www.schoolofvisualarts.edu

President:
David John Rhodes................................212-592-2350

Simmons Institute of Funeral Service Inc
1828 South Ave at West Brighton
Syracuse, NY 13207
315-475-5142 Fax: 315-475-3817
Web site: www.simmonsinstitute.com

President/CEO:
Maurice C Wightman..............................315-475-5142
e-mail: mcwightman20@aol.com

Technical Career Institutes Inc
320 W 31st St
New York, NY 10001
212-594-4000 Fax: 212-967-9453
e-mail: admissions@tcicollege.edu
Web site: www.tcicollege.edu

Acting President:
Karen Romaine....................................212-594-4000
e-mail: kromaine@tcicollege.edu

Utica School of Commerce
201 Bleecker St
Utica, NY 13501
315-733-2307 Fax: 315-733-9281
Web site: www.uscny.edu

President:
Philip M Williams 315-733-2307
e-mail: pwilliams@uscny.edu
Executive VP Adminstration:
John L Crossley 315-733-2307
e-mail: jcrossley@uscny.edu

Wood Tobe-Coburn
8 E 40th St
New York, NY 10016
212-686-9040 or 800-394-9663 Fax: 212-686-9171
Web site: www.woodtobecoburn.edu

President:
Sandi Gruninger 212-897-0101
e-mail: sgruninger@woodtobecoburn.edu

PUBLIC SCHOOL DISTRICTS

School District Administrators

ALBANY

Albany City SD
Eva Joseph, Superintendent
Academy Park, Albany, NY 12207-1099
518-462-7200 Fax: 518-462-7295
e-mail: mjohnson@albany.k12.ny.us
Web site: www.albanyschools.org

Berne-Knox-Westerlo CSD
Steven M Schrade, Superintendent
1738 Helderberg Trl, Berne, NY 12023-2926
518-872-1293

Bethlehem CSD
Leslie Loomis, Superintendent
90 Adams Pl, Delmar, NY 12054-3297
518-439-7098

Cohoes City SD
Charles S Dedrick, Superintendent
7 Bevan St, Cohoes, NY 12047-3299
518-237-0100 Fax: 518-233-1878
e-mail: cdedrick@cohoes.org

Green Island UFSD
Herb Perkins, Superintendent
171 Hudson Ave, Green Island, NY 12183-1293
518-273-1422

Guilderland CSD
Gregory Aidala, Superintendent
6076 State Farm Rd, Guilderland, NY 12084-9533
518-456-6200

Maplewood Common SD
Jerome D Steele, Superintendent
32 Cohoes Rd, Watervliet, NY 12189-1898
518-273-1512

Menands UFSD
Mary Veitch Gridley, Superintendent
19 Wards Ln, Menands, NY 12204-2197
518-465-4561

North Colonie CSD
Randy A Ehrenberg, Superintendent
91 Fiddler's Ln, Latham, NY 12110-5349
518-785-8591 Fax: 518-785-8502
e-mail: rehrenberg@ncolonie.org
Web site: www.northcolonie.org

Ravena-Coeymans-Selkirk CSD
Vicki Wright, Superintendent
26 Thatcher St, Selkirk, NY 12158-0097
518-756-5200 Fax: 518-767-2644
e-mail: vwright@rcscsd.org

South Colonie CSD
Thomas Brown, Superintendent
102 Loralee Dr, Albany, NY 12205-2298
518-869-3576

Voorheesville CSD
Alan McCartney, Superintendent
432 New Salem Rd, Voorheesville, NY 12186-0498
518-765-3313

Watervliet City SD
Carol Carlson, Superintendent
2557 Tenth Ave, Watervliet, NY 12189-1798
518-629-3200 Fax: 518-273-8009
e-mail: ccarlson@vliet.neric.org

ALLEGANY

Alfred-Almond CSD
Richard A Nicol, Superintendent
6795 Rt 21, Almond, NY 14804-9716
607-276-2981

Andover CSD
William C Berg, Superintendent
31-35 Elm St, Andover, NY 14806-0508
607-478-8491

Belfast CSD
Robert D'Angelo, Superintendent
1 King St, Belfast, NY 14711-0336
585-365-9940

Bolivar-Richburg CSD
Joseph DeCerbo, Superintendent
100 School St, Bolivar, NY 14715-1235
585-928-2561 Fax: 585-928-2411
e-mail: jdecerbo@brcs.wynric.org
Web site: www.brcs.wynric.org

Canaseraga CSD
Terrence L Wissick, Superintendent

Offices and agencies appear in alphabetical order.

4-8 Main St, Canaseraga, NY 14822-0230
607-545-6421

Cuba-Rushford CSD
Anne S Brungard, Superintendent
5476 Rt 305, Cuba, NY 14727-1014
585-968-1556

Fillmore CSD
David Hanks, Superintendent
104 Main St, Fillmore, NY 14735-0177
585-567-2251

Friendship CSD
Robert Mountain, Superintendent
46 W Main St, Friendship, NY 14739-9702
716-973-3534

Genesee Valley CSD
Michael Taylor, Superintendent
1 Jaguar Dr, Belmont, NY 14813-9788
585-268-7900

SCIO CSD
Michael J McArdle, Superintendent
3968 Washington St, Scio, NY 14880-9507
716-593-5510

Wellsville CSD
Byron Chandler, Superintendent
126 W State St, Wellsville, NY 14895-1358
585-596-2170

Whitesville CSD
Charles E Cutler, Acting Superintendent
692 Main St, Whitesville, NY 14897-9706
607-356-3301 Fax: 607-356-3598

BROOME

Binghamton City SD
Peggy J Wozniak, Superintendent
164 Hawley St, Binghamton, NY 13901-2126
607-762-8100

Chenango Forks CSD
Ellen O'Donnell, Superintendent
One Gordon Dr, Binghamton, NY 13901-5614
607-648-7543

Chenango Valley CSD
Carmen A Ciullo, Superintendent
1160 Chenango St, Binghamton, NY 13901-1653
607-779-4710

Deposit CSD
Kraig D Pritts, Superintendent

171 Second St, Deposit, NY 13754-1397
607-467-5380 Fax: 607-467-5535
e-mail: kraig@pobox.com
Web site: www.depositcsd.org

Harpursville CSD
Kathleen M Wood, Superintendent
54 Main St, Harpursville, NY 13787-0147
607-693-8101

Johnson City CSD
Lawrence A Rowe, Superintendent
666 Reynolds Rd, Johnson City, NY 13790-1398
607-763-1230 Fax: 607-763-8761

Maine-Endwell CSD
Joseph F Stoner, Superintendent
712 Farm-to-Market Rd, Endwell, NY 13760-1199
607-754-1400

Susquehanna Valley CSD
Richard T Stank, Acting Superintendent
1040 Conklin Rd, Conklin, NY 13748-0200
607-775-9100

Union-Endicott CSD
James P Coon, Superintendent
1100 E Main St, Endicott, NY 13760-5271
607-757-2112

Vestal CSD
Mark Capobianco, Superintendent
201 Main St, Vestal, NY 13850-1599
607-757-2241

Whitney Point CSD
Carol A Eaton, Superintendent
10 Keibel Rd, Whitney Point, NY 13862-0249
607-692-8202 Fax: 607-692-4434
e-mail: ceaton@wpcsd.org

Windsor CSD
Richard Montgomery, Superintendent
215 Main St, Windsor, NY 13865-4134
607-655-8216 Fax: 607-655-3553
Web site: www.windsor-csd.org

CATTARAUGUS

Allegany - Limestone CSD
Stephen J Troskosky, Superintendent
3131 Five Mile Rd, Allegany, NY 14706-9627
716-375-6600

Cattaraugus-Little Valley CSD
Louis C McIntosh, Superintendent
207 Rock City St, Little Valley, NY 14755-1298
716-938-9155

Ellicottville CSD
Patricia Haynes, Superintendent

Offices and agencies appear in alphabetical order.

5873 Route 219, Ellicottville, NY 14731-9719
716-699-2368

Franklinville CSD
Terence M Dolan, Superintendent
31 N Main St, Franklinville, NY 14737-1096
716-676-8029

Gowanda CSD
Charles J Rinaldi, Superintendent
10674 Prospect St, Gowanda, NY 14070-1384
716-532-3325 Fax: 716-995-2156
e-mail: crinaldi@gowcsd.org

Hinsdale CSD
Dennis W Senn, Superintendent
3701 Main St, Hinsdale, NY 14743-0278
716-557-2227

Olean City SD
Mark J Ward, Superintendent
410 W Sullivan St, Olean, NY 14760-2596
716-375-8018

Portville CSD
Peter A Tigh, Superintendent
500 Elm Street, Portville, NY 14770-9791
716-933-7141

Randolph Academy UFSD
John Hogan, Superintendent
336 Main Street E, Randolph, NY 14772-9696
716-358-6866

Randolph CSD
Sandra M Craft, Superintendent
18 Main St, Randolph, NY 14772-1188
716-358-7005 Fax: 716-358-7072
e-mail: scraft@rand.wnyric.org
Web site: www.randolph.wnyric.org

Salamanca City SD
Rick T Moore, Superintendent
50 Iroquois Dr, Salamanca, NY 14779-1398
716-945-2403

West Valley CSD
Edward Ahrens, Superintendent
5359 School St, West Valley, NY 14171-0290
716-942-3293

Yorkshire-Pioneer CSD
Jeffrey Bowen, Superintendent
12125 County Line Rd, Yorkshire, NY 14173-0579
716-492-9304

CAYUGA

Auburn City SD
John B Plume, Superintendent

78 Thornton Ave, Auburn, NY 13021-4698
315-255-8835

Cato-Meridian CSD
Deborah D Bobo, Superintendent
2851 NYS Rt 370, Cato, NY 13033-0100
315-626-3439

Moravia CSD
William P Tammaro, Superintendent
68 S Main St, Moravia, NY 13118-1189
315-497-2670

Port Byron CSD
Neil F O'Brien, Superintendent
30 Maple Ave, Port Byron, NY 13140-9647
315-776-5728

Southern Cayuga CSD
Peter F Cardamone, Superintendent
2384 Rt 34B, Aurora, NY 13026-9771
315-364-7211

Union Springs CSD
Linda Rice, Superintendent
239 Cayuga St, Union Springs, NY 13160
315-889-4101

Weedsport CSD
Stephen V Hubbard, Superintendent
2821 E Brutus St, Weedsport, NY 13166-9105
315-834-6637

CHAUTAUQUA

Bemus Point CSD
Albert D'Attilio, Superintendent
3980 Dutch Hollow Rd, Bemus Point, NY 14712-0468
716-386-2375

Brocton CSD
Jack J Skahill Jr., Superintendent
138 W Main St, Brocton, NY 14716-9779
716-792-2173 Fax: 716-792-7944
e-mail: jskahill@roc.wynric.org

Cassadaga Valley CSD
John Brown, Superintendent
Rt 60, Sinclairville, NY 14782-0540
716-962-5155

Chautauqua Lake CSD
Benjamin Spitzer, Superintendent
100 N Erie St, Mayville, NY 14757-1098
716-753-5808 Fax: 716-753-5813
Web site: www.clake.wnyric.org

Clymer CSD
Ralph Wilson, Superintendent

Offices and agencies appear in alphabetical order.

8672 E Main St, Clymer, NY 14724-0580
716-355-4444

Dunkirk City SD
Carl Militello, Superintendent
620 Marauder Dr, Dunkirk, NY 14048-1396
716-366-9300

Falconer CSD
Jane R Fosberg, Superintendent
2 East Ave N, Falconer, NY 14733-1395
716-665-6624 Fax: 716-665-9265
e-mail: jfosberg@falcon.wynric.org

Forestville CSD
John O'Connor, Superintendent
12 Water St, Forestville, NY 14062-9674
716-965-2742

Fredonia CSD
Paul Di Fonzo, Superintendent
425 E Main St, Fredonia, NY 14063-1496
716-679-1581

Frewsburg CSD
Stephen Vaustrom, Superintendent
26 Institute St, Frewsburg, NY 14738-0690
716-569-9241

Jamestown City SD
Raymond J Fashano, Superintendent
201 E Fourth St, Jamestown, NY 14701-5397
716-483-4420

Panama CSD
Carol S Hay, Superintendent
41 North St, Panama, NY 14767-9775
716-782-2455

Pine Valley CSD (South Dayton)
Vincent J Vecchiarella, Superintendent
7755 Rt 83, South Dayton, NY 14138-9698
716-988-3293

Ripley CSD
John P Hamels, Superintendent
12 N State St, Ripley, NY 14775-0688
716-736-6201
e-mail: jhamels@ripley.wnyric.org

Sherman CSD
Howard R Ferguson, Superintendent
127 Park St, Sherman, NY 14781-0950
716-761-6122

Silver Creek CSD
Gordon Salisbury, Superintendent

1 Dickinson St, Silver Creek, NY 14136-0270
716-934-2603 Fax: 716-934-7597
Web site: www.silvercreek.wnyric.org

Southwestern CSD at Jamestown
Robert S Guiffreda, Superintendent
600 Hunt Rd, Jamestown, NY 14701-5722
716-484-1136

Westfield CSD
Laura Chabe, Superintendent
203 E Main St, Westfield, NY 14787-1199
716-326-2151

CHEMUNG

Elmira City SD
Laura E Sherwood, Superintendent
951 Hoffman St, Elmira, NY 14905-1715
607-735-3010

Elmira Hts CSD
Mary Beth Fiore, Superintendent
100 Robinwood Ave, Elmira Heights, NY 14903-1598
607-734-7114 Fax: 607-734-7134
Web site: www.heightsschools.com

Horseheads CSD
William Congdon, Superintendent
One Raider Ln, Horseheads, NY 14845-2398
607-739-5601

CHENANGO

Afton CSD
Elizabeth A Briggs, Superintendent
29 Academy St, Afton, NY 13730-0005
607-639-8229

Bainbridge-Guilford CSD
Roger A Hutchinson, Superintendent
18 Juliand St, Bainbridge, NY 13733-1097
607-967-6321 Fax: 607-967-4231

Georgetown-South Otselic CSD
Jane A Collins, Superintendent
125 County Rd 13A, South Otselic, NY 13155-0161
315-653-7591

Greene CSD
Frederick F Tarolli, Superintendent
40 S Canal St, Greene, NY 13778-1281
607-656-4161

Norwich City SD
Robert L Cleveland, Acting Superintendent

19 Eaton Ave, Norwich, NY 13815
607-334-1600

Oxford Academy & CSD
Grayson Stevens, Superintendent
12 Fort Hill Park, PO Box 192, Oxford, NY 13830-0192
607-843-7185

Sherburne-Earlville CSD
Steven Szatko, Superintendent
15 School St, Sherburne, NY 13460-0725
607-674-7300

Unadilla Valley CSD
Charles E Stratton, Superintendent
4238 State Hwy 8, New Berlin, NY 13411-0606
607-847-7500

CLINTON

Ausable Valley CSD
Linda M Langevin, Superintendent
1273 Rt 9N, Clintonville, NY 12924-4244
518-834-2845

Beekmantown CSD
Mark A Sposato, Superintendent
37 Eagle Way, West Chazy, NY 12992-2577
518-563-8250 Fax: 518-563-8132
e-mail: sposato.mark@bcsdk12.org
Web site: www.bcsdk12.org

Chazy UFSD
Gerald L Blair, Superintendent
609 Miner Farm Rd, Chazy, NY 12921-0327
518-846-7135

Northeastern Clinton CSD
Robert J Hebert, Superintendent
103 Route 276, Champlain, NY 12919
518-298-8242

Northern Adirondack CSD
William F Scott, Superintendent
Rt 11, Ellenburg Depot, NY 12935-0164
518-594-7060

Peru CSD
A Paul Scott, Superintendent
17 School St, Peru, NY 12972-0068
518-643-6000

Plattsburgh City SD
Michelle M Kavanaugh, Superintendent
49 Broad St, Plattsburgh, NY 12901-3396
518-957-6002

Saranac CSD
Michael J Derrigo, Superintendent

32 Emmons St, Dannemora, NY 12929
518-565-5600

COLUMBIA

Berkshire UFSD
Claudia F Kauffman, Superintendent
13640 Rt 22, Canaan, NY 12029-0370
518-781-3500

Chatham CSD
Marilyn Barry, Superintendent
50 Woodbridge Ave, Chatham, NY 12037-1397
518-392-1501 Fax: 518-392-2413

Germantown CSD
Donald E Gooley, Superintendent
123 Main St, Germantown, NY 12526-5326
518-537-6280

Hudson City SD
James B Clarke Jr., Superintendent
621 State Rt 23B, Hudson, NY 12534-4011
518-828-4360

Kinderhook CSD
Daralene C Jewell, Superintendent
2910 Rt 9, Valatie, NY 12184-0137
518-758-7575

New Lebanon CSD
Patrick Gabriel Jr., Superintendent
14665 Route 22, New Lebanon, NY 12125-2307
518-794-9016

Taconic Hills CSD
David A Paciencia, Superintendent
73 County Rt 11A, Craryville, NY 12521-5510
518-325-0313 Fax: 518-325-3557
Web site: www.taconichills.k12.ny.us

CORTLAND

Cincinnatus CSD
Cheryl Dudley, Superintendent
2809 Cincinnatus Rd, Cincinnatus, NY 13040-9698
607-863-3200

Cortland City SD
John Lutz, Superintendent
1 Valley View Dr, Cortland, NY 13045-3297
607-758-4100

Homer CSD
Douglas Larison, Superintendent
80 S West St, Homer, NY 13077-0500
607-749-7241

Marathon CSD
Timothy Turecek, Superintendent

Colleges,
Universities &
School Districts

Offices and agencies appear in alphabetical order.

1 E Main St, Marathon, NY 13803-0339
607-849-3251

McGraw CSD
Maria S Fragnoli-Ryan, Superintendent
10 W Academy St, PO Box 55, McGraw, NY 13101-0556
607-836-3636 Fax: 607-836-3635
e-mail: msfryan@mcgrawschools.org
Web site: www.mcgrawschools.org

DELAWARE

Andes CSD
John M Bernhardt, Superintendent
85 Delaware Ave, PO Box 248, Andes, NY 13731-0248
845-676-3167 Fax: 845-676-3181
e-mail: jbernhardtcatskill.net

Charlotte Valley CSD
Mark R Dupra, Superintendent
15611 St Hwy 23, Davenport, NY 13750-0202
607-278-5511

Delhi CSD
Maria Rice, Superintendent
2 Sheldon Dr, Delhi, NY 13753-1276
607-746-1300 Fax: 607-746-6028
Web site: www.delhischools.org

Downsville CSD
Robert J Mackey, Superintendent
14784 State Highway 30, Downsville, NY 13755-0912
607-363-2101

Franklin CSD
Michael Shea, Superintendent
26 Institute St, Franklin, NY 13775-0888
607-829-3551

Hancock CSD
Terrance Dougherty, Superintendent
67 Education Ln, Hancock, NY 13783-1196
607-637-1301

Margaretville CSD
John P Riedl, Superintendent
415 Main St, Margaretville, NY 12455-0319
845-586-2647

Roxbury CSD
Craig Carr, Superintendent
53729 NYS Route 30, Roxbury, NY 12474-0207
607-326-4151

Sidney CSD
Dominic A Nuciforo Sr., Superintendent
95 W Main St, Sidney, NY 13838-1699
607-563-2135

South Kortright CSD
Benjamin C Berliner, Superintendent

58200 State Hwy 10, South Kortright, NY 13842-0113
607-538-9111 Fax: 607-538-9205
e-mail: berliner@dmcom.net
Web site: www.southkortrightcs.org

Stamford CSD
Joseph P Beck, Superintendent
1 River St, Stamford, NY 12167-1098
607-652-7301

Walton CSD
Jonathan W Buhner, Superintendent
47-49 Stockton Ave, Walton, NY 13856-1493
607-865-4116

DUTCHESS

Arlington CSD
Frank Pepe Jr., Superintendent
696 Dutchess Tpke, Poughkeepsie, NY 12603
845-486-4460

Beacon City SD
Vito P DiCesare Jr., Superintendent
10 Education Dr, Beacon, NY 12508-3994
845-838-6900

Dover UFSD
Craig T Onofry, Superintendent
2368 Rt 22, Dover Plains, NY 12522
845-832-4500

Hyde Park CSD
Carol Pickering, Superintendent
11 Boice Rd, Hyde Park, NY 12538-1632
845-229-4000

Millbrook CSD
W Michael Mahoney, Superintendent
PO Box AA-3323 Franklin, Millbrook, NY 12545-0127
845-677-4200
Web site: www.millbrookcsd.org

Northeast CSD
Richard N Johns, Superintendent
194 Haight Rd, Amenia, NY 12501-0405
845-373-4100

Pawling CSD
Frank De Luca, Superintendent
7 Haight St, Pawling, NY 12564-1146
845-855-4600

Pine Plains CSD
Linda Kaumeyer, Superintendent
2829 Church St, Pine Plains, NY 12567-5504
518-398-7181

Poughkeepsie City SD
Robert C Watson Sr., Superintendent

Offices and agencies appear in alphabetical order.

11 College Ave, Poughkeepsie, NY 12603-3313
845-451-4950

Red Hook CSD
Jan Volpe, Superintendent
7401 South Broadway, Red Hook, NY 12571-9446
845-758-2241

Rhinebeck CSD
Joseph L Phelan, Superintendent
45 North Park Rd, Rhinebeck, NY 12572-0351
845-871-5520

Spackenkill UFSD
Lois C Colletta, Superintendent
15 Croft Rd, Poughkeepsie, NY 12603-5028
845-463-7800

Wappingers CSD
Richard A Powell, Superintendent
29 Marshall Rd, Wappingers Falls, NY 12590-3296
845-298-5000

ERIE

Akron CSD
Ronald G Decarli, Superintendent
47 Bloomingdale Ave, Akron, NY 14001-1197
716-542-5101

Alden CSD
Donald W Raw Jr., Superintendent
13190 Park St, Alden, NY 14004-1099
716-937-9116

Amherst CSD
Dennis Ford, Superintendent
55 Kings Hwy, Amherst, NY 14226-4330
716-362-3051 Fax: 716-836-2537
Web site: www.amherstschools.org

Buffalo City SD
Yvonne Hargrave, Superintendent
712 City Hall, Buffalo, NY 14202-3375
716-851-3575 Fax: 716-851-3033

Cheektowaga CSD
Delia G Bonenberger, Superintendent
3600 Union Rd, Cheektowaga, NY 14225-5170
716-686-3606

Cheektowaga-Maryvale UFSD
Gary L Brader, Superintendent
1050 Maryvale Dr, Cheektowaga, NY 14225-2386
716-631-7407 Fax: 716-635-4699
Web site: www.maryvale.wnyric.org

Cheektowaga-Sloan UFSD
James P Mazgajewski, Superintendent

166 Halstead Ave, Sloan, NY 14212-2295
716-891-6402

Clarence CSD
Thomas G Coseo, Superintendent
9625 Main St, Clarence, NY 14031-2083
716-407-9102

Cleveland Hill UFSD
Bruce Inglis, Superintendent
105 Mapleview Rd, Cheektowaga, NY 14225-1599
716-836-7200

Depew UFSD
Robert F Defilippo, Superintendent
591 Terrace Blvd, Depew, NY 14043-4535
716-686-2251

East Aurora UFSD
Donald H Belcer, Acting Superintendent
430 Main St, East Aurora, NY 14052-1750
716-687-2302

Eden CSD
Robert E Zimmerman, Superintendent
3150 Schoolview Rd, Eden, NY 14057-0267
716-992-3629

Evans-Brant CSD (Lake Shore)
Kenneth J Connolly, Superintendent
959 Beach Rd, Angola, NY 14006-9690
716-926-2201 Fax: 716-549-6407
e-mail: kjc@lakeshore.wnyric.org
Web site: www.lakeshore.wnyric.org

Frontier CSD
Robert S Guiffreda, Superintendent
S 5120 Orchard Ave, Hamburg, NY 14075-5657
716-926-1711 Fax: 716-926-1776
e-mail: gcooper@fronier.whyric.org
Web site: www.frontier.wnyric.org

Grand Island CSD
Thomas Ramming, Superintendent
1100 Ransom Rd, Grand Island, NY 14072-1460
716-773-8801

Hamburg CSD
Peter Roswell, Superintendent
5305 Abbott Rd, Hamburg, NY 14075-1699
716-646-3220

Holland CSD
Garry Stone, Superintendent
103 Canada St, Holland, NY 14080-9645
716-537-8222

Hopevale UFSD at Hamburg
David S Frahm, Superintendent

3780 Howard Rd, Hamburg, NY 14075-2252
716-648-1930

Iroquois CSD
Neil Rochelle, Superintendent
2111 Girdle Rd, Elma, NY 14059-0032
716-652-3000

Kenmore-Tonawanda UFSD
Steven A Achramovitch, Superintendent
1500 Colvin Blvd, Buffalo, NY 14223-1196
716-874-8400

Lackawanna City SD
Paul G Hashem, Superintendent
30 Johnson St, Lackawanna, NY 14218-3595
716-827-6767

Lancaster CSD
Thomas J Markle, Superintendent
177 Central Ave, Lancaster, NY 14086-1897
716-686-3200

North Collins CSD
Jack Mann, Superintendent
2045 School St, North Collins, NY 14111-0740
716-337-0101

Orchard Park CSD
Paul Grekalski, Superintendent
3330 Baker Rd, Orchard Park, NY 14127-1472
716-209-6280

Springville-Griffith Inst CSD
Brenda Peters, Superintendent
307 Newman St, Springville, NY 14141-1599
716-592-3230

Sweet Home CSD
Geoffrey M Hicks, Superintendent
1901 Sweet Home Rd, Amherst, NY 14228-3399
716-250-1402 Fax: 716-250-1374
e-mail: ghicks@shs.k12.ny.us
Web site: www.sweethomeschools.com

Tonawanda City SD
George W Batterson, Superintendent
202 Broad St, Tonawanda, NY 14150-2098
716-694-7784

West Seneca CSD
James K Brotz, Superintendent
1397 Orchard Park Rd, West Seneca, NY 14224-4098
716-677-3101

Williamsville CSD
Howard S Smith, Superintendent

105 Casey Rd, East Amherst, NY 14051-5000
716-626-8005

ESSEX

Crown Point CSD
Shari L Brannock, Superintendent
2758 Main St, Crown Point, NY 12928-0035
518-597-4200

Elizabethtown-Lewis CSD
Gail J Else, Superintendent
7530 Court St, Elizabethtown, NY 12932-0158
518-873-6371

Keene CSD
Cynthia Ford-Johnston, Superintendent
33 Market St, Keene Valley, NY 12943-0067
518-576-4555 Fax: 518-576-4599
e-mail: cjohnsto@kcs.neric.org
Web site: www.neric.org

Lake Placid CSD
Ernest H Stretton, Superintendent
50 Cummings Rd, Lake Placid, NY 12946-1500
518-523-2475

Minerva CSD
Ann A Jaeger, Superintendent
1466 County Rt 29, Olmstedville, NY 12857-0039
518-251-2000 Fax: 518-251-2395
e-mail: jaegera@minervasd.org

Moriah CSD
Harold Bresett, Superintendent
39 Viking Ln, Port Henry, NY 12974-9702
518-546-3301 Fax: 518-546-7895

Newcomb CSD
John Mulholland, Superintendent
5535 Rt 28 N, Newcomb, NY 12852-0418
518-582-3341

Schroon Lake CSD
Michael Bonnewell, Superintendent
1125 US Rt 9, Schroon Lake, NY 12870-0338
518-532-7164

Ticonderoga CSD
John C McDonald Jr., Superintendent
9 Amherst Ave, Ticonderoga, NY 12883-1444
518-585-6674

Westport CSD
Paul D Savage II, Superintendent
25 Sisco St, Westport, NY 12993-0408
518-962-8244 Fax: 518-962-4571
e-mail: savagep@westportcs.org

Willsboro CSD
Steven D Schoonmaker, Superintendent

Offices and agencies appear in alphabetical order.

18 Farrell Rd, Willsboro, NY 12996-0180
518-963-4456

FRANKLIN

Brushton-Moira CSD
Earle S Gregory, Superintendent
758 County Rt 7, Brushton, NY 12916
518-529-8948 Fax: 518-529-6062
e-mail: egregory@mail.fehb.org
Web site: www.bmcsd.org

Chateaugay CSD
Patrick J Calnon, Superintendent
42 River St, Chateaugay, NY 12920-0904
518-497-6420

Malone CSD
Wayne C Walbridge, Superintendent
42 Huskie Ln, PO Box 847, Malone, NY 12953-1118
518-483-7800 Fax: 518-483-3071

Salmon River CSD
Glenn R Bellinger, Superintendent
637 County Rt 1, Fort Covington, NY 12937-9722
518-358-6610

Saranac Lake CSD
Scott Amo, Superintendent
79 Canaras Ave, Saranac Lake, NY 12983-1500
518-891-5460

St Regis Falls CSD
Patricia A Dovi, Superintendent
92 N Main St, St Regis Falls, NY 12980-0309
518-856-9421

Tupper Lake CSD
Michael Hunsinger, Superintendent
294 Hosley Ave, Tupper Lake, NY 12986-1899
518-359-3371

FULTON

Broadalbin-Perth CSD
Robert C Munn, Superintendent
14 School St, Broadalbin, NY 12025-9997
518-954-2500

Gloversville City SD
Daniel T Connor, Superintendent
243 Lincoln St, PO Box 593, Gloversville, NY 12078-0005
518-775-5600 Fax: 518-725-3611

Johnstown City SD
John S Whelan, Superintendent

2 Wright Dr Ste 101, Johnstown, NY 12095-3099
518-762-4611

Mayfield CSD
Ralph Acquaro, Superintendent
27 School Street, Mayfield, NY 12117-0216
518-661-8207

Northville CSD
Dan M Russom, Superintendent
131 S Third St, Northville, NY 12134-0608
518-863-7000

Oppenheim-Ephratah CSD
Charles A Molloy, Acting Superintendent
6486 State Hwy 29, St Johnsville, NY 13452-9309
518-568-2014

Wheelerville UFSD
Robert A Delilli, Superintendent
2417 State Hwy 10, Caroga Lake, NY 12032-0325
518-835-2171

GENESEE

Alexander CSD
Dick L Young, Superintendent
3314 Buffalo St, Alexander, NY 14005-9769
585-591-1551

Batavia City SD
Richard G Stutzman Jr., Superintendent
39 Washington Ave, Batavia, NY 14021-0677
585-343-2480

Byron-Bergen CSD
Gregory C Geer, Superintendent
6917 W Bergen Rd, Bergen, NY 14416-9747
585-494-1220

Elba CSD
Joan Cole, Acting Superintendent
57 S Main St, Elba, NY 14058-0370
585-757-9967

Le Roy CSD
Mary Jane Brooke, Superintendent
2-6 Trigon Park, Le Roy, NY 14482-1204
585-768-8133

Oakfield-Alabama CSD
Robert McIntosh, Superintendent
7001 Lewiston Rd, Oakfield, NY 14125-0210
585-948-5211

Pavilion CSD
Edward J Orman, Superintendent

Colleges, Universities & School Districts

7014 Big Tree Rd, Pavilion, NY 14525-9111
585-584-3115

Pembroke CSD
Gary T Mix Sr., Superintendent
Rt 5 & 77, PO Box 308, Corfu, NY 14036-0308
585-599-4525

GREENE

Cairo-Durham CSD
William Zwoboda, Superintendent
424 Main St, Cairo, NY 12413-0780
518-622-8534

Catskill CSD
Charlotte Gregory, Acting Superintendent
343 W Main St, Catskill, NY 12414-1699
518-943-4696

Coxsackie-Athens CSD
L Jeffrey Baltes, Superintendent
24 Sunset Blvd, Coxsackie, NY 12051-1132
518-731-1710

Greenville CSD
John Oates, Superintendent
4976 Route 81, Greenville, NY 12083-0129
518-966-5070

Hunter-Tannersville CSD
Ralph Marino Jr., Superintendent
6094 Main St, Tannersville, NY 12485-1018
518-589-5400

Windham-Ashland-Jewett CSD
John Wiktorko, Superintendent
5411 State Route 23, Windham, NY 12496-0429
518-734-3403

HAMILTON

Indian Lake CSD
Mark T Brand, Superintendent
28 W Main St, Indian Lake, NY 12842-9716
518-648-5024 Fax: 518-648-6346
e-mail: brandm@ilcsd.org
Web site: www.ilcsd.org

Inlet Common SD
Alana Kempf, Superintendent
220 Rt 28, Inlet, NY 13360-0207
315-369-3222

Lake Pleasant CSD
John E Brewer Jr., Superintendent

Elm Lake Rd, Speculator, NY 12164-0140
518-548-7571

Long Lake CSD
Lawrence C Patzwald, Acting Superintendent
1 School St, Long Lake, NY 12847-0217
518-624-2147 Fax: 518-624-3896
e-mail: kslentz@mail.fehb.org
Web site: www.longlakecsd.org

Piseco Common SD
Peter J Hallock, Superintendent
Rt 8, Piseco, NY 12139-0007
518-548-7555 Fax: 518-548-5310
e-mail: bogriver13@yahoo.com

Raquette Lake UFSD
John W Simons, Superintendent
115 Rt 28, Raquette Lake, NY 13436-0010
315-354-4733

Wells CSD
Paul G Williamsen, Superintendent
Route 30, PO Box 300, Wells, NY 12190-0300
518-924-6000

HERKIMER

Bridgewater-West Winfield CSD
Lawrence Zacher, Acting Superintendent
500 Fairground Rd, West Winfield, NY 13491-0500
315-822-6161

Dolgeville CSD
Sharon S Colpoys, Superintendent
38 Slawson St, Dolgeville, NY 13329-1298
315-429-3155

Frankfort-Schuyler CSD
Robert Reina, Superintendent
605 Palmer St, Frankfort, NY 13340-1310
315-894-5083

Herkimer CSD
Robert J Moorhead, Superintendent
801 W German St, Herkimer, NY 13350-2199
315-866-2230

Ilion CSD
Robert J Service, Superintendent
1 Golden Bomber Dr, Ilion, NY 13357-0480
315-894-9934

Little Falls City SD
William A Gokey, Superintendent
15 Petrie St, Little Falls, NY 13365-1657
315-823-1470 Fax: 315-823-0321
Web site: www.lfcsd.com

Mohawk CSD
Joyce M Caputo, Superintendent

Offices and agencies appear in alphabetical order.

28 Grove St, Mohawk, NY 13407-1782
315-867-2904

Poland CSD
John W Stewart, Superintendent
74 Cold Brook St, Poland, NY 13431-0008
315-826-0203

Town of Webb UFSD
Alana Kempf, Superintendent
3002 Main St, Old Forge, NY 13420-0038
315-369-3222

Van Hornesville-Owen D Young CSD
James Christmann, Superintendent
2316 State Rt 80, Van Hornesville, NY 13475-0125
315-858-0729

West Canada Valley CSD
Kenneth Slentz, Superintendent
5447 State Rt 28, Newport, NY 13416-0360
315-845-6800

JEFFERSON

Alexandria CSD
Myrajean Koster, Superintendent
34 Bolton Ave, Alexandria Bay, NY 13607-1699
315-482-9971

Belleville Henderson CSD
Robert R Ike, Superintendent
8372 County Rt 75, Belleville, NY 13611-0158
315-846-5411

Carthage CSD
Carl P Mangee, Superintendent
25059 County Rt 197, Carthage, NY 13619-9527
315-493-5000

General Brown CSD
Stephan J Vigliotti Sr., Superintendent
17643 Cemetery Rd, Dexter, NY 13634-9731
315-639-4711

Indian River CSD
Roger W Adams, Superintendent
32735-B County Rt 29, Philadelphia, NY 13673-0308
315-642-3481

La Fargeville CSD
Susan Whitney, Superintendent
20414 Sunrise Ave, La Fargeville, NY 13656-0138
315-658-2241

Lyme CSD
Donnalee Dodson, Superintendent

11868 Academy St, Chaumont, NY 13622-0219
315-649-2417

Sackets Harbor CSD
Suzanne C Tingley, Superintendent
215 S Broad St, Sackets Harbor, NY 13685-0290
315-646-3575

South Jefferson CSD
Jamie A Moesel, Superintendent
13180 US Rt 11, PO Box 10, Adams Center, NY 13606-0010
315-583-6104

Thousand Islands CSD
John E Slattery, Superintendent
8483 County Rt 9, Clayton, NY 13624-1000
315-686-5594

Watertown City SD
Terry N Fralick, Superintendent
376 Butterfield Ave, Watertown, NY 13601-4593
315-785-3700

LEWIS

Beaver River CSD
Gerald Crowell, Superintendent
9508 Artz Rd, Beaver Falls, NY 13305-0179
315-346-1211

Copenhagen CSD
Lisa A Parsons, Superintendent
3020 Mechanic St, Copenhagen, NY 13626-0030
315-688-4411

Harrisville CSD
Rolf Waters, Superintendent
Mill St, PO Box 200, Harrisville, NY 13648-0200
315-543-2707

Lowville Academy & CSD
Kenneth J McAuliffe, Superintendent
7668 State St, Lowville, NY 13367-1397
315-376-9000

South Lewis CSD
Frank C House, Superintendent
4264 East Rd, Turin, NY 13473-0010
315-348-2500

LIVINGSTON

Avon CSD
Bruce Amey, Superintendent
191 Clinton St, Avon, NY 14414-1495
585-226-2455

Caledonia-Mumford CSD
David V Dinolfo, Superintendent

Colleges,
Universities &
School Districts

99 North St, Caledonia, NY 14423-1099
585-538-3400

Dalton-Nunda CSD (Keshequa)
Lucinda Miner, Acting Superintendent
15 Mill St, Nunda, NY 14517-0517
585-468-2541

Dansville CSD
Adele Bovard, Superintendent
284 Main St, Dansville, NY 14437-1199
585-335-4000 Fax: 585-335-4002

Geneseo CSD
Jon G Hunter, Superintendent
4050 Avon Rd, Geneseo, NY 14454-9799
585-243-3450

Livonia CSD
David Deloria, Superintendent
6 Puppy Ln, PO Box E, Livonia, NY 14487-0489
585-346-4000 Fax: 585-346-6145

Mt Morris CSD
Kathleen M Farrell, Superintendent
30 Bonadonna Ave, Mount Morris, NY 14510-1498
585-658-2568

York CSD
Thomas Manko, Superintendent
2578 Genesee St, Retsof, NY 14539-0102
585-243-1730 Fax: 585-243-5269
e-mail: tjmanko@yorkcsd.org
Web site: www.yorkcsd.org

MADISON

Brookfield CSD
Gerard O'Sullivan, Superintendent
1910 Fairground Rd, Brookfield, NY 13314-0060
315-899-3323

Canastota CSD
Frederick J Bragan, Superintendent
120 Roberts St, Canastota, NY 13032-1198
315-697-2025

Cazenovia CSD
Robert Dubik, Superintendent
31 Emory Ave, Cazenovia, NY 13035-1098
315-655-1317

Chittenango CSD
Thomas E Marzeski, Superintendent
1732 Fyler Rd, Chittenango, NY 13037-9520
315-687-2669

De Ruyter CSD
Bruce R Sharpe, Superintendent

711 Railroad St, Deruyter, NY 13052-0000
315-852-3410

Hamilton CSD
Edmund P Backus, Superintendent
47 W Kendrick Ave, Hamilton, NY 13346-1299
315-824-3721

Madison CSD
Cynthia DeDominick, Superintendent
7303 State Route 20, Madison, NY 13402
315-893-1878

Morrisville-Eaton CSD
Nelson K Bauersfeld, Superintendent
5061 Fearon Rd, Morrisville, NY 13408-0990
315-684-9300

Oneida City SD
Ronald R Spadafora Jr., Superintendent
565 Sayles St, Oneida, NY 13421-0327
315-363-2550

Stockbridge Valley CSD
Randy C Richards, Superintendent
6011 Williams Rd, Munnsville, NY 13409-0732
315-495-4400 Fax: 315-495-4492
e-mail: rrichards@stockbridge-csd.moric.org

MONROE

Brighton CSD
Henry J Peris, Superintendent
2035 Monroe Ave, Rochester, NY 14618-2027
585-242-5080 Fax: 585-242-5212

Brockport CSD
James C Fallon, Superintendent
40 Allen St, Brockport, NY 14420-2296
585-637-1810

Churchville-Chili CSD
Annemarie Spadafora, Superintendent
139 Fairbanks Rd, Churchville, NY 14428-9797
585-293-1800 Fax: 585-293-1013
e-mail: aspadafora@cccsd.org
Web site: www.cccsd.org

East Irondequoit CSD
John Abbott, Acting Superintendent
600 Pardee Rd, Rochester, NY 14609-2898
585-339-1210

East Rochester UFSD
Howard S Maffucci, Superintendent
222 Woodbine Ave, East Rochester, NY 14445-1860
585-248-6302

Fairport CSD
William Cala, Superintendent

Offices and agencies appear in alphabetical order.

38 W Church St, Fairport, NY 14450-2130
585-421-2004

Gates-Chili CSD
Richard A Stein, Superintendent
910 Wegman Rd, Rochester, NY 14624-1440
585-247-5050

Greece CSD
Steven Walts, Superintendent
750 Maiden Ln, Rochester, NY 14615-1296
585-621-1000

Hilton CSD
C Todd Eagle, Superintendent
225 West Ave, Hilton, NY 14468-1283
585-392-1000

Honeoye Falls-Lima CSD
Diane E Reed, Superintendent
20 Church St, Honeoye Falls, NY 14472-1294
585-624-7010

Penfield CSD
G Susan Gray, Superintendent
2590 Atlantic Ave, Penfield, NY 14526-0900
585-249-5700

Pittsford CSD
Mary Alice Price, Superintendent
42 W Jefferson Rd, Pittsford, NY 14534-1978
585-218-1004 Fax: 585-218-1088
e-mail: maryalice_price@pittsford.monroe.edu
Web site: www.pittsfordschools.com

Rochester City SD
Manuel J Rivera, Superintendent
131 W Broad St, Rochester, NY 14614-1187
585-262-8378

Rush-Henrietta CSD
Kenneth Graham, Superintendent
2034 Lehigh Station Rd, Henrietta, NY 14467-9692
585-359-5012

Spencerport CSD
Phillip Langton, Superintendent
71 Lyell Ave, Spencerport, NY 14559-1899
585-349-5102 Fax: 585-349-5011
Web site: www.spencerportschools.org

Webster CSD
Thomas J Strining, Superintendent
119 South Ave, Webster, NY 14580-3594
585-265-3600

West Irondequoit CSD
Jeffrey B Crane, Superintendent

95 Stanton Ln, Rochester, NY 14617-3093
585-342-5500 Fax: 585-266-1556
Web site: www.westirondequoit.org

Wheatland-Chili CSD
Thomas Gallagher, Acting Superintendent
940 North Rd, Scottsville, NY 14546-1299
585-889-6246 Fax: 585-889-6284
Web site: www.wheatland.k12.ny.us

MONTGOMERY

Amsterdam City SD
Ronald E Limoncelli, Superintendent
11 Liberty St, Amsterdam, NY 12010-0670
518-843-5217 Fax: 518-842-0012
e-mail: rlimoncelli@gasd.org
Web site: www.gasd.org

Canajoharie CSD
Richard Rose, Superintendent
136 Scholastic Way, Canajoharie, NY 13317-1197
518-673-6302 Fax: 518-673-3177
e-mail: rrose@canajoharie.k12.ny.us
Web site: www.canajoharie.k12.ny.us

Fonda-Fultonville CSD
Glenn G Goodale, Superintendent
112 Old Johnstown Rd, Fonda, NY 12068-1501
518-853-4415

Fort Plain CSD
Douglas C Burton, Superintendent
25 High St, Fort Plain, NY 13339-1218
518-993-4000

St Johnsville CSD
Christine Battisti, Superintendent
61 Monroe St, St Johnsville, NY 13452-1111
518-568-7023 Fax: 518-568-5407

NASSAU

Baldwin UFSD
Kathy Weiss, Superintendent
960 Hastings St, Baldwin, NY 11510-4798
516-377-9271 Fax: 516-377-9421
e-mail: weiss@baldwin.k12.ny.us
Web site: www.baldwin.k12.ny.us

Bellmore UFSD
Sheldon Dumain, Superintendent
580 Winthrop Ave, Bellmore, NY 11710-5099
516-679-2909

Bellmore-Merrick Central HS District
Thomas Caramore, Superintendent

Colleges,
Universities &
School Districts

1260 Meadowbrook Rd, North Merrick, NY 11566-9998
516-992-1001

Bethpage UFSD
Richard S Marsh, Superintendent
10 Cherry Ave, Bethpage, NY 11714-1596
516-644-4001

Carle Place UFSD
Patricia B Hansen, Superintendent
168 Cherry Ln, Carle Place, NY 11514-1788
516-622-6442

East Meadow UFSD
Robert R Dillon, Superintendent
718 The Plain Road, Westbury, NY 11590
516-478-5776

East Rockaway UFSD
Arnold Dodge, Superintendent
443 Ocean Ave, East Rockaway, NY 11518-1299
516-887-8300

East Williston UFSD
Carolyn S Harris, Superintendent
11 Bacon Rd, Old Westbury, NY 11568-1599
516-333-3758 Fax: 516-333-1937

Elmont UFSD
Maria Palandra, Superintendent
135 Elmont Rd, Elmont, NY 11003-1609
516-326-5500 Fax: 516-326-5574
Web site: www.elmontschools.org

Farmingdale UFSD
Roberta A Gerold, Superintendent
50 Van Cott Ave, Farmingdale, NY 11735-3742
516-752-6510

Floral Park-Bellerose UFSD
William J McDonald, Superintendent
One Poppy Pl, Floral Park, NY 11001-2398
516-327-9300

Franklin Square UFSD
Timothy E Lafferty, Superintendent
760 Washington St, Franklin Square, NY 11010-3898
516-505-6975

Freeport UFSD
Eric L Eversley, Superintendent
235 N Ocean Ave, Freeport, NY 11520-0801
516-867-5205 Fax: 516-623-4759
Web site: www.freeportschools.org

Garden City UFSD
Stephen I Leitman, Superintendent

56 Cathedral Ave, Garden City, NY 11530-0216
516-478-1010

Glen Cove City SD
Jerry Cicchelli, Superintendent
150 Dosoris Ln, Glen Cove, NY 11542-1237
516-759-7217

Great Neck UFSD
Ronald L Friedman, Superintendent
345 Lakeville Rd, Great Neck, NY 11020-1606
516-773-1405 Fax: 516-773-6685
e-mail: rfriedman@greatneck.k12.ny.us
Web site: www.greatneck.k12.ny.us

Hempstead UFSD
Susan Thompson, Superintendent
185 Peninsula Blvd, Hempstead, NY 11550
516-292-7001

Herricks UFSD
John E Bierwirth, Superintendent
999 B Herricks Rd, New Hyde Park, NY 11040
516-248-3105

Hewlett-Woodmere UFSD
Lester M Omotani, Superintendent
1 Johnson Pl, Woodmere, NY 11598-1312
516-374-8100

Hicksville UFSD
Maureen K Bright, Superintendent
200 Division Ave-Adm, Hicksville, NY 11801-4800
516-733-6600

Island Park UFSD
Edward Price, Superintendent
150 Trafalgar Blvd, Island Park, NY 11558-1798
516-431-7268 Fax: 516-431-7550
Web site: www.ips.k12.ny.us

Island Trees UFSD
James Parla, Superintendent
74 Farmedge Rd, Levittown, NY 11756-5205
516-520-2100

Jericho UFSD
Henry L Grishman, Superintendent
99 Cedar Swamp Rd, Jericho, NY 11753-1202
516-203-3600

Lawrence UFSD
John T Fitzsimons, Superintendent
195 Broadway, Lawrence, NY 11559-0477
516-295-7030

Levittown UFSD
Herman A Sirois, Superintendent

Offices and agencies appear in alphabetical order.

150 Abbey Ln, Levittown, NY 11756-4042
516-520-8300 Fax: 516-520-8314
Web site: www.levittownschools.com

Locust Valley CSD
Anthony L Singe, Superintendent
22 Horse Hollow Rd, Locust Valley, NY 11560-1118
516-674-6310

Long Beach City SD
Robert Greenberg, Superintendent
235 Lido Blvd, Long Beach, NY 11561-5093
516-897-2104

Lynbrook UFSD
Philip S Cicero, Superintendent
111 Atlantic Ave, Lynbrook, NY 11563-3437
516-887-0253

Malverne UFSD
Mary Ellen Freeley, Superintendent
301 Wicks Ln, Malverne, NY 11565-2244
516-887-6405

Manhasset UFSD
Lawrence Bozzomo, Superintendent
200 Memorial Pl, Manhasset, NY 11030-2300
516-627-7705 Fax: 516-627-8158
Web site: www.manhasset.k12.ny.us

Massapequa UFSD
Lawrence Pereira, Superintendent
4925 Merrick Rd, Massapequa, NY 11758-6298
516-797-6160

Merrick UFSD
Ranier W Melucci, Superintendent
21 Babylon Rd, Merrick, NY 11566-4547
516-992-7240

Mineola UFSD
Lorenzo Licopoli, Superintendent
200 Emory Rd, Mineola, NY 11501-2361
516-237-2001 Fax: 516-237-2008

New Hyde Park-Garden City Park UFSD
Joseph Rudaitis, Superintendent
1950 Hillside Ave, New Hyde Park, NY 11040-2607
516-352-6257

North Bellmore UFSD
Dominic Mucci, Superintendent
2616 Martin Ave, Bellmore, NY 11710-3199
516-992-3000

North Merrick UFSD
David S Feller, Superintendent

1057 Merrick Ave, Merrick, NY 11566-1047
516-292-3694 Fax: 516-292-3097

North Shore CSD
Edward K Melnick, Superintendent
112 Franklin Ave, Sea Cliff, NY 11579-1706
516-705-0350

Oceanside UFSD
Herb R Brown, Superintendent
145 Merle Ave, Oceanside, NY 11572-2206
516-678-1215

Oyster Bay-East Norwich CSD
Phyllis Harrington, Superintendent
1 McCouns Ln, Oyster Bay, NY 11771-3105
516-861-3227

Plainedge UFSD
John A Richman, Superintendent
241 Wyngate Dr, North Massapequa, NY 11758-0912
516-992-7455 Fax: 516-992-7445
Web site: www.plainedgeschools.org

Plainview-Old Bethpage CSD
Martin Brooks, Superintendent
106 Washington Ave, Plainview, NY 11803-3612
516-937-6301

Port Washington UFSD
Geoffrey N Gordon, Superintendent
100 Campus Dr, Port Washington, NY 11050-3719
516-767-5005

Rockville Centre UFSD
William H Johnson, Superintendent
128 Shepherd St, Rockville Centre, NY 11570-2298
516-255-8920 Fax: 516-255-8810

Roosevelt UFSD
Ronald O Ross, Superintendent
240 Denton Pl, Roosevelt, NY 11575-1539
516-867-8616 Fax: 516-379-0178
e-mail: maedavis@rooseveltufsd.com
Web site: www.rooseveltschools.net

Roslyn UFSD
David J Helme, Superintendent
300 Harbor Hill Rd, Roslyn, NY 11576-1531
516-625-6303

Seaford UFSD
George Duffy III, Superintendent
1600 Washington Ave, Seaford, NY 11783-1998
516-592-4001

Sewanhaka Central HS District
John R Williams, Superintendent

Offices and agencies appear in alphabetical order.

77 Landau Ave, Floral Park, NY 11001-3603
516-488-9800

Syosset CSD
Carole G Hankin, Superintendent
99 Pell Ln, PO Box 9029, Syosset, NY 11791-9029
516-364-5605

Uniondale UFSD
William K Lloyd, Acting Superintendent
933 Goodrich St, Uniondale, NY 11553-2499
516-560-8824

Valley Stream 13 UFSD
Elizabeth Lison, Superintendent
585 N Corona Ave, Valley Stream, NY 11580-2099
516-568-6100 Fax: 516-825-2537
e-mail: elison@valleystream13.com
Web site: www.valleystream13.com

Valley Stream 24 UFSD
Edward M Fale, Superintendent
75 Horton Ave, Valley Stream, NY 11581-1420
516-256-0153

Valley Stream 30 UFSD
Lawrence R McGoldrick, Superintendent
175 N Central Ave, Valley Stream, NY 11580-3801
516-285-9881

Valley Stream Central HS District
Marc F Bernstein, Superintendent
One Kent Rd, Valley Stream, NY 11580-3398
516-872-5601 Fax: 516-872-5658
e-mail: bernstem@vschsd.org
Web site: www.vschsd.org

Wantagh UFSD
Carl Bonuso, Superintendent
3301 Beltagh Ave, Wantagh, NY 11793-3395
516-679-6300

West Hempstead UFSD
Carol D Eisenberg, Superintendent
252 Chestnut St, West Hempstead, NY 11552-2455
516-390-3107 Fax: 516-489-1776

Westbury UFSD
Constance R Clark, Superintendent
2 Hitchcock Ln, Old Westbury, NY 11568-1624
516-876-5016 Fax: 516-876-5187
e-mail: cclark@westburyschools.org
Web site: www.westburyschools.org

NEW YORK CITY

NYC Chancellor's Office
Joel I Klein, Chancelor

52 Chambers St, New York, NY 10007
212-374-0200 Fax: 212-374-5763

NYC Region 1
Irma Zardoya, Regional Superintendent
1 Fordham Plz, Rm 81, Bronx, NY 10458
718-741-7090

NYC Region 10
Lucille Swarns, Regional Superintendent
4360 Broadway, Rm 52, New York, NY 10033
917-521-3700

NYC Region 2
Laura Rodriguez, Regional Superintendent
1230 Zerega Ave, Bronx, NY 10462
718-828-2440

NYC Region 3
Judith Chin, Regional Superintendent
30-48 Linden Pl, Flushing, NY 11354
718-281-7575

NYC Region 4
Reyes Irizarry, Regional Superintendent
28-11 Queens Plz N, Long Island City, NY 11101
718-391-8300

NYC Region 5
Kathleen M Cashin, Regional Superintendent
82-01 Rockaway Blvd, Ozone Park, NY 11416
718-270-5800

NYC Region 6
Gloria Buckery, Regional Superintendent
5619 Flatlands Ave, Brooklyn, NY 11234
718-968-6100

NYC Region 7
Michelle Fratti, Regional Superintendent
715 Ocean Terr, Rm 1, Staten Island, NY 10301
718-556-8350

NYC Region 8
Marcia Lyles, Regional Superintendent
131 Livingston St, Brooklyn, NY 11201
718-935-3900

NYC Region 9
Peter Heaney Jr., Regional Superintendent
333 7th Ave Rm 712, New York, NY 10001
212-356-7500

NIAGARA

Barker CSD
Steven J La Rock, Superintendent

Offices and agencies appear in alphabetical order.

1628 Quaker Rd, Barker, NY 14012-0328
716-795-3832

Lewiston-Porter CSD
Whitney Vantine, Superintendent
4061 Creek Rd, Youngstown, NY 14174-9799
716-286-7266

Lockport City SD
Bruce T Fraser, Superintendent
130 Beattie Ave, Lockport, NY 14094-5099
716-478-4835

Newfane CSD
James Mills, Superintendent
6273 Charlotteville Rd, Newfane, NY 14108-9709
716-778-6850 Fax: 716-778-6852
e-mail: jmills@newfane.wnyric.org
Web site: www.newfane.wnyric.org

Niagara Falls City SD
Carmen A Granto, Superintendent
607 Walnut Ave, Niagara Falls, NY 14302-0399
716-286-4205 Fax: 716-286-4283
e-mail: cgranti@nfschools.net
Web site: www.nfschools.net

Niagara-Wheatfield CSD
Judith H Howard, Superintendent
6700 Schultz St, Niagara Falls, NY 14304
716-215-3003 Fax: 716-215-3039
e-mail: jhoward@nwcsd.wnyric.org
Web site: www.nwcsd.k-12.ny.us

North Tonawanda City SD
John George, Superintendent
175 Humphrey St, North Tonawanda, NY 14120-4097
716-807-3500

Royalton-Hartland CSD
Paul J Bona Jr., Superintendent
54 State St, Middleport, NY 14105-1199
716-735-3031

Starpoint CSD
C Douglas Whelan, Superintendent
4363 Mapleton Rd, Lockport, NY 14094-9623
716-210-2352

Wilson CSD
Michael Wendt, Superintendent
412 Lake St, PO Box 648, Wilson, NY 14172-0648
716-751-9341

ONEIDA

Adirondack CSD
Oren Cook, Superintendent

110 Ford St, Boonville, NY 13309-1200
315-942-9200 Fax: 315-942-5522
e-mail: ocook@adirondackcsd.org
Web site: www.adirondackcsd.org

Camden CSD
Rocco J Longo, Superintendent
51 Third St, Camden, NY 13316-1114
315-245-4075

Clinton CSD
Jeffrey H Roudebush, Superintendent
75 Chenango Ave, Clinton, NY 13323-1395
315-557-2253 Fax: 315-853-8727
e-mail: clinton@ccs.edu
Web site: www.ccs.edu

Holland Patent CSD
Kathleen Davis, Superintendent
9601 Main St, Holland Patent, NY 13354-4610
315-865-7221

NY Mills UFSD
David Langone, Superintendent
1 Marauder Blvd, New York Mills, NY 13417-1566
315-768-8127

New Hartford CSD
Robert L Bradley, Superintendent
33 Oxford Rd, New Hartford, NY 13413-2699
315-624-1218

Oriskany CSD
Michael S Deuel, Superintendent
1313 Utica St, Oriskany, NY 13424-0539
315-768-2058

Remsen CSD
Ann P Turner, Superintendent
Davis Dr, PO Box 406, Remsen, NY 13438-0406
315-831-3797

Rome City SD
Thomas Gallagher, Superintendent
112 E Thomas St, Rome, NY 13440-5298
315-338-6500 Fax: 315-334-7409
e-mail: tgallagher@romecsd.org
Web site: www.romecsd.org

Sauquoit Valley CSD
Deborah S Flack, Superintendent
2601 Oneida St, Sauquoit, NY 13456-1000
315-839-6311

Sherrill City SD
Norman Reed, Superintendent
5275 State Rt 31, Verona, NY 13478-0128
315-829-2520

Utica City SD
Daniel G Lowengard, Superintendent

Offices and agencies appear in alphabetical order.

1115 Mohawk St, Utica, NY 13501-3709
315-792-2222

Waterville CSD
James Van Wormer, Superintendent
381 Madison St, Waterville, NY 13480-1100
315-841-3900

Westmoreland CSD
Antoinette Kulak, Superintendent
5176 Rt 233, Westmoreland, NY 13490-0430
315-557-2601

Whitesboro CSD
Arnold L Kaye, Superintendent
67 Whitesboro St, PO Box 304, Yorkville, NY 13495-0304
315-266-3303

ONONDAGA

Baldwinsville CSD
Jeanne M Dangle, Superintendent
29 E Oneida St, Baldwinsville, NY 13027-2480
315-638-6043

East Syracuse-Minoa CSD
Frederick N Thomsen, Superintendent
407 Fremont Rd, East Syracuse, NY 13057-2631
315-656-7205 Fax: 315-656-3241
Web site: www.esmschools.org

Fabius-Pompey CSD
Martin L Swenson, Superintendent
1211 Mill St, Fabius, NY 13063-8719
315-683-5301

Fayetteville-Manlius CSD
Philip Martin, Superintendent
8199 E Seneca Tpke, Manlius, NY 13104-2140
315-682-1200

Jamesville-Dewitt CSD
Alice Kendrick, Superintendent
6845 Edinger Dr, Dewitt, NY 13214-0606
315-445-8304

Jordan-Elbridge CSD
Marilyn Dominick, Superintendent
9 Chappell St, Jordan, NY 13080-0902
315-689-3978 Fax: 315-689-0084
e-mail: mdominick@jecsd.org

La Fayette CSD
Mark P Mondanaro, Superintendent
5955 Rt 20 W, Lafayette, NY 13084-9701
315-677-9728

Liverpool CSD
Jan Matousek, Superintendent

195 Blackberry Rd, Liverpool, NY 13090
315-622-7125

Lyncourt UFSD
Michael Sandore, Superintendent
2707-2709 Court St, Syracuse, NY 13208-3234
315-455-7571

Marcellus CSD
Timothy H Barstow, Superintendent
2 Reed Pkwy, Marcellus, NY 13108-1199
315-673-0201

North Syracuse CSD
Kathleen B Gramet, Superintendent
5355 W Taft Rd, North Syracuse, NY 13212-2796
315-452-3128

Onondaga CSD
Carolyn F Costello, Superintendent
4466 S Onondaga Rd, Nedrow, NY 13120-9715
315-492-1701

Skaneateles CSD
Walter J Sullivan, Superintendent
49 E Elizabeth St, Skaneateles, NY 13152-1398
315-291-2221

Solvay UFSD
Thomas G Helmer, Superintendent
103 3rd St, Solvay, NY 13209-1532
315-468-1111

Syracuse City SD
Stephen C Jones, Superintendent
725 Harrison St, Syracuse, NY 13210-2325
315-435-4161 Fax: 315-435-4015
Web site: www.syracusecityschools.com

Tully CSD
Lawrence A Dismore, Superintendent
20 State St, PO Box 628, Tully, NY 13159-0628
315-696-6204

West Genesee CSD
Rudolph Rubeis, Superintendent
300 Sanderson Dr, Camillus, NY 13031-1655
315-487-4562

Westhill CSD
Stephen A Bocciolatt, Superintendent
400 Walberta Rd, Syracuse, NY 13219-2214
315-426-3218

ONTARIO

Canandaigua City SD
Stephen J Uebbing, Superintendent

Offices and agencies appear in alphabetical order.

143 N Pearl St, Canandaigua, NY 14424-1496
585-396-3700

East Bloomfield CSD
Frederick A Wille, Superintendent
21 Oakmount Ave, East Bloomfield, NY 14443-0098
585-657-6121

Geneva City SD
Larry Pederson, Acting Superintendent
649 S Exchange St, Geneva, NY 14456-3492
315-781-0276

Gorham-Middlesex CSD
Keith R Eddinger, Superintendent
4100 Baldwin Rd, Rushville, NY 14544-9799
585-554-4848

Honeoye CSD
William F Schofield, Acting Superintendent
8576 Main St, Honeoye, NY 14471-0170
585-229-4125

Manchester-Shortsville CSD
Robert E Leiby, Superintendent
1506 Rt 21, Shortsville, NY 14548-9502
585-289-3964

Naples CSD
Brenda C Keith, Superintendent
136 N Main St, Naples, NY 14512-9201
585-374-7900

Phelps-Clifton Springs CSD
Michael J Ford, Superintendent
1490 Rt 488, Clifton Springs, NY 14432-9334
315-548-6420

Victor CSD
Timothy J McElheran, Superintendent
953 High St, Victor, NY 14564-1167
585-924-3252

ORANGE

Chester UFSD
Judy L Waligory, Superintendent
64 Hambletonian Ave, Chester, NY 10918
845-469-5052

Cornwall CSD
Timothy J Rehm, Superintendent
24 Idlewild Ave, Cornwall on Hudson, NY 12520
845-534-8009

Florida UFSD
Douglas Burnside, Superintendent

51 N Main St, PO Box 7, Florida, NY 10921-0757
845-651-3095

Goshen CSD
Roy Reese, Acting Superintendent
227 Main St, Goshen, NY 10924-2158
845-294-2410

Greenwood Lake UFSD
John Guarracino, Superintendent
80 Waterstone Rd, Greenwood Lake, NY 10925-0008
845-477-7395

Highland Falls CSD
Bruce H Crowder, Acting Superintendent
21 Morgan Rd, Fort Montgomery, NY 10922
845-446-9575

Kiryas Joel Village UFSD
Steven Benardo, Superintendent
51 Forest Rd, Ste 315, Monroe, NY 10950-0398
845-782-2300

Middletown City SD
Kenneth Eastwood, Superintendent
223 Wisner Ave Ext, Middletown, NY 10940-3240
845-341-5691

Minisink Valley CSD
Dr Martha Murray, Superintendent
Rt 6, PO Box 217, Slate Hill, NY 10973-0217
845-355-5110

Monroe-Woodbury CSD
Frank L Moscati, Superintendent
278 Rte 32, Education Ctr, Central Valley, NY 10917-1001
845-928-2321

Newburgh City SD
Annette M Saturnelli, Acting Superintendent
124 Grand St, Newburgh, NY 12550-4600
845-563-3500

Pine Bush CSD
Rose Marie Stark, Superintendent
156 State Rt 302, PO Box 700, Pine Bush, NY 12566-0700
845-744-2031

Port Jervis City SD
Joseph Dilorenzo, Superintendent
9 Thompson St, Port Jervis, NY 12771-3058
845-858-3175

Tuxedo UFSD
Joseph P Zanetti, Superintendent
Route 17, Box 2002, Tuxedo Park, NY 10987-2002
845-351-4799

Valley CSD (Montgomery)
Richard M Hooley, Superintendent

Colleges,
Universities &
School Districts

Offices and agencies appear in alphabetical order.

944 State Rt 17k, Montgomery, NY 12549-2240
845-457-2400

Warwick Valley CSD
Joseph Natale, Superintendent
225 West St Ext, Warwick, NY 10990-0595
845-987-3010

Washingtonville CSD
Harvey Hilburgh, Acting Superintendent
52 W Main St, Washingtonville, NY 10992-1492
845-497-2200

ORLEANS

Albion CSD
Ada Grabowski, Superintendent
324 East Ave, Albion, NY 14411-1697
585-589-2056

Holley CSD
Mary Anne Kermis, Superintendent
3800 N Main St, Holley, NY 14470-9330
585-638-6316

Kendall CSD
Michael C O'Laughlin, Superintendent
1932 Kendall Rd, Kendall, NY 14476-0777
585-659-2741

Lyndonville CSD
Christine J Tibbetts, Superintendent
25 Housel Ave, Lyndonville, NY 14098-0540
585-765-3101

Medina CSD
Richard Galante, Superintendent
One Mustang Dr, Medina, NY 14103-1845
585-798-2700

OSWEGO

Altmar-Parish-Williamstown CSD
Deborah Haab, Superintendent
639 County Rt 22, Parish, NY 13131-0097
315-625-5251

Central Square CSD
Walter J Doherty, Superintendent
642 S Main St, Central Square, NY 13036-3511
315-668-4220

Fulton City SD
Michael J Egan, Superintendent
167 S Fourth St, Fulton, NY 13069-1859
315-593-5510

Hannibal CSD
Michael J DiFabio, Superintendent

928 Cayuga St, Hannibal, NY 13074-0066
315-564-7900

Mexico CSD
G Scott Hunter, Superintendent
40 Academy St, Mexico, NY 13114-3432
315-963-8400

Oswego City SD
David Fischer, Superintendent
120 E 1st St, Oswego, NY 13126-2114
315-341-2001

Phoenix CSD
Rita Racette, Superintendent
116 Volney St, Phoenix, NY 13135-9778
315-695-1555

Pulaski CSD
Marshall Marshall, Superintendent
2 Hinman Rd, Pulaski, NY 13142-2201
315-298-5188

Sandy Creek CSD
Stewart R Amell, Superintendent
124 Salisbury St, Sandy Creek, NY 13145-0248
315-387-3445

OTSEGO

Cherry Valley-Springfield CSD
Nicholas J Savin, Superintendent
597 County Hwy 54, Cherry Valley, NY 13320-0485
607-264-9332

Cooperstown CSD
Mary Jo A McPhail, Superintendent
39 Linden Ave, Cooperstown, NY 13326-1496
607-547-5364

Edmeston CSD
David Rowley, Superintendent
11 North St, Edmeston, NY 13335-0529
607-965-8931

Gilbertsville-Mount Upton CSD
Douglas A Exley, Superintendent
693 State Hwy 51, Gilbertsville, NY 13776-1104
607-783-2207

Laurens CSD
Romona N Wenck, Superintendent
55 Main St, Laurens, NY 13796-0301
607-432-2050

Milford CSD
Peter N Livshin, Superintendent

Offices and agencies appear in alphabetical order.

42 W Main St, Milford, NY 13807-0237
607-286-3341

Morris CSD
Michael Virgil, Superintendent
65 Main St, Morris, NY 13808-0040
607-263-6100

Oneonta City SD
James C Piscitelli, Superintendent
189 Main St, Ste 302, Oneonta, NY 13820-1142
607-433-8232

Otego-Unadilla CSD
Rexford A Hurlburt Jr., Superintendent
2641 State Hwy 7, Otego, NY 13825-9795
607-988-5038

Richfield Springs CSD
Robert Barruco, Superintendent
93 Main St, Richfield Springs, NY 13439-0631
315-858-0610

Schenevus CSD
Edmund G Shultis, Superintendent
159 Main St, Schenevus, NY 12155-0008
607-638-5530

Worcester CSD
Maureen McNolty, Superintendent
198 Main St, Worcester, NY 12197
607-397-8785

PUTNAM

Brewster CSD
Mark S Lewis, Superintendent
30 Farm-to-Market Rd, Brewster, NY 10509-9956
845-279-8000

Carmel CSD
Marilyn C Terranova, Superintendent
81 South St, Patterson, NY 12563-0296
845-878-2094

Garrison UFSD
Gary Loewenberg, Superintendent
1100 Rt 9 D, Garrison, NY 10524-0193
845-424-3689

Haldane CSD
John J Dinatale, Superintendent
15 Craigside Dr, Cold Spring, NY 10516-1899
845-265-9254

Mahopac CSD
Robert J Reidy Jr, Superintendent

179 East Lake Blvd, Mahopac, NY 10541-1666
845-628-3415

Putnam Valley CSD
Gary Tutty, Superintendent
146 Peekskill Hollow Rd, Putnam Valley, NY 10579-3238
845-528-8143

RENSSELAER

Averill Park CSD
Michael J Johnson, Superintendent
8439 Miller Hill Rd, Averill Park, NY 12018-9798
518-674-7055

Berlin CSD
Maria A Diamond, Superintendent
53 School St, Berlin, NY 12022-0259
518-658-2690

Brunswick CSD (Brittonkill)
Teresa Thayer Snyder, Superintendent
3992 NY Rt 2, Troy, NY 12180-9034
518-279-4600

East Greenbush CSD
Terrance Brewer, Superintendent
29 Englewood Ave, East Greenbush, NY 12061-2213
518-477-2755

Hoosic Valley CSD
James A Seeley, Superintendent
2 Pleasant Ave, Schaghticoke, NY 12154-9702
518-753-4450

Hoosick Falls CSD
Roger E Thompson, Superintendent
21187 NY Rt 22, Hoosick Falls, NY 12090-0192
518-686-7012

Lansingburgh CSD
Lee Bordick, Superintendent
576 Fifth Ave, Troy, NY 12182-3295
518-233-6850

North Greenbush Common SD (Williams)
Joseph Padalino, Superintendent
476 N Greenbush Rd, Rensselaer, NY 12144
518-283-6748

Rensselaer City SD
Gordon F Reynolds, Superintendent
555 Broadway, Rensselaer, NY 12144-2694
518-465-7509

Schodack CSD
Douglas B Hamlin, Superintendent

Colleges, Universities & School Districts

1216 Maple Hill Rd, Castleton, NY 12033-1699
518-732-2297

Troy City SD
Armand Reo, Superintendent
1728 Tibbits Ave, Troy, NY 12180-7013
518-271-5210

Wynantskill UFSD
Christine Hamill, Superintendent
East Ave, PO Box 345, Wynantskill, NY 12198-0345
518-283-4679

ROCKLAND

Clarkstown CSD
William B Heebink, Superintendent
62 Old Middletown Rd, New City, NY 10956
845-639-6419

East Ramapo CSD (Spring Valley)
Jason P Friedman, Superintendent
105 S Madison Ave, Spring Valley, NY 10977-5400
845-577-6011

Edwin Gould Academy-Ramapo UFSD
Patricia M McLeod, Superintendent
681 Chestnut Ridge Rd, Chestnut Ridge, NY 10977-6222
845-573-5020

Haverstraw-Stony Point CSD
Dodge R Watkins, Superintendent
65 Chapel St, Garnerville, NY 10923-1280
845-942-3000

Nanuet UFSD
Mark S McNeill, Superintendent
101 Church St, Nanuet, NY 10954-3000
845-627-9888

Nyack UFSD
Roberta R Zampolin, Superintendent
13a Dickinson Ave, Nyack, NY 10960-2914
845-353-7010

Pearl River UFSD
Frank V Auriemma, Superintendent
275 E Central Ave, Pearl River, NY 10965-2799
845-620-3900

Ramapo CSD (Suffern)
Robert B Macnaughton, Superintendent
45 Mountain Ave, Hillburn, NY 10931-0935
845-357-7783

South Orangetown CSD
Joseph Zambito, Superintendent

160 Van Wyck Rd, Blauvelt, NY 10913-1299
845-680-1050

SARATOGA

Ballston Spa CSD
John R Gratto, Superintendent
70 Malta Ave, Ballston Spa, NY 12020-1599
518-884-7195

Burnt Hills-Ballston Lake CSD
James Schultz, Superintendent
50 Cypress Dr, Scotia, NY 12302-4398
518-399-9141

Corinth CSD
Matthew F Breitenbach, Superintendent
105 Oak St, Corinth, NY 12822-1295
518-654-2601

Edinburg Common SD
Margaret A McCullough, Superintendent
4 Johnson Rd, Edinburg, NY 12134-5390
518-863-8412

Galway CSD
Clifford Moses, Superintendent
5317 Sacandaga Rd, Galway, NY 12074-0130
518-882-1033

Mechanicville City SD
Michael J McCarthy, Superintendent
25 Kniskern Ave, Mechanicville, NY 12118-1995
518-664-5727

Saratoga Springs City SD
John E Macfadden, Superintendent
3 Blue Streak Blvd, Saratoga Springs, NY 12866-5967
518-583-4708

Schuylerville CSD
Leon J Reed, Superintendent
14 Spring St, Schuylerville, NY 12871-1098
518-695-3255

Shenendehowa CSD
John O'Rourke, Acting Superintendent
5 Chelsea Pl, Clifton Park, NY 12065-3240
518-881-0610

South Glens Falls CSD
James P McCarthy, Superintendent
6 Bluebird Rd, South Glens Falls, NY 12803-5704
518-793-9617

Stillwater CSD
Donald Flynt, Superintendent

Offices and agencies appear in alphabetical order.

334 N Hudson Ave, Stillwater, NY 12170-0490
518-373-6100

Waterford-Halfmoon UFSD
Carl J Klossner, Superintendent
125 Middletown Rd, Waterford, NY 12188-1590
518-237-0800

SCHENECTADY

Duanesburg CSD
Mark A Villanti, Superintendent
133 School Dr, Delanson, NY 12053-0129
518-895-2279

Niskayuna CSD
Kevin S Baughman, Superintendent
1239 Van Antwerp Rd, Schenectady, NY 12309-5317
518-377-4666

Rotterdam-Mohonasen CSD
L Oliver Robinson, Superintendent
2072 Curry Rd, Schenectady, NY 12303-4400
518-356-8200

Schalmont CSD
Valerie Kelsey, Superintendent
401 Duanesburg Rd, Schenectady, NY 12306-1981
518-355-9200

Schenectady City SD
John Falco, Superintendent
108 Education Dr, Schenectady, NY 12303-3442
518-370-8100

Scotia-Glenville CSD
Michael J Marcelle, Superintendent
900 Preddice Pkwy, Scotia, NY 12302-1049
518-382-1215

SCHOHARIE

Cobleskill-Richmondville CSD
Samuel A Shevat, Superintendent
155 Washington Ave, Cobleskill, NY 12043-1099
518-234-4032

Gilboa-Conesville CSD
Matthew Murray, Superintendent
132 Wyckoff Rd, Gilboa, NY 12076-9703
607-588-7541

Jefferson CSD
Edward J Roche, Superintendent
1332 St Rt 10, Jefferson, NY 12093-0039
607-652-7821

Middleburgh CSD
John G Metallo, Superintendent

168 Main St, Middleburgh, NY 12122
518-827-5567

Schoharie CSD
Carmine Giangreco, Superintendent
136 Academy Drive, PO Box 430, Schoharie, NY 12157-0430
518-295-8132

Sharon Springs CSD
Linda Tharp, Acting Superintendent
514 State Rt 20, Sharon Springs, NY 13459-0218
518-284-2266

SCHUYLER

Odessa-Montour CSD
Carol Boyce, Superintendent
300 College Ave, Odessa, NY 14869-0430
607-594-3341

Watkins Glen CSD
Mary Ellen Correa, Superintendent
303 12th St, Watkins Glen, NY 14891-1699
607-535-3219

SENECA

Romulus CSD
Casey W Barduhn, Superintendent
5705 Rt 96, Romulus, NY 14541-9551
607-869-5391

Seneca Falls CSD
Gerald Macaluso, Superintendent
98 Clinton St, Seneca Falls, NY 13148-1090
315-568-5818

South Seneca CSD
Janie L Nusser, Superintendent
7263 Main St, Ovid, NY 14521-9586
607-869-9636

Waterloo CSD
Randy Bos, Superintendent
109 Washington St, Waterloo, NY 13165
315-539-1500

ST. LAWRENCE

Brasher Falls CSD
Alan M Tessier, Superintendent
1039 State Hwy 11C, Brasher Falls, NY 13613-0307
315-389-5131

Canton CSD
Katrina Jacobson, Superintendent

Colleges,
Universities &
School Districts

99 State St, Canton, NY 13617-1099
315-386-8561

Clifton-Fine CSD
Paul J Alioto, Superintendent
11 Hall Ave, Star Lake, NY 13690-0075
315-848-3335

Colton-Pierrepont CSD
Martin Bregg, Superintendent
4921 State Hwy 56, Colton, NY 13625-0005
315-262-2100

Edwards-Knox CSD
William Cartwright, Superintendent
2512 County Hwy 24, Russell, NY 13684-0630
315-562-8326

Gouverneur CSD
Christine J Larose, Superintendent
133 E Barney St, Gouverneur, NY 13642-1100
315-287-4870

Hammond CSD
Dennis Johnson, Superintendent
51 S Main St, Hammond, NY 13646-0185
315-324-5931

Hermon-Dekalb CSD
Ann M Adams, Superintendent
709 E Dekalb Rd, Dekalb Junction, NY 13630-0213
315-347-3442

Heuvelton CSD
Clive B Chambers, Superintendent
87 Washington St, Heuvelton, NY 13654-0375
315-344-2414

Lisbon CSD
Ernest L Witkowski, Superintendent
6866 County Rt 10, Lisbon, NY 13658-0039
315-393-4951

Madrid-Waddington CSD
Kendall C Straight, Superintendent
2582 State Hwy 345, Madrid, NY 13660-0067
315-322-5746

Massena CSD
Douglas W Huntley, Superintendent
84 Nightingale Ave, Massena, NY 13662-1999
315-764-3700

Morristown CSD
Beverly L Ouderkirk, Acting Superintendent
408 Gouverneur St, Morristown, NY 13664-0217
315-375-8814

Norwood-Norfolk CSD
James Short, Superintendent

7852 St Hwy 56, Box 1, Norwood, NY 13668-0194
315-353-9951

Ogdensburg City SD
William H Flynn, Superintendent
1100 State St, Ogdensburg, NY 13669-3398
315-393-0900

Parishville-Hopkinton CSD
A Jay Kilcoyne, Superintendent
12 County Rt 47, Parishville, NY 13672-0187
315-265-4642

Potsdam CSD
Sylvia A Root, Superintendent
29 Leroy St, Potsdam, NY 13676-1787
315-265-2000

STEUBEN

Addison CSD
Betsey A Stiker, Superintendent
1 Colwell St, Addison, NY 14801-1398
607-359-2244

Arkport CSD
William S Locke, Superintendent
35 East Ave, Arkport, NY 14807-0070
607-295-7471

Avoca CSD
R Christopher Roser, Superintendent
17-29 Oliver St, Avoca, NY 14809-0517
607-566-2221

Bath CSD
Marion Tunney, Superintendent
25 Ellas Ave, Bath, NY 14810-1107
607-776-3301

Bradford CSD
Lynn Lyndes, Superintendent
2820 Rt 226, Bradford, NY 14815-9602
607-583-4616

Campbell-Savona CSD
Scott E Layton, Superintendent
8455 County Rt 125, Campbell, NY 14821-9518
607-527-4548

Canisteo-Greenwood CSD
Karen J Moon, Superintendent
84 Greenwood St, Canisteo, NY 14823-1299
607-698-4225

Corning City SD
Judith P Staples, Superintendent

Offices and agencies appear in alphabetical order.

165 Charles St, Painted Post, NY 14870-1199
607-936-3704

Hammondsport CSD
Christopher R Brown, Superintendent
8272 Main St Ext, Hammondsport, NY 14840-0368
607-569-5240

Hornell City SD
David C Smith, Superintendent
25 Pearl St, Hornell, NY 14843-1504
607-324-1302

Jasper-Troupsburg CSD
Chad C Groff, Superintendent
3769 State Route 417, Jasper, NY 14855-0081
607-792-3675

Prattsburgh CSD
Jeffrey A Black, Superintendent
1 Academy St, Prattsburgh, NY 14873-0249
607-522-3795

Wayland-Cohocton CSD
Robert Cownie, Superintendent
2350 Rt 63, Wayland, NY 14572-9404
585-728-2211

SUFFOLK

Amagansett UFSD
Judith S Wooster, Superintendent
320 Main St, PO Box 7062, Amagansett, NY 11930-7062
631-267-3572

Amityville UFSD
Brian M Desorbe, Superintendent
150 Park Ave, Amityville, NY 11701-3195
631-598-6507

Babylon UFSD
William Bernhard, Superintendent
50 Railroad Ave, Babylon, NY 11702-2221
631-893-7925

Bayport-Blue Point UFSD
Richard W Curtis, Superintendent
189 Academy St, Bayport, NY 11705-1799
631-472-7860

Bayshore UFSD
Evelyn Blose Holman, Superintendent
75 W Perkal St, Bayshore, NY 11706-6696
631-968-1117

Brentwood UFSD
Les A Black, Superintendent

52 Third Ave, Brentwood, NY 11717-6198
631-434-2325

Bridgehampton UFSD
Dianne B Youngblood, Superintendent
2685 Montauk Hwy, PO Box 3021, Bridgehampton, NY 11932-3021
631-537-0271

Brookhaven-Comsewogue UFSD
Richard T Brande, Superintendent
290 Norwood Ave, Port Jefferson, NY 11776-2999
631-474-8105

Central Islip UFSD
Fadhilika Atiba-Weza, Superintendent
50 Wheeler Road, Central Islip, NY 11722-9027
631-348-5001

Cold Spring Harbor CSD
Frederick D Volp, Superintendent
75 Goose Hill Rd, Cold Spring Harbor, NY 11724-9813
631-692-8036

Commack UFSD
James H Hunderfund, Superintendent
480 Clay Pitts Rd, East Northport, NY 11731-3828
631-912-2010

Connetquot CSD
Alan B Groveman, Superintendent
780 Ocean Ave, Bohemia, NY 11716-3629
631-244-2211

Copiague UFSD
William R Bolton, Superintendent
2650 Great Neck Rd, Copiague, NY 11726-1699
631-842-4015

Ctr Moriches UFSD
Donald A James, Superintendent
529 Main St, Center Moriches, NY 11934-2206
631-878-0052

Deer Park UFSD
Richard E Organisciak, Superintendent
1881 Deer Park Ave, Deer Park, NY 11729-4326
631-274-4010

East Hampton UFSD
Raymond D Gualtieri, Superintendent
4 Long Ln, East Hampton, NY 11937
631-329-4104

East Islip UFSD
Dennis P Maloney, Superintendent
1 C B Gariepy Ave, Islip Terrace, NY 11752-2820
631-224-2000

East Moriches UFSD
John P Roche, Superintendent

Colleges,
Universities &
School Districts

9 Adelaide Ave, East Moriches, NY 11940-1320
631-878-0162

East Quogue UFSD
Joseph F Donovan, Superintendent
6 Central Ave, East Quogue, NY 11942-9632
631-653-5210 Fax: 631-653-3752

Eastport-South Manor CSD
B Allen Mannella, Superintendent
149 Dayton Ave, Manorville, NY 11949-9469
631-874-6720 Fax: 631-878-6308
e-mail: mannella@esmonline.org
Web site: www.esmonline.org

Elwood UFSD
William J Swart, Superintendent
100 Kenneth Ave, Greenlawn, NY 11740-2900
631-266-5402

Fire Island UFSD
Wendell Chu, Superintendent
Surf Rd, PO Box 428, Ocean Beach, NY 11770-0428
631-583-5626 Fax: 631-583-5167
e-mail: wchu@fi.k12.ny.us

Fishers Island UFSD
Jeanne F Schultz, Superintendent
Greenwood Rd, PO Drawer A, Fishers Island, NY 6390
631-788-7444

Greenport UFSD
Charles Kozora, Superintendent
720 Front St, Greenport, NY 11944-1599
631-477-1950 Fax: 631-477-2164
Web site: www.greenport.k12.ny.us

Half Hollow Hills CSD
Sheldon Karnilow, Superintendent
525 Half Hollow Rd, Dix Hills, NY 11746-5899
631-592-3008

Hampton Bays UFSD
Joanne S Loewenthal, Superintendent
86 E Argonne Rd, Hampton Bays, NY 11946-1739
631-723-2100 Fax: 631-723-2109
Web site: www.hamptonbays.k12.ny.us

Harborfields CSD
Raymond A McCloat, Superintendent
2 Oldfield Rd, Greenlawn, NY 11740-1235
631-754-5320

Hauppauge UFSD
Peter C Scordo, Superintendent
495 Hoffman Lane, Hauppauge, NY 11788-3103
631-265-3630

Huntington UFSD
John J Finello, Superintendent

50 Tower St, Huntington Station, NY 11746
631-673-2038

Islip UFSD
Alan Van Cott, Superintendent
215 Main St, Islip, NY 11751-3435
631-859-2209 Fax: 631-859-2224

Kings Park CSD
Mary Derose, Superintendent
101 Church St, Kings Park, NY 11754-1769
631-269-3210

Lindenhurst UFSD
Neil Lederer, Superintendent
350 Daniel St, Lindenhurst, NY 11757-0621
631-226-6511 Fax: 631-226-6865
e-mail: nlsupt@optonline.net

Little Flower UFSD
George Grigg, Superintendent
2460 N Wading River Rd, Wading River, NY 11792-0547
631-929-4300

Longwood CSD
Candee A Swenson, Superintendent
35 Yaphnk-Mid Isl Rd, Middle Island, NY 11953-2369
631-345-2172

Mattituck-Cutchogue UFSD
Kenney W Aldrich, Superintendent
385 Depot Ln, Cutchogue, NY 11935
631-298-4242

Middle Country CSD
Leonard Adler, Superintendent
Eight 43rd St, Admin Office, Centereach, NY 11720-2325
631-285-8005

Miller Place UFSD
Donald K Carlisle, Superintendent
275 Route 25A, Miller Place, NY 11764-2036
631-474-2733

Montauk UFSD
J Philip Perna, Superintendent
50 S Dorset Rd, Montauk, NY 11954-5057
631-668-2474

Mt Sinai UFSD
Jonathan Van Eyk, Superintendent
150 N Country Rd, Mount Sinai, NY 11766-0397
631-870-2550 Fax: 631-473-0905

New Suffolk Common SD
Richard Olcott, Acting Superintendent

Offices and agencies appear in alphabetical order.

1295 4th St, New Suffolk, NY 11956-0111
631-734-6940 Fax: 631-734-6940
e-mail: teach46@optonline.net

North Babylon UFSD
John Micciche, Superintendent
5 Jardine Pl, North Babylon, NY 11703-4203
631-321-3226

Northport-East Northport UFSD
William J Brosnan, Superintendent
158 Laurel Ave, Northport, NY 11768-3455
631-262-6604

Oysterponds UFSD
Rita Mattus, Superintendent
23405 Main Rd, Orient, NY 11957-1135
631-323-2410

Patchogue-Medford UFSD
Veronica McDermott, Superintendent
241 S Ocean Ave, Patchogue, NY 11772-3787
631-687-6380

Port Jefferson UFSD
Edward J Reilly, Superintendent
550 Scraggy Hill Rd, Port Jefferson, NY 11777-1969
631-476-4404

Quogue UFSD
Richard J Benson, Superintendent
10 Edgewood Rd, PO Box 957, Quogue, NY 11959-0957
631-653-4285 Fax: 631-653-4864
e-mail: rbenson@quogueschool.com

Remsenburg-Speonk UFSD
Katherine M Salomone, Superintendent
11 Mill Rd, Remsenburg, NY 11960-0900
631-325-0203 Fax: 631-325-8439
e-mail: ksal22@aol.com

Riverhead CSD
Paul R Doyle, Superintendent
700 Osborne Ave, Riverhead, NY 11901-2996
631-369-6716

Rocky Point UFSD
James Gerardi, Superintendent
170 Rt 25A, Rocky Point, NY 11778-8401
631-744-1600

Sachem CSD
James A Ruck, Superintendent
245 Union Ave, Holbrook, NY 11741-1890
631-471-1336 Fax: 631-471-1341
e-mail: ruck@sachem.edu
Web site: www.sachem.edu

Sag Harbor UFSD
Kathryn Holden, Superintendent

200 Jermain Ave, Sag Harbor, NY 11963-3549
631-725-5300

Sagaponack Common SD
Lee Ellwood, Superintendent
Main St, PO Box 1500, Sagaponack, NY 11962-1500
631-537-0651 Fax: 631-537-2342
e-mail: esagapon@optonline.net

Sayville UFSD
Rosemary F Jones, Superintendent
99 Greeley Ave, Sayville, NY 11782-2698
631-244-6510 Fax: 631-244-6504
e-mail: drrfjones@aol.com
Web site: www.sayville.k12.ny.us

Shelter Island UFSD
Kenneth A Lanier Sr., Superintendent
33 North Ferry Rd, Shelter Island, NY 11964-2015
631-749-0302

Shoreham-Wading River CSD
Robert W Pellicone, Superintendent
250B Rt 25A, Shoreham, NY 11786-2192
631-821-8105 Fax: 631-929-3001
e-mail: swrcsd@yahoo.com
Web site: www.swrcsd.org

Smithtown CSD
Charles A Planz, Superintendent
26 New York Ave, Smithtown, NY 11787-3435
631-382-2005 Fax: 631-382-2010
e-mail: cplanz@smithtown.k12.ny.us
Web site: www.smithtown.k12.ny.us

South Country CSD
Michael C La Fever, Superintendent
189 N Dunton Ave, East Patchogue, NY 11772-5598
631-730-1510

South Huntington UFSD
Thomas C Shea, Superintendent
60 Weston St, Huntington Station, NY 11746-4098
631-425-5300

Southampton UFSD
Linda J Bruno, Superintendent
70 Leland Ln, Southampton, NY 11968-5089
631-591-4510

Southold UFSD
Christopher Gallagher, Superintendent
420 Oaklawn Ave, PO Box 470, Southold, NY 11971-0470
631-765-5400 Fax: 631-765-5086

Springs UFSD
Thomas R Quinn, Superintendent

Colleges, Universities & School Districts

Offices and agencies appear in alphabetical order.

48 School St, East Hampton, NY 11937-1698
631-324-0144

Three Village CSD
Frank J Carasiti, Superintendent
200 Nicolls Rd, Stony Brook, NY 11790-3410
631-730-4010 Fax: 631-474-7784
e-mail: fcarasit@3villagecsd.k12.ny.us

Tuckahoe Common SD
Linda J Rozzi, Superintendent
468 Magee St, Southampton, NY 11968-3216
631-283-3550

Wainscott Common SD
Dominic Annacone, Superintendent
47 Main St, PO Box 79, Wainscott, NY 11975-0079
631-537-1080

West Babylon UFSD
Melvin S Noble, Superintendent
10 Farmingdale Rd, West Babylon, NY 11704-6289
631-321-3142

West Islip UFSD
Beth V Blau, Superintendent
100 Sherman Ave, West Islip, NY 11795-3237
631-893-3200

Westhampton Beach UFSD
Lynn Schwartz, Superintendent
340 Mill Rd, Westhampton Beach, NY 11978-2045
631-288-3800

William Floyd UFSD
Richard J Hawkins, Superintendent
240 Mastic Beach Rd, Mastic Beach, NY 11951-1099
631-874-1201 Fax: 631-281-3047

Wyandanch UFSD
Frank Satchel Jr., Superintendent
1445 Straight Path, Wyandanch, NY 11798-3997
631-491-1013

SULLIVAN

Eldred CSD
Ivan J Katz, Superintendent
600 Rt 55, Eldred, NY 12732-0249
845-557-6141

Fallsburg CSD
Walter Milton Jr., Superintendent
115 Brickman Rd, PO Box 124, Fallsburg, NY 12733-0124
845-434-5884

Liberty CSD
Lawrence A Clarke, Superintendent

115 Buckley St, Liberty, NY 12754-1600
845-292-6990 Fax: 845-292-1164

Livingston Manor CSD
Debra Lynker, Superintendent
19 School St, Livingston Manor, NY 12758-0947
845-439-4400 Fax: 845-439-4717

Monticello CSD
Eileen P Casey, Superintendent
237 Forestburgh Rd, Monticello, NY 12701
845-794-7700

Roscoe CSD
George Will, Superintendent
6 Academy St, Roscoe, NY 12776-0429
607-498-4126

Sullivan West CSD
Alan R Derry, Superintendent
10494 Rt 97, Callicoon, NY 12723
845-887-5300

Tri-Valley CSD
Nancy S George, Superintendent
34 Moore Hill Rd, Grahamsville, NY 12740-5609
845-985-2296

TIOGA

Candor CSD
Jeffrey J Kisloski, Superintendent
80 Main St, Candor, NY 13743-0145
607-659-5010

Newark Valley CSD
Mary Ellen Grant, Superintendent
79 Whig St, Newark Valley, NY 13811-0547
607-642-3221

Owego-Apalachin CSD
Mychael Willon, Superintendent
36 Talcott St, Owego, NY 13827-9965
607-687-6224

Spencer-Van Etten CSD
C Thomas Bailey, Superintendent
16 Dartts Crossroad, Spencer, NY 14883
607-589-7100

Tioga CSD
Patrick Dougherty, Superintendent
3 Fifth Ave, Tioga Center, NY 13845-0241
607-687-8000

Waverly CSD
Michael W McMahon, Superintendent

Offices and agencies appear in alphabetical order.

15 Frederick St, Waverly, NY 14892-1294
607-565-2841

TOMPKINS

Dryden CSD
Mark Crawford, Superintendent
2127 Drydn Rd, Route 38 Box 88, Dryden, NY 13053
607-844-5361

George Junior Republic UFSD
J Brad Herman, Superintendent
24 McDonald Rd, Freeville, NY 13068-9699
607-844-6200

Groton CSD
Gary P Smith, Superintendent
400 Peru Rd, Groton, NY 13073-1297
607-898-5301

Ithaca City SD
Judith C Pastel, Superintendent
400 Lake St, Ithaca, NY 14851-0549
607-274-2101

Lansing CSD
Corliss Kaiser, Superintendent
264 Ridge Rd, Lansing, NY 14882-9021
607-533-4294

Newfield CSD
William Hurley, Superintendent
247 Main St, Newfield, NY 14867-9313
607-564-9955

Trumansburg CSD
Cosimo Tangorra Jr., Superintendent
100 Whig St, Trumansburg, NY 14886-9179
607-387-7551

ULSTER

Ellenville CSD
Lisa A Wiles, Superintendent
28 Maple Ave, Ellenville, NY 12428-2000
845-647-0100

Highland CSD
John McCarthy, Superintendent
320 Pancake Hollow Rd, Highland, NY 12528-2317
845-691-1012

Kingston City SD
Gerard M Gretzinger, Superintendent
61 Crown St, Kingston, NY 12401-3833
845-339-3000

Marlboro CSD
Julie V Amodeo, Superintendent

50 Cross Rd, Marlboro, NY 12542-6009
845-236-5802

New Paltz CSD
Edward Rhine, Acting Superintendent
196 Main St, New Paltz, NY 12561-1200
845-256-4020

Onteora CSD
Justine Winters, Superintendent
4166 Rt 28, Boiceville, NY 12412-0300
845-657-6383

Rondout Valley CSD
Marilyn Pirkle, Superintendent
122 Kyserike Rd, Accord, NY 12404-0009
845-687-2400

Saugerties CSD
Richard R Rhau, Superintendent
310 Washington Ave Ext, Saugerties, NY 12477-0577
845-247-6500

Wallkill CSD
Donald V Andrews, Superintendent
19 Main St, Wallkill, NY 12589-0310
845-895-7101

West Park UFSD
Maureen Abramoski, Superintendent
2112 Rt 9w, West Park, NY 12493-0010
845-384-6412

WARREN

Bolton CSD
Raymond Ciccarelli Jr., Superintendent
26 Horicon Ave, Bolton Landing, NY 12814-0120
518-644-2400

Glens Falls City SD
Thomas F McGowan, Superintendent
15 Quade St, Glens Falls, NY 12801-2725
518-792-1212

Glens Falls Common SD
Ella W Collins, Superintendent
120 Lawrence St, Glens Falls, NY 12801-3758
518-792-3231

Hadley-Luzerne CSD
Irwin H Sussman, Superintendent
27 Ben Rosa Park, Lake Luzerne, NY 12846-0200
518-696-2112

Johnsburg CSD
Michael Markwica, Superintendent

Colleges, Universities & School Districts

Offices and agencies appear in alphabetical order.

165 Main St, North Creek, NY 12853-0380
518-251-2814

Lake George CSD
Bruce Levin, Superintendent
381 Canada St, Lake George, NY 12845-1197
518-668-5456

North Warren CSD
Joseph R Murphy, Superintendent
6110 State Rt 8, Chestertown, NY 12817
518-494-3015

Queensbury UFSD
Brian Howard, Superintendent
429 Aviation Rd, Queensbury, NY 12804-2914
518-742-6000

Warrensburg CSD
Timothy D Lawson, Superintendent
103 Schroon River Rd, Warrensburg, NY 12885-4803
518-623-2861

WASHINGTON

Argyle CSD
Ryan Sherman, Superintendent
5023 State Rt 40, Argyle, NY 12809-0067
518-638-8243

Cambridge CSD
Frank Greenhall, Superintendent
23 W Main St, Cambridge, NY 12816-1118
518-677-2653

Fort Ann CSD
Steven Black, Superintendent
One Catherine St, Fort Ann, NY 12827-5039
518-639-5594

Fort Edward UFSD
Stanley W Maziejka, Superintendent
220 Broadway, Fort Edward, NY 12828-1598
518-747-4594

Granville CSD
Daniel A Teplesky, Superintendent
58 Quaker St, Granville, NY 12832-1596
518-642-1051

Greenwich CSD
Susanne Fulmer, Superintendent
10 Gray Ave, Greenwich, NY 12834-1107
518-692-9542

Hartford CSD
Thomas W Abraham, Superintendent

4704 State Rt 149, Hartford, NY 12838-0079
518-632-5931

Hudson Falls CSD
Mark E Doody, Superintendent
1153 Burgoyne Ave, Hudson Falls, NY 12839-0710
518-747-2121

Putnam CSD
Kent F Cauley, Superintendent
126 County Rt 2, Putnam Station, NY 12861-0091
518-547-8266

Salem CSD
Richard Wheeler, Superintendent
41 E Broadway, Salem, NY 12865-0517
518-854-7855

Whitehall CSD
James Watson, Superintendent
87 Buckley Rd, Whitehall, NY 12887-3633
518-499-1772

WAYNE

Clyde-Savannah CSD
Richard A Drahms, Acting Superintendent
215 Glasgow St, Clyde, NY 14433-1222
315-902-3000

Gananda CSD
Thomas A Cox, Superintendent
1500 Dayspring Rd, Walworth, NY 14502-9518
315-986-3521

Lyons CSD
James O Derusha, Acting Superintendent
9 Lawrence St, Lyons, NY 14489-1496
315-946-2200

Marion CSD
J Richard Boyes, Superintendent
4034 Warner Rd, Marion, NY 14505-0999
315-926-2300

Newark CSD
Robert W Christmann, Superintendent
100 E Miller St, Newark, NY 14513-1599
315-332-3217

North Rose-Wolcott CSD
Daniel Starr, Superintendent
11669 Salter-Colvin Rd, Wolcott, NY 14590-9398
315-594-3141

Palmyra-Macedon CSD
James A Tobin, Superintendent

Offices and agencies appear in alphabetical order.

151 Hyde Pkwy, Palmyra, NY 14522-1297
315-597-3401

Red Creek CSD
David G Sholes, Superintendent
6815 Church St, Red Creek, NY 13143-0190
315-754-2010

Sodus CSD
Susan Kay Salvaggio, Superintendent
6264 Route 88, Sodus, NY 14551-0220
315-483-5201

Wayne CSD
Michael Havens, Superintendent
6076 Ontario Ctr Rd, Ontario Center, NY 14520-0155
315-524-1001

Williamson CSD
Maria Ehresman, Superintendent
4148 Miller St, Williamson, NY 14589-0900
315-589-9661

WESTCHESTER

Abbott UFSD
Michael P Frazier, Superintendent
100 N Broadway, Irvington, NY 10533-1254
914-591-7428

Ardsley UFSD
Richard Maurer, Superintendent
500 Farm Rd, Ardsley, NY 10502-1410
914-693-6300

Bedford CSD
Debra Jackson, Superintendent
632 Route 172, Bedford, NY 10506-0173
914-241-6010

Blind Brook-Rye UFSD
Ronald D Valenti, Superintendent
390 North Ridge St, Rye Brook, NY 10573-1105
914-937-3600

Briarcliff Manor UFSD
Frances G Wills, Superintendent
45 Ingham Rd, Briarcliff Manor, NY 10510-2221
914-941-8880

Bronxville UFSD
Warren H Gemmill, Superintendent
177 Pondfield Rd, Bronxville, NY 10708-4829
914-395-0500

Byram Hills CSD
John A Chambers, Superintendent

10 Tripp Ln, Armonk, NY 10504-2512
914-273-4082

Chappaqua CSD
James F Donovan, Superintendent
66 Roaring Brook Rd, Chappaqua, NY 10514-1703
914-238-7200

Croton-Harmon UFSD
Marjorie E Castro, Superintendent
10 Gerstein St, Croton-on-Hudson, NY 10520-2303
914-271-4793

Dobbs Ferry UFSD
Sidney Freund, Superintendent
505 Broadway, Dobbs Ferry, NY 10522-1118
914-693-1506

Eastchester UFSD
Robert C Siebert, Superintendent
580 White Plains Rd, Eastchester, NY 10709
914-793-6130

Edgemont UFSD
Nancy L Taddiken, Superintendent
300 White Oak Ln, Scarsdale, NY 10583-1725
914-472-7768

Elmsford UFSD
Carol Franks-Randall, Superintendent
98 South Goodwin Ave, Elmsford, NY 10523-3711
914-592-8440

Greenburgh CSD
Josephine N Moffett, Superintendent
475 W Hartsdale Ave, Hartsdale, NY 10530-1398
914-761-6000

Greenburgh Eleven UFSD
Sandra G Mallah, Superintendent
Children's Vlg Campus-W, PO Box 501, Dobbs Ferry, NY
10522-0501
914-693-8500

Greenburgh-Graham UFSD
James G Donlevy, Superintendent
One S Broadway, Hastings-on-Hudson, NY 10706-3809
914-478-1106

Greenburgh-North Castle UFSD
Robert Maher, Superintendent
71 S Broadway, Dobbs Ferry, NY 10522-2834
914-693-4309

Harrison CSD
Louis N Wool, Superintendent
50 Union Ave, Harrison, NY 10528-2032
914-630-3002

Hastings-On-Hudson UFSD
John J Russell, Superintendent

Colleges, Universities & School Districts

Offices and agencies appear in alphabetical order.

27 Farragut Ave, Hastings-on-Hudson, NY 10706-2395
914-478-6200

Hawthorne-Cedar Knolls UFSD
Mark K Silverstein, Superintendent
226 Linda Ave, Hawthorne, NY 10532-2099
914-773-7345

Hendrick Hudson CSD
Joan Thompson, Superintendent
61 Trolley Rd, Montrose, NY 10548-1199
914-736-5200

Irvington UFSD
Kathleen Matusiak, Superintendent
40 N Broadway, Irvington, NY 10533-1328
914-591-8501

Katonah-Lewisboro UFSD
Robert V Lichtenfeld, Superintendent
One Shady Lane Rt 123, South Salem, NY 10590-1930
914-763-7001

Lakeland CSD
Barnett Sturm, Superintendent
1086 Main St, Shrub Oak, NY 10588-1507
914-245-1700

Mamaroneck UFSD
Sherry P King, Superintendent
1000 W Boston Post Rd, Mamaroneck, NY 10543-3399
914-220-3005

Mt Pleasant CSD
Alfred Lodovico, Superintendent
825 Westlake Drive, Thornwood, NY 10594-2120
914-769-5500

Mt Pleasant-Blythedale UFSD
Ellen Bergman, Superintendent
95 Bradhurst Ave, Valhalla, NY 10595-1697
914-347-1800

Mt Pleasant-Cottage UFSD
Norman Freimark, Superintendent
1075 Broadway, Pleasantville, NY 10570-0008
914-769-0456

Mt Vernon City SD
Brenda L Smith, Superintendent
165 N Columbus Ave, Mount Vernon, NY 10553-1199
914-665-5201

New Rochelle City SD
Linda E Kelly, Superintendent
515 North Ave, New Rochelle, NY 10801-3416
914-576-4200

North Salem CSD
Peter Litchka, Superintendent

230 June Rd, North Salem, NY 10560-1211
914-669-5414

Ossining UFSD
Robert J Roelle, Superintendent
190 Croton Ave, Ossining, NY 10562-4599
914-941-7700

Peekskill City SD
Judith Johnson, Superintendent
1031 Elm St, Peekskill, NY 10566-3499
914-737-3300

Pelham UFSD
Charles T Wilson, Superintendent
661 Hillside Rd, Pelham, NY 10803
914-738-3434

Pleasantville UFSD
Donald Antonecchia, Superintendent
60 Romer Ave, Pleasantville, NY 10570-3157
914-741-1400

Pocantico Hills CSD
Thomas C Elliott, Superintendent
599 Bedford Rd, Sleepy Hollow, NY 10591-1215
914-631-2440

Port Chester-Rye UFSD
Charles D Coletti, Superintendent
113 Bowman Ave, Port Chester, NY 10573-2851
914-934-7901

Rye City SD
Edward J Shine, Superintendent
324 Midland Ave, Rye, NY 10580-3899
914-967-6108

Rye Neck UFSD
Peter J Mustich, Superintendent
310 Hornidge Rd, Mamaroneck, NY 10543-3898
914-777-5200

Scarsdale UFSD
Michael V McGill, Superintendent
2 Brewster Rd, Scarsdale, NY 10583-3049
914-721-2410

Somers CSD
Joanne Marien, Superintendent
110 Primrose, PO Box 620, Lincolndale, NY 10540-0620
914-248-7872

Tuckahoe UFSD
Michael Yazurlo, Superintendent
65 Siwanoy Blvd, Eastchester, NY 10707-3841
914-337-5376

UFSD - Tarrytown
Howard W Smith, Superintendent

Offices and agencies appear in alphabetical order.

200 N Broadway, Sleepy Hollow, NY 10591-2696
914-631-9404

Valhalla UFSD
Thomas M Kelly, Superintendent
316 Columbus Ave, Valhalla, NY 10595-1300
914-683-5040

White Plains City SD
Timothy P Connors, Superintendent
5 Homeside Ln, White Plains, NY 10605-4299
914-422-2019

Yonkers City SD
Angelo Petrone, Acting Superintendent
1 Larkin Center, Yonkers, NY 10701-2756
914-376-8100

Yorktown CSD
Gordon Bruno, Superintendent
46 Triangle Center, Yorktown Heights, NY 10598-4104
914-243-8001

WYOMING

Attica CSD
Bryce L Thompson, Superintendent
3338 E Main St, Attica, NY 14011-9699
585-591-0400

Letchworth CSD
Joseph W Backer, Superintendent

5550 School Rd, Gainesville, NY 14066-9788
585-493-5450

Perry CSD
Dennis G Kenney, Superintendent
33 Watkins Ave, Perry, NY 14530-1198
585-237-0270

Warsaw CSD
Philip D D'Angelo, Superintendent
153 W Buffalo St, Warsaw, NY 14569-1295
585-786-8000

Wyoming CSD
Sandra B Duckworth, Superintendent
1225 Route 19, Wyoming, NY 14591-0244
585-495-6222

YATES

Dundee CSD
Nancy R Zimar, Superintendent
55 Water St, Dundee, NY 14837-1099
607-243-5533

Penn Yan CSD
Tiffany Phillips, Acting Superintendent
One School Dr, Penn Yan, NY 14527-1099
315-536-3371

BOCES District Superintendents

Albany-Schoharie-Schenectady BOCES
Barbara Nagler
1031 Watervliet-Shaker Rd, Albany, NY 12205-2106
518-456-9215 Fax: 518-456-9299
e-mail: bnagler@gw.nelic.org

Broome-Delaware-Tioga BOCES
Joseph R Busch
435 Glenwood Rd, Binghamton, NY 13905-1699
607-763-3309 Fax: 607-763-3691
Web site: www.btboces.org

Cattaraugus-Allegany-Erie-Wyoming BOCES
Robert D Olczak
Center at Olean, 1825 Windfall Rd, Olean, NY 14760-9303
716-376-8200 Fax: 716-376-8452
Web site: www.caew-boces.wnyric.org

Cayuga-Onondaga BOCES
Gary A Gilchrist

5980 South St Rd, Auburn, NY 13021-5699
315-253-0361 Fax: 315-252-6493
Web site: www.cayboces.org

Clinton-Essex-Warren-Washington BOCES
Craig L King
1585 Military Tpk, PO Box 455, Plattsburgh, NY 12901-0455
518-561-0100 ext 6 Fax: 518-562-1471
Web site: www.cves.org

Delaware-Chenango-Madison-Otsego BOCES
Alan D Pole
6678 County Rd #32, Norwich, NY 13815-3554
607-335-1233 Fax: 607-334-9848
e-mail: polea@dcmoboces.com
Web site: www.dcmoboces.com

Dutchess BOCES
John C Pennoyer

Colleges,
Universities &
School Districts

5 Boces Rd, Poughkeepsie, NY 12601-6599
845-486-4800 Fax: 845-486-4981
e-mail: drjcp@admin.dcboces.org
Web site: www.dcboces.org

Eastern Suffolk BOCES
Gary Bixhorn
James Hines Administration Ctr, 201 Sunrise Hwy, Patchogue, NY 11772-1868
631-289-2200 Fax: 631-289-2381
Web site: www.esboces.org

Erie 1 BOCES
Donald A Ogilvie
355 Harlem Rd, West Seneca, NY 14224-1892
716-821-7000 Fax: 716-821-7242
Web site: www.erie1boces.org

Erie 2-Chautauqua-Cattaraugus BOCES
Richard G Timbs
8685 Erie Rd, Angola, NY 14006-9620
716-549-4454 or 800-228-1184 Fax: 716-549-5181
Web site: http:\\e2ccboces.wnyric.org

Franklin-Essex-Hamilton BOCES
David J DeSantis
3372 State Rte 11, PO Box 28, Malone, NY 12953-9608
518-483-6420 Fax: 518-483-2178
e-mail: dcurrant@mail.fehb.org
Web site: www.fehb.org

Genesee-Livingston-Steuben-Wyoming BOCES
Michael Glover
80 Munson St, Le Roy, NY 14482-8933
585-658-7900 Fax: 585-344-7909
Web site: www.gvboces.org

Hamilton-Fulton-Montgomery BOCES
Geoffrey H Davis
25 West Main St, PO Box 665, Johnstown, NY 12095-0665
518-762-4634 Fax: 518-762-4724
Web site: www.hfmboces.org

Herkimer-Fulton-Hamilton-Otsego BOCES
Sandra A Simpson
352 Gros Blvd, Herkimer, NY 13350-1499
315-867-2023 Fax: 315-867-2002
Web site: www.herkimer-boces.org

Jefferson-Lewis-Hamilton-Herkimer-Oneida BOCES
Jack Boak
20104 State Rte 3, Watertown, NY 13601-5560
315-779-7000 or 800-356-4356 Fax: 315-779-7009
e-mail: jboak@mail.boces.com
Web site: www.boces.com

Madison-Oneida BOCES
Jacklin G Pexton

4937 Spring Rd, PO Box 168, Verona, NY 13478-0168
315-361-5510 Fax: 315-361-5517
e-mail: districtsuperintendent@moboces.org
Web site: www.moboces.org

Monroe 1 BOCES
Gregory J Vogt
41 O'Connor Rd, Fairport, NY 14450-1390
585-377-4660 Fax: 585-383-6404
e-mail: gregory_vogt@boces.monroe.edu
Web site: www.monroe.edu

Monroe 2-Orleans BOCES
Christopher B Manaseri
3599 Big Ridge Rd, Spencerport, NY 14559-1799
585-352-2400 Fax: 585-352-2442
Web site: www.monroe2boces.org

Nassau BOCES
James D Mapes
71 Clinton Rd, PO Box 9195, Garden City, NY 11530-4757
516-396-2500 Fax: 516-997-8742
e-mail: jmapes@mail.naboces.org
Web site: www.nassauboces.org

Oneida-Herkimer-Madison BOCES
Howard D Mettleman
Box 70 Middle Settlement Rd, New Hartford, NY 13413-0070
315-793-8561 Fax: 315-793-8541
e-mail: hmettelman@oneida-boces.org
Web site: www.oneida-boces.org

Onondaga-Cortland-Madison BOCES
Jessica F Cohen
6820 Thompson Rd, PO Box 4754, Syracuse, NY 13221-4754
315-433-2602 Fax: 315-434-9347
Web site: www.ocmboces.org

Orange-Ulster BOCES
Robert J Hanna
53 Gibson Rd, Goshen, NY 10924-9777
845-291-0100 Fax: 845-291-0129
Web site: www.ouboces.org

Orleans-Niagara BOCES
Clark J Godshall
4232 Shelby Basin Rd, Medina, NY 14103-9515
800-836-7510 x 2201 Fax: 585-798-1317
Web site: www.onboces.org

Oswego BOCES
Joseph P Camerino
179 County Rte 64, Mexico, NY 13114-4498
315-963-4222 Fax: 315-963-7131
Web site: www.oswegoboces.org

Otsego-Delaware-Schoharie-Greene BOCES
Marie Warchol

Offices and agencies appear in alphabetical order.

159 W Main St, Frank W Cyr Center, Stamford, NY 12167-1027
607-652-7531 Fax: 607-652-1215
Web site: www.oncboces.org

Putnam-Northern Westchester BOCES
James T Langlois
200 Boces Dr, Yorktown Heights, NY 10598-4399
914-248-2302 Fax: 914-248-2308
Web site: www.pnwboces.org

Rensselaer-Columbia-Greene (Questar III) BOCES
James N Baldwin
10 Empire State Blvd, Castleton, NY 12033-2692
518-477-8771 Fax: 518-477-9833
Web site: www.questar.org

Rockland BOCES
James M Ryan
65 Parrott Rd, West Nyack, NY 10994-0607
845-627-4701 Fax: 845-624-1764
e-mail: jryan@rboces.lhric.org
Web site: www.rocklandboces.org

Schuyler-Chemung-Tioga BOCES
Anthony J Micha
459 Philo Rd, Elmira, NY 14903-1089
607-739-3581 Fax: 607-795-5304
Web site: www.sctboces.org

Southern Westchester BOCES
Ronald L Smalls
17 Berkeley Dr, Rye Brook, NY 10573-1422
914-937-3820 Fax: 914-937-7850
e-mail: rsmalls@swboces.org
Web site: www.swboces.org

St Lawrence-Lewis BOCES
Linda R Gush
139 Outer State Rd, PO Box 231, Canton, NY 13617
315-386-4504 Fax: 315-386-2099
e-mail: info@sllboces.org
Web site: www.sllboces.org

Steuben-Allegany BOCES
Anthony J Micha, Interim Superintendent

6985 Technology Way, PO Box 586, Hornell, NY 14843
607-324-7880 Fax: 607-324-0201
e-mail: tcagle@saboces.org
Web site: www.saboces.org

Sullivan BOCES
Martin D Handler
6 Wierk Ave, Liberty, NY 12754-2151
845-292-0082 Fax: 845-292-8694
e-mail: mhandler@scboces.org
Web site: www.scboces.org

Tompkins-Seneca-Tioga BOCES
Gary A Gilchrist, Interim Superintendent
555 Warren Rd, Ithaca, NY 14850-1833
607-257-1551 Fax: 607-257-2825
Web site: www.tstboces.org

Ulster BOCES
Martin Ruglis
175 Rte 32 North, New Paltz, NY 12561-1034
845-255-3040 Fax: 845-255-7942
e-mail: mruglis@mhric.org
Web site: www.ulsterboces.org

Washington-Saratoga-Warren-Hamilton-Essex BOCES
John L Stoothoff
1153 Burgoyne Ave, Ste 2, Fort Edward, NY 12828-1134
518-746-3310 or 518-581-3310 Fax: 518-746-3319
e-mail: jstoothoff@wswheboces.org
Web site: www.wswheboces.org

Wayne-Finger Lakes BOCES
Joseph J Marinelli
131 Drumlin Ct, Newark, NY 14513-1863
315-332-7400 Fax: 315-332-7425
Web site: www.wflboces.org

Western Suffolk BOCES
Vacant
507 Deer Park Rd, PO Box 8007, Dix Hills, NY 11746-5207
631-549-4900 Fax: 631-423-1821
e-mail: centraladmin@wsboces.org
Web site: www.wsboces.org

Offices and agencies appear in alphabetical order.

FINANCIAL PLAN OVERVIEW

This information is excerpted from the New York State 2005-2006 Executive Budget, Appendix II, published 1/18/2005.
All Governmental Funds combines activity in the four governmental fund types: the General Fund; Special Revenue Funds;
Capital Projects Funds; and Debt Service Funds.

NEW YORK STATE CASH DISBURSEMENTS BY FUNCTION
ALL GOVERNMENTAL FUNDS
(thousands of dollars)

	2003-2004 Actual	2004-2005 Estimated	2005-2006 Recommended
ECONOMIC DEVELOPMENT AND GOVERNMENT OVERSIGHT			
Agriculture and Markets, Department of	68,780	86,302	81,962
Alcoholic Beverage Control	10,558	10,446	11,471
Banking Department	55,868	59,923	80,331
Consumer Protection Board	3,113	2,438	2,575
Economic Development, Department of	131,877	207,978	329,114
Empire State Development Corporation	52,074	36,975	264,200
Energy Research and Development Authority	29,557	26,123	26,006
Housing Finance Agency	0	0	0
Housing and Community Renewal, Division of	250,348	218,008	208,106
Insurance Department	105,913	137,349	151,444
Olympic Regional Development Authority	7,575	7,750	7,750
Public Service, Department of	47,080	56,259	56,800
Science, Technology and Academic Research, Office of	39,304	72,245	64,639
Functional Total	802,047	921,796	1,284,398
PARKS AND THE ENVIRONMENT			
Adirondack Park Agency	4,207	4,664	4,758
Environmental Conservation, Department of	795,259	910,179	923,971
Environmental Facilities Corporation	6,788	13,744	6,414
Parks, Recreation and Historic Preservation, Office of	196,921	230,253	229,175
Functional Total	1,003,175	1,158,840	1,164,318
TRANSPORTATION			
Motor Vehicles, Department of	203,748	225,512	282,085
Thruway Authority	2,865	4,000	4,000
Transportation, Department of	4,923,094	5,223,558	5,470,221
Functional Total	5,129,707	5,453,070	5,756,306
HEALTH AND SOCIAL WELFARE			
Advocate for Persons with Disabilities, Office of	1,213	4,075	0
Aging, Office for the	177,333	175,592	179,963
Children and Family Services, Office of	3,365,235	3,133,154	3,114,406
Health, Department of	31,567,174	33,449,683	36,056,490
Medical Assistance	27,643,723	29,447,466	30,989,058
Medicaid Administration	578,628	577,400	589,500
All Other	3,344,823	3,424,817	4,477,932
Human Rights, Division of	14,067	15,328	15,119
Labor, Department of	882,065	1,017,503	894,781
Prevention of Domestic Violence, Office of	2,063	2,164	2,235

	2003-2004 Actual	2004-2005 Estimated	2005-2006 Recommended
HEALTH AND SOCIAL WELFARE (Continued)			
Temporary and Disability Assistance, Office of	4,224,108	4,455,430	4,756,977
Welfare Assistance	2,876,620	3,100,802	3,385,656
Welfare Administration	378,024	342,533	359,550
All Other	969,464	1,012,095	1,011,771
Welfare Inspector General, Office of	892	1,106	1,124
Workers' Compensation Board	130,832	755	766
Functional Total	40,364,982	42,254,790	45,021,861
MENTAL HEALTH			
Mental Health, Office of	2,138,308	2,191,254	2,236,667
Mental Hygiene, Department of	1,654	4,750	4,800
Mental Retardation and Developmental Disabilities, Office of	2,623,994	2,816,190	2,922,882
Alcohol and Substance Abuse Services, Office of	474,930	467,249	481,507
Developmental Disabilities Planning Council	3,270	3,739	3,679
Quality of Care for the Mentally Disabled, Commission on	9,722	11,376	13,492
Functional Total	5,251,878	5,494,558	5,663,027
PUBLIC PROTECTION			
Capital Defenders Office	12,519	12,694	10,916
Correction, Commission of	2,503	2,511	2,510
Correctional Services, Department of	2,131,272	2,272,941	2,198,965
Crime Victims Board	63,192	62,059	62,478
Criminal Justice Services, Division of	309,208	302,479	314,199
Homeland Security	25,769	152,804	238,516
Investigation, Temporary State Commission of	3,071	3,513	3,652
Judicial Commissions	2,298	2,604	2,703
Military and Naval Affairs, Division of	1,639,924	127,199	135,722
Parole, Division of	188,005	181,667	182,352
Probation and Correctional Alternatives, Division of	80,814	75,557	0
Public Security, Office of	0	0	0
State Police, Division of	512,740	492,591	511,473
Functional Total	4,971,315	3,688,619	3,663,486
EDUCATION			
Arts, Council on the	45,949	46,003	44,134
City University of New York	1,220,761	1,027,315	1,361,579
Education, Department of	22,969,248	23,167,976	24,075,147
School Aid	15,561,534	17,636,096	18,303,517
STAR Property Tax Relief	2,819,455	3,072,000	3,202,000
Handicapped	1,344,140	1,538,359	1,653,373
All Other	3,244,119	921,521	916,257
Higher Education Services Corporation	881,988	1,016,445	927,845
State University Construction Fund	8,184	9,256	10,480
State University of New York	4,497,866	4,834,556	4,989,413
Functional Total	29,623,996	30,101,551	31,408,598

	2003-2004 Actual	2004-2005 Estimated	2005-2006 Recommended
GENERAL GOVERNMENT			
Audit and Control, Department of	148,963	182,508	240,088
Budget, Division of the	28,955	43,714	43,399
Civil Service, Department of	20,148	22,241	25,199
Elections, State Board of	3,356	3,711	151,525
Employee Relations, Office of	3,298	3,752	3,768
Executive Chamber	12,458	15,729	15,580
General Services, Office of	200,233	218,353	242,479
Inspector General, Office of	5,194	5,605	6,017
Law, Department of	149,095	174,910	178,245
Lieutenant Governor, Office of the	358	487	485
Lottery, Division of	159,224	174,220	177,264
Racing and Wagering Board, State	13,734	16,770	125,902
Real Property Services, Office of	46,108	52,790	51,299
Regulatory Reform, Governor's Office of	3,227	3,472	3,554
State Labor Relations Board	3,262	3,669	4,605
State, Department of	125,628	185,816	190,622
Tax Appeals, Division of	2,676	2,812	2,994
Taxation and Finance, Department of	344,957	345,923	343,784
Technology, Office for	32,737	20,197	20,076
TSC Lobbying	1,044	1,336	1,376
Veterans Affairs, Division of	10,953	12,293	12,835
Functional Total	1,315,608	1,490,308	1,841,096
ALL OTHER CATEGORIES			
Legislature	202,252	201,629	207,622
Judiciary (excluding fringe benefits)	1,431,275	1,543,984	1,604,166
World Trade Center	0	1,688,125	149,000
Local Government Assistance	824,372	972,661	1,023,650
Long-Term Debt Service	3,351,303	3,807,373	3,841,998
General State Charges/Miscellaneous	3,054,632	2,829,997	2,897,621
Functional Total	8,863,834	11,043,769	9,724,057
TOTAL ALL GOVERNMENTAL FUNDS SPENDING	97,326,542	101,607,301	105,527,147

BIOGRAPHIES

Executive Branch

GEORGE E PATAKI (R)

George Pataki was elected Governor of New York State in November 1994, and re-elected in November, 1998 and 2002. He is the state's first Republican-Conservative chief executive. Mr Pataki received his BA in 1967 from Yale University, where he was Ranking Scholar, and his JD from Columbia Law School in 1970, where he was a member of the Board of Editors of the *Columbia Law Review*. He was engaged in the private practice of law from 1970 to 1989. He has been a continuous member of the Peekskill Republican City Committee since 1974, including a term as Chairman from 1977 to 1983, and he was a member of the New York State Republican Committee from 1980 to 1985. After serving as Mayor of the City of Peekskill from 1981 to 1984, he served in the State Assembly (1984-1993) and the State Senate (1993-1994). He has also served as special counsel to the New York State Judiciary Committee, counsel to the Select Task Force on Court Reorganization, and counsel to the New York State Senate Child Care Committee. Following the attacks of September 11, the Governor led the state through memorials and remembrance, and on to a period of rebirth and rebuilding. To honor the memories of those lost in the attacks and to move the state forward, he has dedicated himself to rebuilding Lower Manhattan and to launching a comprehensive effort to revitalize the economy and restore stability to the state's finances. One goal is to make New York a powerhouse in high technology research and job creation, and the centerpiece of this effort is a one billion high-tech biotechnology Center of Excellence initiative, anchored by major research centers in locations around the state. He has also consistently fought for a cleaner environment, being active in preserving open space and cleaning up the Hudson River and Long Island Sound. Governor Pataki continues as a co-proprietor of his family's farm. He and his family live in Garrison, New York.

RANDY A DANIELS (R)

Randy A Daniels was appointed New York State Secretary of State by Governor George E Pataki on April 12, 2001. He holds a Bachelor's degree in Government and Journalism from Southern Illinois University. Before entering politics, he acquired extensive experience in journalism. He was a reporter for WVON Radio in Chicago from 1970 to 1972, correspondent for CBS News in Chicago from 1992 to 1997, Foreign Correspondent for CBS in Nairobi, Kenya from 1977 to 1980, and Managing Director of Jacaranda Nigeria Limited—a television training program for Nigerian television—from 1982 to 1984. He joined the public sector as Director of Communications for the New York City Council President's Office from 1986 to 1988, Press Secretary to the Prime Minister of the Bahamas from 1988 to 1992, and Vice President of Hirschfeld Realty in New York City from 1993 to 1995. He served under Governor Pataki

from 1995 to 1999 as Senior Vice President and Deputy Commissioner of Economic Revitalization at the Empire State Development Corporation. Here he oversaw the Harlem Community Development Corporation and coordinated New York State's role in the Federal Empowerment Zone program and Enterprise Community program. In 1997 Governor Pataki nominated Secretary Daniels to the State University of New York (SUNY) Board of Trustees and later nominated him Vice Chairman. He continues to serve as Chairman of the Investment Committee, Co-Chair of the Committees on General Education and Charter Schools, and he is a member of the Executive and Finance Committees. He has also been an adjunct journalism professor at both the City College of New York and Columbia University's Graduate School of Journalism.

MARY O DONOHUE (R)

Mary O Donohue was elected Lieutenant Governor in 1998 and re-elected in 2002. Following graduation from the College of New Rochelle in 1968, she taught elementary and junior high school in the Albany and Rensselaer County school districts for ten years, and she earned a Master's of Science in Education from Russell Sage College in Troy (1973). In 1980, she entered law school at Albany Law School of Union University, where she earned a JD degree in 1983. During law school she served as a law clerk and intern in the US Attorney's Office in Albany and also worked on the staff of Senator Joseph L Bruno. She was an associate attorney with O'Connell & Aronowitz PC until 1988, when she began her own practice in Troy. From 1990 to 1992, she also served as Assistant Rensselaer County District Attorney. In 1992 she was elected as Rensselaer County's first female District Attorney, and she won re-election in 1995. During her tenure, she achieved convictions in over ninety percent of the cases she handled, and she gained wide respect for her expertise in the areas of domestic violence, child abuse, juvenile justice, and the death penalty. In 1996 she was elected to the State Supreme Court for the seven-county Third Judicial District. In 1999 Governor Pataki appointed her to chair the Governor's Task Force on School Violence. As a result of public hearings, forums, and one-on-one meetings with students over a year's time, the Governor was able to sign into law the Safe Schools Against Violence Act in 2000. She was appointed to chair the Governor's Task force on Quality Communities in 2000, and the Task Force on Small Business in 2003. In 1994, Ms Donohue was appointed to the Transition Team for Criminal Justice; and in 1996, she was appointed Chair of the Capital District Women's Advisory Council. She was born and raised in Rensselaer County, where she still resides.

ALAN G HEVESI (D)

Alan G Hevesi was elected as New York State Comptroller in 2002. He holds a PhD in Public Law and Government. From 1967 through 1993, he was a member of the Queens College faculty and later was an adjunct professor at Fordham Law School and Columbia University's School of International and Public Affairs. He spent twenty-two years in the State Assembly, where he authored 103 laws and established himself as a champion of affordable health care, education reform, and the rights of people with disabilities. He also fought to keep New York City's water clean. He blocked the proposed sale of the City's water system and held up a $2.2 billion watershed agreement until he won substantial improvements. Just prior to becoming State Comptroller, he served two terms (starting in 1993) as New York City's 41st Comptroller. During his tenure, the City's five pension funds grew from $49 billion to more than $80 billion. Mr Hevesi more than doubled the number of audits conducted by his Office, identifying hundreds of millions of dollars in savings. He is a lifelong resident of Queens.

ELIOT SPITZER (D)

Eliot Spitzer was elected Attorney General in November 1998. Establishing a pattern of success early on, he received top academic honors from Princeton University and graduated from Harvard Law School where he was Editor of the *Harvard Law Review*. He served as clerk to US Judge Robert W Sweet. He was an associate of Paul, Weiss, Rifkind, Wharton & Garrison, and later at Skadden, Arps, Slate, Meagher & Flom. Prior to his election as Attorney General, he was a partner in Constantine & Partners in New York. He served as Assistant District Attorney in Manhattan from 1986 to 1992. As

Attorney General, he investigated conflicts of interest by investment banks, illegal trading practices by mutual funds, and bid rigging in the insurance industry. He has recovered billions of dollars for small investors and other consumers in these cases and was the catalyst for industry-wide reforms. He sued Midwest power plants and achieved significant reductions in the emissions that are responsible for acid rain and smog in the Northeast. He exposed the dangerous practice by pharmaceutical companies of concealing information about the clinical trials of drugs and helped develop new disclosure policies in the industry. He has gained national acclaim for his efforts. Also active throughout his career in civic affairs, he was the founder of the non-profit Center for Community Interest which represented neighborhood groups. He was a Trustee of the Montefiore Medical Center and chair of a community preservation corporation. As an authority on prosecution and public interest law, Mr Spitzer has been a regular analyst and commentator on national news programs, including: NBC's *Today Show, CNN's Burden of Proof, CNBC, and Court TV*. In addition, he has published numerous articles in leading newspapers and legal journals on a range of public policy issues. He lives in Manhattan and maintains a residence in Columbia County.

New York State Assembly

PETER J ABBATE, JR (D-I)
49th - Part of Kings County

6419 11th Avenue, Brooklyn, NY 11219
718-232-9565/fax: 718-837-2526

8500 18th Avenue, Brooklyn, NY 11214
718-236-1764/fax: 718-234-0986

Peter Abbate was first elected to the New York State Assembly in 1986. He entered St. John's University in 1967 and graduated with a BA in Political Science. From 1974 to 1975, he was Legislative Assistant to Assemblyman Stephen J Solarz and from 1975 to 1985 was District Representative for Mr Solarz while Mr Solarz was a US Congressman. Mr Abbate has been an active member of the Civitan Club of Brooklyn, the Boy Scouts of America, the Kiwanis Club of 18th Ave, the Statewide Homeowners & Tenants Assn, and the Guild for Exceptional Children. In 2002 he was appointed chairman of the Assembly Committee on Governmental Employees, after earlier serving as chairman of the Committee on Real Property Taxation and the Committee on Cities. Mr Abbate is a lifelong resident of Bensonhurst.

PATRICIA L ACAMPORA (R-I-C-WF)
1st - Suffolk County

400 West Main Street, Suite 201, Riverhead, NY 11901
631-727-1363/fax: 631-369-3869

Patricia Acampora was first elected to the New York State Assembly in a November 1993 special election. Raised in Long Island, she attended local schools. She later graduated from the IBM Institute in Manhattan and attended Suffolk Community College and Dowling

College. Before being elected to the Assembly, she was assistant to Suffolk County Executive Robert Gaffney where she initiated and headed the county's Internship Program and served on the Family Violence Task Force and the Legal System Committee. From 1983 to 1990, she served as executive assistant to Joseph Sawicki, her predecessor in the Assembly. During her own tenure in the Assembly, she has been a tireless advocate for the environment, better health care, and improved public safety and education. She resides in Mattituck with her husband, Alan Croce.

THOMAS W ALFANO (R-I-C-WF)
21st - Part of Nassau County

Citibank Bldg, 925 Hempstead Turnpike, Franklin Sq, NY 11010
516-437-5577/fax: 516-354-2551

Thomas Alfano was first elected to the New York State Assembly in 1996. He received his undergraduate and JD degrees from Fordham University, following which he worked as an attorney in several prominent New York City law firms. He is currently a counselor in the law firm of Entwistle & Cappucci, LLP, where he specializes in civil litigation. From 1988 to 1996, Mr Alfano served as staff counsel to NYS Senator Dean G Skelos, and from 1990 to 1996 he was also chairman of the Town of Hempstead Public Employees Relations Board. He has been active in the area of education, and his efforts have been recognized extensively by the groups, schools, and educational organizations throughout the 22nd Assembly district. He has been president of the North Valley Stream Kiwanis Club, and he is an advisory Board Member of United Cerebral Palsy Association of Nassau County. He resides in North Valley Stream and is active in youth athletic leagues in his community.

CARMEN E ARROYO (R-D-L)
84th - Part of Bronx County

384 E 149th St, Ste 608, Bronx, NY 10455
718-292-2901/fax: 718-993-6021

Carmen Arroyo was elected to the New York State Assembly in a special election in February 1994, the first and only Puerto Rican/Hispanic woman elected to the NY State Assembly. Born in Puerto Rico, she arrived in the US in 1964. In 1966 she founded the South Bronx Action Group, in which she expanded the notion of tenant advocacy to include the interrelated services of employment, health, adult education, and welfare. In 1978 she became Executive Director of the South Bronx Community Corporation. At the same time, she continued her education, receiving her Associate of Arts degree from Eugenio Maria de Hostos Community College in 1978 and her BA from the College of New Rochelle's School of New Resources in 1980. She served as member and president of Community School Board #7 and was a member of the Lincoln Hospital Community Advisory Board for seventeen years. She is currently the President of Puerto Rican Women in Political Action and is also a member of the Black & Puerto Rican Caucus, the Women's Caucus, the NYS Assembly/Senate Puerto Rican/Hispanic Task Force, and the National Order of Women Legislators. She continues to reside in the South Bronx.

DARREL J AUBERTINE (D-I-G-WF)
118th - Parts of Jefferson & St Lawrence Counties

200 Washington St, Ste 404B, Watertown, NY 13601
315-786-0284/fax: 315-786-0287

17 Hodskin St, Canton, NY 13617
315-386-2037/fax: 315-386-2041

Darrel J Aubertine was first elected to the New York State Assembly in November 2002. Prior to his election, he was a full-time dairy farmer for over thirty years at his family's Triple A Aubertine Farm, a sixth-generation Heritage Farm. He began public service in 1994-95 as a member of the Cape Vincent Town Board. In 1996 he became the Jefferson County Legislator for District 1, and he was elected chairman of the Jefferson County Board of Legislators in 1998 and 1999. As a lifelong resident of northern New York, his chief concern during his tenure in the State Assembly has been improvement of the economic climate in the North Country. He currently resides in the town of Cape Vincent.

JEFFRION L AUBRY (D-L-WF)
35th - Part of Queens County

98-09 Northern Blvd, Corona, NY 11368
718-457-3615/fax: 718-457-3640

Jeffrion Aubry was first elected to the New York State Assembly in a special election on January 3, 1992. He attended the College of Santa Fe, where he received his BA degree in 1969. He was employed by Elmcor Youth and Adult Activities, a not-for-profit multi-service corporation, for sixteen years, holding various positions including Executive Director. He also worked as a teacher in the New Mexico State Penitentiary for Eastern New Mexico University and as a consultant for Massand Associates, an engineering firm. He is former Director of Economic Development for the Borough President's Office of Queens, former Queens representative to the

Economic Development Corporation of the City of New York, and former Chairman of the Small Business Development Center's Advisory Board at York College. Currently, he is a member of several organizations, including the New York State Association of Black and Puerto Rican Legislators, the New York State Assembly Puerto Rican/Hispanic Task Force, the Medicaid Working Group, and the Assembly Majority Worker's Compensation Reform Task Force.

JAMES G BACALLES (R-C)
136th - Steuben and Yates Counties

103 Gansevoort Street, Bath, NY 14810
607-776-9691/fax: 607-776-9691

James Bacalles was elected to the New York State Assembly in 1995 in a special election. A graduate of Ithaca College, he began a ten-year stint in 1979 as an elected member of the former Steuben County Board of Supervisors. He was appointed to the Medicaid and Welfare Reform Task Force of the New York State Association of Counties (NYSAC). He also served on the Steuben County committee studying alternate forms of government, leading to the transformation of the County Board of Supervisors into the Steuben County Legislature. He was a member of that Legislature until 1989. He is involved in scouting activities: he served as lodge adviser of the Order of the Arrow, scouting's national honor society, and he is currently President of the Five Rivers Council. He has dedicated many hours to the Board of Directors of the Corning Hospital/Founders Pavilion, the Steuben County Youth Board, the Corning Area Youth Center, and the United Way. He is a lifelong resident of Corning.

WILLIAM A BARCLAY (R-I-C)
124th - Parts of Onondaga & Oswego Counties

200 North Second St, Fulton, NY 13069
315-598-5185/fax: 315-592-2359

William A Barclay was first elected to the New York State Assembly in November 2002. A graduate of St. Lawrence University and Syracuse University College of Law, Mr Barclay served as a clerk for Judge Roger Minor of the US Court of Appeals, Second Circuit, in Albany and New York City. He is currently a partner in the law firm of Hiscock and Barclay, specializing in business law, and he serves as a board member of Panthis Corporation and QMP Enterprises, Inc. He is on the boards of directors for the Friends of the Rosamond Gifford Zoo at Burnet Park, the Everson Museum of Art, and Northern Oswego County Health Services. Until his election to the Assembly, he was a member of the SUNY Oswego College Council. He represents the eighth generation of his family living in Pulaski, Oswego County, where he now lives with his wife Margaret and their two children.

ROBERT D BARRA (R-I-C)
14th - Nassau County

534 Merrick Rd, Lynbrook, NY 11563
516-561-8216/fax: 516-561-8223

Robert Barra was first elected to the New York State Assembly in November 2000. He earned his BA degree in Communications/Journalism from Hofstra University. He served as a councilman in the Town of Hempstead; while on the Town Board he also served as District Chief of Staff to State Senator Dean Skelos. He has been a Lynbrook Village Trustee and District Director for former Nassau

Biographies

Congressman David Levy. An active member of his community, Mr Barra is a former member of the board of directors for the Nassau County Health Care Corporation, a former member of the St. Raymond School Board, an honorary member of the Lynbrook Fire Department, Tally-Ho Engine Co #3, and a charter member of the Lynbrook Kiwanis Club. He and his wife Celeste and their two daughters live in North Lynbrook.

THOMAS F BARRAGA (R-I-C-RL-WF)
8th - Part of Suffolk County

187 Sunrise Highway, Suite C, West Islip, NY 11795
631-422-1321/fax: 631-422-6085

Born in Brooklyn, Thomas Barraga was first elected to the New York State Assembly in 1982. He holds a BBA in Marketing from St John's University and an MAB from Long Island University; in 1981 he received his PhD in Business and Public Administration from Columbia Pacific University. He served six years in the United States Marine Corps Reserves and was honorably discharged in August 1966. He worked in the private sector for thirteen years, holding various administrative and sales positions with the American Can Company, Dun and Bradstreet, and Pfizer Pharmaceuticals. In 1977 he was appointed to the position of Town Clerk of the Town of Islip, and he was elected to this office in 1977, 1979, and 1981. He is former Vice Chairman of Trustees of Suffolk Community College. Currently he is a member of the Sons of Italy-Giuseppe A Nigro Lodge #2234, Brentwood; the American Legion-West Islip Post #1738; and the Suffolk Chapter of the Vietnam Veterans of America. He lives with his wife in West Islip; they have two children and four grandchildren.

MICHAEL R BENEDETTO (D)
82nd - Part of Bronx County

Albany Office: LOB 919, Albany, NY 12248
518-455-5296

Michael R Benedetto was first elected to the New York State Assembly in 2004. He received his BA in History/Education from Iona College in 1969 and in 1971 earned an MA in Social Studies/Education. He has spent his entire career as a teacher. In 1974 he joined the New York City Public School system as a teacher of mentally and physically challenged students; in 1977 he was assigned to PS 160, the Walt Disney School, and in 1988 became coordinator of the special education unit. He is currently on the staff of Mercy College as an adjunct instructor. While with the NYC schools, he ran the first "very special" Olympics for multiply handicapped children; he became an "in-service" instructor, teaching other teachers about special education; and he worked as a mentor teacher and taught in his schools' talented and gifted program. In his community, he established the Throggs Neck Community Players community theater and served as member of Community Planning Board #10. He also started the Bronx Times Reporter, which became the largest community paper in the Bronx. He has received awards from such organizations as the New York Lung Association and the NYC Adaptive Physical Education Department, and in 1993 received the FIAME (Federation of Italian-American Educators) Excellence in Teaching Award. He has also received New York State and Congressional citations for his teaching achievements. He is a lifelong resident of Northeast Bronx.

MICHAEL A BENJAMIN (D-R-WF)
79th - Part of Bronx County

540 E 169th St, Bronx, NY 10456
718-588-3119/fax: 718-588-3317

Michael A Benjamin was first elected to the New York State Assembly in a special election in February 2003. He earned a BA in Political Science from Syracuse University and completed the Master of Science Program in Urban Affairs at Hunter College. Prior to his election to the Assembly, he served as Deputy Chief Clerk on the Bronx Board of Elections, the first African-American to head the Board. He was Vice President of the 44th Precinct Community Council and a member of the Local Draft Board. He has worked for three members of the Assembly: Hector Diaz, Jose Serrano, and Aurelia Greene. He also served as President of the Board of Directors for Sherman Terrace Co-op, Inc. He is a member of the Bronx Branch of the NAACP, which has honored him for his work, as has the New Covenant Board of Christian Education, the Bronx Unity Democratic Club, and many other organizations. Mr Benjamin was born in the Bronx and is a lifelong resident of New York.

WILLIAM F BOYLAND, JR (D-L)
55th - Part of Kings County

467 Thomas S Boyland St, Brooklyn, NY 11212
718-498-8681/fax: 718-498-1796

William F Boyland, Jr was first elected to Assembly in a special election held on February 25, 2003. Born in Brooklyn, he was initiated into public service by his father, William F. Boyland, Sr and his uncle, Thomas S. Boyland, both distinguished Assembly members. He attended Virginia State University, during which time worked for Virginia Governor Douglas Wilder and was also an intern in the offices of two US Congressmen, Major R Owens and Congressman Edolphus "Ed" Towns. Returning to New York, he began his career as a community activist. As a member of Local 371, he was an eligibility specialist with the Department of Social Services. He has also worked on behalf of Wayside Baptist Church, the NAACP, among other organizations. Born in Brooklyn, Mr Boyland is a lifelong resident of New York.

ADAM T BRADLEY (D-I-WF)
89th - Part of Westchester County

4 New King St, Town of North Castle, White Plains, NY 10604
914-686-7335/fax: 914-666-0046

Adam T Bradley was first elected to the New York State Assembly in November 2002. He received his BA and JD from Pace University, and he is an attorney in private practice specializing in family law. Prior to his election to the Assembly, he gained extensive governmental and legislative experience through his service as an Assistant County Attorney in Westchester County and as Counsel to Assemblyman Richard L Brodsky, where he was responsible for drafting legislation, working with lobbyists, and addressing public groups on the Assemblyman's behalf. He has also handled many high-profile Election Law matters at trial and appellate courts, and he has acted as a consultant to numerous candidates. He is a member of the Advisory Board of the Coachman Family Center, the treasurer of the WCLA-PAC, and a member of the Board of Directors of the Law Guardian Association. He is a lifelong resident of New York and is currently residing in Westchester County.

RICHARD L BRODSKY (D-I-WF)
92nd - Part of Westchester County

5 West Main Street, Ste 205, Elmsford, NY 10523
914-345-0432/fax: 914-345-0436

Richard Brodsky was first elected to the New York State Assembly in November 1982. He is a graduate of Brandeis University and Harvard Law School. First elected to public office in 1975, he served four terms on the Westchester County Board of Legislators. In the Assembly, he chaired the Committee on Environmental Conservation from 1993 to 2002, and he has led efforts to investigate the Indian Point nuclear power plants. He has also been active on a national level, serving as co-chair of CLEAN (Coalition of Environmental Legislators for Environmental Action Now) and NCEL (National Coalition of Environmental Legislators). Assemblyman Brodsky has received many awards in recognition of his service to his community, including the Martin Luther King, Jr, Award; the United Service Medal; the Jewish Council of Yonkers Appreciation Award; the American Arab Council Distinguished Service Award; the United Federation of Teachers' Friend of Education Award; the New York State Federation of Police Legislative Excellence Award; the Westchester Distinguished Service Medal; and the New York State Audubon Society's William B Hoyt Environmental Award. Mr Brodsky was born in Brooklyn. His family later moved to Westchester County. He and his wife have two daughters.

JEFFREY D BROWN (R)
121st - Part of Onondaga County

201 S Main St, Room 200, North Syracuse, NY 13212
315-452-1115/fax: 315-452-1119

Jeffrey D Brown was first elected to the New York state Assembly in November 2002. He graduated from Cornell University School of Hotel Administration and the Syracuse University College of Law. In 1997 he became Regional Attorney for the New York State Department of Environmental Conservation. In the State Assembly, his focus has been on economic development and job growth. As a captain with the 174th Fighter Wing, New York Air National Guard, he is also founder of the bi-partisan New York State Armed Forces Legislative Caucus comprising State Senate and Assembly members who have served in the military. Active in community groups, he is past President of the Syracuse affiliate of the Cerebral Palsy Association and a member of the Fayetteville-Manlius School District's Advisory Council on Special Education. He is a recipient of M&T Bank's 40 Under 40 award, honoring Central New Yorkers for their success and contributions. Born and raised in DeWitt, he has lived in Central New York for more than thirty years.

DANIEL J BURLING (R-I-C)
147th - Parts of Allegany, Genesee, Livingston & Wyoming Counties

2371 N Main St, Warsaw, NY 14569
585-786-0180/fax: 585-786-0182

Daniel J Burling was first elected to the New York State Assembly in 1998. After high school, he served in the United States Marine Corps from 1965 to 1969, which included a tour in Vietnam. He earned an honorable discharge as a Sergeant E-5m and then attended the Empire State Military Academy, graduating with a commission as a 2nd Lieutenant in the US Army Reserve in 1976. He graduated from Herkimer County Community College and received his BS degree from the University of Buffalo School of Pharmacy. A New York State registered pharmacist, Mr Burling has been president and owner of Burling Drug since 1987. He has also served as an Intern/Staff Pharmacist at Genesee Memorial Hospital and as a consulting pharmacist for the Genesee County Nursing Home. Prior to his election to the Assembly, Mr Burling served on the Genesee County Legislature. He is a licensed private pilot and aircraft mechanic and served as airport manager for Nellis Airport in Fort Plain in 1972. He is a Charter Boat Captain and owner/operator of Medicine Man Charters since 1985. Mr Burling is a member of the New York Pharmacists' Association, the National Association of Retail Druggists, and the Pharmacy Association of Western New York. Recently he accepted a commission as Lieutenant Colonel in the New York Guard. Assemblyman Burling was born in Batavia, and he and his wife of thirty years now live in the Town of Alexander.

MARC W BUTLER (R-I-C)
117th - Parts of Fulton, Herkimer & Otsego Counties

235 Prospect Street, Herkimer, NY 13350
315-866-1632/fax: 315-866-5058

33-41 East Main St, Johnstown, NY 12095
518-762-6486/fax: 518-762-2720

Marc Butler was elected to the New York State Assembly in 1995. He holds a BA in English from SUNY at Potsdam. A reporter from 1976 to 1986 for the Utica Observer-Dispatch, he spent most of his time in the newspaper's Herkimer County Bureau Office, where he reported on local government and politics. In 1986, he joined Utica National Insurance as a Corporate Communications Specialist. Prior to election to the Assembly, his political career had included service as a Newport Village Trustee and Deputy Mayor and two terms in the Herkimer County Legislature, where he was Majority Leader after 1993. He served as the Greater Utica United Way SEFA (State Employees Federated Appeal) Regional Chairman and the Valley United Way Chairman for the 2003 to 2004 campaign. In 2003 he was selected as the annual "Good Citizen" by VFW Post 7220, Middleville. A lifelong resident of the Mohawk Valley, he currently resides in the Village of Newport.

KEVIN A CAHILL (D-I-WF)
101st - Dutchess & Ulster County

Gov Clinton Bldg, 1 Albany Ave, Ste G-4, Kingston, NY 12401
845-338-9610/fax: 845-338-9590

Kevin Cahill was first elected to the New York State Assembly in 1992. A graduate of SUNY New Paltz and Albany Law School, he had served from 1986 to 1992 in the Ulster County Legislature, where he was Minority Leader. He left the State Assembly in 1994 and directed a Medicare health plan under contract with the Federal Health Care Financing Administration. In 1998 he was returned to the Assembly as the candidate for the Democratic, Independence, and Liberal parties, and he was reelected in 2000 as candidate for the Democratic, Independence, and Working Families parties. He has amassed a strong record in the Assembly on environmental issues, civil rights, labor, and women's issues, and he is a vigorous advocate for local real property tax reform. Mr Cahill has two daughters and is a lifelong resident of Kingston, New York.

Biographies

NANCY CALHOUN (R-I-C)
96th - Parts of Orange & Rockland Counties

1002 World Tradeway, Stewart International Airport, New Windsor, NY 12553
845-564-1330/fax: 845-564-1347

Nancy Calhoun was elected to the New York State Assembly in November 1990. Born in Suffern, NY, she attended Empire State College, where she majored in Public and Business Administration. Prior to her election to the Assembly, Ms Calhoun was Supervisor of the Town of Blooming Grove from 1986 to 1990, Councilwoman for the Town of Blooming Grove from 1982 to 1985, Blooming Grove Assessor's Clerk from 1978 to 1981, and Washington Central School District Tax Collector from 1976 to 1984. She has served as President of the Orange County Supervisors and Mayors Association (1988-1989), Orange County Community Development Advisory Board Member (1987-1989), Orange Municipal Planning Federation Director, and member of Orange County Solid Waste Citizens Advisory Committee. Currently she is executive member of the Women's Legislative Caucus, secretary to the American-Irish Legislators Society, and Assembly Minority Leader Nesbitt's representative on the Hudson River Valley Greenway Council. She is married and lives in Washingtonville. She has two sons and one daughter, and five grandchildren.

RONALD J CANESTRARI (D-I)
106th - Parts of Albany, Rensselaer & Saratoga Counties

Legislative Office Bldg, Rm 717, Albany NY 12248
518-455-4474/fax: 518-455-4727

Ronald Canestrari was first elected to the New York State Assembly in 1988. He is a graduate of Fordham College and Fordham University School of Law, a member of the New York State Bar Association, and a former member of the Bar of the District of Columbia. He served in the US Army from 1969 to 1971 and worked as an attorney with the federal government in Washington, DC. Prior to his election to the Assembly, he was Mayor of the City of Cohoes for thirteen years. He currently serves as the Assembly's Deputy Majority Leader as well as the Chairman of the Higher Education Committee. In the Assembly, he serves as a member of the Standing Committee on Rules, Ways and Means, Banks, Labor, and Local Government. As chair of the Assembly Working Group on Television Coverage, he has made Assembly Session footage available throughout the State. He is the recipient of an Honorary Doctorate of Laws from Manhattan College.

ANN-MARGARET E CARROZZA (D-I-WF)
26th - Part of Queens County

33-17 Francis Lewis Blvd, Bayside, NY 11358
718-321-1525/fax: 718-321-2071

Ann-Margaret E Carrozza was elected to the New York State Assembly on November 5, 1996. She received her JD from Hofstra University, where she served on the Law Review. She is a member of the New York State Bar Association-Trusts and Estates and Elder Law sections, the Queens County Bar Association-Elderly and Disabled Committee, the Association of the Bar of the City of New York-Surrogates Court Committee, and the National Committee of Elder Law Attorneys. In the Assembly, she has sponsored numerous pieces of legislation focusing on health law issues, trusts and estates, and senior citizens' rights. Ms Carrozza is the host of a weekly cable television program in which she discusses budget & policy initiatives with guests.

PAT M CASALE (R-C-RL)
108th - Parts of Albany, Columbia, Greene & Rensselaer Counties

4 Normanskill Blvd, Delmar, NY 12054
518-439-1926/fax: 518-455-5923

Pat Casale was first elected to the New York State Assembly in 1992. After graduating from LaSalle Institute in Troy, he enlisted in the US Army, where he served in the 69th Infantry Division in Korea. Upon receiving an honorable discharge, he went on to graduate from Hudson Valley Community College and pursued a career in retail. Prior to election to the Assembly, Mr Casale served as Councilman in the City of Troy for twelve years, and in 1985 was elected to the Office of Rensselaer County Clerk, a position he held until 1992. He is active in community and professional organizations, including the NYS county Clerks Association (NYSACC), the Center for Economic Growth, the Commission on Economic Opportunity, the National Association of State Legislators. He has received the Christian Coalition/Friends of Family Award, the Uncle Sam Citizen of the Year Award, and many other honors.

JOAN K CHRISTENSEN (D-WF-VE)
119th - Part of Onondaga County

4317 E Genesee St, Rm 103, Syracuse, NY 13214
315-449-9536/fax: 315-449-0712

Joan Christensen was first elected to the New York State Assembly in 1990. She is a graduate of Metropolitan Business College in Chicago and attended the Independent Studies Program at Syracuse University. Starting in 1984 she served two terms on the City of Syracuse Board of Assessment Review and three terms on the Syracuse Common Council. In the Assembly, she served as chair of the Assembly's Task Force on Women's Issues from 1995 to 2000 and two terms as the elected Chair of the Legislative Women's Caucus. More recently she has chaired the Assembly's Administrative Regulation Review Commission (ARRC). She belongs to many organizations, including Women in Government (serving on its Board of Directors), the National Order of Women's Legislators, Delta Kappa Gamma, and the Metropolitan Business and Professional Women's Club of Syracuse. Her numerous awards include a citation as Feminist Legislator of Honor from the Central New York Chapter of NOW, a Certificate of Recognition from the Upstate Medical University and its United University Professions, the Vietnam Veterans of America Central New York Chapter 103 Veterans' Advocacy Award, and many others. She has four children and lives in Syracuse.

BARBARA M CLARK (D-L-WP)
33rd - Part of Queens County

97-01 Springfield Blvd, Queens Village, NY 11429
718-479-2333/fax: 718-464-7128

Barbara Clark was first elected to the New York State Assembly in November 1986, following a career devoted primarily to civil service on behalf of her southern Queens community. She served as school safety supervisor for the New York Division for Youth Services. She founded Community Care Development, Inc, and was instrumental in the establishment and development of the Family Preservation Center. She was a prime sponsor of the New York City School Governance Law, mandating parental involvement in matters affecting the schools. In the Assembly, she has served as Chair of the Committee on Aging (1997-2000) and Chair of the New York State Legislative Caucus. Her more recent Assembly Committee assignments include Children and Families, Education, and Labor. She and her husband, Thomas Clark, Jr, have four grown children and a granddaughter.

ADELE COHEN (D-WF)
46th - Part of Kings County

2823 West 12th Street, Suite 1F, Brooklyn, NY 11224
718-266-0267/fax: 718-648-6549

Adele Cohen was first elected to the New York State Assembly in 1998. She received her BA degree in History from Brooklyn College and an MA in Education from Long Island University. She taught in the New York City public school system on the elementary and junior high school levels for five years. In 1976, she began an eight-year tenure with the International Ladies' Garment Workers' Union (ILGWU), as the Office Manager and Benefits Director for Local 99. Then, fulfilling a lifelong goal, she attended New York Law School at night (supporting herself and her children with paralegal work) and received her JD in 1987. From 1988 through 1998, she worked as an attorney for District Council 37 Legal Services, representing working union members in a variety of civil matters and specializing in will preparation, estate planning, and elder law. Her community involvement include membership in the Shorefront Democratic Club, the Committee to Preserve Brighton Beach and Manhattan Beach, the National Women's Political Caucus (former New York State President), Hadassah (life member), the Brooklyn Women's Bar Association, and the Brooklyn Bar Association. She was born and raised in Brooklyn.

WILLIAM COLTON (D-L-WF)
47th - Part of Kings County

211Kings Highway, Brooklyn, NY 11223
718-236-1598/fax: 718-236-6507

William Colton was elected to the New York State Assembly in November 1996. He received a BA degree from St John's University and an MS degree in Urban Education from Brooklyn College. He was a public school teacher for eleven years, serving as a UFT Chapter Chairperson for six years. While teaching, he attended St John's School of Law, receiving a JD degree in 1978. Long active in community affairs, Mr Colton was co-founder and organizer of the Bensonhurst Tenants Council and a member of the Bensonhurst Straphangers Committee for improving public transit. He fought for more money for public schools in Districts 20 and 21, as well as for numerous improvements such as traffic lights and pest control. He has been a member of the Board of Trustees of the Verrazano Lodge of the Order of the Sons of Italy and a member of the Board of Directors of the Cardinal Stritch Knights Corporation of the Cardinal Stritch Knights of Columbus Council. He has received many honors, including Outstanding Teacher of the year in PS 56, the United Federation of Teachers of District 13 Political Action Award, and many other awards. He currently serves as Vice Chair of the Assembly's Minority Conference. A lifelong resident of his district, he is married and has two stepchildren.

JAMES D CONTE (R-I-C)
10th - Parts of Nassau & Suffolk Counties

1783 New York Ave, Huntington Station, NY 11746
631-271-8025/fax: 631-424-5984

James Conte was first elected to the New York State Assembly in a special election on March 15, 1988. After earning a BA degree in Economics and Political Science from SUNY at Stony Brook, he began his career as an intern to State Senator James Lack and subsequently worked for Senator Martin Knorr and Assemblywoman Toni Rettaliata. He was later employed as an intergovernmental analyst for the office of the Suffolk County Executive Intergovernmental Relations Unit, acting as liaison between the State Legislature and executive departments. In the Assembly, he rose to become the Ranking Minority Member of the Education Committee. Recipient of a kidney transplant, he was appointed by Governor Pataki to the New York State Transplant Council in 1997 and reappointed in 2001. He is a member of the Huntington Historical Society, Huntington Elks Club, and Constantino Brumidi Lodge Sons of Italy in Deer Park. Born in Huntington Station, he lives there now with his wife and three children.

VIVIAN E COOK (D-L)
32nd - Part of Queens County

142-15 Rockaway Blvd, Jamaica, NY 11436
718-322-3975/fax: 718-322-4085

Vivian Cook was elected to the New York State Assembly in 1992. She was born in Rock Hill, South Carolina, and graduated from DeFrans Business Institute. She has served as District Leader of Queens County for over 25 years. She is Chairwoman of the Queens County Democratic Committee, founder and executive member of the Allied Regular Democratic Club, and founder and Chairperson of the Board of Directors of the South Ozone Park Women's Association. She has helped in the construction or rebuilding of numerous parks and recreational areas in her community, and she supported community housing programs that provide residents with affordable homes. She has also obtained improved benefits, housing, and medical services for senior citizens. Some of the numerous awards she has received include the Sojourner Truth Award from the National Association of Negro Business and Professional Women's Club, the Rockaway Boulevard Senior Citizens Golden Kiwanis Community Service Award, the Friends of Arts Award, the Military Women of NYC Award, the Forestdale Foster and Adoptive Parents Association Award, the Neighborhood Housing Services of Jamaica Award, and the Zeta Phi Beta Sorority Finer Womanhood Week Award. She resides in Jamaica, Queens County.

CLIFFORD W CROUCH (R)
107th - Broome, Chenango, Delaware & Ulster Counties

7 Kattelville Rd, Ste 1, Binghamton, NY 13901
607-648-6080/fax: 607-563-9854

Clifford Crouch was elected to the New York State Assembly in a special election November 1995. A 1965 graduate of Cornell University, he was owner and operator of a farm from 1967 to 1989. He and his wife currently are owners of Country Settings, a furniture and gift store in the Town of Bainbridge. He served as Councilman for the Town of Bainbridge from 1982 to 1986 and Supervisor from 1986 until his election to the Assembly. He also served from 1992 until

687

1995 as Chairman of the Board of Supervisors in Chenango County. He has served on numerous committees throughout his career, such as the Chenango County Solid Waste Committee, the Human Resources Committee, the Planning and Safety Committee, and the Personnel Committee. He has been a member of the Bainbridge Local Development Corporation, the Board of Directors of the Broome Cooperative Fire Insurance Company, the American Agriculturist Foundation, the Bainbridge Lions Club, and the Bainbridge Methodist Church. He and his wife reside in the Town of Bainbridge and have three children and two grandchildren.

MICHAEL J CUSICK (D-I-C-WF)
63rd - Part of Richmond County

1911 Richmond Ave, Staten Island, NY 10314
718-370-1384/fax: 718-370-2543

Michael Cusick was first elected to the New York State Assembly in November 2002. A 1991 graduate of Villanova University, he has had valuable experience at all levels of government. He began his public career shortly after graduation as Special Assistant to former President of the City Council Andrew J Stein. Later, he was chief of Staff to former Staten Island Assemblyman Eric N. Vitaliano. Finally, just before election to the Assembly, he served as Director of Constituent Services for U.S. Senator Charles E Schumer, overseeing a vast caseload of constituent needs and serving as Senator Schumer's liaison to all federal agencies. He has also been active in Democratic politics, serving as president of New York State Young Democrats from 1997 to 2000. He is a member of the New York State Democratic Committee representing the 63rd district. His civic interests include the Staten Island Board of Directors of the Catholic Youth Organization and the Boy Scouts of America. He currently lives with his wife in the Silver Lake neighborhood of Staten Island.

STEVEN H CYMBROWITZ (D-WF)
45th - Kings County

1800 Sheepshead Bay Rd, Brooklyn, NY 11235
718-743-4078/fax: 718-368-4391

Steven Cymbrowitz was first elected to the New York State Assembly in November 2000. He holds a BA from CW Post College, a Master's degree in Social Work from Adelphi University, and a law degree from Brooklyn Law School. He has devoted his professional career to improving housing and protecting neighborhoods. Before his election to the Assembly, he served as Executive Director of the North Brooklyn Development Corporation, Director of Housing and Community Development for the Metropolitan New York Coordinating Council on Jewish Poverty, Assistant Commissioner of the Division of Homeless Housing Development for the New York City Department of Housing Preservation and Development (HPD), Assistant Commissioner of the Division of Housing Production and Finance for HPD, and Deputy Commissioner of Development at HPD. He also served as the New York City Housing Authority's Director of Intergovernmental Relations.

RoANN M DESTITO (D-I-WF)
116th - Part of Oneida County

101 West Liberty St, Rome, NY 13440
315-338-5779/fax: 315-732-1413

207 Genesee St, Rm 401, State Office Bldg, Utica, NY 13501
315-732-1055/fax: 315-732-1413

RoAnn Destito was first elected to the New York State Assembly in 1992. She earned her BS degree in Industrial Relations at LeMoyne College. In the Assembly she has worked to improve the local economy and educational system and to provide quality affordable health care. She secured over $50 million to help redevelop the former Griffiss Air Force Base. She was part of the team that helped convince the Federal Base Realignment and Closure Commission (BRACC) to keep the Air Force Research Laboratory in Rome intact. She was appointed to the Budget Reform Conference Committee. Active in her community, Ms Destito has served on the board of the Senior Citizens Council of Rome and was one of the founders of the Mid-York Child Care Coordinating Council. She has worked with the project DARE, the Oneida County Teen Pregnancy Coalition, the Muscular Dystrophy Association, the Oneida County Runaway and Homeless Youth Advisory Board, and the National Council on Alcoholism. She has received community service awards from the New York State Correctional Officers & Police Benevolent Association, the Oneida County Historical Society, the New York Farm Bureau, and the YWCA. Born in Utica, she now lives with her husband and their son in Rome, New York.

THOMAS P DiNAPOLI (D-I-L-WF)
16th - Part of Nassau County

11 Middle Neck Rd, Suite 200, Great Neck, NY 11021
516-482-6966/fax: 516-482-6975

Thomas DiNapoli was first elected to the New York State Assembly in 1986. He earned a BA degree in History from Hofstra University and a Masters Degree from New School University. In 1972, at the age of eighteen, he was elected a Trustee of the Mineola Board of Education. He served for ten years on the school board, including two terms as its president. In the Assembly, he has championed environmental causes, chairing the Environmental Conservation Committee and crafting the landmark "Long Island Pine Barrens Protection Act." He has been recognized for his achievements by the Council of State Governments, the Healthy Schools Network, and the NYS Audubon Society. Born in Rockville Centre, he grew up in Albertson and currently resides in Great Neck.

JEFFREY DINOWITZ (D-L-WF)
81st - Part of Bronx County

3107 Kingsbridge Ave, Bronx, NY 10463
718-796-5345/fax: 718-796-0694

Jeffrey Dinowitz was first elected to the New York State Assembly in February 1994. He is a graduate of the Bronx High School of Science, City University, and Brooklyn Law School. Prior to his election to the Assembly, he was an Administrative Law Judge for the State of New York for ten years. He has served in a myriad of community organizations. He was Vice President of the Riverdale Community Council and a member of Bronx Area Policy Board #7. He was a member of the Boards of Directors for the Bronx High school of Science Foundation and for the Bronx Council for Environmental Quality. He is a former officer of the New York Teaching Housing Corporation, and is a member of Riverdale Senior Services, the Riverdale Mental Health Association, the Riverdale YM-YWHA, and the Bronx Historical Society. He is on the Executive Committee of the Riverdale-Hudson Chapter of B'nai B'rith. In addition he has been a member of District Council 37 and the Public Employees Federation. A lifelong resident of the Bronx, he has been married to Sylvia Gottlieb since 1978. They have two children.

PATRICIA A EDDINGTON (D-I-WF)
3rd - Part of Suffolk County

38 Oak Street, Suite 5, Patchogue, NY 11772
631-207-0073; fax: 631-207-2206

Patricia Eddington was first elected to the New York State Assembly in November 2000. She holds a BA in Political Science from SUNY at Stony Brook and an MA from the SUNY-Stony Brook School of Social Welfare. She is a NYS Certified Social Worker. Prior to her election, she was an Associate Professor of Philosophy and Women's Studies at Suffolk County Community College (where she earned an AA Degree) and also a social worker in the Islip School District. She served as a Patchogue-Medford school board member from 1980 to 1989 and for five years was a member of the Patchogue-Medford library board. She is past president of NOW mid-Suffolk Chapter, as well as former Vice President of the National Women's Political Caucus, Suffolk County Chapter. She has received several awards for her work in education. She is a lifelong resident of New York and currently resides in Medford.

STEVEN C ENGLEBRIGHT (D-I-G-WF)
4th - Part of Suffolk County

149 Main Street, E Setauket, NY 11733
631-751-3094/fax: 516-751-3082

Steven Englebright was elected to the New York State Assembly in a special election in February 1992. He holds a BS degree from the University of Tennessee and an MS in Paleontology/Sedimentology from SUNY-Stony Brook. Early in his career he was Founding Director of the Museum of Long Island Natural Sciences at SUNY-Stony Brook. First elected to public office in 1983, he served for five terms in the Suffolk County Legislature, where he was the chief architect of the County's Water Quality Protection and Open Space programs, which effectively doubled the size of Suffolk's Park System. In the New York State Assembly, Mr Englebright chairs the Committee on Aging and has advocated for important senior-related problems. He has also fought to maintain funding for education and to keep college affordable for the children of working-class families; his efforts have twice earned him the Student Association of the State University (SASU) Legislator of the Year Award. A Setauket homeowner since 1973, he has two daughters.

JOSEPH A ERRIGO (R-C)
130th - Parts of Livingston, Monroe & Ontario Counties

3045 East Henrietta Road, Henrietta, NY 14467
585-334-5210

Joseph Errigo was first elected to the New York State Assembly in November 2000. He graduated from Aquinas Institute in 1956 and joined the US Marine Corp Reserves, where he served until his Honorable Discharge in 1962. From 1965 until his retirement in 1995, he worked as an official Court Reporter for the State of New York in the Supreme, County, Family, and Surrogate Courts. This led to his first business venture (with two partners), Tiro Reporting Service, which existed until 1999; he still serves as a consultant for Midtown Reporting, Inc. He also started another small business, Errigo Sand

& Gravel in 1995, and the company is still operating successfully. In 1999, Mr Errigo was appointed Livingston County Commissioner to the Rochester Genesee Regional Transportation Authority, where he served for 20 months. He also served on the Judicial Screening Committee of Livingston County. After joining the Assembly, he was appointed Ranking Minority Member on the Children and Families Committee, and as a result of his experience in the private sector, he was also appointed to the Economic Development, Job Creation, Commerce and Industry Committee. Born and raised in Rochester, he now lives with his wife Cathy in Conesus, where they operate a small family farm. They have three grown children and five grandchildren.

ADRIANO ESPAILLAT (D-L-WF)
72nd - Part of New York County

210 Sherman Ave, Ste A, New York, NY 10034
212-544-2278/fax: 212-544-2252

Adriano Espaillat was first elected to the Assembly in 1996, the first Dominican-American to be elected to a state house in the United States. He earned his BS degree in Political Science from Queens College and later completed postgraduate courses in Public Administration at the NYU Leadership for Urban Executives Institute. In 1980 he joined the New York City Criminal Justice Agency where he worked as the Manhattan Court Services Coordinator for eight years. In 1991 he was chosen as a member of Governor Cuomo's Dominican Advisory Board, on which he served for two years. The following year, he was elected Democratic District Leader for the 72nd Assembly District Part-A, and he was reelected in 1995. From 1992 to 1994, he served as Director of the Washington Heights Victim Services Community Office and, in 1994, became Director of Project Right Start. Since 1986, he has actively served on Community Planning Board 12 as a member of the Executive Board, working on tenants' behalf and successfully petitioning for greater police services in the community.

HERMAN D FARRELL, JR (D)
71st - Part of New York County

2541-55 Adam Clayton Powell Jr Blvd, New York, NY 10039
212-234-1430/fax: 212-234-1868

250 Broadway, 22nd Floor, New York, NY 10007
212-312-1441/fax: 212-312-1445

Herman Farrell was first elected to the New York State Assembly in 1974. Prior to his election, he served as Assistant Director of the Mayor's Office in Washington Heights. He has also been a Confidential Aide to a State Supreme Court Judge. In 1970 Mr Farrell was elected a Democratic State Committeeman, and in 1973 he was elected Democratic District Leader. In April 1981 he was elected County Leader of the New York County Democratic Committee. From 1981 to 1982 he served as Chairman of the Sub-Committee on Financial Institutions of the National Conference of State Legislators, and in 1983 he was elected Vice-Chair of the Democratic State Party, a position he held for ten years. He has served as a member of the Democratic National Committee since 1988. He has been honored by numerous organizations, including the Harlem Committee, New York State Psychiatric Institute, State university of New York Educational Opportunity Center, New York State Affirmative Action Council, and the New York State Court Clerks Association. He was chosen Man of the Year by the New York State Supreme Court Officers Association, and he is a recipient of the Muriel Silberberg Award. He is the father of two children and has two granddaughters.

DONNA FERRARA (R-I-C-WF)
15th - Part of Nassau County

150 Post Avenue, Westbury, NY 11590
516-338-2693/fax: 516-338-2696

Donna Ferrara was elected to the New York State Assembly in November 1992. She received her BA degree in Business and English from SUNY at Albany and a JD in 1984 from St John's University School of Law. She began her career as a Legislative Aide to Senator Norman Levy in Albany. Upon admission to the state bar, she served as Legislative Counsel to Senator Kemp Hannon on Long Island. Thereafter, she was a Deputy Town Attorney for the Town of Hempstead, where she was the Town's Freedom of Information Officer. She was also Counsel to both the Map Committee and the Department of Planning and Economic Development. During her first term in the Assembly, she was responsible for landmark statewide legislation prohibiting discrimination by insurance companies against breast cancer victims. In 1996, she was ranked first among the 211 legislators by the Environmental Advocates Group for her exceptional voting on environmental issues. She has also been a recipient of the Profiles in Green Courage Award. The Nassau County Police recognized her contributions to crime prevention and victims' rights legislation by naming her Honorary Law Enforcement Officer of the Year in 1996. She is married to Robert Gregory, Executive Director of the New York State Association of Counties; they have two children, a daughter and a son.

GINNY FIELDS (D-WF)
5th - Suffolk County

2 So Main St, Ste 2, Sayville, NY 11782
631-589-8685/fax: 631-589-2947

Assemblywoman Ginny Fields was elected to the Assembly in a special election on March 9, 2004. She was a health care administrator for thirty-seven years. She began elected public service in the Suffolk County Legislature in November 1999, where she served two terms and sponsored a bill requiring Suffolk County to make available to the public comparison prices from local pharmacies for the top twenty-five drugs used by seniors. She is co-founder of the Oakdale Civic Association, and she has served on the Board of Directors of the Sayville Chamber of Commerce. She is a former chair of the Suffolk County Legislature's Health Committee. She also worked as a grassroots leader and activist for many years. She has been concerned with wetlands, habitat and open space and served as president of the Great South Bay Audubon Society. In 1999 she championed the acquisition by New York State of Benton Bay, comprising 127 acres of wetlands, after working for ten years to facilitate preservation of the parcel. A lifelong resident of Suffolk County, she is the mother of two sons and a homeowner in Oakdale.

GARY D FINCH (R-I-C)
123rd - Cayuga County & parts of Broome, Chenango, Cortland & Tioga Counties

69 South Street, Auburn, NY 13021
315-255-3045/fax: 315-255-3048

Gary Finch was first elected to the New York State Assembly on November 2, 1999. He attended Cayuga Community College and received a degree from the Simmons School of Mortuary Science in Syracuse in 1966. He also earned a BS degree in Public Administration and Political Theory from SUNY Empire State College in 1989. Since 1970, Finch has been owner and operator of Brew-Finch Funeral Homes. He was first elected to public office in 1979 as a Village of Aurora Trustee, and in 1982 he was elected Mayor, a post he held until 1990. He is heavily involved in community service. He has been chair of the Board of Trustees at Cayuga Community College. He has served as Cayuga County United Way's president and campaign chair and member of its executive and finance committees. He is past member of Leadership Cayuga's Curriculum Program; former chair of the membership committee for the Cayuga County Chamber of Commerce; and a charter member, past president, and big brother for Big Brothers and Big Sisters. He was named Assemblyman of the Year by the NYS Association of Big Brothers and Big Sisters. Born in Aurora, he lives with his wife in Springport. They have raised two children.

MICHAEL J FITZPATRICK (R-C-RL)
7th - Part of Suffolk County

50 Rte 111, Ste 202, Smithtown, NY 11787
631-724-2929/fax: 631-724-3024

Michael J Fitzpatrick was first elected to the New York State Assembly in November 2002. A graduate of St Michael's College in Vermont with a BA in Business, he is an investment associate with UBS Financial Services Inc in its Port Jefferson office. Prior to joining the Assembly, he served on the Smithtown Town Board for 15 years. During his first term in the Assembly, he served as Ranking Minority Member on the Tourism, Arts and Sports Development Committee. Serving his community, Mr Fitzpatrick is a member and past president of the Board of Trustees for the Cleary School for the Deaf in Nesconset, and he has also been the Major Gifts Chairman for the Smithtown YMCA's capital campaign. He is past president of the Suffolk County Charter Revision Commission and the Human Resources Committee of Catholic Charities, Diocese of Rockville Center. He is currently a member of the Knights of Columbus, Council 3958; the Ancient Order of Hibernians; the Board of Directors of the Suffolk Sports Hall of Fame; and the Advisory Board of the Academy of St Joseph in Brentwood. Born in Jamaica, Queens, and raised in Hauppauge, Long Island, he now resides in St. James. He is married and has two children.

SANDRA R GALEF (D-I-WF)
90th - Parts of Putnam & Westchester Counties

2 Church Street, Ossining, NY 10562
914-941-1111/fax: 914-941-9132

Sandra Galef was first elected to the Assembly in 1992. She graduated from Purdue University and earned a Master's degree in Education at the University of Virginia. Before coming to the Assembly, she served as a County Legislator for 13 years and as Minority Leader of the Westchester County Board of Legislators for 8 years. She also served as president of the New York State Association of Counties, and on the national level as chairperson of the Labor and Employee Benefits Steering Committee Chair of the National Association of Counties. In the Assembly, she has been a leading advocate for legislative reform and has been involved in matters pertaining to education, taxes, energy, health, and senior citizens.

She has been president of the League of Women Voters of Briarcliff-Ossining, president and board member of the United Way of Northern Westchester. She has been honored by many organizations, including the American Cancer Association, New York State Association of Counties, New York State Federation of Police, and the United Way. Born in LaCross, Wisconsin, she has lived in Westchester County since 1944. She currently resides in Ossining.

DAVID F GANTT (D)
133rd - Part of Monroe County

74 University Ave, Rochester, NY 14605-2928
585-454-3670/fax: 585-328-6118

David Gantt was first elected to the New York State Assembly in 1983. He attended Roberts Wesleyan College and the Rochester Institute of Technology. His professional experience has included service as Youth Counselor for the City of Rochester and as administrator for the Anthony L. Jordan Health Center. He has also been an active member of the Lithographers & Photoengravers International Union Local 230. Before joining the Assembly, he served nine years in the Monroe County Legislature. In the Assembly he has been author of bills aimed at expanding anti-drug efforts, improving safety on the state's roads and bridges, and promoting minority businesses. He has been honored by such organizations as the Upstairs Youth Agency, the Mt Vernon Baptist Church, the Monroe county Board of Elections, and the NYS Association of Counties.

MICHAEL N GIANARIS (D-WF)
36th - Part of Queens County

21-77 31st Street, Suite 107, Astoria, NY 11105
718-545-3889/fax: 718-545-7306

Michael Gianaris was first elected to the New York State Assembly in November 2000. He received a Bachelors Degree in Economics and Political Science from Fordham University and his JD degree from Harvard Law School. He practiced law as a litigator in private practice for two years. He began his career in public service as an aide to Congressman Thomas Manton, and he later served as Governor Cuomo's Queens County Regional Representative. Prior to his campaign and election to the Assembly, he served as Associate Counsel to the Assembly Committees on Consumer Affairs and Protection, Governmental Operations, Veterans Affairs, and Agriculture and Markets. He has served as a member of Queens Community Planning Board #1, as Legal Counsel to the United Community Civic Association, and as a board member of the Eastern Orthodox Lawyers Association. He is a lifelong resident of Astoria, New York.

DEBORAH J GLICK (D-WF)
66th - Part of New York County

853 Broadway, Suite 2120, New York, NY 10003
212-674-5153/fax: 212-674-5530

Deborah Glick was first elected to the Assembly in 1991, the first openly lesbian or gay member of the State Legislature. She graduated from the City University of New York and earned her MBA from Fordham University. She owned and managed a small printing business in TriBeCa before becoming Deputy Director of General Services at the City Department of Housing, Preservation and Development, a position she held until May 1990. She has also served on Manhattan's Community Board #2 and has worked with the National

Organization for Women, the Women's Political Caucus, and the National Abortion and Reproductive Rights Action League. Her priorities in the State Assembly have included passage of the Sexual Orientation and Nondiscrimination Act (SONDA), which was signed into law in December 2002, and passage of the Women's Heath and Wellness Act, which became law on January 1, 2003. Appointed Chair of the Social Services Committee in 2001, she has been concerned with protection of the state's most vulnerable citizens. She has served as the Chair of the National Conference of State Legislatures' (NCSL) Standing Committee on Human Services and Welfare and as a member of the NCSL Task Force on Welfare Reauthorization. A lifelong resident of New York, she lives in Greenwich Village.

DIANE M GORDON (D)
40th - Part of Kings County

669 Vermont Street, Brooklyn, NY 11207
718-257-5824/fax: 718-257-7084

Diane Gordon was first elected to the New York State Assembly in November 2000. She received her degree in Business Administration from New York City Technical College in 1985 and is certified by the American Business Institute in Business Mathematics. Her civic involvement began in 1985, when she founded the Save our Homes Organization of East New York. She has worked in daycare, taught fifth and sixth grades, and served as a senior-citizen caseworker and community liaison. She served on the Community School Board of District 19, was elected to the area policy board of Community Planning Board 5, and has been elected as New York State Committeewoman since 1996. She is currently a member of the New York State Black, Puerto Rican and Hispanic Legislative Caucus, the Puerto Rican/Hispanic Task Force, the Legislative Women's Caucus, the Democratic Study Group, and the Brooklyn Delegation of the New York State Assembly (Kings County). Born in Hemingway, South Carolina, she grew up in the East New Nork and Brownsville section of Brooklyn.

RICHARD N GOTTFRIED (D-L-WF)
75th - Part of New York County

242 W 27th Street, New York, NY 10001
212-807-7900/fax: 212-243-2035

Richard Gottfried was first elected to the New York State Assembly in 1970 at the age of 23. He graduated from Cornell University in 1968 and Columbia Law School in 1973. He is a lawyer but since 1973 has worked full-time as a legislator. He is a leading state health policy-maker and was a major architect of New York's managed care reforms. He is a Fellow of the New York Academy of Medicine, and a member of the American Public Health Association, the New York Civil Liberties Union, the Association of the Bar of the City of New York, the Art Students League of New York, Stephen Wise Free Synagogue, and The China Institute. He is head of the Manhattan Assembly Democratic Delegation. He has repeatedly been honored by the New York Civil Liberties Union Roll and the Family Planning Advocates, and he was named Environmental Legislator of the Year by the Environmental Planning Lobby. Born in New York, he lives in Manhattan.

ALEXANDER B "PETE" GRANNIS (D-WF)
65th - Part of New York County

Biographies

1672 First Avenue, New York, NY 10128
212-860-4906/fax: 212-996-3046

Pete Grannis was first elected to the Assembly in 1974. He is a graduate of Rutgers University and the University of Virginia Law School and has taken graduate courses in tax law at New York University Law School. Prior to entering the Assembly, he practiced law in New York City and served as Compliance Counsel for the NYS Department of Environmental Conservation. In the Assembly, as chair of the Insurance Committee, he authored landmark legislation on behalf of consumers, including New York's precedent-setting Community Rating/Open Enrollment law, which revolutionized the way small-group and individual health insurance policies are sold in the state. On account of his work, New York banned discrimination in the individual and small-group markets and provided for portability of health insurance coverage. He served ten years as Chairman of the Assembly Housing Committee, working on behalf of tenants' rights and affordable housing. He has been honored by the Environmental Planning Lobby, the Audubon Society, the Environmental Action Coalition, and Environmental Advocates for support of measures dealing with acid rain and clean air and water. Born in Chicago, he lives in Manhattan.

ROGER L GREEN (D-WF)
57th - Part of Kings County

55 Hanson Place, Brooklyn, NY 11217
718-596-0100/fax: 718-834-0865

Roger L. Green was first elected to the Assembly in 1980. He attended Wilberforce University in Ohio and Southern Illinois University, from which he received a BS in 1973. In the Assembly, he co-authored the Supplemental Tuition Assistance Program (STAP), providing financial assistance to poor and working-class students attending undergraduate colleges in New York State. He also co-authored the Prenatal Care legislation that was signed into law by Governor Mario Cuomo. He is founder of several social service groups, including the Latimer-Woods Economic Development Association, the Jackie Robinson Center for Physical Culture, and the Center for Law and Justice. He is former Chairman of the NYS Black and Puerto Rican Caucus. He was born in Brooklyn.

AURELIA GREENE (D-WF)
77th - Part of Bronx County

930 Grand Concourse, Ste E, Bronx, NY 10451
718-538-2000/fax: 718-538-3310

Aurelia Greene was elected to the New York State Assembly in 1982. She graduated from Livingston College at Rutgers University, where she majored in Community Development. She is a former public agency administrator and public official. She has taught at Antioch College, lectured at numerous universities in the metropolitan area, served as a major proposal writer, and is an experienced counselor. In the Assembly, she is the first woman to chair the powerful Assembly Standing Committee on Banks. She has been responsible for many landmark bills, including the Motor Vehicle Leasing Act (part of the Omnibus Consumer Credit, Disclosure, and Deregulation Act of 1994). For her work on behalf of bicycle helmet legislation, she was awarded a Gold Helmet by the NYS Head Injury Association. She has received the NAACP's Woman of the Year Award, the Morrisania Education Council's Distinguished Community Leadership Award, the New York State's Brotherhood Award,

and numerous other honors. A native of the Bronx, she is married to the Honorable Jerome A Greene and is the mother of two and grandmother of seven.

AILEEN M GUNTHER (D-C)
98th - Sullivan County and Part of Orange County

19 South Street, Middletown, NY 10940
845-342-9304

20 Anawana Lake Road, Monticello, NY 12701
845-794-5807/fax: 845-794-5910

In November 2003, Aileen Gunther was elected to fill the vacancy created by the untimely death of her husband, Assemblyman Jake Gunther. She grew up in Orange County, received her nursing degree from Orange County Community College, and studied liberal arts at the State University of New York at New Paltz. She is a registered nurse and the former Director of Performance Improvement and Risk Management for Catskill Regional Medical Center. She was named a member of the Sullivan County Local Emergency Preparedness Council following the September 11, 2001 terrorist attacks. She became a member of the AIDS Task Force in 1996 and has been a trained HIV Counselor since 1998. She is a member of the Mid-Hudson Chapter Association of Infection Control Practitioners; she is also Vice-President of the Mid-Hudson Chapter of Association of Infection Control Practitioners, President of the Mid-Hudson Chapter of Infection Control Preparedness, and the New York State Government Liaison for the Mid-Hudson Chapter of Infection Control Practitioners. She lives in the Sullivan County hamlet of Forestburgh.

JAMES P HAYES (R-C-WF)
148th - Erie & Niagara Counties

5555 Main St, Amherst, NY 14221
716-634-1895/fax: 716-634-1250

James Hayes was first elected to the New York State Assembly in 1998 and is Minority Whip. He holds a BA in political science from Canisius College in Albany. He is a fundraising and marketing consultant and a former director of alumni relations and admissions officer at his alma mater. Prior to his election to the Assembly, he served as legislative assistant to former US Representative Bill Paxon in 1989. He served as trustee for the Village of Williamsville and as the village's deputy mayor from 1991 to 1993. He was elected member of the Amherst Town Board in 1993 and reelected in 1997. During his tenure, he was the Board's liaison to the highway department, the public library, the Amherst Museum, and citizen-based environmental and safety Committees. From 1995 until his election to the Assembly, he served as first director of development for Catholic Charities of Buffalo, and in 1996 helped to found the Catholic Charities of Buffalo, NY, Foundation. Born and raised in Erie County, he lives in Amherst.

CARL E HEASTIE (D-WF)
83rd - Part of Bronx County

1351 East Gun Hill Road, Bronx, NY 10469
718-654-6539/fax: 718-654-5836

Carl E Heastie was first elected to the New York State Assembly in November 2000. He holds a BS degree in Applied Mathematics and Statistics from the State University of New York at Stony Brook, and he is presently enrolled in Baruch College's MBA program. Prior to joining the Assembly, he served as a Democratic State Committeeman for eight years and was employed as a Budget Analyst in the Office of the New York City Comptroller for eight years. He is a member of the Williamsbridge Branch of the NAACP, the National Council of Negro Women, and the Grace Baptist Church. He is a lifelong resident of New York.

ANDREW HEVESI (D-WF)

28th - Parts of Queens County (Forest Hills, Glendale, Kew Gardens, Kew Garden Hills,. Maspeth, Middle Village, Rego Park, South Jamaica)

98-08 Metropolitan Avenue, Forest Hills, NY 11375
518-455-4926/fax: 518-455-5173

Andrew Hevesi was first elected to the New York State Assembly in a special election held May 2005 to fill the seat left vacant when former Assemblyman Michael Cohen resigned for family reasons. Andrew is the son of State Comptroller Alan Hevesi, who represented the same district in the Assembly for many years. His older brother, Daniel, served in the State Sentae for four years. Born and raised in Forest Hills, Andrew has lived there all his life. He attended PS 144 in Forest Hills and also the Garden School in Jackson Heights. He competed in local youth athletic leagues, and he now gives back to the children of his community by serving as Director of the Forest Hills Youth Athletic Leargue Basketball Clinic. Prior to his election to the Assembly, he served as Chief of Staff to former New York State Assemblyman Jeff Klein and Director of Community Affairs for New York City Public Advocate Betsy Gottbaum. He also worked as a paralegal in the Queens County District Attorney's Office, Domestic Violence Bureau.

DOV HIKIND (D-R)

48th - Part of Kings County

1310 48th Street, Brooklyn, NY 11219
718-853-9616/fax: 718-436-5734

Dov Hikind was first elected to the New York State Assembly in 1982. He attended Brooklyn and Queens Colleges where he received his BA in Political Science and his MA in Urban Administration. From 1973 to 1980, he was a history teacher in Yeshiva Toras Emes. He was formerly a Senior Legislative Financial Analyst. A spokesman against discrimination of any kind, Assemblyman Hikind chaired the Subcommittee on Human Rights and published an in-depth study of the effects of the quota system and reverse discrimination on education, business, and the civil service. After the Crown Heights riots in 1991, he joined forces with other Jewish leaders and elected officials to address issues stemming from the violence. In 1996, he founded the United New York Democratic Club, a political action group dedicated to bipartisan support of candidates in major city and state races who are committed to quality of life concerns and promoting greater unity and understanding within New York's diverse communities. He has helped form, and served for a time as Executive Director of the Jewish Neighborhood Action Council. He is also the founder of the United Jewish Coalition. He was born in New York.

DANIEL L HOOKER (R)

127th - Schoharie County & parts of Chenango, Columbia, Delaware, Greene, Otsego & Ulster Counties

45 Five Mile Woods Rd, Ste 2, Catskill, NY 12414
518-943-1371/fax: 518-943-0223

21 Liberty St, Sidney, NY 13838
607-563-2919/fax: 607-563-9310

Daniel L Hooker was first elected to the New York State Assembly in November 2002. After two years at Virginia Military Institute, where he was ranking cadet, he earned a BA at Cornell, and he is currently completing his MBA at the College of Saint Rose in Albany. Prior to taking his seat in the Assembly, he was a Senior Vice President of Farm Family Holdings, Inc, and he also served as Director of Member Services for New York Farm Bureau Member Services, Inc. He was a Councilman in the Town of Nelson in Madison County. A veteran of the Gulf War, he volunteered again for active duty after the September 11 attacks; during Operation Iraqi Freedom he was stationed in Albany, working with the families of Marines while carrying on his duties as Assemblyman. He is a member of the Schoharie County Farm Bureau, the AMVETS of Schoharie County, the Irish Cultural Center, and the Knights of Columbus. He is a Life Member of the Veterans of Foreign Wars, the American Legion, and the Marine Corps League. He has served on the Rip Van Winkle Council Boy Scout Executive Board. He is a former volunteer fireman and presently a Major in the Marine Corps Reserve. He and his family reside in Saugerties.

EARLENE HOOPER (D-I-L)

18th - Part of Nassau County

80 N Franklin St, Hempstead, NY 11550
516-489-6610/fax: 516-538-3155

Earlene Hooper was elected to the New York State Assembly in a special election on March 15, 1988. She earned a BA in English from Norfolk University and a Master's degree in Social Work from Adelphi University. She served as an administrator in the NYS Department of Social Services' Division of Child and Family Services. As Legislative delegate of the Nassau County Chapter of Jack and Jill of America, she established the DEALS project (Developing and Expanding Adult Life Skills). In the Assembly her priorities have been aid to schools, drug law enforcement, and safe housing. She is a member of the Assembly Task Force on Women's Issues and the NYS Black and Puerto Rican Legislative Caucus. In January 2001, she was appointed Chair, Majority Conference, by Sheldon Silver. She is an active member of the NAACP, the Central Nassau Chapter of the Negro Business and Professional Women's Association and Delta Sigma Theta Sorority.

WILLIAM B (SAM) HOYT, III (D-I-L-WF)

144th - Part of Erie County

Donovan State Office Bldg, 125 Main Street, Rm 257,
Buffalo, NY 14203
716-852-2795/fax: 716-852-2799

William Hoyt was first elected to the New York State Assembly in May 1992. He graduated from SUNY College at Buffalo with a BA degree in Political Science. Prior to his election, he served as Western New York regional director for Senator Daniel P Moynihan. In the Assembly, he has introduced legislation to encourage a "Smart Growth" approach to combating urban sprawl. He has been one of the legislature's leading opponents of legalizing casino gambling, which he views as an economic threat to the region. He has introduced bills designed to combat date rape, school violence, vandalism, high-speed police chases, arson, professional dealers of illegal fireworks, and many other crimes. He has sponsored important legislation on domestic violence, elder abuse, and health clinic access, in addition to supporting educational initiatives to combat teen pregnancy. In 2001 he was named to chair the Assembly's committee on Alcoholism and Drug Abuse. He received the SUNY Chancellor's Recognition Award in 1992. Other awards include National Family Planning & Reproductive Health Association's Distinguished Public Service Award, the National Association for Mental Illness Public Service Award, and the PEF Quality Service Award. He was born and raised on Buffalo's West Side.

VINCENT IGNIZIO (R-I-C-RL)
62nd - Part of Richmond County

Legislative Office Building, Room 531, Albany, NY 12248
518-455-4495

Vincent Ignizio was elected to the Assembly in 2004. He earned his Bachelor's degree in communications and journalism from Rider University, Lawrenceville, New Jersey. Prior to joining the Assembly, he served as chief of staff for former New York City Councilman Stephen Fiala and later was appointed administrator for the 51st Council District by then Speaker Peter Vallone. He went on to serve as chief of staff for Councilman Andrew J. Lanza for nearly seven years, during which time he handled over $50 million in capital projects and more than $3.5 million in expense monies. Over the past seven years, he has been working with Assemblyman Matthew Mirones (R-C-I Staten Island, Bay Ridge), State Sen John Marchi (R-C Staten Island), U.S. Congressman Vito Fossella (R-NY 13), Councilman Lanza, and Councilman James Oddo to solve many of the South Shore's most pressing issues. Recently, he served on the subcommittee for the Growth Management Task Force and co-authored five major down-zonings for the South Shore to make it illegal to build thousands of new houses. He serves on the boards of Crossroads Foundation and the YMCA South Shore Center, and has been involved with the soccer community on Staten Island for most of his life. He resides in Annandale.

RHODA S JACOBS (D-L)
42nd - Part of Kings County

2294 Nostrand Avenue, Brooklyn, NY 11210
718-434-0446/fax: 718-421-4396

Rhoda Jacobs was first elected to the New York State Assembly in 1978. She received her Bachelors degree from Brooklyn College. She is currently Assistant Speaker in the Assembly. In the past, she has been chair of the Social Services Committee and Assistant Speaker Pro Tempore and Chair of the Majority Program Committee. She operates a full-time Community Services Office, and she has served on the boards of community development corporations and hospitals. A former officer of the National Association of State Legislators, she served as Treasurer of the National Association of Jewish Legislators and is currently still a member. Ms Jacobs was co-founder and co-director of the Brooklyn College Day Care Center and serves on the Board of Directors of the Brooklyn College Alumni Association and the Hillel Foundation. She was a leader of the Coalition Against Redlining. She is affiliated with the Brooklyn Women's Political Caucus, the National Organization of Women, the Jewish Women's Leadership Caucus, and the National Association of Jewish Legislators. She was born and raised in Brooklyn.

SUSAN V JOHN (D)
131st - Part of Monroe County

840 University Ave, Rochester, NY 14607
585-244-5255/fax: 585-244-1635

Susan John was first elected to the New York State Assembly in 1991. She earned her Bachelor's degree in Public Affairs from George Washington University and her JD from Syracuse University. She subsequently practiced law with a firm in Rochester. As a strong supporter of affordable medical care, she was a staunch advocate of the Women's Health and Wellness Act of 2002. In 2003 she fought for Upstate New York to receive its fair share of state funding for staff investment in hospitals and nursing homes. She authored New York State's Anti-Stalking Law and subsequent laws relating to clinic access and stalking. She is a member of the Office for the Prevention of Domestic Violence Advisory Council and the Visiting Committee for the State Archives. Additionally, she is the Eastern Regional Board Member of the Women's Legislative Network of the National Conference of State Legislatures.

RYAN S KARBEN (D-I)
95th - Part of Rockland County

1 Blue Hill Plaza, Ste 1116, PO Box 1549, Pearl River, NY 10965
845-624-4601/fax: 845-624-2911

Ryan Scott Karben was first elected to the New York State Assembly in 2002. He received his BA in English (magna cum laude) from Yeshiva University in 1996 and a JD from the Columbia University School of Law (Harlan Fiske Stone Scholar). He is currently a member of the firm of Kurtzman, Matera Gurock Scuder & Karben, LLD. Prior to joining the Assembly, he served on the Planning Board of the Town of Ramapo and then in 1997 was elected to represent Ramapo in the Rockland County Legislature. As a member of the State Assembly's Energy Committee, he has taken a leadership role in investigating utility companies. In his community, he has served on Board of Directors of the UJA-Federation of Rockland County and on the Advisory Boards of the Martin Luther King Multi-Purpose Center, Big Brothers/Big Sisters of Rockland, and Ramapo Little League. He is also a member of the Arts Council of Rockland, NAACP-Spring Valley Branch, and the Rockland County Conservation Association. Born in the Bronx, he resides in Monsey.

THOMAS J KIRWAN (R-C-RL)
100th - Parts of Dutchess, Orange and Ulster Counties

190 South Plank Road, Newburgh, NY 12550
845-562-0888/fax: 845-561-5218

Thomas Kirwan was first elected to the Assembly in 1995. He received a BA degree in History & Political Science from Mount Saint Mary College in 1970. He served with the New York Police for twenty-eight years and retired as a Lieutenant with the Bureau of Investigations. He spent his last four years in Manhattan with the New York Drug Enforcement Task Force investigating mid- to upper-level drug dealers in New York City. In the Assembly, he has been Ranking Minority Member of the Committee on Cities and a member of the committees on Education, Ways and Means, and Alcoholism and Drug Abuse. He is a member of the Board of Directors of Our Lady of Comfort, a women's shelter, and a member of the civic organization UNICO in Newburgh. He is a lifelong resident of Newburgh.

BRIAN M KOLB (R-I-C-RL)
129th - Cayuga, Cortland, Onondaga, Ontario & Seneca Counties

607 W Washington St, Ste 2, Geneva, NY 14456
315-781-2030/fax: 315-781-1746

Brian Kolb was elected to the Assembly in a special election held in February 2000. He holds a both a BS and MS from Roberts Wesleyan College. Prior to joining the Assembly, he was Supervisor for the Town of Richmond, Chairman of Leadership Rochester's Board of Directors, and a member of both the Ontario County Revolving Loan Fund Committee and the Ontario County Board of Supervisors. In the private sector, he is former President of Refraction Technologies and a co-founder of the North American Filter Corporation, and he is currently affiliated with Stone Bridge Business Partners of Rochester. He is also Adjunct Professor of Adult and Graduate Education at Roberts Wesleyan College, and he was formerly a member of the Honeoye Central School Board and the Finger Lakes Community College Board of Trustees. Other community affiliations include the Canandaigua Rotary Club, the Honeoye Chapter of the Sons of the American Legion, the New York Guard and Ontario Charities Classic Board of Directors. He is a member of the Board of Directors of Thomas Health system Senior Living Services. He lives in Canandaigua.

DAVID R KOON (D-I-WF)
135th - Part of Monroe County

268 Fairport Village Landing, Fairport, NY 14450
585-223-9130/fax: 585-223-5243

David Koon was elected to the New York State Assembly in a special election held in February 1996. A graduate of Fairmont State College in West Virginia, Mr Koon began his career at Kelly Springfield Tire Company in Cumberland, Maryland. In 1982 he joined Bausch and Lomb as an Industrial Engineer in Oakland Maryland. Here he served his community as a Cub Scout Master, PTA President, and an active member of the Lions Club. In 1989 Bausch & Lomb moved him to the Rochester office, and he settled in the suburb of Fairport. In 1994 he was appointed to Rochester Mayor William Johnson's transition team on crime and violence, and he eventually became Co-Chair of the Task Force to Reduce Violence. He also helped to organize the Rochester Challenge against violence. In 2004 he received the "911 Professional Award" for his work on wireless enhanced 911 issues in New York. He and his wife, Suzanne, residents of Fairport, have a son Jason. In honor of their deceased daughter, David and Suzanne created the Jennifer Paterson Koon Peacemaking Foundation through St John Fisher College.

IVAN C LAFAYETTE (D-L-WF)
34th - Queens County

33-46 92nd St, Ste 1-W, Jackson Heights, NY 11372
718-457-0384/fax: 718-335-8254

Ivan Lafayette was elected to the New York State Assembly in November 1976. He attended Brooklyn College and served in the US Army from 1952 to 1954. He is a former Democratic District Leader and State Committeeman. In the Assembly, he is Speaker Pro Tempore and Dean of the Queens Delegation. He has sponsored hundreds of bills that are now law, including the nationally acclaimed Truth in Testing Law for college applicants, the Uninsured Motorist Law, the Red Light Camera Law, and several laws on banking. He has served

as the Honorary President of the Jackson Heights/Elmhurst Kehillah and Trustee of the North Queens Homeowner and Civic Association. He is a member or former member of the Executive Committee of the Health Planning Task Force, Kiwanis Club of Jackson Heights, and Advisory Board of Jackson Heights Community Development Corporation. He has served on the Faculty Advisory Board of the LaGuardia Community College Secretarial Science Department and was responsible for the formation of the Air Services Committee for LaGuardia and Kennedy Airports under the Queens Office of the Economic Development Corporation. He resides in Jackson Heights.

GEORGE S LATIMER (D)
91st - Part of Westchester County

933 Mamaroneck Ave, Ste 102, Mamaroneck, NY 10534
914-777-3832

George Latimer was elected to the New York State Assembly in 2004. He holds a BA from Fordham University and a Masters Degree in Public Administration from New York University's Wagner School. By profession, he is a marketing executive with over twenty years of experience working with major corporations that included Nestle, AT&T, ITT, IBM, and the former Shearson Lehman. His two decades of public service include a term on the Rye City Council (1988-1991) and seven terms as a Westchester County Legislator (1992-2004). From 1998 to 2001, he served as Chairman of the Westchester County Board of Legislators. He has received public recognition and awards from numerous Westchester and Hudson Valley organizations. He and his family are active volunteers in their home community in Rye.

JOHN W LAVELLE (D-WF)
61st - Part of Richmond County

114 Central Avenue, Staten Island, NY 10301
718-442-9932/fax: 718-442-9942

John Lavelle was first elected to the New York State Assembly in 2000. Before reaching the Assembly, he was active for over twenty years in his community. He is a founding member of the Brighton Kiwanis Club. He chaired the Staten Island Continuum of Education, the Silver Lake Area Committee of Community Board One, and the Board of the Veterans Action Coalition. In 1993 Governor Mario Cuomo appointed him to the New York State Charter Commission for the City of Staten Island. He also has a longstanding interest in health issues: He served on the Community Advisory Board for the Sisters of Charity Health Care System at St Vincent's Medical Center; he also created a monthly recreation program at the Sea View Hospital Rehabilitation Center and Home and served as Chair of the Center's Advisory Board. Since taking his seat in the Assembly, he has made education a top priority; in 2002 to 2003, he worked to secure an additional $600 million for New York City schools. He resides in West Brighton.

CHARLES DE LAVINE (D)
61st - Part of Nassau County

Legislative Office Building 325, Albany, NY 12248
518-455-5456

Charles D Lavine was elected to the New York State Assembly in 2004. He earned a BA in English from the University of Wisconsin in 1969 and a JD from New York Law School in 1972. From 1972 to

1976, he was a staff attorney for the Legal Aid Society of the City of New York. From 1977 to 1995, he was a partner in Grossman, Lavine & Rinaldo in Forest Hills, and since 1996 he has been a sole practitioner specializing in criminal defense work. Active in his community, he has served as counsel for the Glen Cove Community Development Agency and the Industrial Development Agency. In 2000 he was appointed to the Glen Cove Planning Board, and in 2003 he was selected to fill a vacancy on the Glen Cove City Council, a position to which he was subsequently elected. He has received an award from the Queens County Bar Association for instructing on the defense of federal criminal cases, and he also serves as an instructor at Cardozo Law School's Intensive Trial Advocacy Program. He has been a resident of Glen Cove since 1980.

JOSEPH R LENTOL (D)
50th - Part of Kings County

619 Lorimer Street, Brooklyn, NY 11211
718-383-7474/fax: 718-383-1576

Joseph Lentol was first elected to the New York State Assembly in 1972. Educated at the University of Dayton, St John's University Law School, and the Baltimore University School of Law, he served as Kings County Assistant District Attorney from 1971 to 1972, prior to joining the Assembly. In his thirty-two years of service in the Assembly, he has been singled out for many honors. In 2000 he was one of only two Assembly Members chosen by the Assembly Speaker and Governor Pataki to participate in the Election Modernization Task Force. In 2001 he was elected by his colleagues to direct the Brooklyn Assembly Delegation, responsible for making decision and advocating for funds and activities that benefit all areas of the borough. In the same year, he was appointed to the City's Community Action Board. He has worked to preserve and enhance the waterfront in his North Brooklyn district, improve tenants' rights, deter crime, and revitalize commercial corridors. He is a lifelong resident of New York City.

BARBARA S LIFTON (D-WF)
125th - Cortland & Tompkins Counties

106 E Court St, Ithaca, NY 14850
607-277-8030/fax: 607-277-8033

Barbara Lifton was first elected to the New York State Assembly in November 2002. She received a BA degree from SUNY Geneseo with certification to teach Secondary English in 1973 and an MA in English in 1985. She taught English at Geneseo High School from 1976 to 1982 and in Ithaca schools from 1985 to 1988. She was also a member of the New York State United Teachers, the Ithaca Teachers Association, the PTA and the Ithaca Hockey Boosters. For fourteen years prior to joining the Assembly, she served as Chief of Staff to Assemblyman Marty Luster. She was a longtime member of the steering committee of the Tompkins County Nuclear Weapons Freeze Campaign and worked for many years with Justice for All, a local group that fought cuts to Medicare and Social Security. She co-founded the Coalition for Community Unity in 1998 to combat hate groups. She served for two years on the Cornell/Community Waste Management Committee and was a member of the Ithaca Area Health Care Network. She resides in Ithaca.

VITO J LOPEZ (D-L)
53rd - Part of Kings County

434 South Fifth St, Brooklyn, NY 11211
718-963-7029/fax: 718-963-6942

Vito Lopez was first elected to the New York State Assembly in 1984. He graduated from Long Island University with a BS in Business Administration and in 1970 received his Master's degree in Social Work from Wurzweiler School of Social Work, Yeshiva University. He served as a part-time Adjunct Professor of Human Services at LaGuardia College and was also an Instructor at Molloy College, Empire State College, and Yeshiva University. In the Assembly, Mr Lopez represents a diverse community with one of the largest Latino/Puerto Rican districts in the state. He has emerged as a leader on issues of aging: He founded the Ridgewood Bushwick Senior Center, City-Wide Advocates for Seniors, North Brooklyn Senior Citizens Coalition, and the Ridgewood Bushwick Senior Citizens Council. He has also established a community-based education program in Bushwick through Long Island University, giving district residents the chance to obtain an affordable college education. He helped establish Brooklyn Unidos, a leading advocacy group for Latinos within his district. He was born and raised in Brooklyn.

DONNA LUPARD (D)
126th - Part of Broome County

Binghamton State Office Building, 17th Fl, Binghamton, NY 13901
607-723-9047

Donna A. Lupardo was elected to the New York State Assembly in 2004. Originally from Staten Island, she graduated from Wagner College and earned an MA degree in Philosophy at SUNY Binghamton. She stayed on as an adjunct faculty member in the School of Education & Human Development for ten years before dedicating herself to community education and public service. Prior to being elected to the Assembly, she served as the Director of Education for the Mental Health Association of the Southern Tier, working to address community mental health needs such as teen suicide prevention and elderly depression. She served on the Broome County Legislature from 1999 to 2000. She is the first woman to represent Broome County in the State Legislature. She is the recipient of the American Cancer Society Leadership Award, YWCA Alice Mills Award, Mental Health Association of New York State's Esther Mallach Staff Leadership Award, and the New York State Theatre Educators Association's Administrator of the Year. She resides in Endwell, New York.

WILLIAM MAGEE (D-I)
111th - Madison County & parts of Oneida & Otsego Counties

214 Farrier Avenue, PO Box 417, Oneida, NY 13421
315-361-4125/fax: 315-361-4222

William Magee was elected to the New York State Assembly in 1990. He graduated from Cornell University in 1961 with a degree in Agricultural Economics. After graduating from the Reish American School of Auctioneering, he became an auctioneer and small businessman in Madison County. In 1972 he was elected Supervisor for the Town of Nelson, where he served for nineteen years until his election to the Assembly. From 1985 to 1990 he was also employed at the New York State Fair in Syracuse. In the Assembly he has sponsored and led the fight for approval of the Northeast Interstate Dairy Compact to provide a stable milk price for dairy farmers all over the state, and he led the rally for the passage of the Farmland

Viability Act, which provides assistance to farmers. He currently serves as a member of the SUNY Morrisville College Council and the Board of Directors of both the Community Memorial Hospital and the Crouse Community Center. He is also a member of the Cazenovia Civic Club and the Hamilton Lions Club. He is a lifelong resident of Madison County.

WILLIAM B MAGNARELLI (D-WF-VE)
120th - Part of Onondaga County

State Office Building, 333 East Washington St, Rm 840, Syracuse, NY 13202
315-428-9651/fax: 315-428-1279

William Magnarelli was first elected to the New York State Assembly in 1998. He attended Syracuse University where he received a BA in history and a JD degree. Upon graduating, he entered the Army Reserves, retiring after six years with the rank of Captain. Prior to his election to the Assembly, he was elected to the Syracuse Common Council and served as Majority Leader. In the Assembly, he made job creation and medical care his top priorities. He brought home $2.5 million for the Workforce Development Initiative to help train and place workers. He also secured $2.33 million for the establishment of the New York Indoor Environment Quality Center (NYIEQ). He helped pass Family Health Plus, which brings health coverage to one million uninsured New Yorkers, and helped expand the Elderly Pharmaceutical Insurance Coverage (EPIC) program to make 215,000 seniors eligible for low-cost prescriptions. His community involvement include serving on the board of the Arthritis Foundation and as president of Our Lady of Pompeii Church Parish Council. He is a lifelong resident of Syracuse.

PATRICK R MANNING (R)
103rd - Parts of Columbia and Dutchess Counties

872 Rte 376, Wappingers Falls, NY 12590
845-221-3400/fax: 845-221-1131

444 Warren St, Hudson, NY 12534
518-822-8904/fax: 518-828-0901

Patrick Manning was elected to the New York State Assembly in 1994. He attended the Maxwell School of Citizenship at Syracuse University and graduated from Vassar College in 1986 with a BA in Political Science. He earned his Master's degree in Public Administration from Marist College in 2002. Prior to his election to the New York State Assembly, he was an Executive Aide for then Assemblyman Glenn E Warren and a Dutchess County Legislator for the 20th District. In 1993 he established and served on the Hudson Valley Stadium Corporation. He is a licensed real estate broker, and he continues to work at his family's firm, Rand Manning Real Estate. He is President of the Board of the Wappingers Education Foundation and a board member with the Dutchess County unit of the American Cancer Society, Dutchess County YMCA, Stony Kill Foundation, Inc, and the Hudson Valley Land Trust, which he co-founded. He is also involved with the Mid-County Improvement Association, Sigma Alpha Mu Fraternity, and Colombia County Association in the City of New York. He resides in the Town of East Fishkill.

MARGARET M MARKEY (D)
30th - Part of Queens County

55-19 69th St, Maspeth, NY 11378
718-651-3185/fax: 718-651-3027

Margaret Markey was first elected to the New York State Assembly in 1998. She is a graduate of the Berkeley School of New York City. She began her civic involvement as a member of Community Board 2, and after new geographical lines were implemented she served on Community Board 5. In 1981 she returned to the salaried work force as Account Executive for Projects In Knowledge, a pharmaceutical educational and firm. Then, turning her marketing skills to public service, she joined the office of the Queens Borough President as the Assistant Director of Economic Development. She helped establish an Office of Tourism in Queens and was promoted to Director of Tourism, a position she held until running for State Assembly in 1998. She continues serving her community as Democratic District Leader and is a member of the Maspeth Chapter of Kiwanis. She is a lifelong resident of Maspeth, where her family has lived for four generations.

NETTIE MAYERSOHN (D-L-WF)
27th - Part of Queens County

159-06 71st Ave, Flushing, NY 11365
718-969-1508/fax: 718-358-1979

Nettie Mayersohn was elected to the New York State Assembly in November 1982. She received a BA degree from Queens College in 1978. Prior to her election to the Assembly, Ms Mayersohn was the Executive Director of the New York State Crime Victims Board; she was also Chairperson of the Pomonok Community Center and founded and helped organize the Pomonok Neighborhood Center. In the Assembly, she is well known for the passage of the Baby AIDS law, which requires that parents be notified when their newborns test positive for HIV, and she was prime sponsor of the HIV Partner Notification Law. She is a member of the Eastchester Jewish Center and the Israel Center of Hillcrest Manor, and she is a member of the Board of Directors of the Harry Van Arsdale Jr Memorial Association. She has been a resident of the Eastchester Cooperative in Flushing, Queens, for forty-five years.

ROY J McDONALD (R-I-C)
112th - Washington County and parts of Rensselaer & Saratoga Counties

383 Broadway, Rm 202, Fort Edward, NY 12828
518-747-7098/fax: 518-747-7202

Roy McDonald was elected to the New York State Assembly in a special election in February 2002. He received his Bachelor's and Masters degrees from SUNY at Oneonta. Professionally, he is a vice president and public finance investment banker for Paine Webber's Municipal Securities Group. Prior to joining the Assembly, he served as the Town and County Supervisor of Wilton in Saratoga County. He is currently a member of the Saratoga VFW, Saratoga/Wilton Elks, Vietnam Veterans of America, SUNY-Oneonta President's Advisory Committee, Saratoga Economic Development Corporation, and Saratoga County Chamber of Commerce. He has received many awards, including Distinguished Service Awards from both the Saratoga Vietnam Veterans of America and the Saratoga County ARC. He is a native of the Lansingburgh section of Troy, New York, and a lifelong resident of the state.

Biographies

DAVID G McDONOUGH (R-C-I)
19th - Part of Nassau County

3000 Hempstead Turnpike, Ste 110, Levittown, NY 11756
516-731-8830/fax: 516-731-8845

David G. McDonough was elected to the New York State Assembly in a special election held in February 2002. He holds a BA in Economics from Columbia University, and he has served in the US Coast Guard and Air Force. He is past president of the Nassau County Council of Chambers of Commerce, and he headed the Committee for the Merrick Downtown Revitalization Project. He is founding member and continuing board member of the Bellmore-Merrick Community Wellness Council and a member and past president of the Kiwanis Club of Merrick. In the 2005 Assembly, he is Ranking Minority Member of the Consumer Affairs and Protection Committee and a member of the Transportation, Education, and Tourism committees. He is Vice Chairman of the Assembly Minority Task force on Sex Crimes against Children and Women and a member of the Task Force on Successful New York Schools. He has lived in Merrick for thirty-six years.

JOHN J McENENY (D-I-L-WF)
104th - Part of Albany County

Legislative Office Bldg, Rm 648, Albany, NY 12248
518-455-4178/fax: 518-455-7537

John McEneny was first elected to the Assembly in 1992. He holds a BA in History from Siena College and Certificates in Community Development and Public Administration from New Mexico State University School of Agriculture and the Kennedy School of Government at Harvard. He served in the Peace Corps in Colombia, and he has been a social services caseworker, a counselor, and a director of the Albany County Neighborhood Youth Corps. In 1984 he became a local services coordinator for the Governor's Job Training Partnership Council, and in 1985 he became Director of the State Urban Cultural Parks Program. From 1989 to 1991 he was Assistant Albany County Executive, and in 1991 he won election to the Albany County Legislature. In 1992 he was appointed Chief of Staff to State Assemblyman Richard J. Connors, D-Albany, and following Connor's decision not to seek re-election in 1992, he ran and was elected to the State Assembly. He currently serves as President of the New York State American-Irish Legislators Society and is a member of the Commission for the Restoration of the Capitol. He resides in Albany.

BRIAN M McLAUGHLIN (D-L-WF)
25th - Part of Queens County

163-13 Depot Rd, Flushing, NY 11358
718-762-6575/fax: 718-762-0917

Brian McLaughlin was elected to the New York State Assembly in 1992. He worked as an apprentice in the Electrical Union Training Program and became a journeyman electrician in 1977. While working as an electrician, he continued his education, receiving a BS degree from Empire State College in 1981 and a Master's degree in Industrial Labor Relations from the New York Institute of Technology in 1988. Prior to joining the Assembly, he was Pension Director of the electrical industry, a member of the Board of Directors of the Queens Overall Economic Development Corporation, a member of Community Board 8, and an officer of a local little league. In the Assembly, he has authored more than a dozen state laws. He continues to be a leading labor activist, serving as the president of the New York City Central Labor Council and a Business Representative of Local Union 3 of the International Brotherhood of Electrical Workers, AFL-CIO. He serves on the boards of the United Way of Greater New York and other civic organizations, and he has been honored by dozens of organizations. He resides in Flushing.

JIMMY K MENG (D-I-L-WF)
22 ND - Part of Queens County

Legislative Office Bldg, Rm 920, Albany, NY 12248
518-455-5411

Jimmy Meng was elected to the New York State Assembly in 2004, the first Asian-American elected to that body. Born in Shandong Province in China, Meng received his bachelor's degree from the National Taiwan Normal University. He came to the United States in 1975. He later earned his master's degree from Audrey Cohen College. He has long worked to improve the Flushing Community, serving as the President of the Flushing Business Association and as a member of former Mayor Rudolph Giuliani's Small Business Advisory Council. He authored the original plan to create a downtown Flushing Business Improvement District. He also raised over $150,000 in 9/11 relief funds for the families of police and firefighters and helped the 109th Precinct raise money for winter coats and bicycles as part of their crime-fighting programs. In recognition of his contributions to the community, Meng was awarded the 2004 Ellis Island Medal of Honor, the Outstanding Community Service Award from former Mayor Rudolph Giuliani, and the Person of 1998 Award from Governor George E. Pataki. He has lived in Queens for over twenty-five years.

JOEL M MILLER (R-C)
102nd - Part of Dutchess County

3 Neptune Road, Suite A19E, Poughkeepsie, NY 12601
845-463-1635/fax: 845-463-1638

Dr Joel Miller was elected to the State Assembly in 1995. He earned a BS degree (Phi Beta Kappa) from the City College of New York in 1965 and a DDS from Columbia University's School of Dental and Oral Surgery in 1967. He joined the military in 1963 and served on active duty in the US Air Force from 1967 to 1969. He remained in the Air Force reserve as a Captain until 1977. In 1969, he established a dental practice in the Town of Poughkeepsie. He has been a member of the Executive Committee of the Dutchess County Dental Society for twenty-six years, serving as Treasurer for five years and President for two years. Additionally, he served as President of the Mid-Hudson Dental Management and Marketing Corporation for five years and remains a member of its Executive Committee. Currently Dr Miller is a Major in the New York State Guard. He is a member and past president of the Harding Club, a philanthropic and social organization, as well as a member of the American Legion and several local Chambers of Commerce. He resides in the Town of Poughkeepsie.

JOAN L MILLMAN (D-WF)
52nd - Part of Kings County

District Office: 341 Smith St, Brooklyn, NY 11231
718-246-4889/fax: 718-246-4895

Joan Millman was elected to the New York State Assembly in a special election on February 18, 1997. She holds a Bachelor's degree from Brooklyn College, a Master's degree in Library Science from Pratt Institute, and a Professional Diploma from Long Island University, Brooklyn Campus. She taught elementary school and served as school librarian at PS 10 in Brooklyn from 1964 to 1984. From 1985 to 1996 she was an educational consultant to New York City Council President Carol Bellamy and Senator Marty Connor. From 1995 to 1996, she was a member of the Citywide Advisory Committee on Middle School Initiatives. In the Assembly, she has sponsored legislation to reform the Rockefeller Drug Laws, the Women's Health and Wellness Bill, and the Safe Weapon Storage Act. She was an early advocate for the creation of the Brooklyn Bridge Park and has worked to revitalize all of Brooklyn's waterfront. She was born in Brooklyn and is a lifelong resident.

MATTHEW MIRONES (R-I-C-RL)
60th - Parts of Kings & Richmond Counties

34 Dumont Avenue, Staten Island, NY 10305
718-667-5891/fax: 718-667-5879

Matthew Mirones was elected to the New York State Assembly in a special election in February 2002. He received a BS from NYU Medical School in Prosthetics and Orthotics, and for more than twenty-five years he has practiced in the field of prosthetic rehabilitation. He is a member of numerous professional organizations and has lectured at NYU Medical School. In the State Assembly he has worked to ensure that quality health care is available, particularly to children and seniors. In 2003, responding to disproportionately high smoking rates for Richmond and Kings Counties, he arranged for the availability of free smoking cessation nicotine patch kits to be distributed under the auspices of Staten Island University and Victory Memorial hospitals. In addition to his health-care related activities, Assemblyman Mirones is a Trustee of the Staten Island Institute of Arts and Sciences, a member of the Brooklyn and Staten Island Chambers of Commerce, a trustee of the Staten Island Institute of Arts & Sciences, and a member and past president of the Grasmere Civic Association.

JOSEPH D MORELLE (D)
132nd - Part of Monroe County

1945 East Ridge Road, Rochester, NY 14622
585-467-0410/fax: 585-467-0410

Joseph Morelle was elected to the Assembly in 1991. He received his Bachelor's degree from the State University College at Geneseo, and he is working toward a Master's degree in Information Technology. He is president and CEO of MMI Technologies, Inc, a Rochester-based computer software development company. From 1983 to 1990, he served in the Monroe County Legislature. In the Assembly, he worked on the Speaker's Task Force on Budget Reform and was co-chair of the Assembly's Welfare Reform Task Force. He wrote the Eastridge Law, mandating stiffer penalties for juveniles bringing firearms to schools. In 1997 he was selected by the NYS Small Business Development Center to participate in a trade mission to the People's Republic of China. He is a member of the Greater Rochester Metro Chamber of Commerce, the National Federation of Independent Businesses, and the New York State Library Association. He resides in Eastridge.

LOUIS A MOSIELLO (R)
93rd - Part of Westchester County

35 East Grassy Sprain Rd, 4th Fl, Yonkers, NY 10710
914-779-8805

Louis A. Mosiello was elected to serve the 93rd Assembly District in 2004. He is a graduate of Roosevelt High School and attended Westchester Community College. He formerly held the rank of Sergeant in the Mamaroneck Police Department. He was elected five times to the Westchester County Legislature, where he chaired the Committee on Transportation and the Committee on Cities. In the State Assembly, he was selected in March 2005 to serve on the Education and Cities Committees, and he has also been appointed to serve as Ranking Minority Member of the Governmental Operations Committee. Active in his community throughout his career, Assemblyman Mosiello founded and was President of the Grassy Sprain Civic Association. In addition, he founded and served as honorary Chairperson of the Yonkers Great Hunger Memorial Committee. He has served as a member of the New York State Assembly Community Advisory Board, the State Legislative Advisory Committee, and as Vice-Chairman of the Yonkers City Council Charter Revision Commission. He resides in Yonkers.

CHARLES H NESBITT (R-I-C)
139th - Parts of Genesee, Monroe, Niagara and Orleans Counties

121 N Main Street, Ste 100, Albion, NY 14411
585-589-5780/fax: 585-589-5813

Charles Nesbitt was elected to the New York State Assembly in 2002. A Vietnam Veteran, he was decorated as a combat helicopter pilot with the 57th Assault Helicopter Co; he served ten years on active and reserve duty. Prior to becoming an Assemblyman, he was for many years general sales manager at Moore Nesbitt Inc and Nesbitt Chrysler Plymouth Dodge Inc. He held various local government positions: he was Councilman on the Albion Town Board, Chairman of the Town of Barre Planning Board, and Chairman of the Orleans County Planning Board. In the Assembly, he has served as the Ranking Member of the Veterans Affairs Committee and as a member of the NYS Veterans Affairs Commission. In 2003 he helped create the Patriot Plan, a comprehensive assistance package extended to members of the National Guard and Reserve, and in 2004 he worked with Governor Pataki on Patriot Plan II to further extend benefits. He is a member of the Genesee Community College Advisory Board, Elks Lodge 1006, the American Legion Sheret Post 35, Vietnam Veterans of America Chapter 193, and the VFW Post 202. He is also past president of both the Orleans County Heart Association and the Albion Chamber of Commerce. He resides in Albion.

CATHERINE T NOLAN (D-WF)
37th - Part of Queens County

45-25 47th Street, Woodside, NY 11377
718-784-3194/fax: 718-417-1982

61-08 Linden Street, Ridgewood, NY 11385
718-456-9492/fax: 718-417-4982

Catherine Nolan was elected to the New York State Assembly in 1984. She graduated from New York University with a BA degree (cum laude) in Political Science and attended the NYU Graduate

School of Public Administration. From 1987 to 1994 she chaired the Assembly's Subcommittee on Mass Transit; she was honored by the Coalition of MTA Employee Unions and cited by the NYS Environmental Planning Lobby for her efforts on behalf of public transit. In 1994 she was appointed Chair of the Committee on Labor. In 2003 Speaker Sheldon Silver appointed her Chair of the Assembly's Committee on Banks. She is the Assembly's representative to the MTA Capital Program Review Board, where she successfully signed the third MTA Capital Plan, driving millions of dollars to mass transit. Ms Nolan is a member of the Ridgewood Democratic Club, 9th CD Democratic Club, and the West Queens Independent Democratic Club. She lives in Ridgewood.

CLARENCE NORMAN, JR (D-WF)
43rd - Part of Kings County

1218 Union Street, Brooklyn, NY 11225
718-756-1776/fax: 718-778-3010

Clarence Norman was elected to the New York State Assembly in 1982. He graduated from Howard University in 1972 with a BA degree in Political Science and received a JD from St John's University Law School. He began his professional career in 1976 as Legal Counsel to the New York State Assembly Subcommittee on Probation and Parole, and he also worked for five years as a trial attorney with the Kings County District Attorney's office. For seven years while he was in the State Assembly (1987 to 1993), he served as State Committeeman (District Leader) of the 43rd Assembly District. In 1990 he was elected Chairman of the Executive Committee for the Kings County Democratic Committee, the largest Democratic county organization in the country. He is the Assembly's Deputy Speaker. He served on the Board of the Bedford-Stuyvesant Lawyers Association, was First Vice-President of the 77th Precinct Community Council in Brooklyn, and was Chairman of the Housing Committee for Community Planning Board #8. Mr Norman has also served as a member of the Brooklyn Overall Economic Development Association, and the NAACP.

ROBERT C OAKS (R)
128th - Wayne County and parts of Cayuga & Oswego Counties

10 Leach Rd, Lyons, NY 14489
315-946-5166/fax: 315-946-5229

Robert Oaks was first elected to the New York State Assembly in 1992. He earned a Bachelor's degree in Political Science from Colgate University in 1974 and a Master's degree in Recreation Administration from the University of Montana in 1976. Also in 1976, he became Assistant Director of the Continuing Education Program for the Greece Central School District. In 1978 he was appointed Director of the Wayne County Youth Bureau. He was elected Wayne County Clerk in 1982, a post he held until 1992. He served as a member of the New York State Republican Committee from 1985 to 1992, on the Wayne County United Way Board of Directors for nine years, and as a member of the Macedon Recreation Commission and the Wayne County Youth Board. Assemblyman Oaks is a fifth-generation resident of Wayne County. He presently serves on the Board of Directors of the Finger Lakes Council Boy Scouts of America and the Wayne Community Endowment Advisory Board. He resides in Macedon.

MAUREEN C O'CONNELL (R-I-C)
17th - Part of Nassau County

224 Seventh St, 2nd Fl, Garden City, NY 11530
516-739-5119/fax: 516-228-8044

Maureen O'Connell was elected to the Assembly in a February 1998 special election. She graduated in 1971 from the Flushing Hospital and Medical Center School of Nursing; she then designed and implemented a home-based system for the management of oncology patients at the North Shore University Hospital, where she worked from 1971 to 1985. She also co-authored numerous articles on hospice care. In 1984, Ms O'Connell graduated from St Joseph's College in Patchogue, New York, with a BS degree in Health Care Administration; she received her JD from St John's University School of Law. She practiced law in the areas of civil litigation, elder law, and health regulatory compliance in what was then the second largest law firm in Nassau County. From 1991 to 1998 she served as Trustee/Deputy Mayor of the Village of East Williston. She is a member of the Nassau County Bar Association, the Medical-Legal and Elder Law Committees, and the Oncology Nursing Society; and has also served Nassau County as a member of the Mercy League of Roslyn and the Willistons, and the American Cancer Society Breast Cancer Detection Team. A lifelong resident of Nassau County, she lives in East Williston.

DANIEL J O'DONNELL (D-WF)
69th - Part of New York County

245 West 104th St, New York, NY 10025
212-866-3970/fax: 212-864-1095

Daniel J O'Donnell was first elected to the New York State Assembly in November 2002. He holds a BA in Public Affairs from George Washington University and a law degree from CUNY Law School. Prior to his election, he opened his own public-interest law firm, a community practice that includes representation of tenants and civil rights cases ranging from employment discrimination to First Amendment Issues. He is a founding member of the New York City Chapter of Citizen Action and the Morningside Heights Historic District Committee. He has held leadership roles as the former chair of the Community Board 9 Housing and Land Use Committee. Born in Queens, he has resided in Morningside Heights for more than a decade.

Thomas F O'Mara (R)
137th - Chemung County and parts of Schyler and Tioga County

333 E Water St, 3rd Fl, Ste 301, Elmira, NY 14901
607-732-3500

Thomas F. O'Mara was elected to the New York State Assembly in 2004. He holds a BA degree from the Catholic University of America and a JD degree from Syracuse University School of Law. A former Chemung County District Attorney, he has also served as Chemung County Attorney, Assistant District Attorney in both the New York County and Chemung County District Attorney's Office, and counsel to the Chemung County Industrial Development Agency. Active in his community, Assemblyman O'Mara is a member of the Southern Tier Economic Growth Board of Directors, Southern Tier Organization to Reform Medicaid, Schuyler County Partnership for Economic Development, and the New York State Judicial Screening Committee for Chemung County. He is also a member and Secretary of the St. Joseph's Hospital (Elmira) Board and a Trustee of the Horseheads Free Library. A native of Chemung County, Mr O'Mara presently lives in Horseheads.

FELIX W ORTIZ (D-I-L-WF)
51st - Part of Kings County

404 55th Street, Brooklyn, NY 11220
718-492-6334/fax: 718-492-6435

Felix Ortiz was elected to the New York State Assembly in November 1994. He graduated from Boricua College in 1983 with a BS degree in Business Administration and received his Master's degree in Public Administration from New York University in 1986. From 1996 to 1998, he served in the US Army and was honorably discharged. Prior to his election to the Assembly, he served as an Administrative Manager in the office of the Bronx Borough President and as a Senior Budget Analyst for the Administration of Criminal Justice in the New York City Mayor's Office. Active in community and political affairs, he served as Democratic District Leader of the 51st Assembly District from 1992 to 1994, a member of Community Board #7, Chair of the Public Safety Committee, President of the 33rd Street Block Association, and as a member of 72nd Precinct Community Council. Born and raised in Salinas, Puerto Rico, he moved to New York City in 1980.

GEORGE CHRISTIAN ORTLOFF (R-I-C)
114th - Clinton & Franklin Counties and part of Essex County

176 US Oval, Suite 1000, Plattsburgh, NY 12903
518- 562-1986/fax: 518-563-8970

North Country Community College, 75 Williams St,
Reshetkina Hall, Malone NY 12953
518-483-9930/fax: 518-483-8599

George Christian Ortloff was elected to the New York State Assembly in a special election in February 1986. He earned his BS degree from Rensselaer Polytechnic Institute in 1969 and his MA degree in Journalism and Political Science from the University of Michigan in 1975. He also studied at the University of California at Berkeley, Solano Community College, and the Defense Language Institute. He served in the US Air Force from 1970 to 1973. A career journalist, he covered the Apollo and Skylab manned space programs for National Public Radio in the mid 1970s; he has worked in newspapers, radio, and as Managing Editor of WPTZ-TV news in Plattsburgh (1981-1985). Mr Ortloff has written two books, *Lake Placid: The Olympic Years, 1932-1980*, and *A Lady in the Lake*. He has won four New York State Broadcasters Association awards, two Detroit Press Club Association awards, and a New York State Publishers Association award. In 1977 he was elected Village Trustee in Lake Placid, later becoming a county committeeman until, in 1981, he was appointed District Field Assistant for Congressman David O'B Martin. Active in sports, he was Chief of Ceremonies and Awards for the XIII Olympic Winter Games at Lake Placid. Born in Lake Placid, he currently resides in Plattsburgh.

WILLIAM L PARMENT (D-I)
150th - Part of Chautauqua County

Hotel Jamestown Bldg, Rm 809, Jamestown, NY 14701
716-664-7773/716-672-7050 (North County)/fax: 716-483-0299

William L Parment was first elected to the New York State Assembly in 1982. He graduated from Jamestown Community College, received an AAS degree from State University Agricultural and Technical College in Farmingdale, and a BS degree from SUNY New Paltz. After graduating from college, he worked as a civil technician in the construction industry and as a facilities planner for the state university. For twelve years, he was employed by Chautauqua County, first as a planner, then as Deputy Director of Planning and Development. For six years, he was employed as Director of Public Works. His other government activities include former membership on the County Board of Health, several years of service on the Southern Tier West Regional Planning Board, and membership on the Chatauqua County Charter Commission. Mr Parmenter is a sixth-generation Chatauqua County native.

AMY R PAULIN (D-I-WF)
88th - Part of Westchester County

700 White Plains Road, Suite 252, Scarsdale, NY 10583
914-723-1115/fax: 914-723-2665

Amy Paulin was first elected to the New York State Assembly in November 2000. She earned a Master's degree in Criminal Justice from the State University of New York at Albany. Prior to joining the Assembly, she served for four years (1995-1999) as a Scarsdale village trustee. She is a founder and former Chair of the Westchester Women's Agenda, and she helped establish a Human Rights Commission and a Domestic Violence Council. She served as President of the Westchester League of Women Voters from 1992 to 1995, and also served as Vice President of the League of Women Voters of New York State, where she was in charge of the League's issue advocacy. She is currently active in the Westchester chapter of New Yorkers Against Gun Violence, the Scarsdale Arts Council, the Westchester County Legislative Committee on Families, the Westchester Children's Association and the Westchester AIDS Council. She now lives in Scarsdale.

CRYSTAL D PEOPLES (D-I-L)
141st - Part of Erie County

792 E Delavan Ave, Buffalo, NY 14215
716-897-9714/fax: 716-897-1154

Crystal Davis Peoples was first elected to the New York State Assembly in November 2002. She received a Bachelor of Science in Elementary Education and Master's Degree in Student Personnel Administration from Buffalo State College. Prior to her election to the Assembly, she was the 7th District Erie County Legislator from 1993 to 2002; she was Majority Leader and Chairperson of the Legislature's Finance Committee for five of the nine years she was in office. She sponsored public education campaigns that addressed social ills, housing and economic development; she also played an integral role in the inter-governmental economic-development collaboration that brought a food market to an area where over 113,000 people had no immediate access to fresh meats, fruits, or vegetables. She is a lifelong resident of the city.

JOSE R PERALTA (D-WF)
39th - Part of Queens County

82-11 37th Ave, Jackson Heights, NY 11372
718-458-5367/fax: 718-458-0855

Jose Peralta was first elected to the New York State Assembly in November 2002. He graduated from Queens College, where he was the first Latino Student Body President and also represented over 200,000 students within the CUNY system as a member of the University Student Senate. Before coming to the State Assembly, he served as a community liaison for Assemblyman Brian McLaughlin. He was subsequently Director of the Commission on the Dignity for Immigrants at the New York City Labor Council, representing over 1.5 million immigrants. The Commission is a partnership between the labor unions and the Archdiocese of New York. He is a member of the Northside Democratic Club, the New Century Democratic Club, the JFK Democratic Club, the Dominican American Society, the Gran Alliance of Queens, the Dominican American Hispanic Congress, Community Board 3, and the Inter-American Political and Civic Parliament.

N NICKOLAS PERRY (D-WF)
58th - Part of Kings County

903 Utica Avenue, Brooklyn, NY 11203
718-385-3336/fax: 718-385-3339

N Nick Perry was elected to the New York State Assembly in 1992. Born in Jamaica, he moved to the United States in 1971. Drafted into the US Army in 1972, he was on active duty for two years and on inactive reserve until 1978. He attended Brooklyn College, where he earned a BA in political science and later an MA in Public Policy and Administration. He worked as a volunteer in several political campaigns, and in 1983 he was appointed a member of Community Board 17. He was unsuccessful in two bids for District Leader, but he served during this period as a member of the Executive Board of the 67th Police Precinct Community Council and as a director of the Flatbush East Community Development Corp. In 1988 he was elected Chairman of Community Board #17 (after having served one term as Second Vice-Chairman), and he also became a member of the Brooklyn Borough Board. He is a life member of Disabled American Veterans, and a former member of the Board of Directors of Nazareth Regional High School, Caribbean Action.

AUDREY I PHEFFER (D-L-WF)
23rd - Part of Queens County

108-14 Crossbay Blvd, Ozone Park, NY 11417
718-641-8755/fax: 718-945-9549

90-16 Rockaway Beach Blvd, Rockaway Beach, NY 11693
718-945-9550/fax: 718-945-9549

Audrey Pheffer was first elected to the New York State Assembly in a special election on April 28, 1987. She graduated cum laude from Queens College of the City of New York in 1982. Her community involvement spans four decades. In 1963 she joined the Association for the Help of Retarded Children (AHRC)-Rockaway Auxiliary. From 1973 to 1977, she worked at the Rockaway Occupational Training Center where she advocated for special education and job placement for the mentally disabled. In 1977 she joined the New York City Commission on Human Rights-Neighborhood Stabilization Program and was promoted to the position of Acting Director of the Far Rockaway Office. In 1980 she served as Executive Assistant to State Senator Jeremy S Weinstein, and in 1986 she joined the staff of New York City Council President Andrew Stein as a Special Assistant. In 1982 she was elected Democratic State Committeewoman and a year later she was elected District Leader.

ADAM CLAYTON POWELL, IV (D-L-WF)
68th - Part of New York County

107 East 116th Street, New York, NY 10029
212-828-3953/fax: 212-828-2807

Adam Clayton Powell IV was first elected to the New York State Assembly in November 2000. Born in Puerto Rico, he graduated from Howard University and earned a law degree from the Fordham University School of Law. From 1992 to 1997 he served on the New York City Council representing East Harlem and parts of the Upper West Side and South Bronx. He has served as Assistant District Attorney in the Bronx. He has formed coalitions for the Federal Emergency Management Agency (FEMA) to bring order and hope to communities decimated by natural disasters; in 1998 he went to Puerto Rico and spent four months there helping victims of Hurricane George. He has appeared on a variety of television programs as a commentator on civil and political rights. He is bi-cultural and bi-lingual and uses his African American and Latino heritages to bring further parity to those communities. He currently is a member of the National Black Leadership Commission on AIDS and the Harlem Chapter of the American Red Cross.

JAMES GARY PRETLOW (D-I-WF)
87th - Part of Westchester County

48 North Broadway, Yonkers, NY 10701
914-375-0456

6 Gramatan Ave, Mount Vernon, NY 10550
914-667-0127/fax: 914-667-0209

J Gary Pretlow was elected to the New York State Assembly in 1992. He earned a BA degree in Business Administration from Baruch College in 1972, and he is a licensed stockbroker and insurance agent. Before entering politics, he was the manager of Accounting for Bloomingdales Department Store. In 1980 he joined The Limited, a national retail company, as the Assistant Controller, and in 1985 started a partnership, Moncur-Pretlow & Company, a financial-planning and management-consulting firm. He was elected to the Mount Vernon City Council and served until his election to the Assembly. He is a member of the Association of Black & Puerto Rican Legislators and the New York State Senate and Assembly Hispanic Task Force, and he has received numerous awards for his outstanding civic service.

JACK QUINN (R)
146th - Part of Erie County

3812 South Park Ave, Blasdell, NY 14219
716-826-1878

Jack Quinn was elected to the State Assembly in 2004. He earned a BA from Siena College and a JD from University at the Buffalo Law School, where he graduated with honors. While in law school, he worked at various law firms in the Buffalo and Washington, DC, areas, researching and writing on a variety of issues including labor, the environment, crime, and the military. In addition, Assemblyman Quinn interned in the Washington, DC, office of Congressman James Walsh, where he focused on constituent, lobbyist, and citizen action relations. He served with the New York State Office of Science, Technology, and Academic Research and then joined the Erie County District Attorney's office as a prosecutor. As an Assistant

District Attorney, he brought numerous criminals to justice, garnering an impressive record of convictions in Buffalo's city courts. Active within his community, Assemblyman Quinn is a member of the St. Francis High School Alumni Association, the University at Buffalo Law School Alumni Association, and the Erie County and the New York State Bar Associations. A lifelong resident of Erie County, he currently resides in Hamburg, NY.

ANN G RABBIT (R)
97th - Parts of Orange and Rockland Counties

41 High St, Goshen, NY 10924
845-291-3631

Annie Rabbitt was elected to the New York State Assembly in 2004. A third-generation woman business owner, Assemblywoman Rabbitt owns O'Hare's Pub in Greenwood Lake and is the Past President of the Greenwood Lake Chamber of Commerce. She is also a member of the Restaurant, Bar & Tavern Association. She brings a wealth of local government experience to the Assembly: She has served as the Deputy Supervisor of the Town of Warwick since 2003, and she also served as both a Village Trustee and as Deputy Mayor, where she was responsible for the Department of Public Works. She organized a Home Owners Association to improve Greenwood Lake and worked to establish a Bi-State Commission to fund and regulate cleanup of the lake. She has been recognized for her dedication to serving her community, receiving the Outstanding Citizen Achievement Award in 1998 from the Orange County Chamber of Commerce as well as the New York State Woman of Distinction Award from the New York State Senate. In the Assembly her concerns are for better education and increased communication between local and state governments. She resides in Greenwood.

ANDREW P RAIA (R-C)
9th - Part of Suffolk County

75 Woodbine Ave, Northport, NY 11768
631-261-4151/fax: 631-261-2992

Andrew P Raia was first elected to the New York state Assembly in November 2002. He received a BA from SUNY at New Paltz. Prior to his election to the Assembly, he served as the Chief of Staff to Suffolk County Legislator Allan Binder. He had also worked in the offices of New York State Assemblymen John C Cochrane and John Behan, and New York State Senator Carl Marcellino, and New York State Senate Majority Leader Ralph Marino. In the Assembly he serves as the Ranking Minority Member on the Aging Committee. Mr Raia serves on the Executive Boards of the Huntington Boys and Girls Club, the Huntington Freedom Center, the Huntington Station Enrichment Center, and Perspectives on Youth. He is also a member of both the Huntington and the East Northport Chambers of Commerce.

PHILIP R RAMOS (D-WF)
6th - Part of Suffolk County

1010 Suffolk Ave, Brentwood, NY 11717
631-435-3214/fax: 631-435-3239

Phil Ramos was first elected to the New York State Assembly in November 2002. He began his working career as a therapy aid and Emergency Medical Technician. In 1979 he joined the Suffolk County Police Department and worked an undercover officer in the

Narcotics Unit before being promoted to detective. He joined with other Latino police officers to found the Suffolk County Police Hispanic Society; in 1993 he was elected the Society's president. He also worked with the Long Island Guardians to create a mentoring program for Latino police officers to serve as role models for Latino and African American children. Ramos was born in the Bronx and is a lifelong resident of New York.

WILLIAM REILICH (R-C-I)
134th - Part of Monroe County

2300 W Ridge Rd, Rochester, NY 14626
585-225-4190/fax: 585-225-6502

Bill Reilich was first elected to the New York State Assembly in 2002. His district includes the towns of Greece, Ogden, and Sweden in Monroe County. A businessman, he is the former owner of the Reilich Corporation, which he founded in 1975 as Upstate Alarm. Prior to joining the Assembly, he served as a member of the Greece Chamber of Commerce and as a Captain of the Marine Volunteer Fire Department. From 1997 to 2002, he was a Monroe County Legislator, serving as Chairman of the Ways and Means Committee and as Vice Chairman of the Intergovernmental Relations Committee. He lives with his family in Greece.

ROBERT B REILLY (D)
109th - Parts of Albany and Suffolk Counties

5 Halfmoon Executive Park Dr, Clifton Park, NY 12085
518-371-0568

Robert P. Reilly was elected to the New York State Assembly in 2004. He received his BA from Notre Dame and his Master's from the College of Saint Rose; he completed all coursework for a PhD at Rensselaer Polytechnic Institute. He is chairman and CEO of Technofuture Enterprises Inc and 30-year owner of the Partridge Pub. He has taught in both public and private schools and also taught a stint in East Africa. He also served as director of the NYS Public Broadcasting Office for the State Education Department. A devoted runner, he was a cross country track coach at Siena College for seventeen years. Before election to the State Assembly, he was an Albany County Legislator, where he was the major force behind adoption of a new County Charter. He also initiated and chaired the OTB Committee, which eventually led to needed OTB reform. He has been president of the Shaker Heritage Society, and he has been a member of the National Erie Canal Commission, the Mohawk Valley Heritage Corridor Commission, Albany County Alternatives to Incarceration, and the Region 4 Fish and Wildlife Management Board. He resides in Latham.

JOSE RIVERA (D-L)
78th - Part of Bronx County

2488 Grand Concourse, Room 416, Bronx, NY 10458
718-933-2204/fax: 718-993-2535

Jose Rivera was first elected to the New York State Assembly in 1982. He served for five years, after which he left office and was re-elected in 2000. Born in La Perla, Puerto Rico he was educated in the public schools of New York and hardened in the steel plants of Brooklyn. He has devoted his life to helping the people of the Bronx in their struggle for jobs, better housing and social justice. In 1975, he founded the United Tremont Trades and secured jobs for Latino,

Biographies

African-Medallion Taxicab Industry and the "Bodegueros" of New York, and also sponsored the 12% Construction Set-Aside Bill for minority contractors. In 1980, the attention of the entire world focused on the South Bronx, through Rivera's now legendary People's Convention on Charlotte Street. From 1982 to 1987 in the Assembly, he was Treasurer, Vice Chair and eventually Chairman of the Black and Puerto Rican Caucus. He was instrumental in helping to establish the Martin Luther King holiday in the state of New York. In 1987 he became a Council Member for the 15th District in the Bronx. In this capacity, he was the President of the Black and Latino Caucus of the City Council and Chairman of the Council's Civil Service and Labor Committee and State and Federal Legislation Committee. He also served on the Governmental Operations and Health Committees. In November 2000 he was re-elected to the New York State Assembly by a huge margin. He is on the Board of The Puerto Rican/Hispanic Task Force and the Black and Puerto Rican/Hispanic Legislative Caucus. His daughter, Naomi Rivera, was elected to the Assembly in 2004.

NAOMI RIVERA (D)
80th - Part of Bronx County

Legislative Office Building 530, Albany, NY 12248
518-455-5844

Naomi Rivera was elected to the New York State Assembly in 2004. She had a ten-year career in accounting with large multinational corporations such as Sumitomo before she turned to public service. As Director of Special Events for the Bronx Borough President's Office, she managed the borough's cultural affairs, developing new events such as the Bronx Food and Art Festival and the Puerto Rican Film Festival. She also produced the borough's annual ethnic pride celebrations. More recently, she served as the Deputy Chief Clerk of the Bronx Board of Elections. She is the co-chair of the Bronx Domestic Violence Advisory Council. She is the creator of "DiVA" (Domestic Violence Awareness), a campaign designed to maximize community outreach through special events. Strongly committed to the arts in children's education, she collaborated with the "VH1 Save the Music Foundation" and other organizations to ensure that Bronx schools were the recipients of musical instruments. She also served as Founder and Executive Director of the Children's Traveling Theater Project. She and her husband, Antonio Rodriguez, reside in the Morris Park section of the Bronx.

PETER M RIVERA (D)
76th - Part of Bronx County

1262 Castle Hill Ave, Bronx, NY 10462
718-931-2620/fax: 718-931-2915

Peter Rivera was elected to the New York State Assembly in 1992. Born in Ponce, Puerto Rico, he migrated to New York City at an early age. He earned a BA degree in Business Administration from Pace College in 1968 and a JD degree from St John's Law School in 1974. His career in public service began in the late 1960s as a police officer in the South Bronx. He rose to the rank of detective, and then became a federal agent with the DEA. Upon graduating from law school, he joined the Bronx District Attorney's Office, working as an Assistant District Attorney in the Homicide Bureau. Since 1978 he has practiced law privately. In the Assembly, he is Chairman of the Puerto Rican/Hispanic Task force. Mr Rivera has served on the Mayor's Committee on City Marshals, the Gateway National Recreation Area Commission, the Spanish Progress Foundation, El Comite

de la Providencia, the Governor's Committee on the Judiciary, and the Board of Directors of OTB.

ANNETTE M ROBINSON (D-WF)
56th - Part of Kings County

1360 Fulton Street, Rm 417, Brooklyn, NY 11216
718-399-7630/fax: 718-399-7690

Annette M Robinson was elected to the New York State Assembly in a special election in February 2002. She received both her BS and Master's Degree from New Hampshire College. She has devoted most of her life to community affairs. In 1977, she was elected as a member of the Community School Board of District 16, a post she held for three terms. She served as Coordinator and Liaison for former NYC Comptroller Harrison J. Goldin, and after six years of service, she became District Director for US Congressman Major R. Owens. She was elected to the New York City Council in 1991. As the representative of the 36th Council District, she served as chairperson of the Subcommittee on Juvenile Justice. In the Assembly, Ms Robinson is a District Leader/State Committeewoman for her District and has served as the Vice-Chairperson of the New York State Council of Black Elected Democrats. She is also a national speaker on religious, cultural, and political issues, appearing on the Ricky Lake Show and numerous times on NYI BCAT Cable Television, and various radio stations. Born in Harlem and raised in Brooklyn, she is a lifelong resident of New York.

JOSEPH S SALADINO (R-C-I)
12th - Part of Nassau County

200 Boundary Avenue, Massapequa, NY 11758
516-844-0635/fax: 516-844-0364

Assemblyman Joseph Saladino was elected in a special election held in March 2004. He studied at Tulane University and holds undergraduate and Masters degrees from New York Institute of Technology. He brings sixteen years of government experience to the Assembly. Most recently, he was the Director of Operations for the Town of Oyster Bay and formerly served as Executive Assistant for the Town of Hempstead. Previously he had a career in broadcast journalism, working as a news anchor and broadcaster for some of Long Island's largest television and radio stations. He also worked with an engineering firm where he learned many aspects of civil construction and environmental engineering. He has been a member of the Massapequa Kiwanis Club for sixteen years, where he has served as President and has received the distinguished award of "Kiwanian of the Year." He is also a member of the Sons of Italy-Columbus Lodge, a former trustee of the Massapequa Historical Society, and co-founder of the Massapequa Anti-Graffiti Involvement Committee. Assemblyman Saladino has presented lectures to youth and community groups concerning conservation, catch and release fishing techniques, the proper disposal of pollutants, and protecting and conserving our potable ground water supply. He has been instrumental in providing video programs, radio talk shows and newspaper articles about Long Island's aquifer and has taken a lead role in protecting it. He is a lifelong resident of Massapequa.

STEVEN SANDERS (D-L-WF)
74th - Part of New York County

201 East 16th Street, 4th Fl, New York, NY 10003
212-979-9696/fax: 212-979-0594

250 Broadway, Rm 2234, New York, NY 10007
212-319-1464/fax: 212-312-1479

Steven Sanders was first elected to the New York State Assembly in a special election in February 1978. He graduated from City College with a degree in Government in 1973. Before his election to the State Assembly, he served as president of the Stuyvesant Town Tenants Association. In the Assembly, he has long championed educational reform and tenants' and civil rights. As Chairman of the Assembly's Committee on Education, much of his work has involved advocacy for equitable funding for school districts and reforms that support educational quality. He helped negotiate an agreement with Mayor Bloomberg in June 2002 to dramatically restructure the governance of New York City's Board of Education. Mr Sanders is a leading advocate for tenants, seniors and persons with disabilities and has a highly distinguished legislative and community record of accomplishment in these areas. He was a prime sponsor of the State's Hate Crimes Law, is an ardent and vocal defender of women's reproductive freedom, and a proponent of enhanced services, including housing, for people with AIDS. He is the pre-eminent legislator advocating for improved health care and appropriate educational programs for the deaf, deaf-blind and hard of hearing. He has been honored by many organizations, including the New York Civil Liberties Union, the United Jewish Appeal, and Common Cause, which made him its first ever "Ethical Legislator of the Year." He is a lifelong resident of New York City.

TERESA R SAYWARD (R)
113th - Hamilton & Warren Counties, most of Essex County & part of Saratoga County

7559 Court St, Rm 203, PO Box 217, Elizabethtown, NY 12932
518-873-3803

21 Bay St, Ste 206, Glens Falls, NY 12801
518-792-4546/fax: 518-792-5584

Teresa R Sayward was first elected to the New York State Assembly in November 2002. Prior to her election, she served as Town Supervisor in Willsboro, NY. She served on the Board of Supervisors for Essex County for eleven years and as chairwoman for two years. Ms Sayward served as chairwoman of the Inter-Governmental Affairs Committee at New York State Association of Counties, the North County Advisory Council for the New York State Division for Women, and the Essex County Board of Supervisors' Legislative Committee, and in that role served as the lobbyist in Albany for Essex County. She also served as chairwoman of Willsboro's Zoning Board of Appeals. Assemblywoman Sayward served as director on the Adirondack Association of Towns and Villages, director on the Plattsburgh North County Regional Chamber of Commerce, a member of the Board of Directors of the Smith House Health Care Center, a member on the Board of Directors for Cornell Cooperative Extension Soil and Water Conservation District and a member of the Adirondack North County Association. Ms Sayward was born in Willsboro and is a lifelong resident of New York.

WILLIAM D SCARBOROUGH (D-L-WF)
29th - Part of Queens County

114-52A Merrick Blvd, St Albans, NY 11434
718-657-5312/fax: 718-657-7365

William Scarborough was first elected to the New York State Assembly in 1994. He holds a BA degree in Psychology and Political Science from Queens College of the City University of New York, His political career began when he was elected to Community School Board #28. In that post, he shared responsibility for over twenty-two elementary and middle schools with a budget of approximately $30 million. He was also District Manager of Community Board 12, where he coordinated and monitored the delivery of municipal services to residents of the Community Board. During his tenure as District Manager, he was also Chairman of the Board's Human Services Cabinet, increasing the availability of primary health care in the area. He served as Chairman of Area Policy Board 12 and was a member from 1983 to 1994. In the Assembly, Mr Scarborough has focused his efforts in the areas of health care, education, and youth services. He has funded and sponsored many education and youth programs. He also was a sponsor of bills protecting HMO customers, a bill to create a permanent summer jobs program, bills increasing penalties for child abuse, and bills reducing air and noise pollution around New York City's two major airports. He was raised in Jamaica, Queens, and has since lived in St Albans and Rosedale.

ROBIN L SCHIMMINGER (D-I-C)
140th - Parts of Erie & Niagara Counties

3514 Delaware Ave, Ste 201, Kenmore, NY 14217
716-873-2540/fax: 716-873-5675

Robin Schimminger was elected to the New York State Assembly in 1976. He earned a BA degree from Canisius College in Buffalo and also studied at Ireland's William Butler Yeats International School of Literature and the University College, Dublin. He received his JD degree from New York University Law School. Before joining the Assembly, he was twice elected to the Erie County Legislature, in 1973 and 1975; there he served as Chairman of the Public Health Commission. In the Assembly, he was named the first chairman of the new Assembly Standing Committee on Small Business in 1985 and continued to serve until 1997, at which time he was named to chair the Assembly Standing Committee on Economic Development, Job Creation, Commerce and Industry. Among his legislative accomplishments is his Omnibus Procurement Act, which maximizes the opportunity for in-state firms to do business with New York State. His Linked Deposit Program, a low-interest loan program for small and medium sized businesses has been singled out for national recognition by the Small Business Administration. He has also been active in other areas such as toxic waste and teenage driving and alcohol programs. He has served on the boards of numerous civic, community, educational, and cultural organizations. He is a co-founder of the Buffalo Dortmund Sister City Committee and is on the Board of Directors of Junior of Western New York. Born in North Tonawanda, New York, he now lives in Kenmore, New York.

MARK J F SCHROEDER (D-L-WF)
145th - Part of Erie County

Legislative Office Building, Rm 323, Albany, NY 12248
518-455-4691

Mark Schroeder was elected to the New York State Assembly in 2004. He holds a Bachelor's Degree from Empire State College. Prior to joining the Assembly, he served for three years on the Erie

County Legislature, during which time he amassed a number of accomplishments. He started the South Buffalo Education Center, which offers free GED and computer classes. To date more than 90 students have earned their G.E.D at the school and more than 700 have completed the computer training. The school also has the highest graduation and retention rates of any G.E.D. school in the county. He also started The Greater South Buffalo Chamber of Commerce, which now has more than 150 members, and he spearheaded the Seneca Street Redevelopment Project, a multi-million dollar project that will completely remake the strip. An avid runner, Schroeder has run several marathons, including the 1999 Dublin, Ireland Marathon, where he raised more than $3,000 for the Sisters of Mercy. He grew up and now lives in South Buffalo.

DIERDRE K SCOZZAFAVA (R-C)
122nd - Lewis County and parts of Jefferson, Oswego & St Lawrence Counties

93 East Main St, Gouverneur, NY 13642
315-287-2384/fax: 315-287-2895

Dierdre "Dede" Scozzafava was first elected to the New York State Assembly in 1998. She holds a BS degree from Boston University School of Management and a Masters in Business Administration from Clarkson Graduate School of Management. She is an investment adviser for RBC Dain Ruasher Inc in Watertown, New York. Prior to her election to the Assembly, Ms Scozzafava served as a Village of Gouverneur Trustee for four years and as Mayor of the Village of Gouverneur from 1993 until her election to the Assembly. As Mayor, she carried the town budget from a deficit to a positive fund balance while also creating the Gouverneur Area Microenterprise Revolving Loan Fund to stimulate local job growth. In the Assembly, she was appointed Ranking Member of the Local Governments Committee. She served on the Task Force on Education Standards and the Nursing Shortage Task Force. She is also an active member of the First United Methodist Church, having served as chairperson of the Board of Trustees. In addition, she is a member of the Gouverneur Business Women and an associate member of the Gouverneur Arts Club. She was also President of the St Lawrence County Mayors Association. Assemblywoman Scozzafava was born in Buffalo and is a lifelong resident of New York.

FRANK R SEDDIO (D-I)
59th - Part of Kings County

2424 Ralph Ave, Brooklyn, NY 11234-5517
718-968-2770/fax: 718-968-2773

Frank Seddio was first elected to the New York State Assembly in 1998. He attended Brooklyn College and is a graduate of St John's University School of Law. He began his professional career as a member of the New York Police Department, first as Operations officer and then as Community Affairs Officer for Brooklyn South, the police borough headquarters. Starting in 1985, he served in the NYC Department of Transportation as Director of the Transportation Intelligence Division, Assistant Commissioner for Enforcement, and First Assistant Commissioner, before retiring in 1991 to begin a private law practice. He also served as District Manager of Community Board 18 from 1980 to 1985, then as Chairman of CB 18 in 1995 to 1998. He currently serves as a legal counsel to and member of the West Indian American Day Carnival Association. Involved in civic affairs for over thirty years, he has served as the grand knight of the St Pius X Council Knights of Columbus, founding member and first

elected president of the Canarsie Volunteer Ambulance Corps, member of the board of Canarsie AWARE, president of the Thomas Jefferson Democratic Club, honorary member of the Midget Squadron Yacht Club, member of the Friends United Community Association, and board member of the Canarsie Mental Health Clinic. He is a lifelong resident of Brooklyn.

ANTHONY S SEMINERIO (D-C)
38th - Part of Queens County

107-05 Jamaica Ave, Richmond Hill, NY 11418
718-847-0770/fax: 718-847-9346

68-28 Myrtle Ave, Glendale, NY 11385
718-366-6725/fax: 718-336-6751

Anthony Seminerio was elected to the New York State Assembly in 1978. He holds a BS degree from the New York State Institute of Technology. Prior to his election to the Assembly, he served as a Corrections Officer in the New York City Corrections System. In 1972 he was elected to serve as a union executive board member for the Corrections Officers Benevolent Association. He served as a collective bargaining negotiator for members of the Department of Correction with the City of New York. He was also a Founder and Treasurer of the New York State Peace Officers Association. He is involved in the Holy Name Society of Our Lady of Perpetual Help, the Boy Scouts, the Columbia Association of the Department of Corrections, and the New York State PTA. He has received awards that include the Man of the Year from the Crime Victims Political Platform and the Queens Soccer Club, and achievement awards from the Long Island Correctional Association, the Columbia Association of Corrections Officers, and the Forest Park Senior Center. He is a talk radio show host on WABC in New York and a part-time actor.

SHELDON SILVER (D-L-WF)
64th - Part of New York County

250 Broadway, Suite 2307, New York, NY 10007
212-312-1420/fax: 212-312-1425

Sheldon Silver was elected to the New York State Assembly in 1976. He is a graduate of Yeshiva University and Brooklyn Law School. In 1968, he began his professional career with the New York City law firm of Schecter and Schwartz. In 1971, Mr Silver was appointed Law Secretary to Civil Court Judge Francis N Pecora, a position he held until 1976. Assemblyman Silver has served as Speaker of the Assembly since 1994. From the outset, he has made education the hallmark of his tenure as speaker. His comprehensive education initiative, LADDER (Learning, Achieving, Developing by Directing Educational Resources), has emphasized standards and the importance of early childhood learning to educational success. Through LADDER, New York State has established the first pre-kindergarten program for all four-year olds in the nation. The program has also targeted resources at reducing class size and making necessary school infrastructure repairs to ensure classroom facilities that meet 21st century educational needs. In working to adopt his first state budget as speaker in 1994, he succeeded in winning critical funding for education and health care programs. Other significant achievements include his major victory over efforts to end rent control in 1997, in which Speaker Silver saved thousands of middle-class families in the New York City Metropolitan region from losing their homes, and his success in restoring vital funding for the state's breast cancer mapping program in the 1998 state budget. The Speaker's public service career has been marked by numerous awards and honors, including the United Jewish Appeal Citation for his humanitarian efforts, the Legislator of the Year Award from the Environmental Planning Lobby and the Distinguished Public Service Award by the Federation of Jewish Philanthropies. Speaker Silver also was the recipient of the first annual Chinese Journalist Association's Award and has been recognized for his outstanding legislative record by the Lower Manhattan Loft Tenants and the Greater New York Hospital Association, and received the Distinguished Lawmaker of the Year Award from the Long Island Breast Cancer Action Coalition.

WILLIS H STEPHENS, JR (R-I-C)
99th - Parts of Putnam, Dutchess and Westchester Counties

DBS Gov't Center Bldg 2, 110 Old Rte 6, Carmel, NY 10512
845-225-5038/fax: 914-225-5160

Willis Stephens was first elected to the Assembly in 1995. In 1997 he received a BA degree from Cornell University, where he studied government and politics, and he earned a JD degree in 1980 from St John's University of Law. He is a member of the law firm of Stephens and Charbonneau in Brewster, New York. He served as counsel to the Town of Southeast and as a member of the Charter Revision Commission of Westchester County. In 1985 he was appointed Assistant Counsel to Senate Majority Leader Warren M Anderson. After Senator Anderson's retirement in 1987, he was reappointed by former Majority Leader of the Senate, Ralph J Marion. He advised the Senate Majority in the areas of transportation and environmental law, contributing to passage of the Clean Air Act implementing legislation, the recodification of the DWI laws, and a $21 billion financing package for transportation. He is a member of the Board of Directors of the Putnam Hospital Center Foundation, Ronald McDonald House at the Maria Fareri Children's Hospital, and a former advisory committee member of the Board of Trustees of Trinity-Pawling School in Pawling. Born in Mount Kisco, he resides in Brewster, New York.

SCOTT M STRINGER (D-L-WF)
67th - Part of New York County

230 West 72nd Street, Ste 2F, New York, NY 10023
212-873-6368/fax: 212-873-6520

Scott Stringer was elected to the New York State Assembly in November 1992. He received a BA degree in Government Studies from John Jay College. Prior to his election, he spent eight years in the office of Assemblyman Jerry Nadler, beginning as a constituent worker and eventually serving as housing coordinator and then chief of staff. Among his notable accomplishments in the Assembly are laws to protect victims of domestic abuse. In 1994 his bill to mandate that police officers serve orders of protection to battered women was signed into law. He also authored the bill banning insurance discrimination against victims of domestic violence, which became law in 1996. His law to allow battered women work release when their crimes were committed under abusive duress became law in 2002. In 2003 Speaker Sheldon Silver appointed him Chair of the Cities Committee.

ROBERT K SWEENEY (D-I-WF)
11th - Part of Suffolk County

270-B N Wellwood Ave, Lindenhurst, NY 11757-3708
631-957-2087/fax: 516-957-2998

Robert Sweeney was elected to the New York State Assembly in a special election in March 1988. A graduate of Adelphi University, he earned his Master's degree in Public Administration at CW Post. Prior to his election to the Assembly, Mr Sweeney served as Lindenhurst Village Clerk for fourteen years, during which time he received his designation as a Certified Municipal Clerk (CMC), held by less than five percent of all municipal clerks in New York State. He is also a former president of the New York State Association of City and Village Clerks. In the Assembly, he has been actively involved in health care, authoring legislation dealing with health insurance and care for diabetes. In 1993 he was elected to the Board of Directors of the American Diabetes Association, Long Island Chapter, and in 1995 he received the National Public Policy Leadership Award from the American Diabetes Association. He sponsored boating safety legislation and he worked to expand the law on drug-free school zones to include day care centers, Pre-K, and kindergarten programs. A strong supporter of higher education, he received the 1996 Friend of SUNY Award and the 2001 Friend of SUNY Farmingdale Award. In 2005 he was ranked as the second most prolific Assemblyman of 2004, with thirty-one of his bills signed into law during that year. He has served on the Board of Directors of the Literacy Volunteers of America, Suffolk County; as a member of the advisory board of Children and Parents Together, Family Service League of Suffolk County; and on numerous other organizations. He is a lifelong resident of Babylon Town.

JAMES N TEDISCO (R-I-C)
110th - Parts of Schenectady and Saratoga Counties

12 Jay Street, Suite 1, Schenectady, NY 12305
518-370-2812/fax: 518-370-2862

James Tedisco was elected to the New York State Assembly in 1982. He received a graduate degree in Special Education from the College of St Rose following his undergraduate studies in Psychology at Union College. He worked in the field of education from 1973 to 1982; first as guidance counselor, varsity basketball coach and athletic director at Notre Dame-Bishop Gibbons High School in Schenectady; then as special education teacher, resource room instructor and varsity basketball coach at Bethlehem Central High School in Delmar. He also served as a Schenectady City Councilman from 1977 to 1982. Elected at the age of 27, he was, at the time, the youngest City Councilman in Schenectady's history. In the Assembly, he is a member of numerous committees and was elevated in 2002 to the position of Assistant Minority Leader Pro Tempore. He is a member of the Sons of Italy, Schenectady Lodge 321, the Ballston Spa NY Elks Lodge No 2619, the Schenectady Rotary Club, the Union College Alumni Association and Friends of Union Athletics, Schenectady Big Brothers/Big Sisters, and Friends of the Schenectady Museum. He lives in Schenectady.

FRED W THIELE, JR (R-I-WF)
2nd - Part of Suffolk County

2302 Main Street, Box 3062, Bridgehampton, NY 11932
631-537-2583/fax: 516-537-2836

Fred Thiele was elected to the New York State Assembly in a special election in March 1995. He attended Cornell University and in 1976 received a BA degree (summa cum laude) in Political Science and

History from Southampton College of Long Island University. In 1979 he received his law degree from Albany Law School. He served as a counsel to former Assemblyman John L Behan from 1979 to 1982, and from 1982 to 1987 he served as Southampton Town Attorney. He was elected to the Suffolk County Legislature in 1987. As a freshman legislator, he was appointed chairman of the County Legislature's Public Works and Transportation Committee. In 1991 he was elected Southampton Town Supervisor. Upon joining the State Assembly in 1995, he was appointed to the Assembly's Environmental Conservation, Election Law, and Agriculture Committees. In 2004, he served as Ranking Minority Member of the Assembly's Judiciary Committee. He lives in Sag Harbor, New York.

MICHELE R TITUS (D-L-WF)
31st - Part of Queens County

19-31 Mott Avenue, Rm 301, Far Rockaway, NY 11691
718-327-1845/fax: 718-327-1878

Michele Titus was elected to the New York State Assembly in 2002. She received a Bachelor of Arts degree in Political Science from SUNY Binghamton, and a law degree from Albany Law School. She went to work for NY State Senator Ada L Smith as Chief of Staff, and then served as the Executive Director of the New York State Black and Puerto Rican Legislative Caucus. She was an attorney for the New York City Board of Education, where she specialized in special education law. Other legal experiences included the Consumer Frauds Bureau of the NYS Attorney General's office and the Integrity Bureau at the Queens County District Attorney's office. In the Assembly, she has served with the Committees on Children and Families; Codes; Judiciary; Local Governments; Small Businesses, and the Subcommittee on Airports. She is a member of the Black and Puerto Rican Legislative Caucus, the Women's Legislative Caucus, the New York State Puerto Rican/Hispanic Task Force, the council of black elected Officials, and the New York state Trial Lawyers Association. She is a lifelong resident of Queens.

PAUL A TOKASZ (D-I-C-WF)
143rd - Part of Erie County

Gen Donovan State Office Bldg, 125 Main St, Buffalo, NY 14203
716-852-2791/fax: 716-852-2794

Paul Tokasz was first elected to the New York State Assembly in 1983. He received his BA degree in History from Hobart College, and his Master's degree in Education from Buffalo State College in 1968. He has also completed courses in education at Canisius College and course work in business administration at SUNY at Buffalo. Mr Tokasz was an elementary school teacher in the City of Buffalo from 1968 to 1977. He served as Deputy County Clerk in charge of the Erie County Auto Bureau from 1977 to 1986. He also served as Clerk of the Erie County Legislature during 1977. From 1987 to 1998, he was First Deputy County Clerk in the Erie County Clerk's Office. In the State Assembly, he was appointed Majority Leader in January 2001, thereby making him the floor leader responsible for day-to-day operations in the legislative session in the chamber. Mr Tokasz serves on the Fireman's Association of New York State and the Cheektowaga Chamber of Commerce. He has received numerous awards, including the 2000 Golden Trumpet Award from the Firemen's Association of the State of New York, the University of Buffalo Legislative Action Committee Award, and the 1999 William Hoyt Advocacy Award, He has also been recognized by the Environ-

mental Planning Lobby and other organizations for his passionate support of important environmental issues.

PAUL D TONKO (D-L-I-WF)
105th - Montgomery County & part of Schenectady County

Guy Park Manor, 366 West Main Street, Amsterdam, NY 12010
518-843-0227/fax: 518-843-0049

Paul Tonko was first elected to the New York State Assembly in 1983. He attended Clarkson University and graduated with a BS degree in Mechanical and Industrial Engineering. He worked as an engineer for the New York State Dept. of Transportation, as well as on the staff of the Dept. of Public Service, prior to being elected to the Assembly. He was elected to the Montgomery County Board of Supervisors in 1975, and served as chair in 1981. In the Assembly, he has gained a national reputation as an expert and utility issues. He is the author of comprehensive energy legislation that deregulates the electric industry in New York State. Since 1992 he has served as Chairman of the Assembly Standing Committee on Energy. Active in civic affairs, Mr Tonko is a member of the Knights of Columbus Council 209, the BPOE Lodge 101, Kiwanis Club of Amsterdam, the Montgomery County Chamber of Commerce, and the Wildwood Program. He also serves on the Board of Directors for Hispanic Outreach Services, the Horace J Inman Senior Citizens Center, the Montgomery Red Cross, and the Montgomery County Unit of the American Cancer Society. He has received the New York State Conference of Mayors' Legislative Award for his continuing commitment to local government issues.

DARRYL C TOWNS (D-I-L-WF)
54th - Part of Kings County

840 Jamaica Avenue, Brooklyn, NY 11208
718-235-5627/fax: 718-235-5966

Darryl Towns was elected to the New York State Assembly in 1993. He is a 1990 graduate of North Carolina Agricultural & Technical State University with a degree in Economics. Mr Towns served in the United States Air Force. Prior to his election to the Assembly, He was Director of Community Affairs at Interfaith Hospital. In the Assembly, his ANCHOR Program bill, which was unanimously supported in both houses of the Legislature, is aimed at bolstering commercial revitalization in residential communities throughout New York City and supporting increased housing developments. He is Chair of the New York State Assembly Legislative Commission on Science and Technology and Chair of the Subcommittee on Mass Transit. He is a member of the National Black Caucus for State Legislators, New York State Black, Puerto Rican & Hispanic Legislative Caucus, and the New York State Assembly & Senate Hispanic/Puerto Rican Task Force. He lives in Brooklyn.

DAVID R TOWNSEND, JR (R-C-I-WF)
115th - Parts of Oneida & Oswego Counties

4767 State Rte 233, PO Box 597, Westmoreland, NY 13490
315-853-7260/fax: 315-853-4609

David Townsend was first elected to the New York State Assembly in November 1990. In 1966 he joined the Rome Police Department, and the following year, was appointed to the New York State Police. In January 1979 he was appointed a Deputy Sheriff in the Law Enforcement Division of the Oneida County Sheriff's Department. Between January 1982 and April 1989, he worked as an undercover narcotics agent and was assigned to the Federal Drug Enforcement Administration Task Force in Syracuse in 1987. During this time he was elected president of the Oneida County Deputy Sheriffs Benevolent Association and president of the New York State Deputy's Association, positions he held until 1990. In the Assembly, he serves as Minority Whip. He is the only Assembly member since January 1, 1991 to have never missed a vote in the Assembly. He was the recipient of the Federal Teddy Roosevelt Conservation Award in October 1992, and in 1995 he was honored by the Metropolitan Police Conference as Assemblyman of the Year. He resides in the Town of Lee.

HELENE E WEINSTEIN (D-WF)
41st - Part of Kings County

3520 Nostrand Avenue, Brooklyn, NY 11229
718-648-4700/fax: 718-769-4846

Helene Weinstein was first elected to the New York State Assembly in 1980. Ms Weinstein received a Bachelor's degree in Economics from American University and a law degree from the New England School of Law. In the Assembly, she has been a longtime advocate for children and families: she sponsored New York's landmark Family Protection and Violence Intervention Act and the child Support Standards Act. She is a member of the Leadership Council of NYC Chapter of the NYS Alzheimer's Association, the New York State Labor Commissioner's Task Force on Displaced Homemakers, the Brooklyn Women's Political Caucus, the Holocaust Survivors Assn - The Next Generation, the Jewish Women's Leadership Caucus, and the Brooklyn Bar Association; she is also a member of the board of the Center for Women in Government. She has been honored for her outstanding achievements with such awards as the Legislator of the Year Award from NYS Coalition Against Domestic Violence, NYS Bar Association's Howard A. Levine Award, Legislative Leader Award from the Kings Count Council of Jewish War Veterans, and the Margaret Sanger Award presented by Family Planning Advocates.

HARVEY WEISENBERG (D-I-L)
20th - Part of Nassau County

20 West Park Ave, #201, Long Beach, NY 11561
516-431-0500/fax: 516-431-0412

Harvey Weisenberg was elected to the New York State Assembly in a special election in February 1989. He attended Niagara University, graduated from New York University with a BS degree, and received an MS degree from Hofstra University. He also has a Professional Diploma in Administration from CW Post University. A former police officer in Long Beach, Mr Weisenberg has bee involved the field of education for over 20 years as a teacher and an administrator. He was elected to the Long Beach City Council in 1976, and served as president of that body in 1977 and 1980. In the Assembly, he has championed the needs of the disabled, and he is a staunch supporter of anti-drug programs. He chaired the Committee on Alcoholism and Drug Abuse until January of 2001, when Speaker Sheldon Silver appointed him to the post of Deputy Majority Whip. In 2003 he was appointed Assistant Speaker Pro Tempore. He is active in the Lions Club, Kiwanis, the Long Beach Chamber of Commerce, the Nassau County Juvenile Diabetes Foundation, Long Beach Hospital, Long Beach Breast Cancer Coalition, the American Legion, the Association for Help of Retarded Children, the Long Island Arthritis Foundation, the Alliance for the Mentally Ill, the March of Dimes, and the

US Lifeguard Association. He has been honored by by the Federal and State Departments for the innovative drug programs he has created. He lives in Long Beach.

MARK S WEPRIN (D-L-WF)
24th - Part of Queens County

56-21 Marathon Parkway, Little Neck, NY 11362
718-428-7900/fax: 718-428-8575

Mark Weprin was first elected to the New York State Assembly in March 1994 to fill the seat left vacant by the death of his father, Assembly Speaker Saul Weprin. In 1983 he received a BA from SUNY-Albany in 1983 and his JD from Brooklyn Law School in 1983. Between college and law school, he was a public relations executive (1983-1989), then Legislative Representative in the office of former Mayor Edward Koch (1986-1989). After law school he joined the firm of Shea and Gould. In the Assembly he has been a leading advocate for senior citizens as former Chair of the Subcommittee for Outreach and Oversight of Senior Citizens Programs. He is a member of the Hillcrest Jewish Center, the Independence Democratic Club, and the Eastern Queens Democratic Club. Assemblyman Weprin is a leader in the autistic community and has been acknowledged for his commitment with the Guardian Angel Award by the NY Families for Autistic Children and by Family and Friends for Autism Research. He was born and raised in Queens.

SANDRA LEE WIRTH (R-C-RL)
142nd - Parts of Erie & Niagara Counties

5763 Seneca St, Elma, NY 14059
716-675-7170/fax: 716-675-1608

Sandra Lee Wirth was elected to the New York State Assembly in 1994. She was an Erie County Legislator from 1992 to 1994. She has been Owner/Broker of Metro Sandra Lee Wirth, Realtor since 1980. In the Assembly, she has been appointed Ranking Minority Member on the Real Property Taxation Committee. She was also appointed to the Administrative Regulations Review Commission and the Legislative Commission on Skills Development & Vocational Education. She is active in her community as Chairman and Past President of the West Seneca Drug Abuse Prevention Council. She is also a sponsor of the "Call Home Free" program and the National Crime Prevention Council's "National Night Out." She is a member of the Greater Buffalo Association of Realtors, the National Association of Realtors, the New York State Association of Realtors, the West Seneca and Clarence Chambers of Commerce, and the Elma Business Association. She has been the recipient of numerous professional honors including President of the Greater Buffalo Association of Realtors, Elma Business Person of the Year, and Vigilant Fire Company Citizen of the Year Award.

KEITH L T WRIGHT (D-L-WF)
70th - Part of New York County

163 W 125th St, Ste 920, Adam Clayton Powell Jr Bldg, New York, NY 10027
212-866-5809/fax: 212-864-1368

Keith Wright was first elected to the Assembly in 1993. He attended Tufts University, where he received a Bachelor's and Master's degree, then earned a JD degree from Rutgers University in 1982. Prior to his election to the Assembly, he was an associate in the Law Office of Ruffin H Cotton, Jr. In 1983 he joined the staff of Human Resources Administration (HRA) as a Special Assistant to the General Counsel. He served in this capacity until 1986, when he left the HRA to join the staff of then Mayor David N Dinkins. He then became Assistant Director of Government Relations at the New York City Transit Authority. In the Assembly, he has been on the Special Task Force on Criminal Just Reform, the Black and Puerto Rican Caucus, and the Puerto Rican/Hispanic Task Force. A strong opponent of the death penalty and an advocate for criminal justice reform, he introduced legislation to prevent "no knock" search warrants, which became part of the Community Relations Policing Package. Assemblyman Wright was born and raised in Harlem.

KENNETH P ZEBROWSKI (D)
94th - Part of Rockland County

67 N Main St, New City, NY 10956
845-634-9791

Kenneth P Zebrowski was elected to the New York State Assembly in 2004. He attended Fordham University and received a degree from New York Law School in 1970. After being employed by a law firm in Nyack, New York, he started his own law firm in 1972 with Francis A. Nicolai, now the Administrative Judge of the 9th Judicial District. Mr Zebrowski is a practicing trial attorney in Rockland County and former adjunct professor at Long Island University's graduate program, and he serves as counsel to the Rockland County Public Administrator. Before election to the State Assembly, he served in the Rockland County Legislature and was chairman of the Legislature for four terms. During this time, he strengthened the County's effort to prevent domestic violence and sexual assault, and he sponsored and passed legislation that banned the use of the drug ephedra and the sale of synthetic steroids to minors. He also participated in many civic organizations. He has served as assistant coach of the New City Girls Softball League, board member and coach of the New City Rams (Pop Warner Youth Football), and assistant coach of the New City Little League (Boys). He has been a board member of Venture and chairman of its finance committee. He has been board member of Volunteer Counseling Service, Jawanio, and the Association of Retarded Citizens. He was chairman of the Nyack Board of Trustees and acting president of Nyack Hospital.

New York State Senate

JAMES S ALESI (R-I-C)
55th - Part of Monroe County

220 Packett's Landing, Fairport, NY 14450
585-223-1800/fax: 585-223-3084

James S Alesi was first elected in a special election in February 1996. A graduate of St John Fisher College, Senator Alesi owns and operates Allstate Commercial Laundries, Inc, and Statewide Laundry Services, which operates in upstate New York. Prior to his election to the Senate, he served in the Monroe County Legislature from 1989 to 1992 and then in the State Assembly from 1993 to 1996. In the Assembly, he was elected President of his class of Freshman Legislators. Currently, he chairs the Senate's Commerce, Economic Development and Small Business committee. Senator Alesi is active in numerous local community organizations, and has served on the Board of Directors of Big Brothers-Big Sisters, Mercy Flight, and Rochester Italian Charities. He is a lifelong resident of East Rochester.

CARL ANDREWS (D-WF)
20th - Part of Kings County

572 Flatbush Ave, Brooklyn, NY 11225
718-284-4700/fax: 718-282-3585

Carl Andrews was elected to the New York State Senate in a special election in February 2002. He received a Bachelor of Arts degree from Medgar Evers College and his Master's Degree from the State University of New York at Albany. Prior to his election, he had served as Director of Intergovernmental Relations for Attorney General Eliot Spitzer, Director of New York City Government Operations for the State Senate's Office of the Minority Leader, and Special Assistant to the State Secretary of State. Currently, Senator Andrews serves as Minority Whip as well as the Ranking Minority Member on the Senate's Civil Service and Pensions Committee. He has served as a member of Community Board 8, the Coalition for Community Empowerment, Brooklyn Coalition of African-American Clergy and Elected Officials, and the Society for the Preservation of Weeksville and Bedford-Stuyvesant History. He also served on the New York City's School Chancellor's Redesign Committee for High Schools.

MICHAEL A L BALBONI (R-I-C-WF)
7th - Part of Nassau County

151 Herricks Rd, Ste 202, Garden City Park, NY 11040
516-873-0736/fax: 516-873-0759

Michael A L Balboni was elected to the New York State Senate in 1997. He graduated from Adelphi University with honors and earned his JD from St John's University School of Law. He began his career in public service as counsel to former Senator John R Dunne, then became Counsel to the New York State Judiciary Committee. In 1987 he was appointed Deputy County Attorney in Nassau County until he was elected to the State Assembly, where he served eight years. Currently, Senator Balboni chairs the Senate Committee on Veterans, Homeland Security, and Military Affairs. In 2004, he was appointed by former U.S. Secretary of Homeland Security Tom Ridge to a national task force that examined the flow of homeland security funding from the federal government to local communities. He also co-chaired the National Conference of State Legislatures (NCSL) Task Force on Protecting Democracy and now chairs its Law and Justice Committee. He is a lifelong resident of Long Island and currently lives in the town of East Williston.

JOHN J BONACIC (R-I-C)
42nd - Delaware, Sullivan and parts of Orange and Ulster Counties

279 Main Street, Suite 202, New Paltz, New York, NY 12561
845-255-9656/fax: 845-255-9262

John Bonacic was first elected to the New York State Senate in 1998. He received his BA in Economics from Iona College, and his Doctorate of Law from Fordham Law School. Prior to his election to the Senate, he served seventeen years as an Orange County Legislator. In addition, he served as Assistant District Attorney for Orange County. In 1990 he was elected to the New York State Assembly, where he served until his election to the Senate. Currently, Senator Bonacic chairs the Senate's Housing, Construction and Community Development Committee and is Co-Chairperson of the Senate Task Force on Health and Wellness. In the latter position, he successfully steered the Women's Health and Wellness Act into law in 2002. He lives in the Town of Mount Hope in Orange County, New York.

NEIL D BRESLIN (D-I-WF)
46th - Albany County

414 State Capitol Bldg, Albany, NY 12247
518-455-2225/fax: 518-426-6807

Neil Breslin was first elected to the New York State Senate in 1996. The Albany native graduated from Fordham University in 1964 with a BS degree in Political Science and received his JD from the University of Toledo in Toledo, Ohio. In 1981 he formed a partnership, the Breslin Law Firm, with his two brothers. In the Senate, he currently serves as the Finance Committee's Ranking Minority Member. In addition, he is a member of the Executive Committee and formerly chaired the State/Federal Relations Committee of the National Conference of Insurance Legislators. He has served on the Board of Arbor House, a women's residence facility, including seven years as its president. In addition, he has the attorney for St Anne's Institute in Albany. He also is active within the New York State Bar Association and is currently of counsel to the law firm of Girvin and Ferlazzo. He is a lifelong resident of Albany.

BYRON W BROWN (D-I-C-W)
60th - Parts of Niagara and Erie Counties

65 Court Street, Room 213, State Ofc Bldg, Buffalo, NY 14202
716-854-8705/fax: 716-854-3051

Byron W Brown was first elected to the New York State Senate in November 2000. He holds a dual Bachelor of Arts degree in Political Science and Journalism from Buffalo State College and completed a certificate program for senior executives in state and local government at Harvard University's John F Kennedy School of Government. Prior to being elected to the Senate, he served on key staff positions with the president of the Buffalo City Council, the Chair of the Erie County Legislature and the Deputy Speaker of the New York State Assembly. His first elected office came in 1995, when he represented the Masten District on the City of Buffalo Common Council. Currently, Senator Brown serves as Ranking Minority Member of the Senate's standing Cities Committee. He also sits on the boards of Western New York Public Broadcasting Services (PBS), the Boy Scouts Council of Western New York, the Community Action Organization of Erie County and the Humboldt Branch of the YMCA. He is a native of Queens.

JOSEPH L BRUNO (R-I)
43rd - Rensselaer County and part of Saratoga County

368 Broadway, Saratoga Springs, NY 12866
518-583-1001/fax: 518-583-4458

Senate Majority Leader Joseph L Bruno was first elected to the Senate in 1976. He holds a BS degree in Business Administration from Skidmore College and served in the Korean conflict as an infantry sergeant. In 1966 Mr Bruno was on the campaign staff of Governor Nelson Rockefeller, and from 1969 to 1974 he served as Special Assistant to Speaker of the Assembly Perry B. Duryea. Senator Bruno was elected Temporary President of the New York State Senate in January, 1995 and re-elected to that position in 1997, 1999, 2001, 2003, and 2005. In this capacity, he serves as Chairman of the Rules Committee and as an ex officio member of all of the Senate's standing committees and statutory commissions. Among his economic development initiatives is the 2002 Gen*NY*sis program for capital investment of more than $225 for bio-technology research and development. In addition, Senator Bruno has led the effort to reform the budget process so that new budgets are on time each year. Under his leadership, the Senate has passed comprehensive budget reform legislation to ensure that a new budget is on time every year - a goal reached in 2005 for the first time in twenty years.

MARTIN CONNOR (D-WF)
25th - Part of Kings and New York Counties

250 Broadway, Suite 2011, New York, NY 10007
212-298-5565/fax: 212-298-5574

Martin Connor was first elected to the Senate in a special election held in 1978. He has a BA in Politics and in 1970 received a JD from Catholic University of America in Washington, DC. Between 1970 and 1974, Senator Connor was associated with the large Wall Street law firm White & Case, where he practiced corporate and anti-trust litigation. In 1974 he joined the office of the General Counsel of Xerox Corporation, where he practiced antitrust law. In 1977 he left private practice upon his appointment as Assistant Counsel to the State Comptroller, a post he resigned upon his election to the Senate. Formerly the Senate Minority Leader for eight years, Senator Connor is the Ranking Minority Member of the Senate's standing Local Government Committee. He resides in Brooklyn Heights.

JOHN A DeFRANCISCO (R-I-C-W)
50th - Most of Onondaga County

800 State Office Bldg, 333 East Washington St, Syracuse, NY 13202
315-428-7632/fax: 315-472-4157

John A DeFrancisco was elected to the New York State Senate in 1992. The Syracuse native graduated with a BS degree from Syracuse University's College of Engineering and received his JD degree from Duke University in Durham, NC. Senator DeFrancisco worked in the law firm of Simpson, Thatcher and Bartlett in New York City before serving as a Judge Advocate in the United States Air Force from 1972 to 1975. He served as Assistant District Attorney in Onondaga County from 1975 until 1977. From 1978 to 1990 he was an Adjunct Professor of Law at the Syracuse University College of Law and he has maintained a private practice since 1977. Prior to his election, he served eleven years on the Syracuse Common Council. Currently, he chairs the Senate's Standing Committee on Judiciary. In addition, he is the Deputy Majority Leader for Intergovernmental Affairs. He sat on the Joint Legislative Committee on Rockefeller Drug Law Reform in 2004, which worked to reach an agreement resulting in the Rockefeller Drug Law Reform Bill in December of that year. He resides in Syracuse.

Biographies

711

RUBIN DIAZ, SR (D)
32nd - Part of Bronx County

1750 Westchester Ave, Bronx, NY 10472
718-892-7513/fax: 718-892-8224

Rubin Diaz Sr was first elected to the New York State Senate in November 2002. Prior to his election, he served on the New York City Council representing the 18th District in the Bronx. In the Senate, he currently serves as the Ranking Minority Member of the Committee on Mental health and Developmental Disabilities. Born in Bayamon, Puerto Rico, he served in the US Army before moving to New York City in 1965. He received a BA Degree from Herbert H Lehman College in 1976 and a Theological Degree from The Damascus Bible Institute in 1978, becoming an ordained Minister of the Church of God. He founded and until recently has served as the Executive Director for the Christian Community Benevolent Association Inc, and he is also founder and pastor of the Christian Community Neighborhood Church.

MARTIN M DILAN (D-WF)
17th - Part of Kings County

786 Knickerbocker Ave, Brooklyn, NY 11207
718-573-1726/fax: 718-573-2407

Martin M Dilan was first elected to the New York State Senate in November 2002. He is a graduate of Brooklyn College, where he participated in the Special Baccalaureate Degree Program. Currently, he serves as the Ranking Minority Member of the Senate Committee on Elections. Prior to his election, he was a member of the New York City Council representing the 37th Council District. He served as a member of Community School Board #32 for fourteen years, seven as the Chair. He served as a Legislative Assistant for the US House of Representatives, as a Democratic District Leader, and as a Democratic State Committeeman.

THOMAS K DUANE (D-WF)
29th - Part of New York County

494 8th Avenue, Ste 503, New York, NY 10001
212-268-1049/fax: 212-564-1003

Thomas Duane was first elected to the New York State Senate in 1998. He was the first openly gay and HIV-positive person elected to the State Senate. He earned a Bachelor's degree from in Urban Studies and American Studies from Lehigh University. Prior to his election to the Senate, he served seven years in the New York City Council. He currently serves as the Ranking Minority Member of the Senate Codes Committee, and the Senate Crime Victims, Crime and Corrections Committee. In 2002, he advocated for passage of the Sexual Orientation Non-Discrimination Act (SONDA), which was signed into law. The lifetime New Yorker has lived in Chelsea since 1976, and served four terms as Male Democratic District Leader in the 64th Assembly District starting in 1982. In addition, he served seven years on his local community board.

HUGH T FARLEY (R-I-C)
44th - Schenectady, Montgomery and Fulton Counties, and part of Saratoga County

2430 Riverfront Center, Amsterdam, NY 12010
518-843-2188/fax: 518-843-8363

Senator Farley was elected to the New York State Senate in 1976 and was chosen Majority Whip in 1995. He holds a BS degree from the University of Albany, and also graduated from Mohawk Valley Community College. He received his JD degree from the American University Law School in Washington, DC. Senator Farley served in the US Army in Germany and has been a high school teacher. In 1965 he was appointed to the faculty of the State University at Albany's School of Business, where he became Full Professor, Law Area Coordinator, and in 2000 was named Professor Emeritus of Business Law. In addition, he has served on the university's University Senate. First elected to public office in 1970, Senator Farley originally served as a Councilman and, later, Majority Leader in the Town of Niskayuna. He currently chairs the Senate Banks Committee. Senator Farley is a member of the Executive Committee of the National Conference of State Legislatures and the Governing Board of the Council of State Governments.

JOHN J FLANAGAN (R-I-C-WF)
2nd - Part of Suffolk County

260 Middle Country Rd, Ste 203, Smithtown, NY 11787
631-361-2154/fax: 631-361-5367

John J Flanagan was first elected to the New York State Senate in November 2002. Senator Flanagan received a BA in Economics from the College of William and Mary in Williamsburg, Virginia, and a law degree from Touro Law School in Huntington. He is Chairman of the Senate Committee on Elections and Co-chairman of the Administrative Regulations Review Commission and therefore works with state agencies to review rules with an eye toward a rule's statutory authority, compliance with legislative intent, and other impacts. Also, Senator Flanagan served as Chairman of the Senate Committee on Ethics. Prior to his election, he served in the New York State Assembly for sixteen years. In 1997 he was appointed Assistant Minority Leader Pro Tempore in the Assembly. In 1998 he was appointed Ranking Republican member of the Assembly's Ways and Means Committee. He practices law in the firm of Forchelli, Curto, Schwartz, Mineo, Carlino & Cohen LLP. He lives in East Northport, New York.

CHARLES J FUSCHILLO, JR (R-I-C)
8th - Part of Nassau and Suffolk Counties

30 South Ocean Avenue, Suite 305, Freeport, NY 11520
516-546-4100/fax: 516-546-4334

Charles J Fuschillo, Jr, was first elected to the New York State Senate in 1998. Senator Fuschillo received his Bachelor's of Business Administration from Adelphi University. Prior to his election, he was the Chief Operating Officer for a private, non-profit family service agency. Currently, Senator Fuschillo chairs the Senate's Consumer Protection Committee, and is author of the state's Telemarketer "Do Not Call" Registry. Senator Fuschillo is active in his community, and serves on the board of directors and is a member of organizations including Ascent: A School for Individuals with Autism, Kiwanis, the Community Wellness Council, Italian Americans in Government, and Order Sons of Italy in America.

MARTIN J GOLDEN (R-I-C)
22nd - Part of Kings County

7403 5th Avenue, Brooklyn, NY 11209
718-238-6044/fax: 718-238-6170

Martin J Golden was first elected to the New York Senate in November 2002. He attended John Jay College and St John's University, where he received an Associate's Degree. He serves as Chairman of the Aging Committee, where he has worked on issues such as assisted living, Senior Bill of Rights, and long-term care reform. Prior to his election, he served on the New York City Council representing the 43rd Council District. He is a former New York City police officer who retired after suffering a serious injury. He and his family later purchased the Brooklyn catering hall called Bay Ridge Manor.

EFRAIN GONZALEZ, JR (D)
33rd - Part of Bronx County

1780 Grand Concourse, 1st Floor, Bronx, NY 10457
718-299-7905/fax: 718-583-8249

Efrain Gonzalez was elected to the New York State Senate in 1989. At the age of 20, Senator Gonzalez was elected Union Representative for the Transport Worker's Union; he later served as Union Representative for Local 820 of the International Brotherhood of Teamsters. He is now Chairman of the New York State Senate Democratic Task Force on International Trade Development. In addition, Senator Gonzalez serves as Chair of the Minority Conference. He is founding member and Chairman Emeritus of the National Hispanic Caucus of State Legislators (NHCSL). He also is Chairman of the New York State Senate Puerto Rican/Hispanic Task Force, President of the National Hispanic Policy Institute, Inc, and member of the Senate Minority Task Force on Education and the Senate Minority Task Force on Financing of Affordable Housing and of the Senate Minority Task Force on Education. Senator Gonzalez was born in Coamo, Puerto Rico and has lived in the Bronx since he was six months old.

KEMP HANNON (R-I-C)
6th - Part of Nassau County

224 Seventh St, 2nd Fl, Garden City, NY 11530
516-739-1700/fax: 516-747-7430

Kemp Hannon was first elected to the New York State Senate in November 1989. He graduated from Boston College and holds a JD degree from Fordham Law School. In the Senate, he currently serves as Assistant Majority Whip, Chair of the Senate Committee on Health, and Chair of the Health Budget Subcommittee. His interest in health care has led him to various positions with the National Conference of State Legislators, including Chair of its Health Committee. He has been deeply involved with the New York State Health Care Reform Act and advocates for the re-examination and re-authorization of the HCRA in 2005. During his Senate tenure, he has served as Chairman of the Committee for Housing and Minority Leader Pro Tempore in the Assembly. He lives in Garden City, New York.

RUTH HASSELL-THOMPSON (D-I-WF)
36th - Parts of Bronx and Westchester Counties

767 East Gunhill Road, Bronx, NY 10467
718-547-8854/ fax: 718-515-2718

Ruth Hassell-Thompson was first elected to the New York State Senate in 2000. She is an alumna of Bronx Community College. Prior to her Senate service, in 1993, Senator Hassell-Thompson was elected to the Mount Vernon City Council, where she served as both Council President and Acting Mayor. She currently sits on the Senate Banks and the Senate Veterans, Homeland Security and Military Affairs committees as their Ranking Minority Member. Senator Hassell-Thompson's career also includes service as Executive Director of the Westchester Minority Contractors' Association and President and CEO of Whart Development Company, Inc, a real estate development company. She is also retired nurse and counselor, specializing in helping women with substance abuse issues. She has served as President and CEO of The Gathering, a volunteer-staffed women's center in Mount Vernon that provides counseling and support services. Senator Hassell-Thompson was also a health educator for the Mount Vernon Neighborhood Health Center's initiative working with persons affected by HIV/AIDS. She is the recipient of two Honorary Doctorates: Mercy College, Doctor of Humane Letters; and Eastern Theological Consortium, Faculty of Arts and Sciences, Christ Theological Seminary, Doctor of Humanities.

OWEN H JOHNSON (R-I-C-WF)
4th - Part of Suffolk County

23-24 Argyle Square, Babylon, NY 11702
631-669-9200/fax: 631-669-9007

Owen Johnson was first elected to the New York State Senate in 1972. Senator Johnson graduated from Hofstra University in 1956 with a BA degree in History-Political Science after being honorably discharged from service with the US Marine Corps. Since 2003, he has served as Chairman of the Senate Finance Committee. He also serves on the New York State Public Authorities Control Board and co-chairs the Legislative Audit Committee. He is also Chairman of the Senate Subcommittee on the Long Island Marine District, a Commissioner on the Atlantic States Marine Fisheries Commission, and Vice-Chair of the Legislative Commission on Government Administration. He is a National Director of the American Legislative Exchange Council, an organization for which he previously served as National Chairman. He is a member of Cross of Christ Lutheran Church in Babylon. He lives in West Babylon.

JEFFREY D KLEIN (D)
34th - Parts of Bronx and Westchester Counties

415 Legislative Office Building, Albany, New York 12247
518-455-3595

Jeffrey D "Jeff" Klein was first elected to the New York State Senate in 2004. The lifelong Bronx resident received a BA from Queens College, an MPA from Columbia University School of International and Public Affairs, and a JD from the City University of New York Law School. Currently, he serves as the Ranking Minority Member of the Senate's Consumer Protection Committee. Prior to his election, Senator Klein spent ten years as a New York State Assemblyman, where he served as Chairman of the Subcommittee on Crime and the Elderly, the Committee on State-Federal Relations, and the Committee on Oversight, Analysis and Investigations. He has also served as Chief of Staff to Congress James Scheuer. Among his community and civil affiliations is membership on the New York regional board of the Anti-Defamation League. He is a lifelong resident of the northeast Bronx.

LIZ KRUEGER (D-WF)
26th - Part of New York County

211 East 43rd St, Ste 1300, New York, NY 10017
212-490-9535/fax: 212-490-2151

Liz Krueger was elected to the New York State Senate in 2002. Senator Krueger graduated from Northwestern University in Chicago, Ill. with a Bachelors degree in Social Policy and Human Development. She also holds a Masters degree from the University of Chicago's Harris Graduate School of Public Policy. She chairs Minority Program Development and is the ranking Democrat on the Senate Committee on Housing, Construction and Community Development. She also serves as Chair of the Senate Minority Task Force on Legislative and Budgetary Reform. Prior to her election, Senator Krueger was the Associate Director of the Community Food Resource Center (CFRC) for 15 years and the founding Director of the New York City Food Bank. She has served as Chair of the New York City Food Stamp Task Force, Co-Facilitator of the New York City Welfare Reform Network, and served as a board member on both the City-Wide Task Force on Housing Court and the New York City Federal Emergency Management Agency Emergency Food and Shelter Program administered by the United Way of Greater New York.

CARL KRUGER (D-R)
27th - Part of Kings County Secretary

2201 Avenue U, Brooklyn, NY 11229
718-743-8610/fax: 718-743-5958

Senator Carl Kruger was first elected to the New York State Senate in 1994. Mr Kruger holds a BS degree in Political Science. Prior to his election, Mr Kruger served as an Assistant Director of Member Services for the New York State Assembly and for ten years was the Chairperson of Community Board #18. He currently serves as Secretary to the Minority Conference and is the Ranking Minority Member of the Senate's Aging Committee. Senator Kruger is a member of the SUNY Health Science Center Advisory Board, the Board of Trustees of the Flatlands Volunteer Ambulance Corporation, the Advisory Board of Visions and is Vice President of the Georgetowne Civic Association. Senator Kruger is also a member of the Flatbush Park Jewish Center, the Knights of Pythias Excelsior Lodge, and a former board member of Temple Hillel.

WILLIAM J LARKIN, JR (R-C)
39th - Parts of Orange and Ulster Counties

1093 Little Britain Road, New Windsor, NY 12553
845-567-1270/fax: 845-567-1276

Senator Larkin was first elected to the New York State Senate in 1990. Mr Larkin graduated from LaSalle Institute in Troy and also attended the University of Maryland and the University of Denver. He currently serves as the Chair of the Senate Committee on Racing, Gaming and Wagering, and has served in key positions relating to the insurance industry, including a year long presidency of the National Conference of Insurance Legislators starting in 2001. Prior to his election to the Senate, Mr Larkin served twelve years in the State Assembly, where he served as Assistant Minority Leader Pro Tempore. Senator Larkin is a veteran of 23 years of active military duty including combat assignments during World War II and the Korean War. He retired from the United States Army in 1967 with the rank of Lieutenant Colonel. Following his military service, Senator Larkin served as an Executive Assistant in the New York State Senate and as Supervisor of the Town of New Windsor in Orange County. Senator Larkin is a member of the Knights of Columbus, Veterans of Foreign Wars, the American Legion, and the Disabled American Veterans.

KENNETH P LaVALLE (R-I-C)
1st - Part of Suffolk County

325 Middle Country Road, Suite 4, Selden, NY 11784
631-696-6900/fax: 631-696-2307

Kenneth P LaValle was first elected to the New York State Senate in 1976. He holds an undergraduate degree from Adelphi College, a degree in Education from the State University College at New Paltz, and a JD degree from Touro College Jacob D Fuchsberg Law Center. Senator LaValle also has completed extensive graduate study in Government and International Relations at New York University. He is a former Executive Director of the Senate Education Committee. He currently serves as Chair of the Majority Conference, and chairs the Senate Committee on Higher Education. He has worked to establish a Burn Unit at University Hospital in Stony Brook. He also authored the Pine Barrens Preservation Act of 1993. He is a practicing attorney with Twomey, Latham, Shea & Kelley.

VINCENT L LEIBELL, III (R-I-C)
40th - Putnam County, parts of Dutchess andWestchester Counties

1441 Route 22, Suite 205, Brewster, NY 10509
845-279-3773/fax: 845-279-7156

Vincent L Leibell was first elected to the New York State Senate in 1994. He holds a Bachelor's Degree in Economics, a Law degree from St John's University and a Master's degree in Public Administration from New York University. He currently serves as Chair of the Senate's Corporations, Authorities and Commissions Committee. Prior to his election, he served as an Associate Counsel to the New York State Senate, County Attorney of Putnam County, and as an Assistant District Attorney in Westchester County. From January 1983 until his election to the Senate, he served in the State Assembly and became Assistant Minority Leader Pro Tempore. The Navy veteran has commanded a U.S. Naval Reserve Unit in upstate New York. He lives in Patterson, New York.

THOMAS W LIBOUS (R-C)
52nd - Broome, Tioga and part of Chenango County

1607 State Ofc Bldg, 44 Hawley Street, Binghamton, NY 13901
607-773-8771/fax: 607-773-3688

Senator Thomas W Libous was first elected to the New York State Senate in 1988. He graduated from Broome Community College and the State University of New York at Utica. He currently serves as Assistant Majority Leader, House Operations, as well as Chair of the Transportation Committee. In the past, he has chaired the Mental Health and Developmental Disabilities Committee, as well as the Alcoholism and Drug Abuse Committee. The Binghamton resident also worked to see the American Hockey League affiliate to the Ottawa Senators locate in his hometown. Prior to his election, he was employed by Chase-Lincoln First Bank and Johnson City Publishing.

ELIZABETH O'CONNOR LITTLE (R-I-C)

45th - Clinton, Essex, Franklin, Hamilton, Warren & Washington Counties

21 Bay Street, Glens Falls, NY 12801
518-743-0968/fax: 518-743-0336

Elizabeth O'Connor Little was first elected to the New York State Senate in November 2002. She graduated from the College of Saint Rose with a degree in Elementary Education. Currently, she chairs the Senate's Local Government Committee, and thereby oversees committee work on legislation that affects local government entities, including counties, towns, villages, school districts, fire districts and special districts. Prior to her Senate election, she served in the New York State Assembly for seven years. She also has served as At-Large-Supervisor to the Warren County Board of Supervisors for the Town of Queensbury and Chair of the Town of Queensbury Recreation Commission. She is also now serving as a member of the Hudson-Fulton-Champlain Quadricentennial Commission planning and developing the 400th anniversary celebration of the historic discoveries of Henry Hudson and Samuel de Champlain, and also the 200th anniversary of Robert Fulton's landmark steamship voyage up the Hudson River.

SERPHIN R MALTESE (R-I-C)

15th - Part of Queens County

71-04 Myrtle Avenue, Glendale, NY 11385
718-497-1800/fax: 718-386-7803

Serphin R Maltese was first elected to the New York State Senate in 1988. He holds a BA degree from Manhattan College. The Infantry veteran of the Korean War was awarded a War Service Scholarship and received his LLB and JD degrees from Fordham University Law School. Currently, he chairs the Senate's Cities Committee. Previously, he has chaired the Senate's Committee on Veterans and Committee on Consumer Protection. He is currently a member of the American Legion's National Legislative Council. Prior to his election, Senator Maltese served as Queens Assistant District Attorney and Deputy Chief of the Homicide Bureau. He also has previously served as Counsel to US Senator Alfonse M D'Amato. As co-founder of the New York State Conservative Party in 1962, he went on to become State Chairman of the party from 1986 until his election to the Senate. The Senator's extensive civil and community organization affiliations include the Glendale Kiwanis, Queens Chamber of Commerce, Sons of Italy-Mario Lanza Lodge, Americans of Italian Heritage. The Senator also previously served as counsel to the New York State Commission on the Deaf and Multiply Impaired. He is also a member of the American Legion, Catholic War Veterans, Korean War Veteran's Association, and Veterans of Foreign Wars.

CARL LOUIS MARCELLINO (R-I-C-WF)

5th - Parts of Nassau and Suffolk Counties

250 Townsend Square, Oyster Bay, NY 11771
516-922-1811/fax: 516-922-1154

Carl Louis Marcellino was first elected to the New York State Senate in March 1995. He received his BA and MS degrees from New York University, and received his Professional Diploma in Administration and Supervision from St John's University. Currently, he chairs the Senate's Environmental Conservation Committee. Senator

Marcellino is a former teacher and education administrator and served as Oyster Bay Town Clerk prior to his election to the Senate. Senator Marcellino is Chairman of the Oyster Bay Western Waterfront Committee, a founding member of the State Advisory Board of the National Environmental Policy Institute, and former President of the New York Conference of Italian American State Legislators. He is a longtime resident of Syosset.

JOHN J MARCHI (R-D-I-C)

24th - Part of Richmond County

358 St Marks Place, Staten Island, NY 10301
718-447-1723/fax: 718-981-1270

John J Marchi was first elected to the Senate in 1957. He was born in Staten Island and attended local schools and Manhattan College from which he graduated with first honors. He holds a JD degree from St John's University School of Law, and a Doctor of Juridical Science degree from Brooklyn Law School. Currently the Assistant Majority Leader on Conference Operations, Senator Marchi also has served as Assistant Majority Whip, Chairman of the Senate Committee on Corporations, Authorities and Commissions, and Vice President Pro Tempore. He also chaired the Finance Committee for eighteen years. Senator Marchi served in the Coast Guard during World War II and was on combat duty in the Atlantic, the Pacific and in Asia. He retired in 1982 from the Active Reserve. Senator Marchi is a member of numerous religious, veteran, professional and civic associations, including the Richmond County and American Bar Associations and the American Judicature Society.

GEORGE D MAZIARZ (R-I-C-WF)

62nd - Orleans County and parts of Monroe and Niagara Counties

2578 Niagara Falls Blvd., Wheatfield, New York 14304
716-731-8740fax: 716-438-0955

George D Maziarz was elected to the New York State Senate in March 1995. He holds a BA degree in History from Niagara University. He was appointed City Clerk of North Tonawanda in 1978 and served in that capacity until elected Niagara County Clerk in 1989. He currently chairs the Senate's Labor Committee, and is also a member of the New York State Workforce Investment Board. Previously, he chaired the Committee on Tourism, Recreation and Sports Development, and the Senate Aging Committee. Senator Maziarz also has served as President of the Chamber of Commerce of the Tonawandas, has served on the board of directors of the United Way of the Tonawandas, and the corporate advisory board of DeGraff Memorial Hospital. Senator Maziarz also is a past officer and twenty-nine year member of Live Hose Co #4. He resides in Newfane, New York.

RAYMOND A MEIER (R-C)

47th - Lewis County and parts of Oneida and St Lawrence Counties

State Office Building, 207 Genesee St, 4 Fl, Utica, NY 13501
315-793-9072/fax: 315-793-2723

Raymond Meier was first elected to the New York State Senate in 1996. He holds a BA degree in Political Science and a JD degree from Syracuse University. He currently chairs the Social Services, Children and Families Committee. Prior to his election to the Senate, Mr Meier served as Oneida County Legislator and as Oneida County Executive. He also has served as Deputy Onondaga County Attorney; Legislative Counsel to the late Senator James H Donovan; and Corporation Counsel for the City of Rome. Currently, he is of counsel to the law firm of Saunders, Kahler, Amoroso and Locke in Utica. He also serves as an at-large member of the National Conference of State Legislatures' Executive Committee. He is a resident of Western, New York.

VELMANETTE MONTGOMERY (D-WF)
18th - Part of Kings County

30 3rd Ave, 6th Fl, Rm 615, Brooklyn, NY 11217
718-643-6140/fax: 718-237-4137

Velmanette Montgomery was first elected to the New York State Senate in 1984. She received her Master's degree in Education from New York University and studied at the University of Accra in Ghana. She currently serves as the Ranking Minority Member on the Senate's Social Services, Children and Families Committee, and is Assistant Minority Leader for Floor Operations. Before her election to the State Senate she was a Revson Fellow at Columbia University and received the Institute for Educational Leadership Fellowship. Prior to becoming a Legislator, Senator Montgomery was a teacher, an adjunct professor, and a day care director. She co-founded the Day Care Forum of New York City. She also served as president of Community School Board 13.

THOMAS P MORAHAN (R-I-C-WF)
38th - Rockland County and part of Orange County

158 Airport Executive Park, Nanuet, NY 10954
845-425-1818/fax: 845-425-6473

Senator Thomas P Morahan was first elected to the New York State Senate in May 1999. Senator Morahan attended Rockland Community College and served in the United States Army. He currently serves as Chair of the Senate Committee on Mental Health and Development Disabilities. He previously served as Chairman of the Elections Committee. Senator Morahan began his political career as a member of the Clarkstown Zoning Board of Appeals, and was elected to the Rockland County Legislature in 1977. He was elected to the New York State Assembly in 1980. In 1984 he returned to the Rockland County Legislature, culminating in his election as Chairman of the Legislature in 1996.

MICHAEL F NOZZOLIO (R-I-C)
54th - Seneca and Wayne Counties and parts of Cayuga, Monroe, Ontario and Tompkins Counties

119 Fall Street, Seneca Falls, NY 13148
315-568-9816/fax: 315-568-2090

Michael F Nozzolio was first elected to the New York State Senate in 1992. He received a BS degree in Labor Relations and an MS degree in Public Administration and Agricultural Economics from Cornell University. He also earned a JD degree from the Syracuse University College of Law. Currently, he serves as Chairman of the Senate Crime Victims, Crime and Correction Committee. He is also a Commander in the New York Naval Militia. Prior to his Senate service, Mr Nozzolio served in the State Assembly for ten years. While in the Assembly, he served as Deputy Minority Leader. Senator Nozzolio serves on the Board of the Cornell Agricultural and Food Technology Park and the Seneca Museum of Waterways and Industry.

GEORGE ONORATO (D)
12th - Part of Queens County

28-11 Astoria Boulevard, Long Island City, NY 11102
718-545-9706/fax: 718-267-9094

George Onorato was elected to the New York State Senate in 1983. He received a Presidential Citation while serving in the US Army, 118th Medical Battalion from 1950 to 1952. Currently, Senator Onorato is Vice Chair of the Minority Conference, and is a member of the Senate Minority Task Force on Waterfront Development. He is the Ranking Minority Member of the Senate's Insurance Committee. In addition, he serves as Co-Chair of the New York State Armed Forces Legislative Caucus. In addition, he is past Treasurer and Past President of the Conference of Italian American Legislators. He served as Secretary/Treasurer of Bricklayer's Local #41 in 1968, where he served until his election to the State Senate. He is a lifelong resident of Astoria.

SUZI OPPENHEIMER (D-WF)
37th - Part of Westchester County

222 Grace Church Street, 3rd Floor, Port Chester, NY 10573
914-934-5250/fax: 914-934-5256

Suzi Oppenheimer was first elected to the New York State Senate in 1984. Senator Oppenheimer received her BA degree in Economics from Connecticut College for Women, and a Master's degree from Columbia University's Graduate School of Business., Senator Oppenheimer served four terms as Mayor of the Village of Mamaroneck. She also served as President of the Westchester Municipal Officials Association, the Westchester Municipal Planning Federation, and the Mamaroneck League of Women Voters. She currently serves as Deputy Minority Whip, Ranking Minority Member on the Senate's standing Education Committee, and chairs the Senate Democratic Task Force on Women's Issues. Prior to her election to the Senate, Senator Oppenheimer served four terms as Mayor of the Village of Mamaroneck. She sits on the board of the Child Care Action Campaign, the Westchester Community Opportunity Program, and the Mental Health Association of Westchester. She is a resident of Mamaroneck, New York.

FRANK PADAVAN (R-I-C)
11th - Part of Queens County

89-39 Gettysburg Street, Bellerose, NY 11426
718-343-0255/fax: 718-343-0354

Frank Padavan was first elected to the New York State Senate in 1972. He holds a Bachelor's degree in Electrical Engineering from the Polytechnic Institute of Brooklyn and Master's degree in Business Administration from New York University. Prior to his election to the Senate, Mr Padavan was employed by Westinghouse Electric Corporation for fourteen years. He also served as Deputy Commissioner of the New York City Department of Buildings. Senator Padavan currently serves as the Senate's Vice President Pro Tempore, and in late 2004 was appointed to Co-Chair the New York State Senate Task Force on Government Reform. He also chairs the Senate Majority Task Force on Immigration. He was a Colonel in the Army Corps of Engineers. Senator Padavan is credited with establishing the Northeast Queens Nature and Historic Preserve Commission and is a member of the American Institute of Electronic and

Electrical Engineers, the Army Reserve Officers Association, and the American Legion, among other civic organizations.

KEVIN S PARKER (D-WF)
21st - Part of Kings County

4515 Avenue D, Brooklyn NY 11203
718-629-6401/fax: 718-629-6420

Kevin S Parker was first elected to the New York State Senate in 2002. He received a Bachelor of Science Degree in Public Service from Penn State University and a Master of Science Degree from the New School for Social Research Graduate School of Management and Urban Policy. He is currently pursuing a doctoral degree in Political Science at the City University of New York Graduate School and University Center. Senator Parker currently serves as the Ranking Minority Member of the Senate's Energy and Telecommunications Committee. Prior to his election, he served as Special Assistant to former New York State Comptroller H Carl McCall. As a New York City Urban Fellow, he served as a Special Assistant to Manhattan Borough President Ruth Messinger. Also, he was Legislative Aide to former New York City Council Member Una Clarke and Special Assistant to Assemblyman Nick Perry. He served as Project Manager with the New York State Urban Development Corporation. Mr Parker is a member of the Community Service Society's Associates program and the Children's Defense Fund's Community Crusade for Children.

DAVID A PATERSON (D-WF)
30th - Part of New York County

Adam Clayton Powell SOB, 163 West 125th St, Suite 932, New York, NY 10027
212-222-7315/fax: 212-678-0001

David A Paterson was first elected to the New York State Senate in 1985. He is a graduate of Columbia University and Hofstra Law School. He has served as the Senate Minority Leader since 2002, which makes him the state's highest-ranking African-American elected official. The job also means is he is an ex official member of all of the Senate's standing committees. He is also the Ranking Minority Member of the Rules Committee. Senator Paterson, who is legally blind, also advocates on behalf of visually and physically challenged people. This has led him to service as a member of the American Foundation for the Blind. He lives in Harlem.

MARY LOU RATH (R-I-C)
61st - Genesee and part of Erie Counties

5500 Main Street, Suite 260, Williamsville, NY 14221
716-633-0331/fax: 716-633-0830

Mary Lou Rath was first elected to the New York State Senate in 1993. She holds a BS degree from Buffalo State Teachers College. Prior to her election to the Senate, Senator Rath served as a Legislator in Erie County for fifteen years, four as the Republican Leader of the Erie County Legislature. She currently chairs the Senate's Tourism, Recreation and Sports Development Committee, and also chairs the Long-Term Care Subcommittee of the Senate Task Force on Medicaid Reform. She founded the Senate's Women of Distinction program, which honors New York's women. She resides in Williamsville, New York.

JOSEPH E ROBACH (R-I-C-WF)
56th - Part of Monroe County

2300 West Ridge Road, Rochester, NY 14626
585-225-3650/fax: 585-225-3661

Joseph E Robach was first elected to the New York State Senate in November 2002. Senator Robach is a graduate of the State University of New York College at Brockport, where he received his Bachelor of Science and Master of Public Administration degrees. Currently, he chairs the Senate's Civil Service and Pensions committee. Prior to his election, he served as the New York State Assemblyman for the 134th Assembly District for eleven years. Previously, he served as Contract Administrator for the Monroe County Department of Social Services, a General Manager for the Public Abstract Information Services and a variety of positions in the Monroe County Department of Public Safety. He also served on State Senator Ralph Quattrochiocchi's adjunct staff. Senator Robach's extensive civic activity includes his being named an Honorary Member of the Board of Directors of the Rochester Vietnam Veteran's Memorial. Also, he is a Paul Harris Fellow, which is the Rotary's highest award. He is also past Chairman of the Rochester Chamber of Commerce Safety Council Highway and Traffic Safety Committee. He lives in the Town of Greece.

JOHN D SABINI (D-WF)
13th - Part of Queens County

35-07 88th St, Jackson Heights, NY 11372
718-639-8469/fax:718-639-9026

John D Sabini was first elected to the New York State Senate in 2002. Prior to his election, he served as a New York City Council Member. Mr Sabini graduated from New York University's College of Business Administration and attended its Graduate School of Public Administration. He currently serves as Ranking Minority Member on two committees: Racing, Gaming and Wagering, and the Transportation Committee. Prior to his election to the Senate, Senator Sabini served on Community Board No 3-Q and the Community Advisory Board at Elmhurst Hospital. He also served as District Administrator for Congressman James H Scheuer and Stephen J Solarz, Director of the State Assembly's Subcommittee on Senior Citizen Facilities, and Vice President of the MWW Group. Mr Sabini is a lifelong resident of Jackson Heights, New York.

STEPHEN M SALAND (R-C)
41st - Columbia and part of Dutchess Counties

3 Neptune Road, Suite A19B, Poughkeepsie, NY 12601
845-463-0840/fax: 845-463-3438

Stephen M Saland was first elected to the New York State Senate in 1990. He graduated from the University of Buffalo, and from Rutgers Law School. In addition to serving as Deputy Majority Leader for State/Federal Relations, Senator Saland is Chairman of the Senate Education Committee. He also serves on the Joint Legislative Conference Committee on Budget Reform. He previously served as Chairman of the Children and Families Committee. Prior to his Senate election, Senator Saland served as a Councilman for the Town of Wappinger, and was a member of the State Assembly from 1980 through 1990. He is previous president of the National Conference of State Legislatures, and is now president of the NCSL Foundation for State Legislatures. Senator Saland is of counsel to the law firm of Gellert & Klein, P.C. He has won many awards from numerous organizations, including the New York State School Boards Association, the Metropolitan Police Conference, and the Federation on Child Abuse and Neglect. He lives in the Town of Poughkeepsie.

JOHN L SAMPSON (D-WF)
19th - Part of Kings County

9114 Flatlands Avenue, Brooklyn, NY 11236
718-649-7653/fax: 718-649-7661

John Sampson was first elected to the New York State Senate in 1996. He graduated from Brooklyn College in 1967 with a BA degree in Political Science. In 1991, he graduated from Albany Law School. He currently serves as the Ranking Minority Member of the Senate Health Committee. In addition, he is a member of the Administrative Regulations Review Commission. Prior to his election, Senator Sampson worked as a staff attorney for the Legal Aid Society of New York. He has been an attorney at the law firm of Alter and Barbaro, Esqs, since 1993, where he represents clients in real estate, criminal, and election matters. He has received numerous awards and he is a member of the Board of Trustees of Albany Law School.

DIANE J SAVINO (D-WF)
23rd District - Part of Kings and Richmond Counties

36 Richmond Terrace, 1st Floor, Staten Island, New York 10301
718-727-9406

Diane Savino was first elected to the New York State Senate in 2004. She graduated from St. John's University and the Cornell School of Industrial and Labor Relations. In the Senate, she currently serves as the Ranking Minority Member of the Labor Committee and she is on the Committees for Civil Service and Pensions; Environmental Conservation; Housing, Construction and Community Development; Judiciary; Tourism; Recreation and Sports Development; and Transportation. She began her career as a caseworker for New York City's Child Welfare Administration, providing direct assistance to abused and neglected children in the Agency's Division of Foster Care and Adoption. While on the job, she quickly became involved in her local labor union, rising through the ranks to Vice President for Political Action & Legislative Affairs of the Social Service Employees Union, Local 371, DC 37 of AFSCME. In this capacity, she represented 16,000 public sector workers and their families at City Hall and the State Capital. She lives in the Fort Wadsworth section of Staten Island.

ERIC T SCHNEIDERMAN (D-WF)
31st - Parts of Bronx and New York Counties

80 Bennett Avenue, Ground Fl, New York, NY 10033
212-928-5578/fax: 212-928-0396

Eric Schneiderman was first elected to the New York State Senate in November 1998. Senator Schneiderman graduated from Amherst College with degrees in English and Asian studies and received his JD from Harvard Law School. He became Deputy Minority Leader in 2003, a position that means he leads Senate debate on behalf of the Minority Conference. During the first term of his tenure in the Senate, he was instrumental in passing the first pro-choice legislation in decades - the Clinic Access bill — as well as a Hate Crimes law and a historic package of gun control legislation. Prior to his Senate election, he clerked in the U.S. District Court for the Southern Dis-

trict of New York and later became partner at the firm of Kirkpatrick and Lockhart. He founded the Attorney General's Anti-Crime Advocates program and was lead counsel for the New York Urban League and the Straphangers Campaign in a lawsuit against the MTA to halt proposed a fare increase in public transportation. He resides on the Upper West side of Manhattan.

JOSE M SERRANO (D-WF)
28th - Parts of Bronx and New York Counties

706 Legislative Office Building, Albany, New York 12247
518-455-2795

Senator Jose M. Serrano was first elected to the New York State Senate in 2004. He graduated from Manhattan College with a B.A. in Government. Currently he serves as Ranking Minority Member of the Senate's Tourism, Recreation and Sports Development Committee. Prior to his election to the Senate, he served on Community Board 4 and as Chairman of the Board for the Institute of Family Health. In 2003 he was elected to the New York City Council for District 17, and in this capacity served as Chair of the Council's Committee on Cultural Affairs, Libraries, and International Inter-group relations. He led the fight against devastating budget cuts to libraries and the city's cultural institutions. Senator Serrano also worked for the New York Shakespeare Festival after graduating from college. He lives in the South Bronx.

JAMES L SEWARD (R-I-C)
51st - Cortland, Greene, Herkimer, Otsego, Schoharie, and parts of Chenengo and Tompkins Counties

41 South Main Street, Oneonta, NY 13820
607-432-5524/fax: 607-432-4281

James L Seward was first elected to the New York State Senate in 1986. He holds a BA degree from Hartwick College in political science, and he also studied at the Nelson Rockefeller Institute of Government at SUNY Albany. Currently, he chairs the Senate Committee on Insurance. He won passage of legislation in 2002 that extends group health insurance offered by chambers of commerce to sole proprietors of business. He has also served as Chairman of the Senate Majority Task force on Volunteer Emergency Services. Senator Seward is a former Milford Town Justice. He serves on the board of Pathfinder Village and the Catskill Symphony, is a trustee to Glimmerglass Opera, and is a director of Wilber National Bank. In 1999 Hartwick College awarded him an honorary Doctor of Laws degree. He lives in Milford, New York.

DEAN G SKELOS (R-I)
9th - Part of Nassau County

55 Front Street, Rockville Centre, NY 11570
516-766-8383/fax: 516-766-8011

State Senator Dean G Skelos was first elected to the New York State Senate in 1984. He received a BA in History from Washington College in Chestertown, Maryland in 1970, and in 1975 he received his JD degree from Fordham University School. He currently serves as Deputy Majority Leader, which means he is an ex officio member of all Senate committees and numerous Senate Majority Task Forces. In addition, he chaired the New York State Senate's NextGen Task Force, and in that capacity crafted a strategy to encourage creation of well paying technology jobs. He also chaired the Senate Standing

Committee on Aging for ten years. Prior to his election to the Senate, he was a member of the New York State Assembly for two years, representing the 19th District. He is a member of the State Legislative Leaders Foundation, National Conference of State Legislators, and the National Conference of Insurance Legislators. He is of counsel to the firm of Ruskin Moscou Faltischeck PC. He lives in Rockville Centre, New York.

ADA L SMITH (D-I-WF)
10th - Part of Queens County

116-43 Sutphin Blvd, Jamaica, NY 11434
718-322-2537/fax: 718-322-8417

Senator Ada L Smith was first elected to the New York State Senate in 1988. She is a graduate of CUNY's Baruch College. In the Senate, she has served as Assistant Minority Leader for Policy and Administration since 2004, and also has served as Minority Whip and Minority Conference Chair. She is the Ranking Minority Member of the Senate Committee on Corporations, Authorities and Commissions. Prior to her election, she served as Deputy City Clerk of the City of New York. Senator Smith is a former President of the Baruch College Alumni Association and former Trustee and Life Director of the Baruch College Fund. She also has been active in the New York State Black and Puerto Rican Legislative Caucus. She is the recipient of many honors, including the Baruch College's Outstanding Achievement Award, CUNY'S President's Medal, and the NAACP's Woman of the Year Award.

MALCOLM A SMITH (D-R-C-WF)
14th - Part of Queens County

205-19 Linden Blvd, St Albans NY 11434
718-528-4290/fax: 718-528-4898

Malcolm A Smith was first elected to the New York State Senate in 2000. He received a BA in Economics from Fordham University and has done graduate work at Fordham, NYU, and the New School of Social Research. He is a real estate developer by profession. Prior to his election, Senator Smith was Chief Aide to NYC Councilman Archie Spigner and later the Procurement Manager for the NYC Office of Economic Development Division of Small and Minority Business. He served as District Manager for Congressman Floyd H Flake from 1986. In his first year as State Senator (2000-2001), he secured $10 Million dollars from the MTA for much-needed improvement of their LIRR Stations within his District. In the same year a collaboration with Assemblywoman Barbara Clarke secured $1 Million for the Jamaica Clinic in Hollis Queens. In his second year (2001-2002), collaboration with city and state officials engineered an agreement that yielded $10 million to clean up the Westside Corporation Toxic Site in Jamaica, Queens. Currently, he is Ranking Minority Member of the Senate Judiciary Committee.

NICHOLAS A SPANO (R-I-C)
35th - Part of Westchester County

1 Executive Blvd, Yonkers, NY 10701
914-969-5194/fax: 914-969-4031

Nicholas A Spano was first elected to the New York State Senate in November 1996. He holds a BA from Iona College in New Rochelle. Head of the Westchester Delegation to the Senate, he serves as Senior Assistant Majority Leader and Liaison to the Executive Branch

and chairs the Senate Standing Committee on Investigations, Taxation and Government Operations. He previously chaired the Senate Labor Committee and the Mental Health Committee on which he still sits as a member. Prior to joining the Senate, he served in the State Assembly for eight years. He is a lifelong resident of Yonkers.

WILLIAM T STACHOWSKI (D-I-C-WF)
58th - Part of Erie County

2030 Clinton Street, Buffalo, NY 14206
716-826-3344/fax: 716-826-6372

William T Stachowski was first elected to the New York State Senate in 1981. He holds a BA degree in Political Science from College of the Holy Cross in Worcester, MA. He currently serves as the Ranking Minority Member on the Investigations and Government Operations Committee and Ethics Committee. Prior to his election, Senator Stachowski was a teacher/counselor at St Ann's Roman Catholic School in Buffalo and an assistant football coach at St Francis High School in Athol Springs. He was named to the Erie County Legislature (3rd District) in December 1974, where he served until November 1981. Senator Stachowski serves on the City of Buffalo's Inner Harbor Task Force, the Ilio DiPaolo Scholarship Committee, and the Western New York Delegation Hydro Re-Allocation Committee. He is a member of numerous organizations, including the Southtowns Walleye Association, the Erie County Fire Chief's Mutual Aid Program, and Friends of the Buffalo River. He was the 1990 recipient of the New York State Sheriff's Award "Friend of Law Enforcement" and the 1993 recipient of the Hilbert College Fellows Medal, and he has been honored by many other organizations.

TOBY ANN STAVISKY (D-WF)
16th - Part of Queens County

144-36 Willets Point Blvd, Flushing, NY 11357
718-445-0004/fax: 718-445-8398

Toby Ann Stavisky was first elected to the Senate in 1999. She received her Bachelor's degree from Syracuse University and completed graduate school at Hunter and Queens Colleges. In the Senate, she was appointed Assistant Minority Whip in 2003, and she also currently serves as Ranking Minority Member of the Senate Committee on Higher Education. Prior to entering public life, Senator Stavisky worked in the actuarial department of a major insurance company and taught Social Studies in the New York City high schools, including Brooklyn Technical, Haaren, and Thomas Edison. She also served as District Manager in Northeast Queens for the 1980 Census. Senator Stavisky was a founder of the North Flushing Senior Center and served on its Board of Directors. She serves as an honorary trustee of the Whitestone Hebrew Center where she and her husband, the late State Senator Leonard Price Stavisky, were honored as "Couple of the Year."

CAESAR TRUNZO (R-I-C-WF)
3rd - Part of Suffolk County

NYS Office Bldg, Veterans Memorial Hwy, Hauppauge, NY 11788
631-360-3236/fax: 631-360-3386

Caesar Trunzo was first elected to the New York State Senate in 1972. He served in the US Army during World War II and graduated from Heffley & Browne Business College in 1946. Currently, he is Deputy Majority Whip and previously served as Chairman of the

Senate Transportation Committee and Chairman of the Civil Service and Pensions Committees. He also is Chair of the Majority Program Development Committee. Before his election to the Senate, Mr Trunzo was an Accounting Supervisor of Fairchild Stratos Corp, Bay Shore, New York, and Chief Accountant and Assistant Treasurer of Dayton T Brown, Inc, Bohemia, New York. He served as a member of the Islip Planning Board from 1959 until he became Councilman of the Town of Islip in 1965. He is a member of the Brentwood Lions Club, the Sons of Italy, the St Anne's Holy Name Society, and the St Anne's Council Knights of Columbus. He lives in Brentwood, New York.

DAVID J VALESKY (D-WF)
49th - Madison County and parts of Cayuga, Oneida and Onondaga Counties

805 State Office Building, 333 East Washington St, Syracuse, NY 13202
315-478-8745

Senator David J Valesky was elected to the New York State Senate in 2004. He received his Bachelor's degree from SUNY Potsdam and his Master's degree from the University of Connecticut. He currently serves as the Ranking Minority Member of the Senate's Committee on Agriculture and the Ranking Minority Member of the Senate Committee on Environmental Conservation. Prior to his election, Senator Valesky served as an aide to former State Assembly Majority Leader Michael Bragman. He then became Vice President of Communications at WCNY, the public television and radio station of Central New York, a post he occupied from 1995 to 2004. There, he hosted the midday talk show HOUR CNY. He lives in the Madison County city of Oneida.

DALE M VOLKER (R-I-C-WF)
59th - Wyoming & parts of Erie, Livingston & Ontario Counties

4729 Transit Road, Suite 6, Depew NY 14043
716-656-8544/fax: 716-656-8961

Dale M Volker was first elected to the New York State Senate in 1975. He attended Niagara University and graduated from Canisius College. Subsequent to graduation, Senator Volker worked full time as a police officer in the Village of Depew while studying law at the University of Buffalo. After graduating, he continued to serve with the Depew Police Department for six years. Throughout his law enforcement career, he was a member of the Depew Police Benevolent Association and served a term as its President. Prior to his Senate election, Mr Volker served three years in the Assembly. Active in his community and in his church, he has directed the United Fund Appeal in Depew and has served as Chairman of the Catholic Charities Appeal. He is a member of numerous civic organizations and sits on the Board of Regents-Canisius College. He lives in the village of Depew.

GEORGE H WINNER, JR (R-I-C)
53rd - includes Chemung, Schuyler, Steuben and Yates counties and part of Tompkins County

228 Lake Street, P.O. Box 588, Elmira, NY 14902
607-732-2765

George H. Winner, Jr. was elected to the New York State Senate in 2004. He graduated from St Lawrence University and was admitted to practice law in New York after completing a legal clerkship. Currently, he chairs the Senate Ethics Committee. Prior to his election to the Senate, Senator Winner spent twenty-six years in the New York State Assembly. There, he served as Minority Leader Pro Tempore, Deputy Minority Leader, and Ranking Minority Member of the Assembly Judiciary Committee. Before being elected to public office himself, Senator Winner was counsel and legislative assistant to then-Senate Deputy Majority Leader William T. Smith from 1971 to 1978. He is a partner in the law firm of Keyser, Maloney, Winner LLP in Elmira, where he lives with his family.

JAMES W WRIGHT (R-I-C)
48th - Jefferson, Oswego and parts of St Lawrence Counties

State Office Bldg, 317 Washington St, 4th Floor, Watertown, NY 13601
315-785-2430/fax: 315-785-2498

James Wright was first elected to the New York State Senate in November 1992. He graduated from the State University of New York at Oswego in 1971 and attended the Maxwell School of Public Administration at Syracuse University. He was selected to participate in the Local Government Public Administration Internship at Harvard University's Kennedy School of Government Program for Senior Executives, and in the United States Army War College National Security Seminar. He has also served as an adjunct faculty member and a private consultant. In the Senate, he is currently Deputy Majority Leader for Policy and chairs the Senate Energy and Telecommunications Committee. He began his career as a caseworker in child protective services in Oswego County, then became the first County Administrator of Oswego County, a post he held until his appointment as first County Administrator of Jefferson County. He was honored by Oswego State with the Lifetime Award of Merit in 2002.

CATHARINE M YOUNG (R-C-I)
149th - Parts of Allegany, Cattaraugus & Chautauqua Counties

700 Westgate Plaza, W State St, Olean, NY 14760
716-373-7103/fax: 716-373-7105

Catharine Young was first elected to the New York State Assembly in 1998. She attended SUNY-Fredonia and earned a BA (magna cum laude) in Mass Communication from St Bonaventure University. Prior to the State Assembly, she served as a Cattaraugus County legislator, representing the City and Town of Olean, and became Majority Whip within her first eighteen months of service. She was appointed Chairperson of the Development and Agriculture Committee and was a member of the County Board of Health. Ms Young served as Director of Communications & Development for the Rehabilitation Center, and has also worked as a newspaper staff reporter and a freelance writer for national and local publications. In the Assembly she has served as Ranking Minority Member on the Housing Committee, and she serves on the Task Forces on the State of New York Agriculture and the Task Force on Sex Crimes Against Women and Children. She has served on numerous boards in her community, including the Cattaraugus County American Red Cross, and the Olean Chamber of Commerce. She was president of the Olean Rotary Club, and a teacher at St Mary of the Angels parish for four years. She is a past member of the Greater Olean executive committee and was an Olean YMCA volunteer. She is a lifelong resident of New York.

U.S. Senate: New York Delegation

HILLARY RODHAM CLINTON (D)

476 Russell Senate Office Bldg, Washington, DC 20510
202-224-4451/fax: 202-228-0282

780 Third Avenue, Suite 2601, New York, NY 10017
212-688-6262/fax: 212-688-7444

Leo O'Brien Fed Ofc Bldg, 1 Clinton Sq, Rm 821, Albany, NY 12207
518-431-0120/fax: 518-431-0128

J M Hanley Fed Bldg, 100 South Clinton St, PO Box 7378, Syracuse, NY 13261-7378
315-448-0470/fax: 315-448-0476

Guaranty Bldg, Suite 208, 28 Church Street, Buffalo, NY 14202
716-854-9725/fax: 716-854-9731

Keating Fed Ofc Bldg, 100 State St, Rm 3280, Rochester, NY 14614
585-263-6250/fax: 585-263-6247

PO Box 273, Lowville, NY 13367
315-376-6118/fax: 315-376-8230

PO Box 617, Hartsdale, NY 10530
914-725-9294/fax: 914-472-5073

155 Pinelawn Rd, Ste 250 N, Melville, NY 11747
631-249-2825/fax: 631-249-2847

Hillary Rodham Clinton was first elected to the United States Senate in November 2000. She is the first First Lady elected to the United States Senate. She attended Wellesley College and is a graduate of Yale Law School. In 1977 she was appointed chair of the Legal Services Corporation by President Jimmy Carter. From 1986 to 1989, she chaired the board of the Children's Defense Fund. She also served as chair of the American Bar Association Commission on Women in the Profession in 1987. In 1988 and 1991, she was named one of the National Law Journal's 100 Most Influential Lawyers in America. While serving as First Lady in 1993, Senator Clinton was appointed by President Clinton to chair the Task Force on National Health Care. She led the fight to pass the Children's Health Insurance Program, which provides health insurance for millions of working families, and to increase funding for breast cancer research and treatment. She also worked to pass strong anti-crime measures, including the Brady Bill and the assault weapons ban. In the US Senate, Senator Clinton serves on the Committees for Environment and Public Works; Health, Education, Labor and Pensions; and is the first New York Senator to serve on the Senate Armed Services Committee. After 9/11 she worked to secure $21.4 billion to assist cleanup and recovery and since then has closely monitored the disbursement of funds. Working on behalf of the economy in New York and elsewhere, she led a bipartisan effort to bring next-generation broadband access to rural communities; co-sponsored the 21st Century Nanotechnology Research and Development Act; won an extension of Unemployed Insurance for displaced workers; and spoke out against tax breaks for the wealthiest Americans. She has visited troops in Afghanistan and Iraq. An advocate for children and families for more than thirty years, she wrote the best-selling book, *It Takes A Village: And Other Lessons Children Teach Us*, contributing nearly $1 million of author proceeds to charities assisting children and families. Her latest book, *Living History*, sold more than 1.5 million copies in the US and another 1.5 million abroad.

CHARLES E SCHUMER (D)

313 Hart Senate Office Bldg, Washington, DC 20510
202-224-6542/fax: 202-228-3027

757 Third Avenue, Suite 17-02, New York, NY 10017
212-486-4430; TDD: 212-486-7803/fax: 212-486-7693

Leo O'Brien Federal Building, Room 420, Albany, NY 12207
518-431-4070/fax: 518-431-4076

111 West Huron Street, Room 620, Buffalo, NY 14202
716-846-4111/fax: 716-846-4113

100 State Street, Room 3040, Rochester, NY 14614
585-263-5866/fax: 585-263-3173

100 S Clinton St, Rm 841, Syracuse, NY 13261-7318
315-423-5471/fax: 315-423-5185

15 Henry St., Rm B6, Binghamton, NY 13901
607-772-6792/fax: 607-772-8124

145 Pine Lawn Rd., #300, Melville, NY 11747
631-753-0978/fax: 631-753-0997

PO Box A, Red Hook, NY 12571
914-285-9741/fax: 845-758-1043

Charles Schumer was first elected to the United States Senate in November 1998. He is a graduate of Harvard University and Harvard Law School. He was elected to the State Assembly in 1974 and the US House of Representatives in 1980. Since his election to the Senate, Senator Schumer has made improving New York's economy his top priority. He has been successful in bringing affordable air service to Upstate New York, and he initiated a comprehensive effort to attract new businesses and financial resources to that area. Improving access to quality education is another priority. He is working to make college tuition tax deductible for most American families and has developed a plan to provide a series of incentives to attract the best and brightest to teaching. Senator Schumer is also working to ensure that all Americans have quality health care and access to affordable prescription drugs. He has fought to restore hospital cuts inflicted by the 1997 Balanced Budget Act, to provide seniors with a prescription drug benefit under Medicare, and to remove barriers that delay generic medications from coming to the marketplace. He now leads the fight against privatization of Social Security and to ensure the solvency of the program through a bipartisan solution. He is working to retain Medicaid funding and the deductibility of state and local taxes on federal tax returns. Born in Brooklyn, he is a lifelong resident of New York.

Biographies

U.S. House of Representatives: New York Delegation

GARY L ACKERMAN (D)
5 - Queens & Nassau Counties

2243 Rayburn House Office Bldg, Washington, DC 20515
202-225-2601/fax: 202-225-1589

218-14 Northern Blvd, Bayside, NY 11361
718-423-2154/fax: 718-423-5053

Gary Ackerman was first elected to Congress in a special election in 1983. He graduated from Queens College and taught Social Studies and Math at New York Junior High School. In 1970 he left his teaching position to start a weekly newspaper in Queens, which is now part of the largest community news group in the New York Metropolitan area. He was first elected to public office in 1978 as a member of the New York State Senate. As a US Congressman and chair of the Subcommittee on Asia and the Pacific, he made history in October 1993 by traveling to North Korea to discuss the framework under which North Korea would agree to cease building nuclear weapons. Mr Ackerman is also well known for his efforts to feed the starving people of Ethiopia and for playing a leading role in the rescue of Ethiopian Jews and their emigration to Israel. He also convinced the German government to establish a $10 million fund to compensate 18,000 Holocaust survivors and to investigate whether 3,300 former Nazi soldiers collecting German pensions in the US are war criminals. He was successful in getting Medicare to cover testing for prostate cancer and persuaded the National Cancer Institute to fund and undertake the nation's first ever study of environmental factors causing breast cancer. Congressman Ackerman was born in Brooklyn and is a lifelong resident of New York.

TIMOTHY H BISHOP (D)
1 - Parts of Suffolk County

1113 Longworth House Office Bldg, Washington, DC 20515-3201
202-225-3826/fax: 202-225-3143

3680 Route 112, Ste C, Coram, NY 11727
631-696-6500/fax: 631-696-4520

33 Flying Point Rd, Ste 104A, Southampton, NY 11968
631-259-8450

Timothy H Bishop was first elected to Congress in 2002. Mr Bishop earned a Bachelor's degree in History from Holy Cross College and a Masters degree in Public Administration from Long Island University. Prior to his election, he served as Provost at Southampton College. During his twenty-nine years at the college, he held a variety of positions. In Congress he serves on the powerful Transportation and Infrastructure Committee and the Education and Workforce Committee. Congressman Bishop has been chair of the Scholarship Committee for the Southampton Rotary Club, chair of the Southampton Town Board of Ethics, a member of the Board of Directors and Treasurer of the Bridgehampton Childcare and Recreation Center, and a board member of the Eastern Long Island Coastal Conservation Alliance. He was born in Southampton and is a lifelong resident of New York.

SHERWOOD L BOEHLERT (R)
24 - Broome, Cayuga, Chenango, Cortland, Herkimer, Oneida, Ontario, Otsego, Seneca, Tioga & Tompkins Counties

2246 Rayburn House Office Bldg, Washington, DC 20515
202-225-3665/fax: 202-225-1891

10 Broad St, Utica, NY 13501
315-793-8146/fax: 315-798-4099

21 Lincoln St, Auburn, NY 13021
315-255-0649/fax: 315-255-1369

45 Church St, Cortland, NY 13045
607-758-3918/fax: 607-758-9007

Sherwood Boehlert was first elected to Congress in 1982. Mr Boehlert served in the US Army from 1956 to 1958 and holds a BA from Utica College. He was Manager of Public Relations for Wyandotte Chemicals Corp from 1961 to 1964. From 1964-1972 he served as Chief of Staff for Congressman Alexander Pirnie, and from 1973 to 1979 he served as Chief of Staff for Congressman Donald Mitchell. He was elected Oneida County Executive in 1979. In Congress, Mr Boehlert chairs the Science Committee, which has jurisdiction over all federal nonmilitary scientific and technology research and development programs including NASA, the National Science Foundation, and research and development initiatives within the Environmental Protection Agency, the Department of Energy, and the Department of Commerce. He is a member of the Select Committee on Intelligence, where he is on the front line of important intelligence decisions faced by Congress; he is also a delegate to the NATO Parliamentary Assembly, where he serves as chairman of the Assembly's Scientific and Technology Committee. Congressman Boehlert was born in Utica and is a lifelong resident of New York. He and his family currently live in New Hartford, New York.

JOSEPH CROWLEY (D)
7 - Queens & Parts of Bronx Counties

312 Cannon House Office Bldg, Washington, DC 20515
202-225-3965/fax: 202-225-1909

82-11 37th Avenue, Ste 607, Jackson Heights, NY 11372
718-779-1400/fax: 718-505-0156

2114 Williamsbridge Rd, Bronx, NY 10461
718-931-1400/fax: 718-931-1340

Joseph Crowley was first elected to Congress in November 1998. A graduate of Queens College, he had previously served in the New York State Assembly. Congressman Crowley has been an outspoken advocate for strong leadership by the United States to improve human rights and foster democracy throughout all of Latin America. In addition to leadership for justice and equality throughout all of Ireland, he has been a leader in support of Israel including sponsorship of legislation to guarantee Israel fair and equal treatment at the United Nations. In 2000, as a freshman member, Congressman Crowley passed his amendment to appropriate $25 million to the United Nation's Population Fund (UNFPA) to improve the health of over one million women and children in Third World nations. In 2003 he was selected to serve as Deputy Chief Whip, making him the highest-ranking New York Member of the Democratic Leadership. Other appointments include the Committees on Financial Services and on International Relations. On the domestic front, he has made fighting to improve the quality of life for families in Queens and the Bronx his first priority. At his request, former President Clinton appointed a federal coordinator for virus prevention and control efforts on the national, state, and local levels. Mr Crowley's other goals for New Yorkers include education funding to allow New York to rebuild and rehabilitate its aging schools, a strong Health Care Bill of Rights to protect New Yorkers in managed care plans and a long-term solution to save Social Security. A lifelong resident of New York, Congressman Crowley lives in Woodside, New York.

ELIOT L ENGEL (D)
17 - Bronx, Rockland & Westchester Counties

2161 Rayburn House Office Bldg, Washington, DC 20515
202-225-2464/fax: 202-225-5513

3655 Johnson Ave, Bronx, NY 10463
718-796-9700/fax: 718-796-5134

261 West Nyack Rd, West Nyack, NY 10994
845-735-1000/fax: 845-735-1963

6 Gramatan Ave, Ste 205, Mt Vernon, NY 10550
914-699-4100/fax: 914-699-3646

Eliot Engel was first elected to the Congress in November 1988. He graduated from Hunter-Lehman College with a BA in History. He holds a Master's degree in Guidance and Counseling from Herbert H Lehman College of the City University of New York and a law degree from New York Law School. Prior to his election to Congress, he was a teacher and guidance counselor in the New York City public school system and then served twelve years in the New York State Assembly (1977-1988). In Congress, Mr. Engel has authored landmark housing and education legislation and advocated increasing funding for the war on drugs. He has also authored legislation on US trade policy, education reform, long-term health care, and domestic terrorism. He was the prime sponsor of the Congressional resolution recognizing Jerusalem as the undivided capital of Israel. He also authored the legislation designating October as Italian American Cultural and Heritage Month. Congressman Engel is a lifelong resident of the Bronx.

VITO J FOSSELLA (R)
13 - Richmond County & parts of Kings County

1239 Longworth House Office Bldg, Washington, DC 20515
202-225-3371/fax: 202-226-1272

9818 Fourth Ave, Brooklyn, NY 11209-8102
718-630-5277/fax: 718-630-5388

4434 Amboy Road, 2nd Floor, Staten Island, NY 10312
718-356-8400/fax: 718-356-1928

Vito Fossella was first elected to Congress in a special election in November 1997. He holds a BS degree from the University of Pennsylvania's Wharton School, and a JD degree from Fordham University's School of Law. His political career began in 1994, when he was elected to the New York City Council. In that capacity, he secured funding for construction of the first schools built on Staten Island in over a decade and initiated the "Readers Are Leaders"

program, challenging fourth graders to read ten books in six weeks. He also introduced the first landfill closure bill, paving the way for the historic agreement to close Fish Kills landfill, and he authored a variety of proposals to eliminate or reduce business taxes. In Congress, his priorities continued to be pro-growth economic strategies and efforts to improve our children's education system. As a member of the Transportation and Banking Committee, he secured funding for a new Staten Island Ferry, the construction of ferry terminals, and a new commissary at Fort Hamilton. In 2002 he authored the Investor and Capital Markets Fee Relief Act. Also active in foreign affairs, he emerged as a national spokesman in 1999, when he opposed the offer of clemency to terrorists affiliated with the FALN. Currently he is a member of the Committee on Energy and Commerce and Vice Chairman of its Environment Subcommittee, and also a member of the Committee on Financial Services. Congressman Fossella is a native of Staten Island.

BRIAN HIGGINS (D)
27 - Chautauqua & Erie Counties

431 Cannon House Office Bldg, Washington, DC 20515-3227
202-225-3306/fax: 202-226-0347

Larkin Bldg, 726 Exchange St, Ste 601, Buffalo, NY 14210
716-8523501/fax: 716-852-3929

Fenton Bldg, Ste 300, 2 E Second St, Jamestown, NY 14701
716-484-0729/fax: 716-484-1049

Brian Higgins was first elected to the United States Congress in 2004. He received his undergraduate and graduate education at Buffalo State College, studying political science and history, respectively. From 1987 to 1993 he served in the Buffalo Common Council, where he earned a reputation for intelligence, hard work, effectiveness, and honesty. In 1995 he was admitted to Harvard on the inaugural Western New York Harvard Graduate Fellowship, and he received an MA in Public Policy and Administration from the JFK School of Government in 1996. He lectured for a time at Buffalo State College, and in 1998 was elected to the NYS Assembly, where his priorities were economic development and job creation in western New York and the revitalization of Buffalo's waterfront. In the US Congress, he continues to make economic development and job creation a priority throughout Chautauqua and Erie Counties. He serves on the Committee of Transportation and Infrastructure and on the T&I Subcommittee on Highways, Transit and Pipelines; Water Resources and Environment; and Coast Guard and Maritime Transportation. He also serves on the Committee on Government Reform, and on its subcommittees on Energy and Resources and on National Security, Emerging Threats, and International Relations. He lives in South Buffalo.

MAURICE D HINCHEY (D)
22 - Ulster, Sullivan, Orange, Dutchess, Delaware, Broome, Tioga & Tompkins Counties

2431 Rayburn House Office Bldg, Washington, DC 20515
202-225-6335/fax: 202-226-0774

100A Federal Building, Binghamton, NY 13901
607-773-2768/fax: 607-773-3176

123 South Cayuga Street, Suite 201, Ithaca, NY 14850
607-273-1388/fax: 607-273-8847

Biographies

291 Wall St, Kingston, NY 12401
845-331-4466/fax: 845-331-7456

City Hall, 3rd Fl, 16 James St, Middletown, NY 10940
845-344-3211/fax:845-342-2070

Maurice Hinchey was first elected to Congress in 1992. He served in the US Navy after high school and then worked two years as a laborer before attending SUNY-New Paltz, where he earned both his Bachelor's and Master's degrees. He later pursued advanced graduate studies in Public Administration and Economics at SUNY-Albany. In 1975 he began an eighteen-year tenure in the New York State Assembly, where he chaired the Environmental Conservation Committee. Under his leadership, the committee conducted a successful investigation of Love Canal, one of the nation's first major toxic dumpsites, and developed the nation's first law to control acid rain. He also led an investigation into organized crime control of the waste-hauling industry that led to the conviction of more than twenty criminal figures. He was also responsible for the development of the statewide system of urban parks, now called heritage areas, and was the author of the act that created the Hudson River Greenway. In the US Congress, Mr Hinchey's top priorities have been ensuring economic security for working families, strengthening our education system, and protecting our environment. He has also focused on job creation, economic development, and deficit reduction. He sponsored successful legislation that secured 1,000 defense jobs in his district. Congressman Hinchey was born on Manhattan's Lower West Side and was raised in Saugerties. He and his family now reside in Hurley, New York.

STEVE ISRAEL (D)
2 - Parts of Nassau & Suffolk Counties

432 Cannon House Office Bldg, Washington, DC 20515
202-225-3336/fax: 202-225-4669

150 Motor Pkwy, Ste 108, Hauppauge, NY 11788
631-951-2210; 516-505-1448/fax: 631-951-3308

Steve Israel was first elected to Congress in November 2000. His long record of public service began in 1980 when he handled foreign policy, national security, and human rights issues for former Congressman Richard Ottinger. In that role, Mr Israel drafted legislation to protect Catholic employees in US-owned firms in Northern Ireland and developed many initiatives to protect human rights in Bolivia, Chile, Guatemala, North Korea, South Africa, and the former USSR. He also served as Majority Leader on the Huntington Town Board. In that role, he reduced and stabilized taxes for seven consecutive years, brought Huntington's bond rating from worst to first in the entire region, and passed an historic $15 million environmental protection program. In the US Congress, he quickly rose to leadership positions. In his second term, he was tapped for a position as Assistant Democratic Whip, and he also served on the important House Armed Services Committee; in his third term he was appointed Chair of the House Caucus Democratic Task Force on Defense and the Military. Congressman Israel was raised on the South Shore of Long Island. He currently resides in the Town of Huntington.

SUE W KELLY (R)
19 - Dutchess, Orange, Putnam, Rockland & Westchester Counties

2182 Rayburn House Office Bldg, Washington, DC 20515
202-225-5441/fax: 202-225-3289

21 Old Main St, Room 107, Fishkill, NY 12524
845-897-5200/fax: 845-897-5800

Orange County Government Center, 255 Main St, 3rd Fl, Goshen, NY 10924
845-291-4100/fax: 845-291-4164

2025 Crompond Rd, Yorktown Heights, NY 10598
914-962-0761/fax: 914-962-9537

Sue Kelly was first elected to Congress in 1994. She graduated from Denison University in Ohio with a BA degree in botany and bacteriology and earned a Master's degree in Health Advocacy from Sarah Lawrence College. Prior to serving in public office, she worked as an educator, small business owner, patient advocate, and rape crisis counselor. Since her election to Congress, her accomplishments have been significant and diverse. She pushed legislation providing $11 million for habitat restoration along the Hudson River; her legislation to guarantee women reconstructive surgery following a mastectomy became law in 1998; and she championed legislation, which is now law, relieving most homeowners of capital gains taxation when they sell their principal residence. Ms Kelly spearheaded the effort to bring home $27 million for a new veterans' nursing home in Montrose, New York, and successfully secured $35 million in important transportation infrastructure projects in the Hudson Valley. She continues to work in support of numerous federal grant programs, which help Hudson Valley communities address issues ranging from local law enforcement needs to clear water projects for municipalities. She is committed to giving teachers and local administrators the flexibility to decide how best to use federal resources in meeting the education needs of students. She supports health care reforms to ensure that health care decisions are made by the patients and their doctors, not by insurance company bureaucrats. She has also reintroduced the Women's Health and Cancer Rights Act and legislation to ensure insurance coverage for children in need of reconstructive surgery due to congenital defects such as cleft palates. She resides in Katonah, New York.

PETER T KING (R)
3 - Nassau County

436 Cannon House Office Bldg, Washington, Dc 20515
202-225-7896/fax: 202-226-2279

1003 Park Blvd, Massapequa Park, NY 11762
516-541-4225/fax: 516-541-6602

Peter King was first elected to Congress in 1992. He is a graduate of St Francis College, Brooklyn and University of Notre Dame Law School. He began his political career in November 1977 by winning election to the Hempstead Town Council. Subsequently, he was elected to three terms (1981, 1985, 1989) as Comptroller of Nassau County. As the county's chief fiscal watchdog, he initiated official audits and investigations that resulted in millions of dollars in savings to local taxpayers. In Congress, he serves on the Financial Services Committee and the International Relations Committee. He is an advocate of relieving the tax burdens of working families, safeguarding Social Security and Medicare, and strengthening our national defense. He is a lifelong resident of New York and has lived in Nassau County for more than thirty years.

JOHN R "RANDY" KUHL

29 - Allegany, Cattaraugus, Chemung, Monroe, Ontario, Schuyler, Steuben & Yates Counties

1505 Longworth House Office Bldg, Washington, DC 20515-3229
202-225-3161/fax: 202-226-6599

32 Denison Pkwy West, Corning, NY 14830
607-937-3333/fax: 607-937-6047

Westgate Plaza, 700 W State St, Olean, NY 14760
800-562-7431

Randy Kuhl was first elected to the United States Congress in 2004. He received a BS in Civil Engineering from Union College in 1966 and a JD from Syracuse College of Law in 1969. After serving in the NYS Assembly from 1980 to 1986, he was elected to the State Senate, where he was Assistant Majority Leader from 1995 to 2004. As a freshman Member of the US Congress, he serves on three key Committees: Transportation and Infrastructure, where he is Vice Chair of the Aviation Subcommittee and a member of the Economic Development Subcommittee; Agriculture, where he is a member of the Livestock and Horticulture Subcommittee; and Education and the Workforce, where he is a member of the Education Reform and 21st Century Competitiveness Subcommittee. He is the former State Chairman of the American Legislative Exchange Council (ALEC) and was vice chairman of the National Conference of State Legislatures' (NCSL) Wine Industry Task Force. He is a member of the Advisory Committee of the Five Rivers Council of the Boy Scouts of America and the Executive Committee of the Steuben County Republican Committee. He lives in Hammondsport, New York.

NITA M LOWEY (D)

18 - Rockland & Westchester Counties

2329 Rayburn House Office Bldg, Washington, DC 20515
202-225-6506/fax: 202-225-0546

15 Third St, Ste 2, New City, NY 10956
845-639-3485/fax: 845-639-3487

222 Mamaroneck Ave, Ste 310, White Plains, NY 10605
914-428-1707/fax: 914-328-1505

Grinton I. Will Library, 1500 Central Park Ave, Yonkers, NY 10710
914-779-9766 (by appointment)

Nita Lowey was first elected to Congress in 1988. She received her Bachelors degree from Mt Holyoke College and in May 1989 was awarded an honorary Doctor of Laws degree from Pace University. Prior to her election to Congress, she served in the NY Department of State from 1975 to 1987. She was Assistant Secretary of State from 1985 to 1987. She also served on the NYS Child Care Commission and was a founder of the NYS Association of Women Office Holders. In Congress she has taken a leadership role on a wide range of issues. Under her leadership, federal funding for after-school programs has increased from $1 million in 1996 to $1 billion today. She staunchly defended the Public Broadcasting System (PBS), even "inviting" Muppets Bert and Ernie to a Congressional hearing, and she has been equally strong in her defense of the National Endowment of the Arts (NEA). Her legislation requiring labeling of all food products with the eight most common food allergens became law in 2004.

She has given priority to national security and the fight against terrorism. In 2003 she was chosen by her colleagues to serve on the Select Committee on Homeland Security. Outside Congress, Congresswoman Lowey has long been active in community and civic activities. She served as PTA President of PS 178 and was a 20-year member of the Hillcrest Jewish Center. Congresswoman Lowey was born in the Bronx and is a lifelong resident of New York.

CAROLYN B MALONEY (D)

14 - Kings & Queens Counties

2331 Rayburn House Office Bldg, Washington, DC 20515
202-225-7944/fax: 202-225-4709

28-11 Astoria Blvd, Astoria, NY 11102-1933
718-932-1804/fax: 718-932-1805

1651 3rd Avenue, Suite 311, New York, NY 10128-3679
212-860-0606/fax: 212-860-0704

Carolyn Maloney was first elected to Congress in November 1992. A graduate of Greensboro College, she came to New York City in 1970 and worked for several years as teacher and administrator for the NYC Board of Education. In 1977 she went to work for the NYS Legislature, serving as a legislative aide and senior program analyst in the NYS Assembly and as Director of Special Projects for the Minority Leader in the NYS Senate. In 1982 she won a seat on the New York City Council and served for ten years. In the US Congress, she has worked to ensure that New York's recovery from 9/11 is completed; in 2004 she obtained health monitoring and treatment for the workers at Ground Zero after 9/11. She was named Chair of the Democratic Caucus Task force on Homeland Security in June 2003. She spearheaded passage of the Debbie Smith Act to expedite use and processing of DNA rape kits. She founded the bi-partisan Congressional Working Group on Parkinson's Disease to increase awareness of the disease and to coordinate efforts to increase research funding. A staunch supporter of key US allies, she passed legislation cracking down on the Arab boycott of Israel and has championed the cause of justice in Ireland and Greece. She is a member of the Congressional Caucus on Women's Issues, the Congressional Arts Caucus, and the Executive Committee of the Democratic Study Group. She has received the Military Order of the Purple Heart for Meritorious and Conspicuous Service for Veterans, as well as numerous other awards. She lives in New York City.

CAROLYN McCARTHY (D)

4 - Nassau County

106 Cannon House Office Bldg, Washington, DC 20515
202-225-5516/fax: 202-225-5758

200 Garden City Plaza, Ste 320, Garden City, NY 11530
516-739-3008/fax: 516-739-2973

Carolyn McCarthy was elected to her first term in Congress in 1996. She is a licensed practical nurse with over thirty years of experience working in the health-care field. After her husband was killed and her son injured in the 1993 Long Island Railroad massacre, she turned her tragedy into a public campaign against gun violence, speaking out across the country on its roots and causes. In the US Congress, she has addressed not only gun issues but also health and education issues. Serving on the Education and Workforce Committee and the Financial Services Committee, she advances her goals to provide working families tax cuts, stimulate the economy, protect Long Islanders' savings and pensions, and ensure every child a top

Biographies

725

education. She was a key figure in the passage of the Elementary and Secondary Education Act, which contained her provisions to fund school nurses, after-school care, and mentoring programs. She has received many honors, among them being named one of Newsday's 100 Long Island Influentials, Congressional Quarterly's 50 Most Effective Legislators in Congress, one of Ladies' Home Journal's America's 100 Most Important Women, and Advertising Age's list of "Most Impact by Women in 1999." Before her election in 1996, she had never run for public office. She is a lifelong resident of Mineola, New York.

JOHN M McHUGH (R)
24 - Clinton, Lewis, Essex, Jefferson, Franklin, Oswego, Fulton, St Lawrence, Hamilton, Madison & Herkimer Counties

2333 Rayburn House Office Bldg, Washington, DC 20515
202-225-4611/fax: 202-226-0621

28 North School St, PO Box 800, Mayfield, NY 12117-0800
518-661-6486/fax: 518-661-5704

104 Federal Building, Plattsburg, NY 12901-9723
518-563-1406/fax: 518-561-9723

120 Washington St, Ste 200, Watertown, NY 13601-3370
315-782-3150/fax: 315-782-1291

205 S Peterboro St, Canastota, NY 13032-1312
315-697-2063/fax: 315-697-2064

John McHugh was first elected to Congress in 1992. He received a BA in Political Science from Utica College of Syracuse University in 1970, and earned a Master's degree in Public Administration from SUNY's Nelson A Rockefeller Graduate School of Public Affairs in 1977. He began his career in public service in 1971 in Watertown, where he served for five years as confidential assistant to the city manager. Thereafter, he joined the staff of NYS Senator H Douglas Barclay, where he acted as chief of Research & Liaison with local government for nine years. Elected to the 46th State Senate District seat in 1984, he served four terms in the legislature's upper house. In the US Congress, he has been a champion of fiscal responsibility, lower taxes, stronger schools, and protection of Social Security and Medicare. He has fought to help farmers secure better prices, rallying Congressional members from across the country to enact the Option 1-A pricing system, which provides higher payments to farmers for their milk. He is a member of the House Armed Services Committee, the House Government Reform Committee, and the House Permanent Select Committee on Intelligence. A lifelong resident of New York, Congressman McHugh was born in Watertown and now lives in Pierrepoint Manor in Jefferson County.

MICHAEL R McNULTY (D)
21 - Albany, Fulton, Montgomery, Rensselaer, Saratoga, Schenectady, Schoharie & Counties

2210 Rayburn House Office Bldg, Washington, DC 20515
202-225-5076/fax: 202-225-5077

O'Brien Fed Bldg, Room 827, Albany, NY 12207518-465-0700/fax: 518-427-5107

2490 Riverfront Center, Amsterdam, NY 12010-4612
518-843-3400/fax: 518-843-8874

US Post Office, Schenectady, NY 12305-1982
518-374-4547/fax: 518-374-7908

33 Second St, Troy, NY 12180-3975
518-271-0822/fax: 518-273-6150

Fulton Co Ofc Bldg, 223 W Main St, Rm 10, Johnstown, NY 12095
518-762-3568/fax: 518-736-2004

Michael McNulty was first elected to Congress in 1988. He is a graduate of St Joseph's Institute, Loyola University Rome Center, and the College of Holy Cross, where he earned a BA degree in Political Science. He is also a graduate of the Hill School of Insurance. He was first elected to public office in November 1969, as Town Supervisor of Green Island. After eight years as Supervisor, he was elected Mayor of the Village of Green Island and served in that capacity until he won election to the 106th New York State Assembly District NY in 1982. In Congress, after having served as Freshman Majority Whip for the northern region of the country during the first session of the 101st Congress, he was named to the position of Majority Whip-At-Large and served in that capacity through the 103rd Congress. He now serves as At-Large-Whip. He has served on numerous committees: Armed Services, Small Business, International Relations, and Post Office and Civil Service. He serves on the House Ways & Means Committee and is Ranking Democratic Member of the Subcommittee on Select Revenue Measures. He also serves on the Committee on Oversight. In 1991, he was awarded a Doctorate of Human Letters (Honoris Causa) by the College of St Rose. Congressman McNulty is a lifelong resident of New York.

GREGORY W MEEKS (D)
6 - Queens County

1710 Longworth House Office Bldg, Washington, DC 20515
202-225-3461/fax: 202-226-4169

196-06 Linden Boulevard, Saint Albans, NY 11412
718-949-5600/fax: 718-949-5972

1931 Mott Ave, Rm 305, Far Rockaway, NY 11691
718-327-9791/fax: 718-327-4722

106-11 Liberty Ave, 2nd Fl, Richmond Hill, NY 11417
718-738-4200/fax: 718-738-5588

Gregory W Meeks was first elected to Congress in a special election In 1982 he ran for public office to win a seat on the New York City Council. He received his BA degree in History with a minor in Political Science from Adelphi University and his JD from Howard University School of Law. After working as an Assistant District Attorney in Queens, he left this position to become Special Narcotics Prosecutor for the City of New York. He later joined the State Investigations Commission responsible for investigations of public officials, state employees, and organized crime. He eventually became Supervising Judge for the New York State Works Compensation System. Starting in 1982, he served five years in the NYS Assembly. His leadership and consensus-building skills were further demonstrated when he was elected by his colleagues as chair of the Council of Black Elected Democrats (COBED), a statewide organization consisting of New York legislators and public officials. In Congress, Mr Meeks serves on the House Financial Services Committee and two of its subcommittees. He is the author of a major revision of the federal statutes governing predatory lending practices. He has balanced his support of labor by supporting trade, business development, and global economics. Active in his community, he founded the Jesse L Jackson Independent Democratic Club, which was renamed the Thurgood Marshall Regular Democratic Club. He is a member of the 100 Black Men, the NAACP, the United Black Men of Queens, and the National Black Caucus of State Legislators, Inc. Born in East Harlem, he is a lifelong resident of New York and currently resides in Far Rockaway.

JERROLD L NADLER (D)
8 - New York & Kings Counties

2334 Rayburn House Office Bldg, Washington, DC 20515
202-225-5635/fax: 202-225-6923

445 Neptune Ave, Brooklyn, NY 11224
718-373-3198/fax: 718-996-0039

201 Varick St, Ste 669, New York, NY 10014
212-367-7350/fax:212-367-7356

Jerrold Nadler was elected to Congress in 1992. He graduated from Columbia University and Fordham Law School. In 1976, after a stint as a legislative assistant, he was elected to the New York State Assembly, where he served for sixteen years, during which time he was credited with authoring much of the state's body of law on domestic violence and child support enforcement and was one of the architects of the landmark "Child Support Adjustment Act." In Congress he is perhaps best known as a prominent member of the Judiciary Committee. As Ranking Member on the Constitution Subcommittee, he has dealt with such issues as constitutional rights, federal civil rights laws, abortion, gay rights, and government ethics. He is also a highly regarded expert on infrastructure. After his district was attacked on 9/11, he dedicated his efforts to the residents, employees, and small businesses there, and he has also taken the lead in the continuing fight to protect air quality in Lower Manhattan. He is known nationwide as a champion of progressive causes and has a rating of 100% from such organizations as Planned Parenthood and the NAACP. He is a member of the National Governing Council of the American Jewish Congress and of the US Holocaust Memorial Council. He serves as a member of the NYS Board of Directors of the National Abortion Rights Action League and of Americans for Democratic Action. He is a past president of District 7-A of the Zionist Organization of America, and he formerly served as a member of the board of the Women's Interarts Center. Born in Brooklyn, he currently resides on Manhattan's West Side.

MAJOR R OWENS (D)
11 - Kings County

2309 Rayburn House Office Bldg, Washington, DC 20515
202-225-6231/fax: 202-226-0112

1414 Cortelyou Rd, Brooklyn, NY 11226
718-940-3213/fax: 718-940-3217

289 Utica Ave, Brooklyn, NY 11213
518-773-3100/fax: 718-735-7143

Major Owens was first elected to the US House of Representatives in 1982. Born in Memphis, Tennessee, he received his Bachelors degree in Mathematics from Morehouse College in Atlanta and his Master's Degree in Library Science from Atlanta University. He held a number of specialized and supervisory positions in the Brooklyn Public Library, and he has taught at Columbia University in one of the nation's top library schools. His involvement in politics is partially a result of his work as chair of the Brooklyn Congress of Racial Equality, as Vice President of the Metropolitan Council on Housing, and as the Commissioner of the New York City Community Development Agency. In 1974, he was elected to the NYS Senate and remained in this position until 1982. In the US Congress he is a member of the Education and Workforce Committee, which guides federal involvement in education, job training, labor law, employee safety and pensions, and programs for the aging and people with disabilities. As Ranking Democrat on its Subcommittee for Workforce Protections, he has fought for minimum wage increases, blocked the attempt to eliminate cash payments for overtime, and defeated the conspiracy to dismantle the Occupational Safety and Health Administration. As Chairman of the Congressional Black Caucus on Haiti, he led the successful three-year fight to restore that nation's democratically elected President.

CHARLES B RANGEL (D)
15 - New York County

2354 Rayburn House Office Bldg, Washington, DC 20515
202-225-4365/fax: 202-225-0816

163 W 125th St, Suite 737, New York, NY 10027
212-663-3900/fax: 212-663-4277

Charles Rangel was first elected to Congress in November 1970. Following high school, he joined the US Army, serving with the Seventh Infantry Division in Korea. He earned a BS degree from New York University in 1957 and a JD from St John's University School of Law. In 1961 he was appointed assistant US attorney in the Southern District of New York by then US Attorney General Robert Kennedy. He was appointed by President Johnson as general counsel to the National Advisory Commission on Selective Service in 1966 and was elected to the first of two terms in the New York State Assembly that same year. In the US Congress, he has amassed a record of accomplishments in economic development, housing, health care, education, veterans' affairs, drug abuse, and crime prevention. He is a founding member and former chairman of the Congressional Black Caucus; he was also chairman of the NYS Council of Black Elected Democrats and was a member of the House Judiciary Committee during the hearings on the articles of impeachment against President Richard Nixon. Later, as Chairman of the Select Committee on Narcotics Abuse and Control, he emerged as a leading fighter against drug addiction. As the senior Democratic member of the Ways and Means Committee, he continues to address the vital needs of his district. He is the principal author of the $5 billion dollar federal empowerment zone demonstration project to revitalize urban neighborhoods throughout America. He is also the author of the Low Income Housing Tax Credit. He was born in Harlem and still lives there.

THOMAS M. REYNOLDS (R)
26 - Seneca, Wayne, Wyoming, Erie, Genesee, Ontario, Monroe, Livingstone & Cayuga Counties

332 Cannon House Office Bldg, Washington, DC 20515
202-225-5265/fax: 202-225-5190

500 Essjay Rd, Suite 260, Williamsville, NY 14221
716-634-2324/fax: 716-631-7610

1577 West Ridge Rd, Rochester, NY 14615
585-663-5570/fax: 585-663-5711

Thomas Reynolds was first elected to Congress in 1998. Educated at Springville-Griffith Institute and Kent State University, he is a licensed real estate and insurance broker. He served in the NY Air National Guard from 1970 to 1976, where he rose to the rank of Sergeant. After serving on the Concord Town board from 1974 to 1982, he joined the Erie County Legislature from 1982 to 1988. In 1988, he was elected to the NYS Assembly, where he became the Assembly Republican Leader in 1995. While in the Assembly, he served as Chair of the Assembly Minority Affordable Housing Task Force and was honored as Legislator of the Year by the American Legislative Exchange Council. He served as Erie County Republican Chair from 1990-1996. In Congress, Mr Reynolds has earned a reputation as a champion of veterans' issues, working to strengthen facilities such as the Canandaigua VA Medical Center and Batavia Veterans Home, and improving health care services for veterans across western New York and the Finger Lakes district. He has seen several of his legislative initiatives signed into law, including the State Flexibility Clarification Act, which makes it more difficult of the federal government to impose unfunded mandates on state and local governments, and the Smith-Reynolds bill, which is intended to ease border congestion between the US, Canada, and Mexico. He lives in Clarence, New York.

JOSE E SERRANO (D)
16 - Bronx County

2227 Rayburn House Office Bldg, Washington, DC 20515
202-225-4361/fax: 202-225-6001

788 Southern Blvd, Bronx, NY 10455
718-620-0084/fax: 718-620-0658

890 Grand Concourse, Bronx, NY 10451
718-538-5400/fax: 718-620-0658

Jose E Serrano was first elected to Congress in a special election early in 1990. Born in Mayaguez, Puerto Rico, he moved to the Bronx as a young boy. Following high school, he served in the 172nd Support Battalion of the US Army Medical Corps, was employed by Community School Board #7, and was Chair of the South Bronx Community Corp. He was elected to the NYS Assembly in 1974. In 1980, President Jimmy Carter appointed him one of the first members of the Intergovernmental Advisory Council on Education. In Congress, he serves on the House Appropriations Committee as a member of the Subcommittee on Science, State, Justice, and Commerce and the Subcommittee on Homeland Security. As an appropriator, he has managed to secure millions of dollars in federal funding for his Bronx district; perhaps the most significant project has been the environmental restoration of the Bronx River. He has been a leading voice on preserving civil liberties in the wake of 9/11 and the strong law-enforcement provisions of the PATRIOT Act. He is architect of the English-Plus resolution, calling on government to encourage all Americans to learn and use multiple languages, in addition to English. Since his earliest days in Congress, he has supported lifting the embargo against Cuba. He also proposed the bill, signed into law as part of a larger bill, which grants posthumous citizenship to non-citizens who died as a result of the 9/11 attack and who had already initiated the process to become US citizens.

LOUISE McINTOSH SLAUGHTER (D)
28 - Erie, Monroe, Niagara & Orleans Counties

2469 Rayburn House Office Bldg, Washington, DC 20515
202-225-3615/fax: 202-225-7822

3120 Federal Bldg, 100 State St, Rochester, NY 14614
585-232-4850/fax: 585-232-1954

465 Main St, Ste 105, Buffalo, NY 14203
716-853-5813/fax: 716-853-6347

1910 Pine Ave, Niagara Falls, NY 14301
716-282-1274/fax: 716-283-2479

Louise McIntosh Slaughter was first elected to Congress in 1986. She attended the University of Kentucky, where she received a BS degree in Microbiology and a Master's degree in Public Health. Entering politics in the early 1970s, she has served in three different legislatures: the Monroe County Legislature (1976-1979), the NYS Assembly (1982-1986), and currently the US House of Representatives. She is the Ranking Member of the Committee on Rules, the first woman ever to hold this position. In this capacity, she has fought for the integrity of the democratic process: In March 2005 she unveiled a Congressional report detailing erosion of the legislative process in the last decade. A leading advocate for women's rights, she was co-chair of the Congressional Caucus for Women's Issues during the 108th Congress, and she co-authored the Violence Against Women Act in 1994. A member of the House Budget Committee in the early 1990s, she secured the first $500 million earmarked for breast cancer research at the National Institute of Health (NIH). As longtime co-chair of the Congressional Arts Caucus, she leads the fight for funding of the arts; in 2004 she won an additional $10 million for the National Endowment for the Arts (NEA) and $3.5 million for the National Endowment for the Humanities (NEH). She has won numerous awards. She was the first member of Congress to win the Sydney R Yates National Arts Advocacy Award, presented by the National Assembly of State Arts Agencies. In 2003 she was named as Humane Legislator of the Year by the American Humane Association. Born in Harland County, Kentucky, she lives in Fairport, a suburb of Rochester.

JOHN E SWEENEY (R)
20 - Columbia, Delaware, Dutchess, Essex, Greene, Otsego, Rensselaer, Saratoga, Washington & Warren Counties

416 Cannon House Office Bldg, Washington, DC 20515
202-225-5614/fax: 202-225-6234

939 Rte 146, Ste 430, Clifton Park, NY 12065
518-371-8839/fax: 518-371-9509

111 Main St, Delhi, NY 13753
607-746-9700/fax: 607-746-9747

21 Bay St, Glens Falls, NY 12801
518-792-3031

7578 N Broadway, Redhook, NY 12571
845-758-1222/fax: 845-758-2870

John Sweeney was first elected to Congress in 1998. He received his Bachelors degree in Political Science and criminal justice from Russell Sage College. A year after graduating, he was appointed head of the Rensselaer County DWI prevention program, which under his direction became the most successful program of its type in New York State. While still working, he attended law school, receiving his JD degree from the Western New England School of Law in 1990. He was selected to serve as both executive director and counsel to the New York State Republican Party in 1992. In 1995, he became NYS Commissioner of Labor, and in 1997 he was appointed deputy secretary to the Governor. In the US Congress, he serves on the powerful House Appropriations Committee. He is Vice Chairman of the Transportation, Treasury and HUD Appropriations Subcommittee, and he has also been assigned to the Homeland Security and the Foreign Operations Subcommittees. In 2004 he led the charge to ban dangerous steroids and steroid precursors. Born in Troy, he is a lifelong resident of New York, currently living in Clifton Park.

EDOLPHUS TOWNS (D)
10 - Kings County

2232 Rayburn House Office Bldg, Washington, DC 20515
202-225-5936/fax: 202-225-1018

1670 Fulton St, Brooklyn, NY 11213
718-774-5682/fax: 718-774-5730

26 Court St, Ste 1510, Brooklyn, NY 11241
718-855-8018/fax: 718-858-4542

1110 Pennsylvania Ave, Store 5, Brooklyn, NY 11207
718-272-1175/fax: 718-272-1203

2294 Nostrand Ave, Brooklyn, NY 11210
718-434-7931/fax: 718-774-5730

Edolphus Towns was first elected to Congress in November 1982. He served on active duty in the US Army from 1956 to 1958. He earned his Bachelor's degree from North Carolina A&T University and is a member of the Phi Beta Sigma Fraternity. He also holds a Master's degree in Social Work from Adelphi University. He has taught in the NYC public school system and is a former professor at Medgar Evers College in Brooklyn. He also has been a director at the Metropolitan Hospital, the assistant administrator at Beth Israel Hospital from 1965 to 1975, and in 1978 he became the borough president of Brooklyn. Throughout his years in the US Congress, his work in education, telecommunications, health care, and financial services has won him numerous awards. He is a member of the Energy and Commerce Committee, where he is on the Commerce, Trade and Consumer Protection Subcommittee, the Health Subcommittee, and the Telecommunications and the Internet Subcommittee. He is committed to protecting our national parks and creating open space throughout Brooklyn, including the Brooklyn Bridge Park Project, of which he was an original incorporator. Mr Towns serves on the Board of Directors of the American Red Cross, the Board of Directors of Kings County Boy Scouts, and the advisory board of Medgar Evers College, is a former president of the Association of the Study of Afro-American Life and History, and is a member of Adelphi University Alumni Association Academy of Distinction. He was born in Chadbourn, North Carolina and lives in the Cypress Hills section of Brooklyn.

NYDIA M VELAZQUEZ (D)
12 - New York, Queens & Kings Counties

2241 Rayburn House Office Bldg, Washington, DC 20515
202-225-2361/fax: 202-226-0327

268 Broadway, 2nd Fl, Brooklyn, NY 11211
718-599-3658/fax: 718-599-4537

173 Avenue B, New York, NY 10009
212-673-3997/fax: 212-473-5242

16 Court Street, Suite 1006, Brooklyn, NY 11241
718-222-5819/fax: 718-222-5830

Nydia Velazquez was first elected to Congress in 1992. Born in Yabucoa, Puerto Rico, she attended the University of Puerto Rico in Rio Piedras, where she graduated magna cum laude in 1974. In 1976 she earned her Master's degree from New York University. From 1976 to 1981, she was a member of the faculty of the University of Puerto Rico, Humacao Campus, in the Social Sciences department, where she became the chair of the department in 1977. She also was an adjunct professor in the Black and Puerto Rican Studies Department at Hunter College of the CUNY. Her political career began in 1983 with her appointment as special assistant to Congressman Edolphus Towns. In 1984 she became the first Latina ever to be elected to the New York City Council. In 1986 she was the Director of the Department of Puerto Rican Affairs in the United States, where she initiated one of the most successful employment empowerment programs in the nation's history. As a member of Congress, she has worked to promote economic development, to protect community health and the environment, and to secure access to affordable housing, quality education, and health care for all New York families. As Ranking Member of the House Small Business Committee, she has been an advocate of American small business and entrepreneurship. She was recently named as the inaugural "Woman of the Year" by Hispanic Business Magazine.

JAMES T WALSH (R)
25 - Cayuga, Monroe, Onondaga & Wayne Counties

2369 Rayburn House Office Bldg, Washington, DC 20515
202-225-3701/fax: 202-225-4042

PO Box 7306, Syracuse, NY 13261
315-423-5657/fax: 315-423-5669

James Walsh was first elected to Congress in 1988. He earned his Bachelor's degree in history from St Bonaventure University, and he served in the Peace Corps as an agricultural extension agent in Nepal. He worked for New York Telephone and NYNEX, and for his last two years with the company he was on loan to the State University of New York as an instructor. At the same time he was director of the Telecommunications Institute at the Utica College of Technology. For eleven years before going to Congress, he served as president of the Syracuse Common Council and district councilor. In Congress, he is nationally recognized as a leader in child nutrition through his support of the WIC (Women, Infants, and Children) Program and EFAP (The Emergency Food Assistance Plan). In 1999 he was author and primary sponsor of the Newborn and Infant Screening and Intervention Program Act, to assist in screening newborns for hearing loss. Today, close to ninety-five percent of all infants are screened at birth. Congressman Walsh is also Chairman of the Friends of Ireland, a bipartisan working group involved in Irish-American relations. For his work in promoting peace in Ireland, he was presented with the 2002 Ellis Island Medal of Honor by the National Ethnic Coalition of Organizations. He lives in the Town of Onondaga, a suburb of Syracuse.

ANTHONY D WEINER (D)

9 - Kings & Queens Counties

1122 Longworth House Office Bldg, Washington, DC 20515
202-225-6616/fax: 202-225-4183

1800 Sheepshead Bay Rd, Brooklyn, NY 11235
718-743-0441/fax: 718-520-9010

80-02 Kew Gardens Rd, Ste 5000, Kew Gardens, NY 11415
718-520-9001/fax: 718-520-9010

90-16 Rockaway Beach Blvd., Rockaway, NY 11693
718-318-9255/fax: 718-520-9010

Anthony Weiner was first elected to Congress in 1998. Previously, he served as an aide to then-Representative Charles Schumer from 1985 to 1991. He was a member of the New York City Council from 1992 through 1998, where he was chair of the Subcommittee on Safety in Public Housing and later the chair of the Subcommittee on Federal Affairs. As a Congressman, he was the only New Yorker appointed by House leadership to the Homeland Security Task Force. He is a member of the Judiciary Committee. As a member of the Science Committee, Subcommittee on Space and Aeronautics, he was a moving force behind investigation of the Columbia Disaster. He also serves on the Transportation and Infrastructure Committee, working to reduce airport air noise. He is a lifelong resident of New York.

Name Index

Name Index

Name Index

Brandt, Dorothy K Chin, 61
Brandt, Florence, 68
Brandt, Marc N, 283
Brandwene, Merle, 310
Brannen, Rita A, 401
Branning, Susan, 563
Brannock, Shari L, 648
Brannon, Patsy, 616
Bransten, Eileen, 58
Braslow, Stephen L, 68
Brassell Jr, Robert, 547
Brathwaite Nelson, Valerie, 60
Braun, Evelyn L, 60
Braun, Richard F, 58
Brauth, Sorelle, 168
Braverman, Robert, 370
Bray, Jeffrey, 580
Bray, Sarah, 594
Breaux, Antoine, 452
Brecher, Charles, 291, 330, 467
Bredhoff, Nancy, 189, 224
Breen, Carol, 606
Breen, Cathleen, 492
Breen, Dorothy, 533
Breen, J Timothy, 68
Breen, Peg, 233, 304
Breese, James R, 421
Bregg, Martin, 664
Brehm, Robert A, 159
Breig, Thomas, 325
Breiner, Charles, 308
Breitbart, Vicki, 486
Breitenbach, Matthew F, 662
Brello, Lori L, 570
Brencick, William J, 204
Brennan, Charles J, 520
Brennan, James, 201
Brennan, James F, 38, 46, 47, 51, 52
Brennan, John, 368
Brennan, Lawrence J, 66
Brennan, Megan, 203
Brennan, Michael J, 58
Brennan, Patricia, 141, 432
Brennan, Patrick H, 80, 104, 169, 230, 302
Brennan, Teresa A, 3
Brennan, Thomas A, 423
Brennan, Thomas F, 6, 285, 294
Brennan, Wendy, 513
Brennan, William J, 17, 363
Brenner, Adele, 370
Brenner, Barbara S, 472, 547
Brenon, Joan M, 440
Breselor, Frank, 460
Bresett, Harold, 648
Bresler, Barry M, 101, 327
Breslin, Dennis, 129
Breslin, Ellen, 21, 35, 377·
Breslin, Katherine, 470
Breslin, Michael G, 398
Breslin, Neil D, 20, 22, 25, 26, 27, 29, 30,
   31, 201, 291, 328, 711

Breslin, Richard W, 400
Breslin, Thomas A, 63
Bresnan, James J, 119, 354
Bressman, Susan B, 225
Brettschneider, Eric B, 315
Brettschneider, Stanley, 561
Brew, Lee, 399
Brewer Jr., John E, 650
Brewer, Aida, 17, 101, 327
Brewer, Beth A, 599
Brewer, Douglas J, 403
Brewer, Marie, 64
Brewer, Terrance, 661
Brewer, Vincent, 194
Brewer-Shelton, Valencia, 526
Brewster, Paul, 182
Breyman, Steve, 189
Brez, Wendy J, 346
Briand, Elizabeth, 527
Briccetti, Heather, 27, 30
Briccetti, Heather C, 519
Brick, Andrew, 438
Brickman, Ellen, 513
Bridenbecker, Terri, 577
Bridgen, Margot, 84
Briffault, Richard, 163, 292
Briganti-Hughes, Mary, 60
Briggs, Daniel L, 411
Briggs, Elizabeth A, 644
Briggs, R Michael, 444, 449
Briggs, Ronald J, 402
Briggs, Vernon, 273
Bright, Joan H, 425
Bright, Maureen K, 654
Bright, Terri, 439
Brill, Jo, 467
Brill, Joseph A, 600
Brilliant, Elizabeth, 447
Brilling, Jaclyn A, 15, 168
Brindle, Buzz, 610
Brining, Donald R, 410
Brinkley, Alan, 533
Brinthaupt, John A, 400
Brisson, Michael, 197
Bristol, Daniel S, 434
Brizell-Delise, Hillary, 499
Brizzell, Mary, 418
Broadbooks, John, 605
Brockman, Edward J, 413
Brockway, David M, 64
Broder, John P, 225
Broderick, David S, 406
Broderick, Kathleen M, 13, 280
Broderick, Michael, 26, 27, 30
Broderick, Peter L, 66
Brodhagen, Patricia, 482
Brodsky, Richard L, 38, 45, 46, 53, 102,
   201, 356, 685
Brodt, John, 457
Brody, Gary, 92
Brody, Stuart, 445

Broitman, Elana, 530
Bronat, Gary, 568
Brondolo, Thomas, 431
Bronfenbrenner, Kate, 273, 298
Brongo, Richard J, 417
Brongo, William, 65
Bronheim MD, David S, 561
Bronheim, David S, 558
Bronson, Harry, 50, 141
Bronstein, Richard W, 304
Brooke, Mary Jane, 649
Brooks, Albert, 196
Brooks, Greg, 426
Brooks, Helen, 474
Brooks, Kermit, 252
Brooks, Maggie, 405
Brooks, Martin, 655
Brooks, Michael J, 578
Brooks, Pamela, 580
Brooks, Paul C, 577
Brooks, Richard H, 271
Brooks, Roberta, 77
Brooks, Russell, 440
Brooks, Stan, 610
Brooks, Stephen, 115, 256
Brooks, Tracey, 46, 47, 48
Brooks, Wayne, 443
Brophy, Patrick W, 566
Brosnahan-Sullivan, Mary, 469
Brosnan, William J, 667
Brotz, James K, 648
Brown Clemens, Terryl, 12
Brown Clemons, Terryl, 89, 99, 133, 167,
   177, 214, 227, 236, 252, 268, 300, 325
Brown, Byron W, 20, 22, 25, 26, 27, 29, 30,
   31, 103, 291, 711
Brown, Carolyn, 477
Brown, Christopher R, 665
Brown, Conchetta M, 68
Brown, Corrine, 396
Brown, Cynthia, 359
Brown, Dan, 498, 581
Brown, David, 89, 99, 134, 252, 301, 325
Brown, David J, 423
Brown, Donald, 10
Brown, Earl D, 398, 434
Brown, Frank, 345
Brown, Gary, 253, 598
Brown, Gordon, 449
Brown, Henry, 396
Brown, Herb R, 655
Brown, Holly E, 429
Brown, Ifigenia, 15, 288, 301, 326
Brown, James F, 438
Brown, Jane, 466
Brown, Jeffrey, 47, 53, 364
Brown, Jeffrey D, 38, 48, 49, 53, 685
Brown, Jeffrey S, 66
Brown, John, 643
Brown, Joseph, 638
Brown, Joyce F, 480, 619

Name Index

Name Index

Name Index

Fontaine, Monita W, 561
Fonti, Robert, 471
Fonzo, Paul Di, 644
Forand, Douglas, 196, 289
Forbes, David, 578
Forbes, Gordon G, 542
Forbes, Michael P, 583
Ford, Carl F, 351
Ford, Dennis, 647
Ford, Henry, 444
Ford, Michael J, 659
Ford, Mike, 578
Ford, Tanya L, 421
Ford-Johnston, Cynthia, 648
Forma, Joseph, 59
Forman, Dan, 613
Forman, Peter M, 64
Formel, Ann F, 12, 244, 266
Foro, Daniel, 8, 132, 250, 286
Forrest, Linda A, 156
Forrest, Steven W, 71
Forrestel, II, E Peter, 92
Forsline, Philip, 79
Forst, Donald H, 602
Fortino, Jessica, 107, 544
Fortuna, Diana, 467
Fortuna, Jane B, 72
Fosberg, Jane R, 644
Fosbrook, Leonard, 593
Fosco, Maria, 467
Foskey, Carnell, 66
Fosler, Gail, 107
Fossella, Vito, 91, 105, 170, 184, 217, 231,
    247, 391, 392
Fossella, Vito J, 384, 723
Foster, Greg, 607
Foster, Phyllis M, 132, 250, 286
Foster, Ruth, 480
Fountain, Raymond H, 592
Fowler, Jerry L, 79
Fowler, Jr, William E, 356
Fowler, Rick, 456
Fox, Charles, 4, 166, 175, 349
Fox, James P, 125, 355
Fox, John, 607
Fox, Michael, 26, 28, 31
Fox, Thomas J, 51
Foxman, Abraham H, 239
Foy, James, 5, 306, 626
Foy, Joseph, 329
Foy, Veronica J, 366
Fragnoli-Ryan, Maria S, 646
Frahm, David S, 647
Fraites, Aisha, 492
Fralick, Terry N, 651
Frame, Lawrence, 124, 338, 354
Francis, Margaret E, 557
Francis, Will, 78
Franco, Victor, 54
Francy, Don, 492
Franczyk, David, 417

Franczyk, Thomas P, 70
Frand, Deni, 570
Frank, Barney, 91, 230, 246, 392
Frank, Charmaine, 432
Frank, Gregory R, 435
Frank, Lisa, 509
Frank, Paul M, 259
Frank, Peter M, 500
Frank, Ronald L, 548
Frankel, Sandra L, 416
Franklin, Carol A, 156
Franks, Martin, 171
Franks-Randall, Carol, 671
Franzese, Nicole, 579
Franzese, Robert, 566
Fraser, Bruce T, 657
Fraser, Carl, 455
Fraser, Charles, 433
Fraser, Lori, 243
Fraser, Michael, 176, 375
Frateschi, Timothy A, 424
Fratti, Michelle, 656
Frayler, Jeff, 455
Frazee, Evelyn, 59
Frazer, Michael, 10
Frazier, Adolphus C, 467
Frazier, Diane E, 459
Frazier, Michael P, 671
Frazier, Pauline, 212
Freda, William, 537
Frederick, Bruce, 132, 251, 287
Frederick, Gary, 350
Frederick, John A, 43
Fredericks, Albert, 497
Fredericks, K L, 104
Fredsall, David, 88
Freed, Adam, 197
Freed, Kathryn E, 61
Freedman, Corri, 42
Freedman, Fran, 221
Freedman, Helen E, 58
Freedman, Holly, 589
Freedman, Jo, 481
Freedman, Lynn P, 219, 239
Freeley, Mary Ellen, 655
Freeman, Edward, 209, 276, 307
Freeman, Henry, 598
Freeman, Janeene, 470
Freeman, Linda, 486
Freeman, Lynn, 581
Freeman, Nora L, 62
Freeman, Robert J, 198, 290
Freidmutter, Cindy, 431
Freilich, Joan, 498
Freimark, Norman, 672
Freitag, Amy, 431
French, Daniel, 487
French, Douglas E, 158
French, Richard, 612
Frescatore, Donna J, 211
Fresina, Anthony M, 555

Freund, Jack, 522
Freund, Sidney, 671
Freundlich, David, 68
Frey, Joseph P, 144
Frey, Thomas, 304, 331
Freyberg, Caridad, 526
Fricano, Amy J, 59
Fricke, Jr, Greg S, 569
Friday, Shirley, 68
Fried, Bernard J, 62
Frieden, Thomas R, 428
Friedland, Edward A, 11, 235
Friedlander, Mark, 60
Friedman, Andrew, 504, 605
Friedman, Dana, 466
Friedman, David, 57
Friedman, Donald, 470
Friedman, Eby, 99, 147
Friedman, Jason P, 662
Friedman, Larry, 403
Friedman, Lucy, 451
Friedman, Marcy S, 61
Friedman, Michael, 90, 126, 229, 509
Friedman, Rhea G, 62
Friedman, Ronald L, 654
Friedman, Thomas, 508
Friello, Carolyn, 438
Frier, Raymond, 471
Fries, Sue A, 156
Friia, JoAnn, 74
Frisch, Debra L, 198
Frisch, Kevin, 598
Friscia, Richard, 416
Friscoe, Louis, 510
Friske, William, 281
Froehlich, Richard, 118, 228
Frohman, Sherry, 14, 135, 312, 469
Froikin, Sara, 523
Fromberg, Allan J, 433
Frommer, Charles, 560
Frommer, Ross, 533
Frost, Jacqueline R, 500
Frost, Jerome K, 408
Frost, Martin, 395
Fruci, William, 159
Frungillo, John, 600
Fryda, Diana, 492
Frye, Celeste, 466
Frye, Mary B, 286, 294
Frye, Robert W, 125, 355
Fuchs, Ester, 425
Fuchs, Jim, 433
Fugolo, Rev Joseph, 239
Fuleihan, Dean, 36, 53
Fuller, Brian, 481
Fuller, Michael, 42, 466
Fuller, Paul, 227
Fuller, Tuulia, 481
Fullwood, Michael, 489
Fulmer, Susanne, 670
Fung, Margaret, 239, 260, 319

Name Index

Name Index

Name Index

Irizarry, Reyes, 656
Irvin, Thomas, 3
Irving, Lisa, 17, 236, 312
Irwin, Julie, 363
Isaacs, Steve, 595
Isakson, Johnny, 388
Iselin, Harold, 487
Ishmael, Cheryl, 121, 148, 200, 214
Ison, Jeanne, 125, 181, 382
Israel, Doug, 474
Israel, Steve, 91, 231, 247, 366, 384, 391,
    392, 724
Issa, Darrell, 393
Issac, Ernesto, 526
Istomin, Marta C, 630
Iulo, Robert, 426
Ivanoff, Nick, 358
Ives, Kirk, 23
Ives, Lisa, 580
Ivey, Mary E, 302, 350
Iwanicki, Stan, 82
Iwanowicz, Peter, 453
Izeman, Mark A, 486
Izquierdo, Richard, 37
Izyk, Edward, 436
Izzo, Cynthia, 251
Jablonski Ryman, Dawn, 14
Jacangelo, Dominic, 13, 178, 335
Jaccarino, Thomas M, 435
Jaccoma, Barbara, 502
Jack, Howard A, 185
Jack, Joanne, 308
Jack, Kevin, 267
Jackier, Diane, 430
Jackman-Brown, Pam B, 61
Jackson, Brad W, 580
Jackson, Carol, 467
Jackson, Deborah A, 303
Jackson, Debra, 671
Jackson, Edison O, 467, 624
Jackson, Edna, 26
Jackson, Helen Cash, 334
Jackson, Jill W, 561
Jackson, Josephine, 155
Jackson, M Randolph, 58
Jackson, Marvin, 79, 103
Jackson, Melissa C, 62
Jackson, Patricia A, 203, 238
Jackson, Shirley Ann, 522, 633
Jackson, Terri, 481
Jackson, Thomas H, 633
Jackson, Wayne P, 35
Jackson-Grove, Amy D, 357
Jackson-Lee, Sheila, 394
Jacob, Andrew T, 176
Jacob, Col Andrew, 124, 181
Jacob, Phyllis Gangel, 58
Jacobie, John, 363
Jacobosky, Anne, 313
Jacobs, Alex, 146
Jacobs, Ann, 141

Jacobs, Frederick J, 491
Jacobs, Jay, 446
Jacobs, Judith A, 405
Jacobs, Matt, 462
Jacobs, Pamela R, 615
Jacobs, Rhoda S, 35, 40, 45, 49, 50, 52, 694
Jacobsen, Susan, 132, 251, 287
Jacobson, Jonathan G, 446
Jacobson, Katrina, 663
Jacobson, Laura Lee, 58
Jacobson, Michael, 141, 264
Jacobson, Philip, 271
Jacobson, Ted, 562
Jacques, Keith R, 491
Jaeger, Ann A, 648
Jaeger, Kathleen, 221
Jaeger, Steven M, 66
Jaffe, Barbara, 61
Jaffe, Dana M, 69
Jaffe, Robert, 512
Jafri, Ali, 236
Jagow, Wayne F, 406
Jaker, William, 612
James, Debra A, 61
James, Donald A, 665
James, Francine, 12, 252
James, Kathryn, 158
James, Nathaniel, 367
James, Yvette, 509
Jamieson, Linda S, 59
Jamison, Gy Sgt John, 365
Jamison, Julie, 526
Janczak, Susan P, 67
Janeczek, Kathy, 423
Janer, Fernando, 526
Janey, Kerry, 526
Jannetty, Karen L, 530, 562
Jaquith, Grant C, 137, 258
Jaracka-Maher, Wendy, 14
Jardine, Anne, 133, 214, 252
Jarman, Richard, 467
Jaromin, Marc, 614
Jaros, Susan K, 415
Jarvis, Gary, 410
Jarvis, Lucinda A, 159
Jason, Paul S, 566
Jaspan, Arthur W, 566
Jauch, Deborah, 308
Jaunzemis, Candace, 531
Jayson, Larry, 232
Jecen, James R, 71
Jeffers, Darrell E, 539
Jeffords, H Susan, 298
Jeffords, James, 185, 358, 387
Jeffords, James M, 330, 388
Jeffrey, Kevin, 431
Jeffries Jr, Ross E, 572
Jeffries, Roger, 8, 132, 251, 287
Jenik, Peter, 429
Jenkins, Caroll, 16, 326
Jenkins, Connie, 604

Jenkins, Harriet L, 156
Jenkins, Joan, 481
Jenkins, Lew, 481
Jenkins, William, 184, 390
Jennings, Dr Ralph, 608
Jennings, Gerald D, 415
Jennings, Gerald J, 503
Jennings, Jim, 346
Jennings, Teresa, 91
Jenny, Richard, 177, 213
Jensen, Genevieve M, 635
Jerome, Marc M, 639
Jerome, Stephen J, 639
Jerominek, Maribel, 479
Jerrett, Theodore I, 407
Jersey, Dennis, 288, 301, 326
Jess, A Sam, 403
Jewell, Daralene C, 645
Jewett, Andrew, 30
Jezer, Rhea, 529
Jicha, Jean, 73
Jimenez, Dawn M, 61
Jimenez, Jenny P, 563
Jimenez-Hernandez, Iris, 429
Jiminez, Angela, 14, 134
Jimino, Kathleen M, 408
Jobson, Douglas J, 409
Joch, Nancy M, 68
Jochnowitz, Jay, 597
Jockers, Kenneth, 261
Joel, Richard M, 636
Joerg, Claude A, 406
Johansen, Lawrence A, 123, 149, 296
John, Dennis B, 399
John, Susan V, 40, 47, 48, 50, 51, 237, 246,
    270, 296, 694
Johns, Richard N, 646
Johnson III, Daniel E, 572
Johnson Jr, Peter J, 568
Johnson, Adrienne, 43
Johnson, Allan C, 160
Johnson, Andrew, 309
Johnson, Brian A, 550
Johnson, Bruce C, 456
Johnson, Carl, 10, 175
Johnson, Catherine, 226
Johnson, Celeste M, 212
Johnson, Charlotte, 31
Johnson, Chris, 499
Johnson, Craig, 439
Johnson, Daniel, 145, 277, 311
Johnson, David, 21, 142, 145, 374
Johnson, Dennis, 467, 664
Johnson, Diana A, 58
Johnson, Doris, 481
Johnson, Eddie Bernice, 185, 396
Johnson, James C, 591
Johnson, Jeanine, 42
Johnson, Jeanne, 67
Johnson, Joan, 211, 499
Johnson, Joan B, 422

Name Index

Name Index

Loglisci, David, 16, 197
Logus, Maria, 254
Loiodice, Charles L, 244, 266
Lollie, Alvin, 310
Lombardi, Diane C, 39
Lombardi, Francis J, 125, 355
Lombardi, III, Tarky, 553
Lombardi, Jr, Tarky, 476
Lombardi, Judith K, 582
Lombardi, Michael, 117, 353
Lombardo, Barbara A, 604
Lometti, William V, 184
Lomma, Debra, 308
Lonczak, Bill, 325
Londa, Ivan, 639
Lonergan, John, 509
Lonergan, Vincent, 21
Long, Daniel, 480
Long, Gregory, 460
Long, Janet, 481
Long, Jim, 28, 32
Long, Michael R, 443
Long, Richard B, 126, 200, 256, 383
Long, Susan, 533
Long, Thomas M, 444
Long-Chelales, Eileen, 203, 302
Longhurst, Richard, 455
Longo, Angela Pedone, 158
Longo, John, 35, 377
Longo, Rocco J, 657
Longo, Stephen M, 39
Longstaff, Patricia, 100, 228, 288
Longworth, Sandra, 306
Lonnen, Carol R, 407
Lonzano, Zorayda, 526
Loomis, David, 8, 131, 311
Loomis, Leslie, 641
Loomis, Peter, 17, 351
Loomis, Peter S, 351
Loper, William, 367
Lopes, Nelson, 309
Lopez, Destiny, 512
Lopez, Edgardo, 309
Lopez, Felix, 527
Lopez, Gene R, 62
Lopez, Norma, 426
Lopez, Peter D, 409
Lopez, Robert, 145
Lopez, Stephen, 236
Lopez, Vito J, 41, 47, 49, 52, 230, 237, 270, 291, 302, 313, 696
Lopez, Wilfredo, 428
Lopez-Summa, Gina M, 11, 236
Lopiccolo, Karen, 308
Lopinski, John A, 113, 352
LoPrimo, Laurie, 429
Lordahl, Gerard, 232
Lorenz, Jack A, 542
Lorenz, Len, 325
Lorenz, Michael J, 569
Lorenzo, Albert, 60

Lorey, Scott, 451
Lorey, Thomas, 402
Loria, Anne L, 637
Lorigo, Ralph C, 443
Lorito, Thomas F, 59
Lorow, Catherine, 155
Losinski, Elilzabeth, 463
Losquadro, Steven, 112, 336
Loss, Mandi, 3
Loszynski, Joseph F, 135
Lott, Plummer E, 58
Lott, Trent, 387, 389
Lotto, Steven A, 69
Lotz, Christina L, 410
Loughlin, Daniel J, 60
Loughney, Robert, 472
Loughren, Thomas, 400
Louizou, Thomas M, 358
Loukmas, Heather, 499
Louloudes, Virginia P, 342
Lounsbury, Lee, 308
Lounsbury, Peggy A, 560
LoVallo, Sharon M, 70
Loveday Jr, William, 402
Lovejoy, Mary Beth, 455
Lovelett, Steven S, 198
Lovell, Jeffrey, 4, 77, 88, 96, 142, 166, 175, 209, 226, 235, 243, 250, 266, 276, 285, 294, 300, 306, 324, 333, 349, 362
Lovell, Kelly, 100, 147
Lovell, Kelly A, 107
Lowder, Brian, 605
Lowe, Kim, 613
Lowe, Richard B, 58
Lowengard, Daniel G, 657
Lowey, Nita M, 81, 170, 204, 329, 384, 390, 393, 397, 725
Lowman, Wayne, 602
Lowman, Wayne K, 601
Lowrie, Stuart, 494
Lowry, Marcia Robinson, 239, 317
Loyola, Guido A, 73
Lozito, Gaetan B, 70
Lozzi, Dave, 608
Lubin, Alan, 478, 572
Lubin, Alan B, 513
Lubov, Heather, 431
Lubow, Fran L, 62
Lucarelli, Michael, 582
Lucas, Frank D, 390
Lucey, Brian J, 538
Lucia, Janene, 84
Lucia, Richard B, 579
Luciano, Daniel F, 57
Luciano, Mark, 41
Luck, Candace, 198
Ludgate, Kathleen, 104
Ludington, Spencer J, 71
Ludmer, Audrey C, 560
Ludovic, Blain, 475
Ludwig, Arnold J, 568

Ludwig, Joseph, 422
Lugar, Richard G, 105, 388
Luisi-Potts, Billie, 345
Lukas, Susan, 370
Lukens, Daniel, 316
Luker, John, 78
Luks, Allan, 316
Lundberg, Marc G, 46
Lundberg, Mark G, 49, 50, 52, 53
Lundgren, Dan, 204, 393
Lundstedt, Scott, 522
Lungen, Stephen F, 411
Lunn, Robert J, 59
Lupardo, Donna, 41, 48, 49, 51, 53, 696
Lupi, Patricia, 74
Lupinetti, Pat, 133, 214, 252
Lupkin, Stanley N, 138
Lupuloff, Karen, 133, 214, 251
Lupuloff, Karen I, 61
Lurie, Alvin D, 273
Lurie, David L, 581
Lurie, Edward S, 20, 21
Luryi, Serge, 99, 147
Lusk, Jared C, 436
Lussier, Nancy, 176
Luster, Martin A, 422
Lustig, Esther, 503
Luther, Carole, 22, 31
Luther, Joan F, 158
Luthin, Catherine, 503
Lutton, Jim, 614
Lutz, David, 188
Lutz, John, 645
Luvera, Joseph V, 194, 300
Luvison, Kelly, 600
Lux, Michael, 542
Luxenberg, Arthur M, 555
Lydic, Pamela S, 577
Lyles, Marcia, 656
Lyman, James, 140
Lyman, Stephen P, 407
Lynam, Elizabeth, 467
Lynaugh, Barbara, 68
Lynch, Harold J, 62
Lynch, James, 194, 300
Lynch, John, 363
Lynch, John J, 491
Lynch, John P, 318
Lynch, Kenneth, 176
Lynch, Margaret, 169
Lynch, Mark, 510
Lynch, Patricia, 503
Lynch, Patrick, 140, 299
Lynch, Stephen, 393
Lynch, Steve, 415
Lynch, William, 503
Lynch-Landy, Virginia, 491
Lyndes, Lynn, 664
Lynker, Debra, 668
Lynn, Andrew, 504
Lynn, Roxanne R, 69

Name Index

Indexes &
Demographic
Maps

Name Index

Ruddock, Charmaine, 461
Ruddy, Cort, 25
Ruderman, Hon Terry Jane, 261
Ruderman, Terry J, 61
Rudgers, Nathan, 5, 77, 306
Ruditzky, Howard A, 58
Rudnick, Andrew J, 577
Rudnick, Tracey, 468
Rudolph, Elnatan, 529
Rudolph, Kenneth W, 59
Rudolph, Richard, 402
Rudy, Harry, 363
Ruest, Penny, 160
Ruff, Edwin, 18, 245, 269
Ruggieri, Bernard, 520
Ruggiero, Joseph, 445
Ruggiero, Steve, 203, 302
Ruglis, Martin, 675
Ruhlmann, Dandrea L, 65
Ruiz, Hilda, 527
Ruiz, Norma, 60
Ruiz, Sandra, 468
Rumpler, Kurt, 12, 244, 266
Rumsey, Philip R, 59
Runion, Kenneth, 421
Runkel, Jay, 209, 276, 307
Runyan, John C, 554
Runyon, Dave, 6, 166, 193
Rupert, Clarke, 114, 179, 378
Rupert, Peter, 26, 31
Rupert, Peter L, 20
Ruppert, David, 213, 268
Rupprecht, Mark J, 418
Rush, Andrew, 3, 373
Rush, James, 213, 268
Rush, Kenneth E, 407
Rushdoony, Jonathan, 91
Ruskay, John, 530
Ruskay, John S, 305
Ruskin, Lea, 69
Ruslander, Betsey R, 254
Russ, Linda, 24
Russell, Barrett, 10, 194
Russell, Cynthia M, 72
Russell, John J, 671
Russell, Mark, 441
Russell, Patrick E, 403
Russell, Peter, 81
Russell, Robert T, 70
Russell, Theresa A, 545
Russianoff, Gene, 360, 492
Russo, Alisha, 473
Russo, Christopher, 419
Russo, James, 421
Russo, Jerry, 427
Russo, Joe, 608
Russo, Pasqualino, 17, 199, 313
Russo, Stephen, 71
Russo, Theresa, 539
Russom, Dan M, 649
Rustum, Youcef, 213

Rutherford, Clyde, 83
Rutigliano, Christine, 196, 289
Rutkowski, Edward J, 336
Rutnik, Douglas P, 525
Ruttan, Julie, 509
Rutter, Hillary, 218
Ruzow, Daniel A, 191, 293
Ryan, Alison, 611
Ryan, Bill, 413
Ryan, Daniel J, 146, 311
Ryan, Dennis, 12, 245, 267, 312, 362
Ryan, Dennis V, 157
Ryan, Edward F, 406
Ryan, Elsie, 370
Ryan, Garry P, 89, 123, 229
Ryan, Jack, 432
Ryan, James M, 675
Ryan, John, 419
Ryan, Kevin K, 64
Ryan, Kurt J, 444
Ryan, Mary Ann, 575
Ryan, Maryann, 611
Ryan, Melissa, 33, 55, 202
Ryan, Robert, 3, 96, 250, 324
Ryan, Thomas, 213
Ryan, Tim, 627
Ryan, Tom, 562
Ryan, VADM John R, 619
Rybczynski, Catherine A, 421
Ryder, Melanie, 579
Rydl, Lubomira, 80
Ryerson, Lisa Marsh, 636
Ryerson, Lorraine, 66
Ryman, Dawn Jablonski, 167
Rynasko, Michael, 478
Rzepka, Patricia L, 40
Sabesta, Rebecca, 198
Sabin, Deborah A, 295
Sabini, John, 356
Sabini, John D, 24, 27, 28, 29, 31, 32, 328, 340, 717
Sabo, Martin O, 390
Sabo, Michael A, 366
Sabol, Sharon, 304
Sacco, Elizabeth, 487
Sachs, Jeffrey, 533
Sack, Robert L, 350
Sacket, James L, 409
Sackett, Robert A, 60
Sackman, Bobbie, 473
Sacks, Barry, 71
Sacks, Burton, 512
Sadhwani, Gouri, 497
Sagara, Kyoko, 527
Saginaw, Carol, 320, 466, 499
Sahrle, Mike, 614
Saidel, Judith R, 208
Saillant, Roger, 472
Sais, Michael, 40
Saitta, Wayne P, 58
Sakac, Sister Ann, 631

Saks, Alan J, 60
Sakwrai, Motoatsu, 583
Salaberrios, Rafael, 434
Saladino, Joseph S, 43, 48, 296, 704
Salamone, Frank, 606
Saland, Stephen M, 19, 24, 26, 27, 28, 29, 30, 31, 149, 717
Salandy, Sabine, 470
Salerno, George D, 60
Sales, Angela, 468
Sales, Frederick A, 455
Salhaus, Steve, 268
Salinitro, Barbara, 63
Salins, Peter D, 615
Salis, Harry, 59
Salisbury, Gordon, 644
Salkin, Andrew, 433
Salkin, Patricia, 205
Salman, Barry, 60
Salomon, Susan, 113, 135, 255
Salomone, John, 415
Salomone, Katherine M, 667
Salotti, Mary Q, 158
Saltzman, Robert J, 207
Salvage, Lynn, 639
Salvaggio, Susan Kay, 671
Salvione, Sherri, 469
Salzman, Joan R, 426
Sama, Jeffrey, 176
Samaniuk, John, 351
Samaroo, Veria, 466
Same, Peter W, 410
Same, Ruth V, 160
Samers, Audrey M, 11, 243
Sammakia, Bahgat, 100, 147
Sammarco, Valentino T, 64
Sammons, Ann, 132, 251, 287
Sammons, James, 475
Sammons, Robert, 244, 266, 375
Sample, Jeanne, 132, 250, 286
Sampson, Brian, 495
Sampson, Christian G, 437
Sampson, Frederick D R, 60
Sampson, John, 718
Sampson, John L, 24, 27, 28, 29, 31, 32, 33, 215
Sampson, Rick J, 110, 346, 560
Samuels, Barry, 595
Samuels, Chuck, 613
Samuels, Debrarose, 61
Samuels, Paul N, 139, 262, 499
San Filippo, Andrew A, 417
Sanchez, Fernando, 104
Sanchez, Loretta, 204, 397
Sanchis, Frank, 512
Sander, Lucia, 74
Sanders, Bernard, 392
Sanders, Judy, 611
Sanders, Lewis W, 157
Sanders, Steven, 43, 46, 47, 50, 52, 149, 704

Schlotter, Mary A, 41
Schlueter, Thomas, 273
Schmelzer, Patricia A, 398
Schmetterer, Jerry, 404
Schmick, Janet, 590
Schmidt Jr, Benno C, 623
Schmidt, Bruce, 448
Schmidt, David, 61
Schmidt, Robert W, 57
Schmidt, Sue, 31
Schmidt, Warren G, 443
Schmitt, Peter J, 405
Schmitt, Tim, 604
Schnabel, Martin, 117, 353
Schneer, Errol, 219
Schneider, Evan, 41
Schneider, Howard, 600
Schneider, Jean T, 62
Schneider, Maureen, 584, 585
Schneider, Norman, 487
Schneider, Philip, 512
Schneider, Reed, 433
Schneider, Rev Msgr Francis J, 634
Schneider, Wayne, 123, 149, 296
Schneiderman, Eric T, 20, 24, 27, 28, 30, 31, 32, 718
Schneier, Martin, 58
Schnell, William A, 528
Schoch, Amy, 9, 98, 175
Schoelle, Jr, Robert L, 419
Schoelles, Patricia A, 634
Schoen, Neal W, 349
Schoenberg, Daniel, 454
Schoenberger, Ilan, 437
Schoenfeld, Martin, 58
Schoetz, Kenneth, 253
Schofield, Daniel A, 398
Schofield, Rob, 578
Schofield, William F, 659
Scholz, Robert, 533
Schonfeld, Mark, 105
Schoolman, Maureen, 54, 103, 149
Schoonmaker, Steven D, 648
Schoonover, Laura M, 157
Schorno, Edmond, 125, 355
Schorsch, Ismar, 629
Schrade, Steven M, 641
Schrader, Scott, 401
Schrafroth, Jessica, 505
Schramm, Jane M, 582
Schreck, Wayne J, 65
Schreiber, Jane, 254
Schreiber, Michelle D, 62
Schroeder, David E, 632
Schroeder, Lee, 463
Schroeder, Mark, 43
Schroeder, Mark J, 50, 51, 52, 53
Schroeder, Mark J F, 705
Schroeffel, Bruce, 526
Schruers, Terry, 455
Schubel, David C, 407

Schuchman, David, 637
Schuffler Jr, David, 450
Schuh, Sherry, 429
Schuhle, Anne, 599
Schuler, Kevin, 509
Schulman, Clifford A, 551
Schulman, Martin J, 60
Schultz, Daniel, 150
Schultz, James, 662
Schultz, Jeanne F, 666
Schultz, Susan, 130
Schulz, William F, 239
Schumer, Charles, 397
Schumer, Charles E, 91, 138, 205, 231, 259, 341, 384, 386, 387, 389, 721
Schuppenhauer, John A, 70
Schuster, Bill, 231
Schuster, Robert, 366
Schutte, Thomas F, 633
Schutz, Lisa, 70
Schwab, Kevin, 613
Schwartz, Amy, 487
Schwartz, Andrew, 432
Schwartz, Arthur Z, 556
Schwartz, Barry K, 563
Schwartz, Ira, 143
Schwartz, Joe, 600
Schwartz, John R, 73
Schwartz, Lawrence, 413
Schwartz, Lynn, 668
Schwartz, Michael, 72
Schwartz, Richard, 494
Schwartz, Richard J, 7, 333
Schwartz, Rita, 108, 359
Schwartz, Sheldon, 329
Schwarz, Bernard, 429
Schwarz, Jr, Frederick A O, 426
Schwarz, Richard, 330, 462
Schwarz, Thomas J, 618
Schweich, Thomas A, 204
Schwenk, Edwin M, 516
Schwenzfeier, Eric, 251
Schwerzmann, Peter A, 65
Sciacca, Jim, 166, 193
Sciandra, Russell, 460
Sciarrino Jr, Matthew, 61, 62
Scicchitano, Gregory, 419
Scida, Louis, 117, 353
Sciglibaglio, Eleanor, 158
Sciolino, Anthony J, 65
Sciortino, Franklin J, 104
Sciotti, Nicholas A, 410
Sclar, Gordon, 366
Scofield, Robert, 230
Scola, Philip M, 368
Sconiers, Rose H, 59
Scoppetta, Nicholas, 428
Scorcia, John, 203, 302
Scordo, Peter C, 666
Scott, A Paul, 645
Scott, Brian Y, 212

Scott, Clarence W, 351
Scott, Karen, 613
Scott, Loretta, 437
Scott, Mark, 608
Scott, Paul R, 603
Scott, Robert A, 625
Scott, Robert C, 138, 394
Scott, Valerie, 415
Scott, William F, 645
Scova, Patricia June, 424
Scozzafava, Deirdre K, 45
Scozzafava, Dierdre, 136, 257
Scozzafava, Dierdre K, 43, 46, 48, 54, 291, 706
Screnci, Diane P, 169
Scriber, William W, 159, 446
Scripps, James E, 97
Scuccimarra, Thomas H, 61
Scudder, Henry J, 58
Scullin, Jr, Frederick J, 257
Scully, Peter A, 114, 176, 179
Sculti, Christine, 97
Scuti, Christine, 167
Seaman, David E, 66
Seaman, Marietta, 439
Searles, John R, 399
Searles, Michael, 98
Sears, Lawrence, 130
Seay, J David, 283, 512
Seay, Millard, 117, 353
Sebastian, Blair W, 234
Sebastian, Kris, 605
Secor, Sharon L, 410
Seddio, Frank R, 43, 45, 50, 53, 54, 706
Sederer, Lloyd, 428
Sedita, Frank A, 59
Sedor, Dennis, 156
Seebold, Kelly, 10, 211
Seeley, James A, 661
Seeley, Joe, 12, 325
Seeley, Mary, 479
Seeley, Teresa B, 71
Seemann, Lisa, 50
Seereiter, Micheal, 509
Seewald, Robert G, 62
Segal, Jay, 487
Segal, Marvin E, 60
Segalla, David, 146
Segermeister, David, 203, 302
Seggos, Basil, 523
Segui, Gail, 557
Sehr, Gregory, 457, 535
Seibert, Harry W, 67
Seidel, Elizabeth, 530
Seiden, Adam, 72
Seidenfeld, Stanley, 230
Seidman, A Alan, 407
Seifried, E William, 102, 114, 228
Seiter Jr, Norman W, 59
Sejan, John, 156
Selleck, Bruce, 186

Indexes &
Demographic
Maps

Name Index

Smith, Bruce W, 350
Smith, Christopher, 366, 490
Smith, Christopher H, 393
Smith, Clay D, 444
Smith, Dana, 130
Smith, David C, 665
Smith, David K, 552
Smith, Donald Blaine, 408
Smith, Donald F, 616
Smith, Donna M, 313
Smith, Ellen, 533
Smith, Frederick W, 335
Smith, G Mike, 351
Smith, Gary P, 669
Smith, George Bundy, 57
Smith, Gerald L, 157
Smith, Gordon, 217, 387, 388, 389
Smith, Guy, 402
Smith, Hal, 278
Smith, Howard S, 648
Smith, Howard W, 672
Smith, III, Arthur J, 446
Smith, James E, 436
Smith, Jamie, 30
Smith, JoAnn M, 220, 240, 318
Smith, John, 611
Smith, Joseph, 130
Smith, Joseph V, 245, 269
Smith, Joyce, 98
Smith, Judy, 213
Smith, Karen, 61
Smith, Karen J, 638
Smith, Kevin T, 545
Smith, Kimberleigh, 481
Smith, Lamar S, 394
Smith, Larry, 563
Smith, Leta, 310
Smith, Linda, 349
Smith, Lisa, 122, 148
Smith, Lorrie, 38
Smith, Luther A, 434
Smith, Lynn, 594
Smith, M Kathryn, 63
Smith, M Patricia, 134, 245, 253, 268
Smith, Malcolm, 30
Smith, Malcolm A, 24, 27, 28, 29, 31, 32,
   257, 719
Smith, Martin E, 63
Smith, Marty, 447, 448
Smith, Marty L, 157
Smith, Mary H, 59
Smith, Michael C, 432
Smith, Michael J, 637
Smith, Nancy A, 64
Smith, Nancy E, 57
Smith, Nancy L, 158
Smith, Onnolee, 295
Smith, Patricia M, 429
Smith, Patrick, 524
Smith, Perry F, 211
Smith, Peter R, 121, 168, 180

Smith, Rex, 597
Smith, Rhonda, 466
Smith, Richard, 486
Smith, Richard L, 460
Smith, Richard M, 606
Smith, Richard P, 525
Smith, Robert, 134, 448
Smith, Robert A, 408
Smith, Robert S, 57
Smith, Ruth E, 61
Smith, Timothy G, 483, 550
Smith, Valarie, 150
Smith, Vincent M, 326
Smith, Wallace, 341
Smith, Wallace D, 450
Smith, William N, 92
Smith-Caronia, Terri, 493
Smith-Socaris, Christian, 517
Smits, Stephen M, 279
Smoczynski, Karl, 196, 289
Smolka, Mary Ellen, 468
Smolkin, Stanley A, 72
Smulian, Dan, 493
Smyth, Andrea, 469, 530
Snavley, Larry, 522
Snell Jr, Joseph F, 417
Snively, Randy, 607
Snively, Rick, 607
Snowe, Olympia J, 105, 185, 272, 387, 389
Snyder, Barry, 208
Snyder, Bill, 608
Snyder, Jackie, 425
Snyder, Michael J, 194, 335
Snyder, Patricia Di Benedetto, 345
Snyder, Phyllis, 240, 320
Snyder, Richard, 602
Snyder, Teresa Thayer, 661
Snyder, Vic, 391
Snyder, William F, 615
Soares, P David, 398
Sobelski, Stan, 611
Sobin, Melinda, 492
Sobol, Thomas, 154
Soderberg, Carl-Axel P, 183
Soffel, Denise, 470
Sofield, Sr, Thomas R, 423
Sohluger, Neil, 453
Sohn, Anita, 482
Sohn, Harold, 482
Sokolow, Alan V, 206, 292, 330
Sola, David A, 150
Solano, Socrates, 545
Solarz, Ron, 284
Solecky, Richard, 198
Solis, Hilda L, 184, 392
Solis, Salvador, 466
Sollazzo, Robert A, 105
Soloff, Brenda S, 62
Solomkin, Bruce, 146
Solomon, Amy, 195
Solomon, Charles H, 62

Solomon, David L, 203
Solomon, Jane S, 61
Solomon, Jerry, 133, 214, 252
Solomon, Mark J, 262
Solomon, Martin M, 58
Solomon, Michael, 197
Soloway, Ronald, 322
Sombke, Lawrence, 16, 100, 178, 197, 290,
   376
Somers, Bob, 77
Somers, Susan, 308
Sommer, Brett M, 435
Sommer, Jeffrey, 121, 200, 327, 381
Sommer, Judah C, 93, 551
Sommers, Michael, 78
Son, Shin, 319
Sonberg, Michael R, 62
Song, Mina, 527
Sonn, Paul, 460
Sonneborn, James, 466
Sonnenblick, Arthur I, 305
Sontz, Marvin, 559
Sopak, Sandra K, 399
Sorady, Karen, 88
Sorendo, Lou, 603
Sorensen, Jon, 7, 97, 167, 374
Soria, Rosa, 462
Soriano-Tavera, Alexandra, 555
Sorin, Martin, 177, 213
Sorrell, Duayne, 469
Sorrentino, Vincent J, 421
Sosa-Lintner, Gloria, 63
Soscia, Michael F, 350
Sossei, Steve, 196, 289
Soto Ruiz, Nilda, 623
Soto, Faviola, 61
Sottile, James M, 423
Souder, Mark Edward, 393
Soule, Norman, 343
Southard, Rebecca, 53
Sovas, Gregory H, 190
Spacher, Kevin, 436
Spada, Albert, 412
Spadafora Jr., Ronald R, 652
Spadafora, Annemarie, 652
Spahr, Stephen M, 117, 354
Spain, Edward O, 58
Spalter, Ronald, 623
Spano, Andrew J, 413
Spano, John J, 10, 194
Spano, Leonard N, 413
Spano, Linda, 245, 269
Spano, Nicholas A, 19, 24, 28, 29, 30, 31,
   32, 34, 55, 201, 719
Spano, Nicolas A, 181
Spargo, Thomas J, 59
Spas Ervin, Jennifer, 278, 311
Spear, Susan, 446
Spears, Brenda S, 62
Specter, Arlen, 138, 205, 386, 389
Specter, Marvin M, 263

Name Index

Name Index

Organization Index

Includes the names of the top three levels in all New York State executive departments and agencies; public corporations; authorities; commissions; all organizations listed in the Private Sector sources segment of each policy chapter; lobbyist organizations; political action committees; chambers of commerce; newspapers; news services; radio and television stations; SUNY and CUNY locations; and private colleges.

Organization Index

Organization Index

Indexes &
Demographic
Maps

835

Montgomery County Chamber of Commerce/ Montgomery County Partnership, In, 586
Monticello CSD, 668
Monticello Raceway, 344
Monticello Raceway Management Inc, 474
Monument Builders Assn (NYS), 516
Monument Industry PAC, 557
Moody's Investors Service, Public Finance Group, 292, 331
Morano, Regina G, 510
Moravia Chamber of Commerce, 586
Moravia CSD, 643
Morello, Charles J, 511
Morgan Associates, 511
Morgan Stanley, 94, 539
Morgante, Samuel, 511
Moriah CSD, 648
Morris & McVeigh LLP, 511
Morris & McVeigh NYS PAC, 557
Morris CSD, 661
Morris Heights Health Ctr, 510
Morris, Mark, 511
Morristown CSD, 664
Morrisville State College, 618
Morrisville-Eaton CSD, 652
Morse, Alan, 511
Mortgage Insurance Companies of America, 499
Mosholu Montefiore Community Ctr, 503
Mothers Against Drunk Driving (MADD) of NYS, 140
Mothers Against Drunk Driving-NYS Office, 507
Motion Picture Assn of America Inc, 458
Motley, Duane R, 511
Motor Truck Assn (NYS), 503
Motor Vehicle Operators Union, Local 983, DC-37, AFSCME, 534
Motor Vehicles Department, 13, 349, 376
   Administration, Office for, 349
   Appeals Board, 349
   Governor's Traffic Safety Committee, 349
   Legal Affairs, Office for, 349
   Operations & Customer Service, Office for, 349
   Safety, Consumer Protection & Clean Air, Office for, 349
Motorola, Inc, 474, 487
Mount Kisco Chamber of Commerce, 586
Mount Pleasant, Town of, 424
Mount Saint Mary College, 631
Mount Sinai Medical Center, 222, 509, 511
Mount Sinai School of Medicine, 631
Mount Vernon, 72
   Civil & Criminal Courts, 72
Mount Vernon Chamber of Commerce, 586
Mount Vernon Ind Dev Agency (City of), 586
Mount Vernon, City of, 424
Mountaintop Democratic Club, 557

Movers & Warehousemen Political Action Committee, 557
Movers' & Warehousemen's Assn Inc (NYS), 489
Moving Image (The) (dba The Film Forum), 536
MRH & Company, Inc, 504
Mt Morris CSD, 652
Mt Pleasant CSD, 672
Mt Pleasant-Blythedale UFSD, 672
Mt Pleasant-Cottage UFSD, 672
Mt Sinai Hospital of Queens, 540
Mt Sinai UFSD, 666
Mt Vernon City SD, 672
MTA (Metropolitan Transportation Authority), 116
MTA Bridges & Tunnels, 116, 352, 379
MTA Long Island Bus, 116, 353, 379
MTA Long Island Rail Road, 117, 353, 379
MTA Metro-North Railroad, 117, 353, 379
MTA New York City Transit, 117, 353, 379
MTA Office of the Inspector General, 117
Muhs, Robert E, 511
Mulholland & Knapp, LLP, 207
Mullane, Robert A, 511
Multi Housing Laundry Assn, 535
Multimedia Games Inc, 521
Mulvihill ICS Inc, 516
Municipal Art Society, 512
Municipal Assistance Corporation for the City of New York, 89, 118, 290, 379
Municipal Credit Union, 94
Municipal Electric Utilities Assn of NYS (MEUA), 512
Municipal Electric Utilities Association, 173
Murphy, Daniel C, 512
Murphy, Robert J, 512
Murphy, Thomas V, 512
Murray, Claire, 512
Museum Association of New York, 345
Museum for African Art, 536
Museum of Arts & Design, 496
Museum of Modern Art (The), 471, 523
Mutual Redevelopment Houses Inc, 459
My-T Acres Inc, 84
NAMI-NYS, 283, 512
Nanuet UFSD, 662
Naples CSD, 659
Naral Pro Choice New York, 505
Naral Pro-Choice NY, 504
NARAL Pro-Choice, New York, 512
NARAL Pro-Choice, NY, 512
NARAL/Pro/Choice Multicandidate PAC, 557
Nasca, Samuel J, 513
Nassau BOCES, 674
Nassau Community College, 482, 620
Nassau Council of Chambers, 586
Nassau County, 66, 69, 405
   1st, 2nd & 3rd District Courts, 69

County & Surrogate's Courts, 66
   Family Court, 66
   Supreme Court, 66
Nassau County Detectives Association Inc, 561
Nassau County Ind Dev Agency, 586
Nassau County PBA PAC, 561
Nassau County PHCC, 534
Nassau County Village Officials Assn, 475
Nassau Regional Off-Track Betting Corporation, 118, 337, 379, 459, 501
Nassau-Suffolk Hospital Council Inc, 474
NASW-NYS Political Action Committee, 557
Nat'l Assn of Energy Service Companies, 485
Nat'l Assn of Social Workers - New York City Chapter, 561
Nat'l Electric Manufacturers Assoc, 487
Nat'l Federation of Independent Business/ NY Save America's Free Enterpri, 561
National Academy of Forensic Engineers, 263
National Alliance for the Mentally Ill of NYC, Inc, 513
National Amputation Foundation Inc, 222, 369
National Archives & Records Administration, 149, 340
   Franklin D Roosevelt Presidential Library & Museum, 149, 340
National Assn of Chain Drug Stores, 513
National Assn of Health Underwriters, 479
National Assn of Marine Manufacturers (Ahern, Barbara J), 459
National Assn of Professional Employer Organizations, 464
National Assn of Social Workers (NYC Chapter), 474
National Assn of Social Workers (NYS Chapter), 513, 518
National Assn of Theatre Owners of NYS (NATO), 458
National Association of Black Accountants, NY Chapter, 110
National Association of Social Workers, NYS Chapter, 320
National Basketball Association, 345
National Center for Disability Services, 475
National Cleaners Assn, 495
National Coffee Association, 85
National Conference of Insurance Guaranty Funds, 488
National Council of Jewish Women, 240, 320
National Council to Prevent Delinquency Inc, 517
National Credit Union Administration, 91
   Albany Region, 91
National Economic Research Associates, 173, 360

Organization Index

Organization Index

Organization Index

Organization Index

Organization Index

Geographic Index

Includes the names of the top three levels in all New York State executive departments and agencies; public corporations; authorities; commissions; all organizations listed in the Private Sector sources segment of each policy chapter; lobbyist organizations; political action committees; chambers of commerce; newspapers; news services; radio and television stations; SUNY and CUNY locations; and private colleges.

Arkansas

Little Rock
Entergy Corporation Political Committee NY (ENPAC-NY), 549

California

Cupertino
Apple Computer, Inc, 454

Encino
NY Film PAC, 558

Los Angeles
Assn of Independent Commercial Producers Inc PAC, 543

San Francisco
Working Assets Funding Service Inc, 540

Connecticut

Danbury
Rouse, James, 524

Essex
JLW Consulting, LLC, 494

Farmington
NY Region 9A UAW PAC Cmte, 558

Greenwich
500 Club, 542
The Nestle Waters North America, Inc Political Action Com, 570

Hartford
Allegue, Raul R, 452
Hartford Advocates Fund (The), 551
Hartford Financial Svcs Group Inc, 489
US Treasury Department
Area 1 Director's Office, 329

Monroe
Army Aviation Association of America (AAAA), 367

Shelton
Perkins, Janice C, 517

Suffield
CIGNA Corporation Political Action Committee, 544

Trumbull
Oxford Health Plans Inc-NY Cmte for Quality Health Care, 564
United Healthcare Services, Inc (FKA Oxford LLC), 534

Waterford
Trading Cove NY, LLC, 532
Weekley, Daniel A, 537

Windsor
US Postal Service
NORTHEAST AREA (Includes part of New York State), 203

Woodbury
Dierks, John W, 476

District of Columbia

Washington
21st Century Democrats, 542
Aetna Inc PAC, 542
Amalgamated Transit Union, 452
American Continental Group, 453
American Express Company PAC (AXP PAC), 542
American Federation of Teachers, 273
American Insurance Assn New York PAC, 542
American Resort Dev/Assn Resort Owners' Coalition PAC, 543
Atlantic States Marine Fisheries Commission, 112, 179
ATU-NY Cope Fund, 542
Baker & Hostetler, LLP, 456
Ciccone, Stephen J, 467
Cohen, Marsha A, 469
Consumer Advocacy PAC, 547
Corning Incorporated Employees PAC, 547
CTIA - The Wireless Assn, 463
D.R.I.V.E.-Democratic, Republican, Independent Voter Education, 547
Democratic Congressional Campaign Committee, 163
Democratic Governors' Assn - NY, 548

Dewey Ballantine LLP Political Action Committee-New York, 548
Eastman Kodak Company, 108
Emily's List, 163, 549
Facer & Stamoulas, PC, 479
Federal Communications Commission
Office of Media Relations, 169
Federal Election Commission, 162
Gay and Lesbian Victory Fund, 550
General Motors Corporation Political Action Committee-N, 551
Gibson Dunn & Crutcher, LLP, 485
Glover Park Group, Inc (The), 485
Goldman Sachs & Co, 93
Goldman Sachs NY PAC, 551
Governor's Office
New York State Office of Federal Affairs, 4, 192
Green Worlds Coalition Fund, 551
HillPAC-NY, 552
Holch, Neils, 491
Honda North America Inc, 492
Hotel Employees Restaurant Int'l Union Tip Edu Fund, 552
HSBC North America, Inc PAC (H-PAC), 551
International Paper Political Action Committee, 554
International Union o, 554
Ironworkers Political Action League, 554
Jewish War Veterans of the USA, 368
Landau-Painter, Cathy, 498
Morgante, Samuel, 511
National Guard Association of the US (NGAUS), 369
National Transportation Safety Board
Office of Administrative Law Judges, 356
National Wildlife Federation, 188
NYSE State PAC, 561
Ocean Conservancy (The), 515
Reserve Officers Association (ROA), 370
Scripps Howard News Service, 607
SEIU PEA State Fund, 568
Solowan, Richard, 530
Sommer, Judah, 530
UFCW Active Ballot Club, 571
US Commission on Civil Rights
EASTERN REGION (includes New York State), 162, 237
US Department of Energy
Office of External Affairs, 169

Geographic Index

Detroit
Cingular Wireless LLC EPAC, 545
Dominion PAC-NY, 548
Ford Motor Company Civic Action Fund, 550
General Motors Corporation, 484
Professionals Political Action committee-NY, 566

Harper Woods
Ciaravino, Anthony S, 467

Missouri

St Louis
Enterprise Rent-A-Car Company NY PAC, 549

New Hampshire

Dover
Air Force Sergeants Association (AFSA), Division 1, 367

New Jersey

Avon by the Sea
Luthin Associates, Inc, 503

Bedminster
AT&T Corporation, 171

Bridgewater
Fleet Bank of New York PAC, 550

Cherry Hill
Compac, NJ, 546
Freedom America, 550

Clark
AeA New York Council, 106, 171

East Rutherford
New York Giants, 346

Edison
US Environmental Protection Agency
Division of Environmental Science & Assessment (DESA), 183

Englewood Cliff
Port Authority PBA, Inc State of New York PAC, 566

Flanders
Humane Society of the United States, Mid Atlantic Regional Office, 84, 319

Florham Park
Friedman, John P, 483

Fort Lee
Port Authority Sergeants Benevolent Assn PAC, 566

Iselin
Cobb Jr, James H, 469
Federal Mediation & Conciliation Service
Northeastern Region, 270
New York Shipping Association Inc, 360

Jersey City
Dow Jones Newswires (Dow Jones & Company), 606
US Treasury Department
Northeast Region (serving NY), 91

Lindhurst
US Department of Homeland Security (DHS)
Newark Asylum Office-Including NYS not served by New York City, 203, 238

Madison
Watkins, James, 536
WYETH Good Gov't Fund, 572

Monroe Twp
Local 23-25, Unite State & Local Campaign Cmte, 555

Morristown
NYS Bar Assn, Federal Constitution & Legislation Cmte, 264
Pitney Hardin et al, 264

New Brunswick
Johnson & Johnson Employees' Good Gov't Fund PAC, 554

New York
Bristol-Myers Squibb Co Employee PAC, 544

Newark
Commonwealth Business Media, 601
Journal of Commerce, 601
Keyspan Services PAC, 554
Prudential New York Political Action Committee, 566

Paramus
Hartman & Winnicki, PC, 108, 261
Liantonio, John J, 501
NYS Bar Assn, Intellectual Property Law Section, 108, 261

Parsippany
Cendant Corporation NY PAC, 545
Hastings, Jamie, 489
Muhs, Robert E, 511
National Transportation Safety Board
Aviation Division, Northeast Regional Office, 356

Secaucus
WWOR (UPN 9), 613

Springfield
IUOE Local 825 Political Action & Education Cmte, 553

Teaneck
Latina Political Action Committee, 555

Watervliet
Murray, Claire, 512

Wayne
Enterprise Rent-A-Car, 479

West Trenton
Delaware River Basin Commission, 114, 179

New York

Accord
Rondout Valley CSD, 669

Adams
South Jefferson Chamber of Commerce, 591

Adams Center
South Jefferson CSD, 651

Addison
Addison CSD, 664

Afton
Afton CSD, 644

Akron
Akron CSD, 647
Bank of Akron, 92
New York State Travel & Vacation Association, 347
Save American Jobs PAC, 568

Albany
3rd Department, 57
Adirondack Mountain Club Inc, 185, 341, 451
Advocate for Persons with Disabilities, Ofc of, 373
Advocate for Persons with Disabilities, Office of, 4, 235, 276
AFGI PAC, 542
AFSCME District Council 37, 297
AFSCME, New York, 297
Aging, Office for the, 4, 306
Agostine Jr, Joseph A, 451
Agriculture & Markets Department, 5, 77, 306
Soil & Water Conservation Committee, 78

Geographic Index

Geographic Index

Buffalo Territory, 329
Western NY Majority Leader PAC, 572

Cherry Valley
Cherry Valley-Springfield CSD, 660

Chester
Chester UFSD, 659

Chestertown
North Warren Chamber of Commerce, 587
North Warren CSD, 670

Chestnut Ridge
Edwin Gould Academy-Ramapo UFSD, 662
NYS Laborers' PAC, 560

Chittenango
Chittenango CSD, 652

Churchville
Churchville-Chili CSD, 652

Cicero
Cicero, Town of, 417

Cincinnatus
Cincinnatus CSD, 645

Clarence
Clarence Chamber of Commerce, 578
Clarence CSD, 647
Clarence Ind Dev Agency (Town of), 578

Clarksville
American Motorcyclist Assn PAC, 543

Claverack
Children & Family Services, Office of
Brookwood Secure Center, 309
Rural Water Association, 190

Clay
Clay, Town of, 418

Clayton
Clayton Chamber of Commerce, 578
Thousand Islands CSD, 651

Clifton Park
Army Aviation Association of America (AAAA), Western NY Chapter, 367
Boltz, John J Consulting, 459
Clifton Park, Town of, 418
Coalition for Education Reform & Accountability, 469
Coalition of Fathers & Families NY, 219, 317, 546
Coalition of Fathers & Families NY, PAC, 205, 260
CP Rail System, 359
DKI Engineering & Consulting USA, PC, Corporate World Headquarters, 359
Doherty, C R & Co, 476

Empire State Association of Adult Homes & Assisted Living Facilit, 220
Fitzgerald, Gary J, 482
Franco, William A, 482
Ianniello, Anderson & Reilly, PC, 493
Iroquois Healthcare Alliance, 221
New York Long-Term Care Brokers Ltd, 249
Newcomb, Lisa, 514
Nurse Practitioners Assn of NYS (The), 224, 515
Nurse Practitioners of NYS PAC, 564
NYS Car Wash PAC, 559
Shenendehowa CSD, 662
Southern Saratoga County Chamber of Commerce, 591
UHAP PAC, 571

Clifton Springs
Clifton Springs Area Chamber of Commerce, 578
Phelps-Clifton Springs CSD, 659

Clinton
Clinton Chamber of Commerce Inc, 578
Clinton CSD, 657
Hamilton College, 628

Clintonville
Ausable Valley CSD, 645

Clyde
Clyde Industrial Dev Corp, 578
Clyde-Savannah CSD, 670

Clymer
Clymer CSD, 643

Cobleskill
Cobleskill College of Agriculture & Technology, 618
Cobleskill-Richmondville CSD, 663
Northeast Organic Farming Association of New York, 86
Schoharie County Ind Dev Agency, 590

Cohoes
Anderson, David, 454
Cohoes
Civil, Criminal & Traffic Courts, 70
Cohoes Chamber of Commerce, 578
Cohoes City SD, 641
Cohoes Ind Dev Agency (City of), 578
Cohoes, City of, 418

Cold Spring
Haldane CSD, 661

Cold Spring Harbor
Cold Spring Harbor CSD, 665
Cold Spring Harbor Fish Hatchery & Aquarium, 343
Watson school of Biological Sciences at Cold spring Harbor, 636

Collins
Correctional Services Department
Collins Correctional Facility, 129

Colton
Colton-Pierrepont CSD, 664

Commack
Long Island Association, 502, 584
Long Island Business Institute-Commack, 639
Mental Retardation & Developmental Disabilities, Office of
Long Island Developmental Disabilities Services Office, 280

Comstock
Correctional Services Department
Great Meadow Correctional Facility, 129
Washington Correctional Facility, 130

Congers
Reserve Officers Association (ROA), Department of NY, 370

Conklin
Susquehanna Valley CSD, 642

Cooperstown
Cooperstown Chamber of Commerce, 579
Cooperstown CSD, 660
Elections, State Board of
Otsego, 159
New York Center for Agricultural Medicine & Health, Bassett He, 85
New York, Susquehanna & Western Railway, 360
NY State Historical Association/The Farmers' Museum, 345
Otsego County, 407
Supreme, County, Family & Surrogate's Courts, 67

Copenhagen
Copenhagen CSD, 651

Copiague
Copiague UFSD, 665

Coram
US Department of the Interior
Coram Sub-District Office, 183

Corfu
Pembroke CSD, 650

Corinth
Corinth CSD, 662
Corinth Ind Dev Agency (Town of), 579

Corning
Convention Centers & Visitors Bureaus
Steuben County Conference & Visitors Bureau, 339
Corning

NYS College of Human Ecology at Cornell University, 616

NYS College of Veterinary Medicine at Cornell University, 616

NYS School of Industrial & Labor Relations at Cornell University, 616

NYS Water Resources Institute of Cornell University, 188

Prisoners' Legal Services of New York, 140, 264

Science, Technology & Academic Research, Office of
Center for Advanced Technology in Life Science Enterprise, 99, 147

Tompkins County, 411
Supreme, County, Family & Surrogate's Courts, 68

Tompkins County Area Dev, 593

Tompkins County Chamber of Commerce, 593

Tompkins Trustco Inc, 95

Tompkins-Seneca-Tioga BOCES, 675

True, Walsh & Miller LLP, 225

US Department of Agriculture
Cornell Cooperative Extension Service, 80

US Department of the Interior
Ithaca Sub-District Office, 183

WHCU (870 AM), WTKO (1470 AM), WYXL (97.3 FM), WQNY (103.7 FM), 609

Jackson Heights

British Airways PLC, 359

Plaza College, 639

Queens Chamber of Commerce (Borough of), 589

United Spinal Assn (FKA Eastern Paralyed Veterans Assn), 534

United Spinal Association, 370

Jamaica

Browne, Brian, 461

Civil Court, NYC
Queens County, 61

CUNY York College, 624

Family Court, NYC
Queens County, 62

Federal Maritime Commission
New York Area Office, 356

Filipino American Human Services Inc, 240, 318

Health Department
New York State Veterans' Home at St Albans, 212, 362

Housing & Community Renewal, Division of
Rent Administration, 227

Jamaica Chamber of Commerce, 583

Jamaica Dev Corp (Greater Jamaica), 583

MTA Long Island Rail Road, 117, 353

New York City

Library, Queens Borough Public, 431

New York Racing Association, 346

New York Thoroughbred Horsemen's Assn, Inc Political Action Committe, 563

Queens County
Supreme & Surrogate's Courts, 67

Queens Educational Opportunity Center, 622

St John's University, 634

St John's University, School of Law, 190

Unified Court System
11th Judicial District (Judicial Department 2), 255

US Department of Agriculture
JFK International Airport Inspection Station, 80

US Department of Health & Human Services
New York Quarantine Station, 216, 314
Northeast Region, 216, 314

US Department of Homeland Security (DHS)
JFK International Airport Area Office, 81, 202

US Justice Department
Investigations Division, 258
JFK/LGA, 137

US Transportation Department
Federal Aviation Administration-Eastern Region, 357

Workers' Compensation Board
Queens, 246, 269

Jamestown

Chautauqua County Chamber of Commerce, 577

Chautauqua County Ind Dev Agency, 578

Jamestown
Civil & Criminal Courts, 71

Jamestown Business College, 639

Jamestown City SD, 644

Jamestown Community College, 620

Jamestown, City of, 422

Post-Journal, 600

Southwestern CSD at Jamestown, 644

WKZA (106.9 FM), 609

Jamesville

I Love Good Government, 553

Parks, Recreation & Historic Preservation, NYS Office of
Central Region, 335

Jasper

Jasper-Troupsburg CSD, 665

Jefferson

Jefferson CSD, 663

Jericho

Jericho UFSD, 654

New York Community Bank, 233

Johnson City

Davis College, 627

Johnson City CSD, 642

WBNG (12), WBXI (11), 611

Johnstown

Children & Family Services, Office of
Tryon Girls Center, 310
Tryon Residential Center, 310

Correctional Services Department
Hale Creek ASACTC, 130

Elections, State Board of
Fulton, 157

Fulton County, 402
Family Court, 64
Supreme, County & Surrogate's Courts, 64

Fulton County Economic Dev Corp, 580

Fulton County Ind Dev Agency, 580

Fulton-Montgomery Community College, 620

Hamilton-Fulton-Montgomery BOCES, 674

Johnstown
Civil & Criminal Courts, 71

Johnstown City SD, 649

Jordan

Jordan-Elbridge CSD, 658

Keene Valley

Keene CSD, 648

Kendall

Kendall CSD, 660

Kenmore

Kenmore-Town of Tonawanda Chamber of Commerce, 583

Metro/Colvin Realty Inc, 304

Metro/Horohoe-Leimbach, 304

Tonawanda, Town of, 439

Keuka Park

Keuka College, 629

Kew Gardens

Criminal Court, NYC
Queens County, 62

Elections, State Board of
Queens, 158

New York City Boroughs
Queens (Queens County), 434

Queens County (NYC Borough of Queens), 408

Kinderhook

US Department of the Interior
Martin Van Buren National Historic Site, 340

Kings Park

Kings Park Chamber of Commerce, 583

Kings Park CSD, 666

Sullivan County Chamber of Commerce,
592
Sullivan County Chamber of Commerce &
Industry, Inc, 532

Lima
New York Forest Owners Association Inc,
189

Limestone
Children & Family Services, Office of
Cattaraugus Residential Center, 309

Lincolndale
Somers CSD, 672

Lindenhurst
Babylon, Town of, 416
Education Department
Long Island Regional Office, 146
Lindenhurst UFSD, 666
Lindenhurst, Village of, 423

Lisbon
Empire State Honey Producers Association,
83
Lisbon CSD, 664

Little Falls
Evening Times (The), 600
Liberty Group Publishing, 600
Little Falls
Civil & Criminal Courts, 72
Little Falls City SD, 650
NYS Association for Health, Physical
Education, Recreation & Dance, 152

Little Valley
Cattaraugus County, 399
Supreme, County & Surrogate's Courts,
63
Cattaraugus-Little Valley CSD, 642
Elections, State Board of
Cattaraugus, 156

Liverpool
Bryant & Stratton College-North Campus,
637
Greater Syracuse Association of Realtors
Inc, 303
Insurance Fund (NYS)
Syracuse, 244, 267
Liverpool Chamber of Commerce (Greater
Liverpool), 584
Liverpool CSD, 658
Local #30 PAC, 555
Mullane, Robert A, 511
Municipal Electric Utilities Association,
173
Northeast Equipment Dealers Association
Inc, 110
Salina, Town of, 438

Livingston Manor
Livingston Manor CSD, 668

Livonia
Livonia CSD, 652

Loch Sheldrake
Sullivan County Community College, 621

Lockport
Ayers, Deborah, 456
Elections, State Board of
Niagara, 158
Greater Niagara Newspapers, 600
Lockport
Civil & Criminal Courts, 72
Lockport City SD, 657
Lockport Ind Dev Agency (Town of), 584
Lockport Union-Sun & Journal, 600
Lockport, City of, 423
Niagara County, 406
County, Family & Surrogate's Courts, 66
Starpoint CSD, 657
TOW PAC, 570

Locust Valley
Locust Valley CSD, 655

Lodi
Venture Vineyards Inc, 87

Long Beach
Lancer Insurance Co/Lancer Compliance
Services, 274
Long Beach
Civil & Criminal Courts, 72
Long Beach Chamber of Commerce, 584
Long Beach City SD, 655
Long Beach, City of, 423

Long Island
Long Island Council of Dedicated
Merchants Chamber of Commerce, 584

Long Island City
Asbestos Workers Local 12 Political Action
Committee, 543
Bricklayers & Allied Craftsmen Local
Union 1 PAC, 544
Correctional Services Department
Queensboro Correctional Facility, 130
DeVry Institute of Technology, Long Island
City Campus, 638
Donnellan, James, 476
Elevator Constructors Union Local No 1
Political Action Committee, 548
Environmental Conservation Department
Region 2, 176
Fiorello H LaGuardia Community College,
624
MetLife, 248
Metlife Inc Emplyees' Political
Participation Fund A, 557
MetLife Ins Co Political Fund B, 556

Modutank Inc, 188
New York City
Design & Construction, Dept of, NYC,
427
Educational Construction Fund, NYC,
427
New York City School Construction
Authority, 118, 148
New York Metropolitan Transportation
Council, 354
NYC Region 4, 656
Osborne Association/South Forty, 140, 275
Sheet Metal Workers Int'l Assn Local 137
PAL Fund, 568
Steamfitters' Union Local 638 PAC, 569
Tile Layers Subordinate Union Loacal 7 of
New York and New, 570
Transportation Department
Region 11, 351

Long Lake
Long Lake CSD, 650
New York State Snowmobile Association,
346

Loudonville
Brescia, Richard, 461
Family Physicians PAC, 550
NYS Academy of Family Physicians, 222
Professional Insurance Agents of New York
Political Action Committ, 566
Siena College, 634

Lowville
Elections, State Board of
Lewis, 157
Lewis County, 404
Supreme, County, Family & Surrogate's
Courts, 65
Lewis County Chamber of Commerce, 584
Lewis County Ind Dev Agency, 584
Lowville Academy & CSD, 651
NYS Weights & Measures Association, 85

Lynbrook
Disabled American Veterans, Department of
New York, 368
Lynbrook P.B.A. PAC, 556
Lynbrook UFSD, 655

Lyndonville
Lyndonville CSD, 660

Lyon Mountain
Correctional Services Department
Lyon Mountain Correctional Facility,
130

Lyons
Elections, State Board of
Wayne, 160
Lyons CSD, 670
Wayne County, 412

Geographic Index

Geographic Index

Wallkill CSD, 669

Walton
Walton CSD, 646

Walworth
Gananda CSD, 670

Wampsville
Elections, State Board of
Madison, 157
Madison County, 404
*Supreme, County, Family & Surrogate's
Courts, 65*

Wantagh
New York State Park Police PBA PAC Inc,
563
Wantagh Chamber of Commerce, 593
Wantagh UFSD, 656

Wappingers Falls
Southern Dutchess Chamber of Commerce
(Greater Southern Dutchess), 591
Wappingers CSD, 647

Wards Island
Mental Health, Office of
Kirby Forensic Psychiatric Center, 278
Manhattan Psychiatric Center, 278

Warrensburg
Warrensburg Chamber of Commerce, 594
Warrensburg CSD, 670

Warsaw
Elections, State Board of
Wyoming, 161
Warsaw Chamber of Commerce (Greater
Warsaw), 594
Warsaw CSD, 673
Wyoming County, 413
*Supreme, County, Family & Surrogate's
Courts, 69*

Warwick
Correctional Services Department
Mid-Orange Correctional Facility, 130
NYS Plumbing, Heating & Cooling
Contractors PAC, 560
Warwick Valley Chamber of Commerce,
594
Warwick Valley CSD, 660

Washingtonville
Blooming Grove Chamber of Commerce,
576
Washingtonville CSD, 660

Wassaic
Mental Retardation & Developmental
Disabilities, Office of
*Taconic Developmental Disabilities
Services Office, 280*

Waterford
Parks, Recreation & Historic Preservation,
NYS Office of
Field Services, 178, 335
Historic Sites Bureau, 178, 335
Waterford-Halfmoon UFSD, 663

Waterloo
Elections, State Board of
Seneca, 159
Finger Lakes PAC, 550
Seneca County, 410
*Supreme, County, Family & Surrogate's
Courts, 68*
Seneca County Ind Dev Agency, 591
Waterloo CSD, 663

Watertown
Correctional Services Department
Watertown Correctional Facility, 130
Development Authority of the North
Country, 101, 114, 228, 579
Elections, State Board of
Jefferson, 157
Empire State Development Corporation
North Country Region (Watertown), 98
Environmental Conservation Department
Region 6, 176
Jefferson Community College, 620
Jefferson County, 403
Family & Surrogate's Courts, 65
Supreme & County Courts, 65
Jefferson-Lewis-Hamilton-Herkimer-Oneid
a BOCES, 674
Johnson Newspaper Corp, 605
Law Department
Watertown, 253
New York State Tug Hill Commission, 124,
181
NYS Council of Machinists, 274
State Department
Watertown, 198
Transportation Department
Region 7, 352
Watertown
Civil & Criminal Courts, 74
Watertown City SD, 651
Watertown Daily Times, 605
Watertown, City of, 440
Watertown-North County Chamber of
Commerce (Greater Watertown), 594
WFRY (97.5 FM), 611
WWNY (7), 614
WWTI (50), 614

Waterville
Waterville CSD, 658

Watervliet
Maplewood Common SD, 641
US Defense Department
Watervliet Arsenal, 364

Watervliet
Civil & Criminal Courts, 74
Watervliet City SD, 641

Watkins Glen
Elections, State Board of
Schuyler, 159
Farm Sanctuary, 83
Schuyler County, 410
*Supreme, County, Family & Surrogate's
Courts, 67*
Schuyler County Chamber of Commerce,
591
Schuyler County Ind Dev Agency, 591
Schuyler County Partnership for Econ Dev,
591
Watkins Glen CSD, 663

Waverly
Waverly CSD, 668

Wayland
Wayland-Cohocton CSD, 665

Webster
Webster Chamber of Commerce, 594
Webster CSD, 653
Webster, Town of, 440

Weedsport
Weedsport CSD, 643

Wells
Wells CSD, 650

Wellsville
Liberty Group Publishing, 605
Wellsville Area Chamber of Commerce,
594
Wellsville CSD, 642
Wellsville Daily Reporter/Spectator, 605

West Amherst
Buffalo Niagara Builders' Assn Build PAC,
544

West Babylon
Federation of Organizations Inc, 282
Kaplan, Randy L, 495
West Babylon UFSD, 668

West Brentwood
Mental Health, Office of
Pilgrim Psychiatric Center, 279

West Chazy
Beekmantown CSD, 645

West Coxsackie
Correctional Services Department
Coxsackie Correctional Facility, 129

West Haverstraw
Health Department
Helen Hayes Hospital, 211

World Wide Web (URL) Index

Air Force Women Officers Associated (AFWOA) . . . . www.afwoa.org
Albany City SD. . . . . www.albanyschools.org
Albany College of Pharmacy . . . . www.acp.edu
Albany County . . . . www.albanycounty.com
Albany County Airport Authority. . . . . www.albanyairport.com
Albany County Convention & Visitors Bureau . . . . www.albany.org
Albany County Ind Dev Agency. . . . . www.albanycounty.com/IDA
Albany County Rural Housing Alliance Inc. . . . . www.timesunion.com/communities/acrha
Albany Housing Coalition Inc . . . . www.timesunion.com/communities/ahc
Albany Ind Dev Agency (City of) . . . . www.albanyny.org
Albany Law School . . . . www.als.edu
Albany Medical College. . . . . www.amc.edu/academic
Albany Port District Commission. . . . . www.portofalbany.com
Albany, City of . . . . www.albanyny.org
Albany-Colonie Regional Chamber of Commerce. . . . . www.ac-chamber.org
Alcoholic Beverage Control, Division of . . . . www.abc.state.ny.us
Alcoholism & Substance Abuse Services, Office of . . . . www.oasas.state.ny.us
Alesse, Mark . . . . www.nfib.com
Alexandria Bay Chamber of Commerce. . . . . www.alexbay.org
Alfred State College of Technology . . . . www.alfredstate.edu
Alfred University . . . . www.alfred.edu
Allegany County. . . . . www.alleganyco.com
Alliance Bank . . . . www.alliancebankna.com
Alliance for the Arts . . . . www.allianceforarts.org
Alliance of American Insurers . . . . www.allianceai.org
Alliance of NYS Arts Organizations . . . . www.thealliancenys.org
Alliance of Resident Theatres/New York (ART/New York) . . . . www.offbroadwayonline.com
ALSTOM Transportation Inc . . . . www.transport.alstom.com
Altria Corporate Services . . . . www.altria.com
Alzheimer's Association, Northeastern NY . . . . www.alzneny.org
AMAC, Association for Metroarea Autistic Children . . . . www.amac.org
AMDeC Foundation . . . . www.amdec.org
Amdursky Pelky Fennell & Wallen . . . . apfwlaw.com
Amerada Hess Corporation. . . . . www.hess.com
American Academy McAllister Institute of Funeral Service . . . . www.a-a-m-i.org
American Cancer Society-Eastern Division . . . . www.cancer.org
American Chemistry/American Plastics Council . . . . www.americanchemistry.com
American College of Nurse-Midwives, NYC Chapter. . . . . www.nysmidwives.org; www.nyc.org
American College of Ob & Gyn, District II/NY. . . . . www.acog.org/goto/nys
American College of Physicians, New York Chapter . . . . www.acponline.org/chapters/ny
American Continental Group . . . . www.acgrep.com
American Council of Engineering Companies of NY (ACECNY) . . . . www.acecny.org
American Express Company. . . . . www.americanexpress.com
American Farmland Trust, Northeast Regional Office. . . . . www.farmland.org
American Federation of Musicians, Local 802. . . . . www.local802afm.org
American Federation of Teachers. . . . . www.aft.org
American Heart Assn/American Stroke Assn. . . . . www.americanheart.org; www.strokeassociation.org
American Heart Association Northeast Affiliate . . . . www.americanheart.org
American Infertility Association. . . . . www.americaninfertility.org
American Institute of Architects (AIA) New York State Inc . . . . www.aianys.org
American Insurance Assn . . . . www.aiadc.org
American International Group Inc . . . . www.aig.com
American Jewish Committee . . . . www.ajc.org
American Lawyer Media Inc . . . . www.law.com
American Legion, Department of New York . . . . www.ny.legion.org
American Liver Foundation, Western NY Chapter . . . . www.liverfoundation.org

American Lung Association of NYS Inc . . . . www.alanys.org
American Management Association International . . . . www.amanet.org
American Military Retirees Association Inc. www.amra1973.org
American Museum of Natural History . . . . www.amnh.org
American Red Cross in Greater New York . . . . www.nyredcross.org
American Resort Dev/Assn Resort Owners' Coalition PAC . . . . www.arda.org
American Society for the Prevention of Cruelty to Animals (ASPCA) . . . . www.aspca.org
Amherst Chamber of Commerce . . . . www.amherst.org
Amherst CSD . . . . www.amherstschools.org
Amherst Ind Dev Agency (Town of) . . . . www.amherstida.com
Amherst, Town of . . . . www.amherstny.us
Ammann & Whitney . . . . www.ammann-whitney.com
Amnesty International USA . . . . www.amnestyusa.org
Amsterdam City SD . . . . www.gasd.org
Amsterdam Ind Dev Agency . . . . www.amsterdamedz.com
Animal Plant Health Inspection Service . . . . www.aphis.usda.gov
Antalek & Moore Insurance Agency . . . . www.antalek-moore.com
Anti-Defamation League . . . . www.adl.org
Aon Group Inc . . . . www.aon.com
Apple Assn, Inc (NY) . . . . www.nyapplecountry.com
Apple Banking for Savings . . . . www.applebank.com
Apple Computer, Inc. . . . . www.apple.com
Appraisal Education Network School & Merrell Institute . . . . www.merrellinstitute.com
Arcade Area Chamber of Commerce . . . . www.arcadechamber.org
Army Corps of Engineers . . . . www.usace.army.mil
Art & Science Collaborations Inc . . . . www.asci.org
Art Commission, NYC . . . . www.nyc.gov/artcommission
Art Institue of New York City (The) . . . . www.ainyc.aii.edu
ArtsConnection Inc (The) . . . . www.artsconnection.org
Asciutto, Georgia M big5schools.home.mindspring.com
Asian American Federation of New York . . . . www.aafny.org
Asian American Legal Defense & Education Fund Inc . . . . www.aaldef.org
Asian Americans for Equality . . . . www.aafe.org
ASPIRA of New York Inc . . . . www.nyaspira.org
Assn for Community Living . . . . www.aclnys.org
Assn of Community & Residential Agencies (NYS) . . . . www.nysacra.org
Assn of Counties & Its Affiliated Organizations (NYS) . . . . www.nysac.org
Assn of School Business Officials (NYS) . . . . www.nysasbo.org
Associated Builders & Contractors, Construction Training Center of NYS . . . . www.abc.org/newyork
Associated General Contractors of America, NYS Chapter . . . . www.agcnys.org
Associated Licensed Detectives of New York State . . . . www.aldonys.org
Associated Medical Schools of New York . . . . www.amsny.org
Associated New York State State Food Processors Inc . . . . www.nyfoodprocessors.org
Associated Press (Albany/Upstate Bureau) . . . . www.ap.org
Associated Risk Managers of New York Inc . . . . www.armnortheast.com
Association Development Group, Inc. . . . . www.adgcommunications.com
Association for a Better New York . . . . www.abny.org
Association for Addiction Professionals of New York . . . . www.aapnycounselor.com
Association for Community Living . . . . www.aclnys.org
Association for Eating Disorders - Capital Region . . . . www.geocities.com/craedny
Association for Neighborhood & Housing Development . . . . www.anhd.org
Association for the Help of Retarded Children . . . . www.ahrcnyc.org
Association of Fire Districts of the State of NY Inc . . . . www.firedistnys.com
Association of Government Accountants, NY Capital Chapter . . . . www.aganycap.org
Association of Graphic Communications . . . . www.agcomm.org
Association of Independent Video & Filmmakers (AIVF), (The) . . . . www.aivf.org

Indexes &
Demographic
Maps

Coalition of Voluntary Mental Health Agencies, Inc (The) . . . . www.cvmha.org
Cobleskill College of Agriculture & Technology . . . . www.cobleskill.edu
Cochran School of Nursing . . . . www.riversidehealth.org
Cohen, Marsha A . . . . www.reinsurance.org
Cohoes Chamber of Commerce . . . . www.cohoeschamber.com
Cohoes Ind Dev Agency (City of) . . . . www.ci.cohoes.ny.us
Cohoes, City of . . . . www.cohoes.com
Cold Spring Harbor Fish Hatchery & Aquarium . . . . www.cshfha.org
Coleman, Elizabeth . . . . www.nystla.org
Colgate Rochester Crozer Divinity School . . . . www.crcds.edu
Colgate University . . . . www.colgate.edu
Colgate University, Department of Geology . . . . departments.colgate.edu/geology
Collective Bargaining, Office of, NYC . . . . www.ocb-nyc.org
College of Mount Saint Vincent . . . . www.mountsaintvincent.edu
College of New Rochelle (The) . . . . www.cnr.edu
College of Saint Rose (The) . . . . www.strose.edu
College of Westchester (The) . . . . www.cw.edu
Colliers ABR Inc . . . . www.colliersabr.com
Colonie, Town of . . . . www.colonie.org
Columbia County . . . . www.columbiacountyny.com
Columbia County Chamber of Commerce . . . . www.columbiachamber-ny.com
Columbia Hudson Partnership . . . . www.chpartnership.net
Columbia Law School, Legislative Drafting Research Fund . . . . www.law.columbia.edu
Columbia University . . . . www.columbia.edu
Columbia University, Exec Graduate Pgm in Public Policy & Administration . . . . www.columbia.edu/~sc32
Columbia University, Mailman School of Public Health . . . . cpmcnet.columbia.edu/dept/sph/popfam
Columbia University, Mailman School of Public Health, Center for Public Health . . . . . . www.cpmcnet.columbia.edu/dept/sph
Columbia University, School of the Arts . . . . www.columbia.edu/cu/arts
Columbia University, Science & Technology Venture . . . . www.stv.columbia.edu
Columbia-Greene Community College . . . . www.sunycgcc.edu
Commission on Economic Opportunity for the Greater Capital Region . . . . www.ceo-cap.org
Commission on Independent Colleges & Universities . . . . www.cicu.org
Commissioned Officers Assn of the US Public Health Service, Inc (COA) . . . . www.coausphs.org
Committee of Methadone Program Administrators Inc of NYS (COMPA) . . . . www.compa-ny.org
Commodity Futures Trading Commission . . . . www.cftc.gov
Commodore Applied Technologies Inc . . . . www.commodore.com
Common Cause/NY . . . . www.commoncause.org/ny
Commonwealth Business Media . . . . www.joc.com
Commonwealth Fund . . . . www.cmwf.org
Communications Workers of America, District 1 . . . . www.cwa-union.org
Community Advocacy & Advisory Services . . . . www.communityadvocacy.com
Community Bankers Assn of NY State, Accounting & Taxation Cmte . . . . www.greenpoint.com
Community Bankers Assn of NY State, Bank Operations & Admin Cmte . . . . www.northcountrysavings.com
Community Bankers Assn of NY State, Banking Law & Regulations Cmte . . . . www.astoriafederal.com
Community Bankers Assn of NY State, Government Relations Cmte . . . . www.pioneersb.com
Community Bankers Assn of NY State, Mortgages & Real Estate Cmte . . . . www.mynycb.com
Community Bankers Association of NY State . . . . www.cbanys.org
Community Health Care Assn of NYS . . . . www.chcanys.org
Community Healthcare Network . . . . www.chnnyc.org
Community Housing Improvement Program (CHIP) . . . . www.chipnyc.org
Community Preservation Corp . . . . www.communityp.com
Community Service Society of New York . . . . www.cssny.org
Comptroller of the Currency . . . . www.occ.treas.gov
Comptroller, NYC . . . . www.comptroller.nyc.gov
Concordia College . . . . www.concordia-ny.edu
Conference Board (The) . . . . www.conference-board.org

Dakota Software Corporation . . . . www.dakotasoft.com
Dale Carnegie & Associates Inc . . . . www.dale-carnegie.com
Dansville Chamber of Commerce. . . . . www.dansvilleny.net
Davenport, Nancy . . . . www.acli.com
Davis College . . . . www.davisny.edu
Day, Berry & Howard LLP. . . . . www.dbh.com
Debevoise & Plimpton LLP . . . . www.debcoise.com
Decision Strategies Group . . . . www.decisionstrategiesgroup.com
DeGraff, Foy, Kunz & Devine, LLP. . . . . www.degraff-foy.com
Delaware . . . . www.co.delaware.ny.us
Delaware County Chamber of Commerce . . . . www.delawarecounty.org
Delaware River Basin Commission . . . . www.drbc.net
Delaware-Chenango-Madison-Otsego BOCES . . . . www.dcmoboces.com
Delhi CSD. . . . . www.delhischools.org
Democrat and Chronicle. . . . . www.democratandchronicle.com
Democratic Congressional Campaign Committee . . . . www.dccc.org
Democratic Governors' Assn - NY. . . . . www.democraticgovernors.org
Dental Hygienists' Association of the State of New York Inc . . . . www.dhasny.org
Deposit Chamber of Commerce . . . . www.tds.net/depositchamber
Deposit CSD. . . . . www.depositcsd.org
Design & Construction, Dept of, NYC. . . . . www.nyc.gov/html/ddc
Detectives' Endowment COPE. . . . . www.nycdetectives.org
Deutsche Bank . . . . www.db.com
Development Authority of the North Country . . . . www.danc.org
Development Counsellors International . . . . www.aboutdci.com
Developmental Disabilities Planning Council . . . . www.ddpc.state.ny.us
DeVry Institute of Technology, Long Island City Campus . . . . www.ny.devry.edu
DeWitt, Town of. . . . . www.townofdewitt.com
Digiovanni, Joseph . . . . www.libertymutual.com
Dionondehowa Wildlife Sanctuary & School - Not For Profit. . . . . www.dionondehowa.org
Disabilities, Mayor's Office, for People with. . . . . www.nyc.gov/html/mopd
Disabled American Veterans, Department of New York . . . . www.davny.org
District Council 37, AFSCME www.district37.net
District Council 37, AFSCME, AFL-CIO www.dc37.net
DKI Engineering & Consulting USA, PC, Corporate World Headquarters. . . . . www.dkitechnologies.com
Doctors Without Borders USA. . . . . www.doctorswithoutborders.org
Dolan Media Co . . . . www.nydailyrecord.com
Dominican College . . . . www.dc.edu
Donnelly, Edwin . . . . www.nysaflcio.org
Donohue, Gavin J . . . . www.ippny.org
Dorothea Hopfer School of Nursing at Mount Vernon Hospital . . . . www.ssmc.org
Dow Jones & Company . . . . www.wsj.com
Dow Jones Newswires (Dow Jones & Company) . . . . www.djnewswires.com
Dowling College. . . . . www.dowling.edu
Downtown-Lower Manhattan Assn . . . . downtownny.com
Doyle, Michael R . . . . www.api.org
Drug Enforcement Administration - New York Task Force . . . . www.usdoj.gov/dea/deahome.html
Drum Major Institute for Public Policy - Not For Profit . . . . www.drummajorinstitute.org
Dupee, Dupee & Monroe, PC. . . . . www.dupeelaw.com
Dutchess . . . . www.dutchesselections.com
Dutchess BOCES . . . . www.dcboces.org
Dutchess Community College . . . . www.sunydutchess.edu
Dutchess County. . . . . www.dutchessny.gov
Dutchess County Economic Dev Corp. . . . . www.dcedc.com
E-3 Communications www.e3communications.com
East Aurora Chamber of Commerce (Greater East Aurora). . . . . www.eanycc.com

Indexes &
Demographic
Maps

Great Lakes United	www.glu.org
Great Neck Chamber of Commerce	www.greatneckchamber.org
Great Neck UFSD	www.greatneck.k12.ny.us
Greater New York Hospital Association	www.gnyha.org
Greater Niagara Newspapers	www.journal-register.com
Greater NY Automobile Dealers' Assn Inc	www.gnyada.com
Greater Rochester Association of Realtors Inc	www.homesteadnet.com
Greater Rochester Visitors Assn	www.visitrochester.com
Greater Syracuse Association of Realtors Inc	www.cnyrealtor.com
Greater Upstate Law Project Inc	www.gulpny.org
Greece Chamber of Commerce	www.greecechamber.org
Greece, Town of	www.townofgreece.org
Green Chimneys School-Green Chimneys Children's Services Inc	www.greenchimneys.org
Greenberg Traurig, LLP	www.gtlaw.com
Greenburgh, Town of	www.greenburghny.com
Greene County	www.discovergreene.com
Greene County Soil & Water Conservation District	www.gcswcd.com
Greene County Tourism Promotion	www.greenetourism.com
Greenmarket/Council on the Environment of NYC	www.cenyc.org
GreenPoint Bank	www.greenpoint.com
Greenport UFSD	www.greenport.k12.ny.us
Greenport-Southold Chamber of Commerce	www.greenportsoutholdchamber.org
GreenThumb	www.greenthumbnyc.org
Greenvale Chamber of Commerce (Greater Greenvale)	www.greenvalechamber.com
Greenville Area Chamber of Commerce	www.greenville-ny.com
Greenwich Chamber of Commerce (Greater Greenwich)	www.greenwichchamber.org
Greenwich Village-Chelsea Chamber of Commerce	www.gvccc.com
Greenwood Lake Chamber of Commerce	www.greenwoodlakeny.org
Grossman Strategies	www.grossman.net
Guide Dog Foundation for the Blind Inc	www.guidedog.org
Guilderland Chamber of Commerce	www.guilderlandchamber.com
Guilderland Ind Dev Agency (Town of)	www.guilderland.org
GVA Williams	www.gvawilliams.com
H J Kalikow & Co LLC	www.hjkalikow.com
Hager, Susan	www.uwnys.org
Hamburg Chamber of Commerce	www.hamburg-chamber.org
Hamburg Ind Dev Agency	www.townofhamburgny.com
Hamilton College	www.hamilton.edu
Hamilton-Fulton-Montgomery BOCES	www.hfmboces.org
Hampton Bays Chamber of Commerce	www.hamptonbayschamber.com
Hampton Bays UFSD	www.hamptonbays.k12.ny.us
Hancock Area Chamber of Commerce	www.hancockareachamber.com
Hannan, K T Public Affairs Inc	www.kthpa.com
Harlem Chamber of Commerce (Greater Harlem)	www.harlemdiscover.com
Harris Beach LLP	www.nysba.org
Harris Interactive Inc	www.harrisinteractive.com
Harrison, Town/Village of	www.townharrison.org
Harter Secrest & Emery, LLP	www.hartersecrest.com
Hartman & Winnicki, PC	www.hartmanwinnicki.com
Hartwick College	www.hartwick.edu
Harvestworks	www.harvestworks.org
Hastings-on-Hudson Chamber of Commerce	www.hastingsgov.org
Haverstraw, Town of	www.townofhaverstraw.us
Hawk Creek Wildlife Center, Inc	www.hawkcreek.org
Hawkins Delafield & Wood LLP	www.hawkins.com
HBA of CNY Local Build PAC	www.hbaofcny.com

Indexes &
Demographic
Maps

949

Indexes & Demographic Maps

Indexes & Demographic Maps

New York Civil Liberties Union . . . . www.nyclu.org
New York Civil Rights Coalition . . . . www.nycivilrights.org
New York College of Health Professions . . . . www.nycollege.edu
New York College of Podiatric Medicine . . . . www.nycpm.edu
New York Committee for Occupational Safety & Health . . . . www.nycosh.org
New York Community Bank . . . . www.mynycb.com
New York Community Trust (The) . . . . www.nycommunitytrust.org
New York Convention Center Operating Corp . . . . www.javitscenter.com
New York Counties Registered Nurses Association www.nysna.org/districts/13.htm
New York County (NYC Borough of Manhattan) . . . . www.manhattanbp.org
New York Daily News . . . . www.nydailynews.com
New York Farm Bureau . . . . www.nyfb.org
New York Field Corn Growers Association . . . . www.nycorn.org
New York Forest Owners Association Inc . . . . www.nyfoa.org
New York Foundation for the Arts . . . . www.nyfa.org
New York Giants . . . . www.giants.com
New York Hall of Science . . . . www.nyscience.org
New York Health Plan Association . . . . www.nyhpa.org
New York Holstein Association . . . . www.nyholsteins.com
New York Immigration Coalition (The) . . . . www.thenyic.org
New York Independent System Operator - Not For Profit . . . . www.nyiso.com
New York Institute of Technology . . . . www.nyit.edu
New York Insurance Association Inc . . . . www.nyia.org
New York Islanders . . . . www.newyorkislanders.com
New York Jets . . . . www.newyorkjets.com
New York Landmarks Conservancy . . . . www.nylandmarks.org
New York Law Journal . . . . www.law.com
New York Law School . . . . www.nyls.edu
New York Lawyers for the Public Interest . . . . www.nylpi.org
New York Library Association (The) . . . . www.nyla.org
New York Long-Term Care Brokers Ltd . . . . www.nyltcb.com
New York Magazine (New York Metro LLC) . . . . www.newyorkmetro.com
New York Marine Trades Association . . . . www.nymta.com
New York Medical College . . . . www.nymc.edu
New York Mercantile Exchange Inc . . . . www.nymex.com
New York Metropolitan Transportation Council . . . . www.nymtc.org
New York Mets . . . . www.mets.com
New York Municipal Insurance Reciprocal (NYMIR) . . . . www.nymir.org
New York Network . . . . www.nyn.suny.edu
New York Newspaper Publishers Association . . . . www.nynpa.com
New York Observer (The) . . . . www.nyobserver.com
New York Post . . . . www.nypost.com
New York Power Authority . . . . www.nypa.gov
New York Presbyterian Hospital . . . . www.med.cornell.edu; www.nyp.org
New York Press Photographers Association . . . . www.nyppa.org
New York Public Interest Research Group . . . . www.nypirg.org
New York Public Interest Research Group Straphangers Campaign . . . . www.straphangers.org; www.nypirg.org
New York Public Welfare Association . . . . www.nypwa.com
New York Racing Association . . . . www.nyra.com
New York Retailers for Effective Government . . . . www.retailcouncilnys.com
New York School of Interior Design . . . . www.nysid.edu
New York Schools Insurance Reciprocal (NYSIR) . . . . www.nysir.org
New York Seed Improvement Project, Cornell University, Plant Breeding Depar . . . . SeedPotato.NewYork.cornell.edu
New York Shipping Association, Inc . . . . www.nysanet.org
New York Society for the Deaf . . . . www.nysd.org
New York State Air Force Association . . . . www.nysafa.org

New York State Assessors' Association. . . . . www.nyassessor.com
New York State Assn of Fire Districts . . . . www.firedistnys.com
New York State Association of Agricultural Fairs Inc. . . . . www.nyfairs.org
New York State Association of Family Services Agencies, Inc. . . . . www.nysafsa.org
New York State Association of Independent Schools . . . . www.nysais.org
New York State Association of Insurance & Financial Advisors Inc . . . . www.nysaifa.com
New York State Athletic Commission . . . . www.dos.state.ny.us/athletic.html
New York State Auto Dealers Association. . . . . www.nysada.com
New York State Board of Law Examiners . . . . www.nybarexam.org
New York State Bridge Authority . . . . www.nysba.net
New York State Canal Corporation . . . . www.canals.state.ny.us
New York State Catholic Conference. . . . . www.nyscatholic.org
New York State Citizens' Coalition for Children Inc. . . . . www.nysccc.org
New York State Commission of Correction. . . . . www.scoc.state.ny.us
New York State Commission on Quality of Care for the Mentally Disabled . . . . www.cqc.state.ny.us
New York State Community Action Association. . . . . www.nyscaaonline.org
New York State Congress of Parents & Teachers Inc . . . . www.nypta.com
New York State Conservation Council. . . . . www.nyscc.com
New York State Council of Churches. . . . . www.nyscommunityofchurches.org
New York State Council of School Superintendents . . . . www.nyscoss.org
New York State Credit Union League Inc . . . . www.nyscul.org
New York State Dairy Foods Inc . . . . www.nysdfi.org
New York State Democratic Committee . . . . www.nydems.org
New York State Directory . . . . www.greyhouse.com
New York State Disaster Preparedness Commission . . . . www.nysemo.state.ny.us
New York State Dormitory Authority . . . . www.dasny.org
New York State Electric & Gas Corporation (NYSEG). . . . . www.nyseg.com
New York State Energy Research & Development Authority . . . . www.nyserda.org
New York State Environmental Facilities Corp . . . . www.nysefc.org
New York State Ethics Commission . . . . www.dos.state.ny.us/ethc/ethics.html
New York State Financial Control Board. . . . . www.fcb.state.ny.us
New York State Government Finance Officers Association Inc . . . . www.nysgfoa.org
New York State Health Facilities Association . . . . www.nyshfa.org
New York State Higher Education Services Corp (NYSHESC) . . . . www.hesc.org
New York State Hospitality & Tourism Association . . . . www.nyshta.org
New York State Housing Finance Agency (HFA) . . . . www.nyhomes.org
New York State Judicial Conduct Commission . . . . www.scjc.state.ny.us
New York State Law Reporting Bureau. . . . . www.courts.state.ny.us/reporter
New York State Law Revision Commission . . . . www.lawrevision.state.ny.us
New York State Liquor Authority . . . . www.abc.state.ny.us
New York State Mortgage Loan Enforcement & Administration Corporation . . . . www.empire.state.ny.us
New York State Motor Truck Association . . . . www.nytrucks.org
New York State Nurses Association. . . . . www.nysna.org
New York State Olympic Regional Development Authority . . . . www.orda.org
New York State Ophthalmological Society . . . . www.nysos.com
New York State Osteopathic Medical Society . . . . www.nysoms.org
New York State Petroleum Council . . . . www.api.org
New York State Podiatric Medical Association . . . . www.nyspma.org
New York State Public Employees Federation (PEF) . . . . www.nyspef.org
New York State Rehabilitation Association . . . . www.nyrehab.org
New York State Republican Party . . . . www.nygop.org
New York State Restaurant Association. . . . . www.nysra.org
New York State Rural Housing Coalition Inc . . . . www.ruralhousing.org
New York State School Boards Association . . . . www.nyssba.org
New York State School Music Association (NYSSMA) . . . . www.nyssma.org
New York State Snowmobile Association . . . . www.nyssnowassoc.org

Indexes &
Demographic
Maps

NYC Board of Education Employees, Local 372/AFSCME, AFL-CIO www.local372.com
NYC Campaign Finance Board . . . . www.nyccfb.info
NYC Coalition Against Hunger . . . . www.nyccah.org
NYC District Council of Carpenters' PAC . . . . www.nycdistrictcouncil.com
NYC Neighborhood Open Space Coalition . . . . www.treebranch.com; www.walkny.org
NYMAGIC Inc . . . . www.nymagic.com
NYP Holdings Inc . . . . www.nypost.com
NYS Academy of Family Physicians . . . . www.nysafp.org
NYS AFL-CIO COPE . . . . www.nysaflcio.org
NYS Agricultural Society . . . . www.nysagsociety.org
NYS Alliance for Arts Education . . . . www.nysaae.org
NYS Arborists . . . . www.newyorkstatearborists.com
NYS Architects PAC . . . . www.aianys.org
NYS Association For Food Protection . . . . www.foodscience.cornell.edu/nysfsanit/index.html
NYS Association for Health, Physical Education, Recreation & Dance . . . . www.nysahperd.org
NYS Association for the Education of Young Children . . . . www.nysaeyc.org
NYS Association of Area Agencies on Aging . . . . www.nysaaaa.org
NYS Association of Chiefs of Police Inc . . . . www.nychiefs.org
NYS Association of Community & Residential Agencies . . . . www.nysacra.org
NYS Association of Counties . . . . www.nysac.org
NYS Association of County Health Officials . . . . www.nysacho.org
NYS Association of Criminal Defense Lawyers . . . . www.nysacdl.org
NYS Association of Electrical Contractors . . . . www.nysaec.org
NYS Association of Fire Chiefs . . . . www.nysfirechiefs.com
NYS Association of Health Care Providers . . . . www.nyshcp.org
NYS Association of Library Boards . . . . www.nysalb.org
NYS Association of Realtors . . . . www.nysar.com
NYS Association of School Business Officials . . . . www.nysasbo.org
NYS Association of Service Stations & Repair Shops . . . . www.nysassrs.com
NYS Association of Solid Waste Management . . . . www.newyorkwaste.org
NYS Bar Assn, Civil Rights Cmte . . . . www.proskauer.com
NYS Bar Assn, Court Structure & Judicial Selection Cmte . . . . www.mgglaw.com
NYS Bar Assn, Diversity & Leadership Development Cmte . . . . www.woh.com
NYS Bar Assn, Environmental Law Section . . . . www.farrellfritz.com
NYS Bar Assn, Federal Constitution & Legislation Cmte . . . . www.mklex.com
NYS Bar Assn, Intellectual Property Law Section . . . . www.hartmanwinnicki.com
NYS Bar Assn, Judicial Campaign Monitoring Cmte . . . . rlodmo.lawoffice.com
NYS Bar Assn, Lawyer Referral Service Cmte . . . . apfwlaw.com
NYS Bar Assn, Legal Aid Cmte/Funding for Civil Legal Svcs Cmte . . . . www.lshv.org
NYS Bar Assn, Media Law Cmte . . . . www.newyorker.com
NYS Bar Assn, President's Cmte on Access to Justice . . . . www.boylanbrown.com
NYS Bar Assn, Public Trust & Confidence in the Legal System . . . . www.debcoise.com
NYS Bar Assn, Review Attorney Fee Regulation Cmte . . . . www.nysba.org
NYS Bar Assn, Review Judicial Nominations Cmte . . . . www.englertcoffeymchugh.com
NYS Bar Assn, Review the Code of Judicial Conduct Cmte . . . . www.bondmarkets.com
NYS Bar Assn, Tax Section . . . . www.sullcrom.com
NYS Bar Assn, Tort System Cmte . . . . www.binghamtonlaw.com
NYS Bar Assn, Torts, Insurance & Compensation Law Section . . . . www.connorscorcoran.com
NYS Bar Assn, Trial Lawyers Section . . . . www.connorslaw.com
NYS Bar Assn, Trusts & Estates Law Section . . . . www.dbh.com
NYS Berry Growers Association . . . . www.nysbga.org
NYS Broadcasters Association . . . . www.nysbroadcastersassn.org
NYS Builders Association Inc . . . . www.nysba.com
NYS Chapter AGC PAC . . . . www.agcnys.org
NYS Cheese Manufacturers Association, Department of Food Science . . . . www.newyorkcheese.org
NYS Child Care Coordinating Council . . . . www.nyscccc.org

Indexes & Demographic Maps

Indexes &
Demographic
Maps

State University College of Technology at Delhi . . . . www.delhi.edu
State University Construction Fund . . . . www.sucf.suny.edu
State University Empire State College . . . . www.esc.edu
State University Health Science Center Upstate Medical University . . . . www.upstate.edu
State University Institute of Technology . . . . www.sunyit.edu
State University of New York at Albany . . . . www.albany.edu
State University of New York at Binghamton . . . . www.binghamton.edu
State University of New York at Buffalo . . . . www.buffalo.edu
State University of New York at Stony Brook . . . . www.sunysb.edu
State University of New York College of Environmental Science & Forestry . . . . www.esf.edu
State University of New York Downstate Medical Center. . . . . www.downstate.edu
State University of New York Maritime College . . . . www.sunymaritime.edu
Staten Island (Richmond County). . . . . www.statenislandusa.com
Staten Island Advance. . . . . www.silive.com
Staten Island Chamber of Commerce . . . . www.sichamber.com
Staten Island Economic Dev Corp . . . . www.siedc.net
Staten Island Zoo . . . . www.statenislandzoo.org
Statewide Black & Puerto Rican/Latino Substance Abuse Task Force . . . . www.nytaskforce.org
Statewide Corporate Strategies Inc. . . . . www.statewidestrat.com
Statewide Emergency Network for Social & Economic Security (SENSES) . . . . www.sensesny.org
Statewide Youth Advocacy, Inc . . . . www.syanys.org
Statistics . . . . www.nass.usda.gov/ny
Statue of Liberty National Monument & Ellis Island . . . . www.nps.gov/stli/
Steuben . . . . www.steubencony.org
Steuben County Conference & Visitors Bureau . . . . www.corningfingerlakes.com
Steuben County Ind Dev Agency . . . . www.steubencountyida.com
Steuben-Allegany BOCES . . . . www.saboces.org
Stuto, Diane D. . . . . www.licony.org
Subcontractors Trade Assn Inc State PAC . . . . www.stanyc.com
Suffern Chamber of Commerce . . . . www.suffernchamberofcommerce.org
Suffolk County . . . . www.co.suffolk.ny.us
Suffolk County Assn of Municipal Employees' PAC Inc . . . . www.scame.org
Suffolk County Chapter Nat'l Womens Political Caucus . . . . www.nwpc.org
Suffolk County Community College . . . . www.sunysuffolk.edu
Suffolk County Correction Officers' Assn PAC . . . . www.sccoa.net
Suffolk County Deputy Sheriffs Benevolent Assn Inc PAC . . . . www.scdsba.com
Suffolk Regional Off-Track Betting Corp . . . . www.suffolkotb
Sullivan BOCES . . . . www.scboces.org
Sullivan County . . . . www.co.sullivan.ny.us
Sullivan County Chamber of Commerce . . . . www.catskills.com
Sullivan County Community College. . . . . www.sullivan.suny.edu
Sullivan County Visitors Association . . . . www.scva.net
Sunbridge College. . . . . www.sunbridge.edu
Sunwize Technologies LLC . . . . www.sunwize.com
SUNY at Albany, Center for Technology in Government . . . . www.ctg.albany.edu
SUNY at Albany, Center for Women in Government & Civil Society . . . . www.cwig.albany.edu
SUNY at Albany, Nelson A Rockefeller College. . . . . www.albany.edu/rockefeller
SUNY at Albany, Professional Development Program, NE States Addiction . . . . www.pdp.albany.edu
SUNY at Albany, School of Public Health, Center for Public Health Preparedness . . . . . . www.ualbanycphp.org
SUNY at Buffalo, Research Institute on Addictions . . . . www.ria.buffalo.edu
SUNY at Cortland, Center for Environmental & Outdoor Education . . . . www.cortland.edu
SUNY at New Paltz, College of Liberal Arts & Sciences . . . . www.newpaltz.edu
SUNY Board of Trustees . . . . www.suny.edu
SUNY Buffalo Human Rights Center . . . . wings.buffalo.edu/law/bhrlc
SUNY Metropolitan Recruitment Center . . . . www.suny.edu
SUNY System Administration & Executive Council . . . . www.suny.edu

Tonawanda (Town Of) Dev Corp . . . . www.tonawanda.com
Tonawanda News . . . . www.tonawanda-news.com
Tonawanda, Town of . . . . www.tonawanda.ny.us
Tonawandas, Chamber of Commerce of the . . . . www.the-tonawandas.com
Touro College . . . . www.touro.edu
Transport Workers Union of America, AFL-CIO . . . . www.twu.com
Transportation Alternatives . . . . www.transalt.org
Transportation Department . . . . www.dot.state.ny.us
Transportation, Department of, NYC . . . . www.nyc.gov/dot
Tranter, G Thomas, Jr . . . . www.corning.com
Trees New York . . . . www.treesny.com
Tri-State Transportation Campaign . . . . www.tstc.org
Tribeca Film Institute . . . . www.tribecafilminstitute.org
Trocaire College . . . . www.trocaire.edu
Trooper Foundation-State of New York Inc . . . . www.nystrooperfoundation.org
Troy, City of . . . . www.troyny.org
True, Walsh & Miller LLP . . . . www.twmlaw.com
Tupper Lake Chamber of Commerce . . . . www.tupperlakeinfo.com
Tyson, Lisa . . . . www.lipc.org
UA Plumbers & Pipefitters LU 773 Voluntary NYS PAC Fund www.lu773.org
UFT COPE Local . . . . www.uft.org
UHAP PAC . . . . www.upstatehealthcare.org
Ulster BOCES . . . . www.ulsterboces.org
Ulster County . . . . www.co.ulster.ny.us
Ulster County Chamber of Commerce . . . . www.ulsterchamber.org
Ulster County Community College . . . . www.sunyulster.edu
Ulster County Dev Corp/Ulster County Ind Dev Agency . . . . www.ulsterny.com
Ulster Savings Bank . . . . www.ulstersavings.com
Unification Theological Seminary . . . . www.uts.edu
Unified Court System . . . . www.courts.state.ny.us
Uniformed Fire Officers Association . . . . www.ufoa.org
Union College . . . . www.union.edu
Union Local Dev Corp (Town of) . . . . www.townofunion.com
Union of Needletrade, Textile & Industrial Employees (UNITE!) . . . . www.uniteunion.org
Union State Bank . . . . www.unionstate.com
Union Theological Seminary . . . . www.uts.columbia.edu
Union, Town of . . . . www.townofunion.com
UNITE HERE and Local Election & Political Education Fund . . . . www.unitehere.org
United Federation of Teachers . . . . www.uft.org
United Food & Commercial Workers Local 1 . . . . www.ufcwone.org
United Hospital Fund of New York . . . . www.uhfnyc.org
United Jewish Appeal-Federation of Jewish Philanthropies . . . . www.ujafedny.org
United Nations Development Corporation . . . . www.undc.org
United Neighborhood Houses - Not For Profit . . . . www.unhny.org
United New York Ambulance Network (UNYAN) . . . . unyan.net
United Restaurant, Hotel & Tavern Association of NY Statewide PAC . . . . . . www.esrta.org
United Spinal Association . . . . www.unitedspinal.org
United Transportation Union . . . . www.utu.org
United University Professions . . . . www.uupinfo.org
United Way of Central New York . . . . www.unitedway-cny.org
United Way of New York City . . . . www.unitedwaynyc.org
Unity Mutual Life Insurance Co . . . . www.unity-life.com
Unity PAC . . . . www.unity-life.com
University at Buffalo . . . . www.government.buffalo.edu
University of Rochester School of Medicine www2.envmed.rochester.edu
Upstate Farms Cooperative Inc . . . . www.upstatefarms.com

Indexes & Demographic Maps

Indexes & Demographic Maps

977

Universal Reference Publications
Statistical & Demographic Reference Books

Profiles of New York, 2005/06 ♦ Profiles of Florida, 2005/06 ♦ Profiles of Texas, 2005/06

Packed with over 50 pieces of data that make up a complete, user-friendly profile of each state, these directories go even further by then pulling selected data and providing it in ranking list form for even easier comparisons between the 100 largest towns and cities! The careful layout gives the user an easy-to-read snapshot of every single place and county in the state, from the biggest metropolis to the smallest unincorporated hamlet. The richness of each place or county profile is astounding in its depth, from history to weather, all packed in a easy-to-navigate, compact format. No need for piles of multiple sources with this volume on your desk. Here is a look at jus a few of the data sets you'll find in each profile: History, Geography, Climate, Population, Vital Statistics, Economy, Income, Taxes, Education, Housing, Health & Environment, Public Safety, Newspapers, Transportation, Presidential Election Results, Information Contacts and Chambers of Commerce. As an added bonus, there is a section on Selected Statistics, where data from the 100 largest towns and cities is arranged into easy-to-use charts. Each of 22 different data points has its own two-page spread with the cities listed in alpha order so researchers can easily compare and rank cities. A remarkable compilation that offers overviews and insights into each corner of the state, *Profiles of New York*, *Profiles of Florida* and *Profiles of Texas* go beyond Census statistics, beyond metro area coverage, beyond the 100 best places to live. Drawn from official census information, other government statistics and original research, you will have at your fingertips data that's available nowhere else in one single source. Data will be published on additional states in 2006 and 2007.

Profiles of New York, 2005/06: 800 pages; Softcover ISBN 1-59237-108-6; $129.00
Profiles of Florida, 2005/06: 800 pages; Softcover ISBN 1-59237-110-8; $129.00
Profies of Texas, 2005/06: 800 pages; Softcover ISBN 1-59237-111-6; $129.00

America's Top-Rated Cities, 2005

America's Top-Rated Cities provides current, comprehensive statistical information and other essential data in one easy-to-use source on the 100 "top" cities that have been cited as the best for business and living in the U.S. This handbook allows readers to see, at a glance, a concise social, business, economic, demographic and environmental profile of each city, including brief evaluative comments. In addition to detailed data on Cost of Living, Finances, Real Estate, Education, Major Employers, Media, Crime and Climate, city reports now include Housing Vacancies, Tax Audits, Bankruptcy, Presidential Election Results and more. This outstanding source of information will be widely used in any reference collection.

> *"The only source of its kind that brings together all of this information into one easy-to-use source. It will be beneficial to many business and public libraries." —ARBA*

2,500 pages, 4 Volume Set; Softcover ISBN 1-59237-076-4, $195.00

America's Top-Rated Smaller Cities, 2004/05

A perfect companion to *America's Top-Rated Cities*, *America's Top-Rated Smaller Cities* provides current, comprehensive business and living profiles of smaller cities (population 25,000-99,999) that have been cited as the best for business and living in the United States. Sixty cities make up this 2004 edition of *America's Top-Rated Smaller Cities*, all are top-ranked by Population Growth, Median Income, Unemployment Rate and Crime Rate. City reports reflect the most current data available on a wide-range of statistics, including Employment & Earnings, Household Income, Unemployment Rate, Population Characteristics, Taxes, Cost of Living, Education, Health Care, Public Safety, Recreation, Media, Air & Water Quality and much more. Plus, each city report contains a Background of the City, and an Overview of the State Finances. *America's Top-Rated Smaller Cities* offers a reliable, one-stop source for statistical data that, before now, could only be found scattered in hundreds of sources. This volume is designed for a wide range of readers: individuals considering relocating a residence or business; professionals considering expanding their business or changing careers; general and market researchers; real estate consultants; human resource personnel; urban planners and investors.

> *"Provides current, comprehensive statistical information in one easy-to-use source…*
> *Recommended for public and academic libraries and specialized collections." —Library Journal*

1,100 pages; Softcover ISBN 1-59237-043-8, $160.00

To preview any of our Directories Risk-Free for 30 days, call (800) 562-2139 or fax to (518) 789-0556

The Comparative Guide to American Suburbs, 2005

The Comparative Guide to American Suburbs is a one-stop source for Statistics on the 2,000+ suburban communities surrounding the 50 largest metropolitan areas – their population characteristics, income levels, economy, school system and important data on how they compare to one another. Organized into 50 Metropolitan Area chapters, each chapter contains an overview of the Metropolitan Area, a detailed Map followed by a comprehensive Statistical Profile of each Suburban Community, including Contact Information, Physical Characteristics, Population Characteristics, Income, Economy, Unemployment Rate, Cost of Living, Education, Chambers of Commerce and more. Next, statistical data is sorted into Ranking Tables that rank the suburbs by twenty different criteria, including Population, Per Capita Income, Unemployment Rate, Crime Rate, Cost of Living and more. *The Comparative Guide to American Suburbs* is the best source for locating data on suburbs. Those looking to relocate, as well as those doing preliminary market research, will find this an invaluable timesaving resource.

"Public and academic libraries will find this compilation useful…The work draws together figures from many sources and will be especially helpful for job relocation decisions." – Booklist

1,700 pages; Softcover ISBN 1-59237-004-7, $130.00

The Asian Databook: Statistics for all US Counties & Cities with Over 10,000 Population

This is the first-ever resource that compiles statistics and rankings on the US Asian population. *The Asian Databook* presents over 20 statistical data points for each city and county, arranged alphabetically by state, then alphabetically by place name. Data reported for each place includes Population, Languages Spoken at Home, Foreign-Born, Educational Attainment, Income Figures, Poverty Status, Homeownership, Home Values & Rent, and more. Next, in the Rankings Section, the top 75 places are listed for each data element. These easy-to-access ranking tables allow the user to quickly determine trends and population characteristics. This kind of comparative data can not be found elsewhere, in print or on the web, in a format that's as easy-to-use or more concise. A useful resource for those searching for demographics data, career search and relocation information and also for market research. With data ranging from Ancestry to Education, *The Asian Databook* presents a useful compilation of information that will be a much-needed resource in the reference collection of any public or academic library along with the marketing collection of any company whose primary focus in on the Asian population.

1,000 pages; Softcover ISBN 1-59237-044-6 $150.00

The Hispanic Databook: Statistics for all US Counties & Cities with Over 10,000 Population

Previously published by Toucan Valley Publications, this second edition has been completely updated with figures from the latest census and has been broadly expanded to include dozens of new data elements and a brand new Rankings section. For ease-of-use, *The Hispanic Databook* presents over 20 statistical data points for each city and county, arranged alphabetically by state, then alphabetically by place name. Data reported for each place includes Population, Languages Spoken at Home, Foreign-Born, Educational Attainment, Income Figures, Poverty Status, Homeownership, Home Values & Rent, and more. Next, in the Rankings Section, the top 75 places are listed for each data element. These easy-to-access ranking tables allow the user to quickly determine trends and population characteristics. This kind of comparative data can not be found elsewhere, in print or on the web, in a format that's as easy-to-use or more concise. A useful resource for those searching for demographics data, career search and relocation information and also for market research.

"This accurate, clearly presented volume of selected Hispanic demographics is recommended for large public libraries and research collections."-Library Journal

1,000 pages; Softcover ISBN 1-59237-008-X, $150.00

Ancestry in America: A Comparative Guide to Over 200 Ethnic Backgrounds

Never before has this kind of information been reported in a single volume. Section One, Statistics by Place, is made up of a list of over 200 ancestry and race categories arranged alphabetically by each of the 5,000 different places with populations over 10,000. The population number of the ancestry group in that city or town is provided along with the percent that group represents of the total population. This informative city-by-city section allows the user to quickly and easily explore the ethnic makeup of all major population bases in the United States. Section Two, Comparative Rankings, contains three tables for each ethnicity and race. These easy-to-navigate tables allow users to see ancestry population patterns and make city-by-city comparisons as well. Plus, as an added bonus with the purchase of *Ancestry in America*, a free companion CD-ROM is available that lists statistics and rankings for all of the 35,000 populated places in the United States. This brand new, information-packed resource will serve a wide-range or research requests for demographics, population characteristics, relocation information and much more. *Ancestry in America: A Comparative Guide to Over 200 Ethnic Backgrounds* will be an important acquisition to all reference collections.

"This compilation will serve a wide range of research requests for population characteristics … it offers much more detail than other sources." –Booklist

1,500 pages; Softcover ISBN 1-59237-029-2, $225.00

To preview any of our Directories Risk-Free for 30 days, call (800) 562-2139 or fax to (518) 789-0556

The Value of a Dollar 1860-2004, Third Edition

A guide to practical economy, *The Value of a Dollar* records the actual prices of thousands of items that consumers purchased from the Civil War to the present, along with facts about investment options and income opportunities. This brand new Third Edition boasts a brand new addition to each five-year chapter, a section on Trends. This informative section charts the change in price over time and provides added detail on the reasons prices changed within the time period, including industry developments, changes in consumer attitudes and important historical facts. Plus, a brand new chapter for 2000-2004 has been added. Each 5-year chapter includes a Historical Snapshot, Consumer Expenditures, Investments, Selected Income, Income/Standard Jobs, Food Basket, Standard Prices and Miscellany. This interesting and useful publication will be widely used in any reference collection.

"Recommended for high school, college and public libraries." –ARBA

600 pages; Hardcover ISBN 1-59237-074-8, $135.00

The Value of a Dollar 1600-1859, The Colonial Era to The Civil War

Following the format of the widely acclaimed, T*he Value of a Dollar, 1860-2004*, *The Value of a Dollar 1600-1859*, *The Colonial Era to The Civil War* records the actual prices of thousands of items that consumers purchased from the Colonial Era to the Civil War. Our editorial department had been flooded with requests from users of our Value of a Dollar for the same type of information, just from an earlier time period. This new volume is just the answer – with pricing data from 1600 to 1859. Arranged into five-year chapters, each 5-year chapter includes a Historical Snapshot, Consumer Expenditures, Investments, Selected Income, Income/Standard Jobs, Food Basket, Standard Prices and Miscellany. There is also a section on Trends. This informative section charts the change in price over time and provides added detail on the reasons prices changed within the time period, including industry developments, changes in consumer attitudes and important historical facts. This fascinating survey will serve a wide range of research needs and will be useful in all high school, public and academic library reference collections.

600 pages; Hardcover ISBN 1-59237-094-2, $135.00

Working Americans 1880-1999
Volume I: The Working Class, Volume II: The Middle Class, Volume III: The Upper Class

Each of the volumes in the *Working Americans 1880-1999* series focuses on a particular class of Americans, The Working Class, The Middle Class and The Upper Class over the last 120 years. Chapters in each volume focus on one decade and profile three to five families. Family Profiles include real data on Income & Job Descriptions, Selected Prices of the Times, Annual Income, Annual Budgets, Family Finances, Life at Work, Life at Home, Life in the Community, Working Conditions, Cost of Living, Amusements and much more. Each chapter also contains an Economic Profile with Average Wages of other Professions, a selection of Typical Pricing, Key Events & Inventions, News Profiles, Articles from Local Media and Illustrations. The *Working Americans* series captures the lifestyles of each of the classes from the last twelve decades, covers a vast array of occupations and ethnic backgrounds and travels the entire nation. These interesting and useful compilations of portraits of the American Working, Middle and Upper Classes during the last 120 years will be an important addition to any high school, public or academic library reference collection.

"These interesting, unique compilations of economic and social facts, figures and graphs will support multiple research needs. They will engage and enlighten patrons in high school, public and academic library collections." –Booklist

Volume I: The Working Class ◆ 558 pages; Hardcover ISBN 1-891482-81-5, $145.00
Volume II: The Middle Class ◆ 591 pages; Hardcover ISBN 1-891482-72-6; $145.00
Volume III: The Upper Class ◆ 567 pages; Hardcover ISBN 1-930956-38-X, $145.00

Working Americans 1880-1999 Volume IV: Their Children

This Fourth Volume in the highly successful *Working Americans 1880-1999* series focuses on American children, decade by decade from 1880 to 1999. This interesting and useful volume introduces the reader to three children in each decade, one from each of the Working, Middle and Upper classes. Like the first three volumes in the series, the individual profiles are created from interviews, diaries, statistical studies, biographies and news reports. Profiles cover a broad range of ethnic backgrounds, geographic area and lifestyles – everything from an orphan in Memphis in 1882, following the Yellow Fever epidemic of 1878 to an eleven-year-old nephew of a beer baron and owner of the New York Yankees in New York City in 1921. Chapters also contain important supplementary materials including News Features as well as information on everything from Schools to Parks, Infectious Diseases to Childhood Fears along with Entertainment, Family Life and much more to provide an informative overview of the lifestyles of children from each decade. This interesting account of what life was like for Children in the Working, Middle and Upper Classes will be a welcome addition to the reference collection of any high school, public or academic library.

600 pages; Hardcover ISBN 1-930956-35-5, $145.00

Working Americans 1880-2003 Volume V: Americans At War

Working Americans 1880-2003 Volume V: Americans At War is divided into 11 chapters, each covering a decade from 1880-2003 and examines the lives of Americans during the time of war, including declared conflicts, one-time military actions, protests, and preparations for war. Each decade includes several personal profiles, whether on the battlefield or on the homefront, that tell the stories of civilians, soldiers, and officers during the decade. The profiles examine: Life at Home; Life at Work; and Life in the Community. Each decade also includes an Economic Profile with statistical comparisons, a Historical Snapshot, News Profiles, local News Articles, and Illustrations that provide a solid historical background to the decade being examined. Profiles range widely not only geographically, but also emotionally, from that of a girl whose leg was torn off in a blast during WWI, to the boredom of being stationed in the Dakotas as the Indian Wars were drawing to a close. As in previous volumes of the *Working Americans* series, information is presented in narrative form, but hard facts and real-life situations back up each story. The basis of the profiles come from diaries, private print books, personal interviews, family histories, estate documents and magazine articles. For easy reference, *Working Americans 1880-2003 Volume V: Americans At War* includes an in-depth Subject Index. The *Working Americans* series has become an important reference for public libraries, academic libraries and high school libraries. This fifth volume will be a welcome addition to all of these types of reference collections.

600 pages; Hardcover ISBN 1-59237-024-1; $145.00
Five Volume Set (Volumes I-V), Hardcover ISBN 1-59237-034-9, $675.00

Working Americans 1880-2005 Volume VI: Women at Work

Unlike any other volume in the *Working Americans* series, this Sixth Volume, is the first to focus on a particular gender of Americans. *Volume VI: Women at Work*, traces what life was like for working women from the 1860's to the present time. Beginning with the life of a maid in 1890 and a store clerk in 1900 and ending with the life and times of the modern working women, this text captures the struggle, strengths and changing perception of the American woman at work. Each chapter focuses on one decade and profiles three to five women with real data on Income & Job Descriptions, Selected Prices of the Times, Annual Income, Annual Budgets, Family Finances, Life at Work, Life at Home, Life in the Community, Working Conditions, Cost of Living, Amusements and much more. For even broader access to the events, economics and attitude towards women throughout the past 130 years, each chapter is supplemented with News Profiles, Articles from Local Media, Illustrations, Economic Profiles, Typical Pricing, Key Events, Inventions and more. This important volume illustrates what life was like for working women over time and allows the reader to develop an understanding of the changing role of women at work. These interesting and useful compilations of portraits of women at work will be an important addition to any high school, public or academic library reference collection.

600 pages; Hardcover ISBN 1-59237-063-2; $145.00
Six Volume Set (Volumes I-VI), Hardcover ISBN 1-59237-063-2, $810.00

The Comparative Guide to American Elementary & Secondary Schools, 2004/05

The only guide of its kind, this award winning compilation offers a snapshot profile of every public school district in the United States serving 1,500 or more students – more than 5,900 districts are covered. Organized alphabetically by district within state, each chapter begins with a Statistical Overview of the state. Each district listing includes contact information (name, address, phone number and web site) plus Grades Served, the Numbers of Students and Teachers and the Number of Regular, Special Education, Alternative and Vocational Schools in the district along with statistics on Student/Classroom Teacher Ratios, Drop Out Rates, Ethnicity, the Numbers of Librarians and Guidance Counselors and District Expenditures per student. As an added bonus, *The Comparative Guide to American Elementary and Secondary Schools* provides important ranking tables, both by state and nationally, for each data element. For easy navigation through this wealth of information, this handbook contains a useful City Index that lists all districts that operate schools within a city. These important comparative statistics are necessary for anyone considering relocation or doing comparative research on their own district and would be a perfect acquisition for any public library or school district library.

"This straightforward guide is an easy way to find general information. Valuable for academic and large public library collections." –ARBA

2,400 pages; Softcover ISBN 1-59237-047-0, $125.00

The American Tally: Statistics & Comparative Rankings for U.S. Cities with Populations over 10,000

This important statistical handbook compiles, all in one place, comparative statistics on all U.S. cities and towns with a 10,000+ population. *The American Tally* provides statistical details on over 4,000 cities and towns and profiles how they compare with one another in Population Characteristics, Education, Language & Immigration, Income & Employment and Housing. Each section begins with an alphabetical listing of cities by state, allowing for quick access to both the statistics and relative rankings of any city. Next, the highest and lowest cities are listed in each statistic. These important, informative lists provide quick reference to which cities are at both extremes of the spectrum for each statistic. Unlike any other reference, *The American Tally* provides quick, easy access to comparative statistics – a must-have for any reference collection.

"A solid library reference." –Bookwatch

500 pages; Softcover ISBN 1-930956-29-0, $125.00

To preview any of our Directories Risk-Free for 30 days, call (800) 562-2139 or fax to (518) 789-0556

Profiles of America: Facts, Figures & Statistics for Every Populated Place in the United States

Profiles of America is the only source that pulls together, in one place, statistical, historical and descriptive information about every place in the United States in an easy-to-use format. This award winning reference set, now in its second edition, compiles statistics and data from over 20 different sources – the latest census information has been included along with more than nine brand new statistical topics. This Four-Volume Set details over 40,000 places, from the biggest metropolis to the smallest unincorporated hamlet, and provides statistical details and information on over 50 different topics including Geography, Climate, Population, Vital Statistics, Economy, Income, Taxes, Education, Housing, Health & Environment, Public Safety, Newspapers, Transportation, Presidential Election Results and Information Contacts or Chambers of Commerce. Profiles are arranged, for ease-of-use, by state and then by county. Each county begins with a County-Wide Overview and is followed by information for each Community in that particular county. The Community Profiles within the county are arranged alphabetically. *Profiles of America* is a virtual snapshot of America at your fingertips and a unique compilation of information that will be widely used in any reference collection.

A Library Journal Best Reference Book "An outstanding compilation." –Library Journal

10,000 pages; Four Volume Set; Softcover ISBN 1-891482-80-7, $595.00

The Environmental Resource Handbook, 2005/06

The Environmental Resource Handbook is the most up-to-date and comprehensive source for Environmental Resources and Statistics. Section I: Resources provides detailed contact information for thousands of information sources, including Associations & Organizations, Awards & Honors, Conferences, Foundations & Grants, Environmental Health, Government Agencies, National Parks & Wildlife Refuges, Publications, Research Centers, Educational Programs, Green Product Catalogs, Consultants and much more. Section II: Statistics, provides statistics and rankings on hundreds of important topics, including Children's Environmental Index, Municipal Finances, Toxic Chemicals, Recycling, Climate, Air & Water Quality and more. This kind of up-to-date environmental data, all in one place, is not available anywhere else on the market place today. This vast compilation of resources and statistics is a must-have for all public and academic libraries as well as any organization with a primary focus on the environment.

"…the intrinsic value of the information make it worth consideration by libraries with environmental collections and environmentally concerned users." –Booklist

1,000 pages; Softcover ISBN 1-59237-090-X, $155.00 ◆ Online Database $300.00

Weather America, A Thirty-Year Summary of Statistical Weather Data and Rankings

This valuable resource provides extensive climatological data for over 4,000 National and Cooperative Weather Stations throughout the United States. *Weather America* begins with a new Major Storms section that details major storm events of the nation and a National Rankings section that details rankings for several data elements, such as Maximum Temperature and Precipitation. The main body of *Weather America* is organized into 50 state sections. Each section provides a Data Table on each Weather Station, organized alphabetically, that provides statistics on Maximum and Minimum Temperatures, Precipitation, Snowfall, Extreme Temperatures, Foggy Days, Humidity and more. State sections contain two brand new features in this edition – a City Index and a narrative Description of the climatic conditions of the state. Each section also includes a revised Map of the State that includes not only weather stations, but cities and towns.

"Best Reference Book of the Year." –Library Journal

2,013 pages; Softcover ISBN 1-891482-29-7, $175.00

To preview any of our Directories Risk-Free for 30 days, call (800) 562-2139 or fax to (518) 789-0556

Older Americans Information Directory, 2004/05

Completely updated for 2004/05, this Fifth Edition has been completely revised and now contains 1,000 new listings, over 8,000 updates to existing listings and over 3,000 brand new e-mail addresses and web sites. You'll find important resources for Older Americans including National, Regional, State & Local Organizations, Government Agencies, Research Centers, Libraries & Information Centers, Legal Resources, Discount Travel Information, Continuing Education Programs, Disability Aids & Assistive Devices, Health, Print Media and Electronic Media. Three indexes: Entry Index, Subject Index and Geographic Index make it easy to find just the right source of information. This comprehensive guide to resources for Older Americans will be a welcome addition to any reference collection.

"Highly recommended for academic, public, health science and consumer libraries..." –Choi

1,200 pages; Softcover ISBN 1-59237-037-3, $165.00 ◆ Online Database $215.00 ◆ Online Database & Directory Combo $300.00

The Complete Directory for Pediatric Disorders, 2004/05

This important directory provides parents and caregivers with information about Pediatric Conditions, Disorders, Diseases and Disabilities, including Blood Disorders, Bone & Spinal Disorders, Brain Defects & Abnormalities, Chromosomal Disorders, Congenital Heart Defects, Movement Disorders, Neuromuscular Disorders and Pediatric Tumors & Cancers. This carefully written directory offers: understandable Descriptions of 15 major bodily systems; Descriptions of more than 200 Disorders and a Resources Section, detailing National Agencies & Associations, State Associations, Online Services, Libraries & Resource Centers, Research Centers, Support Groups & Hotlines, Camps, Books and Periodicals. This resource will provide immediate access to information crucial to families and caregivers when coping with children's illnesses.

"Recommended for public and consumer health libraries." –Library Journal

1,200 pages; Softcover ISBN 1-59237-045-4, $165.00 ◆ Online Database $215.00 ◆ Online Database & Directory Combo $300.00

The Complete Directory for People with Rare Disorders

This outstanding reference is produced in conjunction with the National Organization for Rare Disorders to provide comprehensive and needed access to important information on over 1,000 rare disorders, including Cancers and Muscular, Genetic and Blood Disorders. An informative Disorder Description is provided for each of the 1,100 disorders (rare Cancers and Muscular, Genetic and Blood Disorders) followed by information on National and State Organizations dealing with a particular disorder, Umbrella Organizations that cover a wide range of disorders, the Publications that can be useful when researching a disorder and the Government Agencies to contact. Detailed and up-to-date listings contain mailing address, phone and fax numbers, web sites and e-mail addresses along with a description. For quick, easy access to information, this directory contains two indexes: Entry Name Index and Acronym/Keyword Index along with an informative Guide for Rare Disorder Advocates. The Complete Directory for People with Rare Disorders will be an invaluable tool for the thousands of families that have been struck with a rare or "orphan" disease, who feel that they have no place to turn and will be a much-used addition to the reference collection of any public or academic library.

"Quick access to information... public libraries and hospital patient libraries will find this a useful resource in directing users to support groups or agencies dealing with a rare disorder." –Booklist

726 pages; Softcover ISBN 1-891482-18-1, $165.00

The Directory of Drug & Alcohol Residential Rehabilitation Facilities

This brand new directory is the first-ever resource to bring together, all in one place, data on the thousands of drug and alcohol residential rehabilitation facilities in the United States. *The Directory of Drug & Alcohol Residential Rehabilitation Facilities* covers over 1,000 facilities, with detailed contact information for each one, including mailing address, phone and fax numbers, email addresses and web sites, mission statement, type of treatment programs, cost, average length of stay, numbers of residents and counselors, accreditation, insurance plans accepted, type of environment, religious affiliation, education components and much more. It also contains a helpful chapter on General Resources that provides contact information for Associations, Print & Electronic Media, Support Groups and Conferences. Multiple indexes allow the user to pinpoint the facilities that meet very specific criteria. This time-saving tool is what so many counselors, parents and medical professionals have been asking for. *The Directory of Drug & Alcohol Residential Rehabilitation Facilities* will be a helpful tool in locating the right source for treatment for a wide range of individuals. This comprehensive directory will be an important acquisition for all reference collections: public and academic libraries, case managers, social workers, state agencies and many more.

"This is an excellent, much needed directory that fills an important gap..." –Booklist

300 pages; Softcover ISBN 1-59237-031-4, $135.00

To preview any of our Directories Risk-Free for 30 days, call (800) 562-2139 or fax to (518) 789-0556

Sedgwick Press
Hospital & Health Plan Directories

The Comparative Guide to American Hospitals

This brand new title is the first ever resource to compare all of the nation's hospitals by 17 measures of quality in the treatment of heart attack, heart failure and pneumonia. This data is based on the recently announced Hospital Compare, produced by Medicare, and is available in print and in a unique and user-friendly format from Grey House Publishing, along with extra contact information from Grey House's *Directory of Hospital Personnel*. *The Comparative Guide to American Hospitals* provides a snapshot profile of each of the nations 6,000 hospitals. These informative profiles illustrate how the hospital rates in 17 important areas: Heart Attack Care (% who receive Aspirin at Arrival, Aspirin at Discharge, ACE Inhibitor for LVSD, Beta Blocker at Arrival, Beta Blocker at Discharge, Thrombolytic Agent Received, PTCA Received and Adult Smoking Cessation Advice); Heart Failure (% who receive LVF Assessment, ACE Inhibitor for LVSD, Discharge Instructions, Adult Smoking Cessation Advice); and Pneumonia (% who receive Initial Antibiotic Timing, Pneumococcal Vaccination, Oxygenation Assessment, Blood Culture Performed and Adult Smoking Cessation Advice). Each profile includes the raw percentage for that hospital, the state average, the US average and data on the top hospital. For easy access to contact information, each profile includes the hospitals address, phone and fax numbers, email and web addresses, type and accreditation along with 5 top key administrations. These profiles will allow the user to quickly identify the quality of the hospital and have the necessary information at their fingertips to make contact with that hospital. Most importantly, *The Comparative Guide to American Hospitals* provides an easy-to-use Ranking Table for each of the data elements to allow the user to quickly locate the hospitals with the best level of service. This brand new title will be a must for the reference collection at all public, medical and academic libraries.

2,500 pages; Softcover ISBN 1-59237-109-4 $175.00

The Directory of Hospital Personnel, 2005

The Directory of Hospital Personnel is the best resource you can have at your fingertips when researching or marketing a product or service to the hospital market. A "Who's Who" of the hospital universe, this directory puts you in touch with over 150,000 key decision-makers. With 100% verification of data you can rest assured that you will reach the right person with just one call. Every hospital in the U.S. is profiled, listed alphabetically by city within state. Plus, three easy-to-use, cross-referenced indexes put the facts at your fingertips faster and more easily than any other directory: Hospital Name Index, Bed Size Index and Personnel Index. *The Directory of Hospital Personnel* is the only complete source for key hospital decision-makers by name. Whether you want to define or restructure sales territories... locate hospitals with the purchasing power to accept your proposals... keep track of important contacts or colleagues... or find information on which insurance plans are accepted, *The Directory of Hospital Personnel* gives you the information you need – easily, efficiently, effectively and accurately.

"Recommended for college, university and medical libraries." –ARBA

2,500 pages; Softcover ISBN 1-59237-065-9 $275.00 ◆ Online Database $545.00 ◆ Online Database & Directory Combo, $650.00

The Directory of Health Care Group Purchasing Organizations

This comprehensive directory provides the important data you need to get in touch with over 800 Group Purchasing Organizations. By providing in-depth information on this growing market and its members, *The Directory of Health Care Group Purchasing Organizations* fills a major need for the most accurate and comprehensive information on over 800 GPOs – Mailing Address, Phone & Fax Numbers, E-mail Addresses, Key Contacts, Purchasing Agents, Group Descriptions, Membership Categorization, Standard Vendor Proposal Requirements, Membership Fees & Terms, Expanded Services, Total Member Beds & Outpatient Visits represented and more. Five Indexes provide a number of ways to locate the right GPO: Alphabetical Index, Expanded Services Index, Organization Type Index, Geographic Index and Member Institution Index. With its comprehensive and detailed information on each purchasing organization, *The Directory of Health Care Group Purchasing Organizations* is the go-to source for anyone looking to target this market.

"The information is clearly arranged and easy to access...recommended for those needing this very specialized information." –ARBA

1,000 pages; Softcover ISBN 1-59237-036-5, $325.00 ◆ Online Database, $650.00 ◆ Online Database & Directory Combo, $750.00

To preview any of our Directories Risk-Free for 30 days, call (800) 562-2139 or fax to (518) 789-0556

The HMO/PPO Directory, 2005

The HMO/PPO Directory is a comprehensive source that provides detailed information about Health Maintenance Organizations and Preferred Provider Organizations nationwide. This comprehensive directory details more information about more managed health care organizations than ever before. Over 1,100 HMOs, PPOs and affiliated companies are listed, arranged alphabetically by state. Detailed listings include Key Contact Information, Prescription Drug Benefits, Enrollment, Geographical Areas served, Affiliated Physicians & Hospitals, Federal Qualifications, Status, Year Founded, Managed Care Partners, Employer References, Fees & Payment Information and more. Plus, five years of historical information is included related to Revenues, Net Income, Medical Loss Ratios, Membership Enrollment and Number of Patient Complaints. Five easy-to-use, cross-referenced indexes will put this vast array of information at your fingertips immediately: HMO Index, PPO Index, Other Providers Index, Personnel Index and Enrollment Index. *The HMO/PPO Directory* provides the most comprehensive information on the most companies available on the market place today.

> *"Helpful to individuals requesting certain HMO/PPO issues such as co-payment costs, subscription costs and patient complaints. Individuals concerned (or those with questions) about their insurance may find this text to be of use to them." –ARBA*

600 pages; Softcover ISBN 1-59237-057-8, $275.00 ◆ Online Database, $495.00 ◆ Online Database & Directory Combo, $600.00

The Directory of Independent Ambulatory Care Centers

This first edition of *The Directory of Independent Ambulatory Care Centers* provides access to detailed information that, before now, could only be found scattered in hundreds of different sources. This comprehensive and up-to-date directory pulls together a vast array of contact information for over 7,200 Ambulatory Surgery Centers, Ambulatory General and Urgent Care Clinics, and Diagnostic Imaging Centers that are not affiliated with a hospital or major medical center. Detailed listings include Mailing Address, Phone & Fax Numbers, E-mail and Web Site addresses, Contact Name and Phone Numbers of the Medical Director and other Key Executives and Purchasing Agents, Specialties & Services Offered, Year Founded, Numbers of Employees and Surgeons, Number of Operating Rooms, Number of Cases seen per year, Overnight Options, Contracted Services and much more. Listings are arranged by State, by Center Category and then alphabetically by Organization Name. Two indexes provide quick and easy access to this wealth of information: Entry Name Index and Specialty/Service Index. *The Directory of Independent Ambulatory Care Centers* is a must-have resource for anyone marketing a product or service to this important industry and will be an invaluable tool for those searching for a local care center that will meet their specific needs.

> *"Among the numerous hospital directories, no other provides information on independent ambulatory centers. A handy, well-organized resource that would be useful in medical center libraries and public libraries." –Choice*

986 pages; Softcover ISBN 1-930956-90-8, $185.00 ◆ Online Database, $365.00 ◆ Online Database & Directory Combo, $450.00

Sedgwick Press
Education Directories

Educators Resource Directory, 2005/06

Educators Resource Directory is a comprehensive resource that provides the educational professional with thousands of resources and statistical data for professional development. This directory saves hours of research time by providing immediate access to Associations & Organizations, Conferences & Trade Shows, Educational Research Centers, Employment Opportunities & Teaching Abroad, School Library Services, Scholarships, Financial Resources, Professional Consultants, Computer Software & Testing Resources and much more. Plus, this comprehensive directory also includes a section on Statistics and Rankings with over 100 tables, including statistics on Average Teacher Salaries, SAT/ACT scores, Revenues & Expenditures and more. These important statistics will allow the user to see how their school rates among others, make relocation decisions and so much more. For quick access to information, this directory contains four indexes: Entry & Publisher Index, Geographic Index, a Subject & Grade Index and Web Sites Index. *Educators Resource Directory* will be a well-used addition to the reference collection of any school district, education department or public library.

> *"Recommended for all collections that serve elementary and secondary school professionals." –Choice*

1,000 pages; Softcover ISBN 1-59237-080-2, $145.00 ◆ Online Database $195.00 ◆ Online Database & Directory Combo $280.00

To preview any of our Directories Risk-Free for 30 days, call (800) 562-2139 or fax to (518) 789-0556

Grey House Publishing
Business Directories

The Directory of Business Information Resources, 2006

With 100% verification, over 1,000 new listings and more than 12,000 updates, this 2006 edition of *The Directory of Business Information Resources* is the most up-to-date source for contacts in over 98 business areas – from advertising and agriculture to utilities and wholesalers. This carefully researched volume details: the Associations representing each industry; the Newsletters that keep members current; the Magazines and Journals - with their "Special Issues" - that are important to the trade, the Conventions that are "must attends," Databases, Directories and Industry Web Sites that provide access to must-have marketing resources. Includes contact names, phone & fax numbers, web sites and e-mail addresses. This one-volume resource is a gold mine of information and would be a welcome addition to any reference collection.

"This is a most useful and easy-to-use addition to any researcher's library." –The Information Professionals Institute

2,500 pages; Softcover ISBN 1-59237-078-0, $195.00 ◆ Online Database $495.00

Nations of the World, 2005 A Political, Economic and Business Handbook

This completely revised edition covers all the nations of the world in an easy-to-use, single volume. Each nation is profiled in a single chapter that includes Key Facts, Political & Economic Issues, a Country Profile and Business Information. In this fast-changing world, it is extremely important to make sure that the most up-to-date information is included in your reference collection. This 2005 edition is just the answer. Each of the 200+ country chapters have been carefully reviewed by a political expert to make sure that the text reflects the most current information on Politics, Travel Advisories, Economics and more. You'll find such vital information as a Country Map, Population Characteristics, Inflation, Agricultural Production, Foreign Debt, Political History, Foreign Policy, Regional Insecurity, Economics, Trade & Tourism, Historical Profile, Political Systems, Ethnicity, Languages, Media, Climate, Hotels, Chambers of Commerce, Banking, Travel Information and more. Five Regional Chapters follow the main text and include a Regional Map, an Introductory Article, Key Indicators and Currencies for the Region. New for 2004, an all-inclusive CD-ROM is available as a companion to the printed text. Noted for its sophisticated, up-to-date and reliable compilation of political, economic and business information, this brand new edition will be an important acquisition to any public, academic or special library reference collection.

"A useful addition to both general reference collections and business collections." –RUSQ

1,700 pages; Print Version Only Softcover ISBN 1-59237-051-9, $145.00 ◆ Print Version and CD-ROM $180.00

The Grey House Performing Arts Directory, 2005

The Grey House Performing Arts Directory is the most comprehensive resource covering the Performing Arts. This important directory provides current information on over 8,500 Dance Companies, Instrumental Music Programs, Opera Companies, Choral Groups, Theater Companies, Performing Arts Series and Performing Arts Facilities. Plus, this edition now contains a brand new section on Artist Management Groups. In addition to mailing address, phone & fax numbers, e-mail addresses and web sites, dozens of other fields of available information include mission statement, key contacts, facilities, seating capacity, season, attendance and more. This directory also provides an important Information Resources section that covers hundreds of Performing Arts Associations, Magazines, Newsletters, Trade Shows, Directories, Databases and Industry Web Sites. Five indexes provide immediate access to this wealth of information: Entry Name, Executive Name, Performance Facilities, Geographic and Information Resources. *The Grey House Performing Arts Directory* pulls together thousands of Performing Arts Organizations, Facilities and Information Resources into an easy-to-use source – this kind of comprehensiveness and extensive detail is not available in any resource on the market place today.

"Immensely useful and user-friendly ... recommended for public, academic and certain special library reference collections." –Booklist

1,500 pages; Softcover ISBN 1-59237-023-3, $185.00 ◆ Online Database $335.00

International Business and Trade Directories

Completely updated, the Third Edition of *International Business and Trade Directories* now contains more than 10,000 entries, over 2,000 more than the last edition, making this directory the most comprehensive resource of the worlds business and trade directories. Entries include content descriptions, price, publisher's name and address, web site and e-mail addresses, phone and fax numbers and editorial staff. Organized by industry group, and then by region, this resource puts over 10,000 industry-specific business and trade directories at the reader's fingertips. Three indexes are included for quick access to information: Geographic Index, Publisher Index and Title Index. Public, college and corporate libraries, as well as individuals and corporations seeking critical market information will want to add this directory to their marketing collection.

"Reasonably priced for a work of this type, this directory should appeal to larger academic, public and corporate libraries with an international focus." –Library Journal

1,800 pages; Softcover ISBN 1-930956-63-0, $225.00 ◆ Online Database (includes a free copy of the directory) $450.00

To preview any of our Directories Risk-Free for 30 days, call (800) 562-2139 or fax to (518) 789-0556

The Grey House Safety & Security Directory, 2005

The Grey House Safety & Security Directory is the most comprehensive reference tool and buyer's guide for the safety and security industry. Arranged by safety topic, each chapter begins with OSHA regulations for the topic, followed by Training Articles written by top professionals in the field and Self-Inspection Checklists. Next, each topic contains Buyer's Guide sections that feature related products and services. Topics include Administration, Insurance, Loss Control & Consulting, Protective Equipment & Apparel, Noise & Vibration, Facilities Monitoring & Maintenance, Employee Health Maintenance & Ergonomics, Retail Food Services, Machine Guards, Process Guidelines & Tool Handling, Ordinary Materials Handling, Hazardous Materials Handling, Workplace Preparation & Maintenance, Electrical Lighting & Safety, Fire & Rescue and Security. The Buyer's Guide sections are carefully indexed within each topic area to ensure that you can find the supplies needed to meet OSHA's regulations. Six important indexes make finding information and product manufacturers quick and easy: Geographical Index of Manufacturers and Distributors, Company Profile Index, Brand Name Index, Product Index, Index of Web Sites and Index of Advertisers. This comprehensive, up-to-date reference will provide every tool necessary to make sure a business is in compliance with OSHA regulations and locate the products and services needed to meet those regulations.

"Presents industrial safety information for engineers, plant managers, risk managers, and construction site supervisors…" –Choice

1,500 pages, 2 Volume Set; Softcover ISBN 1-59237-067-5, $225.00

The Grey House Homeland Security Directory, 2005

This updated edition features the latest contact information for government and private organizations involved with Homeland Security along with the latest product information and provides detailed profiles of nearly 1,000 Federal & State Organizations & Agencies and over 3,000 Officials and Key Executives involved with Homeland Security. These listings are incredibly detailed and include Mailing Address, Phone & Fax Numbers, Email Addresses & Web Sites, a complete Description of the Agency and a complete list of the Officials and Key Executives associated with the Agency. Next, *The Grey House Homeland Security Directory* provides the go-to source for Homeland Security Products & Services. This section features over 2,000 Companies that provide Consulting, Products or Services. With this Buyer's Guide at their fingertips, users can locate suppliers of everything from Training Materials to Access Controls, from Perimeter Security to BioTerrorism Countermeasures and everything in between – complete with contact information and product descriptions. A handy Product Locator Index is provided to quickly and easily locate suppliers of a particular product. Lastly, an Information Resources Section provides immediate access to contact information for hundreds of Associations, Newsletters, Magazines, Trade Shows, Databases and Directories that focus on Homeland Security. This comprehensive, information-packed resource will be a welcome tool for any company or agency that is in need of Homeland Security information and will be a necessary acquisition for the reference collection of all public libraries and large school districts.

"Compiles this information in one place and is discerning in content. A useful purchase for public and academic libraries." –Booklist

800 pages; Softcover ISBN 1-59237-057-8, $195.00 ◆ Online Database (includes a free copy of the directory) $385.00

The Grey House Transportation Security Directory & Handbook, 2005

This brand new title is the only reference of its kind that brings together current data on Transportation Security. With information on everything from Regulatory Authorities to Security Equipment, this top-flight database brings together the relevant information necessary for creating and maintaining a security plan for a wide range of transportation facilities. With this current, comprehensive directory at the ready you'll have immediate access to: Regulatory Authorities & Legislation; Information Resources; Sample Security Plans & Checklists; Contact Data for Major Airports, Seaports, Railroads, Trucking Companies and Oil Pipelines; Security Service Providers; Recommended Equipment & Product Information and more. Using the *Grey House Transportation Security Directory & Handbook*, managers will be able to quickly and easily assess their current security plans; develop contacts to create and maintain new security procedures; and source the products and services necessary to adequately maintain a secure environment. This valuable resource is a must for all Security Managers at Airports, Seaports, Railroads, Trucking Companies and Oil Pipelines.

800 pages; Softcover ISBN 1-59237-075-6, $195

To preview any of our Directories Risk-Free for 30 days, call (800) 562-2139 or fax to (518) 789-0556

The Directory of Venture Capital & Private Equity Firms, 2005

This edition has been extensively updated and broadly expanded to offer direct access to over 2,800 Domestic and International Venture Capital Firms, including address, phone & fax numbers, e-mail addresses and web sites for both primary and branch locations. Entries include details on the firm's Mission Statement, Industry Group Preferences, Geographic Preferences, Average and Minimum Investments and Investment Criteria. You'll also find details that are available nowhere else, including the Firm's Portfolio Companies and extensive information on each of the firm's Managing Partners, such as Education, Professional Background and Directorships held, along with the Partner's E-mail Address. *The Directory of Venture Capital & Private Equity Firms* offers five important indexes: Geographic Index, Executive Name Index, Portfolio Company Index, Industry Preference Index and College & University Index. With its comprehensive coverage and detailed, extensive information on each company, *The Directory of Venture Capital & Private Equity Firms* is an important addition to any finance collection.

"The sheer number of listings, the descriptive information provided and the outstanding indexing make this directory a better value than its principal competitor, Pratt's Guide to Venture Capital Sources. Recommended for business collections in large public, academic and business libraries." –Choice

1,300 pages; Softcover ISBN 1-59237-062-4, $450.00 ◆ Online Database (includes a free copy of the directory) $889.00

The Directory of Mail Order Catalogs, 2005

Published since 1981, this 2005 edition features 100% verification of data and is the premier source of information on the mail order catalog industry. Details over 12,000 consumer catalog companies with 44 different product chapters from Animals to Toys & Games. Contains detailed contact information including e-mail addresses and web sites along with important business details such as employee size, years in business, sales volume, catalog size, number of catalogs mailed and more. Four indexes provide quick access to information: Catalog & Company Name Index, Geographic Index, Product Index and Web Sites Index.

"This is a godsend for those looking for information." –Reference Book Review

1,700 pages; Softcover ISBN 1-59237-066-7 $250.00 ◆ Online Database (includes a free copy of the directory) $495.00

Thomas Food and Beverage Market Place, 2005

Thomas Food and Beverage Market Place is bigger and better than ever with thousands of new companies, thousands of updates to existing companies and two revised and enhanced product category indexes. This comprehensive directory profiles over 18,000 Food & Beverage Manufacturers, 12,000 Equipment & Supply Companies, 2,200 Transportation & Warehouse Companies, 2,000 Brokers & Wholesalers, 8,000 Importers & Exporters, 900 Industry Resources and hundreds of Mail Order Catalogs. Listings include detailed Contact Information, Sales Volumes, Key Contacts, Brand & Product Information, Packaging Details and much more. *Thomas Food and Beverage Market Place* is available as a three-volume printed set, a subscription-based Online Database via the Internet, on CD-ROM, as well as mailing lists and a licensable database.

"An essential purchase for those in the food industry but will also be useful in public libraries where needed. Much of the information will be difficult and time consuming to locate without this handy three-volume ready-reference source." –ARBA

8,500 pages, 3 Volume Set; Softcover ISBN 1-59237-058-6, $495.00 ◆ CD-ROM $695.00 ◆
CD-ROM & 3 Volume Set Combo $895.00 ◆ Online Database $695.00 ◆ Online Database & 3 Volume Set Combo, $895.00

Sports Market Place Directory, 2005

For over 20 years, this comprehensive, up-to-date directory has offered direct access to the Who, What, When & Where of the Sports Industry. With over 20,000 updates and enhancements, the *Sports Market Place Directory* is the most detailed, comprehensive and current sports business reference source available. In 1,800 information-packed pages, *Sports Market Place Directory* profiles contact information and key executives for: Single Sport Organizations, Professional Leagues, Multi-Sport Organizations, Disabled Sports, High School & Youth Sports, Military Sports, Olympic Organizations, Media, Sponsors, Sponsorship & Marketing Event Agencies, Event & Meeting Calendars, Professional Services, College Sports, Manufacturers & Retailers, Facilities and much more. *The Sports Market Place Directory* provides organization's contact information with detailed descriptions including: Key Contacts, physical, mailing, email and web addresses plus phone and fax numbers. Plus, nine important indexes make sure that you can find the information you're looking for quickly and easily: Entry Index, Single Sport Index, Media Index, Sponsor Index, Agency Index, Manufacturers Index, Brand Name Index, Facilities Index and Executive/Geographic Index. For over twenty years, *The Sports Market Place Directory* has assisted thousands of individuals in their pursuit of a career in the sports industry. Why not use "THE SOURCE" that top recruiters, headhunters and career placement centers use to find information on or about sports organizations and key hiring contacts.

1,800 pages; Softcover ISBN 1-59237-077-2, $225.00 ◆ CD-ROM $479.00

To preview any of our Directories Risk-Free for 30 days, call (800) 562-2139 or fax to (518) 789-0556

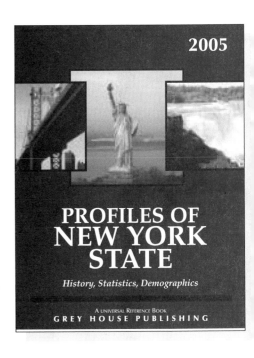

DEMOGRAPHIC MAPS

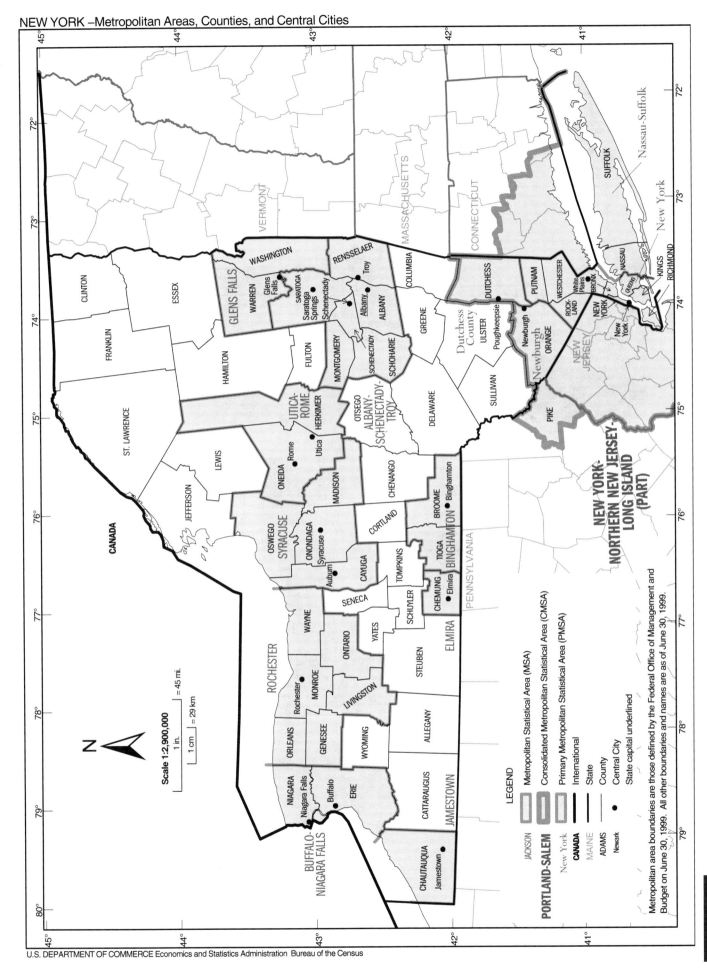

NEW YORK-
NORTHERN NEW JERSEY-
LONG ISLAND
(PART)

Metropolitan area boundaries are those defined by the Federal Office of Management and
Budget on June 30, 1999. All other boundaries and names are as of June 30, 1999.

CANADA

Scale 1:2,900,000

1 in. = 45 mi.

1 cm = 29 km

N

LEGEND

Metropolitan Statistical Area (MSA)

Consolidated Metropolitan Statistical Area (CMSA)

Primary Metropolitan Statistical Area (PMSA)

International

State

County

Central City

State capital underlined

JACKSON

New York

CANADA

MAINE

ADAMS

Newark

PORTLAND-SALEM

Indexes &
Demographic
Maps

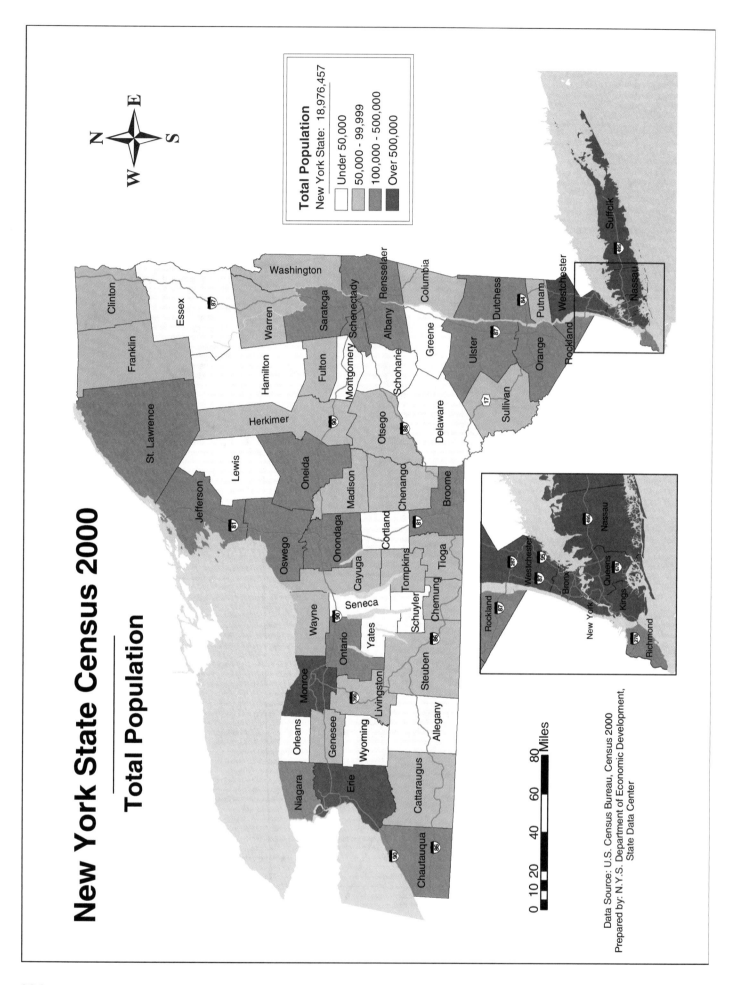

New York State Census 2000

Total Population

Total Population
New York State: 18,976,457

Under 50,000
50,000 - 99,999
100,000 - 500,000
Over 500,000

Clinton

Essex

Franklin

St. Lawrence

Hamilton

Herkimer

Lewis

Jefferson

Oneida

Oswego

Onondaga

Madison

Cayuga

Seneca

Wayne

Monroe

Orleans

Genesee

Wyoming

Niagara

Erie

Cattaraugus

Chautauqua

Allegany

Livingston

Ontario

Yates

Steuben

Schuyler

Chemung

Tioga

Tompkins

Cortland

Chenango

Broome

Washington

Warren

Saratoga

Schenectady

Rensselaer

Albany

Columbia

Greene

Schoharie

Delaware

Sullivan

Ulster

Dutchess

Putnam

Orange

Rockland

Westchester

Montgomery

Fulton

Otsego

Suffolk

Nassau

Rockland

Westchester

Bronx

New York

Queens

Kings

Richmond

Data Source: U.S. Census Bureau, Census 2000
Prepared by: N.Y.S. Department of Economic Development,
State Data Center

0 10 20   40   60   80 Miles

994

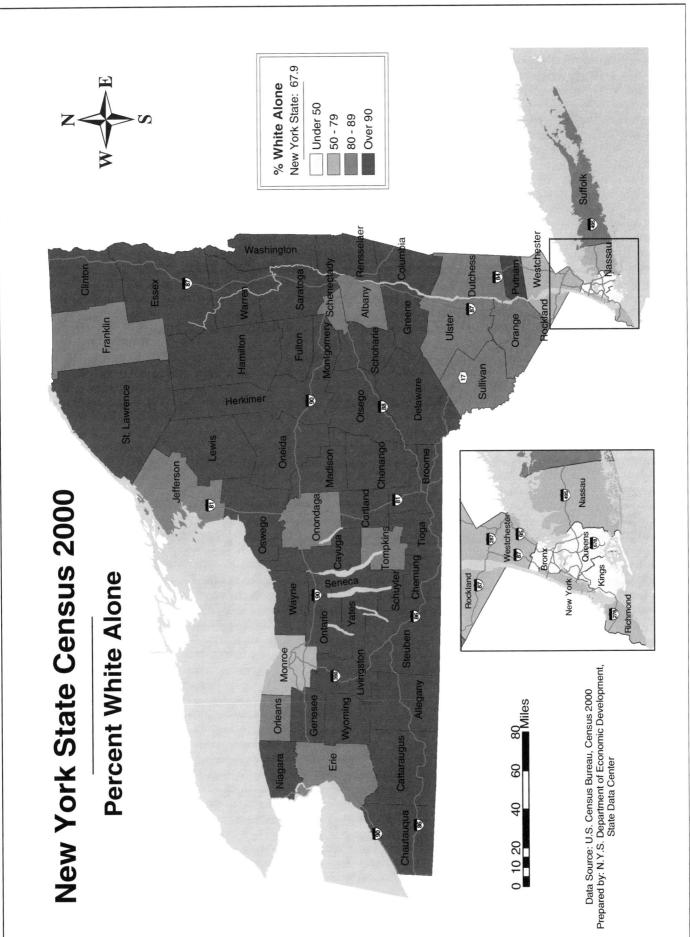

New York State Census 2000

Percent White Alone

% White Alone
New York State: 67.9

- Under 50
- 50 - 79
- 80 - 89
- Over 90

Data Source: U.S. Census Bureau, Census 2000
Prepared by: N.Y.S. Department of Economic Development,
State Data Center

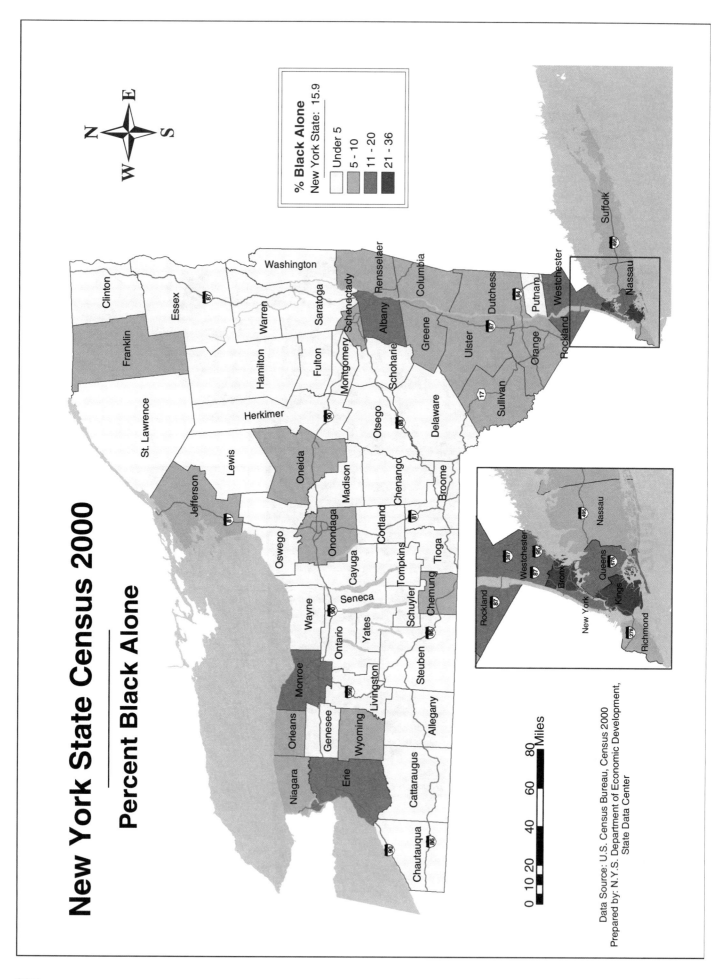

New York State Census 2000

Percent Black Alone

% Black Alone
New York State: 15.9

- Under 5
- 5 - 10
- 11 - 20
- 21 - 36

Data Source: U.S. Census Bureau, Census 2000
Prepared by: N.Y.S. Department of Economic Development,
State Data Center

0 10 20 40 60 80 Miles

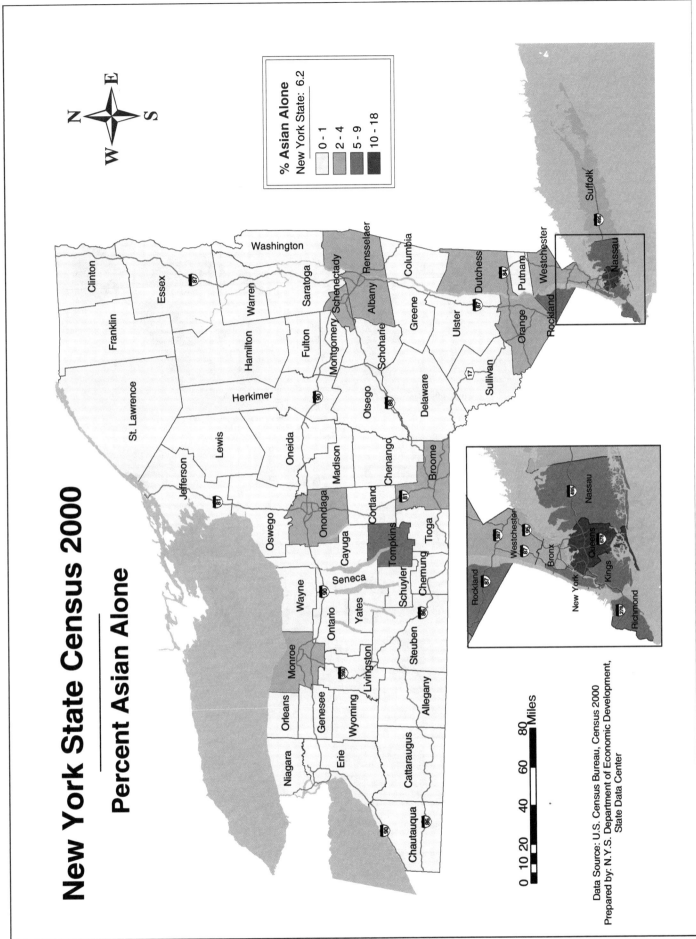

New York State Census 2000

Percent Asian Alone

% Asian Alone
New York State: 6.2

- 0 - 1
- 2 - 4
- 5 - 9
- 10 - 18

N
W E
S

Clinton
Essex
Franklin
Warren
Washington
Saratoga
Schenectady
Rensselaer
Columbia
Hamilton
Fulton
Montgomery
Albany
Greene
Dutchess
Putnam
Westchester
St. Lawrence
Schoharie
Ulster
Orange
Rockland
Herkimer
Otsego
Delaware
Sullivan
Lewis
Oneida
Jefferson
Madison
Chenango
Broome
Oswego
Onondaga
Cortland
Tioga
Cayuga
Tompkins
Chemung
Seneca
Schuyler
Wayne
Ontario
Yates
Steuben
Monroe
Livingston
Orleans
Genesee
Wyoming
Allegany
Niagara
Erie
Cattaraugus
Chautauqua

Suffolk
Nassau
Westchester
Rockland
Bronx
New York
Queens
Kings
Richmond

Data Source: U.S. Census Bureau, Census 2000
Prepared by: N.Y.S. Department of Economic Development,
State Data Center

0 10 20   40   60   80 Miles

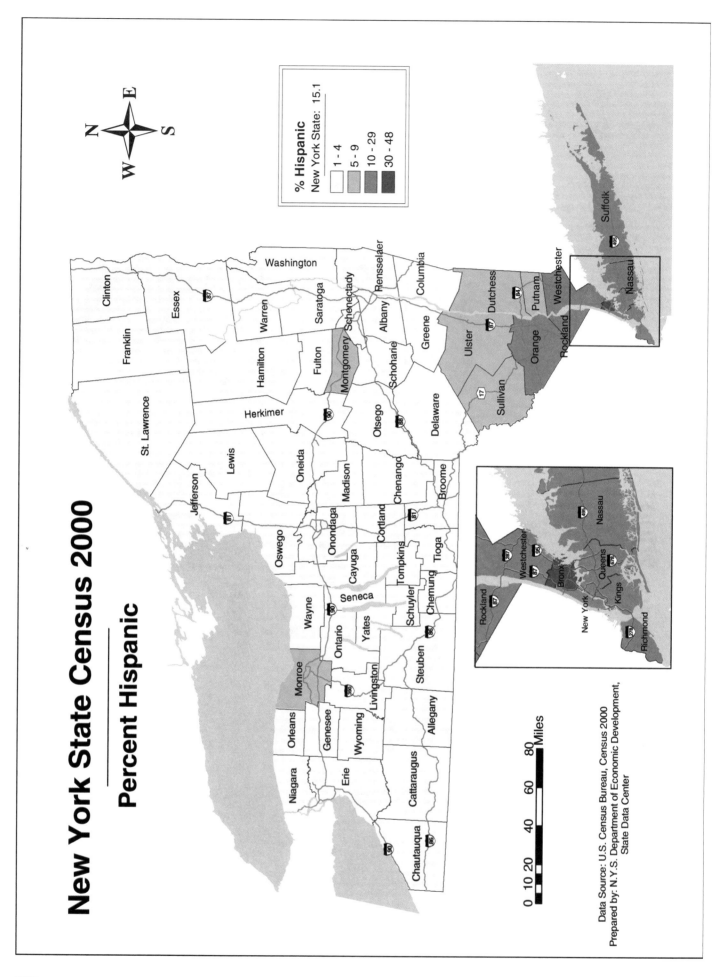

New York State Census 2000

Percent Hispanic

% Hispanic
New York State: 15.1

- 1 - 4
- 5 - 9
- 10 - 29
- 30 - 48

Data Source: U.S. Census Bureau, Census 2000
Prepared by: N.Y.S. Department of Economic Development,
State Data Center

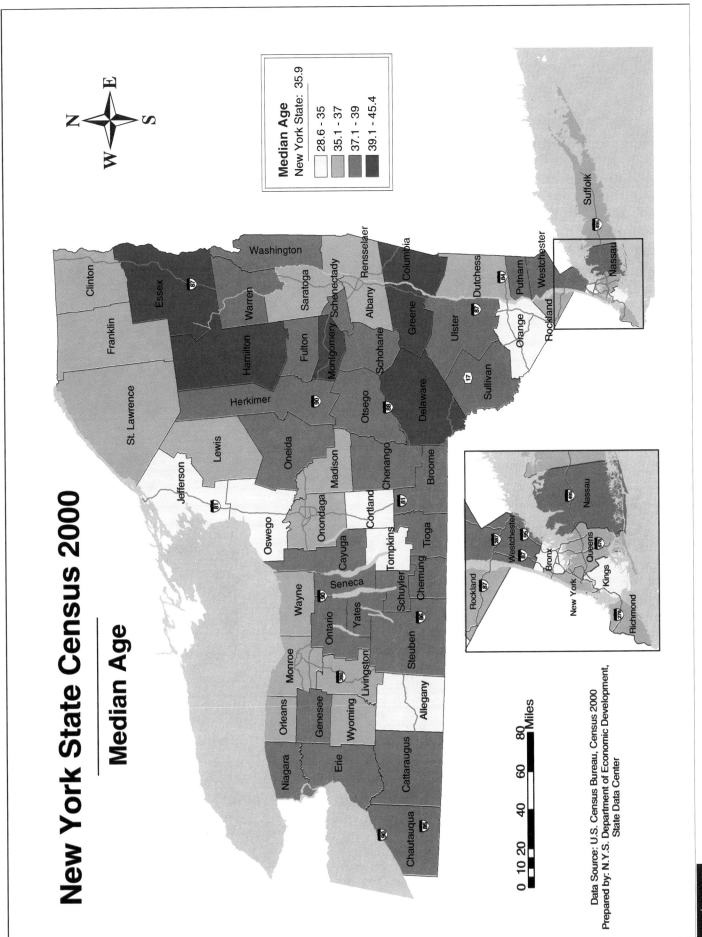

New York State Census 2000

Median Age

Median Age
New York State: 35.9

	28.6 - 35
	35.1 - 37
	37.1 - 39
	39.1 - 45.4

Data Source: U.S. Census Bureau, Census 2000
Prepared by: N.Y.S. Department of Economic Development,
State Data Center

0 10 20   40   60   80 Miles

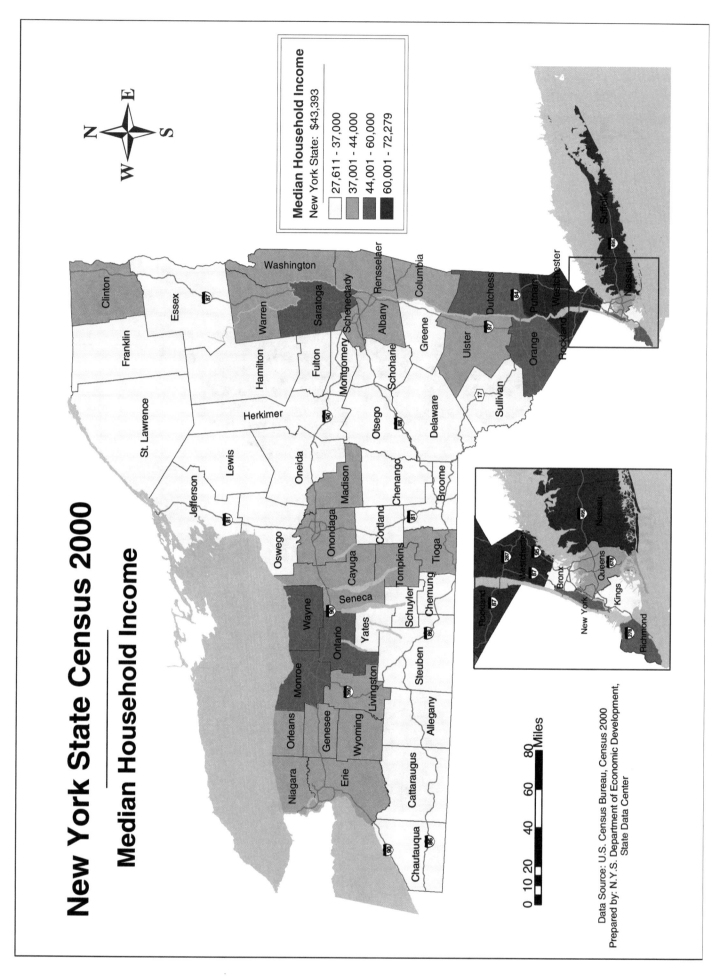

1000

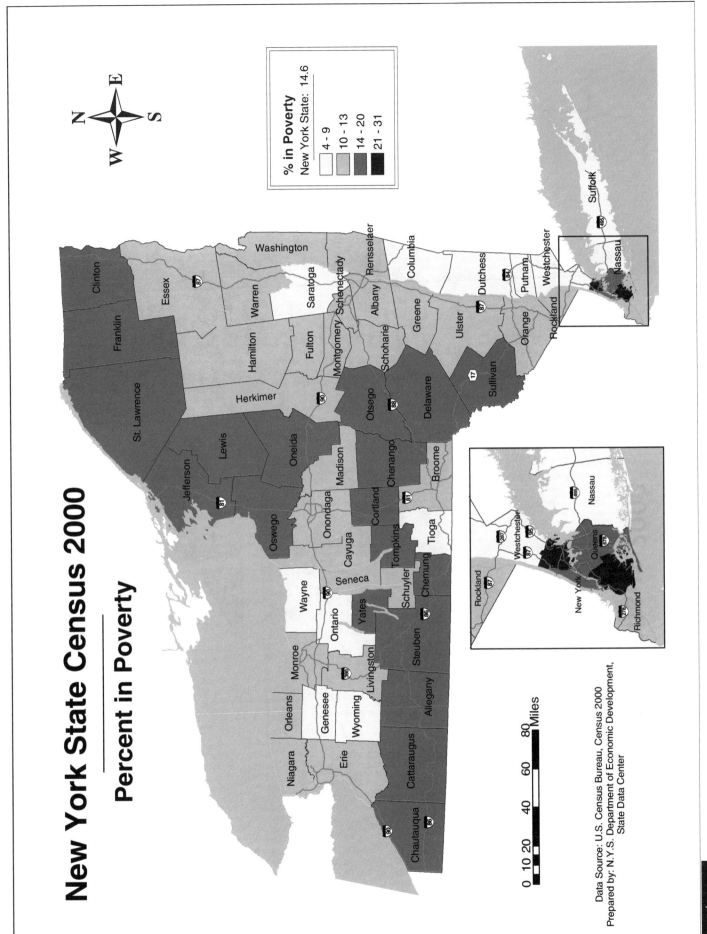

New York State Census 2000

Percent in Poverty

% in Poverty
New York State: 14.6

4 - 9
10 - 13
14 - 20
21 - 31

Data Source: U.S. Census Bureau, Census 2000
Prepared by: N.Y.S. Department of Economic Development,
State Data Center

0 10 20   40   60   80 Miles

Indexes &
Demographic
Maps

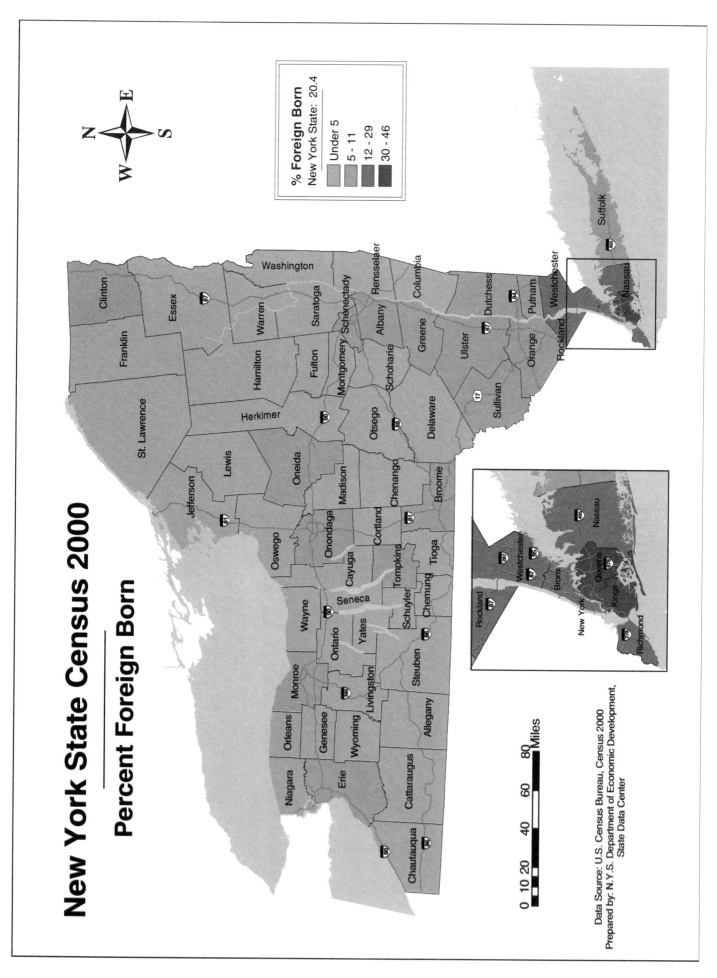

New York State Census 2000

Percent Foreign Born

% Foreign Born
New York State: 20.4

- Under 5
- 5 - 11
- 12 - 29
- 30 - 46

Data Source: U.S. Census Bureau, Census 2000
Prepared by: N.Y.S. Department of Economic Development,
State Data Center

0 10 20   40   60   80 Miles

1002

New York State Census 2000

Percent Speaking Language Other Than English

% Language Other Than English
New York State: 28

- Under 6
- 6 - 20
- 21 - 30
- 31 - 50

N
W E
S

Clinton
Essex
Franklin
St. Lawrence
Washington
Warren
Hamilton
Saratoga
Schenectady
Rensselaer
Columbia
Albany
Greene
Montgomery
Fulton
Schoharie
Ulster
Dutchess
Putnam
Orange
Rockland
Westchester
Sullivan
Delaware
Otsego
Herkimer
Lewis
Oneida
Madison
Chenango
Broome
Jefferson
Oswego
Onondaga
Cortland
Tioga
Cayuga
Tompkins
Chemung
Seneca
Schuyler
Wayne
Ontario
Yates
Steuben
Monroe
Livingston
Orleans
Genesee
Wyoming
Allegany
Niagara
Erie
Cattaraugus
Chautauqua

Suffolk
Nassau

Rockland
Westchester
Nassau
New York
Bronx
Queens
Kings
Richmond

0 10 20   40   60   80
Miles

Data Source: U.S. Census Bureau, Census 2000
Prepared by: N.Y.S. Department of Economic Development,
State Data Center

Indexes &
Demographic
Maps

1003

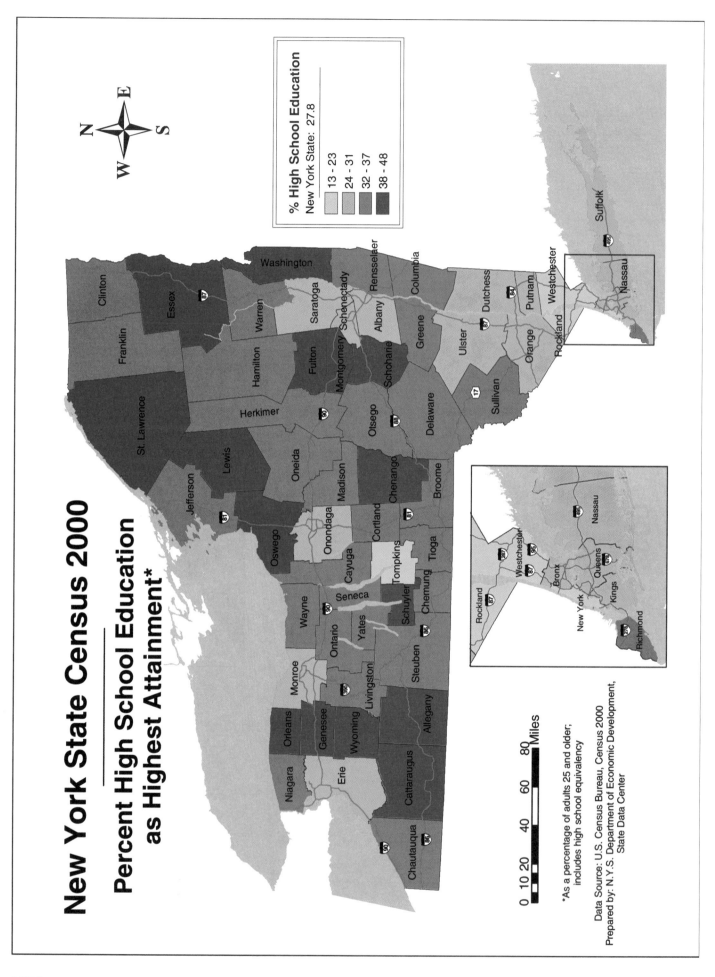

New York State Census 2000

Percent High School Education as Highest Attainment*

% High School Education

New York State: 27.8

- 13 - 23
- 24 - 31
- 32 - 37
- 38 - 48

0 10 20 40 60 80 Miles

*As a percentage of adults 25 and older; includes high school equivalency

Data Source: U.S. Census Bureau, Census 2000
Prepared by: N.Y.S. Department of Economic Development, State Data Center

New York State Census 2000

Percent Bachelor's Degree or Higher*

% Bachelor's Degree or Higher
New York State: 27.4

- 12 - 16
- 17 - 19
- 20 - 29
- 30 - 49

N
E
S
W

*As a percentage of adults 25 and older

0 10 20   40   60   80 Miles

Data Source: U.S. Census Bureau, Census 2000
Prepared by: N.Y.S. Department of Economic Development,
State Data Center

Clinton
Essex
Franklin
St. Lawrence
Hamilton
Warren
Washington
Saratoga
Schenectady
Rensselaer
Columbia
Fulton
Montgomery
Schoharie
Albany
Greene
Herkimer
Lewis
Jefferson
Oneida
Madison
Otsego
Delaware
Ulster
Dutchess
Putnam
Westchester
Rockland
Orange
Sullivan
Oswego
Onondaga
Cortland
Chenango
Broome
Cayuga
Tompkins
Tioga
Chemung
Seneca
Schuyler
Wayne
Ontario
Yates
Steuben
Livingston
Monroe
Orleans
Genesee
Wyoming
Allegany
Niagara
Erie
Cattaraugus
Chautauqua

Suffolk
Nassau
Rockland
Westchester
Bronx
New York
Queens
Kings
Richmond

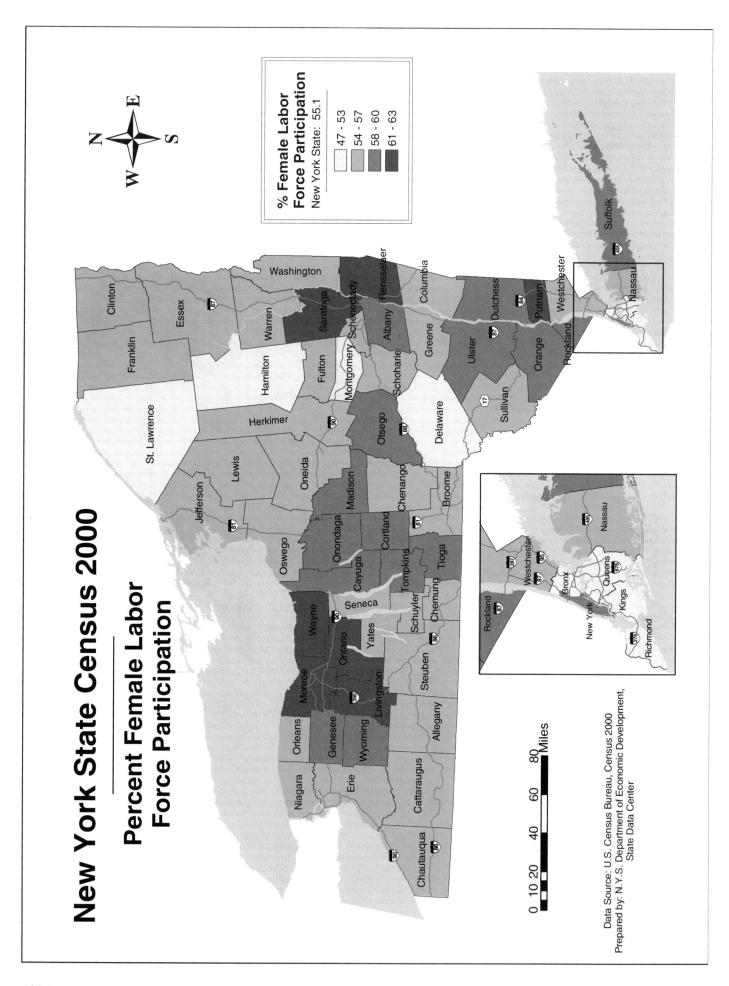

New York State Census 2000

Percent Female Labor Force Participation

% Female Labor Force Participation
New York State: 55.1

- 47 - 53
- 54 - 57
- 58 - 60
- 61 - 63

N E S W

Data Source: U.S. Census Bureau, Census 2000
Prepared by: N.Y.S. Department of Economic Development,
State Data Center

0 10 20   40   60   80 Miles

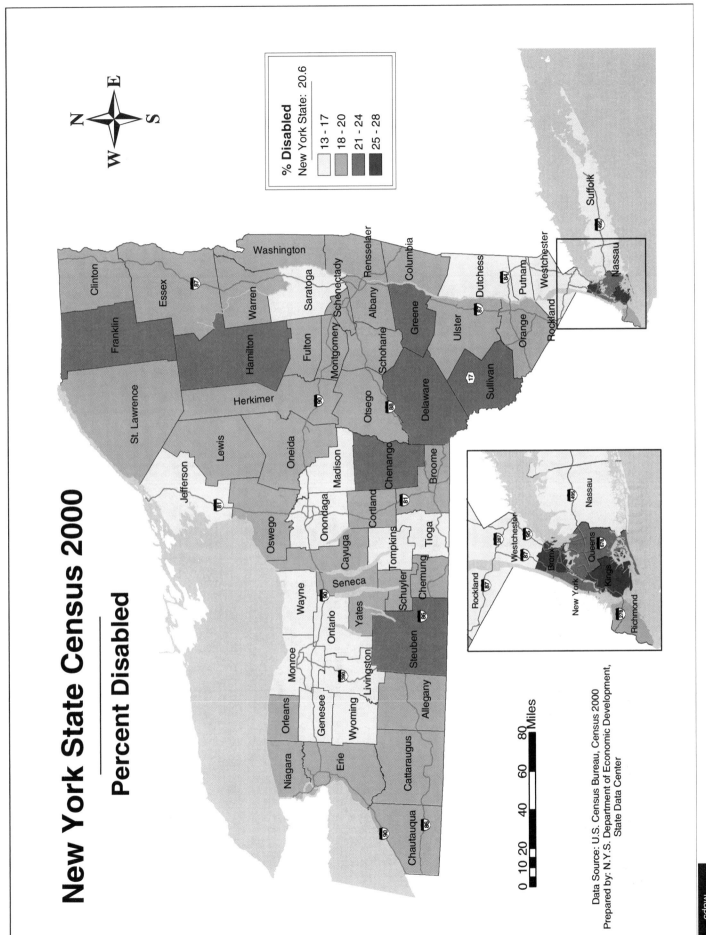

New York State Census 2000

Percent Disabled

% Disabled
New York State: 20.6

- 13 - 17
- 18 - 20
- 21 - 24
- 25 - 28

Data Source: U.S. Census Bureau, Census 2000
Prepared by: N.Y.S. Department of Economic Development,
State Data Center

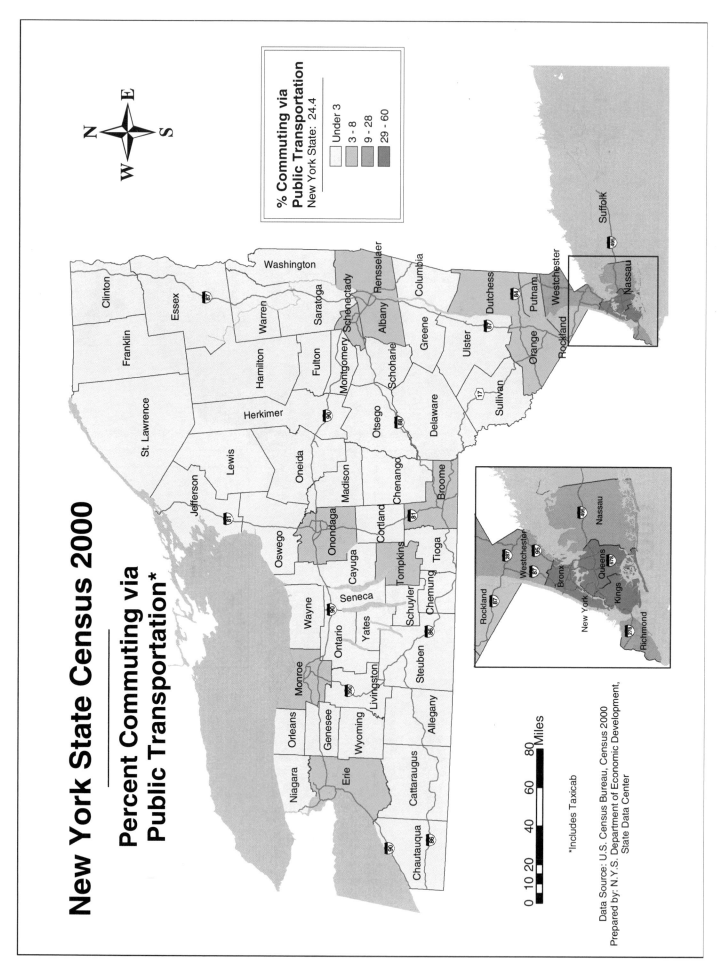

New York State Census 2000

Percent Commuting via Public Transportation*

% Commuting via Public Transportation
New York State: 24.4

- Under 3
- 3 - 8
- 9 - 28
- 29 - 60

Miles
0 10 20 40 60 80

*Includes Taxicab

Data Source: U.S. Census Bureau, Census 2000
Prepared by: N.Y.S. Department of Economic Development,
State Data Center